プログレッシブ
英語コロケーション辞典

著者　塚本倫久
英文校閲　Jon Blundell

小学館

電子編集＆ＤＴＰ	鈴木さゆみ
本文デザイン	利根川裕 (glove)
装丁	利根川裕 (glove)
イラスト	祖敷大輔
制作	川又繁夫
資材	森　雅彦
制作企画	金田玄彦
販売	前原富士夫　福島真実
宣伝	浦城朋子
編集	三谷博也
編集協力	塩澤信司／桂川千津子

まえがき

　国際社会の中で日本人もますます発信する力が求められています．英語を読んだり，聞いたりはできても，話したり書いたりするときに自然な英語が出てこないことがあります．その原因の一つは母語である日本語の干渉です．たとえば「明るい未来」「電話に出る」「ピクニックをする」「水と油」「損益」などは日常生活の中でしばしば使われる表現ですが，英語の表現はすぐには出てこないかもしれません．それぞれ a bright future, answer the phone, have a picnic, oil and water, profit and loss のように言います．「明るい未来」は bright がすぐ思い浮かべば問題ありません．「電話に出る」の「出る」は answer を使います．「ピクニックをする」の「する」は必ずしも「宿題をする do homework」のように do と結びつくわけではないので注意が必要です．「水と油」「損益」は日本語と順序が逆です．さらに a strong position「強い立場」の反対は a weak position「弱い立場」ですが，a strong wind「強風」の反対は a weak wind ではなく a light wind「微風」です．

　語と語の結びつきには相性があり，そのような「語と語の慣習的な結びつき」はコロケーション（連語）と呼ばれます．ネイティブスピーカーに近い自然な英語を使うためには，コロケーションの知識がとても重要です．本辞典は，学習者がまず使えるようにしておきたい基本語のコロケーションをわかりやすく示しました．英語の自然な語と語の結びつきを確認して，語感を身につけ，英会話や英作文などに役立てていただくことを目的としています．従来あまり取り上げられてこなかった highly successful（大成功の），absolutely delighted（心から喜んで），openly discuss（率直に議論する）など程度や感情を表す-ly 副詞と連結する形容詞や動詞のコロケーションも豊富に示しました．

　コロケーションは一般に語彙的コロケーションと文法的コロケーションに分けられます．語彙的コロケーションは a lovely girl, have a dream, absolutely right のような「形容詞＋名詞」「動詞＋名詞」「副詞＋形容詞」の連結です．いっぽう文法的コロケーションは believe that…, provide A with B のように動詞，名詞，形容詞が前置詞，不定詞，節など文法構造を従えるものです．従来のコロケーション辞典はどちらかといえば語彙的コロケーションを中心に編纂されていますが，日本人学習者が話したり，書いたりする際には文法的コロケーションも合わせて学習することが重要であることから，本辞典では文法的コロケーションも記述しました．

　見出し語の選定にあたっては，文部科学省の中学校，高等学校教科書の語彙選定基準，大学英語教育学会基本語リスト「JACET8000」，British National Corpus（BNC）の高頻度語をもとに，コロケーションの観点から重要な約2500語を選定し，BNCの頻度情報などに基づいて基本的なコロケーションを示しました．

　用例には BNC などコーパス（実際に使われた自然言語データ）を利用しましたが，学習者にふさわしい実際の場面を彷彿とさせるような用例を提供するために，外国人に対する英語教育の経験豊かな同僚の Jon Blundell 氏に協力いただき，用例に綿密な検討を加えるとともに，作成にも携わっていただきました．

　最後に著者を辞書の世界へと導いてくださった恩師岡田尚先生，在外研修中にコーパス言語学についてご指導いただいた Charles Owen 先生に心よりお礼申し上げます．

　本辞典が英語の発信力を高めたいと願っている高校生，大学生，一般の読者の方々に少しでもお役に立つことができるならば，著者として望外の喜びです．Let's collocate!

２０１２年４月
塚本倫久

この辞典の使い方

1．見出し語
★名詞・形容詞・動詞から選んだ基本語約2,500語を収録し，アルファベット順に配列した．同じつづりで品詞が異なる語も別見出しとして扱った．アメリカ英語とイギリス英語でつづりが異なる場合，見出し語は米国つづりで示し，訳語のあとにイギリスつづりを注記で示した．

2．発音
★国際音標記号を用いて /･･･/ に入れて示した．米式発音と英式発音が異なる場合，米式と英式を | で区切って米式，英式の順に示した．

3．訳語
★原則としてコロケーションとして取り上げた訳語のみを示した．おもに米国で用いる語義は《米》，おもに英国で用いる語義は《英》，おもに話しことばで用いる語義は《話》，くだけた場面で用いる語義は《略式》とした．

4．コロケーション表
★見出し語が多義語の場合，語義ごとにコロケーションを二重線で分けた．コロケーションが同義・反対義の場合や，関連するコロケーションは破線で示した．
★表に出てくる名詞は無冠詞あるいはa, an, the, one's, A'sをつけて示した．one'sは主語と同じ人称，A'sは主語とは異なる人称を示す．ただし冠詞は代表的なものを示してあるので，表では不定冠詞で示されていても，用例の中では文脈で限定されて定冠詞になることも多い．
★語彙的コロケーション：名詞の見出しでは「動詞＋名詞」「形容詞＋名詞」「名詞＋名詞」を中心に示した．
　　動詞の見出しでは「副詞＋動詞」を中心に示した．「副詞＋動詞，動詞＋副詞」の連結における副詞の位置は，前後どちらか一方しかとれない場合，両方可能な場合もあるが，その場合に前後どちらが優勢かはそれぞれのコロケーションやコンテキストなどによっても異なる．表では一般的な位置を示した．
　　形容詞の見出しでは「動詞＋形容詞」「副詞＋形容詞」を中心に示した．
★文法的コロケーション：本書では発信に必要な文法的コロケーションも示した．Cは補語を示す．それぞれの品詞で取り上げたおもなコロケーションは次のとおり．
　　動詞の見出しでは「動詞＋to do / doing」「動詞＋that」「動詞＋名詞＋前置詞＋名詞」
　　形容詞の見出しでは「形容詞＋前置詞」「形容詞＋doing / to do」「形容詞＋that / wh-節」
　　名詞の見出しでは「名詞＋to do」「名詞＋that節」「名詞＋前置詞 / 前置詞＋名詞」
★用例中でコロケーションは太字で，共起する前置詞のうち特に注意したいものは斜体で示した．
★コロケーションにさらに別の要素が加わった固定表現は適宜♦で目立たせた．

5．PHRASES PHRASES〉
★日常の話しことばで使われる文単位の固定表現を，ニコニコマーク😊をつけて示した．
★I'm afraid (that)... や It's fair to say (that)... のような導入節も示した．

A

abandon /əbǽndən/ 動 捨てる，断念する

completely	abandon	完全に断念する
never	abandon	決して断念しない
largely	abandon	ほぼ断念する
virtually	abandon	事実上断念する
effectively	abandon	
finally	abandon	ついに断念する

▷I have **never abandoned** my dream to go abroad. 外国へ行く夢を捨てたことはない
▷The project was **finally abandoned**. その計画はついに断念された

ability /əbíləti/ 名 能力，才能；学力

have	the ability	能力がある
demonstrate	one's ability	能力を示す
show	one's ability	
develop	one's ability	能力を伸ばす
enhance	one's ability	
lack	the ability	能力を欠く
lose	one's ability	能力がなくなる
affect	A's ability	能力に影響を及ぼす
doubt	A's ability	能力を疑う
assess	A's ability	学力評価をする
test	A's ability	学力を試す

▷How can I **develop** this **ability**? どうしたらこの能力を伸ばせますか
▷Drugs were used to **enhance** athletic **abilities**. 運動能力を高めるのに薬物が使われた
▷Laura **lacks** the **ability** to care about people. ローラには人を気遣う能力が欠けている

an exceptional	ability	並外れた能力
an extraordinary	ability	
a remarkable	ability	すばらしい能力
a great	ability	
a natural	ability	天賦の能力
an innate	ability	
intellectual	ability	知的能力
linguistic	ability	言語能力
artistic	ability	芸術的才能
physical	ability	身体能力
athletic	ability	運動能力
high	ability	高い学力
low	ability	低い学力
average	ability	平均的学力

▷He was a writer of **exceptional ability**. 彼は並外れた才能のある作家だった
▷Tony, you have a **natural ability** to help people. トニー，きみには人を助ける才能が生まれながらにあるね
▷Mike is a student of **average ability**. マイクは平均的な学力の生徒だ

ability	to do	…する能力

▷He had the **ability to** read a situation. 彼には状況を読む能力があった

able /éibl/

形 (be able to do で)…できる；有能な

barely	able to do	ほとんど…できない
hardly	able to do	
better	able to do	よりよく…できる
more	able to do	
the most	able	最も有能な
less	able	能力の劣る

▷I feel **better able to** make these comments now. いまではもっとうまくこういう論評ができると思う
▷He was **the most able** boy John had ever taught. 彼はジョンがそれまで教えた中で最も優秀な少年だった

absence /ǽbsəns/ 名 不在，欠席；欠如

a long	absence	長い不在
a prolonged	absence	長引いた不在
a temporary	absence	一時的な不在
unauthorized	absence	無断欠席，無断欠勤
a complete	absence	まったくの欠如
a total	absence	
a conspicuous	absence	目立つ欠如

▷She came back to work after a **long absence**. 久しぶりに彼女は仕事に復帰した
▷The problem is that there is a **complete absence** of political leadership. 問題は政治的な指導力が完全に欠けていることだ

absence	from A	Aを欠席すること

▷I imagine you'll be taking quite a long **absence from** the office. あなたはかなり長期にわたって会社を休むことになるんだろうね

in	A's absence	留守中に

▷What has happened **in** my **absence**? 私のいないときに何があったの

3

absent /ǽbsənt/ 形 不在の, 欠席の

entirely	absent	まったくない
totally	absent	
conspicuously	absent	不在が目立つ

▷The latest figures were **entirely absent** from the report. 最新の数値が報告からまったく抜け落ちていた
▷Paul's name was **conspicuously absent** from the list. ポールの名前がリストにないのが目立った

absent	from A	Aを欠席している；Aに欠けている

▷She was **absent from** school for 3 days. 彼女は3日間学校を休んだ(★会話ではしばしば not at..., not there を用いる：I telephoned him at work, but he wasn't there. 彼の職場に電話したが, 席を外していた)

absorb /æbsɔ́ːrb | əb-/ 動 吸収する；合併する

easily	absorb	簡単に吸収する
quickly	absorb	すばやく吸収する
rapidly	absorb	

▷Calcium in milk is **easily absorbed** by the body. 牛乳中のカルシウムは体に吸収されやすい

absorb	A into B	AをBに吸収する

▷You get drunk when too much alcohol is **absorbed into** the blood. 大量のアルコールが血液に吸収されると酔いが回る

absorbed /æbsɔ́ːrbd | əb-/ 形 夢中になった

totally	absorbed	すっかり夢中になった
completely	absorbed	

▷Jill was **completely absorbed** in her work. ジルは仕事にすっかり夢中になっていた

absorbed	in A	Aに夢中になった

▷He was totally **absorbed in** his computer and didn't hear anything. 彼はコンピュータにすっかり夢中になっていて何も耳に入らなかった

abstract /ǽbstrækt | ⵪/ 形 抽象的な

highly	abstract	きわめて抽象的な
purely	abstract	まったく抽象的な
entirely	abstract	

▷This is a **highly abstract** argument. これはきわめて抽象的な議論だ

abuse /əbjúːs/ 名 虐待；乱用

prevent	abuse	虐待を防ぐ；乱用を防ぐ
open to	abuse	乱用されやすい

▷What can be done to **prevent abuse** of the elderly? 高齢者への虐待を防ぐために何がなされうるか(★「虐待を受ける」は動詞 abuse を用いて次のようにいう：Some children are **abused by** their parents. 両親から虐待を受ける子どももいる)

alcohol	abuse	アルコールの乱用
drug	abuse	麻薬の乱用
substance	abuse	薬物乱用
sexual	abuse	性的虐待
sex	abuse	
child	abuse	児童虐待
verbal	abuse	ことばの暴力

accept /æksépt/ 動 受け入れる, 容認する

fully	accept	全面的に受け入れる
readily	accept	快く受け入れる
reluctantly	accept	しぶしぶ受け入れる
be generally	accepted	一般に受け入れられている
be widely	accepted	

▷I didn't want to **fully accept** what had happened. 起きてしまったことを心底から受け入れたくはなかった
▷She quite **readily accepted** his proposal of marriage. 彼女は彼からの結婚の申し込みを二つ返事で受けた

accept	A as B	AをBとして認める

▷I've **accepted** it **as** my fate. それを自分の運命として受け入れた

accept	that...	…ということを受け入れる

▷He doesn't **accept that** he's too old to go skydiving. スカイダイビングをするには年をとりすぎているということを彼は頑として認めない

♦**It is accepted that...** …だと受け入れられている ▷It was accepted that there was nothing more we could do. これ以上打つ手はないという意見がみんなに受け入れられていた

| be prepared to | accept | 受け入れる用意が |
| be willing to | accept | ある |

▷I was **prepared to accept** her offer. 彼女の申し出を受け入れる用意はあった

acceptable /ækséptəbl/ 形 容認できる

generally	acceptable	一般に容認できる
perfectly	acceptable	完全に容認できる
mutually	acceptable	双方が容認できる
socially	acceptable	社会的に容認できる
morally	acceptable	道徳的に容認できる
widely	acceptable	広く受け入れられる

▷That's **perfectly acceptable**. それは完全に納得できるよ
▷We hope we'll be able to find a **mutually acceptable** solution. お互いに納得できる解決法が見つかるといいですね
▷Violence is not **socially acceptable**. 暴力は社会的に容認されるものではない

| acceptable | to A | Aに受け入れられる |

▷His conclusion is **acceptable to** most people. 彼の結論はほとんどの人に受け入れられる

access /ǽkses/ 名 接近；通路

gain	access	近づける, 立ち入れる
get	access	
deny A	access	A(人)にアクセスを拒む

▷Hackers can't **gain access** to our credit card information. ハッカーたちはクレジットカードの情報を手に入れることはできない
▷I was **denied access** to the website of the City Hall. 市役所のホームページへのアクセスを拒否された

easy	access	至便, 楽な利用
public	access	一般の立ち入り
unauthorized	access	不正アクセス
Internet	access	ネット接続

▷Since my room was on the top floor, I had **easy access** to the roof. 私の部屋は最上階だったので, すぐ屋上に出られた
▷There is no **public access** to that parking lot. その駐車場は一般の人は立ち入れない

accident /ǽksədənt/ 名 事故；偶然

have	an accident	事故にあう
be involved in	an accident	
cause	an accident	事故を引き起こす
avoid	an accident	事故を避ける
prevent	an accident	事故を防ぐ
investigate	an accident	事故を調査する

▷I'm afraid he **had** an **accident** last night. 彼は昨夜事故にあったんです
▷We didn't know what **caused** the **accident**. 事故の原因はわからなかった
▷The police are having a campaign to **prevent accidents**. 警察は事故防止キャンペーンの実施中だ
▷Police are **investigating** the **accident**. 警察はその事故を捜査中だ

| an accident | happened | 事故が起きた |
| an accident | occurred | |

▷The **accident occurred** about 9 p.m. Wednesday. その事故は水曜日の午後9時ごろ起きた

a terrible	accident	ひどい事故
a bad	accident	
a serious	accident	重大な事故
a tragic	accident	痛ましい事故
a fatal	accident	死亡事故
a minor	accident	小さな事故
a nuclear	accident	原子力事故
a car	accident	自動車事故
a road	accident	交通事故
a traffic	accident	

▷"What's wrong with you?" "There's been a **terrible accident**."「どうしたの」「大変な事故があったんだ」
▷I had a **bad accident** when I was young. 若いころひどい事故にあった
▷35% of **serious accidents** are caused by bad driving. 大事故の35％は運転ミスが原因だ
▷He was involved in a **fatal accident** in Italy. 彼はイタリアで死亡事故に巻き込まれた

| an accident | involving A | Aがかかわる事故 |

▷Most **accidents involving** children happen on journey to or from school. 子どもが関係する事故のほとんどは学校の行き帰りに起こる

| in | an accident | 事故で |
| by | accident | たまたま, 偶然に；誤って |

▷His mother was killed **in an accident** eight years ago. 彼の母親は8年前に事故で亡くなった
▷Sorry, I pushed the button **by accident**. ごめん, うっかりボタンを押しちゃった

| accord |

PHRASES

it is no accident 偶然ではない ▷It's no accident that all your friends are here. Surprise party! Happy Birthday! きみの友人がそろっているのは偶然じゃないよ。びっくりパーティーさ。誕生日おめでとう

accord /əkɔ́ːrd/ 名 一致, 調和; 合意, 協定

reach	an accord	合意に達する
sign	an accord	協定に調印する

▷Southeast Asian countries and China **signed an accord** to create the world's biggest free trade area. 東南アジア諸国と中国は世界最大の自由貿易市場をつくる協定に調印した

an accord	between A	Aの間の合意

▷It's going to be very difficult to **reach an accord between** the USA and China. 米国と中国が合意に達するのはきわめて難しくなりそうだ

in	accord with A	Aと一致して
of	one's own accord	自発的に

▷Nobody forced the Prime Minister to resign. He did it **of his own accord**. 首相が辞任したのはだれかに強制されたわけではなく, 自らの意思によるものだった

account /əkáunt/

名 口座; 勘定書, 会計簿, 記述, 報告, 説明

open	an account	口座を開く
close	an account	口座を解約する
credit to	an account	口座に入金する
withdraw from	an account	口座から引き落とす
settle	an account	貸借を清算する
give	an account	報告する
provide	an account	
take A into	account	Aを考慮に入れる

▷I'd like to **open an account**. 口座を開きたいのですが

▷He **gave** a fascinating **account** *of* his journey around Europe. 彼はヨーロッパ中を旅行したときの興味深い話をしてくれた

▷We need to **take into account** the fact that he was under a great deal of stress. 彼がかなりストレスを感じていたことを考慮する必要がある

a bank	account	銀行口座
a savings	account	普通預金口座
a checking	account	当座預金口座
a current	account	
a full	account	詳しい報告
an eyewitness	account	目撃情報

▷I'll put the money into your **bank account**. お金をあなたの銀行口座に振り込んでおきます

▷He gave me a **full account** of the race. 彼はレースの模様を詳しく話してくれた

by	all accounts	だれに聞いても
on	A's account	A(人)のために
on	account of A	Aが理由で
on	that account	そのために
on	this account	このために

▷Tony was, **by all accounts**, a bright child. トニーはだれに聞いても頭のよい子だった

▷School was closed **on account of** the typhoon. 学校は台風のせいで休みになった

▷We couldn't meet the deadlines. It was **on that account** that we lost the contract. 締め切りに間に合わなかった。契約をとれなかったのはそのためだ

account /əkáunt/ 動 (account for A で) A

を説明する; Aの割合を占める

fully	account for A	Aを十分説明する
partly	account for A	Aを一部説明する
still	account for A	いまなおAを占める

▷Coffee **still accounts for** more than 40% of Rwanda's exports. コーヒーはいまなおルワンダの輸出の40%以上を占めている

accurate /ǽkjurət/ 形 正確な, 精密な

fairly	accurate	かなり正確
reasonably	accurate	
highly	accurate	非常に正確な
not completely	accurate	厳密には正確で
not strictly	accurate	はない
historically	accurate	歴史的に正確な

▷Your guess was **fairly accurate**. あなたの推測はかなり正確だった

▷I'm sure this is a **historically accurate** depiction. これは歴史的に正確な描写だと思う

accurate	to A	Aまでの精度がある

▷This digital thermometer is **accurate to** within one hundredth of a degree. このデジタル温度計は100分の1度までの精度がある

accuse /əkjúːz/ 動 告発する, 起訴する

falsely	accuse	不当に告発する
wrongly	accuse	
publicly	accuse	公に非難する

▷ She **falsely accused** him of stealing some money from her handbag. 彼女はハンドバッグからお金を盗んだと彼を犯人扱いした

accuse	A of B	A(人)をBで告発する
accuse	A of doing	A(人)を…したと非難する

▷ She **accused** him **of** sexual harassment. 彼女は彼をセクハラで訴えた

ache /éik/ 名 痛み

have	an ache	痛い
feel	an ache	

▷ I **have** an ache *in* my back. 腰が痛い

ache	in A	Aの痛み

▷ I felt a dull **ache in** my stomach. 胃に鈍痛があった

aches and pains	体中の痛み

▷ I feel very tired and have lots of **aches and pains**. とても疲れていて体中が痛い

ache /éik/ 動 痛む

ache	badly	ひどく痛む
ache	terribly	
ache	fiercely	激しく痛む
ache	a bit	少し痛い
ache	all over	体中が痛い
really	ache	すごく痛む

▷ My head **ached badly**. 頭がひどく痛んだ
▷ I'm **aching all over**. 体中が痛い
▷ My knees **really ache** this morning. けさはひざがすごく痛い

ache	from A	(体の一部が)Aで痛い

▷ Her legs were **aching from** the long walk. 長い距離を歩いたので彼女は足が痛かった

achieve /ətʃíːv/ 動 達成する, 成し遂げる

fail to	achieve	達成できない
try to	achieve	達成しようとする

★ try のほか aim, hope, want, attempt など積極的な行動を表す動詞と連結する

▷ She **failed to achieve** good results in her exams. 彼女は試験でよい結果を出せなかった
▷ What are you **trying to achieve**? 何を成し遂げようとしているのですか

achievement /ətʃíːvmənt/

名 業績; 達成

a great	achievement	偉大な業績
a tremendous	achievement	
a major	achievement	大きな業績
a remarkable	achievement	めざましい業績
a notable	achievement	
the main	achievement	主要業績
educational	achievement	学業成績
academic	achievement	

▷ Breaking two world records was a **remarkable achievement**. 世界記録を2つも破るなんてすごかった

measure	(an) achievement	業績を評価する
recognize	(an) achievement	業績を認める

▷ This award **recognizes** outstanding **achievement** in science. この賞は科学の世界での大きな業績に対して贈られる

a sense of	achievement	達成感
levels of	achievement	達成度

▷ Gardening gives me a **sense of achievement** and satisfaction. ガーデニングは達成感と満足感を与えてくれる

acknowledge /æknálidʒ | -nɔ́l-/

動 認める

reluctantly	acknowledge	しぶしぶ認める
officially	acknowledge	公式に認める
be generally	acknowledged	広く認められている
be widely	acknowledged	

▷ Julia is **widely acknowledged** *as* an expert on modern American literature. ジュリアはアメリカ現代文学の専門家だということはだれもが認めている

acknowledge that...	…だと認める

| acquaintance |

▷He finally **acknowledged that** I was right. 私が正しいと彼はとうとう認めた

be acknowledged	as C	Cと認められる

▷She's **acknowledged as** an expert on art. 彼女は美術の専門家として認められている

acquaintance /əkwéintəns/

名 知り合い，知人；面識

make	A's acquaintance	Aと知り合いになる
renew	acquaintance	旧交を温める

▷I **made** the **acquaintance** of a man called Phillip Adams. フィリップ・アダムズという男と知り合いになった
▷I was glad to **renew acquaintance** *with* Christine. クリスティンと旧交を温められてうれしかった

a casual	acquaintance	ちょっとした知人
a business	acquaintance	仕事上の知人
a mutual	acquaintance	共通の知人
a personal	acquaintance	個人的知り合い

▷We had a **mutual acquaintance**, a man named Tim. 私たちには共通の知り合いでティムという男がいた

on	first acquaintance	初めて会ったとき

▷**On first acquaintance** he seemed a really nice guy. 初めて会ったとき彼はとてもよい人に思えた

friends and acquaintances	友人知人

▷Tom held a big party for all his **friends and acquaintances**. トムは友人知人のために盛大なパーティーを開いた

acquire /əkwáiər/ 動 取得する；習得する

easily	acquire	簡単に習得する
rapidly	acquire	すばやく獲得する
recently	acquired	最近取得した
newly	acquired	新しく取得した

▷Our office **recently acquired** two new computers. 最近うちのオフィスに新しいコンピュータを2台入れた

act /ækt/ 名 行為，行い

a criminal	act	犯罪行為
an unlawful	act	不法行為
an illegal	act	
a wrongful	act	不当行為
a conscious	act	意識的な行為
a deliberate	act	意図的な行為
a physical	act	肉体的行為
the sexual	act	性行為
a balancing	act	うまくバランスをとること

▷Do they realize they are committing an **illegal act**? 自分たちのやっているのが不法行為だと彼らはわかっているのか
▷That is not an accident but a **deliberate act** of violence. それは偶然の事故ではなく、計画的な暴力行為だ
▷I need to study hard at school and also do my part-time job. It's a tough **balancing act**! 学校で懸命に勉強してアルバイトもする必要がある。両方のバランスをとるのは難しい

in	the act of doing	…しているところを

▷Ben was caught **in** the **act of** stealing a motorbike. ベンはバイクを盗んだ現行犯でつかまった

act /ækt/ 動 行動する；効く；演じる

act	quickly	すばやく行動する
act	illegally	違法な行為をする
act	reasonably	分別ある行動をとる
act	responsibly	責任ある行動をとる
act	strangely	奇妙な行動をとる
act	suspiciously	あやしい行動をとる
act	independently	自主的に行動する
act	accordingly	ふさわしい行動をとる

▷It is necessary for Japan to **act independently** of U.S. policies. 日本は米国の政策から独立した行動をとる必要がある
▷You're a guest. So I expect you to **act accordingly**! あなたはお客さんなんだから，お客さんらしくふるまってね

act	for A	A(人)の代理を務める
act	on A's behalf	

▷My wife can't be here today so I'm **acting on** her **behalf**. 妻がきょうは来られませんので私が代わりを務めます

act	as if	…のようにふるまう

▷She **acted as if** she was the host. 彼女はまるでホストのようにふるまった

action /ækʃən/ 名 行動, 行為, 活動；訴訟

take	action	行動を起こす

swing into	action	すばやく動く
put A into	action	Aを実行に移す
bring A into	action	
bring	an action	訴訟を起こす

▷It's no good just talking. We need to **take action**. 話しているだけではだめだ．行動に出なくては
▷I'm **putting** my plan **into action**. 計画を実行に移す予定だ
▷He **brought** an **action** *against* his former employers. 彼は以前の雇用主を訴えた

decisive	action	断固とした行動
immediate	action	すばやい行動，迅速
urgent	action	な行動
prompt	action	
concerted	action	協調行動
political	action	政治的行動
disciplinary	action	懲戒処分
legal	action	訴訟，裁判
civil	action	民事裁判
criminal	action	刑事裁判
class	action	集団訴訟

▷**Immediate action** is needed to rescue the survivors. 生存者を救うには迅速な対応が必要とされる
▷This is the time for **prompt action**. すばやい行動をとるときだ
▷I joined an antiwar demonstration. It was the first **political action** of my life. 戦争反対デモに参加した．生まれて初めての政治活動だった
▷The company has taken **disciplinary action** against the employee. 会社は社員を懲戒処分にした
▷They're really angry. I think they're going to take **legal action** against us. 連中はかんかんに怒っているよ．こっちを訴えてくるんじゃないか

a course of	action	行動方針
a man of	action	活動家，行動派

▷What do you think the best **course of action** is? どのような行動方針が最善だと思いますか
▷That's so unlike you! You're a **man of action**. あなたらしくないね．行動的な人なのに

in	action	活動中で，交戦中で
out of	action	活動しない；機能しない

▷She wanted to come and see the project **in action**. 彼女は進行中のプロジェクトを見に来たかった ♦**killed in action** 戦死した ▷He was killed in action in the Second World War. 彼は第2次世界大戦で戦死した
▷He has been **out of action** since August with a knee injury. 彼はひざを痛めて8月から試合を休んでいる
(PHRASES)
Let's have some action. / Let's see some action. ☺ (もたもたしている人に)何かしろよ

active /ǽktiv/ 形 活動的な，積極的な

become	active	活動的になる
remain	active	依然として活発だ

▷Tom **remained active** even after he retired. トムは退職後も依然として活動的だ

physically	active	体をよく動かす
sexually	active	性的に盛んな
economically	active	勤労所得のある
extremely	active	非常に活発な
increasingly	active	ますます活発な

▷I'm not a very **physically active** person at all. あまり体を動かすタイプではない
▷In 1972 only 57 percent of women were **economically active**. 1972年には働いて所得を得ていた女性は57%だけだった
▷She's playing an **increasingly active** role in society. 彼女は社会でますます積極的に活動している

active	in A	Aに積極的な

▷I was very **active in** politics in my twenties. 20代のころ，政治に積極的に参加していた

activity /æktívəti/ 名 活動，活気，活況

conduct	activities	活動を行う
perform	activities	
be involved in	activities	活動にかかわる
take part in	activities	
monitor	activity	活動を監視する

▷It appears these guys were **involved in** criminal **activities**. こいつらは犯罪にかかわっていたようだ
▷We are constantly **monitoring activity** in criminal areas. 犯罪がよく起こる地域を絶えず監視している

criminal	activity	犯罪(行為)
terrorist	activity	テロ活動
mental	activity	精神活動
physical	activity	身体活動
commercial	activity	商業活動
economic	activity	経済活動
political	activity	政治活動
military	activity	軍事活動
seismic	activity	地震活動
volcanic	activity	火山活動

▷He was involved in **criminal activity**. 彼は犯罪

| add |

に巻き込まれた
▷ Recently **economic activity** has been increasing. 最近の経済活動は上向きになってきている
▷ The **volcanic activity** still continues. 火山活動はいまなお続いている

an area of	activity	活動分野
a hive of	activity	活気に満ちた場所

▷ The office was a **hive of activity** as everybody rushed to meet the deadline. 締め切りに間に合わせようとみんな忙しくしていて、オフィスは活気にあふれていた

add /ǽd/ 動 加える

add	considerably	大幅に付け加える
add	hastily	急いで付け加える
add	quickly	

▷ If we stay in a five-star hotel it will **add considerably** to the cost of our holiday! 5つ星ホテルに泊まれば休暇の費用がかなりかさむぞ
▷ "Of course, when I said 'stupid,' I didn't mean you!," he **added hastily**. 「ばかな、と言ったのはもちろんきみのことを言ったのではない」と彼は急いで付け加えた

add A	to B	AをBに加える

▷ Don't **add** any more wine **to** that soup! これ以上ワインをそのスープに加えないで

add	that...	付け加えて…と言う

▷ I'd like to **add that** I totally disagree. 付け加えて申しますが、私は絶対反対です

addition /ədíʃən/

名 付加されたもの；付け加えること；足し算

make	an addition	加える
include	an addition	追加が含まれる
build	an addition	建て増しする
do	addition	足し算する

▷ Ella wants to come on the trip to Hawaii, too, so we need to **make** an **addition** to the list. エラもハワイ旅行に行きたがっているのでリストに加える必要がある
▷ I plan to **build** an **addition** to my house. 家の建て増しを計画している

the latest	addition	最近加わったもの
a recent	addition	
a new	addition	新たな追加、新人
a welcome	addition	ありがたい追加

▷ These are the **new additions** to the contract. 契約の新しい追加条項です
▷ India will be a **welcome addition** to ASEAN. インドが東南アジア諸国連合に加わるのは歓迎すべきことだ

an addition	to A	Aへの追加
in	addition	さらに、その上

▷ China is an **addition to** the list. 中国がリストに追加される
▷ If we're going to Hokkaido, **in addition**, we'll need some warm clothes. 北海道に旅行するなら、暖かい服がさらに必要だ ♦**in addition to** A Aに加えて
▷ In addition to English, she also speaks French. 英語のほかに彼女はフランス語も話す

address /ədrés/ 名 住所；演説

give	one's address	住所を教える
give	an address	演説をする
deliver	an address	

▷ I can **give** you my home **address**. 自宅の住所を教えてあげてもいいですよ
▷ Mr. Cosby stood up to **give** the opening **address**. コスビー氏は開会の辞を述べるために立ち上がった

one's home	address	自宅の住所
one's business	address	職場の住所
a return	address	差出人住所
one's email	address	Eメールアドレス
Web	address	ウェブアドレス
an inaugural	address	就任演説
a keynote	address	基調演説
one's opening	address	開会の辞

▷ What did you feel about President Obama's **inaugural address**? オバマ大統領の就任演説をどのように感じましたか

no fixed	address	住所不定

★新聞記事で用いる

▷ The name of the accused is Paul Robinson, 45, of **no fixed address**. 被告人の名前はポール・ロビンソン 45歳、住所不定

adequate /ǽdikwət/ 形 十分な、適した

perfectly	adequate	まったく十分な
quite	adequate	
barely	adequate	十分ではない
hardly	adequate	

no longer	adequate	もはや十分でない
more than	adequate	十分すぎるほどだ

▷That is a **perfectly adequate** answer to the question. それは質問に対する申し分のない答えだ
▷In Tokyo 100,000 yen is **barely adequate** to live on in a month. 東京で暮らすのに月10万円ではとても足りない
▷Parking space was **more than adequate** to meet the user's needs. 駐車スペースは利用者のニーズを十分満たしていた

be considered	adequate	十分だと考えられる

▷In the West a 10% tip is usually **considered adequate**. 西洋ではふつうチップは1割で十分とされる

adequate	for A	Aに適した

▷The instant camera I bought was **adequate for** most purposes. 私が買ったインスタントカメラはたいていの目的に適っていた

adequate	to do	…するのに十分な

▷The data wasn't **adequate to** draw conclusions. そのデータは結論を出すのに十分でなかった

adjust /ədʒʌ́st/ 動 調整する；順応する

automatically	adjust	自動的に調節する
carefully	adjust	注意深く調節する
easily	adjust	簡単に順応する
quickly	adjust	すぐ順応する

▷Temperatures **automatically adjust** to comfort conditions. 温度は快適な状態に自動的に調節されます
▷Allison **easily adjusted** to the new environment. アリソンは容易に新しい環境に順応した

adjust	to A	Aに順応する
adjust	A to B	AをBに合わせて調整する
adjust	A for B	

▷My eyes quickly **adjusted to** the darkness. 私の目はすぐ暗さに慣れた
▷I **adjusted** the radio **to** the correct station. ラジオ(の周波数)を正しい局に合わせた
▷The interest rate should be **adjusted for** inflation. 金利はインフレに合わせて調整すべきだ

admission /ædmíʃən/ əd-/

名 入るのを許可すること；認めること

apply for	admission	入る申し込みをする
gain	admission	入るのを許可される
refuse	admission	入るのを断る
make	an admission	認める

▷She **applied for admission** to the University of Toronto. 彼女はトロント大学に入学願書を出した
▷I hope to **gain admission** to a foreign university. 外国への大学の入学を希望している
▷He **made** an **admission** of guilt. 彼は罪を認めた

emergency	admission	緊急入院
hospital	admission	入院

▷**Hospital admissions** have increased by thirty percent. 入院患者数は3割増えた

admission	to A	Aへ入るのを許可されること；Aの入場料

▷She died three days after her **admission to** hospital. 彼女は入院の3日後に亡くなった

admit /ædmít/ əd-/ 動 認める

freely	admit	包み隠さず認める
openly	admit	率直に認める
readily	admit	喜んで認める
finally	admit	最後には認める

▷I **freely admit** that may be true. それが真実だろうと率直に認めます
▷He **finally admitted** he'd made a mistake. 間違いを犯したと彼は最後には認めた

admit	(that)...	…だと認める
admit	doing	…したと認める

▷They never **admitted stealing** the money. 彼らは金を盗んだことを決して認めなかった

admit	A to B	A(人)をBに入院させる；入場を可能にする

▷He was **admitted to** hospital with heart problems. 彼は心臓病で入院した

not admit	or deny	認めも否定もしない

▷The bank **didn't admit or deny** fault. 銀行は過失を肯定も否定もしなかった

have to	admit	認めるしかない
must	admit	

▷I **must admit** that I regret not going to university. 大学に行かなかったのを後悔していると認めざるをえません

adopt /ədápt | ədɔ́pt/ 動 採用する, 採択する

formally	adopt	正式に採用する
unanimously	adopt	満場一致で採用する
recently	adopted	最近採用した

▷Our company **formally adopted** a new accounting system last month. わが社は先月新しい会計システムを正式に採用した
▷The motion was **unanimously adopted**. 動議は満場一致で採択された

advance /ædvæns | ədvɑ́:ns/

名 前進；発展, 進歩；前払い金

make	an advance	前進する；発展する

▷India has **made** great **advances** in recent years. インドは近年急速に発展した

a great	advance	大きな進歩
a major	advance	
a significant	advance	著しい
a rapid	advance	急速な進歩
recent	advances	最近の進歩
medical	advances	医学の進歩
scientific	advances	科学の進歩
technical	advances	技術の進歩
technological	advances	科学技術の進歩

▷**Major advances** in technology began in the 1970s. 科学技術の大きな発展は1970年代に始まった
▷Can you keep up with the speed of **technological advances**? 科学技術の進歩についていけるかい

advance	in A	Aの進歩
advance	on A	Aの前払い金
in	advance	前もって

▷**Advances in** medicine are increasing life expectancy. 医学の進歩で平均寿命が伸びつつある
▷Can I get an **advance on** my pay? 給料の前払いをお願いできますか
▷I'll let you know **in advance**. 前もってあなたにお知らせします

advance /ædvæns | ədvɑ́:ns/

動 前進する, 前進させる；進歩する, 進歩させる

advance	rapidly	早く進む；急速に発展する
advance	cautiously	注意深く進む
advance	slowly	ゆっくり進む

▷Toyota's car sales have **advanced rapidly** in the US. トヨタ車の米国での販売数は急速に伸びた

advance	on A	Aに進撃する
advance	into A	Aに侵入する
advance	toward A	Aの方へ進む

▷The Russians **advanced into** Poland in 1944. ロシアは1944年ポーランドに侵攻した
▷She slowly **advanced toward** me. 彼女はゆっくり私の方へやってきた

advanced /ædvænst | ədvɑ́:nst/

形 進歩した, 発展した；上級の

highly	advanced	高度に進んだ
technically	advanced	技術的に進んだ
technologically	advanced	科学技術が進んだ

▷She's able to use **highly advanced** technology. 彼女はきわめて高度な科学技術を使いこなせる
▷My son is much more **technologically advanced** than I am. うちの息子は私よりずっと科学技術に通じている

advantage /ædvæntidʒ | ədvɑ́:n-/

名 優位, 利点, 有利

have	the advantage	優位な点がある
enjoy	an advantage	優位がある
gain	an advantage	優位を得る
give	an advantage	優位を与える
offer	an advantage	優位をもたらす

▷My house **has** the **advantage** *of* being close to everywhere I want to go. 私の家はどこでも行きたい所に近いという利点がある
▷We **gained** a technological **advantage** over our rivals. 科学技術の面でライバルより優位に立った

a distinct	advantage	明かな優位
a significant	advantage	著しい優位
an unfair	advantage	不当な優位
a comparative	advantage	比較優位
a competitive	advantage	競争優位
a political	advantage	政治的優位

▷Sportsmen who take drugs have an **unfair advantage**. 薬を服用する運動選手は不当に優位に立っている

advantage and disadvantage	長所と短所

▷Getting married has both **advantages and disadvantages**. 結婚するのは一長一短だな

[PHRASES]

take advantage of A A(人)につけ込む; A(機会など)を利用する(★advantage は full, maximum, complete とよく結びつく) ▷Tiger Woods took full advantage of the fact that his rivals were nervous. タイガー・ウッズは対戦相手たちが緊張しているのを最大限に利用した

advertisement /ædvərtáizmənt | ədvə́:tis-/

名 広告, 宣伝

place	an advertisement	広告を出す
put	an advertisement	
run	an advertisement	広告を掲載する
publish	an advertisement	
see	an advertisement	広告を見る

▷He **placed an advertisement** in the local newspaper asking for volunteers. 彼はボランティアの募集広告を地元の新聞に出した

▷For further details, **see advertisement**. さらに詳細については広告をご覧ください

an advertisement	appears	広告が出る
an advertisement	features A	広告がAを起用する

▷The **advertisement appeared** on the website last month. その広告は先月ウェブに載った

▷**Advertisements featuring** Ichiro will run in national newspapers. イチローを起用した広告が全国紙に掲載される

an advertisement	for A	Aの広告

▷There are many **advertisements for** part-time jobs in the local newspaper. 地方新聞にはアルバイトの募集広告がたくさん出ている

a full-page	advertisement	全面広告
a newspaper	advertisement	新聞広告
a television	advertisement	テレビ広告
a web	advertisement	ウェブ広告
a job	advertisement	求人広告

advice /ædváis | əd-/ 名 忠告, 助言

give	advice	助言を与える
offer	advice	
get	advice	助言をもらう
obtain	advice	
receive	advice	助言を受ける
seek	advice	助言を求める
ask for	advice	
take	advice	助言を受け入れる
accept	advice	
follow	advice	助言に従う
act on	advice	
disregard	advice	助言を無視する
ignore	advice	
reject	advice	助言をはねつける

▷Could you **give** me some **advice**? 助言をいただけませんか

▷May I **offer** you a piece of **advice**? ひとつ忠告してもいいですか

▷You can **obtain advice** for any problems. どんな問題でも助言を得られる

▷I'm going to **seek advice** from my lawyer. 弁護士に助言を求めるつもりです

▷**Take** my **advice**, go and see a doctor. 私の言うことを聞いて医者に行きなさい

▷If you **follow** my **advice**, you might get the job. 私の言うとおりにすれば仕事が見つかるよ

practical	advice	実際的な助言
general	advice	一般的な助言
impartial	advice	公平な助言
expert	advice	専門家の助言
professional	advice	
financial	advice	財政上の助言
legal	advice	法律上の助言
medical	advice	医学上の助言

▷Where can I get **professional advice** on this? この件に関する専門家のアドバイスはどこで受けられるかな

advice	about A	Aについての助言
advice	on A	

▷Could you give me some **advice on** how to improve my English? どうしたら英語が上達するか助言をいただけませんか

on	A's advice	助言に従って
against	A's advice	助言に逆らって

▷He continued smoking **against** the **advice** *of* his doctor. 彼は医者の忠告も聞かずにたばこを吸い続けた

a piece of	advice	ひとつの助言
a word of	advice	

▷Let me give you a **piece of advice**. ひとつ忠告をさせてください

advise /ædváiz | əd-/ 動 忠告する, 助言する

| affair |

strongly	advise	強く勧める
be well	advised to do	…するのがいい
be ill	advised to do	…するのはまずい

▷I **strongly advise** against visiting that place. その場所へは行かないよう強く勧める
▷You would be **well advised to** start job-hunting immediately. すぐ就職活動を始めるのがいいだろう

advise	A to do	A(人)に…するよう忠告する
advise	A that...	A(人)に…と忠告する

▷I **advised** her **to** speak to her boss. 彼女に上司に話すよう助言した
▷I **advised** him **that** he should take it easy. 彼にのんびりやれと忠告した

affair /əféər/

名 事件；情事；(affairs で)業務, 事情, 情勢

handle	the affair	事件を処理する
investigate	the affair	事件を調査する
have	an affair	浮気する
conduct	one's affairs	業務を行う
manage	one's affairs	業務を処理する
run	one's affairs	

▷His resignation is all very unfortunate. I really don't know how to **handle** the **affair**. 彼の辞任は誠に残念なことだ。どう事態に対処したらよいかわからない
▷Are you going to **have** an **affair** with Robert? ロバートと浮気するつもりなの？
▷Now we're free to **run** our own **affairs**. これで自分たちの業務に取り組める

a love	affair	情事, 浮気
current	affairs	時事問題
public	affairs	公務
domestic	affairs	内政問題
internal	affairs	
foreign	affairs	外交
international	affairs	国際問題

▷The discussion was about **domestic affairs** rather than **international affairs**. 議論は国際問題よりむしろ内政問題についてだった

a state	of affairs	事態, 状況

▷This is a terrible **state of affairs**! ひどい事態だ

affect /əfékt/ 動 影響を及ぼす；心を動かす

significantly	affect	著しい影響を与える
directly	affect	直接の影響を与える
adversely	affect	悪い影響を与える
badly	affect	
seriously	affect	深刻な影響を与える
affect	deeply	深く心を突き動かす

▷Violence in video games **adversely affects** young people. テレビゲームの中の暴力は若者に悪影響を及ぼす
▷The village was **badly affected** by floods. その村は洪水の大被害を受けた
▷Drugs can **seriously affect** your health. 薬物は健康に深刻な影響を及ぼすことがある

afraid /əfréid/ 形 恐れて, 怖がって；心配して

terribly	afraid	とても恐れて

▷I was **terribly afraid** of losing her. 彼女を失うのが怖くてたまらなかった

afraid	of A	Aを恐れる
afraid	of doing	…するのを恐れる
afraid	to do	

▷I can't look down! I'm **afraid of** heights. 下を見られないよ。高所恐怖症なんだ
▷Aren't you **afraid of** dying? 死ぬのが怖くないのかい
▷I'm **afraid to** take risks. 危険を冒すのが怖い

afraid	that...	…ではないかと心配して

▷She was **afraid that** something was going to happen to Charles. 彼女はチャールズに何か起こるのではないかと心配していた

PHRASES
Don't be afraid to do ☺ …するのを恐れるな ▷Don't be afraid to ask questions. 質問するのを恐れるな
I'm afraid (that)... ☺ (好ましくないことについて)…と思う, 残念ながら(…だ) ▷I'm afraid I have some bad news (for you). 悪い知らせがあります ▷I'm afraid I'm very busy. 申し訳ありませんがとても忙しいのです
♦**I'm afraid so.** ☺ 残念ながらそうです ▷"Do you really have to go now?" "I'm afraid so." 「本当に行かなくちゃいけないの」「残念ながらそうなんです」
♦**I'm afraid not.** ☺ 残念ながらそうではありません ▷"So you can't help me?" "I'm afraid not." 「それじゃ, 私を助けてくれないの？」「悪いけど無理です」
♦**I'm afraid to say (that)...** 申し上げにくいのですが…です ▷I'm afraid to say I'll have to cancel our appointment. 約束をキャンセルしなければなりません

age /éidʒ/ 名 年齢；時代；長い間

reach	the age of A	Aの年齢に達する
act	one's age	年相応にふるまう
look	one's age	年相応に見える
feel	one's age	年齢を感じる
raise	the age of A	Aの年齢を引き上げる
lower	the age of A	Aの年齢を引き下げる

▷ I've **reached** the **age** of fifty. 私は50歳になった
▷ Can't you **act** your **age**? 年相応にふるまえないのか
▷ **Raising** the **age** of retirement won't solve the problems. 退職年齢を上げても問題は解決しないだろう

a young	age	若い年齢
an early	age	
middle	age	中年
old	age	老年
a ripe (old)	age	高齢, 老齢
working	age	生産年齢
an average	age	平均年齢
a golden	age	黄金時代
the Ice	Age	氷河期
the Stone	Age	石器時代

▷ I got married at the very **young age** of 18. 私は18という若さで結婚した
▷ He showed his talent for music at an **early age**. 彼は幼くして音楽の才能を示した ▷ George Martin died of **old age**. ジョージ・マーティンは老衰で亡くなった
▷ He died at the **ripe old age** of 90. 彼は90歳という高齢で亡くなった ▷ At the **ripe old age** of 22, I thought I knew everything. 22という円熟の年齢なら何でもわかると思っていたよ(★ユーモアで若い人にも用いる)
▷ The **average age** of the group is 45. グループの平均年齢は45歳だ
▷ The first **golden age** was in the '30s and '40s. 最初の黄金時代は30年代, 40年代だった

at	the age of A	Aの年齢で
over	the age of A	Aの年齢を超えて
under	the age of A	Aの年齢未満で

▷ He left home **at** the **age of** eighteen. 彼は18歳で家を出た
▷ Travel is free to all people **over** the **age of** 65. 乗り物は65歳を超えた方は無料です
▷ Children **under** the **age of** eight must be accompanied by an adult. 8歳未満のお子様は大人の同伴が必要です

for	ages	長い間
for	one's age	年の割に
with	age	年とともに
of	all ages	あらゆる年代の

▷ I haven't seen you **for ages**. お久しぶりです
▷ She looks young **for** her **age**. 彼女は年の割には若く見える
▷ Wisdom comes **with age**. 知恵は年とともに身についてくる
▷ Love songs are popular with people **of all ages**. ラブソングはあらゆる年代の人々に人気がある

aggressive /əgrésiv/

形 攻撃的な；積極的な

become	aggressive	攻撃的になる
get	aggressive	
look	aggressive	攻撃的に見える

▷ When my dog meets another dog she immediately **becomes aggressive**. うちの犬はほかの犬と出会うとすぐ攻撃する

extremely	aggressive	非常に攻撃的な
highly	aggressive	かなり攻撃的な
particularly	aggressive	特に攻撃的な
increasingly	aggressive	ますます攻撃的な

▷ My grandson's behavior has become **increasingly aggressive**. 孫の態度がますます攻撃的になった

aggressive	toward A	Aに対して攻撃的な

▷ Why is she so **aggressive toward** David? なぜ彼女はデイビッドに対してそんなに攻撃的なのか

agree /əgríː/ 動 同意する, 賛成する

totally	agree	まったく賛成する
entirely	agree	
wholeheartedly	agree	心から賛成する
finally	agree	とうとう賛成する
reluctantly	agree	しぶしぶ賛成する
be generally	agreed	広く同意される

★ entirely, completely, reluctantly, wholeheartedly は動詞の後でも用いる

▷ I **totally agree** with you. まったくあなたに賛成です
▷ I **agree wholeheartedly** with the ideas you expressed in your report. 報告書であなたが表明した考えに心から賛成します
▷ Troy **agreed reluctantly** to attend the party. トロイはしぶしぶパーティーへの出席に同意した
▷ It's **generally agreed** that global warming is a major problem. 地球温暖化が重大な問題であることでほぼ意見が一致している

agree	with A	Aに賛成する

| agreement |

agree	on A	Aについて合意する
agree	about A	
agree	to A	Aに同意する

▷I **agree with** you about the danger of smoking. 喫煙の危険性についてあなたと同意見です
▷OK! OK! I'll **agree to** anything. Just leave me alone! わかった，わかった．何にでも賛成するからほうっておいてくれ

agree	that...	…ということに賛成する
agree	to do	…することに賛成する

▷It was **agreed that** we should advertise for more staff. スタッフ増員の募集を出すことで意見が一致した
▷They **agreed to** give me a chance. 彼らはぼくにチャンスを与えることに同意した

PHRASES
Don't you agree? 😊 そう思わないか ▷Life is full of mysteries, don't you agree? 人生は不思議なことだらけだね，そう思わないか
I couldn't agree more. 😊 まったく賛成だ

agreement /əgríːmənt/

名 協定，契約；意見の一致，同意

enter into	an agreement	契約を締結する
conclude	an agreement	契約を結ぶ
reach	an agreement	
sign	an agreement	契約に署名する
have	an agreement	契約がある
violate	an agreement	契約に違反する
reach	(an) agreement	合意に達する
come to	an agreement	

▷We're delighted to have **reached** an **agreement** with management. 経営側と協定を結べて喜んでいる
▷We **had** an **agreement** to pay £500 a month to him. 彼に月500ポンド払うことになっていた
▷We have **signed** an **agreement** with that company. その会社との合意書に署名した

a peace	agreement	平和協定
a trade	agreement	貿易協定

▷Finally the two countries signed a **peace agreement**. ついに両国は平和協定に署名した

in	agreement	同意して
under	an agreement	協定に基づいて

▷Emily nodded **in agreement**. エミリーは同意してうなずいた
▷**Under** an **agreement** signed in 1950, the United States had been supplying economic aid to Laos. 1950年に調印された協定に基づいて米国はラオスに経済援助をしていた

aid /éid/ 名 援助，支援；補助となるもの

provide	aid	援助する
give	aid	
receive	aid	援助を受ける
get	aid	
seek	the aid of A	A(人)に援助を求める
enlist	the aid of A	
go to	A's aid	A(人)に援助に行く
come to	A's aid	

▷We **provided aid** to the tsunami victims. 津波の犠牲者に援助をした
▷3% of people **received aid** from the government. 3％の人が政府から援助を受けた

emergency	aid	緊急援助
humanitarian	aid	人道的援助
economic	aid	経済的援助
financial	aid	財政的援助
medical	aid	医療援助
military	aid	軍事援助
foreign	aid	海外援助
overseas	aid	
international	aid	国際援助
teaching	aids	教材

▷The U.S. provides **foreign aid** to India. 米国はインドに海外援助をしている

in	aid of A	Aを援助するための
with	the aid of A	Aの助けを借りて
without	the aid of A	Aの助けを借りずに

▷On Sunday we'll have a charity concert **in aid of** the victims. 日曜日に犠牲者を援助するためのチャリティコンサートを行います
▷He slowly stood up **with** the **aid of** his cane. 彼は杖に頼ってゆっくり立ち上がった

aim /éim/ 名 目的，目標，ねらい；的(まと)

achieve	one's aim	目標を達成する
fulfill	one's aim	
pursue	one's aim	目標を追求する
take	aim	ねらいを定める

▷We hope to **achieve** our **aim** by 2013. 2013年ま

でに目標を達成させたいと思っている
▷He **took aim** *at* the target and fired. 的にねらいを定めて撃った

the main	aim	主要目標
the principal	aim	
the primary	aim	第一の目標
the ultimate	aim	究極の目標
a long-term	aim	長期目標
a short-term	aim	短期目標

▷The **main aim** of this event is to get to know each other. この催しの主要目的はお互いに親しくなることです
▷As a **long-term aim**, the government will seek to raise the employment rate to 80%. 長期目標として政府は就業率を80％まで上げることを目指すだろう

with	the **aim of** do**ing**	…する目的で

▷I stayed in Australia for two years **with** the **aim of** study**ing** business English. ビジネス英語を勉強する目的でオーストラリアに2年間滞在した

aim /éim/ 動 目標にする, 目指す；ねらう

aim	**to** do	…しようとする

▷That's what I **aim to** do. それが私の目標です

aim	**at** A	Aをねらう
aim	**for** A	Aをねらう；Aを目指す

▷We're **aiming for** a big improvement in sales this year. 今年度の売上高の大幅な改善を目指している
(PHRASES)
be aimed at A Aを対象にしている

be aimed	**primarily at** A	おもにA向けである
be aimed	**mainly at** A	
be aimed	**specifically at** A	特にA向けである

★これらの副詞はそれぞれ動詞の前でも用いる

▷Our sales campaign was **aimed primarily at** young teenagers. われわれの販売キャンペーンはおもに10代の若者を対象にしている

air /έər/ 名 空気, 大気；空中, 空

breathe in	the air	空気を吸い込む
fill	the air	辺りを満たす
hang in	the air	辺りにただよう

▷The smell of strawberry **filled** the **air**. イチゴのにおいが辺りに満ちた

clean	air	きれいな空気
fresh	air	新鮮な空気
damp	air	湿った空気
thin	air	薄い大気

▷Let's go out and get some **fresh air**. 外に出て新鮮な空気に触れよう

by	air	飛行機で, 航空便で
in	the air	空中に
into	the air	
on	(the) air	放送中で
off	(the) air	放送されていない

▷How long do you think it would take **by air** to Sidney? 飛行機でシドニーまで何時間くらいかな
▷He threw it high **in** the **air**. それを空高く投げた
▷The CTV Network goes **on air** in September. CTVネットワークは9月に放送を開始する

alarm /əlá:rm/ 名 警報器, 目覚まし；不安

cause	alarm	不安を引き起こす
raise	the alarm	警告を発する
sound	the alarm	
set off	an alarm	警報器を鳴らす
trigger	an alarm	
set	the alarm	目覚ましをセットする

▷There's a fire! Quick! **Raise** the **alarm**! 火事だ, 急げ. 警報を出して
▷I **set off** the **alarm** as soon as I realized the situation. 状況を把握してすぐ警報器を鳴らした
▷I **set** my **alarm** *for* seven o'clock. 7時に目覚ましをセットした

an alarm	goes off	アラームが鳴る
an alarm	sounds	
an alarm	rings	

▷My alarm didn't **go off**. 目覚ましが鳴らなかった

a false	alarm	誤った警報, 誤報
a fire	alarm	火災報知機
a smoke	alarm	煙探知機
a burglar	alarm	盗難警報器

▷It turned out to be a **false alarm**. 誤報だとわかった

album /ǽlbəm/ 名 アルバム

make	an album	アルバムをつくる
record	an album	アルバムを録音する
release	an album	アルバムを発売する

▷He recently **released** an **album** of his own songs. 彼は最近，自作曲を入れたアルバムをリリースした

| an album | comes out | アルバムが発表される |

▷The album **comes out** tomorrow. そのアルバムはあす出ることになっている

a debut	album	デビューアルバム
a solo	album	ソロアルバム
the latest	album	最新アルバム
a photo	album	写真アルバム

▷His **latest album** contains 22 tracks. 彼の最新アルバムには22曲入っている

alert /ələ́ːrt/ 名 警戒態勢，警戒警報

issue	an alert	警戒警報を出す
put out	an alert	
trigger	an alert	警戒態勢を敷く

▷The local government has **issued** a new **alert** about flu. 地方自治体はインフルエンザに関する新たな警戒警報を出した

(a) red	alert	厳戒態勢
(a) flood	alert	洪水警報
a smog	alert	スモッグ警報
a security	alert	警戒警報
a terror	alert	テロ警戒警報

▷The airport was on a **red alert**. 空港は厳戒態勢をとっていた
▷Many parts of Britain were put on **flood alert**. イギリスの多くの地域に洪水警報が出されていた

| on | the alert | 待機して，備えて |
| on | (full) alert | 厳戒態勢をとって |

▷The police were **on full alert**. 警察は厳戒態勢をとっていた

alive /əláiv/ 形 生きている；現存の

stay	alive	生き延びる
keep A	alive	A(人)を生かしておく
be buried	alive	生き埋めになる
come	alive	活気づく，生き生きする

▷Please doctor, **keep** him **alive** somehow. 先生，なんとか彼の命を救ってください
▷Your sister **comes alive** when she performs on stage, doesn't she? きみの姉さんは舞台で演じているとき生き生きしているね

| still | alive | まだ生きている |
| very much | alive | 元気そのもので |

▷He looks **very much alive**. 彼は元気そのものだ

| alive and well | | 生き残って，健在な |
| alive and kicking | | 元気な，ぴんぴんした |

▷Thank goodness you're **alive and well**. あなたが無事に生きていてくれてよかった
▷He wasn't dead. He was **alive and kicking**. 彼は死んだどころか，元気でぴんぴんしていた

| alive | with A | Aでにぎわっている |
| alive | to A | Aに敏感な |

▷Her eyes were **alive with** happiness. 彼女の目は幸せでいっぱいだった
▷Employers should be **alive to** their responsibilities. 雇用者は自らの責任について敏感でなくてはならない

| lucky | to be alive | 幸運にも生き延びる |

▷You're **lucky to be alive**. あなたは幸運にも生き延びた

PHRASES⟩
Look alive! ☺ しゃきっとしなさい

allow /əláu/ 動 許す

| allow | A to do | A(人)に…するのを許す |

▷You know my parents don't **allow** me **to** smoke. たばこはだめって親が言うんだよ

| allow | A in | Aが入るのを許す |
| allow | A out | Aが出るのを許す |

▷She **allowed** him **in** the apartment. 彼女を彼をアパートに入れた

alone /əlóun/ 形 一人の，単独の；ただ…だけの

all	alone	まったくひとりの，
completely	alone	まったく孤独の
quite	alone	

▷I was left **all alone**. 私はひとり取り残された
▷She was **completely alone** in the dark. 彼女は暗がりの中でまったくひとりぼっちだった

leave A	alone	Aをそのままにしておく
let A	alone	
stand	alone	孤立している

▷**Leave** me **alone**! ほうっておいてくれ
▷Remember. You don't **stand alone**. All your friends are supporting you. 覚えておいて，きみはひとりじゃないんだ．友人たちみんなが応援しているよ

alone	with A	Aと二人きりで

▷Do you mind if I speak **alone with** Laura for a moment? ローラと二人だけでちょっと話してもいいですか

alone	in the world	天涯孤独で

▷She had lost everything. She was **alone in the world**. 彼女はすべてを失って，天涯孤独だった

PHRASES
You're not alone. 😊 あなただけではありません ▷Still nervous? Don't worry. You're not alone. まだ緊張しているの？心配いらないよ，みんな同じだから

alter /ɔ́ːltər/ 動 変える，改める

radically	alter	根本的に変える，
drastically	alter	大きく変える
significantly	alter	

▷The attacks of 9/11 **radically altered** the security situation. 9.11のテロ攻撃以降，警備体制は抜本的に見直された
▷The Meiji Restoration **significantly altered** the culture and life style of the Japanese. 明治維新は日本人の文化や生活様式を大きく変えた

alternative /ɔːltə́ːrnətiv | ɔːl-/

名 選択肢，代案；新しい手段

provide	an alternative	代案を提示する
offer	an alternative	

▷Rail travel could **offer** a cheaper **alternative** *to* air travel. 鉄道の旅は空の旅に代わる，より安価な手段となるだろう

a good	alternative	よい代案
an effective	alternative	有効な代案
a suitable	alternative	適切な代案

a practical	alternative	実際的な代案
a viable	alternative	実現可能な代案

▷I'm looking for any other **viable alternative**. ほかの実現可能な代替手段を探している

alternative	to A	Aの代わりの手段

▷There's no **alternative to** closing down the business. 廃業する以外に選択肢はない

ambition /æmbíʃən/ 名 野心，大望

have	(an) ambition	野心がある
achieve	one's ambition	念願を達成する
fullfill	one's ambition	
realize	one's ambition	

▷I **have** big **ambitions** in my life. 私には人生に大きな野心がある
▷I chose to move here to **fulfill** a lifetime **ambition**. 一生の念願を達成するためにここに移る選択をした

(a) big	ambition	大きな野心
(a) great	ambition	
(a) burning	ambition	燃えるような野心
(a) lifelong	ambition	生涯にわたる野心
(a) personal	ambition	個人的な野心
(a) political	ambition	政治的な野心

▷Do you know what the **biggest ambition** of my life was? 私の人生最大の野心は何だったかわかるかい
▷She had no **personal ambitions** or dreams. 彼女には個人的な野心や夢はなかった

ambition	to do	…するという野心

▷Fred has a burning **ambition to** be a professional engineer. フレッドはプロのエンジニアになりたいという燃えるような志をもっている

ambulance /ǽmbjuləns/ 名 救急車

call	an ambulance	救急車を呼ぶ
get	an ambulance	

▷**Call** an **ambulance**! 救急車を呼べ

by	ambulance	救急車で

▷He was taken **by ambulance** to the nearest hospital. 彼は救急車でいちばん近くの病院に運ばれた

amount /əmáunt/ 名 量

increase	the amount	量を増やす
reduce	the amount	量を減らす

▷You need to **reduce** the **amount** of fast food that you eat. あなたは食べるファーストフードの量を減らす必要がある

a considerable	amount	かなりの量
a substantial	amount	
an enormous	amount	大量
a huge	amount	
a large	amount	
a small	amount	少量
an equal	amount	同量
a reasonable	amount	まずまずの量
a generous	amount	豊富な量
the full	amount	総額；総量
the total	amount	
a maximum	amount	最大限の量
a minimum	amount	最小限の量
a certain	amount	ある一定量

★ amount of の後には money など不可算名詞がくる。数えられる名詞のときは a large number of students のように number を用いる

▷I've spent a **considerable amount** of time thinking about it. それについて考えるのにかなりの時間を費やした
▷We've managed to save a **reasonable amount** of money. なんとかまずまずのお金を節約した
▷This stew tastes better if you sprinkle in a **generous amount** of salt. 塩をたっぷりかけるとこのシチューはさらに味がよくなる
▷We still don't know the **total amount** of money that has been stolen. 盗まれた総額はまだわからない
▷If he'd made a **minimum amount** of effort, he would have passed the exam. 最小限の努力でもしていたら彼は試験に合格していただろう
▷He has a **certain amount** of talent. 彼にはある程度の才能がある

analysis /ənǽləsis/ 名 分析

make	an analysis	分析する
perform	an analysis	
carry out	an analysis	

▷It's always better to **make** an **analysis** of past projects. 過去の事業計画を分析することは常により好ましいことだ

(a) careful	analysis	念入りな分析
(a) detailed	analysis	詳細な分析
(a) systematic	analysis	系統的な分析
(a) comparative	analysis	比較分析
(a) quantitative	analysis	定量分析
(a) qualitative	analysis	定性分析
(a) statistical	analysis	統計的分析
(a) theoretical	analysis	理論的分析
(a) historical	analysis	歴史的分析
(a) data	analysis	データ分析
(a) chemical	analysis	化学的分析

▷I have a **detailed analysis** of all the possibilities. あらゆる可能性について詳細な分析結果をもっている
▷These surprising results were obtained from a **statistical analysis** of the data. これらの驚くべき結果はデータの統計的分析から得られた
▷We need a more thorough **data analysis** than this. これよりさらに十分なデータ分析が必要だ

angry /ǽŋgri/ 形 怒った

get	angry	怒る
become	angry	
feel	angry	怒りを感じる
look	angry	怒っているようだ
sound	angry	
make A	angry	A(人)を怒らせる

▷There's no point in **getting angry**. 怒ってもむだだ
▷Don't **make** him **angry**. He has a terrible temper! 彼を怒らせるな．すごく短気だから

really	angry	ひどく怒っている
extremely	angry	
furiously	angry	怒り狂っている

▷Mac was **extremely angry** with Jake. マックはジェイクのことをすごく怒っていた
▷He was **furiously angry** and even violent. 彼は怒り狂って，いまにも暴力をふるいそうだった

angry	about A	Aに腹を立てる
angry	at A	
angry	with A	A(人)に腹を立てる

▷I'm sorry you feel so **angry about** what I did. 私の行為にご立腹されたようで申し訳ありません
▷I thought you were really **angry at** Kate. きみがケイトのことをすごく怒っていると思ったよ
▷Simon, please don't get **angry with** me. サイモン，お願いだからぼくのことを怒らないで

ankle /ǽŋkl/ 名 足首, くるぶし

break	an ankle	足首を骨折する
injure	an ankle	足首をけがする
sprain	an ankle	足首をねんざする
twist	an ankle	

▷I **broke** my **ankle** and couldn't walk for a week. 足首を骨折して1週間歩けなかった
▷I fell and **sprained** my **ankle**. 転んで足首をねんざした

anniversary /æ̀nəvə́ːrsəri/ 名 記念日

mark	the anniversary	記念日を祝う
celebrate	the anniversary	

▷Next year **marks** the 50th **anniversary** *of* our company. 来年はわが社の50周年だ

A's wedding	anniversary	結婚記念日
A's golden	anniversary	結婚50周年記念

▷It's Tom and Sarah's **wedding anniversary** tomorrow. あすはトムとサラの結婚記念日だ

announce /ənáuns/ 動 発表する, 公表する

recently	announced	最近発表した

▷Ford **recently announced** it will close four factories. フォードは4つの工場を閉鎖すると近ごろ発表した

announce	that...	…と発表する

▷I'd like to **announce that** Phillip and I have become engaged. フィリップと私との婚約をお知らせいたします

announcement /ənáunsmənt/ 名 発表

make	an announcement	発表する

▷Ladies and gentlemen, I would like to **make** an **announcement** to all of you. 皆さん、お知らせしたいことがあります

an official	announcement	公式発表
a public	announcement	一般向け発表

▷The **official announcement** will be made tomorrow morning. 公式発表はあすの朝です

announcement	about A	Aについての発表
announcement	by A	Aによる発表
announcement	from A	Aからの発表

▷No **announcement about** an investigation has been made. 調査についてまだ何の発表もない

an announcement	that...	…という発表

▷There was a sudden **announcement that** the next train was delayed by 20 minutes due to the snow. 次の列車は雪で20分遅れるとのアナウンスが突然あった

answer /ǽnsər | áːn-/ 名 答え, 返事

get	an answer	返事をもらう
receive	an answer	
wait for	an answer	返事を待つ
give	an answer	返事をする；答えを示す
provide	an answer	
have	an answer	返事がある；答えがある
know	the answer	返事がわかる；答えがわかる
find	an answer	答えを見つける

▷I'll call you back when I **get** an **answer** from her. 彼女から返事をもらったら折り返しきみに電話するよ
▷Come on, **give** me a straight **answer**. おい、率直に答えてくれよ
▷I cannot **provide** an **answer** to explain how it happened. なぜそんなことが起こったのか説明できる答えがない
▷I don't need to ask her. I already **know** the **answer**. 彼女に聞く必要はない。もう返事はわかっているよ

a short	answer	短い返事
a straight	answer	率直な返事
a clear	answer	明快な返事；明確な答え
an obvious	answer	
a simple	answer	単純な答え
the perfect	answer	完璧な答え
the right	answer	正しい答え
a correct	answer	

▷My **obvious answer** is "No." 私の明確な返事はノーです
▷Does anyone know the **right answer**? だれか正答を知っていますか

the answer	to A	Aに対する答え

▷I want to know the **answer to** the question. その問題の解答を知りたい

| answer |

answer /ǽnsər | ά:n-/ 動 答える；解く

answer	correctly	正確に答える
answer	immediately	すぐ答える
answer	quickly	
answer	simply	簡単に答える
answer	truthfully	正直に答える
answer	honestly	

★correctly, immediately, quickly, simply, truthfully, honestly は動詞の前でも用いる

▷She wouldn't give any reasons why, she **simply answered** "No." 彼女は理由を言おうとせず，簡単に「ノー」と答えただけだった

answer	that...	…だと答える

▷He quickly **answered that** everything was going great. すべてとても順調だと彼は即答した

anxious /ǽŋkʃəs/ 形 心配な；切望して

become	anxious	心配になる
get	anxious	
feel	anxious	心配する
look	anxious	心配そうに見える

▷I **feel** really **anxious** about going to the dentist. 歯医者に行くのが本当に心配だ

desperately	anxious	切に願っている
particularly	anxious	特に願っている

▷He was **particularly anxious** to meet you. 彼は特にあなたに会いたがっていた

anxious	about A	Aのことが心配な
anxious	for A	Aを切望して

▷I'm a little **anxious about** the coming meeting. 今度の会議のことが少し心配だ
▷He was **anxious for** her answer. 彼は彼女の返事を待ち望んでいた

anxious	to do	…することを願っている
anxious	that...	…であることを願っている

▷John's **anxious that** everything should be perfect. ジョンは何の手落ちもないよう願っている

apartment /əpά:rtmənt/ 名 アパート

look for	an apartment	アパートを探す
rent	an apartment	アパートを借りる
move into	an apartment	アパートに引っ越す
leave	an apartment	アパートから引っ越す
move out of	an apartment	
share	an apartment	アパートに共同で住む

▷Tony has **moved into** a small **apartment**. トニーは小さなアパートに引っ越した
▷I'll be **sharing** a three-bedroom **apartment** with Bobby. 3部屋のアパートをボビーと共同で使うことになるだろう

a high-rise	apartment	高層アパート
a luxury	apartment	豪華なアパート
a rented	apartment	賃貸アパート
a self-catering	apartment	自炊式の宿泊施設

▷My family lives in a huge **high-rise apartment**. 私の家族は大きな高層アパートに住んでいる
▷Accommodation in a **self-catering apartment** for seven cost €220 each. 7人用の自炊式アパートの宿泊費用はひとり220ユーロだった

apologize /əpάlədʒáiz | əpɔ́l-/ 動 謝る

apologize	sincerely	心から謝る
apologize	profusely	深くわびる
apologize	unreservedly	全面的に謝る
apologize	personally	個人的に謝る
apologize	publicly	公式に謝る

▷I **apologize unreservedly** *for* what I did. 私の行為を全面的におわびします

must	apologize	謝らなければならない

▷I'm sorry I'm late. I really **must apologize**. 遅れてすみません．ほんとうに申し訳ありません

apologize	for A	Aを謝る
apologize	to A	A(人)に謝る

▷I want to **apologize to** you, Jake. ジェイク，あなたに謝りたいの

apology /əpάlədʒi | əpɔ́l-/ 名 謝罪，陳謝

make	an apology	謝罪する
demand	an apology	謝罪を求める
accept	A's apology	謝罪を受け入れる

▷I think you should **make** an **apology**. あなたは謝ったほうがいいと思う
▷Please **accept** my **apologies**. おわび申し上げます

a public	apology	公の謝罪
one's sincere	apologies	心からの謝罪

▷The government minister was forced to make a **public apology**. 大臣は公式に謝罪せざるをえなかった
▷I'd like to offer my **sincere apologies**. 心から謝罪申し上げます

an apology	for A	Aに対する謝罪
an apology	from A	Aからの謝罪
apologies	to A	Aへの謝罪

▷I think you owe me an **apology for** rudeness. 失礼な態度をとったことを私に謝ってもらいたい
▷We've received a written **apology from** the company. 会社から書面で謝罪を受け取った

a letter of	apology	わび状

▷I think we need to write a **letter of apology**. わび状を書く必要があると思う

apparent /əpǽrənt/ 形 明らかな,明白な

immediately	apparent	すぐに明らかな

▷The mistakes in the design of the car were not **immediately apparent**. 車の設計ミスはすぐには明らかにならなかった

apparent	that...	…は明らかな

▷If you read the essay it's clearly **apparent that** it has been copied from the Internet. そのレポートを読めばインターネットからコピーしたことがよくわかる

appeal /əpíːl/ 名 訴え,懇願;魅力;上訴

have	appeal	人気がある
broaden	one's appeal	人気を広める
widen	one's appeal	
make	an appeal	懇願する,訴える
launch	an appeal	呼びかける
lodge	an appeal	上訴する
dismiss	the appeal	上訴を棄却する

▷That story **had** particular **appeal** *for* young female readers. その物語は若い女性の読者に特に人気があった
▷He **made** an **appeal** *for* more money. 彼はさらなる資金援助を訴えた
▷The agency **launched** an urgent **appeal** *for* donations to help the victims. その機関は犠牲者を援助するために緊急の募金を呼びかけた
▷The court **dismissed** the **appeal**. 裁判所は上訴を棄却した

popular	appeal	大衆的な人気
broad	appeal	幅広い人気
sex	appeal	性的魅力
an urgent	appeal	緊急の訴え

▷Miyazaki's movies have wide **popular appeal**. 宮崎の映画は大衆的な人気がある
▷Leonardo DiCaprio has lots of **sex appeal**. レオナルド・ディカプリオは性的魅力にあふれている

an appeal	for A	Aを求める訴え
an appeal	to A	Aへの訴え

▷They put **appeals for** information into the newspapers. 情報提供の呼びかけを新聞に出した

appeal /əpíːl/ 動 求める,頼む;訴える

appeal	directly	直訴する
appeal	strongly	強く訴える
urgently	appeal	緊急に訴える

▷He **appealed directly** to the company president to improve working conditions. 彼は労働条件の改善を社長に直訴した

appeal	to A	A(人)に訴える
appeal	for A	Aを求める

▷Your sense of humor doesn't quite **appeal to** me. きみのユーモアセンスはいまひとつぼくにはピンと来ない
▷He **appealed to** us **for** help. 彼はわれわれに助けを求めた

appeal	to A to do	A(人)に…するよう求める

▷We **appeal to** everybody **to** support this event. この催しを支持してくださるようみなさんに強く訴えます

appear /əpíər/

動 …のように見える,らしい;現れる;出演する

suddenly	appear	突然現れる
appear	regularly	定期的に出演する

▷Oprah Winfrey **appears regularly** on American TV. オプラ・ウィンフリーはアメリカのテレビにレギュラー

| appearance |

出演している

appear	to do	…するように見える
It appears	that...	…と見える

▷He **appeared to** ignore her. 彼は彼女を無視しているように見えた
▷**It appears that** I was wrong. 私は間違っていたようだ

appearance /əpíərəns/

名 現れること，出現，出演；外見，外観

give	the appearance of A	Aに見せかける
keep up	appearances	外見を繕う
improve	(A's) appearance	外見をよくする
make	an appearance	顔を出す；出演する
put in	an appearance	顔を出す

▷He **gave** the **appearance of** being wealthy. 彼は金持ちのように見せかけた
▷He tried his best to **keep up appearances**. 彼は体裁をつくろうのに必死だった
▷The party will be held next Saturday. We have to **make** an **appearance**. パーティーが次の土曜日にあるので，顔を出さなければなりません

an attractive	appearance	魅力的な外見
physical	appearance	容姿
personal	appearance	身だしなみ
one's first	appearance	初登場
a public	appearance	公の場への登場
a television	appearance	テレビ出演
a TV	appearance	

▷Maybe she doesn't care about your **physical appearance**. たぶん彼女はきみの容姿は気にしていないよ
▷He paid little attention to his own **personal appearance**. 彼は自分の身なりにほとんど気を配らなかった
▷I don't really like to make **public appearances**. 人がたくさんいる場所に顔を出すのは好きではない
▷Justin often makes **TV appearances**. ジャスティンはしばしばテレビに出ている

in	appearance	見たところ，外見上
by	all appearances	どう見ても
to	all appearances	

▷Everyone lives a happy life, at least **in appearance**. みんな幸せな人生を送っている，少なくとも見た目にはそう映る
▷Jack was **to all appearances** asleep. ジャックはどう見ても眠っていた

appearance and behavior	身なりとふるまい

▷Every detail of his **appearance and behavior** was noted in her mind. 彼の身なりとふるまいは細部に至るまで彼女の心に刻み込まれた

appetite /ǽpətàit/ 名 食欲；欲求，欲望

have	an appetite	食欲がある；欲求がある
lose	one's appetite	食欲をなくす；欲求をなくす
ruin	one's appetite	食欲をなくさせる
spoil	one's appetite	
give	an appetite	食欲を出させる；欲求を与える
whet	A's appetite	欲求をそそる
satisfy	A's appetite	食欲を満たす；欲求を満たす

▷He **has** a good **appetite** and loves roast chicken dinners. 彼は食欲が旺盛で，ローストチキンのディナーが大好きだ
▷The champagne **gave** me an **appetite**. シャンパンを飲んだら食欲が出た
▷I think that article on Bali will **whet** your **appetite**. バリ島に関するその記事はあなたの欲求をかき立てるだろう

a good	appetite	旺盛な食欲
a healthy	appetite	
a big	appetite	
an insatiable	appetite	すごい食欲；飽くなき欲求
a poor	appetite	あまりない食欲
a voracious	appetite	激しい食欲
a great	appetite	
an increasing	appetite	高まる欲求
sexual	appetite	性欲

▷They all ate and drank with a **great appetite**. 彼らは旺盛な食欲で飲み食いした
▷They have an **insatiable appetite** *for* fame and success. 彼らには名声と成功への飽くなき欲求がある
▷I have a **poor appetite**. 食欲があまりない
▷The public showed an **increasing appetite** *for* light comedy on TV. 一般の人々はますますテレビで軽いコメディーを見たがるようになった

a loss of	appetite	食欲不振
a lack of	appetite	

▷You should see a doctor about your **loss of ap-**

petite. 食欲不振の原因を医者に診てもらったほうがいい

application /æpləkéiʃən/

名 申し込み，申請；申込書；適用，応用

make	an application	申請をする
submit	an application	申請書を提出する
fill out	an application	申請書に記入する
《英》fill in	an application	
accept	an application	申請を受ける
approve	an application	申請を認める
grant	an application	
turn down	an application	申請を拒絶する
reject	an application	
run	applications	アプリを実行する

▷She **made** an **application** *for* a visa. 彼女はビザの申請をした
▷The company **submitted** a planning **application** to the City Hall. 会社は計画の申請書を市役所に提出した

practical	application	実地への応用，実用化

▷We have to consider the **practical application** of this discovery. われわれはこの発見の実用化を検討しなくてはならない

the application	for A	Aの申し込み

▷We've received over 200 **applications for** this job. この仕事に200を超える申し込みがあった

apply /əplái/

動 申請する；当てはまる；適用する；塗る

apply	equally	等しく当てはまる
apply	directly	直接塗る
apply	evenly	均等に塗る
successfully	apply	うまく応用する
no longer	apply	もはや当てはまらない

▷His comment **applies equally** *to* non-Japanese citizens. 彼のコメントは日本人でない人にも同様に当てはまる
▷These cosmetics are **applied directly** *to* your skin. これらの化粧品は直接お肌に塗っていただけます
▷The theory has been **successfully applied** in business. その理論はビジネスにうまく応用された
▷The old rules **no longer apply**. 古いルールはもはや当てはまらない

apply	for A	Aを申し込む

apply	to A	Aに出願する；Aに適用できる
apply	A to B	AをBに応用する；AをBに塗る

▷This passport is out of date. You'll need to **apply for** a new one. このパスポートは期限切れです。新しいのを申請する必要があります
▷I **applied to** Embry College. エンブリーカレッジに出願した
▷We **applied** the technology **to** other areas. その科学技術を他分野に応用した

appointment /əpɔ́intmənt/

名 予約，約束；任命，職

have	an appointment	予約がある
make	an appointment	予約する
get	an appointment	予約をとる；任命される
keep	an appointment	約束を守る
cancel	one's appointment	予約を取り消す

★医者・美容室などの予約は appointment，ホテル・レストランの予約は reservation を用いる

▷I **have** an **appointment** with Mr. Jones. ジョーンズ氏と約束があります
▷If you want to see me, **make** an **appointment** with my secretary. 私と面会なさりたいなら，秘書に予約をとってください
▷I'm going to go to the doctor as soon as I can **get** an **appointment**. 予約がとれ次第，お医者さんに診てもらうつもりです
▷Anna called me to **cancel** her **appointment**. アンナは約束をキャンセルすると電話してきた

appreciate /əprí:ʃieit/

動 十分に認識する，評価する；感謝する

really	appreciate	本当に評価する；とても感謝する
fully	appreciate	十分評価する；十分認識する
greatly	appreciate	とても感謝する
very much	appreciate	

▷At that time I didn't **fully appreciate** his help. あの当時は彼の援助のありがたみが十分にはわかっていなかった
▷I'd **very much appreciate** it if you would help me. 助けてくだされば，本当に感謝します

| approach |

begin to	appreciate	理解し始める
fail to	appreciate	理解できない

▷I **began to appreciate** that there were many other viewpoints. ほかの見方がたくさんあることがよくわかり始めた

appreciate	that...	…をよく認識する
appreciate	wh-	…かよく認識する

★wh- は how, why, what など

▷I **appreciate that** you're all concerned about me. みんなが私のことを心配してくださっていることはよくわかっています

▷I hope he **appreciates what** I'm doing. 私の行為を彼が評価してくれるといいのですが

approach /əpróutʃ/ 名 接近法, 扱い方

adopt	an approach	方法をとる
take	an approach	
develop	an approach	方法を練り上げる
follow	an approach	方法に従う
try	an approach	方法を試みる
make	an approach	働きかける；接近する

▷I can't understand some of the **approaches adopted** by the European Union. EUが採択した政策の中にはよくわからないものがある

▷Why not **try** a new **approach**? 新しい方法を試してみたらどうかな

a traditional	approach	伝統的手法
an alternative	approach	代わりの方法
a new	approach	新たな手法
a positive	approach	積極的な手法
a basic	approach	基本的な手法

▷There are several **alternative approaches** I could take. とりうるいくつかの代案がある

▷You should always take a **positive approach** to training your dog. 飼い犬を訓練するには常に積極的に犬に働きかけるべきだ

approach	to A	Aに対する方法；Aに近づく道

appropriate /əpróupriət/ 形 適切な

be considered	appropriate	適切と考えられる
be thought	appropriate	

▷I don't think wearing jeans at a wedding would be **considered appropriate**. 結婚式にジーンズを着るのはふさわしくないと思う

entirely	appropriate	まったく適切な
particularly	appropriate	特に適切な

▷I don't know whether that's **entirely appropriate**. それがまったく適切かどうかわからない

appropriate	for A	Aにふさわしい
appropriate	to A	

▷The house must be **appropriate to** our lifestyle. 家はライフスタイルに合ったものでなければならない

It is appropriate	that...	…は適切だ

▷**It's appropriate that** we should thank him formally for all he has done. 彼がいろいろやってくれたことに対しぜひ正式に感謝の意を表すべきだ

approval /əprúːvəl/ 名 承認；賛同, 賛成

require	approval	承認を必要とする
seek	approval	承認を求める
receive	approval	承認を得る
win	approval	
give	approval	承認する
grant	approval	
nod in	approval	賛成してうなずく

▷Passage **requires approval** by two thirds of the members. 可決には委員の3分の2の賛成を必要とする

▷We **received approval** for our building plans. 建設計画の認可を得た

▷Last week the town council **gave approval** to the development project. 先週, 市議会は開発事業を認可した

final	approval	最終的な承認
prior	approval	事前の承認
formal	approval	正式の承認
official	approval	公式の承認
congressional	approval	議会の承認
parliamentary	approval	

▷Japan has given **final approval** for financial aid to developing countries. 日本は発展途上国に対する財政支援を最終的に認可した

▷He ordered staff not to speak to outsiders without **prior approval**. 事前の許可なく外部に話を漏らさないよう彼はスタッフに命じた

▷We need **parliamentary approval** for this project. この計画には議会の承認が必要だ

approval	for A	Aに対する承認, 賛同
on	approval	試用販売の条件で

▷We've just received **approval for** extending the house. 家の増築を認可されたところだ
▷The company is quite willing to send goods **on approval**. その会社は試用販売の条件で積極的に商品を配送している(★商品を試してみた上でよければ購入すること)

approve /əprúːv/ 動 認める；賛成する

formally	approve	公に賛成する
finally	approve	最終的に賛成する
unanimously	approve	満場一致で賛成する

▷We have to wait until the plans are **formally approved**. 計画が公に承認されるまで待たねばならない
▷The meeting **unanimously approved** the decision to employ more staff. 職員の雇用を増やす決定を委員会は満場一致で認めた

approve	of A	Aに賛成する

▷My parents don't **approve of** my new boyfriend. 両親は私の新しいボーイフレンドを認めてくれない

area /ɛ́əriə/ 名 地域, 区域；領域, 分野

cover	an area	地域を範囲に含む；範囲を扱う
identify	areas	領域を特定する

▷Topics are wide and **cover areas** such as Business Planning, Marketing, the Internet, etc. 話題は幅広く, ビジネス計画, 市場戦略, インターネットなどの領域を扱っている

the surrounding	area	周辺地域
a rural	area	田園地帯, 田舎
a metropolitan	area	首都圏
an urban	area	都市部, 市街地
an industrial	area	工業地域
a residential	area	住宅地
a conservation	area	保護地域
a nonsmoking	area	禁煙区域
designated	areas	指定区域
a play	area	遊び場
a picnic	area	ピクニック場
a growth	area	成長分野

▷The national park is one of the biggest wildlife **conservation areas** in the world. その国立公園は世界で最も大きな野生動物保護地域のひとつだ

argue /áːrɡjuː/ 動 言い争う；議論する

argue	fiercely	激しく言い争う
argue	strongly	力強い議論をする
argue	forcefully	
argue	passionately	熱く議論する
argue	convincingly	説得力ある議論をする
argue	persuasively	
successfully	argue	うまく論じる

▷In his book he **argues strongly** against capital punishment. 著書の中で彼は強く死刑反対論を述べている

argue	over A	Aについて言い争う
argue	about A	
argue	with A	A(人)と言い争う
argue	for A	Aに賛成意見を述べる
argue	against A	Aに反対意見を述べる

▷They were **arguing over** me. 彼らは私のことで言い争いをしていた
▷I'm not here to **argue for** or **against** that point. その点への賛否を論じるためにここにいるのではない

argue	that...	…だと論じる

▷The Christian religion **argues that** we are not just animals. キリスト教は人間がただの動物ではないと主張する

argument /áːrɡjumənt/

名 口論, 言い争い；論拠, 議論

have	an argument	口論する
get into	an argument	口論になる
win	an argument	口論に勝つ
lose	an argument	口論に負ける
make	an argument	議論する
develop	an argument	議論を展開する
support	an argument	論拠を支持する
accept	an argument	論拠を受け入れる
reject	an argument	論拠を拒否する

▷Kay **had** an **argument** *with* her mother about the wedding plans. ケイは結婚式の計画について母親と口論した
▷Scott and I **got into** a heated **argument**. スコットと私は熱い口論になった

| arise |

▷John explained the data to **support** his **argument**. ジョンは彼の論拠を支持するデータについて説明した

a heated	argument	熱い口論
a powerful	argument	力強い議論
a logical	argument	論理的な議論
a reasoned	argument	筋の通った議論
a political	argument	政治論議

▷There's a **powerful argument** for introducing identity cards. 身分証明書を導入すべきだという主張には強力な論拠がある

▷I don't think one can make a **reasoned argument** against gay marriage. 同性愛者の結婚への反対を論じ出すと筋の通った議論になりにくい

argument	about A	Aについての口論
argument	over A	
argument	for A	Aへの賛成論
argument	in favor of A	
argument	against A	Aへの反対論

▷What was the **argument about**? 何のことで口論になったの？

▷There are strong **arguments for** and **against** each view. それぞれの見解に賛否両論ある

argument	that...	…という議論

▷There's an **argument that** a big earthquake can happen in the near future. 大地震が近い将来にも起こりうるという議論がある

a line of	argument	議論の方向

arise /əráiz/ 動 起こる，生じる

inevitably	arise	必然的に起きる
arise	naturally	自然に起きる
arise	spontaneously	自然に発生する

▷If the Prime Minister keeps refusing to give press interviews problems will **inevitably arise**. 首相が記者会見を拒否し続けるとどうしても問題になるだろう

arise	from A	Aから起こる，生じる
arise	out of A	

▷I understand that most problems **arise from** the lack of communication. たいていの問題はコミュニケーション不足から起きるんですよね

arm /á:rm/ 名 腕

lower	one's arm	腕を下げる
raise	one's arm	腕を上げる
twist	A's arm	腕をねじあげる
stretch out	one's arm	腕を伸ばす
cross	one's arms	腕を組む
fold	one's arms	
grab	A's arm	腕をつかむ
grasp	A's arm	

▷He **twisted** my **arm** behind my back. 彼は私の腕を後ろ手にねじあげた

▷He **stretched out** his **arm** toward me. 彼は腕を私の方へ伸ばした

▷She sat back in her chair and **folded** her **arms** across her chest. 彼女は椅子に深々と腰かけ腕組みした

by	the arm	手を
in	A's arms	両手に
under	A's arm	脇の下に

▷Toby gently took the man **by** the **arm** and helped him stand up. トビーはやさしく男の腕を取って助け起こした

▷She took the baby **in** her **arms**. 彼女は赤ん坊を腕に抱きしめた

at	arm's length	手を伸ばしたところに

★keep, put, hold などと連結する

▷She held the smelly cheese **at arm's length** and dropped it into a trash can. 彼女は手を伸ばしたままにおいの強いチーズをつかみ，ゴミ箱にポイと捨てた

arrange /əréindʒ/

動 準備する，手配する；配列する

carefully	arrange	きちんと整える
neatly	arrange	

▷The furniture was very clean and **neatly arranged**. 家具は実にきれいに整えられていた

arrange	for A	Aを手配する
arrange	(for A) to do	(A(人)が)…するよう手配する

▷I thought you **arranged for** a taxi. きみがタクシーを手配してくれると思っていた

▷I'll **arrange for** you **to** meet up with them. あなたが彼らと会えるよう手配します

| arrange | that... | …ということを手配する |

▷ I'll try to **arrange that** we should leave at five o'clock. 5時に出られるよう手配してみます

| as | arranged | 手配したとおり |

★ as previously arranged, as originally arranged の結びつきが多い

▷ If we can't meet on Friday, let's meet on Wednesday **as** originally **arranged**. 金曜日に会えないなら，当初の設定どおり水曜日に会おう

arrangement /əréindʒmənt/

名 準備，手配；取り決め，協定；配列

make	an arrangement	手配する；取り決める
have	an arrangement	取り決めがある
come to	an arrangement	合意する

▷ I've **made** an **arrangement** to see John on Saturday. 土曜日にジョンと会うことになっている
▷ We **have** an **arrangement with** the university to use their classrooms. 教室を使用するための取り決めを大学としてある

| a reciprocal | arrangement | 相互取り決め |
| a flower | arrangement | 生け花 |

▷ There are some **reciprocal arrangements** between the UK and EU countries. 英国とEU諸国の間にはいくつかの相互取り決めがある

| arrangements | for A | Aの準備 |
| arrangements | with A | Aとの取り決め |

▷ How are the **arrangements for** the wedding? 結婚式の準備はどうですか
▷ Aren't you forgetting your **arrangement with** Jack? ジャックとの取り決めを忘れているんじゃないか

arrive /əráiv/ **動** 到着する，着く

arrive	safely	無事に着く
finally	arrived	ついに到着した
eventually	arrived	

▷ I'm so glad you **arrived safely**. 無事に到着なさってよかったです
▷ I **finally arrived** in New York. ついにニューヨークに着いた

arrive	at A	Aに着く
arrive	in A	
arrive	from A	Aから着く

▷ When we **arrived at** the station, it was seven thirty. 駅に到着したのは7時半だった
▷ He just **arrived from** America. 彼はアメリカから到着したところだ

art /ɑːrt/ **名** 芸術，美術；技術，こつ

| master | the art | こつを身につける |

▷ He **mastered** the **art** of cooking. 彼は料理のこつを覚えた

fine	arts	芸術
abstract	art	抽象芸術
modern	art	近代美術
contemporary	art	現代美術

▷ Julie majored in **fine arts** at Stanford University. ジュリーはスタンフォード大学で芸術を専攻した

article /ɑ́ːrtikl/ **名** 記事，論文；項目

contribute	an article	記事を寄稿する
publish	an article	論文を発表する
submit	an article	論文を提出する

▷ She has **contributed articles** *to* the magazine. 彼女は論文をその雑誌に寄稿している
▷ The first **article** was **published** in the Dec. 2007 issue. 最初の論文は2007年12月号に発表された

a feature	article	特集記事
a front-page	article	一面記事
an editorial	article	社説
a related	article	関連記事
a magazine	article	雑誌記事
a newspaper	article	新聞記事

▷ See the **front-page article** in today's New York Times. きょうのニューヨークタイムズの一面記事を見てください

| an article | on A | Aについての記事 |
| an article | about A | |

▷ Could you check out the **article on** Bali? バリ島に関する記事を調べていただけませんか

ask

ask /ǽsk | άːsk/ 動 尋ねる；頼む，求める

ask	softly	優しく尋ねる
ask	gently	
ask	politely	丁寧に尋ねる
ask	anxiously	不安げに尋ねる
ask	curiously	興味ありげに尋ねる

▷"Are you feeling better now?," she **asked softly**.「もうだいじょうぶなの」と彼女は優しく尋ねた
▷"Have you seen my purse anywhere," she **asked anxiously**. 「私の財布をどこかで見なかった？」と彼女は不安げに尋ねた

ask	(A) about B	(A(人)に)Bについて尋ねる
ask	(A) for B	(A(人)に)Bを求める

▷Did you **ask** Catherine **about** her new boy friend? キャサリンに新しいボーイフレンドのことを聞いてみたかい
▷You should **ask** your mother for advice. お母さんに助言を求めたほうがいいよ ▷Jennie **asked for** a double espresso. ジェニーはエスプレッソのダブルを頼んだ

ask	A to do	A(人)に…するように頼む

▷Would you **ask** him **to** call me, please? 電話をくれるよう彼に伝えていただけますか

ask	(A) wh-	(A(人)に)…かを尋ねる

★wh- は why, how, whether など

▷Can I **ask what** a cream tea is? 教えてほしいんですがクリームティーって何ですか

asleep

asleep /əslíːp/ 形 眠って

fall	asleep	眠り込む

▷The last time you went to the movies you **fell asleep**. この前映画に行ったとき，きみは寝ちゃったね

fast	asleep	ぐっすり眠って
sound	asleep	
half	asleep	半分眠って

▷"Where's your son now?" "He's **fast asleep** in his bed." 「息子さんはどこだい」「ベッドでぐっすり寝ているよ」

aspect

aspect /ǽspekt/ 名 局面，様相；外観

consider	an aspect	側面を検討する
discuss	an aspect	側面を論じる
deal with	an aspect	側面を扱う
focus on	an aspect	側面に焦点を当てる

▷We have another **aspect** of this matter to **consider**. この件をもうひとつの側面からも検討すべきだ

an important	aspect	重要な側面
a key	aspect	
a significant	aspect	重大な側面
an interesting	aspect	興味深い側面
a financial	aspect	財政的側面
the safety	aspect	安全面

▷Another **important aspect** is that everything should be organized. もうひとつ大事な要素がある．すべてを組織化することだ
▷Music is a **key aspect** of the film. 音楽は映画の重要な側面だ

associate

associate /əsóuʃièit/ 動 結びつける

be closely	associated	密接に結びつく
be strongly	associated	強く結びつく
be usually	associated	ふつう結びつく
be normally	associated	

▷Psychiatry is **closely associated** with psychology. 精神医学は心理学と密接に結びついている
▷Passive smoking is **strongly associated** with increased risk of heart disease. 受動喫煙は心臓病のリスク増大と強く関連づけられる
▷Country and western music is **usually associated** with cowboys. カントリーアンドウェスタンというと普通カウボーイを連想する

associate	A with B	AでBを連想する

▷I always **associate** green apples **with** stomachache. 青いリンゴというといつも腹痛を連想する

assume

assume /əsúːm | əsjúːm/

動 想定する；引き受ける；ふりをする

automatically	assume	機械的に想定する
generally	assume	一般に想定する
usually	assume	
widely	assume	広く想定する
safely	assume	…と思っていい

▷Why do you **automatically assume** I'm like everybody else? 私がほかの人たちと同じだとなぜ頭から決めてかかるのか

▷It is **generally assumed** that old people are wiser than young people. 高齢者は若者より思慮分別があると一般に思われている

assume	(that)...	当然…だと思う

▷I **assume** it was Helen who recruited Steven to the project. スティーブンをそのプロジェクトに誘い入れたのはヘレンだったと思う

be reasonable to	assume	…と想定するのは理にかなっている

▷It is **reasonable to assume** that some workers retire at 60 because of failing health. 健康の衰えから60歳で退職する人がいると想定するのは理にかなったことだ

assumption /əsʌ́mpʃən/

名 仮定, 想定, 前提；就任

make	an assumption	想定する
challenge	an assumption	想定に異議を唱える
question	an assumption	

▷Don't **make** too many **assumptions**. あまりあれこれ憶測しないように
▷My professor advised me to **challenge assumptions** and get more data. 前提を疑ってもっとデータを得るよう先生は私に助言してくれた

an underlying	assumption	根底にある想定
a fundamental	assumption	想定
an implicit	assumption	暗黙の想定
a false	assumption	誤った想定
a wrong	assumption	

▷An **implicit assumption** of this article is that changes will usually be smooth. この記事が暗黙の前提としているのは変化はたいてい円滑に進むということだ
▷These facts seem to be based on **false assumptions**. これらの事実は誤った前提に基づいているようだ

assumption	about A	Aに関する想定

▷I don't think we can make any **assumptions about** getting the contract. 契約をとれるかどうかまだ何とも言えないと思う

on	the assumption that...	…との想定に基づいて

▷I agreed to do overtime **on** the **assumption that** I would be paid extra money. 余分に支払いがあると見込んで残業するのに同意した

atmosphere /ǽtməsfìər/

名 雰囲気；大気, 空気

create	an atmosphere	雰囲気を作り出す
have	an atmosphere	雰囲気がある

▷We **created** an **atmosphere** that feels very comfortable. とても心地よい雰囲気を作り上げた
▷That restaurant **has** a great **atmosphere**. そのレストランは雰囲気がとてもいい

a friendly	atmosphere	友好的な雰囲気
an informal	atmosphere	打ち解けた雰囲気
a relaxed	atmosphere	くつろいだ雰囲気
a general	atmosphere	全体の雰囲気
the whole	atmosphere	
the upper	atmosphere	高層大気

▷The meeting was held in a very **relaxed** and **informal atmosphere**. 会議はリラックスした打ち解けた雰囲気で開かれた
▷She loved the **whole atmosphere** of Regent Street. 彼女はリージェントストリートの全体的な雰囲気が好きだった
▷Ozone in the **upper atmosphere** protects life on earth. 高層大気中のオゾンが地上の生物を守っている

attach /ətǽtʃ/ 動 つける, 添える

firmly	attach	しっかりつける

▷The lid was **firmly attached** to the ice-cream tub. アイスクリームのふたはぴったり容器にはまっていた

attach	A to B	AをBにつける

▷You should **attach** a label with your name and address **to** your baggage. 名前と住所を書いた札を荷物につけたほうがいいよ

attack /ətǽk/ 名 攻撃, 非難；発作

carry out	an attack	攻撃する
make	an attack	
suffer	an attack	攻撃を受ける
launch	an attack	攻撃を仕かける
mount	an attack	
lead	an attack	攻撃を指揮する
have	an attack	発作を起こす
suffer	an attack	発作に苦しむ

▷They have **made an attack** *on* the eastern border.

| attack |

彼らは東側の国境を攻撃した
▷ The city **suffered** a terrorist **attack**. 街はテロ攻撃に見舞われた
▷ The Republican Party **launched** an aggressive **attack** on the Democrats. 共和党は民主党を激しく攻撃した
▷ My dad's in hospital. He **had** a heart **attack**. 父は心臓発作を起こして入院中です

an attack	happens	攻撃がある
an attack	takes place	
an attack	occurs	

▷ When the **attack happened**, where were you? 攻撃があったときあなたはどこにいましたか

a violent	attack	激しい攻撃
a racist	attack	人種差別的攻撃
an arson	attack	放火事件
a terrorist	attack	テロ攻撃
an air	attack	空爆
a bomb	attack	爆弾攻撃
a missile	attack	ミサイル攻撃
a rocket	attack	ロケット攻撃
a nuclear	attack	核攻撃
a revenge	attack	報復攻撃
a frontal	attack	正面攻撃
a fierce	attack	辛辣な非難
a bitter	attack	
a personal	attack	個人攻撃
an asthma	attack	ぜん息の発作
a heart	attack	心臓発作

▷ He carried out his **violent attacks** in streets. 彼は路上で暴力行為を振るった
▷ **Racist attacks** and bullying in schools are on the increase. 学校での人種差別的攻撃といじめが増加している
▷ The police are investigating the incident as an **arson attack**. 警察はその事件を放火として捜査中だ
▷ The threat of **nuclear attack** is greater than ever before. 核攻撃の脅威が以前より大きくなっている
▷ I used to have **asthma attacks**. かつてぜん息の発作がよくあった

under	attack	攻撃を受けて
attack	on A	Aに対する攻撃
attack	against A	

▷ When you're **under attack**, the best defense is to counterattack. 攻撃を受けたとき, 最大の防御は反撃だ
▷ Have you heard of the recent **attack on** the American embassy? アメリカ大使館への最近の攻撃について聞いたかい

attack /ətǽk/ 動 攻撃する, 襲う;非難する

brutally	attack	ひどく攻撃する
immediately	attack	即座に攻撃する
bitterly	attack	痛烈に非難する
fiercely	attack	
strongly	attack	強く非難する

▷ He was **bitterly attacked** by the critics. 彼は批評家から酷評された

attack	A with B	A(人)をBで襲う
attack	A for doing	Aを…したと非難する

▷ Why were they **attacking** him **for losing** the game? 試合に負けたことでなぜ彼が非難されたのか

attempt /ətémpt/ 名 試み, 企て

make	an attempt	試みる, 企てる
fail in	an attempt	試みに失敗する

▷ Caroline **made** no **attempt** to do as I said. キャロリンは何ひとつ私の言うとおりにしようとしなかった
▷ A fifteen-year-old boy **failed in** an **attempt** to rob a taxi driver. 15歳の少年がタクシー運転手から金を奪おうとして失敗した

a successful	attempt	成功した試み
an unsuccessful	attempt	失敗した試み
a vain	attempt	むなしい試み
a serious	attempt	真剣な試み
a brave	attempt	果敢な試み
a desperate	attempt	必死の試み
an assassination	attempt	暗殺の企て
a rescue	attempt	救出の試み
a suicide	attempt	自殺未遂
a murder	attempt	殺人未遂
a robbery	attempt	強盗未遂

▷ After four **unsuccessful attempts**, he finally won gold. 4回も取り損ねた末に彼はようやく金メダルをとった
▷ He made a **vain attempt** to persuade his brother to come back to Australia. 彼は弟にオーストラリアに戻ってくるよう説得したがむだだった
▷ We can now launch a **rescue attempt**. 救出活動に入れる態勢だ

an attempt	at A	Aへの試み

▷ Fred was making an **attempt at** trying not to laugh. フレッドは何とか笑いをこらえようとしていた

an attempt	to do	…する試み

▷I made an **attempt to** make friends with her. 彼女と友だちになろうとした

attend /əténd/ 動 出席する

regularly	attend	定期的に参加する
well	attended	集まりがよい
poorly	attended	集まりが悪い

▷I **regularly attend** monthly community meetings. 月ごとの地域の会合にきちんと出席している
▷The show was well received and **well attended**. そのショーは評判もよく，客の入りもよかった

attention /əténʃən/ 名 注意，注目；世話

pay	attention	注意を払う
give	attention	
attract	(A's) attention	注意を引く
get	(A's) attention	
catch	(A's) attention	
receive	attention	注目を浴びる
focus	attention	注意を集中させる
hold	attention	注意を払い続ける
keep	attention	
turn	one's attention	注意を向ける
draw	(A's) attention	注意を向けさせる
call	(A's) attention	
distract	attention	注意をそらさせる
divert	attention	

▷**Pay attention** to every detail! 細部の隅々にまで注意を払いなさい
▷Chapter 8 **gives attention** to democratic policies. 8章では民主的政策に着目する
▷Shh, don't shout! I don't want to **attract attention**! シーッ，大声を出さないで．人の目を引きたくないの
▷The composer began to **receive attention** *from* abroad in the 1950's. その作曲家は1950年代に海外から注目され始めた
▷He **drew** everyone's **attention** to himself. 彼はみんなの注意を自分に向けさせた
▷One of the pickpockets **distracted** my **attention** while the other stole my wallet. スリの一人が私の注意をそらし，もう一人が私の財布を盗んだ

full	attention	全身全霊での注意
undivided	attention	
careful	attention	入念な注意
close	attention	細心の注意
particular	attention	特別の注意
media	attention	メディアの注目
public	attention	世間の注目
medical	attention	治療

▷It's necessary to pay **careful attention**. 入念な注意を払う必要がある
▷**Media attention** will help to solve this case. メディアが注目すればこの事件の解決に役立つだろう
▷The true facts never came to **public attention**. 真実は決して公にはならなかった
▷Seek **medical attention** as quickly as possible. できるだけ早く医者に診てもらいなさい

PHRASES
Attention, please! ☺(館内放送で)お知らせいたします
Thank you for your kind attention. ☺ご清聴ありがとうございました

attitude /ǽtitjùːd | -tjùːd/ 名 態度；意見

adopt	an attitude	態度をとる
have	an attitude	
take	an attitude	
change	an attitude	態度を変える

▷I feel it's important that we **adopt** a positive **attitude**. 積極的な態度をとるのが大事だという気がする
▷**Having** a good **attitude** to work is very important. 仕事によい態度で臨むのがとても大事だ
▷I've tried to **change** my **attitude** toward her. 彼女に対する態度を変えようとした

a good	attitude	よい態度
a positive	attitude	積極的な態度
a bad	attitude	悪い態度
a negative	attitude	消極的な態度
an aggressive	attitude	攻撃的な態度
a critical	attitude	批判的な態度
a relaxed	attitude	落ち着いた態度
a responsible	attitude	責任ある態度

▷Why does he have such a **negative attitude**? 彼はなぜあんな消極的な態度をとっているのか
▷We expected the company to take a **responsible attitude**. その会社が責任ある態度をとるものと期待していた
▷Keep a positive **mental attitude**. 積極的な心構えを保ちなさい

attitude	to A	Aに対する態度
attitude	toward A	

▷Western **attitudes to** Japan have changed. 日本に

| attract |

対する西洋の態度が変わった
▷I think you should change your **attitude toward** her. 彼女への態度を変えたほうがいいよ

a change of	attitude	態度の変化
a change in	attitude	

▷What's with the sudden **change of attitude**, Ken? ケン，急に態度を変えるなんてどうかしてるんじゃないか

with	(an) attitude	突っ張った態度で；奇異をてらった

▷**With** an **attitude** like that, it's no wonder you have so many enemies. そんな態度じゃ，きみに敵が多いのも当然だ

attract /ətrǽkt/ 動 引きつける，魅惑する

be sexually	attracted	性的に引かれる
be strongly	attracted	強く引かれる

▷I don't think she was **sexually attracted** to me. 彼女が私に性的魅力を感じたとは思わない
▷I'm **strongly attracted** to his work. 彼の作品にすごく魅力を感じる

attract	A to B	A(人)をBに引きつける

▷Do you know what **attracted** me **to** you in the first place? そもそもきみのどこにぼくが引かれたかわかるかい

attractive /ətrǽktiv/ 形 魅力的な

look	attractive	魅力的に見える
make A	attractive	Aを魅力的にする

▷Those leaves **look** particularly **attractive** in autumn. 木々の葉は秋には特にきれいだ
▷We wanted to change the design and **make** it more **attractive** to everyone. デザインをだれにとってももっと魅力あるものに変えたいと望んでいた

extremely	attractive	非常に魅力的な
particularly	attractive	特に魅力的な
stunningly	attractive	驚くほど魅力的な
sexually	attractive	性的に魅力的な
increasingly	attractive	ますます魅力的な

▷San Francisco is **increasingly attractive** as a place to live. サンフランシスコは暮らす場所としてますます魅力的になっている

audience /ɔ́ːdiəns/ 名 聴衆；視聴者

address	an audience	聴衆に話しかける
attract	an audience	聴衆を引きつける
reach	an audience	聴衆に届ける

▷Mr. Prescott **addressed** an **audience** of business leaders yesterday. プレスコット氏はきのう財界の指導者たちを前に演説した
▷The magazine **reached** an **audience** estimated at twenty-five thousand readers worldwide. その雑誌の購読者数は世界で2万5千人に達したと推定される

a large	audience	多くの聴衆
a mass	audience	
a wide	audience	幅広い聴衆
a small	audience	少ない聴衆
a target	audience	対象となる聴衆
a television	audience	テレビ視聴者

▷There was a **large audience** at the concert. 音楽会の聴衆は多かった
▷We need to find a **wider audience**. われわれはもっと視聴者の数を増やす必要がある
▷The politician's speech was well-suited for the **target audience**. その政治家の演説は対象とする聴衆にぴったりだった

authority /əθɔ́ːrəti | ɔːθɔ́r-/

名 権威，権力；権限；当局

have	the authority	権限がある
give	the authority	権限を与える
assert	one's authority	権限を主張する
exercise	authority	権限を行使する
accept	the authority	権限を受け入れる
undermine	the authority	権限を脅かす

▷I don't **have** the **authority** to do so. 私にはそうする権限がない
▷Who **gave** him the **authority** to do that? だれが彼にそうする権限を与えたのか
▷The government can **exercise authority** over security matters. 政府は安全保障上の問題に関して権限を振るえる

political	authority	政治の権威
presidential	authority	大統領権限
(a) public	authority	公的機関
regulatory	authority	監督官庁機関
government	authority	政府当局
police	authority	警察当局

a local	authority	地方自治体
the authorities	concerned	関係当局

▷The government now has no **political authority** to do anything. 政府はいまや政治的権限をなくし, 何もできない
▷You will find the address of your **local authority** in the phone book. 地方自治体の住所は電話帳でわかります
▷The **authorities concerned** refused to accept responsibility. 関係当局は責任を受け入れるのを拒否した

in	authority	権限をもった
with	authority	威厳をもって
authority	over A	Aに対する権限
an authority	on A	Aについての権威

▷In those days we used to trust people **in authority**. 当時は権力者を信頼したものだ
▷He spoke **with authority**. 彼は威厳をもって話した
▷You have no **authority over** me. あなたには私に対して何の権限もない
▷He is an **authority on** American literature. 彼はアメリカ文学の権威だ

available /əvéiləbl/

形 手に入る;利用できる;手が空いている

become	available	利用可能になる
make	available	利用可能にする

▷A new type of mobile phone will **become available** next month. 新型の携帯電話が来月利用可能になります

readily	available	簡単に手に入る
freely	available	
widely	available	広く手に入る
generally	available	
commercially	available	市販されている
currently	available	現在手に入る

▷This software is **freely available** on the Internet. このソフトウェアはインターネットで簡単に手に入る
▷The book is now **widely available** in a new American edition. その本は現在新しいアメリカ版で幅広く入手可能です
▷Almost all **commercially available** trout are farmed. 市場に流通しているマスのほとんどは養殖物です

available	for A	Aに利用できる
available	to A	
available	from A	Aから手に入る

▷I thought it would be a good idea to make the data **available to** the public. データを一般に利用できるようにするのはよい考えだと思った
▷Tickets are **available from** the stadium shop. 切符はスタジアムのショップで入手可能だ

available	to do	…する都合がつく

▷Are you **available to** come for a meeting on Thursday? 木曜の会議には出られますか

average /ǽvəridʒ/ 名 平均, 平均値

an annual	average	年間平均
the national	average	全国平均
an overall	average	全体平均
a weighted	average	加重平均

▷An **annual average** of 30,000 people immigrated to the U.S. in those years. 当時は年間平均3万人が米国に移住した
▷The unemployment rate in this city is above the **national average**. この街の失業率は全国平均より高い
▷This figure is slightly higher than the **overall average**. この数字は全体平均よりやや高い

above	(the) average	平均以上の
below	(the) average	平均以下の
on	average	平均して

▷The total rainfall was 37% **above** the **average**. 全降水量は平均を37%上回った
▷I receive **on average** 30 emails a day. 1日平均30通のEメールを受け取る

avoid /əvɔ́id/ 動 避ける, 回避する

carefully	avoid	注意深く避ける
deliberately	avoid	
narrowly	avoid	かろうじて免れる
best	avoided	絶対に避けるべき

▷She **carefully avoided** eye contact with him. 彼女は極力, 彼と目を合わせないようにした
▷I **narrowly avoided** crashing into the car at the intersection. 交差点で危うく車と衝突するところだった
▷That place is **best avoided**, there are much better places to visit. その場所は絶対に避けるべきです. もっとずっといいところがあります

avoid	doing	…するのを避ける

▷I'm on a diet. I'm trying to **avoid** eating chocolate. ダイエット中で, チョコレートを食べないようにしています

| awake |

be difficult to	avoid	避けるのは難しい

▷ It's **difficult to avoid** that sort of problem. そのような問題を回避するのは難しい

awake /əwéik/ 形 目を覚まして

stay	awake	起きている, 目を覚ましている
keep	awake	

▷ I think I'll go to bed. Sorry, I can't **stay awake** any longer. もう寝るよ。ごめん, これ以上は起きていられないよ

award /əwɔ́:rd/ 名 賞, 賞品, 賞金

present A with	an award	Aに賞を贈る
give A	an award	
win	an award	賞をとる
receive	an award	

▷ The National Museum **presented** him **with an award** for lifetime achievement. 国立美術館は長年の業績に対して彼に賞を贈った
▷ Michael and his friends were **given awards** for their brave actions. マイケルと彼の友人たちの勇敢な行為に対し賞が贈られた

a special	award	特別賞
a top	award	最高賞
an Academy	Award	アカデミー賞

▷ Lynch was nominated for an **Academy Award** for Best Director. リンチはアカデミー賞監督賞にノミネートされた

aware /əwέər/

形 気づいている；意識に目覚めた

acutely	aware	よく知っている
well	aware	
fully	aware	
painfully	aware	痛感している
vaguely	aware	うすうす気づいている
uncomfortably	aware	気づいて落ち着かない
increasingly	aware	だんだん目覚めた
politically	aware	政治に目覚めた

▷ He is **acutely aware** of the bad effects of alcohol. 彼はアルコールの悪影響を痛感している
▷ She was **well aware** of the rules. 彼女はその規則を熟知していた
▷ She's now **painfully aware** of her limits. 彼女はいま自分の限界を痛感している
▷ He became **uncomfortably aware** of the pain in his side. 彼は脇腹に痛みを感じて不安を覚えた

aware	of A	Aに気づいた

▷ He became **aware of** shouts from above. 彼は上からの叫び声に気づいた

aware	that...	…ということに気づく

▷ I was very **aware that** she needed support. 彼女が援助を必要としているのは十分に承知していた

awful /ɔ́:fəl/ 形 ひどい, いやな；恐ろしい

smell	awful	いやなにおいがする
taste	awful	ひどい味がする

▷ These clothes **smell awful**. They need to be washed. この服はひどいにおいがする。洗濯しなくては

really	awful	実にひどい
pretty	awful	かなりひどい
absolutely	awful	とてもひどい

▷ That food tasted **absolutely awful**! 料理はまったくひどい味だった

PHRASES
How awful! 😊 なんてひどい

awkward /ɔ́:kwərd/

形 気まずい；ぎこちない；やっかいな

feel	awkward	気まずく感じる

▷ I **felt** a bit **awkward**, but nodded and smiled back at her. ちょっと気まずく感じたが, うなずいて彼女にほほえみ返した

extremely	awkward	ひどく気まずい；ひどくぎこちない
rather	awkward	かなり気まずい
a bit	awkward	少し気まずい；少しぎこちない
slightly	awkward	

▷ I'm in a **rather awkward** position. 私はかなりやっかいな立場にある

B

baby /béibi/ 名 赤ん坊, 赤ちゃん

have	a baby	赤ん坊を産む
give birth to	a baby	
be expecting	a baby	出産予定である
lose	a baby	流産する
look after	a baby	赤ん坊の世話をする
hold	a baby	赤ん坊を抱く
pick up	a baby	

▷Mommy is going to **have a baby**; you're going to be a big sister.　ママに赤ちゃんが生まれるの, あなたはお姉ちゃんになるのよ
▷Jane **gave birth to** a **baby** girl, named Chelsea.　ジェーンは女の子を産んで, チェルシーと名づけた
▷Did you know she's **expecting a baby**?　彼女に子どもが生まれることを知っていましたか
▷She **lost a baby** at 20 weeks.　彼女は20週で流産した
▷She was **holding** a **baby** in her arms.　彼女は赤ん坊を腕に抱いていた

a baby	is due	赤ん坊が生まれる予定だ
a baby	is born	赤ん坊が生まれる

▷Jenny's **baby is due** soon.　ジェニーの赤ちゃんもうすぐ生まれる予定だ

a new	baby	生まれたばかりの赤ん坊
a newborn	baby	新生児
a tiny	baby	ちっちゃな赤ん坊
a premature	baby	未熟児
a ten-month-old	baby	生後10か月の赤ん坊
a healthy	baby	健康な赤ん坊

▷She has a **new baby** and needs more time off.　彼女は赤ん坊が生まれたばかりで, もっと休みが必要だ
▷She picked up her **tiny baby** and laid him gently in the cradle.　彼女はちっちゃな赤ん坊を抱き上げると, 優しく揺りかごに寝かせた

like	a baby	赤ん坊のように

▷He was crying **like a baby**.　彼は赤ん坊のように泣いていた

back /bæk/ 名 背中; 後ろ, 後部

break	one's **back**	背骨を折る; 一生懸命に努力する
turn	one's **back**	背を向ける

▷She wasn't going to **break** her **back** trying to help Ken.　彼女はケンを助けるために骨折るつもりはなかった
▷She **turned** her **back** *on* me to talk to the girl.　彼女は私に背を向けてその女の子と話し出した

lower	back	腰
upper	back	背中
a broad	back	幅の広い背中
a bad	back	腰痛

▷I felt a sharp pain in my **lower back**.　腰に鋭い痛みを感じた
▷Robert had a **bad back**.　ロバートは腰痛を患っていた

at	the **back**	後ろに, 後部に
in	the **back**	
behind	A's **back**	陰で
on	one's **back**	あおむけに
on	the **back**	裏側に
《英》**back**	to front	(服を)後ろ前に

▷I hope she hasn't been talking about me **behind** my **back**.　私の知らないところで彼女が私のうわさをしていないといいのだけど
▷Ted lay **on** his **back** in the bed.　テッドはベッドにあおむけに寝た
▷Write your name and address **on** the **back** of the envelope.　封筒の裏に名前と住所を書いてください
▷I put my T-shirt on **back to front**.　Tシャツを後ろ前に着た(★《米》では I put my T-shirt on backward. という)

back /bǽk/ 動 後援する, 支持する; 後退させる

back	hastily	急いで後退する
back	slowly	ゆっくり後退する
back	away	後ずさりする
back	off	下がる; やめる
back	up	バックさせる; 支持する

▷She screamed and **backed away** slowly.　彼女は悲鳴をあげ, ゆっくり後ずさりした
▷Emma **backed off** a few steps.　エマは数歩後ずさりした
▷Good work Bob, you've finally got proof to **back up** this theory.　よくやった, ボブ. きみはついにこの理論の裏づけとなる証拠を得たぞ

background /bǽkgràund/ 名 背景; 経歴

form	a background	背景をなす
provide	a background	

▷In 1978 he went to China, which was to **form the background** *to* his first novel. 1978年に彼は中国に行き，それが第一作の小説の背景となった
▷Chapter 1 **provides** some historical **background** *to* the research. 第1章では研究の歴史的背景を示す

family	background	家庭環境
educational	background	学歴
social	background	社会的背景
cultural	background	文化的背景

▷They asked me about my **family background**. 家庭環境について尋ねられた
▷With a strong **educational background**, my future may look reasonably bright. 学歴さえしっかりしていれば私の将来もそこそこ明るいかもしれない
▷They come from a wide range of **social backgrounds**. 彼らの社会的背景は多岐にわたる

against	a background of A	Aを背景に
in	the background	背景に；背後に

▷The story is set **against** the **background of** Paris in the 1920s. その物語は1920年代のパリが背景となっている
▷I heard some voices **in** the **background**. 背後で人の声が聞こえた

bad /bǽd/ 形 悪い；ひどい；腐った

look	bad	悪そうである
get	bad	悪くなる
go	bad	腐る；傷む
taste	bad	ひどい味がする
smell	bad	ひどいにおいがする

▷The situation in Afghanistan **looks bad**. アフガニスタンの情勢はよくなさそうだ
▷The weather **got** very **bad**. 天気がとても悪くなった

extremely	bad	非常に悪い
particularly	bad	特に悪い
especially	bad	
quite	bad	かなり悪い

▷The weather was **extremely bad**. 天候は非常に悪かった
▷He suffered from a **particularly bad** heart attack a few weeks ago. 彼は数週間前に特にひどい心臓発作を起こした

bad	at A	Aが苦手な
bad	for A	Aにとってよくない

▷I'm really **bad at** cooking. 料理は本当に苦手だ（★atの次は名詞・動名詞がくる）
▷Smoking is **bad for** your health. 喫煙は健康によくない

PHRASES⟩
(That's) too bad. ☺ それはいけませんね，残念なことだ

bag /bǽg/ 名 袋；かばん，ハンドバッグ

carry	a bag	かばんを持ち歩く
grab	a bag	かばんをつかむ
sling	a bag	かばんをかける
pack	a bag	かばんに荷物を詰める

▷I always **carry** a **bag** with me wherever I go. どこに行くにもかばんを持ち歩いている
▷He **grabbed** a **bag** of cookies and opened it. 彼はクッキーの袋をつかみ取って，開けた

a bag	containing A	Aが入ったかばん
a bag	full of A	Aでいっぱいのかばん

▷He came back with a **bag full of** food. 彼は袋にいっぱい食べ物を詰めて帰ってきた

a shopping	bag	買い物袋
a paper	bag	紙袋
a plastic	bag	ビニール袋
a garbage	bag	ごみ袋
a sleeping	bag	寝袋
a leather	bag	革のかばん

balance /bǽləns/

名 釣り合い，均衡；差引残額

keep	one's balance	バランスを保つ
maintain	one's balance	
lose	one's balance	バランスを崩す
achieve	a balance	バランスをとる
strike	a balance	
find	a balance	バランスを見つける
alter	the balance	バランスを変える
upset	the balance	バランスを狂わせる
recover	one's balance	バランスを取り戻す
redress	the balance	
tip	the balance	バランスを傾ける

▷Linda walked slowly trying to **keep** her **balance**.

| bargain |

リンダはバランスをなんとか保ちながらゆっくり歩いた
▷He **lost** his **balance** and fell to the ground. 彼はバランスを崩して地面に倒れた
▷The question is how do we **achieve** a **balance**. 問題はどうやってバランスをとるかだ
▷I've decided to **strike** a **balance** between my parents' wishes and mine. 両親の希望と自分の希望をうまく両立させることに決めた
▷These factors, in my view, **tip** the **balance** slightly in favor of the defendant. これらの要素は私の見るところ,被告人にやや有利に働く

off	balance	バランスを失って

▷I tried to grab it but I fell **off balance**. それをつかもうとしたがバランスを崩した

a sense of	balance	バランス感覚

▷I don't have such a good **sense of balance**. それほどバランス感覚がよくない

trade	balance	貿易収支
a bank	balance	銀行預金残高

ball /bɔ́ːl/ 名 ボール,球;球状のもの

hit	a ball	ボールを打つ
kick	a ball	ボールをける
throw	a ball	ボールを投げる
bounce	a ball	ボールを弾ませる
pass	a ball	ボールをパスする
catch	a ball	ボールを捕る
miss	the ball	ボールを取り損なう;ボールを打ち損じる
drop	the ball	ボールを落とす
play	ball	野球をする

▷Lewis **passed** the **ball** accurately to Owen. ルイスはオーウェンにボールを正確にパスした
▷The captain tried to tackle from behind but **missed** the **ball**. キャプテンが後方からタックルしようとしたがボールを取り損なった

bank /bǽŋk/ 名 銀行;土手,岸

borrow from	a bank	銀行から借りる
rob	a bank	銀行強盗をする
burst	its bank(s)	堤防を決壊させる

▷They have to **borrow from** the **bank** to build a new building. 新ビル建設のために銀行から融資を受けなければならない
▷The man was accused of **robbing** the **bank**. その男は銀行強盗の罪で告訴された
▷The river **burst** its **banks** and flooded surrounding areas. 川は堤防を決壊させ,周辺地域を水浸しにした

an investment	bank	投資銀行
the opposite	bank	向こう岸
the far	bank	
a river	bank	川岸
the left	bank	左岸
the right	bank	右岸
a grassy	bank	草の生い茂る土手

▷He heard shouting from the **opposite bank**. 彼は対岸からの叫び声を聞いた

in	a bank	銀行に

▷One million US dollars will be deposited **in** your **bank**. 100万米ドルがあなたの銀行に振り込まれます

bankrupt /bǽŋkrʌpt/ 名 破産

go	bankrupt	破産する
be declared	bankrupt	破産宣告を受ける

▷Another company **went bankrupt** this week. 今週もう1社が倒産した
▷The company was **declared bankrupt** last week. その会社は先週破産宣告を受けた

bar /báːr/ 名 酒場;カウンター;軽食堂;棒

in	a bar	酒場で
at	the bar	カウンターの前に

▷He is too young to drink **in** a **bar**. 彼はまだ酒が飲める年齢ではない
▷Ray was sitting **at** the **bar** drinking beer. レイは酒場のカウンターの前に座ってビールを飲んでいた

a hotel	bar	ホテルのバー
a wine	bar	ワインバー
a coffee	bar	カフェバー
a salad	bar	サラダバー
a friendly	bar	くつろげるバー

bargain /báːrɡən/

名 買い得品,掘り出し物;交渉,取引,商談

look for	a bargain	掘り出し物を探す
pick up	a bargain	掘り出し物を見つける
make	a bargain	取引を決める
strike	a bargain	

▷For people **looking for** a **bargain**, we're offering discounts of up to 50%. 掘り出し物をお探しの方には最大で5割まで割引します
▷He needed financial support. So he and Benson **struck** a **bargain**. 彼は経済的支援を必要としていたので，ベンソンと取引した

a good	bargain	得な買い物
a real	bargain	すごいお買い得
a grand	bargain	大きな商談

▷Emma has an eagle eye for a **good bargain**! エマは掘り出し物に目が利く
▷I got that DVD for around $20. It was a **real bargain**. そのDVDを20ドルほどで手に入れたけど，本当に掘り出し物だった
▷The representative from Korea lacked the authority to strike a **grand bargain** with Washington. 韓国からの代表は米国政府と大きな商談ができるほどの立場にはなかった

PHRASES

That's a bargain. / It's a bargain. ☺ それで決まりだ ▷She said it was a bargain, so everything was okay after that. 「これで交渉成立」と彼女が言ってくれたので，その後はすべてうまくいった

base /béis/

图 土台，基礎；基盤；基地；(野球の)塁

provide	a base	基盤を提供する
broaden	a base	基盤を広げる
build	a base	基地をつくる
establish	a base	基地を設置する
steal	a base	盗塁する
get to	first base	1塁に出る
load	the bases	満塁にする

▷The President needed to **broaden** his political **base**. 大統領は政治基盤を広げる必要があった
▷He has enough speed to **steal** a **base**. 彼には盗塁をねらうだけの脚力がある

a firm	base	しっかりした基礎
a solid	base	
an economic	base	経済基盤
a financial	base	財政基盤
an industrial	base	産業基盤
a customer	base	顧客基盤

a military	base	軍事基地
an air	base	空軍基地
a naval	base	海軍基地
a missile	base	ミサイル基地
a stolen	base	盗塁

▷You have to establish your own **economic base**. 経済的な基盤を築かなければならない
▷The company has expanded its **customer base** from 5,000 in 1995 to over 10,000. 会社の顧客基盤は1995年の5千から1万以上に拡大した
▷Soriano had 24 homers and 25 **stolen bases**. ソリアーノは24ホームラン，25盗塁だった

at	the base	基部に

▷She sat **at** the **base** of the sacred tree. 彼女は神聖な木の根元に座った

on	base	出塁して
off	base	塁を離れて；間違って

▷With two men **on base**, Ichiro hit a three-run home run. 2人の走者を塁に置いてイチローはスリーランを放った
▷Please correct me if I'm **off base** here. 私が間違っていたら訂正してください

basis /béisis/ 图 基礎，根拠；基準

form	the basis	基礎をなす
establish	the basis	
provide	a basis	基礎となる
lay	a basis	基礎を築く

▷Agriculture **forms** the **basis** *of* our economy. 農業は経済の基盤をなしている
▷His Australian experiences **provided** a **basis** *for* his new project. オーストラリアでの経験は彼の新しい事業の基礎となった

a firm	basis	確固とした基礎
a sound	basis	
a theoretical	basis	理論的な根拠

▷A good primary education gives children a **firm basis** *for* the future. 初等教育をしっかり受けさせることは子どもたちの未来に向けたきちんとした土台となる
▷His claims have no **theoretical basis**. 彼の主張は理論的な根拠がない

on a regular	basis	定期的に
on an annual	basis	1年単位で
on a daily	basis	1日単位で
on a day-to-day	basis	

on a monthly	basis	1か月単位で
on a weekly	basis	1週間単位で
on a permanent	basis	継続的に
on a temporary	basis	臨時に
on a casual	basis	臨時雇いで
on a part-time	basis	パートで
on a global	basis	世界規模で

▷Do you take any medicines **on** a **regular basis**? 何か薬を常用していますか
▷I have visited New Zealand **on** an **annual basis** for several years. 数年間，毎年ニュージーランドを訪れている
▷She was employed **on** a **part-time basis**. 彼女はパートタイムで雇われた
▷We will have to deal with this issue **on** a **global basis** in the 21st century. 21世紀にはこの問題に世界規模で取り組まなければならないだろう

on	the basis of A	Aに基づいて
on	the basis that...	…に基づいて

▷Decisions will be made **on** the **basis of** each individual case. 決定は個々の事例に基づいてなされる

bath /bǽθ | bɑ́ːθ/ 名 入浴，ふろ；浴槽，浴室

take	a bath	入浴する
have	a bath	
run	a bath	浴槽に湯を張る
lie in	a bath	湯につかる
soak in	a bath	
give A	a bath	Aをふろに入れる

▷Do you want to **take** a **bath** after supper? 夕食の後にふろに入りたいですか
▷I'll go and **run** a **bath**. ふろの湯を入れてくるよ
▷**Soaking in** a **bath** helps me to relax. ふろにつかるとリラックスする
▷Let me help you **give** the baby a **bath**. 赤ん坊をふろに入れるのを手伝わせて

a hot	bath	(熱い)ふろ
a bubble	bath	泡ぶろ
a steam	bath	スチームバス，蒸しぶろ
a whirlpool	bath	ジェットバス

▷I'm going to take a long, **hot bath**. ゆっくり，熱いふろに入ってくるよ

a room	with bath	バスつきの部屋

▷Twin, three-bedded **rooms with bath** or shower are available. バスあるいはシャワーつきのツイン，スリーベッドの部屋が利用可能です

bathroom /bǽθrùːm | bɑ́ːθ-/
名 浴室；《米》トイレ

go to	the bathroom	トイレに行く

▷I felt very sick so I **went to** the **bathroom**. ひどく吐き気がしてトイレに駆け込んだ

[PHRASES]
May I use your bathroom? 《米》トイレをお借りしていいですか

battle /bǽtl/ 名 戦闘，戦い；闘争

do	battle	戦う
fight	a battle	
lose	a battle	戦いに負ける
win	a battle	戦いに勝つ

▷Instead of **doing battle** *with* business rivals he is now enjoying being a family man. 仕事上のライバルたちとの競争よりも，いまの彼には家庭が大事だ
▷His mother **lost** a **battle** *against* cancer. 彼の母親はがんとの戦いに負けた

a battle	begins	戦いが始まる
a battle	takes place	戦いが起こる
a battle	rages	戦いが激しく続く
a battle	ends	戦いが終わる

▷The **battle took place** at Stamford Bridge 12 miles east of York. その戦いはヨークの東12マイルのスタンフォードブリッジで起こった
▷For four hours a pitched **battle raged** outside the embassy. 4時間の間，激しい戦いが大使館の外で続いた

a bitter	battle	激戦，激しい戦い
a fierce	battle	
a bloody	battle	血みどろの戦い
a desperate	battle	必死の戦い
a decisive	battle	勝敗を決める戦い
a constant	battle	絶え間ない戦い
an uphill	battle	困難な戦い
a losing	battle	勝ち目のない戦い
a legal	battle	法廷闘争

▷The two candidates fought a **bitter battle** throughout the election campaign. 2人の候補者は選挙運動の最初から最後まで激しい戦いを繰り広げた
▷The rescue services were facing an **uphill battle** from the start. 救助隊は最初から困難な戦いに直面していた
▷He fought his **legal battle** for 22 years and won. 彼は法廷闘争を22年間戦い，勝った

in	battle	戦争で

▷He was killed **in battle**. 彼は戦死した

a battle	with A	Aとの戦い
a battle	against A	
a battle	between A	Aの間の戦い
a battle	for A	Aを求める戦い

▷Children are often caught up in the **battle between** their fathers and mothers. 子どもたちはしばしば夫婦間の争いに巻き込まれる

a battle	to do	…する戦い

▷We won the **battle to** save the local hospital. 地元の病院を存続させる戦いに勝った

beach /bíːtʃ/ 名 浜; 海辺

a sandy	beach	砂浜
a pebbly	beach	小石の多い浜辺
a deserted	beach	だれもいない浜辺
a private	beach	個人所有の浜辺

▷They were sitting on a **deserted beech** watching the sunset together. 彼らはいっしょに夕焼けを見ながら人気のない浜辺に座っていた

at	the beach	海辺で
on	the beach	
along	the beach	浜辺に沿って

▷We spent our summer holidays in a small guesthouse **at** the **beach**. 夏の休暇を海辺の小さなゲストハウスで過ごした ▷Let's go swimming **at** the **beach**. 海に泳ぎに行こう(★ swim との連続では on より at が好まれる)
▷I lay **on** the **beach** all afternoon. 午後ずっと浜辺に寝そべって過ごした(★ × lie at a beach とはいわない)

bear /béər/ 動 耐える, 負う; 我慢する

can't	bear doing	…するのに耐えられない
can't	bear to do	
can	hardly bear to do	…するのにとうてい耐えられない

▷I **can't bear** watch**ing** this DVD any longer. It's much too violent. これ以上このDVDを見ていられない. あまりにも暴力的だ
▷I **can't bear to** disappoint him now. 彼をいま失望させるのは耐えがたい

beat /bíːt/

動 打つ, たたく; 打ち負かす; かきまぜる, 泡立てる

easily	beat	簡単に打ち負かす
narrowly	beat	きわどく打ち負かす
be well	beaten	完敗する
be badly	beaten	ひどく殴られる
be severely	beaten	
beat	well	よく泡立てる

▷He **easily beat** the national champion. 彼は簡単にナショナルチャンピオンを破った
▷Canada **narrowly beat** the United States in the final. カナダは決勝でかろうじてアメリカを破った
▷Jack has been **badly beaten** on his chest and stomach. ジャックは胸と腹をひどく殴られた
▷Add the flour and the egg yolks and **beat well**. 小麦粉と卵黄を加えてよく泡立ててください

| beat A | at B | Bの試合でAを破る |
| beat A | by B | Bの差でAを破る |

▷She's a great swimmer, but she got **beaten by** half a length. 彼女はすごい水泳選手だが, 体半分の差で敗れた

beautiful /bjúːtəfəl/ 形 美しい, きれいな

| look | beautiful | 美しく見える |

▷You **look** absolutely **beautiful** today. きょうはほんとうにきれいだね

extremely	beautiful	すごく美しい
extraordinarily	beautiful	並はずれて美しい
absolutely	beautiful	実に美しい
breathtakingly	beautiful	はっとするほど美しい
strikingly	beautiful	
particularly	beautiful	とりわけ美しい

▷She was tall and **breathtakingly beautiful**. 彼女は背が高くて息をのむほど美しかった

beauty /bjúːti/ 名 美, 美しさ; 美人

great	beauty	大変な美しさ
outstanding	beauty	傑出した美しさ
sheer	beauty	美そのもの
natural	beauty	自然の美しさ
physical	beauty	肉体美
a great	beauty	絶世の美女
a real	beauty	すごい美人; すてきな物

▷Nepal is a country of outstanding **natural beauty**.
ネパールは非常に美しい国だ
▷She was a **real beauty** with black hair and dark eyes. 彼女は黒髪で黒い目のすごい美人だった

bed /béd/ 名 ベッド

go to	bed	寝る
get into	bed	ベッドに入る
climb into	bed	ベッドにもぐり込む
get out of	bed	ベッドから出る
climb out of	bed	ベッドからはい出す
lie in	bed	ベッドに横になる
stay in	bed	ベッドで寝ている
put A to	bed	Aを寝かしつける
share	a bed	同じベッドに寝る
make	the bed	ベッドを整える

▷I **go to bed** around 11pm. 11時ごろ寝る
▷I set the clock for eight and **got into bed**. 時計を8時にセットして寝た
▷I **climbed into bed** and fell asleep. ベッドにもぐり込んで眠り込んだ
▷Nick **got out of bed** to go to the toilet. ニックはトイレに行くために起きた
▷Helen **lay in bed** and tried to sleep. ヘレンはベッドに横になって、眠ろうとした
▷You look tired. You should **stay in bed**. 疲れているみたいだね。ベッドで休んでいなさい
▷Can you **put** the children **to bed**? 子どもたちを寝かしつけてくれるかい
▷Okay, you two boys can **share** a bed. じゃ、きみたち男の子2人は同じベッドに寝てね

in	bed	ベッドに入って
out of	bed	ベッドから出て

▷Julie can't come this evening. She's **in bed** with the flu. ジュリーはインフルエンザで寝込んでいるので今夜は来られないよ

a flower	bed	花壇

PHRASES
(**It's**) **time for bed.** ☺ 寝る時間だ

begin /bigín/ 動 始まる；始める

immediately	begin	すぐに始まる
suddenly	begin	急に始まる
slowly	begin	ゆっくり始まる
soon	begin	まもなく始まる

begin	again	再び始まる

★immediately, slowly は動詞の後でも用いる

▷If everything is ready, let's **begin immediately**! 準備ができているならすぐ始めよう
▷I was **slowly beginning** to realize that nobody was listening to me. だれも私の話を聞いていないことに徐々に気づき始めていた
▷She took a deep breath and **began again**. 彼女は深呼吸をして再び始めた

begin	doing	…し始める
begin	to do	

▷He sat down and **began** talk**ing** to Allison. 彼は座ってアリソンに話し始めた
▷Slowly she was **beginning to** understand the situation. ゆっくりと彼女には状況がわかり始めていた

begin	by doing	…することから始める
begin	with A	Aから始める

▷Let me **begin by** tell**ing** you a little about Roy. まず始めにロイのことについて少し話させてください

beginning /bigíniŋ/ 名 始め, 最初, 始まり

mark	the beginning	始まりを告げる
see	the beginning(s)	始まりがわかる

▷When the plum blossom comes out it **marks** the **beginning** of spring. 梅の花が咲き出すと春の訪れだ
▷I could **see** the **beginning** of tears in her eyes. 彼女の目に涙があふれてくるのがわかった

a new	beginning	新たな出発
small	beginnings	小さな始まり

▷Now is the time for a **new beginning**. 今が再出発の時だ
▷She grew her business from **small beginnings** at home. 彼女は自宅で立ち上げた小さな事業を大きく育てた

at	the beginning (of A)	(Aの)初めに
in	the beginning	初めは
from	beginning to end	初めから終わりまで
from the very beginning		いちばん初めから
right from the beginning		

▷They're getting married **at** the **beginning of** next year. 彼らは来年の初めに結婚する予定だ
▷Why didn't you say that **in** the **beginning**? なぜ最初にそう言わなかったの

| behave |

▷I hope you all enjoy the show **from beginning to end**. みなさん，ショーを最後まで存分にお楽しみください
▷You should have told me **right from the beginning**. いちばん最初に私に話しておくべきだった

PHRASES
This is only the beginning. ☺これはほんの始まりにすぎない

behave /bihéiv/ 動 ふるまう，態度をとる

behave	well	行儀よくふるまう
behave	badly	無作法にふるまう
behave	properly	きちんとふるまう
behave	responsibly	責任をもってふるまう
behave	strangely	奇妙なふるまいをする
behave	differently	別のふるまいをする

▷How was it? Did Andy **behave well**? どうだった？アンディはお行儀よくしていたかい
▷I want you to **behave properly**, understand? きちんとふるまってよ，わかった？
▷Perhaps you would **behave differently** if you knew the true facts. 真実を知っていたなら，あなたはたぶん別の行動をとっただろう

behave	in a ... way	…にふるまう

★…には particular, similar, foolish などがくる

▷If you want him to help you, you need to **behave in a particular way**. 彼に手助けしてもらいたいのなら，それなりのふるまい方がある

behave	as if	…であるかのようにふるまう
behave	as though	
behave	like A	Aのようにふるまう
behave	toward A	A(人)に対してふるまう

▷She was **behaving as if** nothing had happened. 彼女は何事も起こらなかったかのようにふるまっていた
▷Stop **behaving like** a child! 子どもみたいなふるまいはやめなさい
▷How does she **behave toward** her colleagues? 彼女は同僚にどのようにふるまっているのか

behavior /bihéivjər/

名 態度，ふるまい，行動(★(英)つづりは behaviour)

affect	A's behavior	行動に影響する
observe	A's behavior	行動を観察する
change	one's behavior	行動を改める

▷Nothing that we say to him **affects** his **behavior**. 彼に何を言っても彼の行動に影響はない
▷After the boss spoke to him he completely **changed** his **behavior**. 上司が彼に話すと彼はすっかり態度を改めた

good	behavior	よいふるまい
bad	behavior	悪いふるまい
aggressive	behavior	攻撃的なふるまい
violent	behavior	暴力的なふるまい
human	behavior	人間の行動
sexual	behavior	性行動
social	behavior	社会的行動

▷I must apologize for my **bad behavior**. 私の態度が悪かったことを謝らなければなりません
▷We don't allow any **aggressive behavior** here. ここではいかなる攻撃的なふるまいも許さない
▷**Human behavior** is so variable from person to person. 人間の行動は人によって実にさまざまだ

a pattern of	behavior	行動様式

▷Habits and regular **patterns of behavior** make us feel comfortable. 習慣や規則正しい行動様式のおかげで我々の気持ちは落ち着く

behavior	toward A	Aに対する態度

▷I suppose your **behavior toward** me will never change. あなたの私に対する態度は決して変わらないだろうと思う

behavior and attitudes		態度と行動

★attitudes and behavior ともいう

▷We are twins and both similar in our **attitudes and behavior**. 私たちは双子で，態度や行動が似ている

belief /bilíːf/ 名 信念；信条，信仰

have	a belief	信念がある
hold	a belief	信念を抱く
express	one's belief	信念を表明する

▷She **has** a strong **belief** in her ability to do well. 自分はきちんとやれると彼女は強く信じている

a firm	belief	強い信念
a strong	belief	
a general	belief	一般に信じられていること
a popular	belief	
a widespread	belief	広く信じられていること
a widely-held	belief	
a growing	belief	広がりつつある見方

personal	belief	個人的な信念
a false	belief	勘違い
a mistaken	belief	

▷Contrary to **popular belief**, a sleeping mind is often busier than one that's awake. 一般に思われているのに反して，起きているときより睡眠中のほうが精神活動はより活発だ

▷The man was shot dead by police in the **mistaken belief** that he was a suicide bomber. その男は自爆テロ犯と勘違いされて警察に射殺された

| a belief | in A | Aを信じること |
| beyond | belief | 信じられないほど |

▷I have a strong **belief in** God. 神を強く信じている
▷Julia was shocked **beyond belief**. ジュリアは信じられないほどショックを受けた

believe /bilíːv/ 動 信じる

firmly	believe	固く信じている
really	believe	
genuinely	believe	心から信じている
truly	believe	
no longer	believe	もはや信じていない
still	believe	まだ信じている
can hardly	believe	ほとんど信じられない
be widely	believed	多くの人が信じている
be generally	believed	

▷I **firmly believe** that I'm doing the right thing. 自分は正しいことをしていると固く信じている
▷Do you **really believe** what you said? 自分の言ったことを本当に信じているの？
▷I **could hardly believe** what I had just heard! 自分の耳がほとんど信じられなかった
▷It is **widely believed** that Mars once had seas. 火星にはかつて海があったと広く信じられている

| find it hard | to believe | …とは信じられ |
| find it difficult | to believe | ない |

▷I **found it difficult to believe** that he would do such a thing. 彼がそんなことをするとは信じられなかった

| believe | (that)... | …だと信じる，思う |

▷I **believe** we've met before. 以前にお会いしたことがありますよね

belt /bélt/ 名 ベルト；地帯

fasten	one's **belt**	ベルトを締める
unbuckle	one's **belt**	ベルトをはずす
undo	one's **belt**	
tighten	one's **belt**	ベルトをきつくする；倹約する
loosen	one's **belt**	ベルトをゆるめる
wear	a **belt**	ベルトをしている

▷**Fasten** your seat **belt**. シートベルトを締めてください
▷He **undid** his seat **belt** and turned off the engine. 彼はシートベルトをはずし，エンジンを止めた
▷She **tightened** the **belt** of her dress. 彼女は服のベルトをきつくした ▷It's time to **tighten** our **belt** financially. 生活を切り詰めるときだ

benefit /bénəfit/

名 利益，恩恵；手当，給付(金)

enjoy	the benefit	利益を享受する
have	the benefit	利益にあずかる
gain	the benefit	利益を得る
reap	the benefit	
bring	benefits	利益をもたらす
offer	the benefit	
claim	(a) benefit	手当を申請する
get	(a) benefit	手当を受ける
receive	(a) benefit	

▷We can no longer **enjoy** the **benefit** *of* overtime pay. もはや残業手当を当てにはできない
▷I've been lucky because I've **had** the **benefit** *of* an experienced coach. 経験豊かなコーチに恵まれて幸運だった
▷New technologies like these **bring benefits** to society. このような新しい科学技術は社会に利益をもたらす
▷If your income is low, you may be able to **claim benefits**. 収入が少なければ給付金を申請できるかもしれない
▷Do you expect to **receive** Social Security **benefits** when you retire? 退職時に社会保障給付を受け取れると思いますか

mutual	benefit	相互利益
the potential	benefits	潜在的利益
public	benefit	公益
fringe	benefits	付加給付
welfare	benefits	福祉手当
child	benefit	児童手当
disability	benefit	障害手当
housing	benefit	住宅手当
sickness	benefit	療養給付
unemployment	benefit	失業手当

▷Doctors are enthusiastic about the **potential bene-**

| best |

fits of the new drug.　新薬がもたらすかもしれない恩恵に医師たちは大きな期待を抱いている
▷Economic growth can bring **social benefits**.　経済成長は社会的利益をもたらしうる

for	A's benefit	Aのために
without	the benefit of A	Aの助けなしに

▷I didn't do it **for** your **benefit**.　あなたのためにそれをしたのではありません
▷She learned French **without** the **benefit of** a teacher.　彼女は先生の世話になることなくフランス語を学んだ

best /bést/ 形 最高の, いちばんの, 最もよい

the very	best	まさに最高の
by far the	best	断然最高の
easily the	best	
probably	best	おそらく最高の

▷Mark got the **very best** education.　マークはまさに最高の教育を受けた
▷It's **probably best** you don't go.　あなたが行かないのがたぶん最善だろう

best	for A	Aにとっていちばんよい

▷I know what's **best for** you.　きみにとっていちばんよいかわかっている

be best	to do	…するのがいちばんだ

▷I decided it was **best to** tell the truth.　本当のことを言うのがいちばんだと心に決めた

better /bétər/ 形 よりよい

feel	better	気分がよくなる
get	better	よくなる; 元気になる

▷A nice cup of tea will make you **feel better**.　おいしいお茶を飲めば気分がよくなるでしょう

considerably	better	ずっとよい
significantly	better	
much	better	
a bit	better	少しよい
a little	better	
slightly	better	

▷His illness became **considerably better**.　彼の病気はかなりよくなった
▷Things are beginning to get **significantly better**.　事態はかなりよくなり始めている
▷He looked **much better** in a suit.　スーツを着ると彼はさらに見栄えがした
▷I feel **a bit better** now.　少し気分がよくなりました
▷If you climb on the roof, you'll see the parade **even better**.　屋上に上がればパレードがさらによく見えるだろう

better	than A	Aよりよい
better	at A	Aがより得意な

▷Your vision is **better than** mine.　あなたは私より視力がいい
▷He was **better at** understanding English than I was at figuring out Chinese.　私の中国語の理解力より彼の英語の理解力のほうが上だった

be better	to do	…するほうがいい

▷It would be **better to** do it now.　それをいまするほうがいいだろう ♦**Wouldn't it be better...?** ☺ …のほうがよくありませんか ▷Wouldn't it be better to leave in the morning?　午前中に出かけたほうがいいんじゃないの？

PHRASES
That's better. ☺ よくなったよ, その調子; 楽になったでしょう ▷I'll add some more salt...That's better.　もう少し塩を加えます. おいしくなりました

bicycle /báisikl/ 名 自転車

ride	a bicycle	自転車に乗る
get on	a bicycle	自転車にまたがる
get off	a bicycle	自転車から降りる
fall off	a bicycle	自転車で転ぶ
pedal	a bicycle	自転車をこぐ

▷I taught her to **ride** a **bicycle**.　彼女に自転車の乗り方を教えた
▷He **fell off** his **bicycle** while riding with friends.　彼は友人たちといっしょに自転車に乗っていて転んだ

big /bíg/ 形 大きい; 年上の

grow	big	大きくなる
seem	big	大きそうだ

▷The world economy **grew bigger** and ever more complex than before.　世界経済は以前にも増して拡大し, はるかに複雑になった
▷When I tried this T-shirt on in the shop it seemed OK, but now it **seems** too **big**.　このTシャツを店で試着したときはよさそうだったのに, どうも大きすぎるみたいだ

fairly	big	かなり大きい

pretty	big	
really	big	すごく大きい
big	enough	十分大きい

▷Sydney has become a **pretty big** city in the last hundred years.　シドニーはこの100年でかなり大きな町になった

▷That apartment isn't **big enough** for both of us.　そのアパートは私たち2人には十分な大きさではない

bill /bíl/

名 請求書；《英》(レストランの)勘定書；法案

pay	a bill	勘定を払う
settle	the bill	
run up	a bill	つけをためる
have	the bill	勘定書を受け取る
split	the bill	割り勘にする
introduce	a bill	法案を提出する
propose	a bill	
approve	a bill	法案を可決する
pass	a bill	
oppose	a bill	法案に反対する

▷Don't worry. I'll **pay** the **bill**.　心配しないで．私が勘定を払うから

▷Could I **have** the **bill**, please?　お勘定をお願いします

▷I'm confident we'll be able to **introduce** a **bill** to Parliament soon.　まもなく法案を国会に提出できると確信している

an electricity	bill	電気代請求書
a phone	bill	電話代請求書

bird /bə́ːrd/ **名** 鳥

feed	a bird	鳥にえさをやる

▷**Feeding birds** is an excellent way for people to learn about wildlife.　鳥にえさをやるのは人が野生動物について学ぶすばらしい方法だ

a bird	flies	鳥が飛ぶ
a bird	sings	鳥がさえずる
a bird	sits	鳥がとまっている

▷The **birds flew** from their nests in the trees.　鳥が木の巣から飛び立った

▷When I looked out the window, a strange, colorful **bird** was **sitting** on a tree branch.　窓の外を見ると変わった色鮮やかな鳥が木の枝にとまっていた

a wild	bird	野鳥
a caged	bird	かごの鳥
a migratory	bird	渡り鳥
an adult	bird	成鳥
a rare	bird	珍しい鳥

▷Let me live as a person, not as a **caged bird**.　かごの鳥のようにではなく，人間としての暮らしをさせて

a flock of	birds	鳥の群れ

▷I watched a large **flock of birds** fly over us.　鳥の大群が私たちの上の方を飛ぶのを見た

PHRASES
a little bird told me (that...) 《略式》だれかさんから聞いたんだけど　▷A little bird told me that you are going out with Helen.　うわさで聞いたんだけどヘレンとつき合っているんだって？

birth /bə́ːrθ/ **名** 誕生；出産；生まれ

give	birth (to A)	(Aを)産む

▷Jane **gave birth to** her child in August.　ジェーンは8月に子どもを出産した

at	birth	出生時に
by	birth	生まれは；生まれながらの
from	birth	生まれたときから

▷I'm a New Yorker **by birth**.　生まれながらのニューヨーカーです

one's date of	birth	生年月日
one's place of	birth	出生地

▷**Date of birth**: July 25, 1988　生年月日：1988年7月25日

▷Please write your **place of birth** here.　ここにあなたの出生地を書いてください

bite /báit/ **名** かむこと；ひと口；虫刺され

have	a bite	ひと口食べる
take	a bite	
grab	a bite	軽く食べる
get	a bite	(蚊などに)食われる

▷Would you like to **grab** a **bite** to eat?　軽く食事をしませんか

another	bite	もうひと口
a big	bite	がぶりとかむこと
a nasty	bite	ひどくかむこと
a mosquito	bite	蚊が刺すこと

| bitter |

▷He took **another bite** of his apple. 彼はリンゴをもうひと口かじった（★ another bite は高頻度で take と連結する）
▷He took a **big bite** *of* his pizza. 彼はピザをがぶりとかじった
▷She had a **mosquito bite** on her right ankle. 彼女は右足首を蚊に刺された

bitter /bítər/ 形 つらい，苦々しい；苦い

| feel | bitter | 苦々しく感じる |
| taste | bitter | 苦い味がする |

▷Mike still **feels bitter** because he wasn't promoted this year. 今年の昇進がなかったのでマイクはまだ苦々しく感じている
▷This dark chocolate **tastes** very **bitter**. このブラックチョコレートはとても苦い

increasingly	bitter	ますます激しい
extremely	bitter	すごくつらい；ひどく苦い
slightly	bitter	少しつらい；少し苦い

▷This espresso coffee tastes **extremely bitter** without sugar. このエスプレッソコーヒーは砂糖なしだとすごく苦い

| bitter | about A | Aに憤慨した |

▷I can't help but be slightly **bitter about** his comments. 彼の発言にいささか腹が立つな

blame /bléim/ 動 非難する；人のせいにする

| partly | blame | 一部…のせいにする |
| be widely | blamed | 広く非難される |

▷He **partly blamed** himself for what happened. 起こったことの責任の一端は自分にもあると彼は思った
▷Passive smoking is **widely blamed** for illness among nonsmokers. 受動喫煙は非喫煙者の健康をも損なうと広く非難されている

blame A	for B	AをBのことで非難する
blame A	on B	AをBのせいにする
be to blame	(for A)	（Aのことで）責めを負うべきだ

▷He **blamed** us **for** her accident. 彼女の事故のことで彼は私たちを責めた
▷I'm sorry (that) I **blamed** everything **on** you. すべてをあなたのせいにしてごめんなさい

don't	blame A	Aを責めない
can't	blame A	Aを責められない
can hardly	blame A	Aをほとんど責められない
can't really	blame A	Aをあまり責められない

▷I **don't blame** you if you want to leave home. お前が家を出たいとしても，責めたりしないよ
▷I **can't blame** him. He's 75 years old. 彼は責められない．75歳なんだから
▷You **can hardly blame** me for getting angry. 私が怒るのも当然だろう

blame /bléim/ 名 責任，非難

get	the blame	責任を負う
take	the blame	責任をとる
put	the blame on A	Aに責任を負わせる
lay	the blame on A	

▷Who **gets** the **blame**? だれが責任を負うのか
▷Don't worry Samantha. I'll **take the blame**. 心配しないでサマンサ．私が責任をとるから
▷She always **puts the blame on** me. 彼女はいつも私のせいにする

blind /bláind/ 名 ブラインド

draw	the blinds	ブラインドを下ろす
pull down	the blinds	
pull up	the blinds	ブラインドを上げる
raise	the blinds	

▷He **drew** the **blinds** and switched on the lights. 彼はブラインドを下ろして照明をつけた
▷She got up and **pulled up** the **blinds**. 彼女は起き上がってブラインドを上げた

block /blák | blɔ́k/

名 ブロック，かたまり；《英》ビル一棟；1区画；障害物

a large	block	大きなブロック
a big	block	
concrete	blocks	コンクリートブロック
a building	block	建築用ブロック
a mental	block	思考停止
writer's	block	物書きのスランプ

▷The wall was constructed from **large blocks** of stone. 壁は大きな石のブロックでできていた
▷She got a **mental block** and completely forgot what she was going to say. 彼女は頭の中が空っぽになり，何をしゃべるつもりだったかすっかり忘れてしまった

| two blocks | away | 2区画先に |

| two blocks | from A | Aから2区画 |

▷ The bank is about three **blocks away** from the police station. 銀行は警察の約3ブロック先です
▷ Go down two **blocks from** here and take a left. ここから2ブロック行って左へ曲がってください

block /blák | blɔ́k/ 動 さえぎる, ふさぐ

completely	block	完全にさえぎる
partially	block	部分的にさえぎる
effectively	block	うまくふさぐ
block	off	閉鎖する, ふさぐ
block	up	

▷ She stood up, **completely blocking** everyone's view from the back. 彼女が立ち上がったため、後ろからはみんな前がまったく見えなくなった
▷ The road was **partially blocked** for a time. 道路は一時的に一部閉鎖された
▷ We need to **block up** the windows with something. 窓を何かでふさぐ必要がある

blood /blʌ́d/ 名 血, 血液；血筋, 血統

lose	blood	出血する
draw	blood	血が出る；採血する
give	blood	献血する
donate	blood	
spit	blood	血を吐く, 吐血する
cough up	blood	

▷ The dog bit me but it didn't **draw blood**. 犬にかみつかれたけど血は出なかった
▷ What percentage of the population **donates blood**? 人口の何パーセントが献血をしているのか
▷ He coughed and **spat blood** on the floor. 彼はせきをして床に血を吐いた

blood	flows	血が流れる
blood	runs	
blood	oozes	血がにじむ

▷ He began to feel **blood flowing** down his leg from a wound. 彼は傷から出る血が脚を流れ落ちるのを感じ始めた
▷ The **blood ran** down his face from the cut on his forehead. 彼の額の傷口から顔に血が流れた

blood	cells	血球
blood	pressure	血圧
a blood	vessel	血管
blood	sugar	血糖(値)

| a blood | transfusion | 輸血 |
| blood | type | 血液型 |

▷ My father has high **blood pressure**. 父は血圧が高い

blow /blóu/ 動 吹く；吹き飛ばす

blow	gently	穏やかに吹く
blow	strongly	強く吹く
blow	hard	

▷ The wind was **blowing strongly** from the northeast. 北東から風が強く吹いていた

| blow | from A | Aから吹く |
| blow | A off B | AをBから吹き飛ばす |

▷ A sudden gust of wind **blew** all the papers **off** his desk. 突風が吹いて彼の机の上の書類がみな吹き飛んだ

board /bɔ́:rd/

名 板；掲示板；委員会, 会議；食事, まかない

| sit on | the board | 取締役である |

▷ He **sat on the board** of the company. 彼は会社の取締役を務めていた

a bulletin	board	掲示板
a management	board	経営会議
chairman of	the board	取締役会会長
a member of	the board	取締役会メンバー

▷ The **members of the board** glanced at one another. 取締役会のメンバーは互いに顔を見合わせた

| full | board | 3食つき宿泊代 |
| half | board | 2食つき宿泊代 |

▷ The price includes **full board**, insurance, airline tickets and airport taxes. 料金には3食つき宿泊代, 保険, 航空券と空港税が含まれます

| on | the board | 掲示板に |
| on | board | 乗り込んで |

▷ How many people are there **on board** that ship? その船には何人が乗っているのか

body /bádi | bɔ́di/ 名 体；死体；本体；団体

| keep | one's body fit | 体を健康に保つ |
| keep | one's body healthy | |

▷I want to do everything I can to **keep** my **body healthy**. 体の健康を保つためにできることは何でもしたい

A's body	aches	体が痛い
a body	was found	死体が見つかった
a body	was discovered	

▷Kelly's **body** was **found** near his home. ケリーの死体は自宅近くで発見された

A's whole	body	全身
the human	body	人体
a dead	body	死体
the main	body	本体, 本文

▷I had a cold and my **whole body** was aching. かぜを引いていて全身が痛かった
▷I guess they hid his **dead body** somewhere else. 彼の死体はどこかほかの場所に隠されているのではないだろうか
▷The **main body** of the text follows the introduction. 本文は導入部の後に来る

| body and soul | 身も心も, 全身全霊で |

▷She threw herself **body and soul** into her work. 彼女は全身全霊を込めて仕事に打ち込んだ

boil /bɔ́il/ 動 沸く, 沸かす；煮える, 煮る

| boil | rapidly | すばやく煮る |
| put A on to | boil | Aを火にかけて沸かす |

▷Chop all veggies into small pieces. **Boil rapidly** for ten minutes stirring well. 野菜をすべて細かく刻んで10分間よくかき混ぜながらすばやく煮てください
▷I **put** the kettle **on to boil**. やかんを火にかけて沸かした

bomb /bám | bɔ́m/ 名 爆弾

place	a bomb	爆弾を仕掛ける
plant	a bomb	
drop	a bomb	爆弾を投下する
a bomb	explodes	爆弾が破裂する
a bomb	goes off	

▷They **planted** a **bomb** under his car. 彼の車の下に爆弾を仕掛けられた
▷A warplane **dropped** a **bomb** on the village. 戦闘機が村に爆弾を落とした

an atomic	bomb	原子爆弾
a nuclear	bomb	核爆弾
an unexploded	bomb	不発弾
a time	bomb	時限爆弾

bomb /bám | bɔ́m/ 動 爆撃する

| be heavily | bombed | 激しい爆撃を受ける |
| be badly | bombed | |

▷Berlin was **heavily bombed** during the Second World War. ベルリンは第2次世界大戦中, 激しい爆撃を受けた

bond /bánd | bɔ́nd/ 名 きずな；債券

form	a bond	きずなを築く
develop	a bond	
strengthen	the bonds	きずなを強める
break	a bond	きずなを断ち切る
issue	bonds	債券を発行する
redeem	a bond	債券を償還する

▷These activities will **strengthen** the **bonds** between members of the community. これらの活動は地域社会のメンバー間のきずなを強めることになるだろう
▷Now is a good time to **issue** government **bonds**. いまが国債を発行するよい時期だ

a corporate	bond	社債
a government	bond	政府債, 国債
a convertible	bond	転換社債
a junk	bond	投資不適格債
a close	bond	密接なきずな
a strong	bond	強いきずな

▷My brother and I had a very **close bond** with my grandmother. 兄も私も祖母との結びつきが強かった
▷They developed a **strong bond** with one another. 彼らは互いに強いきずなを築き上げた

| a bond | between A | Aの間のきずな |
| a bond | with A | Aとのきずな |

▷The report is analyzing the **bond between** parents and children. その報告では親子のきずなが分析してある

bone /bóun/ 名 骨

| break | a bone | 骨を折る |
| crack | a bone | 骨にひびが入る |

▷He has **cracked** a **bone** in his foot. 彼は足の骨にひびが入った

brittle	bones	もろい骨
a broken	bone	折れた骨

▷Her **brittle bones** break easily. 彼女のもろくなった骨は折れやすい
▷Fortunately, he had no **broken bones**. 運のよいことに彼はどこも骨折していなかった

to	the bone	骨の髄まで；徹底的に

▷A cold wind chilled her **to the bone**. 彼女は冷たい風のせいで体の芯まで冷えてしまった

PHRASES
I (can) feel it in my bones. 直感で感じる ▷I feel it in my bones that something bad is going to happen. 何か悪いことが起きるだろうという予感がする

book /búk/ 名 本，書物；巻，編；…帳；帳簿

close	a book	本を閉じる
open	a book	本を開く
publish	a book	本を出版する
revise	a book	本を改訂する
borrow	a book	本を借りる
check out	a book	
lend	a book	本を貸す
finish	a book	本を読み終わる
review	a book	書評する
keep	books	帳簿をつける
do	the books	
close	the books	帳簿を締める
cook	the books	帳簿をごまかす

▷I **opened** the **book** to page 45. 本の45ページを開けた
▷I always **borrow** many **books** *from* the library. いつも図書館からたくさん本を借りる
▷I **lent** that **book** *to* Michael. その本をマイケルに貸した
▷She **reviews books** regularly for the New York Times. 彼女は定期的にニューヨークタイムズに書評を書いている
▷Every taxpayer is required to **keep books**. 納税者はみな帳簿をつける必要がある
▷They helped Steve **cook** the **books**. 彼らはスティーブの帳簿改ざんを手伝った

a new	book	新刊本
a recent	book	近刊本
the latest	book	最新刊
a library	book	図書館の本
an electronic	book	電子書籍
an audio	book	オーディオブック
a comic	book	まんが本
a picture	book	絵本
a reference	book	参考図書
an address	book	住所録

▷His most **recent book** was superb. 彼の近刊の本はすばらしかった
▷**Electronic books** provide a new, environmentally friendly, and inexpensive way to read. 電子書籍のおかげで，新しくて環境に優しくしかも安価な読書法が誕生している

a book	about A	Aに関する本
a book	on A	
a book	by A	Aが書いた本

▷I read a lot of **books about** history. 歴史に関する本をたくさん読んだ

book /búk/ 動 《おもに英》予約する

book	in advance	事前に予約する
book	online	オンライン予約する
be fully	booked	予約でいっぱいだ
be	booked up	

▷It's advisable to **book in advance**. 事前の予約がお勧めです
▷I'm afraid we're **fully booked** this evening. あいにく今夜は予約でいっぱいです

book	A into B	A(人)にB(ホテル)を予約してやる

▷I **booked** him **into** a hotel nearby. 彼に近くのホテルを予約してあげた

border /bɔ́ːrdər/ 名 国境，境界；縁，へり

cross	the border	国境を越える
close	the border	国境を封鎖する
seal	the border	
open	the border	国境の封鎖を解く

▷They **crossed** the **border** to get a better look at Niagara Falls. ナイアガラの滝がもっとよく見えるよう，国境を越えた

across	the border	国境の向こうに
over	the border	
on	the border	境界近くに

▷Perhaps the helicopter will come from **across** the **border**. おそらくそのヘリコプターは国境の向こうからやっ

| boring |

てくるだろう

▷He lives in a small town **on** the **border** between Cambodia and Vietnam. 彼はカンボジアとベトナムの国境に近い小さな町で暮らしている

| the border | between A | Aの間の国境 |
| the border | with A | Aとの国境 |

▷We'll cross the **border between** Manitoba and Ontario in about an hour if we leave soon. いますぐ出発すれば1時間ほどでマニトバ州とオンタリオ州の州境を越えるだろう

| south | of the border | 国境の南側に |
| north | of the border | 国境の北側に |

▷I did a little business just **south of** the **border** in Mexico. メキシコの国境のすぐ南側でちょっとした商売をしていた

boring /bɔ́ːriŋ/ 形 退屈な,つまらない

| dead | boring | まったく退屈な |
| ★ dead boring はくだけた表現 | | |

▷The speech was **dead boring**. 演説はとても退屈だった

born /bɔ́ːrn/ 形 (be bornで)生まれる

be born	in A	A(場所)で生まれる
be born	on A	A(日付)に生まれる
be born	into A	A(家庭)に生まれる

▷Sir Simon Rattle was **born in** Liverpool in 1955. サイモン・ラトルは1955年にリバプールで生まれた
▷I was **born on** November 3rd, 1980. 私は1980年11月3日に生まれました
▷He had been **born into** a wealthy family. 彼は裕福な家庭に生まれた

| be | born and raised | 生まれ育つ |

▷He was **born and raised** in Ohio. 彼はオハイオで生まれ育った

borrow /bárou | bɔ́r-/ 動 借りる

| borrow | heavily | 多額の借金をする |

▷I've **borrowed heavily** *from* the bank to buy a house. 家を買うために銀行からたくさん金を借りた

| borrow | A from B | A(物)をB(人)から借りる |

▷He **borrowed** the umbrella **from** Eric. 彼は傘をエリックから借りた ▷Can I **borrow** the book **from** the library? その本を図書館で借りられるかな

bother /báðər | bɔ́ð-/

動 煩わせる,心配させる;迷惑をかける

| be not particularly | bothered | 特に心配して |
| be not really | bothered | いない |

▷I wasn't particularly bothered by their behavior — I know kids will behave like kids. 子どもたちのふるまいは特に気になりませんでした．子どもは子どもらしくふるまうものだから

| bother | about A | Aを気にする |
| bother | with A | |

▷Don't **bother about** us. 私たちのことはお構いなく
▷Don't **bother with** tidying up the apartment. アパートの片づけのことは気にしないで

| bother | to do | わざわざ…する |

▷He didn't **bother to** lock his bicycle. 彼は自転車の鍵をわざわざかけなかった

bottle /bátl | bɔ́tl/ 名 瓶

an empty	bottle	空瓶
a half	bottle	ハーフボトル
half a	bottle	瓶の半分
a whole	bottle	ひと瓶全部

▷Let's order a **half bottle** of wine. ワインをハーフボトルで注文しよう
▷There's **half** a **bottle** of wine left. ワインが瓶に半分残っている
▷He drank a **whole bottle** of whisky last night. 昨夜彼はウイスキーを1本空けてしまった

| a beer | bottle | ビール瓶 |
| a milk | bottle | 牛乳瓶 |

bottom /bátəm | bɔ́t-/

名 底;下部;最下位;奥;しり

reach	the bottom	底に達する
get to	the bottom	底に達する;真相を究明する
hit	(the) bottom	底をつく

▷She **reached** the **bottom** *of* the stairs and opened

the door quietly. 彼女は階段を降りきってドアを静かに閉めた
▷Eventually he **got to** the **bottom** *of* the problem. とうとう彼は事の真相を突き止めた
▷In early 1997 I lost my full-time job and **hit bottom**. 1997年の初めに常勤の仕事をなくしたころはどん底だった

at	the bottom	底に, 下に；ふもとに
at	bottom	心底は, 本当は
from	the bottom	底から；下から

▷The body of a man was found **at** the **bottom** of the lake. 男の死体が湖底で見つかった
▷**At bottom**, I know you'll always be there for me. 本当はきみがいつも私の力になってくれるとわかっている
▷Thank you **from** the **bottom** of my heart. 心から感謝します
▷Please look at page 10, fourth line **from** the **bottom**. 10ページの下から4行目を見てください

bow /báu/ 名 おじぎ

make	a bow	おじぎをする
give	a bow	

▷The conductor **made** a deep **bow** to the audience who applauded wildly. 指揮者は盛大な拍手にこたえて聴衆に深々とおじぎをした

a little	bow	軽いおじぎ
a slight	bow	
a deep	bow	深いおじぎ

▷He gave a **slight bow** to each guest as they arrived for the wedding ceremony. 結婚式の客が到着すると彼はひとりひとりに軽くおじぎをした

boy /bɔ́i/ 名 男の子, 少年；息子

a big	boy	大きな男の子
a little	boy	小さな男の子
a small	boy	
a baby	boy	男の赤ちゃん
a good	boy	よい子
a bad	boy	いたずらな少年
a naughty	boy	
a clever	boy	賢い少年
a poor	boy	かわいそうな少年

★a small boy は体が普通より小さいというニュアンスを伴うことがある

▷Don't worry, mom. I'm a **big boy** now. 心配しないで, ママ. ぼくはもう大きいんだから
▷Is that **little boy** your son? あの小さな男の子は息子さんですか
▷Be a **good boy**, okay? よい子にしていてね, いい？
▷Our son, Peter... he's a really **naughty boy**. 息子のピーターは本当にいたずらっ子だ
▷I can imagine your shock, **poor boy**. ショックはよくわかるよ, かわいそうに

PHRASES
Boys will be boys. ☺ 男の子はそんなものだ

brain /bréin/ 名 脳；頭脳, 知能

have	a brain	頭がよい
have	brains	
rack	one's brain(s)	知恵を絞る
pick	A's brain(s)	知恵を借りる
use	one's brain(s)	頭を使う

▷She **racked** her **brains** for a solution. 彼女は知恵を絞って解決法を探した
▷Would you mind if I **picked** your **brains** a little? 少しお知恵を拝借できますか
▷**Use** your **brain(s)**! 頭を使えよ

on	the brain	脳に

▷Her doctor told her that she had a tumor **on** the **brain**. 脳に腫瘍があると彼女は医師から言われた
◆**have** A **on the brain** Aのことばかり考えている ▷She's had SMAP on the brain ever since she went to see their concert. 彼女はコンサートを見に行ってからSMAPのことばかり考えている

brake /bréik/ 名 ブレーキ

apply	the brake(s)	ブレーキをかける
put on	the brake(s)	
slam on	the brakes	急ブレーキをかける
jam on	the brakes	
release	the brakes	ブレーキを緩める

▷She **put on** the **brakes**, but couldn't stop in time. 彼女はブレーキをかけたが間に合わなかった
▷James **slammed on** the **brakes** and did a U-turn. ジェームズは急ブレーキをかけてUターンした
▷**Release** the **brakes** and head for the parking lot exit. ブレーキを緩めて駐車場の出口へ行ってください

brake /bréik/ 動 ブレーキをかける

break	hard	急ブレーキをかける
brake	suddenly	

| branch |

brake	to a halt	ブレーキをかけて止まる

▷The bus driver **braked suddenly** and everybody was thrown forward. バスの運転手が急ブレーキをかけると、みんな前方に投げ出された
▷When you come to an intersection you need to **brake to** a halt. 交差点に来たらブレーキをかけて止まる必要がある

branch /bræntʃ | brάːntʃ/

名 枝;支店;部門;支流

a low	branch	低い枝
the topmost	branch	てっぺんの枝
bare	branches	葉を落とした枝
a local	branch	地方支店
an overseas	branch	海外支店
the legislative	branch	立法府
the executive	branch	行政府
the judicial	branch	司法府

▷**Local branches** are listed in the phone book. 地方支社の番号は電話帳に載っている
▷The company has two **overseas branches** in Paris and NewYork. その会社の海外支社は2つで、パリとニューヨークに置かれている

brave /bréiv/ 形 勇敢な, 勇ましい

brave	enough	(…する)勇気がある

▷Bill wishes he were **brave enough** to tell the truth. 真実を話す勇気が自分にあったらよかったのにとビルは思っている

bread /bréd/ 名 パン;糧, 生計

bake	(the) bread	パンを焼く
cut	(the) bread	パンを切る
slice	(the) bread	
toast	(the) bread	パンをトーストする

▷She **baked bread** and cookies this morning. 彼女はけさパンとクッキーを焼いた
▷**Cut the bread** into smaller pieces. パンを小さく何切れかに切ってください

fresh	bread	焼きたてのパン
freshly baked	bread	
toasted	bread	トーストしたパン
brown	bread	黒パン
white	bread	白パン
wholewheat	bread	全粒粉パン
《英》wholemeal	bread	

▷Here's some **freshly baked bread** and a nice cup of tea! 焼きたてのパンとおいしい紅茶をどうぞ
▷Sam ordered a cup of tea, scrambled eggs and **toasted bread**. サムは紅茶、スクランブルエッグとトーストパンを注文した
▷I had a ham sandwich in **brown bread**. 黒パンのハムサンドイッチを食べた

a loaf of	bread	パンひとかたまり
a piece of	bread	一切れのパン
a chunk of	bread	(切りとった)パンの
a hunk of	bread	大きな一片
a slice of	bread	パン1枚

▷He toasted a **piece of bread** and buttered it. 彼はパンの一切れをトーストしてバターを塗った

bread and butter	バターを塗ったパン
bread and jam	ジャムを塗ったパン
bread and cheese	チーズを添えたパン
bread and milk	パンと牛乳
bread and wine	パンとぶどう酒, 聖餐

▷"What would you like for breakfast?" "Only some **bread and butter**, please."「朝食は何がよろしいですか」「バターを塗ったパンだけください」 ◆**earn** one's **bread and butter** 生計を立てる ▷We know we can't earn our bread and butter from rock music alone. ロックミュージックだけでは生計を立てていけないのはわかっている

break /bréik/ 名 休憩, 休暇;中断, 断絶

have	a break	休憩をとる, 休みをとる
take	a break	
need	a break	休暇を必要とする
make	the break	決別する

▷How about we **have a break** for a moment? ちょっと休憩を入れたらどうかな
▷I need to **take a break**. 休憩が必要だ

a short	break	短い休み
a lunch	break	昼休み
a tea	break	ティーブレイク
a coffee	break	コーヒーブレイク
a Christmas	break	クリスマス休暇
a clean	break	きっぱり別れること, 決
a complete	break	別
a commercial	break	コマーシャルによる中断
a career	break	休職

a big	break	幸運
a lucky	break	

▷When's your **lunch break**? 昼休みはいつですか
▷I shouldn't see him ever again. I should make a **clean break**. 彼とは2度と会うまい．きっぱり縁を切ろう
▷Postwar art showed a **complete break** with the past. 戦後の芸術は過去との完全な決別を示した
▷We have to take a quick **commercial break**. ではここでちょっとコマーシャルです(★テレビのキャスターが用いる)
▷I'm waiting for my **big break**. My dream is to become a famous actor. 幸運を待っています．私の夢は有名な俳優になることです

without	a break	休みなし

▷Very often doctors are expected to work 24 hours **without** a **break**. 医者は24時間ぶっ通しで働くものだと思われることが多い

[PHRASES]
Give me a break! 😊 いいかげんにしてくれ

break /bréik/ 動 壊す, 壊れる；中断する

break	in two	半分に割る；半分に
break	in half	割れる
break	up	ばらばらにする

▷The wire **broke in two**. 電線は2つに切れた

breakfast /brékfəst/ 名 朝食

eat	breakfast	朝食をとる
have	breakfast	
cook	breakfast	朝食をつくる
make	breakfast	
skip	breakfast	朝食を抜く

▷We **have breakfast** at 7:30 every morning. 朝食はいつも7時半です
▷I'll **make breakfast** today. きょうはぼくが朝食をつくるよ

a big	breakfast	たっぷりした朝食
a hearty	breakfast	
a light	breakfast	軽い朝食
a continental	breakfast	大陸式朝食
an English	breakfast	英国式朝食
a quick	breakfast	さっととる朝食
an early	breakfast	朝早い朝食
a late	breakfast	遅い朝食

▷I ate a **big breakfast**. I'm still full. 朝食をしっかり食べたので，まだおなかがすいていない
▷Traditional **English breakfast** is delicious. 伝統的な英国式朝食はとてもおいしい
▷In the mornings I just have a **quick breakfast**. 毎日さっと朝食を済ませる
▷We set off after an **early breakfast**. 早めに朝食をとって出かけた

breakfast	in bed	ベッドでとる朝食

▷You don't look well. Don't get up. I'll bring you **breakfast in bed**. 具合が悪そうだね．そのまま寝ていて．ベッドまで朝ご飯を持ってきてあげる

for	breakfast	朝食に

▷What did you have **for breakfast**? 朝食は何を食べたの

breath /bréθ/ 名 息, 呼吸；ひと息

draw	(a) breath	息を吸う
take	a breath	
inhale	a breath	
let out	a breath	息を吐く
exhale	a breath	
hold	one's breath	息を止める
catch	one's breath	呼吸を整える
gasp for	breath	苦しくてハアハアいう
waste	one's breath	むだなことを言う

▷She stopped and **took** a deep **breath**. 彼女は立ち止まって深呼吸した
▷Can you **hold** your **breath** for 15 seconds? 15秒間息を止めていられるかい
▷I sat there for a moment trying to **catch** my **breath**. そこにしばらく腰掛けて呼吸を整えようとした
▷He **gasped for breath** and coughed again. 彼はハアハア息をしてまたせきをした
▷Just leave her alone. Don't **waste** your **breath** on her. 彼女はほうっておけよ．彼女に何を言ってもむだだから

a deep	breath	深呼吸
a long	breath	長い呼吸
a shallow	breath	浅い呼吸
a shaky	breath	震えるような息づかい
a shuddering	breath	
warm	breath	温かい息
bad	breath	くさい息

▷Mark took a **long breath**. マークは長く呼吸した
▷She let out a **shaky breath**. "Wow! That car nearly hit us!" 彼女は声を震わせて言った．「ああ，もう少しで車にはねられるところだった」

| breathe |

▷I could feel her **warm breath** on my cheek. 彼女の温かい息をほおに感じた
▷I hope I don't have **bad breath**. 息がくさくないといいのだけれど

out of	breath	息が切れて
under	one's breath	声をひそめて

▷I was **out of breath** but I kept running. 息切れしたが走り続けた
▷"Damn!" he said **under** his **breath**. 「ちくしょう」と彼は小声で言った

breathe /bríːð/ 動 呼吸する, 息をする

breathe	quickly	速く息をする
breathe	slowly	ゆっくり息をする
breathe	deeply	深呼吸する
breathe	heavily	荒い息づかいをする
breathe	hard	
breathe	easily	ほっと息をつく
breathe	again	
breathe	normally	呼吸を整える
breathe	properly	
breathe	in	息を吸う
breathe	out	息を吐く

▷She started **breathing quickly** and a worried look came across her face. 彼女の息づかいは速くなり, 不安げな表情を顔に浮かべた
▷Close your eyes, and **breathe deeply**. 目を閉じて深呼吸をしてください
▷"This mountain is steeper than I thought," she said, **breathing heavily**. 「この山は思っていたより険しいわ」と彼女は荒い息づかいで言った
▷She had an attack of asthma and couldn't **breathe properly**. ぜんそくの発作がひどくて彼女は呼吸を整えられなかった

bridge /brídʒ/ 名 橋; かけ橋

build	a bridge	橋をかける
cross	the bridge	橋を渡る

▷There's a plan to **build a bridge** across the Mississippi River. ミシシッピ川に橋をかける計画がある
▷Sport can **build** a **bridge** between nations. スポーツは国家間のかけ橋となりうる

over	the bridge	橋の上を
across	the bridge	
under	the bridge	橋の下を
a bridge	over A	Aにかかる橋

a bridge	across A

▷We walked **across** the **bridge** to the Tate Modern. 橋を渡ってテイトモダン(美術館)まで歩いて行った
▷There are 31 **bridges over** the Thames in London. ロンドンのテムズ川には31の橋がかかっている

brilliant /bríljənt/

形 優秀な; 優れた; すばらしい

absolutely	brilliant	実にすばらしい
really	brilliant	とてもすばらしい
technically	brilliant	技術的にすばらしい

▷The TV show was **absolutely brilliant**. すごくいいテレビ番組だった

bring /bríŋ/

動 持ってくる, 連れてくる; 持っていく, 連れていく

bring	A B	A(人)にB(物)を持ってくる
bring	B to A	
bring	B for A	

▷Would you **bring** me another drink, Nick? ニック, もう1杯飲み物を持ってきてもらえますか

broad /brɔ́ːd/ 形 広い; 広範囲な

fairly	broad	かなり広い
rather	broad	
relatively	broad	比較的広い
sufficiently	broad	十分に広い
too	broad	あまりにも広い

★《英》では fairly は肯定的, rather は否定的なニュアンスで用いることがある

▷Our music will appeal to a **fairly broad** range of people. 私たちの音楽はかなり幅広い層の人々の間で人気が出るだろう
▷I don't think the range of exam questions is **sufficiently broad**. 試験問題の範囲はそう広くないと思う
▷The topic is **too broad** for such a short essay. 短いレポートの割にテーマが広すぎる

brother /brʌ́ðər/ 名 兄, 弟, 兄弟

a big	brother	兄
an elder	brother	
an older	brother	

a little	brother	弟
a younger	brother	
a baby	brother	幼い弟

★英語圏ではふつう兄・弟を区別しない．あえて区別するときは上のように表す．話の中で兄・弟に言及するときは名前を言う．sister も同様

▷This is my **elder brother**, Thomas. （人に紹介して）兄のトーマスです
▷I have two **younger brothers**. 弟が2人います

brother and sister	兄弟姉妹，きょうだい

▷How many **brothers and sisters** do you have? きょうだいは何人いますか

budget /bʌ́dʒit/ 名 予算

have	a budget	
set	a budget	予算がある
draw up	a budget	予算を立てる
present	a budget	予算を提出する
submit	a budget	
approve	a budget	予算を承認する
balance	the budget	予算を均衡させる
adhere to	a budget	予算を守る
stick to	a budget	
cut	the budget	予算を削減する
increase	a budget	予算を増額する

▷We **have** a big **budget** for the project. その事業のための潤沢な予算がある
▷My advice is to **set** a **budget** for Christmas shopping and stick to it. 私のアドバイスはクリスマスの買い物の予算を立ててそれを守ることだ
▷It's impossible to **balance** the **budget** unless the government raises taxes. 政府が増税しなければ予算の均衡をとることは不可能だ
▷The government has to **cut** the **budget** by $1.5 billion. 政府は予算を15億ドル削らなければならない

a low	budget	低予算
a tight	budget	緊縮予算
an annual	budget	年度予算
an overall	budget	総予算
the total	budget	
the government	budget	政府予算
a defense	budget	防衛予算
an education	budget	教育予算
an advertising	budget	広告予算
a draft	budget	予算案

▷Where can I buy suitable warm clothes *on* a **tight budget**? かつかつの予算でちょうどいい暖かい服が買えるのはどこかな
▷The **overall budget** is about $300,000. 総予算はおよそ30万ドルです

over	budget	予算を超過して
under	budget	予算以下で
within	(a) budget	予算内で
on	budget	

▷Projects were always huge and **over budget**. 事業は常に巨大で，予算オーバーだった
▷It isn't easy to live **within budget**. 予算内で生活するのは楽ではない

building /bíldiŋ/ 名 建物

design	a building	建物を設計する
construct	a building	建物を建設する
demolish	a building	建物を取り壊す
destroy	a building	
pull down	a building	
restore	a building	建物を修復する
convert	a building	建物を改装する
occupy	a building	建物を占有する；建物を占拠する

★これらのコロケーションは The building was constructed in 1995.（その建物は1995年に建てられた）のような受け身でもよく用いる

▷The firm is **constructing** a new **building** near the station. その企業は駅の近くに新しい建物を建設中だ
▷You need a permit to **demolish** a **building**. 建物を取り壊すには許可が必要だ
▷We need to **pull down** the old **building**. その古い建物を取り壊す必要がある
▷Nearly 200 students **occupied** the **building** in protest. 200人近い学生が抗議の意を表して建物を占拠した

a high-rise	building	高層ビル
a large	building	大きな建物
a tall	building	背の高い建物
a low	building	背の低い建物
a historic	building	歴史的建造物
a 16th century	building	16世紀の建物
a public	building	公共の建物
an office	building	オフィスビル
a school	building	校舎
the main	building	本館

▷Those **historic buildings** have been largely restored. それらの歴史的建造物は大規模に修復された

burn /bə́ːrn/ 動 燃える, 燃やす；やけどさせる

be badly	burned	ひどいやけどを負う
be severely	burned	
be completely	burned	完全に焼ける
burn	down	焼け落ちる
burn	out	燃え尽きる
burn	easily	燃えやすい；日焼けしやすい
burn	brightly	明るく燃える
burn	fiercely	激しく燃える

★過去・過去分詞形は burnt も用いる

▷His hands were **badly burned**. 彼は両手にひどいやけどを負っていた
▷Two houses were **completely burned** to the ground. 2軒の家が全焼した
▷His house **burnt down** at the end of May. 彼の家は5月末に火事で焼けた
▷My skin **burns easily**. 私は日焼けしやすい
▷The blaze broke out at 9:30 a.m. and is still **burning fiercely**. 火災は午前9時半に発生し、まだ激しく燃えている

be burned	to death	焼死する
be burned	to the ground	焼け落ちる

▷At least 28 people were **burned to death**. 少なくとも28人が焼死した

burn	to do	…したいと熱望する

▷Is there anything you're **burning to** do that you haven't yet done? まだしていないことでぜひやりたいことはありますか

burn	with A	A (感情) で燃える

▷His cheeks **burned with** anger. 彼の頬は怒りにほてった

bus /bʌ́s/ 名 バス

go by	bus	バスで行く
travel by	bus	バスで移動する
take	a bus	バスに乗る
ride	a bus	
wait for	a bus	バスを待つ
catch	a bus	バスに間に合う
get on	a bus	バスに乗り込む
get off	a bus	バスを降りる
miss	the bus	バスに乗り遅れる

▷You can **go by bus** to Wellington Zoo. ウェリントン動物園へはバスで行けます
▷Yesterday I spent 40 minutes **waiting for** a bus. きのう40分バスを待った
▷It's too late to **catch** a **bus**. バスに乗るにはもう間に合わない
▷She **got on** a bus to Manhattan. 彼女はマンハッタンへのバスに乗り込んだ
▷I **got off** the bus at Harbone. ハーボーンでバスを降りた
▷We're going to **miss** the **bus** if you don't hurry up. 急がないとバスに乗り遅れるよ

a regular	bus	定期バス
a city	bus	市内バス
a local	bus	路線バス
a school	bus	スクールバス

▷There are **regular buses** from the town center to Clifton. 町の中心からクリフトンまで定期バスがある
▷After 8 p.m. there are no **local buses** or trains. 午後8時以降は路線バスも列車もない

business /bíznis/

名 仕事, 業務；商売；会社, 店

do	business	商売する
conduct	business	
go into	business	事業を始める
set up in	business	事業に乗り出す
go out of	business	廃業する
run	a business	会社を経営する；店を経営する
start	a business	会社を始める
lose	business	業績が悪化する
get down to	business	本題に入る

▷We've **done business** in the U.S. for over 30 years. 米国で30年以上ビジネスをしている
▷Tony and I **went into business** together. トニーといっしょに事業を始めた
▷More than 100 companies **went out of business**. 100以上の会社が倒産した
▷She and her husband **run** a small **business**. 彼女は夫婦で小さな店を経営している
▷He returned to New York where he **started** a **business**. 彼はニューヨークに戻って会社を始めた
▷Some companies are **losing business** because of the economic situation. 経済状況のあおりを受けて業績が悪化している企業もある

big	business	大企業
private	business	私企業
family	business	同族企業

small	business	小企業
core	business	中核事業
international	business	国際業務
show	business	ショービジネス
the music	business	音楽ビジネス
repeat	business	固定客(商売)

▷The importance of the Japanese economy to **international business** is obvious. 国際ビジネスにおける日本経済の重要性は明らかだ

business or pleasure	仕事それとも遊び

▷I love traveling. It doesn't matter if it's for **business or pleasure**. 旅行が好きなので，出張であろうと遊びであろうと構わない

in	business	商売して；準備ができて
on	business	商用で，仕事で

▷We're **in business** to grow and find new customers. さらに商売を広げて新たな販路を見いだす準備ができている
▷My father is away **on business**. 父は仕事で出かけています

PHRASES

Business is business. ☺ 商売は商売だ(情けは禁物)
How's business? ☺ 商売はどうですか
Mind your own business. / It's none of your business. ☺ きみの知ったことじゃない

busy /bízi/ 形 忙しい；混雑した

get	busy	仕事にとりかかる

▷Let's **get busy**! さあとりかかろう

extremely	busy	とても忙しい
fairly	busy	

▷I'm **extremely busy**! とても忙しい

busy	with A	Aで忙しい

▷I'm **busy with** school. 学校のことで忙しい

busy	doing	…するのに忙しい

▷Max was **busy** prepar**ing** the meal. マックスは食事の準備に忙しかった

button /bÁtən/ 名 押しボタン；ボタン

press	a button	ボタンを押す
push	a button	
touch	a button	
do up	a button	ボタンをかける
fasten	a button	
undo	a button	ボタンをはずす

▷**Press** the **button** for the 5th floor. 5階のボタンを押してください(★ Fifth floor, please. 「5階をお願いします」と短く言うことが多い)
▷Sorry I **pushed** the **button** by accident. すみません，誤ってボタンを押してしまいました
▷Just **touch** a **button** and the video camera starts to record. ボタンを押せばビデオカメラが録画を始めます
▷You should **do up** the middle button of your jacket. ジャケットの真ん中のボタンをかけたほうがいい
▷I **undid** the top **button** of my shirt. シャツのいちばん上のボタンをはずした

a button	comes off	ボタンがとれる
a button	falls off	

★「ボタンがとれている」は A button is missing. 「ボタンがとれそうだ」は A button is loose. のようにいう

▷The **buttons** on my sleeves **fell off**. 袖のボタンがとれた

buy /bái/ 動 買う, 購入する；おごる

buy	A B	A(人)にB(物)を買う
buy	B for A	
buy	A for B	A(物)をB(価格)で買う
buy	A from B	A(物)をBから買う

▷He promised to **buy** me that new dress. 私にあの新しい服を買ってくれると彼は約束した
▷Did you **buy** it **for** her? それを彼女に買ってあげたのかい
▷She **bought** the diamond ring **for** $6,000. 彼女はそのダイヤの指輪を6千ドルで買った
▷Do you **buy** your clothes **from** a top store? あなたは服を一流のお店で買いますか

can't afford to	buy	買う余裕がない

▷I **can't afford to buy** a house in the city. 私には都市に家を買うだけの余裕はない

buy and sell	売買する
go (out) and buy	買いに行く

▷Do you know a store where they **buy and sell** secondhand books? 古本を売り買いしている店を知っていますか
▷I'll just **go and buy** some food from the shop. ちょっと食料を買いに店に行ってくるよ

C

cake /kéik/ 名 ケーキ

bake	a cake	ケーキを焼く
make	a cake	ケーキをつくる
cut	the cake	ケーキを切る

▷ My girlfriend **baked** a **cake** for my birthday. ガールフレンドが誕生日にケーキを焼いてくれた
▷ I carefully **cut** the **cake** into triangular pieces. 注意深くケーキにナイフを入れて三角形に切った

a piece of	cake	ケーキ一切れ；朝飯前
a slice of	cake	ケーキ一切れ

▷ Don't worry. Math tests are a **piece of cake**! 心配しないで．数学のテストなんかお茶の子さいさい
▷ Would you like to have another **slice of cake**? ケーキをもう一切れ召し上がりますか

a homemade	cake	自家製ケーキ
a chocolate	cake	チョコレートケーキ
a fruit	cake	フルーツケーキ
a sponge	cake	スポンジケーキ
a birthday	cake	バースデーケーキ
a Christmas	cake	クリスマスケーキ
a wedding	cake	ウェディングケーキ

calculate /kǽlkjuléit/

動 計算する；予測する

accurately	calculate	正確に計算する
mentally	calculate	頭の中で計算する
carefully	calculate	慎重に計算する

★いずれの副詞も動詞の後でも用いる

▷ He **carefully calculated** how much it would cost to move to a larger apartment. もっと広いアパートに引っ越すのにどれくらい費用がかかるか彼は慎重に計算した

calculate	(that)...	…と計算する
calculate	wh-	…か計算する

★ wh- は how, what など

▷ He **calculated that** the plane would land 30 minutes ahead of schedule. 飛行機は予定より30分早く着陸すると彼は計算した
▷ I **calculated how** much money I could afford to spend. 自由に使えるお金がいくらあるか計算した

be calculated	at A	A と計算される
be calculated	according to A	A に従って計算される

▷ Taxes are **calculated at** 36 %. 税金は36％と計算される
▷ The tax is **calculated according to** the value of the property. 税金は財産価値に従って計算される

call /kɔːl/ 名 電話；呼び声

make	a call	電話をかける
give A	a call	A (人) に電話をかける
have	a call	電話がある，電話がかかってくる
get	a call	
take	a call	電話に出る
answer	a call	

▷ Do you mind if I **make** a telephone **call**? 電話をしてもいいですか
▷ I'll **give** you a **call** tomorrow. あす電話します
▷ I **had** a **call** from my daughter today. きょう娘から電話があった
▷ You **got** five phone **calls** while you were out to lunch. きみが昼食に出かけている間に電話が5本あったよ
▷ She **took** a **call** *from* her boss. 彼女は上司からの電話に出た

a long	call	長電話
a quick	call	短い電話
a local	call	市内通話
an international	call	国際電話
a long-distance	call	長距離電話
an incoming	call	着信
an outgoing	call	発信
an emergency	call	緊急電話
a wake-up	call	モーニングコール

▷ Do you mind if I make a **quick** phone **call**? ちょっと電話していいですか
▷ I use my cellphone frequently for **local calls** and **long-distance calls**. 市内通話と長距離電話にしばしば携帯電話を使う
▷ I don't know how to make an **international call** to Australia. オーストラリアへの国際電話のかけ方がわからない

call /kɔːl/ 動 呼ぶ；電話する

be commonly	called	一般に呼ばれる

be frequently	called	よく呼ばれる
be sometimes	called	ときに呼ばれる
be often	called	しばしば呼ばれる

▷Influenza is **commonly called** the "flu." インフルエンザは一般に flu と呼ばれる

call	back	折り返し電話する

▷It's a bad moment now. Can I **call** you **back** in a minute? いまはまずいので,少ししたら折り返しきみに電話していいかな

call	at A	Aを訪ねる;Aに立ち寄る;Aに止まる
call	for A	声を上げてAを呼ぶ

▷I **called at** her house but she wasn't there. 彼女の家を訪ねたが留守だった ▷This train will **call at** Ashbury. この列車はアッシュベリーに止まります
▷**Call for** an ambulance! 救急車を呼んで

call	A B	A(人)のためにBを呼ぶ
call	B for A	

▷Will you **call** a taxi **for** me? タクシーを呼んでくれませんか

calm /káːm/ 形 冷静な, 穏やかな

stay	calm	冷静でいる
remain	calm	
keep	calm	

▷**Stay calm**! Don't panic! 冷静で. パニックにならないで

quite	calm	まったく穏やかな
dead	calm	

▷He seemed to be **quite calm**. 彼はとても穏やかに見えた
▷The sea was **dead calm**. 海はすっかりないでいた

camera /kǽmərə/ 名 カメラ

on	camera	カメラに撮影されて
off	camera	カメラに撮影されないで

▷The robbery was caught **on camera**. 強盗の現場はカメラに写っていた

a digital	camera	デジタルカメラ
a television	camera	テレビカメラ
a video	camera	ビデオカメラ
a hidden	camera	隠しカメラ
a security	camera	防犯カメラ

PHRASES
Look at the camera. カメラを見て(★写真を撮るときのセリフ) ▷Look at the camera and smile. カメラを見て, 笑ってください

campaign /kæmpéin/

名 運動, キャンペーン

launch	a campaign	運動を始める
begin	a campaign	
start	a campaign	
conduct	a campaign	運動を行う
run	a campaign	
lead	a campaign	運動を先導する
join	a campaign	運動に参加する
support	a campaign	運動を支持する

▷They **launched** a **campaign** against smoking in public places. 彼らは公共の場所での喫煙に反対する活動を始めた
▷He **joined** a **campaign** to help save dolphins. 彼はイルカ保護に協力するキャンペーンに加わった
▷Ron is **supporting** a **campaign** to encourage people to recycle their rubbish. ロンはごみのリサイクルキャンペーンを支持している

a campaign	aims at A	運動はAがねらいだ

▷The advertising campaign **aimed at** raising brand awareness. その広告キャンペーンのねらいはブランド認知度を上げることだった

a vigorous	campaign	精力的な運動
an international	campaign	国際的な運動
a national	campaign	全国的な運動
an election	campaign	選挙運動
a political	campaign	政治的運動
a military	campaign	軍事行動
an advertising	campaign	広告キャンペーン
a publicity	campaign	

▷They launched a **vigorous campaign** to clean up the city. 彼らは街をきれいにする精力的な活動を始めた
▷Our **political campaign** was successful. われわれの政治的運動は成功を収めた

campaign	against A	Aに反対する運動
campaign	for A	Aを求める運動

▷We have supported the **campaign against** terror-

| cancel |

ism. われはテロに反対する運動を支持した
▷She started a **campaign for** equal rights. 彼女は同等の権利を求める運動を始めた

| campaign | to do | …する運動 |

▷They started a **campaign to** protect areas of natural beauty. 彼らは自然の景観を守る運動を始めた

cancel /kǽnsəl/ 動 取り消す，中止する

| automatically | cancel | 自動的に取り消す |
| immediately | cancel | すぐ取り消す |

▷If you don't pay the subscription, your membership will be **automatically canceled**. 会費を払わないと会員の権利は自動的に取り消されます
▷She **immediately canceled** her plans. 彼女はすぐ計画を取りやめにした

capable /kéipəbl/ 形 できる；有能な

| seem | capable | 能力があるようだ；能力があるように見える |
| look | capable | |

▷Tom's made a good start in his new job. He **seems capable** of running the department very well. トムは新しい仕事でよいスタートを切った．部をうまく運営していけそうだ

perfectly	capable	完全にできる
quite	capable	
fully	capable	

▷I'm **perfectly capable** of looking after myself. 自分のことはきちんと自分でできますよ

| capable | of A | Aができる |
| capable | of doing | …できる |

▷I didn't believe he was **capable of** such things. 彼にそんなことができるなんて信じられなかった

car /ká:r/ 名 車，自動車

drive	a car	車を運転する
get in	a car	車に乗る
get into	a car	車に乗り込む
get out of	a car	車を降りる
park	a car	駐車する
rent	a car	レンタカーを借りる

▷Do you **drive a car**? あなたは車を運転しますか
▷She **got into** the **car** and started the engine. 彼女は車に乗り込んでエンジンをかけた
▷He **got out of** the **car** and walked up to the house. 彼は車を降りて家の方へと歩いた
▷Where should I **park** the **car**? どこへ駐車したらいいかな

| a car | breaks down | 車が故障する |
| a car | crashes | 車が衝突する |

▷My **car broke down** on the highway. 私の車が高速道路で故障した
▷His **car crashed** into a tree. 彼の車は木に衝突した

an electric	car	電気自動車
a hybrid	car	ハイブリッド車
a luxury	car	高級車
a sports	car	スポーツカー
a police	car	パトカー
a company	car	社用車
a used	car	中古車
a secondhand	car	
a stolen	car	盗難車

▷Half a million **used cars** have been imported from neighboring countries. 50万台の中古車が隣国から輸入された

| by | car | 車で |
| in | a car | 車に乗って |

▷They had to take a cab because it was so far away—20 minutes **by car**. タクシーを拾わなくてはならなった．というのもかなり遠くて，車で20分のところだったから

card /ká:rd/ 名 カード；あいさつ状；トランプ

carry	a card	カードを持ち歩く
hand	a card	カードを手渡す
insert	a card	カードを挿入する
swipe	a card	カードを読取装置に通す
pay by	(a) card	カードで払う
put A on	a card	Aをカードでの支払いに回す
send	a card	カードを送る
get	a card	(お祝いなどの)カードをもらう
receive	a card	
play	cards	トランプをする
shuffle	the cards	トランプを切る
deal	the cards	トランプを配る

▷I **got a card** from Katherine this morning. けさキャサリンからカードをもらった

▷Let's **play cards**! トランプをしよう

an ID	card	身分証明書
an identity	card	
a membership	card	会員証
a business	card	名刺
a greeting	card	あいさつ状

care /kéər/ 名 世話, 介護；注意

take	care	世話をする
provide	care	
need	care	世話を必要とする；
require	care	注意を必要とする
receive	care	世話を受ける

▷Don't worry. I'll **take** good **care** of your cat while you're on holiday. 心配しないで. あなたの休暇中, 猫の世話はしっかりするから
▷She'll **need care** until she gets better. 彼女はよくなるまで介護が必要だ
▷The hospital **provides care** for seriously ill children from all over the country. その病院は全国からやって来る重病の子どもの世話をしている
▷Trees **require care** and attention just like children. 木には子どもと同じように世話と注意が必要だ
▷How often will your parents **receive care**? あなたの両親はどれくらいの頻度で介護を受けられますか

good	care	十分な世話；十分
great	care	な注意
intensive	care	集中治療
medical	care	医療
nursing	care	看護
health	care	健康管理
residential	care	施設介護
primary	care	初期治療

▷She wrapped the present with **great care**. 彼女はプレゼントをていねいに包んだ

with	care	注意して
without	care	注意せずに

▷Please handle these boxes **with care**. 箱を注意して扱ってください
▷He admitted driving **without** due **care** and attention and was fined £250. 彼は不注意運転を認め250ポンドの罰金を科せられた

care /kéər/ 動 気にする, 気にかける

really	care	とても気にする
not much	care	あまり気にしない
care	deeply	非常に気にかける
care	enough	十分気にかける
not care	less	少しも気にしない

★not much care は not care much も用いる

▷The apartment was old and dusty, but Andrew did**n't much care**. アパートは古くてほこりっぽかったがアンドルーはあまり気にしなかった
▷Canadians **care deeply** about the natural environment. カナダ人は自然環境への関心が強い
▷It was nice to have someone who **cared enough** to worry. 気遣っていろいろ心配してくれる人がいてよかった
▷She could**n't care less** about politics. 彼女には政治なんかどうでもよかった

care	about A	Aを気にかける
care	for A	Aを好む；Aの世話をする

▷We **care about** what happens to you. あなたの身に降りかかることが気にかかる
▷Would you **care for** another drink? もう一杯いかがですか ▷Grandfather shouldn't live by himself. He needs someone to **care for** him. 祖父はひとり暮らしをしないほうがいい. だれか世話してくれる人が必要だ

care	to do	…したい

▷Would you **care to** order some wine? ワインを注文なさいますか

care	wh-	…か気にかける

★wh- は who, what, whether, why など

▷I don't **care whether** you agree with me. あなたが賛成であろうがなかろうがどうでもいい

PHRASES
What do you care? ☺ 何を気にしているのか, あなたには関係のないことだ ▷"Are you crying?" "What do you care?"「泣いているの？」「あなたにはどうでもいいことでしょ」

Who cares? ☺ だれも気にするものか ▷"What will my parents think?" "Who cares?"「うちの両親はどう思うかな」「構うもんか」

career /kəríər/ 名 キャリア, 職業, 経歴

make	a career of A	Aを専門の職とする
build	a career	キャリアを築く
pursue	a career	キャリアを積む
begin	one's career	キャリアを積み始める

| careful |

start	one's **career**	
choose	a **career**	キャリアを選ぶ
end	A's **career**	キャリアを終わらせる
ruin	A's **career**	キャリアを台なしにする

▷Anna wants to **build** a **career** in publishing. アンナは出版の世界でキャリアを築きたいと思っている
▷She wants to **pursue** a **career** in medicine. 彼女は医師の仕事に就きたがっている

a successful	career	輝かしいキャリア
a distinguished	career	
A's playing	career	選手としてのキャリア
A's acting	career	俳優としてのキャリア

▷My brother has a **successful career** in the police force. 弟は警察で輝かしいキャリアをもっている

careful /kéərfəl/

形 注意深い；念入りな，綿密な

extremely	careful	非常に気をつける
especially	careful	特に気をつける
particularly	careful	

▷You must be **especially careful** with your user ID and password. ユーザーIDとパスワードには特に気をつけなければならない

careful	**about** A	Aに注意する，気をつける
careful	**of** A	
careful	**with** A	Aの扱いに注意する

▷Be **careful of** the dog. その犬に気をつけて
▷She's very **careful with** her money. 彼女はお金の扱いにすごく注意している

careful	**(that)**...	…に気をつける
careful	**wh-**	…かに気をつける

★wh- は who, what, how など

▷I need to be **careful** it doesn't happen again. 二度とそんなことが起こらないよう気をつける必要がある
▷Be **careful how** you drive on these icy roads. こういった凍った道路の運転には気をつけるように

PHRASES
You can't be too careful. ☺ 用心に越したことはない

case /kéis/ 名 訴訟；事件；論拠；事例；症例

bring	a case	訴訟を起こす
take	a case	訴訟を扱う
consider	a case	訴訟を審理する
hear	a case	
drop	a case	訴訟を取り下げる
dismiss	a case	訴訟を却下する
win	a case	訴訟に勝つ
lose	a case	訴訟に負ける
investigate	a case	事件を捜査する
solve	a case	事件を解決する
present	a case	論拠を提示する
argue	a case	論拠を述べる
show	a case	事例を示す
cite	a case	事例を挙げる
consider	a case	事例を考える
diagnose	a case	症例を診察する
report	a case	症例を報告する

▷Ali **brought** a **case** against two police officers for racist jokes. アリは2人の警察官が人種差別的なジョークを言ったことで告訴した
▷We need a good lawyer to **present** our **case** in court. 法廷でよい弁護士に論点を申し立ててもらう必要がある
▷The lawyers **argued** the **case** for nine days. 弁護士たちは9日にわたって論点を述べた
▷**Consider** the **case** *of* Canada. カナダの場合を考えてみてください

a criminal	case	刑事事件
a civil	case	民事事件
a murder	case	殺人事件
a strong	case	強い論拠
a weak	case	弱い論拠
an extreme	case	極端な事例
a rare	case	まれな事例
a special	case	特別な事例
a severe	case	重症例
a bad	case	

▷This is a book about famous **criminal cases**. これは有名な刑事事件を扱った本だ
▷There's a **strong case** for expanding our workforce. わが社の雇用を拡大すべきとの声が強い
▷In **rare cases** this disease can lead to death. まれにこの病気は死に至ることがある
▷This is a really **special case**. これは実に特別なケースだ

in	that case	そういうことなら，それ
in	which case	なら
as is	the case	よくあることだが

▷You're too busy to order it? OK. **In that case** I'll order it for you. 忙しすぎて注文できないの？ いいよ，じゃぼくが注文してあげる

▷ **As is** often the **case** with rumors, there's some truth to this. うわさというのはそうしたものだが，このうわさにも幾分かの真実が含まれている

case	by case	一件一件
a case	in point	好例，適切な例

▷ These things have to be done on a **case by case** basis. こうしたことには個別に対応しなければならない
▷ Often eastern and western cultures mix successfully. Japan is a **case in point**. しばしば東洋と西洋の文化はうまく融合する。日本がまさに好例だ

cash /kǽʃ/ 名 現金，金

pay (in)	cash	現金で払う
raise	cash	金を集める
be short of	cash	金が不足する

▷ I **paid in cash** and had fifty dollars change. 現金で払って50ドルのおつりをもらった
▷ They organized the event to **raise cash** for charity. 慈善金集めのためのイベントが企画された

extra	cash	追加の金，臨時の金
cash	flow	キャッシュフロー，現金収支

▷ My dad always kept some **extra cash** in his drawer. 父はいつも予備の金を引き出しにしまっていた

cash	on delivery	代引きでの販売

▷ Buyers have a few payment options including personal check, debit card and **cash on delivery**. お支払い方法は小切手，デビットカード，代金引換の中からお選びいただけます

cat /kǽt/ 名 猫

have	a cat	猫を飼っている
keep	a cat	
feed	a cat	猫にえさをやる
stroke	a cat	猫をなでる
pet	a cat	

▷ I **have** a **cat** named Sebastian. セバスチャンという名前の猫を飼っています
▷ I have to go home and **feed** my **cat**. 家に帰って猫にえさをやらなくちゃ
▷ She **stroked** the **cat** gently. 彼女はやさしく猫をなでた

a cat	jumps	猫が飛び跳ねる
a cat	leaps	
a cat	purrs	猫がのどを鳴らす
a cat	meows	猫がニャオと鳴く

▷ My **cat jumped** on my lap. うちの猫が私のひざの上に飛び乗った
▷ The **cat purred** happily in my arms. その猫は私の腕の中でうれしそうにのどを鳴らした

a domestic	cat	飼い猫
a stray	cat	野良猫
a tabby	cat	ぶち猫，とら猫
a fat	cat	金持ち，お偉方

▷ **Domestic cats** eat cat food. 飼い猫はキャットフードを食べる
▷ The place is filled with **stray cats**. その場所は野良猫でいっぱいだ
▷ I don't trust those **fat cats**. ああいう金持ち連中は信用しない

[PHRASES]

(Has the) cat got your tongue? ☺ (親の質問に答えない子どもに向かって) どうして黙っているの (★「猫に舌をとられたのか」が原義) ▷ What's the matter? Cat got your tongue? どうしたの？口がきけなくなったの？

cause /kɔ́:z/ 名 原因；理由；大義

find	a cause	原因を突き止める
investigate	the cause	原因を調査する
advance	a cause	大義を推し進める
champion	a cause	大義を支持する
support	a cause	

▷ I tried to **find** the **cause** of the noise. 騒音の原因を突き止めようとした
▷ Police are **investigating** the **cause** of the accident. 警察は事件の原因を調査中だ

a real	cause	真の原因
the underlying	cause	根底にある原因
an important	cause	重要な原因
the main	cause	主要な原因
the major	cause	大きな原因
a possible	cause	考えうる原因
an immediate	cause	直接の原因
reasonable	cause	もっともな理由

▷ I don't know what the **real cause** was. 真の原因が何だったのか私にはわからない
▷ Jobs, money, family and health were the **main causes** of stress. 仕事，金，家族と健康がストレスの主要原因だった
▷ Research indicates many **possible causes** of lung

| caution |

cancer. 研究の示すところでは，肺がんには多くの原因が考えられる

▷ The **immediate cause** of the accident was that the train passed a signal showing red. 事故の直接の原因は列車が赤信号を無視したことだった

without	good cause	正当な理由もなく
for	a good cause	世のため人のため
in	a good cause	

▷ It was all **in a good cause**, raising money for the Kids Hospital. それは子ども病院の基金を集める慈善事業だった

cause and effect	原因と結果

▷ History is a pattern of **cause and effect**. 歴史とは原因と結果が織りなす模様である

caution /kɔ́ːʃən/ 名 注意，用心

| use | caution | 注意する |
| excercise | caution | |

▷ You must **use** great **caution** when driving in the rain. 雨天での車の運転には十分注意しなければならない

cellphone /séfòun/ 名 携帯電話

pull out	one's cellphone	携帯電話を取り出す
answer	one's cellphone	携帯電話に出る
turn off	one's cellphone	携帯電話の電源を切る
switch off	one's cellphone	
charge	one's cellphone	携帯電話を充電する

▷ She **pulled out** her **cellphone** and dialed a number. 彼女は携帯電話を取り出して番号を入力した
▷ I've rung three times, but he's not **answering** his **cellphone**. 3回電話しているが彼は携帯電話に出ない
▷ I forgot to **turn off** my **cellphone**. 携帯電話の電源を切るのを忘れた
▷ Remember to **charge** your **cellphone**. 忘れずに携帯電話を充電してね

a cellphone	rings	携帯電話が鳴る

▷ The **cellphone** in his pocket **rang**. 彼のポケットの中の携帯電話が鳴った

center /séntər/ 名 中心，中央；中心地；中

心施設(★《英》つづりは centre)

the main	center	おもな中心
a major	center	
the nerve	center	(活動の)中枢
a financial	center	金融センター
an urban	center	都心
《英》city	centre	中心街

▷ London is the nation's **main center** of commerce and finance. ロンドンは国の商業と金融のおもな中心だ
▷ New York City is the world's **financial center**. ニューヨーク市は世界の金融センターだ

in	the center (of A)	(Aの)中心に

▷ He stood **in** the **center of** the stage. 彼は舞台の真ん中に立った

century /séntʃəri/ 名 世紀；100年

the previous	century	前世紀
the following	century	次の世紀
the new	century	新しい世紀
the present	century	今世紀

▷ He heard stories about the two World Wars in the early half of the **previous century**. 前世紀の前半に起きた2つの世界大戦にまつわる話を彼は耳にした
▷ Over the **following centuries** the European and African populations continued to grow. 次の何世紀かの間ヨーロッパとアフリカの人口は増え続けた

the early	twelfth century	12世紀初頭
the mid	twelfth century	12世紀半ば
the late	twelfth century	12世紀後期

▷ In the nineteenth and **early** twentieth **centuries**, magazines were a popular form of entertainment. 19世紀と20世紀初頭において，雑誌は人気のある娯楽形式だった

during	the century	その世紀の間
through	the centuries	何世紀もの間
over	the centuries	

▷ **During** this **century** women have improved their position. 今世紀の間，女性の地位はずっと向上し続けた
▷ The city has changed so much **over** the **centuries**. 街は何世紀もの間に大きく変わった

the turn of	the century	世紀の変わり目

▷ Experts think this picture was painted at the **turn of** the 19th **century**. 専門家の見るところこの絵は19

世紀の変わり目に描かれたものだ

ceremony /sérəmòuni | -məni/

名 式, 儀式, 式典

hold	a ceremony	式を行う
perform	a ceremony	式を執り行う
attend	a ceremony	式に出る

▷ A priest is going to **perform** a **ceremony** at church. 司祭はこの教会で式を執り行う予定です
▷ Thank you all for **attending** this **ceremony**. みなさん, この式にご出席いただきありがとうございます

the ceremony	takes place	式が開かれる

▷ The **ceremony took place** at a famous restaurant in Sydney. 式はシドニーの有名レストランで開かれた

an official	ceremony	公式式典
an opening	ceremony	開会式
a closing	ceremony	閉会式
an awards	ceremony	授賞式
a wedding	ceremony	結婚式
a marriage	ceremony	結婚式
a graduation	ceremony	卒業式

▷ The **official ceremony** will be held in November. 公式式典は11月に開かれる
▷ I enjoyed the Olympic **opening ceremonies**. オリンピックの開会式を楽しんだ

certain /sə́ːrtn/ 形 確信して; 確実な

feel	certain	確信する
make	certain	確かめる; 必ず…する

▷ I'll **make certain** he doesn't forget to ring you. 彼が忘れずにあなたに電話するよう確認しておきます

absolutely	certain	まったく確実な
quite	certain	
by no means	certain	まったく不確実な
almost	certain	ほぼ確実な
virtually	certain	
fairly	certain	かなり確かな
pretty	certain	

▷ Are you **absolutely certain** that you don't know anything else? ほんとうに他には何も知らないのかい
▷ It was **by no means certain** that the ruling party would win this election. 政権党がこの選挙に勝てるかどうかはきわめて不確かだ

▷ She was **almost certain** that he would disapprove. 彼は不賛成だろうと彼女はほぼ確信していた

certain	of A	Aを確信した
certain	about A	

▷ The wedding will be in June, but we're still not quite **certain of** the date. 結婚式は6月ですがまだ日取りは確定していません

certain	(that)...	…と確信した
certain	wh-	…か確信した

★ wh- は who, what, how など

▷ I'm **certain that** I left my wallet on that table. 財布をあのテーブルに置き忘れたのは確かだ
▷ She wasn't **certain what** had happened to her. 彼女は自分に何が起こったのかわかっていなかった

it is certain	that...	きっと…だ
it is not certain	wh-	…か確かでない

★ wh- は who, what, how など

▷ **It** was **not certain whether** the person was alive or dead. その人の生死ははっきりしなかった

for	certain	確かに

★ know, say, tell などと結びつく

▷ I don't **know for certain** whether it's true or not. それが本当かどうかはっきりわからない

chair /tʃéər/ 名 椅子

pull up	a chair	椅子を引き寄せる
pull out	a chair	椅子を引き出す
have	a chair	椅子に座る
take	a chair	
push back	a chair	椅子を後ろへ押す
sit on	a chair	椅子に腰掛ける
sit in	a chair	
sink into	a chair	どすんと椅子に座る
get out of	a chair	椅子から立ち上がる
get up from	a chair	
rise from	a chair	

▷ I **pulled up** a **chair** beside him. 彼の横へ椅子を引き寄せた
▷ Tom **took** a **chair** next to her. トムは彼女の隣の椅子に座った
▷ He **sat in** a **chair** looking out of the window. 彼は椅子に腰掛けて窓の外を眺めていた

▷ She sighed and **sank into** a **chair**. 彼女はため息をついて椅子に沈み込んだ
▷ He **got out of** his **chair** and walked to the door. 彼は椅子から立ち上がってドアの方へ歩いた
▷ My grandmother was so weak that she couldn't **rise from** her **chair**. 祖母は弱っていたので椅子から立ち上がれなかった

a comfortable	chair	座り心地のよい椅子
a rocking	chair	揺り椅子
a swivel	chair	回転椅子
a folding	chair	折り畳み式椅子

▷ She got up from her **comfortable chair**. 彼女は座り心地のよい椅子から立ち上がった

chairman /tʃéərmən/ 名 議長, 司会者 (★ chairperson や chair も用いる); 会長

be appointed	chairman	議長に任命される
be elected	chairman	議長に選ばれる

▷ Mr. McCarthy was **appointed chairman** *of* the committee. マッカーシー氏は委員会の議長に指名された
▷ He was **elected chairman** *of* the council. 彼は理事会の議長に選ばれた

a board	chairman	取締役会会長
a committee	chairman	委員会委員長
the current	chairman	現会長
a former	chairman	元会長, 前会長
a vice	chairman	副会長
a deputy	chairman	副会長, 会長代理

▷ He's a **former chairman** of the Budget Committee. 彼は予算委員会の元委員長だ

challenge /tʃǽlindʒ/ 名 難問; 挑戦

present	a challenge	難問を突きつける
pose	a challenge	
face	a challenge	難問に直面する
meet	a challenge	難問を処理する
respond to	a challenge	
rise to	a challenge	
mount	a challenge	挑戦する
issue	a challenge	
accept	a challenge	挑戦に応じる

▷ So far we have **faced** two **challenges**. これまでのところ2つの難問に直面した
▷ We have to **meet** the **challenge** of international terrorism. 国際テロリズムの難題を処理しなければならない

▷ Fine, Clifford, I **accept** your **challenge**. いいよ、クリフォード. きみの挑戦を受けて立とう

a big	challenge	大きな課題, 難題
a great	challenge	
a real	challenge	まさにやりがいのあるもの
a serious	challenge	
a strong	challenge	手強い挑戦

▷ I had to meet many **big challenges** in my life. 私は人生で多くの難問に出会わなければならなかった
▷ English education in primary school is a **serious challenge** for teachers and society. 小学校での英語教育は教師や社会にとってまさにやりがいのある課題だ
▷ We're going to face **strong challenges** from other companies in the future. 将来は他企業からの手強い挑戦にさらされることになるだろう

challenge /tʃǽlindʒ/ 動 異議を唱える; 挑戦する, 挑む

directly	challenge	真っ向から異議を唱える
seriously	challenge	真剣に異議を唱える

▷ Mr. White's opinion was not **seriously challenged**. ホワイト氏の意見にまともに異議を唱える人はなかった

challenge	A to B	A(人)にBを挑む

▷ I **challenge** you **to** a game of chess. チェスを1局指しましょう

challenge	A to do	A(人)に…するよう要求する

▷ Her eyes **challenged** me **to** reply. 返事をしなさいと彼女は目で促した

chance /tʃǽns | tʃɑ́ːns/ 名 機会; 見込み, 可能性; 偶然

get	a chance	機会を得る
have	a chance	
give (A)	a chance	(Aに)機会を与える
offer (A)	a chance	
seize	the chance	機会をつかむ
jump at	the chance	機会に飛びつく
miss	a chance	機会を逃す
stand	a chance	可能性がある
increase	the chance	可能性を増やす
reduce	the chance	可能性を減らす
decrease	the chance	

take	a chance	一か八かやってみる

▷I didn't **get** a **chance** to apologize. 謝る機会がなかった
▷I haven't **had** a **chance** to talk to Bob yet. ボブと話す機会がまだない
▷Please just **give** me a **chance** to say something. ちょっと言わせてください
▷Now is the time. **Seize** this **chance**! いまがその時だ。このチャンスをつかめ
▷I **missed** a **chance** to be promoted. 昇進のチャンスを逃した
▷I know Tom wants to win the race, but he doesn't **stand** a **chance**. トムがレースに勝ちたいのはわかるが、勝てる可能性はない
▷If you wear a mask, it'll **reduce** the **chances** of catching flu. マスクをすればインフルエンザにかかる可能性が減るだろう
▷"I don't think Kate likes me." "**Take** a **chance**! Ask her for a date."「ケイトに好意をもたれているとは思えないな」「一か八かデートに誘ってみろよ」

a great	chance	絶好の機会
a big	chance	
the only	chance	唯一の機会
the last	chance	最後の機会
another	chance	別の機会
a second	chance	
a good	chance	十分な可能性；よい機会
a fair	chance	
a reasonable	chance	かなりの可能性
a sporting	chance	
little	chance	ほとんどない可能性
a slim	chance	わずかな可能性
a fifty-fifty	chance	五分五分の可能性
an even	chance	
pure	chance	まったくの偶然
sheer	chance	

▷This is the **only chance** you'll ever have to do this in your life. あなたの人生でこれをしなければならない唯一の機会ですよ
▷This is the **last chance**. これが最後のチャンスだよ
▷Give me **another chance**! Please! もう一度チャンスをください。お願いです
▷We've got a **fair chance** of getting to the finals. 決勝に進む可能性は十分ある
▷There's a **reasonable chance** that she'll get a grant to study abroad. 彼女が留学のための奨学金をもらえる可能性は十分にある
▷There is only an **even chance** the global economy will recover this year. 世界経済が今年回復する見込みは五分五分です
▷I met an old school friend in the middle of Tokyo, by **pure chance**. まったく偶然に東京の真ん中で学生時代の友人に会った

by	chance	偶然に，たまたま
by	any chance	ひょっとして

▷I met her **by chance**. たまたま彼女に出会った
▷Do you **by any chance** have an 80-yen stamp? ひょっとして80円切手を持ってないか

PHRASES

No chance! / Fat chance! ☺ そんなことはありえない，まさか ▷Does he think I want to marry him? Fat chance! 私が彼と結婚したがっているとでも彼は考えているのかしら，ありえないわ
(The) chances are (that)... …かもしれない ▷Chances are that Jeff and Christine will get married. ジェフとクリスティンは結婚するかもしれない

change /tʃéindʒ/

名 変化；気分転換；着替え；小銭

make	a change	変更する
cause	a change	変化をもたらす
produce	a change	
undergo	a change	変化を経る
show	a change	変化を示す
reflect	a change	変化を反映する
get	a change	おつりをもらう
keep	the change	おつりをもらっておく

★undergo はふつう great, radical, drastic, tremendous など変化の大きさや状況を表す形容詞との連結で用いる

▷Apparently someone **made** a **change** in the computer data. どうやらだれかがコンピュータのデータを変更したようだ
▷China is **undergoing** tremendous **changes**. 中国は大きな変化を遂げつつある
▷The statement **reflects** a **change** in policy. この声明は政策の変化を反映している

a dramatic	change	劇的な変化
a fundamental	change	根本的な変化
a major	change	大きな変化
a radical	change	抜本的な変化
a significant	change	著しい変化
a minor	change	小さな変化
a sudden	change	突然の変化
climate	change	気候変動
political	change	政治的変革
social	change	社会的変革

▷What has caused this **dramatic change**? こんな劇的な変化はなぜ起きたのか

| change |

▷There're no **major changes**. 大きな変化はなかった
▷There was a **radical change** in the policy of the United States of America. アメリカ合衆国の政策に抜本的な転換があった
▷Were there any **political** or **social changes** during that period? その期間に政治的あるいは社会的な変革はありましたか

a change	in A	Aの変化

▷I didn't understand her **change in** attitude. 彼女の態度の変化が解せなかった

for	a change	変化をつけて

▷Why don't you listen **for** a **change**? たまにはこちらの言うことも聞いてよ

change /tʃéindʒ/

動 変える, 変わる;着替える;両替する

radically	change	根本的に変わる
completely	change	完全に変わる
really	change	すっかり変わる
little	change	ほとんど変わらない
constantly	change	常に変わる
rapidly	change	急速に変化する
suddenly	change	突然変わる
change	dramatically	劇的に変わる
change	significantly	大きく変わる

▷My life has been **radically changed** through the books I've read. 読んだ本を通して私の人生は根本的に変わった
▷What's wrong with you? You've **completely changed**. あなたどうかしたの. すっかり変わってしまって
▷He's **really changed** since I knew him at university. 大学で知り合ったころの彼とはすっかり変わってしまった
▷The village where I was born has **little changed** during the last 100 years. 私が生まれた村はここ100年間ほとんど変わっていない
▷Your opinion is **constantly changing**. きみの意見はころころ変わる
▷The world is **rapidly changing**. 世の中は急速に変化しつつある
▷The weather **changed dramatically**. 天候は急変した
▷Well, I think things have **changed significantly**. 事態は大きく変わったと思いますよ

change	from A to B	AからBに変わる

★change は自動詞・他動詞のどちらもある

▷Her tone **changed from** being warm and friendly **to** cold and commanding. 彼女の口調は温かくやさしかったのに冷たく命令調に変わった

change	A for B	AをBに換える, 両替する
change	A into B	

▷He **changed** the US dollars **into** yen. 彼は米ドルを円に両替した

change	into A	Aに着替える
change	out of A	Aを着替える

▷She **changed into** her jeans and sneakers and went out. 彼女はジーンズとスニーカーに替えて出かけた
▷You should **change out of** that wet clothing. その濡れた服を脱いで着替えたほうがいい

character /kǽriktər/

名 性格;特質, 特徴;登場人物;文字

have	a character	性格をもっている;特質がある
reflect	A's character	性格を反映する
preserve	the character	特徴を失わないようにする
play	a character	人物を演じる
inhabit	a character	役になりきる

★have a character は good, strong など形容詞とともに用いる

▷Do you admit that he **has** a good **character**? 彼の性格はいいと認めますか
▷Steel **plays** two **characters**. スティールは二役を演じる
▷A good actor really **inhabits** the **character** he plays. よい役者は自分が演じる役になりきるものだ

a different	character	異なる性格
a strong	character	強い性格
a weak	character	弱い性格
the main	character	主人公
the central	character	
the leading	character	
a national	character	国民性
Chinese	characters	漢字
a cartoon	character	漫画の登場人物
a fiction	character	フィクションの登場人物

▷Peter and Kate have totally **different characters**. ピーターとケイトは性格がまったく異なる
▷Jackie plays the **main character**. ジャッキーは主人公を演じる

in	character	はまり役の
out of	character	その人らしくない

▷She's a great actress! She's always **in character**. すばらしい女優だ．いつも役にはまっている
▷I was surprised to see her acting so **out of character**. 彼女が柄にもない行動に出たのを見て驚いた

charge /tʃάːrdʒ/

名 料金；非難，告発；責任，監督

make	a charge	代金を請求する
bring	charges	告発する
press	charges	
prefer	charges	
drop	(the) charges	告発を取りやめる
face	a charge	告発を受ける
admit	a charge	容疑を認める
deny	a charge	容疑を否認する
take	charge	担当する

▷The hotel doesn't **make** a **charge** for this service. このサービスにはホテルは代金をいただきません
▷Why didn't Erica **bring charges** *against* Michael? エリカはなぜマイケルを告発しなかったのか
▷She **faced charges** of murdering her husband. 彼女は夫を殺害したとの告発を受けた
▷He **admitted** the **charge** of dangerous driving. 彼は危険運転の容疑を認めた
▷Peter is going to **take charge** *of* our campaign. ピーターは私たちの運動の世話を引き受けるつもりだ

a fixed	charge	固定料金
an annual	charge	年間料金
an extra	charge	追加料金
an additional	charge	
a service	charge	サービス料
an admission	charge	入場料
a criminal	charge	刑事告発
a false	charge	無実の罪

▷**Annual charges** for gas, electricity and water, have all increased compared with last year. ガス，電気，水道の年間料金は昨年と比べてすべて上昇した
▷See if there're **extra charges** for special services. 特別なサービスを頼んだら追加料金がかかるかどうか確かめてみて
▷The investigation led to **criminal charges** against the company. 調査の結果，その会社に対して刑事告発がなされることになった

charge	for A	Aの料金
in	charge	世話して，担当して

▷There's no **charge for** admission. 入場無料です
▷Who is the person **in charge** *of* this project? だれがこの計画の担当者ですか

free of	charge	無料で

▷Tickets to the event are **free of charge**. その催しの券は無料です

chat /tʃǽt/ 名 おしゃべり，雑談

have	a chat	おしゃべりをする

▷I'd like to **have** a **chat** *with* Billy. ビリーとおしゃべりしたい

a cozy	chat	くつろいだ雑談
a friendly	chat	打ち解けた雑談
a little	chat	ちょっとした雑談

▷We were just having a **friendly chat** over a cup of coffee. コーヒーを飲みながら打ち解けておしゃべりしていた

chat /tʃǽt/ 動 おしゃべりする，雑談する

chat	happily	楽しそうにおしゃべりする
chat	quietly	静かにおしゃべりする

▷Tony is **chatting happily** with Helen. トニーはヘレンと楽しそうにおしゃべりしている

chat	about A	Aについておしゃべりする
chat	with A	A(人)とおしゃべりする
chat	to A	

▷What are you **chatting about**? 何を話しているの
▷I've really enjoyed **chatting with** you. あなたとのおしゃべりはとても楽しかった

cheap /tʃíːp/ 形 安い；安っぽい

extremely	cheap	とても安い
really	cheap	実に安い
fairly	cheap	かなり安い
relatively	cheap	比較的安い
comparatively	cheap	

▷The food is **really cheap** and fresh. 食べ物は実に安くて新鮮だ
▷Our country is still **relatively cheap** to live in. 私たちの国は生活費がまだ比較的安い

| check |

cheap and easy	安くて簡単な
《英》cheap and cheerful	安くてそこそこの
《英》cheap and nasty	安かろう悪かろうの

▷ Flights from Birmingham to Copenhagen are **cheap and easy**. バーミンガムからコペンハーゲンまで飛行機で飛ぶのは安くて簡単な移動方法だ
▷ It was a **cheap and nasty** hotel. 安くてひどいホテルだった

check /tʃék/ 名 点検, 検査；阻止；《米》勘定書；小切手(★この語義の《英》つづりは cheque)

have	a check	調べる
make	a check	検査する, チェックする
do	a check	
run	a check	
keep	a check	監視する
write	a check	小切手を切る
present	a check	小切手を渡す
cash	a check	小切手を現金化する
pay by	check	小切手で払う

▷ Thomas **had a check** in his jacket pocket. トマスは自分の上着のポケットを調べた
▷ I **did a check** on some of the things she said. 彼女の発言内容をいくつか調べてみた
▷ It's important to **keep a check** on your blood pressure to prevent a problem such as heart disease. 心臓病などの疾患予防には血圧をチェックするのが重要だ
▷ He **wrote a check** for $2,000. 彼は2千ドルの小切手を切った
▷ I'd like to **cash** these traveler's **checks**. トラベラーズチェックを現金に替えたいのですが
▷ You can **pay by check**. 小切手でお支払いいただけます

a thorough	check	徹底的な点検
a quick	check	あっさりした点検
a regular	check	定期点検
a routine	check	
an annual	check	毎年の点検
a final	check	最終点検
a medical	check	健康診断
a health	check	
a dental	check	歯科検診

▷ I've done a **quick check** to see if anything was missing. 抜け落ちがないかさっと調べた
▷ **Regular checks** are conducted to ensure that the doors are secure. ドアの安全対策がしっかりしているかどうか確認するための定期検査が行われている
▷ He is now busy with a **final check** of his plan. 彼は計画の最終確認で忙しい

hold A in	check	Aを抑える, 食い止める
keep A in	check	

▷ Kevin **held** his anger **in check**. ケビンは怒りを抑えた

check /tʃék/ 動 点検する, 調べる；確かめる

check	regularly	定期的に点検する
check	frequently	たびたび点検する
check	beforehand	前もって点検する
check	carefully	注意深く点検する

▷ ID cards are **checked regularly**. 身分証明書は定期的に調べられる
▷ **Check carefully** before you sign your name. 署名する前に慎重に確かめなさい

check	with A	A(人)に確かめる

▷ Let me **check with** my husband. 夫と相談させてください

check	(that)...	…であることを調べる
check	wh-	…であるか調べる

★ wh- は whether, what, how など

▷ Jenny looked at the map and **checked that** she was going the right way. ジェニーは地図を見て, 道を間違えていないことを確認した
▷ We just wanted to **check whether** or not you were all right. あなたがだいじょうぶかどうか確かめたかっただけです

cheese /tʃíːz/ 名 チーズ

cut	cheese	チーズを切る
slice	cheese	
grate	cheese	チーズをおろす

▷ **Cut** the **cheese** into pieces. チーズを切り分けてください
▷ If you want, you could **grate** the **cheese** into the pasta sauce. お好みでチーズをおろしてパスタソースに入れください

(a) hard	cheese	硬質チーズ
(a) soft	cheese	軟質チーズ
strong	cheese	においの強いチーズ
low-fat	cheese	低脂肪チーズ
grated	cheese	粉チーズ

▷ Cheddar is a **hard cheese**. チェダーは硬質チーズだ

▷I put two slices of **low-fat cheese** in a sandwich. サンドイッチに低脂肪チーズを2切れ入れた

a piece of	cheese	チーズ一切れ
a slice of	cheese	

▷This is a lovely **piece of cheese**. おいしいチーズだね

cheese and biscuits		チーズとビスケット

▷She drank a glass of milk and ate some **cheese and biscuits**. 彼女はコップ1杯の牛乳を飲んでチーズとビスケットを食べた

PHRASES
Say "Cheese"! ☺ (写真を撮る際に)はいチーズ

child /tʃáild/ 名 子ども

have	a child	子どもがいる
have	children	
adopt	a child	子どもを養子にする
raise	a child	子どもを育てる
bring up	a child	

▷I **have** no **children**. 私には子どもがいません(★I have no child. とはふつういわない)
▷Our grandparents live with us and help to **bring up the children**. 祖父母が同居して子育てを手伝ってくれている

a small	child	小さな子ども
a young	child	幼い子ども
a grown-up	child	成人した子ども
a spoiled	child	わがままな子
an only	child	一人っ子
an unborn	child	胎児、おなかの子

▷I've been fluent in French since I was a **young child**. 幼いころからフランス語が流ちょうだった
▷They have two **grown-up children**. 彼らには成人した子どもが2人いる
▷She rubs her stomach, whispering to her **unborn child**. 彼女はおなかをさすって、おなかの子にささやきかけている

chocolate /tʃɔ́:kələt | tʃɔ́k-/
名 チョコレート

bitter	chocolate	ビターチョコレート
dark	chocolate	ブラックチョコレート
《英》plain	chocolate	
hot	chocolate	ココア

▷Do you want a cup of **hot chocolate** or something? 熱いココアか何かほしいですか

a bar of	chocolate	板チョコ一つ
a piece of	chocolate	チョコレート一かけら
a box of	chocolate	チョコレート1箱

▷I bought a **bar of chocolate**. 板チョコを一つ買った
▷Would you like a **piece of chocolate**? チョコレートを一ついかが

choice /tʃɔ́is/ 名 選択;選択権

make	a choice	選ぶ
have	a choice	選択できる
exercise	choice	選択する
give A	the choice	A(人)に選択権を
offer A	the choice	与える

▷It's time to **make a choice**. 選ぶべきときです
▷"Do I **have a choice**?" "No. It's already been decided." 「選択の余地はありますか」「いえ、もう決まっています」 ◆**have no choice (but to do) / have little choice (but to do)** (…するよりほか)選択の自由がない
▷They have no choice but to sell the house. 彼らは家を売るよりほかない
▷I'm going to **give** you two **choices**. 2つから選ばせてあげる

a good	choice	よい選択
the right	choice	正しい選択
a stark	choice	厳しい選択
a hard	choice	難しい選択
personal	choice	個人的選択
a free	choice	自由な選択
first	choice	第1希望
the number one	choice	
a wide	choice	幅広い選択肢
an obvious	choice	当然の選択

▷"I bought some yellow roses at the florist." "Oh, Wendy. **Good choice**." 「花屋さんで黄色いバラを何本か買ったよ」「まあウェンディ、いいのを選んだわね」
▷My **first choice** is to be a lawyer. 第1希望は弁護士になることです
▷Everybody agreed that she was the **obvious choice** for the job. 彼女こそその仕事にうってつけだとみんな賛成した

a choice	between A	Aの間の選択

▷A decision is expected early next week regarding location. The **choice** is **between** Paris and Frankfurt. 場所は来週早々に決まる予定で、パリかフランクフルトの

| choose |

どちらかだ

by	choice	自分の意思で
of	one's choice	自分で選んだ
A of	choice	選ばれるA

▷I'm doing this **by choice**. 私は自らの意思でこれをしています
▷This decision was made **of her own choice**. この決定は彼女が自分で選んだことだ
▷Red was my color **of choice**. 赤が私が選んだ色だった

freedom of	choice	選択の自由

▷Everybody has **freedom of choice** about this. だれでもがこの件で選択の自由がある

choose /tʃúːz/ 動 選ぶ, 選択する；決める

choose	carefully	注意深く選ぶ
choose	wisely	賢明に選ぶ
choose	freely	自由に選ぶ
choose	randomly	無作為に選ぶ
choose A	instead	代わりにAを選ぶ
deliberately	choose	意図的に選ぶ

★carefully, wisely, freely, randomly, deliberately は動詞の前後どちらでも用いる

▷I trust you have **chosen wisely**. きみのことだから賢明な選択をしたと信じているよ
▷You can **choose freely** what you want. ほしいものを自由に選んでいいですよ
▷Ten people were **randomly chosen** from the list. 名簿から10人が無作為に選ばれた
▷He gave her no answer, **choosing instead** to change the subject. 彼は彼女に何も答えず, 代わりに話題を切り替えた

choose	A from B	AをBから選ぶ
choose	between A	Aから選ぶ

▷Bill **chose** a red T-shirt **from** the wardrobe. ビルはたんすから赤いTシャツを選んだ
▷Both candidates were excellent. It was impossible to **choose between** them. どちらの応募者もすばらしく, どちらか一方を選ぶのは無理だった

choose	to do	…するのを選ぶ

▷He **chose to** do nothing. 彼は何もしないことにした

choose	wh-	…か選ぶ

★wh- は which, when, what など

▷I can **choose when** to work and **when** to take a break. いつ働いていつ休憩するか自分で決められる

choose	A as C	AをCに選ぶ

▷Why did you **choose** Australia **as** a place to study? 留学先としてオーストラリアを選んだ理由は何ですか

if A so	choose	A(人)がそう望むなら

★しばしば文尾で用いる

▷You can come with me **if** you **so choose**. 来たいならいっしょに来ていいよ

cigarette /sìɡərét/ 名 たばこ

smoke	a cigarette	たばこを吸う
light	a cigarette	たばこに火をつける
stub out	a cigarette	たばこの火をもみ消す

▷She **lit** a **cigarette** and took a puff. 彼女はたばこに火をつけて吹かした
▷He **stubbed out** his **cigarette** in the ashtray. 彼は灰皿にたばこを押しつけて火を消した

a pack of	cigarettes	たばこ1箱
《英》a packet of	cigarettes	

▷He pulled a **pack of cigarettes** from his pocket. 彼はポケットからたばこの箱を取り出した

circle /sə́ːrkl/ 名 円, 輪；仲間, サークル

draw	a circle	円を描く
form	a circle	輪になる
make	a circle	
join	a circle	サークルに入る

▷I **drew** a **circle** on a sheet of paper. 紙に円を描いた(★×write a circle とはいわない)
▷They **formed** a **circle** around him. 彼を囲んでみんなで輪になった

a wide	circle	幅広い交友関係
a large	circle	
a narrow	circle	狭い交友関係
a small	circle	
academic	circles	学会
literary	circles	文学界
business	circles	実業界
a family	circle	家族の輪
a vicious	circle	悪循環

▷She developed a **large circle** of friends. 彼女は幅広い交友関係を築いた
▷He moved in **literary circles** at that time. 彼はそのころ文学界に出入りしていた
▷The more chocolate I eat, the more chocolate I want to eat! It's a **vicious circle**. チョコレートを食べれば食べるほどもっとほしくなる．悪循環だ

in	a circle	輪になって

▷The children are sitting **in** a **circle**. 子どもたちは輪になって座っている
▷You're never going to get anywhere if you keep running around **in circles** like this. こんなふうに堂々巡りしていてはどうにもならない

a circle	of friends	友人の輪
a circle	of acquaintances	知人の輪

▷I have a wide **circle of acquaintances** in the U.S. 米国に知人があちこちいる

circumstance /sə́ːrkəmstæns | -stəns/

名 事情，状況，情勢；境遇

circumstances	change	状況が変わる

▷Within the last two years, **circumstances** have **changed**. この2年で状況は変化した

normal	circumstances	ふつうの状況
special	circumstances	特別な状況
suspicious	circumstances	不審な状況
different	circumstances	異なる状況
economic	circumstances	経済状況
certain	circumstances	ある状況
particular	circumstances	特定の状況

★ under... circumstances や in... circumstances の結びつきでよく用いる

▷Under **normal circumstances**, late applications will not be accepted. 提出期限を過ぎた申込書はふつう受理しません
▷It's a pity you and I couldn't have met under **different circumstances**. あなたと私がもっと別の状況で出会えていればよかったのに，残念だ
▷In **certain circumstances** we may be able to offer financial aid. 状況によってはお金を援助できるかもしれない

circumstances	surrounding A	Aを取り巻く状況

▷What were the **circumstances surrounding** his death? 彼の死を取り巻く状況はどのようだったのか

given	the circumstances	こういう状況
considering	the circumstances	なので
under	the circumstances	

▷**Given the circumstances**, this decision was understandable. 状況が状況なので無理もない決定だった

under	no circumstances	どんなことがあっ
in	no circumstances	ても…ない

★ not under any circumstances, not in any circumstances も用いる

▷Don't **under any circumstances** ride your motorbike without a crash helmet. どんなことがあってもヘルメットをかぶらずにオートバイに乗るな

citizen /sítəzən/

名 市民；(市民権をもつ)国民

a US	citizen	米国国民
a good	citizen	よき市民
an ordinary	citizen	一般市民
a senior	citizen	高齢者

▷He became a **US citizen**. 彼は(市民権をとって)米国国民になった
▷The Prime Minister talked with many **ordinary citizens** during his election campaign. 首相は選挙期間中，多くの一般市民と話した

city /síti/ 名 都市，都会；市

a big	city	大都会，大都市
a great	city	
a large	city	
a historic	city	歴史的な都市
an old	city	古都
an industrial	city	産業都市
a walled	city	城壁都市
a sister	city	姉妹都市
《英》a twin	city	

▷I don't like living in the country. I want to live in a **big city**. 田舎に住むのはいやだ．大都市に住みたい
▷York is a **historic city**. ヨークは歴史のある街だ

claim /kléim/ 名 主張；権利；要求，請求

make	a claim	主張する

| claim |

deny	a claim	主張を否定する
dispute	a claim	主張に異議を唱える
reject	a claim	
support	A's claim	主張を支持する
make	a claim	請求する
file	a claim	
waive	a claim	請求を放棄する
have	a claim to A	Aを要求する権利がある
have	a claim on A	
lay	claim to A	Aの権利を主張する

▷ The minister **denied claims** that he was going to resign. 大臣は辞任の話を否定した
▷ After his house burned down, he **made a claim** *to* the insurance company. 家が全焼して, 彼は保険会社に請求した ▷ She **made a claim** *for* damages. 彼女は損害賠償を請求した
▷ She **has a claim** *on* her parents' property. 彼女には親の財産を相続する権利がある
▷ Arabs and Israelis both **lay claim to** the ownership of the territories. アラブ人もイスラエル人もどちらも領土の所有権を主張している

the competing	claims	相反する主張
a false	claim	虚偽の主張；不正請求

▷ He made a **false claim** to his insurance company. 彼は保険会社に不正請求をした

claim /kléim/ 動 主張する；要求する

falsely	claim	虚偽の主張をする
claim	back	返還を求める

▷ He **falsely claimed** that he had a degree from Harvard University. 彼はハーバード大学の学位をもっていると偽った
▷ You can **claim back** another £190. さらに190ポンドの返還を求めることができる

claim	(that)...	…と主張する

▷ He **claims that** he was in bed asleep at the time of the murder. 殺害のあった時刻にはベッドで寝ていたと彼は主張している

claim	to do	…すると主張する
claim	to be	…であると主張する

▷ I never **claimed to** know anything about car engines. 車のエンジンについて何か知っていると主張したことなどなかった
▷ He is not the man he **claimed to** be. 彼は彼自身が言っているような人ではない

class /klæs | klɑːs/

名 (学校の)クラス；授業；階級；等級

have	(a) class	授業がある
attend	(a) class	授業に出る
go to	(a) class	
take	(a) class	授業を受ける
cut	(a) class	授業をさぼる
skip	(a) class	
miss	(a) class	授業を欠席する
teach	(a) class	授業を教える
take	(a) class	授業を受け持つ
be late for	class	授業に遅刻する

▷ I **have** six **classes** on Monday. 月曜日は6時間授業がある
▷ I don't feel like **going to a class** today. きょうは授業に出たくない
▷ My teacher told me to stop **cutting classes**. 授業をさぼるのはやめなさいと先生に注意された
▷ Ryan never **missed a class**. ライアンは授業を休んだことはなかった
▷ She **teaches** art **classes** at night school. 彼女は夜間学校で美術の授業を教えている
▷ Let's go now or we'll be **late for class**! さあ行こう, 授業に遅刻するぞ

a French	class	フランス語の授業
a maths	class	数学の授業
an advanced	class	上級クラス
an intermediate	class	中級クラス
(an) evening	class	夜間クラス
lower	class	下層階級
middle	class	中流階級
upper	class	上流階級
working	class	労働者階級
ruling	class	支配階級
social	class	社会階級
first	class	ファーストクラス
business	class	ビジネスクラス
economy	class	エコノミークラス

▷ The British have three main classes, the **upper class**, the **middle class**, and the **working class**. イギリス人には上流階級, 中流階級, 労働者階級と3つのおもな階級がある

in	class	授業で, 授業中に

▷ You're kidding! You fell asleep **in class**! 冗談だろ. 授業中に寝ちゃったのか

clean /klíːn/

形 清潔な, きれいな; 汚れのない, 潔白な

keep A	clean	Aをきれいにしておく
wipe A	clean	Aをきれいに拭く
scrub A	clean	Aをきれいにこする
wash A	clean	Aをきれいに洗う

▷You have to **keep** your room **clean**. 部屋をきれいにしておかなければいけません

perfectly	clean	完璧にきれいな
spotlessly	clean	しみ一つなくきれいな
immaculately	clean	

▷You can use this dish. It's **perfectly clean**. この皿を使ってください. きれいに洗ってありますから
▷Every room was **spotlessly clean**. どの部屋もちり一つなくきれいだった

neat and clean	きちんと整頓された
《英》clean and tidy	

▷She always keeps her room **clean and tidy**. 彼女はいつも部屋をきちんと整頓している

clear /klíər/

形 明快な; 確信した; 澄んだ, 晴れた

seem	clear	明らかと思われる

▷It **seems clear** that we've still got a lot of problems to solve. 解決すべき問題がまだたくさんあるのは明らかだと思われる

fairly	clear	かなり明快な
abundantly	clear	十分に明快な
absolutely	clear	完全に明快な
perfectly	clear	
crystal	clear	
not entirely	clear	必ずしも明快でない

▷I want to make one thing **absolutely clear**. ひとつはっきりさせておきたいのですが
▷The sky was **perfectly clear**. 空は澄み渡っていた
▷I'm **not entirely clear** what you mean. あなたが何を言おうとしているのかわからないところがある

clear and simple	簡単明瞭な

▷It's all here in the instructions. **Clear and simple**. 取扱説明書にすべて説明されています. 簡単明瞭です

make it clear that...	…を明白にする

▷Did you **make it clear that** we didn't agree with her idea? 私たちが彼女の考えに賛成でないことを彼女にきちんと伝えましたか

PHRASES
Is that clear? / Do I make myself clear? ☺ わかったか ▷I don't want to hear another word about it. **Is that clear?** その件については一言も聞きたくない. わかったか

clear /klíər/ 動 片づける; きれいにする

clear	away	取り除く, 片づける
clear	up	片づける, 整頓する

▷Sophie **cleared** the plates **away**. ソフィーは皿を片づけた
▷I **cleared up** the mess on the floor. 散らかった床を片づけた

clear	A of B	AからBを取り除く
clear	B off A	
clear	B from A	

▷I **cleared** the steps **of** snow. / I **cleared** the snow **off** the steps. 階段の雪を取り除いた
▷We need to **clear** the weeds **from** the river. 川の水草を取り除いたほうがいい

clever /klévər/ 形 利口な, 賢い; じょうずな

extremely	clever	とても利口な
really	clever	

▷He was an **extremely clever** child. 彼は子どものころとても賢かった

clever	at doing	…するのがうまい
clever	with A	Aが器用な

▷He was very **clever at** getting what he wanted. 彼はほしいものを手に入れるのがとてもうまかった
▷Cindy is very **clever with** her hands. She has a pottery exhibition next week. シンディは手先がとても器用だ. 来週陶芸の展覧会を開く

climb /kláim/ 動 登る; 上がる

climb	rapidly	急いで登る
climb	steadily	徐々に登りになる; 着実に上がる
climb	steeply	急な登りになる; 急激に上がる

| clock |

▷ Oil prices have **climbed steadily** over the years.
原油価格は何年かにわたって徐々に上がっている

climb	**up** A	Aをよじ登る
climb	**over** A	Aを乗り越える

▷ I **climbed up** the ladder and got to the top. はしごを登り，いちばん上まで行った
▷ He couldn't **climb over** the wall. 彼は壁を乗り越えられなかった

clock /klák | klɔ́k/ 名 時計

set	a clock	時計を合わせる
adjust	a clock	時計を調整する
watch	the clock	時計ばかり気にする

▷ I **set** my alarm **clock** for 5 a.m. 目覚まし時計を朝5時に合わせた
▷ Don't **watch** the **clock**! 時間ばかり気にするな

a clock	strikes	時計が打つ
a clock	chimes	時計が鳴る
a clock	ticks	時計がカチカチいう
a clock	says	時計が…時を指す

▷ The **clock struck** 9. 時計は9時を打った
▷ The **clock says** 6:05. 時計は6時5分を指している

against	the clock	時間に追われて
around	the clock	昼も夜も，24時間
round	the clock	ぶっ通しで

▷ Everything is a race **against** the **clock**. すべては時間との競争だ
▷ She is working **around** the **clock** to resolve this problem. 彼女はこの問題を解決するために昼夜ぶっ通しで働いている

a body	clock	体内時計

close /klóus/ 形 近い，接近した；親密な

extremely	close	とても近い；とても親しい
really	close	
fairly	close	かなり近い
quite	close	かなり近い；かなり親しい
uncomfortably	close	落ち着かないほど近い
close	together	互いに近い
close	enough	十分に近い

▷ We're **really close** to the coast now. すぐそこが海岸というところまで来ている
▷ Emma and I are **fairly close**. We go everywhere together. エマと私はかなり親しい間柄で，どこへでもいっしょに出かける
▷ He was **uncomfortably close**, so I moved away. 彼は不快なほど近づいたので，私は遠ざかった
▷ We both live in the same street. Our houses are **close together**. 私たちは同じ通りに住んでいる．家がすぐ近くだ
▷ Do you think he was **close enough** to hear us? 彼はすぐ近くにいて私たちの話が聞けたかな

close	**to** A	Aに近い

▷ She sat **close to** Steve. 彼女はスティーブの近くに座った ▷ We're all **close to** sixty years old. 私たちはみんな60歳に近い

PHRASES
You are close. ☺ (あなたの推測は)だいたい当たっています ▷ "He's sixty years old, isn't he?" "You're close. Fifty nine."「あの人は60歳かな」「いい線行くね．59歳だよ」

close /klóuz/

動 閉じる；閉める，閉まる；終える，終わる

close	firmly	しっかり閉める
close	tightly	

★どちらの副詞も動詞の前でも用いる

▷ You need to **close** the refrigerator door **firmly**.
冷蔵庫のドアをしっかり閉めないといけない

close	down	閉鎖する
close	off	封鎖する
close	up	ふさがる

▷ They're going to have to **close** the office **down**.
事務所を閉鎖しなければならなくなるだろう
▷ The roads were **closed off** due to the snow. 道路は雪のために封鎖された
▷ Even though it was a deep wound it **closed up** quickly. 傷は深かったが，傷口はすぐふさがった

closed /klóuzd/ 形 閉店して；閉鎖した

remain	closed	閉まったままである

▷ Make sure these gates **remain closed** at all times.
これらの門はいつも閉めておくようにしなさい

closed	**to** A	Aは立ち入り禁止で

▷Broad Street will be **closed to** traffic from 11 a.m. to 5 p.m. ブロードストリートは午前11時から午後5時まで通行止めになります

tightly	closed	しっかり閉まった

▷She kept her eyes **tightly closed** as the roller-coaster went faster and faster. ジェットコースターの速度がどんどん上がってきて，彼女は目をしっかり閉じたままでいた

clothes /klóuz/ 名 衣服

wear	clothes	服を着ている
put on	clothes	服を着る
take off	clothes	服を脱ぐ
change	clothes	着替える
wash	clothes	服を洗う

▷He was **wearing** the same **clothes** as yesterday. 彼はきのうと同じ服を着ていた
▷I want to **put on** some nice **clothes** and go out. すてきな服を着て外出したい
▷He **took off** his **clothes** and put them on the bed. 彼は服を脱いでベッドの上に置いた
▷Let me **change clothes**. 服を着替えさせて

fancy	clothes	はでな服
fashionable	clothes	流行の服
casual	clothes	普段着
everyday	clothes	
baby	clothes	ベビー服
children's	clothes	子ども服
men's	clothes	紳士服
women's	clothes	婦人服
working	clothes	仕事着

▷She was dressed up in **fancy clothes**. 彼女ははでな服を着ていた
▷She was tall, blond and gorgeous and always wore **fashionable clothes**. 彼女は背が高く，金髪美人で，いつも流行の服を着ていた
▷I put on **casual clothes** and decided to stay at home. 普段着を着て家にいることにした

cloud /kláud/ 名 雲；もうもうとした煙

clouds	gather	雲が立ち込める
a cloud	hangs	雲がかかる
a cloud	covers A	雲がAを覆う

▷Dark **clouds gathered** in the sky. 黒い雲が空に立ち込めた

thick	cloud	厚い雲
heavy	cloud	
dense	cloud	
high	cloud	高い雲
low	cloud	低い雲
rain	cloud	雨雲

▷**Thick clouds** covered the sky and blocked the sun. 厚い雲が空を覆い太陽を遮った
▷**Low clouds** hung around the foothills. 低い雲が丘陵に垂れ込めた

club /kláb/ 名 クラブ，同好会

belong to	a club	クラブの一員である
join	a club	クラブに入る
leave	a club	クラブをやめる
run	a club	クラブを運営する

▷I **belong to** a rugby **club**. ラグビー部に所属しています
▷You should **join** the drama **club**. 演劇クラブに入るべきだよ
▷Ever since Bruce **left** the **club**, the team hasn't won a game. ブルースがクラブを抜けて以来，チームは勝ったことがない

a member of	the cub	クラブの会員

▷Are you a **member of** the **club**? あなたはクラブの会員ですか

clue /klú:/ 名 手がかり

have	a clue	手がかりがある
give	a clue	手がかりを与える
provide	a clue	
look for	a clue	手がかりを探る
search for	a clue	
find	a clue	手がかりを見つける

▷Maybe it'll **give** us a **clue** to why he died. それで彼の死因が明らかになるかもしれない
▷History **provides** some **clues** to this puzzle. 歴史はこの謎にいくつかの手がかりを与えてくれる
▷You might **find clues** to where she is now. 彼女の居場所について手がかりが見つかるかもしれない

an important	clue	重要な手がかり
a vital	clue	決定的な手がかり
the only	clue	唯一の手がかり

| coat |

▷TV cameras will provide **vital clues** to his disappearance. 彼の失踪を巡る決定的な手がかりはテレビカメラにある
▷That's the **only clue** we have. われわれが持っている手がかりはそれだけだ

a clue	to A	Aの手がかり
a clue	as to A	
a clue	about A	

▷There're no further **clues as to** what will happen. 今後のなりゆきがどうなるか, それ以上の手がかりはない

coat /kóut/ 名 コート

put on	a coat	コートを着る
throw on	a coat	コートを引っかける
take off	a coat	コートを脱ぐ

▷Outside is very cold. **Put** your **coat on**. 外はとても寒いですからコートを着てください
▷Do you want to **take off** your **coat**? コートを脱ぎますか

coffee /kɔ́:fi | kɔ́fi/ 名 コーヒー

make	coffee	コーヒーをいれる
pour	coffee	コーヒーを注ぐ
drink	coffee	コーヒーを飲む
have	(a) coffee	
sip	one's coffee	コーヒーをすする
finish	one's coffee	コーヒーを飲み終わる

▷I'll **make coffee** as soon as we get back. 家に帰ったらすぐコーヒーをいれるからね
▷Could I **have** a **coffee** please? コーヒーをいただけますか
▷She sat reading the newspaper **sipping coffee**. 彼女は座って新聞を読みながらコーヒーをすすっていた
▷Can we just wait until I **finish** my cup of **coffee**? コーヒーを飲み干すまでみんなちょっと待ってくれるかな

strong	coffee	濃いコーヒー
weak	coffee	薄いコーヒー
black	coffee	ブラックコーヒー
white	coffee	ミルク入りコーヒー
iced	coffee	アイスコーヒー
fresh	coffee	いれたてのコーヒー
instant	coffee	インスタントコーヒー

▷Espresso is a very **strong coffee** and popular throughout Italy. エスプレッソは非常に濃いコーヒーでイタリアの至る所で人気がある
▷There's **fresh coffee** if you'd like some. コーヒーを

いれたところです. よろしければお飲みになりますか

| a cup of | coffee | 1杯のコーヒー |

▷I drink two **cups of coffee** a day. 1日にコーヒーを2杯飲む

cold /kóuld/ 形 寒い；冷たい

| feel | cold | 寒いと感じる |
| get | cold | 寒くなる；冷たくなる |

▷Don't you **feel cold** without a hat? 帽子をかぶらないで寒くありませんか
▷Hurry up! Your dinner's **getting cold**! 急いで. 料理が冷めてしまうよ

extremely	cold	とても寒い
pretty	cold	
freezing	cold	いてつくほど寒い
bitterly	cold	

▷Can we come in? It's **pretty cold** out here. 中に入らない？外はとても寒いもの
▷The night was **bitterly cold**. ひどく寒い夜だった

cold /kóuld/ 名 寒さ；かぜ

keep out	the cold	寒さを防ぐ
catch	(a) cold	かぜを引く
get	a cold	
have (got)	a cold	かぜを引いている

▷Come inside before you **catch** (a) **cold**! かぜを引かないうちに中に入りなさい
▷I think I'm **getting a cold**. かぜを引いたのではないかと思う
▷I **have a cold**. かぜを引いています

bitter	cold	厳しい寒さ
biting	cold	身を切る寒さ
freezing	cold	いてつく寒さ
a bad	cold	ひどいかぜ
a heavy	cold	
a slight	cold	軽いかぜ
a common	cold	普通のかぜ

▷It was **bitter cold** outside. 外は厳しい寒さだった
▷She had a really **bad cold**. 彼女はひどいかぜを引いていた
▷I have a **slight cold**. 少しかぜ気味です
▷The symptoms of the **common cold** are runny nose, sneezing, sore throat and feverishness. 普通のかぜの症状は鼻水, くしゃみ, のどの痛みと発熱だ

colleague /káli:g | kɔ́l-/ 名 同僚

a senior	colleague	先輩の同僚
a junior	colleague	後輩の同僚
a male	colleague	男性の同僚
a female	colleague	女性の同僚
a professional	colleague	職場の同僚
a former	colleague	元同僚

▷I wish to thank my family, friends and **professional colleagues** who have supported me. 私を支えてくれた家族, 友人, 職場の同僚にお礼を言いたいと思います

▷Ken is a **former colleague** and a friend. ケンは元同僚で友人です

collection /kəlékʃən/

名 収蔵物, コレクション；募金

have	a collection	コレクションがある
build up	a collection	コレクションを築く
add to	A's collection	コレクションに加える
make	a collection	募金を集める
take (up)	a collection	

▷He **has a collection** of Japanese woodblock prints. 彼は日本の浮世絵のコレクションをもっている

▷John had **built up a collection** of nearly 2,000 stamps from all over the world. ジョンは世界中から2千近い切手を集めた

▷This album is definitely one to **add to** your **collection**. ぜひこのアルバムをあなたのコレクションにお加えください

▷We **made** a **collection** to buy supplies for the school. 学校の物品を買うために募金を集めた

the collection	contains A	コレクションには
the collection	includes A	Aがある

▷The **collections include** furniture, books, old maps and jewelry. コレクションは家具, 本, 古い地図, 宝石類からなっている

an extensive	collection	膨大なコレクション
a large	collection	
a vast	collection	
a fine	collection	すばらしいコレクション
a unique	collection	ユニークなコレクション
a private	collection	個人コレクション
data	collection	データ収集
garbage	collection	ごみ収集

▷Bruce had a **large collection** of books. ブルースの蔵書は膨大だった

college /kálidʒ | kɔ́l-/ 名 大学；単科大学

attend	college	大学に通う
go to	college	
enter	college	大学に入る
finish	college	大学を卒業する
leave	college	大学をやめる

▷He **attended college** in Ohio. 彼はオハイオの大学に通っていた

▷He **entered college** and chose hotel management as his major. 彼は大学に入り, ホテル経営を専攻に選んだ

▷In my third year I **left college**. 3年生のとき大学をやめた

at	college	大学構内に；《英》大学在学中に
in	college	大学構内に；《米》大学在学中で

▷My son is **in college**. 息子は大学に在学中です

▷I left my books **in college**. 大学に本を置いてきてしまった

color /kʌ́lər/

名 色；顔色；肌色；特色(★《英》つづりは colour)

add	color	色を加える
change	color	色を変える
match	the color	色が合う

▷Her eyes seem to **change color** according to her mood. 彼女の目は気分によって色が変わるみたいだ

▷The curtains **matched** the **color** of the carpet. カーテンの色はカーペットの色と合っていた

a bright	color	鮮やかな色
a dark	color	暗い色
a primary	color	原色
a natural	color	天然色
full	color	フルカラー
local	color	地方色

▷I don't look good in **bright colors**. 私には鮮やかな色は似合いません

▷The book is 180 pages and printed in **full color**. その本は180ページでフルカラー印刷だ

color(s) and shape		色と形

★ shape and color も用いる

▷I like the **color and shape** of your new cellphone.

きみの新しい携帯電話の色と形が好きだ

combine /kəmbáin/

動 結合させる，結合する

successfully	combine	うまく結合させる
combine	well	うまく結びつく

▷He **successfully combined** new and traditional elements. 彼は新しい要素と伝統的な要素をうまく結合させた
▷The team **combined well** and won the match easily. チームはうまく結束して試合に楽勝した

combine	A with B	AとBを結びつける
combine	A and B	

▷Using a hand mixer, **combine** the bananas **with** eggs, buttermilk and vanilla in a mixing bowl. ハンドミキサーを使って，ミキシングボウルでバナナと卵，バターミルク，バニラを混ぜてください

comfort /kʌ́mfərt/ 名 慰め；快適さ

bring	comfort	慰めをもたらす
give	comfort	
offer	comfort	
take	comfort	慰めを得る

▷Her visits **brought** great **comfort** to her grandmother. 彼女がよく来てくれることで彼女の祖母はとても慰められた
▷She tried to **give comfort** to the survivors of the earthquake. 彼女は地震の生存者を慰めようとした
▷I **take comfort** from the fact that although we lost, it was a really close match. 負けたけれど接戦だったということでよしとしよう

a great	comfort	大きな慰め
cold	comfort	慰めにならない慰め

▷It was **cold comfort** to hear that all my friends had passed the exam, but I hadn't. 友人たちがみな試験に受かったと聞いても慰めにはならなかった．だってぼくは落ちたんだもの

comfortable /kʌ́mfərtəbl/

形 快適な；気楽な，くつろいだ；心配のない

feel	comfortable	快適だ；気楽だ

▷I don't **feel comfortable** with my boss. 上司といっしょだと落ち着かない

extremely	comfortable	とても快適な
fairly	comfortable	

▷The bed was huge and **extremely comfortable**. ベッドは大きくてすごく心地よかった

PHRASES
Please make yourself comfortable. ☺ どうぞ楽にしてください

command /kəmǽnd | -máːnd/

名 命令；指揮，支配；自由に使える能力

give	a command	命令を下す
obey	a command	命令に従う
have	command	指揮している
take	command	指揮をとる
have	a command of A	Aを自由にできる

▷It is not hard to train a dog to **obey commands**. 命令に従うように犬を訓練することは難しいことではない
▷The captain had full **command** of the ship. その船長は船を完全に統率していた
▷Yumi **has** an excellent **command** of English. ユミは自由自在に英語を操れる

an excellent	command	自在に使いこなせること
a good	command	
a poor	command	自在に使いこなせないこと
a military	command	軍司令部

▷He has a **poor command** of English. 彼は英語を自在に使いこなせない
▷There was no report from the US **military command** about the attack. その攻撃について米国軍司令部からの報告はなかった

at	A's command	思いのままに
under	A's command	指揮のもと

▷You're a birthday girl, so you get to choose wherever we go today! I'm **at** your **command**! きょうはきみの誕生日なんだからどこへ行くかはきみが決めて，言うとおりにするから

comment /kɑ́ment | kɔ́m-/

名 論評，意見，コメント

have	a comment	コメントがある
make	a comment	論評する，コメントする
pass	comment	

add	a comment	コメントを加える
receive	a comment	コメントをもらう

▷ If you **have** any **comments**, please email us. コメントがおありでしたらEメールをお送りください
▷ I'd like to **make** a **comment** about what Peter just said. ピーターのいまの発言にコメントしたいと思います
▷ I'd like to **add** a few **comments** to the article. その記事に若干のコメントを加えたいと思います

a brief	comment	短い論評
(a) fair	comment	公正な論評
a favorable	comment	好意的な論評
a critical	comment	批判的な論評
a public	comment	公式な論評
further	comment	さらなる論評

▷ I want to make a few **brief comments**. 2, 3短く論評したいと思います
▷ We have received **favorable comments** with regard to its quality. その質に関して好意的なコメントをもらった
▷ I've read **critical comments** by the media about these facts. これらの事実にマスコミが行った批判的コメントを読んだ
▷ Any **further comments** or questions? さらにコメントか質問はありますか

comment	on A	Aについての論評
comment	about A	
comment	from A	Aからの論評

▷ I'd like to hear your **comments on** my lecture. 私の講義についてコメントをお聞かせいただきたいのですが
▷ There was no **comment from** John. ジョンからは何のコメントもなかった

PHRASES
No comment! ☺ 何も話すことはありません

committed /kəmítid/

形 献身的な；かかわった

fully	committed	全面的にかかわった
totally	committed	
firmly	committed	しっかりかかわった

▷ You need to be **fully committed** if you want to become a professional tennis player. プロのテニス選手になりたいなら全力を傾ける必要がある

committee /kəmíti/ 名 委員会

establish	a committee	委員会を設ける
set up	a committee	
chair	a committee	委員会の議長を務める
head	a committee	
be on	a committee	委員会の一員である
sit on	a committee	

▷ The government promised to **establish a committee** to investigate the matter. 政府はその件に関する調査委員会の設置を約束した
▷ He **chaired** a **committee** that demanded political reform. 彼は政治改革を要求する委員会の議長を務めた

a joint	committee	合同委員会
an advisory	committee	諮問委員会
a disciplinary	committee	懲罰委員会

▷ The two countries agreed to set up a **joint committee** on defense. 両国は防衛に関する合同委員会の設置で合意した

common /kάmən | kɔ́m-/

形 普通の，ありふれた；共通の

extremely	common	きわめて普通の
fairly	common	かなり普通の
increasingly	common	ますます普通の
particularly	common	とりわけ普通の

▷ Shortsightedness is **extremely common** among children. 近視は子どもの間でごく普通だ
▷ Internet shopping is becoming **increasingly common**. インターネットショッピングはますます普通になってきている
▷ Flu was **particularly common** this winter. インフルエンザがこの冬特に流行した

common	to A	Aに共通な

▷ Blonde hair and blue eyes are **common to** my family. 私の家族はみな金髪で目が青い

it is common	for A to do	Aが…するのは普通だ

▷ In Japan **it's common for** students **to** work during their school vacations. 日本では学生が学校の休み中にバイトをするのは普通のことだ

communicate /kəmjúːnəkèit/

動 伝達する，伝える，連絡する

communicate	effectively	うまく伝える
communicate	successfully	

| communication |

communicate	directly	直接伝える

▷ Good doctors **communicate effectively** with their patients. よい医師は患者と意思疎通を図るのがうまい
▷ You should **communicate directly** with Susan. スーザンと直接連絡をとったほうがいい

communicate	A to B	AをB(人)に伝える
communicate	with A	A(人)と連絡をとる

▷ We **communicate** well **with** each other all the time. いつも互いによく連絡をとり合っている

communication /kəmjù:nəkéiʃən/

名 伝達, 連絡, 意思疎通；通信システム

have	communication	連絡をとる
improve	communication	伝達をよくする
establish	communications	通信システムを構築する

▷ I haven't **had** any **communication** with Emma for weeks. もう何週間もエマと連絡をとっていない
▷ Our aim is to **improve communication** between people. われわれのねらいは人々の間のコミュニケーションを促進することだ
▷ Up till now, we have **established communications** with eight French universities. これまでにフランスの8大学との通信システムを構築した

effective	communication	効果的な伝達
poor	communication	乏しい伝達
verbal	communication	ことばによる伝達

▷ The first step to **effective communication** is listening. 効果的なコミュニケーションのための第一歩は聞くことだ

a means of	communication	伝達手段

▷ Language is not only a **means of communication** but also a way of expressing identity. 言語はコミュニケーションの手段であるばかりでなく自己表現の方法でもある

communication	between A	Aの間の連絡

▷ There is a total lack of **communication between** our department and human resources. うちの部署と人事課との間はまったく意思疎通が欠如している

communication	skills	伝達能力
communications	system	通信システム
communications	network	通信網

community /kəmjú:nəti/

名 地域共同体, 共同体

a close-knit	community	緊密な共同体
a tightly-knit	community	
the international	community	国際社会
a local	community	地域社会
a rural	community	村落共同体
the whole	community	地域住民全体

▷ The **international community** faces a number of very important challenges. 国際社会は多くの重要な課題に直面している
▷ The **whole community** opposed the proposal for tax increases. 地域住民はみな増税提案に反対した

company /kʌ́mpəni/

名 会社；仲間；同席

form	a company	会社を設立する
set up	a company	
run	a company	会社を経営する
manage	a company	
acquire	a company	会社を買収する
dissolve	a company	会社を解散する
join	a company	入社する
work for	a company	会社で働く
leave	the company	会社を辞める
enjoy	A's company	A(人)と楽しく過ごす
keep A	company	A(人)といっしょにいる

▷ She **formed** her first **company** in 1965. 彼女は最初の会社を1965年に設立した
▷ My dad **runs** his own **company**. 父は企業のオーナーです
▷ David has **joined** the **company** as a sales manager. デイビッドは営業部長としてその会社に就職した
▷ Wendy and I **enjoy** each other's **company**. ウェンディと私はいっしょにいてお互い楽しい
▷ Should we go **keep** her **company**? 彼女といっしょにいたほうがいいかな

a large	company	大企業
a major	company	
a state-owned	company	国有企業
an oil	company	石油会社
an electricity	company	電力会社
an insurance	company	保険会社
a parent	company	親会社

▷ Ron works for an **oil company**. ロンは石油会社に勤務している

competition /kàmpətíʃən | kɔ̀m-/

名 試合；競争

win	a competition	試合に勝つ
lose	a competition	試合に負ける
enter	a competition	試合参加を申し込む
face	competition	競争に直面する
foster	competition	競争を促す

▷This is the first time I've **won** a **competition**. 試合に勝ったのはこれが初めてだ

▷You may get the job, but you **face** stiff **competition**. あなたは仕事を得るかもしれないが，厳しい競争に直面することになる

a great	competition	すごい試合
great	competition	激しい競争
fierce	competition	
intense	competition	

▷Everybody enjoyed it. It was a **great competition**. みんな楽しんだ．すごい試合だった

▷It won't be easy. You can expect **great competition**. 楽じゃないよ．激しい競争になるだろう

competition	between A	Aの間の競争
competition	among A	
in competition	with A	Aと競争して

▷There has always been strong **competition between** me and my brother. 私と兄の間は常に熾烈な競争が続いている

▷I hope we're not going to be **in competition with** each other for this job. この仕事ではお互いに競争したくないものだ

concern /kənsə́ːrn/ 名 懸念，心配；関心事

express	concern	懸念を表明する
voice	concern	

▷The Leader of the Opposition **expressed concern** over the rising level of unemployment. 野党党首は失業率の上昇に懸念を表明した

the main	concern	おもな関心事
the primary	concern	
(a) growing	concern	高まる不安

▷His **main concern** was to finish the project on time. 彼の主要関心事はそのプロジェクトの完成を間に合わせることだった

▷There is **growing concern** for the safety of the mountaineers. 登山家の安全への懸念が高まっている

concerned /kənsə́ːrnd/

形 心配そうな；関係のある

particularly	concerned	特に心配な；特に関係する
primarily	concerned	おもに関係する
mainly	concerned	

▷We're **particularly concerned** *about* the increase in traffic accidents near the school. 学校近辺での交通事故の増加が特に心配だ

▷Today's meeting is **primarily concerned** *with* our company's move to Tokyo. 本日の会議はおもに東京への会社移転に関係します

conclusion /kənklúːʒən/ 名 結論；終結

come to	a conclusion	結論に達する
reach	a conclusion	
draw	a conclusion	結論を引き出す
jump to	a conclusion	結論を急ぐ，早合点する
leap to	a conclusion	
come to	conclusion	終結する

▷The police checked the evidence but couldn't **come to** a **conclusion**. 警察は証拠を調べたが結論に達することはできなかった

▷Don't **jump to conclusions**. 結論を急ぐな

condition /kəndíʃən/ 名 状態；状況；条件

lay down	conditions	条件を課す
impose	conditions	
meet	the conditions	条件を満たす
satisfy	the conditions	
create	the conditions	状況をつくり出す
improve	the condition	状況を改善する

▷Did they **impose** any **conditions** on the loan? 融資には何か条件があるのかい

▷It will be difficult to **meet** the **conditions** of the contract. 契約条件を満たすのは難しいだろう

▷We need to **create** the **conditions** for economic growth. 経済成長のための環境づくりが必要だ

good	condition	よい状態
bad	condition	悪い状態
terrible	condition	
a critical	condition	危篤状態

| difficult | conditions | 困難な状況 |

▷The house was old, dirty and in a **terrible condition**. 家は古く、汚くてひどい状態だった
▷He was still in a **critical condition**. 彼はなお危篤状態にあった

confidence /kánfədəns | kɔ́n-/

名 自信；信頼；確信

have	confidence	自信がある
give A	confidence	Aに自信を与える
gain	confidence	自信を得る
lose	confidence	自信をなくす
undermine	confidence	
have	confidence	信頼する
lose	confidence	信頼をなくす
restore	confidence	信頼を回復する
have	confidence in A	Aを確信する

▷Spending a year in the USA **gave** her **confidence** in speaking English. 米国で1年過ごしたことで彼女は英語を話す自信がついた
▷Losing the tennis match 6-0, 6-0 **undermined** his **confidence**. 6-0, 6-0でテニスの試合に負けて彼は自信をなくした

| great | confidence | 大きな自信；大きな信頼 |
| public | confidence | 国民の信頼 |

▷The Prime Minister has lost **public confidence**. 首相は国民の信頼を失った

| in | confidence | ないしょで |

▷What I'm going to say is **in strict confidence**. 私がこれから言うことは極秘です

| a loss of | confidence | 自信喪失 |

confident /kánfədənt | kɔ́n-/

形 自信がある；確信して

| feel | confident | 自信がある |

▷People want to **feel confident** that they are buying the right product at the right price. 適正な製品を適正な価格で買っているという自信を人々はもちたがる

quietly	confident	自信を秘めた
increasingly	confident	ますます自信を深めた
supremely	confident	最高に自信をもった

conflict /kánflikt | kɔ́n-/

名 紛争；対立, 衝突

| come into | conflict | 衝突する |
| resolve | a conflict | 紛争を解決する |

▷I try not to **come into conflict** with my boss but it isn't easy. 上司と衝突しないようにしているけど簡単じゃないよ

| armed | conflict | 武力紛争 |
| ethnic | conflict | 民族紛争 |

▷**Armed conflict** in the Middle East is looking more likely. 中東で武力紛争が起こりそうだ

| conflict | between A | Aの間の対立 |

▷The **conflict between** the Israelis and the Palestinians shows no sign of ending. イスラエル人とパレスチナ人の対立は終わりの兆しが見えない

connection /kənékʃən/

名 関係, 関連；接続；連絡；縁故

have	connections	関係がある；コネがある
establish	a connection	関係を築く
make	a connection	関連づける
find	a connection	関連を見いだす
see	a connection	関連性を見る
maintain	a connection	関係を維持する
miss	one's connection	（交通機関の）接続を逃す

▷I hear you **have connections** with local politicians. あなたは地元の政治家とコネがあるそうですね
▷The police were unable to **establish** a **connection** between the two crimes. 警察は2つの犯罪の関連を明らかにできなかった
▷Do you **see** a **connection** between Lady Gaga and Madonna's music? レディーガガとマドンナの音楽の間に関連が見てとれますか

a close	connection	密接な結びつき
a direct	connection	直接の結びつき
a spiritual	connection	精神的結びつき
political	connections	政治家とのコネ

▷I have a **close connection** with everyone he works with. 彼の仕事仲間全員と親しくしています
▷Is there a **direct connection** between global warming and powerful hurricanes? 地球温暖化と大きなハリケーンとの間に直接的な関係がありますか

| consequence |

▷If you have good **political connections** it will help your business. 政治家とのしっかりしたコネがあれば商売の助けになるだろう

connection	between A	Aの間の関係
connection	to A	Aとの関係
connection	with A	

▷Is there any necessary **connection between** language and culture? 言語と文化の間には必然的な関係がありますか
▷I don't want to have any **connection to** him in any way. 彼とはいっさいかかわりを持ちたくない

in	this connection	これに関連して

▷**In this connection**, I must mention two things. これに関連して2つ言っておかなければなりません

conscious /kάnʃəs | kɔ́n-/

形 意識している；気づいている

acutely	conscious	鋭く意識する
fully	conscious	十分意識がある
increasingly	conscious	意識が高まった
barely	conscious	ほとんど意識しない
politically	conscious	政治意識の高い
socially	conscious	社会意識の高い

▷I'm **acutely conscious** of that responsibility. その責任を痛いほど意識している
▷She was hit by a car, but don't worry, she is **fully conscious**. 彼女は車にはねられたの。でも心配しないで。意識はしっかりしているから
▷I'm **increasingly conscious** that I'm getting older. 年をとったなあと感じることがだんだん増えてきている
▷I gradually became **politically conscious**. 次第に政治意識が高くなった

conscious	of A	Aを意識している

▷She was barely **conscious of** what she was doing. 自分が何をしているのか，彼女はほとんど意識していなかった

conscious	that...	…を意識している

▷He was **conscious that** they were all watching him. みんなに見られていることを彼は意識していた

consciousness /kάnʃəsnis | kɔ́n-/

名 意識；自覚

lose	consciousness	意識を失う
regain	consciousness	意識を回復する
recover	consciousness	
raise	consciousness	意識を高める

▷Sally **lost consciousness** for a while. しばらくの間サリーは意識を失った
▷When I **regained consciousness**, I was in a hospital. 意識を取り戻すと私は病院にいた
▷What can we do to **raise consciousness** about green issues? 環境保護への意識を高めるために私たちは何をすることができるのか

individual	consciousness	個々の意識
human	consciousness	人間の意識
a collective	consciousness	集団的意識
public	consciousness	公共の意識
national	consciousness	国民的意識
political	consciousness	政治的意識
social	consciousness	社会的意識

▷**Human consciousness** is perhaps the greatest mystery of all. 人間の意識というものはおそらく最大の謎であろう
▷More and more countries have joined the EU. Europe is strengthening its **collective consciousness**. どんどん多くの国々がEUに加盟して，欧州は集団的意識を強めつつある

consequence /kάnsəkwèns | kɔ́nsikwəns/

名 結果，影響；重要性

accept	the consequences	結果を受け入れる
face	the consequences	
suffer	the consequences	
fear	the consequences	結果を恐れる
consider	the consequences	結果を考慮する

▷We took the risk and **suffered** the **consequences**. 私たちは危険を冒し，その結果を受け入れた
▷He doesn't seem to **fear** the **consequences** of his actions. 彼は自分の行動の結果を恐れていないようだ
▷There was no time to **consider** the **consequences**. 結果を考えている時間はなかった

important	consequences	重大な結果
disastrous	consequences	悲惨な結果
serious	consequences	深刻な結果
a direct	consequence	直接の結果
economic	consequences	経済的影響
political	consequences	政治的影響
social	consequences	社会的影響

▷A small error can have **disastrous consequences**. 小さなミスが悲惨な結果を生むことがある

| consider |

▷ The recent financial crisis has had serious **social**, **political** and **economic consequences**.　最近の金融危機は深刻な社会的，政治的，経済的影響をもたらした

as	a consequence	結果として
in	consequence	

▷ You have developed diabetes **as a consequence** of overeating.　あなたは食べ過ぎの結果，糖尿病になった

consider /kənsídər/

動 よく考える，検討する，熟考する；考慮に入れる

carefully	consider	注意深く考える
seriously	consider	真剣に考える
be generally	considered	一般に考えられている
be widely	considered	

▷ He **carefully considered** the question.　彼はその問題を入念に考慮した
▷ Are you **seriously considering** giving up your job?　本気で仕事をやめようと考えているのですか
▷ Canada is **generally considered** a bilingual country.　カナダは一般に2言語使用の国と考えられている

consider	doing	…することを検討する

▷ I hope you'll **consider** giving me a second chance.　もう一度私にチャンスをいただけないでしょうか

consider	that...	…だと見なす
consider	wh-	…か考える

★ wh- は whether, what, how, who など

▷ Do you **consider that** she is a competent leader?　彼女は有能な指導者だと思いますか
▷ She seemed to be **considering whether** or not to trust him.　彼を信用してよいかどうか彼女は迷っているようすだった

consider	A (to be) C	AをCとみなす

▷ Matthew **considered** Charles his best friend.　マシューはチャールズをいちばんの親友と思っていた

consist /kənsíst/

動 (consisit of A で) Aから成る

consist	entirely of A	すべてAから成る
consist	only of A	ただAから成る
consist	simply of A	
consist	largely of A	大部分Aから成る

consist	mostly of A	おもにAから成る
consist	mainly of A	

★ largely は動詞の前でも用いる

▷ My diet **consists entirely of** uncooked fruit, vegetables and nuts.　私の食事は生のフルーツ，野菜とナッツがすべてです
▷ The furniture **consisted only of** a bench and a small table.　家具はベンチが1つと小さなテーブル1つだけだった
▷ The curriculum **consisted largely of** writing, reading and giving presentations.　カリキュラムの大部分は作文，読解とプレゼンテーションだった

constant /kάnstənt | kɔ́n-/

形 一定の，不変の；絶えず続く

remain	constant	一定のままである

▷ The temperature of the nuclear fuel rods should **remain constant** at all times.　核燃料棒の温度は常に一定に保たなければならない

fairly	constant	かなり一定の
reasonably	constant	
relatively	constant	比較的一定の
roughly	constant	ほぼ一定の
almost	constant	ほとんど一定の

▷ Temperatures in Hawaii stay **fairly constant** throughout the year.　ハワイの気温は1年を通してほぼ一定だ
▷ The amount of forest in this area has remained **relatively constant** since the 1970s.　この辺りの森林の量は1970年代以降，比較的一定している

construction /kənstrʌ́kʃən/

名 建設；建築物，建造物；構造

under	construction	建設中で
during	(the) construction	建設中に

▷ Our new home is currently **under construction**.　うちの新居がいま建設中です
▷ It was very noisy **during** the **construction** of the school swimming pool.　学校のプール建設中は騒音がひどかった

consult /kənsʌ́lt/ 動 相談する；診察を受ける

properly	consult	きちんと相談する

consult	widely		広く相談する

★ properly は動詞の後でも用いる

▷The council should have **consulted** the community more **widely** before allowing a nuclear power station to be built. 自治体は原発建設を許可する前に地域社会の意見をもっと幅広く聞くべきだった

consult	A about B	A（人）とBについて相談する
consult	with A	A（人）と相談する

▷I'd like to **consult** you **about** next year's timetables. 来年度の時間割についてあなたと相談したいのですが
▷Please let me **consult with** my parents. 両親と相談させてください

without	consulting A	A（人）との相談なしに

▷You can't make decisions like that **without consulting** me first. 私にまず相談することなしにそのような決定をすることはできません

contact /kάntækt | kɔ́n-/ 图 接触, 連絡

have	contact	連絡をとっている
be in	contact	
come into	contact	知り合う
make	contact	連絡をとる
establish	contact	
get in	contact	
keep	contact	連絡を保つ
maintain	contact	
keep in	contact	連絡をとり続ける
stay in	contact	
lose	contact	連絡がなくなる

▷I have **had** no **contact** with my son for the last six months. 息子とこの半年連絡をとっていない（★ much, some, little, no など「連絡」の程度を表す語とともに用いることが多い）
▷I've been in close **contact** with Jessie for a week. 1週間ジェシーと密に連絡をとり合っている
▷When I was abroad, I **came into contact** with many interesting people. 海外滞在中におもしろい人にいっぱい出会った
▷Did you **make contact** with him? 彼と連絡をとりましたか
▷I can't **get in contact** with him. 彼と連絡がとれない
▷Email is used to **maintain contact** with members. メンバー間の連絡にはEメールが使われている
▷It's difficult for me to **keep in contact** with all of them. 彼らみんなと連絡をとり続けるのは私には難しい
▷Why did they **lose contact** with each other? 彼ら

が互いに没交渉になったのはなぜなのか

close	contact	密接な連絡
regular	contact	定期的な連絡
direct	contact	直接の接触
personal	contact	個人的な接触
physical	contact	肉体的接触

▷I'm still in **close contact** with Kevin. いまもケビンと密に連絡をとっている
▷I think it's better if you make **direct contact** with him yourself. 直接彼と連絡をとるほうがいいと思う
▷**Physical contact** with children is very important. 子どもとのスキンシップはとても重要だ

contact	with A	Aとの連絡
contact	between A	Aとの間の接触

▷The first **contact between** Spain and the Philippines occurred in March of 1521. スペインとフィリピンの最初の接触は1521年3月に起こった

content /kάntent | kɔ́n-/

图 中身；内容；含有量

empty	the contents	中身を全部出す

▷Open the can and **empty** the **contents** into a saucepan. 缶を開け, 中身をソースパンに全部開けてください

digital	content	デジタルコンテンツ
high	content	高い含有量
low	content	低い含有量

contest /kάntest | kɔ́n-/

图 コンテスト, コンクール；競争

have	a contest	コンテストがある
hold	a contest	コンテストを開く
enter	a contest	コンテストに出る
win	a contest	コンテストに勝つ
lose	a contest	コンテストに負ける

▷We'll **have** a karaoke **contest** next month. 来月カラオケコンクールがある
▷I can't believe I **won** this **contest**. このコンテストで優勝したのが信じられない

a close	contest	接戦
presidential	contest	大統領選

▷It was a **close contest** between Obama and Clinton. オバマとクリントンの接戦だった

continue /kəntínjuː/

動 続ける, 続く, 継続する

| continue | doing | …し続ける |
| continue | to do | |

▷ Nancy **continued** reading *Harry Potter* through the night. ナンシーはハリーポッターを夜通し読み続けた
▷ He **continued to** send her emails even though he got no reply. 彼は返事をもらえなくても彼女にEメールを送り続けた

| continue | with A | Aを続ける |

▷ Please **continue with** your story. どうぞ話を続けてください

contract /kάntrækt | kɔ́n-/ 名 契約;契約書

have	a contract	契約している
be awarded	a contract	契約をとる
get	a contract	受注する
win	a contract	
negotiate	a contract	契約交渉をする
make	a contract	契約を結ぶ
sign	a contract	契約書に署名する
renew	a contract	契約を更新する
terminate	a contract	契約を解除する
break	a contract	契約を破る
breach	a contract	契約に違反する
exchange	contracts	契約を取り交わす

▷ He succeeded in **making** a **contract** with Ford. 彼はフォードと契約を結ぶことに成功した
▷ Don't rush into **signing** a **contract**. あわてて契約書にサインするな
▷ The school has **renewed** his **contract** as a teacher. その学校は彼と教員契約を更新した
▷ Next day we were due to **exchange contracts**. 翌日に契約を取り交わす予定だった

a long-term	contract	長期契約
a short-term	contract	短期契約
a five-year	contract	5年契約
a temporary	contract	臨時契約
a formal	contract	正式の契約
an employment	contract	雇用契約

▷ Nick has signed a new **long-term contract**. ニックは新しい長期契約書に署名した
▷ Employees with **temporary contracts** were likely to lose their jobs. 臨時契約の従業員は職を失う可能性があった

| contract | with A | Aとの契約 |
| contract | between A | Aの間の契約 |

▷ I think we should cancel our **contract with** the company. その会社との契約を破棄したほうがいいと思う
▷ There was no **contract between** the two companies. 双方の会社間には何の契約もなかった

contrast /kάntræst | kɔ́ntrɑːst/

名 対照, 対比;著しい差異

| provide | a contrast | 対照をなす |
| make | a contrast | |

▷ The two presidential candidates **provide** a clear **contrast** for the electors. その2人の大統領候補は選挙人たちから見て明らかな対照をなしている

marked	contrast	著しい対照, 際立った対照
sharp	contrast	
stark	contrast	
complete	contrast	まったくの対照

▷ There was thunder and lightening yesterday, but today was a **complete contrast** *with* baking hot sun. きのうは雷鳴と稲光だったが,きょうは焼けつくような太陽でまったく対照的だった

by	contrast	対照的に
in	contrast	
in	contrast to A	Aと対象的に
the contrast	between A	Aの間の相違

▷ Her nose was small **in contrast to** her large brown eyes. 彼女の鼻は小さくて,大きな茶色の目と好対照をなしていた
▷ The **contrast between** life in developed and developing counties is often very great. 先進国と発展途上国の生活の違いはしばしばきわめて大きい

contribute /kəntríbjuːt/

動 貢献する, 寄与する;寄付する

contribute	greatly	大いに貢献する
contribute	significantly	著しく貢献する
contribute	substantially	

▷ She **contributed** greatly **to** the development of the company. 彼女は会社の発展に大きな貢献をした
▷ Charlie Chaplin's funny walk **contributed** signif-

icantly *to* his success. チャップリンが成功を収めたのには，そのおかしな歩き方が大きく関係している

| contribute | to A | Aに寄与する；Aに寄付する |

▷He **contributed** nothing **to** the charity organization. 彼は慈善団体に何も寄付しなかった

contribution /kὰntrəbjúːʃən | kɔ̀n-/

名 貢献，寄与；寄付

| make | a contribution | 貢献する；寄付する |
| pay | a contribution | 寄付する |

▷I'm sure you'll **make** a great **contribution** *to* the team. あなたはきっとチームに大きな貢献をすると思う（★ ˣ do a contribution とはいわない）
▷I was asked to **pay a contribution** to school funds. 学校基金への寄付を頼まれた

an important	contribution	重要な貢献
a significant	contribution	
a great	contribution	大きな貢献
a major	contribution	
a positive	contribution	積極的な貢献
a valuable	contribution	貴重な貢献

▷France has made an **important contribution** *to* the peace process. フランスは和平交渉に重要な貢献をした
▷We want to make a **positive contribution** *to* society. 社会に積極的に貢献したい
▷This book is a **valuable contribution** *to* cultural studies. この本は文化研究に貴重な貢献をしている

| contribution | to A | Aへの貢献；寄付 |

▷Thanks for your great **contribution to** the discussion. 議論に大いに加わっていただきありがとうございます

control /kəntróul/

名 支配，支配権；統制，制御；自制，抑制

have	control	支配している
take	control	支配する，掌握する
gain	control	支配権を獲得する
exercise	control	支配権を行使する
lose	control	支配権を失う；制御できなくなる
regain	control	また制御できるようになる
lose	control	自制できなくなる
keep	control	自制する

▷He didn't like anyone **having control** *over* his life. 彼はだれからも自分の人生を統御されたくなかった
▷Why does he always have to **take control** *of* everything? なぜ彼ばかり何でも取り仕切るのか
▷He's trying to **gain control** of the company. 彼は会社の支配権を得ようとしている

complete	control	完全な支配
direct	control	直接的な支配
effective	control	効果的な支配
strict	control	厳しい管理
quality	control	品質管理
inventory	control	在庫管理

▷I'm not drunk. I'm in **complete control**. 酔ってはいません。まったく正気です
▷We have very **strict control** over the data. データを非常に厳しく管理している

in	control	支配して
out of	control	制御できなくて
under	control	制御して
under	A's control	支配下で
beyond	A's control	力の及ばない

▷I want to be **in control** of my own life. 私は自分の生き方は自分で決めたい
▷My emotions were completely **out of control**. 感情がまったく抑えられなかった
▷It's quite all right. I have everything **under control**. 心配はいらないよ。すべてきちんとしてあるから
▷That decision is **beyond** my **control**. その決定は私にはどうすることもできない

control /kəntróul/

動 支配する；制御する；統制する

carefully	control	注意深く制御する
effectively	control	効果的に制御する
strictly	control	厳しく統制する
tightly	control	

▷The diets were **carefully controlled**. 食事は注意深く管理された
▷The Republicans **effectively controlled** the country. 共和党が国を効果的に支配した
▷The demonstration was **strictly controlled** by the police. デモは警察によって厳しく統制された

convention /kənvénʃən/

名 慣習；大会；協定，条約

| follow | a convention | 慣習に従う |

| conversation |

defy	a convention	慣習を無視する
hold	a convention	大会を開く
organize	a convention	大会を組織する
attend	a convention	大会に参加する
ratify	the convention	協定を批准する
sign	a convention	協定に署名する

▷ When you go to Japan you need to **follow** the **conventions** of Japanese society. 日本に行ったら日本社会のしきたりに従う必要がある
▷ Australia **signed** and **ratified** the UN **Convention** on the Rights of the Child. オーストラリアは国連の子どもの権利条約に署名して批准した

social	conventions	社会慣習
an annual	convention	年次大会
an international	convention	国際大会

▷ You need to understand the **social conventions** of the country you're living in. 住んでいる国の社会慣習を理解する必要がある
▷ I attended the 30th **annual convention**. 第30回の年次大会に出席した

conversation /kànvərséiʃən | kɔn-/

名 会話

have	a conversation	会話をする
hold	a conversation	
carry on	a conversation	
make	conversation	世間話をする
get into	(a) conversation	会話を始める
strike up	a conversation	
overhear	a conversation	会話を偶然耳にする

▷ I met this guy on a train and we **had** a really interesting **conversation**. 列車で出会ったこの男ととてもおもしろい会話を交わした
▷ I **overheard** your **conversation** with Daniel. あなたとダニエルとの会話をたまたま耳にした

general	conversation	普通の会話
a normal	conversation	
casual	conversation	打ち解けた会話
a private	conversation	私的な会話
polite	conversation	儀礼的な会話

▷ It is so annoying. It's hard to have a **normal conversation** with her. いらつくなあ。彼女とは普通の会話もできやしない
▷ We started with some **casual conversation**. 手始めに気の置けない会話を交わした
▷ Nobody knew each other at the party so everybody was making **polite conversation**. お互いに知らない者どうしのパーティーだったので、みんな儀礼的な会話を交わしていた

a conversation	about A	Aについての会話
a conversation	between A	Aの間の会話

▷ We had a **conversation about** a variety of things. いろんなことについて話をした
▷ The **conversation between** my dad and Robin was quite amusing. 父とロビンとの会話はとてもおもしろかった

a topic of	conversation	会話の話題
snatches of	conversation	会話の断片

▷ As usual, the main **topic of conversation** was music. いつものようにおもな話題は音楽だった

convey /kənvéi/

動 伝える,伝達する;運搬する

clearly	convey	明確に伝える
vividly	convey	生き生きと伝える

▷ Her tone of voice **clearly conveyed** that she was angry. 声の調子で彼女が怒っているとはっきり伝わった

try to	convey	伝えようとする
manage to	convey	何とか伝える

▷ I **tried to convey** all my feelings to him. 思いのたけを彼に伝えようとした

convinced /kənvínst/

形 確信した,納得した

fully	convinced	すっかり納得した
totally	convinced	
entirely	convinced	

▷ I'm not **entirely convinced** you're right. あなたが正しいと完全に納得したわけではない

convinced	(that)...	…と確信した

▷ They were **convinced that** I was ill. 彼らは私が病気だと確信していた

convinced	of A	Aを確信した

▷ He was **convinced of** the plan's success. 彼はその計画の成功を確信していた

cook /kúk/ 動 加熱調理する, 料理する

cook	enough	十分に火を通す
cook	gently	弱火で加熱調理する
cook	quickly	手早く加熱調理する

▷This fish is only half-done, it hasn't been **cooked enough**. この魚は半なまで, 十分火が通っていない
▷Put the turkey in the oven and **cook gently** for one and a half hours. 七面鳥をオーブンに入れ弱火で1時間半加熱してください

cook	in A	A(材料・温度)で料理する
cook	for A	A(時間)のあいだ料理する
cook	until...	…になるまで料理する

▷**Cook in** olive oil until soft. 柔らかくなるまでオリーブオイルで料理します
▷The British **cook** vegetables **for** too long, so they lose their taste. イギリス人は野菜の調理時間が長すぎて, 野菜の味が消えてしまう
▷Stir in the lemon juice and **cook until** almost dry. レモン汁を入れてかき混ぜ水分がなくなるまで料理します

cook	A for B	AをB(人)のために料理
cook	B A	する

▷She **cooked** dinner **for** us. 彼女は私たちにディナーを料理してくれた

cooking /kúkiŋ/ 名 料理, 料理法

do	the cooking	料理をする

▷I **do** all the **cooking** and the housework. 料理をつくり家事をするのはすべて私です

home	cooking	家庭料理
Chinese	cooking	中国料理
French	cooking	フランス料理
Italian	cooking	イタリア料理

▷I love **Chinese cooking**. 中国料理が大好きです

cool /kú:l/ 形 涼しい; 冷静な; かっこいい

wonderfully	cool	とても涼しい
slightly	cool	やや涼しい
relatively	cool	比較的涼しい
rather	cool	かなり涼しい
pretty	cool	とても冷静な; とてもかっこいい
extremely	cool	とてもかっこいい
really	cool	

▷It was **wonderfully cool** by the mountain stream even in the middle of summer. 真夏でも渓流沿いはとても涼しかった
▷It's **rather cool** outside. 外はかなり涼しい
▷The air is **relatively cool** tonight. 今夜は空気が比較的ひんやりしています

cool /kú:l/

動 冷やす, 冷ます, 冷える; 冷静にする

cool	completely	すっかり冷ます
cool	rapidly	急に冷ます
cool	slightly	少し冷ます

▷Take the cake out of the oven and let it **cool completely**. ケーキをオーブンから取り出して完全に冷ましてください

allow to	cool	冷ます

▷Remove from the heat and **allow to cool** for ten minutes. 火からおろして10分間冷ましてください
PHRASES
Cool it! ☺ 頭を冷やせ, 落ち着け

cooperate /kouápərèit | -ɔ́p-/ 動 協力する

cooperate	fully	全面的に協力する
cooperate	closely	緊密に協力する

▷We're **cooperating fully** with the police on this matter. この件で警察に全面的に協力している
▷Japan will **cooperate closely** with ASEAN countries on this project. 日本はこの計画でアセアン諸国と緊密に協力するだろう

agree to	cooperate	協力に同意する
be prepared to	cooperate	協力する準備が
be willing to	cooperate	ある
refuse to	cooperate	協力を断る

▷OK. **I agree to cooperate**. What do I have to do? よし, 協力してもいいよ. 何をすればいいかな
▷I'm **willing to cooperate** with your plan. きみの計画に協力しても構わないよ
▷He's still **refusing to cooperate**. 彼はまだ協力を拒んでいる

cooperate	with A	Aに協力する

▷Tommy didn't want to **cooperate with** anyone.

| cooperation |

トミーはだれにも協力したくなかった

cooperation /kouàpəréiʃən | -ɔ́p-/

名 協力

encourage	cooperation	協力を推し進める
promote	cooperation	

▷ The European Union was formed in order to **encourage cooperation** between member states. 欧州連合は加盟国間の協力を推し進めるために設立された

close	cooperation	緊密な協力
full	cooperation	全面的協力
active	cooperation	積極的協力
international	cooperation	国際協力
mutual	cooperation	相互協力
economic	cooperation	経済協力

▷ I still need your **full cooperation**. あなたの全面協力がなお必要です
▷ He required the **active cooperation** of his colleagues. 彼は同僚の積極的な協力を必要とした
▷ **Mutual cooperation** between Japan, China and the US is very important. 日中米間の相互協力がきわめて重要だ

cooperation	between A	Aの間の協力
cooperation	with A	Aとの協力

▷ There should be close **cooperation between** nurses and doctors. 看護師たちと医師たちの間に緊密な協力関係が必要だ

PHRASES
Thank you (very much) for your cooperation. / I'd like to thank you for your cooperation. ☺ ご協力感謝申し上げます

copy /kápi | kɔ́pi/ 名 コピー, 写し; 冊, 部

make	a copy	コピーをとる
send	a copy	コピーを送る
get	a copy	コピーをもらう
receive	a copy	
keep	a copy	コピーを保存する
sell	one million copies	ミリオンセラーになる

▷ **Make** a **copy** and send it to me. コピーをとって私に送ってください
▷ I **received** a **copy** of the report this morning. けさ報告書のコピーを受け取った
▷ I suggest you **keep** a **copy** of this letter. この手紙の控えをとっておいたほうがいいと思うよ

▷ The album **sold** 12 **million copies** worldwide. そのアルバムは世界中で1,200万枚売れた

copy /kápi | kɔ́pi/ 動 コピーをとる；書き写す

copy	down	写しとる
copy	illegally	違法にコピーする

▷ I **copied** the map **down** onto a piece of paper. 地図を紙に写しとった

copy	A from B	AをBからコピーする

▷ She **copied** the answers **from** her friend. 彼女は友人の答案を写した

corner /kɔ́:rnər/ 名 隅, 角；曲がり角

turn	the corner	角を曲がる
round	the corner	

▷ He **turned** the **corner** and saw the Empire State Building in front of him. 角を曲がると彼の前にエンパイアステートビルが見えた

right-hand	corner	右隅
left-hand	corner	左隅
a street	corner	街角
a tight	corner	急な曲がり角；窮地

▷ See the top **left-hand corner**. 左上の隅を見ること
▷ I'm in a bit of a **tight corner**. いまちょっと大変な状況だ

around	the coner	角を曲がって；すぐそばに
round	the corner	

▷ I went **around** the **corner** to the bus stop. 角を曲がってバス停の方へ行った
▷ Fred lived just **round** the **corner**. フレッドはすぐ近くに住んでいた

in	the corner (of A)	(Aの)隅に
on	the corner (of A)	(Aの)角に
at	the corner (of A)	

▷ Simon was sitting **in** the **corner** of the bar. サイモンはバーの隅に座っていた(★部屋などの「隅」には in を用いる)
▷ There's a telephone box **on** the **corner**. 角に電話ボックスがあります(★街の「曲がり角」には on または at を用いる)

correct /kərékt/ 形 正しい, 正確な

absolutely	correct	まったく正しい
perfectly	correct	
entirely	correct	
broadly	correct	大筋で正しい
grammatically	correct	文法的に正しい

▷"The first time we met was in 2003, wasn't it?" "You're **absolutely correct**." 「私たちが出会ったのは2003年でしたね」「そのとおりです」
▷His explanation is **broadly correct**. 彼の説明は大筋で正しい
▷This expression is **grammatically correct**. この表現は文法的に正しい

correspond /kɔ̀:rəspánd | kɔ̀rəspɔ́nd/
動 一致する, 符合する

correspond	closely	ぴったり一致する
correspond	exactly	完全に一致する
correspond	precisely	正確に一致する
correspond	roughly	だいたい一致する

★これらの副詞は動詞の前でも用いる

▷These two diagrams **correspond exactly** *with* one another. これら2つの図表は互いに完全に一致している

| correspond | with A | Aに一致する, 符合する |
| correspond | to A | |

▷What you say now doesn't **correspond with** what you said before. あなたがいま言っていることは前に言ったことと一致していない

cost /kɔ́:st | kɔ́st/ 名 費用, 原価, コスト; 犠牲

cover	the cost	費用をまかなう
meet	the cost	
pay	the cost(s)	費用を支払う
cut	costs	コストダウンする
cut	the cost	
reduce	costs	
increase	costs	コストアップする

▷I don't have enough money to **cover** the **cost** *of* the trip. 旅行費用をまかなうだけの金がない
▷He was ordered to **pay** the **costs** of the trial. 彼は裁判費用を支払うよう命じられた
▷We **cut** the **cost** *of* the advertising in half. 広告費を半分にコストダウンした
▷New technology often **reduces costs**. 新しい科学技術はしばしばコストダウンにつながる

a high	cost	高コスト
a low	cost	低コスト
a total	cost	総額
extra	cost	追加費用
additional	cost	
an average	cost	平均的な費用
an estimated	cost	見積もり
a unit	cost	単位原価
labor	costs	人件費
maintenance	costs	維持費
running	costs	ランニングコスト
fixed	costs	固定費
the social	costs	社会的費用

▷The **total cost** of the project was $5 million. そのプロジェクトの総額は5百万ドルだった
▷We will announce plans to double broadband speed at no **extra cost**. 当社の今度のプランではブロードバンドの速度を追加費用なしで2倍に上げられます
▷The **estimated cost** of repair work is $30 million. 修理の見積もりは3千万ドルだ
▷The **social costs** of alcohol are enormous. アルコールの社会的費用は計り知れない

at	a cost of A	Aの費用で
at	the cost of A	Aを犠牲にして
at	all costs	どんな犠牲を払っても
at	any cost	

▷I bought the car **at** a **cost of** $5,000. 5千ドルでその車を買った
▷He saved her life **at** the **cost of** his own. 彼は自らの命を犠牲にして彼女の命を救った
▷Violence should be avoided **at all costs**. 何としても暴力は避けなくてはいけない

country /kʌ́ntri/ 名 国, 国家; 国民

govern	the country	国を治める
run	the country	
flee	the country	亡命する
leave	the country	出国する
enter	the country	入国する
visit	the country	国を訪れる

▷We need a strong government to **run** the **country**. 国家を治めるために強い政府が必要だ
▷Many people have **fled countries** with a history of war and poverty. 多くの人々が戦争と貧困の歴史にまみれた国を逃げ出した

| couple |

▷She **left** her home **country** at the age of 20 and moved to New York. 彼女は20歳で故国を離れニューヨークに移った

a foreign	country	外国
Western	countries	西洋諸国
European	countries	ヨーロッパ諸国
a developed	country	先進国
a developing	country	発展途上国
the host	country	主催国

▷The **developed countries** in Europe and Asia are closely tied economically with the United States. ヨーロッパとアジアの先進諸国は経済的にアメリカと緊密に結びついている

| across | the country | 国中に，全国に |
| all over | the country | |

▷Police **across** the **country** are looking for the escaped murderer. 全国の警察は逃走中の殺人犯を捜索している

couple /kʌ́pl/ 名 カップル，夫婦；一対，2つ

a happy	couple	幸せなカップル
a young	couple	若いカップル
an elderly	couple	年配のカップル
a married	couple	夫婦
an unmarried	couple	未婚のカップル

▷They seem to be a very **happy couple**. 彼らはとても幸せなカップルに見える
▷You two look like a **married couple**. あなた方お二人はまるで夫婦みたいに見えます

courage /kə́:ridʒ | kʌ́r-/ 名 勇気

have	the courage	勇気がある
take	courage	勇気がいる
lack	the courage	勇気に欠ける
show	courage	勇気を見せる
pluck up	(the) courage	勇気を奮い起こす
summon up	(the) courage	

▷I didn't **have** the **courage** to ask my question aloud. 声を出して質問してみる勇気はなかった
▷It **took** a lot of **courage** to do that. それをするにはとても勇気がいった
▷I **lacked** the **courage** to do what I really wanted to do. 自分が本当にしたいことをする勇気に欠けていた
▷It took me three years to **pluck up** the **courage** to ask her to be my girlfriend. 彼女にガールフレンドになってくれと頼む勇気を奮い起こすのに3年かかった

| great | courage | 大変な勇気 |

▷She fought her illness with **great courage**. 彼女は大変な勇気をもって病気と闘った

course /kɔ́:rs/

名 授業科目，教育課程，コース；進路，経過

attend	a course	授業をとる
take	a course	
do	a course	
offer	a course	授業を設ける
run	a course	
complete	a course	課程を修了する
alter	the course	流れを変える
follow	a course	流れをたどる

▷He's **attending** a **course** on counseling at the institute. 彼は研究所でカウンセリングの授業に出ている
▷They **run** a music **course** so that students can get a job with a record company. 学生にレコード会社での働き口が見つかるよう音楽コースを設けている
▷I believe simple things can **alter** the **course** of your life. ちょっとしたことで人生の流れが変わると思う

an English	course	英語コース
a short	course	短期コース
an advanced	course	上級コース
a training	course	訓練コース
a vocational	course	職業コース
normal	course	自然な成り行き

▷My teacher suggested that I take the **advanced course** offered next semester. 先生は次の学期にある上級コースをとるよう助言してくれた
▷I want to do a **vocational course** and become a computer expert. 職業コースをとってコンピュータの専門家になりたい
▷In the **normal course** of events it should take about 3 weeks to process your visa. 通常ならビザの手続きに3週間ほどかかります

| in | the course of A | Aの間に |
| during | the course of A | |

▷People will change careers three or more times **in** the **course of** their working lives. 人は職業人生の中で3回以上は転職するものだ

court /kɔ́:rt/ 名 裁判所，法廷

go to	court	裁判に訴える
take A to	court	Aを裁判に訴える
bring A to	court	Aを法廷に持ち込む
appear in	court	出廷する
attend	court	
tell	the court	法廷で証言する

▷You need to **go to court** to resolve these problems. これらの問題を解決するには裁判に訴える必要がある
▷She **took** him **to court** for domestic violence. 彼女は彼を家庭内暴力で訴えた
▷Jones **appeared in court** as a witness. ジョーンズは証人として裁判所に出廷した
▷Mr. Jennings didn't **tell** the **court** the truth. ジェニングス氏は法廷で真実を話さなかった

the court	hears	法廷が聴聞する

▷The **court heard** evidence from Mr. Edwards. 裁判所はエドワーズ氏の証言を聴聞した

in	court	法廷で, 裁判で
out of	court	示談で

▷Paul Walker gave evidence **in court**. ポール・ウォーカーは法廷で証言した
▷The matter was settled **out of court**. その件は示談での解決となった

cover /kʌ́vər/

名 保護；(保険による)保障；表紙；カバー, ふた

take	cover	隠れる, 避難する
run for	cover	
give	cover	援護する
provide	cover	保険で保障する

▷The girl **took cover** from the barking dog behind her father. 少女はほえる犬から逃げて父親の後ろに隠れた
▷His insurance company refused to **provide cover**. 彼の保険会社は保障の適用を拒んだ

the front	cover	表紙
the back	cover	裏表紙

▷The picture on the **front cover** is very beautiful. 表紙の絵はとてもきれいだ

under	cover (of A)	(Aに)隠れて
from	cover to cover	初めから終わりまで

▷The attack took place **under cover of** darkness. 攻撃は夜陰に乗じて起こった
▷I read this book **from cover to cover** in one day. この本を1日で読み終えた

cover /kʌ́vər/ 動 おおう；扱う；範囲に含む

adequately	cover	十分カバーする
completely	cover	完全におおう
cover	up	すっかりおおう；隠す

▷The risks are **adequately covered** by insurance. 危険は保険で十分カバーされている
▷The sky was **completely covered** by thick clouds. 空は厚い雲に完全におおわれた
▷Ryan tried to **cover up** his mistake. ライアンは自分の過ちを隠そうとした

cover	A with B	AをBでおおう

▷I **covered** my face **with** my hands. 両手で顔をおおった

crack /krǽk/ 名 割れ目, ひび, 亀裂；鋭い音

have	a crack	ひびが入っている
fill	the crack	亀裂を埋める

▷He **had a crack** in the right wrist. 彼は右の手首にひびが入った
▷The street crew came along and **filled** the **cracks** in the pavement. 道路工事の人たちがやってきて歩道の亀裂を埋めた

a crack	appears	亀裂が現れる

▷A small **crack appeared** in the walls. 小さな割れ目が壁に現れた

fine	cracks	細かなひび
hairline	cracks	

▷It's a really old painting so you can see **fine cracks** in it. とても古い絵画なので細かなひびが見える

crash /krǽʃ/

名 衝突；墜落；暴落；すさまじい音

survive	a crash	衝突事故で生き残る

▷I **survived** the car **crash** with only a little cut. 車の衝突事故にあったが, ほんのかすり傷で助かった

the crash	happens	衝突が起きる
the crash	occurs	

| credit |

▷ The helicopter **crash happened** about 9:30 in the morning.　ヘリコプターの墜落事故が起きたのは朝の9時30分ごろだった

a fatal	crash	死亡事故
a head-on	crash	正面衝突
a car	crash	車の衝突事故
a train	crash	列車事故
an air	crash	飛行機墜落事故
a road	crash	交通事故
a financial	crash	金融恐慌
the stock market	crash	株式市場の暴落
a great	crash	すさまじい音
a loud	crash	

▷ The car was involved in a **fatal crash**.　その車は衝突事故を起こして死者が出た
▷ Three people were injured in the **head-on crash**.　3人が正面衝突で負傷した
▷ **Financial crashes** are often unexpected.　金融恐慌はしばしば予測不可能だ
▷ I heard a **loud crash** of thunder.　大きくとどろく雷鳴を聞いた

in	a crash	衝突事故で

▷ He was seriously injured **in a car crash**.　彼は車の衝突事故で重傷を負った

credit /krédit/ 名 信用；名声, 功績；(大学の)単位；信用供与, クレジット

give A	credit	A(人)の功績を認める
do A	credit	A(人)の名誉となる
get	credit	功績を認められる
take	credit	
deserve	credit	信用に値する
earn	credit	信用を得る
get	a credit	単位をとる
earn	a credit	
obtain	credit	融資を受ける
give	credit	信用貸しにする
extend	credit	信用を供与する

▷ He didn't succeed, but you have to **give** him **credit** for trying.　彼は成功しなかったが, 試みたことだけでもほめてあげないといけない
▷ Your hard work **does** you **credit**.　きみのがんばりは人の認めるところだ
▷ Did Obama **get credit** for improving the economy?　オバマは景気改善の功績を認められたか
▷ I think he **deserves credit**.　彼は信用に値すると思う
▷ You've worked hard! You've **earned** a lot of **credit** with your boss.　がんばって働いたね. これで上司からの覚えがよくなったよ
▷ I've already **earned** enough **credits** to graduate from university.　大学を卒業するのに十分な単位をすでにとった

on	credit	クレジット払いで
in	credit	(口座に)預金残高があって

▷ Nowadays I don't buy anything **on credit**.　最近はクレジットで買い物しないことにしている
▷ I was £600 **in credit** on my account last month.　先月口座に600ポンドの預金があった

credit card /krédit kὰːrd/

名 クレジットカード

pay by	credit card	クレジットカードで払う
use	a credit card	
accept	credit cards	カードでの支払いに応じる
take	credit cards	

▷ Can I **pay by credit card**?　クレジットカードで支払えますか

crime /kráim/ 名 罪, 犯罪

commit	a crime	罪を犯す
carry out	a crime	
investigate	(a) crime	犯罪を捜査する
solve	a crime	犯罪を解決する
fight	(a) crime	犯罪と闘う
combat	(a) crime	
prevent	(a) crime	犯罪を防止する
turn to	crime	犯罪に手を染める

▷ Why are you looking at me like I **committed** some **crime**?　なぜ私が犯罪でもしでかしたみたいに見ているの
▷ The police are **investigating** the **crime** as a robbery.　警察はその犯罪を強盗事件として捜査中だ
▷ We have to **prevent crime** before it happens.　犯罪は起きる前に防がなければならない
▷ He **turned to crime** to pay off his debts.　彼は借金を返済するために犯罪に手を染めた

(a) serious	crime	重大な犯罪
(a) violent	crime	暴力犯罪
organized	crime	組織犯罪
juvenile	crime	青少年犯罪
sex	crime	性犯罪
war	crimes	戦争犯罪
the perfect	crime	完全犯罪

▷If you commit a **serious crime**, you should be punished. 重大な犯罪をしでかせば当然ながら罰せられる
▷**Juvenile crime** in Los Angeles has dropped 25% since 1998. ロサンゼルスの青少年犯罪は1998年以来25％減少した

| a crime | against A | Aへの犯罪 |

▷The slave trade was a **crime against** humanity. 奴隷貿易は非人道的犯罪だった

| the scene of | the crime | 犯行現場 |

▷His fingerprints were found at the **scene of** the **crime**. 彼の指紋が犯行現場で見つかった

criminal /krímənl/ 名 犯罪者

a habitual	criminal	常習犯
a convicted	criminal	有罪判決を受けた者
a notorious	criminal	悪名高い犯罪者

▷In some states in the USA a **convicted criminal** loses the right to vote. アメリカのいくつかの州では有罪判決を受けた者は投票権を失う

crisis /kráisis/ 名 危機, 重大局面

face	a crisis	危機に瀕する
have	a crisis	危機に出会う
suffer	a crisis	危機に見舞われる
cause	a crisis	危機を招く
deal with	a crisis	危機に対処する
resolve	a crisis	危機を乗り切る
solve	a crisis	危機を乗り切る
defuse	a crisis	危機を収拾する

▷Japan **faced** economic **crises** in the 1920s and 1990s. 日本は1920年代と1990年代に経済危機に直面した
▷A successful man of 40 can still **suffer** a midlife **crisis**. 成功した40歳の男性でも中年の危機に見舞われる
▷What **caused** the **crisis**? 危機を招いた原因は何か
▷Do men and women **deal with crises** differently? 危機への対処法は男性と女性で異なりますか
▷Both sides wanted to **resolve** the **crisis** peacefully. 双方とも危機を平和的に乗り切ることを望んだ

a major	crisis	大きな危機
a serious	crisis	深刻な危機
the present	crisis	現在の危機
an economic	crisis	経済危機
a financial	crisis	金融危機
a political	crisis	政治的危機
a currency	crisis	通貨危機
an energy	crisis	エネルギー危機
an oil	crisis	石油危機
a food	crisis	食糧危機
an identity	crisis	自己認識の危機
a midlife	crisis	中年の危機

▷We haven't had a **major crisis** so far. 私たちは今のところ大きな危機には見舞われていない
▷High oil prices have caused a world **economic crisis**. 石油価格の高騰が世界の経済危機を招いた
▷**Financial crisis** can easily spread through the international stock markets. 金融危機は国際株式市場に簡単に拡大する可能性がある
▷Who is responsible for the **present crisis**? 現在の危機はだれの責任なのか

| in | crisis | 危機状態に |

▷Our pension system is **in crisis**. 私たちの年金制度は危機的状況にある

critical /krítikəl/ 形 批判的な；重大な

extremely	critical	非常に批判的な
highly	critical	
strongly	critical	
increasingly	critical	ますます批判的な；ますます重要な
absolutely	critical	きわめて重要な

▷He was **highly critical** of the committee's report. 彼は委員会の報告書に非常に批判的だった
▷The Liberal Democratic Party was **increasingly critical** of the Prime Minister's leadership style. 自民党は首相の主導権の取り方に対する批判をますます強めた

| critical | of A | Aに批判的な |
| critical | to A | Aにとって重大な |

▷I don't mean to be **critical of** you. あなたを批判するつもりはない
▷Protein is **critical to** a healthy diet. たんぱく質は健康な食生活に重要だ

criticism /krítəsizm/ 名 批判；批評

| attract | criticism | 批判を招く |
| come in for | criticism | 批判を浴びる |

| criticize |

come under	criticism	批判を受ける
draw	criticism	
accept	criticism	批判を受け入れる
take	criticism	批判を受け止める
reject	criticism	批判をはねつける

▷The plan will **attract criticism** from environmental groups. その計画は環境団体からの批判を招くだろう
▷Young people sometimes **come in for criticism** about their attitudes. 若者はその態度を批判されることがよくある
▷His remarks have **come under** severe criticism *from* religious groups. 彼の見解は宗教団体から厳しい批判を受けた
▷The manifesto has **drawn criticism** *from* opposition parties. そのマニフェストは野党から批判を受けた

fierce	criticism	痛烈な批判
severe	criticism	厳しい批判
strong	criticism	強い批判
valid	criticism	正当な批判
fair	criticism	
constructive	criticism	建設的批判
considerable	criticism	かなりの批判
increasing	criticism	高まる批判
public	criticism	国民の批判
literary	criticism	文芸批評
social	criticism	社会批評

▷The proposal met with **fierce criticism**. その提案は痛烈な批判にあった
▷I hope you'll accept this as **constructive criticism**. これを建設的な批判として受け入れてほしいと思います
▷Politicians have to fear and respect **public criticism**. 政治家は国民の批判を恐れ、尊重すべきだ
▷He is known for his influential **literary** and **social criticism**. 彼の書く文芸・社会批評は影響力があることで知られる

despite	the criticism	批判にもかかわらず

▷**Despite** the **criticism**, we believe that the conclusions of our study are valid. 批判はあるものの、われわれの研究から導かれた結論は有効だと考えます

criticize /krítəsàiz/

動 批判する，非難する(★《英》つづりは criticise)

heavily	criticize	激しく批判する
severely	criticize	
strongly	criticize	強く批判する

openly	criticize	公然と批判する
be widely	criticized	あちこちで批判される

▷McCain **severely criticized** the media. マケインはメディアを厳しく批判した
▷The newspaper **strongly criticized** the company's financial problems. 新聞はその会社の財政問題を強く批判した
▷His performance in last week's debate was **widely criticized**. 先週の討論会での彼の話しぶりは多くの人から批判された

criticize	A **for** (do**ing**) B	BしたことでA(人)を非難する

▷Don't **criticize** me **for** doing my job. 私の仕事にけちをつけるな

crowd /kráud/ **名** 群衆，観客；大衆

attract	a crowd	観客を集める
draw	a crowd	
disperse	a crowd	群衆を追い払う
address	a crowd	群衆に呼びかける
entertain	the crowd	観客を楽しませる

▷The police **dispersed** the **crowd** with smoke bombs. 警察は発煙筒で群衆を追い払った
▷She **addressed** the **crowd** in a loud voice. 彼女は大声で群衆に呼びかけた

a crowd	gathers	群衆が集まる

▷A crowd **gathered** around him. 群衆が彼を取り囲んだ

a big	crowd	大群衆
a huge	crowd	
a large	crowd	
a good	crowd	
a small	crowd	小規模の群衆
a milling	crowd	ひしめく群衆

▷A **big crowd** gathered at the square in front of the building. 大群衆が建物の前の広場に集まった
▷This bar is very cool; great music and a **good crowd**. このバーはとても雰囲気がよく，音楽もいいし，客も多い
▷He disappeared into the **milling crowd**. 彼はひしめく群衆の中に消えた

in	the crowd	人込みの中で
through	the crowd	人込みをかき分けて

▷Tom tried to follow her but quickly lost her **in** the

crowd. トムは彼女についていこうとしたが，すぐに人込みの中で見失ってしまった

crucial /krúːʃəl/ 形 決定的な，きわめて重要な

| crucial | to (doing) A | A(するの)にきわめて |
| crucial | in (doing) A | 重要な |

▷Your cooperation is **crucial to** the success of this project. この計画の成功にはあなたの協力が欠かせない
▷A proper diet is **crucial in** maintaining your good health. きちっとした食事は健康を維持するのに不可欠だ

| it is | crucial that... | …がきわめて重要だ |

▷**It is crucial that** you reply quickly. すぐ返事するのが大事だ

cry /krái/ 名 叫び声；鳴き声；泣き声

give	a cry	叫び声を上げる
utter	a cry	
hear	a cry	叫び声が聞こえる
have	a cry	泣く

▷Diana **gave** a **cry** of surprise and horror. ダイアナは驚きと恐怖の叫び声をあげた
▷Everybody was panicking. She could **hear** the **cries** of people behind her. みんなパニックに陥っていた．彼女の後ろの方で人々の叫び声が聞こえた
▷Go on. **Have** a good **cry**. It'll do you good. さあ存分に泣けよ．楽になるよ

cry /krái/ 動 泣く；叫ぶ

cry	loudly	声を上げて泣く
cry	silently	静かに泣く
cry	aloud	叫ぶ
cry	out	
nearly	cried	ほとんど泣きそうだった

▷I **cried out** in pain. 痛みで大声を上げた
▷I **nearly cried** with joy. うれし泣きしそうだった

begin to	cry	泣き出す；叫び出す
start to	cry	
make A	cry	A(人)を泣かせる

▷She **began to cry** aloud. 彼女は大声で泣き出した
▷I'm sorry I **made** you **cry**. あなたを泣かせてしまってごめんね

| cry | for A | Aを思って泣く；Aを求めて叫ぶ |
| cry | over A | Aを嘆き悲しむ |

▷When I die there will be no one to **cry for** me. 私が死んでもだれも泣いてくれないだろう ▷**I cried for** help but no one could hear me. 助けを求めて叫んだが，だれにも聞こえなかった
▷There's no need to **cry over** such a trivial matter. そんな些細なことを嘆く必要はない

culture /kʌ́ltʃər/ 名 文化；教養；栽培

dominant	culture	支配的文化
human	culture	人間の文化
Western	culture	西洋文化
youth	culture	若者文化
political	culture	政治文化
corporate	culture	企業風土，社風
popular	culture	大衆文化
mass	culture	

▷Civilization is a form of **human culture** in which many people live in urban centers. 文明とは多くの人々が都市中心に住む人間の文化の一形態である
▷Pop music has been widely accepted as part of **popular culture**. ポップスは大衆文化の一部として幅広く受け入れられてきた

| history and culture | 歴史と文化 |
| language and culture | 言語と文化 |

▷St. Louis is a city rich in **history and culture**. セントルイスは歴史と文化が豊かな街だ

cup /kʌ́p/ 名 カップ；カップ一杯；優勝杯

make	a cup of A	A(茶など)を入れる
pour	a cup of A	A(茶など)を注ぐ
have	a cup of A	A(茶など)を飲む
drink	a cup of A	
win	the cup	優勝する

▷I'll go **make a cup of** coffee for you. コーヒーをお入れしましょう
▷He pulled a coffee mug from the drawer and **poured a cup of** coffee. 彼は引き出しからコーヒーのマグカップを取り出してコーヒーを注いだ
▷Would you like to **drink a cup of** coffee? コーヒーを一杯いかがですか
▷Paul has a good chance of **winning** the **cup**. ポールには優勝するチャンスが十分ある

| cupboard |

the World	Cup	ワールドカップ

▷ Germany will win the **World Cup** final. ドイツがワールドカップ決勝戦で勝つだろう

a cup and saucer		受け皿つきのカップ

▷ She placed her **cup and saucer** on her lap. 彼女は受け皿つきのカップをひざに置いた

cupboard /kʌ́bərd/ 名 食器棚

a built-in	cupboard	つくりつけの食器棚
a locked	cupboard	鍵つきの食器棚

▷ This room has a **built-in cupboard**. この部屋にはつくりつけの食器棚があります
▷ Store medicines safely in a **locked cupboard**. 薬は鍵つきの食器棚にきちんとしまうこと

in	the cupboard	食器棚に

▷ He put the dishes away **in** the **cupboard**. 彼は皿を食器棚に片づけた

cure /kjúər/ 名 治療(薬);回復

look for	a cure	治療法を探す
find	a cure	治療法を見つける

▷ Do you think one day they will **find a cure** for cancer? いつかがんの治療法が見つかると思いますか

an effective	cure	効果的な治療
a miracle	cure	特効薬
a complete	cure	全快

▷ There's no **effective cure** for his illness. 彼の病気には効果的な治療法がない
▷ A **complete cure** may be possible through surgery. 手術すれば完治が可能かもしれない

cure	for A	Aの治療(法)

▷ What is the best **cure for** a hangover? 二日酔いにいちばん効くのは何ですか

curious /kjúəriəs/

形 好奇心の強い;奇妙な

curious	about A	Aを知りたがる

▷ I'm **curious about** what he was saying. 彼が話していたことを知りたい

curious	to do	…したがる

★ do は hear, learn, know, find out など

▷ We're all **curious to** know what is inside. 中に何が入っているのかみんな知りたがっている

it is curious	that...	…は奇妙だ

▷ **It's curious that** I feel no pain. 痛みを感じないのは奇妙だ

currency /kə́:rənsi | kʌ́r-/

名 通貨;流通, 普及

devalue	the currency	通貨を切り下げる
revalue	the currency	通貨を切り上げる
gain	currency	普及する

▷ Brazil **devalued** its **currency** in 1999. ブラジルは1999年に通貨を切り下げた

domestic	currency	国内通貨
foreign	currency	外貨
local	currency	現地通貨
a single	currency	単一通貨
a strong	currency	強い通貨
a weak	currency	弱い通貨

▷ **Foreign currency** is available at the airport. 外貨は空港で入手できる
▷ Britain refused to join the European Euro **single currency** system. イギリスはヨーロッパのユーロの単一通貨制度に加わることを拒んだ
▷ At the moment the dollar is not a **strong currency**. 現在ドルは強い通貨ではない

current /kə́:rənt | kʌ́r-/ 名 流れ;電流

strong	currents	強い流れ
cold	currents	寒流
warm	currents	暖流
tidal	currents	潮流
an electric	current	電流

▷ The **tidal currents** are now quite strong. 潮の流れは今かなり強い
▷ A low-voltage **electric current** runs through the electric fence. 低電圧の電流が電気柵を流れている

curtain /kə́ːrtn/ 名 カーテン

close	the curtains	カーテンを閉める
open	the curtains	カーテンを開ける
draw	the curtains	カーテンを引く、カーテンを閉める
pull	the curtains	
hang	the curtains	カーテンを吊るす

▷ Do you want me to **close** the **curtains** for you? カーテンを閉めてあげましょうか
▷ Andrew shut the windows and **drew** the **curtains**. アンドルーは窓を閉め、カーテンを引いた

custom /kʌ́stəm/ 名 慣習, 習慣

an ancient	custom	古い慣習
an old	custom	
a local	custom	地元の慣習
a social	custom	社会的慣習

▷ It's important to respect **local customs**. 地元の慣習を敬うことが大切だ

it is A's custom	to do	…するのがAの習慣である

▷ **It's** his **custom to** get up at 6 a.m. and run 3 miles before breakfast. 朝6時に起きて朝食前に3マイル走るのが彼の習慣だ

customer /kʌ́stəmər/ 名 客, 顧客

serve	a customer	客に対応する
attract	customers	客を引きつける
get	customers	客を獲得する
win	customers	
lose	cutomers	客を失う
satisfy	a customer	客を満足させる

▷ Anna's busy **serving customers** at the moment. アンナはいま客の対応に追われている
▷ Let's have a sale to **attract** more **customers**. 客をもっと呼ぶためにセールをしよう

a regular	customer	常連客
a repeat	customer	固定客
a new	customer	新規の客
potential	customers	潜在的顧客
prospective	customers	見込み客
a corporate	customer	法人顧客

▷ She's a **regular customer** at that store. 彼女はその店の常連客だ
▷ The first thing you must do is to analyze your **potential customers**. 最初にすべきことは潜在的顧客の分析だ

cut /kʌ́t/ 名 切ること；切り傷；削減, 削除

have	a cut	切り傷がある
make	a cut	切る；削減する
take	a cut	削減を受け入れる

▷ Daniel **has** a **cut** on his face. ダニエルは顔に切り傷がある
▷ The company is not doing well and I've been asked to **take** a **cut** in salary. 会社の業績が悪いので給与カットを求められた

cut /kʌ́t/ 動 切る, 切り分ける

cut	neatly	きれいに切る
cut	away	切り取る
cut	back	刈り込む
cut	down	切り倒す

▷ We need to **cut back** that hedge. あの生垣を刈り込まないと
▷ The trees were all **cut down** and burnt. 木はすべて切り倒されて燃やされた

cut	A in two	Aを半分に切る
cut	A in half	
cut	A into pieces	Aを細かく切る

▷ She **cut** the birthday cake **into** six **pieces**. 彼女はバースデーケーキを6つに切り分けた

cut	out A	Aを切り取る
cut	into A	Aにナイフを入れる

▷ She picked up her knife and fork and **cut into** her pancakes. 彼女はナイフとフォークを取り上げてパンケーキを切った

PHRASES
Cut it out! ☺ いいかげんにしてくれ, やめろよ, 黙れ

damage /dǽmidʒ/

名 損害, 損傷, 被害；(damages で)損害賠償金

cause	damage	損害を与える
do	damage	
suffer	damage	損害を受ける
repair	(the) damage	損害を修復する
claim	damages	損害賠償を請求する
award	damages	損害賠償を認める

★「損害を与える」は ×give damage とはいわない

▷Did the floods **cause** any **damage**? 洪水で被害は出たのですか
▷In the car accident her friend **suffered damage** to her ankle. 自動車事故で彼女の友人は足首に損傷を受けた
▷It'll cost a lot to **repair** the **damage** to the car. 車の破損修理にかなり金がかかるだろう
▷He **claimed damages** of $170,000. 彼は17万ドルの損害賠償を請求した

considerable	damage	かなりの損害
serious	damage	深刻な損害
severe	damage	
extensive	damage	広範な損害
irreparable	damage	回復不能な損害
permanent	damage	恒久的損害
criminal	damage	器物損壊罪
environmental	damage	環境被害
brain	damage	脳損傷
punitive	damages	懲罰的損害賠償

▷A typhoon struck yesterday, but there was no **serious damage**. きのう台風が来たが深刻な被害はなかった
▷There was no **extensive damage** to the house. 家には大きな被害はなかった
▷He was charged with **criminal damage**. 彼は器物損壊罪で起訴された
▷The tsunami caused catastrophic **environmental damage**. 津波は壊滅的な環境被害を与えた

damage /dǽmidʒ/

動 損害を与える, 被害を与える

seriously	damage	深刻な損害を与える
severely	damage	
irreparably	damage	取り返しのつかない
permanently	damage	損害を与える

▷The quarrel **seriously damaged** their relationship. その口論で彼らの関係はひどく傷ついた

dance /dǽns | dάːns/

名 ダンス, 踊り；ダンスパーティー

do	a dance	ダンスをする, 踊る
perform	a dance	
go to	a dance	ダンスパーティーに行く
hold	a dance	ダンスパーティーを催す

▷Look Mommy! I'm going to **do** a little **dance**! ママ見て. ちょっと踊ってみせるから
▷Billy began to **perform** a traditional **dance**. ビリーは伝統的なダンスを踊り始めた
▷Would you like to **go to a dance** with me? いっしょにダンスパーティーに行きませんか

danger /déindʒər/ **名** 危険

face	danger	危険に直面する
pose	a danger	危険をもたらす
recognize	the danger	危険を認識する
realize	the danger	
reduce	the danger	危険を減らす
increase	the danger	危険を増大させる
avoid	(a) danger	危険を避ける

▷The cracks in the building do not **pose** any immediate **danger**. 建物のひび割れはいますぐ危険ということはない
▷We **recognize** the **danger** *of* dumping chemicals. 化学薬品投棄の危険性を認識している

(a) grave	danger	重大な危険
(a) great	danger	大きな危険
(a) real	danger	現実の危険
(a) serious	danger	深刻な危険性
immediate	danger	差し迫った危険
(a) potential	danger	潜在的な危険

▷We're all in **grave danger** now. Please send us some help. 全員きわめて危険な状況だ. 救援を頼む
▷There was no **immediate danger**. 差し迫った危険はなかった
▷With radiation there's always the **potential danger** of cancer. 放射線を浴びるとがんになる潜在的な危険は常にある

in	danger	危険に瀕して
in	danger of A	Aの危険があって
out of	danger	危険を脱して
a danger	that...	…という危険

▷We're **in danger of** losing public support. われわれは公的支援を失う危険がある
▷She's **out of danger** for the moment. 彼女はさしあたり危険を脱している
▷There's always a great **danger that** the exchange rate will change frequently. 為替レートは頻繁に変動する危険性が常に高い

dangerous /déindʒərəs/ 形 危険な

extremely	dangerous	きわめて危険な
highly	dangerous	
particularly	dangerous	特に危険な
potentially	dangerous	潜在的に危険な

▷These kinds of foods are **particularly dangerous** for diabetics. これらの食べ物は糖尿病患者には特に危険だ
▷It was a difficult and **potentially dangerous** situation. 困難で危険をはらむ状況だった

it is dangerous	(for A) to do	(A(人)が)…するのは危険だ

▷**It is dangerous to** walk around this area. この地域を歩き回るのは危険だ

dark /dá:rk/ 形 暗い

get	dark	日が暮れる
grow	dark	
go	dark	急に暗くなる

▷It's **getting dark**. 日が暮れてきた

completely	dark	真っ暗な
really	dark	とても暗い
almost	dark	ほとんど真っ暗な
nearly	dark	

▷The room was **completely dark**. 部屋は真っ暗だった
▷It was **almost dark** outside. 外はほとんど真っ暗だった

dark /dá:rk/ 名 暗がり；日暮れ

after	dark	暗くなってから
before	dark	暗くなる前に
in the	dark	暗闇で

▷I arrived in San Diego **after dark**. 暗くなってからサンディエゴに着いた
▷I'll be back **before dark**. 暗くなる前に戻ります
▷Why are you sitting here **in the dark**? どうしてこんな暗い所に座っているの

data /déitə/ 名 データ, 資料

collect	data	データを収集する
gather	data	
obtain	data	データを入手する
store	data	データを蓄積する
access	data	データにアクセスする
retrieve	data	データを検索する
analyze	data	データを分析する
share	data	データを共有する
provide	data	データを提供する

▷The scientists **collected data** on the lunar environment. 科学者たちは月の環境に関するデータを集めた
▷Can you **store data** on this CD? このCDにデータを保存できますか
▷Computers allow us to **access data** more easily than ever. コンピュータのおかげでいままでより簡単にデータにアクセスできる
▷Johnson **analyzed data** on 300 patients with heart disease. ジョンソンは心臓病をもった300人の患者のデータを分析した

raw	data	生データ
available	data	入手可能なデータ
unpublished	data	非公開データ
personal	data	個人データ
experimental	data	実験データ
basic	data	基礎データ
relevant	data	関連データ
scientific	data	科学的データ
statistical	data	統計データ

▷We've got the **raw data**. Now we need to analyze it on a computer. 生のデータを手に入れた. これからコンピュータで分析する必要がある
▷The **available data** are [is] inadequate for the evaluation. 手に入る限りのデータでは評価を下すには不十分だ(★data は改まった文体では複数扱いで用いることが多い)
▷According to **statistical data**, women live longer than men. 統計データによれば女性は男性より長生きだ

data	from A	Aからのデータ
data	on A	Aに関するデータ

▷Both graphs use **data from** the same experiment. 双方のグラフは同じ実験で得られたデータを使っている
▷We obtained **data on** average July temperatures. 7月の平均気温のデータを入手した

| date |

date /déit/ 名 日付；デート，人と会う約束

fix	a date	日取りを決める
set	a date	
have	a date	デートする
make	a date	人と会う約束をする

▷Have you two **set a date** for the wedding? きみたち2人は結婚式の日取りを決めたのかい
▷I **had a date** with my boyfriend on Sunday. ボーイフレンドと日曜日にデートした

a fixed	date	決まった日
the exact	date	正確な日付
a precise	date	
an earlier	date	もっと早い日
a later	date	もっと後の日
a future	date	
delivery	date	配達日
completion	date	完成日，完了日
arrival	date	到着日
departure	date	出発日

▷There's no **fixed date** for the investigation to finish at the moment. 現在のところ調査の終了日は決まっていない
▷I can't give you a **precise date** yet. まだ正確な日付は言えない
▷We'll confirm the contract *at* a **later date**. 後日，契約を確認します

on	a date	デートに

▷Did you hear? Jake and Julie went **on a date**. 聞いたかい．ジェイクとジュリーはデートしたよ

date	for A	Aの日付

▷The last **date for** applying is April 1. 申し込みの最終日は4月1日です

PHRASES
What's the date today? / **What's today's date?** きょうは何日ですか

daughter /dɔ́ːtər/ 名 娘

have	a daughter	娘がいる

▷She **has a daughter** named Carolyn. 彼女にはキャロリンという娘がいる

a baby	daughter	女の赤ん坊
the only	daughter	一人娘
the eldest	daughter	長女
the youngest	daughter	末娘

▷Sally is Philip's **only daughter**. サリーはフィリップの一人娘だ
▷Deborah and her **eldest daughter** look very much alike. デボラといちばん上の娘は見た目がそっくりだ

day /déi/ 名 日，一日；昼間

the following	day	次の日
the previous	day	前の日
the other	day	先日
one	day	ある日；いつか
some	day	
the very	day	まさにその日
another	day	別の日
a beautiful	day	すばらしい日
a nice	day	すてきな日
a sunny	day	よく晴れた日
a rainy	day	雨の日
a good	day	よい日
a bad	day	ひどい日
a busy	day	忙しい日
a long	day	長い一日
the whole	day	一日中
all	day (long)	
(the) present	day	現代，今日

▷Come and visit **some day**, will you? いつか遊びに来ませんか
▷There was a strike at the airport on the **very day** that we left to go on holiday. 休暇に出かけたまさにその日に空港でストがあった
▷I'm afraid I'm busy tomorrow. How about **another day**? あすは忙しいので別の日はどうですか
▷It's a **beautiful day**! いい天気ですね
▷It's boring to be inside on a **rainy day**. 雨の日に屋内に閉じこもるのは退屈だ
▷I've had a **good day**. 楽しい一日でした
▷Where have you been the **whole day**? 一日中どこへ行っていたの
▷Peter stayed home alone **all day long**. ピーターは一日中一人で家にいた
▷She's studying American history from 1945 to the **present day**. 彼女は1945年から現在までのアメリカ史を勉強している

by	day	日中は，昼間は
during	the day	

▷Jake is a student **by day**, bartender by night. ジェイクは昼間は学生で，夜はバーテンダーをしている
▷Ralph was rarely home **during** the **day**. ラルフは昼間はめったに家にいなかった

the day	before yesterday	おととい
the day	after tomorrow	あさって

▷I arrived in Auckland the **day before yesterday**. 一昨日オークランドに着いた

▷I'm leaving the **day after tomorrow**. あさって立つ予定です

every	day	毎日
every other	day	一日おきに

▷I promise I'll call you **every other day**. 約束する．一日おきにちゃんと電話するよ

day	after day	来る日も来る日も
day	by day	日ごとに

▷She spent **day after day** in the library, researching American history. 彼女は来る日も来る日も図書館でアメリカ史を研究した

▷We're getting older **day by day**. 一日一日と年をとっていく

these	days	近ごろ，最近
in this	day and age	いまどき
in those	days	その当時は

▷What are you doing **these days**? 最近はどうしていますか

▷Lack of sleep is the main problem in teenagers **in this day and age**. 睡眠不足はいまどきの十代の若者の抱える大きな問題だ

▷People had a hard life in the 19th century. **In those days** there was no electricity. 19世紀の人々の生活は大変だった．当時は電気がなかった

PHRASES
Those were the days. ☺ あのころはよかったなあ
What day is it today? きょうは何曜日ですか ▷"What day is it today?" "(It's) Tuesday." 「きょうは何曜日ですか」「火曜日です」

deal

dead /déd/ 形 死んだ

drop	dead	急死する
pronounce A	dead	Aの死亡を宣告する

▷How can a perfectly healthy 28-year-old guy **drop dead**? まったく健康な28歳の男が急死するなんてことがあるだろうか

▷Mr. Smith was **pronounced dead** at the scene at 2:30 a.m. by a doctor. スミス氏は午前2時半に医師によってその場で死亡を宣告された

almost	dead	死んだも同然の
nearly	dead	
already	dead	すでに死んだ
long	dead	ずっと以前に死んだ

▷He looked tired and **almost dead**. 彼は疲れ果ててまるで死人のようだった

▷She stood over the grave of her **long dead** husband. 彼女は遠い昔に亡くなった夫の墓前に立った

dead	or alive	生きているか死んでいるか
dead	and buried	葬り去られて

★ dead or alive は alive or dead も用いる

▷I haven't seen him for twenty years. I don't know if he's **alive or dead**. 彼とはもう20年も会っていない．生死も定かではない

▷All her hopes were **dead and buried** now. 彼女の望みはすべてついえた

deadline /dédlàin/ 名 締め切り，期限

extend	the deadline	締め切りを延ばす
meet	the deadline	締め切りに間に合う
miss	the deadline	締め切りに間に合わない

▷It's impossible to **extend** the **deadline**. 締め切りを延ばすことはできない

▷We'll be in trouble if we **miss** the **deadline**. 締め切りに遅れると困ったことになる

the deadline	passes	締め切りが過ぎる

▷The **deadline** for submission **passed** yesterday. 提出期限はきのうで過ぎた

the deadline	for A	Aの締め切り

▷The **deadline for** application is Aug. 31. 申し込み締め切りは8月31日です

deal /díːl/ 名 取引；扱い，待遇

do	a deal	取引する
make	a deal	
conclude	a deal	取引を成立させる
sign	a deal	取引契約に署名する
strike	a deal	取引をまとめる
have	a deal	取引がある

▷He **signed a deal** with Sony and immediately began recording an album. 彼はソニーとの契約に署名し，直ちにアルバムのレコーディングを始めた

▷The company **had a deal** with General Motors. その会社はゼネラルモーターズと取引があった

the deal	goes through	取引がうまくいく
the deal	falls through	取引がうまくいかない

▷I hope the **deal goes through**. 取引がうまくいくといいけど

a fair	deal	公正な扱い
a raw	deal	不当な扱い
a rough	deal	
a big	deal	《話》大したこと

▷They should have paid you much more money than that. I think you got a **raw deal**. もっと多く支払ってもらうべきだったのに，あなたは不当な扱いを受けたと思いますよ

▷Don't worry about it. It's no **big deal**. 心配しないで．大したことではありませんから

PHRASES

It's a deal. ☺ それで決まりだ ▷"How about you do overtime this weekend and I'll do it next weekend?" "Fine, it's a deal." 「今週末はきみが残業して，来週末はぼくというのでどうだい」「わかった，そうしよう」

death /déθ/ 名 死，死亡；終わり，破滅

cause	death	死を招く
mean	death	死を意味する
face	death	死に直面する
meet	(one's) death	死を迎える
fear	death	死を恐れる
escape	death	死を免れる

▷Does the influenza virus **cause death**? インフルエンザウイルスによって死に至ることがありますか

▷In this country if you're convicted of murder it **means death**. この国では殺人罪で有罪になったら死を意味する

▷During the war he **faced death** many times. 戦争中に彼は何度も死に直面した

▷He **met** his **death** fighting in Iraq. 彼はイラクで戦って死んだ

bleed to	death	出血多量で死ぬ
freeze to	death	凍死する
starve to	death	餓死する
put A to	death	A(人)を処刑する
stab A to	death	A(人)を刺殺する

▷He was stabbed with a knife and **bled to death**. 彼はナイフで刺され，出血多量で死んだ

▷I nearly **froze to death** once on a mountain. 山で凍死しそうになったことがある

▷Some place in the world, a child **starves to death** every two minutes. 世界のどこかで2分ごとに子どもが餓死している

▷Henry VI was **put to death** in the Tower of London. ヘンリー6世はロンドン塔で処刑された

▷Brian was **stabbed to death** last night. ブライアンは昨夜刺殺された

early	death	早すぎる死
(a) premature	death	
sudden	death	突然の死
tragic	death	悲劇的な死
accidental	death	不慮の死，事故死

▷His **early death** was deeply regretted. 彼の早すぎる死は心から惜しまれた

▷Falls are the leading cause of **accidental death** among people aged 75 or older. 転倒が75歳以上の人々の事故死の主要原因だ

death	from A	Aによる死

▷He was ill for a decade before his **death from** cancer. 彼は10年間の闘病生活のあと，がんで亡くなった

debate /dibéit/ 名 議論，討論

have	a debate	議論する
open	a debate	議論を始める
provoke	a debate	議論を巻き起こす
take part in	a debate	討論に参加する

▷Let's **have** a **debate** on economic policy. 経済政策について議論しよう

▷Twenty five students from 15 countries **took part in** the **debate**. 15か国から25名の学生がディベートに参加した

(a) debate	rages	議論が沸騰する
(a) debate	continues	議論が続く

▷The **debate** about global warming has **continued** for many years. 地球温暖化についての論争が何年も続いている

(a) heated	debate	白熱した議論
(a) intense	debate	
(a) fierce	debate	激しい議論
(a) lively	debate	活発な議論
(a) serious	debate	深刻な議論
(a) public	debate	公開討論

▷Having nuclear weapons has sparked **heated debates** since the 1950s. 核兵器の所有を巡って1950年代以来，白熱した議論がなされてきた

▷It is time to have a **serious debate** on tax. 税金に

ついて真剣に論じるべき時だ

debate	about A	Aについての討論
debate	on A	
debate	over A	
debate	surrounding A	Aを巡る討論

▷Bob and I had a big **debate about** capital punishment. ボブと私は死刑について大論争をした
▷There has been considerable **debate surrounding** the government's plans for economic growth. 経済成長に対する政府の計画を巡ってかなりの議論がある

debate /dibéit/ 動 討論する；熟考する

be fully	debated	十分に論議された
be thoroughly	debated	
be hotly	debated	激しく論議された
be fiercely	debated	
be widely	debated	幅広く論議された

▷The question is still **hotly debated**. その問題はいまも激しく論議されている
▷The pension plan has been **widely debated**. 年金制度は幅広い議論の対象となってきた

| debate | wh- (to do) | …(する)か討論する；…(する)か熟慮する |

★wh- は whether, what, how など

▷I **debated whether to** tell him about Gordon. ゴードンのことを彼に話すべきかどうかよく考えた

debt /dét/ 名 債務, 負債, 借金；債券；債権

have	a debt	債務がある
owe	a debt	債務がある
run up	a debt	債務がたまる
repay	a debt	債務を返済する
pay (off)	a debt	
clear	a debt	債務を決済する
settle	a debt	
reduce	a debt	債務を減らす
service	a debt	債務の元利を支払う
write off	a debt	貸し金を償却する
go into	debt	借金をする
get into	debt	

▷She **has debts** of $17,000. 彼女には1万7千ドルの借金がある
▷I **owe** a big **debt** *to* the bank. 銀行からたくさん金を借りている
▷**Repay debts** as quickly as possible. 借金をできるだけ早く返済しなさい
▷He was given 30 days to **settle** his **debts**. 彼は負債を決済するのに30日の猶予が与えられた
▷In America many students **go into debt** when they enter university. アメリカでは大学に入るのに借金をする学生が多い

a large	debt	巨額の債務
an outstanding	debt	未払い債務
a bad	debt	不良債権
total	debt	全債務
a foreign	debt	対外債務
a national	debt	国債

▷The IMF had issued a warning about the government's **outstanding debts**. 国際通貨基金は政府の未払い債務に警告を発した
▷Her **total debt** has now reached £50,000. 彼女の借金はいまや総額5万ポンドに達した

| in | debt | 借金をして |
| in | A's debt | A(人)に恩義があって |

▷I'm deeply **in debt**. ひどい借金苦なんです
▷I don't want to be **in** your **debt**. きみに借りをつくりたくないんだ

decide /disáid/ 動 決める, 決心する

finally	decide	ついに決心する
eventually	decide	
suddenly	decide	突然決心する
obviously	decide	はっきり決心する

▷I **finally decided** that it was time to leave. 出発の時だとようやく決断した
▷Nick has **obviously decided** to follow Mum's advice after all. ニックは結局は母親の忠告に従うことにはっきり決めた

| decide | to do | …する決心をする |

▷I **decided to** go for a walk downtown for an hour or so. 1時間ほど街へ散歩に出かけることにした

| decide | (that)... | …を決心する |
| decide | wh- | …か決める |

★wh- は what, whether, how, when など

▷She **decided that** she would go home early today. 彼女はきょうは早く家に帰ろうと決めた

| decide | against A | Aへの反対を決める |

| decision |

decide	in favor of A	Aへの賛成を決める
decide	on A	Aを決める

▷He considered complaining but **decided against** it. 彼は苦情を言おうかと思ったが, やめることにした
▷Have you **decided on** your major at university? 大学での専攻を決めたかい

decision /disíʒən/ 名 決定, 決心, 結論

make	a decision	決定する
take	a decision	
come to	a decision	決定に至る
reach	a decision	
reverse	a decision	決定をくつがえす

▷You have thirty seconds left. **Make a decision** now! 30秒しか残っていないよ. さっさと決めて
▷Have you **reached a decision**? もう結論に達しましたか
▷You can't **reverse a decision** once it has been signed by the president. いちど社長が署名した決定をくつがえすことはできない

a big	decision	大きな決定
a difficult	decision	困難な決定
a tough	decision	
the right	decision	正しい決定
the wrong	decision	誤った決定
a final	decision	最終決定

▷Was it the **right decision**? それは正しい決断だったのか
▷We definitely made the **wrong decision**. 明らかに決断を誤った

a decision	to do	…する決定

▷I've made a **decision to** stay at the Ritz Hotel for a few more nights. リッツホテルにもう数日滞在することに決めた

a decision	about A	Aについての決定
a decision	on A	

▷Have you made a **decision about** where to go? どこへ行くか決めましたか

declaration /dèkləréiʃən/ 名 宣言; 申告

issue	a declaration	宣言を発する
make	a declaration	宣言する
sign	a declaration	宣言に署名する

▷The United Nations **issued** a **declaration** of human rights in 1948. 国連は1948年に人権宣言を出した

a formal	declaration	公式の宣言
a joint	declaration	共同宣言

▷A **formal declaration** is not required in this case. この件で公式な発表をする必要はない
▷We got agreement on the **joint declaration**. 共同宣言に関して合意を得た

declare /diklέər/ 動 宣言する; 申告する

formally	declare	公式に宣言する
officially	declare	
openly	declare	公然と宣言する
publicly	declare	公の場で宣言する

▷The mayor will cut the ribbon to **officially declare** the new store open. 市長がテープカットして, 新規店の開店を公式に宣言する
▷I **openly declared** my opinion. 率直に自分の意見を発表した
▷He **publicly declared** his innocence. 彼は公式な場で自分が潔白であると述べた

declare	A (to be) C	AがCであると宣言する

▷I **declare** Henry **to be** the winner of this race! このレースの勝者はヘンリーであるとここに宣言します

declare	that...	…と宣言する

▷The doctor officially **declared that** she was brain dead. 彼女は脳死状態にあると医師は正式に断言した

decline /diklái n/ 名 減少, 下落; 衰退, 衰え

fall into	(a) decline	減少する; 衰退する
go into	(a) decline	
suffer	a decline	
reverse	a decline	減少を反転させる
see	a decline	減少を見る
show	a decline	減少を示す

▷As the UK film industry **went into decline**, television expanded. イギリスの映画産業が衰退するにつれてテレビが発展した
▷American music sales **suffered** an almost 10% **decline** in 2005. アメリカの音楽業界は2005年に売上がほぼ1割減った
▷The company succeeded in **reversing** its market-share **decline**. その会社は下がり続けていた市場占有率

を回復させるのに成功した
▷We **saw** a **decline** in world trade for two reasons. 世界貿易は2つの理由で減少した
▷Figure 2 **shows** the steady **decline** in profits. 図2を見ると利益が着実に減ってきていることがわかる

(a) dramatic	decline	劇的な減少
(a) marked	decline	著しい減少
(a) significant	decline	
(a) sharp	decline	急激な減少
(a) steep	decline	
(a) rapid	decline	急速な減少
(a) gradual	decline	緩やかな減少
(a) steady	decline	着実な減少
economic	decline	景気の悪化

▷There's a **marked decline** in the use of public transport. 公共交通の利用が著しく減少している
▷There's been a **steep decline** in the number of jobs available. 求人件数が急激に下がってきている
▷Rail passenger traffic went into **rapid decline**. 鉄道旅客輸送は急速に減少した
▷The lung cancer mortality rate has seen a **gradual decline** since 1980. 肺がん死亡率は1980年から徐々に減少を見せている

in	decline	衰退して
on	the decline	衰えて, 下り坂で

▷Jazz was **on** the **decline**, and pop music was on the rise. ジャズは落ち目でポップスが上り坂だった

a decline	in A	Aの減少

▷A **decline in** imports is improving the trade deficit. 輸入が減ったことで貿易赤字の改善が見られる

decline /dikláin/ 動 減少する；(丁寧に)断る

decline	sharply	急激に減少する
decline	dramatically	劇的に減少する
decline	slightly	わずかに減少する
decline	rapidly	急速に減少する
decline	steadily	着実に減少する
gradually	decline	徐々に減少する

★上の副詞はいずれも動詞の前でも用いる

▷Steel prices have **declined sharply** in most parts of the world. 鉄鋼の価格は世界のほとんどの地域で急激に下がっている
▷Canadian exports to Thailand **declined slightly** in 2007. カナダからタイへの輸出は2007年にやや減少した
▷Smoking rates have **declined rapidly**. 喫煙率は急速に減少してきている

▷The city's population has been **steadily declining** over the past ten years. その都市の人口は過去10年間に確実に減り続けている

decline	by A	A(数量)だけ減少する

▷Domestic beer consumption **declined by** 5% last year. 国内のビール消費量は昨年5％減少した

decline	to do	…するのを断る

▷She smiled and **declined to** comment. 彼女はほほえんで論評するのを断った

decrease /dikríːs/ 動 減少する, 減る

significantly	decrease	著しく減る
markedly	decrease	
slightly	decrease	わずかに減る
rapidly	decrease	急速に減る
steadily	decrease	着実に減る
gradually	decrease	徐々に減る

★上の副詞は動詞の後でも用いる

▷Within 30 minutes the patient's pain **significantly decreased**. 30分もしないうちに患者の痛みは著しく減った
▷The temperature has been **rapidly decreasing** outside. 外は急激に気温が下がってきている
▷The plane **gradually decreased** altitude. 飛行機は徐々に高度を下げた

decrease	by A	A(数値)だけ減る
decrease	in A	A(数など)が減る
decrease	with A	Aとともに減る

★ decrease in A の A は number, size など

▷Taxes **decreased by** 10%. 税金は1割下がった
▷Some animals have been **decreasing in** number due to excessive hunting. 過剰な狩猟によって数が減りつつある動物がいる

defeat /difíːt/ 動 負かす, 破る

easily	defeat	簡単に破る
narrowly	defeat	僅差で破る
finally	defeat	ついに破る
be heavily	defeated	惨敗する

★ defeat はしばしば受け身で用いる

▷I will not be so **easily defeated**! そう簡単には負けないぞ

| defend |

▷ Great Britain **finally defeated** Napoleon in 1815.
英国は1815年ついにナポレオンを破った
▷ In the election last month Wilson was **heavily defeated**. 先月の選挙でウィルソンは惨敗した

| be defeated | by A to B | A対Bで敗れる |

★得点・投票数に用いる

▷ He was narrowly **defeated by** (a vote of) 216 **to** 208. 彼は216対208(票)の僅差で敗れた

defend /difénd/ 動 守る,防御する;擁護する

successfully	defend	うまく守る;防衛に成功する
vigorously	defend	強く擁護する
fiercely	defend	

▷ Labour **successfully defended** 18 out of 20 seats.
労働党は20議席のうち18議席を守った
▷ He **fiercely defended** the government decision.
彼は政府の決定を猛烈に擁護した

| defend | A against B | AをBから守る |

▷ Birds vigorously **defend** their nests **against** foxes.
鳥は巣をキツネから必死で守る

defense /difénts/ 名 防御,守り;弁護, (the defenseで)被告;守備(★《英》つづりはdefence)

come to	A's defense	守りに駆けつける;
rush to	A's defense	弁護する
strengthen	A's defense	防御を強める
make	a defense	弁護する
provide	a defense	弁護の論陣を張る

▷ We have to **strengthen** our homeland **defenses**.
自国の防衛を強化しなければならない
▷ His lawyer was unable to **provide** a good **defense**.
彼の弁護士は弁護の論陣をうまく張ることができなかった

a natural	defense	自然の防御
a strong	defense	強力な防御
national	defense	国防
civil	defense	民間防衛
coastal	defenses	沿岸防衛

▷ The human body has a **natural defense** against germs. 人体には細菌に対する自然防衛機能がある

| defense and security | | 防衛と安全保障 |

▷ He has a job connected with the **defense and security** of the nation. 彼は国の防衛と安全保障に関係した仕事に就いている

| defense | against A | Aに対する防衛 |
| in defense | of A | Aを守るために |

▷ Amanda acted **in defense of** her freedom. アマンダは自らの自由を守るために行動した

deficit /défəsit/ 名 不足(額),赤字

produce	a deficit	赤字を出す
reduce	the deficit	赤字を減らす
cut	the deficit	
show	a deficit	赤字を示す

▷ Finally the Government has managed to **reduce** the **deficit** between imports and exports. 政府はようやく輸入額と輸出額の差を減らすことができた
▷ This year's profits **show a deficit** of 50% compared with last year's. 今年の利益は昨年比で5割減っている

a huge	deficit	巨額の赤字
a fiscal	deficit	財政赤字
a budget	deficit	
a trade	deficit	貿易赤字

▷ The Government's economic policy has produced a **huge** budget **deficit**. 政府の経済政策は巨額の財政赤字を生み出した

define /difáin/ 動 定義する,規定する

accurately	define	正確に定義する
carefully	define	注意深く定義する
precisely	define	正確に定義する
clearly	define	明確に定義する
broadly	define	広く定義する
vaguely	define	大ざっぱに定義する
closely	define	厳密に定義する
strictly	define	

▷ We must **accurately define** our terms. 用語を正確に定義しなければならない
▷ Security is **broadly defined** as a nation's effort to protect its interests from attack. 安全保障を広く定義すると,攻撃から自国の利益を守る努力のことである
▷ Every concept needs to be **strictly defined**. あらゆる概念は厳密に定義される必要がある

| defined | in terms of A | Aの点から定義された |

▷Happiness is **defined in terms of** the satisfaction of desires. 幸福は願望の充足という観点から定義される

define	A as C	AをCと定義する

▷Health is **defined as** a state of complete physical, social and mental well-being. 健康とは肉体的, 社会的, 精神的に完全に快適な状態と定義される

◆**as defined above** 上で定義したように（★論文などで用いる） ▷The term "communication" is used as defined above. 「コミュニケーション」という用語は上で定義したように用いる

definition /dèfəníʃən/ 名 定義

give	a definition	定義を与える
fall within	the definition	定義の範疇に入る
come within	the definition	

▷It's difficult to **give** a precise **definition** of the word "beauty." beauty という語を正確に定義するのは難しい

▷Whales **fall within** the **definition** of mammals. クジラは哺乳類の定義の範疇に入る

a clear	definition	明確な定義
a precise	definition	正確な定義
a broad	definition	広い定義
a wide	definition	
a dictionary	definition	辞書の定義
a legal	definition	法律上の定義

▷There is no **precise definition** of obesity. 肥満の厳密な定義はない
▷Can you give a **broad definition** of feminism? フェミニズムを広く定義してくれるかい
▷What's the **dictionary definition** of "collocation"? コロケーションを辞書はどのように定義していますか
▷What is the **legal definition** of brain death? 脳死を法律的に定義するとどうなりますか

by	definition	定義上；その名が示すとおり

▷Communication is, **by definition**, the transfer of ideas. コミュニケーションとは字義どおり, 考えを伝えることである

degree /digríː/ 名 学位；度；程度

have	a degree	学位をもっている
hold	a degree	
take	a degree	学位をとる
do	a degree	
get	a degree	学位を受ける
obtain	a degree	

▷Bill **has a degree** in history. ビルは歴史の学位をもっている
▷She **took** an MA **degree** in English. 彼女は英語の修士号をとった

a university	degree	大学の学位
a considerable	degree	かなりの程度
a high	degree	高い程度
a greater	degree	より高い程度
a lesser	degree	より低い程度
a certain	degree	ある程度
varying	degrees	さまざまな程度

▷There was a **considerable degree** *of* opposition to the new divorce law. 新しい離婚法に対してかなりの反対があった
▷The factory has achieved a **high degree** *of* production due to automation. その工場は自動化によって高い生産性を達成した
▷Young people find they need a **greater degree** *of* freedom. 若い人々は自分たちにはもっと自由が必要だと考える

to some	degree	ある程度は
to a certain	degree	

▷**To a certain degree**, I understand that. ある程度は理解できます

ten	degrees Celsius	セ氏10度
ten	degrees centigrade	

▷The temperature is about 25 **degrees Celsius** at this time of the year. 1年のこの時期の気温はセ氏25度ぐらいだ

delay /diléi/ 名 遅れ, 遅延

face	(a) delay	遅れが出る
cause	(a) delay	遅れを生む
avoid	(a) delay	遅れを避ける
reduce	(the) delay	遅れを減らす

▷Drivers are **facing** long **delays** because of bad weather. 悪天候のため車の運転に大幅な遅れが出ている
▷Fog **caused** long **delays** at Heathrow Airport. 霧のためヒースロー空港で大幅な遅れが出た

a considerable	delay	かなりの遅れ
a long	delay	大幅な遅れ
a slight	delay	わずかな遅れ
(a) further	delay	さらなる遅れ

| delay |

▷There's a **slight delay** between pressing the button and the photo being taken. ボタンを押して写真が撮れるまでやや時間がずれる

without	delay	直ちに，即刻

▷I must hurry back to the hotel **without delay**. 至急ホテルに戻らなくてはならない

delay /diléi/ 動 延期する，遅らせる

seriously	delayed	ひどく遅れた
further	delay	さらに遅らせる
deliberately	delay	故意に遅らせる

▷If we don't start now, the project will be **seriously delayed**. すぐ始めないとその計画はひどく遅れるだろう

delay	A until B	AをBまで遅らせる

▷The sales figures will be **delayed until** the end of the month. 売り上げ数字が出るのは月末まで遅れるだろう

delicious /dilíʃəs/ 形 とてもおいしい

taste	delicious	おいしい

▷This curry **tastes delicious**! このカレーはおいしい

absolutely	delicious	すごくおいしい
quite	delicious	

★× very delicious とはいわない

▷This meat is **absolutely delicious**! この肉はすごくおいしいですね

▷I did enjoy that wine very much. It was fruity and **quite delicious**. とてもいいワインでした．フルーティでとてもおいしかったです

delight /diláit/ 名 喜び，うれしさ

express	one's delight	喜びを表す
take	(a) delight	喜びを見出す

▷Alan **expressed** his **delight** at the results. アランはその結果をひどく喜んだ

great	delight	大喜び
pure	delight	純粋の喜び
(a) sheer	delight	ただただうれしいこと

▷Skiing was his **great delight**. 彼はスキーが大好きだった

▷She smiled a broad smile of **sheer delight**. 彼女は満面に笑みを浮かべて心からの喜びを表した

with	delight	大喜びで
in	delight	
to	A's delight	うれしいことに

▷People still remember those days **with delight**. 人々はいまなお当時を思い出して喜びにふける

▷**To** my **delight**, I found what I was looking for. うれしいことに探し物が見つかった

delighted /diláitid/ 形 喜んで，うれしがって

absolutely	delighted	心から喜んで
highly	delighted	
obviously	delighted	見るからに喜んで
clearly	delighted	

▷"Did he like your present?" "Yes. He was **absolutely delighted**."「プレゼント気に入ってくれたの，彼？」「ええ，とっても」

▷I am **obviously delighted** to receive this award. この賞を受賞して心からうれしく思います

delighted	with A	Aを喜んで
delighted	at A	
delighted	by A	

▷I'm quite **delighted with** the outcome. 結果をとても喜んでいます

delighted	that...	…を喜んで
delighted	to do	…して喜んで

▷We're **delighted that** Bill is supporting our project. ビルがわれわれの事業を援助してくれているのをとても喜んでいます

▷I'm **delighted to** see you. お目にかかれてうれしい

deliver /dilívər/ 動 配達する；出産する

deliver	free of charge	無料で配達する
deliver	by hand	手渡す
be safely	delivered	無事に出産した

▷She was **safely delivered** of a baby girl. 彼女は女の子を無事に出産した

deliver	A to B	AをBに配達する；伝える

▷Did you **deliver** the message **to** Mike? マイクに伝言してくれたかい

delivery /dilívəri/ 名 配達；出産

make	(a) delivery	配達する
accept	delivery	配達を受け取る
take	delivery	
have	(a) delivery	出産する

▷ We can **accept delivery** between 8 a.m. and 12 o'clock. 配達物は午前8時から12時の間に受け取れます

▷ We can **take delivery** *of* the parcel any time after 10 o'clock. 10時以降はいつでも小包を受け取れる

express	delivery	速達
special	delivery	特別便
late	delivery	配達の遅れ，遅配
free	delivery	無料配達
an easy	delivery	安産
a difficult	delivery	難産

▷ I sent a letter by **special delivery** to William. 手紙を特別便でウィリアムに送った

▷ We apologize for the **late delivery**. 遅配をお詫びいたします

▷ Our company offers **free delivery** on certain purchases. 当社はお買い上げいただく品によっては送料無料です

▷ She had an **easy delivery** in hospital. 彼女は病院で安産だった

demand /dimǽnd | -má:nd/ 名 要求；需要

make	a demand	要求する
meet	a demand	要求を満たす
satisfy	a demand	
reject	a demand	要求を拒む
resist	a demand	
increase	(the) demand	需要を増大させる
reduce	(the) demand	需要を減少させる

▷ The bank robber **made** a **demand** for money. 銀行強盗は金を要求した

▷ The Prime Minister **rejected demands** from Labour MPs. 首相は労働党の国会議員からの要求を拒否した

▷ The new technology **increased** the **demand** for engineers. 新しいテクノロジーによって技術者への需要が増えた

▷ It may be true that high prices have **reduced** the **demand** for organic foods. 価格が高いために自然食品の需要が減っているというのは本当かもしれない

a legitimate	demand	正当な要求
a reasonable	demand	もっともな要求
(a) great	demand	大きな需要
(a) heavy	demand	
(a) high	demand	高い需要
(a) strong	demand	強い需要
(a) growing	demand	増大する需要
(an) increasing	demand	
(an) excess	demand	超過需要

▷ There's a **great demand** for our products. われわれの製品に対する需要は大きい

▷ *Harry Potter* is in **high demand**. 「ハリーポッター」はよく売れている

▷ There was an **excess demand** for their services. 彼らのサービスに対して供給を上回る需要があった

in	demand	需要がある
demand	for A	Aの要求；Aの需要

▷ Healthy food is increasingly **in demand**. 健康食品はますます需要がある

▷ The global **demand for** electricity is expected to increase by 50% by the year 2020. 世界の電力需要は2020年までに50％増えると予想される

demand /dimǽnd | -má:nd/ 動 要求する，問いただす；必要とする

increasingly	demand	ますます必要とする

▷ University posts these days **increasingly demand** a doctorate. 大学で教職に就くには近ごろではますます博士号が必要になりつつある

demand	A of B	AをBに要求する

▷ Her boss **demanded** a great deal **of** her. 上司から彼女への要求は多かった

demand	(that)...	…を要求する
demand	to do	…するよう要求する

▷ I **demand that** you leave here at once! ここをすぐに立ち去ってくれ

▷ She **demanded to** see the boss immediately. 彼女はすぐ上司に面会させろと要求した

democracy /dimákrəsi | -mɔ́k-/ 名 民主主義，民主制；民主主義国家

parliamentary	democracy	議会民主制
representative	democracy	代議民主制
direct	democracy	直接民主制

| democratic |

| liberal | democracy | 自由民主主義国家 |

▷ The United States, Australia and Japan are all **liberal democracies**. 米国，オーストラリア，日本はすべて自由民主主義国家だ

democratic /dèməkrǽtik/ 形 民主的な

truly	democratic	真に民主的な
genuinely	democratic	真に民主的な
fully	democratic	十分に民主的な

▷ If this country was **fully** and **truly democratic**, we wouldn't be in the situation we're in now. この国が十分に，また真に民主主義的だったら，われわれはいまの状況にはいまい

demonstrate /démənstrèit/

動 論証する，説明する；デモをする

| clearly | demonstrate | 明確に論証する |
| demonstrate | peacefully | 平和的にデモをする |

▷ Research has **clearly demonstrated** many people don't understand that new system very well. 調査で明確になったことは，その新しいシステムを理解していない人が多いということだ

| demonstrate | that... | …と証明する |
| demonstrate | wh- | …かを証明する；…かを実演する |

★ wh- は how, what, why など

▷ The report **demonstrates that** a lot of people are dissatisfied. 報告書の示すところでは多くの人々が満足していない
▷ The flight attendant **demonstrated how** to open the emergency exit door. 客室乗務員は非常口のドアの開け方を実演して見せた

| demonstrate | against A | Aに反対のデモをする |

▷ Ten thousand people **demonstrated against** the war. 1万人が反戦デモをした

demonstration /dèmənstréiʃən/

名 デモ；実物説明；論証

hold	a demonstration	デモをする
stage	a demonstration	
join	a demonstration	デモに参加する
take part in	a demonstration	
give	a demonstration	実演をする

★「デモをする」は ×make a demonstration とはいわない

▷ Taxi drivers **held a demonstration** outside City Hall. タクシー運転手たちが市庁舎の外でデモをした
▷ Police say about 3,000 people **joined a demonstration** in London. 警察の発表では約3千人がロンドンのデモに参加した
▷ She **gave a demonstration** of Irish traditional dancing. 彼女はアイルランドの伝統的なダンスを実演した

| a demonstration | takes place | デモが行われる |

▷ A mass **demonstration took place** in front of the Houses of Parliament. 大衆デモが国会議事堂前で行われた

a large	demonstration	大きなデモ
a big	demonstration	
a mass	demonstration	大衆デモ
a public	demonstration	
a peaceful	demonstration	平和的なデモ
a violent	demonstration	暴力的なデモ
a protest	demonstration	抗議デモ
a practical	demonstration	実際にやってみること

▷ In Melbourne there was a **large demonstration** last week. メルボルンで先週大きなデモがあった
▷ A **peaceful demonstration** is being held on Friday. 金曜日に平和的デモが行われることになっている
▷ Can you give us a **practical demonstration**? 実際にやって見せてくれないかな

deny /dinái/ 動 否定する；拒む

strongly	deny	強く否定する
emphatically	deny	
hotly	deny	激しく否定する
strenuously	deny	
categorically	deny	きっぱり否定する
consistently	deny	一貫して否定する

▷ Jackson **strongly denied** the charges. ジャクソンは容疑を強く否定した
▷ The government **categorically denied** reports on Friday by two local newspapers. 金曜日に地方紙2紙が報じた内容を政府はきっぱり否定した
▷ He has **consistently denied** those rumors. 彼は一貫してそれらのうわさを否定した

deny	(that)...	…を否定する
deny	doing	…していないと言う

▷I can't **deny that** I want to go there. そこへ行きたい気持ちを否定のしようもない
♦**There is no denying that...** …は否定できない ▷There is no denying that knowledge is power. 知識は力なりというのは否定できない
▷She **denied** opening my letters. 私の手紙を開封などしていないと彼女は言った

departure /dipáːrtʃər/ 名 出発；試み，逸脱

an abrupt	departure	突然の出発
a sudden	departure	
an early	departure	早めの出発
a late	departure	遅めの出発
a radical	departure	大きな逸脱
a significant	departure	

▷Writing this book was a **radical departure** from his previous career. この本を書くことで彼はそれまでの経歴と完全に決別した
▷Both graphs depict a **significant departure** from expected results. どちらの図表も予想された結果から大きく隔たっている

departure	for A	A（場所）への出発
departure	from A	Aからの出発

▷It has been two weeks since John's **departure from** Paris. ジョンがパリを立ってから2週間になる

depend /dipénd/ 動 (depend on, depend upon で)…次第だ；…に頼る

depend	crucially on A	決定的にA次第だ
depend	entirely on A	完全にA次第だ；完
depend	solely on A	全にAに頼る
depend	largely on A	A次第のところが大
depend	mainly on A	きい
depend	primarily on A	
depend	heavily on A	Aに大きく頼る
depend	partly on A	A次第の部分もある

▷Effective teaching **depends crucially on** the teacher's communication skills. 教育が効果を上げるかどうかは教師のコミュニケーション技術によるところが決定的に大きい
▷It is unwise to **depend solely on** the information contained on websites. ウェブサイトにある情報だけに頼るのは賢明ではない
▷Your choice of hotel **depends largely on** the amount you want to pay. どんなホテルを選ぶかはいくらまでなら払うかに大きく左右される
▷Bone density **depends partly on** the amount of calcium. 骨密度はカルシウム量によって決まる部分もある

it depends (on)		wh-	…か次第だ

★wh- は what, where, how など

▷"I've done something awful. Will you forgive me?" "**It depends what** you did!" 「ひどいことをしてしまったけれど許してくれるかな」「きみが何をやったか次第だね」

deposit /dipázit | -póz-/

名 預金；内金，手付金，保証金

make	a deposit	預金する
have	a deposit	預金がある
pay	a deposit	内金を入れる
put down	a deposit	
pay	a deposit	保証金を払う
leave	a deposit	
lose	a deposit	保証金を没収
forfeit	a deposit	される

▷I want to **make** a **deposit** into my account. 口座に預金したい
▷I **have** a **deposit** of £10,000 in the bank. 銀行に1万ポンドの預金がある
▷You need to **pay** a reservation **deposit**. 予約の内金をお支払いいただく必要があります

a bank	deposit	銀行預金
a time	deposit	定期預金

depression /dipréʃən/

名 憂うつ；不景気，不況

suffer from	depression	うつになる
fall into	depression	うつに陥る
go into	depression	

▷Ryan **suffered from** severe **depression**. ライアンは重度のうつになった

severe	depression	重度のうつ
deep	depression	ひどいうつ
manic	depression	躁うつ病
postnatal	depression	産後うつ病
severe	depression	深刻な不況
economic	depression	経済不況

▷He went into **deep depression**. 彼はひどいうつ状態に陥った
▷The US economy plunged into **severe depression**. 米国経済は深刻な不況に落ち込んだ
▷The **economic depression** lasted throughout the 1990s. 経済不況は1990年代の間ずっと続いた

depth /dépθ/ 名 深さ；奥行き

considerable	depth	かなりの深さ
great	depth	

▷The wreck was located at a **great depth** beneath the ocean. 難破船は海底かなり深くにあった

in	depth	深さは；深く

▷We have discussed it **in depth**. それについて突っ込んだ議論をした

at	a depth of A	Aの深さに
to	a depth of A	Aの深さまで

▷Seeds were sown **at a depth of** 5 cm. 種子は5センチの深さにまかれた
▷Pour the oil **to a depth of** roughly 4 inches in a large, deep saucepan. 大きな深いシチューなべに4インチほどの深さまで油を注ぎます

describe /diskráib/ 動 描写する，述べる，説明する

accurately	describe	正確に描写する
briefly	describe	簡潔に述べる
fully	described	十分説明された
previously	described	前述した
described	above	上述した
described	below	以下で述べた

★accurately, briefly は describe の後，previously は described の後でも用いる

▷She was in shock so she couldn't **accurately describe** what had happened. 彼女はあまりにショックで何が起きたか正確に言えなかった
▷Would you **briefly describe** your view on this issue? この件への見解を簡潔に述べていただけますか
▷The analysis was carried out as **described previously**. 分析は前述のように行われた

describe	A as C	AをCと描写する

▷People **described** her **as** "cute" or "attractive." 人々は彼女のことを「かわいい」とか「魅力的」ということばで説明した

describe	wh-	…かを説明する

★wh- は how, what, who など

▷It's hard to **describe how** she felt. 彼女がどう感じたかを説明するのは難しい

description /diskrípʃən/

名 描写，記述，説明；人相書

give	a description	描写する
provide	a description	
defy	description	とても描写できない
issue	a description	人相書を公表する
fit	the description	人相書に一致する

▷He wrote to me and **gave** a **description** *of* you. 彼はぼくに手紙を書いてきて，きみがどんな人か説明してくれた
▷Mark **provided** a detailed **description** *of* his study. マークは自分の研究について詳しく説明した
▷Police have **issued** a **description** *of* the man. 警察はその男の人相書を公表した

a detailed	description	詳細な描写
a full	description	
an accurate	description	正確な描写
a brief	description	簡潔な描写
a short	description	短い描写
a general	description	概要
an objective	description	客観的な描写

▷Is that an **accurate description** of what was happening? 実際そのとおりのできごとがあったのですか
▷This brochure gives a **short description** of what is worth seeing in Russia. この冊子にはロシアで見る価値のあるものについて短く記述してあります
▷A **general description** can be seen in Figure 1. 概要は図1に示してあります

beyond	description	ことばで表せない

▷Her beauty was **beyond description**. 彼女の美しさは筆舌に尽くしがたかった

deserve /dizə́ːrv/ 動 値する，ふさわしい

richly	deserve	当然ながら値する
fully	deserve	十分に値する
thoroughly	deserve	
well	deserve	

▷Former US President Mr. Jimmy Carter **richly deserves** the Nobel Peace Prize. 元米国大統領ジミー・カーター氏はノーベル平和賞をもらってしかるべきだ
▷She was a wonderful ice skater. Her reputation was **well deserved**. 彼女はすばらしいアイススケーターで，ほめそやされて当然だった

| deserve | better | もっとよい扱いを受けて |
| deserve | more | しかるべきだ |

▷I feel so strongly that this country **deserves better** than what it has now. この国はいまよりもっとよい扱いを受けてしかるべきだと強く感じる

| deserve | to do | …するに値する |

▷Do you think England **deserved to** win the Rugby World Cup? イングランドがラグビーのワールドカップで優勝するほどいいチームだと思っていたかい

design /dizáin/

名 デザイン；設計(図)；模様；計画

| create | a design | デザインを考案する |

▷He **created** a unique **design**. 彼はユニークなデザインをつくり出した

a basic	design	基本的デザイン
an original	design	独創的デザイン
a modern	design	現代的デザイン
the overall	design	全体のデザイン
floral	designs	花模様
geometric	designs	幾何学模様
grand	design	壮大な計画

▷The **basic design** is the same, but the shape has been changed. 基本的デザインは同じだが形が変わった
▷I'm in charge of the **overall design** and production. 全体のデザインと製作を担当しています

| a design | for A | Aの設計図 |

▷Do you have any ideas on a **design for** your garden? 庭の設計図について何かお考えがありますか

design /dizáin/ **動** デザインする，設計する

carefully	designed	入念に設計された
beautifully	designed	美しく設計された
specially	designed	特別に設計された
originally	designed	もともと設計された

▷Everything in the center of the capital is **carefully designed** and built. 首都の中心にあるものはすべて入念に設計され建てられている
▷The book is **beautifully designed**. その本は装丁がきれいだ
▷The building was **originally designed** in the 1950's. その建物はもともと1950年代に設計された

| be designed | to do | …するよう設計される |
| be designed | for A | Aのために設計される |

▷The boat was **designed to** look like a swan. ボートは白鳥の形にデザインされていた
▷Kate stayed at one of the small bedrooms that was **designed for** guests. ケイトが泊まったのは客用に設計された小さな寝室の1つだった

desire /dizáiər/ 名 欲望，願望

feel	a desire	願望を感じる
express	a desire	願望を表明する
indicate	a desire	
satisfy	a desire	願望を満たす
fulfill	a desire	
reflect	a desire	願望を反映する

▷I **felt** the **desire** to hit him. 彼を殴りたくなった
▷Charlie **expressed** a **desire** to stay with us. チャーリーは私たちといっしょにいたいという願望を口にした
▷He had become a doctor in order to **satisfy** his **desire** to save lives. 人の命を救いたいという願望を満たすべく彼は医師になった
▷The walls around the house **reflect** the **desire** to protect the family from the outside world. 家の周りの壁は外の世界から家族を守りたいという願望の反映である

a burning	desire	激しい願望
a great	desire	
a strong	desire	強い願望
an overwhelming	desire	抗しがたい願望
a genuine	desire	心からの願望
a natural	desire	自然な願望
sexual	desire	性欲

▷He has a **burning desire** to become the world number one tennis player. 彼は世界一のテニス選手になりたいと強く願っている
▷My **great desire** is to work for peace and international understanding. 平和と国際理解のために働くことを私は強く望んでいます
▷Suddenly I felt a **strong desire** to eat lots of ice cream. 急にアイスクリームをいっぱい食べたくなった

| have | no desire to do | …する気がない |

▷I honestly **had no desire to** see this film. 正直言って、この映画を見たいとは思わなかった

desk /désk/ 名 机

sit at	one's desk	机に向かっている
leave	one's desk	机を離れる
clear	A's desk	机の上を片づける

▷He was **sitting at** his **desk**. 彼は机に向かっていた
▷I **left** my **desk** and went to the library. 席を立って図書館に行った
▷Mind if I **clear** your **desk**, Alex? きみの机の上を片づけてもいいかい、アレックス

despair /dispéər/ 名 絶望

drive A to	despair	Aを絶望に追い込む

▷Losing his job and getting divorced **drove** him **to despair**. 失業し離婚したことで彼は絶望に追い込まれた

deep	despair	深い絶望
utter	despair	絶望のどん底

▷He saved me from **utter despair**. 彼は絶望のどん底から私を救ってくれた

in	despair	絶望して

▷I shook my head **in despair**. がっかりして首を左右に振った

desperate /déspərət/

形 自暴自棄の、やけになった；必死の

really	desperate	とても自暴自棄の
absolutely	desperate	すっかり自暴自棄の
increasingly	desperate	ますます自暴自棄の

▷The situation is **absolutely desperate**. 状況はまったくどうしようもない
▷She was growing **increasingly desperate**. 彼女はますます自暴自棄になっていた

desperate	for A	Aがほしくてたまらない

▷Andy is really **desperate for** a girlfriend. アンディはガールフレンドがほしくてたまらない

be desperate	to do	必死に…する

▷He was **desperate to** make up for his mistakes. 彼は必死で自分の犯したミスを何とかしようとした

destroy /distrɔ́i/ 動 破壊する

completely	destroy	完全に破壊する
entirely	destroy	
totally	destroy	
effectively	destroy	事実上破壊する
virtually	destroy	
largely	destroy	ほぼ破壊する

▷The bombing **completely destroyed** that building. 爆撃でその建物は全壊した
▷The incident has **effectively destroyed** our confidence in him. その事件でわれわれの彼への信頼は事実上損なわれた
▷Coventry was **largely destroyed** during the Second World War. コベントリーは第2次世界大戦でほとんど破壊し尽くされた

be destroyed	by A	Aで破壊される

★Aは fire, a bomb, an earthquake など

▷The church was **destroyed by** the 1843 earthquake. その教会は1843年の地震で大きな被害を受けた

destruction /distrʌ́kʃən/ 名 破壊

cause	destruction	破滅をもたらす
lead to	the destruction	破壊に至る
prevent	destruction	破壊を防ぐ

▷Floods can **cause** extreme **destruction** to river environments. 洪水で川の環境が大きな被害を被ることもある
▷Global warming will **lead to** the **destruction** of the earth. 地球温暖化は地球破壊をもたらすだろう

total	destruction	完全な破壊
complete	destruction	
wholesale	destruction	
mass	destruction	大量破壊
widespread	destruction	大規模な破壊

▷We don't want to risk **wholesale destruction** of the system. そのシステムが完全に壊れてしまう危険を冒したくはない
▷Some countries still have weapons of **mass destruction**. なお大量破壊兵器を保有している国がいくつかある

detail /ditéil/

名 細かな点, 細部;(details で)詳細

give	details	詳細を示す
provide	details	
go into	detail(s)	詳細に入る
announce	details	詳細を発表する
release	details	
reveal	details	詳細を明かす
contain	details	詳細を含む
include	details	

▷He promised to **give details** later. 彼は後ほど詳細を述べると約束した
▷I won't **go into detail** because I haven't got time. 時間がありませんので詳細には立ち入りません
▷NHK has **announced details** of its brand-new music program. NHKは新しい音楽番組の詳細を発表した

fine	detail(s)	すみずみまでの細部
precise	detail(s)	正確な詳細
full	details	事細かな詳細
further	detail(s)	さらなる詳細

▷The **fine detail** of his comics is clearly illustrated. 彼のコミックスは細部に至るまで鮮明に描かれている
▷There's been an accident, but we don't know the **precise details** yet. 事故があったが, まだ正確な詳細は判明していない
▷I don't know the **full details**. 事細かな詳細までは知らない
▷For **further details** watch their website. 詳細はウェブサイトをご覧ください

| in | detail | 詳細に |

▷He described **in detail** what he had seen and read. 彼は見たこと, 読んだことについて詳細に述べた
♦**in greater detail** / **in more detail** さらに詳細に
▷He explained everything to me in greater detail. 彼は微に入り細をうがって説明してくれた

determine /ditə́ːrmin/

動 決める, 決定する, 確定する

be genetically	determined	遺伝的に決まる
be biologically	determined	生物学的に決まる
be culturally	determined	文化的に決まる
be largely	determined	大きく決まる

▷A characteristic can be **genetically determined**. 特性は遺伝的に決まる可能性がある

▷Pricing is **largely determined** by competition. 価格設定は競争で決まる部分が大きい

| determine | wh- | …か確定する |

★ wh- は how, why, who, what など

▷The police weren't able to **determine how** the fire started. 警察は火事が起きた原因を確定できなかった

develop /divéləp/

動 発展させる, 発展する;開発する

rapidly	develop	急速に発展する
fully	develop	十分に発達させる
be originally	developed	もともと開発された

▷Leeds is **rapidly developing** as a cosmopolitan city. リーズは国際都市として急速に発展しつつある
▷The technology was **originally developed** in the United States. その技術はもともとアメリカで開発された

| develop | from A | Aから発展する |
| develop | into A | Aへと発展する |

▷Many of our projects are **developed from** our employee's ideas. われわれの企画の多くは従業員のアイデアから発展したものだ

developed /divéləpt/

形 発達した, 発展した

highly	developed	高度に発達した
well	developed	よく発達した
fully	developed	十分に発達した
recently	developed	最近発展した;新しく
newly	developed	開発された

▷Japan was the first **highly developed** country in East Asia. 日本は東アジアで最初に高度成長した国だった
▷Genetic engineering is a **recently developed** but highly controversial technology. 遺伝子工学は最近発展した技術だが, 大いに議論の余地がある

development /divéləpmənt/

名 発展, 発達;進展, 展開

encourage	the development	発展を促す
promote	the development	発展を推進する
support	the development	発展を支える
prevent	the development	発展を妨げる

| device |

▷At the moment Thailand vey much **supports** the **development** *of* its tourism industry. いまのところタイは自国の旅行産業への援助を強めている

▷Doctors are doing all they can to **prevent** the **development** *of* diabetes. 糖尿病の進行を食い止めるため医師たちはできることは何でもしている

economic	development	経済発展
industrial	development	産業発展
regional	development	地域発展
urban	development	都市開発
product	development	製品開発
child	development	子どもの発達
significant	development	著しい進展
recent	development	最近の進展
technological	development	技術の進展

▷We have an interest in China's **economic development**. 中国の経済発展に関心をもっている

▷What were the most **significant developments** in the EU during the 1990s? 1990年代のEUにおける最も著しい進展は何でしたか

device /diváis/ 名 装置；工夫

a labor-saving	device	省力化装置
an electronic	device	電子装置
a mechanical	device	機械装置
an explosive	device	爆破装置
a safety	device	安全装置
a storage	device	記憶装置
a nuclear	device	核装置
a rhetorical	device	修辞的な工夫

▷Please turn off any **electronic devices** and put your seats and trays in the upright position. 電子装置の電源を切って椅子とトレイを元の位置に戻してください（★機内アナウンス）

▷He planted an **explosive device** in a garbage bin. 彼はごみ箱に爆破装置を仕掛けた

▷The author uses many **rhetorical devices** such as metaphor and simile. 著者は隠喩や直喩などの修辞的な工夫を多用している

| a device | for A | Aのための装置 |

▷A cellphone is a handy **device for** sending email. 携帯電話はEメールを送るのに手軽な装置だ

devote /divóut/ 動 ささげる；専念する

| devote | exclusively | もっぱら…に充てる |
| devote | entirely | |

▷She **devoted** her time **exclusively** *to* revising for the exam. 彼女はもっぱら試験に備えた復習に時間を充てていた

| devote | A to B | AをBにささげる |

★A は life, time, energy, money, effort など

▷Amanda **devoted** her life **to** her children. アマンダは子どもたちのために人生をささげた

diary /dáiəri/ 名 日記

| keep | a diary | 日記をつける |
| write in | one's diary | 日記に書く |

▷I've **kept** a **diary** since I was ten years old. 10歳の時から日記をつけている

dictionary /díkʃənèri|-ʃənəri/

名 辞書，辞典

use	a dictionary	辞書を引く
consult	a dictionary	
look A up in	a dictionary	辞書でAを調べる
compile	a dictionary	辞書を編む

▷**Consult** your **dictionary** and correct any errors. 辞書を引いて間違いを直しなさい

▷Johnson **compiled** his famous **dictionary** in the 18th century. ジョンソンが，後に有名になった辞書を編纂したのは18世紀のことだ

die /dái/ 動 死ぬ，亡くなる

die	peacefully	安らかに死ぬ
die	suddenly	急死する
die	instantly	即死する
die	prematurely	早すぎる死である
die	young	若くして死ぬ
die	aged 80	80歳で死ぬ
eventually	die	結局は死ぬ

▷His father **died suddenly** when Lenny was eight. レニーが8歳の時，彼の父親は突然亡くなった

▷A drunk driver crashed into the side of his car. He **died instantly**. 酒気帯び運転の車が彼の側面に衝突し，彼は即死した

▷He **died prematurely** of a heart attack. 彼は心臓発作で若すぎる死を迎えた

▷Everyone will **eventually die**. だれでもいつかは死ぬ

| die | of A | Aで死ぬ |
| die | from A | |

be dying	for A	Aがほしくてたまらない
be dying	of A	Aでたまらない

★dying of A の A は boredom, thirst など

▷My mother **died of** old age. 母は老衰で亡くなった
▷He **died from** overwork. 彼は過労死した
▷I've been **dying for** a break. 休憩したくてたまらない
▷Let's find a pub. I'm **dying of** thirst! パブを見つけよう．のどが渇いてたまらない

be dying	to do	…したくてたまらない

▷I'm **dying to** see her again. また彼女に会いたくてたまらない

PHRASES
Never say die! ☺ 弱音を吐くな
You only die once. ☺ 死ぬのは1回きりだ，とにかくやってみよう

diet /dáiət/ 名 食事, 常食；ダイエット

follow	a diet	きちんとダイエットする
go on	a diet	ダイエットを始める
go off	a diet	ダイエットをやめる
come off	a diet	
be on	a diet	ダイエット中である

▷He **follows** his **diet** very strictly. 彼はきびしい食事制限をしている
▷I decided to **go on** a **diet**. ダイエットすることに決めた
▷"Would you like a chocolate?" "No thanks. I'm **on** a **diet**." 「チョコレートはいかがですか」「いえ結構です．ダイエット中なので」

a healthy	diet	健康的な食事
a balanced	diet	バランスのいい食事
a poor	diet	貧しい食事
a staple	diet	主食
a vegetarian	diet	菜食中心の食事
a high-fiber	diet	繊維を多く含む食事
a high-protein	diet	高たんぱく質の食事
a low-fat	diet	低脂肪の食事

▷You need to go on a **healthy diet**. 健康的な食事をしないといけないよ
▷I eat a **balanced diet** consisting of plenty of fresh fruit and vegetables. 新鮮な果物と野菜をたくさん食べてバランスのとれた食事をしています
▷Meat is the **staple diet** of most Europeans. 肉はほとんどのヨーロッパ人たちの主食だ

differ /dífər/ 動 異なる, 違う；意見が合わない

differ	significantly	大きく異なる
differ	considerably	
differ	greatly	
differ	markedly	
differ	slightly	やや異なる

▷Rates of cancer **differ widely** with age. がんの比率は年齢によって大きく異なる
▷The speech of women **differs slightly** from that of men. 女性の話しことばは男性とは少し異なる

beg to	differ	(失礼ながら)意見が違う
agree to	differ	意見の違いを認め合う

▷"I think the Americans should stay in Afghanistan." "Really? I **beg to differ**!" 「アメリカ人はアフガニスタンにとどまるべきだね」「そうかな．ぼくは意見が違うよ」

differ	from A	Aと異なる
differ	with A	A(人)と意見が合わない
differ	on A	Aに関して意見が合わない
differ	over A	

▷I know that your tastes **differ from** mine. きみの好みがぼくとは違うことはわかっているよ
▷I **differ with** you on that point. その点であなたとは意見が違います
▷They **differ over** how serious these problems are. これらの問題がどれほど深刻か彼らの意見に違いがある

difference /dífərəns/

名 違い, 相違；(differences で)意見の違い

make	a difference	違いを生じる
find	any difference(s)	違いを見つける
notice	a difference	違いに気づく
see	the difference	違いがわかる
tell	the difference	
show	the difference	違いを示す
have	one's differences	意見が違う
resolve	one's differences	意見の違いを
settle	one's differences	乗り越える

▷Location can **make** a big **difference** to the success of a company. 立地条件によって会社がうまくいくかどうか，かなりの差が出る
▷No one will **notice** a **difference** except you. 違いに気づくのはきみ以外にはいないだろう
▷Can you **tell** the **difference** *between* butter and margarine? バターとマーガリンの違いがわかりますか
▷Table 2 **shows** the **difference** *in* patients' weight after training. 表2はトレーニング後の患者の体重の違

| different |

いを示している

a big	difference	大きな差異
a huge	difference	
a major	difference	
a great	difference	
a considerable	difference	かなりの差異
a fundamental	difference	基本的な差異
a significant	difference	重大な差異
an important	difference	
the main	difference	主要な差異
a slight	difference	わずかな差異
a subtle	difference	微妙な差異
cultural	difference	文化の違い

▷When you make tea, warming the teapot makes a **big difference**. お茶を入れるときはティーポットを温かくしておくとずいぶん違います

▷There was a **great difference** in personality between the two men. 2人の男は性格が大きく違った

▷What are the **crucial differences** between information and knowledge? 情報と知識の決定的な違いは何ですか

▷He was rich, but I wasn't. That was the **main difference** between us. 彼は金持ちで私はそうではなかった．それが2人の大きな違いだった

▷Nick and I had a **slight difference** of opinion. ニックと私は少し意見が違った

different /dífərənt/ 形 違った；別の

look	different	異なって見える

▷Oh! You **look different**. You've had a haircut! あら、いつもと違って見えるけど、髪を切ったの

significantly	different	著しく違った
completely	different	まったく違った
entirely	different	
totally	different	
rather	different	いくらか違った
somewhat	different	
slightly	different	わずかに違った
subtly	different	微妙に違った

▷His story was **significantly different** from the truth. 彼の話は真実とは著しく異なっていた

▷Your personality is **completely different** from mine. あなたの性格は私とまったく違う

▷He looked **rather different** from usual. 彼はいつもといくらか違って見えた

▷The situation now is **slightly different**. 現在の状況は少し異なっている

different	from A	Aと違う
different	than A	
different	to A	
different	in A	Aの点で違う

▷He seems no **different from** when I met him almost forty years ago. 彼は40年ほど前に会った時とほとんど変わらない

▷You're **different than** any man I have ever met. あなたはこれまで会った男の人たちとは違う

▷Real life is **different to** stories. 実生活は物語とは違う

difficult /dífikʌlt | -kəlt/ 形 難しい，困難な

find A	difficult	Aは難しいとわかる
make A	difficult	Aを難しくする

▷She **found** it extremely **difficult** to understand all of this. 彼女はこれをすべて理解するのはとても難しいことに気づいた

▷She smiled at me and **made** it very **difficult** for me to refuse. 彼女がほほえみかけてきたので、私は断りにくくなった

extremely	difficult	非常に難しい
particularly	difficult	特に難しい
increasingly	difficult	ますます難しい
notoriously	difficult	難しいので有名な

▷Things are becoming **increasingly difficult**. 事態はますます難しくなってきている

▷Latin is a **notoriously difficult** language to learn. ラテン語は知ってのとおり学ぶのが大変だ

it is difficult	(for A) to do	(Aが)…するのは難しい

▷It was **difficult for** me **to** explain the reasons. その理由を説明するのは私には難しかった

difficulty /dífikʌlti | -kəl-/

名 難しさ，困難；問題

have	difficulty	苦労する
experience	difficulty	
face	difficulty	
get into	difficulty	困難に陥る
run into	difficulty	
cause	difficulty	困難を招く
create	difficulty	
cause	a difficulty	問題を生じる
give rise to	a difficulty	

▷ I **had difficulty** *in* sleeping for a few nights. 2, 3日間なかなか眠れなかった
▷ Young people are **experiencing difficulty** in finding jobs. 若者は職探しに苦労している
▷ If you leave before the end of your contract it could **cause** a **difficulty**. 契約が切れる前に辞めると問題になることがある

considerable	difficulty	かなりの困難
great	difficulty	大きな困難
economic	difficulty	経済的困難
financial	difficulty	財政難
practical	difficulties	実際の困難

▷ He had **great difficulty** finishing in time. 時間内に終わらせるのに彼はとても苦労した
▷ Brown is in **financial difficulty**. ブラウンは金に困っている

with	difficulty	苦労して
without	difficulty	苦労なく

▷ I moved the furniture back into her room **with** great **difficulty**. 家具を彼女の部屋に戻すのにすごく苦労した

the difficulty	is...	難しいのは…

▷ The **difficulty is** that my time is limited. 難しいのは私の時間が限られていることだ

dignity /dígnəti/ 名 威厳, 品位, 尊厳

maintain	one's dignity	威厳を保つ
keep	one's dignity	
lose	one's dignity	威厳を失う

▷ You should try not to **lose** your **dignity**. 威厳を失わないようにするべきだ

great	dignity	高い品位
quiet	dignity	静かな威厳
human	dignity	人間の尊厳

▷ Jeff is a man of **great dignity** and pride. ジェフはとても威厳があってプライドの高い人だ

with	dignity	威厳をもって
beneath	A's dignity	体面にかかわる

▷ Do you think we're entitled to choose to die **with dignity**? 私たちには尊厳死を選択する権利があると思いますか
▷ It was **beneath** his **dignity** to ask what conditions were like. どんな条件か聞くのは彼の体面にかかわることだった

dinner /dínər/ 名 ディナー, 夕食(★一日のうちの主要な食事で, ふつうは夕食); 晩餐会

cook	dinner	ディナーをつくる
prepare	dinner	
have	dinner	ディナーをとる
eat	dinner	
have A for	dinner	Aをディナーに食べる
go out for	dinner	ディナーに出かける
go out to	dinner	
invite A to	dinner	Aをディナーに招く

▷ I'd love to help you **cook dinner**. ディナーをつくるのを喜んで手伝うわ
▷ Do you want to **have dinner** *with* me? 私とディナーに行きたいの？
▷ We **had** pizza **for dinner**. 夕食にピザを食べた
▷ We're **going out for dinner** tonight. 今夜はディナーに出かけます
▷ Thank you for **inviting** me **to dinner**. ディナーにお招きいただきありがとうございます

an excellent	dinner	すばらしいディナー
a lovely	dinner	
a good	dinner	おいしいディナー
an early	dinner	早めのディナー
a late	dinner	遅めのディナー
a formal	dinner	正式な晩餐会

▷ I enjoyed an **excellent dinner**. とてもおいしいディナーでした
▷ Let's go out to an **early dinner**. 早めの夕食に出かけよう

direct /dirékt/ 動 向ける; 指示する

be mainly	directed	おもに向けられる
be primarily	directed	
be specifically	directed	特に向けられる

▷ His interest was **mainly directed** *toward* fundamental problems of mathematics. 彼の関心はおもに数学の基礎問題に向けられていた
▷ Domestic violence is **primarily directed** *against* women. 家庭内暴力はおもに女性に向けられる
▷ The Government's advice is **specifically directed** *to* tourists traveling to China. 政府の勧告は特に中国への旅行者向けのものだ

direct	A toward B	AをBに向ける
direct	A at B	
direct	A to B	AにBへの道を教える

| direction |

▷Richard **directed** his anger **toward** me. リチャードは怒りを私に向けた
▷Could you **direct** me **to** her room? 彼女の部屋までの行き方を教えていただけますか

direct	that...	…を指示する
direct	A to do	A(人)に…するよう指示する

▷He **directed** Peter **to** take a right turn when they came to the main road. 幹線道路まで来たら右に曲がるよう彼はピーターに指示した

direction /dirékʃən/

名 方向, 方角；指導；(directions で)指示

change	direction	方向を変える
reverse	direction	方向を逆にする
point in	the direction	方向を指し示す
indicate	the direction	方向を示す
show	the direction	
determine	the direction	方向を定める
give	directions	指示する
follow	directions	指示に従う

▷She **changed direction** and headed to Purcell Park. 彼女は方向を変えてパーセル公園へ向かった
▷Time cannot **reverse direction**. 時間は逆戻りできない
▷This is the most famous mountain in Japan, he said, **pointing in** the **direction** *of* Mt. Fuji. これが日本一有名な山です, と富士山の方向を指しながら彼は言った
▷He **indicated** the **direction** on the map. 彼は地図で方角を示した
▷Barry is 18 years old and has to **determine** his own **direction** in life. バリーは18歳になったので, 自分の人生の方向を決めなければならない
▷He hailed a taxi and **gave directions** for the hotel. 彼はタクシーを止めてホテルへ行ってくれと指示した

all	directions	あらゆる方向
every	direction	
the same	direction	同じ方向
a different	direction	異なった方向
the opposite	direction	反対方向
the right	direction	正しい方向
the wrong	direction	間違った方向
a southerly	direction	南の方向
an easterly	direction	東の方向
a new	direction	新たな方向

▷I looked around *in* **all directions**. あらゆる方向を見回した

▷Oh, no! this man says Powis Castle is that way! We've been walking for 2 hours *in* the **opposite direction**! なんてことだ. この男の人が言うにはポーウィス城はあの方向だって. 2時間も反対方向に歩いてしまった
▷Are we headed *in* the **right direction** for Manchester? マンチェスターへはこの方向で正しいですか
▷I think we're going *in* the **wrong direction**. 向かっている方向が違うんじゃないかな

in	the direction of A	Aの方向に
from	the direction of A	Aの方向から
under	the direction of A	Aの指導のもと

▷He went **in** the **direction of** the library. 彼は図書館の方へ行った (★× went *to* the direction of the library とはいわない)
▷The study was performed **under** the **direction of** Dr. Thomas. その研究はトマス博士の指導のもとで行われた

a sense of	direction	方向感覚

▷We couldn't see in the dark and lost all **sense of direction**. 暗闇で目が見えず方向感覚をまったく失ってしまった

disagree /dìsəgríː/

動 意見が合わない；一致しない

strongly	disagree	強く反対する
totally	disagree	まったく意見が
entirely	disagree	合わない

★strongly は動詞の後にくることもある

▷I **strongly disagree** with your statement. あなたの述べたことに強く反対します
▷I **totally disagree** with you. あなたとはまったく意見が合わない

disagree	about A	Aについて意見が
disagree	on A	合わない
disagree	over A	
disagree	with A	A(人)に反対する

▷My wife and I always **disagreed on** how Kate should be raised. 妻と私はいつもケイトの育て方で意見が合わなかった

disappear /dìsəpíər/

動 見えなくなる, 消える

completely	disappear	完全に見えなくなる

almost	disappear	ほとんど見えなくなる
all but	disappear	
virtually	disappear	
gradually	disappear	徐々に見えなくなる
suddenly	disappear	急に見えなくなる
finally	disappear	ついに見えなくなる
disappear	altogether	完全に消える
disappear	without trace	跡形もなく消える

▷My glasses have **completely disappeared**. 眼鏡が完全にどこかへ行った
▷The sun had **gradually disappeared** over the horizon. 太陽は地平線の向こうに徐々に消えた
▷The mist **suddenly disappeared**. もやが急に晴れた
▷Finally the spots on my face **disappeared altogether**. ようやく顔のにきびがすっかり消えた
▷Mr. Jones recently **disappeared without trace**. ジョーンズ氏は最近すっかり姿を消した

disappear	from A	Aから消える
disappear	into A	Aの中に消える

★into のほか through, under なども用いる

▷The ship moved off and soon **disappeared from** view. 船は沖に出てすぐ見えなくなった
▷She waved and **disappeared into** the house. 彼女は手を振って家の中に姿を消した

disappointed /dìsəpɔ́intid/

形 がっかりした，落胆した

look	disappointed	がっかりしているようだ
seem	disappointed	

▷She **looked disappointed** when she heard you weren't coming to the party. きみがパーティーに来ないと聞いて彼女はがっかりしたようだった

extremely	disappointed	非常にがっかりした
really	disappointed	
bitterly	disappointed	ひどくがっかりした
deeply	disappointed	
desperately	disappointed	
a little	disappointed	少しがっかりした
slightly	disappointed	

▷I'm **extremely disappointed** to have to cancel my travel plans. 旅行の計画を取りやめなくてはいけないのはとてもがっかりだ
▷I was **bitterly disappointed** with the result. その結果にひどく失望した
▷I'm **slightly disappointed** that Alex can't come. アレックスが来られなくて少しがっかりだ

disappointed	with A	Aにがっかりした
disappointed	at A	
disappointed	about A	
disappointed	in A	A(人)に失望する

▷Some people were **disappointed at** the decision. その決定にがっかりした人もいた
▷I'm **disappointed in** you. きみにはがっかりだよ

disappointed	that...	…であることにがっかりした
disappointed	to do	…してがっかりした

▷I'm just **disappointed that** I didn't bring a camera. カメラを持ってこなくて残念だ
▷He was **disappointed to** have lost the opportunity. 彼は機会を失って落胆した

disappointment /dìsəpɔ́intmənt/

名 失望，落胆

feel	disappointment	失望を感じる
express	disappointment	失望を表明する

▷He **expressed disappointment** with the outcome of the negotiations. 彼は交渉結果に失望を表明した

a great	disappointment	大きな失望
a big	disappointment	
a bitter	disappointment	ひどい失望
a deep	disappointment	深い失望
a slight	disappointment	軽い失望

▷The election result was a **great disappointment** for us. 選挙結果はわれわれにとって実に残念だった
▷She felt a **deep disappointment**. 彼女は深い失望を感じた
▷The main dish was fairly good. The only **slight disappointment** was the dessert. メインディッシュはまあまあおいしかったけど，デザートにはちょっとがっかりしました

to	A's disappointment	失望したことには

▷**To** her **disappointment**, there was nothing new in the letter. 彼女ががっかりしたことには手紙には何も目新しいことは書いてなかった

disaster /dizǽstər | -zá:s-/

名 惨事，災害，災難；大失敗

cause	a disaster	惨事を招く
lead to	disaster	

| disciplin |

spell	disaster	惨事となる
avert	(a) disaster	惨事を回避する
avoid	(a) disaster	
face	(a) disaster	惨事に直面する
end in	disaster	惨事になる

▷ Do you know what **caused** this **disaster**? 何がこのような惨事を招いたかわかりますか

▷ We're **facing** financial **disaster**. 財政危機に直面している

▷ Every time you try to help me out, it **ends in disaster**! きみが手伝ってくれようとするといつももんでもないことになる

disaster	strikes	災害が起きる
a disaster	occurs	

▷ You never know when the next **disaster** will **strike**. 次の災害がいつ起きるかはまったくわからない

▷ Sooner or later a **disaster** will **occur**. 遅かれ早かれ災害は起こるものだ

a major	disaster	大災害
a natural	disaster	自然災害
an air	disaster	空の大事故
an ecological	disaster	生態的災害
an environmental	disaster	環境災害
a nuclear	disaster	原子力災害
a tsunami	disaster	津波災害
a financial	disaster	財政破綻
a total	disaster	まったくの大失敗
an absolute	disaster	
a complete	disaster	

▷ Lives could be lost if there was a **major disaster**. 大災害が起きたら人命が失われるだろう

▷ People prepare for hurricanes, earthquakes and other **natural disasters**. 人々はハリケーンや地震、その他の自然災害に備えている

▷ The weather was a **total disaster**. まったくひどい天気だった

▷ This year has been an **absolute disaster** for our team. 今年はうちのチームにとって実にひどい年だった

a recipe for	disaster	災害のもと

▷ In my opinion, that's a **recipe for disaster**. 私が思うにそれは災いのもとだ

discipline /dísəplin/

名 しつけ, 規律, 訓練; 学問分野

impose	(a) discipline	規律を課す
maintain	discipline	規律を保つ

▷ It is important to **impose discipline** *on* your children at an early age. ごく幼いときから子どもをきちんとしつけるのが大事だ

▷ We're doing our best to **maintain discipline**. 全力で規律を保つべく努力している

strict	discipline	厳しい規律
an academic	discipline	学問分野
a scientific	discipline	科学分野
a related	discipline	関連分野

▷ This is a textbook for students of politics and **related disciplines**. これは政治学とその関連分野の学生のためのテキストです

a range of	disciplines	学問領域

▷ Tomorrow's researchers should study a wide **range of disciplines**. あすを担う研究者たちは幅広い学問領域を研究すべきだ

discover /diskʌ́vər/ 動 発見する, わかる

suddenly	discover	突然発見する
later	discover	後に見つかる
recently	discovered	最近発見した

▷ I **suddenly discovered** that I had lost my passport. パスポートをなくしたことに急に気づいた

▷ I **later discovered** her marriage to Tom had ended. 彼女とトムとの結婚が破綻していたと後になって知った

▷ I **recently discovered** the pleasures and dangers of buying at auction. 最近になってオークションで買い物をすることの楽しさと危険に気づいた

discover	that...	…であると発見する
discover	wh-	…か発見する

★ wh- は who, why, how, whether など

▷ I've **discovered that** I know very little about human relationships. 人間関係のことは自分はほとんど知らないというのがわかった

▷ I've **discovered why** Tom was so angry. なぜトムがそんなに怒っているのかわかった

be surprised to	discover	わかって驚く

★ surprised のほかに shocked, horrified, delighted などもよく用いる

▷ He was happily **surprised to discover** his new roommate is Cole. 彼は新しいルームメイトがコールだと知って驚くと同時にうれしかった

discovery /diskʌ́vəri/ 名 発見

make	a discovery	発見をする
lead to	a discovery	発見につながる

▷Thomas **made** an interesting **discovery** about himself. トマスは自分自身についておもしろい発見をした
▷We hope this data will **lead to** many **discoveries**. このデータが多くの発見につながるよう望んでいる

a great	discovery	大発見
an important	discovery	重要な発見
a significant	discovery	重大な発見
an exciting	discovery	胸躍る発見
a new	discovery	新たな発見
a recent	discovery	最近の発見
a scientific	discovery	科学的な発見

▷Some of the **greatest discoveries** resulted by chance or accident. 大発見のいくつかはまったく偶然の結果なされた
▷The cave paintings in Australia are a really **significant discovery**. オーストラリアの洞窟壁画はとても重大な発見だ

a voyage of	discovery	発見の旅

▷Man's journey into space will be a new **voyage of discovery**. 人類の宇宙への旅は新しい発見の旅となるだろう

discrimination /diskrìmənéiʃən/

名 差別

prohibit	discrimination	差別を禁止する
ban	discrimination	
end	discrimination	差別をやめさせる

▷We **prohibit discrimination** based on race, religion and gender. われわれは人種、宗教、性差に基づく差別を禁止する
▷On April 1st 2001 Holland **ended discrimination** against gay people in marriage. 2001年4月1日にオランダは結婚における同性愛者への差別をなくした

sexual	discrimination	性差別
sex	discrimination	
racial	discrimination	人種差別
religious	discrimination	宗教差別
age	discrimination	年齢差別

▷Parker campaigned against **racial discrimination** in the southern United States. パーカーは米国南部で人種差別反対運動を起こした

▷**Religious discrimination** is illegal. 宗教差別は法律違反だ

discrimination	against A	Aへの差別

▷About seventy percent of people in the survey care about **discrimination against** women in the workplace. 調査対象のうち約7割の人が職場での女性差別を気にしている

discuss /diskʌ́s/ 動 議論する, 話し合う

fully	discuss	十分議論する
thoroughly	discuss	
briefly	discuss	簡潔に論じる
openly	discuss	率直に議論する
be widely	discussed	幅広く議論される

▷The issues were **fully discussed** and resolved. それらの問題は十分な論議を経て解決された
▷We will **briefly discuss** some details here. ここでいくつかの詳細について簡潔に論じる
▷The plan was **widely discussed** at the meeting. その計画は幅広く会議で議論された

discuss	A with B	AについてBと話す

▷I've already **discussed** this **with** my father. この件はすでに父と話し合いました

discuss	wh-	…か議論する

★wh- は how, what, who, where など

▷I'm going to **discuss how** to overcome this problem with my colleagues. この問題をどう克服するか同僚と話し合うつもりだ

discussion /diskʌ́ʃən/

名 話し合い, 討論, 議論

have	a discussion	話し合いをする
hold	a discussion	
enter into	discussions	話し合いを始める
take part in	a discussion	話し合いに加わる
begin	a discussion	話し合いを始める
open	a discussion	
conclude	a discussion	話し合いを終える
continue	a discussion	話し合いを続ける

▷Let's not **have** this **discussion** right now. いまはこの議論をするのはやめよう
▷Listeners can **take part in** the **discussion** by phoning in person. リスナー本人が直接電話をかけて

| disease |

議論に参加できる
▷This is a good opportunity to **begin** the **discussion**. これは議論を始めるのによい機会だ
▷I would like to **conclude** these **discussions** over the next 10 days. むこう10日間でこれらの議論の結論を出したいと思います
▷We **continue discussions** tomorrow. あすも議論を続けます

a detailed	discussion	細かな話し合い
a brief	discussion	簡単な話し合い
a public	discussion	公開討論
an informal	discussion	非公式の話し合い
(an) open	discussion	率直な話し合い
a heated	discussion	激しい議論

▷I've had a long and **detailed discussion** with the mayor. 市長と長時間にわたる詳細な議論をした
▷After a **brief discussion**, she agreed to Paul's plan. 少し話し合っただけで彼女はポールの計画に賛成した
▷The company started **informal discussions** with an advertising company. その会社は広告会社と非公式の話し合いを始めた
▷Now is the time for **open discussion**. 率直な話し合いを始める時期だ

a discussion	about A	Aに関する議論
a discussion	on A	
a discussion	with A	A(人)との議論
a discussion	between A	Aの間の議論

▷We had a long **discussion about** politics. 政治について長い議論をした
▷I think we need to hold a **discussion with** Mr. Brown. ブラウンさんと話し合う必要があると思う

| in | discussion with A | Aと話し合い中で |
| under | discussion | 審議中で |

▷Some important issues are still **under discussion**. 重要な案件がまだ審議中だ

disease /dizíːz/ 名 病気

suffer from	a disease	病気を患う
have	a disease	
catch	a disease	病気にかかる
contract	a disease	
die of	disease	病気で死ぬ
die from	(a) disease	
cause	disease	病気を引き起こす
spread	disease	病気を広める
treat	(a) disease	病気を治療する
fight	disease	病気と闘う
combat	disease	
cure	(a) disease	病気を治す
prevent	disease	病気を予防する

▷Peter was **suffering from** a **disease** of the mind. ピーターは心の病を患っていた
▷If I **catch** a **disease**, you'll have to take care of me! 私が病気にかかったら、あんたが私のめんどうを見るんだよ
▷My grandfather **died of** heart **disease**. 祖父は心臓病で亡くなった
▷Can stress **cause disease**? ストレスが病気を引き起こすことはあるか
▷Herbal medicines have been used to **treat disease** in China. 中国では漢方薬が病気の治療に使われてきた
▷The best way to **prevent disease** is to improve one's immune system. 病気を予防する最善の方法は免疫系の機能を高めることだ

(a) serious	disease	重い病気
(a) chronic	disease	慢性の病気
(a) fatal	disease	命にかかわる病気
(an) incurable	disease	不治の病
(an) infectious	disease	感染症
heart	disease	心臓病
liver	disease	肝臓病

▷Diabetes is a **chronic disease**. 糖尿病は慢性の病気だ
▷Malaria is a **serious**, sometimes **fatal disease**. マラリヤは重い、時に命にかかわる病気だ
▷The best medicine for any type of **infectious disease** is always prevention. どんなタイプの感染症であれ、最良の医療は常に予防だ

| with | (a) disease | 病気にかかった |

▷That medicine will be used in the treatment of patients **with** kidney **disease**. その薬は腎臓病の患者の治療に使われるだろう

dish /díʃ/ 名 皿；食器類；料理

do	the dishes	食器を洗う
wash	the dishes	
dry	the dishes	食器をふく
clear	the dishes	食器を片づける

▷Who will **do** the **dishes**? だれが食器を洗うの
▷Can I help you **dry** the **dishes**? 食器をふくのを手伝いましょうか
▷I **cleared** the **dishes** from the table. テーブルの食器を片づけた

a deep	dish	深い皿
a shallow	dish	浅い皿
an ovenproof	dish	耐熱性の皿
a silver	dish	銀の皿
the main	dish	メインディッシュ
A's favorite	dish	好きな料理

▷ What's your **favorite dish**? あなたの好きな料理は何ですか

dish	of the day	本日の料理

▷ This restaurant has a different **dish of** the **day** every day of the week. このレストランは毎日、日替わり定食がある

dismiss /dismís/

動 却下する, 退ける; 解雇する

be easily	dismissed	簡単に退けられる
summarily	dismiss	即座に退ける; 即座に解雇する
be unfairly	dismissed	不当解雇される

▷ The report's findings should not be too **easily dismissed**. 報告書の結論を安易に退けるべきではない
▷ The government **summarily dismissed** the proposal. 政府はその提案を即座に却下した
▷ An employee has the right not to be **unfairly dismissed** by his employer. 被雇用者は雇用者に不当解雇されない権利がある

dismiss	A as B	AをBだとして退ける

▷ He **dismissed** the idea **as** nonsense. 彼はその考えをばかげたものとして退けた

be dismissed	for A	Aを理由に解雇される
be dismissed	from A	Aの職を解かれる

▷ Blackwell was **dismissed from** his post recently. ブラックウェルは近ごろ職を解かれた

disorder /disɔ́ːrdər/

名 (心身の)不調, 障害; 混乱, 騒動

have	a disorder	不調がある
suffer from	a disorder	不調に苦しむ
develop	a disorder	不調が現れる
cause	a disorder	不調を引き起こす
throw A into	disorder	Aを混乱に陥れる

▷ One in five people **have** a sleep **disorder**. 5人に1人は睡眠障害がある
▷ The doctor says I am **suffering from** a stress **disorder**. 私の病気はストレスからくる不調だと医者は言っている
▷ Anxiety can **cause** eating **disorders**. 不安があると摂食障害を引き起こすことがある

an eating	disorder	摂食障害
a mental	disorder	心の不調
a psychiatric	disorder	精神疾患
a personality	disorder	人格障害
public	disorder	社会の混乱
social	disorder	

▷ For the last five years I have been suffering from a **mental disorder**. この5年間心の病に悩まされている
▷ A total of 15 people were arrested for serious **public disorder**. 総計15名が公の秩序を大きく乱したとして逮捕された

display /displéi/

名 陳列, 展示; 演技; 表示装置

go on	display	展示される
put A on	display	Aを展示する
give	a display	披露する

▷ A fine collection of impressionist paintings will **go on display** next month. 印象派絵画のすばらしいコレクションが来月展示される
▷ His drawing was **put on display** at the museum. 彼の描いた絵は美術館に展示された
▷ The Olympic champions **gave** a marvelous **display** of ice dancing. オリンピック優勝者たちがアイスダンスのすばらしい演技を披露した

a dazzling	display	みごとな展示
a fine	display	
a public	display	一般展示
an impressive	display	すばらしい演技
a spectacular	display	
a fireworks	display	花火大会
a visual	display	画像表示

▷ The evening ended with a **dazzling display** of fireworks. 夜会は華やかな花火で幕を閉じた
▷ It was a **fine display** of Irish traditional music. アイルランドの伝統的な音楽が披露された

on	display	展示されて

▷ Over 300 works are **on display**. 300点を超える作品が展示されている

display /displéi/

動 陳列する,展示する;表示する

clearly	display	目立つように展示する
prominently	display	
proudly	display	自慢げに展示する
automatically	display	自動表示する

▷It is very important that prices are **clearly displayed**. 値段をわかりやすく表示するのがとても大事だ
▷Andrew **proudly displayed** his collection of medals. アンドルーはメダルのコレクションを誇らしげに飾っていた
▷We use a CD player that **automatically displays** the song title and artist. 曲名やアーティスト名を自動的に表示するＣＤプレイヤーを使っている

dispute /dispjúːt/

名 論争;紛争, ごたごた, 争議

cause	a dispute	紛争を引き起こす
lead to	a dispute	紛争につながる
spark	a dispute	紛争の発端となる
have	a dispute	紛争を抱えている
resolve	a dispute	紛争を解決する
settle	a dispute	
solve	a dispute	
avoid	a dispute	紛争を避ける

▷We **had** a **dispute** over this issue. この件でごたごたした
▷I have done everything I can to **resolve** this **dispute**. この紛争を解決するためにできる限りのことをした

a bitter	dispute	激しい紛争
an international	dispute	国際紛争
a domestic	dispute	家庭争議
a family	dispute	
an industrial	dispute	労働争議
a labor	dispute	
a territorial	dispute	領土を巡る紛争
a trade	dispute	貿易紛争

▷A **bitter dispute** over who owned the land is to be decided by a court. 土地の所有権を巡る激しい紛争は裁判所で決定を見る予定だ
▷We want to believe that all **international disputes** can be resolved amicably. すべての国際紛争は平和的に解決できると信じたい
▷I don't wish to be involved in a **domestic dispute**. 家庭争議に巻き込まれるのはいやだ
▷Japan and Russia confirmed that the **territorial dispute** between them involves all four islands. 日本とロシアは両国の領土問題は4島すべてを含むことを確認した

a dispute	between A	Aの間の紛争
a dispute	over A	Aを巡る紛争
a dispute	about A	
a dispute	with A	Aとの紛争
beyond	dispute	議論の余地なく
in	dispute	紛争中で

▷Gaps in historical perception have been a source of **dispute between** Japan and South Korea. 歴史認識のずれが日本と韓国のいざこざのもとになってきた
▷I never had a **dispute with** Mr. Brown. ブラウンさんといざこざになったことはない
▷The workers are **in dispute** over unpaid wages dating back for six months. 労働者たちは半年さかのぼっての未払い賃金について紛争中だ

distance /dístəns/ **名** 距離, 道のり;遠距離

walk	distances	距離を歩く
drive	distances	距離を車で行く
travel	distances	距離を移動する
cover	the distance	距離を行く
keep	a distance	距離を保つ
measure	the distance	距離を測る

▷Many people **travel** long **distances** to work. 長距離通勤をしている人が多い
▷**Keep** a safe **distance** between you and the car in front of you. 前の車と安全な車間距離を保ちなさい
▷He **measured** the **distance** with a tape measure. 彼は巻き尺で距離を測った

a long	distance	長い距離
a great	distance	
a considerable	distance	
a short	distance	短い距離
a safe	distance	安全な距離
a far	distance	はるか遠く

▷I'm accustomed to walking **long distances**. 長い距離を歩くのには慣れている
▷I walked the **short distance** to his house. 彼の家まで少しの距離を歩いた
▷In the **far distance**, there seemed to be smoke rising into the air. ずっと向こうの方で煙が上がっているように見えた

at	a distance	距離を置いて
from	a distance	遠くから
in	the distance	遠方に, かなたに

▷**From** a **distance** the tsunami wave didn't seem so big. 遠目には津波はそれほど大きくは見えなかった
▷Sirens could be heard **in** the **distance**. 遠くでサイレンが聞こえた

| within walking | distance | 歩いて行ける距離に |

★walking のほかに driving (車で行ける), hailing (呼べば聞こえる)などがくる

▷The apartment is located **within** easy **walking distance** *of* the university. そのアパートは大学から楽に歩いて行ける所にある

distant /dístənt/ 形 遠い

extremely	distant	とても遠い
increasingly	distant	ますます遠い
relatively	distant	比較的遠い

▷I don't have much contact with Tim now. We've become **increasingly distant**. ティムといまはあまり連絡をとっていない。ますます距離ができてしまった

distinction /distíŋkʃən/

名 区別, 相違点；栄誉

make	a distinction	区別する
draw	a distinction	
gain	the distinction	栄誉を得る

▷Dogs **make** a **distinction** between their owners and other people. 犬は飼い主と他の人を区別する

an important	distinction	重要な区別
a clear	distinction	明確な区別
a sharp	distinction	
a great	distinction	大きな名誉

▷There's no longer a **clear distinction** between the original and the copy. オリジナルとコピーの明確な違いはもはやない
▷There's an **important distinction** between speech and actions. 発言と行動することとの間には大きな違いがある

| with | distinction | 優秀な成績で |
| without | distinction of A | Aの別なく |

▷Susan passed the exam **with distinction**. スーザンは優秀な成績で試験に合格した
▷We should consider the candidates equally **without distinction of** color, sex or age. 肌の色, 性別, 年齢の別なく平等に候補者を見るべきだ

distinguish /distíŋgwiʃ/

動 区別する, 見分ける

clearly	distinguish	明確に区別する
carefully	distinguish	注意深く区別する
easily	distinguish	簡単に区別する
readily	distinguish	

★clearly は動詞の後でも用いる

▷I think it's important that the two aims are **clearly distinguished**. その2つのねらいをはっきり区別するのが大事だと思う

| distinguish | A from B | AとBを区別する |
| distinguish | between A | Aの間を区別する |

▷He has lost his ability to **distinguish** right **from** wrong. 彼は善悪の区別がつかなくなった

distribute /distríbju:t/

動 分配する, 配る；分布させる

be equally	distributed	平等に配られる
be widely	distributed	広く配られる；広く分布する
be evenly	distributed	均等に分布する
be uniformly	distributed	
be unevenly	distributed	不均等に分布する

▷The money was **equally distributed**. その金は平等に分けられた
▷This beetle is **widely distributed** throughout the eastern United States. このカブトムシは米国東部に広く分布している
▷Internet technology is not **evenly distributed** around the world. インターネット技術は国によって浸透の度合いが異なる

| distribute | A among B | AをB(人)に配る |
| distribute | A to B | |

▷Hot soup was **distributed among** homeless people. 熱いスープがホームレスの人々に配られた

distribution /distrəbjú:ʃən/

名 配布, 分配；流通；分布

have	a distribution	分布している
show	the distribution	分布を示す
control	the distribution	流通を管理する

▷Table 1 **shows** the geographic **distribution** *of*

manufacturing in Indonesia. 表1はインドネシアにおける製造業の地理的な分布を示している
▷ Who will **control** the **distribution** of the information? だれが情報配信を管理するのか

equitable	distribution	公平な分配
equal	distribution	平等な分配
unequal	distribution	不平等な分配
a wide	distribution	幅広い分布
geographical	distribution	地理的分布

▷ To avoid future wars, he recommended more **equitable distribution** *of* the world's resources. 将来の戦争を避けるために彼は世界の資源をより公平に分配するよう提案した
▷ Socialism doesn't mean the **equal distribution** *of* wealth. 社会主義だからと言って富が平等に配分されるわけではない

district /dístrikt/ 名 地区, 地域; 区域

a local	district	地方
a metropolitan	district	首都圏
a rural	district	農村地域, 田舎
an urban	district	市街地
a business	district	ビジネス街
a financial	district	金融街
a residential	district	住宅街

▷ Bradford is one of the largest **metropolitan districts** in the country. ブラッドフォードは国で最大の大都市圏の一つだ
▷ The population of **rural districts** has grown by 12% since 1981. 農村地域の人口が1981年以来12パーセント増えた

divide /diváid/ 動 分ける, 分割する

be evenly	divided	均等に分けられた
be equally	divided	平等に分配された
be deeply	divided	激しく意見が分かれた
be sharply	divided	
be bitterly	divided	

▷ The population is **equally divided** between Christians and Muslims. その地の人口はキリスト教徒とイスラム教徒が半々ずつだ
▷ The question of whether or not to join the EU **deeply divided** the country. 欧州連合に加盟するかどうかで国が大きく割れた
▷ Opinions are **sharply divided** on this issue. この件では意見が大きく割れている

divide	into A	Aに分かれる
divide	A between B	AをBの間で分配する
divide	A among B	

▷ Let's **divide into** two groups. 2つのグループに分かれよう
▷ The food was **divided among** those most in need. 食糧は最も困窮している人々で分けられた

be divided	over A	Aについて意見が分かれる
be divided	about A	

▷ The committee were **divided over** who should be appointed chairperson. だれを議長に任命するかで委員会は意見が分かれた

division /divíʒən/ 名 分割; 分裂, 不一致

a deep	division	深刻な分裂
an internal	division	内部分裂

▷ The **internal divisions** among the unions will make it difficult to solve the problem. 労働組合の内部分裂が問題の解決を難しくするだろう

division	of A into B	AのBへの分裂
division(s)	between A	Aの間の分裂
division(s)	within A	A内部の分裂

▷ The Czech Republic was born following the **division of** Czechoslovakia **into** two nations in 1993. チェコ共和国は1993年にチェコスロバキアが2国に分離して生まれた
▷ There were deep **divisions within** the Labour Party. 労働党内に深い対立があった

doctor /dáktər | dɔ́k-/ 名 医者, 医師; 博士

call	a doctor	医者を呼ぶ
get	a doctor	
send for	a doctor	医者を呼びにやる
see	a doctor	医者に診てもらう
go to	a doctor	
consult	a doctor	

▷ Quick! **Get** a **doctor**! 早く。お医者さんを呼んで
▷ Please **send for** a **doctor**! だれか人をやってお医者さんを連れてきて
▷ Do you think I should go and **see** a **doctor**? 医者に行って診てもらったほうがいいかな
▷ If your pain lasts longer than a week, **consult** your **doctor**. 痛みが1週間以上続くようなら医者に診てもらいなさい

a local	doctor	地元の医者
a family	doctor	かかりつけの医者

document /dάkjumənt | dɔ́k-/

名 文書, 書類

draft	a document	文書を起草する
draw up	a document	文書を作成する
produce	a document	文書を提示する
sign	a document	文書に署名する

▷She **drew up** the documents and submitted them to the court. 彼女は文書を作成して裁判所に提出した
▷Please **sign** this **document** right here. 文書のここに署名をお願いします

a confidential	document	機密文書
a classified	document	
a private	document	私文書
an internal	document	内部文書
a forged	document	偽造文書
a legal	document	法律文書
an official	document	正式文書

▷This **confidential document** includes highly sensitive information. その機密文書にはきわめて微妙な情報が含まれている
▷Davis is expected to produce more **legal documents** in court. デイビスはさらに法律文書を法廷に提出するものと見られる

dog /dɔ́:g | dɔ́g/ 名 犬

have	a dog	犬を飼っている
train	a dog	犬を訓練する
feed	a dog	犬にえさをやる
walk	a dog	犬を散歩させる
pet	a dog	犬をなでる

▷Do you **have** a **dog**? 犬を飼っていますか(★ペットとして飼う場合は have がふつう. keep は「(家畜を)飼育する」の意に用いる)
▷Don't forget to **feed** the **dog**. 忘れずに犬にえさをやってね
▷I always **walk** the **dog** late at night. いつも夜遅く愛犬を散歩させます
▷Don't **pet** a **dog** without letting it smell you. 犬をなでるときはまずにおいをかがせなさい

a dog	barks	犬がほえる

▷The **dog barked** furiously. その犬は激しくほえた

a domestic	dog	飼い犬
a stray	dog	野良犬
a faithful	dog	忠犬
a hunting	dog	猟犬
a guide	dog	盲導犬
a police	dog	警察犬
a rescue	dog	救助犬

▷Stay away from **stray dogs**. 野良犬に近づくな
▷Bill was like a **faithful dog**. ビルはまるで忠犬のようにおとなしかった

a dog	on a leash	つながれた犬

▷Harry held the **dog** closely **on the leash**. ハリーは犬をしっかりつないだ

PHRASES
It's a dog's life. ☺ 惨めな生活だよ
That's a good dog. ☺ いい子だ ▷Sit! Sit! I said SIT!!! That's a good dog! お座り. お座り. お座りって言ってるだろ. よし, いい子だ

doll /dάl | dɔ́l/ 名 人形

play with	a doll	人形で遊ぶ

▷I never **played with dolls** during my childhood. 子どものころ人形遊びをしたことがなかった

a rag	doll	ぬいぐるみの人形
a mechanical	doll	機械仕掛けの人形

▷She nodded like a **mechanical doll**. 彼女は機械仕掛けの人形のようにうなずいた

dollar /dάlər | dɔ́lə/ 名 ドル

the U.S.	dollar	米ドル
the Canadian	dollar	カナダドル
a strong	dollar	強いドル
a weak	dollar	弱いドル

▷The **strong dollar** made U.S. products particularly expensive. ドル高で米国製品が特に高価になった
▷A **weak dollar** isn't bad news for everyone. ドル安でみんながみんな困るわけではない

cost	five dollars	5ドルかかる
pay	ten dollars	10ドル払う

▷The cheapest meal here **costs** twenty **dollars**. ここでいちばん安い食事は20ドルだ

dominant /dάmənənt | dɔ́m-/

形 優勢な,支配的な

increasingly	dominant	ますます優勢な
economically	dominant	経済的に優勢な
politically	dominant	政治的に優勢な

▷China will play an **increasingly dominant** role in future political developments. 中国は将来の政治の動きにますます大きな役割を果たすだろう

door /dɔ́:r/ 名 ドア,戸

open	the door	ドアを開ける
close	the door	ドアを閉める
shut	the door	
bang	the door	ドアをバタンと閉める
slam	the door	
lock	the door	ドアの鍵をかける
unlock	the door	ドアの鍵を開ける
leave	the door open	ドアを開けたままにする
keep	the door open	
knock on	the door	ドアをノックする
knock at	the door	
answer	the door	玄関に出る
get	the door	

▷Alex, it's me. **Open** the **door**. アレックス,ぼくだけど.ドアを開けて
▷He quickly **closed** the **door** behind him. 彼は部屋に入ったあと,急いでドアを閉めた
▷She rushed out of the room, **banging** the **door** behind her. 彼女はバタンと音を立ててドアを閉めて,部屋の外へ駆け出した
▷Don't forget to keep the **door locked**! ドアに鍵をかけておくのを忘れないで
▷Can you leave the **door unlocked** in case I'm very late? 帰りがひどく遅くなるかもしれないから,ドアに鍵をかけないでおいてくれるかな
▷I **knocked on** the **door** lightly. 軽くドアをノックした
▷"Michael, could you **answer** the **door**?" "Yes, I've got it." 「マイケル,玄関に出てくれませんか」「わかりました」

live	next door to A	Aの隣に住む

▷I **lived next door to** your sister in New York. 私はニューヨークであなたの妹さんの隣に住んでいた

an open	door	開いたドア
a closed	door	閉まったドア
the front	door	正面玄関
the back	door	裏口
double	doors	両開きのドア
a sliding	door	引き戸
the car	door	車のドア
the driver's	door	運転手席側ドア
the passenger	door	助手席側ドア
the rear	door	後部ドア

▷He heard the **front door** open. 彼は玄関のドアが開く音を聞いた
▷Can you get the **back door** open for me? 裏口の戸を開けてもらえませんか
▷She slammed the **sliding door** with a bang. 彼女は引き戸をバタンと閉めた

the door	leads to A	ドアはAに通じている

▷The **door** on the right **leads to** the kitchen. 右側のドアは台所へ通じている

at	the door	戸口に,玄関に
through	the door	ドアを通って

▷Annie walked in **through** the **door**. アニーはドアから入って来た

doubt /dáut/ 名 疑い,疑念,疑問

raise	doubts	疑念を呼ぶ
have	doubts	疑念がある
express	doubts	疑念を表明する
cast	doubt(s)	疑念を投げかける
throw	doubt(s)	

▷Some people **express doubts** about U.S. military strategy. アメリカの軍事政策に疑念を表明する人もいる
▷A close investigation **threw doubt** *on* the results of the experiment. 綿密な調査によって実験の結果に疑問が投げかけられた

grave	doubt(s)	重大な疑念
serious	doubt(s)	

▷I still have **grave doubts** about the reporting. その報告になお強い疑念がある
▷I have **serious doubts** about my future. 自分の将来に重大な懸念を抱いている

have	no doubt	まったく疑わない
have	little doubt	ほとんど疑わない

▷I have **little doubt** that the venture will be successful. その事業はまず間違いなく成功するだろう

there is	no doubt that...	…は確実だ
there is	little doubt that...	…はほぼ確実だ

▷**There is no doubt that** TV is a very powerful medium. テレビがきわめて有力なメディアであることは疑いようがない

beyond	(any) doubt	疑いもなく,確かに
without	(a) doubt	確かに
in	doubt	疑って;不確かで

▷She couldn't wait to prove **beyond any doubt** that her love was real. 彼女はすぐにでも自分の愛情が本物だとはっきり示したかった
▷Angus! You are **without doubt** the most handsome man in all the world. アンガス,あなたほど顔立ちがきりっとした人は世界中を探しても絶対いないわ
▷When **in doubt**, ask questions. 疑問があれば質問してください

doubt /dáut/ 動 疑う

seriously	doubt	真剣に疑う

▷I **seriously doubt** that what you're saying is true. あなたが言っていることが本当だとはとても思えない

doubt	(that)...	…ではないと思う
doubt	if	…かどうか疑問に思う
doubt	whether	

▷I **doubt that** anybody will believe him. だれも彼を信じないと思う
▷I **doubt if** she can understand me. 彼女にわかってもらえるか疑わしい
PHRASES
I doubt it. 😀 そうは思わない

doubtful /dáutfəl/ 形 疑わしい;疑っている

extremely	doubtful	非常に疑わしい;とても疑っている

▷James is **extremely doubtful** that this is a good idea. ジェイムズにはこれはよい考えだとはとても思えない

it is doubtful	(that)...	…は疑わしい
it is doubtful	whether	…かどうか疑わしい
it is doubtful	if	

▷**It is doubtful that** he will change his mind. 彼が決心を変えることはまずなさそうだ
▷**It is doubtful whether** they will be successful. 彼らが成功するかどうか疑わしい

doubtful	about A	Aについて疑っている

▷Jeff seems to be **doubtful about** how to handle the situation. ジェフはその状況をどう扱ってよいか迷っているようだ

draw /drɔ́ː/ 動 線を引く,描く;引く

draw	beautifully	きれいに描く
draw	well	うまく描く

▷The landscape was **beautifully drawn** in pen and ink. その風景はペンとインクできれいに描かれていた

draw	A from B	AをBから取り出す

▷It took hours to **draw** enough water **from** the well. 井戸から十分な水をくみ出すのに何時間もかかった

dream /dríːm/ 名 夢

have	a dream	夢を見る
wake from	a dream	夢から覚める
awake from	a dream	
fulfill	one's dream	夢を実現する
realize	one's dream	

★「夢を見る」は ˣsee a dream とはいわない

▷I **had** a terrible **dream** last night. 昨夜怖い夢を見た
▷He **awoke from** the **dream** screaming "Help." 夢から目覚めたとき彼は「助けて」と叫んでいた
▷You've got a chance to **fulfill** your **dreams**. きみの夢を実現するチャンスだ
▷Finally I've **realized** my **dream**! ついに夢を実現したぞ

one's dream	comes true	夢がかなう

▷She wanted to be famous and her **dream came true**. 彼女は有名になりたかったが,その夢がかなった(★a dream come true で「かなった長年の夢」の意にもなる.この come は過去分詞)

a bad	dream	悪夢,怖い夢
a terrible	dream	
a strange	dream	不思議な夢
a weird	dream	奇妙な夢
a vivid	dream	鮮明な夢
a recurring	dream	繰り返し見る夢
a lifelong	dream	長年の夢
an impossible	dream	実現不可能な夢
the American	Dream	アメリカンドリーム

▷It seemed to be an **impossible dream**. それはかな

| dress |

わぬ夢のように思えた
▷I woke up from a really **vivid dream** and was thinking about it all morning. すごく鮮やかな夢から覚めて，午前中ずっとそのことを考えていた

| in | a dream | 夢の中で |
| like | a dream | 夢のように |

▷It all seemed **like a dream** to her. 彼女にとってすべては夢のようだった

PHRASES
Sweet dreams. よい夢を(★寝る前の子どもにいう) ▷Good night. Sweet dreams. お休みなさい．いい夢を見てね

dress /drés/

名 婦人服，ドレス(★ふつうワンピース)；衣服，服装

wear	a dress	ドレスを着ている
put on	a dress	ドレスを着る
take off	a dress	ドレスを脱ぐ
try on	a dress	ドレスを試着する

▷"We're going to a nice restaurant." "Do I have to **wear a dress**?" 「出かけるのはすてきなレストランだよ」「ドレスを着なくちゃだめかな」
▷She **put on a dress** and some perfume. 彼女はドレスを着て香水をつけた
▷Jane **took** the **dress off**, hanging it in her closet. ジェインはドレスを脱いでクロゼットにかけた
▷Kathy, **try on** the **dress**. If you like it, I'll buy it for you. キャシー，そのドレスを試着してごらん．気に入ったら買ってあげるよ

a long	dress	ロングドレス
a tight	dress	ぴったりしたドレス
a wedding	dress	ウエディングドレス
(a) formal	dress	正装
full	dress	
evening	dress	夜会服

▷She was dressed in a long black **tight dress**. 彼女は丈の長い，ぴったりした黒のドレスを着ていた
▷We went to the concert in **full dress**. コンサートに正装で出かけた

| in | a dress | ドレスを着て |

▷You'd look so beautiful **in a dress**! ドレスを着るとあなたってほんとにきれい

dress /drés/ 動 服を着る，服を着せる

| get | dressed | 服を着る |

▷Why do girls take so long to **get dressed**? 女の子は服を着るのになぜそう時間がかかるんだ

be elegantly	dressed	上品な服を着た
be neatly	dressed	きちんとした服を着た
be smartly	dressed	
be casually	dressed	カジュアルな服を着た
dress	quickly	さっと服を着る

★casually は dressed の後にもくる

▷The students are all **neatly dressed** in school uniforms. 生徒たちはみなきちんと制服を着ている
▷He was tall and **smartly dressed**. 彼は背が高く，おしゃれな格好をしていた
▷Tom is **dressed casually**, in jeans and T-shirt. トムはジーンズとTシャツでカジュアルな服装をしている
▷I got out of bed and **dressed quickly**. ベッドから出てすばやく服を着た

| dressed | in A | Aを着た |

▷Gary was handsome and was **dressed in** a suit. ギャリーはきりっとした顔立ちで，スーツを着ていた

drink /dríŋk/

名 飲み物，1杯；アルコール飲料，酒

have	a drink	飲み物を飲む；酒を
take	a drink	飲む
go (out) for	a drink	酒を飲みに行く
buy A	a drink	Aに酒をおごる
get	a drink	飲み物を持ってきてあげる；酒を飲む
order	a drink	飲み物を注文する
drive A to	drink	A(人)を酒に走らせる

▷Could I **have a drink** of water, please? 水を1杯いただけますか
▷David **took a drink** of wine. デイビッドはワインをひと口飲んだ
▷Do you want to **go out for a drink** after work? 仕事が終わったら飲みに行くかい
▷Let me **buy** you a **drink**. 1杯おごらせてください

a cold	drink	冷たい飲み物
a hot	drink	熱い飲み物
a non-alcoholic	drink	ノンアルコール飲料
a soft	drink	
an alcoholic	drink	アルコール飲料
a strong	drink	強い酒
a stiff	drink	

▷Would you like some coffee or a **soft drink**? コー

ヒーかノンアルコール飲料はいかがですか
▷I don't drink **alcoholic drinks**. アルコール類は飲みません
▷I can't take **strong drink**: it upsets my stomach. 強い酒は飲めません．胃がむかむかするので

food and drink	飲食物

▷There was lots of **food and drink** at the party. パーティーではたくさんの飲食物が出た

drink /drínk/ 動 飲む；酒を飲む

drink	deeply	ぐっと飲む
drink	down	飲み干す
drink	up	
drink	heavily	大酒を飲む
drink	too much	酒を飲みすぎる

▷He was very thirsty and **drank deeply** from the beer glass. 彼はすごくのどがかわいていたのでビールのグラスをぐっと空けた
▷Anne **drank down** the rest of her coffee. アンは残りのコーヒーを飲み干した
▷Now, **drink up**! さあぐっと空けて
▷I started **drinking heavily** about four years ago. 4年ほど前から大酒を飲むようになった
▷I feel like I **drank too much** last night. 昨夜は飲みすぎたようだ

drink and drive	飲酒運転する
eat and drink	飲食する

▷Don't **drink and drive**! 飲んだら運転するな
▷I shouldn't **eat and drink** so much. 食事も酒も控えめにしないと(★日本語「飲食」と語順が異なる)

something to drink	何か飲むもの

▷Would you like **something to drink**? 何か飲み物はいかがですか

drink	oneself C	酒を飲んでCの状態になる

★Cは unconscious, silly など

▷He **drank** himself unconscious. 彼は酒を飲んで意識がなくなった
PHRASES
I'll drink to that. ☺ 賛成だ，そのとおりだ
What would you like to drink? ☺ 何をお飲みになりますか

drive /dráiv/ 名 ドライブ；精力，やる気

go for	a drive	ドライブに行く
take	a drive	
have	the drive	やる気がある
lack	the drive	やる気に欠ける

▷Why don't you **go for** a **drive**? ドライブに行かないか
▷Do you want to **take** a **drive** with me? いっしょにドライブに行かないか
▷You **have** the **drive** and the passion, but is that enough to get a job? あなたには意欲と情熱はあるけれど，職を得るのにそれで十分だろうか

a... drive	from A	Aから車で…の移動
a... drive	to A	Aまで車で…の移動

▷Stanford is less than an hour's **drive from** San Francisco. スタンフォードはサンフランシスコから車で1時間かからない

drive and determination	やる気と決意

▷We require qualified people with **drive and determination**. 資格があり，やる気と決意もある人を求めています

drive /dráiv/

動 運転する；車で送る；駆り立てる

drive	fast	高速で運転する
drive	slowly	ゆっくり運転する
drive	carefully	慎重に運転する
drive	safely	安全運転する
drive	around	あちこちドライブする
drive	away	車で走り去る
drive	off	
drive	back	車で帰る
drive	out	車で出かける
drive	A home	Aを車で家まで送る

▷Don't **drive** too **fast**! スピードを出しすぎちゃだめだよ
▷He **drove slowly** down the street. 彼は通りに沿ってゆっくり車を走らせた(★slowly は動詞の前でも用いる)
▷Please **drive carefully**. It looks like it's going to storm. 運転に気をつけてね，嵐になりそうだから
▷**Drive safely**. See you soon. 安全運転でね．また会いましょう
▷Let's **drive around** the town for a little bit. ちょっと街をドライブしよう
▷I could hear the car **driving off**. 車が走り去るのが聞こえた
▷She **drove back** to her apartment when she had finished her work. 仕事を終えると彼女は車でアパートに帰った

| driver |

▷We **drove out** to my grandmother's house for a big family dinner. 親族一同が集まる夕食会のために祖母の家まで車で出かけた
▷I'll **drive** you **home**. 家まで車で送るよ

drive	through A	Aを車で通り過ぎる
drive	to A	Aまで車で出かける
drive	A to B	Aを車でBまで送る

▷He **drove through** the police barrier without stopping. 彼は警察の検問を突っ切って走り抜けた
▷We **drove to** the coast. 海岸へ車で出かけた
▷I **drove** her **to** the hospital. 彼女を病院まで車で送って行った

drive	A to do	Aを…するよう駆り立てる

▷I wonder what **drove** him **to** marry her? 彼はなぜ彼女と結婚することにしたのかな

driver /dráivər/ 名 運転手, ドライバー

a careful	driver	慎重なドライバー
a good	driver	優良ドライバー
a drunken	driver	飲酒運転のドライバー
a hit-and-run	driver	ひき逃げのドライバー
a bus	driver	バスの運転手
a cab	driver	タクシー運転手
a taxi	driver	
a truck	driver	トラックの運転手
a train	driver	列車の運転手
a racing	driver	カーレーサー

▷Are you a **good driver**? あなたは運転がうまいの？
▷A **drunken driver** hit her. 飲酒運転のドライバーが彼女をはねた
▷Police are hunting a **hit-and-run driver**. 警察はひき逃げしたドライバーを捜索中だ

drop /dráp|drɔ́p/ 名 落ち込み, 落下

a big	drop	大幅な落ち込み
a sharp	drop	急落
a dramatic	drop	劇的な落ち込み

▷There was a **sharp drop** in temperature this morning and it snowed. けさ気温が急に下がって雪が降った

drop /dráp|drɔ́p/
動 下がる, 下げる；落とす, 落ちる；やめる

drop	dramatically	劇的に下がる
drop	sharply	急激に下がる
drop	slightly	やや下がる
suddenly	drop	急に下がる
accidentally	drop	うっかり落とす

▷Sales and profits **dropped dramatically** in 2007. 売上と利益は2007年に急激に下がった
▷The temperature has **dropped sharply**. 温度が急に下がった

drug /drʌ́g/ 名 麻薬, 覚せい剤；薬

take	drugs	麻薬をやる
use	drugs	
be on	drugs	麻薬をやっている
inject	drugs	麻薬を打つ
smuggle	drugs	麻薬を密輸する
prescribe	drugs	薬を処方する

▷How do you feel when you **take drugs**? 麻薬をやるとどんな感じがしますか
▷Tony had repeatedly **smuggled drugs** into the country. トニーはその国への麻薬密輸を繰り返した
▷We need to examine him first and then **prescribe drugs**. まず彼を検査してから薬を処方する必要があります

illegal	drugs	違法薬物
dangerous	drugs	危険な薬物
hard	drugs	中毒性の強い麻薬

▷Possession of **illegal drugs** may result in heavy fines. 違法薬物を所持していると重い罰金を科せられるおそれがある

dry /drái/ 形 乾いた, 乾燥した；雨が降らない

go	dry	のどが渇く

▷My mouth **went** completely **dry**. のどがからからに渇いた

completely	dry	すっかり乾いた
quite	dry	
mainly	dry	(気象情報で)おおむね
mostly	dry	乾燥した
reasonably	dry	かなり乾いた

▷The paint wasn't **quite dry**. ペンキは完全には乾いていなかった
▷Southern Scotland will be **mainly dry**. スコットランド南部はおおむね雨のない天気になるでしょう
▷It's **reasonably dry** weather at this time of the year. 一年のいまごろはかなり乾いた天候だ

dust /dΛ́st/ 图 ちり, ほこり; 粉末

collect	dust	ほこりをためる
gather	dust	
be covered in	dust	ほこりをかぶる
be covered with	dust	
raise	dust	ほこりを立てる
remove	dust	ほこりを払う

▷The books **gathered dust** for 60 years until they were recently discovered. 60年間ほこりをかぶっていたそれらの本は最近になって発見された
▷The floor was **covered in dust**. 床はほこりだらけだった
▷**Remove dust** periodically by brushing gently. 軽くブラシをかけて定期的にほこりを取り除いてください

the dust	settles	ほこりが収まる

★比喩的に「ごたごたが収まる」の意でも用いる

▷We'll talk about it when the **dust** has **settled**. ごたごたが収まったらその件について話そう

a cloud of	dust	巻き上がるほこり
a layer of	dust	積もったほこり

▷Her feet began kicking up **clouds of dust** as she ran. 彼女が走ると足もとからもうもうと砂ぼこりが巻き上がった
▷A thin **layer of dust** covered the pictures on the wall. 壁の絵にはうっすらほこりがたまっていた

duty /djúːti | djúː-/

图 義務; (duties で)任務, 職務; 税, 関税

have	a duty	義務がある
owe	a duty	義務を負う
do	one's duty	義務を果たす
fulfill	one's duty	
perform	a duty	義務を遂行する
neglect	one's duty	義務を怠る
impose	a duty	義務を負わせる
have	duties	任務がある
carry out	duties	任務を遂行する
perform	duties	
neglect	duties	任務を怠る
impose	duty	税を課す
pay	duty	税金を払う

▷We **had** a **duty** *to* protect him. 私たちには彼を守る義務があった
▷I have to **do** my **duty**. 自分の義務を果たさなければならない
▷You're **neglecting** your **duties** at work. あなたは仕事上の任務を怠っている
▷The President has recovered from his operation and is now able to **carry out** his official **duties**. 大統領は術後の回復が順調で, 現在は公務をこなせる状態だ

a legal	duty	法的責務
a public	duty	公的責務
a moral	duty	道徳的義務
official	duties	公務
customs	duties	関税
import	duty	輸入税

▷I think landlords have a **legal duty** to change locks after a tenant moves. 借家人が引っ越したら鍵を取り替える法的義務が家主にはあると思う
▷Finally at 11:00 p.m. her **official duties** came to an end. ようやく午後11時に彼女の公務が終わった

under	a duty	義務を負って
on	duty	勤務時間中に
off	duty	勤務時間外に

▷Parents are **under** a **duty** *to* their children to protect them. 両親は子どもを保護する義務を負っている
▷I tried to telephone him last night, but he was **on duty**. 昨晩, 彼と電話で話をしようとしたが, 勤務中で話ができなかった

a sense of	duty	義務感

▷He had a strong **sense of duty** to the community. 彼には共同体に対する強い義務感があった

it is the duty	of A to do	…するのはAの
it is A's duty	to do	義務だ

▷**It is** the **duty of** a newspaper **to** report all the facts. 事実をくまなく報道する責務が新聞にはある

E

eager /íːgər/ 形 熱望して, 切望して

only too	eager	すごく熱望して
really	eager	

▷ Julie was **only too eager** to end the conversation with her mother. ジュリーは母親との会話を終わらせたい気持ちでいっぱいだった

eager	to do	しきりに…したがって
eager	for A	Aを熱望して

▷ I was **eager to** see him again. ぜひ彼にまた会いたいと思った

ear /íər/ 名 耳; 聴覚

cover	one's ears	耳をふさぐ
close	one's ears	聞こうとしない
shut	one's ears	
strain	one's ears	耳を澄ます
prick up	one's ears	耳をぴんと立てる
pierce	one's ears	耳にピアスを入れる
clean	one's ear(s)	耳を掃除する
fill	A's ears	耳をつんざく
reach	A's ears	耳に届く
lend	an ear	耳を貸す
bend	A's ear	さんざん話を聞かせる
be all	ears	熱心に聞く

▷ He **covered** his **ears** with his hands. 彼は両手で両耳をふさいだ
▷ The government is **closing** its **ears** to what people really want. 政府は国民が何を望んでいるのかまったく聞こうとしていない
▷ Caroline **strained** her **ears** to hear what they were saying. キャロラインは彼らの話を聞こうと耳を澄ました
▷ I've never had my **ears pierced**. 耳にピアス用の穴を開けたことはない
▷ She's been **bending** my **ear** about her boyfriend for about three months now! 彼女のボーイフレンドの話をこの3か月聞かされっぱなしだ
▷ Tell me more! I'm **all ears**. もっと話して. ぜひ聞きたいです

one's ears	ring	耳鳴りがする
one's ears	prick (up)	耳がそばだつ

▷ After attending the rock concert my **ears** were **ringing**. ロックコンサートに行ったあと耳鳴りがしていた
▷ My **ears pricked up** when I heard my colleagues talking about me to the manager. 同僚たちが私のことを部長に話しているのを聞いて耳をそばだてた

the external	ear	外耳
the inner	ear	内耳
the middle	ear	中耳
a good	ear	いい耳
a sharp	ear	鋭い耳
a sympathetic	ear	親身に耳を傾ける人

▷ She always lends me a **sympathetic ear**. 彼女はいつも親身になって私の言うことを聞いてくれる

by	ear	譜面を見ずに, 暗譜で
in	A's ear	耳元で
an ear	for A	Aを聞き分ける力

▷ She played the piano **by ear**. 彼女は暗譜でピアノを弾いた
▷ She whispered "I love you!" **in** his **ear**. 「愛しているわ」と彼女は彼の耳元でささやいた
▷ She has a good **ear for** music. 彼女は音感がいい

PHRASES

A's **ears are burning**. うわさをされてAの耳がほてる
I couldn't believe my ears. ☺ 自分の耳を疑った
Open your ears. ☺ よく聞きなさい ▷ Open your ears and realize that I'm telling you the truth. よく聞くんだよ. 本当のことを言っているんだから

early /ə́ːrli/ 形 早い

slightly	early	少し早い
a little	early	
fairly	early	かなり早い
relatively	early	比較的早い

▷ His father died at a **relatively early** age. 彼の父親は比較的若くして亡くなった

be in	one's early thirties	30代前半だ

▷ She is **in** her **early** twenties. 彼女は20代前半です

earth /ə́ːrθ/ 名 地球; 大地, 土

the whole	earth	地球全体
the entire	earth	
Planet	Earth	惑星としての地球
Mother	Earth	母なる大地
the bare	earth	むき出しの地面
damp	earth	湿った土
the soft	earth	柔らかい土

▷The satellite can circle the **whole earth** in about one hour. 衛星は約1時間で地球を一周できる
▷There is nothing but **bare earth** in the garden. We haven't had any rain for three months. 3か月の間, 雨が降らず, 庭には草一本生えていない

| on | earth | 地球上に；この世に |

▷He must be the most selfish person **on earth**. 彼ほど自己中心的な人間はこの世にいない
◆**what on earth** いったい全体（★ほかに who, why, where, how などの疑問の強意や nothing, nowhere などの否定の強意に用いる） ▷What on earth are you doing here? いったいここで何をしているんだ

| the surface of | the earth | 地球の表面 |

▷Over the past century, the **surface of** the **earth** has warmed one degree. ここ1世紀の間に地表の温度は1度上昇した

earthquake /ə́:rθkwèik/ 名 地震

cause	an earthquake	地震を引き起こす
feel	an earthquake	地震を感じる
withstand	an earthquake	地震に耐える
predict	an earthquake	地震を予測する

▷If you **feel** an **earthquake** near the coast, you should head for the hills. 海岸近くで地震を感じたら高台に向かったほうがいい
▷We cannot accurately **predict earthquakes**. 地震は正確に予測できない

an earthquake	occurs	地震が起きる
an earthquake	strikes (A)	地震が(Aを)
an earthquake	hits (A)	襲う

▷A major **earthquake** has **struck** Tokyo about every 75 years for the past several centuries. 大地震が数世紀にわたり約75年おきに東京を襲っている

a major	earthquake	大地震
a great	earthquake	
a big	earthquake	
a massive	earthquake	巨大地震
a severe	earthquake	激しい地震
a powerful	earthquake	
a devastating	earthquake	
a minor	earthquake	小さな地震
a small	earthquake	

▷A couple of years ago we had a **big earthquake** in Istanbul. 2, 3年前イスタンブールで大きな地震があった
▷On 17 January1995 a **massive earthquake** hit Kobe killing over 6,000 people. 1995年1月17日, 巨大地震が神戸を襲い6千人以上が死亡した
▷San Francisco recovered from the **devastating earthquake**. サンフランシスコは壊滅的な被害をもたらした地震から復興した

| a magnitude 7.1 | earthquake | マグニチュード7.1の地震 |

★a 7.1 magnitude earthquake, an earthquake of magnitude 7.1, an earthquake with a magnitude of 7.1 などともいう

▷A **magnitude** 6.6 **earthquake** struck Bam in southeast Iran on December 26. マグニチュード6.6の地震が12月26日にイラン南東部のバムを襲った

ease /i:z/ 名 容易さ；気楽さ, 安楽

| with | ease | 容易に, たやすく |

★relative, comparative, apparent, consummate などの形容詞とともに用いることが多い

▷I found his home **with** relative **ease**. 彼の家は比較的簡単に見つかった

| at | ease | 気楽に, くつろいで |
| ill at | ease | 不安で, 落ち着かずに |

▷I feel **at ease** with him. 彼といっしょだと安心だ

easy /i:zi/ 形 楽な, やさしい；安楽な

get	easier	より楽になる
make A	easy	Aを簡単にする
find A	easy	Aを簡単だと思う

▷Life is **getting easier** by the day. 生活は日ごとに楽になりつつある
▷A large sink will **make** it **easier** for you to clean large pots and pans. 大きな流しだと大きな鍋釜類を洗うのがもっと楽だろう
▷She managed to pass the exam. But she didn't **find** it **easy**. 彼女は何とか試験に合格したが一苦労だった

fairly	easy	とても簡単な
quite	easy	
particularly	easy	特に簡単な
relatively	easy	比較的簡単な
surprisingly	easy	驚くほど簡単な
easy	enough	十分簡単な

▷It's **quite easy** to give examples. 例ならいくらでも

| eat |

挙げられる
▷Mexico City is **relatively easy** to explore. メキシコシティは見て回るのが比較的簡単だ
▷It was **easy enough** to understand what they wanted. 彼らが望んでいるのものを見抜くのはごく簡単だった

| easy | to do | 簡単に…できる |

▷His English was **easy to** understand. 彼の英語は理解しやすかった

| it is easy | (for A) to do | (Aが)…するのは簡単だ |

★so, too など強意の副詞とともによく用いる

▷**It's too easy to** say it's all Simon's fault. 全部サイモンのせいにするのはあんまり安易すぎる

PHRASES
I'm easy. ☺ どっちでもいいよ ▷"Do you want to leave now or stay a bit longer?" "I'm easy. Whatever you like."「もう出る？ それとももう少しいる？」「どっちでもいいよ，きみの好きなように」
That's easy. ☺ それなら簡単だよ
Take it easy! ☺ 気楽にやりなさい；じゃあまたね

eat /iːt/ 動 食べる，食事をする

eat	well	よく食べる
eat	healthily	健康によい食事をする
eat	properly	きちんと食事する
eat	quickly	早く食べる
eat	slowly	ゆっくり食べる
eat	regularly	規則正しい食事をする
eat	out	外食する
eat	up	残らず食べる

▷After his illness he **ate well** and put on weight. 病後彼はよく食べたので体重が増えた
▷He is sleeping well and is **eating properly**. 彼はよく寝て，きちんと食べている
▷Make sure you **eat regularly** and have healthy food. 規則正しい食事をし，健康によいものを食べるようにしなさい
▷I'm **eating out** with Emma tonight. 今夜はエマと外食する予定です
▷Here's breakfast. **Eat up!** ☺ さあ朝食です．残さず食べてね

something to	eat	食べ物
a bite to	eat	軽い食べ物
a place to	eat	食事する場所

▷Would you like **something to eat**? 何か食べ物はいかがですか

| eat | like a horse | 大食だ |
| eat | like a bird | 小食だ |

▷I'm so hungry I could **eat like** a **horse**. もう腹ペコでなんでも食べられちゃうよ

PHRASES
What's eating you? ☺ 何を悩んでいるの，何かあったのかい ▷Tell me what's eating you. Maybe I can help you. 何があったか言ってごらん．力になれるから

economical /èkənámikəl | -nóm-/

形 経済的な；節約できる

| extremely | economical | きわめて経済的な |
| highly | economical | |

▷This oil heater is **extremely economical**. この石油ストーブはとても経済的だ

| it is (more) economical | to do | …するのが(より)経済的だ |

▷**It's more economical to** rent a car than to buy one. 車を買うより借りたほうが経済的だ

economy /ikánəmi | ikɔ́n-/

名 経済，景気；節約

run	the economy	経済を動かす
develop	the economy	経済を発展させる
stimulate	the economy	経済を刺激する
revive	the economy	経済を再生する
control	the economy	景気の調整をする
boost	the economy	景気にてこ入れする
spur	the economy	
weaken	the economy	景気の足を引っ張る
stabilize	the economy	景気を安定させる
make	economies	節約する

▷Which party do you trust to **run** the **economy**? 経済運営を安心して任せられるのはどの党ですか
▷Hong Kong's most important challenge is to **develop** its **economy**. 香港の最重要課題は経済を発展させることだ
▷Tax cuts will **boost** the **economy**. 減税は景気のてこ入れになるだろう

the economy	booms	景気が好調だ
the economy	expands	景気が拡大する
the economy	grows	経済が成長する
the economy	shrinks	経済が縮小する

the economy	slows	景気が減速する
the economy	stabilizes	景気が安定する
the economy	recovers	景気が回復する
the economy	remains	景気は依然…だ

▷The **economy grew** by 4.5% in 2005. 2005年には4.5％の経済成長があった
▷The British **economy remains** rather weak. イギリス経済は依然かなり低迷している

a booming	economy	好景気
a bubble	economy	バブル経済
a capitalist	economy	資本主義経済
a market	economy	市場経済
the domestic	economy	国内経済
the global	economy	世界経済
the world	economy	
the international	economy	国際経済
the local	economy	地域経済
a major	economy	経済大国

▷China's role in the **global economy** has changed over the past twenty years. 世界経済における中国の役割はこの20年間で変化した
▷China and India are the world's fastest-growing **major economies**. 中国とインドは世界の経済大国の中で最も成長速度が速い

an economy	based on A	Aに基盤を置く経済

▷The UAE has an **economy based** on oil. アラブ首長国連邦の経済の主体は石油だ

edge /édʒ/ 名 端, へり, 縁；刃；優位

have	an edge	勝る, 優位にある

▷I'm sure we'll **have** an **edge** over the other teams. うちのチームが他チームより優位に立つと確信している

the outer	edge	外縁
the inner	edge	内縁
the top	edge	上端
the bottom	edge	下端
the southern	edge	南端
the western	edge	西端
the water's	edge	水辺
(a) competitive	edge	競争上の優位
the leading	edge	最先端
the cutting	edge	

▷The child suddenly fell over and hit his head against the **top edge** *of* the table. その子は急に転んでテーブルの上端に頭をぶつけた
▷We walked down to the **water's edge**. 水辺まで歩いて行った
▷How do we maintain our **competitive edge**? われわれはどのように競争力を維持するのか
▷Our company is at the **leading edge** *of* technology. 当社は科学技術の最先端にいる

on	the edge of A	Aの端に
at	the edge of A	

▷She was standing **on** the **edge of** a cliff looking down. 彼女は崖っぷちに立って下の方を見下ろしていた

edition /idíʃən/ 名 (刊行物の)版

print	an edition	版を印刷する
publish	an edition	版を出版する
release	an edition	版を発売する

▷About 500 copies of the first **edition** were **printed**. 初版で約500部が印刷された
▷Oxford University Press has **published** a paperback **edition** of his book. オックスフォード出版局は彼の本のペーパーバック版を出した

the first	edition	初版
the latest	edition	最新版
a new	edition	新版
the current	edition	現行版
a limited	edition	限定版
a special	edition	特別版
a hardback	edition	ハードバック版
a paperback	edition	ペーパーバック版
a pocket	edition	ポケット版
a revised	edition	改訂版
an electronic	edition	電子版
an online	edition	オンライン版
(the) morning	edition	朝刊
(the) evening	edition	夕刊
the Sunday	edition	日曜版
the May	edition	5月号

▷I bought the **latest edition** of the *New York Review of Books*. 『ニューヨーク・レビュー・オブ・ブックス』(書評誌)の最新版を買った
▷This **special edition** of the album is a must for collectors. このアルバムの特別版は収集家にはなくてはならないものだ
▷This is a **revised edition** of a book first published in 1985. これは1985年に出版された本の改訂版です
▷The full interview can be read in the **May edition** of the magazine out this Thursday. インタビュー全文は今週木曜日発売の雑誌の5月号で読める

educate /édʒukèit/ 動 教育する

educate	A at B	A(人)をB(大学)で教える
educate	A in B	A(人)にB(教科)を教える；A(人)をB(場所)で教える
educate	A about B	A(人)にBについて教える

▷ She was **educated at** the University of California. 彼女はカリフォルニア大学で教育を受けた
▷ Nick was born in Japan and **educated in** the U.S. ニックは日本で生まれ米国で教育を受けた
▷ We need to **educate** students **about** how to acquire the information they want to find. 求める情報をいかにして得るかを学生に教える必要がある

educate	A to do	…するようA(人)を教育する

▷ We constantly **educate** our people **to** use the latest technology. 社員に最新技術の使い方を絶えず教育している

educated /édʒukèitid/

形 教養のある, 教育のある

highly	educated	高い教育を受けた
well	educated	十分な教育を受けた

▷ He is a **highly educated** person with lots of experience. 彼は高い教育を受け, 経験も豊富だ

education /èdʒukéiʃən/ 名 教育

have	(an) education	教育を受ける
get	(an) education	
receive	(an) education	
provide	(an) education	教育を提供する
continue	one's education	教育を受け続ける
complete	one's education	学業を終える

▷ It is a good sign that many young people **get** their **education** abroad. 多くの若者が海外で教育を受けるのはよい兆候だ
▷ Government has an obligation to **provide** quality **education**. 政府には質の高い教育を提供する義務がある
▷ I want to **continue** my **education** at university. 大学での教育を受け続けたい
▷ After **completing** his **education** at university he worked in a bank. 彼は大学での課程を修了して銀行で働いた

compulsory	education	義務教育
elementary	education	初等教育
《英》primary	education	
secondary	education	中等教育
adult	education	成人教育
continuing	education	
further	education	
higher	education	高等教育
(a) university	education	大学教育
vocational	education	職業教育
sex	education	性教育

▷ **Elementary education** is a six-year program. 初等教育は6年制だ
▷ **Higher education** is no longer a guarantee for a job. 高等教育を受けたからといってもはや仕事に就ける保証はない

effect /ifékt/ 名 効果, 効力, 影響；結果

have	an effect	影響がある
produce	an effect	影響が出る
take	effect	効果を現す
show	the effect	影響を示す
assess	the effect	影響を評価する
examine	the effect	影響を検討する
study	the effect	
reduce	the effect	影響を減らす
come into	effect	施行される
bring A into	effect	Aを施行する
carry A into	effect	

▷ My words **had** no **effect** on him. 私のことばは彼に何の効き目もなかった
▷ World War I **produced** negative **effects** on Germany's economy. 第1次世界大戦はドイツ経済にマイナスの影響を生んだ
▷ The medicine should **take effect** soon. その薬はすぐ効くはずだ
▷ The economy is still **showing** the **effects** of the 2008 economic crisis. 経済にはいまも2008年の経済危機の影響が表れている
▷ The purpose of this research was to **assess** the **effects** of exercise and diet. 調査目的は運動とダイエットの効果を調べることだった
▷ The rules will **come into effect** on September 1. 諸規則は9月1日から実施される
▷ The law was **brought into effect** in 2006. その法律は2006年に施行された

a profound	effect	深刻な影響
an adverse	effect	悪影響
the opposite	effect	逆効果
a positive	effect	プラスの効果
a negative	effect	マイナスの効果
the desired	effect	所期の効果

a direct	effect	直接の影響
side	effects	副作用
the greenhouse	effect	温室効果
special	effects	特殊効果
sound	effects	音響効果
visual	effects	視覚効果

▷Dioxins have an **adverse effect** *on* wildlife. ダイオキシンは野生生物に悪影響を及ぼす
▷The doctor gave me some medicine to make me feel better, but it had the **opposite effect**. お医者さんから気分がよくなる薬をもらったけど逆効果だった
▷The raise in salary had a **positive effect** *on* everybody at work. 賃上げのおかげで職場の全員によい影響があった
▷That email had the **desired effect**. そのEメールにはねらいどおりの効果があった
▷The movie uses **special effects** successfully. その映画は特殊効果をうまく使っている

in	effect	実際には；有効で
to	this effect	こういった趣旨の
to	that effect	そういった趣旨の
to	the effect that...	…といった趣旨の

▷A fire warning is **in effect** for parts of Montana and Idaho tonight. 火災注意報が今夜モンタナとアイダホの一部に出ている
▷She said, "I'm sorry, I can't help it," or words **to that effect**. 「ごめんなさい，私にはどうしようもないの」とか何とかいう意味のことを彼女は言った

effective /iféktiv/ 形 効果的な，有効な

extremely	effective	とても効果的な
highly	effective	きわめて効果的な
particularly	effective	特に効果的な

▷This vaccine is **highly effective** *in* preventing the illness. このワクチンは病気予防に非常に効果的だ

efficient /ifíʃənt/ 形 効率的な；有能な

extremely	efficient	非常に効率的な；非常に有能な
highly	efficient	きわめて効率的な；きわめて有能な

▷Our new boss is **extremely efficient**. 新しい上司は非常に有能な人だ

efficient and economical	効率的かつ経済的な

▷It is the duty of water companies to maintain an **efficient and economical** supply of water. 水の効率的かつ経済的な供給を維持することが水道会社の義務だ

effort /éfərt/ 名 努力，奮闘

make	an effort	努力する
require	effort	努力を必要とする
take	effort	
put in	an effort	努力を注ぐ
spare	no effort	努力を惜しまない
continue	one's efforts	努力を続ける
concentrate	one's effort(s)	努力を集中する

▷They **make** no **effort** to change their way. 彼らは自分の流儀をまったく変えようとしない
▷Physical fitness always **requires effort**. 体の健康のためには常に努力する必要がある
▷You must **concentrate** your **efforts** on improving your English. 英語の上達に全力を集中しなさい

one's best	effort(s)	最大の努力
considerable	effort(s)	多大な努力
a great	effort	
a special	effort	特別な努力
an extra	effort	格別の努力
a determined	effort	懸命な努力
a strenuous	effort	
a concerted	effort	協調行動，力を合わせること
a joint	effort	
a conscious	effort	意識的な努力
a deliberate	effort	
physical	effort	身体的努力
mental	effort	精神的努力

▷Despite my **best efforts**, I was completely ignored. 最大限努力したのに，私はまったく無視された
▷All the museums have put **considerable effort** into providing interesting displays. どの博物館も人の興味を引く展示ができるよう多大な努力を払っている
▷Despite **strenuous efforts**, he only came sixth in the marathon. 彼はすごくがんばったがマラソンで6位がやっとだった
▷The project is a **joint effort** between Japan and Russia. その計画は日露の協同事業だ

with	(an) effort	努力して，なんとか
without	(an) effort	努力せず，楽々と
despite	A's efforts	努力にもかかわらず
in	an effort to do	…しようと努力して

▷**With effort**, Ben controlled his temper. なんとかベンは平静を保った(★ effort に great, much, some, little, no をつけて程度を示すことが多い：**With great effort** he tried to stand. どうにかして彼は耐えようとした)

| egg |

▷He was a genius. He passed all his exams **without effort**. 彼は天才で、どの試験も楽々と合格した
▷Sadly, **despite** all the **efforts** of the medical team, Peter died. 残念ながら医療チームの努力のかいもなく、ピーターは亡くなった
▷He shook his head **in an effort to** clear his head. 頭をすっきりさせようと彼は頭を振った

egg /ég/ 名 卵；(生物の)卵(ら)

lay	an egg	卵を産む
produce	an egg	
hatch	an egg	卵をかえす
boil	an egg	卵をゆでる
break	an egg	卵を割る
beat	an egg	卵をかき混ぜる
whisk	an egg	卵を泡立てる

▷Did you know that penguins **lay eggs**? ペンギンは卵を産むと知っていましたか
▷The mother duck **hatched** her **eggs**. お母さんアヒルは卵をかえしました
▷**Beat eggs** lightly in large bowl. 大きなボウルで卵を軽くかき混ぜてください
▷**Whisk eggs** with milk and cream. 卵を牛乳とクリームで泡立ててください

a fresh	egg	新鮮な卵
a rotten	egg	腐った卵
a boiled	egg	ゆで卵
a fried	egg	フライドエッグ
a poached	egg	ポーチドエッグ
a scrambled	egg	スクランブルエッグ
a beaten	egg	とき卵
an Easter	egg	イースターエッグ
a fertilized	egg	受精卵

▷There is a smell like **rotten eggs**. 腐った卵のにおいがする
▷I'll have sausage, bacon, tomato and **fried egg** please. ソーセージ、ベーコン、トマトとフライドエッグをください

election /ilékʃən/ 名 選挙

hold	an election	選挙を行う
have	an election	
call	an election	選挙の実施を決める
fight	an election	選挙を戦う
contest	an election	
run for	election	選挙に立候補する
(英) stand for	election	

lose	an election	選挙に負ける
win	an election	選挙に勝つ

▷South Africa **held** its first democratic **elections** in 1994. 南アフリカ共和国は1994年に史上初の民主的選挙を行った
▷The Prime Minister will **call** a general **election** by September. 首相は9月までに総選挙の実施を決めるだろう
▷Labour candidates **fought** the **election** successfully. 労働党の候補者たちは選挙を戦って勝った

a free	election	自由選挙
a local	election	地方選挙
a national	election	全国選挙
a general	election	総選挙
a parliamentary	election	議会選挙
a presidential	election	大統領選挙

▷The first **free elections** in Iraq took place on January 1st, 1995. イラクの最初の自由選挙が1995年1月1日に行われた
▷The US **presidential elections** are held every four years. 米国大統領選挙は4年ごとに行われる

electricity /ilektrísəti/ 名 電気, 電力

generate	electricity	発電する, 電気を起こす
produce	electricity	
provide	electricity	電気を供給する
supply	electricity	
conduct	electricity	電気を伝える
use	electricity	電気を使う

▷Solar panels on the roof **generate electricity**. 屋根のソーラーパネルで発電ができる
▷The company **provides electricity** to 2.3 million homes. その会社は230万の家庭に電力を供給している
▷Metal **conducts electricity**. 金属は電気を通す

static	electricity	静電気

▷His T-shirt crackled with **static electricity** as he pulled it over his head. 彼がTシャツを頭から脱ぐとき静電気でぱちぱち音がした

demand for	electricity	電力需要

▷**Demand for electricity** exceeds supply. 電力需要が供給を上回っている

element /éləmənt/ 名 要素, 成分

contain	an element	要素を含む

include	an element	
involve	an element	
combine	elements	要素を組み合わせる
introduce	an element	要素を導入する

▷The movie **contains elements** of satire. この映画には風刺の要素が含まれている
▷Skiing always **involves** an **element** of danger. スキーは常に危険な要素をはらんでいる
▷Hitchcock always **introduced** an **element** of suspense into his movies. ヒッチコックは映画にサスペンスの要素をいつも導入した

a basic	element	基本的要素
a crucial	element	決定的な要素
an essential	element	不可欠な要素
an important	element	重要な要素
the main	element	主要要素
a major	element	大きな要素

▷I'm studying the **basic elements** of criminal law. 刑法の基礎を勉強中だ
▷Photographs are a **crucial element** in the pamphlet. 写真はパンフレットの決定的要素だ

eliminate /ilímənèit/ 動 除く, 除去する

completely	eliminate	完全に除去する
entirely	eliminate	
virtually	eliminate	事実上除去する
largely	eliminate	ほぼ除去する

▷The heat **completely eliminates** bacteria. 熱を加えると細菌は完全に死滅する

eliminate	A from B	AをBから除去する

▷You should **eliminate** the stress **from** your life. 生活のストレスを取り除いたほうがいいよ

email /í:mèil/ 名 Eメール, 電子メール

send	an email	メールを送る
get	an email	メールを受け取る
receive	an email	
check	one's email	メールをチェックする
reply to	an email	メールに返信する
forward	an email	メールを転送する
delete	an email	メールを削除する

▷If you are interested, please **send** an **email** to... 関心のある方は…にメールをお送りください
▷Did you **get** my **email**? 私のメール受け取った?
▷**Check** your **email** at least once a day. 少なくとも1日1回メールをチェックしなさい
▷I **forwarded** the **email** to Dave. デイブにそのメールを転送した

an email	arrives	メールが届く
an email	contains A	メールにAが含まれる

★「メールが届く」は×come ではなく arrive を用いる

▷An **email arrived** this morning from Lynda. けさリンダからEメールが届いた
▷The **email contains** information that I think is shocking. そのEメールはびっくりする情報を含んでいる

(an) unsolicited	email	迷惑メール
(an) unwanted	email	
junk	email	ジャンクメール
spam	email	スパムメール

▷If you get an **unsolicited email**, simply delete it. 迷惑メールを受け取ったら, ただ削除しなさい

an email	with an attachment	添付ファイルのあるメール

embarrassed /imbǽrəst/

形 きまりが悪い, どぎまぎする

feel	embarrassed	きまりが悪い
look	embarrassed	きまりが悪そうだ
get	embarrassed	どぎまぎする

▷She **felt embarrassed** to ask Michael for help again. 彼女はまたマイケルに助けを求めるのを恥ずかしく感じた
▷She **got embarrassed** just thinking about it all again. そのことを思い返すだけで彼女はどぎまぎした

acutely	embarrassed	ひどくきまりが悪い
a little	embarrassed	少しきまりが悪い
slightly	embarrassed	
too	embarrassed	あまりにきまりが悪い
so	embarrassed	

▷Sarah was **acutely embarrassed** to find that everybody knew she was pregnant. 自分が妊娠したことをだれもが知っているのに気づいてサラはひどくきまりが悪かった

embarrassed	to do	…するのはきまりが悪い

▷I'm **embarrassed to** ask for money. お金をくれと頼むのはきまりが悪い

embarrassed	about A	Aはきまりが悪い

▷ I was completely **embarrassed about** what I had done. 自分のしでかしたことでひどく恥ずかしい思いをした

■ emerge /imə́:rdʒ/

動 現れる；頭角を現す；抜け出る

eventually	emerge	ついに現れる
finally	emerge	
gradually	emerge	しだいに現れる
quickly	emerge	すぐに現れる
slowly	emerge	ゆっくり現れる
suddenly	emerge	突然現れる

▷ The lies were uncovered and truth **eventually emerged**. うそが暴露され真実がついに明らかになった
▷ The sun **gradually emerged** from the horizon. 太陽が徐々に地平線から現れた
▷ Beckham had **suddenly emerged** as England's perfect captain. ベッカムはイングランドの文句のつけようのないキャプテンとして突然頭角を現した

begin to	emerge	現れてくる

▷ Slowly the truth is **beginning to emerge**. 徐々に真実が明らかになりつつある

emerge	from A	Aから現れる；Aから抜け出る
emerge	into A	Aの中に現れる
emerge	as A	Aとして頭角を現す

▷ East Asia has begun to **emerge from** economic crisis. 東アジアは経済危機を脱し始めた
▷ When we left the church, we **emerged into** bright sunshine. 教会を後にするとまばゆい陽光に包まれた
▷ She **emerged as** a talented painter in the 1890s. 彼女は1890年代に才能ある画家として登場した

it emerges	(that...)	…が明らかになる

▷ **It emerged that** vehicle fuel prices are likely to rise again next month. 車の燃料費が来月また上がりそうだというのが明らかになった

■ emergency /imə́:rdʒənsi/

名 緊急事態，非常時

deal with	an emergency	緊急事態に対処する
cope with	an emergency	
meet	an emergency	

▷ The ambulance is fully equipped to **deal with emergencies**. 救急車には緊急時に対処する設備が整っている

a medical	emergency	救急医療

▷ A stroke is a **medical emergency**. 脳卒中は救急医療が必要な事態だ

a state of	emergency	非常事態

▷ The government declared a **state of emergency**. 政府は非常事態を宣言した

in	an emergency	緊急の際は
in case of	emergency	

▷ **In** an **emergency** call the police on 999. 緊急時は999をかけて警察へ電話してください

■ emotion /imóuʃən/ **名** 感情；感動

show	emotion	感情を表す
express	one's emotion	
control	one's emotions	感情を抑える
suppress	one's emotion	
hide	one's emotions	感情を隠す
stir (up)	emotion	感情をかき立てる
choke with	emotion	感動でことばが出ない

▷ He wasn't very good at **showing emotion**. 彼は自分の感情を表に出すのがあまり得意ではなかった
▷ She always **controlled** her **emotions** so well. 彼女はいつも感情をうまく抑えていた
▷ Why are you **hiding** your **emotions** from me? なぜ私の前で感情を隠すの
▷ His eyes filled with tears and his voice **choked with emotion**. 彼の目は涙であふれ、感極まって声が出なかった

strong	emotion(s)	激しい感情
intense	emotion(s)	
conflicting	emotions	相反する感情
mixed	emotions	複雑な感情
human	emotion	人間的感情

▷ I'm sure he has **mixed emotions** about me. きっと彼は私に複雑な感情を抱いているのだろう
▷ Fear is a natural **human emotion**. 恐れは本来的に人間に備わった感情だ

■ emphasis /émfəsis/ **名** 強調，重視

give	emphasis	強調する
place	(an) emphasis	
put	(an) emphasis	

| shift | the emphasis | 重点を移す |

▷In his speech the Prime Minister **put** special **emphasis** **on** education. 首相は演説の中で教育を特に強調した

(a) great	emphasis	非常に重視する
a strong	emphasis	こと
(an) increasing	emphasis	ますます重視すること
(a) particular	emphasis	特に重視すること
special	emphasis	

▷There is a **strong emphasis** **on** foreign languages and computer skills in schools. 学校では外国語とコンピュータ技術に非常に重点が置かれている
▷"I'm tired and *hungry*." I placed **particular emphasis** **on** the last word. 「疲れてお腹がすいた」と特に最後のことばを強調した

| with | (the) emphasis on A | Aに重点を置いて |

▷We should redesign this course **with** the **emphasis on** computer skills. コンピュータ技術に重点を置いてこのコースを見直すべきだ

| a change | of emphasis | 重点の変更 |
| a shift | of emphasis | |

▷The **shift of emphasis** from agriculture to industry will require vocational training. 農業から工業へ重点を移すとなれば職業訓練が必要となる

emphasize /émfəsàiz/

動 強調する, 重視する(★《英》つづりは emphasise)

| particularly | emphasize | 特に強調する |
| strongly | emphasize | |

▷In her book she **particularly emphasizes** the need for social reform. 自著の中で彼女は社会改革の必要性を特に強調している
▷Obama **strongly emphasized** the word "change." オバマは「変革」ということばを特に強調した

| emphasize | that... | …ということを強調する |

▷I'd like to **emphasize that** bullying is a serious problem. いじめは深刻な問題だということを強調したいと思います ♦**It should be emphasized that...** …ということは強調しておくべきだ ▷It should be emphasized that smoking is the major cause of lung cancer. 喫煙は肺がんの主要要因だと強調しておくべきだ

employ /implɔ́i/ **動** 雇う；使う

currently	employ	現在雇用している
directly	employ	直接雇用している
be fully	employed	完全雇用される

▷Approximately 700 people are **directly employed** by the company. 約700人がその企業に直接雇用されている
▷In the 1980s the Soviet population was **fully employed**. 1980年代においてソ連の人々の間では完全雇用が実現されていた

| be | employed in A | Aに雇われる |

▷Many people are **employed in** the construction company as day laborers. 多くの人たちがその建設会社に日雇い労働者として雇われている

| employ | A as B | A(人)をBとして雇う |

▷He **employed** Collins **as** an assistant director. 彼はコリンズを副支配人として雇った

| employ | A to do | A(人)を…するのに雇う |

▷I was **employed to** help you. あなたを手助けするために雇われた

employee /implɔ́ii:, èmplɔí:/

名 従業員, 社員, 被雇用者

have	an employee	従業員がいる
hire	an employee	従業員を雇う
dismiss	an employee	従業員を解雇する
fire	an employee	
pay	an employee	従業員に賃金を払う

▷The company **has** over 1,000 **employees**. その会社には千人を超える従業員がいる
▷We can only go on **paying** the **employees** for the next few months. 当社が社員に給与を支払い続けられるのは向こう2, 3か月だけだ

a full-time	employee	常勤従業員
a part-time	employee	パート従業員
a permanent	employee	正社員
a seasonal	employee	期間従業員
a public	employee	公務員
a government	employee	

▷She became a **permanent employee** the following year. 彼女は次の年に正社員になった
▷**Public employees** usually have good job security. 公務員はふつう雇用が保障されている

employer /implɔ́iər/ 名 雇い主, 雇用者

a large	employer	大口雇用者
a major	employer	
a potential	employer	潜在的雇用者
a prospective	employer	将来の雇用主

▷ **Major employers** include the government and the oil and gas industry. 大口雇用者には政府や石油・ガス産業が含まれる
▷ In an interview you should try to show your abilities to your **prospective employer**. 面接では将来の雇用主に能力を見せるようにしたほうがいい

employment /implɔ́imənt/ 名 雇用；職

find	employment	職を見つける
obtain	employment	職を得る
create	employment	雇用を創出する
provide	employment	雇用を提供する

▷ Luckily, she **found employment** at a bank through her friend Laura. 幸運にも彼女は友人のローラを通じて銀行に職を見つけた
▷ After university George **obtained employment** as a teacher. 大学を出たあとジョージは教師の職を得た
▷ He boosted the local economy and **created employment** for local people. 彼は地方経済を活気づけ地元の人々の雇用を生み出した

full-time	employment	常勤の雇用
part-time	employment	パートの雇用
permanent	employment	終身雇用
temporary	employment	一時雇用
full	employment	完全雇用

▷ **Full-time employment** has increased by 18% in the past three years. 常勤の雇用は過去3年で18％増えた
▷ Japanese employers now believe that the age of **permanent employment** is over. 日本の雇用者はいまや終身雇用の時代は終わったと思っている

a contract of employment	雇用契約

▷ His **contract of employment** was terminated on 31 July 2007. 彼の雇用契約は2007年7月31日で切れた

empty /émpti/ 形 からの；空いている

remain	empty	空いたままである
stand	empty	

▷ That factory has **stood empty** for over 3 years. その工場は3年以上空いたままだ

almost	empty	ほとんどからの
nearly	empty	
virtually	empty	
completely	empty	完全にからの
half	empty	半分からの

▷ The train was **nearly empty** at night. 列車には夜はほとんど乗客がいなかった
▷ Is the glass **half empty** or half full? コップに半分しかないか, それともまだ半分あるか(★物事を悲観的にとらえるか楽観的にとらえるかの問いで用いる)

encounter /inkáuntər/

動 遭遇する, 出くわす

frequently	encounter	よく出くわす
regularly	encounter	定期的に出くわす
previously	encountered	以前出くわした

▷ She **frequently encountered** problems with the new staff. 彼女は新人スタッフとの間でよく問題に出くわした

be likely to	encounter	遭遇しそうだ

▷ What sort of problems are they **likely to encounter**? どんな問題にその人たちは遭遇しそうだろうか

encourage /inkə́ːridʒ | -kʌ́r-/

動 励ます, 勇気づける；促進する

actively	encourage	積極的に勧める
be greatly	encouraged	大いに励まされる

▷ He **actively encouraged** her to apply for the job. その仕事に応募するよう彼は彼女に積極的に勧めた
▷ We were **greatly encouraged** to see the improvement in his grades. 彼の成績が上がったのを見てすごく励まされた

encourage	A to do	Aに…するよう励ます

▷ He **encouraged** me **to** develop my musical talent. 彼は私に音楽の才能を伸ばすように勧めた

end /énd/ 名 終わり, 最後；端；目的

come to	an end	終わる
approach	an end	終わりに近づく
draw to	an end	

bring A	to an end	Aを終わらせる
put	an end to A	
mark	the end	終わりを告げる
signal	the end	
reach	the end	端まで来る
achieve	one's end	目的を達成する

▷The song **came to** an **end**, the audience applauded. 歌は終わり聴衆たちは拍手した

▷I'm **approaching** the **end** of my life. 私の人生は終わりを迎えつつある

▷The committee has now decided to **bring** these investigations **to** an **end**. 委員会はこれらの調査を終了する決定をした

▷When we **reached** the **end** of the park, we stood in front of an old movie theater. 公園の端まで来ると、私たちは古い映画館の前に立っていた

the lower	end	下端
the upper	end	上端
the top	end	最上端
the rear	end	後部
the front	end	前部
the far	end	いちばん端
the very	end	
the opposite	end	反対側の端
the other	end	もう一方の端
either	end	どちらかの端、両端
the west	end	西の端

▷House prices are still growing strongly, particularly at the **lower end** of the market. 住宅価格はとりわけ低価格帯でなお大幅に上がっている

▷Sandrine always wears clothes from the **top end** of the market. サンドリーヌは高級品の衣服ばかり身につけている

▷The **front end** of the car was severely damaged. 車の前部がひどく破損した

▷Kate sat at the **far end** of the bar. ケイトはカウンターのいちばん端に坐った

▷Ann and Bobby sat at **opposite ends** of the couch. アンとボビーは長椅子の端と端に坐った

▷There was a laugh at the **other end** of the phone. 電話の向こう側で笑い声が起こった

▷There are exits at **either end** of the station. 駅の両側に出口がある

at	an end	終わって、尽きて
at	the end	最後に;突き当たりに
in	the end	結局、最後には

▷Their marriage is **at** an **end**. 彼らの結婚生活は終わった

▷**At** the **end**, Isabel asked only one question. 最後にイザベラが1つだけ質問した

▷**In** the **end**, I said nothing. 結局私は何も言わなかった

at	the end of A	Aの終わりに
by	the end of A	Aの終わりまでに

★Aにはthe year, the day, the season, January, life, game, courseなど、ある期間やできごとがくる

▷I'll go back to Australia **at** the **end of** January. 1月末にはオーストラリアに戻ります

enemy /énəmi/ 名 敵;敵軍

have	an enemy	敵がいる
make	an enemy of A	Aを敵に回す
make	enemies	敵をつくる
attack	an enemy	敵を攻撃する
destroy	an enemy	敵を倒す
defeat	an enemy	

▷Politicians always **have enemies**. 政治家には常に敵がいる

▷I don't wish to **make** an **enemy** of you. あなたを敵に回したくはない

▷We'll go and **attack** the **enemy** before they attack us. 敵に攻撃される前に敵を攻撃しに行く

a bitter	enemy	憎い敵
the great	enemy	大敵
a sworn	enemy	不倶戴天の敵
a mortal	enemy	
an old	enemy	宿敵、旧敵
a common	enemy	共通の敵
a political	enemy	政敵
an external	enemy	外部の敵

▷Gordon is my **bitterest enemy**. ゴードンというやつは憎んでも憎みきれない

▷Scotland is England's **old enemy**. スコットランドはイングランドの宿敵だ

▷Democrats and Republicans are 100% **political enemies**. 民主党と共和党は完全に政敵だ

▷With the end of the Soviet Union, the US had no **external enemy**. ソ連がなくなって米国には外敵がなくなった

energy /énərdʒi/ 名 精力, 活力;エネルギー

have	energy	精力がある
be full of	energy	精力に満ちている
put	one's energy	精力を注ぐ
devote	one's energy	

| engaged |

produce	energy	エネルギーを生み出す
generate	energy	
release	energy	エネルギーを放出する
provide	energy	エネルギーを供給する
supply	energy	
use	energy	エネルギーを使う
save	energy	エネルギーを節約する
waste	energy	エネルギーを浪費する

▷When we're young, we **have** a lot of **energy**. 若い時には体力がいっぱいある
▷I **put** all my **energy** into my work. 仕事に全精力を注いだ
▷Nuclear fuel is used to **produce energy**. 核燃料がエネルギーを供給するのに使われている
▷Recycling can **save energy**. リサイクルによってエネルギーが節約できる
▷I don't want to **waste** any more **energy** on this matter. この問題にこれ以上は精力を浪費したくない

alternative	energy	代替エネルギー
renewable	energy	再生可能エネルギー
atomic	energy	原子エネルギー
nuclear	energy	核エネルギー
solar	energy	太陽エネルギー

▷There is a need to advance our research on **alternative energy**. 代替エネルギーの研究を推し進める必要がある
▷Wind power is seen as a form of **renewable energy**. 風力は再生可能エネルギーの一つと見られている
▷In 1998 Syria and Russia signed an agreement on the peaceful use of **nuclear energy**. 1998年シリアとロシアは核エネルギーの平和利用に関する合意書に署名した

a burst of	energy	ほとばしり出る活力
a source of	energy	エネルギー源

▷Carbohydrates are an important **source of energy**. 炭水化物は重要なエネルギー源だ

engaged /ingéidʒd/

形 かかわっている，従事している；婚約している

become	engaged	婚約する
get	engaged	

▷Ian **got engaged** to Katharine. イアンはキャサリンと婚約した

actively	engaged	積極的にかかわっている
busily	engaged	忙しくかかわっている
currently	engaged	現在従事している

newly	engaged	婚約したばかりの

▷Most parents are **actively engaged** in their children's education. たいていの親は子どもの教育に積極的にかかわっている
▷We are **busily engaged** in developing a more efficient sales campaign. より効果的な販売キャンペーンを展開すべく鋭意努力中だ

engagement /ingéidʒmənt/

名 婚約；約束

announce	one's engagement	婚約を発表する
break off	one's engagement	婚約を解消する
cancel	one's engagement	
have	an engagement	約束がある

▷Jordan **announced** his **engagement** to Penny. ジョーダンはペニーとの婚約を発表した
▷Christina **broke off** her **engagement** with Malcolm. クリスティーナはマルコムとの婚約を解消した
▷Unfortunately I must leave now. I'm afraid I **have an engagement**. あいにくもう出かけなければなりません．約束がありますので

a prior	engagement	先約
a previous	engagement	
an official	engagement	公式行事への出席
a public	engagement	公の場への出席

▷Due to a **prior engagement** she is unable to attend the party. 先約があって彼女はパーティーに出席できない

engine /éndʒin/ 名 エンジン；原動力

start	an engine	エンジンをかける
turn on	an engine	
cut	an engine	エンジンを切る
turn off	an engine	
run	an engine	エンジンを動かす

▷The driver **started** his **engine** and removed the handbrake. ドライバーはエンジンをかけて，ハンドブレーキをはずした
▷**Turn off** the **engine** before filling up with gas. ガソリンを入れる前にエンジンを切りなさい
▷I pulled over and **cut** the **engine**. 車を道路わきに止めてエンジンを切った

an engine	starts	エンジンがかかる
an engine	runs	エンジンが動く
an engine	stops	エンジンが止まる
an engine	fails	エンジンが動かなくなる

▷I turned the key and the **engine started**. キーを回すとエンジンがかかった
▷The **engine failed** just after the plane had taken off. 飛行機の離陸直後にエンジンが停止した

a powerful	engine	強力なエンジン
a diesel	engine	ディーゼルエンジン
a gasoline	engine	ガソリンエンジン
a steam	engine	蒸気機関
the main	engine	原動力

▷This is the most **powerful engine** Honda has ever built. これはホンダが開発した中で最も強力なエンジンだ（★「強力なエンジン」の意味で a strong engine の頻度は低い）
▷Over recent years consumers have been the **main engine** for UK economic growth. ここ何年か消費者が英国の経済成長の原動力だった

engineer /èndʒiníər/ 名 エンジニア, 技師

a chief	engineer	主任技術者
a consulting	engineer	顧問技師
an electrical	engineer	電気技師
an electronics	engineer	電子工学技師
a civil	engineer	土木技師
a mechanical	engineer	機械技師

▷He worked as a **civil engineer** for a railway company. 彼は鉄道会社で土木技師として働いた

English /íŋɡliʃ/ 名 英語

speak	English	英語を話す
understand	English	英語がわかる
learn	English	英語を学ぶ
study	English	英語を研究する
teach	English	英語を教える

▷She **speaks English** fluently. 彼女は流ちょうに英語を話す
▷She **understands English** but she doesn't speak it very well. 彼女は英語がわかるがうまく話せない
▷Michael is currently **teaching English** at a community college. マイケルは現在コミュニティカレッジで英語を教えている

plain	English	わかりやすい英語
spoken	English	話しことばの英語
written	English	書きことばの英語
American	English	アメリカ英語
British	English	イギリス英語
standard	English	標準英語
business	English	ビジネス英語
good	English	よい英語
perfect	English	完璧な英語
broken	English	片言の英語

▷What does this mean in **plain English**? わかりやすい英語で言うとこれはどういう意味ですか
▷**Spoken English** includes many dialects. 話しことばの英語には多くの方言が含まれる
▷**Standard English** is used for formal communication. 改まったコミュニケーションでは標準英語が用いられる
▷He came up to me and asked in **broken English** if I wanted something. 彼は私のところへやって来て片言の英語で何かほしいか尋ねた

| in | English | 英語で |

▷How do you say "tora" **in English**? トラは英語でどう言いますか

a teacher of	English	英語の先生
a learner of	English	英語学習者
a speaker of	English	英語話者

★それぞれ an English teacher, an English learner, an English speaker のようにもいう

▷This dictionary is aimed at intermediate **learners of English**. この辞書は中級英語の学習者向けです

enjoy /indʒɔ́i/ 動 楽しむ

really	enjoy	すごく楽しむ
thoroughly	enjoy	存分に楽しむ
quite	enjoy	とても楽しむ
always	enjoy	いつも楽しむ

▷She **really enjoyed** talking with you that night. その夜のあなたとの会話を彼女はすごく楽しんだ
▷I **quite enjoyed** the traveling. その旅行はとても楽しかった
▷I **always enjoy** visiting this place. この場所を訪れるのがいつも楽しみです

| enjoy | doing | …して楽しむ |

★ˣenjoy to do とはいわない

▷Did you **enjoy** working with Philip? フィリップとの仕事は楽しかったですか

enter /éntər/ 動 入る; 入学する, 入会する

| finally | | enter | ついに入る |

successfully	enter	うまく入る
illegally	enter	不法に入る

▷ Japan **finally entered** World War II in December 1941. 日本は1941年12月についに第2次世界大戦に突入した
▷ China **successfully entered** the space race last year. 中国は昨年宇宙競争に加わることに成功した
▷ Almost 70 percent of people **illegally entering** the United States are from Mexico. 米国への不法入国者のほぼ7割がメキシコからだ

entertainment /èntərtéinmənt/

名 娯楽

provide	entertainment	娯楽を提供する
enjoy	entertainment	娯楽を楽しむ

▷ Curling is a fun sport that **provides entertainment** for players and spectators alike. カーリングは選手も観客も同じように楽しめるスポーツだ

public	entertainment	一般向け娯楽
mass	entertainment	大衆娯楽
popular	entertainment	人気のある娯楽
family	entertainment	家族向け娯楽
light	entertainment	軽い娯楽

▷ Shakespeare's plays provided **mass entertainment** in the 17th century. シェイクスピアの芝居は17世紀においては大衆に娯楽を提供するものだった

enthusiasm /inθú:ziæzm | -θju-/

名 熱中, 熱意

have	enthusiasm	熱意がある
be full of	enthusiasm	熱意にあふれる
express	enthusiasm	熱意を表す
show	enthusiasm	熱意を示す
share	enthusiasm	熱意を分かち合う
lose	one's enthusiasm	熱意を失う
dampen	A's enthusiasm	熱意をくじく

▷ She **has** incredible **enthusiasm** for her work. 彼女は信じられないほど仕事熱心だ
▷ Fiona was **full of enthusiasm** for the project. フィオナはその事業への熱意にあふれていた
▷ The greatest chess players **show** their **enthusiasm** for the game at a very early age. チェスの名手たちというのはごく幼い時分からチェスに熱中した人たちだ

great	enthusiasm	強い熱意
tremendous	enthusiasm	すごい熱意

genuine	enthusiasm	心からの熱意

▷ Brazilian people have **tremendous enthusiasm** for the game of soccer. ブラジル人はサッカーの試合となると熱狂する
▷ **Genuine enthusiasm** is one of the most powerful forces in business. 心からの熱意がビジネスでは最強の力の一つだ

with	enthusiasm	熱狂的に

▷ The decision was greeted **with enthusiasm** by everyone. その決定はみんなに熱狂的に迎えられた

a lack of	enthusiasm	熱意の欠如

▷ One of the reasons for this **lack of enthusiasm** is lack of communication. 熱意が見られない理由の一つはコミュニケーション不足だ

entrance /éntrəns/

名 入口, 玄関; 入ること, 入学, 入場

make	an entrance	入る, 入場する
gain	entrance	入り込む

▷ Videotapes disappeared as DVDs **made** an **entrance** into the market. DVDが市場に出回るにつれてビデオテープはなくなった

the main	entrance	正面玄関
the back	entrance	裏口
the front	entrance	表玄関

▷ The **main entrance** to the school is situated at the center of the building. 学校の正面玄関は建物の中心に位置している
▷ We entered the building through the **back entrance**. 裏口からその建物に入った

the entrance	to A	Aへの入り口
entrance	into A	Aへ入ること

▷ The only table left was at the **entrance to** the restaurant. ただ一つ残っていたテーブルはレストランの入り口近くだった
▷ The national anthem was played upon the Princess's **entrance into** the hall. 王女が玄関ホールに入ると国歌が演奏された

entry /éntri/

名 入る権利; 入ること, 入場; 参加; 記入; 見出し

make	an entry	入る, 入場する; 記入する
allow	entry	入るのを許可する

gain	entry	入れる
force	an entry	無理に入る
refuse	entry	入るのを断る
deny	entry	
prevent	entry	入れなくする

▷Karen **makes** an **entry** in her diary every day. カレンは毎日日記を書いている
▷Only children aged 16 and over will be **allowed entry**. 16歳以上の子どものみ入場できます
▷It is getting more and more difficult to **gain entry** into universities. 大学へ入学するのがますます難しくなりつつある
▷Cockpit doors on planes were reinforced to **prevent entry** by terrorists. 飛行機のコックピットのドアはテロリストの侵入を防ぐために補強された

free	entry	入場無料
the winning	entry	入賞作品
a dictionary	entry	辞書の見出し語

▷The winners will receive $300 and **free entry** to Disneyland. 勝者には300ドルが与えられ，ディズニーランド入場が無料になります
▷The **winning entries** will be announced on November 15. 入賞作品は11月15日に発表される

envelope /énvəlòup/ 名 封筒

address	an envelope	封筒に宛名を書く
seal	an envelope	封筒に封をする
open	an envelope	封筒を開ける

▷Most people **seal** the **envelope** before posting a letter. たいていの人は手紙を投かんする前に封筒に封をする(★クリスマスカードなどは封をしないまま出すことがある)

an envelope	contains A	封筒にAが入っている

▷Bill handed me an **envelope containing** $2,000 in cash. ビルは私に現金2千ドルの入った封筒を手渡した

a sealed	envelope	封をした封筒

▷I handed a **sealed envelope** to Angus. 封をした封筒をアンガスに渡した

the back of	an envelope	封筒の裏

▷Write your name and address *on* the **back of** the **envelope**. 封筒の裏に名前と住所を書いてください

in	an envelope	封筒に
into	an envelope	封筒の中に
on	an envelope	封筒の上に

▷I put a stamp **on** the **envelope** and posted it. 封筒に切手を貼って投かんした

environment /inváiərənmənt/

名 環境；(the environment で)(自然)環境

create	an environment	環境をつくり上げる
provide	an environment	環境を提供する
protect	the environment	環境を保護する
improve	the environment	環境をよくする
affect	the environment	環境に影響を与える
damage	the environment	環境に害をなす
pollute	the environment	環境を汚染する
destroy	the environment	環境を破壊する

▷How can we **protect** the **environment**? どうすれば環境を保護できるだろうか
▷Pollution has **affected** the **environment**. 公害は環境に影響を与えた
▷Chemicals and oil **polluted** the **environment**. 化学薬品や石油が環境を破壊した
▷Is globalization **destroying** the **environment**? グローバリゼーションによって環境は破壊されつつあるだろうか

a safe	environment	安全な環境
a competitive	environment	競争の厳しい環境
a social	environment	社会環境
a working	environment	作業環境
an economic	environment	経済環境
a political	environment	政治環境
the natural	environment	自然環境
the global	environment	地球環境

▷We're facing a highly **competitive environment**. 非常に厳しい競争環境に直面している
▷Industry needs a stable **political environment**. 産業界は安定した政治環境を必要としている
▷Human activities are changing the **global environment** at all levels. 人間の活動はあらゆるレベルで地球環境を変えつつある

equal /íːkwəl/

形 同等の，対等の，等しい；平等な

become	equal	等しくなる
make A	equal	Aを同等にする

▷It's difficult to **make** everybody **equal**. みんなを同等にするのは難しい

exactly	equal	まったく同じ

| equality |

almost	equal	ほとんど同じ
nearly	equal	
roughly	equal	だいたい同じ
approximately	equal	

▷ Our soccer players have ability **almost equal** to the South Koreans. わが国のサッカー選手の力量は韓国の選手とほぼ同じだ

▷ It was a difficult choice. The two candidates were **roughly equal** in ability. 難しい選択で，2人の志願者の能力はほぼ同じだった

equal	in A	Aが等しい
equal	to A	Aと等しい

★ equal in A のAには length, weight, height, value, size, quality などがくる

▷ Day and night are **equal in** length only twice a year. 昼と夜の長さは1年に2回だけ同じになる

▷ 100 degrees Celsius is **equal to** 212 degrees Fahrenheit. セ氏100度はカ氏212度に等しい

equality /ikwάləti | -wɔ́l-/ 名 平等

achieve	equality	平等を実現する
ensure	equality	平等を確保する

▷ The law should be changed to **ensure equality** of treatment. その法律は待遇の平等が確保できるよう改正されるべきだ

economic	equality	経済的平等
sexual	equality	男女平等
social	equality	社会的平等

▷ As far as possible we should aim to achieve **social equality**. できるだけ社会的平等の達成を目指すべきだ

equipment /ikwípmənt/

名 設備，備品，機器

supply	equipment	機器を提供する
use	the equipment	機器を使う
install	equipment	機器を設置する

▷ Around 70 percent of Americans **use** computer **equipment** at work or home. 約7割の米国人が職場か家でコンピュータ機器を使っている

▷ The school **installed equipment** such as CCTV cameras last year. その学校は昨年CCTVカメラなどの機器を設置した

standard	equipment	標準装備
special	equipment	特殊装置
office	equipment	事務機器
computer	equipment	コンピュータ機器
electrical	equipment	電気機器
electronic	equipment	電子機器
medical	equipment	医療機器
military	equipment	軍事機器
digital	equipment	デジタル機器

▷ DVD drives are becoming **standard equipment** on PCs. DVDドライブはパソコンの標準装備になりつつある

▷ Turn off all **electrical equipment** at night. 夜はすべての電気機器のスイッチを切りなさい

▷ The US has no competitor in high-tech **military equipment**. ハイテクの軍事機器で米国にかなう国はない

a piece of	equipment	一つの機器

▷ This new camera is a fantastic **piece of equipment**. この新しいカメラはすばらしい機種だ

equivalent /ikwívələnt/ 形 同等の

exactly	equivalent	まさに等しい
roughly	equivalent	ほぼ等しい
approximately	equivalent	
broadly	equivalent	

▷ Two languages often do not possess **exactly equivalent** words. 2つの言語間で互いに相当する語がないこともしばしばだ

▷ In size, the country is **roughly equivalent** to the State of Texas. その国の大きさはテキサス州とほぼ同じだ

equivalent	to A	Aと同等の

▷ For a dog, 15 years is **equivalent to** 74 years in a human life. 犬の15年はヒトの人生の74年に相当する

error /érər/ 名 誤り，間違い，ミス；エラー

make	an error	間違いを犯す
contain	an error	間違いがある
correct	an error	間違いを直す

▷ I often **make** small **errors**. よくちょっとしたミスをします

▷ Large databases of information always **contain errors** and outdated information. 巨大な情報データベースには必ず誤りと古くなった情報が入っている

▷ I would like to **correct** one **error** I noticed on page 7. 7ページで気づいた誤りを1つ訂正したいのですが

an error	occurs	間違いが起きる

▷This **error** usually **occurs** when I try to download a huge file. このエラーは大きなファイルをダウンロードしようとするときによく起きます

a serious	error	深刻な間違い
a fatal	error	致命的な間違い
an unexpected	error	予期せぬ間違い
a common	error	よくある間違い
a grammatical	error	文法上の誤り
a spelling	error	スペルミス
a clerical	error	事務的ミス
human	error	人為的ミス
pilot	error	操縦ミス
driver	error	運転ミス

▷Mr. Brown made the **fatal error** of saying what he actually thinks. ブラウン氏は思ったことをそのまま口にするという致命的な過ちを犯した
▷We should never forget that **human error** can occur. 人為的ミスは起こるものだということを忘れるべきではない(★×human mistake とはいわない)

a margin of	error	誤差

▷There's a **margin of error** in his analysis. 彼の分析には誤差がある

in	error	間違って

▷He was arrested **in error**. 彼は誤認逮捕された

escape /iskéip/ 图 逃亡, 脱出

make	one's escape	逃れる, 脱出する
attempt	an escape	脱出を試みる
prevent	an escape	脱出を妨げる
provide	an escape	現実逃避の手段を提供する

▷She finally **made** her **escape** on a flight from Moscow. 彼女はついにモスクワから飛行機で脱出した
▷TV **provided** an **escape** from the deadly dull life. テレビのおかげでひどく退屈な生活から逃れられた

a narrow	escape	かろうじて逃れること
a lucky	escape	幸運にも逃れること
a miraculous	escape	奇跡的に逃れること

▷Four people had a **lucky escape** after a three-car collision. 4人は車3台の衝突事故にあったが幸い無事だった

PHRASES
There is no escape! ☺ もう逃げられないぞ

escape /iskéip/ 動 逃げる, 免れる

narrowly	escape	かろうじて免れる

▷Andy was seriously wounded and only **narrowly escaped** death. アンディは重傷を負ったが命はなんとか助かった

try to	escape	逃げようとする
attempt to	escape	
manage to	escape	なんとか逃げる

▷Don't **try to escape** or you'll be shot. 逃げようとしたら,撃つぞ

escape	from A	Aから逃げる

▷A prisoner **escaped from** the prison where he had been kept for 10 years. 一人の囚人が10年間収監されていた刑務所から脱走した

essential /isénʃəl/

形 欠くことのできない；本質的な

absolutely	essential	きわめて重要な

▷Innovation is **absolutely essential** in an industry. 革新は産業においてきわめて重要だ

essential	to A	Aに不可欠な
essential	for A	

▷Clean water is **essential for** life. きれいな水は生命に欠かせない

it is essential	(that)...	…ということが肝要だ
it is essential	to do	…するのが肝要だ

▷**It is essential that** you consult a doctor immediately. ぜひともすぐ医者に診てもらいなさい
▷**It is essential** for you **to** be there by three o'clock. 3時までには必ずそこに行ってください

establish /istǽbliʃ/

動 設立する；確立する；立証する

be originally	established	元は設立された
clearly	establish	明確に確立する
firmly	establish	しっかり確立する
fully	establish	十分に確立する

▷This company was **originally established** in 1887. この会社は元は1887年に設立された
▷Australia is now **clearly established** as a major

wine producing area. オーストラリアは現在ワインの新しい生産地としての地歩を確立している

▷By the seventh century Buddhism was **fully established** in Japan. 7世紀までに仏教は日本に着実に根を下ろしていた

| establish | A with B | BとBの間にA(関係)を築く |

★Aは a relationship, contact, a friendship など

▷He **established** a friendship **with** Frank. 彼はフランクと友情を結んだ

| establish | that... | …ということを立証する |
| establish | wh- | …かどうかを立証する |

★wh- は whether, how, who など

▷The survey **established that** 21% of those aged 16-20 years were smokers. その調査で16歳から20歳の21％が喫煙者であることが明らかになった

estate /istéit/ 名 地所, 私有地；財産

have	an estate	地所を持っている
own	an estate	地所を所有する
buy	an estate	地所を買う
manage	an estate	地所を管理する
leave	an estate	財産を残す
inherit	an estate	財産を相続する

▷Robin **left** his **estate** to his three sons. ロビンは3人の息子たちに財産を残した

▷Richard **inherited** the family **estate**. リチャードは家督を相続した

a large	estate	大きな地所
personal	estate	動産
real	estate	不動産
《英》a housing	estate	住宅団地

▷The husband will be entitled to all his wife's **personal estate** after her death. 夫は妻の死後, そのすべての動産を得る権利がある

estimate /éstəmət/ 名 見積もり；推定値

make	an estimate	見積もる
give	an estimate	見積もりを出す
provide	an estimate	

▷It's hard to **make** an **estimate** of how many civilians have been killed in the war. その戦争でどれくらいの一般市民が死んだか, はっきり数字を出すのは難しい

▷We have to **provide** an **estimate** of the cost by the end of this month. 今月末までに価格の見積もりを出さなければならない

an accurate	estimate	正確な推定値
a conservative	estimate	控えめな推定値
a rough	estimate	大ざっぱな推定値

▷Let's make a **rough estimate**. 大ざっぱに推定値を出してみよう

estimate /éstəmèit/ 動 見積もる, 推定する

originally	estimate	最初に見積もる
conservatively	estimate	控えめに見積もる
roughly	estimate	大ざっぱに見積もる

▷We **conservatively estimate** the attendance at around 500 people. 約500人と控えめに出席者を見積もっている

| estimate | A at B | AをBと見積もる |

▷The total cost of damage was **estimated at** $2 billion. 被害総額は20億ドルと見積もられた

| estimate | (that)... | …であると推定する |

▷Scientists **estimate that** the Earth was formed around 4.6 billion years ago. 科学者の推定では地球はおよそ46億年前に形成された ♦**it is estimated that...** …と推定される ▷It is estimated that 35% of all marriages ended in divorce in Western Europe. 西ヨーロッパでは結婚の35％が離婚に終わったと推定される

evening /íːvniŋ/ 名 夕方, 晩(★ふつう日没から寝るまで. night は日没から日の出まで)

this	evening	今晩
yesterday	evening	きのうの晩
tomorrow	evening	あすの晩
early	evening	夕方の早い時間
late	evening	夜遅く
the following	evening	その次の晩
the previous	evening	その前の晩
a lovely	evening	すばらしい晩
Friday	evening	金曜の晩
May	evening	5月の晩
a winter	evening	冬の晩

▷Do you have any plan **this evening**? 今晩何か予定はありますか

▷A baby girl was born **yesterday evening**. 女の

赤ちゃんが昨晩生まれた
▷ **Early evening** will be the best time at the shore of the lake. 湖畔がいちばんきれいなのは夕方の早い時間でしょう
▷ The **following evening** I was invited to have dinner with Dennis. 次の晩デニスとの夕食に招かれた
▷ We had a **lovely evening**. すてきな晩でした

in	the evening	夕方に, 晩に
(on)	Friday evening	金曜の晩
on	Saturday evenings	毎週土曜の晩に
on	the evening of A	Aの晩に

▷ **In** the **evening** we drove to Boston. 夕方ボストンに車で行った ◆**late in the evening** 夜遅く ▷ The concert will be broadcast late in the evening on the radio. そのコンサートは夜の遅い時間にラジオで放送される
▷ The annual music festival takes place **on** the **evening of** August 1. 毎年恒例の音楽フェスティバルは8月1日の晩に行われる

event /ivént/ 图 できごと, 事件；行事；種目

organize	an event	行事を催す
stage	an event	
attend	an event	行事に参加する

▷ About 50,000 people are expected to **attend** the **event**. 約5万人がその催しに参加すると予想される

an event	occurs	事件が起きる
an event	takes place	

▷ Three major **events occurred** in my life. これまでの人生で3つ大きなできごとがありました

an important	event	重要なできごと
a major	event	大事件
a historic	event	歴史に残るできごと
a historical	event	歴史上のできごと
a future	event	未来のできごと
an annual	event	年中行事
a social	event	社交行事
a school	event	学校行事
a sporting	event	スポーツ大会

▷ This play is based on **historical events**. この劇は史実に基づいている
▷ The Australian Science Festival is an **annual event** held in Canberra. オーストラリア科学フェスティバルはキャンベラで開催される毎年の恒例行事である
▷ The games are the biggest **sporting event** in the world this year. それらのゲームは今年のスポーツ界最大のイベントだ

in	the event of A	Aの際には
in	the event that...	…である際には
(英) in	the event	実際は
in	any event	とにかく

★Aは death, illness, a crisis など

▷ **In** the **event that** the concert is cancelled we can get our money back. コンサートが中止のときは返金してもらえる
▷ We all took umbrellas with us, but **in** the **event** it didn't rain. みんな傘を持って行ったが, 結局雨は降らなかった
▷ **In any event**, it was extremely difficult to concentrate on the exam. とにかく試験に集中するのがとても難しかった

a chain of	events	一連のできごと
a sequence of	events	
a series of	events	
the course of	events	事の成り行き

▷ In the normal **course of events** I spend my summer holidays abroad. 特にこれといったことがなければ夏休みは海外で過ごす

evidence /évədəns/ 图 証拠, 証言

have	evidence	証拠がある
gather	evidence	証拠を集める
collect	evidence	
find	evidence	証拠を見つける
obtain	evidence	証拠を手に入れる
produce	evidence	証拠を提出する
provide	evidence	証拠を提供する
show	evidence	証拠を示す
give	evidence	証言する
destroy	evidence	証拠を隠滅する

▷ It's not hard to **find evidence** that Chris is right. クリスが正しいという証拠を見つけるのは難しくない
▷ The police were unable to **obtain** enough **evidence**. 警察は十分な証拠を得られなかった
▷ The survey **provides evidence** to support his theories. 調査により彼の学説を支持する事実が出てきている
▷ An accused has the right not to **give evidence** in court. 被告人には法廷で証言しない権利がある

evidence	suggests	証拠が示唆する
evidence	shows	証拠が示す

▷ **Evidence shows** that the potato was being cultivated 2,000 years ago in Peru. ジャガイモは2千年前にペルーで栽培されていたという証拠がある

| evil |

sufficient	evidence	十分な証拠
clear	evidence	明白な証拠
hard	evidence	決定的な証拠
strong	evidence	強力な証拠
insufficient	evidence	不十分な証拠
available	evidence	得られる証拠
further	evidence	さらなる証拠
new	evidence	新たな証拠
circumstantial	evidence	状況証拠
empirical	evidence	実証的な証拠
medical	evidence	医学的証拠
scientific	evidence	科学的証拠

▷There is **sufficient evidence** to suggest that these pictures are fakes. これらの絵が偽物だと示唆する十分な証拠がある
▷I found **strong evidence** that the answer to that question is yes. その質問に対する答えがイエスだという強力な証拠を見つけた
▷**Further evidence** is required to show the US economy is on the upturn. 米国の景気が好転しつつあると言えるためにはさらなる証拠が必要だ
▷There is clear **empirical evidence** against this hypothesis. この仮説に反する明らかな実証的証拠がある

evidence	of A	Aの証拠
evidence	for A	Aのための証拠
evidence	against A	Aに不利な証拠

▷A three-year FBI investigation had found no **evidence of** terrorist activity. 3年間にわたるFBIの調査によってもテロ活動の証拠は見つからなかった
▷Thomson gave **evidence against** Webber in court. トムソンは法廷でウェバーに不利な証言をした

evidence	that...	…という証拠

▷There is no **evidence that** she killed her husband. 彼女が夫を殺害したという証拠は何もない

in	evidence	証拠として
be in	evidence	目立っている

▷Tape recordings cannot always be used **in evidence** in a court of law. 録音テープは証拠として裁判所でいつも使えるとは限らない
▷The effects of the floods are still very much **in evidence** in New Orleans. 洪水の影響はいまなおニューオリンズに色濃く残っている

evil /íːvəl/ 名 邪悪, 悪, 悪事

a great	evil	巨悪
the lesser	evil	(悪い2つの選択肢の)ましなほう
a necessary	evil	必要悪
a social	evil	社会悪

▷If you don't like either presidential candidate you just have to choose the **lesser evil**. どちらの大統領候補も気に入らないなら、ましなほうを選ぶしかない
▷Drink-driving is a serious crime and a **social evil**. 飲酒運転は深刻な犯罪であり社会悪だ

exam /igzǽm/

名 試験, テスト；検査(★ examination の短縮語)

take	an exam	試験を受ける
《英》do	an exam	
pass	an exam	試験に通る
fail	an exam	試験に落ちる
cheat on	an exam	試験でカンニング
《英》cheat in	an exam	する

▷**I took** the **exam** in November and received the results very quickly. 11月に試験を受け結果はすぐ出た
▷Congratulations on **passing** your **exams**! 試験合格おめでとう

an entrance	exam	入学試験
a final	exam	学年末試験；卒業試験
a written	exam	筆記試験

examination /igzæmənéiʃən/

名 試験；検査, 調査

take	an examination	試験を受ける
《英》sit	an examination	
pass	an examination	試験に通る
fail	an examination	試験に落ちる
make	an examination	調査する
require	an examination	検査を必要とする
have	an examination	検査を受ける

▷If **I fail** this **examination**, they won't renew my scholarship. この試験に落ちたら奨学金をもうもらえなくなるだろう

an entrance	examination	入学試験

▷He passed the **entrance examination** to university. 彼は大学の入学試験に合格した

examine /igzǽmin/ 動 調べる；診察する

carefully	examine	注意深く調べる
closely	examine	綿密に調べる
briefly	examine	ざっと調べる
critically	examine	批判的な目で調べる
examine	in detail	詳細に調べる
examine	thoroughly	十分に調べる

★carefully, closely, briefly, critically は動詞の後でも用いる

▷We have **closely examined** the contents of the report. 報告書の内容を綿密に調べた
▷This chapter **briefly examines** the history of the European Union. この章では欧州連合の歴史について簡単に考察する
▷The conclusions drawn from the data must be **examined critically**. そのデータから得られた結論は批判的な目で検討する必要がある
▷We **examined** the cause of the problem **thoroughly**. この問題の原因を十分に調べた

examine	A on B	AにBの試験をする
examine	A in B	
examine	A for B	Bを探してAを調べる

▷The doctor **examined** him **for** signs of illness. 医師は病気の兆候がないか彼を診察した

example /iɡzǽmpl | -záːm-/

名 例, 実例; 手本, 模範

give	an example	例を挙げる
provide	an example	
cite	an example	例を引く
find	an example	例を見つける
set	an example	手本を示す
follow	A's example	見習う

▷Can you **give** an **example**? 例を挙げてくれるかい
▷Parents should **set** a good **example** to their children. 両親は子どもによい手本を示すべきだ
▷I **followed** her **example** and chose to avoid fatty foods. 彼女を見習って脂肪分の多い食品を避けるようにした

a typical	example	典型的な例
a prime	example	
a classic	example	
an excellent	example	すばらしい例
a good	example	よい例
an obvious	example	明快な例
a clear	example	

▷This is a **typical example** of African art. これはアフリカ美術の典型的な作品です

for	example	たとえば

▷I have many hobbies. **For example**, fishing, bird watching and cooking. 趣味は多くて, 釣りやバードウォッチング, 料理などです

exception /iksépʃən/ 名 例外, 特例

make	an exception	特例とする

▷I seldom write to the newspapers, but this time I am **making** an **exception**. めったに新聞に投書したりしないが, 今回は例外だ

an important	exception	大きな例外
a major	exception	
a notable	exception	明らかな例外
a rare	exception	まれな例外
the only	exception	唯一の例外

▷He could trust almost no one. The **only exception** was Jimmy. 彼はだれも信用できなかったが, ただ一人の例外はジミーだった

an exception	to A	Aの例外
with	the exception of A	Aを除いて
without	exception	例外なく

▷There are two **exceptions to** this rule. この規則には例外が2つある
▷**With** the **exception of** Native Americans, the U.S. is a country of immigrants. アメリカ先住民を除くと米国は移民の国だ
▷**Without exception** all fifteen members supported the plan. 15名すべてのメンバーが残らず計画を支持した

exchange /ikstʃéindʒ/

名 交換; 交流; 為替; 口論

cultural	exchange(s)	文化交流
international	exchange	国際交流
foreign	exchange	外国為替
the stock	exchange	証券取引所
a heated	exchange	激しいことばの
an angry	exchange	やりとり

▷**Cultural exchange** aids international understanding. 文化交流は国際理解の助けになる
▷A **heated exchange** took place between them. 激しいことばのやりとりが彼らの間で起こった

an exchange of A		Aの交換

★Aは ideas, views, information など

▷After a free and frank **exchange of** ideas, we reached a compromise. 自由で率直な意見交換をした後に私たちは妥協に達した

in	exchange (for) A	(Aと)引き換えに

▷Some people think you can get whatever you want, **in exchange for** money. お金と引き換えに何でもほしいものが手に入ると思っている人もいる

excited /iksáitid/

形 興奮した, わくわくした

get	excited	興奮する
become	excited	

▷Don't **get** too **excited**! そう興奮するなよ

really	excited	とても興奮した
quite	excited	
increasingly	excited	ますます興奮した
sexually	excited	性的に興奮した

▷Everybody was **quite excited** about the idea. だれもがその考えにわくわくした

excited	about A	Aに興奮した

▷I'm really **excited about** this project. この企画にとてもわくわくしています

excited	to do	…することに興奮した

▷I'm very **excited to** hear that. それはうれしい知らせですね

excitement /iksáitmənt/

名 興奮

cause	excitement	興奮をもたらす

▷His announcement **caused** great **excitement**. 彼の発表は大きな興奮を引き起こした

great	excitement	大きな興奮
high	excitement	
intellectual	excitement	知的興奮
sexual	excitement	性的興奮

▷There was **great excitement** across the country during the Olympics. オリンピック期間中, 国じゅうが大きな興奮に包まれた

▷**Sexual excitement** gets the heart pumping. 性的に興奮すると心臓の鼓動が速くなる

with	excitement	興奮して

▷Jeremy clapped his hands **with excitement**. ジェレミーは興奮して手をたたいた

exciting /iksáitiŋ/

形 興奮させる, わくわくさせる, 刺激的な

sound	exciting	おもしろそうだ
get	exciting	おもしろくなる

▷"We're going to go on an adventure holiday in Canada!" "Really? **Sounds exciting**!"「カナダに冒険旅行に行く予定さ」「ほんとかい. おもしろそうだね」

really	exciting	とても興奮させる
quite	exciting	
tremendously	exciting	すごく興奮させる

▷This breakthrough in technology is **tremendously exciting**. この科学技術上の大発見にはすごく胸が躍る

an exciting	new A	刺激的な新しいA

▷He is one of the most **exciting new** talents in the business. 彼はビジネス界で最も刺激的な新しい才能をもつ一人だ

exclude /iksklú:d/

動 除外する;排除する, 締め出す

totally	exclude	完全に排除する
completely	exclude	
deliberately	exclude	意図的に排除する
expressly	exclude	特に排除する
specifically	exclude	
effectively	exclude	事実上排除する

▷Please tell me why you are **deliberately excluding** me. どうしてわざと私をのけものにしているのか教えて

▷Women were once **effectively excluded** from higher education. 女性はかつて高等教育から事実上, 排除されていた

exclude or restrict		排除あるいは制限する

▷Certain types of insurance claim may be **excluded or restricted**. ある種の保険金請求は排除あるいは制限される場合がある

exclude	A from B	AをBから締め出す

▷As he was not yet sixteen, he was **excluded from**

taking part in the race. 彼は16歳になっていなかったのでレースへの参加を認められなかった

excuse /ikskjúːs/ 名 言い訳, 弁解, 口実

have	an excuse	言い訳がある
make	an excuse	言い訳をする
give	an excuse	
look for	an excuse	言い訳を探す
find	an excuse	言い訳を見つける
use A as	an excuse	Aを言い訳にする

▷ Now you no longer **have** an **excuse** to ignore him! こうなってはもはや彼を無視できないよ
▷ Stop **making excuses**! 言い訳するのはやめなさい
▷ Stop **giving** me **excuses**! きみの言い訳はもうたくさんだ
▷ I tried to **find** an **excuse** for the delay. 遅れた言い訳を見つけようとした

the perfect	excuse	申し分ない言い訳
a good	excuse	うまい言い訳
a reasonable	excuse	もっともな言い訳
a feeble	excuse	へたな言い訳

▷ Winter is coming. It's the **perfect excuse** to stay indoors. 冬がやって来る. それは家の中にいる申し分のない口実になる
▷ Tim missed two lessons without a **reasonable excuse** today. ティムはこれといって理由もないのにきょう2つ授業を休んだ
▷ Feeling tired is a **feeble excuse**. 疲れたなんて理由にもならない言い訳だ

an excuse	for A	Aに対する言い訳

▷ She made **excuses for** why she couldn't see Tom. 彼女はなぜトムに会えないのかあれこれ言い訳した

an excuse	to do	…する言い訳

▷ Saying that he was ill was just an **excuse to** avoid coming to the meeting. 病気だという彼のことばは会議に出ないための口実だった

exercise /éksərsàiz/

名 運動；練習, 練習問題；演習

do	exercise	運動する；練習する；練習問題をする
take	exercise	運動する
get	exercise	
repeat	the exercise	運動を反復する

▷ **Do exercise** every day to keep fit. 健康を保つために毎日運動しなさい
▷ Please open your books and **do Exercise** 1. 本を開いて, 練習問題の1をしなさい

good	exercise	よい運動
strenuous	exercise	激しい運動
vigorous	exercise	
gentle	exercise	軽い運動
light	exercise	
moderate	exercise	適度な運動
regular	exercise	定期的にやる運動
aerobic	exercise	エアロビクス
physical	exercise	体の運動, 体操
mental	exercise	頭の体操
a simple	exercise	簡単な練習問題
a practical	exercise	応用問題
a training	exercise	訓練演習
a military	exercise	軍事演習

▷ I recommend **gentle exercise** such as walking or yoga. 散歩やヨガなど軽い運動を勧めます
▷ **Regular moderate exercise** can reduce body fat. 適度な運動を定期的に行えば体脂肪を落とせる
▷ Let me give you a couple of **practical exercises**. では応用問題を少しやってみましょう

lack of	exercise	運動不足

▷ **Lack of exercise** is the main cause of overweight. 運動不足が太りすぎの主要原因だ

exhibition /èksəbíʃən/ 名 展覧会, 展示会

have	an exhibition	展覧会を開く
hold	an exhibition	
organize	an exhibition	展覧会を準備する
visit	an exhibition	展覧会を見に行く

▷ She **had** a solo **exhibition** in Tokyo last year. 彼女は昨年個展を東京で開いた
▷ Prince Charles **visited** the **exhibition** at the Mall Galleries in London. チャールズ皇太子はロンドンのモール画廊での展示会に訪れた

an international	exhibition	万国博覧会
a special	exhibition	特別展示
a temporary	exhibition	仮設展示

▷ The **international exhibition** will be held at the convention center from Tuesday June 20. 万国博覧会はコンベンションセンターで6月20日火曜日から開かれる

on	exhibition	展示されて

| exist |

▷English paintings are **on exhibition** at Thomas Mclean's Gallery. イギリス絵画の展覧会がトマス・マクリーンギャラリーで開催されている

exist /igzíst/ 動 存在する；生存する

actually	exist	現実に存在する
already	exist	すでに存在する
currently	exist	いま存在する
no longer	exist	もはや存在しない

▷Do you think such a perfect person **actually exists**? そんな完璧な人が現実に存在すると思うかい
▷Unfortunately due to war damage, most of the original buildings **no longer exist**. 残念ながら戦災のために元の建物の大半はもはや存在しない

exist	on A	Aで生きる

▷If you want to **exist** just **on** vegetables, that's your choice. 野菜だけを食べて生きるのを選ぶのならそれはきみの自由だ

existence /igzístəns/

名 存在，生存；生活，生活様式

be in	existence	存在する
have	an existence	存在している
come into	existence	生まれる
go out of	existence	消滅する
deny	A's existence	存在を否定する
confirm	the existence	存在を確かめる
prove	A's existence	存在を証明する
eke out	an existence	何とか食べていく

▷The United Nations has **been in existence** for nearly half a century. 国連が生まれて半世紀近くになる
▷Our solar system **came into existence** 4.6 billion years ago. 私たちの太陽系は46億年前に誕生した
▷Some people are still **denying** the **existence** of global warming. 地球が温暖化していることをいまなお否定する人もいる
▷NASA **confirmed** the **existence** of the ozone hole. NASAはオゾンホールの存在を確かめた

the continued	existence	存続
an independent	existence	独立生活
a hand-to-mouth	existence	食うや食わずの生活
a previous	existence	前世

▷The **continued existence** of terrorism is a major problem. いまなお続くテロは重大な問題だ

▷Since she left home she's been living a completely **independent existence**. 彼女は家を出てから完全に独立した生活をしている

exit /égzit, éksit/ 名 出口

make	an exit	退出する，退場する

▷Any good actor knows when to **make** an **exit**. よい俳優は引き際を知っている

an exit	from A	Aの出口

▷They found their **exit from** the building was blocked. 彼らは建物の出口が塞がれているのに気づいた

an emergency	exit	非常口
a fire	exit	

▷Where's the **emergency exit**? 非常口はどこですか

expand /ikspǽnd/

動 拡大する，拡張する；詳しく説明する

greatly	expand	大幅に拡大する
further	expand	さらに拡大する
rapidly	expand	急速に拡大する
expand	considerably	かなり拡大する

★rapidly は動詞の後でも用いる

▷Trade between Japan and China has **greatly expanded** in the past ten years. 日中貿易は過去10年で大幅に増えた
▷To **further expand** her business, she invested one hundred million yen. ビジネスをさらに拡大するため彼女は1億円を投資した

expand	into A	Aに拡大する
expand	on A	Aについて詳しく説明する
expand	upon A	

▷The company plans to **expand into** Eastern Europe within the next year. その会社は来年中に東ヨーロッパに進出する計画だ
▷Can you **expand on** this idea? この考えについて詳しく説明してくれませんか

expect /ikspékt/ 動 期待する；思う

fully	expect	確信している
half	expect	半信半疑である
really	expect	とても期待する

reasonably	expect	かなり期待する

▷I **fully expect** him to win the game. 彼が試合に勝つと頭から信じている
▷We can't **reasonably expect** him to keep helping us without payment. 報酬もなく彼が私たちを援助し続けるとはあまり期待できない

as	expected	予想どおり

▷**As expected**, the story has spread widely in the press. 予想どおりその話は報道機関に大きく広がった

expect	to do	…するだろうと思う
expect	A to do	Aが…すると思う
expect	(that)...	…だろうと予想する
be expected	to do	…してもらいたい

▷I didn't **expect** him **to** come. 彼が来るなんて思わなかった
▷I **expect that** he will change his mind. 彼は考えを変えると思う
▷Pupils are **expected to** work hard on a large range of subjects. 生徒諸君には幅広い科目を一生懸命に勉強してもらいたい

expect	A of B	BにAを期待する
expect	A from B	

▷We **expect** more **of** you. きみはもっとできると思う

expense /ikspéns/

名 費用, 出費; (expenses で)必要経費

incur	an expense	費用を負担する
cover	an expense	費用をまかなう
meet	an expense	
bear	an expense	
spare no	expense	費用を惜しまない
reimburse	expenses	経費を払い戻す
pay	expenses	
put A on	expenses	Aを必要経費につける

▷Because prices rose we've **incurred** more **expenses** that we expected. 価格が上がったので予想より多くの費用がかかった
▷She **spared no expense** in making her house comfortable. 彼女は家を快適にするための出費を惜しまなかった
▷The company **paid** all my **expenses** to come for an interview. 面接に来るために立て替えた諸費用を会社がすべて払い戻してくれた

(the) additional	expense	追加費用
(an) extra	expense	余計な費用
(an) unnecessary	expense	不必要な出費
living	expenses	生活費
household	expenses	家計費
travel	expenses	旅費；交通費
traveling	expenses	
removal	expenses	引っ越し費用
legal	expenses	訴訟費用
medical	expenses	医療費

▷You can upgrade to a wider range of TV channels without **additional expense**. 追加のお支払いなしでご覧になれるテレビチャンネルをぐんと増やせます
▷You should avoid **unnecessary expense**. 不必要な出費を減らしたほうがいい
▷**Living expenses** in Tokyo are very high. 東京の生活費はとても高い

at	A's expense	Aの負担で
at	the expense of A	Aを犠牲にして

▷*Peter Rabbit* was published **at** the author's own **expense** in 1901. 『ピーター・ラビット』は1901年に自費出版された

expensive /ikspénsiv/ **形** 高価な

become	expensive	高くなる
get	expensive	
find A	expensive	Aを高いと思う

▷Vegetables **became** quite **expensive** due to the floods. 洪水で野菜がとても高くなった(★ quite など expensive を強める副詞とともによく用いる)
▷He **found** the cost of living less **expensive** in Oregon. オレゴン州での生活費はそれほど高くないと彼は思った

extremely	expensive	すごく高い
really	expensive	
prohibitively	expensive	法外に高い
relatively	expensive	比較的高い
increasingly	expensive	ますます高い

▷Good medicine is **extremely expensive**. よい薬はすごく値段が高い
▷Do you think imported cars are **prohibitively expensive**? 輸入車は法外に高いと思いませんか

A is expensive	to do	Aは…するのに高くつく

▷Big old houses are **expensive to** maintain. 大きくて古い家は維持費が高くつく

experience /ikspíəriəns/ 名 経験, 体験

have	(an) experience	経験する
gain	experience	経験を積む
get	experience	
share	(an) experience	経験を話す
describe	(an) experience	経験を語る
learn by	experience	経験から学ぶ
learn from	experience	

★ have, share, describe との連結では「特定の具体的な経験」を表すときは可算名詞

▷ She **had** a terrible **experience** when she was living in New York. 彼女はニューヨークに住んでいたときひどい体験をした
▷ All you need to do is to **gain experience**. きみに必要なのは経験を積み重ねることだけだ
▷ We **shared experiences** of our travels abroad. 海外旅行の体験を語り合った ▷ Please **share** your long **experience** with the new employees. あなたの長い経験を新入社員たちに伝えてください
▷ I **learned** a lot **from** my **experience** as a volunteer. ボランティア経験から多くを学んだ

long	experience	長い経験
limited	experience	限られた経験
past	experience	過去の経験
previous	experience	以前の経験
personal	experience	個人的経験
practical	experience	実地体験
business	experience	実務経験
a bad	experience	いやな経験
a traumatic	experience	つらい経験

▷ I can tell you from **personal experience** that playing golf isn't easy. 個人的経験から言うとゴルフは簡単ではない

a lack of	experience	経験不足

▷ The project didn't go well due to his **lack of experience**. 事業は彼の経験不足のためうまくいかなかった

experiment /ikspérəmənt/ 名 実験

do	an experiment	実験をする
conduct	an experiment	
carry out	experiments	
perform	an experiment	
try	an experiment	実験を試みる
design	an experiment	実験計画を立てる

▷ We've been **doing** a number of **experiments** to understand how the cells work. 細胞の働きを理解するための実験をたくさんしてきている
▷ We **tried** several **experiments** to test the theory. その理論を検証するためにいくつか実験をした
▷ We **designed experiments** to test Hoff's hypothesis. ホフの仮説を検証するために実験計画を立てた

animal	experiments	動物実験
a scientific	experiment	科学実験
a successful	experiment	成功した実験

▷ Charles Irving conducted a **successful experiment** in making fresh water from seawater. チャールズ・アービングは海水から真水をつくる実験に成功した

an experiment	in A	A(分野)の実験
an experiment	on A	Aに関する実験
an experiment	with A	Aを用いた実験

▷ What is the most famous **experiment in** physics? 物理学で最も有名な実験は何ですか
▷ He conducted a series of **experiments with** mice. 彼はマウスを使って一連の実験をした

an experiment	to do	…する実験

★ do は test, see など

▷ Scientists designed **experiments to** test for the presence of life on Mars. 科学者たちは火星に生命が存在するかを調べるための実験を計画した

expert /ékspə:rt/ 名 専門家, 熟練者

a computer	expert	コンピュータ専門家
a financial	expert	金融専門家
a legal	expert	法律専門家
a medical	expert	医療専門家

▷ I'm not a **legal expert**, just a citizen. 私は法律の専門家ではなく、ただの一般市民です

an expert	at doing	…する達人
an expert	in A	Aの専門家
an expert	on A	

★ ×an expert of A とはいわない

▷ She is an **expert at** calculating. 彼女は計算の達人です
▷ Dr. David Gregory is an **expert in** economics. デイビッド・グレゴリー博士は経済学の専門家です

explain /ikspléin/ 動 説明する, 解説する

fully	explain	十分説明する
satisfactorily	explain	満足のいく説明をする
partly	explain	部分的に説明する
briefly	explain	簡潔に説明する
clearly	explain	明確に説明する
easily	explain	楽々と説明する
well	explain	うまく説明する
explain	exactly	正確に説明する
explain	simply	簡単に説明する

▷He couldn't **satisfactorily explain** what had happened. 何が起きたのか彼は満足のいく説明ができなかった
▷He **clearly explained** what we should do in an emergency. 彼は緊急時に私たちがすべきことを明確に説明した
▷This phenomenon is **easily explained**. この現象の説明は簡単だ
▷Let me **explain exactly** what I mean. 私の意図を正確に説明させてください
▷This is a complex issue and hard to **explain simply**. これは複雑な問題で,簡単に説明するのは難しい

explain	A to B	AをB(人)に説明する
explain	about A	Aについて説明する

▷He **explained** everything **to** me slowly and clearly. 彼は何から何までかんで含めるように私に説明してくれた
▷Could you **explain about** why the floods happened in Florida? なぜフロリダで洪水が起きたのか説明していただけませんか

explain	(that)...	…ということを説明する
explain	wh-	…かを説明する

★ wh- は why, how, what など

▷He **explained that** they had known each other for six years. 彼らは6年来の知己だと彼は説明した
▷She couldn't **explain why** she was late. 彼女はなぜ遅刻したのか説明できなかった

as	explained above	上で説明したように
as	explained earlier	前述したように

▷**As explained above**, December was originally the tenth month of the Roman calendar. 上で説明したように,12月はローマ暦では10番目の月だった

explanation /èksplənéiʃən/ 名 説明

have	an explanation	説明できる
offer	an explanation	説明する
provide	an explanation	
give	an explanation	
need	an explanation	説明を必要とする
require	an explanation	
demand	an explanation	説明を要求する
accept	an explanation	説明を受け入れる

▷He **had** no satisfactory **explanation** for the fall in profits. 彼は減益について満足のいく説明ができなかった
▷I guess you don't **need** long **explanations**. 長い説明は必要ないと思います
▷The part written in italics **requires** some **explanation**. イタリックで書かれた部分は説明が必要です
▷Shareholders **demanded** an **explanation** for Mansfield's resignation. 株主たちはマンスフィールドが辞任した理由の説明を求めた
▷My boss refused to **accept** my **explanation**. 上司は私の説明を受け入れるのを拒否した

a satisfactory	explanation	満足のいく説明
a simple	explanation	簡単な説明
an easy	explanation	
a possible	explanation	可能な説明
an alternative	explanation	代わりの説明

▷Let me offer a **simple explanation**. 簡単に説明させてください
▷I have very carefully considered all the **possible explanations**. あらゆる可能な説明をとても注意深く検討した

explanation	for A	Aについての説明

▷He couldn't give a satisfactory **explanation for** his rude behavior. なぜ失礼な態度をとったのか彼は満足のいく説明ができなかった

explode /iksplóud/

動 爆発する,爆発させる;怒りが爆発する

suddenly	explode	突然爆発する;急に怒り出す

▷He said a man was carrying a suitcase and the suitcase **suddenly exploded**. 男がスーツケースを運んでいるとそれが突然爆発したと彼は言った

explode	into A	急にAに発展する
explode	with A	A(感情)を爆発させる

▷Racial tension has **exploded into** anger and violence. 人種間の緊張は突然怒りと暴力へと発展した

explore /iksplɔ́:r/

| explosion |

動 探検する, 探索する, 調査する

fully	explore	十分に探索する
thoroughly	explore	
systematically	explore	体系的に探る
explore	further	さらに探索する

▷To **fully explore** Kyoto, you must always have a complete travel guide. 京都を見尽くすには，京都を隅々まで紹介した旅行案内書がぜひとも必要です

▷This question is **explored further** in the next chapter. この問題は次の章でさらに検討される

explore	wh-	…かを調べる

★wh- は how, what, why など

▷He **explores how** our minds shape our personalities throughout our lives. 彼が探究しているのは，人が生きていく過程で，心はいかに人の性格を形づくるかということだ

explosion /ɪksploʊʒən/

名 爆発；爆発的な増加

cause	an explosion	爆発を引き起こす

▷We are still investigating what **caused** the **explosion**. 爆発の原因をいまなお調査中です

an explosion	occurs	爆発が起きる

▷The **explosion occurred** at around 4:30 a.m. in a shopping mall. 爆発は午前4時30分ごろショッピングモールで起きた

a huge	explosion	大爆発
a loud	explosion	
a big	explosion	
a massive	explosion	
a small	explosion	小規模の爆発
a controlled	explosion	制御された爆発
a nuclear	explosion	核爆発
a population	explosion	人口爆発
a price	explosion	価格の急騰

▷There was a **huge explosion** that shook the building. 建物を揺らす大爆発が起きた

▷Several **loud explosions** were heard in Baghdad. 数回の大爆発音がバグダッドで聞こえた

▷A **nuclear explosion** destroys everything in an instant. 核爆発は一瞬にしてすべてを破壊する

export /ékspɔːrt/

名 輸出；輸出品；輸出高

boost	exports	輸出を増やす
increase	exports	
reduce	exports	輸出を減らす
ban	the export	輸出を禁止する

▷African countries **boosted exports** by an average of 4.3 percent a year. アフリカの国々は年平均4.3パーセント輸出を伸ばした

▷The government **banned** the **export** *of* weapons to other countries. 政府は他国への武器輸出を禁止した

the main	exports	主要輸出品
a major	export	
the principal	exports	
total	exports	輸出総額
agricultural	exports	農産物輸出

▷Chile's **main exports** to the United States are vegetables and fruit. チリの米国への主要輸出品は野菜と果物だ

▷**Total exports** dropped 6.9 percent during the first eight months of this year. 輸出総額は今年に入ってからの8か月間で6.9パーセント下がった

▷One of our major **agricultural exports** is soybeans. われわれのおもな農産物輸出の一つは大豆だ

imports and exports		輸出入

★exports and imports もほぼ同頻度で用いる

▷The gap between **imports and exports** has expanded. 輸出入の差は拡大した

export /ɪkspɔ́ːrt/ **動** 輸出する

illegally	export	不法に輸出する

▷Nearly 90% of Afghan emeralds are **illegally exported** out of the country. アフガニスタン産出のエメラルドの9割近くが国外に不法輸出されている

export	A to B	AをBに輸出する
export	A from B	AをBから輸出する

▷Malaysia **exports** many products **to** Japan. マレーシアは多くの製品を日本へ輸出している

expose /ɪkspóʊz/ **動** さらす；明るみに出す

be fully	exposed	完全にさらされる
be completely	exposed	
be constantly	exposed	絶えずさらされる

▷We were **fully exposed** to attack. 私たちは完全に攻撃にさらされた
▷They were **constantly exposed** to dangerous levels of radiation. 彼らは危険レベルの放射線に常にさらされていた

expose	A to B	AをBにさらす

▷Approximately 20% of children are **exposed to** passive smoking in their homes. およそ2割の子どもたちが自宅で間接喫煙にさらされている

express /iksprés/ 動 表現する，言い表す

openly	express	率直に表現する
clearly	express	はっきり表現する

▷Charles couldn't **openly express** himself. チャールズは自分を率直に表現できなかった
▷He **clearly expressed** what he wanted to say. 彼は言いたいことをはっきり表現した

expression /ikspréʃən/

名 表現，言い回し；表情

find	expression	表出する
give	expression	表現する
use	expressions	表現を使う
have	an expression	表情をする

▷Wordsworth's feelings **find expression** in his poetry. ワーズワースの感情はその詩に表出している
▷These paintings **gave expression** to human emotions. これらの絵は人間の感情を表現した
▷Children often **use expressions** like "Give me!" or "No way!" 子どもは「ちょうだい」とか「いやだよ」のような表現をよく使う
▷He **had** an **expression** of concern on his face. 彼は心配そうな表情をしていた

a clear	expression	明確な表現
(a) concrete	expression	具体的表現
a natural	expression	自然な表現
free	expression	自由な表現
emotional	expression	感情表現
a colloquial	expression	口語表現
facial	expression	顔の表情
a puzzled	expression	困った表情

▷The message was a **clear expression** of annoyance. そのメッセージにはいらだちが明確に表れていた
▷His response was a pretty **natural expression** of his feelings toward Michael. 彼の反応にはマイケルへの感情がとても自然に表れていた
▷The right of **free expression** shall be protected. 自由な表現の権利は保護すべきだ
▷Her **facial expression** and eye movements are remarkable. 彼女の顔の表情と目の動きは驚くべきものだ

freedom of	expression	表現の自由
a means of	expression	表現手段
the expression	on A's face	顔の表情
the expression	in A's eyes	目の表情

▷Everyone has the right to **freedom of expression**. だれもが表現の自由の権利がある
▷He had a sad **expression on** his **face**. 彼は悲しげな表情を浮かべていた

PHRASES
(**if you'll**) **pardon the expression** ☺ こう言っては悪いけど ▷Actually, I think you've got a screw loose, if you'll pardon the expression! ほんとのことを言うときみの頭はねじが緩んでると思うよ．こんなこと言って悪いけどさ

extend /iksténd/

動 拡大する；延長する，延ばす

greatly	extend	大きく拡大する
gradually	extend	徐々に拡大する

▷Modern health care has **greatly extended** our life span. 現代の保健医療は人間の寿命を著しく延ばした

extend	beyond A	Aを超えた範囲に及ぶ
extend	over A	Aの範囲に及ぶ
extend	to A	

★extend to A は extend over A より範囲が限定されている

▷My goal as a teacher **extends beyond** just telling students what to do. 教師としての私の目標は生徒に何をすべきかを教えるだけにはとどまらない
▷The total garden **extends over** 17,000 square meters. 庭の全体の広さは1万7千平方メートルに及ぶ (★「1万7千平方メートル以上に及ぶ」の解釈も可能)

extent /ikstént/ 名 程度，範囲；広さ

to a large	extent	大いに
to a great	extent	
to a considerable	extent	かなりの程度まで
to a significant	extent	
to a lesser	extent	より少ない範囲で

to a limited	extent	限られた範囲で
to an	extent	ある程度まで

▷ **To a large extent** this policy was successful. かなりの程度までこの政策はうまくいった
▷ Prices fell **to a significant extent**. 価格はかなり下がった
▷ Government policies were successful, but only **to a limited extent**. 政府の政策はうまくいったとはいうものの，範囲は限られていた

the full	extent	全容

▷ The **full extent** *of* the problem will not become apparent for another two or three months. 問題の全容はあと2，3か月は明らかにならないだろう

the extent	to which	どの程度…か
to what	extent	どの程度まで

▷ **To what extent** do the people benefit from such policies? そのような政策から人々はどのくらいの利益を得るだろうか

to	the extent that...	…するほどまでに
to	such an extent that...	

▷ The condition had progressed **to such** an **extent that** the pain was too severe to bear. 病状は進行して痛みが耐えられないほどまでになっていた

eye /ái/ 名 目；視力；観察力；見解

A's eyes	blaze	目が輝く
A's eyes	shine	
A's eyes	glitter	

▷ Her dark **eyes** were **blazing** with anger. 彼女の黒い目は怒りに燃えていた
▷ His **eyes** were **shining** excitedly. 彼の目は興奮に輝いていた

open	one's eyes	目を開ける
close	one's eyes	目を閉じる
shut	one's eyes	
raise	one's eyes	目を上げる
lower	one's eyes	目を伏せる
blink	one's eyes	まばたきする
roll	one's eyes	目を白黒させる
narrow	one's eyes	目を細める
strain	one's eyes	目を痛める
rub	one's eyes	目をこする
wipe	one's eyes	目をふく
catch	A's eye	目を引く

look A in	the eye	Aの目を見る
be all	eyes	目を皿にする

▷ **Open** your **eyes**! Don't go to sleep. 目を開けなさい。眠ってはだめ
▷ He **closed** his **eyes** tightly for a few seconds. 彼は数秒間目をしっかり閉じた
▷ "Oh, no! Mr. Bean! Not you again!" said the driving instructor, **rolling** his **eyes**! 「なんてことだ，ミスタービーン。またお前か」と言って，車の教習所の教官は目を白黒させた(★信じられないとき，あきれたときの表情)
▷ Emma **narrowed** her **eyes** suspiciously. エマは疑わしそうに目を細めた(★日本語「目を細める」は喜びの表情だが，英語では疑いを表す)
▷ Lisa stood up and **looked** him **in** the **eye**. リサは立ち上がって彼の目を見た
▷ She was **all eyes** for what her new neighbors would be like. 新しい隣人がどんな人か彼女は目を皿のようにして見た

blue	eyes	青い目
dark	eyes	黒い目
a good	eye	よい視力
a sharp	eye	
the naked	eye	肉眼，裸眼
a watchful	eye	用心深い目

▷ Her wide **dark eyes** brimmed with tears. 彼女の大きな黒い目は涙であふれた
▷ Atoms are invisible *to* the **naked eye**. 原子は肉眼では見えない
▷ I improved my golf under the **watchful eye** of my father. 父親の入念な指導のもとでゴルフが上達した

in	A's eyes	Aの見解では
in	one's mind's eye	心の目で
with	one's own eyes	自分の目で

▷ **In** my **eyes** Beckham has been the most successful of any British soccer player. 私の意見ではベッカムはイギリスのサッカー界で最も成功した選手だと思う
▷ **In** his **mind's eye** he could see her fate all too clearly. 彼の心の目には彼女の運命がありありと浮かんだ
▷ I saw a UFO. You don't believe me? It's true. I saw it **with** my **own eyes**. UFOを見たんだ，信じてくれないのかい。本当だよ。この目で実際に見たんだ

PHRASES

I couldn't believe my eyes! ☺ 自分の目を疑ったよ

F

face /féis/ 名 顔；表情；正面

turn	one's face	顔を向ける
bury	one's face	顔をうずめる
cover	one's face	顔を覆う
hide	one's face	顔を隠す
wash	one's face	顔を洗う
wipe	one's face	顔をふく
make	a face	顔をしかめる
pull	a face	

▷ I **turned** my **face** *to* the window. 顔を窓の方へ向けた
▷ She **buried** her **face** *in* her hands. 彼女は手に顔をうずめた
▷ Tom **covered** his **face** *with* his hands. トムは両手で顔を覆った
▷ Eric **wiped** his **face** *with* a towel. エリックはタオルで顔をふいた
▷ The little boy hid behind the door and **pulled** a **face** *at* the camera. 小さな男の子はドアの後ろに隠れ，カメラにしかめっつらをして見せた

A's face	lights up	表情が輝く
A's face	brightens	
A's face	darkens	表情が曇る
A's face	falls	表情が沈む

▷ Greg's **face lit up** with pleasure and excitement. グレッグの顔は喜びと興奮に輝いた
▷ Rob's **face darkened** *at* the news. その知らせにロブの顔が曇った
▷ Jane's **face fell**, but she recovered quickly. ジェインは気落ちした表情になったが，すぐ気を取り直した

a pretty	face	かわいい顔
a handsome	face	整った顔
a round	face	丸顔
an oval	face	細長い顔
a pale	face	青ざめた顔
a white	face	
a worried	face	心配そうな表情
a long	face	浮かない表情
a familiar	face	なじみの顔
a new	face	新顔
a famous	face	有名人

★「細長い顔」は **a long face** とはいわない

▷ He had a **pale face**, dark eyes and untidy hair. 彼は青白い顔，黒い目をして，髪の毛はぼさぼさだった
▷ Why the **long face**? Come on, smile! You'll feel a lot better, I promise! なぜ浮かない顔をしているの．さあ，笑って．ずっと気分がよくなるよ．本当さ
▷ It's good to see a **familiar face**. なじみの顔に会えてうれしい

face	down	顔をうつぶせに；表を下に

▷ After she fell from the mountain top they found her lying **face down** in the snow. 山頂から転落した彼女は，雪の中で顔をうつぶせにした状態で発見された

in	the face of A	Aに直面して
on	the face of it	表面上は，一見

▷ **In** the **face of** adversity, I think we have to pull together. 逆境にあっては，みんなで力を合わせるべきだと思う
▷ **On** the **face of it**, there seems to be very little difference between the two views. 一見，その二つの見方にはほとんど差がないように見える

fact /fækt/ 名 事実

an important	fact	重要な事実
relevant	facts	関連する事実
basic	facts	基本的事実
the simple	fact	単純な事実
hard	facts	厳然たる事実
the plain	fact	明白な事実
a sad	fact	悲しい事実
a historical	fact	歴史的事実
the mere	fact	単なる事実

▷ May I present a few **relevant facts**? 関連する事実をいくつか提示しても構いませんか
▷ Let's start with some **basic facts**. 基本的な事実から始めましょう
▷ The **plain fact** is *that* there is no more money available. 明白なのは自由になるお金がもうないことだ
▷ Let me point out a couple of **historical facts**. 2, 3の歴史的事実を指摘させてください
▷ The **mere fact** *that* you conclude that she was suspicious is not enough. 彼女が怪しいときみが結論づけるだけでは不十分だ

overlook	the fact	事実を見過ごす
reflect	the fact	事実を反映する

▷ We mustn't **overlook** the **fact** *that* he did his best to help us. 彼が私たちを助けようと最善を尽くしたことを見過ごしてはいけない

| factor |

the fact	remains	事実は残る

▷ I understand what you're saying, but the **fact remains** *that* it's too late to do anything now. あなたが言おうとすることはわかるけど，いまとなっては遅すぎるという事実に変わりはない

know	for a fact	事実として知っている

▷ I **know for** a **fact** that the information is true. その情報が正しいのはわかっている

a fact	about A	Aについての事実
despite	the fact	事実にもかかわらず
in	fact	実際に，事実上；
in	actual fact	実は

▷ This is a good time to discuss **facts about** alcohol such as the long-term and short-term effects. アルコールの長期および短期の影響について議論するよい機会だ
▷ **Despite** the **fact** that he will be 80 next year, he is as active as ever. 来年は80歳だというのに，相変らず彼はかくしゃくとしている
▷ I really like my job. **In fact**, it's one of the most interesting experiences I've ever had. 仕事がとても気に入っています．本当のところ，いままででいちばんおもしろい経験をさせてもらっています

the fact	that...	…という事実

▷ Paul is proud of the **fact that** he is farming as organically as possible. できる限り有機農業を実践していることにポールは誇りをもっている

factor /fǽktər/ 名 要因, 要素, 因子

an important	factor	重要な要因
a major	factor	大きな要因
a crucial	factor	決定的要因
a key	factor	鍵となる要因
a risk	factor	危険要因
economic	factors	経済的要因
social	factors	社会的要因

▷ Calories are the most **important factor** in weight management. カロリーは体重管理で最も重要な要素だ
▷ Education is one of the most **crucial factors** for socioeconomic development. 教育は社会経済の発展のためにきわめて重要な要素の一つだ
▷ There must be some psychological and **social factors** behind the trend. 流行の背景には心理的および社会的要因があるに違いない

a factor	in A	Aの要因

▷ Lifestyle definitely is a **factor in** the risk of cancer. 生活スタイルはがんになる危険度を決定するまさに一つの要因だ

factory /fǽktəri/ 名 工場

build	a factory	工場を建設する
close	a factory	工場を閉鎖する
manage	a factory	工場を経営する

▷ Many global firms have **built** their own **factories** in China. グローバル企業の多くが中国に工場を建設した

a large	factory	大きな工場
a small	factory	小さな工場
a car	factory	自動車工場
a chemical	factory	化学工場

▷ Audi and GM have **large factories** in Hungary. アウディとGMはハンガリーに大きな工場がある

in	a factory	工場で
at	a factory	

▷ She had worked **in a factory** producing computer parts. 彼女はコンピュータ部品を生産する工場で働いていた

faculty /fǽkəlti/ 名 能力, 機能

mental	faculties	心の機能
critical	faculties	批判力

▷ Yoga exercise has the capacity to prevent illness and keep the body fit by evolving a steady balance between the physical and **mental faculties**. ヨガは体と心の機能をバランスよく発達させることで，病気を予防し健康を保つ力がある

the faculty	for A	Aの能力，才能

▷ Jack had a **faculty for** remembering faces. ジャックには顔を覚える才能があった

fade /féid/ 動 色あせる；しおれる

quickly	fade	すぐ色あせる
rapidly	fade	
soon	fade	そのうち色あせる
gradually	fade	徐々に色あせる
slowly	fade	ゆっくり色あせる

never	fade	決して色あせない
fade	away	色あせる, 消える

▷My feelings of annoyance **soon faded** away. いらいらした気持ちはそのうち消えた
▷The happy memories of my school days will **never fade**. 学生時代の幸せな思い出は決して色あせることはないだろう
▷In time the scar will **fade away**. やがて傷跡は消えるだろう

fade	from A	Aから消える
fade	into A	Aの中に消える

▷Martin's smile **faded from** his face. マーティンの顔からほほえみが消えた
▷The soldier's uniform was camouflaged, so that he would **fade into** the background. 軍服が迷彩が施されていたので, 彼は背景に溶け込んでしまうだろう

fail /féil/ 動 失敗する, し損なう; 怠る

fail	miserably	惨めにも失敗する
fail	dismally	
fail	completely	完全に失敗する

▷Despite our best efforts, we **failed miserably**. 最善の努力をしたけれども惨めに失敗した
▷I **failed completely** to find what I was looking for. 探していたものをどうにも見つけられなかった

fail	in A	Aに失敗する; Aを怠る

▷When you **fail in** business you can always try again. 商売で失敗してもいつでもやり直せる

fail	to do	…しない; …し損なう

▷Jackson **failed to** turn up to his father's birthday party at the weekend. ジャクソンは週末にあった父親の誕生パーティーに顔を出さなかった
♦**never fail to** do 必ず…する ▷She rarely plans her concerts, but never fails to delight her audience. 彼女はめったにコンサートを企画しないが, コンサートを開けば必ず聴衆を喜ばせる
♦**I fail to see / I fail to understand** ☺ どうもよくわからない ▷I'm sorry if I fail to understand your situation. どうもあなたの状況が理解できなくて申し訳ありません

failure /féiljər/ 名 失敗; 故障, 不全

be doomed to	failure	失敗する運命にある
end in	failure	失敗に終わる
result in	failure	
cause	a failure	故障を引き起こす
lead to	failure	故障につながる

▷His attempt was **doomed to failure** from the start. 彼の試みは初めから失敗する運命にあった
▷These negotiations **ended in failure**. これらの交渉は失敗に終わった

a total	failure	まったくの失敗
a complete	failure	
a dismal	failure	惨めな失敗
economic	failure	経済破綻
engine	failure	エンジン故障
brake	failure	ブレーキ故障
power	failure	停電
heart	failure	心不全
liver	failure	肝不全
kidney	failure	腎不全

▷The government's attitude toward this issue is a **total failure**. この問題に対する政府の態度はお粗末きわまる
▷The experiment was a **dismal failure**. その実験は惨憺(さん)たる失敗だった

a failure	in A	Aの失敗

▷A **failure in** an exam can be very upsetting. 試験に落ちると動揺するものだ

failure	to do	…しないこと

▷His **failure to** communicate caused many problems. 彼はコミュニケーションがとれなくていろいろ問題を起こした

fair /féər/ 形 公正な, 公平な

perfectly	fair	まったく妥当な
hardly	fair	とても公正とは言えない
pretty	fair	とても妥当な

▷It's **hardly fair** to judge him before you have met him. まだ会ってもいないのに彼のことを判断するのはとても公正とは言えない

PHRASES
fair enough ☺ 結構です, いいですよ ▷"I'll think about it, but I'm not making any promises, OK?" "Fair enough then."「検討はしてみますが, 何もお約束はできません. いいですか」「それで結構です」
It's fair to say (that)... …と言って差し支えない ▷It's fair to say that BBC News 24 offers a generally superb service. BBC News 24はおおむねすばらしいサービスを提供していると言って差し支えない

It's not fair. ☺ それは不公平だ

faith /féiθ/ 名 信頼；信仰；信義

have	faith	信頼している
lose	faith	信頼を失う
put	one's faith	信頼を置く
place	one's faith	
lose	faith	信頼を失う
destroy	A's faith	信頼を崩す
restore	A's faith	信頼を回復する

▷Jane **has** great **faith** in him. ジェインはとても彼を信頼している（★much, great, some, a little, no など程度を表す副詞，形容詞を faith につける）
▷People have **lost faith** in the government. 人々は政府への信頼を失った
▷Many people **place** their **faith** in him. 多くの人が彼を信頼している
▷He **restored** our **faith** in politics. 彼は政治のわれわれの信頼を回復させた

(a) great	faith	大きな信頼
blind	faith	盲目的な信頼
(a) religious	faith	信仰心

▷I have **great faith** in the younger generation. 私はより若い世代に大きな信頼を寄せている
▷Don't have **blind faith** in a computer-based system. コンピュータ支援システムをむやみに信頼してはいけない

faith	in A	Aへの信頼；A(神)への信仰

▷I have total **faith in** God. 神を全面的に信仰している

break	faith with A	Aとの信義を破る
keep	faith with A	Aとの信義を守る

▷He refused to **break faith with** his principles. 彼は自分の原則を曲げるのを拒んだ
▷Fans have **kept faith with** her since her 1995 debut album. ファンは1995年のデビューアルバム以来，彼女を支持し続けている

in	good faith	信義を守って
in	bad faith	信義を破って

▷We have negotiated **in good faith** to solve this problem. この問題を解決するために誠意をもって交渉した

fall /fɔːl/ 名 下落, 低下；落下, 転倒

have	a fall	転倒する
break	A's fall	落下の衝撃を和らげる
cause	a fall	下落を引き起こす
lead to	a fall	下落につながる
show	a fall	落ち込みを示す

▷I **had a fall** and there was slight bleeding in my nose. 転倒して少し鼻血が出た
▷The roof **broke** his **fall**. He was lucky. 屋根が落下の衝撃を弱めてくれた．彼は幸運だった
▷Economic downturn has **caused a fall** in prices. 景気低迷は価格低下を引き起こした
▷Competition will eventually **lead to a fall** in prices for consumers. 競争はやがては消費者にとっては価格下落につながるだろう

a dramatic	fall	劇的な下落
a significant	fall	大幅な下落
a sharp	fall	急激な下落
a steep	fall	
a further	fall	さらなる下落
a slight	fall	わずかな下落

▷The most **dramatic fall** in birth rate occurred between 1981 and 1988. 出生率の劇的な減少が起きたのは1981年から88年にかけてだった
▷The statistics show a **significant fall** in the number of tourists to Japan. 統計によると日本への旅行者数が大幅に減っている
▷Violent crime has fallen every year and police are expecting a **further fall** this year. 凶悪犯罪は毎年減ってきており，今年はさらに減ると警察は予測している

a fall	from A	Aからの落下
a fall	in A	Aの下落

▷He was injured in a **fall from** a roof. 彼は屋根から落ちてけがをした
▷Inflation means a **fall in** the value of money. インフレとは貨幣価値が下がることである

fall /fɔːl/ 動 落ちる；倒れる；下がる

fall	down	転ぶ
fall	over	
fall	dramatically	劇的に下がる
fall	rapidly	急激に下がる
fall	sharply	
fall	slightly	やや下がる

▷He was completely drunk. Every time he tried to stand up, he **fell over**. 彼はすっかり酔っぱらって，立ち上がろうとするたびに転んでしまった

fall	off A	Aから落ちる
fall	down A	Aを転げ落ちる

▷ Steve **fell off** the roof and landed on his head. スティーブは屋根から落ちて地面に頭をぶつけた
▷ My dad **fell down** the stairs and broke his arm. 父は階段を転げ落ちて腕を折った

fall	into A	Aに落ちる；A(グループ)に分かれる
fall	by A	A(数値)だけ下がる

▷ The stone **fell into** the water. 石は水の中に落ちた
▷ Wine generally **falls into** three categories:red, white and rosé. ワインは一般に3つに分類される。赤、白そしてロゼです

false /fɔ́ːls/ 形 誤った；偽の

totally	false	まったく誤りの
completely	false	
entirely	false	
patently	false	明らかに誤りの

▷ "Was it true that you spent a year in prison?" "No. It's **totally false!**" 「1年間刑務所暮らしをしたって本当かい」「そんなのまったくのでたらめさ」
▷ Problem is, that story is **patently false**. 問題はその話はどう見ても間違いだということだ

fame /féim/ 名 名声

achieve	fame	名声を博する
rise to	fame	
shoot to	fame	

▷ Haruki Murakami **achieved** international **fame** with his series of novels. 村上春樹は一連の小説で国際的な名声を博した

fame and fortune	富と名声
★日本語と順序が逆になる	

▷ Meg has left New York to seek **fame and fortune** in Hollywood. メグはニューヨークを後にしてハリウッドに富と名声を求めに行った

familiar /fəmíljər/
形 よく知られている、なじみ深い

vaguely	familiar	漠然と知られた
all too	familiar	あまりに知られた
painfully	familiar	
depressingly	familiar	
familiar	enough	十分知っている

▷ His face looked **vaguely familiar**. 彼の顔にはなんとなく見覚えがあった
▷ Today security is an **all too familiar** issue in many countries. 今日では多くの国々で安全のことを論じるのはごく当たり前のことになっている
▷ I'm not **familiar enough** with the United States educational system to comment. 米国の教育制度についてコメントするほどよくは知りません

familiar	to A	A(人)によく知られている
familiar	with A	A(事)に精通している

▷ The story is **familiar to** most people. その話はたいていの人が知っている
▷ She is **familiar with** the world of Harry Potter. 彼女はハリー・ポッターの世界に精通している

family /fǽməli/ 名 家族；(一家の)子ども

be in	A's family	家族の所有物である
have	a family	子どもがいる
start	a family	子どもをつくる
bring up	a family	子どもを育てる
raise	a family	
support	a family	子どもを養う
feed	a family	

▷ If you **have a family**, you've got to spend time with them. 子どもがいたら子どもと一緒に過ごさなくてはいけない
▷ This amount of money was not enough to **support a family** of five. この金額では5人の子どもを養うのに十分ではなかった

a large	family	大家族；子どもの多い家庭
a small	family	子どもの少ない家庭
a nuclear	family	核家族
an extended	family	拡大家族

▷ I was the fifth son in a **large family**. 私は子どもの多い家庭の5番目の息子だった
▷ The basic family unit is the **nuclear family**—a husband, a wife and their children. 家族の基本単位は夫、妻とその子どもという核家族だ

family and friends	家族と友人
★ friends and family ともいう	

| famous |

▷ **Family and friends** are far more important to her than material wealth. 家族や友人は彼女にとって物質的な豊かさよりもずっと大切だ

a chicken	farm	養鶏場
a dairy	farm	酪農場
a fish	farm	養魚場

famous /féiməs/ 形 有名な, 名高い

| internationally | famous | 国際的に有名な |
| locally | famous | 地元で有名な |

▷ Franklin became **internationally famous** for his experiments on electricity. フランクリンは電気の実験で国際的に有名になった

| famous | as A | A として有名な |
| famous | for A | A で有名な |

▷ Liverpool is **famous as** the home of the Beatles. リバプールはビートルズの故郷として有名だ
▷ The area is **famous for** the autumn colors. その地域は秋の紅葉で有名だ

fascinating /fǽsənèitiŋ/

形 魅惑的な, うっとりさせる

absolutely	fascinating	たまらなく魅力的な
quite	fascinating	
endlessly	fascinating	魅惑してやまない

▷ The film will be **absolutely fascinating** to people who know the town. その映画はその街を知っている人たちにはたまらなく魅力的だろう
▷ I found the book **endlessly fascinating**. その本の魅力は汲めども尽きないほどだと思った

| It is fascinating | to do | …するのは魅惑的だ |

▷ **It's fascinating to** watch animal behavior in the wild. 自然の中で動物の行動を見るのはぞくぞくする

fantastic /fæntǽstik/

形 すばらしい, すてきな

| absolutely | fantastic | とてもすてきな |

▷ It was an **absolutely fantastic** day, one of the happiest days of my life. それまでの人生でいちばん幸せな, すごくすてきな日でした

PHRASES
That's fantastic! / It's fantastic! ☺ それはすてき単に Fantastic! ともいう)

far /fάːr/ 形 遠い, 向こうの

| the far | north | はるか北 |

★ south, east, west も同様に用いる

▷ Hokkaido is an island in the **far north** of Japan. 北海道は日本の北のほうにある島だ

farm /fάːrm/ 名 農場; 飼育場

run	a farm	農場を経営する
work on	a farm	農場で働く
live on	a farm	農場で暮らす

▷ Charles Brown **runs** a **farm** in Vermont. チャールズ・ブラウンはバーモントで農場を経営している
▷ I **worked on** a **farm** for most of my life. 人生のほとんどを農場で働いた

fashion /fǽʃən/

名 流行, ファッション；仕方, やり方, 流儀

be in	fashion	流行している
be back in	fashion	流行が戻る
come into	fashion	流行しだす
come back into	fashion	また流行しだす
go out of	fashion	流行遅れになる
fall out of	fashion	
set	a fashion	流行を作り出す
follow	a fashion	流行を追う
keep up with	the fashion	

▷ Short hair is now **in fashion**. ショートヘアが流行している
▷ Science fiction was **back in fashion**, thanks to Star Wars. スターウォーズのおかげでSFがまたはやりだしていた
▷ In the 1980s, the term "civil society" **came into fashion**. 1980年代に「市民社会」という用語が流行した
▷ Some clothes I wore in the eighties have **come back into fashion** now. 80年代に着た服がまた流行になっている
▷ Who says radio is **going out of fashion**? ラジオが時代遅れになりつつあるなどと言うのはだれだ
▷ In the sixties the Beatles **set a fashion** for Beatle haircuts. 60年代にビートルズはビートルヘアスタイルに先鞭をつけた

▷He **followed** the **fashion** of the time. 彼は時代の流行を追った
▷She has a hard time **keeping up with** the **fashion**. 彼女はなかなか流行についていけない

the current	fashion	今の流行
the latest	fashion	最新の流行
a new	fashion	新しい流行
high	fashion	最先端の流行

▷What are the **current fashion** trends in California? カリフォルニアの現在のファッショントレンドはどんなものですか
▷Do you know about the **new fashion** for autumn 2012? 2012年の秋の新しい流行を知っていますか

| after | a fashion | 一応は, どうにか |
| in | (a)... fashion | …な仕方で |

★ in (a)... fashion は same, similar, orderly, spectacular などと用いる

▷The email service was restored today, **after a fashion**. Eメールのサービスはきょうどうにか回復した
▷If everyone drove **in** an **orderly fashion**, vehicles would move much faster. みんなが整然と運転すれば車はもっと速く進めるのに
▷She won the women's 100 meter butterfly **in spectacular fashion**. 彼女は女子100メートルバタフライで華々しい勝利を上げた

| changes in | fashion | 流行の変化 |

▷He was sensitive to **changes in fashion**. 彼は流行の変化に敏感だった

fast /fæst | fáːst/ 形 速い

extremely	fast	とても速い
really	fast	
too	fast	あまりにも速い

▷The pace of life is **too fast** for me. 生活のペースが私には速すぎる

fat /fæt/ 形 太った

| grow | fat | 太る |

▷I mustn't eat so much. I'll **grow fat**. 食べすぎはだめだ. 太ってしまう

really	fat	すごく太った
enormously	fat	
rather	fat	どちらかと言うと太った

▷I used to be **really fat**. 昔はとても太っていた
▷I was **rather fat** at the time, although I didn't realize it. その頃どちらかと言うと太っていた. 自覚していたわけではなかったが

father /fáːðər/ 名 父, 父親

A's natural	father	実の父
A's real	father	
A's foster	father	育ての父
a good	father	よき父親
an absent	father	家庭に欠けている父親
A's late	father	亡き父
Heavenly	Father	天なる父
Almighty	Father	全能の父

▷My **late father**, Martin Simpson, was a teacher. いまは亡き父, マーティン・シンプソンは教師でした
▷Almighty God, our **Heavenly Father**. 全能の神よ, 天にましますわれらが父よ

| a father | to A | Aの父 |
| a father | of two | 二児の父 |

★ three, four なども用いる

▷I'm the **father of two** children. 二児の父親です

fault /fɔ́ːlt/

名 過失, 誤り;(過失の)責任;欠陥;欠点

| have | a fault | 欠陥がある;欠点がある |
| correct | a fault | 欠陥を修正する |

▷If he **has** a **fault**, it is that he is too idealistic. 彼に欠点があるとしたら, あまりに理想主義的なところだ
▷We need to **correct** the **faults** in the design. デザインの欠陥を修正する必要がある

a serious	fault	重大な欠陥
a common	fault	よくある欠陥
an electrical	fault	電気故障

▷The book has two **serious faults**. その本には重大な欠陥が2つある
▷There is no evidence of any **electrical fault**. 電気故障があった形跡はない

| fault | in A | Aにおける欠陥 |
| fault | with A | Aの欠陥 |

▷Many people pointed out that there was a big

| favor |

fault in the system. 多くの人たちがシステムに大きな欠陥があると指摘した
▷ It was difficult to find **fault with** his argument. 彼の論法に不備な点を探すのは難しかった

| at | fault | 責任がある |

▷ Thousands of people suffered or died for lack of water and food. Who is **at fault**? 何千人もの人々が水と食料の不足に苦しんだり亡くなったりした. だれに責任があるのか

| be | A's fault (that...) | (…は) Aの責任だ |
| be | all A's fault | すべてAの責任だ |

▷ "I'm sorry. I didn't mean to..." "It wasn't your **fault**." 「すみません. そんなつもりでは…」「きみのせいじゃないよ」

| through | no fault of one's own | 自分に何の落ち度もないのに |

▷ He has lost his job **through no fault of** his **own**. 彼は自分には何の落ち度もないのに職を失った

favor /féivər/ 名 好意；支持, 賛成；親切な行為；えこひいき(★《英》つづりは favour)

ask	a favor	頼みごとをする
do	a favor	頼みを聞いてやる
owe A	a favor	Aに恩義がある
return	a favor	恩を返す
find	favor	支持を得る
win	favor	
gain	favor	
curry	favor	機嫌をとる
show	favor	えこひいきする
fall from	favor	人気がなくなる,
fall out of	favor	支持を失う
lose	favor	

▷ May I **ask** a **favor** of you? お願いがあるのですが
▷ Will you **do** me a **favor**? 願いを聞いてくれるかな
▷ I hope that my story will **find favor** with you all. 私の話がみんなに気に入ってもらえるといいのですが
▷ He knew how to **win** the **favor** of his customers. 彼は顧客の支持を得る方法を知っていた
▷ The president was very popular at first, but soon he **fell from favor**. 大統領は当初は非常に人気があったがすぐに国民の支持を失った

| in | favor of A | Aに賛成して；Aのために |
| in | A's favor | Aに有利に |

▷ We are **in favor of** saving pandas. パンダ保護を推し進めるべきだと思う
▷ Luckily the vote went **in** our **favor**. 幸運にも投票結果はわれわれに有利に出た

PHRASES
Do me a favor! 😊 頼むから, お願いだから；《英》ばか言え, とんでもない

favor /féivər/

動 賛成する, 支持する(★《英》つづりは favour)

strongly	favor	強く支持する
particularly	favor	特に支持する
be much	favored	すごく支持される

▷ The group **strongly favor** tax cuts. そのグループは減税を強く支持した
▷ These hotels are very **much favored** by foreign travelers. これらのホテルは外国人旅行者に非常に人気が高い

| favor A | over B | BよりAを支持する |

▷ Investors are **favoring** Singapore **over** Hong Kong. 投資家たちは香港よりシンガポールに注目している

| tend to | favor A | Aを支持する傾向がある |

▷ Japanese **tend to favor** shorter trips. 日本人は小旅行を好む傾向がある

fax /fæks/ 名 ファックス

get	a fax	ファックスを受け取る
receive	a fax	
send	a fax	ファックスを送る

▷ Did you **get** my **fax**? ファックス届いた？
▷ I **received** a **fax** from Mr. Johnson. ジョンソン氏からファックスを受け取った

| an incoming | fax | 受信ファックス |

▷ I check **incoming faxes** every morning when I arrive in my office. オフィスに着くと毎朝受信ファックスを確認します

| by | fax | ファックスで |

▷ Let us know **by fax**. ファックスで知らせてください

| a fax | machine | ファックス機 |
| A's fax | number | ファックス番号 |

▷ What is Robert's **fax number**? ロバートのファックス番号は何番ですか

fear /fíər/ 图 恐れ, 恐怖；不安, 心配

feel	fear	恐れを感じる
express	fears	恐れを表明する
raise	fears	恐れを増す
confirm	one's fears	心配どおりになる
allay	fears	恐怖を和らげる
overcome	one's fear	恐怖を克服する
conquer	one's fear	
dismiss	fears	恐怖心を一掃する

▷I've never **felt fear** like this. このような恐怖を感じたことはない
▷She always **expressed fears** about getting fat. 彼女は太るのが怖いといつも言っていた
▷Human deaths from bird flu **raise fears** of a global outbreak. 鳥インフルエンザにかかった人の中から死者が出るとなると, 世界的大流行が懸念される
▷The government tried to **allay fears** of fuel shortages. 政府は燃料不足への不安を和らげようとした

fears	grow	恐怖が募る

▷**Fears grew** that terrorists planned further attacks. テロリストがさらなる攻撃を計画しているという不安が高まった

(a) great	fear	大きな恐れ
(a) real	fear	本物の恐れ
the worst	fear(s)	最も心配なこと

▷John has a **great fear** of flying in airplanes. ジョンは飛行機に乗るのをすごく怖がっている
▷There are **real fears** that things will get worse. 事態が悪化するの不安は現実味を帯びている

fear	about A	Aについての恐怖
fear	for A	Aへの恐怖, 心配
for	fear of A	Aを恐れて
in	fear	恐怖に
with	fear	恐怖で
without	fear	恐れることなく

▷**Fears for** the Japanese economy are growing. 日本経済への懸念が増しつつある
▷Many parents kept their children at home **for fear of** kidnapping. 誘拐を恐れて子どもを自宅から外に出さない親が多かった
▷Andy trembled **with fear**. アンディは恐怖に震えた

fear	that...	…という心配

▷The incident raised **fears that** violence could spread throughout the region. その事件のせいで地域に暴力が広がる心配が高まった

PHRASES
No fear! ☺ (英) とんでもない, ごめんこうむる(★提案などを拒否するのに用いる)

fear /fíər/ 動 恐れる；心配する

greatly	fear	非常に恐れる

▷I **greatly fear** that an accident is about to take place. 事故が今にも起こるのではないかととても心配だ

fear	for A	Aを心配する

▷Do you **fear for** your own children's future? 子どもたちの将来が心配ですか

fear	that...	…ということを心配する
fear	to do	…するのを恐れる
fear	doing	

▷Many people **fear that** eating before they go to sleep may cause fat gain. 寝る前に食べると脂肪が増えると心配する人が多い
▷That park was the place where people **feared going** to because of crime. その公園は犯罪を恐れてだれも近づこうとしない場所だった

feature /fíːtʃər/

图 特徴；特集記事；顔立ち

have	a feature	特徴がある
include	a feature	特徴を含む
incorporate	features	
add	features	特徴を追加する
do	a feature	特集を組む
run	a feature	特集記事を載せる

▷The Great Barrier Reef **has** many **features** that help to protect it. グレートバリアリーフには多くの特徴があり, その保護に役立っている
▷The garden **incorporated** all the **features** of an English garden. その庭はイギリス風庭園のあらゆる特徴を取り入れていた
▷This version of Internet Explorer **adds** many new **features**. インターネットエクスプローラの今回のバージョンには多くの新しい特徴が加わっている

an essential	feature	本質的特徴
an important	feature	重要な特徴
a key	feature	
the main	feature	主要な特徴
a distinctive	feature	際だった特徴

| feature |

a striking	feature	
a special	feature	目玉；独自の特色
a common	feature	共通の特徴
a new	feature	新しい特徴

▷Wine is an **essential feature** of the image and economy of Bulgaria. ワインはブルガリアのイメージと経済に不可欠な特産品だ
▷Maori culture is recognized as a **distinctive feature** of New Zealand. マオリ文化はニュージーランドの際だった特徴と見なされている
▷A **special feature** of this year's event is the Vintage Car Exhibition. 今年のイベントの目玉はヴィンテージカーの展示会です

a feature	on A	Aの特集

▷CNN did a **feature on** global warming last month. CNNは先月，地球温暖化に関する特集番組を組んだ

feature /fíːtʃər/

動 特集する；主演させる；特色となっている

feature	prominently	大きな特色である
feature	strongly	

★副詞が動詞の前にくることもある

▷Duke Ellington **featured prominently** in her father's record collection. 彼女の父親のレコードコレクションの中ではデューク・エリントンが際だっていた

feature	A as B	AをBとして出演させる
feature	in A	Aの特色になっている

▷This film **features** Mel Gibson **as** Jefferson Smith. この映画ではジェファーソン・スミス役でメル・ギブソンを起用している
▷The photos **featured in** the book. 写真が中心の本だった

fee /fíː/

名 報酬, 謝礼；手数料；料金, 費用

charge	fees	報酬を請求する
pay	fees	報酬を払う
receive	a fee	手数料を受け取る
earn	a fee	手数料を得る

▷Private schools **charge** high **fees** but have smaller class sizes. 私立学校は授業料は高いが，クラスのサイズは小さめだ
▷Mr. Stanley has **received fees** for work carried out for that company. スタンレイ氏はその会社のために行った仕事の報酬を受け取った

a high	fee	高い料金
a large	fee	
a low	fee	安い料金
a small	fee	
a fixed	fee	固定料金
an additional	fee	追加料金
an annual	fee	年会費
an admission	fee	入場料；入会金
an entrance	fee	入場料；入会費
an entry	fee	入会費；参加費
a membership	fee	会費
a license	fee	ライセンス料

▷You're going to pay rather **high fees**. かなり高い料金を払うことになるよ
▷For a **small fee** any book can be ordered from anywhere in the world. わずかな料金でどんな本も世界中どこからでも注文できる
▷There's an **additional fee** of ten dollars. 追加料金が10ドルかかります
▷Members have to pay an $80 **annual fee**. 会員は80ドルの年会費を払わなければならない

feed /fíːd/

動 食べ物を与える, 肥料をやる；供給する

feed A	to B	A（食べ物）をBに与える
feed B	on A	
feed	on A	Aを常食とする
feed A	with B	AにBを提供する
feed A	into B	AをBに入力する

▷I **feed** bread **to** ducks at a nearby pond every morning. 毎朝近くの池でアヒルにパンをやっている
▷Kangaroos **feed on** leaves. カンガルーは葉を常食にしている
▷They **fed** the stove **with** coal. ストーブに石炭をくべた
▷She **fed** the data **into** a computer. 彼女はデータをコンピュータに入力した

feel /fíːl/ 動 感じる；思う, 気がする

no longer	feel	もはや感じない
still	feel	なお感じる

▷The situation has got so bad that they **no longer feel** safe in the city. 状況がひどく悪化して街はもはや安全とは思えない

▷ **I still feel** hungry. まだ空腹感がある

feel	A do	Aが…するのを感じる
feel	A doing	Aが…しているのを感じる
feel	(that)...	…と考える

▷ Ruth **felt** her face go red with anger. ルースは怒りで自分の顔が赤くなるのがわかった
▷ She suddenly **felt** the room shaking. 彼女は突然部屋が揺れているのを感じた
▷ We **feel that** Norma is well qualified. ノーマは十分な資格があると考えられる

PHRASES
How are you feeling? ☺ 気分はどうですか
I feel for you. ☺ お気の毒です
I know how you feel. ☺ お気持ちはわかります

feeling /fíːliŋ/ 名 感情, 気持ち；感じ

get	a feeling	気がする
have	a feeling	
arouse	feelings	感情をかき立てる
express	feelings	感情を表す
show	feelings	
hide	one's feelings	感情を隠す
hurt	A's feelings	感情を傷つける
understand	A's feelings	感情を理解する
share	A's feelings	感情を分かち合う

▷ I **get** the **feeling** that that's exactly the point. そこがまさに大事だという気がする
▷ I couldn't **express** my **feelings** to her. 彼女に自分の気持ちを表せなかった
▷ I'm sorry I **hurt** your **feelings**. 気分を悪くさせてしまってごめんなさい
▷ I want to **share** that **feeling** with other people. その気持ちをほかの人たちと分かち合いたい

a strong	feeling	強い感じ
a bad	feeling	いやな感じ
a strange	feeling	奇妙な感じ
a general	feeling	全体の感じ
strong	feelings	確固とした意見
mixed	feelings	複雑な感情
bad	feelings	悪感情
ill	feelings	
personal	feelings	個人的感情

▷ I have a **strong feeling** that I've met her before. 彼女には以前に絶対会っていると思う
▷ I have a **bad feeling** in my stomach. お腹の調子がよくない
▷ I had a **strange feelings** that something might have happened. 何か起こったのではないかという妙な気持ちがした
▷ What is your **general feeling** about Canadian films? カナダ映画についてのあなたの全般的な印象はどうですか
▷ I have **strong feelings** about capital punishment. 死刑について確固とした意見をもっている
▷ Natalie and Otto got a divorce. I had **mixed feelings** about it. ナタリーとオットーが離婚して、私は複雑な心境だった

feelings	about A	Aについての思い
feelings	for A	Aに対する思い
feelings	toward A	Aへの思い

▷ What are your **feelings about** this book? この本についてどう思いますか
▷ Emma still has a lot of **feelings for** Alex. エマは今でもアレックスのことが大好きだ
▷ I have no negative **feelings toward** him. 彼に否定的な感情は抱いていない

a feeling	(that)...	…だという感じ

▷ Did you get any **feeling that** something was wrong? 何か変だなという感じがありましたか

PHRASES
I know the feeling. ☺ 気持ちはわかるよ
No hard feelings. ☺ 悪く思わないでね

fence /féns/ 名 柵, 塀, 垣根

build	a fence	柵を築く
erect	a fence	
put up	a fence	
climb	a fence	柵に登る
climb over	a fence	柵を乗り越える
jump over	a fence	柵を飛び越える
mend	fences	関係を修復する

▷ Martin **erected** a **fence** around the pond. マーティンは池の周りに柵をつくった
▷ I saw a cat **climbing** the **fence** of Maureen's garden. 猫がモーリンの庭の塀を登っているのを見た
▷ The government is making an effort to **mend fences** with China. 政府は中国との関係修復の努力をしている

a high	fence	高い柵
a low	fence	低い柵
a barbed-wire	fence	有刺鉄線を張った柵
an electric	fence	電気柵

▷ We began by putting up a **high fence** to keep out the goats. まずヤギを寄せ付けないように高い囲いをつくった

| festival |

▷ The purpose of the **electric fence** is to prevent undesired animals from entering the area. 電気柵の目的は好ましくない動物の侵入を防ぐことだ

festival /féstəvəl/ 名 祭り, フェスティバル

hold	a festival	祭りを催す
attend	a festival	祭りに参加する

▷ The **festival** was **held** in Boston April 20 — May 5. フェスティバルは4月20日から5月5日までボストンで開かれた

a festival	takes place	祭りが開かれる
a festival	begins	祭りが始まる
a festival	opens	

▷ An annual jazz **festival takes place** in mid-November. 毎年恒例のジャズフェスティバルが11月中旬に開催される
▷ The film **festival begins** on November 5. その映画祭は11月5日に始まる

a major	festival	大きな祭り
an annual	festival	毎年恒例の祭り
an international	festival	国際フェスティバル
an art	festival	芸術祭
a film	festival	映画祭
a music	festival	音楽祭
a rock	festival	ロックフェスティバル
a religious	festival	宗教的祭り

▷ The Gion Festival in Kyoto is one of the **major festivals** in Japan. 京都の祇園祭は日本の大きな祭りの一つです
▷ Christmas is a **religious festival**. クリスマスは宗教的な祭りだ

field /fi:ld/ 名 競技場; 分野, 領域

take	the field	入場する; 試合を戦う
lead	the field	トップに立つ
enter	the field	入場する; 分野に入る
leave	the field	退場する

▷ Manchester United had to **take** the **field** without their best player. マンチェスターユナイテッドはチーム内で最高のプレーヤー抜きで試合を戦うことを余儀なくされた
▷ The USA **leads** the **field** in rocket science. 米国はロケット科学で最先端に立っている
▷ He **entered** the **field** of music by accident. 彼はたまたま音楽の世界に入った

▷ On 40 minutes Burns **left** the **field** with a rib injury. 40分にバーンズはろっ骨のけがで退場した

a grass	field	草地
an open	field	広々とした野原
a rice	field	田んぼ
a wheat	field	小麦畑
a playing	field	競技場
a baseball	field	野球場
a soccer	field	サッカー場
a specialist	field	専門分野
a wide	field	広い分野

▷ The event was held in an **open field** in Cannon Hill Park. その催しはキャノンヒルパークの広々とした野外で開かれた
▷ His latest report covers a **wide field**. 彼の最新の報告書は幅広い分野に言及している

fight /fáit/ 名 戦い; 格闘, けんか

pick	a fight	けんかを売る
start	a fight	
have	a fight	けんかする
get into	a fight	
win	a fight	けんかに勝つ; 戦いに勝つ
lose	a fight	けんかに負ける; 戦いに負ける

▷ Please don't **pick** a **fight** with me. 頼むからぼくにけんかを売らないでくれ
▷ Did you two **have** a **fight**? きみたち二人はけんかしたのか
▷ The country has **won** the **fight** against inflation. その国はインフレとの闘いに勝った
▷ Charlie **lost** his **fight** against cancer. チャーリーはがんとの闘いに敗れた

a big	fight	大げんか
a real	fight	本物のけんか
a straight	fight	一騎討ち
a hard	fight	厳しい戦い
a tough	fight	
a good	fight	善戦
a brave	fight	

▷ Anne had a **big fight** with her mother. アンは母親と大げんかした
▷ The General Election is a **straight fight** between Labour and Conservatives. 総選挙は労働党と保守党の一騎打ちだ
▷ Mr. Brown faces a **tough fight** to retain his seat in the next election. ブラウン氏は次の選挙で議席を維持するための厳しい戦いを強いられている
▷ We're fighting a **good fight** and we'll win. 私

ちはよく戦っており，きっと勝利するだろう

a fight	between A	Aの間のけんか
a fight	with A	Aとのけんか
a fight	against A	Aとの戦い
a fight	for A	Aを求める戦い

▷He's responsible for the **fight between** Steve and Kate. スティーブとケイトがけんかしたのは彼に責任がある
▷Did you have a **fight with** her yesterday? きのう彼女とけんかしたの？
▷It's possible to win the **fight against** cancer. がんとの闘いに勝つことは可能だ
▷He joined the **fight for** civil rights. 彼は公民権を求める戦いに加わった

fight /fáit/ 動 戦う；殴り合いのけんかをする

fight	bravely	勇敢に戦う
fight	hard	激しく戦う
fight	back	反撃する
fight	desperately	必死で戦う

▷He **fought bravely** for his country. 彼は国のために勇敢に戦った
▷She **fought hard** against the disease. 彼女は病気と精一杯戦った
▷She didn't attempt to **fight back**. 彼女は反撃しようとしなかった
▷Emergency crews **fought desperately** to save her life. 救急隊は彼女の命を救おうと必死の活動を繰り広げた

fight	against A	Aと戦う
fight	for A	Aのために戦う
fight	over A	Aを巡って戦う
fight	with A	A(人)と戦う，口論する

▷We are **fighting for** equal rights. 私たちは権利の平等を求めて戦っている
▷They are still **fighting over** the same issue. 彼らは同じ問題を巡ってなお言い争いをしている
▷I don't want to **fight with** my parents. 両親と口論したくはない

fight	to do	…しようと戦う

▷She **fought to** control her voice. 彼女は必死で声を整えようとした

figure /fígjər | fígə/
名 数字；(人の)姿，スタイル；図形

reach	a figure	数値に達する
release	a figure	数字を発表する
keep	one's figure	体型を保つ
watch	one's figure	体型に気をつける
lose	one's figure	体型が崩れる

▷Final enrollment **figures** will **be released** in November. 最終の入学者数は11月に公表される
▷It's amazing you can **keep** your **figure** eating like that! そんなに食べてスタイルが保てるなんて驚きだ
▷Women **lose** their **figures**, men lose their hair. 女性は体型が崩れ，男性は髪の毛がなくなる

double	figures	2桁台の数字
official	figures	公式の数字
the latest	figures	最新の数字
a key	figure	中心人物
a leading	figure	第一人者
a public	figure	有名人
a popular	figure	人気者
a good	figure	よいスタイル

▷**Official figures** show that crime is falling. 公式の数字では犯罪は減少しつつある
▷Dick was a **key figure** in this debate. ディックはこの討論で中心的な人物だった
▷Matsui is among the most **popular figures** in Japan. He is nicknamed "Godzilla." 松井は日本で最も人気のある人物の一人で，「ゴジラ」の愛称で呼ばれている
▷Mary is attractive and she has a **good figure**. メアリーは魅力的でスタイルがよい

figure /fígjər | fígə/
動 重要な位置を占める；思う

figure	prominently	特に重要な位置を占める

▷Wrestlers from Mongolia **figure prominently** in Japanese sumo. 日本の相撲界ではモンゴル出身力士が特に目立っている

figure	(that)...	…だと思う

▷I **figured** I didn't have much time to prepare for the meeting. 会議の準備をする時間があまりないと思った

PHRASES
Go figure. ☺ どうもよくわからないよ
It figures. / **That figures.** ☺ やっぱり思ったとおりだ，やはりそうか ▷"We shouldn't expand our company too fast. We should do it step by step." "Yes, that figures." 「会社をそんなに早く大きくしないほうがいい．段階を踏むべきだ」「そうだね，そのとおりだね」

file /fáil/

名 (項目別の)書類, 記録；(コンピュータの)ファイル

keep	a file	記録を残す
create	a file	ファイルをつくる
open	a file	ファイルを開く
close	a file	ファイルを閉じる
save	a file	ファイルを保存する
copy	a file	ファイルをコピーする
delete	a file	ファイルを削除する
retrieve	a file	ファイルを検索する

▷**Copy** the **files** to a USB memory drive. ファイルをUSBメモリドライブにコピーしなさい
▷I accidently **deleted** a **file** I've been working on all day. 1日かけて作成していたファイルを誤って削除してしまった
▷**Retrieve** the **file** you wish to copy. コピーしたいファイルを検索しなさい

a personal	file	個人ファイル
a secret	file	秘密ファイル
a large	file	大きなファイル
a data	file	データファイル

▷I have some **large files** to send you by email. Eメールであなたに送る大きなファイルがあります

a file	on A	Aに関するファイル
on	file	ファイルに(して)

▷Police keep **files on** criminals. 警察は犯罪者のファイルを保存している
▷She has 40,000 résumés and photos **on file**. 彼女は4万人の履歴書と写真をファイルに記録している

film /film/

名 《英》映画(《米》movie)；(写真の)フィルム；薄い膜

see	a film	映画を見る
watch	a film	
direct	a film	映画を監督する
make	a film	映画を撮る
shoot	a film	
produce	a film	映画を製作する

▷Every time I **see** that **film**, I think it's just wonderful. その映画を見るたびに, すばらしいと思う
▷I'm **making** a **film** that deals with the life of Shakespeare. シェイクスピアの生涯を題材とした映画を撮影中です
▷**Producing** a **film** can be very expensive. 映画製作には高額な費用がかかることがある

final /fáinl/

名 決勝戦；《米》学年末試験, 《英》最終試験

reach	the final(s)	決勝に進む
make	the final(s)	
make it to	the final(s)	
qualify for	the final(s)	
go through to	the final(s)	
win	the final(s)	決勝で勝つ
take	one's finals	最終試験を受ける

▷Brazil **reached** the **final** by beating Italy last night. ブラジルは昨夜イタリアを破って決勝に進んだ
▷The top six teams **qualify for** the **finals**. 上位6チームが決勝に駒を進める
▷Liverpool went on to **win** the **final** 3-1. リバプールは勝ち続け決勝でも3対1で勝った
▷Emma is due to **take** her **finals** this year. エマは今年, 最終試験を受けることになっている

find /fáind/

動 見つける, 発見する；わかる, 気づく

eventually	find	ついに見つける
never	find	決して見つからない

▷I **eventually found** a good solution. ついによい解決策を見つけた
▷We **never found** any evidence of that at all. その証拠はまったく見つからなかった

find	A B	AにBを見つけてやる
find	A doing	Aが…しているのに気づく

▷I promised him that I would **find** him a job. 彼に仕事を見つけてやると約束した
▷Tom **found** her waiting for him. トムは彼女が彼を待っているのに気づいた ▷He **found** himself getting nervous. 彼は自分が緊張しているのがわかった

find	A C	AがCだと気づく

★Cは difficult, hard, easy, impossible, attractive などの形容詞

▷I **found** it very interesting. それをとてもおもしろいと思った

find	that...	…であるとわかる

▷I **found that** I need our friendly discussions. ざっくばらんな議論が必要だとわかった

fine /fáin/ 形 すばらしい；元気な；細かい

absolutely	fine	実にすばらしい；とても
just	fine	元気な
exceptionally	fine	すごくすばらしい
particularly	fine	とりわけすばらしい
extremely	fine	すごく細かい

▷Everything is **absolutely fine**. 万事まったく順調です
▷John Williams is an **exceptionally fine** guitar player. ジョン・ウィリアムズは並はずれてすばらしいギター奏者だ
▷The weather has been **particularly fine** lately. このところずっとすばらしい天気だ

PHRASES〉
(I'm) fine thanks. ☺ 元気です
A is fine. A（時間・場所など）でいいですよ（★待ち合わせなどの約束に用いる）▷Three o'clock, outside the library is fine. 3時に図書館の外ということで構いません
(No,) I'm fine (thanks). いいえ、もう結構です（★食べ物などを勧められて断るときに用いる）▷"More tea?" "No, I'm fine thanks." 「紅茶をもっといかが？」「いいえ、もうけっこうです」
That's fine. ☺ 大丈夫です、いいですよ ▷"I'm so sorry." "That's fine." 「本当にごめんなさい」「大丈夫ですよ」
You're a fine one to talk! ☺ （自分のことを棚に上げて）よくそんなことが言えるよ

fine /fáin/ 名 罰金

pay	a fine	罰金を払う
impose	a fine	罰金を科す
face	a fine	罰金を科される

▷You'll probably have to **pay a fine**. おそらく罰金ものだよ
▷The US government **imposed a fine** of $168,000 on that company. 米国政府はその会社に16万8千ドルの罰金を科した
▷He now **faces a fine** of up to $1,000. 彼は千ドル以下の罰金を科せられている

a heavy	fine	重い罰金
a substantial	fine	
a maximum	fine	罰金の最高額

▷In Melbourne Australia there is a **heavy fine** for dropping cigarette butts. オーストラリアのメルボルンではたばこの吸い殻を捨てると重い罰金が科せられる

| a fine | for A | Aに対する罰金 |

▷I recently received a **fine for** driving in a bus lane. バスレーンを走行して罰金をくらったばかりだ

finger /fíŋgər/ 名 (手の)指

point	a finger	指をさす
raise	a finger	指を立てる
jam	one's fingers	指を挟む
lick	one's finger	指をなめる
run	one's finger	指を走らせる
drum	one's finger	指でとんとんたたく
tap	one's finger	
snap	one's fingers	指を鳴らす
click	one's fingers	
cut	one's finger	指を切る
burn	one's fingers	指をやけどする；痛い目にあう

▷Davis **raised a finger** to indicate he wanted to respond. デイビスは人差し指を立てて、発言を求めた（★発言を求めるときに人差し指を立てる）
▷"Wow!" "What happened?" "I **jammed** my **fingers** in the door." 「痛い」「どうしたの」「ドアに指を挟んじゃった」
▷She **ran** her **fingers** through my hair. 彼女は私の髪に指を滑らせた
▷Sue **drummed** her **fingers** on the table for a moment. スーは少しの間テーブルを指でとんとんたたいた（★いらだちの動作を表す）
▷"Oh, right!" Jake said, **snapping** his **fingers**. 「そうだ」とジェイクは言って指を鳴らした（★何かを思いついたり、しめた、というときのしぐさ）
▷I tried to put out the fire with a blanket and **burnt** my **fingers**. 毛布で火を消そうとして、指をやけどした ▷The recent stock market in Germany has **burned** many **fingers**. ドイツにおける最近の証券市場で多くの投資家がやけどした

the first	finger	人差し指
the index	finger	
the middle	finger	中指
the ring	finger	薬指
the little	finger	小指
a slender	finger	細い指
a fat	finger	太い指
an accusing	finger	非難の矛先

★「親指」は thumb

▷She has beautiful long **slender fingers**. 彼女の指はほっそりして長い

| finish |

▷He pointed an **accusing finger** at her. 彼は彼女に非難の矛先を向けた

the tips of	A's fingers	指先

▷The **tips of** my **fingers** were freezing with cold. 指先が寒さで凍りそうだった

finish /fíniʃ/ 動 終える；終わる

finally	finish	ついに終わる
nearly	finished	ほぼ終了した
almost	finished	

▷I **finally finished** high school and went on to university. ついに高校を終えて大学に進学した
▷"Do you need a hand?" "No thanks. It's **nearly finished** now."「手伝いましょうか」「いいえ結構です。もうほとんど終わりました」

finish	first	1位になる

★ second, third なども用いる

▷Tom **finished second**. Who was the winner? トムが2位に終わったってことは優勝したのはだれ？

finish	with A	Aで終わる；Aを使い終える

▷The winners **finished with** three points in the final eight minutes. 勝者は最後の8分で3得点して終わった ▷Are you **finished with** the newspaper? 新聞はもうお済みですか

finish	doing	…し終える

★ × finish to do とはいわない

▷I've just **finished** read**ing** *Harry Potter*. ちょうど『ハリー・ポッター』を読み終えたところだ

PHRASES
I'm finished. ☺(何かしていたことが)もう終わりました；ごちそうさまでした
Let me finish. ☺ 最後まで言わせて ▷Wait a minute, Nancy. Let me finish. ちょっと待ってナンシー、最後まで言わせて

fire /fáiər/ 名 火；火事, 火災；発砲, 射撃

catch	fire	火がつく
start	a fire	火事を出す
set A on	fire	Aに放火する
set	fire to A	
put out	a fire	火事を消す
extinguish	a fire	
fight	a fire	消火に当たる
die in	a fire	焼死する
be damaged by	fire	火事の被害を受ける
be destroyed by	fire	焼失する
make	a fire	火を起こす
build	a fire	
light	a fire	火をつける
open	fire	戦火を開く
cease	fire	銃撃をやめる
come under	fire	砲火を浴びる

▷Cigarettes frequently **start** house **fires**. たばこはしばしば住宅火災の原因となる
▷He **set fire to** his neighbor's house. 彼は隣家に放火した
▷I used a fire extinguisher to **put out** the **fire**. 消火器を使って火を消した
▷He died **fighting** a **fire** in a chemical plant. 彼は化学工場の消火活動中に亡くなった
▷At least 12 people **died in** the fire. 少なくとも12名がその火事で死亡した
▷The building was completely **destroyed by** the **fire**. その建物は火事で全焼した
▷Sally **made** a **fire** in the hearth. サリーは炉床に火を入れた
▷I **lit** a **fire** in the fireplace and sat by it. 暖炉に火をつけてそばに腰を下ろした
▷The soldiers didn't hesitate. They **opened fire** immediately. 兵士たちはためらうことなくすぐに発砲を始めた
▷**Cease fire!** 撃ち方やめ
▷The soldiers **came under** heavy **fire**. 兵士たちは激しい銃撃を受けた

a fire	breaks out	火事が発生する
a fire	burns	火が燃える
a fire	goes out	火が消える
a fire	spreads	火が広がる

▷The **fire broke out** at two o'clock in the morning. 火災は夜中の2時に発生した
▷The **fire burnt** brightly. 火は明るく燃えた
▷We get pretty chilly if the **fire goes out**. 火が消えてしまったら寒さにこごえることになる
▷As the **fire spread** rapidly, people in the building rushed outside. 火の回りが早かったので建物内の人は急いで外に出た

a big	fire	大火事
a disastrous	fire	ひどい火災
a forest	fire	森林火災

a blazing	fire	赤々と燃える火
an open	fire	暖炉の火, たき火
friendly	fire	友軍からの誤爆
《英》an electric	fire	電気ヒーター
《英》a gas	fire	ガスヒーター

▷Eight people died in a **big fire** last year. 大火により昨年は8名の死者が出た
▷There is an **open fire** in the living room. 居間では暖炉の火が燃えている

on	fire	燃えて, 火災を起こして

▷When he arrived at home he saw that his house was **on fire**. 帰宅してみると自宅が燃えさかっていた

a line of	fire	銃弾の飛び交う場所

fire /fáiər/ 動 撃つ, 発砲する

fire	blindly	やみくもに発砲する
fire	back	撃ち返す
fire	off	発射する

▷They **fired off** some missiles. ミサイルを何発か発射した

fire	at A	Aをめがけて発射する

▷He grabbed his gun and **fired at** them. 彼は拳銃をつかんで彼らに発砲した

firm /fə́:rm/ 名 企業, 事務所; 会社 (★ふつう会社組織でない企業をさす)

work for	a firm	会社で働く
join	a firm	入社する
leave	a firm	会社を辞める

★「(その日の仕事を終えて)退社する」はふつう leave the office という

▷She previously **worked for** a technology firm in Chicago. 彼女は以前シカゴの技術関連の企業に勤めていた
▷Johnson **joined** the **firm** in November 2005. ジョンソンは2005年11月に入社した
▷He **left** the **firm** to establish his own company. 彼は会社を辞めて自分の事務所を設立した

a large	firm	大会社
a big	firm	
a small	firm	小さな会社

a local	firm	地元の会社
an accounting	firm	会計事務所
a consulting	firm	コンサルティング会社
a law	firm	法律事務所

▷All our **large firms** are now investing abroad. 我が国の大企業はどこも海外投資をしている
▷I'm chairman of a small **consulting firm**. 小さなコンサルティング会社の会長です

a firm	based in A	Aに本拠を置く会社

▷Grant Thornton is an accounting **firm based in** Chicago. グラント・ソーントンはシカゴに本拠を置く会計事務所だ

fist /físt/ 名 握りこぶし

clench	one's fist	こぶしを握り締める
shake	one's fist	(怒って)こぶしを振ってみせる

▷He **shook** his **fist** *at* me. I thought he was going to hit me! 彼はぼくに向かってこぶしを振るってみせた. 殴られると思った

fit /fít/ 動 合う; 合わせる, 適合させる

easily	fit	楽に合う
really	fit	よく合う
fit	neatly	きちんと合う
fit	perfectly	完璧に合う
fit	together	ぴったり合う

▷I wanted a pocket computer that **easily fitted** into my pocket. ポケットに簡単に入る小型コンピュータがほしかった
▷Now that I've lost weight my clothes no longer **really fit** me. 体重が減ったので, いままで着ていた服がぴったり合わなくなってきた
▷These two parts should **fit together**. この2つの部分がぴったり合わなくてはいけない

fit	in A	Aに合う
fit	with A	Aと調和する

★in のほかに into, on なども用いる

▷This key doesn't **fit into** the lock. この鍵は錠前に合わない

fit /fít/ 形 元気な, 健康な; 適した

fully	fit	体調がすっかりよい
physically	fit	体調が整った

▷He needs to be **physically fit** and well-conditioned. 彼は体調を整え，万全なコンディションづくりをしておく必要がある

get	fit	体調を整える
see	fit	適切だと思う，よいと思う
think	fit	

▷He **saw fit** to close the company without any notice. 何の予告もなしにすぐ会社を閉じるのがいいと彼は考えた

fit	and healthy	体調がよく健康な
fit	and proper	きちんとした

▷I wish I was **fit and healthy**. 健康そのものだといいのになあ
▷She wants everything to be done in a **fit and proper** way. 彼女は何から何まで完全にきちんとしていないと気が済まない

fit	for A	Aに合った
fit	to do	…するのに適した

▷He was wearing clothes that weren't **fit for** climbing a mountain. 彼は登山にふさわしくない服装をしていた

flag /flǽg/ 名 旗

fly	a flag	旗を掲げる
raise	a flag	
lower	a flag	旗を降ろす
wave	a flag	旗を振る

▷They are **flying** the Japanese **flag**. 日本の国旗が掲げられている
▷Students practiced **raising** and **lowering** the **flag** for the opening ceremony. 生徒たちは開会式に備えて旗を揚げたり降ろしたりする練習をした
▷Children **waved flags** as they sang our national anthem. 子どもたちは国歌を歌いながら旗を振った

a flag	flies	旗がはためく

▷American **flags** were **flying** in cities and towns all across the country on July 4th. 7月4日には国中の都市や町で星条旗がはためいていた

a national	flag	国旗

▷The Canadian **national flag** is a red maple leaf set against a white background. カナダの国旗は白地に赤のカエデの葉です

under	the flag of A	Aの旗のもとに

▷He is traveling around the world to spread the message of peace **under the flag of** the United Nations. 彼は国連の代表として平和のメッセージを広げるために世界を旅している

flash /flǽʃ/ 名 きらめき，閃光；ひらめき

a blinding	flash	目もくらむ閃光
a bright	flash	きらめく閃光
a sudden	flash	突然のきらめき
a brief	flash	一瞬のきらめき

▷The atomic bomb dropped on Hiroshima at 8:15 am with a **blinding flash**. 原子爆弾は目もくらむ閃光とともに午前8時15分，広島に落ちた
▷I had a **sudden flash** of inspiration. 突然インスピレーションを得た
▷She felt a **brief flash** of disappointment. 彼女は一瞬がっかりした

flash /flǽʃ/

動 ぴかっと光る；さっと通り過ぎる

flash	across A	Aにぱっと現れる；(考えが) Aにひらめく

★「考えがひらめく」の意では into, through も用いる

▷Lightening **flashed across** the sky followed by a crack of thunder. 稲光が空にぱっと走り，続いて雷鳴がとどろいた
▷A brilliant idea **flashed into** his mind. すばらしい考えが彼の頭に浮かんだ

flash	on and off	点滅する

▷I saw lights **flashing on and off**. ライトが点滅しているのが見えた

flat /flǽt/ 形 平らな

fairly	flat	かなり平らな
rather	flat	どちらかと言うと平らな
completely	flat	まったく平らな
almost	flat	ほぼ平らな

▷My speaking voice is **rather flat**, but my singing

voice is good. 私の話す声はどちらかと言うと抑揚がないが，歌うといい声だ

flavor /fléivər/

名 風味；趣，味わい(★(英)つづりは flavour)

have	a flavor	風味がある
give	a flavor	風味をつける；雰囲気
impart	a flavor	を伝える
add	flavor	風味を加える
get	a flavor	雰囲気をつかむ

▷Every leaf **has** its own **flavor**. どの葉にも独自の香りがある
▷That spice **gives** great **flavor** to the curry. そのスパイスはカレーにとてもすばらしい風味を与える
▷Dr. Sinclair's presentation **gave** the **flavor** of his book. シンクレア博士の研究発表はその著作の雰囲気を伝えていた

a good	flavor	よい味
a distinctive	flavor	独特の味
a full	flavor	濃い味
a rich	flavor	
a strong	flavor	
a delicate	flavor	繊細な味
a subtle	flavor	
a sweet	flavor	甘い味
a bitter	flavor	苦い味
a nutty	flavor	ナッツ風味

▷This recipe brings out the **full flavor** of lobster. この調理法はロブスターの味を余すところなく引き出してくれる
▷The steak was very tender with **rich flavor** from the beer. とても柔らかいステーキで，ビールの味が移って，こくがよく出ていた
▷Icelandic caviar has a **subtle flavor**. It's difficult to appreciate it. アイスランドのキャビアは繊細な風味で，堪能するのは難しい
▷Hawaiian sweet potatoes have a slightly **sweet flavor**. ハワイのサツマイモは少し甘い味がする
▷Caffeine itself has a **bitter flavor**. カフェイン自体は苦い味がする

in	flavor	味が

▷This cheese is very mild **in flavor**. まろやかな味のチーズだ

flavor and texture	味と食感

▷These mussels share a delicate **flavor and texture**. これらのムール貝は繊細な味と食感を兼ね備えている

flesh /fléʃ/ 名 肉；皮膚

flesh and blood	血の通った人間；肉親
flesh and bone	肉と骨

▷I love you like my own **flesh and blood**. あなたを肉親のように愛している
▷The tiger attacked him and bit through **flesh and bone**. トラは彼を襲い肉と骨にまでかみついた

flexible /fléksəbl/

形 融通のきく；曲げやすい

extremely	flexible	非常に柔軟な
sufficiently	flexible	十分に融通のきく

▷The system is **extremely flexible** and enables you to make changes at any time. とても柔軟なシステムなので，いつでも変更を加えることができる
▷Our rules are not **sufficiently flexible**. They're much too severe. 私たちの規則は融通があまりきかなくて，あまりに厳しすぎる

flight /fláit/ 名 飛行；(飛行機の)便

catch	a flight	飛行機に間に合う
take	a flight	飛行機に乗る
make	a flight	飛行する；飛行機に乗る
book	a flight	飛行機を予約する

▷I had to get up at 5:30 this morning to **catch** my **flight**. 予約した飛行機に乗るのにけさは5時半に起きなければならなかった
▷If you want to get there more quickly you could **take** a direct **flight** to London. もっと早く着きたいならロンドン行きの直行便に乗ったらどうですか
▷In 1905 they **made** a **flight** covering a distance of 24 miles in almost 40 minutes. 1905年に彼らは24マイルの距離をほぼ40分で飛行した
▷I **booked** a **flight** to Australia. オーストラリアへの飛行機を予約した

a direct	flight	直行便
a non-stop	flight	
a connecting	flight	乗り継ぎ便
an internal	flight	国内便
a domestic	flight	
an international	flight	国際便
a long	flight	長時間の飛行
a short	flight	短時間の飛行
an early	flight	早朝便

| float |

▷There's no **direct flight** from Japan to South Africa. 日本から南アフリカへの直行便はない
▷Fred drove to Denver airport to catch an **internal flight**. フレッドは国内便に乗るためにデンバー空港まで車で行った

float /flóut/ 動 浮く,浮かべる;漂う

| float | around | あたりを漂う |

★ほかに away, up, down なども用いる

▷A lot of garbage was **floating around** on the sea. ごみがたくさん海に漂っていた
▷After the typhoon many boats had **floated away**. 台風が去ったあと,多くの船が岸から流されていた
▷Many bubbles were **floating up** near the hot spring. 温泉近くで泡がたくさん浮かび上がってきていた
▷It became cold and snow flakes began to **float down**. 寒くなって雪片が漂いながら舞い落ち始めた

| float | in A | Aに浮かぶ |
| float | on A | |

▷A lot of oil was **floating on** the water. 大量の油が水に浮かんでいた

flood /flʌ́d/ 名 洪水;氾濫

| cause | a flood | 洪水を引き起こす |

▷Heavy rain **caused floods** in parts of the South. 南部のいくつかの地域で大雨による洪水が起きた

a great	flood	大洪水
a devastating	flood	壊滅的な洪水
a flash	flood	鉄砲水
a sudden	flood	突然の氾濫

▷The bridge was broken down by a **great flood**. 橋は大洪水で流された
▷New Orleans was hit by a **devastating flood**. ニューオーリンズは壊滅的な洪水に襲われた
▷The **sudden flood** of American goods will force domestic prices down. アメリカ製品が急に大量に流入してくれば国内価格は押し下げられることになるだろう

floor /flɔ́:r/ 名 床;(建物の)階

sweep	the floor	床を掃く
mop	the floor	床にモップをかける
scrub	the floor	床をごしごしする
wipe	the floor	床をふく
cover	the floor	床を覆う

▷I regularly **sweep** and **wipe** the **floor**. 定期的に床を掃いて,ふいている
▷I **mopped** the **floor** twice and dried it. 2度床にモップをかけて乾かした
▷I don't want to **cover** the **floor** with cheap rugs. 床を安っぽい敷物で覆いたくない

a polished	floor	磨き上げた床
a wooden	floor	木の床
a tiled	floor	タイル張りの床
the top	floor	最上階
the upper	floor	上の階
the lower	floor	下の階

▷Our new apartment has a beautiful wooden **polished floor**. 新しいアパートは美しい木製のつやつやした床です
▷The living room has a polished **wooden floor**. その居間の木の床はよく磨いてあった(★a wood floor も用いる)
▷My office is on the **top floor**. 私のオフィスは最上階にあります
▷The restaurant on the **upper floor** has great views over the lake. 上の階のレストランは湖の眺めがすばらしい

| on | the floor | 床に;…階に |

▷The dish fell **on** the **floor** and broke. 皿は床に落ちて割れた
▷Jane's sitting **on** the **floor** watching TV. ジェインは床に座ってテレビを見ている
▷I live **on** the third **floor** of this building. このビルの3階に住んでいます

flow /flóu/ 名 流れ;流出,流出量

control	the flow	流れを制御する
increase	the flow	流れをよくする
improve	the flow	
reduce	the flow	流れを悪くする
block	the flow	流れをふさぐ
interrupt	the flow	流れをさえぎる
stem	the flow	流れを抑える
stop	the flow	流れを止める

▷Exercise **increases** blood **flow** of all parts of your body. 運動すれば体中の血行がよくなる
▷Smoking narrows arteries, **reducing** blood **flow** to your feet. 喫煙は動脈を狭くし,足への血行を悪くする

▷I'm sorry to **interrupt** the **flow** of your argument. 議論の流れを妨げて申し訳ありません
▷The new law aims to **stem** the **flow** of illegal immigrants to Europe. 新法にはヨーロッパへの不法移民の流れを食い止めるねらいがある

a constant	flow	絶え間ない流れ
a steady	flow	安定した流れ
information	flow	情報の流れ
traffic	flow	交通の流れ
blood	flow	血流
water	flow	水流
a lava	flow	溶岩流

▷The shop has a **constant flow** of customers. その店には絶え間ない客の出入りがある
▷There's a **steady flow** of tourists from all over the country. 全国各地から刻々と旅行者が訪れてきている

flow /flóu/ 動 流れる

flow	freely	スムーズに流れる
flow	smoothly	
flow	in	流入する
flow	back	逆流する

▷Traffic is **flowing smoothly**. 交通は順調に流れている
▷The company is doing well and a lot of money is **flowing in**. 会社は好調で多額の資金が流入してきている
▷Money is starting to **flow back** into Europe from the US. 資金が米国からヨーロッパへ逆流し始めている

| flow | through A | Aを通って流れる |

★ほかに out of, down, from, into なども用いる

▷The Thames **flows through** London. テムズ川はロンドンを流れている
▷Look! A lot of water is **flowing out of** a hole in that pipe. 見て．水が大量にパイプの穴から流れ出ているぞ
▷When the volcano erupted hot lava **flowed down** the sides of the mountain. 火山が噴火して熱い溶岩が山腹を流れ落ちた

flower /fláuər/ 名 花

produce	flowers	花をつける
bear	flowers	
come into	flower	開花する
plant	flowers	花を植える
cultivate	flowers	花を栽培する
send	flowers	花を送る
pick	flowers	花を摘む
arrange	flowers	花を生ける

▷The sweet peas **produce flowers** in spring. スウィートピーは春に花をつける
▷Daffodils **come into flower** in early spring. 水仙は早春に開花する
▷I **picked** some **flowers** from the garden. 庭の花を摘んだ
▷She **arranged flowers** in the vase for the party. 彼女はパーティー用に花瓶に花を生けた

flowers	appear	花が咲く
flowers	bloom	
flowers	open	花が開く
flowers	grow	花が育つ
flowers	fade	花がしおれる

▷**Flowers bloom** in late spring or early summer. 花々は晩春や初夏に鮮やかに咲く
▷**Flowers open** at dawn and close by night. 花々は明け方に開き夜には閉じる
▷Look at all those beautiful **flowers growing** in that garden! 庭に咲いている美しい花々を見てごらん
▷These **flowers fade** very quickly. これらの花はすぐしおれる

spring	flowers	春の花
wild	flowers	野の花
garden	flowers	庭の花
fresh	flowers	切りたての花
dried	flowers	ドライフラワー
pressed	flowers	押し花
dead	flowers	枯れた花
artificial	flowers	造花

▷It's important to regularly remove **dead flowers**. 枯れた花を定期的に取り除くことが大切だ

| a bouquet of | flowers | 花束 |
| a bunch of | flowers | |

▷Bouquet is a French word for **a bunch of flowers**. ブーケは花束を表すフランス語由来の語だ

| in | flower | 満開で |

▷The roses are **in flower** now. バラはいま満開だ

fly /flái/ 動 飛ぶ；飛行機で行く

| fly | high | 高く飛ぶ |

| focus |

fly	low	低く飛ぶ
fly	away	飛び立つ
fly	off	

▷ The bird **flew away** to another tree. 鳥は別の木へと飛び去った

fly	from A to B	AからBに飛行機で行く
fly	into A	Aに飛行機で乗り入れる；Aに飛び込む
fly	over A	Aの上を飛ぶ

▷ We **flew from** Narita **to** London. 成田からロンドンに飛んだ
▷ Most major airlines **fly into** Heathrow airport. ほとんどの主要航空会社はヒースロー空港に乗り入れている
▷ Two planes **flew into** the Twin Towers on 9/11. 2機の航空機が9月11日ツインタワーに突っ込んだ
▷ They're watching helicopters **flying over** their heads. 彼らは頭上を飛び交う数機のヘリコプターを眺めている

focus /fóukəs/ 名 焦点, ピント

become	a focus	焦点になる
provide	(a) focus	焦点を合わせる
have	a focus	焦点が定まっている
change	the focus	焦点を変える
shift	the focus	焦点を移す
move	the focus	
come into	focus	焦点が合う
bring A into	focus	Aに焦点を合わせる

▷ Ishikawa won a major golf tournament when he was seventeen and **became** the **focus** of much attention. 石川は17歳でメジャートーナメントに勝利し、注目の的になった
▷ Your essay is too general. You need to **have** a **focus**. きみの小論は総論すぎる。焦点を絞らないといけない
▷ Charlie, don't **shift** the **focus** of the conversation. We're still talking about your problems. チャーリー、話をそらすな。まだお前の問題について話しているのだから
▷ Finally I understand. Finally things have **come into focus**. ようやくわかった。やっと事情が飲み込めてきた

the focus	is on A	焦点がAに当たる

▷ The **focus** is **on** developing friendship and communication skills. 友情とコミュニケーション技術を育てることに重点を置いてある

the central	focus	最大の焦点
the main	focus	
the major	focus	
the primary	focus	
a sharp	focus	絞り込んだ焦点
a strong	focus	

▷ This is the **central focus** of this article. これがこの記事のいちばんの論点です
▷ Our **primary focus** is to help the children who are in need of care. 私たちがまず重点を置いているのはケアを必要としている子どもたちを助けることだ
▷ These rumors came into **sharp focus** when they were revealed in the newspapers. 新聞に暴露されてこれらのうわさに当たる焦点が絞れてきた

focus	for A	Aに対する焦点

▷ The **focus for** the November presidential election is the economy and America's role in the world. 11月の大統領選挙の争点は経済および世界におけるアメリカの役割である

in	focus	焦点が合って
out of	focus	焦点がずれて

▷ In the photo the face is **in focus** but the rest is blurred. 写真では顔に焦点が合っているが、その他はぼやけている
▷ His new plan is totally **out of focus**. 彼の新しい計画はまったくのピンぼけだ

focus /fóukəs/ 動 焦点を合わせる

focus	mainly	おもに焦点を当てる
focus	particularly	特に焦点を当てる
focus	exclusively	もっぱら焦点を当てる
focus	entirely	

▷ Joseph's study **focuses mainly** on European paintings. ジョゼフの研究はおもにヨーロッパ絵画を中心にしている
▷ Her interests **focus particularly** on technology and education. 彼女の関心は特に科学技術と教育が中心である
▷ Discussion **focused exclusively** on domestic violence issues. 議論は家庭内暴力の問題にもっぱら集中した

focus	on A	Aに焦点を当てる
focus	upon A	

▷ Sorry, I can't help. I'm too busy **focusing on** my other work. ごめんなさい、お手伝いできません。手を離せないほかの仕事がありまして

fold /fóuld/ 動 折り畳む

carefully	fold	ていねいに折り畳む
neatly	fold	きちんと折り畳む
fold	(A) up	(Aを)折り畳む；折り畳める
fold	(A) down	
fold	(A) away	
fold	A back	Aを折り返す
fold	A in half	Aを半分に折り畳む
fold	A in two	

▷He **carefully folded** the newspaper. 彼は新聞をていねいに折り畳んだ
▷We need to **fold up** the tent. テントを畳む必要がある
▷The rear seats **fold down**. 後部座席は折り畳めます(★他動詞で次のようにもいえる：The rear seats can be folded down.)
▷He **folded** the letter **away** and put it in his pocket. 彼は手紙を折り畳んでポケットに入れた
▷I **folded back** the blanket and rolled up my pajamas. 毛布を畳んでパジャマをくるくる巻いた
▷We **folded** the paper **in half**. 紙を半分に折り畳んだ

follow /fálou | fɔ́l-/ 動 後に続く

closely	follow	ぴったり後に続く
quickly	follow	すぐ後に続く
soon	follow	
immediately	follow	直後に続く

▷It is very important that we **closely follow** the guidelines. ガイドラインに厳密に従うことが非常に重要だ
▷He **quickly followed** her out of the room. 彼は彼女に続いてすぐ部屋を出た

be	followed by A	Aが後に続く

▷In Northern Europe autumn is **followed by** a long, cold winter. 北欧では秋に続いて長く寒い冬が続く

it	follows that...	結果として…になる
it	doesn't necessarily follow that...	必ずしも…ということにはならない

▷Your fingerprints are on the money. So **it follows that** you must have taken it. あなたの指紋が紙幣に残っている．ということはその金をとったのはあなたに違いない

food /fú:d/ 名 食物, 食料；食品

eat	food	食べ物を食べる
prepare	food	食べ物を準備する
provide	food	食べ物を提供する
serve	food	食べ物を出す
produce	food	食料を生産する

▷Whenever you **prepare food**, wash your hands well first. 食べ物を準備するときはまず手をよく洗ってください
▷The United Nations **provided food**, milk and clothing. 国連は食料とミルクと衣類を提供した
▷We are busy **serving food** to customers at lunch time. 昼食時は客に食事を出すのに忙しい

favorite	food	好きな食べ物
health	food	健康食品
fast	food	ファーストフード
junk	food	ジャンクフード
emergency	food	非常食
hot	food	辛い食べ物；熱い食べ物
natural	food	自然食品
organic	food	有機食品
frozen	food	冷凍食品
canned	food	缶詰食品
processed	food	加工食品
fatty	food	脂肪分の多い食品
high-calorie	food	高カロリー食品
spicy	food	辛い食べ物
baby	food	ベビーフード
pet	food	ペットフード
cat	food	キャットフード
dog	food	ドッグフード

▷Teenagers love **fast food**, soft drinks and sweets. 10代の若者たちはファーストフード，ソフトドリンク，菓子が大好きだ
▷Avoid **high-calorie**, **fatty foods**, and you'll lose weight. 高カロリーで脂肪分の多い食べ物を避ければ体重が減るでしょう
▷Beer goes well with **spicy food**. ビールは辛い食事とよく合う(★「辛い」を表すのに hot and spicy の連結もしばしば用いる：hot and spicy food 辛い食べ物)
▷Eat fewer **processed foods** such as potato chips and frozen dinners. ポテトチップスや冷凍食品のような加工食品をなるべく食べないようにしなさい

food and drink(s)		飲食物

▷Don't bring your **food and drinks** into the library! 図書館に飲食物を持ち込まないでください

a supply of	food	食料の供給

▷**Supplies of food** and medicine are running low.

| fool |

食料と薬の供給が乏しくなりつつある

fool /fúːl/ 名 ばか者

| a complete | fool | まったくのばか |

▷There's no point in asking him. The man is a **complete fool**. あいつに聞いてもむださ．まったくばかだから

look (like)	a fool	ばかみたい
feel (like)	a fool	ばかを見る
be	no fool	抜け目がない
make	a fool of A	A(人)をばかにする

▷When you disagreed with me in front of everybody you made me **look a fool**. みんなの前で私に反対してあなたは私の顔をつぶしてくれた
▷He is **no fool**. 彼は抜け目がない
▷He's angry because he thinks you **made a fool of** him. あなたにばかにされたと思って彼は怒っている

foot /fút/ 名 足(足首から下の部分)

get to	one's feet	立ち上がる
rise to	one's feet	
leap to	one's feet	ぱっと立ち上がる
be on	one's feet	立っている
stamp	one's feet	足を踏み鳴らす
tap	one's feet	とんとん足踏みする
drag	one's feet	足を引きずる
wipe	one's feet	足をふく

▷The audience **rose to** its **feet** and applauded. 聴衆は立ち上がって拍手した
▷They **stamped** their **feet** and shouted. 彼らは足を踏み鳴らして叫んだ
▷She **tapped** her **foot** in irritation. 彼女はいらいらして足を踏み鳴らした
▷He's **dragging** his **feet** slightly. 彼は少し足を引きずっている

| foot | slips | 足が滑る |

▷My left **foot slipped** into a hole. 滑って左足が穴にはまり込んだ

| on | foot | 徒歩で |

▷The best way to travel around the city is **on foot**. 街を見て回るのにいちばんよい方法は歩くことだ

force /fɔːrs/ 名 力，暴力；軍隊；影響力

use	force	武力を行使する
resort to	force	力に訴える
come into	force	(法律が)施行される
bring A into	force	Aを施行する
join	forces	力を合わせる
combine	forces	

▷The US finally decided to **use force** against Iraq. 米国はついにイラクに対する武力行使を決定した
▷The new laws **come into force** in one month's time. 新しい法律が1か月後に施行される
▷The Act will be **brought into force** early next year. その法令は来年早々に発効する
▷America and Britain **joined forces** in World War II. 米国とイギリスは第二次世界大戦で協力した

brute	force	腕力
gravitational	force	重力
centrifugal	force	遠心力
the driving	force	原動力
an economic	force	経済力
a political	force	政治力
the labor	force	労働力
the armed	forces	軍隊
military	forces	
nuclear	force	核兵器
peace-keeping	force	平和維持軍
the air	force	空軍

▷Competition is the **driving force** of economic growth. 競争は経済成長の原動力だ
▷The multinational corporations are a powerful **political** and **economic force** in this country. 多国籍企業はこの国において強大な政治力と経済力がある
▷The United States has the most powerful **armed forces** in the world. 米国は世界最強の軍隊を有している
▷Japan has declared that **nuclear force** should never be used. 核兵器の使用は決してあってはならないと日本は宣言した

| by | force | 力ずくで |
| in | force | (法律が)施行されて |

▷Don't do it **by force**, try to persuade them. 力ずくでやるのではなく，彼らを説得するよう努めなさい
▷The rules are not **in force** yet. それらの規則はまだ実施されていない

force /fɔːrs/ 動 強制する

| eventually | force | 結局は強いる |
| finally | force | |

▷The workers were **eventually forced** to accept cuts in their wages. 労働者たちは結局に賃金カットを受け入れざるを得なかった

force A	to do	Aに…するよう
force A	into doing	強いる
force oneself	to do	無理に…する

▷I was **forced to** withdraw money from the ATM. ATMからお金を引き出さざるをえなかった
▷I was really tired, but I **forced** my**self to** stay awake. 疲れ果ててはいたが、無理をして起きていた

| force A | into B | Aを無理やりBに押し込む |
| force A | out of B | Aを無理やりBから追い出す |

▷An eye injury **forced** him **into** early retirement. 目のけがで彼は早期退職に追い込まれた

forest /fɔ́:rist | fɔ́r-/ 名 森, 森林

| walk in | the forest | 森の中を歩く |
| walk through | the forest | |

▷When you are **walking through** the **forest** in South America, be careful of snakes and spiders. 南米の森の中を歩いているときは蛇とクモに気をつけろ

dense	forest	うっそうとした森
a dark	forest	暗い森
tropical	forest	熱帯林

▷In Finland, 76 percent of the nation is covered by **dense forest**. フィンランドは国の76パーセントが深い森に覆われている
▷On the way they had to go through a **dark forest**. 途中、暗い森を通り抜けなければならなかった

forget /fərgét/ 動 忘れる

completely	forget	すっかり忘れる
almost	forget	ほとんど忘れる
never	forget	決して忘れない
soon	forget	すぐ忘れる
easily	forget	簡単に忘れる

▷I **completely forgot** about the problem. その問題のことはすっかり忘れていた
▷I **almost forgot** to say, I'm going away for a few days. 言い忘れるところでしたが数日出かけます
▷I'll **never forget** that experience. その体験を決して忘れないだろう
▷Rules are too **easily forgotten**. 規則はいとも簡単に忘れられる

forget	(that)...	…ということを忘れる
forget	wh-	…かを忘れる
forget	to do	…し忘れる

★wh- は how, why, where, when など

▷Don't **forget** we're going to a movie this evening. 今晩映画を見に行くのよ。忘れないでね
▷He's a little bit crazy, but let's not **forget** the man is a genius. 彼はちょっと変だけど、天才だっていうことを忘れないようにしよう
▷I **forgot where** I put the door key. ドアの鍵をどこへ置いたか忘れてしまった
▷I **forgot to** give you a message from my wife. 忘れてたよ。妻からきみに伝言があったんだ
▷Don't **forget to** post my letter. 手紙を投函するのを忘れないでね

| forget | about A | Aのことを忘れる |

▷**Forget about** Lewis! ルイスのことは忘れろ
PHRASES
Before I forget,... 忘れないうちに言っておきますが ▷Before I forget, Jim rang. He asked you to call him back. そうそう、忘れないうちに伝えておかなくちゃ。ジムから電話があってね。電話してくれってさ
Forget it! ☺ 気にするなよ、もういいよ
Oh! I nearly forgot! ☺ そうだ、もう少しで忘れるところだった

forgive /fərgív/ 動 許す, 大目に見る

| never | forgive | 決して許さない |

▷I'll **never forgive** you! あなたを決して許さないから

| forgive | A for doing | A(人)が…したのを許す |

▷Her mother never **forgave** her **for marrying** Tony. 母親は彼女がトニーと結婚したのを決して許さなかった

| forgive and forget | | 許して忘れる |

▷It's time to **forgive and forget**. そろそろ許して忘れるべき時期だ(水に流してあげよう)
PHRASES
A could be forgiven for thinking... A(人)が…と考えてもおかしくない ▷You could be forgiven for thinking summer was over already. 夏はもう終わったと考えてもおかしくない
Please forgive me! ☺ お願いだから許して

form /fɔ́ːrm/ 名 形；形式，型，形態；書式

take	a form	形式をとる
complete	a form	書式を完成する
fill out	a form	書式に書き込む
fill in	a form	
sign	a form	書式に署名する

▷This book **takes** the **form** *of* a long interview. この本は長いインタビューの形式をとっている
▷Please **complete** the **form** and send it in as soon as possible. 書式を完成させてできるだけ早く提出してください
▷Before you **fill in** the application **form**, you should read through the information. 申込用紙に書き込む前に案内をお読みください
▷He **signed** an application **form**. 彼は申込用紙にサインした

various	forms	さまざまな形式
a simple	form	単純な形式
digital	form	デジタル形式
good	form	好調
poor	form	不調
an application	form	申込用紙
an entry	form	参加申込用紙
an order	form	注文用紙

▷Elaine was a shy girl, who suffered **various forms** of bullying. エレインは内気な少女でさまざまないじめに苦しんだ

in	the form of A	Aの形で

▷The money was received **in** the **form of** checks and cash. 金は小切手と現金の形で受領された

formal /fɔ́ːrməl/ 形 正式の

purely	formal	まったく形式的な

▷"You're asking me a lot of questions, officer." "Don't worry sir. Our inquiry is **purely formal**." 「ずいぶんいろいろ聞いてくるんですね，おまわりさん」「ご心配なく，単にかたちだけの取り調べですから」

former /fɔ́ːrmər/
形 以前の，前の；(代名詞的に)前者

the former... (and) the latter...	前者は…そして後者は…

▷The hotel has a swimming pool and a restaurant. **The former** is recommended, **the latter** is not. ホテルにはプールとレストランがあります．前者はお勧めですが，後者はお勧めしません

fortunate /fɔ́ːrtʃənət/ 形 幸運な

fortunate	to do	幸運にも…する
fortunate	that...	…なのは幸運だ

▷I feel **fortunate to** have grown up in Wales. ウェールズに育ったことを幸運だと感じている
▷I'm **fortunate that** I'm engaged in work that I like. 私は好きな仕事に就けて幸運だ

fortune /fɔ́ːrtʃən/ 名 財産，大金；運，運勢

bring	fortune	幸運をもたらす
tell	A's fortune	運勢を占う
make	a fortune	ひと財産つくる
amass	a fortune	
inherit	a fortune	財産を相続する
lose	a fortune	財産を失う
seek	one's fortune	立身出世を求める
cost	a fortune	大金がかかる
spend	a fortune	大金を使う

▷Lady, you have a lucky face! Want me to **tell** your **fortune**? お嬢さん，いい運勢が顔に出ていますね．占ってあげましょうか
▷His family **made** a **fortune** in steel. 彼の一族は鉄鋼で財産を築いた
▷He has **amassed** a **fortune** estimated at several hundred million dollars. 彼が蓄えた財産は数億ドルと見積もられる
▷Simon **inherited** his **fortune** from his father. サイモンは父親から財産を相続した
▷I didn't come here to **seek** my **fortune**. 立身出世を求めてここへ来たのではない
▷The buildings are old and **cost** a **fortune** to maintain. それらの建物は古くて維持費が莫大だ
▷She **spends** a **fortune** on cosmetics and skin care. 彼女は化粧品とスキンケアに大金を注ぎ込んでいる

good	fortune	幸運
a considerable	fortune	かなりの財産
a large	fortune	
a small	fortune	かなりの大金
economic	fortunes	経済の浮沈
political	fortunes	政治的命運

▷I had the **good fortune** to meet that artist. 幸運にもその芸術家に出会えた

▷He left a **considerable fortune**. 彼はかなりの財産を残した
▷He was a wealthy man and left a **large fortune**. 彼は資産家で巨万の富を残した
▷I've spent a **small fortune** on my house to fix it up. 家の修理にかなりの大金を使った
▷The **economic fortunes** of the region are closely linked to the state of the world oil market. その地域の経済的浮沈は世界の石油市場の状況と密接に結びついている

frame /fréim/ 名 枠；骨組み

a door	frame	ドア枠
a window	frame	窓枠
a photo	frame	写真の額
a picture	frame	額縁
a wooden	frame	木の枠

▷The picture was in an oval **wooden frame**. 写真は楕円形の木のフレームに入っていた

free /frí:/ 形 自由な；無料の；暇な

absolutely	free	無料の
completely	free	無料の；完全に自由
entirely	free	な；すっかり暇な
totally	free	

▷Here's the good news. Entry is **absolutely free**. いい知らせだ．参加は無料だよ
▷Smoking is legal if you are 20 and over. You're **entirely free** to smoke if you choose to. 20歳以上なら喫煙は法律で認められています．吸いたいならどうぞ

free	to do	自由に…できる

▷You are **free to** do what you like. ご自分の好きなようにしてください

free	from A	Aがない
free	of A	

▷Within nine months, I was almost totally **free from** the pain. 9か月も経たないうちに痛みはすっかりなくなった
▷This medicine is relatively **free of** side effects. この薬は副作用が少ないほうだ

feel	free	自由にする
break	free	自由になる
get	free	
set A	free	Aを自由にする

▷**Feel free** to have a cup of coffee. 自由にコーヒーを飲んでください
▷The dog **broke free** of his lead and ran off into the woods. 犬は鎖を振りほどいて森の中に逃げた
▷There wasn't enough evidence to hold the suspects and they were **set free**. 容疑者たちを勾留しておく十分な証拠がなく，釈放された

for	free	ただで，無料で

▷"Will you fix it **for free**?" "Of course."「ただで直してくれるよね」「もちろん」

free and fair		自由で公正な

▷We welcome **free and fair** competition in our own domestic markets. われわれは国内市場での自由で公正な競争を歓迎します

freedom /frí:dəm/ 名 自由；解放

have	(the) freedom	自由がある
enjoy	(the) freedom	自由を享受する
allow	(the) freedom	自由を許す
give	(the) freedom	自由を与える
restrict	(the) freedom	自由を制限する

▷He **had** the **freedom** to do whatever he wanted to do. 彼は何でもしたいことをしてよかった
▷We **enjoy** more **freedom** than ever before. 私たちはこれまでより多くの自由を謳歌している
▷The government **allows freedom** of expression. 政府は表現の自由を認めている
▷Democracy **gives freedom** to people to express their opinions. 民主主義のもとでは国民には意見を自由に表明する自由がある
▷During World War I, the Government **restricted freedom** of speech. 第一次世界大戦中，政府は言論の自由を制限した

great	freedom	大きな自由
individual	freedom	個人の自由
personal	freedom	
academic	freedom	学問の自由
political	freedom	政治的自由
religious	freedom	宗教的自由

▷We live in an era of **great freedom**. われわれは大いなる自由の時代に生きている
▷I think that **individual freedom** needs to be protected. 個人の自由は守られる必要があると思う

freedom	from A	Aからの自由
freedom	of A	Aの自由

| freeze |

★of A の A は speech, choice, information などがくる

▷In 1810, Mexico declared its **freedom from** Spain.　1810年メキシコはスペインからの独立を宣言した
▷Do you support **freedom of speech**?　言論の自由を支持しますか
▷Sweden has perhaps the strongest **freedom of information** laws in the world.　スウェーデンにはおそらく世界で最も徹底した情報公開法がある

freedom	to do	…する自由

▷Give women greater **freedom to work**.　女性の働く自由を拡大せよ

freeze /frí:z/ 動 凍る；ぞっとする

frozen	solid	かちかちに凍った
freeze	over	一面に凍る
freeze	up	凍結する
freeze	to death	凍死する

▷This lake **freezes over** in the winter.　この湖は冬には一面に凍る
▷The water on the lake has **frozen up**. Let's go skating.　湖に氷が張ったよ．スケートに行こう

freeze	with A	A で動けなくなる
frozen	to the spot	その場に釘づけになった

★A には fear, terror, shock などがくる

▷His face **froze with shock**.　彼の顔はショックでこわばった
▷She was **frozen with fear** after one robber held a knife to her neck.　泥棒が彼女の首筋にナイフを当てると，彼女は恐怖に身をすくませた
▷My heart stopped beating. I was **frozen to the spot**.　心臓が止まりそうになって，その場で固まった

frequency /frí:kwənsi/ 名 頻度，回数

increase	the frequency	頻度を増やす
decrease	the frequency	頻度を減らす
reduce	the frequency	
increase	in frequency	頻度が増す
decrease	in frequency	頻度が減る

▷We should **increase** the **frequency** *of* the visits.　訪問の回数を増やしたほうがよいだろう
▷We **reduced** the **frequency** of the meeting to once a week.　会議の頻度を週1回に減らした

great	frequency	高い頻度
high	frequency	高頻度；高周波
low	frequency	低頻度；低周波
relative	frequency	相対頻度
increasing	frequency	増える頻度
alarming	frequency	驚くほどの頻度

★with … frequency でよく用いる

▷The number of people getting divorced has reached a very **high frequency**.　離婚するカップルの件数が非常に多くなった
▷There is a **low frequency** of crime in this area.　このあたりは犯罪の発生頻度が低い
▷Problems of pollution are being reported **with increasing frequency**.　汚染の問題が報告される頻度がますます高くなりつつある
▷The number of serious crimes is increasing **with alarming frequency**.　重大犯罪が起こる頻度が驚くほど高くなりつつある

fresh /fréʃ/ 形 新鮮な

completely	fresh	まったく新鮮な
still	fresh	なお新鮮な

▷I was filled with excitement because I had a **completely fresh** idea.　すっかり興奮していた．というのはすごく新しいアイデアを思いついたからだ
▷The experience is **still fresh** in my memory.　その経験はいまも鮮やかに覚えています

fresh	from A	A から来たばかりの

▷At that time I was 22 and **fresh from** university.　当時22歳で大学を出たばかりだった

friend /fréⁿd/ 名 友人，友だち

become	friends	友人になる
make	friends	親しくなる
have	a friend	友人がいる
lose	a friend	友人を失う
meet	a friend	友人に会う
see	a friend	
visit	a friend	友人を訪ねる
bring	a friend	友人を連れてくる

▷How did you **become friends** *with* Robert?　どんなふうにロバートと友だちになったの？
▷Tell him to **bring** some **friends**. The more the merrier.　友だちを連れてくるよう彼に言って．多ければ

多いほど楽しいから

A's best	friend	いちばんの親友
a close	friend	親友
a great	friend	
a good	friend	いい友だち
a lifelong	friend	生涯の友
an old	friend	古くからの友人
a mutual	friend	共通の友人

▷Jean is my **best friend**.　ジーンは私のいちばんの親友です
▷Glenn and I are **close friends**.　グレンと私は親友です
▷Kevin has three **lifelong friends**.　ケビンには生涯の友が3人いる
▷Jane and Charles met through a **mutual friend** at a party in London.　ジェインとチャールズは共通の友人を介してロンドンのパーティーで出会った

a friend	of mine	私の友人
a friend	of yours	あなたの友人
a friend	of John('s)	ジョンの友人

▷Roger is a **friend of mine**.　ロジャーは私の友人です
[PHRASES]
What are friends for? ☺　何のための友だちなの，友だちじゃないか

friendly /fréndli/

形 親しい；親切な；やさしい

quite	friendly	とても友好的な
environmentally	friendly	環境にやさしい

▷The youth hostel was very nice and everyone was **quite friendly**.　とてもいいユースホステルで，みんなとても親切だった
▷Recycling is the most **environmentally friendly** option.　リサイクルは最も環境にやさしい選択肢だ

friendly	to A	Aに親切な
friendly	with A	Aと親しい

▷I tried to be **friendly to** him and to make him laugh.　親切にして彼を笑わせようとした
▷I became **friendly with** him and his family.　彼やその家族と親しくなった

friendly	and helpful	親切で力になってくれる

▷The staff are **friendly and helpful**.　スタッフはとても親切で快く手伝ってくれる

frightened /fráitnd/

形 おびえた

terribly	frightened	ひどくおびえた
too	frightened	あまりにおびえた

▷People were **too frightened** *to* go through the park at night.　人々はすっかりおびえてしまって夜間にその公園を通り抜けることができなかった

frightened	of A	Aにおびえた
frightened	to do	…するのにおびえた
frightened	(that)…	…であるのにおびえた

▷Are you **frightened of** the police?　お前は警察が怖いのか
▷Women are **frightened to** walk alone after dark.　女性たちは日が暮れてからひとりで歩くのを怖がっている
▷He was often **frightened that** he was losing his memory.　彼は自分が記憶を失いつつあるのがときどき怖くなった

front /fránt/

名 前部，前面，正面；表(紙)；前線

a cold	front	寒冷前線
a warm	front	温暖前線

▷The **cold front** will move down across England.　寒冷前線がイングランドを北から南へ移動するでしょう

on	the front	表に
at	the front	前部に；先頭に
in	the front	前列に
to	the front	前線に

▷Was he **at the front** all the time?　彼はずっと最前列にいたのかい
▷I always like to sit **in the front** when I go to a movie.　映画を見に行くときは前列に座るのが好きだ
▷Those young soldiers were sent directly **to the front**.　若い兵士たちはいきなり前線へ送られた

fruit /frúːt/ 名 果物

bear	fruit	実をつける
produce	fruit	
grow	fruit	果物を栽培する

▷People in rural areas **grow fruit** and vegetables in small private gardens.　田舎の人々は小さな家庭菜園で果物と野菜を栽培している

fresh	fruit	新鮮な果物
ripe	fruit	熟した果物
dried	fruit	ドライフルーツ
canned	fruit	缶詰の果物
citrus	fruit(s)	柑橘類の果物

▷Eat **fresh fruit** and light, easy-to-digest foods. 新鮮な果物と、軽くて消化のよい食べ物を食べなさい
▷**Citrus fruits** like oranges and lemons are rich in vitamin C. オレンジやレモンなどの柑橘類はビタミンCが豊富だ

a piece of	fruit	果物1個

▷It's good for your health to eat at least one **piece of fruit** a day. 1日に最低1個は果物を食べると健康にいい

fruit and vegetables	果物と野菜

▷She eats a lot of **fruit and vegetables**. 彼女は果物と野菜をたくさん食べる

fuel /fjúːəl/ 名 燃料

burn	fuel	燃料を燃やす
use	fuel	燃料を使う
save	fuel	燃料を節約する
run out of	fuel	燃料が切れる
add	fuel to A	A(議論など)をさらに激しくする

▷The pilot continued to circle the airport, trying to **burn fuel** to reduce the risk of fire. パイロットは空港の周りを旋回し、少しでも燃料を消費して火災の危険を減らそうとした
▷You can **save fuel** by shutting off your engine. エンジンを切ることで燃料を節約できる
▷We **ran out of fuel** half way up the mountain. 山を半分まで登ったところで燃料が切れた
▷He **added fuel to** the rumor that there is a political element to the attacks. 襲撃事件には政治的要素が絡んでいるといううわさを彼はさらにあおった

fossil	fuel	化石燃料
solid	fuel	固体燃料
domestic	fuel	家庭用燃料
nuclear	fuel	核燃料
spent	fuel	使用済み燃料
renewable	fuel	再生可能燃料
unleaded	fuel	無鉛燃料

▷The government are going to increase **domestic fuel** prices by an average of 30%. 政府は家庭用燃料の価格を平均3割値上げする
▷**Fossil** and **nuclear fuels** still completely dominate the U.S. energy supply. 化石燃料と核燃料はいまなお米国のエネルギー供給を完全に左右している

full /fúl/ 形 いっぱいの；満腹の

half	full	半分入った
three-quarters	full	4分の3入った

▷The bottle was only **half full**. 瓶の中身は半分しかなかった

full	of A	Aでいっぱいの

▷The kitchen was **full of** the smell of freshly baked bread. キッチンは焼き立てのパンの匂いに包まれていた
PHRASES
I'm full. ☺ お腹がいっぱいです

fun /fán/ 名 おもしろさ, 楽しさ

have	fun	楽しむ

▷We were good friends and we'd **had** a lot of **fun** together at university. 私たちは仲良しで、大学で一緒に楽しい時を過ごした

good	fun	とても楽しいこと
great	fun	
a lot of	fun	
good clean	fun	健全な楽しみ

▷We must come to Disneyland again. It was **great fun**! またディズニーランドに来なくちゃ. すごく楽しかった
▷There was no cigarette smoking and alcohol at the party — just **good clean fun**. たばこを吸う人も酒を飲む人もいない、ごく健全なパーティーだった

for	fun	楽しみのために；冗談で

▷I just wanted to ask you, since you're always so busy, what do you do **for fun**? 前から聞きたいと思っていたのですが、あなたはいつも忙しくしていらっしゃいますね. 気晴らしには何をしているのですか

a sense of	fun	遊び心

▷He is a generous person with a good **sense of fun**. 彼は気前がよくて遊び心にも富んでいる
PHRASES
Sounds like fun. ☺ おもしろそうだ ▷Bungee jump-

ing? Sounds like fun. バンジージャンプだって？おもしろそうだね
That's fun. 😊 それはおもしろい
What fun! 😊 なんておもしろいんだろう

function /fÁŋkʃən/

名 機能，働き；役目；式典，行事

have	a function	機能がある
fulfill	a function	機能を果たす
serve	a function	
perform	a function	

▷ The red button and green button **have** different **functions**. 赤のボタンと緑のボタンの働きは異なる
▷ This button **fulfills** the **function** of starting the engine. このボタンはエンジンをスタートさせる機能を果たしている
▷ This new robot is able to **perform** many **functions**. この新型ロボットは多くの役目を果たせる

an important	function	重要な働き
the main	function	主要な機能
a social	function	社交の集まり

▷ Instead of just passing exams, the **main function** of learning English should be communication. 単に試験に合格するためだけではなく，コミュニケーションを図れるようにすることに英語学習の主眼を置くべきだ
▷ Over sixty guests attended the **social function**. 60人以上の招待客が社交の催しに出席した

fund /fÁnd/ 名 資金，基金；投資信託

set up	a fund	基金を設立する
establish	a fund	
run	a fund	基金を運用する
manage	a fund	
have	funds	資金がある
obtain	funds	資金を確保する
borrow	funds	資金を借り入れる
raise	funds	資金を調達する
allocate	funds	資金を配分する

▷ We can **borrow funds** up to $15 million. 1500万ドルまで資金を借り入れできる
▷ He managed to **raise funds** for a new building. 彼は新ビル建設の資金をなんとか調達できた
▷ The government has **allocated funds** for social welfare. 政府は社会福祉に資金を配分した

an investment	fund	投資ファンド
a social	fund	社会基金
a trust	fund	信託基金
a pension	fund	年金基金
a hedge	fund	ヘッジファンド
sufficient	funds	十分な資金
public	funds	公的資金

▷ The local government has established a **social fund** to help patients and their families. 地方自治体は患者とその家族を支援するための社会基金を設立した
▷ These communities don't have **sufficient funds** to improve their environment. これらの地域社会には環境を整備する十分な資金がない
▷ The research is supported by **public funds**. その研究は公的資金によって支えられている

funds	for A	Aの資金

▷ T-shirts will be sold to raise **funds for** the project. その事業の資金を募るためにTシャツが販売される

a flow	of funds	資金の流れ
a lack	of funds	資金不足
a shortage	of funds	

▷ The US economy depends on a massive **flow of funds** from overseas investors. 米国経済は海外投資家からの巨額な資金の流れに依存している
▷ A **lack of funds** to make the next step is really the problem at the moment. 次の段階に進むための資金不足がまさに当面の問題だ

funeral /fjúːnərəl/ 名 葬式

arrange	a funeral	葬式を手配する
attend	a funeral	葬式に参列する
go to	a funeral	

▷ They are **arranging** the **funeral** for Thursday. 彼らは木曜日の葬儀の手配をしている
▷ Yesterday I **attended** the **funeral** of a friend's mother. きのう友人のお母さんの葬儀に参列した

a state	funeral	国葬

funny /fÁni/ 形 おかしい，こっけいな；奇妙な

really	funny	とてもおかしい
a bit	funny	少し奇妙な

▷ She was **really funny** and entertaining. 彼女はとても愉快でみんなを楽しませてくれた

| furniture |

funny	little	ちょっとおかしな

▷Have you seen Emma's new baby? She's a **funny little** thing! エマの赤ん坊を見た？変わったおちびちゃんね

PHRASES

I thought it was funny. ☺ 変だなと思ったんだ
That's funny. ☺ それはおかしい，不思議だ，どうしたんだろう
That's not funny! / It's not funny! ☺ 笑いごとじゃないぞ
What's so funny? ☺ 何がそんなにおかしいの?

furniture /fə́ːrnitʃər/ 名 家具

antique	furniture	アンティーク家具
bedroom	furniture	寝室用家具

▷The room is decorated with **antique furniture**. その部屋はアンティーク家具で飾られている

a piece	of furniture	家具一点

▷In the corner of my living room there's a nice **piece of furniture**. 私の居間の隅にすばらしい家具があります

furniture	in the room	部屋の家具

▷All the **furniture in** the **room** is completely new. 部屋の家具はどれもまったく新しい

future /fjúːtʃər/

名 (the future で)未来，将来；将来性，前途

look to	the future	これからのことを考える
predict	the future	これからのことを予測する
foretell	the future	
have	a future	前途がある
secure	the future	前途を確かなものにする
consider	the future	前途を考える

▷No one can **predict** the **future**. だれもこれからのことを予測できない
▷Do you think the film world **has a future**? 映画界に未来はあると思いますか
▷I needed to **secure** the **future** of my children. わが子たちの将来を確かなものにする必要があった
▷I have to start **considering** my **future**. 自分の行く末について考え始めなければならない

the near	future	近い将来
the immediate	future	
the foreseeable	future	
the not too distant	future	遠くない将来
the distant	future	遠い将来
a bright	future	明るい将来
a great	future	
a promising	future	有望な将来
a bleak	future	暗い将来
an uncertain	future	不確かな将来
the long-term	future	長期的将来

▷I have no plans to marry *in* the **near future**. 近い将来結婚する予定はありません
▷Something needs to be done *in* the **immediate future**. ごく近い将来に何か手を打つ必要がある
▷The economy is unlikely to improve *in* the **foreseeable future**. 経済は当面は好転しそうにない
▷*In* the **not too distant future**, computer, telephone and video technology may merge into one. 遠くない将来にコンピュータ，電話，ビデオの技術は合体して一つになるかもしれない
▷She is a talented actress with a **bright future**. 彼女は才能ある女優で，未来も明るい
▷He has a **promising future** ahead of him. 彼は前途有望だ
▷Thousands of workers are facing a very **uncertain future**. 何千人もの労働者が先行きのはっきりしない状況に直面している
▷We must do all we can to secure the company's **long-term future**. 会社の将来を長期的に確実なものにするためにできることは何でもやらなければならない

in	(the) future	将来に；これからは

▷If I have the opportunity **in (the) future**, I'll do my best to help you. 将来その機会があれば全力でお力添えします

G

gain /géin/ 名 利益；増加

net	gain	純利益
ill-gotten	gains	不正利益
personal	gain	個人的利益
material	gain	物質的利益
weight	gain	体重増加

▷Don't trust him! He's only doing it for **personal gain**. 彼を信用するな．自分の利益のためにやっているだけだから

gain	from A	Aから得るもの
a gain	in A	Aの増加

▷Ken won his last three matches and is showing a big **gain in** confidence. ケンはここ3試合に勝って大きく自信をつけている

game /géim/ 名 試合；ゲーム，遊び

play	a game	試合をする；ゲームをする
lose	a game	試合に負ける
win	a game	試合に勝つ

▷Let's **play** a **game** of cards. トランプをしよう
▷Japan **won** the **game** against England. 日本はイングランドとの試合に勝った

the game	is played	試合が行われる

▷The **game is played** with 11 players on each side. 試合は両サイド11名で行われる

a ball	game	球技
a board	game	ボードゲーム
a card	game	カードゲーム
a computer	game	コンピュータゲーム
a video	game	テレビゲーム
a big	game	大事な試合
a home	game	本拠地での試合
an away	game	敵地での試合
a good	game	いいゲーム；うまいプレー
a great	game	
the Olympic	Games	オリンピック大会

▷There's a **big game** on Saturday–Manchester United against Liverpool. 土曜日にマンチェスターユナイテッド対リバプールの大事な試合がある
▷It was a **great game**! すばらしい試合だった

the game	against A	Aとの試合
the game	with A	

▷England lost the **game against** Germany. イングランドはドイツとの試合に敗れた

PHRASES
Don't play games with us. ☺ からかわないで
The game is over. ☺ ゲームセットだ
The game is up. ☺ 万事休すだ

gap /gǽp/ 名 すきま；格差；欠落

leave	a gap	すきまを残す
fill	the gap	すきまを埋める
bridge	the gap	格差を埋める
close	the gap	格差を縮める
narrow	the gap	
reduce	the gap	
widen	the gap	格差を広げる

▷Now Hudson's left as sales manager we'll have to find someone else to **fill** the **gap**. ハドソンが営業責任者として異動していったので，だれか穴を埋める人材を探してこないといけない
▷The new tax system will **widen** the **gap** between rich and poor. 新しい税制は貧富の格差を広げるだろう

a big	gap	大きなすきま；大きな格差
a huge	gap	
a wide	gap	
a narrow	gap	狭いすきま
a small	gap	
a long	gap	長い空白期間
a short	gap	短い空白期間

▷There's a **big gap** in the hedge. 垣根に大きなすきまがある
▷The rabbit escaped through a **narrow gap** in the fence. ウサギはフェンスの狭いすきまから逃げた
▷We are happy to see him back here after a **long gap**. 久しぶりに戻ってきた彼に会えてうれしい

a gap	between A	Aとのすきま
a gap	in A	Aのすきま

▷You need to leave a bigger **gap between** paragraphs. 段落間をもっと開ける必要がある
▷After the crash there was a big **gap in** the wall. 衝突で壁に大きな穴が開いていた

garage /gərá:dʒ | gǽrɑ:dʒ/

名 車庫, ガレージ；自動車修理工場

a double	garage	2台用の車庫
a single	garage	1台用の車庫

▷ The house has a **double garage**. その家には2台用の車庫がある

in	a garage	車庫に

▷ It's much safer to put a car **in a garage**. 車を車庫に入れたほうがずっと安全だ

take A	to a garage	Aを修理工場へ持っていく

▷ If you **take** a car **to a garage** it always costs a fortune to have it repaired. 車を修理工場へ持っていくと, 修理代がいつも高くつく

garbage /gá:rbidʒ/ 名 ごみ

take out	the garbage	ごみを出す
dump	garbage	ごみを捨てる
throw	garbage	
leave	the garbage	ごみを残す

▷ Where should we **dump** our **garbage**? どこへごみを捨てればいいのか
▷ Stop **throwing** your **garbage** on roadsides. 道路わきにごみを捨てるのはやめてください

a pile of	garbage	ごみの山

▷ We must not leave any **piles of garbage** in the streets. ごみの山を道路に放置してはならない

garden /gá:rdn/ 名 庭, 庭園

have	a garden	庭がある
do	the garden	庭いじりをする
water	the garden	庭に水をまく
overlook	a garden	庭を見下ろす
go into	the garden	庭に出る

▷ Her house **has** a really large **garden**. 彼女の家にはすごく大きな庭がある
▷ It's too hot to **do** the **garden** today. 庭仕事をするにはきょうは暑すぎる

a botanic	garden	植物園
a botanical	garden	

a flower	garden	花園, 花畑
a vegetable	garden	菜園
a kitchen	garden	家庭菜園
a herb	garden	ハーブ園
a rose	garden	バラ園
the front	garden	前庭
the back	garden	裏庭

▷ The **front garden** has a driveway with space to park two cars. 前庭には車を2台駐車できる私有車道がある

in	the garden	庭で

▷ I spent the afternoon **in** the **garden**. 午後は庭で過ごした

gas /gǽs/ 名 ガス, 気体；ガソリン

give off	gas	ガスを発生させる
turn on	the gas	ガスの火をつける
turn off	the gas	ガスの火を消す

▷ She forgot to **turn off** the **gas**. 彼女はガスの火を消し忘れた

(a) poisonous	gas	有毒ガス
nerve	gas	神経ガス
tear	gas	催涙ガス
(a) greenhouse	gas	温室効果ガス
natural	gas	天然ガス

▷ **Poisonous gas** was escaping from the pipe. 有毒ガスがパイプから漏れていた

gather /gǽðər/ 動 集める, 集まる；思う

gather	around	周りに集まる
《英》gather	round	
gather	together	かき集める
gather	up	

▷ **Gather around** everybody! I've got some important news! みんな集まって。大事なお知らせがあります
▷ She **gathered** her notes **up** and put them in her briefcase. 彼女はメモをかき集めて書類カバンに入れた

gather	(that)...	…だと推測する

▷ I **gathered that** there would be no more problems with the contract. 契約に何もこれ以上問題はないだろうと思った

generate /dʒénərèit/

動 生み出す, もたらす；発生させる

automatically	generate	自動的に生み出す
spontaneously	generate	

▷The computer **automatically generates** a reply. コンピュータは自動的に回答を作成する

be generated	from A	Aから生み出される

▷Electricity for this area is **generated from** a power station in London. この地域の電気はロンドンの発電所から生み出されたものだ

generation /dʒènəréiʃən/

名 世代, 同時代の人々；一世代

belong to	a generation	世代に属する
produce	a generation	世代を生み出す

▷He **belongs to** a "Spend! Spend! Spend!" **generation**. 彼は金を使って使って使いまくる世代に属している

▷The mid-20th century **produced** a **generation** of antiwar protesters in the U.S.A. 20世紀半ば米国では反戦世代が生まれた

a new	generation	新しい世代
the younger	generation	
the older	generation	古い世代
future	generations	未来の世代
a later	generation	後の世代
the next	generation	次の世代
an earlier	generation	前の世代
previous	generations	
the first	generation	第1世代
the second	generation	第2世代

▷We're developing a **new generation** of hybrid cars. 新世代ハイブリッドカーを開発中だ

▷We should try to preserve the Earth for **future generations**. 未来の世代のために地球を守る努力をすべきだ

▷The **next generation** will not thank us for what we are doing. 次世代の人々はわれわれの世代が行っていることに感謝の念を抱かないだろう

▷We have inherited the problems of an **earlier generation**. 私たちは前世代の問題を受け継いでいる

for generations	何世代も

▷This picture by van Gogh has been in our family **for generations**. ゴッホが描いたこの絵は代々わが家に受け継がれてきたものだ

gesture /dʒéstʃər/

名 身ぶり, しぐさ；意思表示

make	a gesture	身ぶりをする

▷He **made** a **gesture** with his hands meaning "I know, I know." 彼は両手で「わかっている, わかっている」というしぐさをした

a dramatic	gesture	芝居がかったしぐさ
a grand	gesture	大げさな意思表示
a small	gesture	ささやかな意思表示
a symbolic	gesture	象徴的な意思表示

▷He donated $10,000 dollars to the charity. He likes to make **grand gestures**! 彼は慈善事業に1万ドル寄付した. 向こう受けをねらったことをやりたがるんだ

in	a gesture	身ぶりで
with	a gesture	

▷Let's send them a bouquet of flowers **in** a **gesture** of appreciation. 感謝のしるしに花束を彼らに送ろう

▷**With** a **gesture** of annoyance she slammed the door behind her. いらだったしぐさで彼女は部屋に入ったあと背後のドアをばたんと閉めた

gift /ɡíft/ **名** 贈り物；才能

make (A)	a gift	(Aに)贈り物をする
give (A)	a gift	
receive	a gift	贈り物を受け取る
accept	a gift	
have	a gift	才能がある；贈り物がある

▷She said she really liked the painting so he **made** a **gift** of it to her. 彼女がその絵をすごく気に入ったと言うので, 彼はプレゼントしてあげた

▷When he retired he **received** many **gifts** from his friends. 退職の際に彼は友人たちからたくさん贈り物をもらった

▷Julie **has** a **gift** for music. ジュリーには音楽の才能がある

a generous	gift	気前のよい贈り物
a special	gift	特別な贈り物
a small	gift	ささやかな贈り物
a free	gift	おまけ, 景品
a Christmas	gift	クリスマスプレゼント
a wedding	gift	結婚祝い

| girl |

a great	gift	すばらしい才能
a rare	gift	まれな才能
a special	gift	特別な才能

▷There's a **free gift** with every packet of cornflakes. すべてのコーンフレークの箱におまけがついている
▷Mozart had a **great gift** for music. モーツァルトには音楽の才能があふれていた

as	a gift	贈り物として
a gift	from A	Aからの贈り物
a gift	to A	Aへの贈り物
a gift	for A	Aの才能

▷Please accept this **as a small gift**. ささやかな贈り物ですがお受け取りください
▷This ring was a **gift from** my mother. この指輪は母からもらったの
▷I bought this Japanese fan as a **gift to** an old friend of mine. 旧友へのプレゼントにこの扇子を買った

girl /gə́ːrl/ 名 少女, 女の子

a baby	girl	女の赤ん坊
a little	girl	幼い女の子
a young	girl	
a small	girl	
a lovely	girl	かわいい女の子
a nice	girl	
a pretty	girl	きれいな女の子
a good	girl	いい子
a big	girl	お姉さん
poor	girl	かわいそうな女の子

▷She could play the piano really well even when she was a **little girl**. 彼女は小さい頃からすでにピアノがとてもうまかった
▷Stop crying! Be a **good girl**! 泣くのはやめなさい. いい子にして
▷How old are you? Four? Wow! You're a **big girl** now! 歳はいくつ？4つ？じゃあもうお姉ちゃんね
▷The **poor girl** had lost all her money. かわいそうにその少女はお金をすっかりなくしてしまった

glance /glǽns | glάːns/ 名 ちらっと見ること

cast	a glance	さっと見る
shoot	a glance	
take	a glance	
throw	a glance	
steal	a glance	盗み見する
exchange	glances	互いに目を合わせる

▷She **cast** a **glance** at Isabel's face. 彼女はイザベルの顔をちらっと見た
▷She **stole** a **glance** at him. He was so good-looking! 彼女は彼を盗み見した. すごくすてきな人だった
▷They **exchanged glances**. Maybe it was the police at the door. 彼らは目配せをした. 玄関にいるのはおそらく警察だ

a quick	glance	すばやく見ること
a backward	glance	後方をちらっと見ること
a sidelong	glance	横目でちらっと見ること
a sideways	glance	

▷I know it's late, but could you take a **quick glance** at this file? もう遅いのはわかっていますが, このファイルにさっと目を通していただけませんか
▷She left the room without a **backward glance**. 彼女は後ろを振り返りもせず部屋を出て行った

a glance	at A	Aをちらっと見ること
at	a glance	一目で
at first	glance	一見して

▷Take a **glance** at this letter. I can't understand a word of it. この手紙をちょっと見て, 何が書いてあるのか全然わからなくて
▷He could tell **at a glance** that something was missing from his desk. 机から何かなくなっていると彼は一目でわかった
▷**At first glance** she seemed much too young to be a grandmother. 第一印象では彼女は孫がいる歳には見えなかった

glance /glǽns | glάːns/ 動 ちらっと見る；さっと目を通す

glance	at A	Aをちらっと見る；Aにさっと目を通す

★over, around, toward なども用いる

▷I **glanced at** my watch. It was still early. ちらっと時計を見たらまだ早かった
▷Maggie **glanced over** her shoulder. マギーは肩越しにちらっと振り返った ▷She **glanced over** a newspaper. 彼女は新聞にさっと目を通した
▷She **glanced around** the room. Everything seemed normal. 彼女は部屋をさっと見回した. 変わったところは何もなかった

glance	quickly	すばやくさっと見る
glance	down	下をちらっと見る
glance	up	上をちらっと見る

▷He **glanced quickly** at the speedometer. 速度計を急いでちょっと見た
▷She **glanced up** from her book. 彼女は本からちらっと目を上げた
▷She **glanced** him **up** and **down**. 彼女は彼を上から下までさっと見た

glass /glæs | glɑːs/

名 ガラス；コップ，グラス；(glasses で)眼鏡

pour	a glass	グラスに注ぐ
fill	a glass	グラスを満たす
drain	one's glass	グラスを空ける
raise	one's glass	乾杯する
wear	glasses	眼鏡をかけている
put on	one's glasses	眼鏡をかける
take off	one's glasses	眼鏡をはずす

▷Can I **pour** you a **glass** of wine? ワインをお注ぎしましょうか
▷He **filled** a **glass** full of whiskey. 彼はグラスにウイスキーをなみなみと注いだ
▷He **drained** his **glass** with one gulp. 彼はぐっと一口でグラスを空けた
▷Let's **raise** our **glasses** to success in the coming year! 来年がよい年になるよう乾杯しよう
▷She **wears glasses**. 彼女は眼鏡をかけている
▷Nancy **put on** her **glasses**. ナンシーは眼鏡をかけた

opaque	glass	不透明ガラス
broken	glass	割れたガラス
bulletproof	glass	防弾ガラス
stained	glass	ステンドグラス
an empty	glass	空のグラス
a beer	glass	ビールグラス
a wine	glass	ワイングラス
a brandy	glass	ブランデーグラス

▷Don't cut yourself on the **broken glass**. 割れたガラスでけがをしないように
▷She put the **empty glasses** in the sink. 彼女は空のグラスを流し台に置いた

a piece	of glass	一片のガラス
a pane	of glass	1枚のガラス
a sheet	of glass	
slivers	of glass	ガラスの破片
a pair	of glasses	一対の眼鏡

▷There were **pieces of glass** all over the road. 道路のあちこちにガラスの破片が散乱していた

glove /ɡlʌv/ 名 手袋

put on	one's gloves	手袋をはめる
pull on	one's gloves	
wear	gloves	手袋をはめている
take off	one's gloves	手袋をはずす

▷**Put on** your **gloves**. It's really cold outside. 手袋をして，外はとても寒いよ
▷Why aren't you **wearing gloves**? It's freezing! どうして手袋をしていないの？凍えるほど寒いのに
▷He **took off** his hat and **gloves**. 彼は帽子を脱ぎ手袋をはずした

a pair of	gloves	一対の手袋

▷I need to buy a new **pair of gloves**. 新しい手袋を買わなくちゃ

leather	gloves	革の手袋
rubber	gloves	ゴム手袋
woolen	gloves	毛糸の手袋

▷She uses **rubber gloves** when she does the washing-up. 食器洗いの際に彼女はゴム手袋を使う
▷You need **woolen gloves** to keep your hands warm in winter. 冬に手を温かくしておくには毛糸の手袋がいる

goal /ɡoʊl/ 名 目標；ゴール，得点

have	a goal	目標がある
set	a goal	目標を定める
establish	a goal	
achieve	one's goal	目標を達成する
reach	a goal	
attain	a goal	
score	a goal	得点を入れる
get	a goal	
concede	a goal	ゴールを許す

▷You have to **set** your **goals** before you can achieve them. 目標を達成するにはまず目標を定めなければならない
▷He'll do anything to **achieve** his **goal**. 彼は目標を達成するためなら何でもするだろう
▷It's a miracle! We've **scored** a **goal**! 奇跡だ，ゴールを決めたぞ
▷England **conceded** a **goal** in the last minute of extra time. イングランドは延長戦の最後でゴールを許した

a common	goal	共通の目標

the ultimate	goal	究極の目標
the winning	goal	決勝ゴール

▷ Let's work together. We have a **common goal**. 力を合わせよう．われわれには共通の目標があるのだ
▷ The **ultimate goal** is to double our sales in 12 months. 究極の目標は12か月で売り上げを2倍にすることだ

a goal	against A	A(相手チーム)に対するゴール
a goal	from A	Aからのゴール

▷ Japan scored a **goal against** Brazil in the last minute. 日本は土壇場でブラジルからゴールを奪った
▷ He scored a **goal from** 30 yards out. 30ヤード離れたところから彼はゴールを決めた

god /gád | gɔ́d/

名 (God で)神；(ギリシャ・ローマ神話の)男神

believe in	God	神を信じる
praise	God	神をほめたたえる
thank	God	神に感謝する
swear to	God	神に誓う
pray to	God	神に祈る

▷ Do you **believe in God**? あなたは神を信じますか
▷ I **swear to God**. Nothing happened! 神にかけて誓うよ．何もなかったんだ
▷ She **prays to God** every night. 彼女は毎晩神に祈りを捧げる

PHRASES
God bless A 《話》Aに神の祝福を；Aはありがたい
▷ **God bless** her! She's given $50,000 to our charity! われわれの慈善事業に5万ドルを寄付してくれた彼女に神の祝福を(★ God Bless America は米国の準国歌の一つ．God save the Queen は英国国歌)

God (only) knows《話》神のみぞ知る ▷"Do you know what he means?" "God knows! I can't understand a word he says!"「彼が言ってることわかるかい」「さっぱりだ．一言も理解できないよ」

gold /góuld/ 名 金；金メダル

strike	gold	金を掘り当てる
produce	gold	金を産出する

▷ There are still places in the world where it's possible to **strike gold**. 世界にはまだ金鉱を掘り当てられる場所がある

pure	gold	純金
real	gold	本物の金
24 carat	gold	24金

▷ Her wedding ring was really expensive. **Pure gold**. 彼女の結婚指輪はすごく高くて，純金だった
▷ Is that **real gold** or just gold plated? それは本物の金ですか，それとも金メッキ？
▷ This bracelet is 18 **carat gold**. このブレスレットは18金だ

gold and silver	金と銀

▷ The thieves stole a lot of **gold and silver** jewelry. 強盗団は大量の金銀の宝飾品を盗んだ

good /gúd/

形 よい；じょうずな；善良な；行儀がいい；役に立つ

feel	good	気分がいい
look	good	よさそうに見える
smell	good	よいにおいがする
sound	good	耳に心地よい
taste	good	おいしい

▷ I like your shirt. It **looks good** on you. いいシャツね．似合っているわ
▷ Mmmm! That coffee **smells good**! うん，いいにおいのコーヒーだ

extremely	good	きわめてよい
really	good	実によい
particularly	good	特によい
perfectly	good	まったくよい
pretty	good	とてもよい
quite	good	かなりいい
good	enough	十分によい

▷ Her exam marks were **extremely good**. 彼女の試験の点数はすごくよかった
▷ This dictionary is **really good**. この辞書はすごくいい
▷ The Prime Minister made a **particularly good** speech last Thursday. 首相は先週の木曜日にとりわけすばらしい演説をした
▷ Really? You think the soup is too salty? It tastes **perfectly good** to me. そうかな．きみにはスープは塩がきつすぎるかい．ぼくにはちょうどいい味なんだけど
▷ Her English is **pretty good**. 彼女の英語はとてもうまい
▷ We have seen some progress. But I'm not satisfied. It's not **good enough**. いくらか進歩はあったけれど，私は満足していません．まだ不十分です

good	for A	A(人)にとってよい

good	to A	A(人)に親切な

▷Don't drink so much alcohol. It's not **good for** you. 酒の飲みすぎはいけないよ．きみにとっていいことではない
▷He's always giving her money and presents. He's very **good to** her. 彼はしょっちゅう彼女に金品をあげている．彼女にずいぶんと親切だ

it is good	to do	…してうれしい
it is good	of A to do	…してくれるとはAは親切だ
it is good	(for A) to do	(Aが)…するのは適切だ

▷**It**'s very **good to** see you, Sam. きみに会えてうれしいよ，サム
▷**It**'s **good of** you **to** help out at the last moment. 土壇場になって手助けしてくれるなんて親切な人だね
▷**It** is not **good for** her **to** be alone. 彼女がひとりでいるのはよくない

good	at A	Aが得意な

▷I didn't know you were **good at** rugby. きみがラグビーが得意とは知らなかった

〉PHRASES〈
Good for you! ☺ よくやった ▷"After failing my driving test four times I finally passed it!" "Good for you!" 「4回運転免許の試験に落ちてようやく受かったよ」「それはよかった」
That's good. ☺ それはいいですね ▷"I have my own flat." "Oh, that's good." 「自分のアパートを持っています」「ああ，それはいいですね」

good /gúd/ 名 利益；善

the common	good	公共の利益
the public	good	
the general	good	

▷Communists believe that everybody in society should work for the **common good**. 共産主義者は社会のみなが公共の利益のために働くべきだと信じている

for	the good of A	Aのために

▷I think the President should resign **for the good of** the nation. 大統領は国民のことを考えて辞職すべきだと思う

do (A)	good	(Aの)ためになる

▷It really **does** me **good** to get out in the fresh air away from the office. オフィスを出て外の新鮮な空気を吸うと本当にすっとする

good and evil		善と悪

▷The forces of **good and evil** are constantly fighting against each other. 善の力と悪の力は絶えず互いに戦い続けている

〉PHRASES〈
What's the good of A? ☺ Aに何の意味があるのか
▷**What's the good of** me writing reports if my boss doesn't read them? どうせ上司が読まないなら，報告書を書いて何の意味があるのか

goods /gúdz/ 名 商品；財産

produce	goods	商品を生産する
sell	goods	商品を売る
supply	goods	商品を供給する
buy	goods	商品を購入する
purchase	goods	
deliver	goods	商品を配達する

▷We need to **produce goods** that will sell internationally. 外国でも売れる製品をつくる必要がある
▷That new department store **sells** all kinds of unusual **goods**. その新しい百貨店ではあらゆる種類の珍しい商品を売っている
▷You can **buy goods** a lot cheaper in a discount shop. ディスカウントショップで商品をずっと安く買える
▷The **goods** won't be **delivered** until the week after next. 商品がお手元に届くのは再来週になります

a range of	goods	品ぞろえ

▷That store carries a wide **range of goods**. その店の品ぞろえは幅広い

consumer	goods	消費財
durable	goods	耐久消費財
capital	goods	資本財
industrial	goods	産業財
household	goods	家庭用品
electrical	goods	電化製品
luxury	goods	高級品
manufactured	goods	工業製品
branded	goods	ブランド品
counterfeit	goods	偽ブランド品
imported	goods	輸入品
stolen	goods	盗品

▷**Electrical goods** are becoming cheaper. 電化製品は安くなっている
▷The police found many **stolen goods** in his house. 警察は彼の家で盗品を数多く見つけた

goods and services		財貨とサービス

▷ **Goods and services** make up a large amount of our economy.　モノ・サービスが経済の大部分を占めている

the supply	of goods	商品の供給
the movement	of goods	商品の移動

▷ The **supply of goods** was interrupted because of production problems.　生産ラインのトラブルで商品の供給が止まった

▷ Free trade means the free **movement of goods** from one country to another.　自由貿易とは国から国への商品の自由な移動ということだ

government /gʌ́vərnmənt/

名 政府；内閣；統治

form	a government	政府をつくる
head	a government	政府を率いる
accuse	the government	政府を非難する
support	the government	政府を支持する
bring down	the government	政府を倒す

▷ After the election it proved very difficult to **form a government**.　選挙が終わってみると政権を発足させるのがきわめて難しいとわかった

▷ The protestors **accused** the **government** of wasting taxpayers' money.　抗議デモ参加者たちは納税者のお金を政府が浪費していると非難した

▷ How can we **support a government** that wasn't democratically elected?　民主的に選出されたわけではない政府をわれわれはどうやって支持できるのか

the government	announces	政府が発表する
the government	claims	政府が主張する

▷ The **government** recently **announced** a rise in the sales tax.　政府は近ごろ売上税のアップを発表した

▷ The **government claims** the newspaper reports are completely untrue.　政府の主張するところでは新聞報道はまったくのでたらめだ

central	government	中央政府
the federal	government	連邦政府
local	government	地方自治体
a minority	government	少数党政府
a coalition	government	連立政権

▷ Some people think **central government** has too much power.　中央政府が権力を握りすぎていると考える人もいる

▷ More and more power is going to **local government**.　地方自治体にどんどん権限が移行しつつある

grade /gréid/

名 等級；成績，評点；学年

a top	grade	最高級
a high	grade	高級
a low	grade	低級
a good	grade	よい成績
a high	grade	
a poor	grade	悪い成績
a low	grade	

▷ He's a **top grade** scientist.　彼は一流の科学者だ

▷ He got a **high grade** in the math exam.　彼は数学の試験で優秀な成績をとった

get	a grade	成績をとる
gain	a grade	

▷ He **got** a good **grade** in his class.　彼はクラスでよい成績をとった

in (the) fifth	grade	5年生で

▷ "What grade are you in?" "I'm **in the** 11th **grade** now."　「何年生ですか」「11年生(高校2年生)です」

greeting /gríːtiŋ/

名 あいさつ；(greetings で)あいさつのことば

exchange	greetings	あいさつを交わす
send	greetings	あいさつ状を送る

▷ I don't know him very well. We just **exchange greetings** on the train every morning.　あの人のことをよく知っているわけじゃないんです。毎朝，列車で会ってあいさつを交わすだけなので

▷ She **sent greetings** to family and friends back home in California.　彼女は故郷のカリフォルニアの家族や友人にあいさつ状を送った

a formal	greeting	改まったあいさつ
a friendly	greeting	気さくなあいさつ

▷ "Dear Sir" is a **formal greeting**. "Hi, Bill" would be informal.　「拝啓」は改まったあいさつなので，「やあ，ビル」とすればくだけた表現になるね

in	greeting	あいさつで

▷ The president raised a hand **in greeting** as he drove through the streets.　通りを車でパレードする大統領は片手を挙げてあいさつした

grip /gríp/ 名 握ること

take	a grip	握る
keep	a grip	握ったままでいる
tighten	one's grip	握りを強める
loosen	a grip	握りを弱める

▷ My mother used to **keep** a firm **grip** on my hand when she took me shopping. 私を買い物に連れて行くとき母は私の手をしっかりつかんでいたものだった

ground /gráund/

名 地面；土地；場所，…場；(grounds で) 根拠

fall to	the ground	地面に落ちる
hit	the ground	地面にぶつかる
touch	the ground	地面につく
leave	the ground	離陸する
get off	the ground	
cover	(the) ground	(距離を)行く；(範囲に)わたる
gain	ground	前進する，よくなる
lose	ground	退却する，負ける

▷ Soon it will be autumn and all the leaves will be **falling to** the **ground**. じきに秋が来て葉はすっかり落ちるだろう
▷ The helicopter **hit** the **ground** only 200 meters from my house. ヘリコプターは私の家からほんの200メートル先に落ちた
▷ He ran so fast that his feet hardly seemed to **touch** the **ground**. 彼が走るスピードはものすごくて，ほとんど足が地面に着いていないみたいだった
▷ The plane **left** the **ground** smoothly with a perfect takeoff. 飛行機は滑らかに飛び立った．完璧な離陸だった
▷ We must **cover** a lot more **ground** tomorrow. あすはずっと長い距離を移動しなくてはならない
▷ Support for the Liberal Democrats has been **gaining ground** recently. 自由民主党への支持が最近伸びている
▷ We need to carry out a new sales campaign. We're **losing ground** to our competitors. われわれは販促キャンペーンを新たに打つ必要がある．ライバル企業に遅れをとりつつあるからだ

solid	ground	固い地面
rough	ground	でこぼこの地面
high	ground	高台
firm	ground	しっかりした立場
shaky	ground	あやうい立場
common	ground	共通の立場
middle	ground	中立の立場；妥協点
reasonable	grounds	正当な理由
economic	grounds	経済的理由

▷ We need to get off this marsh and onto **solid ground**. この湿地を出て足下がしっかりした地面に上がらなくては
▷ Luckily they built this house on **high ground**. There's no danger of floods. 幸い高台に家を建ててあるので洪水の危険はない
▷ We couldn't find any **common ground**. We couldn't agree about anything. われわれは合意点が見いだせず，何ひとつ意見が一致しなかった
▷ There are no **reasonable grounds** to doubt what she says. 彼女の発言を疑う正当な根拠はない

above	ground	地上に
under	ground	地下に
on	the ground	地面に，地べたに

▷ After the accident they found her lying **on** the **ground**, injured. 事故が起きて，けがをした彼女は地面に横たわっていた

on (the)	grounds of A	Aを根拠に；Aのかどで
on the	grounds that...	…との理由で

▷ She took her employers to court **on grounds of** sexual discrimination. 彼女は性差別を理由に雇い主を告訴した
▷ They refused his job application **on the grounds that** he didn't have enough experience. 経験不足という理由で彼は求人応募を断られた

group /grúːp/

名 グループ，集団，群れ；団体

form	a group	グループをつくる
set up	a group	
lead	a group	グループを率いる
join	a group	グループに加わる
belong to	a group	グループに属する

▷ They **formed** a **group** to protest against cuts in wages. 彼らは賃金カットに抗議するグループを結成した
▷ He **led** a **group** of tourists up Mount Fuji. 彼は富士登山客の一行を引率した
▷ She **joined** a **group** of environmentalists. 彼女は環境保護論者のグループに参加した
▷ She **belongs to** a **group** that supports women's rights. 彼女は女性の権利を支援するグループの一員だ

in	groups	グループで

| grow |

into	groups	グループに

▷Should we work **in groups**, or individually? グループで作業したほうがいいですか，それとも一人ひとり作業すべきですか
▷There are a lot of people. I think we should divide **into** two **groups**. 人が多すぎるので2グループに分けたほうがいいと思う

a large	group	大きなグループ
a small	group	小さなグループ
an ethnic	group	民族集団
a social	group	社会集団
a consumer	group	消費者団体
a pressure	group	圧力団体
an interest	group	利益団体
a working	group	作業部会
an environmental	group	環境保護団体

▷Aborigines are a small **ethnic group** in Australia. アボリジニはオーストラリアの少数民族集団である
▷We should form a **working group** to try to solve some of these problems. 作業部会をつくって諸問題のいくつかの解決を図るべきだ
▷The **environmental group** was protesting against global warming. その環境保護グループは地球温暖化に抗議していた

a member	of a group	グループ構成員
the leader	of a group	グループ指導者

▷Not all the **members of** the **group** have the same opinion. グループの全員が同じ意見をもっているわけではない

grow /gróu/ 動 成長する；育つ，育てる

rapidly	grow	急速に成長する
eventually	grow	やがて成長する
grow	fast	急速に成長する
grow	rapidly	
grow	steadily	着実に伸びる
grow	well	よく育つ

▷There were about three groups at the start and it **eventually grew** to 20 groups. 最初は3つほどのグループだったのがやがて20にまで増えた
▷The number of AIDS cases is **growing rapidly** in Africa. エイズ症例数はアフリカで急速に増えつつある
▷Sales have been **growing steadily** during the past six months. ここ半年の売上は着実に伸びている
▷Your tomatoes are **growing well**! あなたのトマトはよく育っていますね

grow	into A	Aへと成長する
grow	in A	Aが増える
grow	by 10%	1割増える

★grow in A の A は number, amount, size など

▷From a cute little girl she's **grown into** a beautiful woman. かわいらしい少女だったのが，おとなになって美しくなった
▷We're expecting traffic accidents to **grow in number** again this year. 交通事故が今年もまた増えると予想される
▷Wow! Your little girl has really **grown in size** since I saw you last. わあ，お嬢ちゃんはこの前見たときよりずいぶん大きくなりましたね

begin to	grow	成長し始める
continue to	grow	成長し続ける

▷If this sunflower **continues to grow**, soon it'll be over 2 meters high! このヒマワリがこのまま育てばすぐ2メートル以上の高さになるだろう

grow	to do	…するようになる

▷She soon **grew to** like living in Japan. 彼女はすぐに日本での暮らしが好きになった

as A	grows	Aが成長するにつれて

▷**As** the children **grow** I get more free time. 子どもの成長につれて自由になる時間が増えてきている

growth /gróuθ/ 名 成長，発展；増大，増加

achieve	growth	成長を達成する
encourage	growth	成長を促す
promote	growth	成長を促進する
stimulate	growth	成長を刺激する
show	growth	成長を示す
stunt	(A's) growth	発育を妨げる

▷Reducing interest rates should **encourage growth** in the economy. 利下げによって経済成長が促されるはずだ
▷Drinking a lot of milk **promotes** healthy **growth** in young children. 牛乳をたくさん飲めば幼い子どもは健康に育つ
▷The economy has **shown growth** during the last quarter. この四半期の経済は伸びを示している

rapid	growth	急速な成長
slow	growth	ゆっくりした成長
steady	growth	着実な成長

economic	growth	経済成長
population	growth	人口増加

▷Sales figures are up. We've just experienced a period of **rapid growth**. 売上高が上がった. わが社はまさに急成長期だ
▷**Economic growth** has slowed down considerably since the financial crisis. 経済成長は金融危機以来かなり減速している

growth	in A	Aの成長

▷Recently there's been a rapid **growth in** unemployment. このところ失業が急に増えてきている

growth and development	成長と発展

▷Recently we have seen a big increase in the **growth and development** of computer technology. このところコンピュータ技術は大きく成長し発展した

a rate of	growth	成長率

▷A child's **rate of growth** can be affected by many different factors. 子どもの成長速度は多くのいろいろな要素に影響を受けることがある

guarantee /gærəntíː/ 名 保証(書)

give	a guarantee	保証する；保証
offer	a guarantee	書をつける
provide	a guarantee	保証する
have	a guarantee	保証書がある

▷Do you **give** a **guarantee** with this product? この商品には保証書がつきますか
▷They **offer** a 5-year **guarantee** with this product. この製品には5年間の保証書がついている

an absolute	guarantee	絶対的保証
constitutional	guarantee	憲法上の保証
personal	guarantee	個人的な保証
a loan	guarantee	融資保証
a five-year	guarantee	5年の保証書

▷There's no **absolute guarantee** that your shares will make money! 株がもうかる保証はまったくない
▷I can give you my **personal guarantee** that your child will be safe in our nursery. 個人的に保証できますが，お子さんをうちの幼稚園に安心して預けていただけますよ
▷This product is covered by a **three-year guarantee**. この製品は3年間の保証つきです

a guarantee	against A	Aに対する保証
a guarantee	for A	

▷There's no **guarantee against** fires, floods, earthquakes, etc. 火災, 洪水, 地震等に対する保証がない
▷Is there a **guarantee for** this product? この製品には保証がついていますか

a guarantee	(that)...	…という保証

▷I can give you a **guarantee that** this product will last for at least 5 years. 保証しますよ．この製品は最低でも5年はもちます

guarantee /gærəntíː/ 動 保証する

absolutely	guarantee	絶対に保証する
almost	guarantee	ほぼ保証する
virtually	guarantee	事実上保証する

▷If you go to the Amazon in South America I can **almost guarantee** that you'll see many rare species of birds and insects. 南米アマゾンに行けばまず間違いなく珍しい鳥や昆虫をたくさん見られるよ
▷If you go to Harvard or Yale it **virtually guarantees** you a top job. ハーバードかイェールに入れば社長の座につくことが約束されたも同然だ

guarantee	to do	…すると保証する
guarantee	(that)...	…と保証する

▷He **guaranteed to** do all repairs free of charge. どんな修理でも無料ですると彼は保証した
▷They **guaranteed that** our guide would be fully experienced. 彼らは私たちのガイドが十分な経験があると保証した

guard /gáːrd/

名 警備員，ガードマン；見張り

post	a guard	警備員を配置する
relieve	the guard	警備を交替する
change	the guard	
stand	guard	見張る
keep	guard	
drop	one's guard	警戒を解く

▷You **stand guard** over our luggage while I look for a taxi. タクシーを探してくるあいだ荷物を見張っていてね
▷Don't **drop** your **guard**. They could attack at any time! 警戒を解いてはいけない．いつ襲撃があるかわからないぞ

an armed	guard	武装警備員
a security	guard	警備員

▷ There was an **armed guard** outside the President's country house. 大統領の別荘の外に武装警備員が一人いた

off	(one's) guard	油断して
on	(one's) guard	警戒して
under	guard	監視されて

▷ I didn't know how to answer his question. I was completely taken **off guard**. 彼の質問にどう答えてよいかわからなかった．不意を突かれてしまった
▷ I don't trust him. Be **on** your **guard**! あいつは信用ならないから警戒しろよ
▷ There's no chance he'll escape. He's **under** a heavy police **guard**. 彼が逃げ出せる見込みはない．警察の厳重な監視下にあるのだから

guard /gáːrd/ 動 守る；見張る，警戒する

carefully	guard	注意深く守る
jealously	guard	油断なく守る
heavily	guarded	厳重に警備された

▷ The secret has been **carefully guarded** to this day. その秘密はきょうまで注意深く守られてきた
▷ This secret recipe for duck sauce has been **jealously guarded** for over 100 years. このカモのソースの秘伝のレシピは百年以上堅く守られてきた

guard	A from B	AをBから守る
guard	against A	Aを警戒する

▷ We have to **guard against** the spread of influenza. インフルエンザの拡大に備えなければならない

guess /gés/ 名 推測，推量

make	a guess	推測する
have	a guess	
take	a guess	
hazard	a guess	当てずっぽうで言う

▷ She **made** several **guesses** but none of them was correct. 彼女はいくつか推測したが，どれも外れていた
▷ From the way Beth keeps looking at Peter I'd **hazard** a **guess** that she really likes him! ベスがピーターをずっと見ているようすから察すると，彼のことを好きなんじゃないかなと思う

a good	guess	みごとな推測，図星
an educated	guess	知識に基づく推測
a rough	guess	当てずっぽう
a lucky	guess	まぐれ当たり

▷ You're right! That was a **good guess**! そうです．図星です
▷ "What's the population of China now?" "I've no idea." "Go on! Make an **educated guess**!"「中国の人口はいまどれだけですか」「わかりません」「いや，目星をつけてみて」
▷ I didn't really know the answer. It was just a **lucky guess**. 実を言うと答えは知らなかったんだ．ただのまぐれ当たりさ

at	a guess	推測では

▷ "How many people came to the wedding?" "**At a guess** I'd say about 500."「結婚式には何人くらい来たの」「だいたい500人ぐらいかな」

[PHRASES]

My guess is that...《話》…だと思う ▷ My guess is that he won't retire until he's 70. ぼくの推測では彼は70歳になるまで退職しないと思うね
Your guess is as good as mine. 😊（何かを聞かれて）私にもわかりません ▷ "Who's going to be the next U.S. President?" "No idea. Your guess is as good as mine."「次の米国大統領はだれがなるかな」「さあね．私にもわかりませんね」

guess /gés/ 動 推測する；思う

already	guessed	すでに推測した
probably	guess	だいたい推測する
guess	correctly	正しく言い当てる
guess	right	

▷ I expect you've **already guessed** what I'm going to say. 私が何を言おうとしているか，もうわかっているよね

guess	at A	Aを推測する

▷ We can only **guess at** what they are talking about. 連中の会話の内容は推測するしかない

guess	(that)...	…だと推測する；…だと思う
guess	wh-	…か推測する

★ wh- は what, who, how など

▷ I **guess** you're right. あなたは正しいと思う
▷ **Guess who** came to the party! だれがパーティーに来たか当ててごらん

not be hard	to guess	推測するのは
not be difficult	to guess	難しくない

▷She's finally decided to quit her job. It's **not hard to guess** the reason! 彼女はついに仕事を辞める決心をした．理由は想像にかたくない

PHRASES

I **can only guess...** 推測するしかない，よくわからない
▷I can only guess how many people went to the demonstration. Maybe 5,000? デモの参加人数はよくわかりません．5千人かな？
Guess what! ☺ 何だと思う，ねえ聞いてよ ▷Guess what! I passed my driving test! I can't believe it! ねえ聞いて．運転免許の試験に通ったよ．信じられない
I guess so. / I guess not. そう思います／そうは思いません ▷"Is he going to call you back?" "I guess not." 「彼は折り返し電話をくれるかな」「くれないと思うよ」
let me guess ☺ 当ててみようか ▷Don't tell me! Let me guess! 言わないで．当ててみるから
you can guess ☺ わかるだろ ▷Dave came home drunk again after a party last night. You can guess what his wife said to him! デイブはきのうもパーティーで酔っぱらってご帰宅さ．奥さんに何て言われたか，お見通しだろ
you'll never guess ☺ 想像もつかないと思うけど ▷You'll never guess who I saw yesterday! きのうだれに会ったと思う？思いも寄らない人だよ

guest /gést/ 名 客；泊まり客；ゲスト

have	a guest	客がある
invite	a guest	客を招待する
entertain	a guest	客をもてなす
greet	a guest	客にあいさつする
welcome	a guest	客を歓迎する
receive	a guest	客を迎える

▷That meal was delicious. You really know how to **entertain** a **guest**! すごくおいしい食事でした．客のもてなし方をよくご存じですね
▷He stood by the door, ready to **greet** the **guests** as they came in. 彼はドアのそばに立って入って来る客にあいさつする準備をした
▷He **welcomed** the **guests** one by one and showed them to their seats. 彼は一人ずつ客を出迎えて席に案内した

an honored	guest	賓客
an unexpected	guest	予期せぬ客
an invited	guest	招待客
a regular	guest	常連客
a special	guest	特別ゲスト

▷Ken Russell was one of the **honored guests** at the festival this year. ケン・ラッセルは今年のフェスティバルの賓客の一人だった
▷I'm afraid you can't come in unless you're an **invited guest**. 招待客でない方はあいにく入場できません
▷She's a **regular guest** at our weekly meetings. 私たちが毎週行っている会議に彼女にいつも出てもらっている
▷Tonight we have a very **special guest**. 今夜は特別なゲストをお呼びしてあります

PHRASES

Be my guest. ☺ どうぞご自由に，ご遠慮なく ▷"Do you mind if I show it to her?" "Be my guest." 「それを彼女に見せてもいいかな」「どうぞご自由に」

guide /gáid/

名 案内書，手引き；指針；案内人，ガイド

provide	a guide	指針となる
produce	a guide	手引きを作成する
use A	as a guide	手引きとして使う

▷These talks aim to **provide** a **guide** for parents in caring for teenage children. これらの講演のねらいは10代の子どものめんどうを見る親たちに指針を与えることだ
▷The council has **produced** a **guide** on consumer rights. 審議会は消費者の権利に関する手引きを作成した
▷This book can be **used as** a **guide** to the main shopping areas in Tokyo. この本は東京の主要なショッピングエリアの案内書として使える

a general	guide	大まかな手引き
a rough	guide	
a good	guide	すぐれた手引き
a practical	guide	実用的な手引き
a reliable	guide	信頼できる手引き
a useful	guide	役立つ手引き
a travel	guide	旅行案内
a mountain	guide	山岳ガイド

▷This leaflet gives you a **rough guide** to the most interesting places to visit in Kyoto. このパンフレットを見れば京都の見所がだいたいわかる
▷This is a really **good guide** to the museum. この本はとてもよい美術館ガイドだ

a guide	to A	Aの手引き

▷For more information on stretching, see *Beginner's **Guide** to Stretching*, page 126. ストレッチについてさらに詳しいことは『ストレッチ入門』126ページを

| guilt |

ご覧ください

guilt /gílt/ 名 自責の念

a sense of	guilt	罪悪感
a feeling	guilt	
guilt and shame		自責の念と恥の感覚

▷ He was overcome with **guilt and shame** at what he had done. 彼は自分のしたことに対して自責の念と恥ずかしいという思いに襲われた

guilty /gílti/

形 罪を犯した；罪の意識がある，やましい

really	guilty	すごく気がとがめる
a little	guilty	少し気がとがめる
slightly	guilty	
rather	guilty	いくぶん気がとがめる

▷ Sorry! I took the last cake! I feel **a little guilty**! ごめん．最後のケーキを食べちゃった．申し訳ないな
▷ He had a **rather guilty** expression on his face. 彼の表情にはいくぶんやましさが表れていた

feel	guilty	罪の意識を感じる
be found	guilty of A	Aの有罪判決を受ける
plead	guilty to A	Aの罪を認める

▷ You don't need to **feel guilty**. You didn't do anything wrong. 罪の意識を感じる必要はないよ．きみは何も悪いことはしていないのだから
▷ He was **found guilty of** murder. 彼は殺人罪で有罪とされた
▷ He **pleaded guilty to** stealing the car. 彼は車の窃盗容疑を認めた

gun /gʌ́n/ 名 銃，拳銃，ピストル

carry	a gun	銃を携帯する
pull (out)	a gun	銃を取り出す
draw	a gun	銃を構える
point	a gun	銃を向ける
fire	a gun	銃を発砲する

▷ It's illegal to **carry** a **gun** without a license. 免許を持たずに銃を所持するのは違法だ
▷ Don't **point** that **gun** at me! It's dangerous! おれに銃を向けるなよ．危ないじゃないか
▷ He was accused of **firing** a **gun** at a policeman. 彼は警官に発砲したとして告訴された

guy /gái/ 名《略式》男；やつ

a nice	guy	いいやつ
a good	guy	
a tough	guy	たくましいやつ，乱暴なやつ

▷ He's a **tough guy**, but he can be sympathetic too. 彼は乱暴者だが，思いやりがある一面もある

H

habit /hǽbit/ 名 習慣, 癖；習性

be in	the habit	習慣がある
have	a habit	
make	a habit	習慣にする
develop	a habit	習慣を身につける
get into	a habit	
acquire	a habit	
become	a habit	習慣になる
break	the habit	習慣をやめる
get out of	the habit	
kick	the habit	
change	habits	習慣を変える

▷He's **in** the **habit** of going jogging every morning at 6:30. 彼は毎朝6時半にジョギングするのを習慣にしている

▷She **made** a **habit** of not leaving the office before everyone else had gone home. 彼女は他の人が帰る前にオフィスを出ないようにしていた

▷Our dog has **developed** the **habit** of jumping onto the sofa to watch television! うちの犬ったらソファに飛び乗ってテレビを見るようになったの

▷When he gave up smoking he **acquired** the **habit** of chewing gum. 彼は禁煙したら代わりにガムをかむ癖がついた

▷She started smoking when she was 18 and she's never been able to **break** the **habit**. 彼女は18歳のときにたばこを吸い始めたが, いまだに禁煙できない

▷I've got to **get out of** the **habit** of eating too much and **into** the **habit** of taking more exercise. 食べ過ぎをやめて, もっと運動する習慣をつけなくちゃ

a bad	habit	悪い習慣
a good	habit	よい習慣
old	habits	古い習慣
a regular	habit	いつもの習慣
eating	habits	食習慣
dietary	habits	
drinking	habits	飲酒の習慣
smoking	habits	喫煙習慣

▷Exercising regularly is definitely a **good habit**. 定期的に運動するのは間違いなくよい習慣だ

▷Going out with my friends to karaoke every weekend has become a **regular habit**. 週末には決まって友人たちとカラオケに行くようになった

▷It's important to have good **dietary habits**. よい食習慣を守るのが大切だ

(from) force of	habit	いつもの癖で
out of	habit	

▷Sorry! I didn't mean to turn left at the traffic lights. **Force of habit**. ごめん. 信号で左に曲がるつもりはなかったんだけど, いつもの癖だね

the habit	of a lifetime	生来の習慣

▷You know from experience that it's not easy to break the **habit of a lifetime**. 生来の癖を直すのは簡単ではないというのはきみも経験からわかるだろ

PHRASES＞
Old habits die hard. 古い習慣はなかなか直らない

hair /héər/ 名 髪の毛；(1本の)毛

lose	one's **hair**	髪が少なくなる
do	one's **hair**	髪を整える
brush	one's **hair**	髪にブラシをかける
comb	one's **hair**	髪をとかす
wash	one's **hair**	髪を洗う
cut	A's **hair**	髪を切る
dry	one's **hair**	髪を乾かす
dye	A's **hair**	髪を染める

▷Ken isn't bald yet, but he's beginning to **lose** his **hair**. ケンははげてはいないが髪が薄くなり始めている

▷Sorry. She'll be another 10 minutes at least. She's **doing** her **hair**. ごめんなさい. 彼女は少なくともあと10分かかります. いま髪を整えていますので

▷He had his **hair cut** regularly. 彼は定期的に髪を刈ってもらっていた

▷You'd better **dry** your **hair**. Otherwise you'll catch cold. 髪を乾かしたほうがいいよ. かぜを引くから

black	hair	黒髪
dark	hair	
blond(e)	hair	金髪
fair	hair	
golden	hair	
brown	hair	褐色の髪, 茶髪
red	hair	赤毛
gray	hair	白髪
white	hair	
curly	hair	カールした髪
straight	hair	ストレートの髪
wavy	hair	ウェーブのかかった髪
dry	hair	乾いた髪
long	hair	長い髪
short	hair	短い髪

▷Did you see a woman with **blond hair** and sun-

glasses go out of the building? サングラスをかけた金髪の女性が建物から出て行くのを見ましたか
▷He is tall and handsome, with **brown hair**. 彼は背が高くてハンサムで髪は褐色です
▷Mum has **long dark hair**. お母さんは黒くて長い髪をしている
▷He found a **gray hair**. Then another. Then another. Three **gray hairs**! 彼は白髪を1本見つけた. それから1本. また1本. 白髪が3本だ (★ hair は髪の毛全体をさすときは不可算名詞で, 一本一本をさすときは可算名詞)
▷John has **curly hair**. ジョンの髪はカールがかかっている

half /hæf | hɑːf/ 名 半分, 2分の1

the lower	half	下半分
the upper	half	上半分
the first	half	前半
the second	half	後半
the latter	half	
the northern	half	北半分

▷The **lower half** of his body was entirely covered with spots. 彼の下半分には発疹がいっぱい出ていた
▷The **upper half** of the building was totally destroyed by fire. 建物の上半分は火事ですっかり焼け落ちた
▷I've only read the **first half** of that book. まだその本の前半しか読んでいない
▷Many important discoveries were made during the **latter half** of the 17th century. 17世紀の後半に多くの重要な発見がなされた

| in | half | 半分に |

▷Let's cut the cake **in half**. ケーキを半分に切ろう

| an hour | and a half | 1時間半 |
| a mile | and a half | 1マイル半 |

▷It takes me at least an hour **and a half** to get from my house to the university. 私の家から大学に着くのに少なくとも1時間半かかる

hall /hɔːl/ 名 玄関; 廊下; 会館

the entrance	hall	玄関広間
the main	hall	メインホール
the dining	hall	ダイニングホール
a concert	hall	コンサートホール
an exhibition	hall	展示会場

▷The concert will be held in the **main hall**. コンサートはメインホールで行われる

| in | the hall | 玄関で, 玄関に |

▷Can you switch on the light **in the hall**? 玄関の明かりをつけてくれませんか

hand /hænd/ 名 手; 手助け

hold	hands	手を握り合う
shake	hands	握手する
put	one's **hand** on A	手をAに置く
raise	one's **hand**	手を挙げる
wave	one's **hand**	手を振る
clap	one's **hands**	手をたたく
rub	one's **hands**	手をこする
wash	one's **hands**	手を洗う
give A	a hand	Aを手伝う
lend	a hand	手を貸す
want	a hand	手助けがほしい
need	a hand	手助けがいる

▷They were **holding hands** as they walked down the street. 彼らは手をつないで道路を行進していた
▷O.K. I'm sorry. Let's **shake hands** and be friends. わかったわ. だけどごめんなさい. 握手して, いままでどおりお友だちでいましょう (★愛を告白されて断る文句)
▷He **put** his **hand on** her shoulder. 彼は彼女の肩に手を置いた
▷Please **raise** your **hand** if you want to ask a question. 質問があれば手を挙げてください
▷She **waved** her **hand**, but he didn't recognize her. 手を振って合図する彼女に彼は気づかなかった
▷She **clapped** her **hands** in delight. 彼女はうれしくて手をたたいた
▷**Wash** your **hands** before you eat. 食事の前に手を洗いなさい
▷It's kind of you to **give** me a **hand**. 手伝ってくれてご親切さま
▷I'd be glad to **lend** a **hand**. 喜んで手を貸します

dirty	hands	汚れた手
clean	hands	きれいな手
an outstretched	hand	伸ばした手
a free	hand	空いた手
one's bare	hands	素手
a helping	hand	援助の手
capable	hands	有能な人の手

▷After the earthquake the rescuers were digging the earth away with their **bare hands**. 地震のあと救助隊は素手で土を払いのけていた
▷Look at this mess! I could use a **helping hand**

to clear it up! なんて散らかりようなの．片づけをだれかに手伝ってもらいたいくらいだわ
▷In his **capable hands** there's no need to worry. 有能な彼の手に委ねれば心配の必要はない

take A	by the hand	Aの手をとる

▷She **took** him **by the hand** and led him into the garden. 彼女は彼の手をとって庭へ案内した

at	hand	手元に
by	hand	手で
in	one's **hand**	手に
off	A's **hands**	A(人)の手を離れて
out of	hand	手に負えない

▷It was lucky there was a rope **at hand**. They were able to use it to pull her to safety. 幸運なことに手元にあったロープを使って彼女を安全な場所に引っ張れた
▷I write **by hand** in small notebooks. 手書きで小さなノートに書いています
▷He had some letters **in** his **hand**. 彼は手紙を何通か手にしていた
▷I'm sorry, I can't help you. Your case is **off** my **hands** now. 助けてあげられなくてごめん．きみの件はもう私の手を離れているので

hand	in hand	手に手を取って

▷They walked along the river bank **hand in hand**. 彼らは川岸を手を取り合って歩いた

on	one's **hands and knees**	四つんばいで

▷She got down **on** her **hands and knees** and started searching for her contact lens. 彼女は四つんばいになってコンタクトレンズを探し始めた

PHRASES
Hands off! 😊 さわるな，手を触れるな；じゃまするな
▷Hands off! That's my piece of cake! さわらないで．私の分のケーキよ

handle /hǽndl/ 名 取っ手, 柄

turn	a handle	取っ手を回す
pull	a handle	取っ手を引く

▷**Turn** the **handle** to the right to open the door. 取っ手を右に回してドアを開けてください
▷**Pull** the **handle** toward you. 取っ手を手元へ引いてください

a door	handle	ドアの取っ手
a broom	handle	ほうきの柄

handle /hǽndl/ 動 処理する；手で扱う

handle	carefully	注意深く扱う
handle	with care	
handle	roughly	ぞんざいに扱う
well	handled	うまい処理の
badly	handled	まずい処理の
easily	handle	簡単に処理する

▷**Handle** this parcel **carefully**. There's glass inside. この小包は取り扱いにご注意ください．中にガラスが入っていますから
▷It's a delicate situation. It needs to be **handled with care**. 微妙な状況なので，注意深く対応する必要がある
▷The whole operation was extremely **well handled**. 作業はすべてきわめて順調に処理された
▷The whole affair was **badly handled**. 何から何までまずい処理がなされた
▷Don't worry. I can **easily handle** the extra work. ご心配なく．余分の業務もうまくこなせますから

be able	to handle	扱える
be difficult	to handle	扱いが難しい
be hard	to handle	
be easy	to handle	扱いが簡単だ

▷I don't think I'll be **able to handle** any more rude customers. 横柄な客の相手はこれ以上ごめんです
▷This car is really **easy to handle**. この車はとても運転しやすい

happen /hǽpən/ 動 起こる

actually	happen	実際に起こる
really	happen	本当に起こる
just	happen	たまたま起きる
never	happen	決して起こらない
usually	happen	たいてい起こる
happen	again	再び起きる

▷I don't believe that was what **actually happened**. そんなことが実際に起きたとは信じられない
▷We'll never know what **really happened**. ことの真相は決してわからないだろう
▷I **just happened** to meet him by chance. 彼に会ったのはほんのたまたまだ
▷That will not **happen again**. それは二度と起きないだろう

see	what happens	ことの成り行きを見る

▷It will be interesting to **see what happens** in the next three years. 向こう3年間のことの成り行きを見

| happy |

るのは興味深い

anything	can happen	何が起きても不思議ではない
what	happens if...	…ならどうなるか
whatever	happens	何が起きようと

▷ It's a really dangerous situation. **Anything can happen**! 非常に危険な状況だ.何が起こっても不思議じゃない
▷ I'll look after you **whatever happens**. 何が起ころうときみのめんどうを見るよ

happen	to A	A(人)に起こる

▷ I'm afraid something has **happened to** him. 彼に何かあったのではないかと心配だ
◆ **What happened to A? / Whatever happened to A?** Aはどうなったんだ ▷ Whatever happened to Kate? She was here a minute ago. ケイトにいったい何があったの？ちょっと前にここにいたのに

happen	to do	たまたま…する

▷ By chance I **happened to** bump into him outside the railway station. たまたま駅の外で彼にばったり会った

PHRASES
What happened? ☺ 何があったの

happy /hǽpi/ 形 幸せな, うれしい; 満足した

look	happy	幸せそうだ; 満足そうだ
seem	happy	

▷ Carolyn **seems** quite **happy** in her new job. キャロリンは新しい仕事にとても満足そうだ

extremely	happy	すごくうれしい
really	happy	
quite	happy	
particularly	happy	とりわけうれしい
perfectly	happy	この上なくうれしい
not at all	happy	まったくうれしくない
not entirely	happy	完全には満足しない
never	happy	決して満足しない

▷ I'm **perfectly happy** with that suggestion. とてもいいご提案をいただきました
▷ They're **not at all happy** with our new product. 我が社の新製品はまったく不評だ
▷ I'm **not entirely happy** with your explanation. あなたの説明に完全に満足しているわけではありません
▷ No matter how hard I try, my boss is **never happy** with my work. どれだけがんばっても上司は私の仕事を認めてくれない

happy	about A	Aをうれしく思う
happy	with A	
happy	for A	A(人)のことをうれしく思う

▷ I am very **happy about** the news. その知らせを本当にうれしく思います
▷ I'm **happy with** my current salary. いまの給料に満足している
▷ I'm **happy for** you. よかったですね; 私もうれしく思います

happy	(that)...	…をうれしく思う
happy	to do	…してうれしい

▷ Thank goodness! I'm **happy that** everything worked out well in the end. やれやれ. 最後にはすべてうまくいってよかった
▷ I'm very **happy to** meet you John. ジョン, あなたに会えてうれしいです

hard /hɑ́ːrd/ 形 難しい; 堅い

extremely	hard	とても難しい
quite	hard	
really	hard	

▷ It's **quite hard** to get a good score in the TOEFL exam. TOEFLの試験でよい点をとるのはとても難しい

hard	on A	A(人)につらくあたる

▷ Don't be so **hard on** yourself. ☺ そんなに自分を責めないで

find A	hard	Aは難しいと思う

▷ I **find** these math problems really **hard** to do. これらの数学の問題はすごく難しいと思う

hard	(for A) to do	(Aにとって)…するのは難しい

▷ He could be American or Canadian. It's very **hard to** say. 彼はアメリカ人かもしれないしカナダ人かもしれない. 何とも言えませんね ▷ It's **hard to** believe. ☺ 信じがたいね

harm /hɑ́ːrm/ 名 害, 損害, 危害

cause	harm	害を及ぼす
do	harm	
prevent	harm	害を防ぐ

▷ Drinking alcohol when you are pregnant can **cause** serious **harm** *to* your baby. 妊娠中の飲酒は

胎児に重大な害を及ぼすことがある
▷It wouldn't **do** any **harm** to write a letter of apology. 詫び状を一筆書いても損はないだろう
◆**do more harm than good** 百害あって一利なし
▷It's better to say nothing. Complaining would do more harm than good. 何も言わないほうがいい。文句を言ったところで一ついいことはない
▷We do all we can to **prevent harm** coming to our employees if they work in dangerous places. 危険な場所で働く従業員に被害が及ばないようできる限りのことをする

great	harm	大きな害
serious	harm	深刻な害
bodily	harm	肉体的危害
physical	harm	

▷Her husband gets angry and shouts at her, but he hasn't done her any **bodily harm**. 彼女の夫は怒って彼女にどなり声を上げることはあっても、彼女の体に危害を加えたことはない

PHRASES
There's no harm in (do)ing A Aしても害はない
▷There's no harm in asking for a rise. He can only say "No!" 賃上げを要求しても害はないさ、あっちは「ノー」と言うだけだね

hat /hæt/ 名 帽子

wear	a hat	帽子をかぶっている
put on	one's hat	帽子をかぶる
remove	one's hat	帽子を脱ぐ
take off	one's hat	
raise	one's hat	帽子を取ってあいさつする

▷She was **wearing** a big **hat** to keep the sun off. 彼女は日よけに大きな帽子をかぶっていた
▷Better **put** your **hat on**. It's cold outside. 帽子をかぶったほうがいいよ、外は寒いから
▷When you enter a church you should **remove** your **hat**. 教会に入るときは帽子をお脱ぎください
▷He's very polite. He **raised** his **hat** to me. 彼はとても礼儀正しくて、帽子を取ってあいさつしてくれた

in	a hat	帽子をかぶった

▷Isn't that Diana? Over there. The woman **in** the **hat**. あれはダイアナじゃない？あそこ、帽子をかぶった女性だよ

a straw	hat	麦わら帽子
a bowler	hat	山高帽
a cowboy	hat	カウボーイハット
a panama	hat	パナマ帽

| head |

hate /héit/ 動 憎む，ひどく嫌う

really	hate	すごく憎む
just	hate	ちょっといやだ
always	hate	いつも憎む
still	hate	まだ憎む

▷She **really hates** being kept waiting. 彼女は待たされるのが大の苦手だ
▷Even though I'm grown up I **still hate** going to the dentist! おとなになってもやっぱり歯医者はきらいだ

hate	to do	…したくない，…するのはいやだ
hate	doing	
hate	A doing	A(人)に…してほしくない

▷I **hate** travel**ing** to work during the rush hour. ラッシュアワーに通勤するなんてまっぴらごめんだ
▷She **hates** me telephon**ing** her at work. 私が彼女の職場に電話すると彼女はいやがる

hate it	when	…はいやだ

▷Don't you just **hate it when** the TV advertisements come on in the middle of a movie? 映画の途中にテレビのコマーシャルが入るのはちょっといやじゃない？

head /héd/ 名 頭，顔；(組織の)長

put	one's head	頭を突き出す
stick	one's head	
turn	one's head	後ろを振り向く
raise	one's head	頭を上げる
bend	one's head	頭を垂れる
bow	one's head	頭を下げる
duck	one's head	首をかがめる
hang	one's head	うなだれる
nod	one's head	同意してうなずく
shake	one's head	首を横に振る
scratch	one's head	頭をかく
bang	one's head	頭をぶつける
use	one's head	頭を使う
come into	A's head	頭に浮かぶ
get it into	one's head	頭にたたき込む
lose	one's head	気が動転する
keep	one's head	冷静を保つ

▷She **stuck** her **head** around the door and said: "Dinner's ready!" 彼女は戸口から顔だけ出して「夕飯ですよ」と言った
▷She **turned** her **head**. The man was still following her. 彼女が振り返ると男はまだ後をつけてきていた
▷He **raised** his **head**. "Listen! Can you hear something?" 彼は顔を上げて言った。「耳を澄ませて。何か

223

| headache |

聞こえる？」
▷**Duck** your **head**! The ceilings here are very low. 頭をかがめて．ここの天井はすごく低くなっているから
▷She **nodded** her **head** in agreement. 彼女は賛成してうなずいた
▷She **shook** her **head**. "I'm definitely not going to the party." 首を振って彼女は言った．「絶対パーティーに行かないわよ」
▷He **scratched** his **head**. "I've no idea what you're talking about." 頭をかきながら彼は言った．「何のことをおっしゃっているのかわかりません」(★困惑・戸惑いのしぐさ)
▷He **banged** his **head** *against* the top of the door frame. 彼はドア枠の上部に頭をぶつけた
▷Come on, Jane, **use** your **head**. さあ，ジェイン，頭を使うんだ
▷A good idea **came into** my **head** this morning. いい考えがけさ頭に浮かんだ
▷Can't you **get it into** your **head** that I don't want to see you any more? 二度とあなたに会いたくないって言ってるのにわからないの
▷I can't believe he resigned. He must have **lost** his **head**. 彼の辞任は信じられない．頭がどうかしていたに違いない

have one's **head** in one's hands		両手に顔をうずめる

★have のほかに hold, put なども用いる

▷She **put** her **head in** her **hands** and started to cry. 彼女は両手に顔をうずめて泣き出した

one's **head**	bows	頭が垂れる
one's **head**	comes up	顔が上がる
one's **head**	turns	顔が向く

▷His **head bowed**. "I'm sorry. It won't happen again." 彼は頭を垂れた．「申し訳ありません．もう二度としません」
▷His **head came up** in surprise. "What did you say?" 彼は驚いて顔を上げた．「何て言った？」
▷His **head turned** to where the sounds were coming from. 音が聞こえてくる方へ彼は顔を向けた

a bald	**head**	はげ頭
a clear	**head**	さえた頭
a cool	**head**	冷静な頭
a former	**head**	元の長

▷The man with the **bald head** is my girlfriend's father. 頭がはげているあの人はぼくのガールフレンドのお父さんです
▷Don't panic! Try to keep a **cool head**. あわてないで．冷静に
▷Mr. Williams has retired now. He's a **former head** of our department. ウィリアムズさんは現在は退職していますが，うちの部署の元部長です

from **head** to	toe	頭の先からつま先まで
from **head** to	foot	

▷She was dressed **from head to toe** in a Minnie Mouse costume. 彼女は上から下までミニーマウスの衣装で着飾っていた

〈PHRASES〉
on your own head be it ☺ どうなろうと私は知らないよ(きみの責任だよ) ▷Well, I think you're making a mistake, but on your own head be it! きみのやっていることは間違っていると思うけど，自分の責任で好きなようにやればいいさ

headache /hédèik/

名 頭痛；頭痛の種

have	a headache	頭痛がする
suffer from	a headache	
cause	a headache	(Aに)頭痛を引き起こす
give A	a headache	

▷I **have** a terrible **headache**. ひどい頭痛がする
▷Recently I've started to **suffer from headaches**. このところよく頭痛がする
▷Reading in poor light can **cause** a **headache**. 照明の悪いところで読書すると頭痛の原因となることがある
▷I wish you'd stop complaining. You're **giving** me a **headache**! 文句を言うのはこれくらいにしてくれないかな．頭が痛くなってくるよ

a bad	headache	ひどい頭痛
a severe	headache	
a terrible	headache	
a major	headache	頭痛の種

▷If you've got a **bad headache** you should take some medicine. ひどい頭痛がするなら薬を飲みなさい
▷I don't know how we can increase sales this year. It's a **major headache**. 今年の売上をどうしたら伸ばせるか，頭の痛いところだ

a headache	for A	Aの頭痛の種

▷They're in financial trouble. It's a bit of a **headache for** them. 資金繰りが苦しくて彼らも頭が痛いところだ

headline /hédlàin/ 名 見出し

grab	the headlines	新聞の見出しを
hit	the headlines	にぎわせる

▷ Yet another scandal about a Hollywood movie star **grabbed the headlines**. ハリウッドの映画スターのスキャンダルがまた新聞をにぎわせた

health /hélθ/ 名 健康, 健康状態

maintain	health	健康を維持する
protect	health	健康を守る
improve	the health	健康を増進する
affect	A's health	健康に影響を及ぼす
damage	A's health	健康を損なう

▷ Regular exercise can **improve the health**. 定期的に運動すれば健康増進に役立つ
▷ He jogs a lot to **maintain** his **health**. 彼は健康維持のためによくジョギングしている
▷ Eating junk food can **affect** your **health**. ジャンクフードを食べると健康に影響を及ぼす可能性がある

ill	health	不健康
mental	health	心の健康
physical	health	体の健康
public	health	公衆衛生

▷ He suffers from **ill health**. 彼は健康がすぐれない
▷ **Mental health** is just as important as **physical health**. 心の健康は肉体の健康と同じくらい大切だ

in good	health	健康状態がよく
in poor	health	健康状態が悪く
good	for one's health	健康によい
bad	for one's health	健康に悪い

▷ He's **in very good health** for a man of eighty. 彼は80歳の割にはとても健康だ
▷ Sarah's been **in very poor health** recently. サラは最近健康がすぐれない
▷ Too much coffee is **bad for** your **health**. コーヒーの飲みすぎは健康によくない

one's **state of**	health	健康状態

healthy /hélθi/ 形 健康な, 健全な

apparently	healthy	見たところ健康な
perfectly	healthy	まったく健康な

▷ There was no problem. The doctor said he was **perfectly healthy**. どこも悪いところはなかった。医師の説明では健康そのものだそうだ

hear /híər/ 動 聞こえる, 聞く

actually	hear	実際に聞く
almost	hear	ほとんど聞こえる
already	heard	すでに聞いた
ever	heard	いままでに聞いた
never	heard	まったく聞いていない

▷ You can **actually hear** the improvement in sound quality. 音質が向上したことを実際に耳でお聞きいただけます
▷ I could **almost hear** what they were saying in the next room. 隣の部屋で連中がしゃべっている内容をほとんど聞けた
▷ It seems he's a famous artist but I've **never heard** of him. 有名なアーティストらしいが彼のことを聞いたことがない

be pleased to	hear	聞いてうれしい
be glad to	hear	
be delighted to	hear	
be surprised to	hear	聞いて驚く
be interested to	hear	ぜひ聞きたい
be sorry to	hear	聞いて残念だ

▷ I was **pleased to hear** that you've been promoted. 昇進されたと伺うれしかったです
▷ I'm **glad to hear** that everything went well. すべてうまくいったと聞いてうれしい
▷ I'd **be interested to hear** what she thinks. 彼女の考えをぜひ聞いてみたい
▷ I'm **sorry to hear** you're not well. 体調がよくないとお聞きしましたが、心配です

hear	**about** A	Aについて聞く
hear	**of** A	Aのことを伝え聞く

▷ Nice to meet you. I've **heard** a lot **about** you. お目にかかれてうれしいです。おうわさはかねがね
▷ I had never **heard of** Lewis before. ルイスのことはそれまで聞いたことがなかった

hear	A do	Aが…するのが聞こえる
hear	A doing	Aが…しているのが聞こえる

▷ She **heard** Bill go out. 彼女はビルが出て行く音を聞いた
▷ I **heard** people talk**ing** in the room below. 下の部屋で話している人たちの声が聞こえた

hear	(that)...	…だと聞く；…とのうわさだ
hear	what	何が…か聞く

▷ "**I hear** Japanese people love working long hours at their companies. Is that true?" "Well, yes and no." 「日本人は会社で長時間働くのが好きだって聞いてるけど、それ本当？」「そうですねえ、どちらとも言えません」

| heart |

PHRASES
(Do) you hear (me)? 😊 聞いてるかい
I hear you. 😊 聞こえてるよ；同感だ

heart /hɑ́ːrt/

名 心臓；心；愛情；勇気；中心，核心

break	A's heart	ひどく悲しませる
open	one's heart	心を開く
win	A's heart	心をつかむ

▷ It would **break** Sally's **heart** if her parents got divorced. 両親が離婚するようなことになったらサリーは心を痛めるだろう
▷ Apparently she had a little too much to drink and **opened** her **heart** to him. どうやら彼女は少し飲み過ぎたようで，彼に心を開いていた
▷ He kept buying her present after present until finally he **won** her **heart**! 彼は彼女にプレゼント攻勢をしかけ，ついには彼女の心をつかんだ

A's heart	beats	心臓が脈を打つ
A's heart	thumps	
A's heart	leaps	心臓が激しく鼓動する
A's heart	jumps	
A's heart	stops	心臓が停止する
A's heart	sinks	心が沈む
A's heart	goes out	心から同情する

▷ When he saw her his **heart** began to **beat** faster! 彼女を見て彼の心臓の鼓動は早まった
▷ It was a very dangerous situation. He could feel his **heart thumping** loudly. とても危険な状況に，彼は心臓が大きく脈打つのを感じた
▷ When she heard that he wasn't married her **heart leaped**. Still a chance! 彼が結婚していないと聞いて彼女の心臓は高鳴った．まだチャンスはあるわ
▷ The news about the big earthquake made her **heart sink**. 大地震のニュースに彼女の心は沈んだ
▷ I feel so sorry for those poor, hungry people in Africa. My **heart goes out** to them. アフリカの貧しく飢餓に苦しむ人々を本当に気の毒に思う．彼らに心から同情する

a warm	heart	優しい心
a broken	heart	傷心
a heavy	heart	沈んだ気持ち
a sinking	heart	
a light	heart	軽やかな気持ち

▷ The news wasn't good. He returned home from the hospital with a **heavy heart**. よくない知らせに彼はふさぎ込んで病院から帰宅した

have	a weak heart	心臓が悪い

have	a bad heart	
have	a kind heart	心が優しい
have	a good heart	
have	a heart of gold	
have	a big heart	心が寛容な
have	a heart of stone	心が冷たい
have	a change of heart	気が変わる

▷ She's so kind to everybody. She's got a **heart of gold**! 彼女はだれにでもとても親切で，思いやりの深い人です
▷ My girlfriend refuses to speak to me. She's got a **heart of stone**! ガールフレンドはぼくに話そうともしない．とても冷たいんだ
▷ At first he was against his daughter's marriage, but then he **had a change of heart**. 当初は娘の結婚に反対していた彼だが，気持ちが変わった

at	heart	心の底は；気持ちは
in	one's heart	内心は
with	all one's heart	心から
at	the heart	中心に

▷ Actually he's quite a sensitive person **at heart**. 実のところ彼は根はとても傷つきやすい人だ
▷ I wish you both happiness **with all** my **heart**. お二人の幸せを心からお祈りします
▷ Germany lies **at the heart** of Europe. ドイツはヨーロッパの中央に位置する ▷ It's lack of money that's **at the very heart** of the problem. 問題の中心は資金不足だ

heart and soul	身も心も
the hearts and minds	心と頭

▷ Whatever Bill does, he puts himself into it **heart and soul**. 何をするにもビルは全身全霊を打ち込んでやる
▷ Politicians have to win the **hearts and minds** of the people. 政治家は人々の心と頭をつかまなければならない

heat /híːt/ 名 熱，熱さ；暑さ

feel	the heat	熱さを感じる
generate	heat	発熱する
reduce	the heat	火を弱くする
turn down	the heat	
turn up	the heat	火を強くする
turn off	the heat	火を止める

▷ I don't think the electric heater is working. I can't **feel** any **heat**. 電気ストーブがきいていないんじゃないかな．ちっとも暖かくないよ
▷ Wind power can be used to **generate heat**. 風力は熱を発生させるのに活用できる

▷ If the sauce starts to boil you should turn down the gas and **reduce** the **heat**. ソースが沸騰しはじめたらガスを小さくして火を弱めなさい
▷ **Turn up** the **heat**. The water's not boiling yet. もっと火を強くして，まだお湯が沸いていないわ
▷ **Turn off** the **heat** and add the tomato sauce. 火を止めて，トマトソースを加えてください

dry	heat	乾いた暑さ
intense	heat	猛烈な暑さ
white	heat	白熱
(a) high	heat	強火
(a) low	heat	弱火
(a) gentle	heat	
(a) moderate	heat	中火
(a) medium	heat	

▷ The **dry heat** of the summer takes away all your energy. 夏の乾いた暑さで体力がすべて奪われてしまう
▷ It's dangerous to work a long time in conditions of **intense heat**. 酷暑の中で長時間働くのは危険だ
▷ Cook over a **low heat** for 10 minutes. 弱火で10分間調理してください

the heat	from A	Aからの熱
in	the heat of A	Aの真っ最中に

▷ The **heat from** the camp fire was enough to keep them warm. キャンプファイヤーの火で彼らは十分に暖かかった
▷ Terrible things are done **in** the **heat of** battle. 戦闘の最中にはとんでもないことが起こる
◆ **in the heat of the moment** ついかっとなって
▷ Forget what I said. I didn't mean it. It was said in the heat of the moment. いまのことばは忘れて．本気じゃなかったの．ついかっとなって言っちゃった

heaven /hévən/ 名 天国；楽園

go to	Heaven	天国に行く

▷ I hope I **go to Heaven** when I die! 死んだら天国に行きたい

in	heaven	天国に；幸せな気分で

▷ He proposed to her in such a romantic way. She was **in heaven**! 彼にとてもロマンチックなプロポーズをされて彼女は天にも登る気持ちだった

heaven	and [or] hell	天国と［か］地獄

▷ When we die some people believe we go to **Heaven or Hell**. 死んだら天国か地獄に行くと信じている人もいる

a heaven	on earth	地上の楽園

PHRASES
Good heavens! / Heavens! ☺ おやおや，これはこれは
▷ Good Heavens! England won the World Cup? I can't believe it! 何だって，イングランドがワールドカップで優勝したって？信じられないな

height /háit/ 名 高さ，高度；身長

measure	the height	高さを測る
reach	a height	高さに達する
gain	height	高度を上げる
lose	height	高度を下げる

▷ He's really tall. I think he's going to **reach** a **height** of over 2 meters. 彼はすごく背が高いね．2メートル以上に背が伸びるんじゃないか
▷ The plane looked to be in trouble, but gradually it **gained height**. トラブルがあったように見えたが，飛行機は徐々に高度を上げた

full	height	ぴんと立ったときの身長
a great	height	高身長；すごい高さ
average	height	平均的な身長
medium	height	
dizzy	heights	目もくらむ高さ

▷ Angrily, she drew herself up to her **full height** and marched out of the room. 怒って彼女はすっくと立ち上がり，部屋から出て行った
▷ The eagle can reach a **great height**. ワシはすごい高空まで飛べる
▷ He's **medium height** with short brown hair. 彼は背丈は中ぐらいで，茶髪を短くしています
▷ She reached the **dizzy heights** of stardom. 彼女はスターの座にのし上がった

in	height	高さ…の
at	a height of A	A(数値)の高度で

▷ He's 1.75 meters **in height**. 彼は身長1メートル75センチです
▷ The airplane flew **at a height of** 25,000 feet. 飛行機は2万5千フィートの高度で飛行した

height and weight		身長と体重

▷ You need to have your baby's **height and weight** measured regularly. 赤ん坊の身長と体重を定期的に測ってもらう必要がある

hell /hél/ 名 地獄；生き地獄

| help |

go to	hell	地獄に行く
go through	hell	さんざん苦労する
make A's life	hell	A(人)をひどい目に遭わせる

▷ When she was at junior high school the other students **made** her **life hell**. 彼女は中学生のときほかの生徒たちからひどい目に遭わされた

hell	on earth	この世の地獄
the A from	hell	最低のA

▷ If nuclear war breaks out it'll be like **hell on earth**. 核戦争が起きたらこの世は地獄と化すだろう
▷ Let's leave. This is the restaurant **from hell**! 出ようよ。ここは最低のレストランだ

PHRASES
Get the hell out of here! ☺ ここから出ていけ
To hell with A! ☺ Aなんかくそくらえ ▷ We've waited nearly an hour and a half for him. To hell with it! I'm going home! 1時間半くらい彼を待ったぞ，ひどいもんだ。ぼくは家に帰るよ
What the hell! ☺ かまうものか，どうだっていいよ

help /hélp/

名 助け, 援助, 手伝い；役立つもの

get	help	援助を受ける
receive	help	
seek	help	援助を求める
ask for	help	
find	help	援助を得る
need	help	援助を必要とする
want	help	援助が欲しい
give	help	援助する
provide	help	
offer	help	援助を申し出る

▷ Quick! **Get** some **help**! There's been an accident. 急いで。助けを呼んで。事故です
▷ He's over eighty, but he's very independent. He never **seeks** any **help**. 80歳を超えてはいるものの彼はまだ自立しており，人の助けを求めない
▷ If you **need** any **help**, please call me. 助けが必要なら，電話してください
▷ We need to **provide** more **help** for the homeless. ホームレスの人たちへの援助がもっと必要だ

a great	help	大きな助け
a big	help	
extra	help	追加の援助
financial	help	資金援助

▷ Thanks a lot. You've been a **great help**. ありがとう。とても助かりました
▷ She says she needs **extra help** at work. 職場にもっと余分に人がいると彼女は言っている
▷ We need to arrange some **financial help**. われわれは財政支援をとりつける必要がある

help and advice	援助と忠告
help and support	助力と支援

▷ He thanked her for her **help and support**. 彼は彼女の助力と支援に感謝した

help	from A	Aからの援助
help	to A	Aへの援助
help	with A	Aでの援助

▷ He got a lot of **help from** his parents. 彼は両親から多くの援助を受けた
▷ He has been a good **help to** you. 彼はあなたをずっとよく助けてきた
▷ Would you like some **help with** the dishes? 皿洗いを手伝いましょうか

with	the help of A	Aの援助により
without	the help of A	Aの援助なしで

▷ **Without** the **help of** United Nations many more earthquake victims would have died. 国連の援助がなかったら地震による死者の数はもっと増えていただろう

help /hélp/ 動 助ける, 手伝う；役に立つ

be greatly	helped	大いに助けられる
really	help	本当に助ける
certainly	help	確実に助ける

▷ The flood victims were **greatly helped** by donations from people all over the world. 洪水の犠牲者たちは世界中の人々からの義援金に大いに助けられた
▷ Thank you. You **really helped** us when we needed it. 感謝します。援助が本当に必要なときに手を貸してくださいました

help A	into B	AがBに入るのを手伝う
help A	out of B	AがBから出るのを手伝う
help A	with B	AのBを手伝う

▷ Can you **help** me **into** my wheelchair? 車椅子に乗るのを手伝ってくれませんか
▷ **Help** me **out of** this mess, John. この窮地から助け出してくれよ，ジョン
▷ Shall I **help** you **with** your homework? 宿題を手伝ってあげようか

help A	(to) do	Aが…するのを助ける
help	(to) do	…するのを手伝う

▷Can you **help** me do the washing-up? 食器洗いを手伝ってくれませんか ▷I'll make a cup of tea. It'll **help** you feel better. お茶をいれよう。気分がよくなるよ ▷He **helped** me **to** follow my dream. 彼は私が夢を追いかけるのを助けてくれた
▷Can you **help** tidy up the kitchen? 台所を片づけるのを手伝ってくれませんか

PHRASES

help oneself (to A) (A(飲食物)を)自由にとって食べる ▷(Please) help yourself. ☺ どうぞご自由にお召し上がりください
It can't be helped. ☺ どうしようもない
May I help you? / Can I help you? ☺ ご用件は何でしょうか;(店で)何を差し上げましょうか ▷"May I help you?" "We're just looking." (買い物で)「お伺いしましょうか」「見ているだけです」

helpful /hélpfəl/

形 役立つ, 有用な; 助けになる

extremely	helpful	非常に役に立つ
quite	helpful	とても役立つ
particularly	helpful	とりわけ役立つ
especially	helpful	

▷The man I spoke to on the telephone was **extremely helpful**. 電話で話した人はとても協力的だった

| helpful | in doing | …するのに役立つ |
| helpful | for doing | |

▷You've been most **helpful in** provid**ing** all that information. いろいろ情報を提供いただき、とても助かりました

| it's helpful | for A to do | A(人)にとって…するのが役立つ |

▷**It's helpful for** children **to** interact with each other at an early age. 幼いころから互いに影響を与え合うのは子どもにとって有益なことだ

| it may be | helpful | 助かるかもしれない |

★may のほかに can, will, might, could, would などの助動詞との連結が多い

▷**It might be helpful** if you waited a little longer. もう少しお待ちいただけると助かるのですが

hesitate /hézətèit/ 動 ためらう

| hesitate | (for) a moment | 一瞬ためらう |
| hesitate | (for) a second | |

▷She **hesitated for a moment** and then said "Ok, I'll do it." 彼女は一瞬ためらったが「いいわ、私がやる」と言った

| hesitate | to do | …するのをためらう |

▷I **hesitated to** go there alone again. また一人でそこへ行くのをためらった

PHRASES

don't hesitate to do 《話》…するのをためらわないで ▷Don't hesitate to ask me questions. 遠慮なく私に聞いてください

hide /háid/ 動 隠す; 隠れる

hide	away	隠す
completely	hidden	すっかり隠れて
well	hidden	
half	hidden	半分隠れて

▷The money was **hidden away** under the floorboards. お金は床下に隠されていた
▷The summit of Mount Fuji was **completely hidden** behind clouds. 富士山頂は完全に雲に隠れていた
▷The police couldn't find the stolen jewelry. It was too **well hidden**. 巧みに隠されていたので警察は盗品の宝飾品を発見できなかった

| hide A | from B | AをBから隠す |

▷He **hid** the letters away **from** her. 彼はそれらの手紙を彼女から隠した

| hide A | in B | AをBに隠す |
| hide | in A | Aに隠れる |

★behind, under なども用いる

▷She **hid** the letters **in** an old box. 彼女は手紙を古い箱に隠した
▷He **hid behind** a tree. 彼は木の後ろに隠れた
▷He **hid** the front door key **under** the flower pot. 彼は玄関の鍵を植木鉢の下に隠した

high /hái/ 形 高い

extremely	high	非常に高い
fairly	high	かなり高い
particularly	high	特に高い
relatively	high	比較的高い

▷The water level in the river is **fairly high** now. 川の水位はかなり増している
▷Prices are **relatively high** compared with last year. 価格は昨年と比べ高めだ

| hint |

be A	high	Aの高さがある

★Aには eight feet などの数値がくる

▷The fence is six feet **high**. そのフェンスの高さは6フィートだ

hint /hínt/

名 暗示，ヒント；わずかな量；気配

give	a hint	ヒントを与える，ほのめかす
drop	a hint	
get	a hint	ヒントを得る
take	a hint	暗示を受ける

▷The professor **gave** us some **hints** about how to write a good essay. 教授はよいレポートの書き方についてヒントをいくつか与えてくれた

▷He wouldn't tell me exactly, but he **dropped** a few **hints**. 彼は正確に言おうとはしなかったが、それとなくほのめかした

▷I pointed to my watch several times, but he wouldn't **take** the **hint**. 何回か時計を指さしたが、彼にはピンとこなかったみたいだ

helpful	hints	有益なヒント
useful	hints	
a strong	hint	強い暗示
a faint	hint	かすかな気配
the slightest	hint	

▷Here are some **helpful hints** that will keep your tree healthy. 木を生き生きと保つための有益なヒントがあります

▷There's a **faint hint** of lavender in your perfume. きみの香水はラベンダーの香りがほのかにするね

▷He didn't give the **slightest hint** that he intended to resign. 辞任の意向があるそぶりを彼はみじんも見せなかった

a hint	on A	Aに関するヒント
a hint	about A	

▷Could you give me some **hints on** how to cook this turkey? この七面鳥をどう調理するかヒントをいただけませんか

history /hístəri/ 名 歴史；歴史書；履歴

go down in	history	歴史に残る
make	history	
trace	A's history	歴史をたどる
write	a history	歴史を書く
have	a history	経歴がある

▷President Obama will **go down in history** as the first black American president. オバマ大統領は米国初の黒人大統領として歴史に残るだろう

▷James Watt **made history** as the inventor of the steam engine. ジェームズ・ワットは蒸気エンジンの発明者として歴史に残っている

▷She **wrote** a **history** of the war in Iraq. 彼女はイラクにおける戦争の歴史を書いた

▷Afghanistan **has** a **history** of many wars during the last 100 years. アフガニスタンにはこの百年間多くの戦争の歴史がある

recent	history	近年の歴史
ancient	history	古代史
medieval	history	中世史
modern	history	近代史
human	history	人類の歴史
recorded	history	記録に残る歴史
a checkered	history	変化に富む歴史
economic	history	経済史
social	history	社会史
past	history	過ぎ去ったこと
a long	history	長い履歴
A's medical	history	病歴

▷Dropping the atomic bomb on Hiroshima was one of the most terrible events in **human history**. 広島への原爆投下は人類の歴史で最も悲惨なできごとの一つだった

▷He has a **long history** of drug abuse. 彼には薬物を乱用した長い履歴がある

▷A patient's **medical history** should be confidential. 患者の病歴は外に漏らしてはならない

history	shows	歴史が示す

▷As **history shows**, wars are inevitable. 歴史が示すように戦争は避けられない

hit /hít/

名 大当たり，ヒット；打撃，衝突

prove	a hit	ヒットとなる
make	a hit	ヒットする；たたく

▷The movie **proved a hit**. その映画はヒットした

▷She really likes you. I think you've **made** a **hit**! 彼女はきみにほれているよ。ぞっこんだよ

a big	hit	大ヒット
a huge	hit	

A's greatest	hits	ベストヒット集
a direct	hit	直撃

▷His first album was a **big hit**. 彼の最初のアルバムは大ヒットした
▷The school received a **direct hit** and was completely destroyed. 学校は直撃を受けて全壊した

hit /hít/ 動 強く当たる；たたく，殴る

almost	hit	もう少しで当たる
be badly	hit	ひどい被害を受ける
be hard	hit	

▷The country's economy has been **badly hit** by the financial crisis. その国の経済は財政危機でひどく痛手を受けた
▷After the rise in sales tax the company's profits were **hard hit**. 消費税の引き上げで会社の収益はひどい損害をこうむった

hit A	on B	A(人)のB(体の部位)
hit A	in B	をたたく
hit A	with B	AをBでたたく

▷Wendy **hit** him **on** the head. ウェンディは彼の頭をたたいた
▷Dave **hit** Bob **with** a baseball bat. デイブはボブを野球のバットで殴った

hold /hóuld/ 名 持つこと，つかむこと

catch	hold	つかむ
grab	hold	
take	hold	
get	hold	
keep	hold	しっかり握っている

▷I **grabbed hold** of him and we sat and talked for a couple of minutes. 彼をつかまえて，座って2，3分ことばを交わした
▷Suddenly, he **took hold** of both her hands. 突然，彼は彼女の両手をつかんだ
▷I **got hold** of her arm. 彼女の腕をつかんだ
▷**Keep hold** of my hand. If you don't you might fall. 私の手をつかんでいて．そうしないと転ぶから

hold /hóuld/

動 しっかり保持する，手に持つ；しっかり支える

hold	tightly	しっかりつかむ
still	hold	なお保っている
be widely	held	広く支持されている
be commonly	held	

▷**Hold** me **tightly**. しっかり抱いて
▷He **still holds** the world record for the 100 meters. 彼はいまも百メートルの世界記録を保持している

hold	A C	AをCの状態に保つ

▷He **held** the door open for her. 彼はドアを開けて彼女を待ってあげた

hold	(that)...	…と考えている

▷In his recent book Stephen Hawking **holds that** the universe could have been created without God. 近著でスティーブン・ホーキング博士が述べているのは，宇宙は神なしに創造されたかもしれないということだ

hole /hóul/ 名 穴，くぼみ

make	a hole	穴を開ける
drill	a hole	
dig	a hole	穴を掘る
cut	a hole	切って穴を開ける
blow	a hole	爆発させて穴を開ける
fill	a hole	穴をふさぐ

▷I need to **make** another **hole** in the strap of this shoulder bag. ショルダーバッグのひもにもう一つ穴を開けなくちゃ
▷They're **digging** a **hole** in the road. 道路に穴を掘っている
▷Can you **cut** another **hole** in this belt for me? このベルトにもう一つ穴を開けてくれないか
▷We need to **fill** this **hole** up with earth. この穴を土でふさぐ必要がある

a big	hole	大きな穴
a large	hole	
a deep	hole	深い穴
a gaping	hole	大きく開いた穴
a small	hole	小さな穴
a tiny	hole	ちっぽけな穴

▷Suddenly a **big hole** appeared in the road. 突然，道路に大きな穴ができた
▷I thought it was cold! There's a **gaping hole** in the tent! 寒いと思ったら，テントに大きな穴が開いているよ

a hole	in A	Aの穴

▷He's digging another **hole in** the ground. 彼は地

holiday /hάlədèi | hɔ́lədèi/

名 祭日, 休暇;《英》(長期の)休暇

take	a holiday	休暇をとる
have	a holiday	
go on	a holiday	休暇に出かける
spend	a holiday	休暇を過ごす

▷ You work too hard. I think you should **take a holiday**. きみは働き過ぎだ。休暇をとったほうがいいよ
▷ I **went on holiday** to Hawaii last summer. 昨年の夏に休暇でハワイに出かけた
▷ How would you like to **spend a holiday** in France? フランスでどのように休暇を過ごされますか

a good	holiday	楽しい休暇
one's annual	holiday	年次休暇
a paid	holiday	有給休暇
the summer	holiday(s)	夏季休暇
the Christmas	holiday(s)	クリスマス休暇
the Easter	holiday(s)	イースター休暇
a public	holiday	国民の祝日
a national	holiday	

▷ Have a **good holiday**, Simon! 楽しい休暇を過ごしてね, サイモン
▷ When are you taking your **annual holiday**? 年次休暇をいつ取るの
▷ Your company is very generous. They offer long **paid holidays**. 気前のいい会社に勤めてるね。長い有給休暇があるんだな
▷ Tomorrow's a **public holiday**. あしたは国民の祝日だ(★《英》では国民の祝日に a bank holiday「一般公休日」,《米》では a legal holiday「法定休日」も使われる)

on	holiday	休暇で

▷ Are you here **on holiday**? ここへは休暇でいらしているのですか ▷ I'm going to Scotland for a week **on holiday**. 休暇で1週間スコットランドに行くつもりです

home /hóum/

名 わが家;家, 家庭;故郷;生息地

be away from	home	家を留守にする
leave	home	家を出る;親元を離れる
run away from	home	家出する
own	a home	家を持つ

buy	a home	家を買う
build	a home	家を建てる
lose	one's home	家を失う

▷ My children have all grown up and **left home**. うちの子どもはみな成長して家を出ました
▷ Apparently she tried to **run away from home** when she was 17 years old. どうやら彼女は17歳のときに家出しようとしたらしい
▷ Many people can't afford to pay their mortgages and are going to **lose** their **homes**. 住宅ローンを払えなくなって家を失うことになる人が多い

a happy	home	幸福な家庭
a family	home	実家
a permanent	home	定住地
one's spiritual	home	心の故郷
a comfortable	home	快適な家
a private	home	個人の家;民宿
a new	home	新築住宅
an existing	home	中古住宅
the ancestral	home	先祖代々の家

▷ She comes from a **happy home**. 彼女は幸福な家庭の出だ
▷ Now we believe we have finally found a **permanent home** at Park Lane. パークレーンこそ私たちの永住の地だと思う
▷ Many **private homes** welcome visitors to stay at a cheap price. 客を安価で滞在させてくれる民宿が多い
▷ Lord Pilkington had to sell the **ancestral home**. ピルキントン卿は先祖代々の家を売却しなければならなかった

at	home	家で;実家で;国内で;本拠地で;くつろいで

▷ I rang the doorbell but nobody was **at home**. ドアのベルを鳴らしたが, 家にはだれもいなかった ▷ The murder was big news both **at home** and abroad. その殺人事件は国の内外で大きなニュースになった ▷ Manchester United are playing Liverpool **at home** next weekend. マンチェスターユナイテッドは来週本拠地でリバプールと試合する予定だ ▷ I feel **at home** here. ☺ ここはくつろげるなあ ▷ Please make yourself **at home**. ☺ どうぞおくつろぎください

honest /άnist | ɔ́n-/ **形** 正直な, 誠実な

quite	honest	まったく正直な
perfectly	honest	
totally	honest	
absolutely	honest	

▷To be **quite honest** I think maybe you should have apologized to her. 率直に言ってきみは彼女に謝るべきだったと思うよ
▷To be **perfectly honest**, I think you'd be crazy to marry him! 正直に言わせてもらえれば、彼と結婚するなんてあなたどうかしてる
▷I don't think he gave a **totally honest** answer. 彼の返事が何から何まで率直なものとは思えない

| honest | enough | 十分正直な |

▷He was **honest enough** to admit he was wrong. 彼は正直に間違いを認めた

| honest | about A | Aを包み隠さない |
| honest | with A | Aに誠実な |

▷I think you should be **honest about** your feelings. 自分の感情を包み隠さないほうがいいよ
▷Be **honest with** him! 彼に対して誠実にしなさい

| open and honest | | 率直で正直な |

▷He's a very **open and honest** kind of guy. 彼はとても率直で正直なやつだ

honor /ánər | ɔ́n-/

名 名誉; (honors で)勲章(★《英》つづりは honour)

be	an honor	光栄である
have	the honor	光栄に浴する
defend	A's honor	名誉を守る
save	A's honor	名誉を守る
share	the honor	名誉を分け合う
win	honor(s)	名誉を得る
receive	honors	勲章を授かる
take	honors	

▷It is an **honor** to meet you, Mr. Kingsley. お会いできて光栄です、キングズリーさん
▷He was forced into a fight to **defend** her **honor**. 彼女の名誉を守るために彼は戦わざるを得なくなった
▷He **received** various **honors** for services to his country. 彼は国への貢献に対しさまざまな勲章を受けた

| (the) guest of | honor | 主賓 |

▷I'd like to introduce this evening's **guest of honor**. 今宵の主賓をご紹介いたします

a great	honor	大きな名誉
top	honors	最高の栄誉; 最優
the highest	honors	秀賞

▷It is a **great honor** to be here this evening. 今晩この場にいられることはとても光栄です
▷Julie received **top honors** for her painting. ジュリーは絵画で最優秀賞をとった

| 《英》with | honours | 優等で |

▷He passed the exam **with honours**. 彼は優等で試験に通った

| in honor | of A | Aに敬意を表して |

▷They decided to hold a huge party **in honor of** his victory. 彼の勝利を記念して盛大なパーティーを開くことが決まった

hope /hóup/ 名 希望, 望み; 見込み

be full of	hope	希望に満ちている
express	hope	希望を表明する
live in	hope	希望を捨てていない
give up	hope	希望を失う
lose	hope	
offer	hope	希望を与える
give	hope	

▷He **expressed** the **hope** that a decision would be made within the next few weeks. 決定は2,3週間以内になされるだろうという希望を彼は表明した
▷We don't think our situation will improve but we **live in hope**. 状況が改善するとは思わないが、それでも希望は捨てていない
▷Don't **give up hope** of receiving an award. 賞をもらえる希望を捨てるな
▷We mustn't **lose hope**. 希望を失ってはいけない
▷Religious belief **offers hope** to many people. 宗教的信念は多くの人々に希望を与える
▷Help from charitable organizations has **given hope** to millions of people. 慈善団体からの援助は何百万の人々に希望を与えた

great	hope	大きな希望
the best	hope	最大の望み
a faint	hope	かすかな望み
a real	hope	本物の希望
a vain	hope	はかない希望
the only	hope	唯一の希望
a new	hope	新たな希望

▷Achieving world peace is the **only hope** for the human race. 世界平和の達成は人類にとって唯一の希望だ
▷The election of Barack Obama gave **new hope** to the world. バラク・オバマの当選は新たな希望を世界に与えた

| hope |

a glimmer of	hope	わずかな希望
a ray of	hope	

▷ She's still holding **a glimmer of hope** that he may still be alive. 彼女は彼がまだ生きているかもしれないとのわずかな希望をもっている

hopes and dreams		夢と希望
hopes and fears		希望と不安

▷ All parents have **hopes and dreams** for their children. 両親はみな我が子に夢と希望を抱いている (★ dreams and hopes も用いるが,日本語とは逆の語順の hopes and dreams のほうが頻度が高い)
▷ Pupils talked about their **hopes and fears** for the future. 生徒たちは将来の希望と不安について話した

hope	for A	Aに対する希望
hope	of doing	…する望み

▷ We mustn't give up **hope for** the future. 未来への希望をあきらめてはならない
▷ She has no **hope of** passing the exam. 彼女は試験に合格する望みはない

in	the hope of doing	…を期待して
in	the hope that...	

▷ He wrote letter after letter **in** the **hope of** persuading her to change her mind. 何とか彼女が決心を変えてくれることを期待して彼は手紙を何通も書いた

hope /hóup/ 動 希望する, 望む

sincerely	hope	心から願う
certainly	hope	
really	hope	
only	hope	望むばかりだ

▷ I **sincerely hope** you'll be happy in your new job. 新しい仕事に満足されることを心から願っています
▷ I **only hope** there's still time to make an application. 申し込みの時間がまだあることを望むばかりだ

hope	for A	Aを望む

▷ What do you **hope for** in the future? 未来に何を望みますか

hope	(that)...	…であることを望む
hope	to do	…することを望む

▷ I **hope** we can help you. お手伝いできるといいのですが

▷ What do you **hope to** do after you graduate? 卒業後は何をしたいですか

PHRASES
I hope not. ☺ そうでないといいんだけど ▷ "I think the movie's already started." "I hope not."「映画はもう始まっているんじゃないか」「まだだといいね」
I hope so. ☺ そうだといいんだけど ▷ "He's probably at the hotel." "I hope so."「彼はたぶんホテルにいるでしょう」「そうだといいね」

horizon /həráizn/ 名 地平線, 水平線

above	the horizon	地平線の上に
below	the horizon	地平線の下に

▷ By that time the sun had set far **below** the **horizon**. そのころには太陽は地平線のはるかかなたに沈んでいた

hospital /háspitl | hɔ́s-/ 名 病院

go to	(the) hospital	入院する
go into	(the) hospital	
be admitted to	hospital	
be taken to	hospital	病院に運ばれる
be rushed to	(the) hospital	病院に急送される
leave	(the) hospital	退院する
be discharged from	hospital	
come out of	(the) hospital	

★ hospital が単に「建物」でなく「診療する所」の意味を表すとき《英》では the を省く傾向がある

▷ He **went into hospital** last week. 彼は先週入院した
▷ After the plane crash the survivors were **taken to** the nearest hospital. 墜落事故後,生存者たちはいちばん近い病院に運ばれた
▷ She was **rushed to hospital** and put in intensive care. 彼女は病院に急送され,集中治療を受けた
▷ He's **leaving hospital** on Tuesday. 彼は火曜日に退院する予定だ

in	(the) hospital	入院して, 病院で

▷ He was **in hospital** for 3 weeks. 彼は3週間入院した ▷ He's being treated **in hospital** for burns. 彼は病院でやけどの治療中だ

a general	hospital	総合病院
a local	hospital	地域病院

| a private | hospital | 私立病院 |
| the university | hospital | 大学病院 |

▷ I don't have enough money to enter a **private hospital**. 私立病院に入院するだけの金がない

hospitality /hàspətǽləti | hɔ̀s-/

名 もてなし，歓待

offer	hospitality	もてなす
provide	hospitality	
extend	hospitality	
enjoy	hospitality	もてなしを受ける

▷ I've really **enjoyed** your kind **hospitality**. 親切なおもてなし本当にありがとうございました
▷ They **provided** warm **hospitality** after the official events concluded. 公式行事終了後，温かいもてなしがあった

PHRASES
Thank you for your hospitality. ☺ おもてなしありがとうございます

host /hóust/ 名 主人役，主催者；司会者

| play | host | 主催する；開催地になる |
| act as | host | |

▷ New York City **plays host** to the Art Show this July. ニューヨーク市は今年7月に美術展を開催する

hot /hát | hɔ́t/ 形 熱い，暑い；辛い

extremely	hot	すごく熱い，すごく暑い；すごく
really	hot	辛い
a little	hot	少し熱い，少し暑い；少し辛い

▷ It gets **really hot** here in summer. 当地は夏はすごく暑い

| hot and dry | | 暑くて乾燥した |
| hot and humid | | 高温多湿の |

▷ The weather has been really **hot and dry** during the last four weeks. ここ4週間，暑くて乾燥した天候が続いている

hotel /houtél/ 名 ホテル

| book | a hotel | ホテルを予約する |
| reserve | a hotel | |

check into	a hotel	チェックインする
check in at	a hotel	
《英》book into	a hotel	
check out of	a hotel	チェックアウトする
stay at	a hotel	ホテルに泊まる
stay in	a hotel	

▷ Have you **checked into** a **hotel** yet? ホテルにもうチェックインしましたか
▷ We can go sightseeing after we've **booked into** the **hotel**. ホテルのチェックインを済ませてから観光に出かけられるよ
▷ We have to **check out of** the hotel by 11:00 a.m. 11時までにホテルをチェックアウトしなくてはならない
▷ We **stayed in** a really nice **hotel**. とてもすてきなホテルに泊まった

a cheap	hotel	安ホテル
a comfortable	hotel	快適なホテル
a friendly	hotel	接客のいいホテル
a luxury	hotel	高級ホテル
a five-star	hotel	五つ星ホテル

▷ It's a really **friendly hotel**. I like staying there. 客への対応がていねいなホテルなので気に入っている
▷ She's staying in a **five-star hotel**. 彼女は五つ星ホテルに宿泊中だ

hour /áuər/ 名 1時間；時刻

| take | two hours | 2時間かかる |
| last | three hours | 3時間続く |

▷ It **takes** me an **hour** and a half to get to university. 大学に行くのに1時間半かかる

a half	hour	30分
half	an hour	
a quarter of	an hour	15分
an hour	and a half	1時間半
one and a half	hours	
every	hour	1時間ごとに

▷ It'll take you about a **half hour** to finish this report. この報告書を仕上げるのに30分くらいかかるね
▷ We're in the country here. A bus only comes **every** four **hours**. いなかに来ているからバスは4時間に1本しかない

| an hour's | drive | 車で1時間 |

★ drive のほか walk, sleep, exercise なども用いる

▷ It's only an **hour's drive** to the coast. 海岸まで車でほんの1時間だ

by	the hour	1時間単位で
per	hour	1時間あたり
an	hour	
for	an hour	1時間のあいだ
in	an hour	1時間したら
on	the hour	毎時0分に
for	hours	長いあいだ

▷He gets paid **by the hour**. 彼は時給で払ってもらっている
▷She'll be here **in an hour**. 彼女は1時間したら着くだろう
▷A bus arrives here **on the hour**. バスは毎時0分にここに着く
▷She's been talking on the phone **for hours**. 彼女はずいぶん長電話している

hour	after hour	何時間も続けて

▷**Hour after hour** went by and still they had no news. 時間が刻々と過ぎてもまだ何の知らせもなかった

business	hours	業務時間, 勤務時間
office	hours	
working	hours	
opening	hours	営業時間
visiting	hours	面会時間
school	hours	授業時間

▷You shouldn't make private phone calls during normal **working hours**. 通常の勤務時間内に私用電話をしてはならない

house /háus/ 名 家, 住宅; 建物

build	a house	家を建てる
demolish	a house	家を取り壊す
renovate	a house	家を改装する
move into	a house	引っ越す
《英》move	house	
rent	a house	家を借りる
share	a house	家を共同で使う

▷They're going to **demolish** this **house** and put up a new apartment building. この家は取り壊されて新しくアパートが建つ予定だ
▷Have you **moved into** your new **house** yet? 新居への引っ越しは済んだかい
▷We're planning to **rent** a **house** in the country. 田舎に家を借りる予定だ
▷She **shares** a **house** with three other students. 彼女は3人の学生とハウスシェアしている

a detached	house	一戸建て
a semi-detached	house	2軒1棟の家
a row	house	テラスハウス
《英》a terraced	house	
a rented	house	貸家
an empty	house	空家
a beach	house	海辺の家
a packed	house	満席
a full	house	

▷They live in a **rented house**. 彼らは貸家住まいだ
▷We've got a **full house** at the moment. いまのところ満席です

housework /háuswə̀ːrk/ 名 家事

do	housework	家事をする

▷In the near future, robots will be **doing** all the **housework**. 近い将来ロボットはあらゆる家事をこなすだろう

human /hjúːmən | hjúː-/

形 人間の, 人類の; 人間らしい

very	human	きわめて人間的な
quite	human	すごく人間味のある
fully	human	いかにも人間らしい
almost	human	ほとんど人間的な

▷It's **very human** to be jealous! 嫉妬するのは人間として当たり前だ
▷Now I've had a shower. I feel **almost human** again! シャワーを浴びてやっと人心地がついた
PHRASES
I'm only human. しょせんただの人間だから ▷You can't blame me for being attracted to her. After all, I'm only human. 彼女に魅力を感じるからってぼくを責められないよ. ぼくだって人間なんだから

humor /hjúːmər | hjúː-/

名 ユーモア, おかしみ; 気分(★《英》つづりは humour)

black	humor	ブラックユーモア
dry	humor	さりげないユーモア
(a) good	humor	上機嫌

▷When he left the party he was **in** a very **good humor**. パーティー会場から出るとき彼は上機嫌だった

a sense of	humor	ユーモアのセンス

▷I like Paul. He's got a great **sense of humor**! ポールは好きだよ．ユーモアのセンスがあるからね

hundred /hʌ́ndrəd/ 名 100

a	hundred		100
one	hundred		
two	hundred		200
three hundred	(and)	five	305
three hundred	(and)	sixty	360

★100の位と10の位あるいは1の位の間に米国ではandを入れないが，英国では入れるのが普通

▷**A hundred** years ago life in the States was entirely different. 百年前の米国の生活はまったく異なっていた

a [one] hundred	thousand	10万
a [one] hundred	million	1億
hundreds	of A	何百というA

▷She won **a hundred thousand** dollars in the lottery. 彼女は宝くじで10万ドル当たった
▷This rock is over **a hundred million** years old. この岩は1億年以上前のものだ
▷There were **hundreds of** people at the wedding. 結婚式には何百人もの人がいた

hungry /hʌ́ŋgri/ 形 空腹の

go	hungry	おなかがすく
feel	hungry	空腹を覚える

▷We can't let the children **go hungry**. 子どもを飢えさせておくわけにはいかない

really	hungry	とても空腹の
still	hungry	まだ空腹の

▷I'm **really hungry**. Let's stop for a meal. すごくおなかがすいちゃった．車を止めて食事しよう
▷That meal was delicious. But I'm **still hungry**. おいしい料理だったけど，まだおなかがすいてるよ

hungry	for A	Aに飢えている

▷That child is always **hungry for** attention. その子はいつも注目されることを求めている

tired and hungry	疲れて空腹の

▷They came down from the mountain **tired and hungry**. 疲れ切って空腹で彼らは下山してきた

hurt /hə́ːrt/ 動 傷める，傷つける；痛む

hurt	badly	ひどく傷める；ひどく痛む
hurt	slightly	少し傷める；少し痛む
seriously	hurt	ひどく傷める
really	hurt	ひどく痛む
hurt	deeply	ひどく心を傷つける

▷My shoulder **hurt badly** but I didn't think it was broken. 肩がひどく痛かったが折れているとは思わなかった
▷It was a bad car crash, but surprisingly she was only **slightly hurt**. ひどい衝突事故だったが，驚いたことに彼女は軽傷で済んだ

hurt	oneself	けがをする

▷Are you OK? Have you **hurt** yourself? 大丈夫かい．けがしちゃった？

PHRASES
I don't want to hurt you. ☺ あなたを傷つけたくはありません

husband /hʌ́zbənd/ 名 夫

leave	one's husband	夫と別れる
lose	one's husband	夫を亡くす

▷She says she's going to **leave** her **husband**. 彼女は夫と別れると言っている
▷She **lost** her **husband** in a road accident. 彼女は夫を交通事故で亡くした
▷She **lost** her **husband** to cancer. 彼女は夫をがんで亡くした（★病気で亡くなるときは to）

her former	husband	前夫
her future	husband	未来の夫
her late	husband	亡夫

▷Her **former husband** still keeps in contact with her. 彼女の別れた旦那からはいまも連絡がある
▷Her **late husband** left her a great deal of money. 彼女の亡夫は彼女に大金を残した

husband and wife	夫婦

★この語順で用い，冠詞はつけない

▷They've been **husband and wife** for over 60 years. 彼らは夫婦になって60年以上だ

| ice |

I

ice /áis/ 名 氷

the ice	forms	氷が張る
the ice	melts	氷が解ける

▷It's so cold that **ice** is **forming** on the windows outside. すごく寒くて窓の外側に氷が張りついている
▷Spring is coming and the **ice** is **melting**. もうすぐ春が来て氷が解ける

thick	ice	厚い氷
thin	ice	薄い氷

▷Antarctica is almost entirely covered by **thick ice**. 南極大陸はほぼ全体が厚い氷に覆われている

a block of	ice	氷の塊
a lump of	ice	

▷It's freezing! My body feels like a **block of ice**. 凍えそうだよ。体が氷の塊みたいだ

idea /aidí:ə | -déə/

名 考え, アイデア；意見, 見解；思想

have	an idea	考えがある
get	an idea	考えを思いつく
get	the idea	《略式》わかる
discuss	the idea	考えについて論じる
exchange	ideas	考えを交換する
give	an idea	考えを与える
develop	the idea	考えを発展させる
introduce	the idea	考えを導入する
express	an idea	考えを表明する
support	the idea	考えを支持する
accept	the idea	考えを受け入れる
reject	the idea	考えを拒否する
abandon	the idea	考えを捨てる

▷I **have** an **idea**. ☺ いい考えがある
▷Do you **have** any **ideas**? 何か考えはありますか
▷I don't know where she **got** the **idea** from, but it's working really well. どこで彼女がそのアイデアを思いついたのかわからないけど, とてもうまくいっているよ
▷So you pull this lever up and press this red button. **Get** the **idea**? このレバーを引き上げて赤いボタンを押すんだよ。わかったかい
▷Let's **discuss** the **idea** again next week. 来週またその案について議論しよう
▷Let's meet over lunch and **exchange ideas**. 昼食会をやりながら意見交換しよう
▷Could you **give** an **idea** of how much you think it will cost? どれくらいコストがかかるか見当を示していただけませんか
▷I think we need to **develop** the **idea** a little more before presenting it to the board of directors. 役員会に提出する前にもう少し考えを練る必要があると思う
▷They were going to set up a second office in London, but now they've **abandoned** the **idea**. ロンドンに第2事務所を開設する予定だったが, 断念した

a good	idea	よい考え
a great	idea	すばらしい考え
a bright	idea	
an excellent	idea	
a brilliant	idea	
an interesting	idea	おもしろい考え
an original	idea	当初の考え
the basic	idea	基本的な考え
a clear	idea	明快な考え
a general	idea	だいたいの見当
a rough	idea	
the main	idea	考えの骨子
the wrong	idea	誤った考え

▷OK! That's a **great idea**! Let's do it! いいね。それはすばらしい考えだ。そうしよう
▷This is completely different from our **original idea**. これは私たちの当初の考えとまったく違います
▷I still don't have a **clear idea** of what changes the company is going to make. 会社がどのような変更を持ち出してくるかまだはっきりとはわからない
▷Can you give me a **rough idea** of how many people are coming to the party? パーティーに何人くらい出るか, ざっと教えてくれるかい

an idea	about A	Aについての考え
an idea	on A	Aに関する考え
an idea	for A	Aに対する考え
the idea	of A	Aの考え
an idea	to do	…する考え

▷I'd appreciate any **ideas on** how to improve service to our customers. 顧客へのサービスをどうやったら改善できるか何かアイデアをもらえるとありがたいのですが
▷It's a good **idea to** go to the doctor. 医者に診てもらうのがいいね

have	no idea	わからない

★that, how, whatなどが後に続く

▷I **had no idea** (*that*) you were so unhappy. きみがそんなに悲しい思いをしているとはわからなかった ▷I **have no idea** *how* this person got my credit card number. この人がどうやって私のクレジットカード番号を

盗んだのかわかりません ▷We **have no idea** what's going on. 何が起こっているのかわからない

PHRASES
That's an idea. 😊 それはいいね
That's the idea! 😊 その調子だ

identify /aidéntəfài/

動 見分ける, 確認する；同じ物とみなす

correctly	identify	正確に見分ける
clearly	identify	はっきり見分ける
easily	identify	簡単に見分ける
readily	identify	
be closely	identified	密接に関係する

▷This type of poisonous mushroom can be **easily identified**. この種の毒キノコは簡単に見分けられる
▷The increase in the ownership of guns is **closely identified** *with* the increase in the number of murders. 銃所有者の増加は殺人件数の増加と密接に関連している

can	identify	確認できる
be able to	identify	
be possible to	identify	確認可能だ
try to	identify	確認しようとする

▷It is **possible to identify** many reasons for the decrease in population. 人口減少の理由の多くは特定可能だ
▷Doctors are **trying to identify** the causes of the influenza outbreak. 医師たちはインフルエンザ大流行の原因を特定しようとしている

identify A	**as** B	AをBだと確信する

▷She was able to **identify** him **as** her attacker. 彼女を襲ったのはその男だと彼女にはわかった

identity /aidéntəti/

名 身元, 正体；独自性, 個性

establish	A's identity	身元を確認する
establish	one's identity	個性を確立する
lose	one's identity	個性を失う
reveal	A's identity	正体を明かす
disclose	A's identity	
discover	the identity	正体を突き止める
know	the identity	正体を知っている
protect	one's identity	身元を隠す
conceal	one's identity	

▷It seems difficult to **establish** the **identity** of the victims. 犠牲者たちの身元確認は難しそうだ

▷He refuses to **reveal** his **identity**. 彼は自分の身元を明かすのを拒否している
▷The police never **discovered** the **identity** of the murderer. 警察は殺人犯の正体を突き止められなかった
▷We **know** the **identity** of three of the terrorists. テロリストたちのうち3名の身元はわかっている

one's true	identity	正体
mistaken	identity	人違い
a corporate	identity	企業イメージ統合戦略
cultural	identity	文化的アイデンティティ
a national	identity	国民のアイデンティティ

▷Her **true identity** will never be known. 彼女の正体は決してわからないだろう
▷We don't know if it was a case of **mistaken identity**. But we're pretty sure it was the same gang. 人違いだったかどうかはわからないが, 一味の仲間であることは間違いない
▷It's important for each country to preserve its **cultural identity**. それぞれの国が文化の独自性を保持するのが大切だ

a sense of	identity	自分らしさの意識

▷If you want to be happy in life you need to develop a **sense of identity** within society. 幸せな人生を送りたければ, 社会の中で自分は自分だという意識をもてるようにする必要がある

ignore /ignɔ́ːr/ 動 無視する

completely	ignore	完全に無視する
totally	ignore	
virtually	ignore	実質的に無視する
largely	ignore	ほとんど無視する
simply	ignore	単に無視する
deliberately	ignore	わざと無視する

★ignore completely も高頻度で用いる

▷He **completely ignored** everything I said. 彼は私の言ったことをまったく無視した
▷I think we can **largely ignore** this report. この報告書の大部分は無視できると思う

ignore	the fact that...	…という事実を無視する

▷We shouldn't **ignore the fact that** he was under a lot of stress at the time. 彼にはそのとき大変なストレスがかかっていたという事実を無視すべきではない

ill /íl/ 形 病気の；吐き気がする

| illness |

become	ill	病気になる; 気分が悪くなる
fall	ill	
get	ill	
be taken	ill	
feel	ill	気分が悪い

▷Nancy **fell ill** after dinner. ナンシーは夕食後, 気分が悪くなった
▷Watching that fish wriggling around on that plate makes me **feel ill**! あんなふうに生きた魚が皿の上でばたばた動いているのを見ると気分が悪くなるよ

critically	ill	危篤の
terminally	ill	末期症状の
seriously	ill	重症の
severely	ill	
desperately	ill	
extremely	ill	
really	ill	
quite	ill	かなり具合が悪い
mentally	ill	心を病んでいる
physically	ill	体を病んでいる

▷He's **critically ill** in hospital. 彼は入院していて危篤状態にある
▷I'm afraid he's **terminally ill**. The doctors can do nothing for him. 彼の病気はもう末期で, 医師たちも手の打ちようがない
▷Tom's not **seriously ill**. Just a cold. トムは重病というわけではなく, ただのかぜだ

ill	in bed	病気で寝込んでいる
ill	in hospital	病気で入院している

▷Carol spent last week **ill in bed**. キャロルは体調を崩して先週は寝て過ごした

ill	with A	Aを病んでいる

▷He's **ill with** influenza. 彼はインフルエンザにかかっている

illness /ílnis/ 名 病気

have	an illness	病気にかかる
suffer from	an illness	
treat	(an) illness	病気を治療する
cause	illness	病気の原因となる
recover from	an illness	病気が治る

▷She's **suffered from** that illness for years. 彼女は数年その病気を患っている
▷A doctor should know how to **treat** all kinds of **illnesses**. 医者たるもの, あらゆる病気の治療法を知っていなければならない
▷Overeating can **cause illness**. 食べ過ぎは病気の元だ

acute	illness	急性の病気
chronic	illness	慢性病, 持病
serious	illness	重い病気
mild	illness	軽い病気
terminal	illness	末期の病気

▷It's a **chronic illness**. She's had it for years. 持病でもう何年も彼女はその病気を患っている
▷It's not a **serious illness**. You'll recover in a couple of weeks. たいした病気ではありません. 2, 3週間で治りますよ

injury and illness	けがと病気

★illness and injury も用いる

▷Are you insured against **illness and injury**? 傷病保険に入っていますか

image /ímidʒ/ 名 イメージ, 像

have	an image	イメージがある
create	an image	イメージを作る
form	an image	
project	an image	イメージを与える
present	an image	
conjure up	an image	イメージが浮かぶ
change	one's image	イメージを変える
improve	one's image	イメージアップする
shed	one's image	イメージを脱ぎ捨てる
shake off	one's image	

▷She **projects** an **image** of a very confident person, but in fact she's not confident at all. 自信家だとの印象を与えようとしているが, 実は彼女は自信がない
▷The movie **conjures up images** of what it was like to live in the USA in the 1930s. その映画は1930年代の米国での暮らしぶりを彷彿とさせてくれる
▷I've **changed** my **image** of Peter. He's actually quite a nice chap. ピーターの見方が変わった. 実はとてもいいやつだ
▷I think you should try to **improve** your **image**. A haircut and a new suit might be a good idea! きみはイメージアップを図ってみたら？散髪して新しいスーツを着てみるなんてどうかな (★×image up とはいわない)

a positive	image	プラスイメージ
a good	image	
a negative	image	マイナスイメージ
a bad	image	

one's	**public**	**image**	世間のイメージ
a	**corporate**	**image**	企業イメージ
a	**mental**	**image**	心像
a	**visual**	**image**	視覚映像
a	**mirror**	**image**	鏡像

▷ Even though he is a positive person he projects a **negative image**. 積極的なタイプだが彼にはマイナスイメージがつきまとう
▷ The recent scandal ruined his **public image**. 最近のスキャンダルで彼の世間的イメージは悪くなった
▷ We need to be very careful about projecting the right **corporate image**. 正しい企業イメージをもってもらえるよう留意する必要がある
▷ She had a **mental image** of how wonderful it would be to live in Hawaii. ハワイに住んだらすてきだろうなと彼女は心の中で考えた

imagine /iméædʒənéiʃən/

[名] 想像, 想像力

have	an **imagination**	想像力がある
not take	much **imagination**	大して想像力はいらない
use	one's **imagination**	想像力を働かせる
capture	A's **imagination**	心をとらえる
catch	A's **imagination**	
fire	A's **imagination**	想像力をかき立てる

▷ It **doesn't take much imagination** to guess what they were doing! 彼らが何をしていたか想像するのに大して想像力はいらない
▷ "I've got no idea what to draw." "**Use** your **imagination**!"「何を描いたらいいかわからないよ」「想像力を働かせなさい」
▷ Her performance really **captured** the **imagination** *of* the audience. 彼女の演技はまさに聴衆の心をとらえた

creative	**imagination**	豊かな想像力
a **fertile**	**imagination**	
a **vivid**	**imagination**	
the **popular**	**imagination**	一般的なイメージ

▷ To be a writer you need a great deal of **creative imagination**. 作家になるには豊かな想像力が必要だ
▷ She's got a very **fertile imagination**. 彼女は実に想像力が豊かな人だ
▷ I can't believe you thought I had two girlfriends at the same time! You must have a very **vivid imagination**! ぼくが二またをかけていると思うだなんて、きみの想像力は旺盛だなあ
▷ Halloween is associated with ghosts in the **popular imagination**. ハロウィーンは一般的なイメージでは幽霊と結びついている

| **in** one's | **imagination** | 想像の中で |
| **with** | **a little imagination** | 少し想像力を働かせれば |

▷ **In** my **imagination** I was 5 years old again. Back in my childhood. 想像の中で5歳の自分に戻っていた. 子どもの自分だ

| **a figment of** | A's **imagination** | 想像の産物 |
| **a lack of** | **imagination** | 想像力の欠如 |

▷ I thought I saw a ghost by the fireplace, but I guess it was just a **figment of** my **imagination**. 暖炉のそばに幽霊を見たと思ったが, 気のせいだったんだろう
▷ I'm afraid he suffers from a **lack of imagination**. 彼には想像力が欠如していると思う

imagine /imédʒin/ [動] 想像する

always	**imagine**	いつも想像する
just	**imagine**	ちょっと想像する
easily	**imagine**	容易に想像する

▷ I **always imagined** he was an honest chap. あいつは正直なやつだとずっと思っていた
▷ **Just imagine** it! ☺ ちょっと考えてもごらん; そんなばかな
▷ I can **easily imagine** how you felt. あなたがどう感じたか簡単に想像できる

| **imagine** | (A) **doing** | (Aが)…するのを想像する |

▷ Can you **imagine** wait**ing** 8 hours for your plane to take off? 飛行機が離陸するのに8時間も待つなんて想像できますか
▷ I can't **imagine** Dave agree**ing** to a divorce. デイブが離婚に同意するとは考えられないな

| **imagine** | (**that**)... | …と想像する |
| **imagine** | **wh**- | …か想像する |

★ wh- は what, why, how など

▷ Now **imagine that** you are alone. さて, ひとりの自分を想像してみてください
▷ It must have been a real shock. **Imagine how** he felt. すごくショックだったはずだよ. 彼の気持ちを想像してもみなよ

| **imagine** | **A as C** | AがCだと想像する |

| immigrant |

▷ I always **imagined** him **as** a helpful person. いつも彼を助けになる人と思っていた

PHRASES
Can you imagine? 😊 想像できますか，考えてごらん

immigrant /ímigrənt/ 名 移民

an illegal	immigrant	不法入国者

▷ Laws against **illegal immigrants** have become more severe recently. 不法入国者を取り締まる法律が近ごろますます厳しくなってきている

an immigrant	from A	Aからの移民
an immigrant	to A	Aへの移民

▷ She's an **immigrant from** Poland, living in London at the moment. 彼女はポーランドからの移民で，現在はロンドンに住んでいる
▷ My grandfather was an **immigrant to** New York in the late 19th century. 祖父は19世紀後半にニューヨークへ渡った移民だった

impact /ímpækt/
名 衝撃，衝突；影響力，インパクト

have	an impact	影響力を及ぼす
make	an impact	
consider	the impact	影響を考える
examine	the impact	影響を調べる
assess	the impact	影響を評価する
reduce	the impact	影響を減らす

▷ What you said **had** an **impact** on him. あなたの言ったことに彼は大きく影響された
▷ We should **examine** the **impact** of violent computer games on young people's minds. 暴力的なコンピュータゲームが若者の心に及ぼす影響を調べるべきだ

a major	impact	大きな影響
a significant	impact	重大な影響
little	impact	ささいな影響
a direct	impact	直接の影響
an immediate	impact	即座の影響
economic	impact	経済への影響
environmental	impact	環境への影響

▷ Advances in computer technology have made a **major impact** on people's lives. コンピュータ技術の進歩は人々の生活に大きな影響を与えた
▷ The financial crisis in America made an **immediate impact** on economies of countries throughout the world. アメリカの財政危機は世界中の国々の経済にすぐ影響を及ぼした

▷ The **environmental impact** of global warming on the earth is frightening. 温暖化が地球環境に与える影響は恐ろしいほどだ

impact	on A	Aへの影響

▷ Terrorism has had a major **impact on** airport security. テロリズムは空港のセキュリティに大きな影響を及ぼしている

import /ímpɔːrt/ 名 輸入；輸入品

boost	imports	輸入を増やす
reduce	imports	輸入を減らす
ban	imports	輸入を禁止する

★ boost [reduce / ban] the import of A も用いられる

▷ Tariffs are intended to **reduce imports**. 関税は輸入を減らすことを意図している
▷ The government is trying to **reduce** the **import** of foreign rice. 政府は外国産のコメの輸入を減らそうとしている

imports	rise	輸入が増加する
imports	increase	
imports	fall	輸入が減少する

▷ **Imports** have **risen** recently compared with exports. このところ輸入が輸出と比べて増加した

agricultural	imports	農産物の輸入
foreign	imports	外国輸入
a major	import	主要輸入品目
total	imports	輸入総額

▷ Beef is a **major import** for Japan. 牛肉は日本への主要輸出品目だ

an import	from A	Aからの輸入品
an import	into A	Aへの輸入品

▷ This cheese is an **import from** Holland. このチーズはオランダからの輸入品だ

import /impɔ́ːrt/ 動 輸入する；持ち込む

illegally	import	不法に輸入する

▷ He was accused of **illegally importing** drugs. 彼は不法に麻薬を輸入して告訴された

import A	from B	AをBから輸入する
import A	into B	AをBに輸入する

▷Japan **imports** a lot of coffee **from** Columbia. 日本はコロンビアから大量のコーヒーを輸入している（★しばしば受け身でも用いる：This rice was **imported from** China. これは中国からの輸入米だ)
▷Many foreign words have been **imported into** Japanese. 多くの外来語が日本語に取り入れられてきた

importance /impɔ́:rtəns/ 名 重要性

increase	in importance	重要性が高まる
attach	the importance	重視する
recognize	the importance	重要性を認める
realize	the importance	重要性に気づく
understand	the importance	重要性を理解する
stress	the importance	重要性を強調する
emphasize	the importance	
underline	the importance	

▷His job has **increased in importance** recently. 彼の仕事の重要性が近ごろ高まっている
▷The Japanese Government **attaches** great **importance** *to* the relationship with the United States. 日本政府は米国との関係が非常に重要と考えている
▷I don't think you **understand** the **importance** of what I'm trying to tell you. これからきみに言おうとしていることがどれほど大事か，きみはわかっていないね
▷The President **stressed** the **importance** of remaining calm at all times. 大統領はいついかなるときも冷静であることの重要性を強調した

of A	importance	重要性がAの

★Aには great, crucial, paramount, particular, vital などの形容詞がくる

▷What you say in your speech tomorrow will be **of** vital **importance** to the country. あすの演説の内容は国家にとってきわめて重要です

a matter of	great importance	きわめて重要なこと

important /impɔ́:rtənt/ 形 重要な

extremely	important	きわめて重要な
particularly	important	とりわけ重要な
especially	important	
increasingly	important	ますます重要な

▷It's **particularly important** that you keep this information secret. あなたは是が非でもこの件を秘密にしておかなければならない

▷It's becoming **increasingly important** to protect our computer system from viruses. コンピュータシステムをウイルスから守るのがますます重要になってきている

important	to A	Aにとって重要な

▷It may not be **important to** you, but it's very important to me. あなたには大事ではないかもしれないけど，私にはとても大事なことです

it is important	(for A) to do	(Aにとって)…するのが重要だ
it is important	(that)...	…が重要だ

▷**It's important to** keep a backup copy of your thesis. 論文のバックアップコピーをとっておくのが大切だ

impossible /impásəbl | -pɔ́s-/

形 不可能な, ありえない

seem	impossible	不可能と思われる
prove	impossible	不可能とわかる
find A	impossible	Aは不可能と思う
make A	impossible	Aを不可能にする

▷I **find** it **impossible** to understand her point of view. 私には彼女の考え方が理解できない
▷They **made** it **impossible** for me to continue working there. 彼らのせいで私はそこでの仕事を続けられなくなった

absolutely	impossible	まったく不可能な
almost	impossible	ほとんど不可能な
practically	impossible	
nearly	impossible	不可能に近い
virtually	impossible	事実上不可能な

▷It's **absolutely impossible** to know what she's thinking. 彼女が何を考えているのかまったく見当もつかない
▷It was an **almost impossible** task. それはほとんど不可能な任務だった
▷It's **nearly impossible** to work over 16 hours a day! 1日に16時間以上働くなんてほとんど不可能だ

it is impossible	(for A) to do	Aにとって…するのは不可能だ

▷**It's impossible for** me **to** complete the essay this week. レポートを今週完成させるのはぼくには無理だ
PHRASES
That's impossible. ☺ それはありえない

impressed /imprést/ 形 感動した

| impression |

deeply	impressed	深く感動した
greatly	impressed	非常に感動した
particularly	impressed	とりわけ感動した

▷She was **deeply impressed** by the little girl's painting. 彼女はその小さな女の子の絵に深く心を動かされた
▷He was **particularly impressed** by your essay on the Edo period. 彼は江戸時代に関するあなたの論文にとりわけ感銘を受けた

be impressed	by A	Aに感銘を受ける
be impressed	with A	

▷He was **impressed by** your questions after the lecture. 彼は講義の後のあなたの質問に感心した
[PHRASES]
I'm so impressed. ☺ 感心しました

■ impression /impréʃən/ 名 印象

get	an impression	印象を受ける
gain	an impression	
have	an impression	
give	an impression	印象を与える
make	an impression	
create	an impression	
convey	an impression	
leave	an impression	印象を残す
confirm	an impression	印象を再確認する
reinforce	an impression	印象を強める

▷I **have** the **impression** that he's not really interested in politics. 彼は政治にあまり興味をもっていないという印象が私にはある
▷He **gave** the **impression** that he knew all about Ancient Greek history. 彼は古代ギリシャの歴史をすべて知っているという印象を与えた
▷It's important to **make** a good **impression** on your teacher. 先生によい印象を与えることが大切だ
▷That just **confirms** the **impression** I had of him earlier. それは彼に対するこれまでの印象を再確認するものだ

a strong	impression	強い印象
a false	impression	誤った印象
a misleading	impression	
a wrong	impression	
a bad	impression	悪い印象
a good	impression	よい印象
a favorable	impression	
an initial	impression	最初の印象
a lasting	impression	忘れられない印象

an overall	impression	全体の印象
a general	impression	

▷I don't want to give you a **false impression**. あなたに誤った印象を与えたくない
▷You made a really **good impression**! きみの与えた印象はほんとによかったよ
▷I got the **general impression** that he didn't really want to continue with the course. 彼は実のところそのコースを続けたくないのだという印象を全体に受けた

under the impression (that)...	…と思い込んで

▷I was **under** the **impression that** you knew all about it. その件をきみはすべて知っていると思い込んでいた

■ impressive /imprésiv/

形 強い印象を与える, 印象的な, みごとな

extremely	impressive	とても印象的な
pretty	impressive	
particularly	impressive	特に印象的な
equally	impressive	同様に印象的な

▷Tom's exam results were **particularly impressive**. トムの試験結果は特によかった
▷I think both candidates were **equally impressive**. どちらの応募者も同じくらいすばらしかったと思う

■ improve /imprúːv/

動 改良する, よくなる; 上達する, 上達させる

considerably	improve	ずいぶんよくなる
dramatically	improve	劇的によくなる
greatly	improve	大幅によくなる
vastly	improve	
significantly	improve	著しくよくなる
certainly	improve	確実によくなる
gradually	improve	徐々によくなる
steadily	improve	着実によくなる

★considerably, dramatically, greatly, significantly, steadilyは動詞の後でも用いる

▷His English has **improved dramatically** since he started taking private lessons. プライベートレッスンを始めてから彼は劇的に英語が上達した
▷The situation has **greatly improved** since the last time we spoke. 前回の話し合い以降, 状況は大きく改善した
▷This year's sales figures have **significantly improved** over last year's. 今年の売上高は昨年と比べ

て著しく増えた

try to	improve	改善しようとする
be designed to	improve	改善するよう工夫してある

▷He's **trying to improve** his backhand. 彼は(テニスの)バックハンドがうまくなるよう練習している

an attempt to	improve	改善の試み
an effort to	improve	改善の努力

▷You really should make more **effort to improve**. きみは上達するようもっと努力すべきだ

inch /ɪntʃ/ 名 インチ(★1インチは12分の1フィート；2.54センチメートル)

an inch	thick	厚さ1インチの
an inch	long	長さ1インチの
an inch	wide	幅1インチの
an inch	high	高さ1インチの

▷We need a five **inch thick** piece of wood. 5インチの厚さの木が必要だ

half	an inch	2分の1インチ
a half	inch	

▷Leave about **half an inch** between your big toe and the end of the shoe. 足の親指と靴の先に2分の1インチぐらいすき間を残しておきなさい

incident /ˈɪnsədənt/ 名 事件

remember	an incident	事件を思い出す
describe	an incident	事件の説明をする
report	an incident	事件を報告する
investigate	an incident	事件を調査する

▷He seemed completely unable to **remember** the **incident**. 彼はその事件をまったく思い出せないようだった
▷Police are **investigating** the **incident**. 警察が事件を捜査中だ

an incident	happens	事件がある
an incident	occurs	事件が起こる

▷Every time an unusual **incident happens** she panics. 普通でないことが起こるたびに彼女はパニックを起こす

a major	incident	大事件
a serious	incident	重大な事件
a minor	incident	小さな事件
a violent	incident	暴力事件
an isolated	incident	単独の事件
a shooting	incident	銃撃事件

▷There have been no **major incidents** of terrorism for the last two months. ここ2か月大きなテロ事件は起きていない
▷Apparently a **serious incident** took place outside the White House. どうやらホワイトハウスの外で重大な事件が起きたようだ

following	an incident	事件の結果
without	incident	何事もなく，無事に

▷A man was arrested **following** an **incident** outside a nightclub. ナイトクラブの外で起きた事件でひとりの男が逮捕された
▷Luckily the demonstration was peaceful and passed **without incident**. 幸いデモは平穏に行われ，何事もなく通り過ぎた

income /ˈɪnkʌm/ 名 収入，所得

have	an income	収入がある
earn	an income	収入を得る
receive	an income	収入を受け取る
increase	an income	収入を増やす
reduce	an income	収入を減らす
supplement	one's income	収入を補う

▷He **has** an **income** of over $100,000 a year. 彼は1年に10万ドル以上の収入がある
▷He **receives** a good **income** from his investments. 彼は投資でよい収入を得ている
▷He had to take on an extra job to **supplement** his **income**. 彼は収入を補うために副業に手を出さなければならなかった

income	falls	収入が下がる
income	rises	収入が上がる

▷Their **income fell** by 50% last year. 彼らの昨年の収入は半減した

a high	income	高い収入
a low	income	低い収入
an annual	income	年間所得
a regular	income	定収入
a total	income	総所得
gross	income	総収入

▷She doesn't have a very **high income**. Just enough to live on. 彼女はそれほど高い収入がない．かつかつに暮らす程度だ

▷ Together they earn a **total income** of around $120,000. 彼らの総所得はひっくるめて12万ドルほどだ

| a source of | income | 収入源 |

▷ She's very rich. She has a private **source of income**. 彼女はとても裕福だ。個人的な収入源がある

increase /ínkri:s/ 名 増加, 増大

see	an increae	増加を見る
show	an increase	増加を示す
cause	an increase	増加を引き起こす
represent	an increase	増加を表す

▷ We're going to **see** a big **increase** in the number of elderly people during the next 10 years. 次の10年で高齢者の数は大きな増加を見るだろう

▷ Our poor service has **caused** an **increase** in complaints. うちのサービスが悪くてクレームが増えた（★ cause an increase はふつうよくないことの増加をさす）

▷ Total profits this year **represent** an **increase** of 72% over last year. 今年度の利益総額は昨年比で72％増えている

a dramatic	increase	劇的な増加
a huge	increase	大幅な増加
a substantial	increase	
a significant	increase	著しい増加
a marked	increase	
a rapid	increase	急速な増加
a sharp	increase	急激な増加
a slight	increase	わずかな増加
pay	increase	賃上げ
price	increase	値上げ
tax	increase	増税
population	increase	人口増加
temperature	increase	気温上昇

▷ We're seeing a **dramatic increase** in global warming. われわれは地球温暖化が劇的に進むのを目の当たりにしている

▷ Exports are not doing well. We need to see a **substantial increase**. 輸出が不調だ。大幅に増やす必要がある

▷ Last month there was a **sharp increase** in sales. 先月の売り上げは急激に増えた

increase	in A	Aの増加
increase	of 30%	3割の増加
on	the increase	増加して

▷ Recently there's been an **increase in** interest in 3D computer games. 最近3Dコンピュータゲームに関心が高まっている

▷ There's going to be an **increase of** 50% in the price of alcohol. アルコール価格は5割上がるだろう

▷ The number of homeless people is **on the increase**. ホームレスの数が増加中だ

increase /inkrí:s/

動 増加する, 増える；増やす

greatly	increase	大幅に増える
significantly	increase	著しく増える
substantially	increase	大きく増える
gradually	increase	徐々に増える
steadily	increase	着実に増える
increase	considerably	大幅に増える
increase	dramatically	劇的に増える
increase	rapidly	急激に増える
increase	sharply	

★ significantly, substantially は高頻度で動詞の後でも用いる

▷ I think your chances of being promoted have **greatly increased**. あなたの昇進のチャンスは大幅に増えたと思う

▷ The number of cases of influenza has **significantly increased** over the past two weeks. インフルエンザの患者数はここ2週間で著しく増えた

▷ Our costs have **increased substantially**. わが社のコストは大きく増えた

▷ The number of visa applications has **increased dramatically**. ビザの申請数が劇的に伸びた

▷ Unless foreign aid **increases rapidly** the number of people dying of hunger will continue to rise. 海外からの援助が急激に増えなければ、飢餓で死ぬ人の数はこれからも増え続けるだろう

increase	by 50%	5割増える
increase from 10	to 20	10から20に増える
increase	in size	大きさが増す
increase	in price	値段が増す
increase	in value	価値が増す

▷ The price of coffee has **increased by** 50% during the last 12 months. コーヒー価格はここ12か月間で5割上昇した

▷ The number of cases of bird flu has **increased from** 5 **to** 17. 鳥インフルエンザの件数は5件から17件に増加した

▷ Gold has greatly **increased in value** recently. 金は近ごろ価値が大きく上がった

independence /ìndipéndəns/

名 独立, 自立

achieve	independence	独立する
gain	independence	独立を勝ち取る
declare	(one's) independence	独立を宣言する
maintain	one's independence	独立を維持する
recognize	independence	独立を認める

▷ The USA **achieved independence** from Britain in 1776. 米国は1776年にイギリスから独立した
▷ Most countries that used to be British colonies have now **gained** their **independence**. かつてイギリス植民地だったほとんどの国はいまでは独立を勝ち取っている

full	independence	完全な独立
economic	independence	経済的独立
political	independence	政治的独立

▷ Many people in Tibet want to claim **full independence** from China. 中国からの完全独立を主張する人がチベットには数多くいる
▷ Many countries have achieved **political independence** during the last 50 years. 多くの国がここ50年の間に政治的独立を達成した

independence	from A	Aからの独立

▷ The Scottish Nationalist Party believes that political **independence from** England is essential. スコットランド国民党はイングランドからの政治的独立が不可欠であると信じている

a declaration of	independence	独立宣言

▷ The **Declaration of Independence** was signed in 1776. アメリカ独立宣言は1776年に署名された

independent /ìndipéndənt/

形 独立した，自立した

fully	independent	完全に独立した
entirely	independent	
totally	independent	
completely	independent	
newly	independent	新たに独立した

▷ Clare doesn't want to live with her parents. She wants to be **fully independent**. クレアは両親のもとで暮らすことを望んでいない．完全に独立したがっている
▷ A **newly independent** country faces many challenges. 新しく独立した国は多くの難題に直面している

independent	of A	Aから独立した
independent	from A	

▷ The inquiry should be **independent of** any government interests. 調査は政府の利害から独立して行われるべきだ

index /índeks/ 名 索引，目録；指数

consult	an index	索引を調べる

▷ She **consulted** an **index** of Scottish surnames. 彼女はスコットランド人の姓の索引を調べた

index	falls	指数が下がる
index	rises	指数が上がる

▷ In May the consumer price **index fell** 0.1 percent. 5月に消費者物価指数は0.1％下がった

an alphabetical	index	アルファベット順索引
body mass	index	体格指数
consumer price	index	消費者物価指数
a stock	index	株価指数

▷ There should be an **alphabetical index** at the back of the book. 巻末にアルファベット順索引があったほうがいい

indicate /índikèit/ 動 指し示す

clearly	indicate	明確に示す
strongly	indicate	

▷ These latest figures **clearly indicate** a significant drop in the birthrate. これらの直近の数字は出生率の著しい減少を明らかに示している

indicate	(that)...	…であることを示す
indicate	wh-	…かを示す

★ wh- は where, what, when など

▷ Recent data **indicates that** the age at which women get married is steadily increasing. 最近のデータは女性の結婚年齢が着実に上がりつつあることを示している

industry /índəstri/ 名 産業，工業

develop	an industry	産業を発展させる

| influence |

▷You need a lot of capital to **develop** an **industry**. 産業を発展させるには多くの資本が必要だ

growing	industry	成長産業
high-tech	industry	ハイテク産業
local	industry	地場産業
private	industry	民間産業
heavy	industry	重工業
light	industry	軽工業
the manufacturing	industry	製造業
the service	industry	サービス産業
primary	industry	第一次産業
secondary	industry	第二次産業
tertiary	industry	第三次産業
the chemical	industry	化学工業
the nuclear	industry	原子力産業
the steel	industry	鉄鋼業
the automobile	industry	自動車産業
the entertainment	industry	娯楽産業
the movie	industry	映画産業
the music	industry	音楽産業

▷The new government grant will greatly help **local industry**. 新たな政府交付金のおかげで地場産業は大いに助かるだろう

▷The **chemical industry** has been responsible for a great deal of pollution. 化学工業のせいで多くの公害が引き起こされた

influence /ínfluəns/

名 影響, 影響力; 影響力のある人

have	an influence	影響力がある
exert	an influence	影響力を及ぼす
exercise	an influence	
use	one's influence	影響力を使う
extend	one's influence	影響力を広げる
increase	one's influence	影響力を増す
show	the influence	影響力を示す

▷Your report definitely **had** an **influence** on his decision. あなたの報告は彼の決定に間違いなく影響を及ぼした

▷I think he should try to **exert** a stronger **influence** over his children. 彼は子どもたちにもっと威厳をもって接するようにすべきだ

▷His father **used** his **influence** to get him the job. 彼の父親は顔をきかせて息子に就職口を見つけた

▷Her paintings **show** the **influence** of Picasso's cubist period. 彼女の絵にはピカソのキュービズム時代の影響が現れている

(a) considerable	influence	かなりの影響力
a great	influence	大きな影響力
a major	influence	
a strong	influence	強い影響力
a direct	influence	直接の影響
undue	influence	不当な影響力
political	influence	政治的影響力

▷He advised her a lot. He was definitely a **great influence**. 彼は彼女にいろいろ助言した. 人への影響力の大きな人だ

▷**Undue influence** was used to prevent the truth from coming out. 真実が表に出るのを防ぐために不当な影響力が行使された

▷He used his **political influence** to get the contract. 彼は自分の政治的影響力を生かして受注を取り付けた

influence	on A	Aへの影響力
influence	over A	

★×influence to A とはいわない

▷Parents seem to have little **influence over** their children these days. 昨今では子に対する親の影響力はごく小さいようだ

under	the influence	影響を受けて

▷He was **under the influence** of drink when he committed the crime. 犯行時に彼は酒に酔っていた

influence /ínfluəns/ 動 影響を及ぼす

deeply	influence	深く影響を及ぼす
profoundly	influence	
greatly	influence	大きく影響を及ぼす
heavily	influence	
strongly	influence	強く影響を及ぼす
directly	influence	直接影響を及ぼす

▷He was **deeply influenced** by his university professor. 彼は大学の教授から深く影響を受けた

▷Experiences in early life **profoundly influence** our characters. 幼いころの経験は性格に深い影響を及ぼす

▷British and American pop music was **heavily influenced** by the Beatles. イギリスとアメリカのポップミュージックはビートルズから大きな影響を受けた

▷The ideas of Confucius **strongly influence** Eastern thought even today. 儒教の考えは東洋の思想に今日でも強く影響を与えている

inform /infɔ́ːrm/ 動 知らせる, 通知する

properly informed	適切な情報を得た
fully informed	十分な情報を得た
well informed	
reliably informed	信頼できる情報を得た

▷Please ensure that I am kept **fully informed** of the situation. 私が常に状況を把握できるようにしておいてください
▷He's very **well informed** about the situation in China. 彼は中国情勢に精通している
▷I am **reliably informed** that he will be arriving on Tuesday. 彼が火曜日に到着するというのは間違いない情報だ

inform A of B	AにBについて知らせる
inform A about B	

▷He **informed** me **of** several interesting facts. 彼は私にいくつか興味深い事実を知らせてきた

inform A (that)...	…とAに知らせる

▷I've **informed** my lawyers **that** I want a divorce. 弁護士たちに離婚の意思を伝えた

information /ɪnfərméɪʃən/

名 情報；案内，案内所

contain	information	情報を含む
have	information	情報がある
store	information	情報を蓄える
find	information	情報を見つける
obtain	information	情報を得る
get	information	
gather	information	情報を集める
collect	information	
receive	information	情報を受け取る
retrieve	information	情報を検索する
access	information	情報にアクセスする
provide	information	情報を提供する
give	information	
release	information	情報を公開する
convey	information	情報を伝える
share	information	情報を共有する
exchange	information	情報を交換する

▷You can **obtain** further **information** by contacting city hall. 市役所に連絡すればさらに情報を得られますよ
▷We need to **gather** more **information**. もっと情報を集める必要がある
▷The hotel receptionist can **provide** more **information**. ホテルの受付係に聞けばもっと詳しいことを教えてくれるでしょう
▷Well, thanks, Tom. You've **given** me some good **information**. ありがとう，トム．きみからいい情報をもらったよ
▷Email is an extremely useful way of **conveying information** quickly. Eメールは情報をすばやく伝える非常に有益な方法だ
▷He's not willing to **share** his **information** with anybody else. 彼は他の人と情報を共有したがらない

accurate	information	正確な情報
relevant	information	関連情報
useful	information	有益な情報
available	information	入手可能な情報
additional	information	追加の情報
further	information	さらなる情報
basic	information	基本的情報
detailed	information	詳しい情報
confidential	information	内密の情報

▷I've collected together all the **relevant information**. 関連情報をすべてかき集めた
▷Please send us all the **available information** as soon as possible. 入手可能な情報を至急すべて送ってください
▷We need some **additional information**. われわれにはさらに情報が必要だ
▷For **further information** contact... お問い合わせは…まで(★広告・パンフレットでしばしば用いる)
▷I hope you understand that this is **confidential information**. この情報は内密ですのでご承知おきください

information	about A	Aに関する情報
information	on A	

▷We have no **information** yet **on** the car accident. 自動車事故に関してまだ何の情報も得ていない

injure /índʒər/ 動 傷つける，痛める

be seriously	injured	重傷を負う
be badly	injured	
be severely	injured	
be fatally	injured	致命傷を負う
be slightly	injured	軽傷を負う

▷He was **badly injured** in a car accident last week. 彼は先週自動車事故で重傷を負った
▷Luckily the people in the bus were only **slightly injured**. 幸いバスの乗客たちは軽傷ですんだ

be killed and [or] injured	死傷する

| injury |

▷ Many people were **killed or injured** in the earthquake. 地震により死傷者が多く出た

injury /índʒəri/ 名 負傷, けが；損害

suffer	an injury	負傷する
receive	an injury	
sustain	an injury	
cause	injury	負傷させる
have	an injury	負傷している
escape	injury	負傷を免れる
avoid	injury	
recover from	an injury	けがから回復する

▷ He **suffered** severe head **injury**. 彼は頭部に重傷を負った
▷ He said it wasn't his intention to **cause** any **injury**. けがを負わせるつもりはなかったと彼は言った
▷ He **had** an **injury** which prevented him from playing in the World Cup. 彼はけがを負ってワールドカップに出られなくなった
▷ Luckily everybody **escaped injury**. 幸いなことに負傷者は出なかった
▷ She's in hospital now **recovering from** an **injury**. 入院中の彼女はけがが回復に向かっている

a serious	injury	重傷
a severe	injury	
a minor	injury	軽傷
a knee	injury	ひざのけが
a head	injury	頭のけが
a leg	injury	脚のけが

▷ He received a **serious injury** in the last five minutes of the game. 彼は試合の最後5分で重傷を負った
▷ Three people received hospital treatment for **minor injuries**. 3名が軽傷で病院治療を受けた

innocent /ínəsənt/ 形 無罪の, 無実の

completely	innocent	完全に無罪の
entirely	innocent	
perfectly	innocent	
totally	innocent	

▷ It turned out that she was **completely innocent**. 彼女は完全に無罪であることが判明した

innocent	of A	A(犯罪)を犯していない

▷ I am **innocent of** all the criminal charges. 刑事罰を受けたことは一度もありません

inquiry /inkwáiəri/ 名 調査；問い合わせ

conduct	an inquiry	調査を行う
hold	an inquiry	
have	an inquiry	
demand	an inquiry	調査を要求する
make	inquiries	問い合わせる
receive	an inquiry	問い合わせを受ける

▷ The police are **conducting** an **inquiry** *into* how the prisoners escaped. 囚人たちがどうやって脱獄したか警察が調査中だ
▷ You need to **make inquiries** about how to apply for a scholarship. 奨学金の応募方法について問い合わせる必要がある

a public	inquiry	公式の調査
an independent	inquiry	独自の調査
an official	inquiry	正式の調査
a government	inquiry	政府調査
a judicial	inquiry	司法調査

▷ The government has agreed to hold an **independent inquiry** *into* the matter. 政府はその件に関して独自調査を行うことに同意した
▷ They are still refusing to hold an **official inquiry**. 彼らは正式な調査を行うことをなお拒否している

an inquiry	into A	Aの調査
an inquiry	about A	Aについての問い合わせ

▷ We've had many **inquiries** recently **about** studying abroad. 最近は留学について多くの問い合わせがある

insist /insíst/ 動 主張する, 言い張る

strongly	insist	強く主張する
still	insist	なお主張する

▷ The unions are **still insisting** *on* a 5% increase in salary. 組合はなお5％の賃上げを主張している

insist	on A	Aを主張する；Aを言って聞かない
insist	upon A	

▷ If you **insist on** interrupting me I'll have to leave the room. どうしても私の話のじゃまをするのなら, 私は部屋から出て行きますよ

insist	(that)...	…だと主張する

▷ He **insisted that** the meeting should be postponed until next week. 会議は来週まで延期すべきだと彼は主張した

| instruction |

PHRASES
I insist! ☺ どうか私の思うようにさせてください ▷ "After you." "No, after you! I insist!"「お先にどうぞ」「とんでもない，あなたこそお先にどうぞ」

install /instɔ́ːl/

動 取り付ける，設置する；インストールする；就任させる

recently	installed	設置したばかりの
newly	installed	

▷ They've **recently installed** two new photocopying-machines in our building. うちのビルには最近，2台の新しいコピー機が設置された

have A	installed	Aを取り付けてもらう

▷ We're **having** a new computer system **installed** next month. 来月に新しいコンピュータシステムをインストールしてもらう予定だ

install A	in B	AをBに設置する

▷ Automatic vending machines are being **installed in** the canteen. 自動販売機が食堂に設置されつつある

install A	as B	A(人)をBに就任させる

▷ Barrack Obama was **installed as** President in January 2009. バラク・オバマは2009年1月に大統領に就任した

instance /ínstəns/ **名** 例, 実例

take	an instance	例を挙げる
remember	an instance	事例を覚えている

▷ I **remember** an **instance** when our village was attacked. うちの村が攻撃された時のことを覚えている

in	one instance	ある一つの場合
in	this instance	この場合
for	instance	たとえば

▷ I don't usually smoke cigars, but **in this instance** I'll make an exception. ふだんは葉巻は吸わないが今回は例外としよう

▷ The euro is used by many countries, **for instance**, France, Germany, Spain, Italy, and so on. ユーロはフランス，ドイツ，スペイン，イタリアなど多くの国で使われている

an instance	when...	…の時のこと
an instance	where...	…の場合

▷ This is the only **instance where** we received a complaint. これが苦情を受けた唯一の例だ

institution /ìnstətjúːʃən | -tjúː-/

名 公共機関, 施設；制度, 慣習

a public	institution	公共機関
an academic	institution	学術機関
an educational	institution	教育機関
a financial	institution	金融機関
a political	institution	政治制度
a social	institution	社会制度

▷ Many **educational institutions** are receiving less financial support from the Government this year. 今年は政府から財政援助を減らされた教育機関が多い
▷ Many people find it difficult to trust the **financial institutions** after the recent financial crisis. 最近の金融危機を受けて，金融機関は信用できないと考える人が多い

instruction /instrʌ́kʃən/

名 使用説明(書)；指示, 指図；指導

give	instructions	指示を与える
have	instructions	指示を受けている
receive	instructions	指示を受ける
issue	instructions	指示を出す
follow	(the) instructions	指示に従う
take	instructions	
give	instruction	指導する
provide	instruction	
receive	instruction	指導を受ける

▷ I **gave** him **instructions on** how to get there. そこへの行き方を彼に指示した
▷ We still haven't **received** any **instructions** from headquarters yet. まだ本社から指示を受けていない
▷ **Follow** the **instructions** below. 下記の指示に従ってください

detailed	instructions	細かな指示
specific	instructions	明確な指示
written	instructions	文書による指示
religious	instruction	宗教教育
moral	instruction	道徳教育

▷ For more **detailed instructions** on how to grow vegetables, click on the link above. 野菜の育て方についての詳細は上のリンクをクリックしてください

251

| instrument |

▷ We should provide clear **written instructions** about what to do in the case of a fire. 火災時にとるべき行動について文書ではっきり指示しておくのがいい
▷ **Religious instruction** is not compulsory in our school. うちの学校では宗教教育は必修ではない

| instructions | on A | Aの取扱説明 |
| instruction | on A | Aについての指導 |

▷ Are there any **instructions on** how to load the software? ソフトウエアを読む込む方法についての取扱説明書はありますか

| under | instructions | 指示のもとで |

▷ He was **under** strict **instructions** to allow no-one to enter the building. 絶対にだれも建物内に入れてはならないとの指示を彼は受けていた

instrument /ínstrəmənt/

名 楽器；器具，機器，道具

| play | an instrument | 楽器を演奏する |
| use | an instrument | 道具を使う |

▷ My mother likes music but she doesn't **play** any **instruments**. 母は音楽好きですが，楽器は弾きません

a brass	instrument	金管楽器
a percussion	instrument	打楽器
a stringed	instrument	弦楽器
a wind	instrument	管楽器
a precision	instrument	精密機器
a measuring	instrument	計測器
an optical	instrument	光学機器
a surgical	instrument	手術器具

▷ She plays a **stringed instrument**—the violin or cello, I think. 彼女は弦楽器を演奏する．バイオリンかチェロかな

insurance /inʃúərəns/ 名 保険；保険金

buy	insurance	保険に入る
take out	insurance	保険を掛ける
have	insurance	保険に入っている
provide	insurance	保険を手配する

▷ It's much more expensive for older people to **buy** life **insurance**. 年配の人が生命保険に入るのはずっと高くつく
▷ The other car driver didn't **have** any **insurance**. 相手方のドライバーは保険に入っていなかった

▷ The company will **provide** free health **insurance**. 会社は無料で健康保険を手配してくれるだろう

| insurance | covers | 保険が補償する |

▷ Your **insurance** will **cover** accidental damage. ご加入の保険では偶発的損害がカバーされます

national	insurance	国民保険
social	insurance	社会保険
life	insurance	生命保険
health	insurance	健康保険
medical	insurance	医療保険
car	insurance	自動車保険
travel	insurance	旅行保険
accident	insurance	傷害保険
fire	insurance	火災保険
unemployment	insurance	失業保険

▷ **Medical insurance** is really expensive these days. 最近の医療保険は非常に高額だ

insurance	against A	Aに対する保険
insurance	for A	Aの保険
insurance	on A	

▷ We need to get **insurance against** fire. 火災保険に加入する必要がある
▷ Do you have **insurance on** your car? 車に保険をかけていますか

intelligence /intélədʒəns/

名 知能，知性；(他国に関する)情報

have	intelligence	知性がある
insult	A's intelligence	知性をばかにする
gather	intelligence	情報を収集する

▷ Don't **insult** my **intelligence**! 私をばかにするな
▷ It's the job of the CIA to **gather intelligence** on possible terrorist attacks. 起こりうるテロ攻撃に関しての情報収集がＣＩＡの仕事だ

artificial	intelligence	人工知能
high	intelligence	高い知能
low	intelligence	低い知能

▷ He's a man of very **high intelligence**. 彼は非常に高い知能の持ち主だ

intelligent /intélədʒənt/ 形 頭のよい

| highly | intelligent | とても頭がよい |

▷My father was **highly intelligent** and very hard-working. 父はとても頭がよく、働き者だった

sensitive and intelligent	気配りがあり頭がよい
thoughtful and intelligent	思いやりがあり頭がよい

▷She was very **sensitive and intelligent**. 彼女はとても気配りがあって頭もよかった

intend /inténd/ 動 意図する

fully	intend	必ず…するつもりだ
clearly	intended	明確に意図した
originally	intended	もともと意図した
never	intended	決して意図していない

▷The bomb was **clearly inteded** to kill and injure as many people as possible. その爆弾は明らかにできるだけ多くの人を死傷させることを意図したものだった
▷The party was **originally intended** for close friends only. そのパーティーはもともと親しい友人だけを呼んで開くつもりだった
▷The elevator was **never intended** to hold 25 people. そのエレベーターは25名も人が乗ることは想定されていなかった

intend	to do	…するつもりである
intend	doing	
intend A	to do	Aに…させるつもりである
intend	that...	…というつもりである

▷After graduating from high school Linda **intends to** go on to university. 高校を卒業したらリンダは大学に進学するつもりだ
▷Bob's father **intended** him **to** take over the family business. ボブの父親は彼に家業を継がせるつもりだった

intend A	as B	AをBのつもりで言う

▷What I said was **intended as** a compliment. あんなふうに言ったのはお世辞のつもりだった

be intended	for A	Aに向けたものだ

▷This water was never **intended for** drinking. この水は飲料用ではなかった

intention /inténʃən/ 名 意図, 意向

announce	one's intention	意向を表明する
express	one's intention	
declare	one's intention	意向を明らかにする
state	one's intention	意向を述べる
indicate	one's intention	意向を示す

▷Did you hear? The president has just **announced** his **intention** to resign. 聞いたかい。社長が辞任する意向を表明したって
▷She **indicated** her **intention** to stand again for parliament this year. 彼女は今年もまた国会議員に立候補する意思を表明した

the original	intention	当初の意図
the true	intention	真意
bad	intentions	悪意
good	intentions	善意

▷Her **original intention** was to leave before the end of the month. 彼女の当初の考えでは月末前に出かける予定だった
▷I know everything went wrong, but I'm sure she had **good intentions**. 何もかもうまくいかなかったけど、きっと彼女はよかれと思ってやったんだよ

intention	that...	…という意図
intention	to do	…する意図

▷It wasn't my **intention that** you should get into trouble. あなたがめんどうなことになるなんて、そんなつもりは私にはなかった

have no intention	of doing	…するつもりはない
with the intention	of doing	…するつもりで

▷I **have no intention of** sitting here doing nothing. 安閑とここに座っているつもりはない
▷I don't think he did it **with** the **intention of** causing trouble. 彼は問題を起こすつもりでやったのではないと思う

interest /íntərəst/

名 興味, 関心；利子, 利息；利益

have	(an) interest	興味がある
feel	(an) interest	
lose	interest	興味を失う
attract	interest	興味を引く
arouse	interest	
show	(an) interest	興味を示す
express	(an) interest	
take	(an) interest	興味をもつ
be of	interest	興味深い
charge	interest	利子を課す
pay	(the) interest	利子を払う
repay with	interest	利子をつけて返済する
earn	interest	利子を稼ぐ

| interested |

protect	A's **interests**	利益を守る
defend	A's **interests**	利益を守る
serve	the **interests**	利益にかなう

▷ Apparently he **has** an **interest** *in* wild birds. 彼は野鳥に興味があるようだ
▷ My son isn't **showing** much **interest** *in* studying. うちの息子は勉強にあまり興味を示していません
▷ It seems she's suddenly **taken** an **interest** *in* kendo. 彼女は急に剣道に興味をもったようだ
▷ I don't have enough money to **pay** the **interest** *on* my loan. ローンの利子を払えるだけのお金がありません
▷ I'd like to do something that **serves** the **interests** of the community. 地域社会の利益にかなうことを何かしたいのです

(a) great	**interest**	大きな興味
(a) special	**interest**	特別の興味
(a) particular	**interest**	
(an) active	**interest**	積極的な興味
(a) common	**interest**	共通の利害
(the) national	**interest**	国益
(the) public	**interest**	公共の利益
annual	**interest**	年利
simple	**interest**	単利
compound	**interest**	複利

▷ She takes a **special interest** in helping the homeless. 彼女はホームレス支援に特別の関心がある
▷ At the Oscar Awards a dress worn by Lady Gaga was of **particular interest**. オスカー受賞式でレディ・ガガが着ていたドレスはとりわけ人々の興味を引いた
▷ The government claimed that a public inquiry was not in the **public interest**. 公開審査会を開くのは公益にかなっていないと政府は主張した

an **interest**	in A	Aへの興味
the **interest**	on A	Aの利子

▷ The **interest on** this loan is 5%. このローンの利子は5パーセントだ

with	**interest**	興味をもって
in	A's **interest(s)**	Aに有利で

▷ Everyone looked at Max **with interest**. みんな興味深げにマックスを見た

interested /íntərəstid/

形 興味をもった，関心のある

deeply	**interested**	深い関心がある
particularly	**interested**	特に興味がある
genuinely	**interested**	心から興味がある
not remotely	**interested**	少しも興味がない
no longer	**interested**	もう興味がない

▷ Apparently he's **deeply interested** in ancient Egyptian history. 彼は古代エジプトの歴史に深い関心があるようだ
▷ She seemed to be **genuinely interested** in our suggestion. 彼女は心底からわれわれの提案に関心があるようだった

interested	in A	Aに興味がある

★ in の後は doing も用いる

▷ Are you **interested in** Japanese culture? 日本文化に興味がありますか
▷ Are you **interested in** going on a trip to Kyoto this weekend? 今週末京都へ旅行に出かける気はないですか

be **interested**	to see	ぜひ見たい
be **interested**	to know	ぜひ知りたい
be **interested**	to hear	ぜひ聞きたい

▷ I'd be **interested to hear** what happens. どんなことになるかぜひ聞いてみたい

interesting /íntərəstiŋ/

形 興味深い，おもしろい

find A	**interesting**	Aをおもしろいと思う

▷ I didn't **find** that book at all **interesting**. その本はちっともおもしろくなかった

really	**interesting**	とても興味深い
particularly	**interesting**	特に興味深い

▷ The exhibition of French impressionist paintings was **particularly interesting**. フランス印象派絵画の展覧会は特に興味深かった

it is **interesting**	that...	…はおもしろい
it is **interesting**	to do	…するのはおもしろい

★ do は note, see, hear, learn など

▷ It's **interesting that** Tom said one thing to you and a completely different thing to me! トムがきみに言ったこととぼくに言ったことがまったく異なるとはおもしろい
▷ It's always **interesting to** hear how our old school friends are getting on. 昔の学校仲間の近況を聞くのはいつも楽しみだ

PHRASES

How interesting! / That's interesting! ☺(相手の

| interview |

話に応じて)それはおもしろい ▷So you've decided to take up golf! How interesting! ゴルフを始めることにしたのか. それはいい

Internet /íntəːrnèt/

名 (the Internet で)インターネット, ネット

access	the Internet	ネットにアクセスする
surf	the Internet	ネットサーフィンをする

▷Every day I **access** the **Internet**. インターネットに毎日アクセスしている

on	the Internet	インターネットで

▷You can get a lot of useful information **on** the **Internet**. 多くの有益な情報をインターネットで得ることができる

interpret /intə́ːrprit/

動 解釈する; 通訳する

correctly	interpret	正しく解釈する
be variously	interpreted	さまざまに解釈される
be widely	interpreted	広く解釈される

▷I don't think you're **correctly interepreting** what I mean. 私の意図をきみは正しく解釈してくれていないと思う
▷His book was **widely interpreted** as an attack on the capitalist society. 彼の著作は資本主義社会を攻撃する書だと一般には受け取られてきた

interpret A	as C	AをCだと解釈する

▷I **interpreted** his silence **as** a refusal to cooperate. 彼が黙っているのを見て協力するのはいやなんだなと思った(★しばしば受け身でも用いる:His silence was **interpreted as** a refusal to cooperate.)

interpretation /intə̀ːrprətéiʃən/

名 解釈, 説明; 通訳

give	an interpretation	解釈する
make	an interpretation	
be open to	interpretation	解釈の余地がある
put	an interpretation on A	Aを解釈する

▷She **gave** an entirely different **interpretation** of what was said at the meeting. 彼女は会議での発言内容に関してまったく異なる解釈をした
▷What makes the ideal parent is completely **open to interpretation**. 理想の親とは何かについてはいろいろ解釈の余地がある
▷He **put** a totally different **interpretation on** the Chairperson's report. 議長報告を彼はまったく別なふうに解釈した(★interpretation の前に different, wrong, one's own などの形容詞がくることが多い)

the correct	interpretation	正しい解釈
a possible	interpretation	可能な解釈
a different	interpretation	異なる解釈

▷There are various **possible interpretations** of the law in this situation. この状況に関してはさまざまな法律解釈が可能だ
▷I had a totally **different interpretation** of what was said. 私は発言内容をまったく別なふうに解釈した

interrupt /intərʌ́pt/

動 じゃまをする; 中断する

rudely	interrupt	ぶしつけに遮る
suddenly	interrupt	急に遮る
temporarily	interrupt	一時中断する
constantly	interrupt	絶えず中断する

▷His speech was **constantly interrupted** by the audience. 彼の演説は絶えず聴衆に中断させられた
PHRASES
Don't interrupt me! ☺ じゃましないで
(I'm) sorry to interrupt (you), (but...) お話し中すみません; お仕事中申し訳ありません ▷I'm sorry to interrupt you, David, but... 話の途中で申し訳ないんだけど, デイビッド

interval /íntərvəl/ 名 間隔

at	fixed intervals	決まった間隔で
at	regular intervals	一定の間隔で

▷I go for a health checkup **at regular intervals**. 定期的に健康診断を受けている

interview /íntərvjùː/

名 会見, インタビュー; 面接

give	an interview	会見する
attend	an interview	会見に出る
conduct	an interview	面接を行う
have	an interview	面接を受ける

255

| introduce |

get	an interview

▷ The Prime Minister refused to **give** an **interview**. 首相は会見を断った
▷ They're going to **conduct** the final **interviews** next week. 最終面接は来週の予定だ
▷ I **had** an **interview** yesterday for a job. きのう就職面接を受けた

a face-to-face	interview	一対一会談
an exclusive	interview	独占会見
a press	interview	記者会見
a television	interview	テレビ会見
a job	interview	就職面接

▷ The leaders of the two main political parties had a **face-to-face interview** on television last night. 2大政党の党首は昨夜テレビで一対一会談を行った
▷ The newspaper succeeded in getting an **exclusive interview** with the President's wife. その新聞は大統領の妻との独占インタビューに成功した

introduce /ìntrədjúːs | -djúːs/

動 紹介する；導入する，取り入れる

be formally	introduced	正式に紹介された
be originally	introduced	元々は導入された
be gradually	introduced	徐々に導入された
recently	introduced	最近導入した

▷ I'm sorry. I don't believe we've been **formally introduced**. 失礼．私たちはお互いにまだ正式に紹介されていませんね
▷ Cats were **originally introduced** into houses to kill mice. 猫はもともとネズミを殺すために家に持ち込まれた
▷ Our company has **recently introduced** a new model of eco-car. わが社は近ごろ新型のエコカーを導入した

introduce A	to B	AをBに紹介する
introduce A	into B	AをBに持ち込む
introduce A	to B	

▷ Let me **introduce** you **to** my sister. 姉に紹介するよ
▷ Several rare birds were bred and **introduced into** the wild recently. 数羽の稀少な鳥を近ごろ繁殖させて野生に放った
▷ Christianity was first **introduced to** Japan in the 16th century. キリスト教は16世紀に最初に日本に伝えられた

[PHRASES]
Let me introduce myself. ☺ 自己紹介させてください ▷ Let me introduce myself. My name is John Hamilton. 自己紹介します．ジョン・ハミルトンです

introduction /ìntrədʌ́kʃən/

名 紹介；導入；手引き，入門；序文

make	the introductions	紹介する
need	no introduction	紹介するまでもない

▷ Would you mind **making** the **introductions**? 紹介していただけませんか
▷ Our speaker today **needs no introduction**. He is known to you all. きょう話をしてくださる方は紹介するまでもありません．みなさんよくご存じの方です

a brief	introduction	短い前置き
an excellent	introduction	よい手引き
a general	introduction	総論的な手引き

▷ This book provides **an excellent introduction** *to* the rules of sumo wrestling. この本は相撲のルールのとてもよい手引きです
▷ This course will give you a **general introduction** *to* mathematics. この講座は数学概論となります

an introduction	to A	Aの序文；Aの入門書

▷ This book offers an excellent **introduction to** psychology. これはとても優れた心理学入門書です

a letter of	introduction	紹介状

▷ Would you like me to write you a **letter of introduction**? 紹介状を書いて差し上げましょうか

invent /invént/ 動 発明する

newly	invented	新たに発明された
be originally	invented	もともと発明された

▷ Bob observed the moon through the **newly invented** telescope. ボブは新しく発明された望遠鏡で月を見た
▷ The submarine was **originally invented** hundreds of years ago by Leonardo da Vinci. 潜水艦はもともとレオナルド・ダビンチが何百年も前に発明した

invention /invénʃən/

名 発明；でっち上げ

a new	invention	新たな発明
the latest	invention	最新の発明
pure	invention	まったくのでっち上げ

▷If it's a **new invention** you need to patent it. 新しい発明なら特許を取る必要がある

investigate /invéstəgèit/

動 調べる，調査する，捜査する

thoroughly	investigate	十分調査する
fully	investigate	
properly	investigate	きちんと調査する
further	investigate	さらに調査する

▷The report was written without **properly investigating** the reasons for the accident. その報告書は事故原因をきちんと調査せずに書かれた

investigate	wh-	…か調査する

★wh-は how, what, why, whether など

▷We need to **investigate how** the report was lost. どのようにその報告書が紛失したのか調査する必要がある

investigation /invèstəgéiʃən/

名 調査；捜査，取り調べ

conduct	an investigation	調査する
carry out	an investigation	
begin	an investigation	調査を始める
launch	an investigation	
order	an investigation	調査を命じる
require	an investigation	調査を要する

▷The bank is **conducting** an **investigation** into how the computer data was lost. コンピュータのデータがどのように失われたのか銀行による調査が進行中だ

▷It's important to **launch** an **investigation** into how so many mistakes were made. どうしてそんなに多くのミスが生じたのか調査を始めるのが大事だ

▷This is a matter which **requires** further **investigation**. この件にはさらなる調査が必要だ

a detailed	investigation	詳細な調査
a full	investigation	十分な調査
a criminal	investigation	犯罪調査
a scientific	investigation	科学捜査

▷A **detailed investigation** took place soon afterward. すぐ後で詳細な調査が行われた

an investigation	into	A	Aの調査
under	investigation		調査中で
on	investigation		調べてみると

▷We should carry out an **investigation into** why the number of homeless people is increasing. ホームレスの数がなぜ増加しているのか調査を進めるべきだ

▷There's nothing I can say at the moment. The matter is still **under investigation**. いまのところ何も申し上げられません．この件はなお調査中です

▷**On investigation**, it was found that they had been given false information. 調査してみると彼らが誤った情報をつかまされていたことが判明した

investment /invéstmənt/ 名 投資

make	an investment	投資する
attract	investment	投資を誘致する
encourage	investment	投資を奨励する
increase	one's investment	投資を増やす

▷He **made** an **investment** in several large oil companies. 彼はいくつかの大手石油会社に投資した

▷It's important for us to **attract** foreign **investment**. われわれにとって重要なのは海外からの投資を誘致することだ

▷Now is not the time to **increase** your **investment**. いまは投資を増やす時期ではない

a good	investment	有利な投資
a safe	investment	安全な投資
capital	investment	設備投資
direct	investment	直接投資
foreign	investment	外国投資
private	investment	民間投資
public	investment	公共投資

▷I think you made a really **good investment**. あなたは実に有利な投資をしましたね

▷It is very important to increase **public investment** in the health service. 医療サービスへの公共投資を増やすことがきわめて重要だ

invitation /invətéiʃən/ 名 招待；招待状

give	an invitation	招待する
extend	an invitation	
receive	an invitation	招待を受ける
get	an invitation	
accept	an invitation	招待に応じる
refuse	an invitation	招待を断る
turn down	an invitation	
decline	an invitation	

▷He **extended** an **invitation** to all his friends on the occasion of his graduation party. 卒業パーティ

| invite |

-にあたり彼は友だち全員を招待した

▷ Please **accept** an **invitation** *to* our wedding. 私たちの結婚式にご招待しますのでぜひお出でください

▷ I'm sorry. I'll have to **decline** your **invitation**. 残念ですがご招待をお受けできません

a formal	invitation	正式な招待

▷ I still haven't received a **formal invitation**. まだ正式な招待を受けていない

invitation	to A	Aへの招待

▷ I just got an **invitation to** dinner from Mike and Helen. マイクとヘレンから夕食の招待を受けたところだ

at	the invitation of A	Aの招きで
at	A's invitation	
by	invitation (only)	招待者に限る

▷ I've come **at** the **invitation of** Professor Thornton. ソーントン教授の招きで参りました

▷ Admission is **by invitation only**. 入場は招待者に限ります

invite /inváit/

動 招待する, 招く；勧める, 促す

formally	invite	正式に招待する
cordially	invite	謹んで招待する
kindly	invite	丁重に招待する
warmly	invite	温かく招待する
invite	along	いっしょに誘う
invite	back	(いっしょに外出した後)自宅に招く
invite	in	家に招き入れる
invite	out	デートに誘う
invite	over	家に招く

▷ We **cordially invite** you to a party at our house on the 28th of this month. 今月28日の当家でのパーティーに謹んでご招待申し上げます

▷ I was **kindly invited** to give a speech at her wedding. 光栄にも彼女の結婚式でスピーチをするよう頼まれた

▷ I think we should **invite** Tom **along** on our trip to Canada. カナダ旅行にトムもいっしょに誘ったらどうかな

▷ After visiting the exhibition, Anna **invited** me **back** for a meal. 展覧会に出かけたあとでアンナは私を自宅での食事に招いてくれた

▷ Tom's **invited** me **out**! Finally!!! トムがデートに誘ってくれたの. 待ちに待ったわ

▷ Would you like to **invite** Eddie **over** for supper tonight? エディーを今夜の夕食に招待したらいかが

invite A	for B	AをBに招待する
invite A	to B	

▷ She **invited** Peter **for** dinner. 彼女はピーターをディナーに招待した

▷ I'd like to **invite** you **to** dinner this weekend. この週末にディナーにご招待したいのですが

invite A	to do	Aに…するよう招く； …するよう求める

▷ They **invited** him **to** stand up and sing another song. 立ち上がってもう一曲歌うよう彼は求められた

▷ He was **invited to** propose a toast. 彼は乾杯の音頭をとるよう求められた

involve /inválv | -vólv/

動 巻き込む, 関与させる；熱中させる

inevitably	involve	必然的に含む
necessarily	involve	

▷ The company's new plan **inevitably involves** job losses. 社の新規計画を進めればいやおうなく職を失う人が出てくる

involve A	in B	AをBにかかわらせる
involve oneself	in A	Aに深くかかわる

▷ I don't want to **involve** her **in** a difficult situation. 彼女を困難な状況に巻き込みたくない

▷ I don't want to **involve** myself **in** your personal affairs. あなたの個人的なことにかかわりたくない

involve	doing	…することを含む

▷ Taking this job has **involved** doing a lot of overtime. この仕事に就いてかなり残業することになった

involved /inválvd | -vólvd/

形 かかわって

closely	involved	密接にかかわって
heavily	involved	深くかかわって
deeply	involved	
actively	involved	積極的にかかわって
directly	involved	直接かかわって

▷ I have been **closely involved** in the work of two committees. 私は2つの委員会の仕事に密接にかかわっている

▷ Jennifer is **heavily involved** in the women's

movement. ジェニファーは女性運動に深くかかわっている

▷He is **actively involved** in the Communist Party. 彼は共産党に積極的にかかわっている

be involved	in A	Aにかかわっている
be involved	with A	
be involved	with A	Aと恋愛関係になる

★ get involved, become involved も用いる

▷More than 5,000 people were **involved in** the demonstration. 5千人以上がデモに加わった

▷He never **gets involved with** his colleagues at work. 彼は職場の同僚とは決して恋愛関係にならない

iron /áiərn/ 名 鉄

iron and steel	鉄鋼

▷The **iron and steel** industries were particularly important in 19th century Britain. 鉄鋼業は19世紀のイギリスでは特に重要だった

island /áilənd/ 名 島

a small	island	小さな島
a remote	island	離島
a tropical	island	熱帯の島
a volcanic	island	火山島
a desert	island	無人島

▷It's only a **small island**, but both countries claim it is theirs. 小さな島にすぎないが、両国はそれが自分たちの島だと主張している

▷Saint Helena is a **volcanic island** in the Atlantic ocean. セントヘレナは大西洋にある火山島です

issue /íʃuː/ 名 問題, 問題点

raise	an issue	問題を提起する
address	an issue	問題に取り組む
consider	an issue	問題を検討する
examine	an issue	
discuss	an issue	問題を議論する
resolve	an issue	問題を解決する
confuse	an issue	問題をぼかす

▷Before we close the meeting I'd like to **raise an issue** if I may... 会議を終える前によろしければ問題を提起したいのですが

▷These days politicians fail to **address** the most important **issues**. 最近の政治家たちは最重要問題に取り組んでいない

a major	issue	大きな問題, 大問題
a big	issue	問題
an important	issue	重要な問題
a key	issue	
the main	issue	主要問題
a central	issue	中心的問題
a fundamental	issue	基本的問題
a thorny	issue	やっかいな問題
an environmental	issue	環境問題
a political	issue	政治問題
a social	issue	社会問題

▷This small problem has now turned into a **major issue**. このささいな問題がいまや大問題になった

▷Abuse of drink and drugs is an important **social issue**. 酒と薬物の乱用は大きな社会問題だ

at	issue	論争中の, 争点の

▷We're all agreed about that. That point is not **at issue**. みなその件には賛成です。そこの点は争点にはなっていません

item /áitəm/ 名 項目；品目；記事

select	an item	品目を選ぶ

▷She **selected** several **items** that were discounted at 50%. 彼女は5割引きの品目をいくつか選んだ

individual	items	個々の項目；個別品目
an agenda	item	議題項目
a news	item	ニュース項目

▷You can either have a set meal or order **individual items**. 定食を選んでもいいし、一皿ずつ選んでもいいよ

item	on A	Aの項目, 品目

▷That **item of** news is of great interest to me. そのニュース記事は私にはとても興味深い

▷Let's move on to the next **item on** the agenda. 議題の次の項目に移りましょう

item by item	品目ごとに, 品目別に

▷The police checked everything in the house **item by item**. 警察は家の中にある物を一つずつ調べた

J

jacket /dʒǽkit/ 名 上着, ジャケット

wear	one's jacket	上着を着ている
put on	one's jacket	上着を着る
remove	one's jacket	上着を脱ぐ
take off	one's jacket	

▷ Why don't you **put on** your **jacket**? It's getting cold. 上着を着たら？寒くなってきたから
▷ Do you mind if I **take off** my **jacket**? 上着を脱いでも構いませんか

a jacket and tie		上着にネクタイ

▷ Dress is formal. **Jacket and tie**. 正装でおいでください．上着にネクタイ着用のこと

a denim	jacket	デニムのジャケット
a leather	jacket	革のジャケット
a tweed	jacket	ツイードのジャケット
a dinner	jacket	タキシード
a life	jacket	救命胴衣

▷ It's a formal dinner. You'd better wear a **dinner jacket**. 正式なディナーなので，タキシードを着なさい

jam /dʒǽm/ 名 ジャム

spread	jam	ジャムを塗る

▷ He likes to **spread** a lot of **jam** on his toast. 彼はトーストにたっぷりジャムを塗るのが好きだ

homemade	jam	自家製ジャム
apricot	jam	アンズジャム
blueberry	jam	ブルーベリージャム
strawberry	jam	イチゴジャム

▷ **Homemade jam** tastes much better than the jam you buy in the shops. 自家製のジャムはお店で買うジャムよりずっとおいしい
▷ I love **strawberry jam** on my toast. トーストにイチゴジャムをつけるのが好きです

a jar of	jam	ジャム一瓶

▷ A **jar of jam** is so expensive these days. 瓶詰めのジャムは近ごろすごく値段が高い

jam /dʒǽm/

動 押し込む；はさむ；ふさぐ；動かなくなる

jam A	into B	AをBに押し込む
be jammed	with A	Aでいっぱいだ

▷ He hurriedly **jammed** all his clothes **into** his suitcase and rushed out of the house. 彼は急いでありったけの服をスーツケースに押し込んで，家を飛び出した
▷ Every bank holiday the roads are **jammed with** traffic. 銀行法定休業日はいつも道路が車で渋滞する

jam	up	動かなくなる
be jammed	together	ぎゅうぎゅう詰めだ

▷ There were far too many people in the elevator. Everybody was **jammed together**. エレベーターに人が乗りすぎて，ぎゅうぎゅう詰めだった

jaw /dʒɔ́ː/ 名 あご

clench	one's jaw(s)	歯を食いしばる
set	one's jaw	

▷ "I'm not going to drink that horrible medicine," said the little girl and **clenched** her **jaws** until they ached! 「あんな薬を飲むのは絶対にいや」と少女は言って，痛くなるくらい歯を食いしばった

the lower	jaw	下あご
the upper	jaw	上あご
a square	jaw	角張ったあご
a broken	jaw	骨の折れたあご
a fractured	jaw	

▷ I can't move my **lower jaw**. 下あごが動かせない
▷ After the car crash they found that he had got a **broken jaw**. 車の衝突事故の後，彼はあごの骨を折っているとわかった

A's jaw	tightens	あごがこわばる
A's jaw	drops	あんぐり口を開ける

▷ Her **jaw dropped** in astonishment. 彼女は驚いて口をあんぐり開けた

job /dʒáb | dʒɔ́b/ 名 仕事, 職；務め

have	a job	仕事に就いている
do	a job	仕事をする
look for	a job	仕事を探す
apply for	a job	求人に応募する
find	a job	仕事を見つける
get	a job	仕事を得る
take	a job	仕事に就く

land	a job	仕事にありつく
lose	one's job	失業する
quit	one's job	仕事を辞める
give up	one's job	
offer	a job	仕事を提供する
create	jobs	雇用を創出する
change	jobs	転職する

▷I **had** a permanent **job** in Chicago. シカゴで定職に就いていました
▷I'm happy to **do** a **job** there. そこで働けてうれしい
▷I'm out of work. I'm **looking for** a **job**. 失業中で仕事を探しています
▷She **applied for** a **job** as a waitress in a restaurant. 彼女はレストランのウエートレスの仕事に応募した
▷She **found** a **job** at the airport. 彼女は空港で仕事を見つけた
▷She **got** a new **job** last month. 彼女は先月新しい仕事に就いた
▷She **took** a **job** as a police officer. 彼女は警察官の仕事に就いた
▷Ken **lost** his **job** last month. ケンは先月失業した
▷I've had enough. I'm going to **quit** my **job**. もうたくさんだ. 仕事を辞めるよ
▷He **offered** me a **job** as his assistant. 彼は助手の仕事を私にくれた

a boring	job	退屈な仕事
a rewarding	job	報われる仕事
a satisfying	job	やりがいのある仕事
a demanding	job	きつい仕事
a well-paid	job	給料のいい仕事
a low-paid	job	給料の悪い仕事
a full-time	job	常勤の仕事
a part-time	job	非常勤の仕事
a steady	job	安定した仕事
a stable	job	
a permanent	job	定職
a temporary	job	臨時の仕事
a proper	job	ちゃんとした仕事
a big	job	大仕事

▷It seems many people can't find **satisfying jobs** right now. 昨今はやりがいのある仕事を見つけられない人が多いようだ
▷It turned out to be a really **demanding job**. それはすごくきつい仕事であるとわかった
▷Teaching is never a very **well-paid job**. 教職は決して給料のよい仕事ではない
▷She's got a **part-time job** at MacDonald's. 彼女はマクドナルドでバイトを見つけた
▷She wants to marry someone with a **stable job**. 彼女は安定した仕事をもった人と結婚したがっている
▷I only have a part-time job now, but want to get a **proper job** as soon as I can. いまはアルバイトだけど, できるだけ早くちゃんとした仕事に就きたい
▷That's a **big job**! それは大仕事だな

| out of | a job | 失業中で |
| on | the job | 仕事中で; 実地で |

▷I'm **out of** a **job** now. いま失業中です
▷He had a heart attack and died **on the job**. 彼は心臓発作を起こして業務中に亡くなった

PHRASES＞
Good job! ☺ よくやった ▷You did really well. Good job! とてもうまくいったね. よくやった
That's my job. それは私の仕事だ

joke /dʒóuk/ 名 冗談, ジョーク

make	a joke	冗談を飛ばす
tell	a joke	
crack	a joke	
enjoy	a joke	冗談を楽しむ
have	a joke	冗談を言い合う
share	a joke	冗談をいっしょに楽しむ
get	the joke	冗談がわかる
take	a joke	冗談を冗談としてとる
play	a joke	からかう

★× say a joke とはいわない

▷He's quite fun to be with. He's always **making jokes**. 彼はいっしょにいるととても楽しいやつで, いつも冗談ばかりだ
▷Mr. Carter is not the best person to **have** a **joke with**. He has no sense of humor at all! カーターさんに冗談を言ってもだめだね. ユーモアのセンスのかけらもない人だから
▷What are you laughing at? Come on! **Share** the **joke**! なぜ笑ってるの？ねえ, 何がおもしろいのか教えて
▷He doesn't like to be laughed at. He can't **take** a **joke**. 彼は笑い者にされるのが好きじゃない. 冗談を冗談として済ませられない人だから
▷He loves **playing jokes** on people. 彼は人をからかうのが好きだ

a good	joke	うまい冗談
a bad	joke	悪い冗談
a silly	joke	ばかげた冗談
a stupid	joke	
an old	joke	言い古された冗談
a cruel	joke	きつい冗談
a sick	joke	趣味の悪い冗談
a dirty	joke	下品な冗談
a practical	joke	悪ふざけ

▷That's a **good joke**! ☺ うまいジョークだね
▷You shouldn't tell **dirty jokes** when there are

| journalist |

women around. 女性のいるところで下品な冗談を言ってはいけません

▷Be careful of Tony! He likes playing **practical jokes**. トニーに気をつけなさい．いたずら好きだから

| a joke | about A | Aについての冗談 |

▷He told me this terrific **joke about** an Englishman and an Irishman. イングランド人とアイルランド人についてのこの傑作ジョークを彼から教えてもらった

PHRASES
It's a joke. ☺ 冗談だよ
It's no joke. ☺ 冗談ではありません

journalist /dʒə́ːrnəlist/
名 ジャーナリスト

a freelance	journalist	フリーの記者
a foreign	journalist	外国人記者
a financial	journalist	経済記者
a political	journalist	政治記者

▷**Foreign journalists** are no longer being allowed into the country. 外国人記者はもはやその国への入国を許可されていない

journey /dʒə́ːrni/ 名 旅行, 移動

make	a journey	旅行する
begin	a journey	旅に出る
go on	a journey	
set out on	a journey	
continue	one's journey	旅を続ける
break	one's journey	旅を中断する
complete	one's journey	旅を終える

▷She's always wanted to **go on a journey** around the world. かねてから彼女は世界一周旅行をしたがっていた

▷Some friends of mine have just **set out on** a **journey** up the Amazon. 友人の何人かがアマゾン川をさかのぼる旅に出発したところだ

▷Finally he **completed** his **journey** around the world. ついに彼は世界一周旅行を成し遂げた

a long	journey	長期の旅行
a short	journey	短期の旅行
a hazardous	journey	危険な旅行
a dangerous	journey	

▷It's quite a **long journey** by car from London to Edinburgh. About 7 hours. ロンドンからエディンバラへ車で移動するのはかなり時間がかかる．だいたい7時間だ

PHRASES
Safe journey! / Have a safe journey. ☺ 道中ご無事で
Safe journey home! / Safe journey back! ☺ 気をつけて帰ってね

joy /dʒɔ́i/ 名 喜び, 歓喜

bring	joy	喜びをもたらす
share	A's joy	喜びを分かち合う
discover	the joy	喜びを発見する

▷Her piano playing **brought joy** to many people. 彼女のピアノ演奏は多くの人たちを喜ばせた

▷The whole nation **shared** her **joy** at winning the world title. 国中が世界タイトルを獲得した彼女と喜びを分かち合った

pure	joy	純粋な喜び
sheer	joy	
a real	joy	本当の喜び
a great	joy	大きな喜び

▷It must have been a **great joy** for them when their baby was born. 赤ん坊の誕生は彼らにとって大きな喜びだったに違いない

| for | joy | うれしくて, うれしさのあまり |
| with | joy | |

▷I'm so happy I could jump **for joy**! とてもうれしくてそこら中を跳び回りたいくらいだ（★ jump のほかに dance, sing, weep などともよく結びつく）

| joy and sorrow | | 喜びと悲しみ |

▷Often **joy and sorrow** seem to go hand in hand. 喜びと悲しみはしばしば手を携えてやってくるようだ

| be a joy | to do | …するのはうれしい |

▷It was a **joy to** see her so happy. 彼女がすごく喜んでいるのを見てうれしかった

justice /dʒʌ́stis/ 名 正義；正当性；司法

ask for	justice	正義を求める
do	justice	公正な扱いをする
administer	justice	裁く
bring A to	justice	Aを裁判にかける
escape	justice	法の裁きを逃れる

▷He didn't **do justice** to all the work that we put in to making that report. その報告書作成に費やしたわれわれの労苦を彼はまったく評価してくれなかった

▷The police spent 3 years looking for the murderer, but finally they **brought** him **to justice**. 殺人犯の捜査に警察は3年かかったが、ついに犯人を司法の手に委ねた

▷He thought he could **escape justice**, but the police caught him. 法の裁きを逃れられると思った彼だったが、警察に捕まってしまった

social	justice	社会正義
civil	justice	民事裁判
criminal	justice	刑事裁判

▷**Social justice** requires that criminals should go to prison. 社会正義からしてみれば犯罪者は投獄するべきということになる

with	justice	公平に、公正に

▷We should deal with criminals firmly but **with justice**. われわれは犯罪者を毅然と、しかし公正に扱うべきだ

a sense of	justice	正義感
a miscarriage of	justice	誤審

PHRASES
There's no justice. この世に正義はない、不公平ばかりだ

K

keen /kíːn/ 形 熱心な

extremely	keen	非常に熱心な
particularly	keen	特に熱心な
especially	keen	

▷We told her she could see some koala bears in the zoo, but she didn't seem **particularly keen**. 動物園でコアラが見られるよと彼女に言ってみたが、気乗り薄なようすだった

keen	on A	Aに熱心な

▷I'm not very **keen on** classical music. クラシック音楽にはあまり興味がありません

be keen	to do	…したがっている
be keen	for A to do	Aが…するのを切望する

▷She's really **keen to** meet you. 彼女はとてもきみに会いたがっている

▷My father is very **keen for** me **to** take the entrance exam to Tokyo University. 父は私の東大受験を強く望んでいる

key /kíː/ 名 鍵、キー；手がかり

insert	a key	鍵を差し込む
put in	a key	
turn	a key	鍵を回す
leave	a key	鍵を置いておく
hold	the key	鍵を握る

▷She **inserted** the **key** but it wouldn't turn. 彼女は鍵を差し込んだが、回らなかった

▷I can't **turn** the **key** in this lock. Maybe it's the wrong one. キーを差し込んでも回らないよ、キーが違うんじゃないかな

▷I'll **leave** a **key** for you on the table. テーブルの上に鍵を置いておきますよ

▷We're sure he **holds** the **key** *to* the mystery. 彼がなぞの鍵を握っているのは確かだ

the key	to A	Aの鍵

▷Hard work is the **key to** success. 勤勉こそ成功の鍵です

a spare	key	予備の鍵
a car	key	車のキー
a door	key	ドアの鍵
a house	key	家の鍵
a room	key	部屋の鍵
the arrow	key	矢印キー
the function	key	ファンクションキー
the return	key	リターンキー

▷Do you have a **spare key**? スペアキーを持ってるかい

a bunch of	keys	鍵束

▷Have you seen a **bunch of keys**? I thought I left them on the table. 鍵束を見なかったかい。テーブルの上に置いておいたと思ったんだが

kick /kík/ 名 けること；興奮、スリル

give A	a kick	A(人・物)をける
take	a kick at A	A(人)をける
aim	a kick	ねらってける
receive	a kick	けられる
take	a kick	
get	a kick out of A	Aに楽しみを覚
get	a kick from A	える

▷Hey! Ref! Did you see that? He just **gave** me a **kick**! ちょっと審判、見たかい。いま彼がぼくをけったよ

▷That horrible little boy just **took** a **kick** *at* me! あのくそがき、おれをけってきやがった

▷ The boy **aimed** a **kick** at the ball but missed. 少年はボールをねらってけったが，けり損ねた
▷ The karate player **took** a **kick** in the stomach. その空手選手は腹にけりを食らった
▷ He **gets** a **kick out of** teasing me. 彼は私をからかっておもしろがっている

a good	kick	うまいキック
a hard	kick	強烈なキック
a powerful	kick	力強いキック
a goal	kick	ゴールキック
a corner	kick	コーナーキック
a penalty	kick	ペナルティキック
a free	kick	フリーキック

▷ The goalkeeper gave the ball a **good kick** and sent it down to the opposite end of the pitch. ゴールキーパーはみごとなキックで敵陣ゴール近くまでボールを戻した

for	kicks	楽しみのために

▷ They didn't realize taking drugs was so dangerous. They just did it **for kicks**. 麻薬をやる危険性をあいつらはわかっていなかった．おもしろ半分でやったのさ

kid /kíd/ 名 子ども；若者

have (got)	a kid	子どもがいる

▷ He **has** a wife and three **kids**. 彼には奥さんと3人の子どもがいる

a little	kid	小さな子ども
a young	kid	幼い子ども
poor	kid	かわいそうな子

▷ Don't hurt him. He's only **a little kid**. その子にけがさせちゃだめだよ．まだほんの子どもなんだから
▷ **Poor kid!** He lost both parents in a car crash. かわいそうに．あの子は両親を自動車事故で亡くしたんだよ

kill /kíl/ 動 殺す

almost	kill	殺しそうになる
be nearly	killed	死にそうになる
be killed	instantly	即死する

▷ Climbing that mountain **almost killed** me! あの山に登って死ぬ思いをした
▷ He was **nearly killed** in a train crash. 列車の衝突事故で彼はあやうく死にかけた
▷ The truck exploded and he was **killed instantly**. トラックは爆発し，彼は即死した

be	killed in A	A(事故など)で死ぬ

▷ The whole family were **killed in** a car crash. 家族全員が自動車事故で亡くなった

A is	killing me	A(体の部位)が死ぬほど痛い

▷ Do we have to walk much further? My legs are **killing me!** まだまだ歩かなくちゃいけないの？脚がひどく痛いんだけど

kilometer /kíloumi:tər/

名 キロメートル(★《英》つづりは kilometre)

square	kilometer	平方キロメートル
cubic	kilometer	立方キロメートル

▷ About five **square kilometers** of forest was destroyed by fire. 約5平方キロメートルの森林が火事で焼き尽くされた

30 kilometers	from A	Aから30キロのところに

▷ Oxford is about 80 **kilometers from** London. オックスフォードはロンドンから80キロほどのところにあります

kind /káind/ 名 種類，種

the same	kind	同じ種類
a different	kind	異なる種類
all	kinds	あらゆる種類
every	kind	
any	kind	
some	kind	ある種類
another	kind	もう一つの種類
various	kinds	さまざまな種類
a particular	kind	ある種類
the right	kind	適切な種類

▷ I want to get the **same kind** of computer as yours. あなたと同じ機種のコンピュータを買いたい
▷ I think this is a **different kind** of rice. このコメは種類が異なると思う
▷ There are **all kinds** of reasons why I don't want to marry him. わたしが彼と結婚したくない理由は山ほどあります
▷ She was bitten by **some kind** of insect. 彼女は何かの虫に刺された
▷ You can buy heaters of **various kinds** in this shop. この店ではいろんな種類の加熱器具が買える
▷ Go to the **right kind** of doctor to find the **right kind** of drug for you. 適切な医師のところへ行ってあ

あなたに合った薬を見つけなさい

a kind	of A	一種のA
the kind	of A	Aのような

▷"What kind of cake?" "It was a **kind of** lemon cake."「どんなケーキ?」「レモンケーキの一種だったよ」
▷He's not the **kind of** person who would tell lies. 彼はうそをつくような人ではありません

that kind	of thing	そのようなこと
this kind	of thing	このようなこと

▷He's very active. He likes snowboarding, skiing, mountaineering – **that kind of thing**. 彼はとても活動的でスノーボード, スキー, 登山といったようなことが好きだ

king /kíŋ/ 名 王, 国王

be crowned	king	王位に就く
become	king	国王になる

▷William was **crowned King** of England on Christmas Day in 1066. ウィリアムは1066年のクリスマスの日にイングランド国王の座に就いた
▷He never thought he would **become king**. 彼は自分が国王になるとはまったく思っていなかった

the late	king	亡き国王
the last	king	前国王
the former	king	元国王
the future	king	未来の国王

▷The **late king** was greatly loved by his people. 亡き国王は国民からとても愛されていた

the King and Queen		王と王妃

▷The **King and Queen** will be arriving shortly. 王と王妃はまもなく到着する予定だ

kiss /kís/ 名 キス

give A	a kiss	A(人)にキスする
drop	a kiss	軽くキスする
plant	a kiss	強くキスする
blow	a kiss	投げキッスする
return	A's kiss	キスを返す

▷He **gave** her a **kiss** on the cheek. 彼は彼女の頬にキスした
▷He **dropped** a **kiss** on the back of her neck. 彼は彼女のうなじに軽くキスした
▷She **blew** a **kiss** to him on the way out. 彼女は出て行くときに彼に投げキッスをした
▷He kissed her but she didn't **return** his **kiss**. 彼は彼女にキスしたが, 彼女は彼にキスを返さなかった

a quick	kiss	すばやいキス
a long	kiss	長いキス
a gentle	kiss	軽いキス
a light	kiss	
a passionate	kiss	激しいキス

▷He gave her a **quick kiss** and rushed back to his car. 彼は彼女にすばやくキスすると急いで車に戻った

kiss /kís/ 動 キスする

kiss	gently	軽くキスする
kiss	lightly	
kiss	passionately	激しいキスをする

▷He **kissed** her **gently** on the cheek. 彼は彼女の頬に軽くキスした

kiss A	goodbye	Aに別れのキスをする
kiss A	goodnight	Aにお休みのキスをする

▷Did you **kiss** her **goodnight**? 彼女にお休みのキスをしたかい

kiss A	on B	A(人)のBにキスする

▷He **kissed** her **on** the forehead. 彼は彼女の額にキスした

knee /ní:/ 名 ひざ

bend	one's knees	ひざを曲げる
straighten	one's knees	ひざを伸ばす
fall to	one's knees	ひざまずく
drop to	one's knees	
sink to	one's knees	

▷If you're going to pick up something heavy you should **bend** your **knees**. 重い物を持ち上げるときにはひざを曲げたほうがいい

on	one's knees	ひざまずいて

▷He was **on** his **knees** hunting for something under the sofa. 彼はひざまずいてソファーの下を何やら探していた
▷He fell **on** his **knees** and begged her not to go. 彼はひざまずいて, 行かないでくれと彼女に懇願した

knife /náif/ 名 ナイフ, 小刀, 短刀

hold	a knife	ナイフを握る
pick up	a knife	ナイフを手にとる
carry	a knife	ナイフを持ち歩く

▷ You **hold** the **knife** in your right hand and the fork in your left. 右手にナイフ, 左手にフォークを持ちます
▷ He **picked up** a **knife** and started waving it around. 彼はナイフを手にとって振り回し始めた
▷ Be careful! He **carries** a **knife**! 気をつけろ. あいつはナイフを持っているぞ

a blunt	knife	刃の鈍いナイフ
a sharp	knife	刃の鋭いナイフ
a kitchen	knife	包丁
a bread	knife	パン切りナイフ
a butter	knife	バターナイフ
a carving	knife	肉切りナイフ
a pocket	knife	ポケットナイフ

▷ I can't cut the bread with this **blunt knife**. このナイフは切れ味が悪くてパンが切れない
▷ We need a **sharp knife**. よく切れるナイフがいる

| a knife and fork | | ナイフとフォーク |

▷ Do you find it easier to eat with a **knife and fork** or chopsticks? ナイフとフォークのほうが食べやすいですか, それとも箸にしますか

| with | a knife | ナイフで |

▷ He cut the rope **with** a **knife**. 彼はロープをナイフで切った

know /nóu/ 動 知っている, わかっている

know	full well	とてもよく知っている
know	perfectly well	
know	very well	
know	exactly	はっきりわかる
hardly	know	ほとんど知らない
be well	known	よく知られている
be best	known	最もよく知られている

▷ You **know full well** that I don't have the money to give you. きみにあげる金はないことはよくわかっているだろ
▷ I didn't **know** Tony **very well**. トニーのことはよく知らなかった
▷ I **know exactly** what you're feeling right now. あなたのいまの気持ちが手にとるようにわかる
▷ I don't love him. I **hardly know** him! 彼を愛してなんかいないわ. 彼のことをほとんど何も知らないのよ
▷ Liverpool is **best known** as the home of the Beatles. リバプールは何よりもビートルズ誕生の地として有名だ

| know A | about B | BについてAがわかっている |

★ A は anything, all, a lot など

▷ Do you **know anything about** his plans? 彼の計画について何か知っていますか ▷ She **knows a lot about** the life of Beatrix Potter. 彼女はビアトリクス・ポターの生涯についてよく知っている

| know | of A | Aのことを(聞いて)知っている |

▷ Do you **know of** anyone who could help me? だれか私を手伝ってくれる人に心当たりはありませんか

know	(that)...	…だとわかっている
know	wh-	…かわかっている
know	whether	…かどうかわかる
know	if	

★ wh- は what, where, why, how など

▷ How did you **know that** I stayed there? 私がそこにいるとどうしてわかったの
▷ Do you **know what** time it is? いま何時かわかる? ▷ I don't **know why** she's angry with me. 彼女がなぜ私のことを怒っているのかわからない ▷ Do you **know where** he lives? 彼がどこに住んでいるか知ってるか ▷ Do you **know how** to get to Forest Lane from here? ここからフォレストレーンへどうやって行くかわかりますか
▷ I don't **know whether** I can come on Thursday. 木曜日に行けるかどうかわかりません

| let A | know | A(人)に知らせる |

▷ Please **let** me **know** when he arrives. 彼が着いたら知らせてね

| be known | as A | Aとして知られている |
| be known | for A | Aで知られている |

▷ Matsui is also **known as** "Godzilla." 松井は「ゴジラ」の愛称でも知られている

PHRASES

Do you know what? / You know what? / Know what? 😊 ちょっと聞いて, あのね ▷ You know what? This is the first time I've ever tried to swim underwater. 白状するけどさ, 潜水は初めてなんだ
How should I know? / How do I know? 😊 私が知っているわけがないでしょう ▷ "How do you say 'Hello' in Russian?" "How should I know? No idea!" 「ロシア語で「こんにちは」ってどう言うの」「私にわかるわけないでしょう. 見当もつかないわ」

I don't know ☺ さあね；知りません ▷"Where do you want to go first?" "I don't know. It's up to you."「まずどこへ行きたい」「わからないな．きみに任せるよ」

I know ☺ (共感・同意を表して)そうだね ▷"It was very cold." "I know, I know." "And snowing..." "I know."「すごく寒かったね」「本当にねえ」「雪も降っていたし」「まったくだね」

Who knows? ☺ そんなのだれにもわからないよ；ひょっとするとそうかも ▷"Where's he going to?" "Who knows?"「彼はどこに行くのかな」「そんなの知らないよ」

Yes, I know. ☺ はい，わかっています ▷"You just have to wait two more years. Know what I mean?" "Yes, I know."「さらにあと2年お待ちいただかないと．言っていることがわかりますか」「はい，わかります」

you know ☺ (適当なことばを探して)ええと，あのう；(文尾で)(意見などを強調して)…なんだよ ▷Well you know–I'm a simple kind of guy. 何と言うか，おれは単純なたちなんだ ▷I don't like Harry, you know. ハリーが好きじゃないんだよ

(You) know what? / (You) know something? ☺ (話題を導入して)ねえ，知ってるかい ▷You know what? I think I'm drunk too. あのね，ぼくも酔っ払っているみたいだ

you never know ☺ (先のことは)わからないけどね，もしかすると ▷You never know. I might marry. 先のことはわからないが，ひょっとすると結婚するかもしれない

knowledge /nάlɪdʒ | nɔ́l-/

名 知識，知っていること

acquire	knowledge	知識を得る
gain	knowledge	
have	some knowledge	知識がある
have	little knowledge	知識がほとんどない
have	no knowledge	知識がない
extend	one's knowledge	知識を広げる
increase	one's knowledge	知識を増やす
require	knowledge	知識を必要とする
share	one's knowledge	知識を共有する

▷He **acquired** quite a lot of **knowledge** of the political system in the USA. 彼は米国の政治制度について相当の知識を得た

▷I **had little knowledge** of East Asian culture. 東アジアの文化について知識がほとんどなかった

▷He wants to **extend** his **knowledge** of the history of Japan. 彼は日本史についての知識を広げたいと思っている

▷Doing accurate research these days **requires** a good **knowledge** of statistics. いまの時代，精密な研究をするには統計学の知識が大いに必要だ

▷He refuses to **share** his **knowledge** with his colleagues. 彼は同僚と知識を共有するのを拒んでいる

common	knowledge	だれでも知っていること
detailed	knowledge	詳細な知識
general	knowledge	一般的知識
personal	knowledge	個人的知識
prior	knowledge	予備知識
previous	knowledge	
medical	knowledge	医学の知識
scientific	knowledge	科学の知識
technical	knowledge	専門知識

★個々の知識をさすときは不定冠詞をつけることがある

▷The fact that smoking causes cancer is **common knowledge** now. 喫煙ががんの原因になるということは今ではだれでも知っている

▷She has a **detailed knowledge** of modern American literature. 彼女は現代アメリカ文学に詳しい

▷I have no **personal knowledge** of her ability as a translator. 彼女の通訳としての能力を個人的に知っているわけではない

▷You shouldn't try to repair electrical faults without **prior knowledge** of electronics. 電子工学の予備知識もないのに電気故障を修理しようとするな

▷We need to employ someone with a good **technical knowledge** of building construction. ビル建設に関する十分な専門知識をもった人を雇う必要がある

knowledge	about A	Aについての知識

▷He has a very good **knowledge about** world history. 彼は世界史に非常に詳しい

knowledge	that...	…という知識

▷He had no **knowledge that** she was already married. 彼女は既婚者だと彼は知らなかった

with	A's knowledge	承知の上で
without	A's knowledge	知らないうちに

▷She dropped out of university **without** her parent's **knowledge**. 彼女は両親の知らないうちに大学を中退した

knowledge and experience	知識と経験
knowledge and skill(s)	知識と技術

★skill(s) and knowledge も用いる

▷He is a great coach who has a lot of **knowledge and experience** about soccer. 彼はサッカーについて豊富な知識と経験をもったすばらしいコーチだ

L

label /léibəl/

名 ラベル，荷札；(レコード会社の)商標，レーベル

carry	a label	ラベルがついている
bear	a label	
put	a label	ラベルを張る
attach	a label	

▷This sweater doesn't **carry** any **label** about how to wash it. このセーターには洗濯方法についてのラベルがついていない
▷I forgot to **attach** a **label** *to* my suitcase. スーツケースにラベルを張り忘れた(★put なら put a label *on*)

an address	label	宛名ラベル
a luggage	label	荷札
a designer	label	デザイナーブランド
a major	label	有名ブランド；メジャーレーベル

▷Write your name and address on the **luggage label**. 荷札に名前と住所を書いてください
▷The coats in this store are really expensive. They're all **major labels**. この店のコートはとても高いが，すべて有名ブランドだ

a label	on A	Aについたラベル

▷The **label on** this sweater says "Wash by hand." セーターのラベルには「手洗い」と書いてある

on	the label	ラベルに

▷There should be some washing instructions **on the label**. ラベルに洗い方が書いてあるはずだ

labor /léibər/

名 労働；労働者(階級)；分娩，陣痛(★《英》つづりは labour)

provide	labor	労働を提供する
reduce	A's labor	仕事を減らす
withdraw	(one's) labor	ストをする
be in	labor	陣痛がある
go into	labor	陣痛が始まる

▷Developing countries often **provide** very cheap **labor**. 発展途上国はかなりの低賃金労働者を供給することが多い
▷Modern inventions such as washing machines and dishwashers greatly **reduce** our **labor**. 洗濯機や食器洗い機のような現代の発明品は労力を大いに軽減してくれる
▷The factory workers are threatening to **withdraw** their **labor**. その工場の労働者はスト突入の構えでいる
▷She was **in labor** for over 16 hours before the baby was born. 彼女は陣痛が始まって出産まで16時間以上かかった

casual	labor	臨時労働者
skilled	labor	熟練労働者
unskilled	labor	未熟練労働者
cheap	labor	低賃金労働者
organized	labor	組織労働者
forced	labor	強制労働
hard	labor	重労働
manual	labor	肉体労働
physical	labor	
a difficult	labor	難産
an easy	labor	安産

▷There's a shortage of **skilled labor**. 熟練労働者が不足している
▷That company won't pay you very much. They're looking for **cheap labor**. あの会社はあまり給料を払ってくれないよ。低賃金労働者を求めているからね
▷They had to work 18 hours a day. It was **forced labor**. 彼らは1日に18時間も働かされた。まるで強制労働だった
▷The judge sentenced him to 5 years **hard labor**. 裁判官は彼に5年の重労働の判決を下した

lack /lǽk/ 名 欠乏，不足

the apparent	lack	明らかな欠如
a complete	lack	まったくの欠如
a total	lack	
a general	lack	全般的な欠如
a relative	lack	相対的な欠如

▷He was shocked by the **apparent lack** of enthusiasm of his students. 自分の学生たちが見るからに熱意を欠いていることに彼はショックを受けた
▷He has a **complete lack** of interest in his job. 彼は自分の仕事にまったく関心がない
▷I'm afraid there's a **general lack** of discipline in this school. この学校では全般的に規律が欠けている

lack	of A	Aの欠如

★Aは interest, confidence, experience, funds, information, knowledge, understanding など

▷Many people died because of the **lack of** good medical care. 十分な医療が受けられなくて多くの人が亡くなった

for	lack of A		Aが不足して
through	lack of A		
by	lack of A		

▷They couldn't complete the project **for lack of** money. 資金不足のため事業を仕上げることができなかった

ladder /lǽdər/ 名 はしご

put up	a ladder	はしごを立てかける
climb (up)	the ladder	はしごを上る
move up	the ladder	
climb down	the ladder	はしごを下りる
descend	the ladder	
fall off	a ladder	はしごから落ちる

▷If we **put a ladder up** *against* the wall we can climb in through the upstairs window. はしごを壁に立てかければ上の階の窓へ登って中に入れる
▷**Climb down** the **ladder** before the fire spreads! 火が回る前にはしごを下りろ
▷"How did he break his leg?" "He **fell off a ladder**." 「彼はどうして足を骨折したの」「はしごから落ちたんです」

the evolutionary	ladder	進化の階段
the social	ladder	社会の階段
the career	ladder	出世の階段

▷He's never been interested in the **career ladder**. He just wants an easy life. 彼は出世の階段に興味をもったことはない. ただ気楽な生活を望んでいるだけだ

the ladder	to A	Aにかけたはしご; Aへの階段

▷He slowly climbed the **ladder to** the roof. 彼は屋根にかけたはしごをゆっくり上った

lady /léidi/ 名 女性; 淑女

an elderly	lady	年配の女性
an old	lady	
a young	lady	若い女性
a lovely	lady	すてきな女性

▷There's a **young lady** waiting outside to see you. 若い女性が外で待って面会を求めています

▷Have you met Ben's wife? She's a **lovely lady**. ベンの奥さんに会ったことがあるかい. すてきな女性だよ

a lady	with A	Aを身につけた女性

▷The **lady with** gray hair and glasses is Emma's mother. 白髪で眼鏡をかけた女性はエマのお母さんです

lake /léik/ 名 湖

overlook	the lake	湖を見下ろす

▷She lives in a beautiful house **overlooking** the **lake**. 彼女は湖を見下ろす美しい家に住んでいる

a large	lake	大きな湖
a big	lake	
a huge	lake	巨大な湖
a small	lake	小さな湖
a man-made	lake	人造湖
an artificial	lake	
a freshwater	lake	淡水湖
a frozen	lake	凍った湖

★「大きな湖」を表すのにはlargeのほうがbigよりもはるかに高い頻度で用いる

▷We live near to a **large lake** in Switzerland. スイスで大きな湖の近くに住んでいます
▷Have you ever skated on a **frozen lake**? 凍った湖でスケートをしたことがありますか

on	the lake	湖で
in	the lake	
at	the lake	
around	the lake	湖の周りを

▷Let's go fishing **on** the **lake**. 湖に魚釣りに行こう (★× to the lakeとはいわない)
▷Let's walk **around** the **lake**. 湖の周りを歩こう

land /lǽnd/

名 土地; 陸, 陸地; 国土

agricultural	land	農地
arable	land	耕作に適した土地
cultivated	land	耕地
adjoining	land	隣接する土地
fertile	land	肥沃な土地
poor	land	やせた土地
industrial	land	工業用地
private	land	私有地

| land |

public	land	公有地
forest	land	森林地帯
open	land	開けた土地
one's **native**	land	故国

▷ There's a lot of **fertile land** near to the river. 川の近くに肥沃な土地がたくさんある
▷ It's **poor land**. Nothing grows well on it. その土地はやせていて，ろくに何も育たない
▷ I live in Japan, but England is my home country—my **native land**. 私は日本に住んでいますが，イギリスが故郷，私の故国です

an area	of land	（一定面積の）土地
a piece	of land	（一区画の）土地

▷ The proposed new town will cover a huge **area of land**. 提案されたニュータウンは広大な専有面積になる予定だ

by	land	陸路で
on	land	陸で

▷ It'll take longer to get there by sea than **by land**. そこへ行くには陸路より海路のほうが時間がかかる
▷ Penguins live half in the sea and half **on land**. ペンギンは海中と陸上で半々ずつ暮らす

■ land /lǽnd/

動 着陸する；上陸する，上陸させる；地面に落ちる

land	safely	無事に着陸する
land	heavily	強く落ちる

▷ Even though one engine was on fire the airplane **landed safely**. エンジンの一つが火を吹いたものの飛行機は無事に着陸した
▷ He fell from the window and **landed heavily** on his back in the garden below. 彼は窓から落ちて，下の庭にあおむけに強く落ちた

land	at A	A（場所）に着陸する

▷ We **landed at** London Heathrow at 8 o'clock in the evening. 晩の8時にロンドンのヒースロー空港に着陸した

■ landing /lǽndiŋ/

名 着陸，着地；（階段の）踊り場

make	a landing	着陸する

▷ The plane **made** a safe **landing**. 飛行機は無事に着陸した

a crash	landing	胴体着陸，不
a forced	landing	時着
an emergency	landing	緊急着陸
a safe	landing	安全な着陸
a soft	landing	軟着陸
the first-floor	landing	1階の踊り場

▷ The plane had to make a **forced landing** because of engine trouble. 飛行機はエンジントラブルのため不時着しなければならなかった

■ landscape /lǽndskèip/

名 風景；風景画；展望，状況

a beautiful	landscape	美しい風景
a rural	landscape	田園風景
an urban	landscape	都市景観
an industrial	landscape	産業景観
the political	landscape	政治的風景
the social	landscape	社会的風景

▷ The English painter, John Constable, loved painting **rural landscapes**. イギリスの画家ジョン・コンスタブルは好んで田園風景を描いた
▷ She hated living in such a small village. She was seeking a wider **social landscape**. 彼女はそんな小さな村に住んでいるのがいやで，もっと幅広い社会的風景を追い求めていた

■ lane /léin/ 名 車線；小道，路地

change	lanes	車線を変更する
turn into	the lane	小道に入る

▷ It's dangerous to keep **changing lanes** when you're driving. 運転中に車線を変えてばかりいるのは危険だ
▷ **Turn into** the **lane** and you'll see the church on the right. 小道に入ると右側に教会が見えます

the fast	lane	高速車線
the slow	lane	低速車線
the inside	lane	内側車線
the middle	lane	中央車線
the outside	lane	外側車線
the passing	lane	追い越し車線
a narrow	lane	狭い小道
a winding	lane	曲がりくねった小道

▷ I don't like driving in the **fast lane**. 高速車線を運転するのは好きではない
▷ Cars were traveling much too fast along the

outside lane.　何台もの車が外側車線をものすごいスピードで走っていた
▷Our car got stuck in a **narrow lane**.　私たちの車は狭い小道で動きがとれなくなってしまった

down	the lane	小道を通って
up	the lane	
along	the lane	小道に沿って

▷She walked **down** the **lane** to the post office.　彼女は小道を歩いて郵便局まで行った

language /læŋgwidʒ/ 名 言語, ことば

learn	a language	ことばを覚える
study	a language	
speak	a language	ことばを話す
understand	the language	ことばを理解する
use	language	ことばを使う

▷It's easier to **learn** a **language** when you're young.　若いときはことばを覚えやすい
▷"Can you **speak** any foreign **languages**?" "Yes, I can speak French and German."「何か外国語が話せますか」「フランス語とドイツ語が話せます」
▷When I arrived in England I couldn't **understand** the **language** at all.　イギリスに着いたときことばがまったくわからなかった

one's native	language	母語
a foreign	language	外国語
an international	language	国際語
the official	language	公用語
a common	language	共通語
spoken	language	話しことば
written	language	書きことば
everyday	language	日常語
body	language	身ぶり言語
sign	language	手話
computer	language	コンピュータ言語

▷We all learn to speak our **native language** without trying very hard.　だれでもみなそれほど苦労せずに母語を話せるようになる(★mother tongue ともいう)
▷In many African countries the **official language** is English.　アフリカの多くの国々では公用語は英語である
▷The **spoken language** is often very different from the **written language**.　話しことばはしばしば書きことばと大きく異なる

〈PHRASES〉
Watch your language! / Mind your language! ☺
ことばに気をつけなさい

| late |

large /láːrdʒ/ 形 大きい, 広い；多い

fairly	large	かなり大きい
relatively	large	比較的大きい
sufficiently	large	十分に大きい

▷A **fairly large** proportion of housewives have part-time jobs.　かなりの割合の主婦がパートの仕事をもっている
▷A **relatively large** percentage of the population supported the government's decision.　比較的多くの住民が政府の決定を支持した

large	enough	十分に大きい

▷This apartment isn't **large enough** for a big family.　このアパートは大家族が住むには広さが十分でない

get	large	大きくなる
grow	large	

last /læst | láːst/ 名 最後, 最後の人〔物〕

the last	to do	…する最後の人〔物〕

▷He was the **last to** arrive.　彼は最後に到着した

the night	before last	一昨晩
the week	before last	先々週
the year	before last	一昨年

▷I'm OK now, but the **night before last** I felt really ill.　もうだいじょうぶですが, 一昨晩はとても具合が悪かった(★「一昨日」は the day before yesterday という. the month before last「先々月」はあまり使わず two months ago ということが多い)

late /léit/

形 遅れた；終わりごろの；最近亡くなった

a bit	late	少し遅い
a little	late	
extremely	late	とても遅い
relatively	late	比較的遅い
too	late	遅すぎる

▷Sorry! I'm a **bit late**. The traffic was terrible.　ごめん, 少し遅れちゃった. 渋滞がひどくて
▷It's **too late** for breakfast and too early for lunch.　朝食には遅すぎるし, 昼食には早すぎる
▷It's **too late** *to* do anything about it now.　それに

271

| laugh |

ついては何をするにしてももう遅すぎる

late	for A	Aに遅れた
late	with A	A（支払いなど）が遅れた

▷Smith! You're **late for** class again! スミス．また授業に遅刻か

late	summer	晩夏
late	2010	2010年後半
the late	eighties	80年代後半
the late	19th century	19世紀後半
one's late	teens	10代後半

▷*In* **late autumn** the tree turns a wonderful red and gold color. 晩秋にその木はすばらしい赤と金色に変わる
▷It was built *in* the **late 19th century**. それは19世紀後半に建てられた
▷The woman is probably *in* her **late twenties**. その女性はおそらく20代後半だ

the late	John Cheever	故ジョン・チーバー
the late	Mr. Cheever	故チーバー氏

★× the late John とはいわない

▷The **late** John Cheever left hundreds of thousands of pounds to charity in his will. 故ジョン・チーバーは遺志により慈善事業に何十万ポンドものお金を寄付した

[PHRASES]
I'm sorry I'm late. / Sorry I'm late. ☺ 遅れて申し訳ない

laugh /læf | lɑːf/ 名 笑い，笑い声

give	a laugh	笑い声を上げる
have	a laugh	笑う
get	a laugh	笑いをとる
raise	a laugh	

▷Brad **gave** a little **laugh**. ブラッドは小さな声で笑った
▷"He's always playing jokes on people." "Yes, he'd do anything to **get a laugh**." 「あいつは人をからかってばかりだ」「そうだね．笑いをとるためなら何だってやるやつだよね」

a good	laugh	大笑い；楽しいこと；愉快な人
a little	laugh	軽い笑い
a short	laugh	短い笑い
a harsh	laugh	とげとげしい笑い

▷Let's get a group together and go to Disneyland! Go on! It'll be a **good laugh**! グループでディズニーランドへ行こうよ．さあ．きっと楽しいよ
▷"If you think you're going to marry my daughter you've made a big mistake," he said, giving a **short laugh**. 「きみが私の娘と結婚することを考えているなら大きな間違いだ」と軽く笑い飛ばしながら彼は言った

laugh /læf | lɑːf/ 動 （声を出して）笑う

laugh	loudly	げらげら笑う
laugh	aloud	
laugh	out loud	
laugh	heartily	心から笑う
laugh	a lot	大いに笑う
laugh	quietly	静かに笑う
laugh	softly	
laugh	nervously	不安げに笑う
laugh	harshly	とげとげしい声で笑う

▷Don't **laugh** so **loudly**! Everybody's looking at you! そうげらげら笑うなよ．みんながきみを見ているよ
▷The book I was reading was so funny that I **laughed out loud**. 読んでいた本がとてもおもしろくて大笑いした
▷"Oh! So you think I'm pretty, then!" she said and **laughed softly**. 「えっ，じゃ私のことをかわいいと思っているのね」と彼女は言ってそっと笑った

begin	to laugh	笑い始める
start	to laugh	
burst out	laughing	急に笑い出す
make A	laugh	Aを笑わせる

▷Tom's a really crazy guy! Once he **begins to laugh** he can't stop! トムは本当におかしなやつだ．一度笑い出すと止まらないんだ
▷When I told my brother that I had just dropped my cellphone down the toilet he **burst out laughing**! 携帯電話をトイレに落としたと弟に言ったら，あいつ吹き出したんだ
▷Don't **make** me **laugh**! ☺ 笑わせないでくれ

laugh	about A	Aのことを笑う
laugh	at A	A を（見て）笑う

▷It seems to be a serious problem now, but in a few days I'm sure we'll all **laugh about** it. いまは深刻な問題に思えるかもしれないが，何日かしたらきっとそのことを笑って話せるだろう
▷I was so embarrassed! Everybody was **laughing at** me! とても気恥ずかしかった．みんなぼくを見て笑っているんだもの

launch /lɔ́:ntʃ/

[動] 発射する, 打ち上げる；売り出す

be officially	launched	正式に始まる
recently	launched	このほど始めた

▷ Our new sales campaign will be **officially launched** next month. 我が社の新しい販売キャンペーンは来月, 正式に始まる予定だ
▷ The Government **recently launched** a new scheme to help the unemployed. 政府はこのほど失業者を支援する新しい仕組みに着手した

law /lɔ́:/

[名] 法, 法律；(個々の)法律, 法規

become	law	(法案が)法になる
enforce	the law	法を執行する
change	the law	法律を改正する
amend	the law	
obey	the law	法律を守る
keep	the law	
break	the law	法律に違反する
violate	the law	

▷ The police are finding it more and more difficult to **enforce** the **law**. 警察にとってその法を執行するのがますます困難になりつつある
▷ Everybody should **obey** the **law**. だれもが法に従う義務がある
▷ **Breaking** the **law** is a very serious matter. 法律違反はたいへんなことだ

civil	law	民事法
commercial	law	商事法
criminal	law	刑事法
common	law	コモンロー
company	law	会社法
copyright	law	著作権法
international	law	国際法
private	law	私法
public	law	公法

▷ She's studying **criminal law** at Cambridge University. 彼女はケンブリッジ大学で刑事法を学んでいる
▷ **International law** is a very complicated subject to study. 国際法という科目は研究するにはとても複雑だ

law and order		法と秩序

▷ The police are responsible for keeping **law and order**. 警察には法と秩序を守る責任がある

against	the law	法に違反して
by	law	法律によって
under	the law	法の下で
within	the law	法の許す範囲で
above	the law	法律が及ばない

▷ It's **against** the **law** to use a cellphone while driving. 運転中に携帯電話を使うのは法律違反だ
▷ In Japan drinking and driving is not allowed **by law**. 日本では飲酒運転は法律で禁じられている
▷ Driving without a license is prohibited **by law**. 無免許運転は法律で禁じられている(★ permitted, protected, obliged なども by law とよく連結する)
▷ The university is **within** the **law** to put up "NO SMOKING" signs. 大学が「禁煙」の標示を掲げるのは法律の許す範囲内だ

lawyer /lɔ́:jər/ [名] 弁護士, 法律家

consult	a lawyer	弁護士に相談する
see	a lawyer	

▷ It'll be expensive if we **consult** a **lawyer**. 弁護士に相談すると高くつくね
▷ You need to **see** a **lawyer**. 弁護士に相談する必要がありますよ

a defense	lawyer	被告側弁護士
a criminal	lawyer	刑事専門の弁護士

lead /líːd/

[名] 先頭, リード；前例, 手本；主役

have	the lead	リードしている
get	the lead	リードする
hold	the lead	リードを保つ
take	the lead	先頭に立つ
lose	the lead	リードを奪われる
regain	the lead	再びリードする
follow	the lead	前例にならう
follow	A's lead	後に続く
give	the lead	手本を示す
play	the lead	主役を演じる

★ have the lead, get the lead はリードしている距離を示す場合は次のようにいう：He has *a* lead of 5 meters. 彼は5メートルリードしている

▷ Jennings **had** the **lead** at the beginning of the race. ジェニングズがレースの初めはリードしていた
▷ Look! The Australian swimmer has **taken** the

| lead |

lead again! ほら，オーストラリアの水泳選手がまた先頭だよ
▷If we can persuade Pete to join our club I'm sure lots of others will **follow** his **lead**. うちのクラブに入るようピートを説得できたら，後に続く人がどっと出るだろう
▷We need somebody to **give** the **lead** and then everybody else will follow. だれかに手本を示してもらう必要がある．そうすればほかのみんながついてくるだろう
▷What's the name of the actor who's **playing** the **lead** in Macbeth? マクベスの主役を演じている俳優の名前は何？

a big	lead	大きなリード
a clear	lead	明らかな優勢
a narrow	lead	わずかなリード
an early	lead	早い段階でのリード

▷In the marathon the British runner got a **big lead**, but then lost it. マラソンで英国の走者が大きくリードしていたが，その後，先頭を奪われた
▷I think Taylor will win the race. He has a **clear lead**. テイラーがレースに勝つさ．明らかに優勢だよ
▷The Japanese team took an **early lead**, but in the end they lost 3-0 to China. 日本チームは試合当初はリードしていたが，結局3対0で中国に負けた

in	the lead	リードして

▷I can't believe it! We're actually **in** the **lead**! 信じられないよ．なんとうちが首位だ
▷Messi scored again before half time to put his team **in** the **lead**. メッシがハーフタイムの前に再び得点しチームが優位に立った

lead	of five points	5点のリード
lead	over A	Aに対するリード

▷The Australian swimmer had a **lead of** nearly 2 meters. オーストラリアの水泳選手は2メートル近くリードしていた
▷The U.S.A. team had a big **lead over** all the other countries. 米国チームは他国に大差をつけていた

lead /líːd/ 動 (先に立って)導く，先導する；リードする；率いる，指導する

easily	lead	簡単に至る
eventually	lead	最終的に導く
ultimately	lead	
inevitably	lead	必然的に導く
lead	directly	直結する

★ eventually, ultimately, inevitably は動詞の後でも用いる

▷If we don't take action now it could **easily lead to** problems in the future. いま何とかしなければ将来何かと問題の種になりかねない
▷The path **eventually led to** a small cottage in the middle of the forest. その道は森の中の小さな山小屋へとつながっていた
▷Many courses at the university **lead directly to** professional qualifications. その大学の講座の多くは専門職の資格と直結している

lead	to A	Aにつながる
lead A	to B	AをBに導く
lead A	into B	

▷I don't think this road **leads to** Oxford. この道はオックスフォードへは通じていないと思う
▷Finally, Beckham **led** his team **to** victory. 最終的にベッカムはチームを勝利に導いた

lead A	to do	Aを…するように仕向ける

▷He **led** everyone **to** believe he was a millionaire! 彼は自分が百万長者だとみんなに信じ込ませた

leader /líːdər/ 名 指導者，リーダー

elect	a leader	リーダーを選出する

▷We need to **elect** a group **leader**. グループリーダーを選ぶ必要がある

the former	leader	前のリーダー
a political	leader	政治指導者
a religious	leader	宗教指導者
the party	leader	党首
an opposition	leader	野党指導者

▷He was the **former leader** of the Labour Party. 彼は労働党の前党首だった

leadership /líːdərʃip/

名 指導者の地位；指導力，統率力

provide	leadership	指導力を発揮する
take over	the leadership	指導者の地位を引き継ぐ

▷In this situation we need someone to **provide good leadership**. この状況ではだれかにすばらしいリーダーシップを発揮してもらう必要がある
▷We need somebody new to **take over** the **leadership** of our party. わが党の指導者の地位を引き継ぐ新たな人物が必要だ

political	leadership	政治的指導力

▷ The Prime Minister showed great **political leadership**. 首相は優れた政治的指導力を発揮した

lack of	leadership	指導力の欠如
A's **style of**	leadership	指導スタイル

▷ Our country has suffered from **lack of leadership** for too many years. 何年にもわたってわが国には指導力が欠けている
▷ The President's **style of leadership** has been very impressive. 大統領の指導スタイルはとてもすばらしい

under	A's leadership	Aの指導力のもとで

▷ The health service was greatly improved **under the leadership** of President Obama. 医療制度はオバマ大統領の指導力のもとで著しく改善された

leaf /líːf/ 名 葉

come into	leaf	葉を出す
shed	leaves	葉を落とす

▷ The trees in our garden are beginning to **come into leaf**. 庭の木々が葉を出し始めている
▷ It's autumn and the trees are beginning to **shed** their **leaves**. 秋が来て木々は葉を落とし始めている

leaves	fall	葉が落ちる
leaves	turn red	紅葉する

▷ Look, Bill! The autumn **leaves** are **falling**! ビル,見てごらん.秋の葉が散っているよ
▷ The **leaves are turning red**. Autumn is coming. 木々が紅葉してもうすぐ秋だ

young	leaves	若葉
autumn	leaves	紅葉
dead	leaves	枯葉
fallen	leaves	落ち葉

▷ Insects prefer to eat **young leaves**. 昆虫は好んで若葉を食べる
▷ **Dead leaves** provide food for next year's plants. 枯葉は翌年に生えてくる植物の肥料になる

leak /líːk/

名 漏れ口;(水・ガスなどの)漏れ;情報漏えい

spring	a leak	漏れ出す
plug	the leak	漏れ口をふさぐ
stop	a leak	漏れを止める

▷ The hosepipe in the garden has **sprung** a **leak**. I'm soaking wet! 庭のホースが漏れ出して,びしょぬれになっちゃった
▷ There's water everywhere! We've got to **plug the leak**! そこらじゅう水びたしだ.漏れ口をふさがなくては

a leak	in A	Aの漏れ口
a leak	from A	Aからの漏れ
a leak	to A	Aへの情報漏えい

▷ Look! There's a **leak in** the water tank. 見て.水槽に漏れ口があるよ

a gas	leak	ガス漏れ
an oil	leak	油漏れ
a radiation	leak	放射能漏れ
a water	leak	水漏れ

▷ I think there's a **gas leak**. Stop! Don't strike any matches! ガスが漏れているよ.待った.マッチをするな

learn /lə́ːrn/ 動 学ぶ, 覚える;知る

soon	learn	すぐ習得する
quickly	learn	
gradually	learn	徐々に習得する
never	learn	何も学ばない

▷ This machine is not so difficult to operate. You'll **soon learn** how to do it. この機械は操作がそれほど難しくないから,やり方はすぐわかるよ
▷ Why did you go out in the freezing cold without a coat? You'll catch a cold! You **never learn**! 凍えるような寒さの中をコートなしでなぜ出かけたの.かぜを引きますよ.懲りない人ね

be surprised to	learn	知って驚く

▷ I was **surprised to learn** that Tom had been married twice before. トムは以前に2度結婚していたと知って驚いた

learn	about A	Aについて知る
learn	of A	

▷ We only **learnt about** her long illness after her death. 彼女の長患いについて知ったのは彼女が亡くなってからだ
▷ It was only after 6 months that we **learned of** his adventures in the Amazon Jungle. 6か月たってやっと彼のアマゾンの密林での冒険のことを知った

| leave |

learn	(that)...	…ということを学ぶ
learn	(how) to do	…することを学ぶ
learn	wh-	…を知る

★wh- は what, who, whether など

▷I **learnt that** when you're angry sometimes it's better to keep quiet and say nothing. 時に怒りを感じても、黙って何も言わないほうがよいことを知った
▷He **learned to** drive a car. 彼は車の運転を習った
▷He **learned how to** read music. 彼は楽譜の読み方を習った
▷We still haven't **learnt** exactly **what** happened. 何が起こったのか正確なところはまだわからない

leave /líːv/

動 去る、離れる；置いておく；…のままにしておく

leave	now	いま去る
leave	soon	すぐ去る
leave	immediately	直ちに去る
always	leave	いつも…のままにする
usually	leave	たいてい…のままにする

▷I'm really sorry, I've got to **leave now**. 申し訳ありませんがもうおいとましなければ
▷Oh! Is that the time? I'm afraid we'll have to **leave soon**. もう時間か。すぐ出かけなくちゃね
▷Why do you **always leave** your room in such a mess? どうしていつも部屋をそんなに散らかしているの

leave	for A	Aへ向けて出発する

▷They **left for** New Zealand last Thursday. 彼らは先週の木曜日にニュージーランドへ向けて出発した

leave	A B	A(人)にBを残す
leave	B to A	

▷Tom **left** Louise a lot of money. トムはルイーズに大金を残した (★Tom left a lot of money to Louise. よりもこの型のほうが頻度が高い)

leave A	to B	AをBに任せる
leave A	to do	Aに任せて…させる

▷**Leave** it **to** me. I'll get it done. 私に任せて。やっておくから
▷"Look at all that mess after the party!" "It's OK. You can **leave** me **to** do the clearing up." 「パーティーの後のあの散らかりようを見て」「だいじょうぶ。片づけは私がやるから」

PHRASES
I'm leaving. ☺ 行ってきます

lecture /léktʃər/ 名 講義、講演；説教

give	a lecture	講義をする
deliver	a lecture	
attend	a lecture	講義に出る
skip	a lecture	講義をサボる
get	a lecture	説教される
give A	a lecture	Aに説教する

▷He **gave** an interesting **lecture on** the English language. 彼は英語に関する興味深い講義をした
▷Hundreds of students **attended** his **lecture**. 何百人もの学生が彼の講義に出た
▷"I heard you had to see the headmaster. What happened?" "Oh, he just **gave** me a **lecture on** the importance of not missing classes!" 「校長先生に呼び出されたって？何があったんだい」「きちんと授業に出るよう説教されただけさ」

an inaugural	lecture	就任講演
a memorial	lecture	記念講演
a public	lecture	公開講演

▷Professor Dalton is giving a **public lecture** next week. ダルトン教授は来週公開講演をします

a course of	lectures	講座
a series of	lectures	一連の講義

▷I'm attending a **course of lectures** at Tokyo University. 東京大学の講座を受講しています
▷She's going to the U.S.A. to deliver a **series of lectures** on global warming. 彼女は地球温暖化について一連の講義をするために米国に出かけるところです

left /léft/ 名 左、左側；(the left で)左翼

on	the left (of A)	(Aの)左側に
to	the left	左の方に

▷Please turn to page 45 and look at the graph **on the left**. 45ページを開けて左のグラフを見てください
▷Sorry! I turned **to** the **left** when I should have turned right. ごめん。右折しなくちゃいけなかったのに左折しちゃったよ

from left	to right	左から右へ
from right	to left	右から左へ

▷The Arabic language is written **from right to left**. アラビア語は右から左へ書く

the far	left	極左、極端な左翼
the extreme	left	

▷Regarding politics, Tom's definitely to **the extreme left**. 政治に関してはトムは明らかに極端な左翼だ

leg /lég/ 名 脚, 足;(椅子などの)脚

cross	one's legs	足を組む
stretch	one's legs	足を伸ばす
swing	one's leg(s)	足をぶらぶらさせる
break	one's leg	足を折る

▷She sat down on the sofa and **crossed** her **legs**. 彼女はソファに腰を下ろして足を組んだ
▷I've been sitting in front of this computer for hours. It's time I **stretched my legs**! もう何時間もパソコンの前に座りっぱなしだ. そろそろ足を伸ばしたいよ
▷You've never ridden a horse before? Just **swing** your **leg** over the saddle! 乗馬は初めてかい？ただ片足を振り上げて鞍にまたがればいいのさ
▷He **broke** his **leg** in a skiing accident. 彼はスキーの事故で足を折った

on	one leg	片足で

▷The flamingo is a strange bird. It likes to stand **on one leg**! フラミンゴは奇妙な鳥だ. 一本足で立つのを好むなんて

a front	leg	前足
a hind	leg	（動物の)後ろ足
the rear	leg	
a broken	leg	骨折した足

▷My dog had a fight recently. His front legs are OK, but one of his **hind legs** is broken. うちの犬ったらこのあいだけんかしちゃって、前足はだいじょうぶだけど、後ろ足の片方が折れたの
▷He's in hospital with a **broken leg**. 彼は足の骨折で入院している

legislation /lèdʒisléiʃən/

名 立法;(制定された)法律

call for	legislation	法律の制定を求める
draft	legislation	法案を起草する
introduce	legislation	法案を提出する
pass	legislation	法案を可決する
adopt	legislation	法案を採択する
enact	legislation	法律を施行する

▷Many have **called for legislation** *against* discrimination at work. 職場での差別を規制する法律の制定を求める者が多い

under	legislation	法律のもとで

▷**Under** current **legislation**, eye tests are compulsory for working people with computers. 現行の法律のもとでは、コンピュータを使った仕事をする人々には目の検査が義務づけられている

leisure /líːʒər | léʒə/ 名 余暇;暇

work and leisure	仕事と余暇

▷It's important to make a distinction between **work and leisure**. 仕事と余暇の区別をするのが大事だ

leisure	facilities	娯楽施設
leisure	industry	レジャー産業
leisure	time	余暇
leisure	activities	余暇の活動

▷How do you spend your **leisure time**? 余暇をどのように過ごしていますか

at	leisure	ゆっくり
at	one's leisure	暇なときに

▷He didn't make any special effort to complete the report. He did it **at leisure**. 彼はレポートを仕上げるのに特別な努力をしたわけではない. のんびりやっていた
▷Completing a jigsaw puzzle is something you can do **at** your **leisure**. ジグソーパズルを完成させるのは暇にまかせてやることだ

length /léŋkθ/ 名 長さ;期間

measure	the length	長さを測る
have	a length	長さがある
reach	a length	長さに達する
extend	the length	長さを延ばす
reduce	the length	長さを減らす
run	the length of A	端から端までAの長さがある
walk	the length of A	Aをくまなく歩く

▷We need to **measure** the **length** before we buy new curtains. 新しいカーテンを買う前に長さを測る必要がある
▷The fish **had** a **length** of over 2 meters. その魚は全長が2メートルを超えた
▷The crack in the ice **reached** a **length** of over 20 meters. 氷の割れ目は20メートルを超える長さに達していた

| lesson |

▷I need to **reduce** the **length** of this dress by at least 4 centimeters. このドレスの丈を少なくとも4センチ短くしなくては
▷This path **runs** the **length of** the stream. この小道は小川の端から端まで延びている
▷We **walked** the **length of** the River Thames from London to Oxford. テムズ川をロンドンからオックスフォードまで歩き通した

the average	length	平均の長さ
considerable	length	かなりの長さ
the whole	length	端から端までの長さ
the full	length	
the entire	length	
the total	length	全長

▷The **average length** of a university lecture is about 1 hour. 大学の講義の平均的な長さは約1時間だ
▷The tsunami swept along the **whole length** of the coast. 津波は海岸全体に押し寄せた
▷He tripped over a chair and fell **full length** onto the floor. 彼は椅子につまずいて床にばったり倒れた

in	length	長さが
at	length	長々と，詳細に；ついに

★at length は 動詞 speak, talk, chat, discuss との連結が多い

▷This rope is useless. It's only 10 feet **in length**. このロープは役立たない，長さが10フィートしかないもの
▷We have to stop now, but we'll discuss this problem again **at length** at our next meeting. 今回はこの辺にして，次回の会議で時間をとってこの問題を議論しましょう
▷I explained and explained and explained! **At length** he understood! さんざん説明を繰り返した末にやっと彼はわかってくれた

for any length	of time	期間の長さを問わず

▷Did you ever live that wonderful kind of life **for any length of time**? たとえわずかの間でもそのようなすばらしい暮らしをしたことがありますか

by	half a length	半身差で

▷She's a great swimmer, but she got beaten **by half a length**. 彼女はすごい水泳選手だが，体半分の差で敗れた

lesson /lésn/ 名 授業，レッスン；教訓

have	a lesson	授業がある
take	a lesson	授業を受ける
give	a lesson	レッスンをする
skip	a lesson	授業をサボる
learn	a lesson	教訓を学ぶ
teach	a lesson	教訓となる

▷I'm going to **have** another German **lesson** on Friday. 金曜日にもも う一つドイツ語の授業を受けます
▷I started **taking** piano **lessons**. ピアノのレッスンを受け始めた
▷Jane **gave** her a **lesson** in good manners. ジェインは彼女に礼儀作法のレッスンをした
▷He'll never do that again. I think he's **learnt** his **lesson**. 彼は二度とあんなことはすまい．教訓になったと思うよ

an English	lesson	英語の授業
a private	lesson	個人レッスン
a valuable	lesson	貴重な教訓

▷Mistakes can often teach us a **valuable lesson**. 誤りはしばしば貴重な教訓を与えてくれる

a lesson	in A	Aの授業，レッスン
a lesson	on A	A(専門分野)の授業

▷If you want a **lesson in** how to deal with people, just look at Helen. 人との接し方を学びたいならヘレンを見てごらん

letter /létər/ 名 手紙；文字

write	a letter	手紙を書く
sign	a letter	手紙に署名する
address	a letter	手紙にあて名を書く
seal	a letter	手紙に封をする
stamp	a letter	手紙に切手をはる
send	a letter	手紙を送る
mail	a letter	手紙を出す
《英》post	a letter	
forward	a letter	手紙を転送する
receive	a letter	手紙を受け取る
get	a letter	
answer	a letter	手紙に返事を出す
reply to	a letter	

▷I've spent the whole morning **writing letters** of invitation. 午前中ずっと招待状を書いて過ごした
▷He **wrote** her a very long **letter**, but she didn't reply. 彼は彼女に長い手紙を書いたが，彼女は返信しなかった(★「彼女に手紙を書く」は write to her ともいう)
▷She **sent** a **letter** *to* the President of the University. 彼女は学長に手紙を送った

▷ We **forwarded** the **letter** *to* Head Office. その手紙を本社へ転送した
▷ We **received** an important **letter** from the bank this morning. けさ銀行から重要な手紙を受け取った
▷ I **answered** the **letter** from that company last week. 先週その会社からの手紙に返事を出した

an anonymous	letter	匿名の手紙
a formal	letter	改まった手紙
an official	letter	公式の手紙
a personal	letter	私信
a thank-you	letter	礼状
a fan	letter	ファンレター
a love	letter	ラブレター
a business	letter	ビジネスレター
a cover	letter	添え状
《英》a covering	letter	
a capital	letter	大文字
a small	letter	小文字
the initial	letter	頭文字

▷ Yesterday I received an **anonymous letter** accusing a member of staff of stealing. きのう職員の一人が窃盗を働いたと告発する匿名の手紙を受け取った
▷ Write your address in **capital letters**, please. 住所を大文字で書いてください

a letter	to A	Aへの手紙

▷ I'm writing a **letter to** my brother. 弟への手紙を書いているところだ

by	letter	手紙で

▷ I think we should answer **by letter**, not by e-mail. Eメールではなく手紙で返事すべきだと思う

level /lévəl/ 名 水準, レベル

achieve	a level	レベルに達する
reach	the level	
remain at	a level	レベルにとどまる
maintain	a level	レベルを維持する
raise	the level	レベルを上げる
increase	the level	
reduce	the level	レベルを下げる
determine	the level	レベルを測る

▷ In the exams she **achieved** a **level** far higher than anybody else. 試験で彼女はほかのだれより高いレベルの成績を収めた
▷ Electricity consumption **remained at** high **levels** in 2005 and beyond. 電気消費は2005年以降依然として高いレベルにとどまった

▷ The entrance exam is much harder now. The university **raised** the **level**. 入学試験は昨今ずっと難しくなっている. 大学が問題のレベルを上げたからだ
▷ How can we help **reduce** the **level** of poverty in developing countries? どうすれば開発途上国における貧困率を下げる手助けができるだろうか
▷ We sent out a questionnaire to **determine** the **level** of support for our policies. われわれの政策がどのくらい支持されているか測るためにアンケートを発送した

a level	rises	レベルが上がる
a level	falls	レベルが下がる

▷ Each year the **level** of our first year students seems to be **rising**. 年ごとに1年生のレベルが上がっているようだ
▷ The **level** of water in the lake is **falling**. We've had no rain for over 3 months. 湖の水位が下がりつつある. 3か月以上も雨が降っていない

a high	level	高いレベル
a low	level	低いレベル
top	level	トップレベル
national	level	全国レベル
a local	level	地方レベル
international	level	国際的なレベル
a general	level	全般レベル
the required	level	要求されるレベル

▷ There's a **high level** of interest in the new type of kitchen robot. 新型の台所用ロボットに高い関心が集まっている
▷ I think the students are very **low level** this year, don't you? 今年の学生はレベルが低いと思わないか
▷ At the moment she plays for a local team, but soon she'll reach **national level**. いまのところ彼女は地方のチームでプレーしているがすぐ全国レベルに達するだろう
▷ He's a good footballer, but maybe he's not **international level** yet. 彼はいいサッカー選手だが, たぶんまだ国際レベルではない
▷ I don't think she'll ever reach the **level required** to be a really good ice-skater. 彼女が傑出したアイススケート選手に求められるレベルに達するとは思えない

at	a level	…のレベルで
on	a level	
above	the level	水準より上で
below	the level	水準より下で

▷ **At** a personal **level** I like him, but I don't think he's the right man for the job. 個人的レベルでは彼のことが好きだが, その仕事に適任とは思わない
▷ Last year's students were definitely **above** the **level** of this year's. 去年の学生は間違いなく今年の学生よりレベルが高かった

▷The money supply was **below** the **level** of the previous December. マネーサプライは前の12月より下がっていた

liberty /líbərti/ 名 自由

protect	liberty	自由を守る
threaten	liberty	自由を脅かす

▷It's very important to **protect** individual **liberty**. 個人の自由を守ることはとても重要だ

civil	liberty	市民としての自由
individual	liberty	個人としての自由
personal	liberty	
political	liberty	政治上の自由
religious	liberty	宗教上の自由

▷**Civil liberty** is closely linked with human rights. 市民としての自由は人権と密接に結びついている
▷**Religious liberty** means that we can choose freely which god or gods we wish to pray to. 宗教の自由とは祈りを捧げたいと思う神を自ら選ぶ自由があることを意味する

at	liberty	自由で, 解放されて
liberty	from A	Aからの自由

▷The United Nations inspectors were **at liberty** to go wherever they wanted in Iraq. 国連査察官はイラク国内のどこに行くのも自由だった

liberty and equality	自由平等

▷Many countries have fought hard for **liberty and equality**. 多くの国々が自由平等を求めて必死に戦ってきた

library /láibrèri | -brəri/

名 図書館, 図書室

use	a library	図書館を利用する
borrow A from	the library	図書館からAを借りる

▷Young people don't **use libraries** so much these days. They prefer to play computer games. 若者は最近あまり図書館を利用しない. コンピュータゲームのほうがお気に入りだ

an academic	library	学術図書館
a university	library	大学図書館
a school	library	学校図書館
a local	library	地元の図書館

a public	library	公共図書館

▷I borrowed these books from our **local library**. これらの本を地元の図書館で借りた

license /láisəns/

名 免許；免許証(★《英》つづりは licence)

issue	a license	免許を発行する
grant	a license	免許を認める
get	a license	免許をとる
obtain	a license	
have	a license	免許がある
hold	a license	
renew	a license	免許を更新する
lose	one's license	免許を取り消される

▷The council have **granted** the pub a **license** to stay open until 2:00 a.m. on Saturdays. 議会は土曜日のパブ営業を深夜2時まで認可した
▷If you want to go fishing in this part of the river you need to **get a license**. この辺の川で魚を釣るには許可証がいる
▷Do you **have** a driver's **license**? 運転免許証をもっていますか
▷He was caught speeding and **lost** his **license**. スピード違反で捕まって彼は免許を取り消された

a license	runs out	免許が失効する
a license	expires	

▷You need to get a new license. This one **ran out** on September 1. 免許を更新していただかないと. この許可証は9月1日で切れていますよ

a provisional	license	(車の)仮免許

▷You need to get a **provisional license** before you can get a full one. 正式の免許をとる前に仮免許をとる必要がある

under	license	許可を得て
without	a license	免許なしで

▷He was prosecuted by the police for driving **without a license**. 彼は無免許運転で警察に起訴された

lie /lái/ 名 うそ

tell (A)	a lie	(Aに)うそをつく
live	a lie	うそをついて生きていく

▷Don't believe him. He's always **telling lies** about me! 彼の言うことを信じちゃだめだよ. ぼくのこと

でいつもうそを並べているんだから
▷ I **told** him a **lie**. ぼくは彼にうそをついた
▷ He told his boss he was very healthy, but actually he was **living** a **lie**. He was seriously ill. 彼は上司には自分はすこぶる健康だと伝えてあったが，実は彼はうそを抱えて生きていた．大病を患っていたのだ

| a pack of | lies | うそ八百 |

▷ We tried to find out the truth, but they just told us a **pack of lies**. 私たちは真相を見いだそうとしたが連中はうそ八百を並べ立てた

a big	lie	大うそ
a blatant	lie	見え見えのうそ
a complete	lie	まったくのうそ
a downright	lie	
a white	lie	罪のないうそ

▷ What? She told you I was married? Unbelievable! That's a **blatant lie**! 何ですって．彼女ったら私が結婚しているって言ったの？信じられない．大うそよ
▷ They told us that nobody would lose their jobs, but it was a **complete lie**. 職を失う者はひとりも出ないと私たちは告げられていたが，まったくのうそだった
▷ She told a **white lie** because she didn't want to upset him. 彼の気分を害したくなくて彼女は差し障りのないうそをついた

lie /lái/ 動 うそをつく

| lie | about A | Aのことでうそをつく |
| lie | to A | A(人)にうそをつく |

▷ How can I **lie about** my age? 年をごまかすなんてできるわけがない
▷ Don't **lie to** me. 私にうそをつかないで

life /láif/

名 生命；生活；生涯，人生；活力；生物

lose	one's **life**	命をなくす
risk	one's **life**	命を危険にさらす
save	A's **life**	命を救う
take	one's (**own**) **life**	(自ら)命を絶つ
have	a **life**	暮らす，生きる
live	a **life**	人生を過ごす
lead	a **life**	
spend	one's **life**	一生を送る
enjoy	**life**	人生を楽しむ
change	A's **life**	人生を変える
come to	**life**	生き返る；動き出す

| bring A to | life | Aに命を吹き込む |

▷ He **lost** his **life** in a mountaineering accident. 彼は山岳事故で命を落とした
▷ Thanks for lending me the taxi fare home last night Stella. You **saved** my **life**! きのうはタクシー代を貸してくれてありがとう，ステラ．おかげで助かったよ
▷ "Did he **take** his **own life**?" "Yes."「彼は自殺したの」「そうなんだ」
▷ He **had** a good **life**. He lived until he was nearly 90, didn't he? 彼の人生はいい人生だった．90歳近くまで生きたんだもの
▷ She **spent** her **life** try*ing* to help poor people in Africa. 彼女はアフリカで貧しい人々を助けることに一生を捧げた
▷ **Enjoy life** while you can! 楽しめるうちに人生を楽しんでおきなさい
▷ He decided to accept a job in Canada and it completely **changed** his **life**. カナダでの仕事を引き受けることにしたために，彼の人生は一変した
▷ It's fascinating watching Miyazaki's animation characters **come to life**. 宮崎アニメのキャラクターたちに命が吹き込まれるのを見ているとわくわくする

one's early	life	子どものころ
one's adult	life	成人のころ
one's later	life	晩年
a long	life	長い人生
a short	life	短い人生
everyday	life	日常生活
daily	life	
family	life	家庭生活
married	life	結婚生活
real	life	実生活
private	life	私生活
one's personal	life	
public	life	公的生活
a happy	life	幸せな生活
a hard	life	つらい生活
a quiet	life	静かな生活
a normal	life	普通の生活
rural	life	田舎の生活
urban	life	都会生活
social	life	社会生活
human	life	人間
animal	life	動物
plant	life	植物
marine	life	海の生物

▷ He wasn't at all interested in art when he was young, but *in* **later life** he took up painting. 彼は若いころは芸術にまったく興味がなかったが，晩年に絵画を始めた
▷ He had a **long life** and a happy one. 彼は長生き

▷These books and drawings give us a very good idea of **everyday life** during the Edo period. これらの本や絵から江戸時代の日常生活がとてもよくわかる
▷Disneyland is a fantasy world. **Real life** is entirely different. ディズニーランドはファンタジーの世界で，実生活はまったく別物だ
▷What I do in my **private life** is none of your business. 私生活で私が何をしようとあなたには何の関係もない
▷My granddad wants to retire and lead a **quiet life** in the country. 祖父は退職して田舎で静かな生活を送りたがっている

the prime	of	life	人生の盛り
the rest	of	one's life	残りの人生，余生
the end	of	one's life	人生の終わり，晩年
the quality	of	life	生活の質
a way	of	life	暮らしぶり

▷Now that I'm retired I'd like to spend the **rest of my life** reading books and playing golf. 退職したいまとなっては余生を読書とゴルフをして過ごしたい
▷At the **end of his life** he suddenly became interested in Christianity. 人生の終幕を迎えて彼は突然キリスト教に興味をもった
▷In many countries the **quality of life** has greatly improved over the last 100 years. 多くの国々ではここ100年で生活の質が著しく向上した
▷I need to change my **way of life**. 暮らしぶりを変える必要がある

all	one's life	一生涯
for	life	一生の，死ぬまで
in	one's life	人生で

▷She spent **all her life** doing her best to help others. 彼女は生涯を全力で人助けに費やした

life and [or] death	生と[か]死
life and work	生涯と仕事
the life and soul	座を楽しませる人気者

▷Quick! Hurry! Get my father to hospital! It's a matter of **life and death**! いますぐ，急いで．父を病院へお願いします．生死にかかわる事態です！
▷This book is about the **life and work** of Albert Einstein. これはアルバート・アインシュタインの生涯と仕事についての本だ
▷Pete is great fun to be with. He's always the **life and soul** of the party! ピートはいっしょにいるととても楽しい人で，いつもパーティーの座を和ませる人気者だ

PHRASES
Get a life! ☺ しっかりと生きなさい，ちゃんとしろ
▷All you do is sit around the house all day doing nothing. Get a life! きみは一日中家でごろごろしているだけじゃないか．しっかりしろよ
How's life (with you)? ☺ どう，最近は？ ▷I'm fine thanks. How's life with you? 私のほうは元気だよ．きみはどうなの
Life is but a dream. ☺ 人生はうたかたの夢だ
Life is short. 人生は短い
Not on your life! ☺ とんでもない，まっぴらだ ▷"I got a great idea! Let's take a ride on a roller coaster!" "No way! Not on your life!" 「いいことを思いついたぞ．ジェットコースターに乗ろうよ」「とんでもない．絶対にいやだ」
That's life. ☺ 人生なんてそんなものだ ▷"Every time things are going well for me something bad suddenly happens." "That's life!" 「万事順調なときに限っていつも突然何か悪いことが起きるんだ」「人生そんなものさ」
This is the life. ☺ これこそ人生だ，極楽だ ▷My father's credit card with no limit and all day to spend in New York! This is the life!!! おやじのクレジットカードでいくらでも金を使えて一日ニューヨークで過ごすなんて．大満足だ
What a life! ☺ 何ということだ ▷We have no job, no money and no hope. What a life! 仕事はないし，金はない，希望もない．ほんとにいやになっちゃうよ

lift /líft/ 名《英》エレベーター(《米》elevator)；《英》(自動車などに)乗せてあげること(《米》ride)

take	the lift	エレベーターに乗る
get	a lift	車に乗せてもらう
give A	a lift	Aを車に乗せてやる
offer A	a lift	車に乗せてあげるとAに申し出る

▷"Let's **take the lift**." "The lift? Oh, you mean the elevator. Americans say 'elevator'!" 「リフトに乗りましょう」「リフト？ああ，エレベーターのことですね．アメリカ人は"elevator"と言います」
▷There's no buses or taxis at this time of night. You need to **get a lift** to the station. 夜のこんな時間にはバスもタクシーもない．車で送ってもらわないと
▷I'll **give** you a **lift** home. 家まで車で送ってあげるよ
▷I **offered** him a **lift**, and he said he wasn't in a hurry. 彼に車で送ってあげようと言ったが，急いでいないからと彼は言った

light /láit/

名 光，光線；明かり，電灯；信号

emit	light	光を放つ
cast	light	
shed	light	

put on	a light	明かりをつける
switch on	a light	
turn on	a light	
put off	a light	明かりを消す
switch off	a light	
turn off	a light	

▷ Can you **turn** the light **on**? 明かりをつけてもらえますか
▷ **Switch off** the **light**, please. 明かりを消してください

light	shines	光が輝く
a light	comes on	明かりがつく
a light	is on	明かりがついている
a light	is off	明かりが消えている
a light	goes down	明かりが弱くなる
a light	goes out	明かりが消える
a light	goes off	

▷ You press the switch and the **light comes on**. スイッチを押すと明かりがつく
▷ Tom must be home. The **light** is **on** in his bedroom. トムは家にいるに違いない。寝室に明かりがついているから
▷ There was a power cut and all the **lights went out**. 停電があって明かりがすべて消えた

bright	light	明るい光
dim	light	かすかな光
natural	light	自然光
infrared	light	赤外光
ultraviolet	light	紫外光
reflected	light	反射光
fluorescent	light	蛍光灯
neon	light	ネオン灯
a street	light	街灯
a warning	light	警告灯
a green	light	青信号
a yellow	light	黄信号
a red	light	赤信号

▷ He didn't stop at a **red light**. 彼は赤信号で止まらなかった

light and shade	光と影, 明暗

▷ Rembrandt's paintings show that he is a master of **light and shade**. レンブラントの絵画は彼が光と影の巨匠であることを示している

a beam of	light	一条の光
a glimmer of	light	きらめく光
the speed of	light	光速

▷ That sports car shot past us *at* the **speed of light**! そのスポーツカーは光速のようなスピードで私たちを追い抜いた

light /láit/ 形 明るい；軽い；わずかな

still	light	まだ明るい
fairly	light	かなり軽い
relatively	light	比較的軽い

▷ We should try to get down the mountain while it's **still light**. まだ明るいうちに下山を試みたほうがいい
▷ This suitcase is **fairly light**. I can carry it easily. このスーツケースはかなり軽くて持ち歩きが簡単だ
▷ These golf clubs are **relatively light**. They're better for a woman. こっちのゴルフクラブは比較的軽めだから女性向きだよ

like /láik/ 動 好きである

always	like	いつも好きだ
never	like	決して好きでない
particularly	like	特に好きだ
especially	like	
really	like	とても好きだ
rather	like	嫌いではない

▷ Our dog **never likes** having a bath. うちの犬はふろに入るのをとてもいやがる
▷ I **particularly liked** the end of your essay. きみのレポートの最後のところが特に気に入った
▷ I **really like** Japanese food. 日本食が大好きです

like	doing	…するのが好きだ
like	to do	
like A	doing	Aに…してもらいたい
like A	to do	

▷ Do you **like to** go to concerts? コンサートに行くのは好きですか
▷ I'd **like** you **to** finish this report by the end of the week. 今週末までにこのレポートを仕上げてもらいたい

like	it when	…の時が好きだ

▷ I **like it when** she sings. 彼女が歌っている時が好きだ

likely /láikli/ 形 ありそうな, らしい

seem	likely	ありそうに思われる

| limit |

▷ It **seems likely** to rain tomorrow.　あすは雨になりそうだ

likely	to do	…しそうである

▷ He's not **likely to** phone now. It's after midnight.　彼がいま電話をかけてくることはないだろう．真夜中過ぎだから

hardly	likely	ありそうにない
quite	likely	かなり可能性が高い

▷ They're **hardly likely** to be open for lunch now. It's nearly 3 o'clock.　店のランチをまだやっているとは思えないよ．ほとんど3時だもの

▷ "Do you think he'll quit his job?" "Yes, **quite likely**. The pay is very low."　「彼は仕事を辞めるかな」「うん，その可能性がかなり高そうだ．給料がとても低いので」

likely	(that)...	…しそうである

▷ It's **likely that** tomorrow's hike will be postponed owing to bad weather.　あすのハイキングは悪天候のせいで延期になりそうだ

more than	likely	ほぼ間違いない

▷ "Do you think the Liberal Democrats will win the next election?" "**More than likely**."　「自民党は次の選挙で勝つと思いますか」「ほぼ確実ですね」

limit /límit/

名 限界，限度；制限；境界，境界線

set	a limit	制限を設ける
impose	a limit	
put	a limit	
reach	one's limit	限界に達する
exceed	the limit	限界を超える
push A to	the limit	A(人)を限界まで追い込む

▷ The police have **set** a new speed **limit** *on* this road of 50 kilometers per hour.　警察はこの道路に新しい速度制限を設けて，時速50キロになった

▷ I think FIFA **imposes** a **limit** *on* the number of tickets that can be sold over the Internet during the World Cup.　FIFAはワールドカップ期間中インターネット上で売られるチケットの枚数を制限していると思う

▷ We've had to **put** a **limit** *on* the number of students that we can accept this year.　今年度の受け入れ学生数に制限を設けなければならなかった

▷ I've tried to be patient, but now I've **reached** my **limit**. I can't take any more.　我慢しようとしたが，限界だ．もうこれ以上は無理だ

an absolute	limit	どうにもならない限界
the lower	limit	下限
the upper	limit	上限
a strict	limit	厳しい制限
an age	limit	年齢制限
a speed	limit	速度制限
a time	limit	時間制限
a weight	limit	重量制限
a financial	limit	財政的な制限
a legal	limit	法定制限

▷ We can contribute $500 to the earthquake disaster fund, but that's the **absolute limit**.　地震災害基金に500ドルは寄付できるが，それがぎりぎりのところだ

▷ A **strict limit** was imposed on the number of immigrants allowed to enter the country this year.　今年はその国への入国を許可される移民の数に厳しい制限が設けられた

▷ Michael was arrested for drunk driving. He was well over the **legal limit**.　マイケルは飲酒運転で逮捕された．法定制限をかなり上回っていた

limit	on A	Aに対する制限
limit	to A	

▷ There is a **limit to** the number of people who can attend the lecture.　講義に出席できる人数に制限がある

beyond	the limit	限度を超えて
over	the limit	
above	the limit	
up to	a [the] limit	限度まで
within	a [the] limit	限度内で
within	limits	適度に，控えめに
without	limit(s)	無制限に

▷ Be careful when you're driving not to go **beyond** the speed **limit**.　運転では制限速度を超えないよう注意しなさい

▷ Don't go **over** the speed **limit**. It's 30 miles an hour and we're doing 45!　制限速度を超えちゃだめだ．時速30マイルが制限なのに45マイル出しているぞ

▷ We can offer financial help **up to a limit** of $50 per student.　学生1名につき50ドルの限度まで経済的な援助を提供できます

▷ He would do anything to get that new contract — **within the limits** of the law.　あの新しい契約をとるためなら彼はどんなことでもするだろう．法律の範囲内でのことではあるが

▷ You can spend as much as you like on your wedding — **without limit**!　結婚式には好きなだけお金を使っていいよ．限度はなしだ

PHRASES

there is no limit to A A に制限はない ▷That country's President is really dangerous. There's no limit to what he'll do to stay in power. その国の大統領は本当に危険だ．権力を維持するためなら何をするかわからない

limit /límit/ 動 制限する

extremely	limited	極端に制限される
severely	limited	厳しく制限される
strictly	limited	
necessarily	limited	どうしても制限される

▷I'm afraid the opportunities for promotion in this company are **extremely limited**. この会社では昇進の機会は極端に限られています

▷It's a small concert hall so tickets are **strictly limited**. 小さなコンサートホールなのでチケットの数はかなり限られている

▷We'd like to do more, but the amount of help we can offer is **necessarily limited**. もっとしてさしあげられるといいのですが，できる援助の量にはどうしても限界があります

limit A	to B	AにBの制限を課す

▷During the emergency, supermarkets **limited** the sale of bottled water **to** 2 bottles per person. 非常事態の間スーパーはボトルウォーターの販売を1人2本に制限した

line /láin/ 名 線；列，行列；(文字の)行；ひも；電話線，回線；路線

draw	a line	線を引く
mark	a line	線を引く；線で印をつける
cross	the line	線を越す
hold	the line	電話を切らないでおく
stand in	line	列に並ぶ
jump	the line	列に割り込む

▷We use a ruler to **draw** a straight **line**. 定規を用いて直線を引く

▷**Hold** the **line**, please. I'm putting you through. 電話を切らずにお待ちください．おつなぎしますので

▷If you go to Expo, you'll probably have to **stand in line** for hours. 博覧会に行けばおそらく何時間も列に並ばなければならないだろう

a straight	line	直線
a diagonal	line	斜線；対角線
a vertical	line	縦線；垂直線
a horizontal	line	横線；水平の線
a dotted	line	点線
parallel	lines	平行線
a fine	line	細い線
a thin	line	
a long	line	長い線；長い列
a short	line	短い線；短い列
the front	line	最前線
a direct	line	直通電話
the main	line	幹線

▷The children queued up in a **straight line** to get their present from Santa Claus. 子どもたちはサンタクロースからプレゼントをもらうためにまっすぐ並んでいた

▷"Have you definitely got that new job?" "Yes. Here's the contract. I've signed on the **dotted line**." 「新しい働き口はちゃんと決まったの」「うん．ほら契約書だよ．点線の上にサインしてあるだろ」

▷There was a **long line** of people waiting to get into the concert. コンサートを待つ人たちの長蛇の列ができていた

▷There was an accident on the **main line** from London to York. ロンドンからヨークへの幹線で事故があった

♦**there is a fine line between** A **and** B AとBとは微妙な差だ ▷There's a fine line between success and failure! 成功と失敗は紙一重

in	(a) line	一列に
in	line	列をつくって；合わせて
out of	line	合わせないで

▷Everybody was waiting **in a line** for the department store to open. デパートの開店をみんな一列になって待っていた

▷Let me know if he steps **out of line**. He has to obey the rules. 人と足並みのそろわない行動を彼がとったら私に知らせてほしい．彼も規則に従わなければならないのだから

link /línk/

名 結びつけるもの［人］，きずな；関連

establish	a link	関連づける
make	a link	
find	a link	関連を見いだす
prove	a link	
have	a link	つながりがある
break	the link	つながりを絶つ
maintain	a link	つながりを維持する
provide	a link	連絡をつける

▷Doctors have **established** a **link** between too

| link |

much exposure to the sun and skin cancer. 日光に当たりすぎることと皮膚がんの関係を医師たちは明らかにした

▷We think he **has a link** with some criminal organizations. 彼は犯罪組織とつながっているとわれわれは考えている

▷We need to **maintain** a **link** with our sister company in New York. わが社はニューヨークの姉妹会社とのつながりを維持する必要がある

▷We need to **provide** a better **link** between our manufacturing department and our sales department. 製造部門と販売部門の連絡をもっとよくする必要がある

close	links	密接な関連
a direct	link	直接の関連
a clear	link	明らかな関連
a strong	link	強い結びつき
a weak	link	弱い結びつき

▷People say he has **close links** *with* top people in the government. 彼は政府のトップの人たちと密接な関係があるとうわさされている

▷We have a **direct link** to our news reporter in Afghanistan. われわれはアフガニスタンにいるレポーターと直接つながっています

▷There's a **strong link** between alcohol and crime. アルコールと犯罪の間には強い関連がある

a link	with A	Aとの結びつき
a link	to A	
a link	between A	Aとの関連

▷Look at these old photos of our town 100 years ago. They provide a real **link with** the past. ほら，この街の100年前の写真だよ．過去とのつながりを実感させてくれるね

▷There's definitely a **link between** hard work and success! 一生懸命がんばれば絶対にうまくいくもんだよ

link /líŋk/ 動 つなぐ，連結する

closely	linked	密接に関連した
intimately	linked	
inextricably	linked	
directly	linked	直接に関連した

▷Poverty is often **closely linked** with crime. 貧困はしばしば犯罪と密接に関連している

▷Doctors say that cigarette smoking is **directly linked** with cancer and heart disease. 医師たちの意見では喫煙はがん，および心臓病と直接の関係がある

link A	to B	AとBをつなげる
link A	with B	

▷The new airport will be **linked to** London by road and rail. 新空港は道路と鉄道でロンドンと結ばれる

lip /líp/ 名 唇

bite	one's lip	唇をかむ
curl	one's lip	唇をゆがめる
lick	one's lips	唇をなめる
smack	one's lips	舌鼓を打つ
purse	one's lips	口をすぼめる
kiss	A's lips	唇にキスする

▷He wanted to disagree violently, but he **bit** his **lip** and said nothing. 彼は強く反対したかったが，唇をかんで何も言わなかった

▷He **smacked** his **lips** over the roast beef. 彼はローストビーフに舌鼓を打った

▷"Could you lend me $500?" he asked. She **pursed** her **lips**. "Well, that might be difficult." she said. 「500ドル貸していただけませんか」と彼が言うと彼女は口をすぼめて答えた．「それは無理かもしれません」

one's lower	lip	下唇
one's bottom	lip	
one's upper	lip	上唇
one's top	lip	

▷Did you hear? Tom was in a fight yesterday! He had a really bad cut on his **lower lip**. 聞いたかい．トムったらきのうけんかして下唇をひどく切ったんだ

list /líst/ 名 一覧表，リスト，名簿

make	a list	リストをつくる
draw up	a list	
compile	a list	

▷When I go shopping I always **make** a **list**. 買い物に出かけるときはいつも買い物リストをつくります

a long	list	長いリスト
a short	list	短いリスト；選抜候補リスト
a detailed	list	詳細なリスト
a full	list	完全なリスト
a complete	list	
a chronological	list	年代順リスト
a mailing	list	郵送先名簿；メーリングリスト

a shopping	list	買い物リスト
a waiting	list	順番待ちリスト
a wine	list	ワインリスト
a word	list	単語リスト

▷I've made a **long list** *of* people to be interviewed. 面接する人たちの長いリストを作成した
▷Maybe you'll get the job. I heard you're on the **short list** *of* applicants. たぶんきみは仕事にありつけるよ．面接の最終候補に残っているらしいから
▷I need a **full list** *of* everyone who will be attending the party. パーティー参加者全員のちゃんとしたリストがいる
▷I couldn't get a flight to London, but I'm *on* the **waiting list**. ロンドン行きの飛行機の座席がとれなかったので，キャンセル待ちなんです

on	a list	リストに

▷My name isn't **on** the **list**. 私の名前がリストにない
◆**high on a list** 優先度の高い

top of	the list	リストの最上位
bottom of	the list	リストの最下位

▷Three people are going to be promoted this year. Congratulations! You're name is **top of** the **list**! 今年の昇進者は3名の予定だが，おめでとう．きみの名前が名簿のトップだよ

listen /lísn/ 動 (注意して)聞く

listen	hard	よく聞く
listen	carefully	注意深く聞く
listen	attentively	
listen	intently	熱心に聞く

▷Please **listen carefully**. I'll only say this one time. よく聞いてね．一度しか言わないから
▷I can't understand why her lecture notes were so bad. She was **listening intently** throughout the lecture. 彼女がなぜあんなひどい講義ノートしかとれないのかわからないな．講義のあいだずっと熱心に聞いていたのに

listen	to A	Aを聞く；A(人)の言うことに耳を傾ける
listen	for A	Aに耳を澄ます

▷I like **listening to** classical music. クラシック音楽を聞くのが好きです
▷**Listen to** me. 私の言うことを聞いて
▷When I play the CD, **listen for** the answers to the questions I've written on the board. CDをかけますから，黒板に書いた質問への答えを聞きとりなさい

PHRASES
Listen (**here**). 😊 いいか，よく聞け
Now listen. 😊 さあ聞いて ▷Now listen carefully! You must hand in your reports by the end of this week. よく聞いて．レポートの提出期限は今週末ですよ

little /lítl/ 形 小さい；わずかな

too	little	あまりにも少ない
very	little	ほとんど…ない
so	little	
relatively	little	比較的少ない
only	a little	ほんのわずかの

▷I couldn't finish the exam. There was **too little** time. 時間があまりに少なすぎて答案を仕上げられなかった
▷We've had **very little** snow this winter. この冬はほとんど雪が降っていない
▷**Only a little** sugar and milk in my tea, please. 紅茶に少しだけ砂糖とミルクを入れてください

tiny	little	ちっぽけな
little	tiny	
lovely	little	かわいらしい
nice	little	すてきなかわいい
pretty	little	かわいらしい
poor	little	かわいそうな
silly	little	たわいない
stupid	little	

★ little の前に感情を示す形容詞がくる

▷They live in a **little tiny** apartment in the middle of Tokyo. 彼らは東京の真ん中のちっぽけなアパートに住んでいる
▷They live in a **lovely little** cottage in the country. 彼らは田舎のすてきなかわいいコテージに住んでいる
▷She's a **pretty little** girl, isn't she? かわいらしい女の子だね
▷**Poor little** thing! She's only four years old and she lost both parents. かわいそうに．ほんの4歳なのに彼女は両親とも亡くしてしまった

little	or no	ほとんどあるいはまったくない

▷There's **little or no** reason to suppose she stole the money. お金を盗んだのは彼女だと推測する理由がほとんど見当たらない

live /lív/ 動 住んでいる；暮らす；生きる

live	alone	ひとり暮らしをする

| living |

live	together	いっしょに住む
actually	live	実際に住んでいる
still	live	まだ住んでいる
live	happily	幸せに暮らす
live	frugally	つましく暮らす

▷Emma **lives alone** in a small apartment in Tokyo.　エマは東京の小さなアパートでひとり暮らしをしている
▷I'm not sure if they're married, but they're **living together**.　二人が結婚しているのかどうかはよく知らないけど，いっしょに暮らしているよ
▷I don't **actually live** in London. I just work there.　実際にロンドンに住んでいるわけではなく，仕事場がロンドンなのです
▷Are you **still living** in Tokyo?　あなたはまだ東京に住んでいるの

live	in A	Aに住む
live	at A	
live	with A	Aといっしょに住む

▷"Where do you live?" "**I live in** New York."　「お住まいはどこですか」「ニューヨークに住んでいます」(★ be living は一時的な居住を意味する：Akiko is living in England. She'll be there for 6 months.　アキコはイングランドに住んでいる．半年滞在する予定だ)
▷He **lives with** his family in Sydney.　彼はシドニーで家族と同居している

live	to be ninety	90歳まで生きる

▷Do you think you want to **live to be** a hundred?　百歳まで生きたいですか

living /lívɪŋ/ 名 生活；生計

earn	a living	生活費を稼ぐ
make	a living	生計を立てる
scrape	a living	どうにか生計を立てる
scratch	a living	

▷He **earns** his **living** doing part-time jobs.　彼はアルバイトをして生活費を稼いでいる
▷He had a really good job, but he lost it and now he **scrapes** a **living** doing a poorly paid part-time job.　彼はすごくよい職に就いていたのだが，失業してしまい，いまは低賃金のアルバイトでどうにか生計を立てている

daily	living	毎日の生活
everyday	living	
a good	living	いい暮らし

▷The stress of **daily living** in New York is very high.　ニューヨークで日々暮らすストレスはとても大きい

▷Famous soccer players and film-stars earn a really **good living**.　有名サッカー選手や映画スターたちは大金を稼いですごくいい暮らしをしている

for	a living	生計のために

▷What do you do **for a living**?　お仕事は何をなさっていますか

the cost	of living	生計費
the standard	of living	生活水準

▷The **cost of living** in Britain has gone up again this year!　イギリスでは今年も生計費が高くなった
▷We have to do something to improve our **standard of living**.　生活水準を上げるために何とかしなければならない

load /lóud/ 名 荷, 積荷；負担, 重荷

carry	a load	荷を運ぶ, 荷を背負う
bear	a load	
lighten	the load	負担を減らす

▷He's responsible for over 750 employees. He **carries** a big **load**.　750名を超える従業員に対する責任が彼にはある．重い荷を背負っているのだ
▷Bob's doing the work of two men. We have to do something to help him **lighten** the **load**.　ボブは2人分の仕事をしており，彼を手伝って負担を軽くするために何とかしなければならない

a heavy	load	重い荷；重い負担
a light	load	軽い荷；軽い負担
a full	load	全負荷；満載

▷The truck was carrying a **heavy load** of rocks.　そのトラックは石をいっぱい積んでいた ▷Now her mother has died, she has to look after her four younger sisters. It's a **heavy load**.　母親が亡くなった今となっては彼女は4人の妹のめんどうを見なければならない．重い負担だ
▷We can't put any more boxes on that truck. It's already got a **full load**.　そのトラックにこれ以上は箱を積めない．もう満載だ

load /lóud/ 動 積む, 載せる；荷物を積む

fully	loaded	満載された
heavily	loaded	重量がいっぱいかかった

▷The truck was **heavily loaded** with bricks.　トラックにはレンガが山積みされていた

load A	into B	AをBに積み込む
load A	onto B	
load B	with A	

▷Can you help me **load** this furniture **onto** the van? この家具をライトバンに載せるのを手伝ってくれるかい
▷They **loaded** the truck (up) **with** furniture. 彼らはトラックに家具を積み込んだ

loan /lóun/ 名 貸付, 融資, ローン

make	a loan	融資をする
provide	a loan	
get	a loan	融資を受ける
take out	a loan	
obtain	a loan	
repay	a loan	融資を返済する
pay off	a loan	融資を完済する

▷The bank will **provide** a **loan**, but the interest rate is very high. 銀行は融資してくれるだろうが利率が非常に高い
▷We don't have enough money to buy that house. We'll have to **take out** a **loan** from the bank. その家を買うにはお金が足りないから銀行から融資を受けることになるだろう
▷It'll take us about 30 years to **repay** the **loan**. 融資返済に30年近くかかるだろう
▷Finally! After 10 years we've finally **paid off** the bank **loan**! やったよ. 10年かかってついに銀行ローンを完済したよ

a large	loan	多額のローン
a long-term	loan	長期融資
a short-term	loan	短期融資
a bridge	loan	つなぎ融資
《英》a bridging	loan	
a bank	loan	銀行ローン
a home	loan	住宅ローン
an interest-free	loan	無利子の貸付
a personal	loan	個人向け融資
a student	loan	学生向けローン

▷He went to the bank to ask for a **long-term loan**. 彼は長期融資の依頼に銀行に行った

on	loan	借りて; 貸して

▷That book's really popular. It's been **on loan** non-stop for 6 months! その本はとても人気があるので, 半年先までずっと貸し出しになっている

a loan	from A	Aからのローン

▷It's now possible to get student **loans from** the government. 現在では政府から学生向け融資を受けることが可能だ

located /lóukeitid | ─ ´ ─/ 形 位置する

centrally	located	中心にある
conveniently	located	便利な所にある
ideally	located	理想的な場所にある

▷The new university campus in Nagoya will be **centrally located**. 名古屋の新しい大学キャンパスは市の中心にできる予定だ
▷Their house is near the railway station. It's very **conveniently located**. 彼らの家は駅の近くでとても便利な所にある
▷Their cottage is in a beautiful village in the Lake District. It's **ideally located**. 彼らの小別荘は湖水地方の美しい村にあって, 理想的な場所に位置している

located	in A	Aに位置する

★at, on や near などの前置詞も用いる

▷Our new office will be **located in** the center of Tokyo. うちの新事務所は東京の中心にできる予定だ
▷The toilets are **located near** the station entrance. トイレは駅の入り口近くにある

location /loukéiʃən/

名 場所, 位置; 野外撮影地, ロケーション

a central	location	中心地
a remote	location	遠隔地
the exact	location	正確な位置
the precise	location	
geographical	location	地理的位置
a secret	location	秘密の場所
a suitable	location	適当な場所

▷The shop is somewhere downtown, but I don't know the **exact location**. その店は繁華街のどこかにあるが正確な場所はわからない
▷This satellite navigation system is capable of finding any **geographical location**. この衛星ナビゲーションシステムはどんな地理的位置でも見つけられる

location	for A	Aにふさわしい場所

▷We've found a really good **location for** building a new hotel. 新しいホテルを建設するのに絶好の場所を

| lock |

見つけた

on	location	ロケ撮影で

▷ They made the film **on location** in South America. その映画は南アメリカでロケ撮影された

lock /lák | lɔ́k/ 名 錠, 錠前

fit	a lock	錠を取りつける
open	a lock	錠を鍵で開ける
turn	a lock	
pick	a lock	錠を鍵以外の物で開ける
break	the lock	鍵をこじ開ける
change	the lock(s)	鍵を変える
replace	the lock(s)	

▷ There's something wrong with this key. It won't **open** the **lock**. この鍵はどうも変だ. 錠がどうしても開かない

▷ My keys to the apartment were stolen, so I think we should **change** the **locks**. アパートの鍵が盗まれたので鍵を変えたほうがいいだろうな

lock /lák | lɔ́k/ 動 鍵がかかる, 鍵をかける

lock	automatically	自動的に鍵がかかる
lock	away	鍵をかけてしまう
be firmly	locked	しっかり鍵がかかっている
remain	locked	鍵がかかったままだ

▷ **Lock away** all your money and jewelry in a drawer. お金と宝石は残らず引き出しの中に鍵をかけてしまっておきなさい

▷ She pushed hard, but the door was **firmly locked**. 彼女は強く押してみたが, ドアにはしっかり鍵がかかっていた

▷ This gate has **remained locked** for over twenty years. この門は20年以上鍵がかかったままだ

close and lock		閉めて鍵をかける

▷ Make sure you **close and lock** the door after you leave. 出かけるときはきちんとドアを閉めて鍵をかけなさい

forget to	lock	鍵をかけ忘れる

▷ Don't **forget to lock** all the doors and windows. ドアと窓にすべて鍵をかけるのを忘れないようにね

lock	A in B	AをBに閉じ込める

▷ The ship was **locked in** ice for several months because of the arctic winter. 北極の冬のために船は数か月氷に閉ざされた

lonely /lóunli/ 形 孤独の；寂しい

be	lonely	孤独である
feel	lonely	孤独を感じる
get	lonely	寂しくなる

▷ I'm **lonely**. I need you. 寂しくて私にはあなたが必要なの

▷ I **felt** really **lonely** when my best friend moved to another town. 親友が別の町に引っ越してしまってとても寂しい思いをした

long /lɔ́ːŋ | lɔ́ŋ/ 形 長い

fairly	long	かなり長い
relatively	long	比較的長い
so	long	すごく長い
long	enough	十分長い

▷ It's a **fairly long** way to the station. I don't think we can walk there. 駅まではかなりの道のりなので歩いては行けないと思うよ

▷ It's **so long** since I saw such a good movie. こんなにいい映画を見たのは久しぶりだ

▷ This rope isn't **long enough**. We'll have to get some more. このロープは長さが足りないのでもう少しもらってこないといけない

A	long	Aの長さの

★Aには two meters, two miles など長さ・距離や an hour など時間がくる

▷ Look at that snake! It must be at least 4 **meters long**! あの蛇を見てごらん. 少なくとも4メートルはあるよ

long and bitter A		長く苦しいA

▷ **Long and bitter** experience has taught me a lot of things. 長くつらい体験は多くのことを私に教えてくれた

PHRASES〉
Long time no see. ☺ 久しぶりだね

look /lúk/

名 見ること；顔つき, 目つき；ようす, 外観

a careful	look	注意して見ること

a close	look	じっくり見ること
a quick	look	さっと見ること
a funny	look	おかしな表情
a puzzled	look	当惑した表情
a strange	look	奇妙な表情
a suspicious	look	怪しげな表情
a worried	look	不安げな表情

▷Take a **careful look** at this report. It's really interesting. この報告書をじっくり見て，とてもおもしろいから
▷Would you mind taking a **quick look** at my essay? 私のレポートにさっと目を通していただけませんか
▷When the Scotsman arrived wearing a kilt, everybody started to give him **strange looks**. そのスコットランド人がキルトを着てやって来ると，だれもが奇妙な表情で彼を見た

have	a look at A	Aを見る
get	a look at A	
take	a look at A	
give A	a look	Aをちらっと見る
shoot A	a look	Aに視線を向ける

▷"Is that somebody at the door?" "I don't know. I'll **have a look**." 「ドアにだれかいるのかな」「わからないな．見てこよう」
▷**Take a look at** this photo. Have you ever seen that man before? この写真を見てください．この男の人を見たことがありますか

from	the look of A	Aのようすから見ると
by	the look of A	

▷**From** the **look of** the program, the concert will be very popular. プログラムから判断するとコンサートはとても人気を呼ぶだろう

look /lúk/ 動 (注意して)見る；…に見える

look	carefully	注意深く見る
look	quickly	さっと見る
look	again	見直す
look	around	見て回る；周りを見る
(英) look	round	
look	away	目をそらす
look	back	振り返る
look	down	下を見る，見下ろす
look	up	見上げる
look	out	外を見る

▷**Look carefully** at this photo. Do you recognize the man on the right? この写真をよく見てください．右の男がだれだかわかりますか
▷Why don't you **look around**? You might see something you like. 見て回ったらどうだい．気に入るものがあるかもしれないよ ▷Don't **look round**, but I think somebody's following us. きょろきょろしないで．だれかにつけられているみたい
▷Don't **look away** from me when I'm talking to you. 私から目をそらしちゃだめ．あなたに話しかけているのよ
▷He **looked back** and saw her waving goodbye. 彼が振り返ると，彼女がさよならと手を振っているのが目に入った
▷"I'm scared of heights!" "Don't **look down**! You'll be OK!" 「高いところが怖いの」「下を見ないで．だいじょうぶだから」 ▷They **looked down** from the roof at the crowd below. 彼らは屋上から下の群衆を見下ろした
▷**Look up** there! There's a man on the top of that building! あそこを見上げてごらん．あのビルの屋上に男の人がいる

look	at A	Aを見る
look	for A	Aを探す
look	out of A	Aの外を見る
look	through A	Aに目を通す

▷"**Look at** that view!" "Yeah. Mountains, lakes... Really beautiful!" 「あの景色を見て」「ええ，山の連なり，湖．実にきれいですね」
▷"What are you **looking for**?" "My glasses." 「何を探しているの」「ぼくの眼鏡だよ」
▷He **looked out of** the window to see if it was still raining. 彼は窓の外を見て，まだ雨が降っているかどうか確かめた
▷I **looked through** the newspaper, but there was nothing interesting. 新聞に目を通したが，おもしろい記事はなかった

look	like A	Aに似ている

▷She **looks like** her mother. 彼女は母親に似ている
▷What does your boyfriend **look like**? あなたのボーイフレンドはどんな人？

it	looks like	…のようだ
it	looks as if	

▷**It looks like** he's not coming. 彼は来ないようだ

look	wh-	…か確かめる

★wh-は where, what, whether など

▷Sorry! I wasn't **looking where** I was going. ごめん．前をよく見ていなかった
PHRASES
I'm just looking. ☺ (店で)ちょっと見ているだけです
▷"Can I help you?" "It's OK, thanks. I'm just looking." 「何かお探しですか」「いえ結構です．ちょっと

| loose |

見ているだけですから」
Look out! 😊 気をつけろ ▷Look out! There's a car coming! 気をつけて，車が来るよ

loose /lúːs/

形 緩い；ゆったりした；結んでいない；つながれていない

come	loose	ほどける，緩む
break	loose	逃げる，自由になる
get	loose	
cut	loose	
let A	loose	Aを放す，逃す

▷Your shoelaces have **come loose**. You'd better do them up. 靴ひもがほどけているよ．結んだほうがいい
▷They tied the dog up with a piece of rope, but he **broke loose** and ran away. 犬はロープでつないであったが，はずして逃げてしまった
▷You shouldn't **let** your dog **loose** on the street. 道で犬を放してはだめです

| rather | loose | かなり緩い |
| too | loose | 緩すぎる |

▷I think we should tighten this rope. It's **rather loose**. ロープをきつく締めたほうがいい．かなり緩いぞ
▷She went on a diet and now all her clothes are **too loose**! ダイエットしたら彼女は服がすべてゆるゆるになった

lose /lúːz/ 動 失う；負ける

almost	lost	ほとんど失った
nearly	lost	
finally	lost	とうとう失った
easily	lose	簡単に失う
never	lose	決して失わない
suddenly	lose	突然失う

▷I **nearly lost** my umbrella yesterday. But I remembered it at the last moment. きのう傘をなくしかけたけど，ぎりぎりで思い出した
▷He waited for her for over an hour, but **finally lost** patience and went home. 彼は彼女を1時間以上待ったが，とうとう待ちきれなくなって家に帰った
▷Don't take your earrings off. You could **easily lose** them. イアリングを外さないで．すぐ失くしてしまうから

lose	to A	(試合などで)Aに負ける
lose	against A	
lose	3 (to) 1	3対1で負ける

▷Japan **lost to** Germany three to one. 日本はドイツに3対1で敗れた
▷"How was the game?" "We **lost 3 to** 1."「試合はどうだったの」「3対1で負けたよ」(★ We lost 3-1. もよく用いられる)

loss /lɔ́ːs | lɔ́s/

名 損失，損害；紛失，喪失；敗北

make	a loss	損を出す
suffer	a loss	
cut	losses	損害を減らす
reduce	losses	
recoup	(one's) losses	損失を取り戻す
mourn	the loss of A	Aの死を悼む

▷Our business **made a loss** last year, but this year we made a profit. うちの事業は昨年は損失を出したが，今年は利益を上げた
▷According to the sales figures the company **suffered a loss** of 30% in profits. 売上高を見ると，会社は30％の減益をこうむった
▷Our company went bankrupt. We just had to **cut** our **losses** and start again. 我が社は倒産した．損害の少ないうちに手を引いて再出発しなければならなかった

a great	loss	多きな損失
a big	loss	
a heavy	loss	
a huge	loss	
a significant	loss	かなりの損失
a substantial	loss	
a total	loss	全損失
economic	loss	経済的損失
financial	loss	財務上の損失

▷When Carter resigned as sales manager it was a **great loss to** the company. カーターが営業責任者を辞任したのは会社にとって大きな損失だった
▷The company had **huge losses** and went bankrupt. 会社は大きな損失を抱えて倒産した
▷Changing from a full-time job to part-time meant that Taylor suffered a **significant loss** in income. 常勤の仕事からパートに変わるということはテイラーには収入がかなり減るということだった
▷Exports fell by over 70% so the country suffered a big **economic loss**. 輸出が7割以上落ち込み，その国は多大な経済的損失をこうむった

| **loss or damage** | 紛失または損害 |

▷Luckily my luggage is insured against **loss or damage**. 幸い私の荷物は紛失または損害の場合の保険がかかっている

a sense of	loss	喪失感

▷After his wife died he felt a deep **sense of loss**. 妻を亡くして彼は深い喪失感を覚えた

at	a loss	途方に暮れて；損をして

▷He was **at** a **loss** to explain how the stolen money was found in his apartment. 盗まれた金がどういうわけで彼のアパートにあったのか，彼は説明に困った
▷The company has operated **at** a **loss** for four consecutive years. その会社は4年連続の赤字営業を続けている

lot /lάt | lɔ́t/ 名 たくさん，多数，多量；(a lot, lots で)(副詞的に)大いに

drink	a lot	たくさん飲む
learn	a lot	よく学ぶ
talk	a lot	たくさん話す

▷"I **drank a lot** last night." "Me, too. I feel terrible!"「きのうはたくさん飲んだよ」「ぼくもだ．気分が悪くて」
▷During his internship he **learnt a lot** about sales techniques. インターンシップの間，販売技術について多くを学んだ
▷He **talked a lot** about a girl called Alison. アリソンという女の子のことを彼はいっぱいしゃべった

an awful	lot	すごくたくさん
a whole	lot	うんと

▷We waste an **awful lot** of time in these meetings. Nobody ever wants to make a decision! こんな会議ばかりでさんざん時間をむだにしている．だれも決定を下したがらないのだから
▷There's a **whole lot** of reasons why I don't want to move to the USA. 米国に移りたくない理由は山ほどある

a lot	better	ずっとよい
a lot	older	ずっと年配の
a lot	younger	ずっと若い

★a lotで比較級を強めて

▷He looked **a lot older** than me. 彼は私よりずっと年配に見えた
▷She's **a lot younger** than I thought. 彼女は思っていたよりずっと若い

loud /láud/ 形 騒々しい，うるさい

get	louder and louder	音がだんだん
grow	louder and louder	大きくなる

▷The sound of thunder **grew louder and louder** as the storm approached. 嵐が近づくにつれて雷の音がだんだん大きくなった

so	loud	あまりに騒々しい
too	loud	騒々しすぎる
deafeningly	loud	耳をつんざくほどうるさい

▷The noise of the airplane was **so loud** that we couldn't hear each other. 飛行機の騒音があまりにも大きかったので，お互いの言うことが聞き取れなかった
▷Can you turn the television down? It's **too loud**. テレビの音を小さくしてくれる？音が大きすぎるよ

love /lΛ́v/ 名 愛，愛情，恋

deep	love	深い愛
great	love	大きな愛
passionate	love	情熱的な愛
real	love	真実の愛
true	love	
unconditional	love	無条件の愛
unrequited	love	報われぬ愛，片思い
lost	love	失恋；失った恋人
first	love	初恋

▷She has a **deep love** of art. 彼女は芸術を深く愛している
▷It's everybody's dream to find **real love** that lasts for ever! 永遠に続く真実の愛を見つけるのはだれにとっても夢だ
▷**True love**? Do you believe in it? 真実の愛だって？そんなものあなたは信じているの
▷Cinderella is such a romantic story! In the end the Prince finds his **lost love** and they live happily ever after! シンデレラってとってもロマンチックなお話よ．最後には王子さまが探していた女性を見つけて，それから二人は幸せに暮らしたの

be	in love	恋している
fall	in love	恋に落ちる
make	love	セックスする

▷I think Tom is **in love** *with* Amanda. トムはアマンダのことが好きだと思う
▷Slowly we **fell in love**. Eighteen months later we got married. 私たちはゆっくりと恋に落ち，1年半後に結婚した ▷I **fell in love** *with* him at first sight. 彼に一目ぼれしたの
▷She would never **make love** *to* him again. 彼女

| love |

は二度と彼と寝ることはないだろう

| love | for A | A(人)に対する愛 |
| love | of A | Aへの愛 |

▷Her **love for** her children was very strong. 自分の子どもたちに対する彼女の愛はとても強かった
▷He has a great **love of** classical music. 彼はクラシック音楽の非常な愛好家だ

| love and respect | | 愛と尊敬 |

▷Martin Luther King had the **love and respect** of so many people. マーティン・ルーサー・キングは多くの人たちから愛され尊敬されていた

love /lˆv/ 動 愛している

always	love	いつも愛している
dearly	love	心から愛している
truly	love	本当に愛している

▷I'll **always love** you. いつまでも愛してる
▷I sometimes wonder whether you do still **truly love** me. あなたがまだ本当に私を愛してくれているのかなと思うことがときどきある

| love | to do | …するのが好きだ |
| love | doing | |

▷He **loves climb**ing mountains. 彼は山登りが好きだ
♦**would love to** do ぜひ…したい ▷I'd love to meet him. すごく彼に会いたい ▷"Would you like to come to our party on Saturday?" "Yes, I'd love to."「土曜日にパーティーにいらっしゃいませんか」「はい，ぜひ」

low /lóu/ 形 低い；(量が)少ない

extremely	low	とても低い
fairly	low	かなり低い
comparatively	low	比較的低い
relatively	low	
generally	low	一般に低い
particularly	low	特に低い

▷The chances of another big earthquake in this region within the next 50 years are **extremely low**. この地域で50年以内にまた大地震が起きる確率はきわめて低い
▷The prices in this supermarket are **comparatively low**. このスーパーマーケットは値段が比較的安い
▷I'm afraid our chances of winning gold at the Olympics are **relatively low**. オリンピックで金をとれ

る可能性は比較的低いと思う
▷The number of tourists is **generally low** at this time of the year. 一年のこの時期には旅行者数は一般に少ない

loyal /lóiəl/ 形 忠実な

| stay | loyal | 忠実であり続ける |

▷Most skillful players used to **stay loyal** *to* one club throughout their careers. 昔は名選手はたいてい生涯1つのチームでずっとプレーしたものだ

| loyal | to A | Aに忠実な |

▷Peter is always **loyal to** his friends. ピーターはいつも友だちに忠実だ

loyalty /lóiəlti/ 名 忠誠，忠実；忠誠心

retain	the loyalty	忠誠を保つ
show	(a) loyalty	忠誠を示す
swear	loyalty	忠誠を誓う
command	loyalty	忠誠を得る

▷We have to make sure we **retain** the **loyalty** of our customers. 顧客にうちの製品をずっとひいきにしてもらえるようにしなければならない
▷He **showed** a **loyalty** to his company even when they were in the wrong. 会社が間違っているときも彼は会社に忠誠を示した

great	loyalty	強い忠誠心
divided	loyalty	分裂した忠誠心
personal	loyalty	個人的な忠誠
political	loyalty	政治的忠誠
brand	loyalty	ブランドロイヤルティ
customer	loyalty	顧客の忠誠

▷When his parents got divorced he felt he had **divided loyalties**. 両親が離婚したとき彼は親への忠誠心が二つに分裂してしまうのを感じた
▷He puts **personal loyalty** before ambition. 彼は野心よりも個人的な忠誠を重んじている

luck /lˆk/ 名 運，幸運

have	much luck	すごく運がある
have	no luck	運がない
bring	luck	運をもたらす
wish A	luck	Aに幸運を願う
push	one's luck	図に乗る

try	one's **luck**	運を試す

▷ I played card games for two hours, but I didn't **have much luck**. カードゲームを2時間したがあまりつきがなかった

▷ This bracelet has always been lucky for me. Please take it. Maybe it'll **bring** you **luck**, too. このブレスレットのおかげでずっと幸運がついて回ったの．あなたにあげる．あなたにも幸運が訪れるかもね

▷ I'm playing a tennis match for the university tomorrow. **Wish** me **luck**! あしたその大学とテニスの試合があるんだ．幸運を祈ってよ

▷ Don't **push** your **luck**. 図に乗ってはいけないよ

▷ "I never win at pachinko." "Go on! **Try your luck**!" 「パチンコでまったく勝てないよ」「続けて運を試してみろよ」

good	luck	幸運
bad	luck	不運
hard	luck	
sheer	luck	まったくの幸運
pure	luck	

▷ They say a four-leafed clover will bring **good luck**. 四つ葉のクローバーは幸福を呼ぶと言われている

▷ "I failed the exam." "Oh! **Hard luck**!" 「試験に落ちちゃった」「ついてなかったね」

beginner's	luck	初心者のまぐれ当たり

▷ "I'd never played golf before and I got a hole in one!" "**Beginner's luck**!" 「ゴルフは初めてだったけど，ホールインワンをしたよ」「ビギナーズラックだね」

a stroke of	luck	思いがけない幸運
a piece of	luck	

▷ "She won 10 million yen on the lottery!" "That was a **stroke of luck**!" 「彼女は宝くじで1千万円当たったよ」「それは思いがけない幸運だったね」

in	luck	運がよくて
out of	luck	運が悪くて
with	luck	運がよければ
with	any luck	
with	a bit of luck	

▷ Professor Taylor's just come back from lunch. If you want to see him, you're **in luck**! テイラー教授は昼食から戻ったところです．お会いになりたいのなら，ちょうどよかったです

▷ **With a bit of luck**, we'll be home in time for supper. うまくいけば夕食までに家に帰れるだろう

PHRASES

Any luck? 😊 うまくいったかい，どうだったの

Better luck next time! 😊 この次はうまくいくといいね

Good luck! / **Best of luck!** 😊 幸運を祈ります ▷ "I'm taking my English exam today." "Good luck!" 「きょう英語のテストがあるんだ」「がんばってね」

Just my luck! 😊 ついてないな ▷ "I'm sorry. All the tickets for the concert are sold out." "Just my luck!" 「申し訳ありませんがチケットは完売です」「ついてないな」

No luck. 😊 だめだった ▷ "Did you find the information you wanted on the internet?" "No luck so far." 「ほしい情報はインターネットで見つかったかい」「いまのところだめだね」

No such luck. 😊 そううまくはいかないよ

What bad luck! 😊 なんてついてないんだ

lucky /lʌ́ki/

形 運のよい，幸運な；幸運をもたらす

lucky	enough	幸運にも

▷ I was **lucky enough** to get two tickets for the World Cup. 運よくワールドカップのチケットが2枚手に入った

be lucky	to do	…して運がよい

▷ You were **lucky to** escape from that terrible car crash. あのひどい交通事故からうまく難を逃れられてよかったね

it is lucky	(that)...	…は運がよい

▷ **It's lucky** you were here. You're the only person who knows first aid. きみがここにいてくれてよかった．応急処置ができるのはきみだけだから

PHRASES

How lucky I am! 😊 なんて幸運なんだ ▷ I can't believe how lucky I am! I won a free holiday for two in Florida! 信じられないくらいついているわ．ペアでフロリダの休日が当たったの

I should be so lucky! / **You should be so lucky!** そんなにうまい話があるはずがない ▷ With chances of 10 million to one you think I can win the lottery? I should be so lucky! 1000万分の1の確率しかないのにぼくがそのくじに当たるっていうの？そんなのありえないよ

Lucky you! 😊 あなたって運がいいね

luggage /lʌ́gidʒ/ 名 手荷物

carry	A's **luggage**	手荷物を運ぶ
collect	A's **luggage**	手荷物を引き取る

▷ Would you like me to **carry** your **luggage**? お荷物を運んで差し上げましょうか

▷ The tourist company will **collect** our **luggage** from the hotel. 旅行会社のほうで荷物をホテルから引

| lunch |

き取ってくれる

| a piece of | luggage | 手荷物一つ |

▷ This is a really heavy **piece of luggage**! この荷物はほんとに重い

| carry-on | luggage | 機内持ち込み手荷物 |
| hand | luggage | |

lunch /lʌ́ntʃ/ 名 昼食

have	lunch	昼食を食べる
eat	one's lunch	
get	lunch	
come to	lunch	昼食を食べに来る
go (out) to	lunch	昼食を食べに出かける
go (out) for	lunch	
meet for	lunch	昼食時に会う
stop for	lunch	昼休みをとる
skip	lunch	昼食を抜く

▷ I **had** a quick **lunch** in the office restaurant. 社内食堂で昼食をさっと済ませた
▷ He **ate** his **lunch** on a park bench. Just sandwiches. 彼は公園のベンチで昼食を済ませた．サンドイッチだけだった
▷ Why don't we go and **get** some **lunch**? 昼食を食べに行きませんか
▷ Lovely to see you. You must **come to lunch** again some time soon. お会いできてうれしいです．近いうちにぜひまた昼食にいらしてください
▷ It's after 12:30. Shall we **go to lunch**? 12時半を回ったよ．昼食を食べに行こうか
▷ Let's **meet for lunch** tomorrow. あす昼食時に会いましょう
▷ I was so busy yesterday that I couldn't even **stop for lunch**. きのうはすごく忙しくて昼食をとることもできなかった

a light	lunch	軽い昼食
a late	lunch	遅い昼食
a picnic	lunch	ピクニックの弁当

▷ I'm starving! I only had a **light lunch**. お腹がペコペコだよ．昼食が軽かったので

after	lunch	昼食後に
before	lunch	昼食前に
at	lunch	昼食に
over	lunch	昼食をとりながら

▷ **After lunch** we'll have a meeting. 昼食後に会議があります
▷ We must get this work finished **before lunch**. 昼食前にこの仕事を片づけなくてはならない
▷ I'm sorry, Mr. Denver is **at lunch** at the moment. 申し訳ありません．デンバーはいま昼食をとっています
▷ Let's talk about the problem **over lunch**. その件は昼食をとりながら話そう

luxury /lʌ́kʃəri/ 名 ぜいたく；ぜいたく品

pure	luxury	まったくのぜいたく
the ultimate	luxury	究極のぜいたく
a small	luxury	ささやかなぜいたく

▷ Drinking champagne in a five star hotel! I can't believe it! **Pure luxury!** 5つ星ホテルでシャンパンを飲むなんて，信じられない．まったくのぜいたくだね
▷ A piece of cheesecake is a **small luxury** when you're on a diet! ダイエット中のチーズケーキ一切れは小さなぜいたくだ

afford	the luxury	ぜいたくする余裕がある
enjoy	the luxury	ぜいたくを楽しむ
live in	luxury	ぜいたくに暮らす

▷ I can't **afford** the **luxury** of traveling first class. ファーストクラスで旅行するようなぜいたくをする余裕はありません
▷ I **enjoy** the **luxury** of not having to worry about money. お金のことを心配する必要がないぜいたくを楽しんでいます
▷ Now she **lives in luxury** in the South of France. いま彼女は南フランスでぜいたくな暮らしをしている

M

machine /məʃíːn/ 名 機械

switch on	the machine	機械のスイッチを入れる
switch off	the machine	機械のスイッチを切る
turn on	the machine	機械を作動させる
stop	the machine	機械を止める
turn off	the machine	機械を止める
operate	a machine	機械を操作する
use	a machine	機械を使う

▷I **switched** the **machine on**, but it doesn't work. 機械のスイッチを入れたが動かない
▷**Turn off** the **machine**. I can't hear what you're saying. 機械を止めて，きみのことばが聞こえないよ
▷I don't know how to **operate** this new **machine**. この新しい機械の操作法がわからない

an answering	machine	留守番電話
a fax	machine	ファックス
a cash	machine	現金自動支払機
an electronic	machine	電子機器
a vending	machine	自動販売機
a sewing	machine	ミシン
a washing	machine	洗濯機
a coffee	machine	コーヒーメーカー

▷She left two messages on my **answering machine**. 彼女は私の留守電にメッセージを2つ残した
▷A personal computer is an example of an **electronic machine**. パソコンは電子機器の一例です
▷You can get a drink from the **vending machine** around the corner. すぐ近くの自動販売機で飲み物を買えます

by	machine	機械で

▷You can't wash this sweater **by machine**. You have to hand-wash it. このセーターは機械で洗えません．手洗いしてください

mad /mæd/ 形 頭が変な；怒った；夢中な

mad	at A	A(人)のことを怒った
mad	with A	
mad	about A	Aに夢中な

▷I'm only ten minutes late. There is no need to get **mad at** me. 10分遅れただけなんだから，私のことを怒る必要ないのに
▷She was **mad with** me for forgetting her birthday. 彼女の誕生日を忘れたので彼女はぼくのことを怒っていた
▷"Do you think she likes me?" "Likes you? She is **mad about** you!"「彼女はぼくのことが好きなのかな」「好きかだって？きみにぞっこんだよ」

be mad	to do	…するとは正気でない

▷I think she was **mad to** pay all that money for a Louis Vuitton handbag! ルイヴィトンのバッグにあんなに金を使うなんて彼女はまともじゃないよ

magazine /mǽɡəzìːn/ 名 雑誌

buy	a magazine	雑誌を買う
get	a magazine	
read	a magazine	雑誌を読む

▷There is no time to **get** a **magazine**. The train's leaving! 雑誌を買っている時間はないよ．列車が出てしまう

a monthly	magazine	月刊誌
a quarterly	magazine	季刊誌
a weekly	magazine	週刊誌
a business	magazine	ビジネス誌
a fashion	magazine	ファッション誌
a literary	magazine	文芸誌

▷I've ordered a **monthly magazine** on world cooking. 世界の料理が載っている月刊誌を注文した
▷He published an article in a **literary magazine**. 彼は文芸誌に論文を発表した

an issue of	the magazine	雑誌の号

▷They're going to announce the prizewinners in the October **issue of** the **magazine**. その雑誌の10月号で受賞者の発表がある

in a	magazine	雑誌で

▷I read about it **in** a **magazine**. それについて雑誌で読んだ

magic /mǽdʒik/ 名 魔法，魔術；手品

use	magic	魔法を使う
work	magic	魔法をかける
believe in	magic	魔法を信じる

do	magic	手品をする
perform	magic	
work	one's magic	すぐれた技を見せる

▷ OK, Harry Potter! Let's see you **use magic** to get us there on time. さあハリー・ポッター．魔法をかけてぼくたちが時間どおりそこに着けるようにして
▷ I don't **believe in magic**. Everything has a logical explanation. 魔法なんか信じない．どんなことも論理的に説明できる
▷ **Do** some **magic** and change him into a white rabbit! 手品で彼を白ウサギに変えてよ
▷ They were losing 3-0, but Beckham **worked** his **magic** and they won the game. 3対0で負けていたが，ベッカムが絶妙の技を見せて彼らは試合に勝った

black	magic	黒魔術
white	magic	白魔術
pure	magic	本物の魔法

▷ Messi ran 50 yards, beat 5 players and put the ball in the net. It was **pure magic**! メッシは50ヤード走って5人をかわし，ゴールを決めた．まるで本物の魔法みたいだった

magnificent /mæɡnífəsnt/

形 壮大な，堂々とした，豪華な

truly	magnificent	まったくすばらしい
really	magnificent	
absolutely	magnificent	

★ ˟ very magnificent とはいわない

▷ She looked **really magnificent** in her wedding dress. ウエディングドレス姿の彼女はすごくきれいだった
▷ That performance of Mozart's 'Marriage of Figaro' was **absolutely magnificent**! モーツァルト「フィガロの結婚」のあの演奏はまったくすばらしかった

mail /méil/

名 郵便物，郵便(制度)；(電子)メール

send	the mail	郵便物を送る
deliver	the mail	郵便物を配達する
forward	A's mail	郵便物を転送する
receive	(the) mail	郵便物を受け取る
open	the mail	郵便物を開封する
read	A's mail	郵便物を読む

▷ Please **send** my **mail** to this address. 私への郵便物はこの住所に送ってください
▷ They **delivered** all my **mail** to the wrong address. 私の郵便物はすべて間違った住所に配達された
▷ I haven't **received** any **mail** for weeks. この数週間私のところにまったく郵便物がきていない

surface	mail	普通郵便
registered	mail	書留郵便
electronic	mail	電子メール
incoming	mail	受信メール
outgoing	mail	送信メール
chain	mail	チェーンメール
fan	mail	ファンレター
junk	mail	くずかごに捨てられてしまう郵便物

▷ It's a very important letter. You'd better send it by **registered mail**. とても大事な手紙だから書留で送ったほうがいい
▷ People don't write letters by hand any more. They use **electronic mail**. 手書きで手紙を書く人はもういなくなって，電子メールを使っている
▷ When I arrive at the office the first thing I do is check my **incoming mail**. オフィスについてまずすることは受信メールのチェックだ

by	mail	郵便で

▷ Send it **by** second-class **mail**. It's not urgent. 第2種郵便物で送ってください．急ぎではないので

a piece of	mail	1通の郵便物

maintain /meintéin/

動 維持する；主張する

easily	maintain	簡単に維持する
properly	maintained	整備が行き届いた
well	maintained	
consistently	maintain	一貫して主張する

▷ Even if you go abroad for a year we can **easily maintain** contact over the Internet. きみが1年間外国にいるとしても，インターネットで簡単に連絡がとれる
▷ The car is old, but in excellent condition. It's been very **well maintained**. 古い車だが状態はいい．メンテナンスが行き届いている
▷ Even while he was in prison he **consistently maintained** that he was innocent. 獄中にあっても彼は一貫して無罪を主張していた

be able to	maintain	維持できる

▷ They were **able to maintain** contact by radio. 彼らは無線で連絡を取り続けることができた(★can との連結より頻度が高い)

maintain	(that)...	…と主張する

▷He **maintains that** he was 50 miles away at the time of the murder. 殺人が起きたとき50マイル離れたところにいたと彼は主張している

maintenance /méintənəns/

名 維持;保守, メンテナンス;扶養

ensure	the maintenance	維持できるようにする
need	maintenance	保守を必要とする
require	maintenance	

▷We did our best to **ensure** the **maintenance** of our good relationship with China. 中国との友好関係を維持できるよう全力を尽くした
▷This elevator **requires** regular **maintenance**. このエレベーターには定期保守が必要だ

annual	maintenance	年1回の保守
regular	maintenance	定期保守
routine	maintenance	日ごろの手入れ
proper	maintenance	適切な保守
preventative	maintenance	予防保守

▷Roller coasters require **regular maintenance**. ジェットコースターは定期保守が必要だ
▷We need to carry out **preventative maintenance** to this machine in order to prevent future problems. 将来の故障に備えて機械の予防保守を行う必要がある

majority /mədʒɔ́:rəti | -dʒɔ́r-/

名 大多数;過半数

gain	a majority	過半数を獲得する
win	a majority	
get	a majority	

▷The democrats failed to **get a majority** of seats in the Congress. 民主党は議席の過半数を獲得できなかった

great	majority	大半
large	majority	
vast	majority	

▷The **great majority** of our investors supported our decision. 投資家の大半がわれわれの決定を支持した
▷A **large majority** of committee members were in favor of the project. 委員会の委員の大半がその事業に賛成だった

in	the majority	大多数で

man /mæn/ 名 (おとなの)男, 男性

a young	man	青年
a middle-aged	man	中年の男性
an elderly	man	初老の男性
an old	man	年配の男性
a poor	man	貧乏な男
a rich	man	金持ちの男
a single	man	独身男性
a married	man	既婚男性
a short	man	背の低い男性
a tall	man	背の高い男性
a fat	man	太った男性
a handsome	man	ハンサムな男性
a nice	man	すてきな男性
a great	man	偉大な男
a wise	man	賢い男

▷Who shall I marry? A **poor, young man**, or a **rich, old man**? Hmm... Difficult! だれと結婚しようかな、貧しくて若い男性か、それともお金持ちで年とった男性か。う〜ん、難しいわ

man and wife	夫婦
men and women	男女

▷They've been together, **man and wife**, for 50 years. 彼らは夫婦として暮らしを共にして50年になる
▷**Men and women** will never be able to understand each other! 男と女は決して互いに理解し合えないだろう

manage /mǽnidʒ/

動 やりくりする;運営する, 経営する, 管理する;操る

finally	manage	最終的にどうにか…する
properly	managed	うまく管理された
well	managed	

▷I **finally managed** to complete my thesis! 最終的にどうにか論文を仕上げた
▷The hotel we stayed at was really **well managed**. The service was great. 私たちが滞在したホテルは管理が行き届いておりサービスがよかった

can	manage	どうにかできる
be able to	manage	

| management |

▷"Shall I help you?" "It's OK, thanks. I **can manage**."「お手伝いしましょうか」「けっこうです。自分でできますから」

manage	to do	どうにか…する

▷How did you **manage to** carry all that luggage? その荷物を全部いったいどうやって運べたの

manage	on A	Aでやりくりする
manage	with A	Aを何とかする
manage	without A	Aなしで何とかする

▷Not everybody can eat out in good restaurants. Some people have to **manage on** a bowl of rice every day. だれもがいいレストランで食事できるわけではない。毎日ご飯一杯でやっていくしかない人もいる
▷I never thought I could **manage without** a car. But it's easy. I use a bicycle! 車なしでやっていけるとは思わなかったが、簡単だった。自転車を使っているよ

learn	(how) to manage	管理法を知っている

▷Our new boss hasn't really **learnt how to manage** other people well. 新しい上司は他の人たちをうまく管理する方法がよくわかっていない

management /mǽnidʒmənt/

名 経営, 管理, 運営；経営者(側)

effective	management	効率的経営
good	management	優れた経営
poor	management	ずさんな経営
middle	management	中間管理職
senior	management	経営上層部
top	management	経営トップ
business	management	企業管理
financial	management	財務管理
personnel	management	人事管理
crisis	management	危機管理
risk	management	リスク管理
data	management	データ管理
information	management	情報管理

▷Our company has been very successful because of **good management**. わが社は優れた経営でとてもうまくいっている
▷**Middle management** can't take any really important decisions. 中間管理職にはいかなる非常に重要な決定も下せない
▷**Senior management** will be holding an important meeting tomorrow. 経営上層部はあす重要な会議を開くことになっている

under	new management	経営者が替わって

★ under the same management は「同じ経営者の下で」

▷This restaurant is much better now. It's **under new management**. このレストランはずっとよくなった。経営者が替わったんだ

management and labor	労使

▷Can **management and labor** ever trust one another? 労使は互いに信頼し合えるものだろうか

manner /mǽnər/

名 方法, やり方；態度；(manners で)行儀, 作法

bad	manners	無作法
good	manners	よい作法；行儀のよさ

▷In England it's **bad manners** to sniffle or sniff when you've got a cold. イギリスではかぜを引いたとき鼻をグズグズいわせたり鼻をすするのは無作法だ
▷John has **good manners**. ジョンは行儀がよい

the manner	of A	Aの仕方

▷The **manner of** choosing the committee seemed very strange. 委員の選び方はすごくおかしく思えた

| in | the manner of A | A風の, Aのような |
| in | a [the]... manner | …のやり方で |

▷That is a painting **in** the **manner of** Gauguin. あれはゴーギャン風の絵だ
▷We should try to deal with complaints **in** a friendly **manner**. クレームには親身になって対処するよう心がけるべきだ
▷Don't be nervous. Just make a speech **in** the usual **manner**. 緊張しないで, いつものようにスピーチしなさい

the manner	in which...	…の仕方

▷I didn't like the **manner in which** he spoke to me. 彼の私への口のきき方が気に入らなかった

map /mǽp/ 名 地図 (★「地図帳」は atlas, 「海図・航空図」は chart)

draw	a map	地図を描く
read	a map	地図を読む
look at	the map	地図を見る
study	a map	地図を調べる

▷Can you **draw** me a **map** of how to get to your house? きみの家までの行き方を地図に描いてくれるかい
▷It's difficult to **read** a **map** while you're driving. 運転中に地図を読むのは難しい

on	the map	地図に

▷This mountain road isn't marked **on** the **map**. この山岳道路は地図に載っていない

a large-scale	map	大縮尺地図
a road	map	道路地図
a street	map	
a tourist	map	観光地図
a world	map	世界地図

march /máːrtʃ/ 名 行進；行進曲

go on	a march	デモ行進する

▷They **went on** a **march** to protest about acid rain and global warming. 彼らは酸性雨と地球温暖化に抗議してデモ行進した

on	the march	行進中で；進展中で

▷Three thousand demonstrators are **on** the **march** to downtown. 3千人のデモ参加者が中心街に向けて行進中だ

a peace	march	平和行進
a protest	march	抗議の行進

march /máːrtʃ/

動 行進する；堂々と歩く，さっさと歩く

march	off	出て行く
march	away	
march	up (and down)	行ったり来たりする

▷She said "I never want to speak to you again!" and **marched off**. 「二度とあなたと話をしたくない」と彼女は言って出て行った

march	into A	Aへさっさと歩いて入って行く
march	out of A	Aからさっさと歩いて出て行く
march	on (to) A	Aに向けて行進する
march	to A	
march	through A	Aを行進する

▷She was so angry that she **marched out of** the room without saying a word. 彼女はひどく怒っていたので，一言も言わずにさっさと部屋から出て行った
▷The soldiers **marched on to** the next village. 兵士たちは隣の村に向かって行進した
▷Thousands of people **marched to** London to protest against cuts in education spending. 何千人もの人々が教育関連支出の削減に抗議して，ロンドンへ向けてデモ行進した

mark /máːrk/

名 跡，しみ；目印；記号；的；《英》点数

make	a mark	しみをつける
leave	a mark	
have	a mark	印がある
bear	a mark	
hit	its mark	的に当たる
find	its mark	
miss	its mark	的を外す
get	... marks	…の点をとる
give A	... marks	Aに…の点を与える

▷I spilt some tomato juice onto my shirt and it **left** a **mark** that I couldn't get out. シャツの上にトマトジュースをこぼしたらしみになって，どうしてもとれなかった
▷A good accent usually **bears** the **mark** of a good education. 発音の仕方がいいというのは通例，ちゃんとした教育を受けた印だ

a distinguishing	mark	目立つ印
a burn	mark	やけどの跡
a scratch	mark	引っかいた跡
full	marks	満点
top	marks	最高点
good	marks	よい点
high	marks	高得点
low	marks	低い点
bad	marks	悪い点
poor	marks	ひどい点
total	marks	合計点数

▷Did the man who attacked you have any **distinguishing marks**? Red hair? Beard? Scar? あなたを襲った人には何か目立つ印がありましたか．赤毛とかひげだとか傷だとか
▷He got **full marks** *in* the English exam! Unbelievable! 彼は英語の試験で満点だったよ．信じられないね
▷I'm sure I'll get **low marks** *in* the math exam. 数学の点はきっと悪いだろう
▷He got thirty-five marks in Part A and forty marks in Part B, so his **total marks** are seventy-five percent. 彼はパートAで35点，パートBで40点を取ったので合計点は75点だ

mark /máːrk/ 動 印をつける，跡をつける；表示する；目立たせる；《英》採点する

be clearly	marked	はっきり示される
be badly	marked	ひどく跡がつく

▷The route we should take is **clearly marked** on this map. 進むべき経路はこの地図にはっきり示されている
▷Be careful with the piano! Oh! Too late! It's already **badly marked**! Please don't drop it again! ピアノを注意して運んでね．ああ遅かった．ひどい跡がついちゃった．二度と落とさないでね

mark A	on B	AのB印をBにつける
mark A	with B	AにBで印をつける

▷**Mark** "true" or "false" **on** this answer paper. この解答用紙に○か×を記入してください
▷On the map, the rivers are **marked with** a blue line. 地図では川は青線で記されている

market /máːrkit/

名 市場(いちば)；市場(しじょう)；販路，需要

go to	(the) market	市場に(買い物に)行く
create	a market	市場をつくる
enter	the market	市場に参入する
develop	a market	市場を開拓する
expand	the market	市場を拡大する
come on	the market	市場に出る
come onto	the market	
put A on	the market	Aを売り出す
dominate	the market	市場を支配する
manipulate	the market	市場を操作する

▷I **go to** the **market** every Wednesday. 毎週水曜日に市場へ買い物に出かける
▷Our company wants to **develop** a **market** in hybrid cars. わが社はハイブリッドカーの市場を開拓したい
▷We've succeeded in **expanding** our **market** by 50% this year. 今年度は5割の市場拡大に成功した
▷A new type of cellphone has **come on** the **market**. 新型の携帯電話が市場に出た
▷We've just **put** our house **on** the **market**. うちの家を売りに出したところです
▷Many companies are trying to **dominate** the **market** in ecocars. エコカー市場を支配しようとしている企業が多い

an active	market	活発な市場
a steady	market	手堅い市場
a buyer's	market	買手市場
a seller's	market	売手市場
the currency	market	為替市場
the financial	market	金融市場
the capital	market	長期金融市場
the money	market	短期金融市場
the foreign exchange	market	外国為替市場
the stock	market	株式市場
the international	market	国際市場
the overseas	market	海外市場
the domestic	market	国内市場
the free	market	自由市場
the export	market	輸出市場
the housing	market	住宅市場
the labor	market	労働市場

▷The **financial market** is up again today. 金融市場はきょう再び上向いている
▷At home we are doing well, but on the **international market** our sales have fallen. 国内では好調だが，国際市場ではうちの売り上げが落ちている
▷Because of the strong yen it's difficult to sell anything on the **overseas market**. 円高のせいで海外市場で物を売るのは難しい

market	for A	Aに対する市場
market	in A	Aの市場
on	the market	売りに出されて

▷There doesn't seem to be a **market for** luxury goods any longer. もはやぜいたく品の市場はないように思われる
▷The **market in** Australian beef has been doing well recently. オーストラリアの牛肉市場はこのところ好調だ
▷Our house is **on** the **market** now. It's a good time to sell. うちの家を売りに出している．ちょうど売り時だ

marriage /mǽridʒ/ 名 結婚；結婚式

celebrate	a marriage	結婚式を執り行う
save	one's marriage	結婚生活を守る

▷She wanted to **save** their **marriage**, but it was too late. They got divorced. 彼女は結婚生活を守りたかったのだが，時すでに遅そく二人は離婚した

a marriage	lasts	結婚が続く
a marriage	breaks up	結婚が破綻する
a marriage	breaks down	
a marriage	ends	結婚が終わる
a marriage	takes place	結婚式が行われる

▷Their **marriage lasted** only two years. 彼らの結婚生活は2年しか続かなかった

▷My first **marriage ended** in divorce. 私の最初の結婚は離婚に終わった
▷The **marriage took place** on June 15, 2002. その結婚式は 2002 年 6 月 15 日に行われた

an early	marriage	早婚
a late	marriage	晩婚
one's first	marriage	初婚
one's second	marriage	再婚
a previous	marriage	前の結婚
a happy	marriage	幸せな結婚
a loveless	marriage	愛のない結婚
a broken	marriage	破綻した結婚
a failed	marriage	
an arranged	marriage	見合い結婚

▷Many people go on to find happiness in their **second marriage**. 再婚して幸せになる人も多い
▷All she wants from life is a **happy marriage** and children. 彼女が人生に望むのは幸せな結婚と子どもだ
▷After two **failed marriages**, Bob still wants to get married again. 結婚に 2 度失敗してもボブはまだ結婚したがっている

marriage	between A	Aの間の結婚

▷Do you think a **marriage between** a soccer star and a pop idol can be successful? 人気サッカー選手とポップスのアイドルとの結婚はうまくいくと思うかい

by	marriage	婚姻による
outside	marriage	非嫡出で；婚外で

▷These days many babies are born **outside marriage**. 近ごろは非嫡出子が多い

married /mǽrid/ 形 結婚している

get	married	結婚する

▷John and I are **getting married** in June. ジョンと私は 6 月に結婚するの
▷She **got married** to Paul last year. 彼女は昨年ポールと結婚した (★× get married with Paul とはいわない)

newly	married	新婚の
recently	married	最近結婚した
happily	married	幸せな結婚生活を送っている

▷That couple over there are **newly married**. The ceremony was only 2 days ago. あそこにいるカップルは新婚で，2 日前に式を挙げたばかりです
▷They've been **happily married** for nearly 50 years. 彼らは 50 年近く幸せな結婚生活を送っている

married	to A	Aと結婚している
married	with children	結婚して子どもがいる

▷Nick is **married to** Helen and they have three children. ニックはヘレンと結婚していて子どもが 3 人いる

marry /mǽri/ 動 結婚する

eventually	marry	ついに結婚する
finally	marry	
never	marry	結婚しない
marry	well	よい相手と結婚する
marry	young	若くして結婚する
marry	late	晩婚である

▷They went out together for over 5 years. Then they **eventually married**. 彼らは 5 年以上つき合って，ついに結婚した

marry A	to B	AをBと結婚させる
marry	A	A(人)と結婚する

★× marry with A とはいわない

▷It's not possible for a priest to **marry** a Christian **to** a Muslim. 司祭がキリスト教徒をイスラム教徒と結婚させることなんてできない
▷Will you **marry** me? ぼくと結婚してくれるかい ▷I wouldn't **marry** Tony, even if he was the last man left on earth! 地球に残った最後の男がトニーだったとしても結婚はしないわ

match /mǽtʃ/ 名 マッチ

strike	a match	マッチをする
light	a match	

▷Can you **strike** a **match**? It's completely dark in here. I can't see anything! マッチをすってよ．まっ暗で何も見えないよ

a box of	matches	マッチ箱

▷I think there's a **box of matches** in that drawer. その引き出しにマッチ箱があると思う

match /mǽtʃ/ 名 試合；似合いの物［人］

have	a match	試合をする
play	a match	
watch	a match	観戦する
see	a match	

| match |

lose	a match	試合に負ける
win	a match	試合に勝つ
meet	one's match	好敵手に出会う

▷ We're **playing** our next **match** on Saturday. 次の試合は土曜日の予定だ
▷ We **lost** the tennis **match** 6-0, 6-0. It was a disaster! 6-0, 6-0 でテニスの試合に負けた. 惨敗だった (★6-0 は six-love と読む)

a big	match	大試合
the final	match	決勝戦
a friendly	match	親善試合
an international	match	国際試合
a boxing	match	ボクシングの試合
a football	match	サッカーの試合
a rugby	match	ラグビーの試合
a good	match	いい組み合わせ
a perfect	match	完璧な組み合わせ

▷ The **final match** takes place next Saturday. 決勝戦は次の土曜日に行われる
▷ I think these curtains would be a **good match** for our wallpaper. このカーテンは壁紙とよく合うと思う
▷ Your new skirt and blouse look great! They're a **perfect match**. あなたの新しいスカートとブラウスはすてき. とてもいい組み合わせね

a match	against A	A との試合
a match	with A	
a match	between A	A の間の試合

▷ Italy's next **match against** Sweden is on Sunday. イタリアとスウェーデンとの次の対戦は日曜日です
▷ I'm looking forward to the **match between** the USA and Brazil. 米国とブラジルの試合を楽しみにしている

match /mætʃ/

動 調和する, 釣り合う; 対戦させる

closely	match	ぴったり合う
exactly	match	
perfectly	match	完璧に合う
not quite	match	うまく合わない
be evenly	matched	互角である

▷ The color of the shoes **exactly matches** your handbag. You have to buy them! その靴の色はあなたのハンドバッグとぴったりよ. 買わなくちゃ
▷ The shoes she was wearing **didn't quite match** her dress. 彼女がはいていた靴は服と合っていなかった
▷ The Wimbledon finalists were **evenly matched**. The match went to 5 sets. ウィンブルドンの決勝戦に出た両選手は実力伯仲で, 試合は第5セットまでもつれ込んだ

match A	with B	A と B を一致させる
match A	to B	
match A	against B	A を B と対戦させる
match A	with B	

▷ You need to **match** the people who come in **with** the names on this list. やってくる人と名簿の名前を照合してください
▷ When you're decorating the house remember that you need to **match** the carpet **to** the curtains. 家を飾りつけるときはカーペットとカーテンを調和させるようにするんだよ
▷ Our judo player was **matched against** a much more experienced opponent. うちの柔道選手の対戦相手はずっと経験豊富だ

material /mətíəriəl/

名 資料; 原料, 材料; 用具, 道具

collect	material	資料を集める
gather	material	
provide	material	資料を提供する
use	material	材料を使う

▷ I'm **collecting material** for my M.A. thesis. 修士論文のための資料を集めている
▷ This book will **provide** some interesting **material** for your essay. この本を読めばレポートを書くいい資料になるだろう

genetic	material(s)	遺伝物質
radioactive	material(s)	放射性物質
recycled	material(s)	リサイクル物質
building	material(s)	建設資材
raw	material(s)	原材料
educational	material(s)	教材
teaching	material(s)	
reading	material(s)	読み物
reference	material(s)	参考資料
research	material(s)	研究資料
writing	material(s)	筆記用具

▷ We are beginning to use **recycled materials** more and more. リサイクル物質の使用が増える一方だ
▷ China supplies some important **raw materials** to Japan for the manufacture of microchips. 中国はマイクロチップ製造のための重要な原材料を日本に供給している

material	for A	A のための資料

▷The editor is always looking for some new **material for** the journal. その編集者はいつも雑誌のための新しいネタを探している

matter /mǽtər/

名 事柄, 問題；物質；(matters で)事情, 事態

raise	a matter	問題を提起する
debate	the matter	問題を論じる
discuss	the matter	
consider	the matter	問題を検討する
investigate	the matter	問題を調査する
handle	the matter	問題を処理する
deal with	the matter	
settle	the matter	問題を解決する
resolve	the matter	
pursue	the matter	問題をさらに追究する

▷I'd like to **raise** a really important **matter**, if I may? きわめて重要な問題を提起したいのですが, よろしいですか

▷We've been **discussing** this **matter** for nearly 3 hours. Let's move on to the next point on the agenda. この問題を議論して3時間近くになります. 次の議題に移りましょう

▷Let's **consider** the **matter** in our next meeting. その件は次の会議で検討しよう

▷My boss promised me that he would **deal with** the **matter** next week. 上司は来週その問題を処理すると私に約束した

▷If an insurance company cannot **settle** the **matter**, it will be handled by a court. 保険会社にその件が解決できなければ裁判所で扱われることになるだろう

an important	matter	重要な問題
a serious	matter	深刻な問題
a delicate	matter	微妙な問題
a personal	matter	個人的な問題
a private	matter	
practical	matters	実際問題
a different	matter	別の問題
an economic	matter	経済問題
environmental	matters	環境問題
financial	matters	財政問題
a legal	matter	法律問題
a political	matter	政治問題
a technical	matter	技術的問題
organic	matter	有機物
printed	matter	印刷物

▷Driving while drunk is a very **serious matter**. 飲酒運転はきわめて深刻な問題だ

▷I'm sorry, I'd rather not talk about it. It's a **personal matter**. 申し訳ありませんがその件はあまり話したくありません. 個人的なことですから

▷If he stays with us for a few days, that's OK. But if it's over a month, that's a **different matter** entirely. 彼がうちに泊まるのが数日だったら問題ないけど, 1か月以上となるとまったく話が別だな(★ that's another matter ともいう)

▷I'm hopeless when it comes to **financial matters**. I leave all that sort of thing to my wife. お金のことになると私はまったく弱くて. そういったことはみな妻に任せています

▷If they find **organic matter** on Mars that means there was life there. 火星に有機物が見つかったら, それは火星に生命があったということだ

be no laughing	matter	笑いごとではない

▷I can't understand why you think it's funny. It's **no laughing matter**. きみがなぜおもしろがっているかわからないな. 笑いごとじゃないんだよ

no matter	wh-	たとえ…でも

★wh- は how, what, where, who など

▷**No matter what** happens, we support you 100%. 何が起きようとも100％あなたを支持します

PHRASES

No matter! ☺ 大したことじゃない, 心配するな
What's the matter? ☺ どうしたのか / **What's the matter with you?** ☺ あなたはどうしてしまったのか
▷What's the matter with you? It's a wonderful opportunity and you're throwing it away! きみはどうかしているんじゃないか. こんなすばらしいチャンスをふいにするなんて

matter /mǽtər/ **動** 重要である, 問題である

A matters	to B	AはB(人)に大事だ

▷Please tell me your opinion. What you think really **matters to** me. きみの意見を聞かせてよ. きみの考えがぼくにはすごく大事なんだ

really	matter	本当に問題だ
hardly	matter	ほとんど問題でない
not much	matter	
no longer	matter	もはや問題でない

▷"I'm so sorry! I broke your vase!" "It **really** doesn't **matter**. I never liked it very much anyway."「本当にごめんなさい. 花瓶を割ってしまって」「大したことありません. その花瓶はあまり気に入っていなかったので」

▷"I think the boss is willing to apologize to you."

"It **hardly matters**. I've decided to quit my job anyway."「ボスはきみに謝ってもいいって言ってるよ」「そんなの関係ないよ．もう辞めるって決めたんだ」

| it doesn't matter | wh- | …かは問題では |
| it doesn't matter | if | ない |

★wh- は what, who, why など

▷**It doesn't matter what** I tell you. You never take any notice! 私が何を言ってもあなたにはどうでもいいのね．ちっとも気に留めてくれないんだもの
▷**It doesn't matter if** you come late. Any time is OK. 遅れてきても構わないよ．いつでもいいんだ

meal /míːl/ 名 食事；1回の食べ物

cook	a meal	食事をつくる
make	a meal	食事をつくる
prepare	a meal	食事を準備する
enjoy	a meal	食事を楽しむ
have	a meal	食事をする
eat	a meal	
serve	a meal	食事を出す
go (out) for	a meal	食事に出かける
skip	a meal	食事を抜く

▷When I get back home I'm too tired to **cook a meal**. 家に帰ると疲れすぎていて食事をつくれない
▷**Enjoy** your **meal**. 食事をお楽しみください（★レストラン従業員が客に言う）
▷We **had** a lovely **meal** at that new Chinese restaurant. あの新しい中華レストランでおいしいものを食べた
▷I'm tired of eating at home. Let's **go out for a meal**. 家で食事をするのは飽きたよ．外に食事に行こう

a good	meal	おいしい食事
a delicious	meal	
a light	meal	軽い食事
a heavy	meal	重い食事
the main	meal	一日でいちばんしっかりとる食事
a hot	meal	温かい食事
a proper	meal	まともな食事

▷We had a very **good meal** at that new Indian restaurant last night. 新しくできたインド料理店できのうの晩とてもおいしい料理を食べた
▷"I'm not very hungry yet." "OK. Let's just have a **light meal** somewhere."「あまりお腹がすいていないんだ」「わかった．どこかで軽い食事をしよう」
▷For me the **main meal** of the day is in the evening. 一日でいちばんしっかり食事をとるのは夜です
▷You can't just eat sandwiches every day. You need a **proper meal**! 毎日サンドイッチばかり食べているわけにはいかないよ．きちんとした食事をしなきゃ

mean /míːn/ 動 意味する；意図する

literally	mean	文字どおり意味する
necessarily	mean	必然的に意味する
probably	mean	おそらく意味する
simply	mean	単に意味する
usually	mean	たいてい意味する

▷Because I say I like golf, it doesn't **necessarily mean** that I'm good at it! 私がゴルフ好きだと言っても，必ずしも得意だということにはならないよ
▷If he says he might not come to the party, it **probably means** he definitely won't come. パーティーに来ないかもしれないと彼が言っているなら，それはおそらく絶対来ないということだろう

| mean | A by B | AをBの意味で使う |

▷What do you **mean by** that? どういうことですか；(怒りを表して)どういうことだ

| mean | (that)... | …ということを意味する |
| mean | to do | …するつもりである |

▷I'm not saying that I won't help you, I just **mean that** I need more time to think about it. きみを手伝わないと言っているんじゃないよ．もっと考える時間が必要だと言っているだけさ ▷This traffic jam goes on for 5 miles. That **means** we're definitely going to miss our plane! この交通渋滞は5マイル続いている．ということは絶対に飛行機に間に合わないよ
▷I didn't **mean to** make her angry. 彼女を怒らせるつもりはなかった

PHRASES

(do) you mean...? ☺(相手の発言を確認して)…のことですか ▷"Who's that famous American film director? You know, ET, Jurassic Park." "Oh, do you mean Steven Spielberg?"「あの有名なアメリカの映画監督はだれだったっけ．ほら，ＥＴやジュラシックパークの」「ああ，スティーブン・スピルバーグのことかい」
I mean (to say) ☺(先の発言を補足・訂正して)つまり，その；いや(そうじゃなくて) ▷When I say it's difficult, I mean to say that it would be impossible. 私が難しいと言ったら，つまりは不可能だろうということだ ▷Take the next on the right... No, sorry. I mean the left! 次を右へ曲がって，いや，すみません．左でした
I know what you mean. / I see what you mean. ☺おっしゃることはわかります ▷I see what you mean, but I don't agree with you. おっしゃることはわかりますが，賛成しかねます
What does A mean? Aはどういう意味ですか ▷What does "serendipity" mean? "serendipity" はどういう意味ですか

You know what I mean? / You see what I mean?
☺(自分の発言を相手に確認して)私の言うことがわかりますね

meaning /míːniŋ/

名 意味；意図, 意義

have	a meaning	意味がある
understand	the meaning	意味を理解する
grasp	the meaning	
convey	the meaning	意味を伝える
explain	the meaning	意味を説明する
take on	a meaning	意味を帯びる
give	a meaning	意味を与える

▷The Japanese word "wa" **has** a special **meaning**. It's difficult to translate into English. 「和」という日本語には特別な意味があり、英語に訳すのは難しい
▷I can't **understand the meaning** of this sentence. この文の意味が理解できません
▷This translation doesn't **convey** the **meaning** of the original text. この翻訳は原文の意味を伝えていない
▷When I started to study Buddhism, it **gave** a whole new **meaning** to my life. 仏教を学び始めたら、私の人生はまったく新しい意味をもつようになった

the exact	meaning	厳密な意味
the precise	meaning	正確な意味
hidden	meaning	隠れた意味
literal	meaning	文字どおりの意味
the original	meaning	元の意味
a figurative	meaning	比喩的な意味
the true	meaning	本当の意味
a different	meaning	異なる意味

▷I know roughly what that word means, but I don't know the **precise meaning**. その語の意味はだいたいはわかりますが、正確な意味はわかりません
▷The **true meaning** of the word "beauty" is difficult to define. 「美」という語の真の意味を定義するのが難しい
▷It's possible for one word to have several **different meanings**. ひとつの語がいくつかの別の意味をもつことがありうる

without	meaning	意味がない

▷I sometimes think that some modern art is totally **without meaning**. 現代美術の中にはまったく意味のないものがあるとときどき思う

means /míːnz/ 名 手段, 方法；資産

provide	a means	手段を提供する
offer	a means	
use	a means	手段を用いる

▷She's over 90 years old. We need to **provide** a **means** of transport for her to get from her house to the hospital. 90歳を超えたおばあさんだから自宅から病院までの交通手段を提供する必要がある
▷We need to **use** a better **means** of improving communication with our customers. 顧客とのコミュニケーションを促進するよりよい手段を用いる必要がある

an alternative	means	代替手段
the best	means	最もよい手段
an effective	means	効果的な手段
a reliable	means	確かな手段

▷The trains have stopped because of the typhoon so we need to find an **alternative means** of getting to Tokyo. 列車が台風で止まったので東京まで行く別の手段を見つける必要がある
▷Raising the price of cigarettes is not always an **effective means** of stopping people from smoking. たばこ値上げは必ずしも人々に禁煙させる効果的な手段ではない

the means	to do	…する資金

▷Our son wants to study in America for a year, but we don't have the **means to** support him. 息子は1年間アメリカで勉強したがっているが、援助する資金がない

no means	of doing	…する手段がない

▷There's **no means of** opening this lock unless you know the number. 番号を知らなければこの錠を開ける手段はない

by	means of A	Aによって
beyond	one's means	収入以上の
within	one's means	収入に見合った

▷The TV program was broadcast **by means of** satellite. そのテレビ番組は衛星によって放送された
▷She lived **within** her **means**. 彼女は身分相応の暮らしをしていた

measure /méʒər/

名 措置, 対策；寸法；計量単位

introduce	measures	対策を導入する
take	measures	対策をとる

▷The government are going to **introduce** meas-

| measure |

ures *to* improve the education system. 政府は教育体系の改善策を導入する予定だ
▷ The police should **take** stronger **measures** *to* control football hooligans. サッカーのフーリガンを規制するために警察はもっと断固とした対策をとるべきだ

an appropriate	measure	適切な措置
a strong	measure	強硬な措置
a drastic	measure	思い切った措置
a temporary	measure	一時的措置
conservation	measures	保護措置
security	measures	安全措置
economic	measures	経済措置

▷ I don't think firing our sales manager is an **appropriate measure**. 営業部長を首にするのは適切な措置ではないと思う
▷ We need to take more **conservation measures** if we are going to save some of our rare animals. 希少動物を保護するつもりならさらに多くの保護措置をとる必要がある

| measures | against A | Aへの対策 |
| a measure | of A | Aの計量単位 |

▷ We need to take **measures against** the possibility of serious flooding. 大洪水が起こるかもしれないので対策をとる必要がある
▷ Kilometers and miles are both **measures of** length. キロメートルもマイルもともに長さの単位だ

measure /méʒər/ 動 測定する, 測る, 計量する; 評価する; …の長さ [大きさ, 分量] がある

measure	accurately	正確に測る
measure	precisely	
measure	directly	直接測る
carefully	measure	注意深く測る

★ accurately measure もほぼ同頻度で用いる

▷ Special cameras are used now to **measure accurately** the speed of passing cars. 通過する車のスピードを正確に測るのに現在は特別なカメラが使われている
▷ We need to **measure** the length of the windows **precisely** before we buy the curtains. カーテンを買う前に窓の長さを正確に測る必要がある

meat /míːt/ 名 (食用の)肉

fresh	meat	新鮮な肉
frozen	meat	冷凍肉
raw	meat	生肉
lean	meat	脂肪の少ない肉, 赤身
potted	meat	瓶詰めの肉

▷ **Fresh meat** always tastes better than meat which has been frozen. 新鮮な肉のほうが冷凍肉よりいつだっておいしい
▷ I don't like meat with fat. I prefer **lean meat**. 脂肪の多い肉は好きではない. 赤身が好きだ

| meat and [or] fish | 肉と [あるいは] 魚 |
| meat and vegetable | 肉と野菜 |

▷ Which would you like, **meat or fish**? 肉と魚のどちらになさいますか

| a piece of | meat | ひと切れの肉 |

▷ That **piece of meat** tasted really good! その肉はとてもおいしかった

medicine /médəsin | médsin/
名 薬; 医学

prescribe	medicine	薬を処方する
take	medicine	薬を飲む
practice	medicine	医者を開業する

▷ The doctor has **prescribed** some new **medicine** for me. 医者は私に新しい薬を処方してくれた
▷ **Take** this **medicine** three times a day. 1日3回この薬を飲んでください
▷ She wants to be a doctor and **practice medicine**. 彼女は医者になって開業したいと思っている

the best	medicine	最良の薬
cough	medicine	せきの薬
prescription	medicine	処方薬
complementary	medicine	代替医療
alternative	medicine	
folk	medicine	民間医療
Chinese	medicine	漢方
Western	medicine	西洋医学

▷ Sleep is **the best medicine** for any diseases. 睡眠はどんな病気にも最良の薬だ
▷ **Chinese medicine** usually works very well. 漢方薬はたいていとてもよく効く

| medicine | for A | Aの薬 |

▷ You need to get some **medicine for** your cough. せきに効く薬を飲む必要がある

| a dose of | medicine | 薬一服 |

▷ If I were you I'd take a **dose of medicine** and go

home to bed. 私だったら薬を一服飲んで家に帰って寝ます

meet /míːt/ 動 会う；面会する

always	meet	いつも会う
rarely	meet	めったに会わない
finally	meet	ついに会う
meet	again	再び会う
meet	frequently	しばしば会う
meet	regularly	定期的に会う

▷We **always meet** on Tuesdays to have lunch together. 私たちはいつも火曜日に会って昼食をいっしょに食べる
▷I've heard so much about you. It's really nice to **finally meet** you. おうわさはかねがね。やっとお目にかかれてとてもうれしいです
▷I hope we **meet again** soon. また近いうちにお目にかかれるといいですね
▷We **meet regularly** every weekend for a game of golf. 私たちは週末ごとに定期的に会ってゴルフをプレーします

meet	at A	A(場所)で会う，A(時間)に会う
meet	on A	A(曜日・日)に会う
meet	with A	A(人)と会見する

▷I'll **meet** you **at** the station in five minutes. 駅で5分後に会おう ▷Let's **meet at** six. 6時に会おう
▷I can't **meet** you **on** Friday. 金曜日にはあなたにお会いできません
▷Some representatives of the Student Union **met with** the Vice Chancellor of the University. 学生自治会の代表の何人かが大学副総長と会合をもった

PHRASES
(It was) nice meeting you. ☺(初対面の人と別れるときに)お会いできてよかったです
Nice to meet you. / Pleased to meet you. ☺ お会いできてうれしいです，はじめまして ▷"This is Tom." "Pleased to meet you."「こちらはトムです」「はじめまして」

meeting /míːtiŋ/

名 会，会議，会合，集会

have	a meeting	会議がある
hold	a meeting	会議を開く
arrange	a meeting	会議を手配する
call	a meeting	会議を招集する
attend	a meeting	会議に出席する
close	a meeting	会議を閉会する
cancel	a meeting	会議を中止する
postpone	a meeting	会議を延期する
chair	a meeting	会議の議長を務める
address	a meeting	会議で演説する

▷We're **holding** a **meeting** next Wednesday. 次の水曜日に会議を開く予定です
▷This month's sales figures are terrible! We need to **call** a **meeting** urgently. 今月の売り上げは散々だった。緊急に会議を招集する必要がある
▷I'm sorry, I can't **attend** the **meeting** next week. すみませんが、来週の会議に出られません
▷We'll have to **postpone** the **meeting** for two weeks. 会議を2週間延期しなければならないだろう
▷"Do you know who's going to **chair** the **meeting**?" "No. The chairperson hasn't been decided yet."「だれが議長を務めるか知っていますか」「いえ、議長はまだ決まっていません」
▷I always feel nervous before I **address** a large **meeting**. 大きな会議で演説する前はいつも緊張する

a meeting	takes place	会議が行われる
a meeting	starts	会議が始まる
a meeting	begins	
a meeting	lasts	会議が続く
a meeting	ends	会議が終わる
a meeting	closes	
a meeting	breaks up	会議が散会する

▷The meeting **took place** on Thursday. 会議は木曜日に行われた
▷The **meeting lasted** three hours. 会議は3時間続いた
▷The **meeting broke up** around 7:00. 会議は7時ごろ散会した

an annual	meeting	年次会議
a monthly	meeting	月例会議
a weekly	meeting	週ごとの会議
regular	meetings	定例会議
a formal	meeting	公式の会議
an informal	meeting	非公式の会議
a general	meeting	総会
a public	meeting	市民集会；意見交換会
a board	meeting	取締役会
a cabinet	meeting	閣議
a summit	meeting	首脳会議

▷We don't need a **weekly meeting**. A **monthly meeting** would be fine. 週ごとの会議は必要ありません。月例会議でいいでしょう
▷We need to hold a **general meeting** of all employees. 全従業員が出る総会を開く必要がある

| member |

▷ A **public meeting** will be held on December 15. 市民集会は12月15日に開かれることになっています

a meeting	with A	Aとの面会
a meeting	between A	Aの間の会議
a meeting	about A	Aについての会議
a meeting	on A	

▷ We've arranged a **meeting with** the Russian President next month. ロシア大統領との会談を来月に設定した

▷ A **meeting between** North Korea and the USA seems unlikely at the moment. 北朝鮮と米国との会議は実現の見込みがなさそうだ

in	a meeting	会議中で
at	a meeting	
during	a meeting	会議の間

▷ "Can I speak to Mr. Davis?" "I'm sorry, he's **in a meeting**. Can I take a message?" (電話で)「デイビスさんをお願いできますか」「申し訳ありません. ただいま会議中で, 伝言を承りましょうか」

▷ Please don't interrupt us with phone calls **during this meeting**. この会議中は電話があっても取り次がないでください

member /mémbər/

名 (組織・集団の)一員, 構成員, 会員

become	a member	一員になる
elect	members	メンバーを選ぶ
include	members	メンバーを含む

▷ She **became a member** of our club two years ago. 彼女は2年前にうちのクラブに入った

▷ We need to **elect** new committee **members** again this year. 今年もまた新しい委員を選ぶ必要がある

▷ Some of the wedding guests **included members** of the royal family. 結婚式の招待客には王室のメンバーも含まれていた

a leading	member	主要メンバー
a prominent	member	
an active	member	活発な会員
an individual	member	個人会員
an honorary	member	名誉会員
a life	member	終身会員
a crew	member	乗組員
a party	member	党員
a union	member	組合員
a family	member	家族の一員
a team	member	チームの一員

▷ He was a **leading member** of the Conservative Party. 彼は保守党の主要メンバーだった

▷ He's an **active member** of the Green Party. 彼は緑の党の活発なメンバーだ

membership /mémbərʃip/

名 会員であること; (集合的に)会員, 会員数

apply for	membership	入会を申し込む
increase	one's membership	会員を増やす
resign	one's membership	退会する
cancel	one's membership	

▷ I'm thinking of **applying for membership** of the debating society. 弁論部に入会を申し込もうと思っている

▷ If we don't **increase** our **membership** we may have to close down. 会員数が増えなければ会は閉じることになるかもしれない

▷ I think I'll have to **resign** my **membership** of the judo club. I don't get enough time to practice anymore. 柔道部を辞めることになると思う. 練習する時間がもう足りないので

associate	membership	準会員
full	membership	正会員
individual	membership	個人会員
a total	membership	全会員数

▷ **Full membership** of the Sports Club is very expensive. スポーツクラブの正会員になるにはかなりお金がかかる

memory /méməri/

名 記憶; 記憶力; 思い出

jog	A's memory	記憶を呼び覚ます
refresh	A's memory	
lose	one's memory	記憶を失う
bring back	memories	思い出を呼び起こす

▷ What you just said about presents just **jogged my memory**. It's my wife's birthday tomorrow! きみがプレゼントのことを口にしたので思い出したよ. あしたは妻の誕生日だった

▷ After the accident he completely **lost** his **memory**. 事故のあと彼はすっかり記憶を失ってしまった

▷ The freezing cold and heavy snow **brought back memories** of her childhood in Canada. 凍えるような寒さと大雪で彼女はカナダで過ごした子どものころを思い出した

| memory | fades | 記憶力が衰える |

▷The older you get, the more your **memory fades**. 年をとればとるほど記憶力は衰える

a vivid	memory	鮮明な記憶
a fond	memory	懐かしい思い出
a good	memory	よい思い出
a happy	memory	幸せな思い出
childhood	memories	子どものころの思い出
long-term	memory	長期記憶
short-term	memory	短期記憶

▷She has **vivid memories** of everybody panicking just after the fire started. 出火直後の, みんながあわてふためいていた姿を彼女は鮮明に記憶している
▷I have **fond memories** of playing with my puppy when I was a child. 子どものころ子犬と遊んだ懐かしい思い出がある
▷She had very **happy memories** of her father. 彼女には父親のことでとても幸せな思い出があった
▷My grandfather's **short-term memory** is getting worse, but his **long-term memory** is still very good. 祖父はすぐ前のことは覚えられなくなってきているが, 昔のことはいまもよく覚えている

have	a good memory	記憶力がいい
have	a bad memory	記憶力が悪い
have	a long memory	昔のことをよく覚えている
have	a short memory	忘れっぽい

▷I **have** a **good memory** for faces. 私は一度顔を見たら忘れません
▷We had a big argument five years ago. He hasn't forgotten. He **has** a **long memory**! ぼくたち5年前にひどい言い争いをしたんだけど, 彼はいまだに忘れていないんだ. 昔のことを根にもつタイプだよ
▷When I learn a new English word, ten minutes later I've forgotten it. I **have** a very **short memory**! 新しい英単語を学ぶと10分後には忘れているんだ. ほんとに忘れっぽくて

a memory	for A	Aの記憶
from	memory	記憶を頼りに
in	memory of A	A(人)を記念して, 追悼して

▷I have a really bad **memory for** names. 名前がなかなか覚えられない
▷He won the speech contest. He recited the whole of "I have a dream" **from memory**! 彼はスピーチコンテストで優勝した. (キング牧師の)「私には夢がある」の全文を暗唱してみせたのだ
▷Church services were held all over the country **in memory of** the President. 大統領を追悼する礼拝が全国で行われた

mention /ménʃən/

動 言及する, 話題に出す; 名を挙げる

mentioned	previously	前述した
mentioned	earlier	
mentioned	above	上で述べた
mentioned	below	下で述べた
mention	briefly	簡単に述べる
specifically	mention	はっきり述べる

▷As Mr. Taylor **mentioned earlier**, we are looking for someone to transfer to our head office in Tokyo. テイラー氏が先ほど言及したように, 東京本社に異動させる人を探しています
▷As I **mentioned above**, this data is not completely reliable. 上述のようにこのデータは必ずしも信用できない
▷Could you **mention briefly** why you decided to apply for this post? このポストに応募することに決めた理由を簡単におっしゃっていただけますか
▷The tour guide **specifically mentioned** that we should bring our own packed lunches. ツアーガイドは弁当を持ってくるようきちんと言った

| mention A | to B | AをB(人)に話す |

▷Please don't **mention** this **to** anyone else! これはほかのだれにも話さないでね

| mention | (that)... | …と言う |

▷She just **mentioned that** she'd got a new job. She didn't give any details. 新しい職が見つかったと言っただけで, それ以上詳しいことは彼女は教えてくれなかった

PHRASES

Don't mention it. ☺ (お礼やおわびへの返事で)どういたしまして, 気になさらないでください ▷"Thanks for all your help." "That's OK. Don't mention it."「いろいろ助けていただきありがとうございます」「いいえ, どういたしまして」

menu /ménjuː/

名 メニュー, 献立表; (コンピュータの)メニュー

offer	a menu	メニューを提供する
study	the menu	メニューをよく見る
select from	the menu	メニューから選ぶ
choose from	the menu	

▷This restaurant **offers** a wide **menu** of Japanese

and Western food. このレストランには日本食から洋食まで幅広いメニューがある
▷He **studied** the **menu** for several minutes before making his choice. 彼は数分じっくりメニューを見てから何にするか決めた
▷If you want to print something out, just **select** "PRINT" **from** the **menu**. 何か印刷したければ、メニューから「印刷」を選んでください

an à la carte	menu	一品料理のメニュー
a special	menu	特別メニュー
dinner	menu	ディナーメニュー
lunch	menu	ランチメニュー
set	menu	定食
the main	menu	メインメニュー
pull-down	menu	プルダウンメニュー

▷I don't want to choose a set. Let's ask for the **à la carte menu**. セットメニューは選びたくないから、一品料理を頼もう
▷Because it's Christmas they have a **special menu**. クリスマスなので特別料理があります

a choice of	menu	メニューの選択

▷As we all like different things, let's go to a place where there's a wide **choice of menu**. みんな好みが違うんだから、メニューの幅広い店に行こうよ

[PHRASES]
Could I have the menu? ☺ メニューを見せていただけますか
What's on the menu? ☺ メニューは何ですか

mess /més/ 名 混乱(状態); 窮地

make	a mess	散らかす
leave	a mess	
clean up	the mess	散らかった物を片付ける
clear up	the mess	
look (like)	a mess	ひどい格好をしている
get into	a mess	困ったことになる
get A into	a mess	A(人)を困らせる

▷Why didn't you clean your shoes outside? Look! You've **made** a **mess** all over the kitchen floor! どうして外で靴をきれいにしなかったの。見てよ。台所の床じゅう汚れちゃったでしょ
▷After the party everybody went home. Nobody helped me to **clean up** the **mess**. パーティーのあと、みんな家に帰ってしまい、片づけをだれも手伝ってくれなかった
▷Give me another 10 minutes to put on my make-up. I can't go out like this. I **look** a **mess**! 化粧にもう10分ちょうだい。こんなひどい格好では出かけられないもの

▷I'm no good at reading maps. Every time I try I **get into** a terrible **mess**! 地図を読むのが苦手で、読もうとするたびにお手上げなんだ
▷Don't **get** me **into** another **mess** like you did last time! このあいだみたいにぼくをまた困らせないでくれ

a complete	mess	ひどい散らかりよう、
an awful	mess	めちゃくちゃな状態
a real	mess	
an economic	mess	経済の混乱

▷"The bathroom's a **real mess**! Water everywhere!" "Sorry, I filled the bath too full!" 「ふろ場がひどいことになってるよ。水浸しだ」「ごめん。おふろをあふれさせちゃった」

in	a mess	散らかって;困って

▷"I'm afraid my room is **in** an awful **mess**!" "I don't think so. You should see mine."「私の部屋はひどく散らかっているんだ」「そんなことはないよ。ぼくの部屋よりましさ」

[PHRASES]
What a mess! ☺ なんて散らかっているんだ;困ったことだ ▷What a mess! Look! I've never seen such an untidy bedroom! なんて散らかりようだ。こんなに散らかった寝室は見たことがないよ

message /mésidʒ/
名 伝言, 言づて; (作品の)意図, メッセージ

convey	a message	伝言を伝える
deliver	a message	
carry	a message	
give	a message	
pass on	a message	
get	a message	伝言を受け取る
receive	a message	
leave	a message	伝言を残す
send	a message	伝言を送る
take	a message	伝言を受ける

▷Could you **give** Sarah a **message** from me? サラに私からの伝言を伝えていただけますか
▷Bill asked me to **pass on** a **message** to you. あなたに伝言するよう私はビルから頼まれた
▷Sorry, I didn't **get** your **message**. 申し訳ありませんがあなたからの伝言を受け取っていません
▷Could I **leave** a **message**? 伝言をお願いできますか
▷I **left** a **message** on her voice mail. 彼女のボイスメールに伝言を残した
▷We should **send** the **message** by email, not by phone. メッセージを電話ではなくEメールで送ったほうがよい

▷Sorry, Tim's not in now. Can I **take** a **message**? ティムは今おりません. 伝言を承りましょうか

an important	message	重要な伝言
an urgent	message	至急の伝言
a personal	message	個人的伝言
a clear	message	明確なメッセージ
a simple	message	単純なメッセージ
a recorded	message	録音メッセージ
a warning	message	警告メッセージ
an error	message	エラーメッセージ

▷We need to send a **clear message**: if you drink and drive, you'll lose your driving license! 飲酒運転をしたら免停になるとの明確なメッセージを送る必要がある
▷**Recorded messages** are useful. You can play them back as often as you like. 録音メッセージは便利で, 好きなだけ聞き直せる

the message	of A	Aの伝言; Aのメッセージ
a message	from A	Aからの伝言
a message	for A	Aへの伝言
a message	to A	Aへの伝言; Aへのメッセージ

▷The **message of** the book is that no-one wins in a nuclear war. その本のメッセージは核戦争にはだれも勝者はいないということだ
▷Oh, there's a **message from** your daughter. そう言えば娘さんから伝言があります
▷I'd like to leave a **message for** Mrs. Bobby Davis. ボビー・デイビス夫人に伝言を残したいのですが
▷John Lennon's song 'Imagine' is a **message to** the world. ジョン・レノンの「イマジン」は世界へのメッセージだ

method /méθəd/ 名 方法, 方式

adopt	a method	方法を採用する
apply	a method	方法を応用する
use	a method	方法を使う
develop	a method	方法を開発する
devise	a method	方法を工夫する

▷We need to **apply** a different sales **method**. This one isn't working. 別の販売方法を用いる必要がある. この方法はうまくいっていない
▷The police are **using** new **methods** to fight against terrorism. 警察はテロと戦うための新しい方法を使っている
▷We need to **devise** a new **method** for advertising our products. うちの製品を広告する新しい方法を工夫する必要がある

a method	is used	方法が使われる
a method	is employed	
a method	has been developed	方法が開発される

▷A simple **method** was **employed** to extract particles of gold from the stream. 小川から金粉を採取するのに単純な方法が使われていた
▷A new **method** has been **developed** for obtaining drinking water from salt water. 海水から飲み水を得る新たな方法が開発された

an effective	method	効果的方法
the principal	method	主要な方法
a new	method	新しい方法
the traditional	method	伝統的方法
a simple	method	簡単な方法
a different	method	別の方法
an alternative	method	代替の方法
various	methods	さまざまな方法
statistical	methods	統計的手法

▷Watching American films can be an **effective method** for improving your English. アメリカ映画を見るのは英語力を高める効果的な方法かもしれない
▷For many years the **principal method** of transportation in the desert was by camel. 何年もの間, 砂漠での主要な運搬方法はラクダによるものだった
▷The ecocar uses a **new method** to power motorcars. エコカーは新しい方法を用いて自動車に動力を供給している
▷There are **various methods** we can use to reduce costs. コスト削減のためにいろんな方法が使える
▷We need to use **statistical methods** to present the results of our survey. 私たちの調査結果を提示するのに統計的方法を使う必要がある

a method	for A	Aのための方法

midnight /mídnàit/ 名 真夜中

at	midnight	真夜中に
by	midnight	真夜中までに
until	midnight	
around	midnight	真夜中ごろに

▷**By midnight** she was beginning to get really worried. 夜の12時になるころにはもう彼女は心配でたまらなくなった
▷I didn't get home **until midnight**. 真夜中まで帰宅しなかった

| mild |

▷I always get hungry **around midnight**. いつも真夜中ごろに腹が減る

mild /máild/ 形 温暖な；穏やかな

relatively	mild	比較的温暖な；比較的穏やかな
unusually	mild	いつになく温暖な
very	mild	とても温暖な；とても穏やかな

▷He's got flu, but it's OK. It's **relatively mild**. 彼はインフルエンザにかかったけどだいじょうぶです．比較的軽い症状です

▷This curry tastes **very mild**. I prefer a really hot Indian curry! このカレーはとても甘口だ．激辛のインドカレーのほうが好きだな

mile /máil/

名 マイル(約1.6km)；(miles で)かなりの距離

3 miles	from A	Aから3マイル
20 miles	away	20マイル離れて

▷My house is about three **miles from** the nearest station. 私の家は最寄り駅から約3マイルです

5 miles	long	長さ5マイルの

★ deep, high なども用いる

▷The hike is only about five **miles long**. We can easily do it in an hour and a half. ほんの5マイルくらいのハイキングだから1時間半で簡単に終わるよ

for	miles	ずっと遠くまで

▷From the top of the mountain you can see **for miles**. 山頂からずっと遠くまで見渡せる

50 miles	per hour	時速50マイル
50 miles	an hour	
20 miles	to the gallon	ガソリン1ガロン当たり20マイル
20 miles	per gallon	
20 miles	a gallon	

▷Jack says his sports car can do over 120 **miles an hour**! ジャックの話では彼のスポーツカーは時速120マイル以上出るんだって

▷The fuel consumption is not very good. Only 20 **miles to the gallon**. 燃費はあまりよくなくて1ガロン当たりわずか20マイルだ

milk /mílk/ 名 牛乳, ミルク

drink	milk	牛乳を飲む
take	milk	牛乳を入れる
add	milk	ミルクを加える
pour	milk	ミルクを注ぐ
spill	milk	ミルクをこぼす

▷"Do you **take milk**?" "Only with tea. Not with coffee, thanks."「ミルクを入れますか」「紅茶には入れますが，コーヒーには入れません」

▷Don't forget to **add** a little **milk** when you make the omelette. オムレツをつくるときは忘れずに牛乳を少し加えなさい

▷Oh, look! You've **spilt milk** all over the table! おい．テーブルじゅうに牛乳をこぼしてるぞ

fresh	milk	新鮮なミルク
hot	milk	熱いミルク
cold	milk	冷たいミルク
cow's	milk	牛乳
goat's	milk	ヤギ乳
condensed	milk	練乳
skim(med)	milk	脱脂乳
breast	milk	母乳

▷I live on a farm, so we always have **fresh milk**. 農場で暮らしているので，いつも絞りたての牛乳を飲んでいます

▷**Skim milk**, please. I hate it, but I'm on a diet! 脱脂乳をください．嫌いなんだけどダイエット中なので

a glass of	milk	ミルク一杯
a liter of	milk	1リットルのミルク

▷Could I have a **glass of milk**, please? ミルクを一杯いただけますか

million /míljən/

名 100万；(millions で)何百万, 無数

a hundred	million	1億

▷Our market is expected to expand to over a **hundred million** people by the year 2025. われわれの市場は2025年までに1億人以上に拡大すると予想される

three million	dollars	300万ドル

▷Her house in Hollywood cost over 6 **million** dollars. ハリウッドにある彼女の家は600万ドル以上した(★ three million のように million の前に数詞がつく場合，s をつけない単数形のほうがふつう)

millions	of A	何百万のA；多数のA

▷I've told you **millions of** times! Wear your slippers when you come into the house! 何度も何度も言っているでしょ．家に入るときはスリッパをはきなさい

mind /máind/ 名 心，頭；精神；知性

bear in	mind	心に留めておく
keep in	mind	
bring A	to mind	Aを思い出す
call A	to mind	
come to	mind	心に浮かぶ
spring to	mind	
cross	A's mind	頭をよぎる
occupy	A's mind	頭を満たす
read	A's mind	心を読む
slip	A's mind	つい忘れる
stick in	A's mind	心にまとわりつく
close	one's mind	心を閉ざす
concentrate	one's mind	頭を集中する
lose	one's mind	正気を失う

▷You don't have to do anything about the problem now, just **bear** it **in mind**. その問題についていまは何もしなくていいです．ただ心に留めておいてください
▷Now that I know you're interested in a part-time job, I'll **keep** you **in mind**. アルバイトに興味があるとのことなので，きみのことを気にかけておくよ
▷I can't **bring** her name **to mind** at the moment. いまのところ彼女の名前が思い出せない
▷I know his name, but it just won't **come to mind**. 彼の名前は知っているんだが，思い出せない
▷My boss asked me if I had any ideas about a new project but nothing immediately **sprang to mind**. 上司から新しい計画について何か考えがないかと聞かれたが，すぐには何も思い浮かばなかった
▷I can't sleep because I think so much. I have so much to **occupy** my **mind**. 考えすぎて眠れないの．頭の中がいろんなことでいっぱいで
▷"Why don't we go to see a movie?" "You must have **read** my **mind**. That's just what I was going to say!"「映画を見に行かないか」「私の心を読んだのね．私も同じことを言おうとしていたの」
▷Sorry I forgot to phone you yesterday. It completely **slipped** my **mind**. きのうきみに電話するのを忘れてごめん．すっかり失念していた
▷My first day at school will always **stick in** my **mind**. 学校での最初の日のことは決して忘れないだろう

one's conscious	mind	意識
one's subconscious	mind	潜在意識
one's unconscious	mind	無意識
a brilliant	mind	優れた知性
a creative	mind	創造力
a closed	mind	閉ざされた心

▷After the accident he was in a coma. His **conscious mind** had stopped working. 事故のあと彼は昏睡状態にあって，意識の働きが止まっていた
▷Like all great writers, he has a very **creative mind**. 偉大な作家がすべてそうであるように，彼は創造力にあふれている
▷Ella's got a **closed mind** when it comes to taking other people's advice. ほかの人の忠告を受け入れる段になるとエラは心を閉ざしてしまう

a frame of	mind	心の状態，気分
a state of	mind	
a change of	mind	心変わり

▷I wouldn't speak to him now, if I were you. He's in an angry **frame of mind**. ぼくがきみならいま彼に話しかけないよ．機嫌が悪いから
▷I regret that he has now had a **change of mind**. 彼が心変わりしてしまったのが残念だ

mind and body	心と体

★body and mind も用いる

▷His **mind and body** had both been exhausted. 彼は心も体も疲れ果てていた

in	mind	心に
in	A's mind	心の中で
on	A's mind	気にかかって

▷I can't offer you a definite job now, but I've something **in mind**. いまはこれといった仕事をあなたに出せませんが，心当たりはあります
▷Thoughts of emigrating to Canada had been going on **in** his **mind** for some time. カナダへの移住を彼はしばらく考えていた
▷What's **on** your **mind**? 何を気にしているの ▷I think Paula's really attractive, don't you? I've **had** her **on** my **mind** all week. ポーラってほんとに魅力的だね．この1週間ずっと彼女のことが頭から離れないんだ

minority /minɔ́ːrəti | mainɔ́r-/

名 少数；少数派

represent	a minority	少数派を代表する

▷I think your opinion **represents** only a **minority** of employees at this company. あなたの意見はこの会社では従業員のほんの少数派だと思う

a small	minority	ごく少数
ethnic	minority	少数民族

| minute |

a minority	group	少数派

▷ Only a **small minority** caused trouble at the soccer game. サッカーの試合で問題を引き起こしたのはごく少数の人たちだった
▷ The opinions of the **ethnic minority** are very important to us. 少数民族の意見は私たちにはとても重要だ

in a [the] minority		少数派で

▷ Only you, me and a few others want to change the system. I'm afraid we're **in a minority**. あなたと私のほか,わずかの人たちが制度を変えたいと思っている.残念ながら私たちは少数派だ

minute /mínit/ 名 分;ちょっとの間

have	10 minutes	10分ある
give A	10 minutes	Aに10分与える
last	10 minutes	10分続く
spend	10 minutes	10分費やす
take	10 minutes	10分かかる
waste	10 minutes	10分むだにする
wait	a minute	ちょっと待つ
hold on	a minute	
hang on	a minute	

▷ We only **have** 10 **minutes** before the train leaves. 列車が出るまで10分しかない
▷ The lecture only **lasted** 20 **minutes**, but it felt like 2 hours! たった20分の講義だったが2時間のように感じた
▷ I **spent** the last 20 **minutes** trying to phone you, but I only got the engaged signal. 20分前からずっときみに電話しているのに,ずっと話し中の音ばかりだったよ
▷ It only **takes** 10 **minutes** from the station to my house. 駅から私の家までは10分しかかからない
▷ We've **wasted** 20 **minutes** looking for your car keys! きみの車のキー探しで20分むだにしたよ
▷ **Wait a minute.** ☺ ちょっと待って ▷ Just a minute! You haven't paid for the cigarettes! **Wait a minute!** Come back! ちょっと,たばこ代をまだいただいていませんよ.ちょっと待って.戻ってきて
▷ **Hold on a minute.** ☺ (電話で)切らずに少々お待ちください

a few	minutes	2, 3分
a couple of	minutes	
a further	5 minutes	さらに5分
another	5 minutes	
several	minutes	数分
final	minutes	終了間際

the last	minute	間際

▷ You need to cook those potatoes for a **further** 5 **minutes**. ジャガイモをさらに5分加熱してください
▷ From there we had to walk **another** 30 **minutes** to get to his house. そこから彼の家に着くまでさらに30分歩かなければならなかった
▷ You go ahead. I'll only be a **couple of minutes**. 先に行って.2, 3分で済むから
▷ In the **final minutes** of play, both sides missed good opportunities. 試合終了間際に両チームとも絶好のチャンスを逃した
▷ Unfortunately, at the **last minute**, I got sick and couldn't go. いよいよというときにあいにく病気になって行けなかった

ten minutes	late	10分遅れで
5 minutes	later	5分後に
ten minutes	long	10分の長さの

▷ She arrived twenty **minutes late** for our appointment. 彼女は約束に20分遅れて着いた
▷ I got on the train and sat down. Ten **minutes later**, I found it was going in the wrong direction! 列車に乗って座ったんだけど,10分後に行き先が違う列車に乗ったのに気づいた
▷ According to the DVD cover this movie is 178 **minutes long**. DVDのカバーによるとこの映画の長さは178分です

five minutes		after ten	10時5分過ぎに
(英) five minutes		past ten	
five minutes		before ten	10時5分前に
(英) five minutes		to ten	
for	a minute		ちょっとの間
for	a few minutes		2, 3分の間
in	5 minutes		5分したら
in	a minute		すぐに
within	minutes		

▷ We arrived at three **minutes after** ten. 10時3分過ぎに着いた
▷ It's seven **minutes to** eight. 8時7分前です
▷ Let me think **for a minute**. ちょっと考えさせて
▷ Would you mind waiting **for a few minutes**? 2, 3分待っていただけませんか
▷ I'll be back **in** ten **minutes**. 10分で戻ります
▷ I'll be back **in a minute**. すぐ戻ります

PHRASES
Do you have a minute? ☺ ちょっと時間がありますか
▷ Do you have a minute? There's something I wanted to ask you. ちょっと時間あるかな.聞きたいことがあるんだ

mirror /mírər/ 名 鏡

look in	the mirror	鏡を見る
glance in	the mirror	鏡をちらっと見る
stand before	a mirror	鏡の前に立つ
stand in front of	a mirror	

▷ "Do I have something in my eye? I can't see anything." "Why don't you **look in** the **mirror**?" 「片方の目に何か入ったかな．何も見えないや」「鏡を見てご覧」

▷ She **glanced in** the rearview **mirror** and saw that a car was about to overtake her. 彼女がバックミラーをちらっと見ると，1台の車が彼女の車を追い越そうとしているのが目に入った

in	the mirror	鏡で

▷ Does this hat look OK on me? I need to see myself **in** the **mirror**. この帽子は私に似合うかな．鏡に映してみなきゃ

▷ She stared at herself **in** the **mirror**. There were red spots all over her face. 彼女は鏡に映った自分をじっと見た．顔中に赤い発疹ができていた

a full-length	mirror	姿見
the bathroom	mirror	浴室の鏡
a rearview	mirror	バックミラー

▷ I think we need a **full-length mirror** in the hallway. 玄関に姿見が必要だな

▷ "You should look in the **rearview mirror** when you're reversing!" "I am. Oh! What was that!" 「バックするときはバックミラーを見たほうがいいよ」「見ているよ．おっと，何だ」

miserable /mízərəbl/ 形 みじめな

feel	miserable	情けない思いをする
make A	miserable	Aをみじめにする

▷ This kind of weather **makes** me really **miserable**. こんな天気で本当にみじめになる

so	miserable	すごくみじめな
thoroughly	miserable	とてもみじめな

▷ Why do you look **so miserable**? なぜそんなにみじめそうにしているの

▷ It rained every day when we were on holiday. We had a **thoroughly miserable** time. 休暇中は毎日雨だった．まったくひどい目にあった

miserable	little	みすぼらしい

▷ The man who worked in the library was a **miserable little** man who never smiled. 図書館で働いていた男はちっとも笑わないみすぼらしい男だった

miss /mís/

動 はずす，はずれる；乗り遅れる；いなくて寂しい

completely	miss	完全にはずす
just	miss	ちょうど乗り損なう
narrowly	miss	危うく…しかける
really	miss	心から寂しく思う
be sorely	missed	いないのが惜しまれる

▷ "Has the 10:45 train to Kyoto left yet?" "Yes. You **just missed** it!" 「10時45分発の京都行きの列車はもう出ましたか」「ちょうど出たところです」

▷ Look where you're going! You **narrowly missed** hitting that car! 周りをよく見ろよ．もうちょっとであの車にぶつけるところだったぞ

▷ I **really miss** you. あなたがいなくて本当に寂しい

▷ We heard that Mr. Petersen died last Sunday. He'll **be sorely missed**. ピーターセンさんがこの前の日曜日に亡くなられたそうです．惜しい方を亡くしました

miss	doing	…できなくて残念だ

▷ It was a great holiday! I **miss** lying on the beach doing nothing all day! すてきな休暇だった．あんなふうに一日中何もせずに浜辺にずっと寝そべっていられたらなあ

PHRASES

I missed that! ☺ 聞き逃してしまったんですが（★もう一度言ってほしいときに用いる） ▷ I'm sorry I missed that. すみません，聞き逃してしまいました

You can't miss it. ☺ すぐにわかります；見逃すはずはありません

missing /mísiŋ/

形 欠けている；行方不明の，紛失した

go	missing	なくなる；行方不明になる

▷ My cellphone has **gone missing**. 携帯電話がどこかへ行っちゃった

still	missing	なお行方不明の

▷ Ten people are **still missing**. 10名がなお行方不明になっている

missing	from A	Aから欠けている

| mist |

▷Why is my name **missing from** the list? なぜ私の名前が名簿にないのかな

mist /míst/ 名 霧, もや

be shrouded	in mist	霧に包まれる

▷In the early morning, Mount Fuji was **shrouded in mist**. 早朝の富士山は霧に包まれていた

a mist	rises	霧が立ち上る
a mist	drifts	霧が漂う
a mist	hangs	霧が立ち込める
a mist	comes down	霧が降りてくる
the mist	clears	霧が晴れる

▷There's a cold **mist** gently **rising** up from the sea. 冷たい霧が海から静かに立ち上っている
▷It's still early in the morning. You can see the **mist** still **hanging** over those trees. まだ早朝で, 木々に霧が立ち込めているのが見える
▷The morning **mist** over the river is beginning to **clear**. 川にかかった朝霧が晴れ始めた

(a) thick	mist	濃霧
(a) heavy	mist	
(a) thin	mist	薄い霧
(a) fine	mist	細かい霧

▷A **thick mist** covered the top of the mountain. 濃い霧が山頂をおおった

mistake /mistéik/ 名 誤り, 間違い

make	a mistake	誤る, 間違える
realize	one's mistake	誤りに気づく
admit	a mistake	誤りを認める
correct	a mistake	誤りを直す
learn from	one's mistakes	過ちから学ぶ
repeat	the mistake(s)	過ちを繰り返す
avoid	the mistake	誤りを避ける

▷With English it's OK to **make mistakes**. That's how you learn! 英語は間違えてもいいんだ. そうやって覚えるんだから
▷When he **realized** his **mistake** it was too late. 彼が自分の誤りに気づいたときにはすでに遅すぎた
▷You have to **learn from** your **mistakes**. 間違いから学ばなければなりません

a big	mistake	大きな間違い
a great	mistake	
a bad	mistake	ひどい誤り

a serious	mistake	
a terrible	mistake	
a common	mistake	よくある間違い
past	mistakes	過去の過ち
the same	mistake	同じ過ち

▷Marrying you was **the biggest mistake** of my life! あなたと結婚したのは私の人生の最大の誤りだったわ
▷The Government has made a **serious mistake** in its foreign policy. 政府は外交政策でひどい誤りを犯した
▷You shouldn't blame him for his **past mistakes**. 過去の過ちで彼を責めないほうがいい

by	mistake	間違って, 誤って

▷Sorry, I opened your letter **by mistake**. ごめん. 間違ってきみの手紙を開封しちゃった

it is a mistake	to do	…するのは間違いだ
make the mistake	of doing	

▷**It** was a **mistake to** ask Tony to give our wedding speech. トニーにぼくたちの結婚式のスピーチを頼んだのは間違いだった
▷I'm afraid you **made** the **mistake of** expecting David to help you. デイビッドが助けてくれると期待するのは間違いだったよ

mix /míks/ 動 混ぜる；混ざる；交わる

mix	thoroughly	十分に混ぜる
mix	well	よく混ぜる
mix	together	混じり合う
mix A	together	Aを混ぜ合わせる
mix	easily	簡単に交わる
mix	freely	自由に交わる

★thoroughly mix, well mix も用いる

▷Add the sugar, butter and eggs and **mix thoroughly** for 2 to 3 minutes. 砂糖, バターと卵を加えて2, 3分よく混ぜてください
▷Oil and water don't **mix together**. 水と油は混じり合わない
▷**Mix** the eggs, flour and water **together**. 卵と小麦粉と水を混ぜ合わせます
▷The children **mixed freely** with each other. 子どもたちは自由に交流し合った

mix A	with B	AとBを混ぜる
mix	with A	A(人)とつきあう

▷**Mix** the eggs **with** flour. 卵を小麦粉と混ぜてください
▷I'm afraid he's **mixing with** the wrong sort of

person. どうも彼は悪そうな人とつきあっている

mix and match		組み合わせる

▷Customers **mix and match** our 21 toppings any way they want on their hot dogs. 当店のホットドッグはどれでもお好きな21のトッピングを組み合わせて召し上がっていただけます

model /mάdl | mɔ́dl/

名 模型；機種；手本，模範；モデル

build	a model	模型をつくる
construct	a model	
make	a model	
develop	a model	機種を開発する
produce	a model	機種を生み出す
provide	a model	モデルとなる

▷We're **building** a **model** of a new type of aircraft. 新型飛行機の模型を製作中なんだ
▷Our company's stopped producing the SS 2000. We're **developing** a new **model** now. わが社はSS 2000の生産を中止し，新機種を開発中だ
▷Our new eco-car should **provide** a **model** for all future cars. わが社の新型エコカーは未来のすべての車のモデルとなるはずだ

a working	model	実用模型
a new	model	新機種
the latest	model	最新機種
a simple	model	簡単なモデル
a standard	model	標準モデル
an alternative	model	代替モデル
a theoretical	model	理論モデル
an economic	model	経済モデル
a fashion	model	ファッションモデル

▷I'm going to sell my car and get a **new model**. いまの車を売って新型車に買い換えるつもりだ
▷This is the **standard model**, but there is a more expensive **alternative model**. これは標準モデルだが，これより高価な代替モデルがある

a model	for A	Aの模範

▷He's a **model for** us all. The perfect husband! 彼は私たちみんなの手本で，夫として完璧だ

moment /móumənt/

名 瞬間，ちょっとの間；(特定の)時期

have	a moment	少し時間がある
take	a moment	少し時間がかかる
wait	a moment	ちょっと待つ
enjoy	every moment	一瞬一瞬を楽しむ
choose	a moment	時期を選ぶ
seize	the moment	時期をとらえる

▷I wanted to ask you a couple of things. Do you **have** a **moment**? 頼みたいことがあったんだけど，ちょっと時間あるかな
▷Would you mind filling in this questionnaire? It won't **take** a **moment**. このアンケートに記入していただいて構いませんか．お時間は取らせません
▷Could you **wait** a **moment**, please? I'll see if Mr. Roberts is in his office. 少々お待ちいただけませんか．ロバーツさんがオフィスにいるかどうか見てみます
▷If you want to talk to him **choose** a **moment** when he's not too busy. 彼に話をしたいならあまり忙しくない時を選びなさい

a brief	moment	ちょっとの間
a spare	moment	暇な時間
the precise	moment	まさにその時
the exact	moment	
the very	moment	
the present	moment	いまこの時
the right	moment	適切な時期
a critical	moment	重大な局面
a crucial	moment	
the last	moment	間際，土壇場

▷At the **precise moment** I walked in, she walked out. ぼくが入って行ったちょうどそのとき彼女は出て行った
▷At the **present moment** we don't know how many people were hurt in the accident. 現時点では事故で何人が負傷したかわからない
▷Sherlock Holmes said: "So the name of the murderer is..." and suddenly, at the **crucial moment**, there was a power cut and the TV went off!「そこで殺人犯の名前だが…」とシャーロック・ホームズが言いかけた肝心なところで急に停電してテレビが消えてしまったんだ
▷She's not coming to the party. She changed her mind at the **last moment**. 彼女はパーティーに来ないよ．間際になって気が変わったんだ

after	a moment	一瞬後に
at	a moment	その瞬間に
for	a moment	ちょっとの間
in	a moment	一瞬で
(up) until	that moment	その時まで

★ **for a moment** は think, hesitate, pause, stand, wait との連結が高頻度

▷ **After** a **moment**, there was complete silence. 一瞬後にまったく何も音がしなくなった
▷ **At** that **moment**, I knew I had made a mistake. その瞬間、間違えたのに気づいた
▷ Mr. Mark, could I speak to you **for** a **moment**? マークさん、ちょっとお話しできますか
▷ I'll be finished **in** a **moment**. すぐに終わります

a moment	ago	ちょっと前に
a moment	later	ちょっと後で

PHRASES

Just a moment. / Wait a moment. ☺ ちょっと待ってください

money /mʌ́ni/ 名 お金, 金銭

make	money	金を稼ぐ
earn	money	
get	money	金を手に入れる
have	money	金がある
cost	money	金がかかる
pay	money	金を払う
borrow	money	金を借りる
lend	money	金を貸す
refund	money	金を返済する
spend	money	金を使う
save	money	金を節約する；貯金する
waste	money	金を浪費する
invest	money	金を投資する
put	money	
lose	money	金を失くす；損を出す
raise	money	募金する；資金を調達する
run out of	money	金がなくなる

▷ Do you know any good ways to **make money** quickly? 手っ取り早く金を稼ぐいい方法を知ってるかい
▷ He didn't **have** much **money**. 彼にはあまり金がなかった
▷ I think John's new car **cost** a lot of **money**. ジョンの新車はとても高かったと思う
▷ I need to **borrow** some **money** *from* the bank. 銀行からお金を借りる必要がある
▷ I don't think that **lending money** to him is a good idea. 彼にお金を貸すのはよくないと思う
▷ I **spent** a lot of **money** on Christmas presents this year. 今年はクリスマスプレゼントにお金をたくさん使った(★ ˣ use money とはいわない)
▷ He **invested** a large sum of **money** in his new project. 彼は新しいプロジェクトに多額の金を投資した
▷ Do you think I should **put** my **money** *into* the stock market? 株に投資したほうがいいかな
▷ I wanted to spend a month in Paris, but after a couple of weeks I **ran out of money**. パリに1か月滞在したかったが、2, 3週間で金が底をついた

big	money	大金
good	money	
pocket	money	小遣い
spending	money	
sufficient	money	十分な金
extra	money	余分な金
easy	money	労せず手に入る金
public	money	公的資金
grant	money	補助金, 奨学金
prize	money	賞金
paper	money	紙幣

▷ Houses in central London cost **big money**. They are very expensive. ロンドン中心部の家はすごく高価で、お金がたくさんかかる
▷ We still haven't got **sufficient money** to start our own business. 自分たちで会社を始めるには資金がまだ足りない
▷ The government has spent a lot of **public money** trying to improve the health service. 政府は医療サービス改善のために多額の公的資金を使った

how much	money	お金をいくら

▷ **How much money** do you have? お金をいくら持っていますか

PHRASES

Money is no object. ☺ 金額は問題ではない(いくらかかっても構わない)
Money isn't everything! ☺ お金がすべてじゃない(お金以外に大切なことがある)
Money talks. ☺ 金がものを言う

month /mʌ́nθ/ 名 (暦の)月

spend	one month	1か月過ごす
take	one month	1か月かかる

▷ She **spent** one **month** lying on a beach with her friends in Thailand. 彼女はタイの海辺で寝そべって友だちと1か月過ごした
▷ We have to order this book from abroad so it will **take** about one **month** to arrive. この本は海外からの注文になるので到着するまで1か月ほどかかる

this	month	今月
next	month	来月
last	month	先月
the month	after next	再来月
the month	before last	先々月

▷ I've been really busy **this month**. 今月は本当に

忙しくしています
▷ I'm going on holiday to Guam **next month**. 来月グアムに休暇に行きます
▷ I saw him **last month**. 先月彼に会った
▷ We're going to move into our new house the **month after next**. 再来月新居に引っ越す予定だ
▷ She started her new job the **month before last**. 先々月彼女は新しい仕事を始めた

every	month	毎月
every other	month	1か月おきに

▷ **Every month** the economy seems to get worse. 月ごとに景気が悪くなっているようだ
▷ This magazine is published **every other month** – six times a year. この雑誌は1か月おき、つまり年6回発行される

the beginning of	the month	月の初め
the end of	the month	月末
the middle of	the month	月半ば
early	this month	今月初旬に
late	this month	今月下旬に

▷ I arrived in Japan at the **beginning of** this **month**. 今月初めに日本に到着しました
▷ I don't get paid until the **end of** this **month**. 月末まで入金の見込みがない
▷ I'll find out if I got the job sometime in the **middle of** this **month**. 今月の中旬あたりに職にありつけたかどうかわかるだろう
▷ We're expecting the baby to be born **early this month**. 今月初旬に赤ん坊が生まれる予定です
▷ We're expecting Bill to arrive from America **late this month**. 今月下旬にビルがアメリカから到着するはずだ

for	a month	1か月の間
over	a month	1か月にわたって
in	a month	1か月で
by	the month	月ぎめで
for	the past six months	ここ6か月間
for	the last six months	

▷ I haven't seen her **for** three **months**. 3か月間彼女に会っていない

mood /múːd/ 名 気分, 機嫌

capture	the mood	気分をとらえる
catch	a mood	
match	one's mood	気分と合う
suit	one's mood	
reflect	a mood	気分を反映する

set	the mood	ムードをつくる

▷ This picture really **captures** the **mood** of Paris in the 1930s. この写真は1930年代のパリの気分をよくとらえている
▷ When Ella plays the piano she always plays music that **matches** her **mood**. ピアノを弾くときエラはいつも自分の気分に合った曲を演奏する
▷ This poem **reflects** a **mood** of deep sadness. この詩は深い悲しみの気持ちを反映している
▷ Buy your girlfriend some chocolate or flowers. It **sets** the **mood** for romance! ガールフレンドにチョコレートと花を買ってあげるよ。ロマンチックな気分になるよ

one's mood	changes	気分が変わる

▷ She's impossible to live with. Her **mood changes** every 5 minutes. 彼女とはいっしょに暮らせない。5分ごとに気分が変わるんだもの

a happy	mood	幸せな気分
a good	mood	上機嫌
a bad	mood	不機嫌
a foul	mood	
a depressed	mood	落ち込んだ気分
a somber	mood	憂うつな気分
an optimistic	mood	楽天的な気分
a relaxed	mood	くつろいだ気分
the present	mood	いまの気分
the public	mood	国民感情
the national	mood	

▷ Better not talk to him. He's in a **bad mood**! 彼に話しかけないほうがいい。ご機嫌斜めだから
▷ The film about the World War II put her in a very **depressed mood**. 第2次世界大戦の映画を見て彼女はとても気分が落ち込んだ
▷ The **present mood** of the country is against immigration. 国全体のいまの気分は移民に反対だ
▷ The President totally misunderstood the **public mood**. 大統領は国民感情を完全に読み間違えた

change	of mood	気分の変化

▷ Let's put on some loud music. This party needs a **change of mood**! にぎやかな音楽をかけよう。パーティーの気分を変えないと

be in	no mood for A	Aの気分ではない
be in	no mood to do	…する気分ではない

▷ Our boss is very angry. He's **in no mood to** talk to anyone. 上司はかんかんで、とても人と話す気分ではない

moon /múːn/ 名 (the moon で) 月

| morning |

the moon	rises	月が昇る
the moon	appears	月が現れる
the moon	comes out	
the moon	shines	月が照る
the moon	disappears	月が隠れる

▷When does the **moon rise** tonight? 今夜の月の出は何時ですか
▷The night sky looks beautiful when the **moon appears** from behind the clouds. 雲間から月が現れるときの夜空はきれいだ
▷The **moon shone** brightly and the stars came out. 月が明るく輝き、星が出た
▷The **moon disappeared** behind the mountain peak. 月は峰の向こうに隠れた

a bright	moon	明るい月
a full	moon	満月
a new	moon	新月
a half	moon	半月
a crescent	moon	三日月
a quarter	moon	上弦の月, 下弦の月

▷**A bright moon** shone over the lake. 明るい月が湖の上に輝いた
▷There's a **full moon** tonight. It's almost like daytime! 今夜は満月で、まるで昼間のようだ

the earth and the moon	地球と月
the sun and the moon	太陽と月

▷**The earth and the moon** are both planets. 地球も月もどちらも惑星だ

morning /mɔ́ːrniŋ/ 名 朝, 午前

all	morning	午前中ずっと
each	morning	毎朝
every	morning	
the following	morning	翌朝
(the) next	morning	
early	morning	朝早く
late	morning	朝遅く
this	morning	けさ
yesterday	morning	きのうの朝
tomorrow	morning	あすの朝
Monday	morning	月曜日の朝
a January	morning	1月の朝
a summer	morning	夏の朝

▷I arrived back home **early yesterday morning**. きのうの朝早く家に戻った
▷Have you seen Tom **this morning**? けさトムを見たかい
▷"Were you late again **this morning**?" "Yes, I'm late **every morning**."「けさも遅刻したのか」「そうさ、毎朝遅刻さ」

in	the morning	朝, 午前中に
from morning	till night	朝から晩まで

▷Kelly bought a newspaper **in the morning**. ケリーは朝、新聞を買った
▷He works 7 days a week **from morning till night**. 彼は朝から晩まで週7日働いている

mother /mʌ́ðər/ 名 母, 母親

a single	mother	未婚の母；母子家庭
a lone	mother	の母親
an unmarried	mother	未婚の母
a widowed	mother	子どものいる未亡人
a working	mother	ワーキングマザー
a foster	mother	養母

▷These days the number of **single mothers** is increasing. 最近シングルマザーの数が増えている
▷After her divorce she got a job in a supermarket and became a **working mother**. 離婚してから彼女はスーパーでの仕事を得て、育児と仕事を両立させた

look like	one's mother	母親に似ている

▷She **looks like** her **mother**. 彼女は母親似だ

one's mother and father	母と父

★one's father and mother も用いる

▷Her **mother and father** are coming to her graduation ceremony. 両親とも彼女の卒業式に来る予定です

mountain /máuntən/ 名 山

climb	a mountain	山に登る
go up	a mountain	
go down	a mountain	下山する
walk down	a mountain	

▷If you're going to **climb** a **mountain** you'll need the proper equipment. 山に登るならきちんとした装備が必要だ
▷**Walking down** a **mountain** is often more dangerous than climbing up. 山は登るより下るほうが危険なことが多い

distant	mountains	遠くの山々
a high	mountain	高い山

▷The view from here is terrific. You can see the **distant mountains** quite clearly. ここからの眺めはすばらしい．遠くの山々がとてもはっきり見える
▷Mount Everest is the world's **highest mountain**. エベレストは世界最高峰の山だ

the top of	a mountain	山の頂上
the slope of	a mountain	山の斜面
the foot of	a mountain	山のふもと

▷There was a wonderful view from the **top of the mountain**. 山頂からの眺めはすばらしかった
▷The **slope** of the **mountain** suddenly became steeper. 山の斜面が急により険しくなった

a mountain	of A	山のようなA

▷He kept borrowing money until finally he had a huge **mountain of** debt. 彼は金を借り続けたあげく最後には山のような借金を抱え込んだ

mouth /máuθ/ 名 口

open	one's mouth	口を開ける
close	one's mouth	口を閉じる
cover	one's mouth	口をおおう
fill	one's mouth	口の中をいっぱいにする
wipe	one's mouth	口を拭く
burn	one's mouth	口をやけどする

▷Please **close** your **mouth** when you're eating! 物を食べるときは口を閉じなさい
▷The little boy kept **filling** his **mouth** with cake. その小さな男の子は口じゅうケーキをほおばっていた
▷"That soup was delicious!" "Yes, but I think you need to **wipe** your **mouth**!" 「おいしいスープだった」「そうね．でも口をふいたほうがいいわよ」
▷Ouch! That tea is really hot! I **burned** my **mouth**! あちっ．お茶が熱すぎて口をやけどしたよ

one's mouth	tightens	口元が引き締まる
one's mouth	twists	口元が歪む
one's mouth	twitches	口元がひくひく動く
one's mouth	goes dry	口が渇く
one's mouth	waters	よだれが出る

▷Her **mouth tightened** in anger. "I told you no smoking in the house!" 怒りで彼女の口元は引きつった．「家の中は禁煙と言ったでしょ」(★相手の態度にむっとしたときのしぐさ)
▷Whenever he gets angry his **mouth twists** with rage. 怒るといつも彼の口元は歪む
▷She was really nervous before the job interview. She felt her **mouth go dry**. 就職面接の前で彼女はとても緊張しており，口が渇くのを感じた
▷Wow! The smell of that freshly baked bread is making my **mouth water**! わあ，焼き立てのパンのにおいによだれが出そうだ

a wide	mouth	(横に)大きな口
a small	mouth	小さな口
a full	mouth	ふっくらした口元
a thin	mouth	薄い口元

▷She has a **wide mouth**. When she smiles you can see her beautiful white teeth. 彼女は口が大きくて，笑うときれいな白い歯が見える

in	one's mouth	口の中で

▷This steak is delicious. It just melts **in** your **mouth**! このステーキはおいしいですよ．まさに口の中でとろけますよ

PHRASES
Shut your mouth! ☺ 黙れ
Watch your mouth! ☺ 口のきき方に気をつけなさい

move /múːv/

動 動かす，動く；引っ越す，移転する

gradually	move	徐々に動く
slowly	move	ゆっくり動く
hardly	move	ほとんど動かない
move	around	あちこち動く
move	back	後ろへ動く
move	closer	近くへ動く
move	forward	前へ動く
move	quickly	すばやく動く
move	swiftly	
move	slowly	ゆっくり動く

▷The day after I ran the marathon I was so stiff that I could **hardly move**. マラソンを走った次の日は筋肉がこわばってほとんど動けなかった
▷Sssssss! I can hear someone **moving around** upstairs! しーっ，だれか上で動き回っている音が聞こえるぞ
▷I can't see from here. Let's **move closer**. ここからは見えないよ．もっと近くに移動しよう
▷Somebody shouted "Fire!" and everybody **moved quickly** toward the exit. だれかが「火事だ」と叫ぶと，みんな出口へと急いだ

move	to A	A(場所)に引っ越す
move	into A	
move	from A to B	AからBへ引っ越す

▷I'm thinking of **moving to** New York. ニューヨークに引っ越そうと考えている
▷Tony and Helen have just **moved into** a new house. トニーとヘレンは新居に引っ越したところです
▷They **moved from** London **to** Oxford. 彼らはロンドンからオックスフォードへ引っ越した

movement /múːvmənt/

名 動き, 動作; 運動; 動向

make	a movement	動きをする
allow	movement	動きを可能にする
control	the movement	動きを制御する
restrict	one's movement	動きを制限する
follow	the movement(s)	動向を追う

▷She **made** a **movement** to leave, but then sat down again. 彼女は出て行くしぐさをしたが, また座った
▷Don't tie the bandage too tight. It needs to be loose enough to **allow movement**. 包帯をあまりきつく結ばないように. 動かせるように緩くしておく必要があります
▷It's important to wear a seat belt in a car, but it **restricts** your **movement**. 車に乗ったらシートベルトをするのが大事だが, 動きが制限される

a forward	movement	前進
a backward	movement	後退
a downward	movement	下降運動
an upward	movement	上昇運動
rhythmic	movement	リズミカルな運動
slow	movement	ゆっくりした動き
a swift	movement	すばやい動き
a sudden	movement	突然の動き
free	movement	自由な移動
democratic	movement	民主化運動
a nationalist	movement	民族主義運動
a political	movement	政治運動
a social	movement	社会運動
a protest	movement	抗議運動
an anti-nuclear	movement	反核運動
an independence	movement	独立運動
a grass-roots	movement	草の根運動
the popular	movement	民衆運動
the labor	movement	組合運動

▷I thought I had put the car into reverse gear, but it suddenly made a **forward movement**. 車をバックギアに入れたと思ったが, 急に前進した
▷He made an **upward movement** with his arm. "Yes. A little higher, Yes. That's it. Stop." 彼は腕を上のほうへ動かした. 「そう, もう少し上. そう, そこです. 止まって」
▷My grandfather is getting old now and is only capable of making **slow movements**. 祖父は高齢になってゆっくりした動作しかできない
▷OK. I'm going to take the photo now. Don't make any **sudden movements**! では写真を撮ります. 急に動かないようにしてください
▷People who live in the European Union have **free movement** from one country to another. EUに住んでいる人々は国から国への移動は自由にできる
▷Have you ever belonged to any **political movement**? いままでに政治運動に属していたことはありますか
▷The **popular movement** *against* nuclear power is gaining support. 原子力に反対する民衆の運動が支持を得つつある

the movement	for A	Aのための運動
the movement	toward A	Aへの動き

▷The **movement for** reforming the present education system is getting stronger. 現行の教育制度を改革しようという動きはますます強まりつつある
▷Do you agree with the recent **movement toward** globalization? 最近のグローバル化への動きに賛成ですか

movie /múːvi/ 名 映画《英》film

go to (see)	a movie	映画を見に行く
go to	(the) movies	
go see	a movie	
see	a movie	映画を見る
watch	a movie	
direct	a movie	映画を監督する
make	a movie	映画を製作する

▷Do you want to **go to** a **movie** this evening? 今夜映画を見に行かないか
▷I haven't **seen** a **movie** for ages. もう何年も映画は1本も見ていない
▷I spent all last night **watching movies** on DVD. 昨夜は一晩中ずっとDVDで映画を見ていた

a good	movie	いい映画
the latest	movie	最新の映画
a new	movie	新作映画
a silent	movie	無声映画
a horror	movie	ホラー映画
a Hollywood	movie	ハリウッド映画
a home	movie	ホームムービー

▷Have you seen Tom Cruise's **latest movie**? It's really great! トム・クルーズの最新の映画を見たかい. とてもいいよ

▷There's a **new movie** on next week. Would you like to go? 来週，新しい映画が封切りになります．見に行きませんか

murder /mə́:rdər/

名 殺人，殺害；殺人事件

commit	(a) murder	殺人を犯す
investigate	a murder	殺人事件を捜査する
witness	a murder	殺人を目撃する
deny	the murder	殺害を否認する
admit	the murder	殺害を認める

▷He **committed** three **murders** in two months. 彼は2か月で3件の殺人を犯した
▷The police are **investigating** a **murder** that took place in the early hours of this morning. 警察は本日早朝に起きた殺人事件を捜査中だ
▷According to newspaper reports he **denied** the **murder** of his wife. 新聞報道によれば彼は妻の殺害を否認した

attempted	murder	殺人未遂
brutal	murder	残忍な殺人
cold-blooded	murder	冷血な殺人
mass	murder	大量殺人
an unsolved	murder	未解決殺人事件

▷He was convicted of **attempted murder**. 彼は殺人未遂で有罪判決を受けた

murder /mə́:rdər/ 動 殺す，殺害する

be brutally	murdered	残忍に殺される
be nearly	murdered	あやうく殺されかける

▷The missing girl was **brutally murdered**. 行方不明の少女は残忍に殺害された
▷The young couple were kidnapped and **nearly murdered**. 若いカップルは誘拐され，あやうく殺害されるところだった

attempt to	murder	殺害を企てる

▷He was charged with **attempting to murder** his wife. 彼は妻に対する殺人未遂で起訴された

be accused of	murdering A	Aを殺害したと
be charged with	murdering A	して起訴される

▷He was **accused of murdering** his whole family. 彼は家族全員を殺害したかどで起訴された

muscle /mʌ́sl/ 名 筋肉

develop	muscles	筋肉を鍛える
pull	a muscle	筋肉を痛める
relax	the muscles	筋肉をほぐす

▷He goes to the gym 5 times a week. He's beginning to **develop muscles**! 彼はジムに週5回通っているから，筋肉がつき始めているよ
▷I heard you **pulled** a **muscle** in your back. How did you do it? 腰の筋肉を痛めたそうだけど，どんなふうに痛めたの
▷You should take a hot bath. It'll **relax** your **muscles**. 熱いふろに入るといい．筋肉がほぐれるよ

a muscle	aches	筋肉が痛む
muscles	relax	筋肉が緩む
muscles	tense	筋肉が緊張する
muscles	tighten	
a muscle	twitches	筋肉が痙攣する

▷My **muscles ached** with fatigue. 疲労で筋肉痛だった
▷You could see that he was angry by the way the **muscles** in his face **tightened**. 顔の強ばりようを見れば彼が怒ったのがわかるだろう

nerve and muscle	神経と筋肉
bone and muscle	骨と筋肉

★muscle and bone も用いる

▷He strained every **nerve and muscle** in his body as he tried to push the broken-down car uphill. 彼は体中の神経と筋肉を振り絞って，故障した車を坂の上へと押し上げようとした

museum /mju:zí:əm/ 名 博物館；美術館

visit	a museum	博物館を訪れる

▷I'm interested in the history of Egypt. I'd like to **visit** a **museum** while we're here. エジプトの歴史に興味があるので，ここに滞在中に博物館に行きたいです

an open-air	museum	野外博物館
a private	museum	個人博物館
an art	museum	美術館
a science	museum	科学博物館

▷Lord Montague has a **private museum** of classic cars. Many are over a hundred years old. モンタギュー卿はクラシックカーの個人博物館を持っており，多くは100年以上前の車だ

music /mjúːzik/ 名 音楽；曲；楽譜

enjoy	music	音楽を楽しむ
listen to	music	音楽を聞く
hear	music	音楽が聞こえる
play	music	演奏する；音楽をかける
write	music	作曲する
compose	music	
dance to	music	音楽に合わせて踊る
read	music	楽譜を読む

▷ One of my favorite hobbies is **listening to music**. 好きな趣味は音楽鑑賞です

▷ They're **playing** some really loud **music** next door. I can't get to sleep. 隣の部屋で騒々しい音楽を流しているので寝つけない

▷ He **composed** some new **music** especially for the Queen's wedding. 彼は女王の結婚式のために特別に新曲をつくった

▷ Unbelievable! I never knew that bears could **dance to music**! 信じられないな．熊が音楽に合わせて踊れるなんて知らなかった

▷ I can't **read music**. 楽譜は読めない

favorite	music	好きな音楽
popular	music	ポピュラー音楽
religious	music	宗教音楽
church	music	教会音楽
traditional	music	伝統音楽
classical	music	クラシック音楽
baroque	music	バロック音楽
chamber	music	室内楽
contemporary	music	現代音楽
choral	music	合唱曲
instrumental	music	器楽曲
electronic	music	電子音楽
vocal	music	声楽
background	music	ＢＧＭ
ballet	music	バレエ音楽
folk	music	民族音楽；民謡

▷ What's your **favorite music**? 好きな音楽は何ですか

▷ I find today's **contemporary music** more difficult to listen to than **classical music**. いまの現代音楽はクラシック音楽より聞きにくいと思う

▷ Do you like **vocal music**? For example, Beethoven's ninth symphony? 声楽は好きですか．例えばベートーベンの交響曲第９番とか

a piece of	music	ひとつの楽曲

▷ Do you know Ravel's 'Bolero'? It's a wonderful **piece of music**. ラベルの「ボレロ」を知っていますか．とてもすばらしい曲ですよ

mystery /místəri/

名 不可解なこと；謎, 神秘

solve	a mystery	謎を解く
resolve	a mystery	
unravel	a mystery	
explain	a mystery	謎を説明する
remain	a mystery	依然として謎だ
shrouded in	mystery	謎に包まれて
cloaked in	mystery	

▷ I've finally **solved** the **mystery** of what happened to my glasses. I found them under the sofa! 眼鏡をどうしたのかようやく謎が解けたよ，ソファーの下にあるのを見つけたんだ

▷ Where my watch has gone to **remains** a **mystery**. 時計がどこへ行ったのか，いまだによくわからない

▷ Exactly what happened on the night of December 22nd 1834 remains **shrouded in mystery**. 1834年12月22日の夜に起こったことは依然として謎に包まれている

the mystery	deepens	謎が深まる

▷ "I lost my wallet. Then I found it with more money in it than before!" "Ha, ha! The **mystery deepens**!"「財布をなくしちゃって，次に見つけたら前よりお金が増えていたんだ」「ほう．謎が深まるねえ」

a complete	mystery	まったくの謎
a real	mystery	本当の謎
a great	mystery	大きな謎
an unsolved	mystery	解けない謎

▷ Where I've put my car keys is a **complete mystery**! どこに車のキーを置いたかまったくわからない

▷ There are many **great mysteries** in the world. 世界には多くの大きな謎がある

a mystery	about A	Aについての謎
mystery	to A	A（人）にとっての謎

▷ "I can't find my umbrella." "Well, there's no **mystery about** that. You probably left it on the train!"「傘が見つからないんだ」「不思議でも何でもないよ．たぶん列車に置き忘れたのさ」

▷ I've no idea where my coat is. It's a complete **mystery to** me. コートがどこかわからない．私にはまったく謎だ

N

nail /néil/ 名 爪；くぎ，びょう

cut	one's **nails**	爪を切る
file	one's **nails**	爪にやすりをかける
paint	one's **nails**	爪にマニキュアを塗る
grow	one's **nails**	爪を伸ばす
bite	one's **nails**	爪をかむ
break	a **nail**	爪を割る
dig	one's **nails**	爪を立てる
drive	a **nail**	くぎを打つ
hammer	a **nail**	
pull out	a **nail**	くぎを抜く

▷She **painted** her **nails** bright red. 彼女は爪に真っ赤なマニキュアを塗った
▷I **grew** my **nails** long. 爪を長く伸ばした
▷When she gets nervous she **bites** her **nails**. 彼女は緊張すると爪をかむ ▷Don't **bite** your **nails**! 爪をかむんじゃないの
▷I **dug** my **nails** into my palm. 手のひらに爪を立てた
▷He **drove** a **nail** *into* the wall. 彼は壁にくぎを打った

a long	nail	長い爪；長いくぎ
a rusty	nail	さびたくぎ
an iron	nail	鉄のくぎ

▷I used to have **long nails**, but now I've cut them short. 爪を伸ばしていたこともあるが，いまは短くしている
▷There's a **rusty nail** sticking up from those old floorboards. 古い床板からさびたくぎが上に突き出ている

name /néim/ 名 名，名前；評判

call	A's **name**	名前を呼ぶ
change	a **name**	名前を変える
forget	A's **name**	名前を忘れる
remember	a **name**	名前を覚えている
give	a **name**	名前をつける
have	a **name**	名前がある
bear	a **name**	名前を担う
have	a **name**	評判がある
get	a **name**	評判を得る
make	one's **name**	名を上げる
make	a **name** for oneself	

▷I'm terribly sorry, I'm afraid I've **forgotten** your **name**. 誠に申し訳ありませんがお名前を失念してしまいました
▷She's really good at **remembering names**. 彼女は人の名前を覚えるのがとても得意だ
▷They haven't **given** their **baby** a name yet. 彼らは赤ん坊にまだ名前をつけていない
▷Ryo Ishikawa has really **made** a **name for himself** as a golf player. 石川遼はゴルフ選手としてまさに名を上げた

a family	name	姓，名字
a last	name	
a first	name	(姓に対して)名
a given	name	
a Christian	name	
a middle	name	ミドルネーム
one's **full**	name	氏名，フルネーム
a maiden	name	旧姓
a married	name	結婚後の姓
a proper	name	本名；固有名(詞)
one's real	name	本名，実名
a false	name	偽名
a stage	name	芸名
a user	name	ユーザーネーム
a brand	name	商標，ブランド名
a company	name	社名
a place	name	地名
a good	name	いい評判
a bad	name	悪い評判
a big	name	有名人
a great	name	
a famous	name	

▷Please write your **full name**, address and telephone number. 氏名，住所と電話番号を書いてください
▷"Godzilla" is just a nickname. His **proper name** is Matsui. ゴジラは単にニックネームで，本名は松井です
▷She refused to tell the police her **real name**. 彼女は警察に自分の実名を言うのを拒んだ
▷"Smith" is a **false name**. His real name is Carter. スミスは偽名で，彼の本名はカーターだ
▷If you keep going out drinking until 1:00 in the morning you'll get a **bad name**. 午前1時まで飲み歩いてばかりいると，悪い評判が立つよ
▷He's a **big name** in the art world. 彼は美術の世界で有名な人だ

name and address	名前と住所
names and faces	名前と顔

▷Could you give me your **name and address**? あなたの名前と住所を教えていただけますか

by	name	名前で；名指しで
by	the name of A	Aという名前の
under	the name (of A)	(Aの)名前で

▷ There are over 60 students in Paul's English class and he knows them all **by name**. ポールの英語クラスには60人以上の学生がいるが, 彼は全員の名前を覚えている
▷ The police say he uses many different names, but at the moment he goes **by** the **name of** Dexter. 警察の説明では彼はいろんな名前を使っているが, 現在はデクスターの名前で通っている
▷ He used to be called Petersen, but now he goes **under** the **name of** Robbins. 彼は以前ピーターセンと呼ばれていたが, いまはロビンズの名で通っている

PHRASES
What's your name? / May I have your name? / May I ask your name? ☺ お名前は？／お名前を伺っていいですか

nap /nǽp/ 名 昼寝, うたたね

take	a nap	昼寝する
have	a nap	

▷ I'm going to **take** a **nap**. Could you wake me up in 10 minutes? 昼寝をするので10分したら起こしていただけますか

a short	nap	仮眠, うたた寝
a little	nap	

▷ You look tired. I think you should have a **little nap**. 疲れているみたいだね, 少し昼寝したほうがいいよ

nation /néiʃən/

名 国, 国家；(集合的に)国民, 民族

divide	a nation	国を分断する

▷ At one time, the question of whether or not to end the Vietnam War **divided** the **nation**. かつてベトナム戦争を終結させるかどうかの問題で国が割れた

a developed	nation	先進国
a developing	nation	発展途上国
an independent	nation	独立国家
an industrial	nation	工業国
an industrialized	nation	
a poor	nation	貧しい国
a rich	nation	豊かな国
the whole	nation	全国民

▷ **Developed nations** should do more to help **developing nations**. 先進国は発展途上国援助のためにもっと多くのことをすべきだ
▷ England became an **industrial nation** during the late 18th and the 19th centuries. イングランドは18世紀後半から19世紀にかけて工業国になった

across	the nation	国じゅうで

natural /nǽtʃərəl/

形 自然の, 天然の；当然の, 当たり前の

completely	natural	まったく天然の
totally	natural	
perfectly	natural	まったく当然の
only	natural	
quite	natural	
natural	enough	十分自然な

▷ When you go abroad for the first time it's **perfectly natural** to feel culture shock. 初めての海外旅行でカルチャーショックを感じるのはごく当然のことだ
▷ It's **quite natural** to be worried before taking your entrance exam. 入学試験の前に不安になるのはきわめて当然だ
▷ "Now that I'm pregnant I feel sick in the mornings." "Well, that's **natural enough**. Nothing to worry about." 「妊娠してから朝, 吐き気がするんです」「よくあることですよ。心配には及びません」

it is natural	(for A) to do	(Aが)…するのは当然だ

▷ **It's natural to** worry before an important exam. 大事な試験の前に不安になるのは当たり前だ

nature /néitʃər/

名 自然；自然現象；性質；本質, 特質

preserve	nature	自然を保護する
destroy	nature	自然を破壊する
change	nature	性質を変える
consider	the nature	性質を考慮する
determine	the nature	性質を特定する
understand	the nature	性質を理解する
depend on	the nature	性質しだいだ

▷ We should **consider** the **nature** *of* the problem before we take any action. 行動に移す前に問題の性質を考慮すべきだ
▷ It seems to be a completely new species. We haven't **determined** the **nature** *of* the insect yet.

まったくの新種のようで，その昆虫の性質はまだ特定できていない

▷Whether the doctor can help you or not **depends on** the **nature** *of* your illness. 医師に助けてもらえるかどうかは病気の性質しだいだ

Mother	Nature	母なる自然
the precise	nature	本質；本性
the exact	nature	
the true	nature	
a general	nature	一般的性質；およそのありよう
a good	nature	よい性質
the complex	nature	複雑な性質
human	nature	人間性

▷We need to understand the **precise nature** of his complaint. 彼がクレームをつけてきた本音を理解する必要がある

▷The **general nature** of his comments was very positive. 彼の論評は全体としてとても好意的だった

▷Don't worry! He won't bite! Labrador dogs have a very **good nature**. 安心して．かまないよ．ラブラドル犬はとても性質がいいから

▷I'm afraid there will always be wars. It's **human nature**. 戦争はいつまでたってもなくならないと思う．それが人間の性(さが)だから

by	nature	生まれつき
by	its (very) nature	本来的に
in	nature	本質は
in	the nature of A	Aの性質を帯びて
in	A's nature	Aの質で
of	... nature	…の種の
given	the nature of A	Aの性質を考慮すると

▷He's **by nature** a very obstinate person. 彼は生まれつきとても頑固だ

▷It's **in** the **nature of** wolves to hunt in packs. 群れで狩りをするのがオオカミの性質だ ▷I'm not **in the nature of** opening other people's letters. 私は人の手紙を開封するような質ではない

▷There are many violent comic books available in Japan, but I don't like reading books **of** that **nature**. 暴力的なコミックが日本ではたくさん手に入るが，私はそういった本は読みたくない

▷**Given** the **nature of** crocodiles it would be unwise to keep one as a pet! ワニの性質を考えるとペットとして飼うのは賢明ではないね

neat /ní:t/ 形 きちんとした，小ぎれいな

neat and clean		きちんとして清潔な
neat and tidy		きちんと整頓された

▷Caroline keeps the house really **neat and clean**. キャロリンはいつも家をきちんときれいにしている

▷Her room is always **neat and tidy**. 彼女の部屋はいつも整然としている

neat	little A	小ぎれいでかわいいA

▷Oh! What a **neat little** kitchen! I love it! まあ，なんて小ぎれいなキッチンだこと．すてき

necessary /nésəsèri | -səri/

形 必要な，欠かせない；必然的な

absolutely	necessary	絶対に必要な
really	necessary	本当に必要な
strictly	necessary	
always	necessary	常に必要な
no longer	necessary	もはや必要ない

▷I'll be in a very important meeting until 3:00. Please don't interrupt me unless it's **absolutely necessary**. 3時まですごく重要な会議に出るので，どうしてもやむをえない場合以外は邪魔しないでくれ

▷Do you think it's **really necessary** to interview all 20 applicants for the job? 仕事に応募してきた20人全員の面接を本当にしなくちゃいけないかな

▷Previous experience with this type of work would be useful, but it's not **strictly necessary**. この種の仕事では前の経験が役には立つだろうが，どうしても必要というわけではない

▷You don't need to go to Tokyo tomorrow. It's **no longer necessary**. あした東京に行かなくていいよ．もう必要なくなったんだ

necessary	for A	Aにとって必要な

▷Do you think it's **necessary for** me to contact head office? 本社と連絡を取る必要があるかな

if	necessary	必要なら
as	necessary	必要なだけ
where	necessary	必要なところに
when	necessary	必要なときに

▷We must get this contract. I'll fly to New York again myself, **if necessary**. この契約はぜひとらなくては．必要なら私がまたニューヨークへ飛びます

▷Please correct the English of this report **where necessary**. 直すところがあればこの報告書の英語を直してください

it is necessary	(for A) to do	(Aが)…することが必要だ

find it necessary	to do	…するのが必要だと気づく
make it necessary	(for A) to do	(A(人)が)…する必要がある

▷I'm afraid **it's necessary for** you **to** double-check all those sales figures.　悪いけど、きみに売上高をすべて再照合してもらう必要があるな
▷I don't see why they **found it necessary to** hold another meeting.　また会議を開くことになった理由がわからない
▷Please don't **make it necessary for** me **to** talk to you again about arriving late for work.　仕事に遅れるなと2度ときみに言わなくて済むようにしてくれよ

necessity /nəsésəti/

名 必要, 必要性；必需品, 不可欠なもの

accept	the necessity	必要性を受け入れる
avoid	the necessity	必要性を避ける
highlight	the necessity	必要性を強調する
stress	the necessity	

▷I don't **accept** the **necessity** of dismissing half our staff.　スタッフの半分を解雇する必要性があるとは思わない
▷We need to **avoid** the **necessity** of closing our business down.　営業停止に追い込まれるのを避ける必要がある
▷The results of this survey **highlight** the **necessity** of changing our company's image.　この調査結果から, わが社の企業イメージを変える必要があるのが明白だ

an absolute	necessity	絶対的必要性
a practical	necessity	実際的必要性
urgent	necessity	緊急の必要性
economic	necessity	経済上の必要性
a basic	necessity	最低限の必需品
the bare	necessity	

▷Today a computer is an **absolute necessity**.　今日コンピュータは絶対に必要だ
▷University fees are quite high, so having a part-time job is a **practical necessity**.　大学の授業料がとても高いので, 現実にはアルバイトをするしかない
▷Providing food and medicine to the earthquake victims is an **urgent necessity**.　地震の被災者に食料や薬を緊急に提供する必要がある
▷Sufficient food and drink are **basic necessities** of life.　十分な食料と飲み物は生きていくのに最低限必要だ

the necessity	for A	Aの必要性
the necessity	to do	…する必要性

▷I'm feeling much better now after that medicine. I don't see the **necessity for** canceling our holiday.　あの薬を飲んでずっと気分がよくなったので, 休暇をキャンセルする必要はないと思う
▷There's no **necessity to** get so angry! I was only joking!　そんなに怒る必要はないじゃないか. 冗談で言っただけさ

of	necessity	必然的に
out of	necessity	必要に迫られて
through	necessity	

▷Many chickens had to be destroyed **out of necessity** because of the danger of bird flu.　鳥インフルエンザの脅威から, 多くの鶏を殺処分せざるをえなかった

neck /nék/ 名 首

break	one's neck	首の骨を折る
wring	A's neck	首を絞める
crane	one's neck	(見ようと)首を伸ばす

▷He **broke** his **neck** in a skiing accident.　彼はスキー事故で首の骨を折った
▷I **craned** my **neck** to look over the other people's heads, but I still couldn't see anything.　他の人々の頭越しに見ようと首を伸ばしても何も見えなかった

a short	neck	短い首
a long	neck	長い首
a thick	neck	太い首
a thin	neck	細い首
a stiff	neck	肩こり

▷I've had a **stiff neck** for the last 10 days.　この10日間, 肩こりが治らない

around	one's neck	首の周りに
by	a neck	首差で；僅差で
neck and neck		接戦で

▷**Around** Melissa's **neck** was a beautiful pearl necklace.　メリッサの首には美しい真珠のネックレスがかかっていた

the nape	of the neck	襟首, うなじ
the scruff	of the neck	首根っこ, 襟首

▷His hand touched the **nape of** her **neck**.　彼の手が彼女のうなじに触れた
▷Rina picked the little kitten up by the **scruff of** its **neck** and dropped it gently into the basket.　リーナは子猫の首根っこをつかんで持ち上げると, そっとバスケットの中に下ろした

need /níːd/ 名 必要(性), 必要なもの; ニーズ

feel	the need	必要を感じる
meet	the need	必要を満たす
avoid	the need	必要を避ける
eliminate	the need	必要がなくなる
recognize	the need	必要性を認識する
stress	the need	必要性を強調する
satisfy	A's need	ニーズを満たす
suit	A's need	ニーズにかなう

▷ If you **feel** the **need** to get some more information call me. さらに情報が必要とお感じになったら電話をください

▷ If you want to **avoid** the **need** to wash the dishes, you should buy paper dishes. 皿を洗う手間を省きたいなら, 紙の皿を買いなさい

▷ The popularity of low-cost airlines is **eliminating** the **need** for long-distance train travel. 低価格の航空機に人気が出たせいで, 長距離列車で移動する必要がなくなりつつある

▷ The government **recognizes** the **need** to create more jobs. 政府はさらに雇用を創出する必要性を認めている

▷ The report **stresses** the **need** for immediate action. その報告書ではすぐ行動を起こす必要性が強調してある

a great	need	大きな必要性
a desperate	need	切迫した必要性
an urgent	need	緊急の必要性
a real	need	現実の必要性
a growing	need	高まる必要性
an increasing	need	
basic	needs	基本的なニーズ
particular	needs	特定のニーズ
special	needs	特別なニーズ
educational	needs	教育的ニーズ
social	need(s)	社会的ニーズ

▷ The situation after the floods is very serious. There's a **great need** for volunteers to help as much as possible. 洪水後の状況はきわめて深刻で, できる限り援助してくれるボランティアたちが大いに必要だ

▷ There's a **desperate need** to help people suffering from hunger and disease in Africa. 飢えや病気に苦しむアフリカの人々を何としても助ける必要がある

▷ There's an **urgent need** for talks to take place between the USA and China. 米中間対話を緊急に行う必要がある

▷ There's a **growing need** for an increase in the number of police officers. 警察官の数を増やす必要がますます高まっている

▷ In poor countries people often don't have enough money to take care of their **basic needs**. 貧しい国々では人々はしばしば基本的なニーズを満たすのに十分なお金がない

the need	for A	Aの必要性
in	need	困っている

▷ When Obama was elected President he stressed the **need for** change. 大統領に選ばれたオバマは変革の必要性を強調した

▷ There's a real **need for** more nurses in the health service. 医療サービスに従事する看護師を増やす必要がまさにある

▷ After the earthquake we need to take care of many people **in need**. 地震の後で困っているたくさんの人々を世話する必要がある

the need	to do	…する必要性

▷ The Principal stressed the **need to** get regular feedback from our students. 校長は定期的に生徒たちから意見を吸い上げる必要性を強調した

▷ There's no **need to** tell Laura. Let's keep it a secret between the two of us! ローラに言う必要はない. ぼくたち2人の秘密にしておこう

need /níːd/ 動 必要とする; 必要がある

desperately	need	切実に必要だ
really	need	本当に必要だ
urgently	need	緊急に必要だ
certainly	need	必ず必要だ
probably	need	おそらく必要だ
still	need	なお必要だ
no longer	need	もはや必要ない

▷ I **desperately need** to go to the toilet! トイレに行かないともうだめだ

▷ That convenience store **urgently needs** two part-time workers. Why don't you apply? あのコンビニではバイトを2名急募しているよ. 応募してみないか

▷ With a bad cut like that you **certainly need** to go to hospital. そんなにひどい切り傷では絶対に病院に行かなくちゃ

▷ Thanks for offering, but we **no longer need** your help. 申し出てくれてありがたいけど, もう助けは必要ないんだ

need	to do	…する必要がある
need A	to do	A(人)に…してもらう必要がある

▷ Your hair's really long. You **need to** get it cut. ずいぶん髪が伸びたね. カットしてもらわないと

▷ Tony? Are you there? I **need** you **to** help me

| needle |

wash the dishes. トニー，いるの？皿洗いを手伝ってほしいんだけど

need	doing	…される必要がある
need	to be done	
need	not have done	…する必要はなかったのに

▷ You can't wear that sweater. It **needs** wash**ing**. [=It **needs to be** washed.] そのセーターは着られないよ．洗濯しないと
▷ I **needn't have** taken my umbrella with me this morning. It didn't rain. けさは傘を持ってくる必要はなかった．雨は降らなかった

PHRASES
Who needs it? 😊 そんなものだれが必要とするのか

needle /níːdl/ 名 針；注射針

thread	a needle	針に糸を通す
insert	a needle	注射針を挿入する
stick	a needle	注射針を刺す
share	a needle	注射針を使い回す

▷ I can't **thread** this **needle**. The hole isn't big enough. この針には糸が通せないよ．穴の大きさが足りないもの
▷ The nurse **inserted** a **needle** *into* the vein to take a blood sample. 看護師は血液サンプルを取るために静脈に注射針を挿入した
▷ The nurse **stuck** a **needle** *into* me. It really hurt! 看護師に注射針を刺されて痛かったのなんのって

| a needle and thread | 糸を通した針，針と糸 |

▷ I always carry a **needle and thread** with me when I go abroad. 海外に出かけるときはいつも針と糸を持っていく

| the eye | of a needle | 針の穴 |

▷ It says in the Bible that it is easier for a camel to pass through the **eye of a needle** than for a rich man to enter the kingdom of God. 聖書には「金持ちが神の国に入るよりも，ラクダが針の穴を通るほうがまだ易しい」と書いてある

negative /néɡətiv/

形 否定の；不賛成の，反対の；消極的な；陰性の

entirely	negative	まったく否定的な
totally	negative	まったく否定的な
extremely	negative	非常に否定的な
slightly	negative	やや否定的な

▷ The results of the survey were not **entirely negative**. 調査結果は完全に否定的なものではなかった
▷ This product has received a **slightly negative** response from our customers. この製品への消費者の反応はやや否定的だった

| negative | about A | Aに対して否定的な |
| negative | for A | Aに対して陰性の |

▷ Try to be less **negative about** the situation. Things may improve. 状況についてあまり否定的にならないようにしよう．事態は好転するかもしれないし
▷ The medical tests were **negative for** Mrs. Roberts, but positive for Mrs. Carter. 医学検査の結果はロバーツ夫人は陰性，カーター夫人は陽性と出た

| positive and [or] negative | 正と負，肯定的と否定的 |

★ negative and [or] positive も用いる

▷ There are both **positive and negative** points about living abroad. 外国暮らしにはプラス面とマイナス面がある

neglect /niɡlékt/

動 怠る，ほったらかしにする；無視する

totally	neglect	まったく無視する
largely	neglect	ほとんど無視する
deliberately	neglect	故意に無視する
be sadly	neglected	ひどく無視された
be much	neglected	
be unjustly	neglected	不当に無視された

▷ This garden is a mess! It's been **totally neglected** for the last 10 years! この庭はひどいありさまだ．この10年すっかりほったらかしだったから

| neglect | to do | …するのを忘れる |

▷ Thank you everybody. That's all for today… Oh! Sorry! I **neglected to** mention — our next meeting will be on July 16th. 皆さんありがとうございました．きょうはこれで終わりです．あ，すみません，言い忘れました．次の会議は7月16日の予定です

| tend | to neglect | 無視しがちである |

▷ Williams has great ideas for the company, but he **tends to neglect** the details. ウィリアムズは会社に壮大なアイデアを出しはするが細部を無視しがちだ

negotiation /nigòuʃiéiʃən/

名 交渉, 協議, 話し合い

conduct	negotiations	交渉を行う
open	negotiations	交渉を始める
start	negotiation	
enter into	negotiation(s)	交渉に入る
continue	negotiations	交渉を続ける
resume	negotiations	交渉を再開する
break off	negotiations	交渉を打ち切る
be open to	negotiation	交渉の余地がある
be subject to	negotiation	

▷The superpowers will start **conducting negotiations** on Monday. 超大国間の交渉が月曜日から始まる
▷The Government still refuses to **open negotiations** with terrorists. 政府はなおテロリストと交渉に入ることを拒否している
▷The USA and Russia will **resume negotiations** in the New Year. 米ロは新年に交渉を再開する
▷If we don't come to an agreement soon the other side say they will **break off negotiations**. 早急に合意に達しなければ交渉を打ち切ると相手は言っている
▷The hijackers haven't refused to talk to us. They say they're still **open to negotiation**. ハイジャック犯はわれわれと話すのを拒否しておらず, なお交渉に応じる準備があると言っている

bilateral	negotiations	二国間交渉
direct	negotiation(s)	直接交渉
protracted	negotiation(s)	長引く交渉
peace	negotiations	和平交渉
trade	negotiations	貿易交渉
wage	negotiation(s)	賃金交渉

▷**Bilateral negotiations** will take place between North and South Korea later in the month. 北朝鮮と韓国の二国間交渉は月の後半に行われる
▷**Direct negotiation** with hostage-takers is unacceptable. 人質犯との直接交渉は受け入れられない

negotiation(s)	between A	A間の交渉
negotiation(s)	on A	Aに関する交渉
negotiation(s)	over A	
negotiation(s)	with A	Aとの交渉

▷**Negotiations between** the police and the kidnappers have been going on all week. 警察と誘拐犯との交渉が1週間続いている
▷Management refuses to have any more **negotiation on** staff salaries. 経営者側は職員給与についてこれ以上の交渉を拒否している

in	negotiation	交渉中で
under	negotiation	

▷Developed and developing countries are still **in negotiation** *with* each other over the problem of global warming. 先進国と発展途上国は地球温暖化の問題について互いになお交渉中だ
▷The exact terms of the contract are still **under negotiation**. 契約条件の詳細についてはなお交渉中である

A **of negotiation**(s)	Aにわたる交渉

★Aは months, years など

▷After six months **of negotiations** we're still no farther forward. 交渉は6か月にわたったが, 何も進んでいない

neighbor /néibər/

名 近所の人, 隣人; 隣国 (★(英)つづりは neighbour)

a good	neighbor	近所づきあいのよい人
one's immediate	neighbor	すぐ隣の人
a near	neighbor	近所の人
a close	neighbor	
one's next-door	neighbor	隣家の人
one's European	neighbors	ヨーロッパ近隣諸国

▷We're lucky. We have very **good neighbors**. They're always very considerate. うちは運がよく, 近所はいい人ばかりで, いつもとても気を配ってくれます
▷Our **immediate neighbor** is driving us crazy! He plays loud music until 3:00 in the morning. うちのすぐ隣の人には頭にくる. 朝3時まで大きな音で音楽を流すんだ
▷Actually, our **nearest neighbor** is over three miles away. 実を言うと, うちからいちばん近いお隣さんの家は3マイル以上も離れています
▷Mrs. Davis is our **next-door neighbor**. デービス夫人はうちの隣に住んでいる
▷Joining the European Union meant that Britain had more contact with her **European neighbors**. EU加盟によって英国はヨーロッパ近隣諸国との接触が増すこととなった

nerve /nə́ːrv/

名 神経; (nerves で)神経過敏; 勇気, 度胸

calm	one's **nerves**	神経を静める
steady	one's **nerves**	
fray	one's **nerves**	神経をすり減らす
have	the **nerve**	度胸がある, ずぶとい

| nervous |

keep	one's **nerve**	平静を保つ
lose	one's **nerve**	怖じ気づく

▷ Drink this whiskey. It'll help you **calm** your **nerves**. ウイスキーを飲んで. 神経を静めてくれるよ
▷ Lena insisted on taking a taxi all the way home and when we arrived she **had** the **nerve** to ask me to pay for it. 家までタクシーで帰ろうと言ったのはレナなのに、着いたらぼくに金を払えなんて図々しいよね
▷ Jet-skiing is not so difficult. You just need to **keep** your **nerve**. ジェットスキーはそれほど難しくない. 平静を保てばいいんだ
▷ She was skiing quite well downhill, but then she **lost** her **nerve** and crashed into a tree. 彼女はなかなかじょうずにスキーで斜面を下っていたが、怖じ気づいてしまって木にぶつかった

a bag of	nerves	緊張の固まり
a bundle of	nerves	
a battle of	nerves	神経戦
a war of	nerves	

▷ Anne had another driving lesson today. The instructor shouted at her and now she's a **bag of nerves**! アンはきょうもまた運転教習があった. 教官にどなられてから彼女は神経がぴりぴりしているんだ

the nerve	to do	…する勇気

▷ I don't know how you found the **nerve to** ask me to lend you more money. You still owe me $500 dollars! もっと金を貸してくれなんてよく頼めたものだね. きみにはまだ500ドル貸してあるんだよ
PHRASES
What a nerve! 😊 なんて図々しい

nervous /nə́ːrvəs/

形 神経質な, びくびくした, 緊張した

feel	nervous	不安に感じる
get	nervous	緊張する
make A	nervous	Aを不安にさせる

▷ I **get nervous** when I have to walk home alone late at night. 夜遅く一人で歩いて帰宅する時は緊張する
▷ Job interviews always **make** me **nervous**. 就職の面接はいつも緊張します

extremely	nervous	非常に緊張した
really	nervous	すごく緊張した
highly	nervous	ひどく緊張した
a little	nervous	やや緊張した
slightly	nervous	

▷ I don't think I did well in the interview. I was **extremely nervous**. 面接のできはよくなかった. ひどく上がってしまって

nervous	about A	Aのことで心配だ
nervous	of A	

▷ She's never traveled by air before so she's a bit **nervous about** the flight. 彼女は飛行機で旅行したことがないので、空の旅が少し心配だ

nest /nést/ 名 巣

build	a nest	巣を作る
construct	a nest	
make	a nest	
leave	the nest	巣立つ；親元を離れる
fly	the nest	

▷ I think those birds are **building** a **nest** in our roof. あの鳥たちはうちの屋根に巣を作っていると思う
▷ The young chicks have learnt how to fly now and have **left** the **nest**. 飛び方を覚えたばかりの幼鳥たちは巣を飛び立った

net /nét/ 名 網, ネット

cast	a net	網を打つ
mend	one's nets	網を修理する
spread	a net	網を広げる

▷ The fishermen **cast** their **nets** in a new area and made a very good catch. 漁師たちは新たな漁場に網を打ち、豊漁だった
▷ The fishermen sat on the shore **mending** their **nets**. 漁師たちは海岸に座って網を修理していた

a drift	net	流し網
a fishing	net	魚網
a mosquito	net	蚊帳(か)
a safety	net	転落防止ネット

network /nétwəːrk/

名 網の目状のもの, 網状組織；放送網；ネットワーク

establish	a network	ネットワークを築く
build	a network	
develop	a network	

▷ She quickly **established** a **network** of people who could be useful to her in her job. 彼女は自分の仕事上で役立つ人のネットワークをすぐ築いた

| news |

▷It's important in business to **develop** a **network** of contacts. ビジネスでは人脈のネットワークを広げるのが大事だ

a large	network	大規模なネットワーク
an international	network	国際ネットワーク
a national	network	全国ネットワーク
a local	network	地方のネットワーク
a support	network	支援ネットワーク
the rail	network	鉄道網
a road	network	道路網
a television	network	テレビ放送網
a distribution	network	販売流通網

▷This airline has established a widespread **international network**. この航空会社は幅広い国際ネットワークを築いた
▷These timetables contain details of all the **national networks** for rail, buses and coaches. この時刻表には鉄道, バスおよび長距離バスの全国路線網が詳しく載っている
▷It's a small company, but it's developed a good **local network** of influential businessmen. 小さな会社だが, 地元の有力ビジネスマンたちと有益なネットワークを築いた

new /njúː | njúː/ 形 新しい；新型の

completely	new	まったく新しい
entirely	new	
totally	new	
brand	new	真新しい, 新品の
spanking	new	
fairly	new	かなり新しい
relatively	new	比較的新しい

▷My car broke down last weekend. I took it to the garage and they said it had to have a **completely new** engine. 車が先週末に故障したので修理工場へ持って行った, エンジンをすっかり取り替えないとだめだって
▷Why does this machine keep breaking down? It's **relatively new**. この機械はなぜ故障ばかりしているのかな. 比較的新しいのに

new	to A	A(人)にとって新しい

▷Everything was **new to** me. すべてが私にとって目新しかった
PHRASES
What's new? ☺ 元気かい, 何か変わったことあるかい

news /njúːz | njúːz/

名 ニュース, 報道；知らせ, たより

get	the news	知らせを受ける
receive	the news	
hear	the news	知らせを聞く
bring	news	ニュースを持ってくる
break	the news	悪い知らせを届ける
make	news	ニュースになる
read	the news	ニュースを読む
watch	the news	ニュースを見る

▷I've **got** some bad **news** for you. お伝えしなくてはならないことがあります
▷I hope Bob and Helen arrived safely in Toronto. We haven't **heard** any **news** yet. ボブとヘレンが無事トロントに到着したならよいのだが, まだ知らせがない
▷Lisa's just arrived. She's **brought** some good **news**. リサがやって来て, いい知らせを持ってきたよ
▷You know the ice skater, Mao Asada? She **made news** yesterday. アイススケート選手の浅田真央を知っているかい. きのうのニュースになっていたよ

bad	news	悪い知らせ
terrible	news	ひどい知らせ
sad	news	悲しい知らせ
good	news	よい知らせ
great	news	すごいニュース
wonderful	news	
welcome	news	歓迎すべき知らせ
the latest	news	最新ニュース
local	news	地元ニュース
national	news	全国ニュース
foreign	news	海外ニュース
world	news	世界のニュース
radio	news	ラジオニュース
television	news	テレビニュース
the ten o'clock	news	10時のニュース

▷I have some **good news** for you. あなたにいい知らせがあります
▷"Did you hear? I passed the exam to get into Tokyo University!" "Oh, **great news!**" 「聞いて. ぼく東大の入試に受かったんだよ」「すごい. 大ニュースだな」
▷Have you just come back from the hospital? How's Paula? What's the **latest news**? 病院から戻ったところなの？ ポーラはどう？ 近況を教えて
▷I check the **foreign news** every morning on the Internet. 毎朝インターネットで海外ニュースをチェックします
▷Did you watch the 10 **o'clock news** last night? 昨夜10時のニュースを見たかい

news	about A	Aについての知らせ

| newspaper |

news	from A	Aからの知らせ

▷ "Is there any **news about** the train crash?" "Not yet, I'm afraid."「列車事故の続報はあるかい」「まだないよ」
▷ We still haven't heard any **news from** the police. 警察からまだ何も知らせを受けていません

on	the news	ニュースで
in	the news	

★ on はテレビ・ラジオなど, in は新聞など

▷ Did you hear? They're going to increase the tax on tobacco! It was **on** the **news** this morning. 聞いたか．たばこ税が上がるって．けさニュースになってたよ

a bit of	news	1本のニュース, ニュース一項目
a piece of	news	
an item of	news	

▷ We had two **pieces of** interesting **news** yesterday. きのうはおもしろいニュースが2本あった

news	that...	…という知らせ

▷ I'm not surprised at the **news that** the Government is going to raise the sales tax. 政府が売上税を上げるというニュースに私は驚かない

PHRASES
No news is good news. ☺ 便りのないのはよい便り
That's news to me. ☺ それは初耳だ

newspaper /njúːzpèipər | njúːz-/

名 新聞; 新聞紙

a daily	newspaper	日刊紙
a morning	newspaper	朝刊
an evening	newspaper	夕刊
a Sunday	newspaper	日曜紙
a local	newspaper	地方紙
a national	newspaper	全国紙
a quality	newspaper	高級紙
a tabloid	newspaper	タブロイド紙

▷ Do you read a **daily newspaper**? 日刊紙を読んでいますか
▷ If you want to find a part-time job why don't you look in the **local newspaper**? アルバイトを探したければ地元の新聞を見てみたら

in	the newspaper	新聞で

▷ Look! There's a photo of you **in** the **newspaper**! 見て．新聞にきみの写真が出ているよ

nice /náis/ 形 すてきな; やさしい; おいしい

extremely	nice	とてもすばらしい
really	nice	本当によい

▷ It's a **really nice** house, much nicer than the house we live in now. 本当にすてきな家だね．私たちがいま住んでいる家よりずっといいよ

nice and clean	とても清潔でよい
nice and warm	とても暖かくてよい

★ nice and /náisənd/ と発音する

▷ Singapore is a beautiful city. It's **nice and clean**. シンガポールは美しい都市でちり一つ落ちていない
▷ Come in out of the cold. It's **nice and warm** inside. 外は寒いから中へお入りください．中はとても暖かくていいですよ

nice	to A	A(人)に親切な

▷ It was great to meet your family. They were really **nice to** me. あなたのご家族にお会いできてよかった．本当によくしていただきました

it is nice	of A to do	A(人)が…してくれてありがたい

▷ It was really **nice of** you **to** send me a birthday card. 誕生カードを送ってくれてありがとう

PHRASES
Nice to meet you. ☺ はじめまして
Nice to see you again! ☺ またお会いしましたね
That's nice! ☺ それはいい ▷ "My boyfriend's going to take me to Disneyland on my birthday!" "Oh, that's nice."「ボーイフレンドと誕生日にディズニーランドに行くの」「それはよかったね」
What a nice A! ☺ なんていいA ▷ What a nice surprise! あらびっくり(うれしいな)

night /náit/ 名 夜, 晩, 夜間; 夕方

spend	a night	一夜を過ごす, 泊まる
stay	the night	

▷ It was great to **spend** a **night** in a five-star hotel yesterday. きのう五つ星ホテルに泊まってとてもよかった
▷ Do you have to leave this evening? Why don't you **stay** the **night**? 今夜立たなければいけないの？泊まっていったら？

every	night	毎夜

last	night	昨夜
yesterday	night	
tomorrow	night	あすの夜
the previous	night	前の夜
the next	night	次の夜
the other	night	先日の夜
the whole	night	一晩中
an early	night	早寝
a late	night	夜更かし
a bad	night	眠れない夜

▷There's a great movie on TV **tomorrow night**. あすの夜テレビでとてもいい映画があるよ
▷I spent the **whole night** writing my report. 一晩中レポートを書いて過ごした
▷I'm feeling a bit tired. I think I'll get an **early night**. 少し疲れたので，今夜は早く寝るよ
▷Last night I had a really **bad night**. I couldn't get any sleep at all. 昨夜はまったく眠れなかった．一睡もできなかった

day and night		昼夜
night and day		
night after night		毎晩毎晩
all night (long)		一晩中

▷Tom's been working **day and night** on that project for the last two weeks. トムはここ2週間そのプロジェクトのために昼も夜も仕事をしている
▷**Night after night** our neighbor's dog keeps us awake howling. 毎晩のように隣の家の犬が遠吠えするせいで眠れない
▷The baby cried **all night**. We didn't get any sleep at all. 赤ん坊に一晩中泣かれて，一睡もできなかった

at	night	夜に，夜は
by	night	夜は，夜間は
during	the night	夜間に，夜のうちに
in	the night	

▷If you sleep a lot during the day you won't be able to sleep **at night**. 昼間に寝すぎると夜に眠れないよ
▷They rested during the day and traveled **by night**. 彼らは昼は休んで夜に移動した
▷The burglars must have come in **during the night** while we were asleep. 強盗たちは私たちが寝ていた夜間に侵入したに違いない
▷Oh, look! Santa Claus came **in** the **night** and brought you some presents! 見てごらん．サンタクロースが夜の間にやって来て，プレゼントを持って来てくれたよ

in	the middle of the night	真夜中に
in	the dead of night	
on	Saturday night	土曜日の夜

on	the night of October 14	10月14日の夜に

▷I woke up suddenly **in** the **middle of** the **night**. I could hear somebody downstairs. 真夜中に突然目が覚めて，だれかが階下にいるのが聞こえた
▷What are you doing **on Saturday night**? 土曜の夜は何をしているの
▷The earthquake occurred **on** the **night of** December 15. その地震は12月15日の夜に起きた

PHRASES
Good night. お休みなさい ▷Good night. See you tomorrow. お休みなさい．またあした
Night night! 😊 お休みなさい(★子どもが，または子どもに用いる) ▷Night night, Mommy! Night night, Daddy! お休みなさい，ママ．お休みなさい，パパ

noise /nɔ́iz/ 名 物音，騒音；雑音

make	a noise	騒音を立てる
cause	a noise	騒音を出す
hear	a noise	物音が聞こえる
reduce	the noise	騒音を減らす
shut out	the noise	騒音を遮断する

▷This photocopier is **making** a lot of **noise**. I think there's something wrong with it. このコピー機はガタガタいっている．故障じゃないかな
▷Who's **causing** all that **noise** in the classroom? 教室でうるさくしているのはだれだ
▷The machines in this factory are really loud. Can't we do something to **reduce** the **noise**? この工場の機械が出す音は大きすぎる．何とか騒音を減らせないか
▷We closed all the windows and doors in order to try to **shut out** the **noise**. 騒音を遮断しようと窓やドアをすべて閉めた

a loud	noise	大きな音
a big	noise	
a terrible	noise	ひどい音
a low	noise	低い音
a strange	noise	妙な音
a funny	noise	
background	noise	周囲の騒音
engine	noise	エンジン音

▷Suddenly, there was a **loud noise** from outside. Two cars had crashed into each other. 突然外で大きな音がした．2台の車が衝突したのだ
▷We live near an airport. The planes make a **terrible noise** as they take off and come in to land. 空港のそばに住んでいて，離着陸のときに飛行機がものすごい音を出す
▷The washing machine is making a **strange noise**.

I think we need to buy a new one. 洗濯機が変な音を立てている．新しいのを買わないと

above	the noise	騒音の中で
over	the noise	

▷When Japan won the Asian Cup, you couldn't hear the announcement **above** the **noise** of the crowds celebrating. 日本がアジアカップで優勝したとき，お祭り騒ぎをする群衆の歓声でアナウンスが聞こえなかった

noon /núːn/ 名 正午

at	noon	正午に
just after	noon	正午少し過ぎに
shortly after	noon	
just before	noon	正午少し前に
shortly before	noon	

▷There was a serious earthquake in the Philippines **just before noon** today. きょう正午前にフィリピンで大地震があった

twelve	noon	正午
high	noon	正午ぴったり

normal /nɔ́ːrməl/ 形 普通の，標準の

perfectly	normal	まったく普通の
quite	normal	
fairly	normal	かなり普通の
apparently	normal	見たところ普通の

▷It's **perfectly normal** to be nervous before a big match. 大きな試合の前に緊張するのはまったく普通のことだ
▷Your blood pressure is **fairly normal**. あなたの血圧はごく正常です
▷Her temperature is **apparently normal**, although she has a bad cough. 彼女の体温は見たところ正常だ．ただ，ひどいせきをしているが

it is normal	(for A) to do	(Aが)…するのはごく普通だ

▷It's **normal for** security checks **to** be carried out at airports. 空港で手荷物検査が行われることはごく普通のことだ

north /nɔ́ːrθ/ 名 北，北部

far	north		はるか北

▷In the **far north** temperatures are much colder than in the far south. 北の果てでは気温は南の果てよりずっと低い

in	the north (of A)	(Aの)北側部分に
to	the north (of A)	(Aの)北の方角に
from	the north (of A)	(Aの)北から

▷Morocco is **in** the **north of** Africa. モロッコはアフリカ北部に位置する
▷Scotland lies **to** the **north of** England. スコットランドはイングランドの北の方角に位置する
▷There's a cold wind blowing **from** the **north**. 冷たい風が北から吹いている

fifty miles	north of A	Aの50マイル北

▷Oxford is about 50 **miles north of** London. オックスフォードはロンドンの北およそ50マイルのところにある

north, south, east and west	東西南北

★日本語と順序が異なる

nose /nóuz/ 名 鼻

blow	one's nose	鼻をかむ
wipe	one's nose	鼻を拭く
pick	one's nose	鼻をほじる
wrinkle	one's nose	鼻にしわを寄せる

▷Do you have a tissue? I need to **blow** my **nose**. ティッシュ持ってる？鼻をかまなきゃ
▷Here. Use my handkerchief to **wipe** your **nose**. ほら，私のハンカチで鼻をふいて
▷"Stop it, Ben! It's rude to **pick** your **nose**!" "Sorry, mummy!"「やめなさい，ベン．鼻をほじるのは行儀が悪いわよ」「ごめんママ」
▷She **wrinkled** her **nose**. "What's that terrible smell?" 彼女は鼻にしわを寄せた．「あのひどいにおいは何かしら」

one's nose	is running	鼻水が出ている
one's nose	wrinkles	鼻にしわが寄る
one's nose	bleeds	鼻血が出る

▷It's so cold my **nose is running**! あんまり寒くて鼻水が出るよ
▷Her **nose wrinkled**. "Can you smell something burning?" 彼女の鼻にしわが寄った．「何かこげているにおいがしない？」(★クンクンにおいをかぐときのしぐさ)

a big	nose	大きな鼻
a large	nose	
a long	nose	高い鼻
a small	nose	低い鼻
a sharp	nose	尖った鼻
a hooked	nose	かぎ鼻
a straight	nose	鼻筋の通った鼻
a red	nose	赤らんだ鼻
a blocked	nose	詰まった鼻
a runny	nose	鼻水の出ている鼻
a broken	nose	骨折した鼻

★鼻が「高い」,「低い」に high, low は用いない

▷Tom has a **big nose**. トムは鼻が大きい
▷Typically Westerners have **longer noses** than Asian people. 概して西洋人はアジアの人たちより鼻が高い
▷He had a **sharp nose** and a bright red face. 彼は鼻が尖っていて赤ら顔をしていた
▷I think he's very handsome. A **straight nose**, a strong chin and a nice smile. 彼はとてもハンサムだと思う. 鼻筋が通って,力強いあごをしているし,ほほえみもすてきだ
▷My cold's no better. I've still got a **blocked nose** and a cough. かぜがよくならないんだ. まだ鼻が詰まってせきが出るよ
▷Rod was in a fight last night. He has a **broken nose** and two black eyes. ロッドは昨夜けんかをし, 鼻を骨折して両目にあざができている

the bridge	of the nose	鼻柱
the end	of the nose	鼻先
the tip	of the nose	

▷She had a big red spot at the **end of** the **nose**. 彼女は鼻先に大きな赤いにきびがあった
▷It's so cold! The **tip of** my **nose** is frozen! すごく寒いよ. 鼻先が凍るようだ

through	the nose	鼻から

note /nóut/

名 走り書き, メモ;注釈;音調, 調子

write	a note	走り書きする
scribble	notes	
send	a note	メモを送る
receive	a note	メモを受け取る
leave	a note	メモを残す
make	a note	メモをとる
keep	a note	
take	notes	
compare	notes	意見交換する
take	note	注目する

▷I **scribbled** these **notes** during the lecture, but now I can't read them! 講義中にメモを走り書きしたんだけど, いまになってみると読めないや
▷Look, dad! Mom has **left** a **note** on the table. She's gone shopping. ほらパパ, テーブルの上にママのメモが置いてあるよ. 買い物に出かけたのよ
▷The police told us to **keep** a **note** of anything unusual that happens. 何か普段と違うことがあったらメモしておくようにと警察から言われた
▷OK. Now that we've interviewed everybody, let's **compare notes**. さてと, 全員への面接が終わったので意見交換しよう
▷**Take** careful **note** of what the sales manager says. 営業部長の言うことによく留意しなさい

a brief	note	簡単なメモ
a suicide	note	遺書
a cheerful	note	明るい調子
a positive	note	前向きな調子
a high	note	高い音
a low	note	低い音

note /nóut/

動 注意する, 気づく;書き留める

note	down	書き留める
as noted	above	上述したように
as noted	earlier	前に述べたように
as noted	previously	

▷Please **note down** my address. 私の住所を書き留めてください
▷**As noted above**, smart phones are becoming very popular. 上述したようにスマートフォンの人気が上がりつつある

note	that...	…に気づく;…に留意する
note	wh-	…か留意する

★wh- は who, what, how など

▷She **noted that** there were two expensive-looking paintings in the committee room. 彼女は会議室に高そうな絵画が2枚あるのに気づいた
▷Please **note how** important it is to use fresh vegetables to prepare this dish. この料理をつくるには新鮮な野菜を使うのがポイントですのでお忘れなく

be worth	noting	注目に値する

| notice |

▷ It's **worth noting** that the deadline for applications is December 31st. 申込期限が12月31日だということに注意しておいたほうがいい

notice /nóutis/

名 掲示；通知, 通告；注意

serve	notice	通知する
have	notice	通知を受ける
receive	notice	
give (A)	notice	(Aに)解雇を通知する
take	notice	気に留める
come to	A's notice	目に留まる
escape	A's notice	目に留まらない

▷ They **served notice** to their employees that the staff canteen would close down next month. 社員食堂が来月閉鎖になるとの通知が従業員にあった

▷ It's important for our staff to **have notice** of any changes that may be introduced. 導入される変更点についてうちの職員には前もって知らせるべきだ

▷ The company is closing down. They **gave** 200 people **notice** last week. 会社を閉じることになって先週200名に解雇通知が出た

▷ "That man's waving at us. Do you know him?" "No. Don't **take** any **notice**. Come on. Let's go!"「あの男の人, 私たちに手を振っているわ. 知ってる人？」「いいえ. 無視して. さあ行きましょう」(★ take notice はしばしば take any notice of A, take no notice of A で用いる)

▷ It has **come to the notice** of the headmaster that one or two boys sometimes smoke a cigarette in school. 学校で時々たばこを吸っている生徒が1, 2名いることに校長が気づいた

▷ I broke my boss's special teacup two days ago. But he hasn't said anything. So far it has **escaped his notice!** 2日前に上司の大事な茶碗を割ったのに何も言われないんだ. まだ気づいていないんだな

advance	notice	予告, 事前の通告
reasonable	notice	しかるべき通知
written	notice	書面による通知
public	notice	世間の注目

▷ We've just had **advance notice** that the government is going to raise the sales tax next year. 政府は来年売上税を上げる予定だとの通告を事前に受けたところだ

▷ If you decide to leave the company we expect you to give us **reasonable notice**. 会社を辞める場合にはしかるべき事前通告をしてもらいたい

▷ We understand that you wish to leave, but we have not received any **written notice** from you yet. あなたが辞めたがっていることはわかっているが, まだ書面による通知を受け取っていません

on short	notice	時間をおかずに, いきなり
at short	notice	
3 months'	notice	3か月前の事前通告

▷ We need someone to go and work in our head office **at short notice**. だれかに至急, 本社勤務をしてもらう必要がある

▷ They can't fire you now. They need to give you **3 months' notice**. いまあなたを解雇はできない. 3か月前に事前通告する必要がある

notice /nóutis/ **動** 気づく

not even	notice	気づきさえしない
hardly	notice	ほとんど気づかない
never	notice	決して気づかない

▷ I changed my hairstyle and my boyfriend did**n't even notice**! 髪型を変えたのに私の彼ったら気づきさえしなかったのよ

▷ "There's a big red spot on my chin!" "It's not so big. You can **hardly notice** it!"「あごに大きな赤いニキビがあるの」「そんなに大きくないよ. ほとんど気がつかないよ」

| notice A | doing | Aが…しているのに気づく |

▷ I didn't **notice** him leav**ing**. 彼が出て行くのに気づかなかった

notice	(that)...	…であることに気づく
notice	wh-...	…かに気づく

★ wh- は how, what, who など

▷ After about 10 minutes he **noticed that** she was really angry. 10分ほどして彼は彼女がとても怒っているのに気づいた

▷ I'm in big trouble! I didn't **notice when** she arrived, **how** she looked or **what** she was wearing! 困っちゃったな. 彼女がいつ着いて, どんなようすで, 何を着ていたか気づかなかったよ

number /nʌ́mbər/

名 数, 数字；番号；総数, 数量

count	the number	数を数える
increase	the number	数を増やす
reduce	the number	数を減らす
limit	the number	数を制限する
get	a number	番号をもらう

| give | a number | 番号を教える |
| identify | a number | 番号を確認する |

▷ I had a part-time job **counting** the **number** of cars that drove past during the rush hour. ラッシュアワーに通る車の台数を数えるアルバイトをした

▷ We need to **increase** the **number** of parking spaces in our company. 我が社は駐車スペースの数を増やす必要がある

▷ We have to **limit** the **number** of circle members to 25. サークルのメンバーの数を25名に制限する必要がある

▷ In the hospital they **give** you a **number** and you have to wait until you're called. 病院では番号を渡されて，呼ばれるまで待たなければなりません

▷ I saw the car drive away after the accident, but I couldn't **identify** the **number**. 事故のあと，車が走り去るのを見たがナンバー確認できなかった

the number	falls	数が減る
the number	reduces	
the number	increases	数が増える
the number	grows	
the number	rises	

▷ The college needs more students. If the **number falls** again this year, we could be in trouble. 大学は学生数を増やす必要がある．今年度も数が減ったら困ったことになる

▷ The **number** of applicants has **increased** by 45% compared with last year. 志願者数は昨年と比べ45％増えた

a large	number	大きい数
a great	number	
a high	number	
a huge	number	巨大な数
a small	number	小さな数
a low	number	
a limited	number	限られた数
a significant	number	かなりの数
a considerable	number	
an increasing	number	増大する数
a growing	number	
the average	number	平均の数
the minimum	number	最小数
the maximum	number	最大数
an equal	number	同数
the total	number	総数
an even	number	偶数
an odd	number	奇数
a three-digit	number	3桁の数

▷ A **large number** of housewives do part-time jobs. かなりの数の主婦がパートの仕事をしている

▷ A **great number** of new projects had to be canceled. 多くの新たな計画が中止を余儀なくされた

▷ It was early so only a **small number** of people had arrived. 早かったので着いていたのは少数だけだった

▷ A **significant number** of women are waiting until later to get married compared with 10 years ago. 10年前と比べてかなりの数の女性が晩婚になっている

▷ An **increasing number** of people are using new hybrid cars. 新しいハイブリッドカーを使用する人の数が増えている

▷ The **minimum number** of students we need to arrange this trip is eight people. この旅行を手配するのに必要な最小限の生徒の人数は8名だ

▷ The **maximum number** of people allowed in this elevator is fifteen. このエレベーターに乗れる最大人数は15人です

▷ There were an **equal number** of boys and girls in the group. そのグループは男の子と女の子は同数だった

▷ We are still not sure of the **total number** of people who died in the train crash. 列車事故で死んだ人の総数はまだわからない

a room	number	部屋番号
a telephone	number	電話番号
a fax	number	ファックス番号
the wrong	number	間違い番号

▷ Sorry. You have the **wrong number**. あなたのおかけになった番号は違っています

| an increase | in numbers | 数の増加 |
| a drop | in numbers | 数の減少 |

▷ There was an **increase in numbers** of house fires this year. 今年は住宅火災の件数が増加した

| in number | 総計で；数では |

▷ Our supporters were low **in number**, but high in enthusiasm! われわれのサポーターは数は少なかったが，士気は高かった

O

obey /oubéi | əb-/

動 従う, 服従する;(法律・規則を)守る

always	obey	常に従う
immediately	obey	すぐ従う
instantly	obey	
meekly	obey	おとなしく従う

▷ **Always obey** the safety rules when you operate this machine. この機械を動かすときには常に安全規則を守ること
▷ If you get an order you should **immediately obey** it. 命令を受けたらすぐ従ったほうがいい
▷ He told her to sit down and she **meekly obeyed**. 彼が座るように言うと彼女はおとなしく従った

refuse to	obey	従うのを拒否する

▷ My dog is so disobedient! I keep telling him to sit, but he **refuses to obey**. うちの犬はすごく反抗的で、いくらお座りと言っても言うことを聞こうとしない

an obligation	to obey	従う義務

▷ Everybody has an **obligation to obey** the law. すべての人に法律を順守する義務がある

object /ábdʒikt | ɔ́b-/

名 物, 物体;対象, 的;目的;目的語

become	an object	対象になる
achieve	one's object	目的を達成する

▷ When she joined the pop group she **became** a great **object** of envy of her schoolmates. ポップスグループに入ると彼女は学校の仲間内で羨望(せんぼう)の的になった
▷ She finally **achieved** her **object** of winning a gold medal at the Olympic games. オリンピックで金メダルをとるという目標を彼女はついに達成した

an inanimate	object	無生物
a physical	object	物体
a solid	object	固体
the main	object	主目的
one's sole	object	唯一の目的
a direct	object	直接目的語
an indirect	object	間接目的語

▷ He treats me as if I'm an **inanimate object**. I'm not a piece of wood! あいつったらぼくのことを物扱いするんだ. ぼくはでくの坊じゃない
▷ She was able to move **physical objects** by telepathy. 彼女はテレパシーで物体を動かせた
▷ The **main object** of this training program is to test your ability to work together as a team. この研修プログラムのおもな目的はきみにチームの一員としてやっていく能力があるかどうかテストすることだ

object /əbdʒékt/ **動** 反対する

strongly	object	強く反対する

★ object strongly も用いる

▷ "I **strongly object** to the decision to close down our branch in Sydney." "Yes, I strongly object, too!" 「シドニー支店を閉鎖する決定に強く反対します」「はい, 私も強く反対です」

object	to A	Aに反対する

▷ I **object to** another rise in gasoline prices! ガソリンの値段がまた上がるのは反対だ

object	that...	…だと言って反対する

▷ She **objects that** the government hasn't done more to help the homeless. 政府はホームレス救済のためにそれだけしかしなかったと言って彼女は反対している

PHRASES
I object to that! ☺ 異議あり

objection /əbdʒékʃən/ **名** 反対, 異議

make	an objection	反対する
raise	an objection	
voice	an objection	
have (got)	an objection	反対がある
have	no objection	異議がない
meet	an objection	反対意見に対処する
withdraw	one's objection	反対を取り下げる

▷ He **made** various **objections** to the new plans. 彼は新しい計画にいろんな点で反対した
▷ Excuse me, I'd like to **raise an objection**. 申し訳ありませんが異議を唱えたいと思います
▷ **Has** anybody **got** any **objections**? だれか反対意見はありますか
▷ So, if you **have no objection** we'll postpone a decision until our next meeting. では異議がなければ次の会議まで決定を延期します
▷ Various proposals have been made to **meet** their

objections. 彼らからの反対意見に対処すべくさまざまな提案がなされた

a strong	objection	強い反対
a serious	objection	
the main	objection	主要な反対
a possible	objection	ありうる反対意見

▷The union has **strong objections** to the proposed salary cuts. 組合は給料カットの提案に強く反対している

▷I can't understand. What **possible objection** could you have? You'll make a big profit! わからないな．あなたが反対する理由があるでしょうか．あなたは大儲けするんですよ

an objection	to A	Aへの反対
an objection	against A	

▷The main **objection to** your plan is that it's too expensive. きみの計画に反対するおもな理由は金がかかりすぎることだ

objective /əbdʒéktiv/ 名 目標，目的

have	an objective	目標がある
set	an objective	目標を設定する
pursue	an objective	目的を追求する
achieve	an objective	目標を達成する
meet	an objective	

▷Don't sit around doing nothing. You need to **have** an **objective** in life! ただ無為に過ごしていてはいけない．人生に目的をもつことが必要だ

▷You need to **set** an **objective**. What do you want to be doing in 5 years' time? 目標を設定する必要がある．5年後には何をしていたいですか

▷Madonna **pursued** her **objective** to become a famous pop star. マドンナは有名なポップスターになるという目標を追い求めた

▷He **achieved** his **objective** of becoming sales manager in 5 years. 彼は5年で営業部長になる目標を達成した

a clear	objective	明確な目的
a specific	objective	
the main	objective	主要目的
the major	objective	大きな目的
the primary	objective	第一の目的
the ultimate	objective	究極の目的

▷Don't be vague. Decide a **clear objective** and then go for it! あいまいにしておくな．明確な目標を定めてがんばれ

▷Her **main objective** in life was to find a rich husband! 彼女にとっての人生の主要目的は金持ちの夫を見つけることだった

▷She's a senator now, but I think her **ultimate objective** is to become President. 彼女はいまは上院議員だが，究極の目標は大統領になることだと思う

objective /əbdʒéktiv/ 形 客観的な

completely	objective	完全に客観的な
purely	objective	
totally	objective	

▷Are you sure that your opinion is **completely objective**? あなたの意見が完全に客観的だという自信がありますか

obligation /àbləgéiʃən | ɔ̀b-/

名 (法律・道徳上の)義務，責任

have	an obligation	義務がある
impose	an obligation	義務を課す
meet	an obligation	義務を果たす
fulfill	an obligation	

▷We have to recall our cars and offer free repair. We **have** an **obligation** to our customers. わが社の車をリコールして無料修理を行わなければならない．われわれには顧客に対する義務がある

▷If we sign the contract we must make sure that we can **fulfill** all our **obligations**. 契約書にサインするからには，課せられた義務をすべて果たせるようにしておかなければならない

a contractual	obligation	契約上の義務
a legal	obligation	法律上の義務
a moral	obligation	道徳的責任

▷I promised I would help her so now I'm under a **moral obligation** to do so. 彼女を助ける約束をしたからには，私にはそうする道義上の責任がある

an obligation	to A	Aに対する義務
under	an obligation	義務を負って

▷She helped me, so I feel **under** an **obligation** to help her. 彼女が私を助けてくれたので私は彼女を助ける義務があると感じている

an obligation	to do	…する義務

▷We are under no contractual **obligation to** pay them any money. 彼らに金を払ういかなる契約上の義務もない

| a sense of | obligation | 義務感 |

▷ She helped Dave a lot after his divorce and now he's helping her out of a **sense of obligation**. 離婚後にデイブは彼女からずいぶん助けられたので，義務感から今度は彼が助けている

observation /ὰbzərvéiʃən | ɔb-/

名 観察，観測；(観察に基づく)意見，所見

| make | an observation | 意見を述べる |

▷ I'd like to **make** an **observation** about the importance of motivating our students. 学生への動機づけの重要さについて意見を述べたいと思います

careful	observation	注意深い観察
a detailed	observation	詳細な観察
direct	observation	直接の観察
empirical	observation	経験的な観察

▷ After **careful observation** over many years, the volcano was declared inactive. 何年にもわたる注意深い観察の後に，その火山は休火山であると宣言された
▷ Are these news reports based on rumors or **direct observation**? これらの報道はうわさに基づくものか，それとも直接の観察に基づくものなのか

an observation	about A	Aに関する意見
an observation	on A	
for	observation	観察のために
under	observation	観察下に；監視下に

▷ The doctors are not sure what's wrong with Ted. They're keeping him in hospital **for observation**. 医師たちはテッドのどこが悪いのか確信がもてず，観察入院を続けさせている

| powers of | observation | 観察力 |

▷ Sherlock Holmes had amazing **powers of observation**! シャーロック・ホームズは驚くべき観察力をもっていた

observe /əbzə́:rv/

動 観察する；気づく；(観察に基づいて)述べる

actually	observe	実際に観察する
carefully	observe	注意深く観察する
directly	observe	直接観察する
be widely	observed	幅広く観察される

▷ I **actually observed** the volcano in Iceland erupting from about 2 miles away. アイスランドの火山が噴火しているのを約2マイル離れた場所から実際観察した
▷ The police need to find someone who **directly observed** the robbery. 警察は強盗の現場を直接目撃した人を見つける必要がある
▷ The UFO was **widely observed** by many people in the south of England. 未確認飛行物体はイングランド南部で多くの人に幅広く目撃された

| observe | A doing | Aが…しているのに気づく；…しているところを観察する |

▷ I **observed** someone break**ing** in through a window. だれかが窓から侵入するところを目撃した
▷ Looking out of her window she **observed** a marching band go**ing** past. 窓の外を眺めながら彼女はマーチングバンドが通り過ぎて行くのを見た

| observe | that... | …であると気づく；…であると述べる |
| observe | wh- | …かを観察する |

★wh- は what, how, where など

▷ She **observed that** all the sandwiches had been eaten after ten minutes. 彼女がふと気づくとサンドイッチは10分後には残らず平らげられていた
▷ Caroline spent 3 months in Africa **observing how** gorillas behave in the wild. キャロリンは3か月アフリカで過ごして，野生のゴリラがどのように行動するか観察した

obtain /əbtéin/ 動 得る，手に入れる

| be easily | obtained | 簡単に手に入る |

▷ We don't have the part to repair your car, but it can be **easily obtained**. ここにはきみの車を修理する部品がないが，簡単に手に入る

| obtain A | from B | BからAを得る |

▷ I **obtained** this beautiful vase **from** an antique shop in Beijing. 北京の骨董店でこの美しい花瓶を手に入れた

obvious /άbviəs | ɔ́b-/ 形 明らかな，明白な

| seem | obvious | 明らかに思われる |

▷ Now that you tell me, it all **seems** so **obvious**. あなたが教えてくれたおかげで事情がはっきりしたよ

| fairly | obvious | かなり明らかな |

| occupation |

quite	obvious	
glaringly	obvious	火を見るより明らかな
immediately	obvious	直ちに明らかな

▷ It was **fairly obvious** that she was embarrassed. 彼女が当惑しているのはかなり明らかだった
▷ When Don arrived at the fire it was **immediately obvious** it was serious. ダンが火災現場に到着すると, 事態が深刻であるのがすぐわかった

it is obvious	that...	…なのは明らかだ

▷ Helen started to cry. **It was obvious that** she was upset. ヘレンは泣きだした. 彼女が取り乱しているのは明らかだった

obvious	from A	Aから明らかだ
obvious	to A	A(人)に明らかだ

▷ It's **obvious from** your enthusiasm that you really want the job. あなたがその仕事を本気でやりたがっているのは熱意を見ればよくわかる
▷ It's **obvious to** everybody except you that you're making a mistake. あなたが間違いを犯しているのはあなた以外のだれの目にも明らかだ

occasion /əkéiʒən/

名 時, 折, 時期；機会；行事, 催し

recall	an occasion	その時のことを
remember	an occasion	思い出す
mark	the occasion	行事を祝う
celebrate	the occasion	

▷ We've been married for over 60 years now, but I can still clearly **recall** the **occasion** that we first met. 結婚して60年以上になりますが, いまでも最初に会った時のことをはっきり思い出せます
▷ It's your 17th birthday on Saturday, isn't it? I think we should hold a party to **mark** the **occasion**. 土曜日はきみの17歳の誕生日だね. お祝いのパーティーを開くつもりなんだ

many	occasions	よくある折
numerous	occasions	
several	occasions	何度かの折
a rare	occasion	まれな折
a particular	occasion	特別な折
a different	occasion	別の折
a previous	occasion	以前の折
a big	occasion	大きな催し
an important	occasion	重要な催し
a memorable	occasion	忘れられない催し
a special	occasion	特別な催し

a social	occasion	社交の催し

▷ You've been late for work on **many occasions**. きみはしょっちゅう会社に遅刻するね
▷ Kumiko's been late for class on **several occasions**. 久美子は何回か授業に遅刻している
▷ I don't think we'd better go to Hokkaido by boat. On a **previous occasion** you were seasick. 北海道へ船で行くのはやめたほうがいいと思うよ. 以前きみは船酔いしたからね
▷ The wedding was a really **big occasion**. They invited over 500 guests. すごく盛大な結婚式で, 500人を超える招待客だった
▷ The royal wedding is going to be a really **special occasion**. 王室の結婚式は実に特別な催しになるだろう
▷ The Oscar award ceremony is a fabulous **social occasion**. オスカー授賞式はすばらしい社交の催しだ

an occasion	to do	…する機会

▷ The Christmas party will be a good **occasion to** announce our engagement. クリスマスパーティーはぼくたちの婚約を発表するよい機会だろう

on	one occasion	ある折に
on	this occasion	この折に
on	that occasion	あの折に
on	occasion(s)	時折
on	the occasion of A	Aを祝って

▷ I'm afraid granddad is getting forgetful. **On one occasion** last week he went out into the street wearing his pajamas! 祖父は忘れっぽくなってきていて, 先週なんかパジャマを着たまま通りに出ちゃった
▷ "Do you get really bad headaches?" "Yes, **on occasions**. But not all the time." 「頭痛がひどいですか」「ええ, 時々なんですが, いつもというわけではありません」
▷ I'd like to present you with a bottle of champagne **on** the **occasion of** your 10th wedding anniversary. あなたの結婚10周年祝いにシャンパンをプレゼントしたい

a sense of	occasion	時と場所をわきまえる感性

▷ Our boss dressed up as Santa Claus at our Christmas party this year! He has a real **sense of occasion**. うちの上司は今年のクリスマスパーティーでサンタクロースに扮したよ. 実に時と場所をわきまえているね

occupation /àkjupéiʃən | ɔ̀k-/

名 職業, 仕事；占有, 占拠, 占領

find	an occupation	職を見つける

▷ I think you should stop doing your part-time job

| occupy |

and **find** a proper **occupation**. アルバイトはやめて，ちゃんとした仕事を見つけるべきだと思うよ

a professional	occupation	専門職
a skilled	occupation	熟練労働
a manual	occupation	肉体労働
illegal	occupation	不法占拠

▷ **Professional occupations** are usually well-paid: lawyers, doctors, for example. 専門職はたいてい給料がいい．例えば弁護士や医者です

| during | the occupation | 占領の間 |
| under | occupation | 占領下で |

▷ The French had a difficult time **during** the **occupation** of France by Germany in the Second World War. 第2次世界大戦中，ドイツ占領下のフランスでフランス人はつらい目にあった
▷ Poland was **under** the **occupation** of Germany during the Second World War. ポーランドは第2次世界大戦中ドイツ占領下にあった

PHRASES

What's your occupation? 😊 ご職業は何ですか

occupy /ákjupài | ɔ́k-/

動 占領する，占拠する，占める

be fully	occupied	完全に手が塞がっている
now	occupy	現在占拠する
still	occupy	なお占拠する

▷ "You're really busy at work now, aren't you?" "Oh, yes. But it's no problem. I like to be **fully occupied**."「ずいぶんとご多忙ですよね」「ええ，でもいいんです．忙しくしているのが好きですから」
▷ A large family **now occupies** the apartment above us. 大家族がアパートの上の部屋に入居中です

| be occupied | with A | Aで忙しくしている |
| occupy oneself | with A | |

▷ If you have to wait a long time at the dentist you should **occupy** yourself **with** something. Read a book! 歯医者で長いこと待たされるなら，何かすればいいじゃないか．本を読めよ

occur /əkə́ːr/

動 起こる；生じる；(考えなどが)浮かぶ

commonly	occur	よく起こる
usually	occur	たいてい起こる
never	occur	決して起こらない
actually	occur	実際に起こる
occur	frequently	頻繁に起こる
occur	naturally	自然に起こる
occur	spontaneously	
occur	simultaneously	同時に起こる

▷ These kinds of problems **commonly occur** when you start a new job. こうした問題は新しく仕事を始めるとよく起きるものだ
▷ We have to make sure that this dangerous situation **never occurs** again. こんな危険な状況には決して二度とならないようにすべきだ
▷ Some people say that the American moon landing never **actually occurred**. アメリカ人による月面着陸は実際にはなかったと言う人たちもいる
▷ Earthquakes **occur frequently** in parts of Southeast Asia. 東南アジアには地震が頻発する地域がある
▷ Two explosions **occurred simultaneously** at 12:15 p.m. 2件の爆発が午後12時15分に同時に起きた

occur	during A	Aの間に起きる
occur	after A	Aの後で起きる
occur	before A	Aの前に起きる

▷ The robbery **occurred during** the night. 強盗事件は夜の間に起きた

odd /ád | ɔ́d/ 形 奇妙な；奇数の

| a little | odd | 少し奇妙な |
| distinctly | odd | 明らかに奇妙な |

▷ "Nick's usually home by 8:00. He's still not back and it's nearly ten now." "Mmm. That's **a little odd**."「ニックはふだん8時には家に帰っているのに，まだなの．そろそろ10時よ」「うーん，ちょっと変だね」

| odd or even | 奇数あるいは偶数の |
| odd and even | 奇数と偶数の |

★ even or [and] odd も用いる

▷ Could you check this list of people we've invited to the dinner party? Are the numbers **odd or even**? ディナーパーティーに招いた人たちの名簿をチェックしていただけませんか．数字は奇数ですか，偶数ですか

| it is odd | (that...) | …は奇妙だ |

▷ "I've been calling Della on her mobile phone all day, but no reply." "Yes, **it's odd that** she doesn't answer."「デラの携帯電話に一日中かけているのに出ないんだ」「変だね，彼女が出ないなんて」

the odd thing is	that...	奇妙なのは…だ

▷"Did you hear that Lea is going to marry Brad?" "Yes, but the **odd thing is that** last week she told me she hated him!"「リーがブラッドと結婚するって聞いた？」「ええ，でも変なんだけど，先週はあんな男，大嫌いって私に言ってたのよ」

PHRASES
That's odd. ☺ 変だな

offense /əféns/ 名 罪，犯罪，違反；感情を害すること，侮辱；攻撃(★《英》つづりは offence)

cause	offense	怒らせる
give	offense	
take	offense	怒る
commit	an offense	罪を犯す
constitute	an offense	犯罪を構成する
convict	A with an offense	Aを罪に問う

▷I'm sorry I didn't mean to be rude. Please don't **take offense**. ごめんなさい．失礼なことを言うつもりはなかったの．気分を悪くしないで

▷If you **commit** a serious **offense** you'll have to go to prison. 重罪を犯せば刑務所行きだよ

▷Free speech **constitutes** an **offense** in certain parts of the world. 世界には自由な言論が犯罪になる地域もある

a first	offense	初犯
a second	offense	再犯
a minor	offense	軽犯罪
a serious	offense	重罪
a sexual	offense	性犯罪

▷Parking your car in the wrong place is a **minor offense**. 正しい場所に駐車しないのは軽犯罪だ

▷Drunk driving is an extremely **serious offense**. 飲酒運転はきわめて重い犯罪だ

it is an offense	to do	…するのは違反である

▷In many countries **it**'s an **offense to** drop litter in the street. 多くの国では道路にごみを捨てるのは違反だ

PHRASES
No offense. ☺ 悪気はありません

offer /ɔ́:fər | ɔ́f-/ 名 申し出；条件提示

make	an offer	申し出る
consider	an offer	申し出を検討する
receive	an offer	申し出を受ける
accept	an offer	申し出を受諾する
take (up)	an offer	
refuse	an offer	申し出を断る
decline	an offer	
turn down	an offer	
reject	an offer	申し出を拒絶する
withdraw	an offer	申し出を撤回する

▷"I'm afraid, $200,000 is too much for us to pay." "OK, then. **Make** an **offer**."「こちらはとても20万ドルも支払えません」「わかりました．では，そちらから数字を提示してください」

▷They won't **accept** an **offer** of less than $150,000 for their house. 家の買い値の申し出が15万ドル未満では彼らは受諾しないだろう

▷They offered us $20,000 for our yacht, but now they've changed their minds and **withdrawn** their **offer**. うちのヨットに彼らは2万ドル提示していたのに，心変わりして申し出を撤回してしまった

a generous	offer	気前のよい申し出
a job	offer	求人
a good	offer	よい条件提示
a special	offer	特価提供

▷I think $50,000 is a **generous offer**. We won't get any more. We should take it. 5万ドルというのは気前のいい申し出だと思う．これ以上は無理だろう．この申し出を受け入れよう

▷These toys are under **special offer**: 50% off. これらのおもちゃは特価中で，5割引きです

office /ɔ́:fis | ɔ́f-/

名 事務所，営業所；役職，公職，任務

go to	the office	会社に行く
leave	the office	会社を出る
open	an office	事務所を開く
run for	office	公職に立候補する
take	office	公職に就く
come into	office	
be in	office	公職にある
be out of	office	公職から離れている
hold	office	公職に就いている
remain in	office	
leave	office	公職を辞す

▷We're thinking of **opening** an **office** in Shanghai. 上海事務所の開設を考えている

▷The senator intends to **run for office** again next year. その上院議員は来年再び選挙に出馬する意向だ

▷The President **came into office** at a very difficult

time. 大統領はきわめて困難な時期に就任した
▷ The Prime Minister has been **in office** for two years now. 首相の在任期間は2年に及んでいる
▷ The President is hoping to **hold office** for another 4 years. 大統領はあと4年間在職することを望んでいる
▷ After the scandal it was difficult for him to **remain in office**. スキャンダルを受けて彼が公職にとどまるのは困難だった
▷ When the Prime Minister **left office**, the country was in a better economic situation. 首相が退陣して国の経済状況は好転した

the head	office	本社
the main	office	
a regional	office	支社, 支店
a local	office	
a branch	office	
public	office	公職

▷ The **head office** is moving to Osaka. 本社は大阪に移転します

oil /ɔ́il/ 名 石油；食用油；オイル

produce	oil	石油を生産する
drill for	oil	石油を掘削する
add	the oil	油を加える
heat	the oil	油を加熱する

▷ Saudi Arabia **produces** a huge amount of **oil**. サウジアラビアは莫大な量の石油を生産している
▷ **Drilling for oil** in the sea can cause severe pollution. 海での石油掘削はひどい公害を引き起こす可能性がある
▷ **Heat** the **oil** in a large frying pan. 大きなフライパンで油を加熱してください

crude	oil	原油
heavy	oil	重油
light	oil	軽油
cooking	oil	食用油
salad	oil	サラダオイル
vegetable	oil	植物油
an essential	oil	精油

▷ **Crude oil** is found naturally in the ground. You need to refine it to make petroleum. 原油は天然の状態で地中にある．石油にするには精製する必要がある

oil and water	水と油
★通例この語順で日本語とは逆	

▷ Bob and Dave really don't get on with each other. They're like **oil and water**! ボブとデイブは互いにうまくやっていけない．まるで水と油だ

old /óuld/ 形 年とった；…歳の；古い

grow	old	年をとる
look	old	年をとって見える

▷ During the past year he seems suddenly to have **grown old**. この1年で彼は急に老けたみたいだ

a little	old	少し年とった
a bit	old	
really	old	とても年とった
much	older	…よりずっと年とった
slightly	older	…より少し年とった

★ much, slightly は比較級と連結する

▷ Granddad! You're 72! Don't you think it's **a little old** to climb Mount Fuji! おじいちゃん．もう72歳なんだよ．富士山に登るには少し年をとりすぎたと思わない？
▷ Sally's husband is **much older** than I thought he would be. He must be over 50. サリーの旦那は私が思っていたよりずっと年配だ．きっと50歳を越えている
▷ I'd like to marry a man **slightly older** than me. Maybe 2 or 3 years older. 少し年上の人と結婚したいの．2つか3つくらい上の人と

old enough	to do	…にふさわしい年齢の
too old	to do	…するには年をとりすぎて

▷ I'm not **old enough to** have a driving license yet. I have to wait 2 more years. まだ運転免許をとれる年齢に達していない．あと2年待たないといけない

how	old	何歳か；どれくらい古いか

▷ **How old** is this Chinese vase? この中国の花瓶はどれくらい古いものですか

be ten years old	10歳だ
ten-year-old	10歳の

▷ I'm eighteen **years old**. 私は18歳です
▷ A thirteen-**year-old** girl shouldn't be out late at night alone. 13歳の少女が夜遅くひとりで出歩いてはいけない

open /óupən/ 動 開く，開ける；開店する

slowly	open	ゆっくり開く
suddenly	open	急に開く
officially	open	正式に開店する
formally	open	

newly	opened	新しく開店した
recently	opened	最近開店した
open	out	広げる
open	up	開ける

▷Sarah woke up in hospital. She **slowly opened** her eyes and looked around. サラは病院で目を覚ました． 彼女はゆっくり目を開けて周りを見回した
▷The door **suddenly opened** and the teacher appeared looking angry. ドアが突然開いて，先生が怒った表情で現れた
▷The new supermarket **officially opened** yesterday. 新しいスーパーマーケットがきのう正式に開店した
▷A new cake shop **recently opened** near our house. 新しいケーキ屋さんがうちの近くに最近開店した
▷I knocked on the door of the shop but it was after closing time and they wouldn't **open up**. 店のドアをノックしたが，閉店後だったので開けてくれなかった

open	＋日時	…に開く

▷Most stores **open at 9:30** in the morning. ほとんどの店は朝9時半に開店する
▷Shops **open until 8 p.m.** on Saturday. 土曜日は店が夜の8時まで開いている
▷The museum **opened in 1971**. その美術館は1971年に開館した

try to	open	開けようとする
be due to	open	開く予定である
plan to	open	開く計画をしている

▷I **tried to open** the door again, but it was impossible. 再びドアを開けようとしたが開けられなかった
▷The new library is **due to open** in June. 新しい図書館は6月に開館予定だ

open /óupən/

[形] 開いている，開いた；公開中の，営業中の；率直な

stay	open	開いている
remain	open	開いている
stand	open	開いたままだ

▷I think the pharmacy **stays open** until 10 p.m. 薬局は午後10時まで開いているはずだよ

wide	open	広く開いた
half	open	半分開いた
slightly	open	やや開いた
always	open	いつも開いている
now	open	公開中の，営業中の

▷Look, the baby's not asleep. Her eyes are **wide open**. ほら，赤ちゃんは寝ていないよ．大きく目を開けてる
▷No wonder it's cold. Look! The window's **half open**! どうりで寒いはずだ．ほら，窓が半分開いている
▷That shop on the corner is **always open** until 10:00 at night. あの角の店はいつも夜10時まで開いている
▷Our office is **now open** in the morning from 9:30 to 12:30, Monday to Friday. うちの事務所は現在は月曜から金曜まで午前9時半から12時半まで開いています

open	to A	Aに公開されている
open	about A	Aについて率直な
open	with A	A(人)に率直な

▷These gardens are private. They're not **open to** the public. これらの庭は個人のもので一般には公開していない
▷I will be **open with** you **about** that matter. その件については隠し立てしません

operate /ɑ́pəreit | ɔ́p-/

[動] 動く，動かす；手術する

operate	effectively	効率的に動く
operate	independently	独立して動く
operate	properly	正確に動く
operate	successfully	うまく動く

▷There's something wrong with this machine. It's not **operating effectively**. この機械はどこかおかしい．きちんと作動していない
▷I used to work for the police, but now I **operate independently** as a private investigator. 昔は警察で働いていたが，いまは独立して私立探偵をやっている
▷He **operates successfully** as a financial consultant. 彼は経済コンサルタントとして順調にいっている

continue to	operate	活動し続ける

▷Our business may go bankrupt. I'm not sure how long we can **continue to operate**. うちの社は倒産するかもしれない．どれくらい経営が続けられるかわからない
▷We can no longer **continue to operate** this bus service. このバスの運行はもう続けられない

how to	operate	操作法

▷You'll need to learn **how to operate** these machines. これらの機械の操作法を学ぶ必要がある

own and operate	所有し経営する

▷She **owns and operates** her own company. 彼女は自分で会社を所有し経営している

operate	on A	A（人・体の部位）に手術をする
operate	on A	Aで動く
operate	at A	

▷ The surgeon **operated** successfully **on** his patient. その外科医は患者の手術に成功した
▷ This car **operates on** electricity. この車は電気で動く
▷ Computers these days **operate at** incredibly high speed. 最近のコンピュータは驚くほど処理速度が速い

operation /ὰpəréiʃən | ɔ́p-/

名 実施，活動；作戦；手術

be in	operation	実施中である
come into	operation	実施される
put A into	operation	Aを実施する
perform	an operation	手術を行う
carry out	an operation	
do	an operation	
have	an operation	手術を受ける
undergo	an operation	

▷ A new train timetable will be **in operation** next month. 新しい鉄道時刻表が来月から適用される
▷ The new laws on sales tax **come into operation** at midnight. 売上税に関する新たな法律が午前零時に施行される
▷ JR are going to **put** the first of their new bullet trains **into operation** next month. ＪＲは新型新幹線の初列車を来月運行する予定である
▷ The doctors decided to **perform** an **operation** immediately. 医師たちは直ちに手術をする決断をした
▷ Bill has to go into hospital next week to **have** an **operation**. ビルは来週入院して手術を受けなければならない

a successful	operation	成功した作戦
a military	operation	軍事作戦
a business	operation	事業活動
a rescue	operation	救出活動
a relief	operation	救援活動
a major	operation	大手術
a knee	operation	ひざの手術
a heart	operation	心臓の手術

▷ We had to carry out a carefully planned **military operation**. 綿密に練った軍事活動を遂行しなければならなかった
▷ Jane had heart surgery yesterday. It was a **major operation**. ジェインはきのう心臓の手術を受けたが，大手術だった

opinion /əpínjən/

名 意見，見解；世論；評価

have	an opinion	意見がある
hold	an opinion	
form	an opinion	意見をまとめる
express	an opinion	意見を述べる
give	an opinion	
voice	an opinion	意見を表明する
ask for	A's opinion	意見を求める

▷ Do you think we should accept their offer? Peter, do you **have** an **opinion**? 向こうの申し出を受け入れるべきだろうか．ピーター，意見はあるかい
▷ We don't have sufficient information yet to **form** an **opinion**. 情報がまだ不十分で見解がまとまらない
▷ Everybody has the right to **express** their **opinion**. だれもが自分の意見を述べる権利をもっている
▷ Why don't you **voice** your **opinion** in the next meeting? 次の会議できみの意見を言ってみたらどうかな
▷ I think we should **ask for** her **opinion** before we do anything. 行動に出る前に彼女の意見を求めたほうがいいと思う

the general	opinion	大方の意見
popular	opinion	よくある意見
public	opinion	世論
a professional	opinion	専門家の意見
expert	opinion	
a strong	opinion	強硬な意見
a personal	opinion	個人的な意見
a good	opinion	高い評価
a high	opinion	
a poor	opinion	低い評価
a low	opinion	

▷ The **general opinion** seems to be that we need better sports facilities. 大方の意見はもっとよいスポーツ施設が必要だということのようだ
▷ According to **popular opinion**, the Prime Minister should definitely resign. 首相は絶対に辞任するべきだというのが大方の意見だ
▷ She has very **strong opinions** on equality for women. 女性の平等に関して彼女はとても強硬な意見の持ち主だ
▷ Your teacher has a very **good opinion** of you. 先生はきみのことをとても高く買っている

a matter	of opinion	意見の分かれるところ
a difference	of opinion	意見の違い
the climate	of opinion	世論の動向

▷ That's a **matter of opinion**. そこは意見の分かれるところだ

▷ They had a **difference of opinion** two years ago and have never spoken to each other since. 2年前に意見を異にして以来，彼らは互いに一度も口をきいたことがない

▷ The Government wanted to continue with nuclear power, but the **climate of opinion** was against them. 政府は原子力を継続したかったが，世論の動向は政府に反対だった

opinion	on A	Aに関する意見
opinion	about A	
in	A's opinion	Aの意見では

▷ What's your **opinion on** capital punishment? 死刑についてあなたはどのような意見ですか

▷ **In** my **opinion**, Jack is very stubborn. ジャックはすごく頑固だというのが私の意見だ

the opinion	that...	…という意見

▷ Do you agree with the **opinion that** society is becoming more violent? 社会がますます暴力的になりつつあるという意見に賛成ですか

opponent /əpóunənt/

名 相手；反対者，敵

a formidable	opponent	手ごわい相手
a leading	opponent	おもな対抗者
the main	opponent	
a political	opponent	政敵

▷ "I'm not sure if Japan can beat Italy in the World Cup." "I agree. The Italians are **formidable opponents**." 「日本がワールドカップでイタリアに勝てるかどうかわからないな」「同感だね．イタリアは手ごわい相手だから」

▷ The Prime Minister gave an excellent speech against his **political opponents**. 首相は政敵を批判するすばらしいスピーチをした

opportunity /àpərtjúːnəti | ɔ̀pətjúː-/

名 機会，チャンス

have	an opportunity	機会がある
find	an opportunity	機会を見つける
get	an opportunity	機会を得る
give	an opportunity	機会を与える
offer	an opportunity	
provide	an opportunity	
seize	an opportunity	好機をつかむ
grasp	an opportunity	

take	the opportunity	機会を利用する
miss	an opportunity	機会を逃す
lose	an opportunity	

▷ I never **had** an **opportunity** to work abroad. 私には海外で働く機会がなかった

▷ I'm hoping to **get** an **opportunity** to study in the USA. 米国で勉強する機会を得たいと望んでいる

▷ Studying abroad in Canada for 6 months **gave** me an **opportunity** to improve my English. カナダへの半年の留学は英語上達の機会を私に与えてくれた

▷ My job **offers** an **opportunity** to travel regularly to the USA. 仕事で米国に行く機会がよくある

▷ I'd like to **take** this **opportunity** to thank everybody for their kind help. この機会を利用して親切に支援してくださったすべての人に感謝したいと思います

▷ I don't want to **miss** an **opportunity** to go to Korea! 韓国へ行く機会を逃したくない

an opportunity	exists	機会がある
an opportunity	arises	機会が訪れる
an opportunity	comes up	

▷ An **opportunity exists** for you to work in the USA. あなたには米国で働く機会がある

▷ There are no more internships abroad available at the moment, but we'll let you know if an **opportunity arises**. いまのところ海外でのインターンシップはもうありませんが，機会があればお知らせします

ample	opportunity	十分な機会
a great	opportunity	絶好の機会
an excellent	opportunity	
a golden	opportunity	
the perfect	opportunity	
a good	opportunity	よい機会
a unique	opportunity	またとない機会
a missed	opportunity	逃した機会
equal	opportunity	機会均等
educational	opportunity	教育機会
a business	opportunity	商機
an investment	opportunity	投資機会
a photo	opportunity	写真撮影の機会
an employment	opportunity	雇用機会，求人
a job	opportunity	
a career	opportunity	

▷ We've given that student **ample opportunity** to improve, but he never gets any better. その学生に上達の機会を存分に与えてきたが，ちっともよくならない

▷ She's going to spend a year doing research at a university in Canada. It's a **great opportunity**! 彼女は1年間カナダの大学に研究をしにいく予定だが，すばらしい機会だ

▷ It's a **unique opportunity**. Don't let it go. チャン

| oppose |

スだから逃すな

▷ Our company believes in **equal opportunity** for men and women. わが社は男女の機会均等が大事と考えている

an opportunity	for A	Aのための機会

▷ My boss told me today that there was an **opportunity for** promotion. 私に昇進のチャンスがあると上司はきょう話してくれた

an opportunity	to do	…する機会

▷ Dave never misses an **opportunity to** tell a joke. Unfortunately none of them are very funny! デイブは機会があればジョークを言うが,残念ながらおもしろいものは一つもない

at	every	opportunity	あらゆる機会に
at	the earliest	opportunity	できるだけ早い
at	the first	opportunity	機会に

▷ That man was so rude. He kept interrupting the meeting **at every opportunity**. あの男はとても失礼で,事あるごとに会議を中断させた

▷ We should reply to this letter **at the earliest opportunity**. できるだけ早い機会にこの手紙に返事をしたほうがいい

oppose /əpóuz/ 動 反対する;抵抗する

bitterly	oppose	激しく反対する
vehemently	oppose	
strongly	oppose	強く反対する
diametrically	oppose	真っ向から反対する
consistently	oppose	一貫して反対する

▷ I **strongly oppose** any changes to the present voting system. 現行の投票制度のいかなる変更にも強く反対する

▷ In politics, he's far left and I'm far right. Our views **diametrically oppose** each other. 政治的信条として彼は極端な左で私は極端な右だから,真っ向から意見が対立する

opposed /əpóuzd/ 形 反対の

strongly	opposed	強く反対の
totally	opposed	まったく反対の
diametrically	opposed	真っ向から反対の

▷ Our boss is **totally opposed** to changing the overtime system. うちの上司は残業制度を変えることにまったく反対だ

be opposed	to A	Aに反対である

▷ 90% of the public are **opposed to** cuts in the health service. 国民の9割が公共医療サービスの削減に反対だ

opposition /àpəzíʃən | ɔ̀p-/

名 反対, 対立; (the opposition で)相手チーム; 野党

express	one's opposition	反対を表明する
face	opposition	反対にあう
meet	opposition	
arouse	opposition	反対を引き起こす

▷ I think we should hold a demonstration to **express our opposition** to the new motorway. 新しい高速道路に対して反対を表明するためにデモをすべきだと思う

▷ If the government raises the sales tax again it will **face strong opposition**. 政府がまた売上税を上げたら強い反対にあうだろう

▷ If we tell anybody now it will only **arouse opposition**. いまだれかに言ってみても反対を引き起こすだけだ

considerable	opposition	かなりの反対
fierce	opposition	激しい反対
strong	opposition	強い反対
stiff	opposition	
political	opposition	政治的敵対勢力
public	opposition	一般市民の反対

▷ President Obama became President of the USA despite **strong opposition** from the Republican Party. オバマは共和党からの強い反対にもかかわらず米国の大統領になった

▷ The Prime Minister finally had to resign because of the great amount of **political opposition** to his policies. 首相の政策に反対する大きな政治勢力のため,首相はついに辞任を余儀なくされた

opposition	from A	Aからの反対
opposition	to A	Aへの反対

▷ If we increase the tax on gasoline, there will be a lot of **opposition from** the public. ガソリン税を上げれば国民から多くの反対が出るだろう

order /ɔ́:rdər/ 名 命令;秩序;順序;注文

give	an order	命令を出す
issue	an order	
obey	orders	命令に従う
follow	orders	

disobey	orders	命令に背く
take	orders	指図を受ける
place	an order	注文する
make	an order	注文する
receive	an order	注文を受ける
take	A's order	注文をとる
maintain	order	秩序を維持する
restore	order	秩序を回復する

▷I don't like my boss. He's very strict. He **gives** us **orders** all the time. 上司が嫌いだ．とても厳しいし，いつも命令ばかりなんだもの
▷If you're in the army you can't refuse to **obey orders**! 陸軍にいれば命令に従うことを拒否できないんだぞ
▷I'm not going to **place** any more **orders** with that store. They never deliver on time. あの店にはもう注文しないぞ．時間どおりに配達してくれないもの
▷May I **take** your **order**, ma'am? ご注文を伺ってもよろしいでしょうか
▷It took several hours before the police could **restore order**. 警察が秩序を回復するのに数時間かかった

alphabetical	order	アルファベット順
numerical	order	数字順
reverse	order	逆の順序
chronological	order	年代順
economic	order	経済秩序
social	order	社会秩序
the established	order	既成秩序
the existing	order	
public	order	公共秩序
mail	order	通信販売
a purchase	order	発注書

▷This list should be in **alphabetical order**: A, B, C, etc... このリストはＡＢＣというふうにアルファベット順にすべきだ
▷It is the duty of the police to prevent violence and keep **public order**. 暴力を防止し，公共の秩序を守るのが警察の義務だ

in	order	順序正しく；整然と；調子よく
out of	order	順序が狂って；不調で
on	order	注文中の
an order	for A	Aの注文

▷These files have got mixed up. Could you put them **in order**? ファイルがごちゃごちゃだ．整理していただけますか
▷These files are **out of order**. これらのファイルは順序がばらばらだ ▷This vending machine doesn't work. It's **out of order**. この自動販売機は動かない．故障だ

▷We've just received an **order for** 25 of our new eco-cars. 新しいエコカーの注文を25台受けたところだ

in	order of A	Aの順に

★A frequency, importance, priority など

▷I have listed complaints from the customers **in order of frequency**. 顧客からのクレームを頻度順に一覧表にした
▷There are four things that you need to do **in order of importance**. 案件が4つあり，重要度の順にこなす必要がある

organization /ɔ̀ːrɡənizéiʃən | -naiz-/

名 組織；編成；団体(★《英》つづりは organisation)

found	an organization	組織を設立する
set up	an organization	
run	an organization	組織を運営する
join	an organization	組織に加わる
strengthen	an organization	組織を強化する

▷She **runs** an **organization** that helps homeless people. 彼女はホームレスの支援組織を運営している
▷We need to attract more members to **strengthen** our **organization**. われわれの組織を強化するためにもっとメンバーを引き込む必要がある

a large	organization	大組織
an international	organization	国際組織
a national	organization	全国組織
a business	organization	事業組織
a political	organization	政治団体
a voluntary	organization	任意団体
a nonprofit	organization	非営利団体

▷There's an **international organization** in our town that promotes cultural exchange between foreign countries. うちの町には外国の国々との文化交流を推進する国際組織がある
▷I want to work for a **business organization**. 企業で働きたいと思っている

organized /ɔ́ːrɡənàizd/ 形 組織化された；計画された，整った(★《英》つづりは organised)

highly	organized	きちんと組織化された
well	organized	用意周到な

▷There was recently a **highly organized** demonstration against nuclear energy. このあいだ反原発の大きなデモがあった

▷ The sports events were **well organized**. スポーツ大会は用意周到に準備された

origin /ɔ́:rədʒin | ɔ́r-/

名 起源, 由来, 原因; 出自, 素性

have	its origin(s)	起源がある
trace	the origin	起源をたどる
owe	its origin	起源とする

▷ The French language **has** its **origins** *in* Latin. フランス語はラテン語に起源をもつ
▷ Many people in the African village suddenly became very sick. Finally doctors **traced** the **origin** of the problem back to a polluted well water. アフリカの村で急に多くの重病人が出た. 最終的に医師たちは汚染された井戸水が原因であることを突き止めた

common	origin	共通の起源
unknown	origin	未知の起源
ethnic	origin	民族的出自
social	origin	社会的出自
humble	origins	卑しい出自

▷ The radio signal we received coming from space is of **unknown origin**. 宇宙から受信された電波信号の出所は不明である
▷ Even today, people of **ethnic origin** often suffer discrimination. 今日もなお少数民族出身の人々はしばしば差別を被っている

the country of	origin	原産国
the place of	origin	原産地

▷ This vase seems to be Japanese, but actually its **country of origin** is China. この花瓶は日本製に見えるが, 実は原産国は中国だ

of...	origin	…起源の

▷ Pheasants are birds **of** Asian **origin**. キジはアジア起源の鳥だ

original /ərídʒənl/ **形** 最初の; 独創的な

highly	original	独創性の高い

▷ Pablo Picasso produced some **highly original** paintings. パブロ・ピカソは独創性の高い絵画を何点か生み出した

outcome /áutkʌ̀m/ **名** 結果, 結末

predict	the outcome	結果を予想する
affect	the outcome	結果に影響する
influence	the outcome	
determine	the outcome	結果を決める

▷ At the moment it's impossible to **predict** the **outcome**. 今のところ結果を予想するのは不可能だ
▷ One of our players was sent off 20 minutes before the end of the match, but luckily it didn't **affect** the **outcome**. 選手の一人が試合終了20分前に退場させられたが, 運よく結果に影響は出なかった

the likely	outcome	起こりそうな結果
a possible	outcome	起こりうる結果
a satisfactory	outcome	満足のいく結果
a successful	outcome	上できの結果
the final	outcome	最終的な結果

★ the likely outcome は a possible outcome よりも起こる可能性が高い

▷ If we raise the price of our lunchboxes, the most **likely outcome** is that we will sell fewer and lose money. 弁当の値段を上げたら, 売れ行きが落ちて損が出る可能性がいちばん高い

outline /áutlàin/

名 概要, 概略; 輪郭, 略図

give	an outline	概要を述べる
provide	an outline	
draw	the outline	輪郭を描く
trace	the outline	輪郭をたどる
see	the outline	輪郭が見える

▷ This handout will **give** you an **outline** of the main points of my presentation. お手元のこの資料に私の発表の主要な論点を大まかに示してあります
▷ She **drew** the **outline** of the main Japanese islands on a piece of paper. 彼女は紙に日本本土の略図を描いた
▷ It's very misty, but in this photo you can just **see** the **outline** of Mount Fuji. 霧がかなりかかってはいるものの, この写真の富士山は輪郭がきちんと映っている

the bare	outline	骨子
a brief	outline	簡単な概略
a rough	outline	
a broad	outline	おおよその概略
a general	outline	
a vague	outline	ぼんやりした輪郭
a dim	outline	

▷She drew a **rough outline** of the coastline of Japan on the whiteboard. 彼女はホワイトボードに日本の海岸線の輪郭をおおざっぱに描いた
▷I can only give you a **broad outline** of the project at the moment. I'll give you the details later. いまは計画の大略しか示せません．詳細は後ほど知らせます

| in | outline | 概略は；輪郭は |

▷Those, **in outline**, are my ideas for improving sales figures. 以上が，概略ですが売り上げを伸ばすための私の考えです

oven /ʌ́vən/ 名 オーブン，天火，かまど

| preheat | the oven | オーブンをあらかじめ熱する |

▷**Preheat** the **oven** *to* 150℃. オーブンをセ氏150度まであらかじめ熱してください

| in | the oven | オーブンで |

▷Bake **in** the **oven** about 30 minutes. オーブンで30分ほど焼いてください

| a gas | oven | ガスオーブン |
| a microwave | oven | 電子レンジ |

overcome /òuvərkʌ́m/ 動 克服する，乗り越える；(be overcome で)打ちのめされる，圧倒される

easily	overcome	やすやすと乗り越える
eventually	overcome	ついには乗り越える
finally	overcome	

▷No problem. These are difficulties that we can **easily overcome**. 問題ないよ．手こずっても乗り越えられることだよ
▷We've had a lot of problems, but we've **finally overcome** them. 多くの問題を抱えていたが，最後には克服した

| be overcome | by A | A(煙など)にやられる |
| be overcome | with A | A(感情)に満たされる |

▷When they entered the building two or three firefighters were **overcome by** smoke. 建物に入ったとき消防士たちの2，3名が煙に巻かれた
▷When she won the Olympic Gold Medal she was **overcome with** emotion. オリンピックで金メダルを獲得した彼女は感極まってしまった

owe /óu/

動 借金がある；恩恵をこうむっている

| owe | much to A | Aに負うところ |
| owe | a great deal to A | 大である |

▷I **owe a great deal to** my professor at university. 大学で教授にとても世話になっている

owe	A B	A(人)にB(金)を借りている；A(人)にB(感謝・謝罪など)の義務を負う
owe B	to A	
owe B	to A	BをAに負っている

▷Bill **owes** me twenty pounds. ビルはぼくに20ポンドの借りがある
▷I think you **owe** her an apology. きみは彼女に謝らなくちゃいけないよ
▷He **owes** money **to** the bank. 彼は銀行からお金を借りている
▷I **owe** my success **to** my family and friends. 私が成功したのは家族と友人たちのおかげだ

PHRASES
How much do I owe you? ☺(代金は)いくらですか
I owe you one. ☺ ひとつ借りができたね；恩に着るよ

P

pace /péis/ 图 歩調, 速度；一歩, 歩幅

increase	one's pace	ペースを上げる
quicken	one's pace	
step up	the pace	
gather	pace	加速する
slow	one's pace	ペースを緩める
slacken	one's pace	
set	the pace	ペースを設定する
keep	pace	ついて行く
keep up	pace	ペースを守る
take	a pace	一歩進む
step back	a pace	一歩退く

▷She could hear footsteps coming up behind her so she **increased** her **pace**. 背後からやってくる足音が聞こえたので，彼女は歩調を早めた
▷The marathon runner tried to **quicken** his **pace**, but he was too tired. そのマラソン走者はペースを上げようとしたが，あまりに疲れていた
▷Support for the President is beginning to **gather pace**. 大統領への支持は勢いを増しつつある
▷Our company is **setting** the **pace** for selling eco-cars. わが社はエコカー販売で他社を先導している
▷Computer technology is developing so fast these days. I can't **keep pace** *with* all the changes. コンピュータ技術は近ごろものすごい速さで発展しているので，とてもすべての変化について行けない
▷**Keep up** the **pace**! Don't slow down! Our university can win this race! ペースを守れ．スピードを落とすな．このレースはうちの大学の勝ちだ
▷The dog growled at her and she **took** a **pace** back. その犬にうなられて，彼女は一歩後ろへ下がった
▷Don't make a quick decision. **Step back** a **pace** and think a little more about it. 即断をしてはいけない．一歩退いてその件をもう少し考えなさい

a brisk	pace	きびきびしたペース
a fast	pace	速いペース
a rapid	pace	
a leisurely	pace	のんびりしたペース
a slow	pace	ゆっくりしたペース
a moderate	pace	適度なペース
a steady	pace	着実なペース

★at a ... pace でよく用いる

▷Take it easy! We can walk *at* a more **leisurely pace**! 無理しないで．もっとのんびりしたペースで歩けるから
▷If we continue *at* this **steady pace** we'll be home before dark. この着実なペースを続ければ，暗くなる前に家に着くだろう

at	one's **own** pace	自分のペースで

▷I like to work **at** my **own pace**. 自分のペースで仕事をするのが好きだ

the pace	of A	Aのペース

★A は life, change, development など

▷These days the **pace of** life is so fast! 近ごろは生活のペースがあまりにも早い

pack /pǽk/ 图 包み，箱；荷物；群れ

lead	the pack	群れをリードする

▷It's always the strongest dog that **leads** the **pack**. 群れをリードするのはいつもいちばん強い犬だ

the pack	contains	箱には…が入っている
the pack	includes	

▷This **pack contains** everything you need in case of medical emergencies. この箱には緊急医療の際に必要な物すべてが入っている

a pack of	A	Aの一組；Aの群れ

★A は cards, cigarettes や hounds, wolves など

▷He went out to buy a **pack of cigarettes**. 彼はたばこを一箱買いに出かけた

pack /pǽk/ 動 荷造りする；詰める

pack	away	収納する
pack	up	荷造りする
densely	packed	ぎっしり詰まった
tightly	packed	

▷Your bedroom is really untidy. Can you **pack** your clothes **away** somewhere? きみの寝室はひどく散らかっているね．服をどこかに収納できないの
▷The square was **densely packed** with protesters against the government. 広場は政府に抗議する人々でぎっしり埋まった
▷We'll never get through this crowd. It's really **tightly packed**. この人込みを通り抜けるのは無理だ．ぎゅうぎゅう詰めだ

pack	A **in** B	AをBに詰め込む
pack	A **into** B	

pack	into A	Aに詰めかける
be packed	with A	Aでいっぱいだ

▷I can't **pack** any more things **into** this suitcase. There's no room. このスーツケースにはこれ以上は入らないよ. すき間がないもの
▷I hate traveling during the rush hour. Everybody **packs into** the train. ラッシュアワーに移動するのはいやだ. みんなが列車に乗り込んでくるから
▷The bus was **packed with** commuters. バスは通勤客でいっぱいだった

pack	A B	BをA(人)のために詰める
pack B	for A	

▷Can you **pack** my suitcase **for** me? 私のスーツケースを詰めてくれるかな

package /pǽkidʒ/

名 包み, 小包；箱；総合政策

send	a package	小包を送る
deliver	a package	小包を配達する
receive	a package	小包を受け取る

▷The postman has just **delivered** a big **package** for you. 郵便屋さんが大きな小包をきみに届けてくれたよ

a package	of A	Aの1パック；一組のA(政策など)

▷We need to get two or three **packages of** sugar from the supermarket. スーパーマーケットで砂糖を2, 3箱買ってこなきゃ
▷The government has just announced a new **package of** economic reform. 政府は経済改革の新政策パッケージを発表したところだ

an aid	package	支援パッケージ
a rescue	package	
a training	package	研修パッケージ

page /péidʒ/ 名 ページ

turn	a page	ページをめくる
flip through	the pages	ページをぱらぱらめくる
flick through	the pages	
see	page 20	20ページを参照
turn to	page 20	

▷Jim wasn't listening. He just **turned** the **page** of his book and continued to read. ジムは聞いていなかった. ただ本のページをめくって読み続けた
▷She didn't look at the book carefully. She just **flipped through** the **pages**. 彼女はその本を注意深く見たわけではなく, ページをぱらぱらめくっただけだった
▷If you want more information on robots **see page** 20 of your textbooks. ロボットについての詳細はテキストの20ページを参照(★ pp.15-20 (15ページから20ページ)は pages fifteen to twenty と読む)

the front	page	(新聞の)一面
the opposite	page	対向ページ
the facing	page	
the following	page	次のページ
the previous	page	前のページ
the sports	page	スポーツ面
a Web	page	ウェブページ

▷The news about the royal wedding was so important that it was on the **front page** of every newspaper. ロイヤルウェディングについての重大ニュースだったので, どの新聞も一面に載せていた
▷You can find instructions on how to cook pasta on the **following page**. パスタの調理法は次のページに載っています
▷Please look at the graph on the **previous page**. 前ページのグラフを見てください

at the top	of the page	ページの上に
at the bottom	of the page	ページの下に
on	page 20	20ページに
to	page 35	35ページを
《英》at	page 35	
from	page 5	5ページから

▷Please look at paragraph one **at the top of the page**. ページ上の第一段落を見てください
▷There's an interesting photograph **on page** 20. 20ページにおもしろい写真があります
▷Open your textbook **to page** 35. 教科書の35ページを開けなさい
▷Please continue to read **from page** 5. 5ページから続けて読んでください

pain /péin/ 名 痛み, 苦痛

be in	pain	痛みがある
have	(a) pain	
feel	pain	痛みを感じる
cause	pain	痛みを引き起こす
inflict	pain	痛みを与える
ease	(the) pain	痛みを和らげる
relieve	(the) pain	
kill	the pain	痛みを抑える
endure	(the) pain	痛みに耐える

▷Bill had terrible toothache. He was **in a lot of pain**. ビルは虫歯がひどくて、すごく痛がった
▷**I have a pain** in my chest, doctor. 先生、胸のあたりが痛いんです
▷Please tell me if you **feel any pain**. 痛みを感じたら教えてください
▷Sometimes strong light **causes pain** in my eye. 強い光を浴びると目が痛くなることがある
▷If you take this medicine it should **ease the pain**. この薬を飲めば痛みが和らぎますよ
▷He took some tablets to **kill** the **pain**. 彼は痛みを抑えるために錠剤を飲んだ

(a) severe	pain	ひどい痛み
(a) terrible	pain	
a searing	pain	激痛
(an) acute	pain	
unbearable	pain	耐えがたい痛み
a sharp	pain	鋭い痛み
(a) dull	pain	鈍い痛み
constant	pain	絶え間ない痛み
physical	pain	肉体的苦痛
(a) real	pain	本物の痛み；頭痛の種
abdominal	pain	腹部の痛み
stomach	pain	腹痛
back	pain	腰痛
chest	pain	胸部痛

▷He felt a **severe pain** in the neck. 彼は首にひどい痛みを感じた
▷She's in **terrible pain**. We have to get her to hospital. 彼女はひどく痛がっている。病院に連れて行かなくちゃ
▷He felt a **sharp pain** in his leg. 彼は脚に鋭い痛みを感じた
▷My grandmother is very ill. She's in **constant pain**. 祖母は重い病気にかかっていて、ずっと痛みが消えない
▷I've been lucky all my life. I've never suffered any **real pain**. 私のこれまでの人生は幸運続きだった。本物の痛みなど感じたことがない

a pain	in A	Aの痛み
in	pain	痛くて
with	pain	

▷She was complaining of a **pain in** her **stomach**. 彼女は腹の痛みを訴えていた
▷He was hurt so badly that he was screaming **with pain**. 彼はひどいけがをして、苦痛の声を上げていた

aches and pains	あちこちの痛み
pain and suffering	苦痛

▷When you get older you start suffering from all kinds of **aches and pains**! 年をとるとあちこちが痛くなりだす

painful /péinfəl/ 形 つらい，苦しい；痛い

extremely	painful	ひどく痛む
terribly	painful	
unbearably	painful	耐え難いほど痛い

▷The joint becomes red, swollen and **extremely painful**. 関節は赤くなり，腫れて極度の痛みを伴う

long and painful	長くてつらい

▷My uncle suffered for a long time with a **long and painful** illness. おじは長患いにずっと苦しんだ

it is painful for A (to do)	(…するのは) A (人) にはつらい

▷**It**'s **painful for** me **to** tell you this, but I think you should start looking for a new job. 言いづらいんだけど，きみは新しい仕事を探し始めたほうがいいね

paint /péint/

名 ペンキ，塗料；(paints で) 絵の具

apply	paint	ペンキを塗る
spray	paint	ペンキをスプレーする

▷Joe **applied paint** to the wall. ジョーは壁にペンキを塗った (★「壁にペンキをスプレーする」なら spray paint *on* the wall となる)
▷Look! Somebody's **sprayed paint on** my car! ありゃあ，ぼくの車にペンキをスプレーしたやつがいる

paint	flakes off	ペンキがはがれる
paint	peels off	

▷The outside of the house looks terrible. Most of the paint has **peeled off**. 家の外側がひどいありさまだ。ペンキがほとんどはがれている

a can of	paint	ペンキ一缶
a coat of	paint	ペンキ一塗り

▷We need to get another **can of paint**. ペンキがもう一缶必要だ
▷The front door is really dirty. We should give it a new **coat of paint**. 玄関のドアがひどく汚れているから，ペンキを塗り直したほうがいい

pale /péil/ 形 青白い；淡い

look	pale	顔色が悪い
turn	pale	青ざめる
go	pale	

▷You're **looking pale** today. Do you feel ill? きょうは顔色が悪いけど，具合でも悪いの ▷The boy's complexion **turned pale**. 少年の表情は青ざめた

palm /pá:m/ 名 手のひら

place	one's **palms**	両手を合わせる
press	one's **palm**	手のひらを押しつける
read	A's **palm**	手相を見る

▷I closed my eyes and **placed** my **palms** together in prayer. 目を閉じ両手を合わせて祈った
▷Sarah **pressed** the **palms** of her hands to her cheeks. サラは手のひらを自分の頬に押しつけた
▷Look! That lady's a fortune teller! Why don't you ask her to **read** your **palm**? ほら，占い師の女性よ．手相を見てくれるよう頼んでみたら

paper /péipər/ 名 紙；新聞；論文；(papersで)書類；《英》試験問題，答案

deliver	**papers**	新聞を配達する
sign	the **papers**	書類にサインする
present	a **paper**	論文を口頭発表する
《英》mark	the **papers**	答案を採点する

▷When I was a schoolboy I had a part-time job **delivering papers**. 学生のころ新聞配達のアルバイトをしていた
▷Our teacher is very busy this week **marking** the **papers**. 先生は今週答案の採点で忙しい（★ mark exam papers ともいう）
▷We've just bought a new house. We're going to **sign** the **papers** tomorrow morning. 新居を購入したばかりで，あすの午前中に書類にサインする予定だ

a daily	paper	日刊紙
a morning	paper	朝刊
an evening	paper	夕刊
a Sunday	paper	日曜紙
a quality	paper	高級紙
a local	paper	地方紙
a national	paper	全国紙
today's	paper	きょうの新聞
recycled	paper	再生紙
wrapping	paper	包装紙
writing	paper	便箋
toilet	paper	トイレットペーパー
an exam	paper	問題用紙

▷*The Times* is a well-known British **national paper**. 『ザ・タイムズ』は英国の有名な全国紙だ
▷I try to use **recycled paper** whenever I can. できる限り再生紙を使うよう努めている

a piece	of paper	紙1枚
a sheet	of paper	

▷Could I have a **piece of paper**? 紙を1枚いただけますか

a paper	on A	Aについての論文
in	the paper	新聞で
on	paper	書面の形で；理屈では

▷I read about it **in** the **paper** this morning. その件はけさ新聞で読んだ
▷Think twice before you put your thoughts **on paper**. じっくり考えてから考えを書き留めるようにしなさい

paragraph /pǽrəgræf | -grà:f/

名 段落，パラグラフ

a new	paragraph	新しい段落
the following	paragraph	次の段落
the previous	paragraph	前の段落
the preceding	paragraph	
the final	paragraph	最後の段落

▷Your essay's quite good, but you need to begin a **new paragraph** here. きみのレポートはよく書けているが，ここから新しい段落を始める必要があるね
▷The answer to the question isn't in this paragraph. It's in the **previous paragraph**. 問題の答えはこの段落にはなくて，前の段落にある

parent /péərənt/ 名 親

natural	parents	実の親
birth	parents	
adoptive	parents	養父母
foster	parents	里親
a single	parent	片親，一人で子育てする親
《英》a lone	parent	
an absent	parent	家庭に欠けている親
an elderly	parent	高齢の親

▷Bringing up a child can be so difficult if you're a **single parent**. 片親では子育てがとても難しいことが

ある
▷ Pam is finding it more and more difficult to look after her **elderly parents**. パムは年老いた両親を世話するのがますます難しくなりつつあると感じている

park /pá:rk/

名 公園, 遊園地；競技場；駐車場

a national	park	国立公園
an amusement	park	遊園地
a theme	park	テーマパーク
an industrial	park	工業団地

★(ニューヨークの)セントラルパーク Central Park や(ロンドンの)ハイドパーク Hyde Park のように公園の名前には the がつかない

▷ Many beautiful areas in England have been made into **national parks**. イングランドの多くの美しい地域は国立公園になった

in	the park	公園で

▷ At lunchtime I like to walk **in** the **park**. お昼時に公園を歩くのが好きだ

part /pá:rt/

名 部分, 一部；部品；役目, 役割；(芝居の)役；(本などの)部

play	a part	役割を果たす；役を演じる
take	a part	役割を果たす
form	part	一部を構成する

▷ Sport **plays** an important **part** in his life. スポーツは彼の人生で重要な役割を果たしている
▷ Peter **played** the **part** of Hamlet in the school play. ピーターは学校劇でハムレットを演じた
▷ Results from a recent Government survey **formed** a large **part** of her lecture. 彼女の講演は政府が行った最近の調査結果の紹介にほとんど終始した

a large	part	大部分
the greater	part	
a major	part	主要な部分
a substantial	part	実質的な部分
a small	part	小さな部分
an important	part	重要な部分
an essential	part	不可欠な部分
a vital	part	
an integral	part	
the best	part	最良の部分
the worst	part	最悪の部分
the early	part	初めの部分
the latter	part	後半の部分
the first	part	最初の部分
the last	part	最後の部分
the upper	part	上の部分
the lower	part	下の部分
the eastern	part	東部分
a major	part	大きな役割
a big	part	
an important	part	重要な役割
an active	part	積極的な役割

▷ A **large part** of the money was given to charity. お金の相当部分が慈善事業に寄付された
▷ A **major part** of this thesis has been copied from the Internet. この論文の大部分はインターネットからコピーしたものだ
▷ A **substantial part** of our success was due to your efforts. われわれが成功できたのはほとんどあなた方の努力のおかげだ
▷ Field work is an **integral part** of this course. It's not just theory. 野外調査はこの講座のなくてはならない部分で, ただ理論だけを扱う講座ではない
▷ The **early part** of the movie was rather boring, but it got better after a while. 映画の初めのほうはちらかと言うと退屈だったが, しばらくするとよくなった
▷ The **upper part** of the building was destroyed by fire. 建物の上部は火事で焼失した
▷ The **eastern part** of the island was hit badly by an earthquake. 島の東部分はひどい地震に見舞われた

(a) part	of A	Aの一部
in	part	ある程度, 一部
in	parts	ところどころ

▷ I think **part of** my tooth has broken off. 歯の一部が欠けちゃったんじゃないかな
▷ I agree **in part** with what you say. あなたの発言に賛成する部分もあります

participate /pa:rtísəpèit/

動 参加する, 加わる

participate	fully	本格的に参加する
participate	actively	積極的に参加する

▷ Your daughter is very popular, Mrs. Taylor. She **participates actively** in many of our clubs. お宅のお嬢さんは人気者です, テイラーさん. うちのクラブの多くに積極的に参加していますよ

participate	in A	Aに参加する

▷ William doesn't seem to **participate in** class very much. ウィリアムはあまり授業に参加していないようだ

| the opportunity | to participate | 参加する機会 |

▷It would be great if we got the **opportunity to participate** in the World Cup again next year. 来年もまたワールドカップに出場する機会が得られればすばらしいことだ

| be invited to | participate | 参加を求められる |
| refuse to | participate | 参加を断る |

▷We've been **invited to participate** in the final stages of the cheerleading contest! チアリーディングコンテストの決勝ステージへの出場を求められたの
▷Kumiko **refused to participate** in the English Speaking Contest. 久美子は英語弁論大会への参加を断った

particular /pərtíkjulər/

形 特別の；独特の；特定の，まさにその

| this | particular A | とりわけこのA |
| that | particular A | とりわけそのA |

▷**This particular** essay is one of the best I have ever read. 中でもこのレポートはいままでに読んだ最良のものの一つだ

party /pá:rti/ 名 パーティー；党，政党

have	a party	パーティーを開く
give	a party	
hold	a party	
throw	a party	
attend	a party	パーティーに出る
form	a party	党を結成する
join	a party	入党する
leave	a party	離党する

▷We're **giving** a **party** next weekend. Would you like to come? 次の週末パーティーを開く予定です，いらっしゃいませんか
▷We're going to **attend** a **party** in London next week. 来週ロンドンでのパーティーに出るつもりだ

a birthday	party	誕生会
a Christmas	party	クリスマスパーティー
an engagement	party	婚約パーティー
a surprise	party	びっくりパーティー
a dinner	party	夕食会
a farewell	party	送別会
a garden	party	園遊会
a political	party	政党

the main	party	大政党，主要政党
the major	party	
the ruling	party	与党
the opposition	party	野党

▷Which **political party** do you support? どの政党を支持していますか
▷The Green party isn't really one of the **main parties** in our country yet. 緑の党はわが国ではまだ主要政党というわけではない
▷The **ruling party** is making many changes in the law. 与党は法律に大きく変更を加えつつある

pass /pǽs | pá:s/ 名 通行証；(ボールの)パス

a free	pass	無料入場券
a three-day	pass	3日間有効の乗車券
a bus	pass	バス定期券
a boarding	pass	搭乗券

pass /pǽs | pá:s/ 動 通る；(時が)過ぎる；(法案などが)通る；渡す，パスする

| pass | quickly | 早く過ぎる |
| pass | unanimously | 全会一致で通る |

▷The day **passed quickly**. その日は早く過ぎた

| let A | pass | Aをそのままにする |

▷I'm not entirely happy with this, but I'll **let** it **pass**. これで完全に満足というわけではないが，よしとしよう

| pass | A B | A(人)にBを渡す |
| pass B | to A | |

▷Could you **pass** me the salt, please? 塩を取っていただけますか
▷Giggs **passes** the ball **to** Rooney and Rooney scores! GOOOOOAAAAAL!!! ギグスがルーニーにボールをパス，そしてルーニーが得点だ．ゴール(★実況中継)
PHRASES〉
I'll pass (this time). ☺ (今回は)パスします ▷ "Would you like another drink?" "No, thanks. I'll pass this time." 「もう一杯いかがですか」「結構です，もう遠慮しておきます」

passenger /pǽsəndʒər/ 名 乗客

| pick up | passengers | 乗客を乗せる |

| passport |

carry	passengers	乗客を運ぶ
drop (off)	passengers	乗客を降ろす

▷ The bus was completely full so it couldn't stop to **pick up** any more **passengers**. バスは超満員だったので，停車してそれ以上乗客を乗せられなかった
▷ This bus can **carry** up to 42 **passengers**. このバスには42名まで乗客が乗れる
▷ The coach driver will **drop passengers off** near their homes. その長距離バスの運転手は乗客をそれぞれの自宅のそばで降ろしてくれるだろう

airline	passengers	飛行機の乗客
first class	passengers	ファーストクラスの乗客
business class	passengers	ビジネスクラスの乗客
bus	passengers	バスの乗客
rail	passengers	列車の乗客
a fellow	passenger	同乗者

▷ I had a really interesting conversation with a **fellow passenger** on the plane back to New York. ニューヨークへ帰る飛行機で乗り合わせた客の一人ととてもおもしろい会話をした

passengers and crew	乗客と乗務員

▷ Both **passengers and crew** put on their seat belts when the plane was hit by a storm. 飛行機が嵐に遭って乗客たちも乗務員たちもシートベルトを締めた

passport /pǽspɔːrt | pάːs-/
名 パスポート，旅券

apply for	a passport	旅券を申請する
renew	a passport	旅券を更新する
issue	a passport	旅券を発行する
get	a passport	旅券を取得する
obtain	a passport	
carry	a passport	旅券を持っている
have	a passport	
hold	a passport	
check	a passport	旅券を調べる
stamp	A's passport	旅券にスタンプを押す

▷ I need to **apply for** a new **passport**. 新しい旅券を申請する必要がある
▷ We don't know who he is. He doesn't **carry** a **passport** or a driver's license. 男の身元はわからない．パスポートも運転免許証も携帯していないので
▷ She **holds** a **passport** from two different countries. 彼女は2か国のパスポートを持っている
▷ You can't enter the country before they've **stamped** your **passport**. 旅券にスタンプを押してもらわないと入国できない

a valid	passport	有効なパスポート

past /pæst | pάːst/ 名 過去，昔；歴史

the distant	past	遠い過去
the recent	past	近い過去

▷ I remember meeting you *in* the **distant past**. Maybe 10 years ago at Tessa's wedding? 遠い昔にお会いしたのを覚えています．たぶん10年前のテサの結婚式でじゃなかったかな
▷ My grandfather's memory is not so good now. He can't even remember things *in* the **recent past**. 祖父は記憶力が落ちて，少し前のことでも思い出せない

look back	on the past	過去を振り返る
cling to	the past	過去にしがみつく

▷ When I **look back on** the **past** I wish I had traveled around the world more. 過去を振り返るともっと世界を旅行しておけばよかったと思う

in	the past	過去に，昔は
into	the past	過去へと
from	the past	過去の

▷ **In** the **past**, traditional steakhouses were very popular places. かつては伝統的なステーキハウスはすごく人気のある場所だった
▷ Yesterday I found an old doll that I had when I was a child. It really took me back **into** the **past**. 子どものころに持っていた古い人形をきのう見つけた．おかげですっかり過去の思い出にふけってしまった

past and present	過去と現在

▷ In the art gallery you can see paintings of many famous people **past and present**. その画廊では古今の多くの有名な人々の絵画を見ることができる

a break with	the past	過去との決別
a thing of	the past	過去のこと

▷ After my divorce I need a complete **break with** the **past**. 離婚した以上は過去ときっぱり縁を切る必要がある
▷ I used to love windsurfing when I was young, but now that's a **thing of** the **past**. 若いころはウインドサーフィンが大好きだったが，それもいまは昔のことだ

past /pæst | pάːst/

| pattern |

形 過去の；ここ…，過去…

the past ... days	ここ…日

★days のほか weeks, months, years なども用いる

▷I haven't seen Tom for the **past** three **days**. この3日間トムを見かけない
▷I've been living in Paris for the **past** three **years**. ここ3年パリに住んでいます

path /pǽθ | pɑ́ːθ/ 名 小道；通り道

follow	the path	道をたどる
block	A's path	道をふさぐ

▷If you **follow** the **path** along the cliff you'll come to an old church. 崖に沿って道をたどると古い教会に着きます
▷As I drove around the corner I saw that a large truck was **blocking** my **path**. 車で角を曲がると大きなトラックが道をふさいでいるのが見えた

a narrow	path	狭い道
a steep	path	急な小道
a coastal	path	海岸の小道
a coast	path	
a garden	path	庭の小道
flight	path	飛行経路
a career	path	職業人としての進路

▷Let's take this **narrow path** across the field. 野原を横切るこの狭い道を行こう

a path	through A	Aを抜ける小道
a path	to A	Aに通じる小道
along	a path	小道に沿って
down	a path	小道を下って
up	a path	小道を上って

▷We went along a **path through** the woods. 森を抜ける小道を行った
▷This is the **path to** the back door of the cottage. この小道は山小屋の裏口に通じている
▷Better not walk **along** this **path**. It's dangerous. It's too close to the cliff. この小道を歩かないほうがいい．崖が迫っていて危険だから

patience /péiʃəns/

名 忍耐(力)，我慢，辛抱強さ

have	the patience	忍耐力がある
need	patience	忍耐を必要とする
require	patience	
lose	patience	我慢できなくなる
run out of	patience	
try	A's patience	忍耐力を試す

▷He doesn't **have** the **patience** to deal politely with customers. 彼には丁寧に客に応対するだけの忍耐力がない
▷Raising a child can often **require** a lot of **patience**. 子育てにはかなり忍耐力が必要なこともある
▷Some of our customers are difficult, but you should try not to **lose** your **patience**. 気難しい客もいるが，堪忍袋の緒を切らしてはだめだ

patience	for A	Aに対する辛抱
patience	with A	

▷Bob deals with complaints from our customers. You need a lot of **patience for** a job like that. ボブは客からのクレームに対応している．かなりの忍耐力を必要とする仕事だ
▷Mandy is a troublemaker. I have little **patience with** her. マンディはごたごたを起こしてばかりだ．彼女には我慢できないよ

time and patience	時間と忍耐
patience and understanding	辛抱と理解

▷Doing a jigsaw puzzle requires a lot of **time and patience**. ジグソーパズルをするには多くの時間と忍耐を必要とする
▷Thank you for your **patience and understanding**. ご辛抱とご理解に感謝いたします

PHRASES
Have patience! ☺ 我慢しなさい

patient /péiʃənt/ 名 患者

a cancer	patient	がん患者
an AIDS	patient	エイズ患者

▷The number of **cancer patients** has been on the increase. がん患者の数が増加傾向にある

a patient	with A	Aのある患者

▷We give drugs to **patients with** severe **pain**. 痛みがひどい患者に薬を投与する

examine	a patient	患者を診察する
see	a patient	

pattern /pǽtərn | pǽtən/

名 型，様式，パターン；模様，柄

363

establish	a pattern	パターンを確立する
set	a pattern	パターンを確立する
follow	a pattern	パターンに従う
show	a pattern	パターンを示す
change	a pattern	パターンを変える
have	a pattern	模様がある

▷We need to **set a pattern** for doing homework. Maybe 2 hours after supper, 3 nights a week? 宿題をするパターンを決める必要がある．夕食後2時間，週に3晩ぐらいかな

▷These robberies seem to **follow** a **pattern**. They all occur on a Friday night. これらの強盗事件はあるパターンに従っているようだ．すべて金曜の夜に起こっている

▷Which curtains do you prefer? The plain ones or the ones that **have** a **pattern**? どちらのカーテンが好みですか．無地ですかそれとも模様があるほうですか

a basic	pattern	基本的パターン
the normal	pattern	通常のパターン
a set	pattern	決まったパターン
a fixed	pattern	決まったパターン
the same	pattern	同じパターン
a similar	pattern	似たパターン
a changing	pattern	変化するパターン
a complex	pattern	複雑なパターン
behavior	patterns	行動パターン
sleep	patterns	睡眠パターン

▷These figures show a **complex pattern** in the rise and fall of gasoline prices over the last 2 years. この数字を見ればここ2年間のガソリン価格が複雑に上下動しているのがわかる

pause /pɔ́ːz/ 動 中断する，一息つく

pause	briefly	少し中断する
pause	momentarily	
pause	for a moment	
pause	here	ここで中断する

▷He asked her: "Shall we take a taxi together?" She **paused momentarily** and then said, "OK, fine." 「いっしょにタクシーに乗ろうか」と彼が尋ねると，彼女は一瞬間を置いて答えた．「ええ，いいわよ」

▷Let's **pause here** for a short break. I'll continue the lecture again in 10 minutes' time. ここでちょっと中断して休憩しましょう．10分後に講義を再開します

| pause | to do | 少し休んで…する |

▷We need to **pause** for a moment **to** check that everybody has understood everything. 少し間を置いて，みんなにわからないところがないか確認する必要がある

| pause | for breath | 一息つく |

▷When you sing this song you need to know exactly where to **pause for breath**. この歌を歌うにはどこで息つぎするか正確に知っておく必要がある

pay /péi/ 動 支払う

well	paid	賃金が高い
highly	paid	
poorly	paid	賃金が低い
be fully	paid	全額支払われる
pay	up	借金を全額払う

▷I do a part-time job, but it's very **poorly paid**. アルバイトをしているがバイト代はすごく安い

▷We still haven't been **fully paid** for the work we did last year. 昨年やった仕事に対してわれわれはまだ全額支払ってもらっていない

▷We've sent bills to this customer 5 times, but he still hasn't **paid up**. この客には請求書を5回も送っているが，いまだに払ってくれない

| pay | for A | Aの代金を払う |
| pay A | for B | A(人)にBの代金を払う |

▷How much did you **pay for** your new sports car? 新しいスポーツカーはいくらで買ったの

▷You don't have to **pay** us for the repair. Your TV is still under guarantee. 修理代をお支払いいただく必要はありません．お宅のテレビはまだ補償期間中ですので

| pay A | to do | A(人)に金を払って…してもらう |

▷Tell Pete I'll **pay** him **to** wash my car. 車を洗ってくれたらお金を払うとピートに言ってくれ

peace /píːs/ 名 平和，和平；平穏

bring about	peace	平和をもたらす
keep	the peace	平和を守る
maintain	peace	平和を維持する
promote	peace	平和を促進する
restore	peace	平和を回復する
disturb	the peace	平穏を乱す
make	peace	和解する

▷A series of meetings was held to try to **bring about peace** in the region. その地域に平和をもたらすべく一連の会議が開かれた

▷The United Nations is trying to **maintain peace**

in that area. 国連はその地域の平和を維持しようとしている
▷After 25 years of war, **peace** was finally **restored** in the region. 25年間にわたる戦争ののち、ついにその地域に平和が取り戻された
▷The police arrested him for **disturbing** the **peace**. 警察は治安を乱したかどで彼を逮捕した
▷She wants to be friends with you again. I think you should **make peace** *with* her. 彼女はまたきみと友だちになりたがっているよ。仲直りしたほうがいいね

peace and quiet	平穏無事
peace and traquillity	
peace and security	平和と安全

▷The children have gone to bed. Finally some **peace and quiet**! 子どもたちが寝てくれて、やっと静かな平穏が戻った
▷Everybody hopes for **peace and security** in the world. だれもが世界の平和と安全を望んでいる

peace of mind	心の平静

▷I wish I could stop worrying. I can't get any **peace of mind** until I know my exam results. 気をもむのはもういやだ。試験の結果がわかるまで気持ちが落ち着かないよ

at	peace	平和に;死んで
in	peace	平穏に
peace	with A	Aとの平和
peace	between A	Aの間の平和

▷After a long war, finally the two countries are **at peace** *with* each other. 長い戦争の末に両国はようやく友好な関係を打ち立てた
▷She doesn't want to talk to anybody. I think we should leave her **in peace**. 彼女はだれとも話したくないんだ。そっとしておいてあげたほうがいいよ

lasting	peace	恒久平和
world	peace	世界平和

peak /píːk/

名 頂点, 絶頂, ピーク;山頂, 峰

reach	a peak	ピークに達する

▷Sales **reached** a **peak** in mid-December. 売り上げは12月半ばにピークに達した

at	one's peak	絶好調で

▷Most boxers are **at** their **peak** in their mid-twenties. ほとんどのボクサーは20代半ばにピークを迎える

peaks and troughs	(グラフなどの)山と谷

▷On this graph you can see the **peaks and troughs** of the economy over the last 20 years. このグラフにこ20年間の経済の山と谷が示されている

pen /pén/ 名 ペン

pick up	a pen	ペンを持つ
take up	a pen	
write	with a pen	ペンで書く
write	in pen	
put	one's pen down	ペンを置く

▷She **picked up** a **pen** and started taking notes. 彼女はペンを取ってメモを取り始めた
▷Please **write with** a **pen**, not pencil. 鉛筆ではなくペンで書いてください
▷Stop writing and **put** your **pens down**, please. 書くのをやめてペンを置いてください

a ballpoint	pen	ボールペン
a felt(-tip)	pen	フェルトペン
a fountain	pen	万年筆

penalty /pénəlti/

名 刑罰, 処罰;罰金;ペナルティ;ペナルティキック

impose	a penalty	刑罰を課す
carry	a penalty	刑罰を伴う
pay	the penalty	報いを受ける
award	a penalty	ペナルティキックを与える
kick	a penalty	ペナルティキックをける
take	a penalty	
miss	a penalty	ペナルティキックをはずす

▷The government **imposes** strict **penalties** on factories that pollute the environment. 政府は環境を汚染する工場に厳しい刑罰を科している
▷He didn't work hard enough before the exams and **paid** the **penalty**. 彼は試験前に一生懸命勉強しなかったので、その報いを受けた
▷Liverpool were **awarded** a **penalty** in the last minute of the game. リバプールは試合終了直前にペナルティキックを与えられた
▷Manchester United **missed** a **penalty** at the beginning of the game. マンチェスター・ユナイテッドは試合冒頭にペナルティキックをはずした

a heavy	penalty	重い処罰
a severe	penalty	厳しい処罰

stiff	penalties	
a tough	penalty	
the maximum	penalty	罰金の最高額
the death	penalty	死刑

▷There's a **severe penalty** for drinking and driving. 飲酒運転への罰則は厳しい
▷I had to pay the **maximum penalty** for not renewing my driving license. 運転免許証を更新していなかったので罰金の最高額を科せられた

penalty	for A	Aに対する処罰；Aの報い

▷You have to pay a **penalty for** illegal parking. 不法駐車には罰金を科される

pencil /pénsəl/ 名 鉛筆

hold	a pencil	鉛筆を持つ
write with	a pencil	鉛筆で書く
write in	pencil	
sharpen	a pencil	鉛筆を削る

▷You should learn how to **hold** a **pencil** properly! 鉛筆の正しい持ち方を学びなさい

a colored	pencil	色鉛筆
a mechanical	pencil	シャープペンシル

▷Do you have any **colored pencils**? 色鉛筆を持っていますか

a paper and pencil		紙と鉛筆

▷Could you lend me a **paper and pencil**? 紙と鉛筆を貸していただけませんか

pension /pénʃən/ 名 年金, 恩給

get	a pension	年金を受け取る
draw	a pension	
receive	a pension	
provide	a pension	年金を支給する

▷After I retired I **got** a good **pension**. 退職後に十分な年金をもらった
▷We **provide** excellent **pensions** for our employees. 従業員に対してわが社は優れた年金を提供している

the basic	pension	基礎年金
an occupational	pension	職域年金
a personal	pension	個人年金

a public	pension	公的年金
《英》a state	pension	

▷He gets an **occupational pension** as well as one from the government. 彼は政府からの年金だけでなく職域年金ももらっている

percent /pərsént/

名 パーセント(★《英》では per cent ともつづる)

10 percent	of A	Aの10パーセント

★動詞の形はAの数に一致させる

▷Eighty **percent of** our students are female. うちの学生の8割は女子だ ▷Seventy **percent of** the land in Japan is mountainous. 日本の国土の7割が山だ

a 10 percent	rise in A	Aの1割増加
a 10 percent	increase in A	
a 10 percent	decline in A	Aの1割減少

▷There was a 50% **increase in** the demand for smartphones last year. 昨年スマートフォンの需要は5割増えた

percentage /pərséntidʒ/

名 百分率, パーセント；割合

calculate	the percentage	百分率を計算する
show	the percentage	百分率を示す

▷These figures don't seem right. Could you **calculate** the **percentage** again? 数字が間違っているようだ．パーセンテージを計算し直していただけますか
▷This table **shows** the **percentage** increase in profits over the last 5 years. この表はここ5年間の利益率の伸びを示している

a greater	percentage	より大きな割合
a high	percentage	大きな割合
a large	percentage	
a low	percentage	小さな割合
a small	percentage	

▷A **high percentage** of 3rd year students have already started job-hunting. 3年生のうち職探しを始めている学生が大きな割合を占めている
▷Only a **small percentage** of women have top jobs in companies. 社長の座に就いている人のうち女性が占める割合はごく小さい

in	percentage terms	パーセンテージで表すと

▷Unemployment has halved. **In percentage terms** that's a decrease of 50%. 失業率は半分になった。パーセンテージで表すと5割の減少だ

perfect /pə́ːrfikt/

形 完全な, 完璧な；最適の

absolutely	perfect	まったく完璧な
almost	perfect	ほぼ完璧な
far from	perfect	完璧とはほど遠い

▷Everything is **absolutely perfect**. すべてまったく完璧だ
▷You got an **almost perfect** score in your last test. この間のテストできみはほぼ満点だった
▷I've been practicing this difficult piano piece for a month now, but it's still **far from perfect**. この難しいピアノ曲をもう1か月も練習しているが, まだ完璧とはほど遠い

| perfect | for A | Aに最適な |

▷I think this dress would be absolutely **perfect for** your sister. このドレスはあなたの妹にまさにぴったりだよ

PHRASES

That's perfect. ☺ 完璧だ ▷"Is the picture on the TV screen OK now?" "Yes. That's perfect." 「テレビ画面の画像はもうだいじょうぶかい」「はい, 完璧です」

perform /pərfɔ́ːrm/

動 遂行する, 成し遂げる；演じる, 上演する；演奏する

| perform | well | うまくいく |
| perform | poorly | できがお粗末だ |

▷Japan **performed** really **well** in the World Cup. 日本はワールドカップでとてもよい成績を収めた

performance /pərfɔ́ːrməns/

名 演技, 演奏, 上演；公演；実績；性能

give	a performance	上演する, 演奏する
affect	a performance	演技に影響を与える；性能に影響が出る
assess	A's performance	演技を評価する；性能を評価する
improve	one's performance	演技の質を高める；性能を高める

▷The pianist **gave** a wonderful **performance** of Chopin's piano music. そのピアニストはショパンのピアノ作品をみごとに演奏した
▷The ice-skater was very nervous so it **affected** her **performance**. そのアイススケート選手は緊張しすぎて演技に影響が出た
▷I'll have to train harder to **improve** my **performance**. 演技の質を高めるためにもっとハードな訓練が必要だ

live	performance	ライブ演奏
good	performance	よい演技；よいでき
poor	performance	ひどいでき
economic	performance	経済実績
financial	performance	財務実績
sales	performance	販売実績
high	performance	高性能

▷Our school members gave a very **good performance** at the speech contest. うちの学校の生徒たちはスピーチコンテストのできがすばらしかった
▷Our company's **financial performance** was very poor this year. わが社の今年度の財務実績はきわめて悪い
▷The new Japanese bullet train has very **high performance**. It can travel at over 300 kilometers per hour. 今度できた新幹線はとても高性能で, 時速300キロを超える速度で走行できる

perfume /pə́ːrfjuːm/ 名 香水

| wear | perfume | 香水をつけている |
| smell | perfume | 香水のにおいをかぐ |

▷Are you **wearing** a new **perfume**? 新しい香水をつけているの？
▷**Smell** this **perfume**! Do you like it? この香水のにおいをかいでみて。好き？

| (an) expensive | perfume | 高価な香水 |
| (a) strong | perfume | 強い香水 |

▷Amanda wears really **expensive perfume**. アマンダはすごく高価な香水をつけている
▷My sister uses a really **strong perfume**. 姉はすごく強い香水を使っている

| a bottle | of perfume | 香水瓶 |

▷I got this **bottle of perfume** for my birthday. 誕生日にこの香水瓶をもらった

period /píəriəd/ 名 期間, 時期；時代

| permission |

cover	a period	期間にわたる
enter	a period	時期に入る
extend	the period	期間を延長する

▷His research **covers** the **period** from 1945 up to the present day. 彼の研究は1945年から現在までの期間にわたっている
▷In 2011 the Arab World **entered** a **period** of revolution. 2011年にアラブ世界は改革の時期に入った
▷I asked the bank to **extend** the **period** of the loan for another 6 months. 銀行にローン期間をあと半年延長してもらうよう頼んだ

a long	period	長期間
a short	period	短期間
a brief	period	
a limited	period	限られた期間
an early	period	初期
a late	period	後期
a transition	period	移行期間；過渡期
a trial	period	試用期間

▷We're offering this product at half price, but only for a **limited period**. この商品を半額で提供していますが、限定期間のみです
▷When the government fell there was a **transition period** before a new government was formed. 政府が倒れ、新政府が発足するまで移行期間があった

after	a period	期間の後
during	the period	期間中に
for	a period	期間に
in	the period	
within	the period	期間内に
over	a period	期間にわたって

▷**After** a **period** *of* very cold weather, spring finally arrived. 厳しい寒さが続いた後についに春が訪れた
▷It will be spring term soon. **During** that **period** a school trip has been arranged. もうすぐ春学期だ。学期中に学校の遠足が準備されている
▷The doctor says I'll have to stay in hospital **for** a **period** of at least 2 weeks. 医師の話では少なくとも2週間は入院しなければならない
▷**In** the **period** 1970–1980 the women's rights movement in the USA became much stronger. 1970年から80年の期間に米国における女権運動はますます強くなった
▷**Over** a **period** *of* 5 years he was promoted from sales assistant to sales manager. 5年間に彼は販売員から販売部長へ昇進した

permission /pərmíʃən/ 图 許し, 許可

apply for	permission	許可を申請する
ask (for)	permission	許可を求める
request	permission	
seek	permission	
give	permission	許可を与える
grant	permission	
refuse	permission	許可を拒否する
get	permission	許可を得る
obtain	permission	
have	permission	許可を得ている

▷You need to **apply for permission** to extend your visa. ビザを延長するには許可を申請する必要がある
▷You should **ask permission** to leave the classroom. 教室を出る許可を求めたほうがいい
▷He's **requested permission** to use the company car park. 彼は会社の駐車場の使用許可を求めた
▷We can't build a factory there. The council won't **give permission**. そこに工場を建てることができない。議会がどうしても認可してくれない
▷I asked my boss for an extra day's holiday, but he **refused permission**. 上司にあと1日の休暇を願い出たが、許可してくれなかった
▷You'll need to **get permission** from your boss. 上司から許可をもらう必要があるよ
▷We couldn't **obtain permission** to build on this piece of land. この土地に建物を建てる許可が得られなかった

official	permission	正式の許可
prior	permission	事前の許可
special	permission	特別許可
temporary	permission	一時的な許可
written	permission	文書による許可

▷We need to get **official permission** to use the school gym for basketball practice. バスケットボールの練習に体育館を使う正式な許可をとる必要がある
▷If you want to use these tennis courts you have to get **prior permission**. このテニスコートを使いたいなら事前に許可をとらなければならない
▷If you want to join our school trip abroad you need to get **written permission** from your parents. 海外への修学旅行に参加したいなら、両親から文書で許可をもらってください

permission	for A	Aの許可
without	permission	許可なしで

▷Have you got **permission for** this demonstration? このデモを行う許可は得てありますか
▷You can't camp here **without permission**. 許可なしにここでキャンプはできない

permission	to do	…する許可

▷Do you have **permission to** fish here? ここで魚を釣る許可を得ていますか

person /pə́ːrsn/ 名 人

an elderly	person	高齢者
a disabled	person	体の不自由な人
the average	person	平均的な人
a qualified	person	有資格者
the right	person	適任者
a business	person	ビジネスマン
a morning	person	朝型人間
a night	person	夜型人間

▷The **average person** is much taller now than 50 years ago. いまや50年前より平均身長はずっと高くなっている
▷She's definitely the **right person** for the job. 彼女はその仕事にまさに適任だ

in	person	本人が, 自ら
per	person	一人につき

▷Don't just send your boss an email about this problem. Go and see him **in person**. この件について上司にＥメールを送って済ませるのではなく, 直接本人に会ってきなさい
▷This 5-day package tour will cost about $1,000 **per person**. 5日間のこのパック旅行は一人あたり千ドルぐらいかかる

personal /pə́ːrsənl/ 形 個人的な, 個人の

highly	personal	きわめて個人的な
purely	personal	純粋に個人的な

▷I'm sorry, I can't give you that information. It's **highly personal**. その件はお教えできません。きわめて個人的なことなので
▷Her reasons for leaving are **purely personal**. It's nothing to do with the job. 彼女が辞める理由はまったく個人的なことで, 仕事とは関係ありません

personality /pə̀ːrsənǽləti/

名 人格, 性格；個性

develop	one's **personality**	人格を形成する
express	one's **personality**	人格を表す
reflect	A's **personality**	人格を反映する

▷It's wonderful to see how babies gradually **develop** their **personality**. 赤ん坊が徐々に人格を形成していくようすを見るのはすばらしいことだ
▷I'm afraid the poor quality of his work **reflects** his lazy **personality**. 彼の仕事がお粗末なのは怠惰な性格を反映していると思う

a strong	personality	強い個性
a powerful	personality	
individual	personality	独特の性格
multiple	personality	多重人格
a split	personality	二重人格
a sports	personality	スポーツ選手
a TV	personality	テレビタレント

★× a TV talent とはいわない

▷He's a natural leader. He has a really **strong personality**. 彼は生まれついての指導者だ。実に強い個性の持ち主だ
▷In Japan **individual personality** is considered less important than in the West. 日本では独特な個性は西洋ほど重要とはみなされていない

perspective /pərspéktiv/

名 視点；正しい見通し

an international	perspective	国際的視点
a historical	perspective	歴史的視点

▷From an **international perspective** the yen is highly overvalued. 国際的に見ると円は過大評価されている

persuade /pərswéid/ 動 説得する

easily	persuade	簡単に説得する
finally	persuade	最終的に説得する
eventually	persuade	
successfully	persuade	うまく説得する

▷I'm sure she can be **easily persuaded** to change her mind. 彼女を説得して考えを変えさせるのは簡単だと思う
▷After months of negotiations we **finally persuaded** them to sign the contract. 数か月の交渉を経てついに彼らを説得して契約書へのサインにこぎつけた

persuade	A **to** do	A(人)に…するよう説得する
persuade	A **of** B	A(人)にBを納得させる
persuade	A (**that**)...	A(人)に…だと納得させる

▷Finally she **persuaded** him **to** give up smoking. ついに彼女は彼を説得してたばこをやめさせた
▷It was difficult to **persuade** him **of** the impor-

tance of making a quick decision. すぐ決断するのが大事だと彼に納得させるのは難しかった
▷I tried to **persuade** him that he should stop working so hard. 働きすぎはやめるよう彼に説得を試みた

try to	persuade	説得を試みる
attempt to	persuade	
seek to	persuade	
hope to	persuade	説得したいと思う
manage to	persuade	何とか説得する
fail to	persuade	説得に失敗する

▷We **tried to persuade** her to change her mind. われわれは彼女が考えを変えるよう説得しようとした
▷We **managed to persuade** her to come with us on holiday to Guam. 彼女を何とか説得してグアムにいっしょに遊びに行く気にさせた

an attempt to	persuade	説得の試み
an effort to	persuade	説得する努力

▷We should have made more of an **effort to persuade** her to apply to university. 彼女が大学受験をするようもっと説得の努力をすべきだった

pet /pét/ 名 ペット, 愛玩動物

have	a pet	ペットを飼っている
keep	a pet	
make	a good pet	いいペットになる
make	an excellent pet	
make	a superb pet	

▷Did you **have** a **pet** when you were a child? 子どものころペットを飼っていましたか
▷Labradors **make** very **good pets**. ラブラドル犬はとてもいいペットになる

a domestic	pet	家庭用ペット
a family	pet	

▷No **domestic pets** are allowed in this apartment. いかなる家庭用ペットもこのアパートでは禁止です

phase /féiz/ 名 局面, 段階

a new	phase	新たな局面
a final	phase	最終局面

▷The US presidential campaign has entered its **final phase**. 米国の大統領選は最終段階に入った

phenomenon /finámənàn | -nɔ́minən/

名 現象(★複数形は phenomena)

explain	the phenomenon	現象を説明する

▷There are still many natural **phenomena** that scientists are unable to **explain**. 科学者たちが説明できない多くの自然現象がいまもある

a natural	phenomenon	自然現象
a social	phenomenon	社会現象
a rare	phenomenon	珍しい現象
a recent	phenomenon	最近の現象

▷The Northern Lights are a beautiful **natural phenomenon**. オーロラは美しい自然現象だ
▷The huge popularity of the Beatles during the 1960s and 70s was an unusual **social phenomenon**. 1960年と70年代のビートルズの人気のすごさは尋常でない社会現象だった
▷The widespread use of cellphones is a fairly **recent phenomenon**. 携帯電話が広く使われるようになったのはかなり最近の現象だ

philosophy /filásəfi | -lɔ́s-/

名 哲学; 人生観

Western	philosophy	西洋哲学
moral	philosophy	道徳哲学
natural	philosophy	自然哲学
political	philosophy	政治哲学
educational	philosophy	教育哲学

▷**Natural philosophy** deals with how we perceive the world through our five senses. 自然哲学が扱うのは人間が五感を通して世界をどのように認識するかだ
▷My brother is studying **political philosophy** at university. 弟は大学で政治哲学を専攻している

a philosophy	of life	人生哲学

▷His **philosophy of life** seems to be to enjoy himself as much as possible! 彼の人生哲学はできるだけ楽しく過ごすことのようだ

phone /fóun/

名 電話機; 電話(★telephone よりくだけた言い方)

answer	the phone	電話に出る
get	the phone	
pick up	the phone	受話器をとる
hang up	the phone	受話器を置く
put down	the phone	
replace	the phone	

slam down	the phone	受話器をガチャンと置く
use	the phone	電話を借りる；電話を使う

▷Could you **answer** the **phone**, please? 電話に出ていただけますか
▷Can somebody **get** the **phone**? だれか電話に出てくれませんか(★ get a phone は「電話機を買う」)
▷She **picked up** the **phone** and dialed the police. 彼女は受話器をとって警察に電話をかけた
▷Don't **hang up** the **phone**! 電話を切らないで
▷Sorry, I can't talk any longer. I'll have to **put** the **phone down**. ごめん．おしゃべりはおしまい．電話を切らないと
▷He **slammed** the **phone down** angrily. 彼は怒って電話をガチャンと切った
▷I don't **use** the **phone** so much now. I do a lot of texting. 近ごろは電話はあまり使わないな．メールが多いね

the phone	rings	電話が鳴る
the phone	goes dead	電話が切れる

▷If the **phone rings**, could you answer it? 電話が鳴ったら出ていただけますか
▷We were in the middle of a conversation when suddenly the **phone went dead**. 話の最中だったのに急に電話が切れた

on	the phone	電話に出て；電話で
over	the phone	電話で
by	phone	

▷She was **on** the **phone** for nearly an hour. I can't talk about it **over** the **phone**. 彼女は1時間近くも電話中だったので，その件をまだ電話で話せていない

a cellular	phone	携帯電話
《英》a mobile	phone	

photograph /fóutəgræf | -grɑ̀:f/

名 写真(★短縮形は photo)

take	a photograph	写真を撮る
pose for	a photograph	写真のポーズをとる

▷I want to have my **photograph taken** by a professional photographer. プロの写真家に私の写真を撮ってもらいたい
▷They **posed for** a **photograph** in front of the Eiffel Tower. 彼らはエッフェル塔の前で写真のポーズをとった

a recent	photograph	最近の写真
an old	photograph	古い写真
a color	photograph	カラー写真
a black-and-white	photograph	白黒写真
a family	photograph	家族写真
a framed	photograph	額入り写真
an aerial	photograph	航空写真
a satellite	photograph	衛星写真

▷You have to attach a **recent photograph** to this application form. この応募用紙に最近撮った写真を貼らなければならない
▷There was a **framed photograph** of their wedding on the mantelpiece. 彼らの結婚式の写真がマントルピースの上に額入りで飾ってあった

picnic /píknik/ 名 ピクニック, 遠足

go on	a picnic	ピクニックに出かける
go for	a picnic	
have	a picnic	ピクニックをする

★× do a picnic とはいわない

▷I don't think we can **go for** a **picnic**. It's going to rain. ピクニックには行けないよ．雨になるから
▷It's a lovely day. Let's **have** a **picnic** on the beach. 天気のいい日だ．浜辺でピクニックしよう

picture /píktʃər/ 名 絵；写真；描写

paint	a picture	絵を描く
draw	a picture	
take	a picture	写真を撮る

▷There's a wonderful view from the top of this cliff. I'd like to **paint** a **picture** of it. この崖の上からの眺めはすばらしい．絵に描いてみたい
▷I need to have my **picture taken** for a new passport. 新しい旅券用の写真を撮ってもらわなくては

the overall	picture	全体像
a complete	picture	
the whole	picture	
an accurate	picture	正確な描写
a mental	picture	頭の中のイメージ

▷Concerning the tsunami in Miyagi I don't know the details, but the **overall picture** doesn't look very good. 宮城での津波について詳細はわからないが，全体の状況は深刻なようだ
▷This book gives us an **accurate picture** of life in Britain in the 19th century. この本は19世紀のイ

| piece |

ギリスの生活を正確に伝えている
▷She had a **mental picture** of everybody applauding as she received first prize in the speech contest. 彼女は自分が弁論大会で優勝して, みんなに拍手されているようすを心に描いた

a picture	by A	A(人)が描いた絵

▷This exhibition has many **pictures by** Picasso. この展覧会にはピカソの絵がたくさん出品されている

piece /píːs/

名 一片；断片；作品；部品, (セットの)1点

a piece of	bread	パン一切れ
a piece of	toast	トースト一切れ
a piece of	cake	ケーキ一切れ
a piece of	meat	肉一切れ
a piece of	equipment	一つの備品
a piece of	land	土地1区画
a piece of	paper	紙1枚
a piece of	information	(1件の)情報
a piece of	news	(1件の)ニュース
a piece of	advice	一つのアドバイス
a piece of	evidence	一つの証拠
a piece of	music	1曲
a piece of	furniture	家具1点
a piece of	work	作品1点

★a piece of は数えられない名詞につける。「紙2枚」は two pieces of paper という

▷Would you like a **piece of cake**? ケーキを一切れいかが
▷"I heard **two interesting pieces of news** this morning." "Really? Go on, then! Tell me!"「けさ, おもしろいニュースを2つ聞いたよ」「ほんと？じゃ教えてよ」

piece by piece		一つずつ

▷She picked the broken glass up from the floor **piece by piece**. 彼女は割れたガラスを床から一つずつ拾った

in	pieces	ばらばらになって
to	pieces	ばらばらに, 粉々に

▷He dropped the vase and it smashed **to pieces**. 彼が落とした花瓶は粉々に割れた

pile /páil/ 名 積み重ね, 山

a huge	pile	大きな山
a big	pile	
a large	pile	
a small	pile	小さな山
a little	pile	

▷There was a **huge pile** of letters lying on the floor. 手紙が山ほど床に置いてあった
▷There was a **small pile** of papers on his desk. 彼の机の上には書類の小さな山があった

the top	of the pile	積み上げた物の最上部
the bottom	of the pile	積み上げた物の最下部

★比喩的に「社会の最上層部」「社会の最下層部」の意味でも用いる

▷My essay was at the **top of** the **pile** on the teacher's desk. 先生の机に積まれたレポートのいちばん上に私のがあった

pity /píti/ 名 哀れみ, 同情；残念なこと

feel	pity	同情する
show	pity	同情を示す

▷We **feel pity** *for* the boy. その少年をかわいそうだと思う

a great	pity	とても残念なこと

▷Yesterday's concert was fantastic. It was a **great pity** you couldn't come. きのうのコンサートはすばらしかったわ. あなたが来られなかったのはとても残念ね

it's a pity	(that)...	…とは残念だ
it's a pity	to do	…するのは残念だ

▷This steak's delicious. **It's a pity** you don't eat meat. とてもおいしいステーキなのに, きみが肉を食べないのは残念だね

out of	pity	気の毒に思って

▷She gave that man $10 **out of pity** for him. 彼女はその男を気の毒に思って10ドルあげた

an object	of pity	哀れみの対象

▷The last thing he wants is to become an **object of pity**. 彼は哀れみの対象にだけはなりたくない

PHRASES
What a pity! ☺ 本当に残念だ / **That's a pity.** ☺ それは残念だ ▷"Pete can't come to the party." "Oh, what a pity! I was hoping to meet him."「ピートはパーティーに来られないの」「それは残念, 彼と会いたかったのに」

place /pléis/ 名 場所；地域；席；箇所；住まい，家；職，身分，地位；順位

change	places	席を替わる
swap	places	
know	one's place	身の程を知る
get	a place	メンバーに選ばれる
lose	one's place	メンバーからはずれる；席[順番]を人にとられる；どこまで読んだか[話したか]わからなくなる
save	A's place	席[順番]をとっておいてやる
keep	A's place	

▷Would you like to **change places**? You can see better from here. 席を替わりましょうか．ここからのほうがよく見えますよ

▷I just heard I **got a place** in our school soccer team. 聞いたばかりの話だけど，ぼくは学校のサッカーチームのメンバーに選ばれたんだ

▷I don't think Ted really **knows** his **place**. He's always arguing with the boss. テッドはまったく身の程を知らないな．上司と言い争ってばかりだもの

▷I can't remember which page I was reading in this book. I've **lost** my **place**. この本をどのページまで読んだかなあ．わからなくなっちゃった ▷I don't want to **lose** my **place** in the queue. (せっかく並んでいたのに)順番を人にとられたくない

a good	place	よい場所
a perfect	place	完璧な場所
a safe	place	安全な場所
a quiet	place	静かな場所
a crowded	place	混雑した場所
a public	place	公共の場所
the right	place	正しい場所
the wrong	place	間違った場所
a meeting	place	待ち合わせ場所

▷Auckland is a **good place** to live. オークランドは暮らすのによいところです

▷This is the **perfect place** for a holiday. ここは休暇には最適なところだ

▷You should keep your money in a **safe place**. 安全な場所にお金をしまっておいたほうがいい

▷It's not polite to use your mobile phone in a **public place**. 公共の場所で携帯電話を使うのは礼儀に反する

▷We've been waiting over half an hour for Tom. Are you sure this is the **right place**? 30分以上トムを待っているよ．場所はほんとうにここかい

▷You were in the **wrong place**. I said in front of the cinema, not inside. きみは場所を間違えたね．ぼくは映画館の前って言ったよ，中じゃないよ

a place	for A	Aのための場所
in	place	あるべき場所に；うまくいって
out of	place	場違いで

▷This park has become a **place for** homeless people. この公園はホームレスの人々の場所になった

▷Can you hold the ladder **in place** while I climb it? ぼくが登るあいだ，はしごをきちんと支えていてくれるかな

▷I was the only person not wearing a suit. I really felt **out of place**. スーツを着ていないのは私だけだったので，すごく場違いだと感じた

a place	to do	…する場所

▷Seattle is a beautiful **place to** live. シアトルは暮らすのに美しい街だ

a [the] place	where	…の場所
a [the] place	in which	

▷This is the **place where** I was born. ここが私の生まれた場所です

▷For this year's holiday we need to find a **place in which** the whole family can have a good time. 今年の休暇に家族みんなで楽しく過ごせる場所を見つけなくてはならない

in	the first place	第一に
in	the second place	第二に

▷You want to know why I'm angry? Well, **in the first place**, you're half an hour late, and **in** the **second place**... 私がなぜ怒っているか聞きたい？一つ目は30分も遅れたこと，二つ目は…

place /pléis/ 動 置く，据える

be well	placed	いい場所にある
be conveniently	placed	便利な場所にある
be ideally	placed	理想的な場所にある

▷The bank is **ideally placed** for commerce. その銀行は商売のためには理想的な場所にある

place A	on B	AをBに置く
place A	at B	
place A	in B	

▷"Happy birthday!" she said, and **placed** a large box **on** the table. 「誕生日おめでとう」と言うと彼女は大きな箱をテーブルに置いた

plain /pléin/ 形 明白な；質素な，地味な

| plan |

plain and simple	単純明白に

▷ If you're late for work again you'll lose your job **plain and simple**. また仕事に遅刻したらあっさり仕事を失うよ

it is plain	that...	…は明白だ
make it plain	that...	…を明白にする

▷ **It**'s **plain that** you haven't understood anything that I've been saying. 私が言ってきたことをきみが少しもわかっていなかったのは明らかだ
▷ The teacher **made it plain that** he needed to work harder to pass the course. その課程の単位をとるには彼はもっとがんばって勉強しなくてはいけないと先生は明言した

plan /plǽn/ 名 計画, 案; 設計図, 図面

have	a plan	計画がある
make	a plan	計画を立てる
work out	a plan	
draw up	a plan	
announce	a plan	計画を発表する
approve	a plan	計画を承認する
carry out	a plan	計画を実行する
change	one's plans	計画を変更する
cancel	a plan	計画を取りやめる

▷ Do you **have** any **plans** this summer? この夏は何か予定がありますか
▷ We need to **make** a **plan** for our trip to Europe. ヨーロッパ旅行の計画を立てなきゃ
▷ The Government has **announced** a **plan** to build two more nuclear power stations. 政府はさらに2基の原子力発電所を建設する計画を発表した
▷ Our **plan** to open a factory in Osaka has been **approved**. 大阪に工場を開設するというわれわれの計画は承認された

a detailed	plan	詳細な計画
a future	plan	将来の計画
a long-term	plan	長期計画
one's original	plan	当初の計画
a business	plan	事業計画
a development	plan	開発計画
a recovery	plan	復興計画
a peace	plan	和平計画
a pension	plan	年金制度

▷ We need a more **detailed plan** to present to the committee tomorrow. あす委員会に出すためのもっと詳細な計画が必要だ
▷ I don't know my **future plans** yet. 将来の計画は未定だ
▷ I think our **original plan** was better than this one. 原案はこれよりよかったと思う

a plan	for A	Aの計画

▷ Do you have any **plans for** this weekend? この週末は何か予定がありますか

a plan	to do	…する予定

▷ I need a **plan to** help me lose weight. 減量に役立つ計画が必要だ

a change of	plan	計画の変更

▷ There's been a **change of plan**. We're not going to Australia after all. 計画の変更があり, オーストラリアへは結局行かない

plane /pléin/ 名 飛行機

catch	a plane	飛行機に乗る
board	a plane	飛行機に搭乗する
get on	a plane	
get off	a plane	飛行機から降りる
fly	a plane	飛行機を操縦する
land	a plane	飛行機を着陸させる

▷ The passengers are already **boarding** the **plane**. 乗客たちはすでに飛行機への搭乗を始めている
▷ We can't fly direct to Los Angeles. We have to **get on** another **plane**. ロサンゼルスへの直行便はないので, 乗り換えなくてはならない
▷ My dad's a pilot. He **flies planes** all over the world. 父はパイロットで, 世界中を飛び回っている

a plane	takes off	飛行機が離陸する
a plane	lands	飛行機が着陸する

▷ The plane **took off** from Paris for Tokyo at 7:00 p.m. 飛行機は午後7時にパリから東京へ飛び立った

by	plane	飛行機で
on	the plane	機内で

▷ I think we should travel **by plane**. It's much quicker. 飛行機で行くべきだと思う. そのほうがずっと早い
▷ The food and service was very good **on** the **plane**. 機内の食事もサービスもとてもよかった

a fighter	plane	戦闘機
a transport	plane	輸送機
a cargo	plane	

plant /plǽnt | plάːnt/ 名 植物；工場

grow	plants	植物を育てる
cultivate	plants	植物を栽培する
water	the plants	植物に水をやる
build	a plant	工場を建てる

▷We're **growing** lots of **plants** in the greenhouse. 温室でたくさん植物を育てている
▷Did you remember to **water** the **plants**? 忘れずに植物に水をやりましたか

wild	plants	野生植物
a rare	plant	珍しい植物
flowering	plants	花の咲く植物
an industrial	plant	工場
a chemical	plant	化学工場
a power	plant	発電所
a nuclear	plant	原子力発電所

▷There are many **wild plants** growing in the garden. 野生植物が庭にたくさん生えている
▷The government is planning to build a **nuclear plant** in our area. 政府は私たちの地域に原子力発電所を建てる計画だ

plant /plǽnt | plάːnt/ 動 植える；据える

firmly	planted	しっかり固定された

▷"I'm not moving!" she said, her feet **firmly planted** on the ground. 「動かないから」と彼女は言ってしっかり大地を踏みしめた

plant A	with B	AにBを植える

▷We **planted** the vegetable patch **with** potatoes. 野菜畑にジャガイモを植えた ▷This part of the garden is **planted with** tomatoes and lettuce. 庭のこの部分にはトマトとレタスが植えられている

plate /pléit/

名 (底の浅い)皿；金属板，プレート

clear	a plate	皿の料理を平らげる

▷She was so hungry that she **cleared** the **plate** in less than a minute. 彼女はあまりに腹ぺこだったので1分もかからずに皿の料理を平らげた

on	a plate	皿に

▷Can you put this cheesecake **on** a **plate**? このチーズケーキを皿によそってくれるかな

a dinner	plate	ディナー用の大皿
a paper	plate	紙皿
a license	plate	ナンバープレート
《英》a number	plate	
a name	plate	ネームプレート

play /pléi/ 名 劇；遊び；競技，プレー

write	a play	劇を書く
produce	a play	劇を演出する
perform	a play	劇を上演する
put on	a play	
see	a play	劇を見る

▷Shakespeare **wrote** many famous **plays**. シェイクスピアは有名な劇をたくさん書いた
▷The drama club needs someone to **produce** a **play**. 演劇部はだれかに芝居の演出をしてもらう必要がある
▷Our school's going to **put on** a **play** at the end of term. うちの学校は学期末に劇を上演する予定だ
▷We **saw** a terrific **play** last night. 昨夜すばらしい芝居を見た

fair	play	フェアプレー
foul	play	反則，不正行為
rough	play	荒っぽいプレー
a new	play	新作
a stage	play	舞台劇
a school	play	学校劇
a radio	play	ラジオ劇

▷The referee is there to ensure **fair play**. 審判は試合が公正に行われるためにいるのだ
▷The police found a dead body near the river. They suspect **foul play**. 警察は川の近くで死体を発見したが，殺人の疑いがあると見ている

in	a play	劇で
at	play	遊んで

▷When I was in junior high school I appeared **in** a school **play**. 中学校のとき学校劇に出た

play /pléi/ 動 遊ぶ；競技をする；演奏する

play	fair	正々堂々と戦う
play	safe	安全策をとる

▷It's best to **play safe** rather than get into an argument. 言い争うより当たり障りなくやるのがいい

| please |

play	with A	Aで遊ぶ
play	against A	Aと対戦する
play	for A	Aのチームで試合に出る

▷I think the children are in their bedroom **playing with** their toys. 子どもたちは寝室でおもちゃ遊びしていると思う
▷We have to **play against** a really good team on Saturday. 土曜日に強豪チームと戦わなければならない
▷David Beckham used to **play for** Manchester United. デイビッド・ベッカムはかつてマンチェスターユナイテッドでプレーしていた

play	A B	A(人)にB(いたずらなど)
play	B on A	をする

▷She had **played** a trick **on** him by pretending to be in love with him. 彼女は彼を愛しているふりをして彼の心をもてあそんだ

please /plíːz/ 動 喜ばせる；人の気に入る

be hard	to please	気難しい
be difficult	to please	
be anxious	to please	人当たりがいい,
be eager	to please	愛想がいい

▷My teacher is very strict. He is really **hard to please**. 先生はとても厳しくて、ほんとに気難しい
▷I like your new secretary. She's very **anxious to please**. きみの今度の秘書はいいね。人当たりがすごくいいよ
▷That new hotel receptionist is very nice. She's always helpful and **eager to please**. あの新しいホテルの受付係はとてもいい。いろいろ手伝ってくれるし愛想もいい

a desire	to please	人を喜ばせようという気持ち

▷In the service industry it's very important to have a **desire to please** your customers. サービス産業ではお客に喜んでもらう気持ちをもつのが大事だ

PHRASES
Please yourself! ☺ 好きにしたら ▷"I really don't feel like going out this evening." "OK. Please yourself. I'll be back around midnight." 「今夜はほんとに出かけたくないの」「いいよ。好きにして。真夜中近くに戻るから」

pleased /plíːzd/ 形 喜んだ、うれしい

look	pleased	うれしそうだ
seem	pleased	

▷Ken **looks pleased**. He must have passed his exam! ケンはうれしそうな顔をしているね。きっと試験に受かったんだよ

extremely	pleased	非常に喜んだ
really	pleased	とても喜んだ
only too	pleased	
well	pleased	
particularly	pleased	とりわけ喜んだ

▷He's **really pleased** that we are coming! 私たちがやって来るのを彼はすごく喜んでいる
▷No problem. I was **only too pleased** to help. 構いませんよ。お手伝いできてよかったです
▷The football manager said he was **well pleased** with the result of the game. 試合結果に十分満足しているとフットボールの監督は語った
▷We're **particularly pleased** with the way you've been working recently. このところのきみの働きぶりを特にうれしく思っているよ

be pleased	at A	Aに満足した
be pleased	with A	
be pleased	about A	Aのことがうれしい

▷Your father was very **pleased at** your exam results. お父さんはきみの試験の結果にとても満足だった
▷Amanda was very **pleased with** her birthday presents. アマンダはいくつも誕生プレゼントをもらってとても満足した
▷Anna was really **pleased about** getting her snorkeling certificate. アンナはシュノーケルの免許がとれてとてもうれしかった

be pleased	to do	…してうれしい
be pleased	that...	…がうれしい

▷She was very **pleased to** receive your present. 彼女はあなたから贈り物をもらってとても喜んでいた
▷She was **pleased that** he hadn't forgotten their wedding anniversary. 彼が二人の結婚記念日を忘れていなかったのが彼女はうれしかった

PHRASES
Pleased to meet you, Mr. Gordon. ☺ ゴードンさん、初めまして

pleasure /pléʒər/ 名 喜び、楽しさ；快楽

get	pleasure from A	A(事)から喜び
get	pleasure out of A	を得る
derive	pleasure from A	
give	pleasure to A	A(人)に喜びを
bring	pleasure to A	与える

| point |

take	pleasure in A	A(事)を楽しむ
find	pleasure in A	
have	the pleasure	光栄に浴する

▷She **gets** a lot of **pleasure from** eating out with her friends. 彼女は友人との外食を大いに楽しんでいる
▷She **derives** a lot of **pleasure from** doing volunteer work. 彼女はボランティアの仕事で多くの喜びを得ている
▷Your visits to the old people's home **give** them a lot of **pleasure**. 高齢者施設にあなたが何度も訪問することでお年寄りたちはとても喜んでいる
▷He **takes pleasure in** playing practical jokes on people. 彼は人に悪ふざけして喜んでいる(★否定的な文脈で用いることが多い)
▷Today I **have** the **pleasure** of announcing the winner of our photography competition. 本日,写真コンテストの受賞者を発表できることは光栄です

great	pleasure	大きな喜び
enormous	pleasure	
real	pleasure	本物の喜び
sheer	pleasure	この上ない喜び

▷It was a **great pleasure** to meet you. あなたにお目にかかれてとても光栄でした
▷It was a **real pleasure** to be here. ここに来られてとてもよかった
▷"I won the lottery! Yeeeeaaah!" She laughed out loud in **sheer pleasure**. 「宝くじが当たった.やったあ」と言って笑いながら,彼女は大喜びした

[PHRASES]
(**It's) my pleasure.** ☺ どういたしまして(★お礼を言われたときの返答) ▷"Thanks for picking me up from the airport." "No problem. It's my pleasure." 「空港まで出迎えに来てくれてありがとう」「いえ,どういたしまして」
(**It's a) pleasure to meet you.** ☺ お目にかかれて光栄です ▷How do you do? It's a pleasure to meet you. 初めまして.お目にかかれて光栄です

pocket /pάkit | pɔ́k-/ 名 ポケット

put A	into a pocket	Aをポケットに入れる
take A	out of a pocket	Aをポケットから出す
reach	into one's pocket	ポケットに手を入れる
search	in one's pocket	ポケットの中を探す
empty	one's pockets	ポケットの中身を全部出す
turn out	one's pockets	

▷She **put** her hand **into** her jacket **pocket**. 彼女は手を上着のポケットに入れた
▷She **reached into** her **pocket** and brought out a small notebook. 彼女はポケットに手を入れて小さなノートを取り出した
▷He **searched in** his **pockets**, but he couldn't find his railway ticket. 彼はポケットの中を探したが電車の切符が見つからなかった

an inside	pocket	内ポケット
an inner	pocket	
a top	pocket	上ポケット
a back	pocket	尻ポケット
a hip	pocket	
a breast	pocket	胸ポケット
a zipped	pocket	チャックつきポケット
a jacket	pocket	上着のポケット
a coat	pocket	コートのポケット
a shirt	pocket	シャツのポケット
a jeans	pocket	ジーンズのポケット
a trouser	pocket	ズボンのポケット

▷Where's my wallet? I thought it was in my **inside pocket**. 財布はどこかな.内ポケットに入れたと思っていたけど
▷He was wearing a handkerchief in the **top pocket** of his suit. 彼はスーツの上ポケットにハンカチを挿していた
▷Charles kept his money in his **back pocket**. チャールズはお金を尻ポケットに入れていた

in	A's pocket	ポケットに
out of	A's pocket	ポケットから
from	A's pocket	
from out of	A's pocket	

▷How much money do you have **in** your **pocket**? ポケットにいくらお金を持っていますか
▷He pulled a clean handkerchief **from out of** his pocket and gave it to her. 彼はポケットからきれいなハンカチを取り出して彼女に渡した

point /pɔ́int/ 名 論点;(話の)核心;段階;目的;地点;(目盛りの)点;得点

raise	the point	論点を提起する
illustrate	the point	論点を説明する
emphasize	the point	論点を強調する
come to	the point	話の核心に入る
get to	the point	
miss	the point	肝心な点がわからない
reach	a point	段階に達する
score	a point	得点を入れる

| point |

▷I think it's very important to **raise** the **point** at our next meeting.　次の会議でその論点を提起するのが大事だと思う
▷I'd like to **emphasize** the **point** that everybody is expected to attend next week's lecture.　来週の講義には全員が出席することになっているという点を強調したい
▷She said she understood but actually she completely **missed** the **point**.　わかったと言ったものの，実のところ彼女は肝心のところがまったくわかっていなかった
▷We haven't **scored** a **point** yet.　私たちはまだ得点を入れていなかった

a good	point	よい点
an important	point	重要な点
a crucial	point	非常に重大な点
a key	point	キーポイント
a major	point	主要な点
a strong	point	強み
a weak	point	弱み
boiling	point	沸点
freezing	point	氷点
melting	point	融点
a high	point	最高の状態
a low	point	最悪の状態
a focal	point	焦点
a turning	point	転換点
a meeting	point	待ち合わせ場所

▷"How can we go to the movies if we don't have any money?" "**Good point!**"　「お金がないのにどうやって映画を見に行けるの」「いいとこ突いているね」
▷Ted looks really angry! I think he's almost reached **boiling point**!　テッドはとても怒っているみたいだ．いまにも爆発しそうだ
▷The **freezing point** of water is 0 degrees centigrade.　水の氷点はセ氏0度だ
▷The guest appearance of Harrison Ford was the **high point** of the evening.　ハリソン・フォードがゲストとして登場したのがその晩のハイライトだった
▷Being sent by his company to Canada was a **turning point** in his career.　会社からカナダへ派遣されたことが彼の経歴の転換点だった

at	this point	この時点で
at	that point	その時点で
at	one point	ある時点で
up to	a point	ある程度まで
to	the point of A	Aの程度まで

▷**At this point**, I think we'd better stop for a break.　この辺で一休みしたほうがいいんじゃないかな
▷**At one point** I thought we were going to lose the game.　いっとき試合に負けると思った
▷I agree with you **up to** a **point**.　ある程度はきみに賛成だ

the point is	that...	要するに…だ

▷The **point is that** it's too late now to do anything about it.　要するに何をするにももう手遅れだ

PHRASES

I see your point. / I take your point. / I get your point.　きみの言いたいことはわかる　▷"If we don't do something about it now it will be too late!" "Yes, I see your point, but what can we do?"　「いま何か手を打たないと手遅れになるよ」「言いたいことはわかるけど，私たちに何ができるかな」
That's not my point. ☺　私が言いたいのはそういうことではない
There is no point in doing　…してもむだだ　▷She's not going to come. There's no point in waiting any longer.　彼女は来ないよ．これ以上待ってもむだだ
What's the point of doing　…して何の意味があるのか　▷What's the point of taking the exam? I know I won't pass!　試験を受けて何になるだろう．どうせ受かりっこないのに
What's your point? ☺　何が言いたいのですか　▷Yes, I understand all that, but what's your point?　おっしゃることはわかりますが，要するに何がお望みですか

| **point** /pɔ́int/ 動 指さす，指し示す

point	at A	Aを指さす
point	to A	
point	toward A	Aの方を指さす

▷Stop it Jason. It's rude to **point at** people!　やめなさい，ジェイソン．人を指すのは失礼だぞ
▷"Look. We can sit there." He **pointed to** two empty seats in the back row.　「ほら，そこに座れる」と彼は後列の空席2つを指さした
▷"I think we go out this way," she **pointed toward** an exit sign on the right.　「出口はこっちだと思う」と言って彼女は右手の出口表示を指さした

| **police** /pəlíːs/

名 警察(★ふつう the police で複数扱い)

call	the police	警察に通報する
contact	the police	警察に連絡する
tell	the police	警察に話す
report A to	the police	警察にAを通報する

▷Someone's broken into our house! **Call** the **police**!　強盗に家に入られた．警察を呼んでくれ
▷If you think someone stole your wallet you should **tell** the **police**.　財布を盗まれたと思うなら警察に言うべきだ
▷If you see anything suspicious you should **report**

it **to** the **police**. 不審物を見かけたら警察に通報すべきだ

the police	appeal for A	警察がAを強く求めている
the police	arrest A	警察がAを逮捕する
the police	investigate A	警察がAを捜査する

▷ The **police** are **appealing for** information. 警察は情報の提供を強く求めている
▷ The **police arrested** him for driving without a license. 警察は彼を無免許運転で逮捕した
▷ The **police** are **investigating** the murder. 警察は殺人事件を捜査中だ

armed	police	武装警官
the local	police	地元の警察
the secret	police	秘密警察

▷ There were many **armed police** patrolling the airport. 多くの武装警官が空港を巡回していた
▷ Our **local police** are always very helpful. うちの地元の警察はいつもめんどう見がいい

political /pəlítikəl/ 形 政治の, 政治的な

social and political	政治社会的
political and economic	政治経済的

★ political and social, economic and political も用いられる

▷ If the government raises the sales tax it will have both **social and political** consequences. 政府が売上税を上げれば政治的にも社会的にも影響があるだろう
▷ We need to have both **political and economic** reform. 政治経済改革の必要がある

politics /pálətiks | pɔ́l-/

名 政治, 政界；政治学

enter (into)	politics	政界に入る
go into	politics	
be involved in	politics	政治に携わる
dominate	politics	政治を支配する
leave	politics	政界を去る
discuss	politics	政治を論じる

▷ He decided to **enter politics** when he was very young. 彼は非常に若くして政界に入る決心をした
▷ She was **involved in politics** from a very early age. 彼女はごく若いころから政治に携わっていた
▷ It's always dangerous to **discuss politics** with someone you don't know! 知らない人と政治を論じるのは常に危険だ

domestic	politics	国内政治
national	politics	国政, 国内政治
local	politics	地方政治
democratic	politics	民主政治

▷ **National politics** sometimes make it difficult for EU members to agree with each other. それぞれの国内政治のせいでＥＵ加盟国が互いに合意できないことがある
▷ In many countries **democratic politics** does not exist. 民主的な政治が存在していない国が多くある

poor /púər/ 形 貧しい；劣った；かわいそうな

desperately	poor	ひどく貧しい；とても
extremely	poor	ひどい
pretty	poor	かなり貧しい；かなり
rather	poor	ひどい

▷ His marks in the exam were **extremely poor**. 彼の試験の点数はとてもひどかった
▷ The rice crop this year was **pretty poor**. 今年の米はとても不作だった

poor	little A	かわいそうなA
poor	old A	

▷ The baby's been crying all day **poor little** thing. あの赤ん坊は一日中泣いている. かわいそうに(★ poor little との頻度の高い連結はほかに girl, boy, chap, child)
▷ Look at that **poor old** man. He's shivering with cold. かわいそうなあの人を見て. 寒さで震えているよ (★ poor old との頻度の高い連結はほかに man, chap)

popular /pápjulər | pɔ́p-/

形 人気のある；大衆的な

become	popular	人気が出る
prove	popular	人気があるとわかる

▷ It's difficult to say why manga has **become** so **popular** in Japan. 日本で漫画がなぜこれほど人気が出たのか理由を説明するのは難しい

extremely	popular	非常に人気のある
immensely	popular	
highly	popular	人気の高い
particularly	popular	特に人気のある
especially	popular	
increasingly	popular	ますます人気のある

| population |

▷Smartphones are becoming **extremely popular**. スマートフォンの人気がとても高まってきている
▷Everybody loves Amy. She's **particularly popular** at school. エイミーはみんなから愛されており、学校の人気者だ
▷Pete is **highly popular** among his friends. ピートは友だちの間で大の人気者だ
▷This new TV series is becoming **increasingly popular**. この新しいテレビシリーズはますます人気が出てきている

popular	with A	A(人)に人気の
popular	among A	A(人)の間で人気の

▷Even today, the Beatles are still **popular among** some young people in Japan. 今日もなおビートルズは日本の一部の若者に人気がある

population /pàpjuléiʃən | pɔ̀p-/

名 人口;(the population で集合的に)住民

a large	population	多くの人口
a small	population	少ない人口
the total	population	総人口
the urban	population	都市人口
the rural	population	農村人口
the local	population	地元住民
the whole	population	全住民
half	the population	住民の半分

▷China has always had a **large population**. 中国は常に多くの人口を抱えてきた(★ ×many population, few population とはいわない)
▷A large percentage of the **total population** of Australia is centered in the cities. オーストラリアの総人口の大部分は都市に集中している
▷The **local population** wants to have a new factory built in their area. 地元住民は地元への新工場建設を願っている
▷After the typhoon the **whole population** had no electricity for several days. 台風の後、全住民に数日間電気が来なかった
▷By 2040 nearly half the **population** will be over the age of 60. 2040年までに国民のほぼ半分が60歳を超えているだろう

position /pəzíʃən/

名 位置, 姿勢;立場, 見解;役職, 地位

change	one's position	姿勢を変える
take	a position	見解をもつ
adopt	a position	
consider	the position	立場を考える
occupy	a position	地位を占める
hold	a position	地位にある
maintain	a position	地位を維持する
apply for	a position	地位に応募する
take up	a position	地位に就く
accept	a position	地位を引き受ける

▷He usually **takes** a moderate **position** on political issues. 彼は政治的問題についてはたいてい穏健な態度をとっている
▷You should **consider** the **position** you're in carefully. きみが置かれている立場をもっとよく考えろ
▷Ms. Taylor **occupies** a very important **position** within the company. テイラーさんは会社内でとても重要な地位を占めている
▷She **holds** the **position** of managing director in her company. 彼女は会社で常務取締役の地位にある
▷She **took up** a **position** as hotel manager last month. 彼女は先月ホテル支配人の職に就いた

an upright	position	まっすぐな位置
a comfortable	position	楽な姿勢
a dominant	position	支配的な立場
a good	position	有利な立場
a strong	position	強い立場
a unique	position	独自の立場
the present	position	現在の地位;いまの状況
a financial	position	財政状況
A's social	position	社会的地位

▷Put your seat in an **upright position**. 座席をまっすぐに戻してください
▷We've maintained a **dominant position** in the market during the last 6 months. ここ半年われわれは市場で支配的な立場を維持している
▷I think we should ask for more money. We're in a very **strong position**. もっとお金を要求したほうがよいと思う。私たちはとても強い立場にいるのだから
▷The President is in a **unique position**. He can change the course of history. 大統領は独自の立場にある。歴史の流れを変えることができるのだから
▷Could you give us an update on the **present position**? いまの状況について最新情報をいただけますか
▷These newspaper stories are certain to affect her **social position**. これらの新聞記事が彼女の社会的地位に影響を与えるのは確かだ

in	a position	立場に
in	position	所定の位置に
into	position	
out of	position	所定の位置から外れて

▷I'm sorry. I'm afraid I'm not **in a position** to help

you. 申し訳ありません．あいにくあなたを助ける立場にはありません
▷ Everything's **in position**. We're ready to start. すべて整って，開始する準備ができている

positive /pάzətiv | pɔ́z-/

形 積極的な；確信している；肯定的な；陽性の

positive	about A	Aを確信した；Aに前向きな

▷ I like Debby. She's always so **positive about** everything. デビーが好きだ．彼女は何につけても常にとても前向きだ

be positive	(that)...	…と確信している

▷ I'm **positive that** I left my watch on this table. 確かに私はこのテーブルに腕時計を置き忘れた

test	positive (for A)	(A(薬物)の)陽性反応が出る

▷ Unfortunately the Olympic Games athlete **tested positive for** drugs. 残念だがそのオリンピック選手は薬物の陽性反応が出た

positive and negative		プラスとマイナスの

▷ I think there are both **positive and negative** points about going to live in Canada. カナダに移り住むのはプラスの面とマイナスの面があると思う

possession /pəzéʃən/

名 所有，所持；所有物

take	possession	手に入れる
come into	A's possession	所有物になる

★ come into (the) possession of A も用いる

▷ The bank **took possession** *of* his house last week. 銀行は先週彼の家を差し押さえた
▷ How did this jewelry **come into** your **possession**? あなたはどのようにしてこの宝石を手に入れたのですか

exclusive	possession	占有
personal	possessions	個人の所有物
a prized	possession	大事な所有物
a treasured	possession	

▷ Both countries claim **exclusive possession** of the island. 両国ともその島の占有を主張している
▷ You can put your **personal possessions** in this locker. 個人の所有物はこのロッカーに入れていいですよ

in	possession of A	Aを所有して
in	one's possession	所有して

▷ The police charged him with being **in possession of** stolen goods. 警察は盗品を所持していた容疑で彼を告発した
▷ He has a beautiful painting by Chagall **in** his **possession**. 彼はシャガールの美しい絵を1枚所有している

possibility /pὰsəbíləti | pɔ̀s-/

名 可能性，見込み；ありそうなこと，起こりうること

offer	the possibility	可能性を提供する
open	the possibility	可能性を開く
open up	possibilities	
suggest	the possibility	可能性を示唆する
consider	the possibility	可能性を考える
discuss	the possibility	可能性を論じる
explore	the possibility	可能性を探る
investigate	the possibility	
reduce	the possibility	可能性を減らす
rule out	the possibility	可能性を排除する
exclude	the possibility	

▷ We haven't found any evidence **suggesting** the **possibility** of a missile launch. ミサイル発射の可能性を示唆するいかなる証拠もまだ見つかっていない
▷ We should **consider** the **possibility** of trying to extend our bank loan. 銀行ローンを延長してみる可能性を考えたほうがいい
▷ I think we should **explore** the **possibility** of merging with another company. ほかの会社と合併する可能性を探るべきだと思う
▷ I think we should install more alarms to **reduce** the **possibility** of theft. 泥棒に入られる可能性を減らすためにもっと警報器を設置すべきだと思う

a strong	possibility	高い可能性
a great	possibility	大きな可能性
a real	possibility	現実の可能性
a distinct	possibility	確かな可能性
a remote	possibility	わずかな可能性
another	possibility	もう一つの可能性
other	possibilities	ほかの可能性

★「高い可能性」は ˣa high possibility とはいわない

▷ There's a **real possibility** that she'll have to stay in hospital for 2 or 3 months. 彼女は2，3か月入院する見込みが強い
▷ There's a **distinct possibility** that you'll be pro-

| possible |

moted next year. きみは来年昇進する可能性が高い
▷There's only a **remote possibility** that our boss is going to leave. うちの上司が辞める可能性はわずかだ
▷**Another possibility** is to cancel the trip. もう一つの可能性は旅行を取りやめることだ

| possibility | for A | Aの可能性 |
| possibility | of doing | …する可能性 |

▷Our company is doing well, but there's still **possibility for** further development. わが社は順調だがさらに発展する可能性がまだある
▷There is no **possibility of** getting any tickets for the show. All the seats are sold out. ショーのチケットが手に入る可能性はない．全席売り切れだ

| possibility | that... | …という可能性 |

▷The **possibility that** he could lose the race never occurred to him. レースに負けることもありうるなどとは彼は思ってもみなかった

possible /pɑ́səbl | pɔ́s-/

形 可能な；起こりうる，ありうる

perfectly	possible	まったく可能な
quite	possible	十分に可能な
still	possible	なお可能な
theoretically	possible	理論的に可能な
always	possible	いつも可能な
not always	possible	いつも可能とは限らない
no longer	possible	もはや不可能な

▷It's **perfectly possible** that I made a mistake. 私が誤りを犯したこともまったくありうる
▷It's **not always possible** to get what you want. ほしいものがいつも手に入るとは限らない
▷We have concluded that it is **no longer possible** to reach an agreement. 合意に達するのはもはや不可能だという結論を出した

if (at all)	possible	できるなら，可能なら
when(ever)	possible	可能ならいつでも
where(ever)	possible	可能ならどこでも

▷**If possible**, could you complete the report by the end of this week? できれば今週末までに報告書を仕上げていただけませんか
▷I visit my grandmother in hospital **whenever possible**. 可能ならいつでも病院に祖母を見舞いに行っています

it is possible	(for A)	(A(人)が)…する
	to do	のは可能だ
it is possible	that...	…はありうる
make it possible	(for A)	(A(人)が)…する
	to do	のを可能にする

▷**Is it possible to** have some extra lessons in English? 英語の補習授業をしてもらえますか
▷Her teacher **made it possible for** her **to** study in the USA. 先生のおかげで彼女は米国に留学できた

as soon as	possible	できるだけ早く
as quickly as	possible	
as far as	possible	できる限り

▷Can you try to get here **as soon as possible**? できるだけ早くここに来られますか
▷Could you ask him to call me back **as quickly as possible**? できるだけ早く折り返し電話がほしいと彼にお伝えくださいませんか
▷I think we should cooperate with them **as far as possible**. できるだけ彼らに協力すべきだと思う

post /póust/

名 地位，職；《英》郵便；郵便物《米》mail》

apply for	a post	職に応募する
get	a post	職を得る
take up	a post	職に就く
hold	a post	職に就いている
leave	a post	職を辞す
resign	one's post	

▷I'm going to **apply for** a **post** as marketing manager. 販売部長の職に応募するつもりだ
▷Tom's found a job. He's **got** a **post** with a trading company. トムは仕事を見つけたよ．貿易会社に職を得たんだ
▷He **holds** a **post** as company director. 彼は会社取締役の地位にある
▷He **resigned** his **post** as Foreign Minister. 彼は外相の職を辞した

an administrative	post	管理職，行政職
a senior	post	上級職
a key	post	要職

▷I applied for an **administrative post** at my old university. 母校の大学の行政職に応募した
▷He holds a **key post** in the US government. 彼は米国政府の要職に就いている

| by | post | 郵便で |

| in | the post | 郵送されて；郵送中に |

▷You don't have to take these heavy books with you. I'll send them **by post**. これらの重い本を持っていく必要はありません．郵便で送ってあげます
▷Your check's **in** the **post**. 小切手をすでに郵送しています

power /páuər/

名 権力，政権；力，能力；大国；エネルギー

come to	power	政権に就く
be in	power	政権に就いている
get	power	政権を握る
seize	power	
take	power	
return to	power	政権に復帰する
exercise	power	権力を行使する
use	power	
abuse	one's power	権力を乱用する
lose	power	権力を失う
have	the power	力をもっている
extend	the power	力を拡大する
increase	the power	力を増す
retain	the power	力を維持する
provide	the power	エネルギーを供給する

▷The present government has been **in power** for much too long. いまの政府は政権に就いてから長すぎる
▷Colonel Qaddafi **seized power** in Libya many years ago. カダフィ大佐がリビアの権力を掌握したのは何年も前だ
▷After such a large defeat it will be difficult for our party to **return to power**. あんな大敗北を喫したわが党が政権に復帰するのは難しいだろう
▷I'm afraid I don't **have** the **power** to help you. 残念ながら私にはあなたを助ける力がない
▷If you push that switch it **increases** the **power** of the hairdryer. そのスイッチを押せばヘアドライヤーの勢いが強くなります
▷This generator will **provide** the **power** if there's an electricity cut. 停電のときにはこの発電機が電力を供給する

considerable	power	大きな力
real	power	実権
economic	power	経済力
political	power	政治力
purchasing	power	購買力
a great	power	大国，強国
an economic	power	経済大国
electric	power	電力
nuclear	power	原子力
wind	power	風力
full	power	全出力
high	power	高出力
low	power	低出力

▷She worked her way up from nothing to a position of **considerable power**. 彼女はゼロからスタートして，かなり力のある地位にまで登り詰めた
▷It's the people behind the Prime Minister who have the **real power**. 実権を握っているのは首相の背後にいる国民だ
▷The Prime Minister has a lot of **political power**. 首相のもつ政治力は大きい
▷Britain used to be a **great power** in the 19th century. 英国は19世紀には強国だった
▷The vacuum cleaner is on **full power** but it's not sucking up any dirt. その掃除機は全出力になっているのに，ほこりを吸っていない
▷You can switch this machine to **high power** or **low power**. この機械のスイッチを入れて高出力にも低出力にもできる

| power | over A | Aへの影響力 |

▷He does everything she tells him to do. She seems to have some **power over** him. 彼は彼女がやれと命じたことは何でもやる．彼女は彼に対してなかなかの力を握っているようだ

| the power | to do | …する能力 |

▷She has the **power to** decide who gets the job. その仕事にだれが就くか決める力が彼女にはある

| the balance of | power | 力の均衡 |

▷The **balance of power** will shift to the East as India and China continue to grow. インドや中国の発展が続くにつれ，力の均衡は東洋に傾くだろう

powerful /páuərfəl/

形 強力な；勢力のある，有力な

extremely	powerful	非常に強力な
immensely	powerful	
particularly	powerful	とりわけ強力な
increasingly	powerful	ますます強力な

★powerful はおもに機械を表す名詞(machine, engine, vacuum cleaner, computer など)と結合するのに対し，strong はおもに生き物にかかわる名詞(man, horse, body, arms, teeth など)と結合する．a powerful man は「影響力のある男」で，a strong man は「体が頑丈な男」)

| practical |

▷ The engine on this new bullet train is **extremely powerful**. 新型新幹線のエンジンは非常に強力だ
▷ Supporters of the Green Party are becoming **increasingly powerful**. 緑の党の支持者はますます力を増しつつある

| powerful | enough | 十分に強力な |

▷ My motor mower isn't **powerful enough** to cut that long grass! 私の電動芝刈り機ではパワーが足りなくてあんな長い草は刈れない

practical /præktikəl/

形 実際的な；実用的な

| highly | practical | 非常に実用的な |
| purely | practical | まったく実用的な |

▷ You don't need to study a lot of theory in this course. It's **highly practical**. このコースでは理論を詰め込む必要はない。非常に実用的なコースです
▷ The work experience on this farm is **purely practical**. この農場での職業経験はまさに実用的だ

practice /præktis/

名 実行, 実践；慣行, やり方；練習

put A	into practice	Aを実行に移す
adopt	the practice	慣行を採用する
follow	the practice	慣行に従う
change	the practice	慣行を変える

▷ I think Mike has some very good ideas. We should **put** them **into practice**. マイクにはとてもよいアイデアがいくつかあると思う。それらを実行に移すべきだ
▷ He's a craftsman. He **follows** the **practice** of hundreds of years of tradition. 彼は職人で, 何百年も続く慣習に従っている
▷ We need to **change** the **practice** of taking an hour and a half for lunch break. An hour is plenty of time. 昼休みを1時間半とる慣行を変える必要がある。1時間で十分だ

current	practice	いまの慣行
common	practice	普通の慣行
standard	practice	
normal	practice	
general	practice	普通の慣行；一般診療
business	practice	ビジネス慣行
management	practice	経営慣行
medical	practice	医院；医療, 診療行為
legal	practice	弁護士事務所；法務, 実務法学
private	practice	個人開業

▷ It's **current practice** for our company to hold a health check every year. わが社では毎年健康診断をするのが恒例だ
▷ It's **common practice** to leave a tip for your waitress in the West. 西洋ではウエートレスにチップを置くのが普通の慣行だ
▷ She wants to be a doctor and go into **medical practice**. 彼女は医者になって医療の仕事に就きたいと思っている

| out of | practice | 練習不足で |
| with | practice | 練習すれば |

▷ I haven't played tennis for ages so I'm afraid I'm rather **out of practice**. 何年もテニスをしていなかったので, かなり練習不足だ

praise /préiz/ 名 称賛

be full of	praise	絶賛する
win	praise	称賛を博する
earn	praise	
receive	praise	称賛を受ける
deserve	praise	称賛に値する
heap	praise	称賛を浴びせる

▷ Your boss was **full of praise** for your recent efforts. 上司はきみの最近のがんばりを絶賛していたよ
▷ Her paintings **won** a lot of **praise**. 彼女の描いた絵画はとても称賛を博した
▷ He **deserves** a lot of **praise** for what he did. 彼の行ったことは大いに称賛に値する
▷ After she won the gold medal for Japan everybody **heaped praise** on her. 日本に金メダルをもたらした彼女にだれもが称賛を浴びせた

| high | praise | 大きな称賛 |

▷ He received **high praise** for winning the 100-meter dash. 彼は百メートル走に勝って大きな称賛を受けた

praise	for A	Aに対する称賛
praise	from A	Aからの称賛
in praise	of A	Aをたたえて

▷ She received special **praise from** the school principal for her essay. 彼女はレポートのことで校長先生からことのほか称賛を受けた
▷ The Minister for Sport made a speech **in praise of** the Olympic team. スポーツ大臣はオリンピックチー

ムをたたえるスピーチをした

praise /préiz/ 動 ほめる, 称賛する

| highly | praise | 大いに称賛する |
| be widely | praised | 広く称賛される |

▷ He was **highly praised** for saving his friend's life. 彼は友人の命を救ってとても称賛された

| praise A | for B | A(人)のBをほめる |

▷ Her teacher **praised** her **for** her homework. 先生は彼女の宿題をほめた ▷ She was **praised for** the high standard of her English essay. 彼女は英語のレポートのできがとてもよくてほめられた

pray /préi/ 動 祈る, 祈願する

| pray | silently | 静かに祈る |
| pray | earnestly | 熱心に祈る |

▷ She went to the church to **pray silently** for her grandmother. 彼女は教会へ行って祖母のために静かな祈りを捧げた

| pray (to A) | for B | (Aに)Bを祈る |

▷ I **prayed for** your recovery. あなたの回復を祈った

| pray | (that)... | …であることを祈る |

▷ I **prayed** to God **that** my family were safe after the earthquake. 地震の後, 家族が無事であってくれと神に祈った

predict /pridíkt/ 動 予言する, 予測する

accurately	predict	正確に予言する
correctly	predict	正しく予言する
confidently	predict	確信をもって予言する
be widely	predicted	大方の予想である

▷ It's difficult to **accurately predict** earthquakes. 地震を正確に予知するのは難しい
▷ We can **confidently predict** that China will become the world's leading economic power. 中国が世界をリードする経済大国になると確信をもって予言できる
▷ It was **widely predicted** that global warming would affect the world's climate. 地球温暖化が世界の気候に影響を与えることは大方の予想するところだった

| preparation |

| predict | (that)... | …と予言する |

▷ We can **predict that** robots will play a large part in our lives in the future. ロボットは将来の私たちの生活に大きな役割を果たすと予想できる

prefer /prifə́:r/ 動 …をより好む

really	prefer	実は…のほうがいい
generally	prefer	一般に…のほうがいい
still	prefer	それでも…のほうがいい

▷ I **generally prefer** to eat at home in the evenings. 普段は晩ご飯は家で食べるのが好きです
▷ I know you like the blue dress, but I **still prefer** the red (one). あなたが青のドレスが気に入っているのは知っているけど, それでも私は赤がいいと思う

| prefer A | to B | BよりAを好む |

▷ When I eat fish I **prefer** white wine **to** red. 魚を食べるとき赤より白ワインのほうが好きです

prefer	(that)...	…であってほしい
prefer	to do	…するほうを好む
prefer	doing	

▷ I'd **prefer that** we meet inside rather than outside the cinema. 映画館の外より中で会えるとありがたいです
▷ I don't think I want to continue working for this company. I'd **prefer** instead **to** find a job somewhere else. この会社で働き続けたくはないな. 代わりにどこか他で仕事を見つけたいよ
▷ I **prefer** eating at home tonight. 今夜は家で食事をするほうがいいな

pregnant /prégnənt/ 形 妊娠している

| get | pregnant | 妊娠する |
| become | pregnant | |

▷ She **became pregnant** *with* her second child. 彼女は二人目の子どもを身ごもった

| heavily | pregnant | 出産間近の |

preparation /prèpəréiʃən/

名 準備, 用意, 支度

| make | preparations | 準備する |
| be in | preparation | 準備中である |

| prepare |

complete	preparations	準備を完了する
require	preparation	準備を必要とする

▷We need to **make preparations** *for* our trip to Guam. グアム旅行の準備をする必要がある
▷The dictionary hasn't been published yet. It's still **in preparation**. その辞書はまだ出版されていない．まだ準備中だ
▷I still haven't **completed preparations** for this evening's party. まだ今晩のパーティーの準備が完了していない
▷If I'm going to give a lecture it will **require** a lot of **preparation**. 講演をすることになったら準備がかなり必要だ

adequate	preparation	十分な準備
careful	preparation	入念な準備
good	preparation	よい訓練の場
final	preparations	最終準備

▷Organizing a class reunion after 20 years will take a lot of **careful preparation**. 20年後に同窓会を開くにはかなり入念な準備が必要だろう
▷Doing an internship is **good preparation** for doing a full-time job. インターンシップをするのは常勤の仕事をするためのよい訓練だ
▷I'm nearly ready. I'm just making the **final preparations**. ほぼ準備ができて，ちょうど最後の仕上げをしているところです

preparation	for A	Aに向けた準備

▷**Preparations for** tomorrow's sports day have just been completed. あしたの運動会の準備がちょうど終わったところだ

in	preparation for A	Aに備えて

▷We had to buy many new things **in preparation for** our new baby! 生まれてくる赤ん坊のために新しく買いそろえなければならないものがいろいろあった

prepare /pripéər/ 動 準備する，用意する

adequately	prepare	十分準備する
busily	prepare	忙しく準備する

▷I'm afraid we didn't **adequately prepare** for this number of guests. 招待客の数の割に準備が足りなかった

prepare	for A	Aの準備をする
prepare A	for B	AをBのために準備する；A(人)にBに備えて準備させる

▷The river is very high. We need to **prepare for** the possibility of flooding. 川の水位が上がっている．洪水の可能性に備える必要がある
▷We need to **prepare** rooms **for** our guests. お客たちのために部屋を準備しなくては ▷It took hours to **prepare** her **for** the wedding. 彼女が結婚式に出る支度をするのに何時間もかかった

prepare	to do	…する準備をする
prepare A	to do	A(人)に…する準備をさせる

▷The phone rang just when we were **preparing to** go out. ちょうど出かけようとしたとき電話が鳴った
▷They tried to **prepare** him **to** hear some bad news. 彼らは彼に悪い知らせを聞かせる心の準備をさせようとした

prepared /pripéərd/ 形 用意ができている

well	prepared	十分準備された
properly	prepared	
badly	prepared	準備が足りない
carefully	prepared	綿密に準備した
freshly	prepared	調理したばかりの

▷It will be snowing on the mountain so we need to be **carefully prepared**. 山では雪になるだろうから，注意深く準備する必要がある
▷These sandwiches are **freshly prepared**. これらのサンドイッチは調理したばかりです

prepared	for A	Aの準備ができて

▷The police were not **prepared for** such a big crowd of people. 警察はあれほどの大群衆への備えができていなかった

present /préznt/ 名 贈り物，プレゼント

make (A)	a present	(A(人)に)贈り物をする
wrap	a present	贈り物を包む
receive	a present	贈り物を受け取る
open	a present	贈り物の包みを開ける

▷I said I liked her Chinese vase and immediately she **made** (me) a **present** of it. 彼女の中国の花瓶が気に入ったと言ったら，彼女はすぐにそれを私にプレゼントしてくれた
▷The shop assistant **wrapped** the **present** beautifully. その店員は贈り物をきれいに包んでくれた
▷Aren't you going to **open** your **present**? プレゼントを開けてみたら？

a present	for A	A(人)への贈り物
a present	to A	

▷I need to buy a **present for** my mom's birthday. 母の誕生日のプレゼントを買わなくちゃ
▷This is a **present to** us all from my uncle Tom. これはトムおじさんから私たちみんなへのプレゼントだ

a Christmas	present	クリスマスプレゼント
a birthday	present	誕生日プレゼント
a wedding	present	結婚祝い

president /prézədənt/

名 大統領；社長, 頭取

the current	president	現大統領
vice	president	副大統領；副社長
acting	president	社長代理
honorary	president	名誉会長

▷The real president is away. I'm just the **acting president** until he returns. 社長本人は不在です。私は社長が戻るまでの単なる代理です

press /prés/

名 (the press で)(集合的に)出版物, 新聞, 雑誌；報道陣(★単数・複数扱い)；(マスコミの)論評；印刷機

leak	to the press	報道機関に漏らす
talk	to the press	報道陣に話す
speak	to the press	
go	to press	印刷に回る

▷We hoped nobody would find out, but unfortunately the story was **leaked to** the **press**. だれにもばれないよう願ったが，残念ながらその記事は報道機関にリークされた
▷He refuses to **talk to** the **press**. 彼は報道機関に話すのを拒否している
▷Finally my book is ready to **go to press**. ようやく私の本は印刷に回せる状態になっている

the press	reports	新聞が報道する

▷The **press reported** last week that there were severe floods in Thailand. タイでひどい洪水があったことを新聞が先週伝えた

the foreign	press	外国紙
the local	press	地元紙
the national	press	全国紙
the popular	press	大衆紙
the tabloid	press	タブロイド紙
the financial	press	経済紙
a good	press	好評
a bad	press	悪評

▷According to the **national press** the number of unemployed is rising. 全国紙によれば失業者数が増加中だ
▷The **popular press** are always interested in publishing the latest scandal. 大衆紙はいつも最新のスキャンダルを公表したがっている
▷This new movie got a very **good press**. この新作映画は大好評を得た

in	the press	報道されて

▷Recently a lot of news about the royal family has been reported **in** the **press**. 近ごろ王室を巡るニュースが数多く新聞で報道されている

press /prés/

動 押す, 押しつける；強いる, 圧力をかける

gently	press	そっと押す
lightly	press	軽く押す
press	firmly	しっかり押す

★press gently, press lightly も用いる

▷Don't press the button too hard. Just **press it lightly**. あまり強くボタンを押さないで，ほんの軽く押してください
▷When you stick the stamp on the envelope **press firmly**. 封筒に切手を張るときはしっかり押さえてください

press A	against B	AをBに押しつける
press A	into B	AをBに押し込む
press	down on A	Aを踏み込む
press	for A	Aを要求する
press	A for B	A(人)にBを要求する

▷She **pressed** her ear **against** the door, trying to hear what they were saying inside. 彼女はドアに耳を押し当てて，中で何をしゃべっているのか聞こうとした
▷I **pressed** the key **into** the lock but it wouldn't turn. 鍵を錠へ差し込んだが，回らなかった
▷He **pressed down on** the brake but nothing happened. 彼はブレーキを踏み込んだが何の反応もなかった
▷The union is **pressing for** an increase in salaries. その組合は賃上げを強く求めている
▷I think we should **press** the government **for** more information. 政府にさらなる情報を要求すべきだ

| press A | to do | A(人)に…するよう迫る |

▷ She kept **pressing** him **to** take her out to dinner. 彼女はディナーに連れて行ってくれと彼にせがみ続けた

pressure /préʃər/

名 プレッシャー, 圧力, 圧迫;(物理的な)圧力

feel	(the) pressure	圧力を感じる
resist	pressure	圧力に抵抗する
withstand	pressure	圧力に耐える
keep up	the pressure	圧力をかけ続ける
give in to	pressure	圧力に屈する
bow to	pressure	
exert	pressure on A	Aにプレッシャーをかける
put	pressure on A	
increase	the pressure	圧力を上げる
reduce	the pressure	圧力を下げる
relieve	the pressure	

▷ So far the Foreign Minister has **resisted pressure** to resign. これまでのところ外相は辞任の圧力に抵抗している

▷ Don't stop writing letters to the manager. We need to **keep up the pressure**. マネジャーに手紙を書くのをやめてはいけない.圧力をかけ続ける必要がある

▷ We need to **exert pressure on** our company to increase salaries. 賃上げを勝ち取るために会社に圧力をかける必要がある

▷ If you open this valve it **reduces** the **pressure** inside the boiler. このバルブを開くとボイラー内部の圧力が減る

considerable	pressure	かなりの圧力
constant	pressure	絶えざる圧力
great	pressure	大きな圧力
strong	pressure	強い圧力
intense	pressure	
severe	pressure	
increasing	pressure	高まる圧力
external	pressure	外部からの圧力
political	pressure	政治的圧力
social	pressure	社会的圧力
financial	pressure	財政圧力
high	pressure	高圧
low	pressure	低圧

▷ Tom's been under **considerable pressure** at work over the last few weeks. トムにはここ2, 3週間仕事でかなりの重圧がかかっている

▷ Doctors are under **constant pressure** to treat more and more patients. 医師たちは増え続ける患者たちを治療するためのプレッシャーに絶えずさらされている

▷ The government is under **severe pressure** to re-examine the use of nuclear power. 原子力の利用を再検討しろとの強い圧力を政府は受けている

▷ When a submarine goes deep the **external pressure** from the sea is very great. 潜水艦が潜行するとき海から受ける圧力はかなり大きい

▷ The government had to hold an election due to **political pressure**. 政府は政治的圧力によって選挙に追い込まれた

under	pressure	プレッシャーを受けて
pressure	for A	Aへの圧力
pressure	from A	Aからの圧力
pressure	on A	Aにかかる圧力

★ **under pressure** は be under pressure, come under pressure, be brought under pressure や place A under pressure, put A under pressure などの連結で用いることが多い)

▷ Sorry I got angry. I've been **under** a lot of **pressure** at work recently. 怒ったりしてごめん.このところ仕事でかなりプレッシャーがかかっていて

▷ We're **coming under** a lot of **pressure** because nearly half the staff have left. スタッフが半分近く辞めたのでわれわれにかかる負担が大きい

▷ There's a strong **pressure for** change within our education system. わが国の教育制度を内部から変えるべきだとの強い圧力がある

pretend /priténd/ **動** ふりをする, 見せかける

pretend	to do	…するふりをする
pretend	to be C	Cのふりをする
pretend	(that)...	…というふりをする

▷ She **pretended to** enjoy the meal, but actually she hated it. 彼女は食事を楽しんでいる風を装ったが,実は嫌いな食べ物だった

▷ "Oh! Really? Are you sure?" said Shirley. She **pretended to be** surprised. 「あら,ほんとう?確かなの?」とシャーリーは言って,驚いたふりをした

▷ Don't **pretend that** you didn't hear me! 私の言うことが聞こえなかったふりをするな

| try to | pretend (that)... | …だというふりをしようとする |

▷ **Try to pretend that** you're enjoying yourself! 楽しんでいるふりをしようとしなさい

pretty /príti/ **形** かわいらしい;すてきな

exceptionally	pretty	並はずれてかわいい
really	pretty	すごくかわいい

▷I think your sister is **exceptionally pretty**. あなたの妹は並はずれてかわいいと思う
▷That dress makes you look **really pretty**! そのドレスを着るときみ、とてもかわいいよ

prevent /privént/ 動 妨げる；防ぐ

effectively	prevent	効果的に防ぐ

▷The new law **effectively prevents** smoking in public places. 新しい法律のおかげで公共の場所での喫煙が効果的に防げている

prevent A	(from) doing	Aが…するのを妨げる

▷The security guard **prevented** him **from** entering the building. 警備員は彼を建物に入れさせなかった

price /práis/

名 価格, 値段；代価

set	prices	価格を設定する
charge	prices	価格をつける
raise	prices	価格を上げる
increase	prices	
cut	prices	価格を下げる
reduce	prices	
affect	prices	価格に影響を及ぼす
keep	prices down	価格を低く抑える
keep	prices low	
pay	the price	(比喩的に)代価を支払う

▷Apparently several petrol companies had a meeting to **set** the same gasoline **prices**. どうやら石油会社数社がガソリンの同一価格を設定しようと会合をもったようだ
▷Some department stores have **cut prices** by up to 50%. 5割まで値下げするデパートもある
▷The increase in demand will **affect prices**. 需要の増加は価格に影響を与える
▷Our company is doing its best to **keep prices down**. わが社は最善を尽くして価格を低く抑えている
▷If you don't give up smoking you'll **pay** the **price** later. たばこをやめなければ後でつけがくるよ

a price	rises	価格が上がる
a price	increases	
a price	goes up	
a price	falls	価格が下がる
a price	goes down	
a price	includes A	価格はAを含む

▷The **price** of electricity is going to **rise** again soon. 電気料金はまたすぐに上がるだろう
▷The **price includes** sales tax. その価格には売上税が含まれる

a high	price	高い価格
a low	price	低い価格
a fair	price	適正価格
a reasonable	price	手ごろな値段
a competitive	price	競争価格
full	price	全額
half	price	半額
a good	price	よい値段, 高値
an average	price	平均価格
a fixed	price	定価, 固定価格
stock	prices	株価
bond	prices	債券価格
house	prices	住宅価格
land	prices	地価
food	prices	食料価格
oil	prices	原油価格
electricity	prices	電気料金
the market	price	市場価格
the purchase	price	仕入れ価格
the retail	price	小売価格

▷You have to pay a very **high price** for some brand goods. ブランド品の中にはとても高くつく品物もある
▷I'm willing to pay a **fair price**. 適正価格を払っても構いません
▷I was able to get a flight back home for a **reasonable price**. 手ごろな値段で帰国便の航空機チケットが手に入った
▷We don't have to pay the **full price** for the hotel. There's a reduction. ホテル代を全額支払う必要はない. 割引がある
▷Today they're selling lots of things off in the supermarket at **half price**. きょうはスーパーで半額セールの品物が多い

a price	for A	Aに対する価格

▷What's the **price for** a week's package tour to South Korea? 韓国への1週間のパックツアーはいくらですか

PHRASES
What price A? 😊 Aはいったい何の価値があるのか；(見込みはなさそうだが)…はどうか ▷"What price a 2-week holiday in Alaska?" "You must be joking! It's the middle of winter!" 「アラスカへ2週間遊びに

| pride |

行くのはどんなもんだろう」「冗談だろ．真冬だよ」

pride /práid/

名 自尊心，誇り，プライド；うぬぼれ

hurt	A's pride	プライドを傷つける
wound	A's pride	
injure	A's pride	
swallow	one's pride	プライドを捨てる
take	pride in A	Aを誇りにする
restore	pride	誇りを取り戻させる
salvage	pride	

▷ When you refused to go on a date with him you **hurt** his **pride**! 彼とのデートをあなたが断ったから彼はプライドが傷ついたのよ
▷ **Swallow** your **pride** and accept the money. プライドを捨ててお金を受け取れよ
▷ Bill **takes** great **pride in** his promotion to Head of the Sales Department. ビルは営業部長に昇進したことをとても誇りに思っている

great	pride	大きな誇り
national	pride	国家の威信

★× big pride とはいわない．「プライドが高い」は be (very) proud を用いて，He is (very) proud. のようにいう

▷ She takes **great pride** in her cooking skills. 彼女は料理の腕に大きな誇りがある
▷ There was a great feeling of **national pride** when Italy won the World Cup. イタリアがワールドカップに勝って国に対する誇りの感情が大きく高まった

A's pride and joy		自慢と喜びの種

▷ Their new baby is their **pride and joy**. 生まれたばかりの赤ん坊は彼らの自慢と喜びの種だ

principle /prínsəpl/

名 原則，原理；主義，方針

establish	a principle	原則を打ち立てる
apply	the principle	原則を適用する
illustrate	the principle	原則を表す
be based on	the principle	原則に基づいている
stick to	one's principles	主義を守り通す
stand by	one's principles	

▷ I think we need to **establish** a **principle** here. こちらで原則を打ち立てる必要がある
▷ I think we should **apply** the **principle** of "first come, first served."「先着順」の原則を適用すべきだと思う
▷ Darwin's theory of evolution is **based on** the **principle** that only the fittest survive. ダーウィンの進化論は適者だけが生き残るという原則に基づいている

a basic	principle	基本原則
a fundamental	principle	
a general	principle	一般原則
a guiding	principle	指針

▷ A **basic principle** of our company is that "the customer is always right." わが社の基本原則の一つは「お客様は常に正しい」ということだ
▷ It's a **general principal** in society that if you break the law you will be punished. 法律に違反すれば罰せられるというのが社会の一般原則だ
▷ Most religions have a set of **guiding principles** that we should follow. たいていの宗教には信者が従う一連の指針がある

in	principle	原則として
on	principle	主義として
against	A's principles	主義に反して

▷ We agree **in principle** to all your requests. あなたが求めていることにすべて大筋で合意します

a matter of	principle	原則の問題

▷ I'm not going to apologize. It's a **matter of principle**. 謝るつもりはない．原則の問題だから

print /prínt/

名 印刷；印刷された字体；印刷物

go into	print	印刷される；出版される

▷ The new dictionary will be **going into print** in early November. 新刊の辞書が11月初旬に出版されることになっている

large	print	大きな活字
small	print	小さな活字
bold	print	太字
color	print	カラー印刷

▷ Does the library have any **large print** books? その図書館には大活字本がありますか
▷ You should read the **small print** before you sign the contract. 契約書にサインする前に細かな文字で印刷された部分を読んだほうがいい

in	print	印刷になって
out of	print	絶版になって

▷It's an old book but it's still **in print**. それは古い本だがまだ出版されている
▷I'm sorry, this book's **out of print**. 申し訳ありません．この本は絶版です

priority /praiɔ́:rəti | -ɔ́r-/

名 優先，優先権；優先事項

give	priority to A	Aを優先する
set	priorities	優先順位を決める
establish	priorities	
take	priority	優先する
have	priority	

▷At airports the staff **give priority to** first-class passengers. 空港ではスタッフはファーストクラスの乗客を優先する
▷Pregnant women and the elderly **take priority** over others on trains and buses. 妊娠中の女性や高齢者は列車やバスで他の乗客たちより優先する
▷We should **have priority**. We were first in line! こっちが先だぞ．列の先頭に並んだんだから

a high	priority	高い優先度
a top	priority	最優先
a low	priority	低い優先度

▷Is staying in a five-star hotel **a high** or **low priority** for you? 5つ星ホテルでの宿泊はあなたにとって優先度は高いですか，低いですか
▷Maintaining our high standard of service is a **top priority** for us. 高水準のサービスを維持することは私たちにとって最優先だ

a list of	priorities	優先リスト
order of	priority	優先順序

▷We can't do everything immediately. We need to draw up a **list of priorities**. 全部をいますぐすることはできない．優先リストをつくる必要がある

prison /prízn/

名 刑務所，監獄；投獄

go to		prison	刑務所に入る
send A to		prison	A(人)を刑務所へ送る
put A in		prison	
escape from		prison	脱獄する
come out of		prison	刑務所から出る
be released from		prison	

▷He **went to prison** for drunken driving. 彼は飲酒運転で刑務所に入った
▷He was **sent to prison** for terrorist activities. 彼はテロ活動を行ったため刑務所に送られた
▷They **put** him **in prison** for selling drugs. 麻薬の売買で彼は投獄された
▷Two terrorists have just **escaped from prison**. テロリストが2名脱獄した
▷He's due to be **released from prison** in three weeks' time. 彼は3週間後には刑務所から釈放されることになっている

in	prison	刑務所に入って

▷The bank robbers were sentenced to eight years **in prison**. 銀行強盗たちに懲役8年の判決が下された

private /práivət/

形 私的な，個人的な；私有の

purely	private	まったく私的な
strictly	private	極秘の；まったく私的な

▷This isn't official. It's **purely** my **private** opinion. これは公式見解ではなく，まったく私の個人的な意見だ
▷This information is **strictly private**. Just between you and me. このことは極秘だよ．ここだけの話にしてよ

public and private	官民の；公私の

★private and public も用いる

▷You should be careful to distinguish between your **public and private** life. 公の生活と私的生活とを注意して区別すべきだ

prize /práiz/ 名 賞，賞品

award	a prize	賞を与える
give	a prize	
present	a prize	賞を贈る
receive	a prize	賞を受ける
win	a prize	賞をとる
get	a prize	
take	a prize	

▷She was **awarded** a **prize** for her graduation thesis. 彼女は卒業論文で賞をもらった
▷The headmaster **presented** a **prize** to my daughter at school today. 校長先生はうちの娘にきょう学校で賞を手渡してくれた

| problem |

▷My son's team **received** a **prize** for their science project. うちの息子のチームは科学プロジェクトで受賞した

▷My brother's really good at sports. He's **won** many **prizes**. 弟はすごくスポーツが得意で,賞をいっぱいとった

a big	prize	大きな賞
a great	prize	
a major	prize	
a special	prize	特別賞
first	prize	1等賞
second	prize	2等賞
third	prize	3等賞
the top	prize	トップ賞

▷It would be great to win a **big prize** on a TV game show. テレビのゲーム番組で高額賞金がもらえたらいいなあ

▷You won a holiday for two in Hawaii? Wow! That's a really **great prize**. ハワイへのカップル旅行が当たったのかい.すごいね,大当たりだね

▷We won the **top prize** in the cheerleading competition! チアリーディング競技でうちのチームはトップ賞を取った

prize	for A	Aに対する賞

▷He won the Nobel **Prize for** Literature. 彼はノーベル文学賞を受賞した

problem /prábləm | prɔ́b-/ 名 問題

have	a problem	問題がある
present	a problem	問題を提起する
pose	a problem	
cause	a problem	問題を引き起こす
face	a problem	問題に直面する
tackle	a problem	問題に取り組む
address	a problem	
deal with	a problem	問題に対処する
overcome	a problem	問題を克服する
solve	a problem	問題を解決する
resolve	a problem	

▷"We **have** a bit of **problem**." "What kind of a problem?"「ちょっと問題があるんです」「どんな問題ですか」

▷Changing the dates of our holiday shouldn't **present** a **problem**. 休暇の日取りを変えたって何の問題もないだろう

▷I don't want to **cause** you any **problems**. あなたにめんどうをかけたくありません

▷We need some help to **tackle** this **problem**. この問題に取り組むには少し手助けがいる

▷We need to try harder to **overcome** our **problems**. 問題克服のためにわれわれはもっと努力が必要だ

▷If we had some more money it would **solve** all our **problems**. もう少しお金があったらわれわれの抱える問題はすべて解決するだろう

a problem	arises	問題が起こる
a problem	lies	問題がある
a problem	remains	問題が残る

▷The **problem lies in** his attitude to work. 問題は彼の勤務態度にある

▷We all agree we need to increase sales, but the **problem remains** how are we going to do it? 売り上げを伸ばす必要がある点ではみんな同意だけど,どうやって伸ばすかの問題は残る

a big	problem	大きな問題
the main	problem	主要な問題
a major	problem	重要な問題
a serious	problem	深刻な問題
a minor	problem	小さな問題
a real	problem	本当の問題
an attitude	problem	問題ある態度
a financial	problem	お金の問題
a social	problem	社会問題

▷The **main problem** is to find a hotel for tonight. 今夜のホテルを見つけるのがさしあたっての主要な問題だ

▷We're having **major problems** at our factory. うちの工場は重要な問題を抱えている

▷I don't have an **attitude problem**! ぼくの態度に問題はないよ

▷Homeless people are becoming an important **social problem**. ホームレスは重要な社会問題になりつつある

the problem	of A	Aの問題
a problem	with A	Aにおける問題

▷Because of heavy rain the **problem of** flooding has increased. 大雨のために洪水の問題が増大した

▷The **problem with** living here is that it takes me over 2 hours to get to work. ここで暮らすことの問題は通勤に2時間以上かかることだ

the problems	associated with A	Aと関連した問題

▷He talked about the familiar **problems associated with** global warming. 彼は地球温暖化と関連してよく取り上げられる問題について話した

a solution to	a problem	問題の解決法

▷We have to find a **solution to** this **problem** quickly. この問題の解決法を早急に見つけなければならない

the problem	is (that)...	問題は…だ

▷**The problem is that** I have no idea where to start. 問題はどこから手をつけてよいかわからないことだ
[PHRASES]
No problem. ☺ 問題ありません ▷"Can we postpone the meeting until tomorrow?" "Sure. No problem."「会議をあすに延ばせますか」「いいですよ，問題ありません」

process /práses | próu-/

名 過程；工程；(時の)経過

begin	the process	過程を始める
start	the process	
complete	the process	過程を完了する
describe	the process	過程を説明する
repeat	the process	過程を繰り返す

▷They're going to **begin** the **process** of interviewing candidates tomorrow. あす応募者への面接が始まる予定だ
▷It took nearly 5 hours to **complete** the **process** of applying for a visa. ビザの申請を完了するのに5時間ほどかかった
▷The scientist **described** the **process** of turning seawater into drinking water. その科学者は海水を飲料水に変える過程について説明した
▷If you don't fill in these forms properly you'll have to **repeat** the whole **process**. 書類にきちんと記入しないと最初からやり直さなければならなくなるよ

a slow	process	ゆっくりした過程
a complex	process	複雑な過程
a natural	process	自然の営み
the aging	process	老化の過程
the democratic	process	民主的過程
the political	process	政治的過程
the learning	process	学習過程
the peace	process	和平過程
the selection	process	選考過程
the manufacturing	process	製造過程
the production	process	生産過程
the whole	process	全過程

▷Making wine is a **complex process**. ワインができるまでの過程は複雑だ
▷Milk can be turned into cheese by a **natural process**. ミルクがチーズになる過程には自然の営みがかかわっている
▷Is it possible to slow the **aging process**? 老化の過程を遅らせることは可能だろうか
▷The President was elected by a **democratic process**. 大統領は民主的な過程を踏んで選ばれた
▷The **whole process** is carried out by computer. 全過程をコンピュータが実行してくれる

in	the process of doing	…する過程で

▷Lots of things were damaged **in** the **process** of mov**ing** house. 引っ越しの過程で多くの物が破損した

product /prádʌkt | pród-/

名 生産物，製品；成果

develop	a product	製品を開発する
design	a product	製品を設計する
produce	a product	製品を生み出す
market	a product	製品を売り出す
supply	a product	製品を供給する
sell	a product	製品を売る
buy	a product	製品を買う

▷It will take a lot of time to **develop** a new **product**. 新製品開発に多くの時間がかかるだろう
▷We need to **produce** a cheaper **product**. もっと安い製品を生み出す必要がある
▷We're having problems **marketing** our **products**. わが社の製品の売り込みに苦労している

the finished	product	完成品
a quality	product	高品質製品
waste	products	廃棄物
agricultural	products	農産物
meat	products	肉製品
dairy	products	乳製品

▷This is where we store the **finished product**. ここに完成品を保管してあります
▷**Agricultural products** have been badly affected by the floods. 農産物は洪水による影響をひどく受けた

production /prədʌ́kʃən/

名 生産，製造，製作；生産物，製品

be in	production	生産されている
go into	production	生産に入る
go out of	production	生産をやめる
start	production	生産を開始する
boost	production	生産を増やす
increase	production	
control	the production	生産を制御する

| profession |

cut	production	生産を減らす
reduce	production	
cease	production	生産を停止する
stop	production	

▷ A new type of smartphone is already **in production**. 新型のスマートフォンがすでに生産されている
▷ More and more 3D TVs are planned to **go into production** next year. 来年は生産を開始する3Dテレビがますます増える予定だ
▷ If demand falls we will have to **cut production**. 需要が落ちたら減産しなければならないだろう
▷ Next year we're planning to **increase production** by 10%. 来年度は生産を1割増やす計画だ

agricultural	production	農業生産
food	production	食糧生産
industrial	production	鉱工業生産
increased	production	増産
mass	production	大量生産
energy	production	エネルギー生産
oil	production	石油生産

▷ **Agricultural production** has increased because of the use of modern machinery. 農業生産高は最新機器の使用のおかげで増加した
▷ The use of robots in our factory has led to **increased production**. 工場でロボットを使うことで増産につながった
▷ **Mass production** helps us to lower costs. 大量生産はコストを抑える助けになる

profession /prəféʃən/

名 職業, 専門職(★弁護士・医師・聖職者・教師など)

enter	a profession	専門職に就く
join	a profession	
go into	a profession	
leave	a profession	専門職を辞める

▷ I want my son to **enter a profession**: teacher, doctor, lawyer. 息子には教員, 医師, 弁護士といった専門職に就いてほしい
▷ My mother used to be a high school teacher, but she **left the profession** two years ago. 母は以前は高校の教師だったが2年前に職を辞した

the legal	profession	法曹界
the medical	profession	医療関係者
the teaching	profession	教職

▷ You'll have to study very hard if you want to enter the **legal profession**. 法曹の仕事に就きたいなら一生懸命に勉強しなければならない

▷ You have to work very long hours if you want to join the **medical profession**. 医療の世界に入りたいなら長時間労働することになるよ

by	profession	職業は

▷ She's a lawyer **by profession**. 彼女の職業は弁護士です

profit /práfit | prɔ́f-/ 名 利益, もうけ

make	a profit	利益を上げる
earn	profits	
show	a profit	利益が出る

▷ My father's business **made** a good **profit** this year. 父の商売は今年かなり利益を上げた
▷ We've been in business for 9 months, but we still haven't **shown a profit**. 商売を始めて9か月になるがまだ利益が出ていない

profits	rise	利益が上がる
profits	increase	
profits	fall	利益が下がる

▷ We're hoping **profits** will start to **rise** again next month. 来月からまた利益が上がり始めると期待している
▷ Our boss is really worried. **Profits** are **falling**. うちの上司はすごく心配している. 利益が下がっているものだから

gross	profit	粗利益
net	profit	純利益
pre-tax	profit	税引前利益
after-tax	profit	税引後利益
operating	profit	営業利益
high	profit	高い利益
low	profit	低い利益
annual	profit	年間利益

▷ The figures look good, but that's just **gross profit**, before tax, etc. 数字はよく見えるが, 税金などを引く前の粗利益にすぎない
▷ Our **net profit**, after tax, etc. is still very good. 税やもろもろを引いた純利益もとてもよい
▷ These sales figures don't show a very **high profit**. これらの売上数字を見るとあまり高い利益は出ていない

profit	from A	Aからの利益
profit	on A	Aでの利益
at a	profit	利益を上げて
for	profit	利益追求のために

▷ **Profits from** our sales abroad are greater than from sales at home. 海外売上から上がる利益のほう

profit and loss	損益
★日本語と語順が逆	

▷These figures show our **profit and loss** over the last 6 months. これらの数字はここ半年の損益を示している

program /próugræm/

名 計画，予定；番組；(催し物の) プログラム；(コンピュータの) プログラム

draw up	a program	計画を立案する
launch	a program	計画を立ち上げる
watch	a program	番組を見る
see	a program	
run	a program	プログラムを実行する

▷Let's **draw up** a **program** of interesting places to visit while we're on holiday. 休暇中に出かける楽しい場所の計画を立てよう

▷"Where's your dad?" "He's **watching** a TV **program**."「お父さんはどこ？」「テレビ番組を見ているよ」

a program	aims to do	計画は…を目指している
a program	includes A	プログラムにAが含まれる

▷This **program aims to** examine the reasons behind the present economic crisis. この番組は現在の経済危機の背景にある理由の分析を目指している

▷The concert **program** this evening **includes** pieces by Beethoven and Mozart. 今晩のコンサートのプログラムにはベートーベンとモーツァルトの曲が含まれている

an economic	program	経済計画
an investment	program	投資計画
a development	program	開発計画
a recovery	program	復興計画
a research	program	研究計画
a conservation	program	保存計画
a nuclear	program	核開発計画
an educational	program	教育課程
a training	program	研修プログラム
a television	program	テレビ番組
a radio	program	ラジオ番組
a news	program	ニュース番組

▷The government's **economic program** has totally failed. 政府の経済計画は完全に失敗した

▷The government has introduced a new **educational program** for elementary schools. 政府は小学校に新教育課程を導入した

▷Our **nuclear program** needs to be carefully reconsidered. われわれの核開発計画は注意深く再考する必要がある

a program	for A	Aのための計画

▷I asked the sports center to draw up a fitness **program for** me. スポーツセンターに自分用のフィットネスプログラムを組んでくれるよう頼んだ

progress /prágres | próu-/

名 進歩，進展；経過

make	progress	進歩する
monitor	A's progress	経過を調べる
track	A's progress	

▷Finally we're **making** some **progress**! とうとう進展があったぞ

▷My aunt is recovering in hospital. The doctors are **monitoring** her **progress**. おばは病院で療養中で、医師たちに経過を診てもらっている

considerable	progress	かなりの進展
good	progress	
significant	progress	
little	progress	少しの進展
rapid	progress	急速な進展
slow	progress	緩慢な進展
steady	progress	着実な進展
further	progress	さらなる進展

▷Every day I practice karate. I think I'm making **good progress**. 毎日空手の練習をしていて，かなり上達していると思う

▷They've been making **rapid progress**. 彼らは急速に上達している

▷I'm making very **slow progress** writing my essay. レポートの執筆が遅々として進まない

progress	toward A	Aに向けての進展
progress	on A	Aでの進展
progress	in A	
in	progress	進行中で

▷Have you made any **progress toward** finding a solution yet? 解決法を見つける筋道は見つかりましたか

▷Have you made any **progress on** your research project yet? あなたは研究プロジェクトで進展がありましたか

| project |

▷The meeting is still **in progress**. まだ会議は進行中だ

| a lack of | progress | 進展不足 |

▷What are the reasons for the **lack of progress**? 進展がない理由は何ですか

project /prάdʒekt | prɔ́dʒ-/

名 事業, プロジェクト

carry out	a project	事業を手がける
undertake	a project	事業に乗り出す
work on	a project	事業を進める
complete	a project	事業を仕上げる
fund	a project	事業に資金を出す
support	a project	事業を支援する

▷We're **carrying out** a **project** on global warming. 地球温暖化に関するプロジェクトを手がけている
▷I think we're **undertaking** a very difficult **project**. 進行中のプロジェクトは困難なものだと思う
▷I'm **working on** a new **project**. 新プロジェクトを進めている
▷We **completed** the **project** last week. プロジェクトは先週完成した
▷We need to find someone to help us **fund** the **project**. プロジェクトの資金手当を助けてくれる人を探す必要がある

a major	project	大プロジェクト
a special	project	特別プロジェクト
a specific	project	特定のプロジェクト
a development	project	開発プロジェクト
an investment	project	投資プロジェクト
a pilot	project	試験プロジェクト
a research	project	研究プロジェクト

▷My boss wants me to work with him on **a major project**. 上司は大プロジェクトで私にいっしょに働いてほしいと思っている

| the aim of | the project | プロジェクトの目標 |

▷The **aim of the project** is to improve service to our customers. プロジェクトの目標は顧客サービスの向上だ

| a project | to do | …する計画 |

▷The group have began a **project to** clean up the lake. その団体は湖をきれいにする計画を始めた

promise /prάmis | prɔ́m-/

名 約束；将来への期待, 見込み

make	a promise	約束する
give	a promise	
fulfill	a promise	約束を果たす；期待に応える
keep	a promise	約束を守る
break	a promise	約束を破る
hold	promise	期待を持たせる
show	promise	

▷She **made** a **promise** to be my best friend for ever. 彼女はずっと私のいちばんの親友であり続けると約束した
▷Everybody thought he would be a great golfer and now he's **fulfilled** that **promise**. だれもが彼は偉大なゴルファーになると思ったが, みごと期待に応えた
▷Don't trust him. He never **keeps** his **promise**. 彼を信じてはいけないよ. 決して約束を守らない男だから
▷I never **break** a **promise**! 私は約束を決して破ったりしない
▷Have you seen Sally run the 100 meters? She **holds a** lot **of promise**. サリーが100メートルを走るのを見たことがあるかい. かなり見込みがあるよ

a broken	promise	破られた約束
a false	promise	偽りの約束
a vague	promise	あいまいな約束
great	promise	有望

▷She left her boyfriend because of all his **broken promises**. 彼女はボーイフレンドがいつも約束を破るので別れた
▷He said he would help me, but it turned out to be a **false promise**. 彼は私を助けると言ったが期待は裏切られた
▷Picasso's early paintings showed **great promise**. ピカソの初期絵画は輝かしい将来を予見させた

| a promise | to do | …する約束 |

▷He gave me a **promise to** email me regularly from Canada. 彼はカナダから定期的に私にメールを送ると約束してくれた

promote /prəmóut/

動 促進する, 推進する；売り込む；昇進させる

| actively | promote | 積極的に推進する |
| heavily | promote | 大いに売り込む |

▷We need to do more to **actively promote** our

product. うちの製品を積極的に売り込むためにもっと手を尽くす必要がある

aim to	promote A	Aの促進をねらう
be designed to	promote A	Aの促進が図られる

▷ We **aim to promote** more information about the dangers of overeating. 食べすぎの危険についてもっと情報を周知させるつもりだ
▷ This government campaign is **designed to promote** healthier lifestyles. この政府キャンペーンはより健康な生活スタイルの促進を目指している

promote A	to B	AをBに昇進させる

▷ Great news! You're going to be **promoted to** section chief. いい知らせだ．きみは課長に昇進だ

promotion /prəmóuʃən/

名 昇進；促進；販売促進

get	promotion	昇進する
win	promotion	
gain	promotion	
deny	a promotion	昇進させない
do	a promotion	販売促進する

▷ Tom's aim is to **get promotion** within 12 months. トムの目標は1年以内に昇進することだ

internal	promotion	内部昇進
rapid	promotion	早い昇進
automatic	promotion	自動的な昇進

▷ She achieved **rapid promotion** within her company. 彼女は社内ですぐに昇進した

proof /prú:f/ 名 証拠，証明，立証

have	proof	証拠がある
give	proof	証拠を提供する
provide	proof	
require	proof	証拠を必要とする

▷ Do you **have proof** of what you're saying? あなたが言っていることに証拠はあるのか
▷ You'll need to **give proof** of your identity. あなたは身元をきちんと証明する必要がある
▷ The police will **require proof** before they arrest her. 警察は彼女を逮捕するのに証拠が必要だ

conclusive	proof	決定的証拠
final	proof	最終的な証拠
further	proof	さらなる証拠
living	proof	生きた証拠

▷ We think she stole the money, but we can't find **conclusive proof**. 彼女が金を盗んだと思うが，決定的な証拠が見つからない
▷ We need **further proof** before we contact the police. 警察に連絡する前にもっと証拠が必要だ
▷ My aunt is **living proof** that it's possible to recover from cancer. おばががんが治るものだという生きた証拠だ

proof	that...	…という証拠

▷ Her face turned bright red. It's **proof that** she was lying! 彼女の顔は真っ赤になった．彼女がうそをついている証拠だ

proper /prápər | prɔ́pə/

形 適切な，ふさわしい；礼儀正しい

perfectly	proper	まったくふさわしい
quite	proper	

▷ I think that it's **perfectly proper** to complain about the noise from your next-door neighbors. 隣家からの騒音に苦情を言うのはまったく正当なことだよ

property /prápərti | prɔ́p-/

名 物件，財産，所有物；不動産，土地；特性

buy	property	物件を買う
sell	property	物件を売る
have	property	物件を所有する
own	property	
obtain	property	物件を手に入れる

★ have より own のほうが改まった言い方

▷ Now is not a good time to **sell property**. いまは物件を売るのによい時期ではない
▷ He **has property** in the middle of Tokyo. 彼は東京の真ん中に不動産を持っている
▷ It's difficult to **obtain property** in the downtown area. 都心で不動産を手に入れるのは難しい

intellectual	property	知的財産
private	property	私有財産，私有地
personal	property	動産，人的財産
stolen	property	盗品

| proportion |

| commercial | property | 商業用不動産 |

▷ If you write a book it's your **intellectual property**. You have copyright. 本を書けばそれはあなたの知的財産だ．あなたに著作権がある
▷ We can't go onto this land. It's **private property**. この土地に立ち入ることはできない．私有地だから
▷ A lot of **stolen property** is kept at the police station. 盗品がたくさん警察署で保管されている

proportion /prəpɔ́ːrʃən/

名 割合，比率；釣り合い

| reach | ... proportions | …の規模に達する |

▷ This year's influenza outbreak has **reached** epidemic **proportions**. 今年はインフルエンザが大流行といえる規模で発生した

a high	proportion	高い割合
a great	proportion	大きい割合
a large	proportion	
a significant	proportion	かなりの割合
a substantial	proportion	
a low	proportion	低い割合
a small	proportion	小さな割合
direct	proportion	正比例
inverse	proportion	反比例

★「割合」の意味では，程度を表す副詞 relatively「比較的」と結びつくことが多い)

▷ Developed nations have a relatively **high proportion** of people over 65. 先進国では65歳を超える人々の割合が比較的高い
▷ A **significant proportion** of the population are now unemployed. 人口のうちかなりの割合が現在失業中だ
▷ Only a **small proportion** of rice is imported from Thailand. タイから輸入される米はごくわずかな割合だ

| in proportion | (to A) | (Aに)比例して |
| out of proportion | (to A) | (Aと)不釣り合いで |

▷ The number of traffic accidents increases **in proportion to** the speed of driving. 交通事故の件数は運転速度に比例して増える
▷ In this painting the nose seems to be **out of proportion to** the rest of the face. この絵では鼻が顔の残りの部分と釣り合いがとれていないようだ

| a sense of | proportion | バランス感覚 |

▷ It's important to keep a **sense of proportion**. バランス感覚を保つのが大事だ

propose /prəpóuz/

動 提案する，申し出る；指名する

| be originally | proposed | もともと提案された |

▷ The same plan was **originally proposed** five years ago. 同じ計画が5年前にも提案されていた

| propose | doing | …するよう提案する |

▷ At the meeting the chairman **proposed** cutting overtime rates. 会議で議長は残業手当の割増率を減らす提案をした

| propose | that... | …と提案する |

▷ I **propose that** we (should) elect a new chairman. 新しい委員長を選出するよう提案します

prospect /práspekt | prɔ́s-/

名 見通し，見込み；期待

have	the prospect	見込みがある
see	the prospect	見通しがある
offer	the prospect	見通しを与える
face	the prospect	見通しに直面する
raise	the prospect	見通しが高まる

▷ If you stay in your present job you **have the prospect** of promotion in the near future. いまの仕事にとどまれば近い将来に昇進の見込みがある
▷ I can **see the prospect** of many people losing their jobs in the near future. 私の見通しでは近い将来多くの人が仕事を失うだろう
▷ My new job **offers the prospect** of a lot of foreign travel. 新しい仕事は頻繁に海外出張がありそうだ
▷ Nearly five million people **face the prospect** of starvation. 500万近い人々が飢餓に直面する見通しだ

economic	prospects	経済見通し
growth	prospects	成長見通し
employment	prospects	雇用見通し
future	prospects	将来見通し
a good	prospect	まずまずの見通し
a reasonable	prospect	

▷ At the moment **economic prospects** do not look very good. いまのところ経済見通しはあまりよくない
▷ The **future prospect** of food shortages is very worrying. 食糧不足の将来予測はとても懸念される(★

複数の見通しが考えられる場合は複数形を用いる：His future prospects look very good. 彼の将来の見通しはとても明るそうだ)

▷There's a **good prospect** that the economy will recover next year. 経済は来年にはまず回復するだろう

the prospect	for A	Aへの見通し

▷The **prospect for** getting a government grant is quite good. 政府奨学金をもらえる見込みが高い

protect /prətékt/ 動 守る，保護する

well	protected	十分に保護された
adequately	protected	
fully	protected	

▷If you're going to play American football your body needs to be **well protected**. アメフトをやるなら体を十分に保護する必要がある

protect A	from B	AをBから守る
protect A	against B	

▷Wear a thick coat and muffler to **protect** you **against** catching cold. かぜを引かないよう厚手のコートとマフラーをしなさい

protection /prətékʃən/ 名 保護

provide	protection	保護する
give	protection	
offer	protection	
need	protection	保護を必要とする

▷You should put on some sun cream to **provide protection** against the sun. 日差しから守るために日焼け止めクリームを塗ったほうがいい

▷If you **need protection** from pollen you should wear a mask. 花粉予防が必要ならマスクをしたほうがいい

environmental	protection	環境保護
legal	protection	法的保護

▷Governments now realize the importance of **environmental protection**. 政府は現在では環境保護の重要性を理解している

▷This insurance policy provides you with **legal protection** if you have a traffic accident. この保険があれば交通事故にあっても法的保護が得られる

protection	against A	Aからの防御,
protection	from A	保護

protection	of A	Aの保護
protection	for A	Aに対する保護
under	the protection of A	Aの保護の下で

▷This spray provides **protection against** mosquito bites. このスプレーをしておけば蚊に刺されにくい

▷Today's lecture is on the **protection of** the environment. きょうの講演は環境保護についてです

▷The government has passed laws that provide **protection for** consumers. 政府は消費者を保護する法律を通過させた

▷These rare birds are **under** the **protection of** strict laws. これらの珍しい鳥は法律で厳しく保護されている

protest /próutest/ 名 抗議，異議

make	a protest	抗議する
stage	a protest	抗議行動を行う
lead	a protest	抗議の先頭に立つ

▷I think it's useless to **make** a **protest**. It won't do any good. 抗議してもむだだと思う．何にもならないだろう

▷People are thinking of **staging** a **protest** about the huge increases in gasoline prices. ガソリン価格の大幅な値上がりに大衆は抗議行動をしようと考えている

▷We need someone to **lead** a **protest** against the building of more nuclear plants. さらなる原子力発電所の建設に反対する抗議活動の先頭に立つ人が必要だ

(a) strong	protest	強い抗議
(a) violent	protest	暴力的抗議行動
(a) mass	protest	集団抗議行動
(a) public	protest	大衆抗議行動
(a) political	protest	政治的抗議行動

▷There'll be a **strong protest** if we raise the age for receiving a pension. 年金受給年齢を引き上げれば強い抗議が出るだろう

▷A **mass protest** is taking place in the main square of the city. 街の中央広場で集団抗議行動が起こっている

(a) protest	against A	Aに対する抗議
(a) protest	at A	
in	protest	抗議して

▷There was a **protest against** the raise in local taxes. 地方税増税に反対の声が上がった

▷Many company employees decided to go on strike **in protest** against restructuring. 従業員たちの多くは

| protest |

リストラ反対のストライキに出ると決めた

a howl of	protest	抗議の叫び
a cry of	protest	
a storm of	protest	抗議の嵐
a letter of	protest	抗議の手紙

▷ When the Prime Minister refused to resign there were **howls of protest**. 首相が辞任を拒否すると抗議の声が続々と上がった
▷ I think we should write a **letter of protest**. 抗議文を書いたほうがいいと思う

▌protest /prətést/

動 抗議する,異議を申し立てる；主張する

| protest | strongly | 強く抗議する |
| protest | loudly | 大声で抗議する |

★副詞は動詞の後で用いることが多い

▷ She **protested strongly,** but the plans for reorganization still went ahead. 彼女は強く抗議したが,再編計画はなおも進んだ
▷ She **protested loudly**, but she was forced to leave the meeting. 彼女は大声で抗議したが,会議を退出させられた

protest	about A	Aについて抗議する
protest	against A	Aに抗議する
protest	at A	

▷ Do you know what the demonstrators are **protesting about**? デモ参加者たちは何に抗議しているのか知っていますか
▷ Many people are **protesting against** the Government's decision. 政府の決定に反対の声を上げる人が多い

| protest | that... | …と主張する |

▷ She **protested that** she hadn't done anything wrong. 何も悪いことはしていないと彼女は主張した

▌proud /práud/ 形 誇りに思う,自慢する

| feel | proud | 誇りを感じる |

▷ You came top in your class. Don't you **feel proud**? クラスでいちばんになってさぞ誇らしいでしょう

extremely	proud	非常に誇りに思う
really	proud	とても誇りに思う
justifiably	proud	誇りに思って当然だ
justly	proud	
particularly	proud	特に誇りに思う

▷ I'm **really proud** of you. きみのことを本当に誇りに思う
▷ She was **justifiably proud** of everything that she had achieved. 成し遂げたことのどれをとっても彼女は誇って当然だった
▷ She was **particularly proud** of getting a black belt for karate. 彼女は空手の黒帯をとったのが特に自慢だった

| proud | of A | Aを誇りに思う |

▷ My mother is **proud of** being a good cook. 母は料理上手が自慢だ

| proud | (that...) | …を誇りに思う |

▷ We're really **proud that** you graduated from university. きみが大学を卒業してくれて私たちはとても誇りに思うよ

| proud | to do | …するのを誇りに思う |

▷ I am **proud to** say that my conscience is completely clear. I've done nothing wrong. 誇りをもって言います。私の良心に何らやましいところはありません。何も悪いことをしていないのですから

▌provide /prəváid/

動 与える,供給する,提供する；備える；規定する

| well | provide | 十分に供給する |

▷ After the tsunami the survivors were **well provided** with food and warm clothes. 津波のあと生存者たちには食糧と暖かな衣類が十分供給された

provide A	with B	A(人)にBを提供する
provide B	for A	
provide A	to B	AをB(人)に提供する

▷ Japanese convenience stores often **provide** their customers **with** chopsticks when they buy food. 日本のコンビニでは食品を買った客によくはしをくれる
▷ We need to **provide** food and water **for** the earthquake survivors. 地震を生き延びた人たちに食糧や水を提供する必要がある

| provide | that... | …と規定する |

▷ The contract **provides that** travel expenses will be paid. その契約書には交通費が支払われると規定してある

provision /prəvíʒən/

名 供給,支給;準備;(法律・契約などの)条項

make	provision(s) for A	A(将来の予定)に備える
contain	provision(s)	条項を含む
include	provision(s)	

▷We need to **make provision for** people who arrive in wheelchairs. 車椅子で来る人たちのために備えておく必要がある
▷The new law **contains provisions** for improving safety in factories. 新たな法律には工場の安全性を改善する条項が含まれている

provision	for A	Aに対する準備

▷Our flight attendants make special **provision for** mothers who travel with young babies. 当機の客室乗務員は小さなお子様連れでご搭乗のお母様方に特別な準備をしております

public /pʌ́blik/

名 大衆,一般の人々;(特定の)層,仲間

be open to	the public	一般公開されている

▷The exhibition will be **open to** the **public** next week. 展覧会は来週に一般公開の予定だ

the general	public	一般大衆
the American	public	一般のアメリカ人
the reading	public	一般読者層
the traveling	public	一般旅行者層

▷This information is not available to the **general public**. この情報は一般大衆の手には入らない
▷The **American public** will want to know the truth. 一般のアメリカ人は真実を知りたがるだろう

in	public	人前で,公然と

▷We think the party leader should apologize **in public**. 党首は公の場で謝罪すべきだと思う

public /pʌ́blik/

形 公の,公共の;広く知れ渡った

go	public	公にする,公表する;株式を公開する
make A	public	Aを公表する

▷She's threatening to **go public** and make a scandal! 公表してスキャンダルにすると彼女は脅している
▷The government is going to **make** the report **public** next week. 政府は来週,報告書を公表する予定だ

publish /pʌ́bliʃ/

動 出版する;発表する,公表する

be recently	published	最近出版された
be originally	published	もともと出版された
be previously	published	以前出版された

▷Have you read this book? It's only **recently published**. この本は読みましたか。最近出たばかりですが
▷This book was **originally published** in 1843. この本はもともと1843年に出版された
▷This paperback was **previously published** as a hardback. このペーパーバックは以前ハードカバーで出版された

punish /pʌ́niʃ/ 動 罰する

be severely	punished	厳しく罰せられた

▷If you don't obey the rules you'll be **severely punished**. 規則に従わなければ厳罰ですよ

punish A	for B	A(人)をB(悪事など)のために罰する
punish A	by B	A(人)にBの罰を課す

▷Why did you **punish** my son **for** being late? It wasn't his fault! うちの息子の遅刻をなぜ罰したのですか。息子のせいではなかったのに ▷He was **punished for** being rude to his teacher. 彼は先生に失礼な態度をとって罰せられた(★しばしば受け身で用いる)
▷They **punished** her **by** making her stay late after class. 罰として彼女に放課後遅くまで居残りさせた

purchase /pə́ːrtʃəs/ 名 購入;買い物

make	a purchase	購入する
finance	the purchase	購入資金を調達する
fund	the purchase	購入資金を出す

▷I **made** several interesting **purchases** in the street market yesterday. きのうの露天市でいくつかいい買い物をした
▷I want to buy my own car, but I don't have enough money to **finance** the **purchase**. マイカーを買いたいが購入資金が足りない

| a major | purchase | 大きな買い物 |

▷Buying a house is a **major purchase** for most consumers. 家の購入はたいていの消費者にとって大きな買い物だ

pure /pjúər/ 形 純粋な；きれいな；澄んだ

| pure and simple | まったくの，ただ単なる |

▷Everything she said was a lie. **Pure and simple**. 彼女が言ったことは全部うそだ．まったくのね

purpose /pə́ːrpəs/ 名 目的，意図

have	a purpose	目的がある
achieve	a purpose	目的を達成する
serve	a purpose	目的を果たす
suit	A's purpose	Aの目的に適う
defeat	the purpose of A	Aの本来の目的を損なう

▷All these rules and regulations **have a purpose**. これらの規則や規定にはすべて目的がある
▷We need to decide what **purpose** we want to **achieve**. 達成したい目的が何なのか決める必要がある
▷It **serves** no **purpose** to complain all the time. 不平ばかり言っていても何の役にも立たない

the main	purpose	主要目的
the primary	purpose	
one's original	purpose	本来の目的
a common	purpose	共通の目的
a specific	purpose	特定の目的
the real	purpose	真の目的

▷The **main purpose** of this meeting is to get to know each other. この会議の主要目的はお互いを知ることだ
▷We mustn't forget what our **original purpose** was. われわれは本来の目的が何だったのか忘れてはならない
▷These tests are designed for a **specific purpose**. これらの試験は特別の目的のために作成されている
▷What's the **real purpose** of your visit? あなたの訪問の本当の目的は何ですか

on	purpose	わざと，故意に
for	the purpose of doing	…するために
a purpose	in A	Aにおける目的

▷You did that **on purpose**! あなた，わざとやったのね

▷This room is used **for** the **purpose of** holding meetings. この部屋は会議用に使われる
▷You need to have a **purpose in** life. 人生に目的をもたなくてはいけない

pursue /pərsúː | -sjúː/
動 追う，追跡する；追い求める

| actively | pursue | 積極的に追い求める |

▷We're **actively pursuing** our plan to open more stores in the center of Tokyo. 東京の中心にさらに店舗をオープンする計画を積極的に推し進めている

put /pút/ 動 置く，入れる；表現する

put	A cleverly	Aをうまく表現する
put	A well	
put	A succinctly	Aを簡潔に表現する
put	A simply	Aを簡単に表現する

▷The Prime Minister **put** the problem very **well**. "No money, no health service!" 首相は「財源がなければ医療サービスもない」と問題をうまいことばで表現した
▷Let me **put** this **simply**. 簡潔に言わせてください

| put A | on B | AをB(場所)に置く |

▷She **put** a vase of flowers **on** the table. 彼女は花瓶をテーブルに置いた

| put A | in B | AをBに入れる |
| put A | into B | |

▷Don't **put** too much sugar **in** your coffee. コーヒーに砂糖を入れすぎないようにしなさい
▷**Put** the flour and salt **into** a bowl. 小麦粉と塩をボウルに入れてください

puzzle /pʌ́zl/ 名 パズル；難問

| solve | a puzzle | パズルを解く |

▷Tim's really good at **solving puzzles**. ティムはパズルを解くのがすごく得意だ

| a crossword | puzzle | クロスワードパズル |
| a jigsaw | puzzle | ジグソーパズル |

Q

qualification /kwɑ̀ləfikéiʃən | kwɔ̀l-/

名 資格；技能；留保(条件)

get	a qualification	資格を得る
gain	a qualification	
obtain	a qualification	
have	a qualification	資格がある
hold	a qualification	
lead to	a qualification	資格につながる
improve	qualifications	技能を高める
lack	qualifications	技能を欠く
require	a qualification	留保を必要とする
need	a qualification	

▷You should try to **get a qualification**. 資格をとるようにしたほうがいい(★ gain, obtain は改まった言い方)
▷Do you **have** any **qualifications**? 何か資格をもっていますか
▷You should do a course that **leads to a qualification**. 資格につながる講座を受けたほうがいい
▷I'm trying to **improve** my **qualifications**. 技能を高めるよう努めています

a formal	qualification	正式な資格
entry	qualifications	入会資格
paper	qualifications	資格証明書
a professional	qualification	専門資格
a vocational	qualification	職業資格
a recognized	qualification	認定資格
academic	qualifications	修了資格

▷She doesn't have any **formal qualifications**. 彼女には正式な資格は何もない
▷Her **paper qualifications** are excellent. 彼女の資格証明書は申し分ない
▷You need to get a **vocational qualification** of some kind. あなたは何らかの職業資格を取得する必要がある

a qualification	for A	Aの資格
a qualification	in A	A(分野)の資格
without	qualification	留保なしの
with	qualifications	留保つきの

▷She has all the right **qualifications for** the job. 彼女にはその仕事に適したあらゆる資格がある
▷If you want to work in the export department you'll need a **qualification in** English. 輸出部門で働きたいのなら英語の資格が必要だろう
▷I agree to your proposal **without qualification**. 留保なしであなたの提案に賛成します

a qualification	to do	…する能力

▷I don't have the **qualifications to** apply for that job. 私にはその仕事に応募する資格がない

qualifications and experience	資格と経験

★ experience and qualifications も用いる

▷They're looking for somebody with **qualifications and experience**. 彼らは資格と経験のある人を探している

qualified /kwɑ́ləfàid | kwɔ́l-/

形 資格のある；条件つきの

well	qualified	十分に資格のある
suitably	qualified	
fully	qualified	正式に資格のある

▷I think you're **well qualified** for the job. あなたはその仕事に十分な資格があると思う
▷Next year she'll be **fully qualified** as a doctor. 来年に彼女は正式な医師の資格を得るだろう

qualified	to do	…する資格のある

▷You're not **qualified to** give advice on this matter. きみにはこの件で忠告する資格はない

quality /kwɑ́ləti | kwɔ́l-/

名 質, 品質；特質, 特性

maintain	(the) quality	質を維持する
improve	(the) quality	質をよくする
enhance	(the) quality	質を高める

▷They were unable to **maintain** the **quality** of their product. 彼らは製品の質を維持できなかった
▷We need to **improve** the **quality** of our service. サービスの質を上げる必要がある
▷Using fresh tomatoes **enhances** the **quality** of the sauce. 新鮮なトマトを使うとソースの質がよくなる

good	quality	良質
high	quality	上質
top	quality	最高品質
poor	quality	低品質
low	quality	

▷This is a cloth of **high quality**. これは上質の生地だ
▷The food at this restaurant is **top quality**. このレ

ストランの食べ物の質は最高だ
▷ This suit is really rather **poor quality**. このスーツはとんでもなく質が悪い

quantity /kwάntəti | kwɔ́n-/

名 量；分量，数量

a large	quantity	大量
a great	quantity	
a huge	quantity	
a vast	quantity	
a considerable	quantity	かなりの量
a substantial	quantity	相当な量
a small	quantity	少量
a sufficient	quantity	十分な量
an unknown	quantity	未知数

★ ×a big quantity とはいわない

▷ Milk contains **large quantities** of calcium. ミルクはカルシウムをたくさん含んでいる
▷ A **huge quantity** of food is wasted and thrown away every day. 大量の食料がむだになって毎日捨てられている
▷ There are still many places where oil exists in **vast quantities**. 石油が大量に存在する場所がいまだにたくさんある
▷ Fishermen have been catching only a **small quantity** of fish recently. 近ごろは漁師はわずかな量の魚しかとれない
▷ An **unknown quantity** of pollution may have got into the sea. 量は不明だが，汚染物質が海に流れ込んだかもしれない

a quantity	of A	Aの量；大量のA
in	quantity	大量に

▷ Avoid eating large **quantities of** food in the evening. 晩にたくさん食べるのは避けなさい
▷ You can get things cheaper if you buy **in quantity**. まとめ買いしていただければ割安になります

quantity and quality		量と質

★ quality and quantity も用いられる

▷ **Quantity and quality** are two very different things. So, please write a shorter, better essay! 量と質とはまるで別のものだから、もっと簡潔にもっとよいレポートを書いてください

quarter /kwɔ́:rtər/

名 4分の1；15分；四半期，3か月

a quarter	of A	Aの4分の1

▷ **A quarter of** our sales are overseas. 売り上げの4分の1が海外だ

a quarter	of seven	7時15分前
(英) a quarter	to seven	
a quarter	after seven	7時15分過ぎ
(英) a quarter	past seven	

▷ It's a **quarter of** seven. 7時15分前です
▷ Let's meet at a **quarter after** seven. 7時15分に会おう

the first	quarter	第1四半期
the second	quarter	第2四半期
the third	quarter	第3四半期
the fourth	quarter	第4四半期
the last	quarter	

▷ Prices rose by 0.5% during the **first quarter** of this year. 今年度の第1四半期に物価が0.5％上がった

question /kwéstʃən/

名 質問；試験問題；懸案，問題；疑問点，疑義

have	a question	質問がある
ask	a question	質問する
address	a question	質問を出す
put	a question	
answer	a question	質問に答える
evade	a question	質問をかわす
raise	a question	問題を提起する
pose	a question	
consider	a question	問題を検討する
address	a question	問題に取り組む
tackle	a question	
call	into question	疑問を投げかける
be open	to question	疑う余地がある

▷ Do you **have** any **questions**? 何か質問がありますか
▷ Can I **ask a question**? 質問してもいいですか
▷ Would anyone like to **put a question** to our guest speaker? 招待講演者に質問なさりたい方はいますか
▷ She refused to **answer** my **question**. 彼女は私の質問に答えるのを拒否した
▷ You **raise** a very interesting **question**. あなたはとても興味深い問題を提起している
▷ You shouldn't have **called** his authority **into question**. 彼の権威に疑問を投げかけるべきではなかった
▷ It's still **open to question** whether he will be promoted next year or not. 来年彼が昇進するかどう

かはまだ疑問の余地がある

an awkward	question	答えにくい質問
an interesting	question	おもしろい質問
a crucial	question	重大な問題
the fundamental	question	根本的な問題
an important	question	重要な問題
a key	question	
a vexed	question	やっかいな問題

▷I think you ask a very **crucial question**. あなたはとても重大な問題を問うていると思う
▷There are several **key questions** that we still haven't answered. われわれがまだ答えを出していない重要な問題がいくつかある

a question	about A	Aに関する質問
a question	on A	
in	question	問題になっている；疑わしい
beyond	question	疑いもなく
without	question	問題なく；口答えせず

▷I have a **question about** the school trip to Kyoto. 京都への修学旅行について質問がある
▷There was a **question on** international law that I couldn't answer. 答えられなかった国際法の試験問題があった
▷Your honesty isn't **in question**. あなたが誠実なのは間違いない
▷I trust her **beyond question**. 頭から彼女を信じている
▷She did everything he said **without question**. 彼が言うことは何でも彼女は何の口答えもせずやった

question(s) and answer(s)	質問と答え

▷This book contains most **questions and answers** about living in the USA. この本は米国での暮らしに関するQ&Aをほぼ網羅している

PHRASES

(That's a) good question. ☺ いい質問です ▷When someone says, "Good question," it usually means they don't know the answer! 「いい質問だね」と人が言うのは、ふつう答えがわからないときだ

queue /kjúː/ 名《英》列

join	a queue	列に並ぶ
stand in	a queue	
jump	the queue	列に割り込む

▷I hate people who **jump** the **queue**. 列に割り込む連中は嫌いだ

quick /kwík/ 形 (動きが)速い

quick	enough	十分速い

▷I tried to get on the train before the doors closed, but I wasn't **quick enough**. ドアが閉まる前に列車に乗ろうとしたが、間に合わなかった

be quick	to do	すぐに…する

▷He was very **quick to** point out my mistakes. 彼はすぐ私の間違いを指摘した

quiet /kwáiət/

形 静かな；平穏な；控え目な、もの静かな

keep	quiet	静かにしている
stay	quiet	

▷**Keep quiet**! I can't hear the television. 静かにしろよ、テレビが聞こえないじゃないか

fairly	quiet	かなり静かな
really	quiet	とても静かな
relatively	quiet	比較的静かな
usually	quiet	ふだん静かな

▷It's been a **fairly quiet** day. Not very busy. とても静かな日で、そう忙しくなかった
▷It's a **relatively quiet** place where I live in the suburbs. 郊外の、比較的静かな場所に住んでいます
▷Why is it so noisy? It's **usually quiet** at this time of night. こう騒々しいのはなぜかな、夜のこの時間はたいてい静かなのに

quiet and gentle	もの静かで優しい
quiet and peaceful	静かでのどかな

▷I love hiking in the woods. It's so **quiet and peaceful**. 森の中のハイキングが好きだ、とても静かでのどかだから

PHRASES

(Be) quiet! ☺ 静かにしろ ▷Be quiet, Mark! マーク、静かにしろ

R

race /réis/ 名 競走, レース；競争；人種

have	a race	競走する
run	a race	
enter	a race	競走に出る
lose	a race	競走に負ける
win	a race	競走に勝つ
come first in	a race	競走で1着になる
come second in	a race	競走で2着になる
finish	a race	完走する

▷ Let's **have** a **race**! 競走しよう
▷ It's too late now to **enter** the **race**. レースに出るにはもう遅すぎる
▷ That horse has **won** a lot of **races** recently. その馬は近ごろ多くのレースに勝っている
▷ Poor Nigel. He came last. He couldn't even **finish** the **race**. かわいそうなナイジェル．彼は最下位で，完走さえできなかった

a big	race	大レース
a close	race	接戦のレース
a hard	race	過酷なレース
a tough	race	
a bicycle	race	自転車レース
a car	race	カーレース
a horse	race	競馬
mixed	race	混血
the human	race	人類

▷ The **big race** is on Saturday! 大事なレースが土曜日にある
▷ It was a **hard race**. You did well to come 3rd. 過酷なレースだった．3位とはよく健闘した

a race	with A	Aとの競走
a race	against A	
a race	for A	Aのための競争

▷ We've entered a **race with** other schools. 他の学校との競走に出た

a race	to do	…する競争

▷ After World War II the world entered a **race to** develop nuclear weapons. 第二次世界大戦後，世界は核兵器の開発競争に入った

class and race	階級と人種
gender and race	性別と人種
sex and race	

★いずれも逆の語順でも用いられる

▷ Her work focuses on issues of **gender and race**. 彼女の仕事はジェンダーと人種の問題に焦点を当てている

radio /réidiòu/ 名 ラジオ（放送）；無線（通信）

turn on	the radio	ラジオをつける
switch on	the radio	
turn off	the radio	ラジオを消す
switch off	the radio	
listen to	the radio	ラジオを聞く

▷ Quick! **Turn on** the **radio**! すぐラジオをつけて
▷ When I'm in my car, I like to **listen to** the **radio**. 車の中でラジオを聞くのが好きだ

local	radio	地元ラジオ放送
national	radio	全国ラジオ放送

▷ Our **local radio** provides a good service. うちの地元のラジオ放送はいい番組を提供している

on	the radio	ラジオで
by	radio	無線で

▷ Are there any good programs **on the radio**? ラジオで何かいい番組があるかな

rain /réin/ 名 雨

look like	rain	雨になりそうだ
get caught in	the rain	雨に降られる
pour with	rain	どしゃ降りの雨が降る
bring	rain	雨をもたらす

▷ It **looks like rain**. 雨になりそうだ
▷ Take an umbrella with you. Don't **get caught in the rain**. 傘を持って行って．雨に遭わないようにね
▷ It's **pouring with rain** outside. 外はどしゃ降りの雨だ
▷ It looks like those clouds are going to **bring rain**. あの雲は雨を降らせそうだ

the rain	falls	雨が降る
the rain	comes down	
the rain	stops	雨がやむ
the rain	begins to fall	雨が降り始める
the rain	starts to fall	

▷ A lot of **rain fell** last night. 昨夜は大雨だった
▷ Has the **rain stopped** yet? 雨はもうやんだのか
▷ Let's go inside before the **rain begins to fall**. 雨になる前に中に入ろう

heavy	rain	大雨
pouring	rain	
torrential	rain	豪雨, どしゃ降り
driving	rain	横殴りの雨
light	rain	小雨
acid	rain	酸性雨

▷ **Heavy rain** is forecast for tomorrow.　あすは大雨の予報だ
▷ There's **torrential rain** outside. I got soaked.　外はどしゃ降りだ. びしょぬれになったよ
▷ **Acid rain** is a major source of pollution.　酸性雨は公害の主要原因だ

in	the rain	雨の中を
after	(the) rain	雨が上がった後に
before	(the) rain	雨が降る前に

▷ Everything smells so fresh **after** the **rain**.　雨の後はすべてがみずみずしくにおう

rain /réin/ 動 雨が降る

rain	heavily	激しく雨が降る
rain	hard	
rain	slightly	少し雨が降る
rain	steadily	雨が本降りである

▷ Better not go outside. It's **raining heavily**.　外に出ないほうがいいよ. 雨がひどいから

start	to rain	雨が降り出す
begin	to rain	
start	raining	
stop	raining	雨がやむ

★ start raining はいまも降り続いていることが暗示されることがある

▷ It's **started to rain**.　雨が降り始めた
▷ I think it's **stopped raining**.　雨はやんだと思う

range /réindʒ/ 名 幅, 多様性；範囲；射程

cover	a range	範囲に及ぶ
extend	the range	範囲を広げる
expand	the range	
broaden	the range	
increase	the range	
limit	the range	範囲を制限する
offer	a range of A	さまざまなAを
provide	a range of A	提供する

▷ The news program **covered** a **range** of topics.　そのニュース番組は幅広い話題を扱った
▷ Car manufacturers are trying to **extend** the **range** of their electric cars.　自動車会社各社は電気自動車のラインナップを拡大しようとしている
▷ If you don't want to spend much money, your **range** of choice is **limited**.　あまりお金を使いたくないなら選択の範囲は限られますよ
▷ The hotel **provides** an excellent **range of** services.　そのホテルは各種のすばらしいサービスを提供している

a great	range	大きな範囲
a vast	range	
a wide	range	広い範囲
a broad	range	
a narrow	range	狭い範囲
a limited	range	限られた範囲
a normal	range	正常範囲
a full	range	全範囲
a whole	range	
a new	range	新しいラインナップ
a good	range	充実のラインナップ
close	range	至近距離
short	range	

▷ They have a very **wide range** of goods in this department store.　このデパートは品ぞろえがとても豊富だ
▷ We only have these sweaters in a **limited range** of colors.　これらのセーターは限られた色しかありません
▷ All your hospital test results are within the **normal range**.　病院の検査結果はすべて正常範囲内です
▷ You can see a **full range** of our products in this catalog.　このカタログで当社の全製品をご覧いただけます
▷ Have you seen our **new range** of cosmetics?　当社の化粧品の新しいラインナップをご覧いただきましたか
▷ We have a **good range** of inexpensive watches.　当店では低価格の時計の品ぞろえが充実しています
▷ The police said he was shot at **close range**.　警察によると彼は至近距離で撃たれた

in	the range of A	Aの範囲で
within	the range of A	Aの範囲内に
in	range	射程内に
within	range	
out of	range	射程外に

▷ We're looking for a house **in** the **range of** $250,000–$300,000.　25万ドルから30万ドルの範囲で家を探している

range /réindʒ/ 動 (範囲が)及ぶ, 広がる

range	widely	広範囲にわたる

▷ Her interest in music **ranges widely** from Mozart to J-pop. 彼女の音楽の興味はモーツァルトからJポップまで多岐にわたっている

range	between A and B	AからBに及ぶ
range	from A to B	

▷ The exam results **range between** very poor **and** excellent. 試験結果は非常に劣るから優までです
▷ At the moment daytime temperatures **range from** 26 **to** 30 degrees centigrade. いまのところ日中の気温はセ氏26度から30度です

rank /rǽŋk/

名 階級, 地位；列；(組織の)仲間, メンバー

reach	the rank	地位に就く
achieve	the rank	
attain	the rank	
hold	the rank	地位に就いている
join	the ranks	仲間入りする
swell	the ranks	仲間を増やす
rise through	the ranks	出世する
break	ranks	列を乱す；結束を乱す
close	ranks	結束を固める

▷ He **reached** the **rank** of colonel in the army. 彼は陸軍で大佐の地位に就いた
▷ I never thought you would **join** the **ranks** of the antigovernment protesters. きみが政府に抗議する人たちの仲間入りをするなんて考えたこともなかった
▷ He went from bellboy to hotel manager. He really **rose through the ranks**. 彼はベルボーイからホテル支配人になった。大した出世だ
▷ We have to stand firm. We mustn't **break ranks**. われわれは足下を固め, 結束を乱してはならない

high	rank	高い階級
senior	rank	
low	rank	低い階級
junior	rank	
social	rank	社会階級
the front	rank	前列
the rear	rank	後列

▷ He has a **high rank** in the police force. 彼は警官隊で高い地位にある
▷ She married a rich man so now her **social rank** is very high. 金持ちと結婚したので, いまや彼女の社会階級はとても高い
▷ He's in the **front rank** of politicians. 彼は政治家の第一線にいる

within	the ranks	集団内部で

▷ I think we have some troublemakers **within** the **ranks**. 集団内にトラブルを起こす人たちが何名かいるね

rank /rǽŋk/ 動 位置づける

rank	high	上位を占める
rank	low	下位に位置する

▷ Finding food and shelter for the flood victims **ranks high** in our list of priorities. 洪水の犠牲者たちに食べ物や避難所を見つけてあげるのを優先している

rank	among A	Aの中に位置づけられる
rank	with A	
rank	as A	Aに位置づけられる

▷ As a golf player, Tiger Woods **ranks with** the best in the world. ゴルフ選手としてタイガー・ウッズは世界最高レベルだ
▷ This earthquake **ranks as** one of the largest in recent years. この地震は近年でも最大のものの一つとして位置づけられる

rapid /rǽpid/ 形 速い；急速な

relatively	rapid	比較的速い

▷ We've been making **relatively rapid** progress, but we still need to go faster. 比較的速い進行できているが, さらにスピードを上げる必要がある

rare /réər/ 形 まれな, 珍しい

extremely	rare	きわめて珍しい
quite	rare	
fairly	rare	かなり珍しい
relatively	rare	比較的珍しい
comparatively	rare	
increasingly	rare	ますます珍しい

▷ It's **extremely rare** for this kind of problem to happen. この種の問題が生じるのはきわめて珍しい
▷ It's **relatively rare** that we receive complaints from our customers. 顧客からクレームを受けるのは比較的珍しい
▷ This species of bird is becoming **increasingly rare**. この鳥はますます珍しくなりつつある種だ

it is rare	(for A) to do	(A(人)が)…するのは珍しい

▷ "Where's Jack?" "**It's rare for** him **to** be late home."「ジャックはどこかな」「ジャックの帰宅が遅くなるのは珍しいね」

rate /réit/ 名 率, レート；料金；速度

increase	rates	率を上げる
raise	rates	
cut	rates	率を下げる
reduce	rates	
affect	rates	率に影響を及ぼす

★ of を伴うときは increase the rate of A のようになる

▷ The government has decided to **cut** interest **rates**. 政府は金利を下げる決定をした
▷ I think the recent high inflation is likely to **affect** the **rate** of interest. このところの高いインフレが金利に影響を及ぼしそうだ

a high	rate	高い率；高利率
a low	rate	低い率；低利率
a fixed	rate	固定金利
an annual	rate	年率；年利率
the average	rate	平均的な率
the birth	rate	出生率
the mortality	rate	死亡率
the death	rate	
the crime	rate	犯罪発生率
the suicide	rate	自殺率
the success	rate	成功率
the growth	rate	成長率
an exchange	rate	為替レート
an interest	rate	金利, 利率
the tax	rate	税率
the unemployment	rate	失業率
a rapid	rate	速い速度, 急速
an alarming	rate	驚くべき速度

▷ Unemployment is at a very **high rate**. 失業率がとても高くなっている
▷ The **annual rate** of interest is now 3%. 現在の年利率は3%だ
▷ Many students are failing this course. What's the **average rate**? このコースを落とす学生が多いが, 平均的な率はどれくらいですか
▷ The water level of the river is rising at a **rapid rate**. 川の水位は急速に上がりつつある

at	a rate of A	Aの割合で

▷ The bullet train was traveling **at a rate of** 300 kilometers per hour. その新幹線は時速300キロで走行していた

reach /ríːtʃ/

動 到着する, 着く；達する；手が届く, 手を差し出す

finally	reach	ついに到達する
eventually	reach	
easily	reach	簡単に到達する
almost	reach	ほぼ到達する
quickly	reach	すぐ到達する
reach	out	手を伸ばす

▷ After 5 hours we **finally reached** the top of the mountain. 5時間後とうとう山頂に到達した
▷ She **reached out** and shook his hand. 彼女は手を伸ばして彼と握手した

reach	for A	Aを取ろうと手を伸ばす
reach	into A	Aの中に手を差し入れる

▷ She **reached for** her cellphone and checked for messages. 彼女は携帯電話に手を伸ばしてメッセージをチェックした
▷ He **reached into** his pocket and brought out a cigarette lighter. 彼はポケットに手を入れてライターを取り出した

react /riǽkt/ 動 反応する；反発する

react	strongly	強く反応する
react	angrily	怒って反応する
react	badly	まずい反応を示す
react	immediately	即座に反応する
react	quickly	すばやく反応する
react	differently	異なる反応をする
react	accordingly	ふさわしい反応をする
react	appropriately	

▷ There's no need to **react** so **angrily**. そんなに怒って反応する必要はない
▷ When the dog ran into the road he **reacted quickly** and stopped the car in time. 犬が道路に飛び出したとき, 彼はとっさに反応して車を緊急停止した
▷ Children tend to **react differently** than adults. 子どもたちはおとなとは異なる反応をするものだ

react	by doing	反発して…する

▷ He **reacted** angrily **by** stand**ing** up and walking out of the room. 彼は憤然と反発し, 立ち上がって部屋を出ていった

react	against A	Aに反発する
react	to A	Aに反応する
react	with A	Aと(化学)反応する

▷How did she **react to** your proposal of marriage? 彼女はきみのプロポーズにどう反応したの
▷Chemicals released by factories **react with** each other in the air to cause global warming. 工場から放出された化学物質は大気中で反応し合って地球温暖化を引き起こす

reaction /riǽkʃən/

名 反応；反発；アレルギー反応；化学反応

get	a reaction	反応を得る
have	a reaction	反応がある
provoke	a reaction	反応を引き起こす
cause	a reaction	
produce	a reaction	
have	a reaction	アレルギー反応が
suffer	a reaction	ある

▷She just sat there and said nothing. I couldn't **get a reaction**. そこに座って無言のままの彼女から何の反応も得られなかった
▷If we increase the price of school meals it's sure to **provoke a reaction**. 学校の給食費を上げたらきっと反発を招くだろう

a reaction	occurs	反応が起きる
a reaction	takes place	

▷You can see a chemical **reaction take place** in this glass tube. このガラス管で化学反応が起きるのを見ることができる

a positive	reaction	肯定的な反応
a negative	reaction	否定的な反応
an adverse	reaction	拒絶反応
immediate	reaction	直接の反応
initial	reaction	最初の反応
a natural	reaction	自然な反応
a chain	reaction	連鎖反応
a chemical	reaction	化学反応
an allergic	reaction	アレルギー反応

▷We're hoping for a **positive reaction** to our plan. われわれの計画に肯定的な反応があることを望んでいる
▷There was an **adverse reaction** to our proposals in the meeting. 会議ではわれわれの提案に拒絶反応があった
▷The explosion was caused by a **chemical reaction**. 爆発は化学反応によって起きた
▷Many people have an **allergic reaction** to pollen. 花粉にアレルギー反応を起こす人は多い

a reaction	against A	Aへの反発
a reaction	to A	Aへの反応
a reaction	between A	Aの間の化学反応

▷There was a big **reaction against** closing down the factory. 工場閉鎖に対して大きな反発があった
▷Fire is a result of a rapid chemical **reaction between** a fuel and oxygen. 火は燃料と酸素の急速な化学反応の結果である

read /ríːd/ **動** 読む

read	aloud	声に出して読む
read out	loud	
read	silently	黙読する
read	carefully	注意深く読む
read	again	もう一度読む
widely	read	幅広く読まれる

★widely read の read は過去分詞

▷Mr. Roberts asked me to **read aloud** in class today. きょう教室でロバーツ先生から朗読を当てられた
▷Make sure you **read** the instructions **carefully**. 説明書を注意深く読むようにしなさい
▷There are so many books that I want to **read again**. 読み返したい本がたくさんある

read and write	読み書きする

▷The child is only four years old, but he is already able to **read and write**. その子はまだ4歳だが，もう読み書きができる

read	about A	Aについて読む
read	of A	
read	from A	Aを拾い読みする
read	through A	Aを読み通す

▷I **read about** it in the paper. それは新聞で読んだ
▷She **reads from** the Bible every night. 彼女は毎晩、聖書を拾い読みしている
▷Could you **read through** my English essay and check it, please? 私の英語のレポートを通読してチェックしていただけませんか

read	A B	A(人)にBを読んで
read	B to A	聞かせる

▷My little daughter likes me to **read** a story **to** her at bedtime. 寝るときに物語を読んで聞かせてとうちの娘からよくせがまれる

read	A as C	AをCだと解釈する

▷I **read** his letter **as** a refusal to help, but maybe I was wrong. 彼からの手紙は援助を拒否していると解釈したが，たぶん私が間違っていた

read	that...	…だと読んで知る

▷Yesterday I **read** in the newspapers **that** there's going to be a shortage of gasoline. きのう新聞で読んだのだが，ガソリンが足りなくなるようだ

reading /ríːdiŋ/ 名 読書；読み物；読み方

extensive	reading	多読
close	reading	精読
careful	reading	
silent	reading	黙読
introductory	reading	入門書
assigned	reading	課題図書
《英》compulsory	reading	
essential	reading	必読書
mandatory	reading	
recommended	reading	推薦図書
suggested	reading	

▷This course requires **extensive reading**. この講座では多読が必要です
▷These books are **essential reading** for your course. これらがこの講座の必読書です

make interesting	reading	読んでみると
make fascinating	reading	おもしろい

▷This book **makes interesting reading**. この本は読んでみるとおもしろい

reading and writing	読み書き

▷For Westerners, **reading and writing** Japanese is much more difficult than speaking. 西洋人にとって日本語を読み書きするのは話すよりずっと難しい

ready /rédi/ 形 準備ができて

almost	ready	ほとんど準備ができて
nearly	ready	
always	ready	いつも準備して

▷Lunch is **almost ready**! 昼食の準備がほぼできたよ
▷If you have any problems, remember, I'm **always ready** to help you. 何か問題があったらいつでも助けてあげるから，忘れないで

ready	for A	Aの準備ができて

▷Get **ready for** a surprise. Bob asked me to marry him! 驚かないでね，ボブが私にプロポーズしたの

get A	ready	Aを準備する
have A	ready	

▷I have to **get** a meal **ready** by 6:00. 6時までに食事の準備をしなくては

ready	to do	…する準備ができて；喜んで…する

▷Are you **ready to** leave yet? もう出かける準備はできていますか

ready and waiting	準備万端整って
ready and willing	進んで，喜んで

▷"Are you ready yet?" "Yes. **Ready and waiting**!" 「準備はいいですか」「はい，準備完了です」
▷I'm **ready and willing** to do anything to help. お役に立つなら喜んで何でもします

PHRASES
Are you ready, Tom? ☺ 準備はできたかい，トム
Ready, set, go! / **Ready, steady, go!** ☺ 位置について，用意，ドン

realistic /rìːəlístik | rìəl-/
形 現実的な，現実をわきまえた

fairly	realistic	かなり現実的な
sufficiently	realistic	十分現実的な

▷The projected figures for next year's profits are not **sufficiently realistic**. 来年度の利益の見込み数字はあまり現実的ではない

realistic	about A	Aに関して現実的な

▷She's not very **realistic about** her chances of being promoted. 彼女は自分の昇進の可能性について現実をわきまえていない

it is realistic	to do	…するのが現実的だ

▷Do you think **it's realistic to** ask for so much money from the bank? そんな多額の融資を銀行に求めるのは現実的だと思いますか

have to	be realistic	現実的にならなければならない
must	be realistic	

▷There's no way we're going to finish in time. We **have to be realistic**. 仕上げはとても間に合いそうにな

| reality |

い．現実的にならなくては

reality /riǽləti/ 名 現実性；現実

become	a reality	現実になる
make A	a reality	Aを現実にする
accept	the reality	現実を受け入れる
face	the reality	現実と向き合う
reflect	the reality	現実を反映する
escape from	reality	現実から逃避する
deny	the reality	現実を否定する
ignore	the reality	現実を無視する

▷ Finally her dream **became** a **reality**. She's a top model in Paris. とうとう彼女の夢は現実になった．いまやパリのトップモデルだ
▷ Why doesn't she **accept** the **reality**? He's not in love with her. 彼女はなぜ現実を受け入れないのだろう．彼に愛されてなんかいないのに
▷ This newspaper report doesn't **reflect** the **reality** of the situation. この新聞報道は現実の状況を反映していない

harsh	reality	厳しい現実
grim	reality	
economic	reality	経済の現実
political	reality	政治の現実

▷ The **economic reality** is that we are in danger of going bankrupt. われわれが倒産の危機にあるというのが経済の現実だ
▷ The **political reality** is that we have little chance of winning the next election. 次の選挙でわれわれが勝つ見込みはほとんどないというのが政治の現実だ

a perception of	reality	現実感
a sense of	reality	

▷ She lives in a dream world. She has no **sense of reality**. 彼女は夢の世界に生きており，現実感というのがない

in	reality	現実には，実際は

▷ Dave and Sarah look very happy, but **in reality** they have quite a lot of problems. デイブとサラはとても幸せそうに見えるが，実際は問題を山ほど抱えている

the reality	is (that)...	現実は…だ

▷ They say they don't want to move to Tokyo, but the **reality is (that)** they don't have enough money. 東京に引っ越したくないと彼らは言うが，現実は十分なお金がないのだ

realize /ríːəlàiz | ríəl-/

動 気づく，悟る；実現する（★《英》つづりは realise）

fully	realize	十分に気づく
suddenly	realize	突然気づく
soon	realize	すぐ気づく
quickly	realize	
immediately	realize	
gradually	realize	次第に気づく
finally	realize	ついに気づく

▷ I don't think you **fully realize** how dangerous the situation is. 状況がどれほど危険なものかきみが十分に理解しているとは思えない
▷ When he tried to pay the bill he **suddenly realized** he'd left his wallet at home. 代金を払おうとして彼は財布を家に忘れてきたことに突然気づいた

realize	(that)...	…だと気づく
realize	wh-	…か気づく

★ wh- は what, how など

▷ Sorry! I've just **realized that** I've made a terrible mistake. ごめん，いま気づいたんだけど，ぼくはひどい間違いをしていたよ
▷ I suddenly **realized what** had happened. 何が起こったのか突然気づいた

reason /ríːzn/ 名 理由，わけ；根拠；理性

see	no reason	理由がわからない
not see	any reason	
know	the reason	理由を知っている
have	a reason	理由がある
give	a reason	理由を挙げる
explain	the reason	理由を説明する

▷ I **see no reason** to postpone the business trip. 出張を延期する理由がわからない
▷ Do you **know** the **reason** (why) she got so angry? 彼女がそんなに怒った理由を知っていますか
▷ I know you don't like him, but do you **have a reason**? きみが彼のことを嫌いなのは知っているが，理由はあるのかい
▷ Could you **explain** the **reason** why you applied for this job? この仕事に応募した理由を説明していただけませんか

(a) good	reason	もっともな理由
the main	reason	おもな理由
a simple	reason	単純な理由
an obvious	reason	明白な理由
a personal	reason	個人的な理由

various	reasons	さまざまな理由

▷ We can't cancel the appointment without **good reason**. もっともな理由もないのに約束を取りやめるわけにはいかない

▷ The **main reason** for going to England is to improve my English. イングランドに行くおもな理由は英語を上達させるためです

▷ The terrorists made a video, but their faces and voices were disguised for **obvious reasons**. テロリストたちはビデオを撮影したが，当然ながら顔や声は偽装されていた

▷ She's requested a transfer to our Tokyo branch for purely **personal reasons**. 彼女はまったく個人的な理由で東京支店への異動願いを出した

the reason	behind A	Aの背景にある理由
the reason	for A	Aの理由

▷ What are the **reasons behind** your decision to go to live in Australia? オーストラリアで暮らすことを決心をした理由の背景には何があるのですか

▷ What is the **reason for** refusing my application? 私の申し出を断る理由は何ですか

for	this reason	こんなわけで
for	that reason	そんなわけで
for	whatever reason	どんな理由であれ
with	reason	もっとも，当然で
within	reason	道理の範囲内で

▷ It is **for this reason** that I have decided to resign. 私が辞める決意をしたのはこういう理由だ

▷ I don't know why, but **for whatever reason**, they refused to sign the contract. なぜだかわからないが，理由はどうあれ彼らは契約書への署名を拒否した

reason	to do	…する理由

▷ She has every **reason to** be annoyed with you. 彼女があなたに腹を立てるのももっともだ

the reason	why ...	なぜ…かという理由
the reason	(that) ...	…だという理由

▷ There's no **reason why** she should be late. 彼女が遅れて来る道理がない

reasonable /rí:zənəbl/

形 理性的な；妥当な；(価格が)手ごろな

seem	reasonable	妥当と思われる

▷ The price they're asking for the house **seems reasonable**. その家の提示価格は妥当と思われる

fairly	reasonable	かなり妥当な
quite	reasonable	
eminently	reasonable	きわめて妥当な
perfectly	reasonable	まったく妥当な

▷ At the moment the air fare from Tokyo to London is **fairly reasonable**. 東京・ロンドン間の現在の航空運賃はかなり手ごろだ

▷ What he's asking you to do is **perfectly reasonable**. 彼があなたに頼んでいることはまったく理にかなっている

it is reasonable	to do	…するのは妥当である

▷ We've been waiting here for over an hour so **it's reasonable to** assume that she's not coming. 1時間以上ここで待っているので，彼女は来ないと考えるのが妥当だな

recall /rikɔ́:l/ 動 思い出す；呼び戻す

still	recall	いまも思い出す
vividly	recall	生き生きと思い出す
vaguely	recall	かすかに思い出す

▷ I can **vividly recall** my first day at school. 初登校の日のことをありありと思い出せる

recall	(that) ...	…を思い出す
recall	wh-	…か思い出す

★ wh- は what, where, why など

▷ I can't **recall that** we've met before. 以前お会いした記憶はありません

▷ She can't **recall what** happened. 何が起こったか彼女は思い出せない

recall	doing	…したのを思い出す

▷ I can't **recall** receiving any letter from her. 彼女から手紙をもらった記憶はない

receipt /risí:t/ 名 領収書，レシート；受領

get	a receipt	領収書を受け取る
have	a receipt	領収書をもらう
keep	a receipt	領収書を取っておく
sign	a receipt	領収書に署名する
acknowledge	receipt	受領を確認する

▷ Don't forget. You need to **get a receipt**. 忘れないで，領収書を受け取るんだよ

| receive |

▷ Could I **have** a **receipt**? 領収書をいただけますか
▷ I **keep** all my **receipts**. 領収書は全部とってあります
▷ Please **acknowledge receipt** *of* this letter as soon as possible. この手紙を受け取った旨をできるだけ早くお知らせください

| on | receipt (of A) | (Aを)受け取り次第 |

▷ **On receipt of** the information, police and fire services rushed to the spot. 情報を受けるとすぐ警察と消防隊が現場に駆けつけた

receive /rɪsíːv/ 動 受け取る;受ける

| recently | received | 最近受け取った |
| be well | received | 好評を博した |

▷ I **recently received** a check for $5,000. 最近5千ドルの小切手を受け取った
▷ The speech you gave was very **well received**. あなたのスピーチはとても好評でした

| receive A | from B | B(人)からAを受け取る |

▷ I still haven't **received** a letter **from** Simon. サイモンからまだ手紙を受け取っていない

recent /ríːsnt/ 形 最近の, 近ごろの

fairly	recent	ごく最近
relatively	recent	比較的最近
comparatively	recent	

▷ This is a **fairly recent** development. これはかなり最近の展開だ
▷ Cellphones are a **relatively recent** invention. 携帯電話は比較的最近の発明だ

in	recent weeks	ここ数週間
in	recent months	ここ数か月
in	recent years	ここ数年

★ **in** のほかに **over** や **during** も用いる

▷ It's been getting more and more humid **in recent weeks**. ここ数週間ますます蒸し暑くなってきている
▷ The cost of living has been rising **over recent months**. 生活費はここ何か月かで上昇している

recognize /rékəgnàɪz/

動 見分けがつく, それとわかる;認識する;認める

easily	recognize	簡単に見分けがつく
immediately	recognize	すぐ見分けがつく
hardly	recognize	ほとんど見分けがつかない
fully	recognize	十分認識する
be generally	recognized	一般に認められる
be widely	recognized	広く認められる

▷ He's tall, with blond hair and glasses. You'll **easily recognize** him. 彼は背が高くて金髪で, 眼鏡をかけています. すぐに彼とわかるでしょう
▷ I **fully recognize** that you're in a difficult situation. あなたが困難な状況にあることは十分認めます
▷ It's **generally recognized** that earthquakes take place frequently in Japan. 日本は地震が多いというのは周知のことだ

| recognize | (that) ... | …だと認める |

▷ I **recognize that** you're working under a lot of pressure at the moment. あなたが現在, 大きなプレッシャーの下で働いていることを承知しています

| recognize A | as B | AをBと認める |

▷ He's widely **recognized as** an expert on foreign policy. 彼は外交政策の専門家として広く認められている

recommend /rèkəménd/

動 勧める;推薦する

highly	recommend	強く勧める
strongly	recommend	
particularly	recommend	特に勧める
thoroughly	recommend	ぜひとも勧める
therefore	recommend	それゆえ勧める

▷ My doctor **highly recommended** joining a fitness club. フィットネスクラブに入るよう医師から強く勧められた
▷ Why don't you try this health drink? I can **thoroughly recommend** it. この健康ドリンクを飲んでみたら？ぜひともお勧めです
▷ There is danger of flooding so we **therefore recommend** that people move to higher ground. 洪水の危険性があるので高台に移るように勧めます

| recommend | (that) ... | …を勧める |

▷ Doctors **recommend that** people take more exercise. もっと運動するよう医師たちは勧めている

| recommend | doing | …するのを勧める |

▷ I **recommend** going on a diet. ダイエットするよう勧めます

recommend

recommend	A for B	A(人)をBに推薦する
recommend	B to A	BをA(人)に推薦する

▷ I'm **recommending** you **for** promotion. あなたを昇進候補に推薦します
▷ When I had toothache my boss **recommended** a good dentist **to** me. 歯痛のとき上司がよい歯医者を推薦してくれた

recommendation /rèkəməndéiʃən/

名 勧告；推薦；推薦状

make	a recommendation	勧告する
accept	a recommendation	勧告を受け入れる
follow	a recommendation	勧告に従う
implement	a recommendation	勧告を実施する

▷ We need to **make** our **recommendations** to the board of directors at the next meeting. 次の会議で取締役会に勧告する必要がある
▷ We'll **accept** a **recommendation** from your previous boss. あなたの前の上司からの勧告を受け入れよう
▷ We've decided to **follow** your **recommendations**. あなたの勧告に従うことにした

detailed	recommendations	詳細な勧告
the main	recommendation	主要な勧告
a specific	recommendation	具体的勧告
a personal	recommendation	個人的推薦

▷ The report made several **specific recommendations**. 報告書ではいくつか具体的な勧告がなされていた
▷ She got the job on my **personal recommendation**. 彼女は私の個人的な推薦で職に就いた

recommendations		for A	Aに対する勧告
one's recommendation		to A	Aへの勧告
a recommendation		on A	Aに関する勧告
on	A's recommendation		Aの勧めで
at	A's recommendation		

▷ What are your **recommendations for** dealing with this crisis? この危機に対処するにあたってあなたは何を勧告されますか
▷ I'm going to take a holiday **on** my doctor's **recommendation**. 医者の勧めで休暇をとる予定だ

recommendation	that ...	…との勧告

▷ Our company has made the **recommendation that** we should employ more part-time staff. もっと多くのパート社員を雇うよう会社は勧告してきた

record /rékərd | -kɔːd/

名 記録；最高記録；成績, 経歴

keep	a record	記録しておく
maintain	a record	
compile	a record	記録をまとめる
break	a record	記録を破る
beat	a record	
set	a record	記録を打ち立てる
hold	a record	記録を保持する

▷ You need to **keep** a careful **record** of your travel expenses. 旅行中に使ったお金を細かく書き留めておく必要がある
▷ She **set** a new world **record** for the marathon. 彼女はマラソンの世界新記録を打ち立てた
▷ She **holds** the **record** for the 100 meters. 彼女は100メートル走の記録を保持している

the record	shows	記録が示している

▷ The **record shows** that he hasn't attended classes for 3 weeks. 彼が授業に3週間出ていないのが記録でわかる

an official	record	公式記録
a written	record	文書に残された記録
historical	record(s)	歴史上の記録
a criminal	record	犯罪歴, 前科
medical	record(s)	病歴, 医療記録
a world	record	世界記録
the current	record	現在の記録
the previous	record	以前の記録

▷ He holds the **official record** for the 10,000 meters. 彼は1万メートル走の公式記録を保持している
▷ They think he has a **criminal record**. 彼には前科があると思われている
▷ Her **medical record** is kept in this file. 彼女の病歴はこのファイルに保存されている
▷ She broke the **previous record** by nearly 4 seconds. 彼女はそれまでの記録を4秒近く破った

record	for A	A(分野など)の記録
record	of A	Aの記録
record	on A	Aにおける実績
on	record	記録の上で

▷ He holds the **record for** this golf course. 彼はこのゴルフコースの記録を保持している
▷ We have no **record** of a Mr. Evans staying at this hotel. エバンスというお名前のお客様がこのホテルに滞在した記録は残っていません
▷ The newspaper reporter attacked the Government **record on** public services. 新聞記者は公共サービス

| recover |

における政府の実績を非難した
▷ It's **on record** as the worst disaster for 50 years. それは50年間で最悪の災害として記録に残っている

recover /rikʌ́vər/

動 回復する, 立ち直る；取り戻す

completely	recover	すっかり回復する
fully	recover	
soon	recover	すぐ回復する
recover	quickly	急速に回復する
recover	sufficiently	十分に回復する
recover	well	順調に回復する

★ recover completely, quickly recover もよく用いる

▷ Liz is out of hospital. She's **completely recovered**. リズは退院しており, すっかり回復している
▷ Tina's **fully recovered** from the accident. ティナは事故のあと, すっかり回復している
▷ I hope you **recover quickly**. すぐ回復されることを祈っています

recover	from A	Aから回復する

▷ She still hasn't **recovered from** the shock! 彼女はまだショックから立ち直っていない

recovery /rikʌ́vəri/ **名** 回復；回収

make	a recovery	回復する
promote	a recovery	回復を促進する

▷ It was a terrible car crash, but he's **made** a full **recovery**. ひどい交通事故だったが, 彼は全治した
▷ The Government are doing all they can to **promote** economic **recovery**. 景気回復を促進するために政府はできることは何でもしている

a complete	recovery	完全な回復
a full	recovery	
a good	recovery	順調な回復
a remarkable	recovery	目覚ましい回復
a speedy	recovery	速い回復
economic	recovery	景気回復
national	recovery	国の復興

▷ We all hope she makes a **full recovery**. 彼女の全快をみんな望んでいる
▷ The doctors had almost given up hope, but she made a **remarkable recovery**. 医師たちはほとんどあきらめていたが, 彼女は目覚ましい回復ぶりを見せた
▷ After the earthquake **national recovery** will take many years. 地震後, 国の復興には何年もかかるだろう

(a) recovery	from A	Aからの回復

▷ **Recovery from** influenza is usually more difficult for the elderly. インフルエンザからの回復はふつう高齢者ほど難しい

on the road	to recovery	回復途上で

▷ I hear you're **on the road to recovery**. あなたは回復に向かっていると伺っています

a sign of	recovery	回復の兆し

▷ I visited her in hospital and she's starting to show **signs of recovery**. 病院に彼女を見舞ったが, 彼女は回復の兆しを見せ始めている

red /réd/ **形** 赤い

go	red	赤くなる
turn	red	

▷ Careful! The traffic lights have **gone red**! 気をつけて. 信号が赤になったよ

reduce /ridjúːs | -djúːs/

動 減らす, 縮小する

considerably	reduce	かなり減らす
drastically	reduce	劇的に減らす
greatly	reduce	大きく減らす
substantially	reduce	かなり減らす
significantly	reduce	著しく減らす
further	reduce	さらに減らす
gradually	reduce	徐々に減らす
slightly	reduce	わずかに減らす

▷ That department store has **drastically reduced** its prices. そのデパートは大幅に値下げした
▷ If you keep fit, the chances of a heart attack are **greatly reduced**. 体調を整えれば心臓発作の可能性は大幅に減少する
▷ I think her fever has **slightly reduced**. 彼女の熱は少し下がったと思う

reduce A	by B	AをBだけ減らす
reduce	from A to B	AからBに減らす

▷ We **reduced** our fuel costs **by** 10%. 燃料費を1割減らした
▷ It's a great diet! I **reduced** my weight **from** 70 kilos **to** 62 kilos in six months! すごいダイエットだ. 半年で体重を70キロから62キロに減らしたんだよ

| reduce or eliminate | | 減らすかなくす |

▷ Many big companies are **reducing or eliminating** traditional pensions. 大企業の多くは伝統的な年金を減らすか廃止しつつある

reduction /rɪdʌ́kʃən/

名 減少, 縮小; 値下げ, 割引

make	a reduction	減らす
cause	a reduction	減少を引き起こす
lead to	a reduction	減少につながる
result in	a reduction	
show	a reduction	減少を示す

▷ We've already **made** a **reduction** in the price of 20%. われわれはすでに価格を2割下げた
▷ The rise in price **led to** a **reduction** in demand. 価格上昇が需要減につながった
▷ The strong yen **resulted in** a **reduction** of exported goods. 円高で輸出が減少した
▷ The latest figures **show** a **reduction** in the number of traffic accidents. 最新数字では交通事故の件数は減少している

a considerable	reduction	かなりの減少
a significant	reduction	著しい減少
a substantial	reduction	大幅な減少
a dramatic	reduction	劇的な減少
a drastic	reduction	
a further	reduction	さらなる減少
a sharp	reduction	急激な減少
cost	reduction	コスト削減
debt	reduction	債務削減
deficit	reduction	赤字削減
a price	reduction	値下げ

▷ There has been a **significant reduction** of foreign tourists visiting our country. わが国を訪れる外国人観光客が著しく減少してきている
▷ You can see from this chart that there was a **sharp reduction** in the number of crimes this year. 今年は犯罪件数が急激に減ったことがこのグラフでわかる

| a reduction | in A | Aの削減 |

▷ There's a **reduction in** the number of jobs available this year. 今年は求人件数が減少している

reference /réfərəns/

名 言及; 参照; 参考文献

| make | reference to A | Aに言及する |

| include | a reference | 言及を含む |

▷ In his speech he **made** no **reference to** the present financial crisis. 演説の中で彼は現在の財政危機について何も言及しなかった

direct	reference	直接的な言及
specific	reference	具体的な言及
particular	reference	特別な言及
special	reference	
passing	reference	短い言及

▷ You should make **direct reference** in your speech *to* all the support you received. あなたが受けたあらゆる援助にスピーチで直接言及したほうがいい
▷ The report made **specific reference** *to* raising the minimum wage. この報告書は最低賃金引き上げに関して具体的に言及した

by	reference to A	Aを参照して
for	future reference	今後の参考のために
in	reference to A	Aに関して
with	reference to A	

▷ The pension is calculated **by reference to** the final salary. 年金給付額は退職時給与を基準に決定される
▷ We need to hold a meeting **with reference to** the recent rise in oil prices. 最近の原油価格の値上がりの件で会議を開く必要がある

reflect /rɪflékt/

動 反映する; 反射する; よく考える; 印象をもたらす

accurately	reflect	正確に反映する
not necessarily	reflect	必ずしも反映しない
simply	reflect	単に反映する
merely	reflect	
partly	reflect	部分的に反映する
reflect	well	よい印象を与える
reflect	badly	悪い印象を与える

▷ This newspaper report does not **accurately reflect** what happened. この新聞報道は起こったことを正確に反映していない
▷ This is my personal opinion and it does **not necessarily reflect** the views of the committee. これは私個人の意見であって，必ずしも委員会の見解を反映してはいない
▷ The fact that we did nothing to help **reflects badly** *on* all of us. 何も援助しなかったことで私たちみんなの評判が悪くなっている

| be reflected | in A | Aに反映している |

reflect	on A	Aをよく考える

▷ The success of our sales campaign is **reflected in** the huge rise in sales this year. 販促キャンペーンの成功は今年度の売り上げの急上昇に反映している
▷ I need some time to **reflect on** what to do. 何をすべきかよく考える時間が必要だ

reflect	that...	…をよく考える
reflect	wh-	…かをよく考える；…かを反映する

★ wh- は what, who, how など

▷ We need to **reflect what** to do if the situation gets worse. 事態が悪化したらどうすべきかよく考える必要がある

reflection /riflékʃən/

名 写った像；反映；反射；よく考えること, 熟慮

catch	a reflection	像が目に入る
see	a reflection	像が見える
look at	a reflection	像を見る
stare at	a reflection	像をじっと見る

▷ They could **see** the **reflection** of the moon in the lake. 湖に月が映っているのが見えた
▷ She **stared at** her **reflection** in the shop window. 彼女は店のウインドーに映る自分の姿をじっと見た

an accurate	reflection	正確な反映
a fair	reflection	正しい反映
a true	reflection	
a sad	reflection	嘆かわしい反映

▷ What you say is a **fair reflection** *of* how the car accident happened. あなたの発言は自動車事故の発生状況を正しく伝えている
▷ It's a **sad reflection** *on* our society today that nobody came to help her. だれも彼女を助けに来なかったのはいまの社会の嘆かわしい反映だ

a reflection	on A	Aについての考察
on	reflection	よく考えてみると,
upon	reflection	熟慮の上で

▷ What are your **reflections on** the present situation in China? 中国の現状をどう考えていますか
▷ **On reflection**, let's wait a couple more months before putting our house on the market. よく考えて家を売りに出すのをもう2, 3か月待とう

reform /rifɔ́:rm/ 名 改革, 改善

introduce	reform(s)	改革を導入する
implement	reform(s)	改革を実行する
support	reform(s)	改革を支援する

▷ It will be difficult to **introduce reform** at this stage. この段階で改革を導入するのは困難だろう
▷ The new Government has already **implemented** several **reforms**. 新政府はすでにいくつか改革を実行した

radical	reform(s)	抜本的な改革
political	reform(s)	政治改革
social	reform(s)	社会改革
structural	reform(s)	構造改革
administrative	reform(s)	行政改革
educational	reform(s)	教育改革
economic	reform(s)	経済改革
tax	reform(s)	税制改革

▷ The Government intends to carry out several **radical reforms** this year. 政府は今年いくつか抜本的な改革を実行する予定だ
▷ What **political reforms** do you feel are necessary? どのような政治改革が必要だと感じますか
▷ China has carried out various **economic reforms** recently. 中国は近年さまざまな経済改革を断行した(★× economical reform とはいわない)

refrigerator /rifrídʒərèitər/

名 冷蔵庫(★口語ではしばしば fridge という)

in	the refrigerator	冷蔵庫に

▷ I keep the eggs **in** the **refrigerator**. 冷蔵庫に卵を保存している

put A	in the refrigerator	Aを冷蔵庫に入れる
take A	out of the refrigerator	Aを冷蔵庫から取り出す

▷ Could you **put** this ice cream **in** the **refrigerator**? このアイスクリームを冷蔵庫に入れていただけますか

refuse /rifjú:z/ 動 拒む, 拒否する；断る

absolutely	refuse	きっぱり断る
steadfastly	refuse	断固として断る
flatly	refuse	あっさり断る
simply	refuse	
consistently	refuse	一貫して断る

▷ She **steadfastly refused** to move into a home for

the elderly. 彼女は高齢者施設に移るのを断固として断った
▷He **flatly refused** to help. 援助はできないと彼はあっさり言った
▷If you don't want to do it **simply refuse**. そうしたくないのなら，あっさり断りなさい

| refuse | to do | …するのを拒む |

▷She **refused to** give him any more money. 彼女は彼にそれ以上お金をあげるのを拒んだ

regard /rigá:rd/ 名 配慮, 考慮；敬意

have	regard	配慮する；敬意を抱く
pay	regard	配慮する
hold A	in high regard	Aを尊敬している
give	one's regards	よろしくと伝える

▷He **has** no **regard** for other people's feelings. 彼は他人の感情など気にかけない
▷She didn't **pay** any **regard** to what her friend told her. 彼女は友人が何を言おうと，われ関せずだった
▷He **holds** you **in** very **high regard**. 彼はあなたをとても尊敬している
▷**Give** my **regards to** Angus when you see him! アンガスに会ったらよろしくお伝えください

particular	regard	特別の配慮
due	regard	相応の配慮
proper	regard	正当な配慮
high	regard	高い評価
great	regard	

▷These new laws have **particular regard** to protecting the environment. これらの新しい法律は環境保護を特に配慮したものだ
▷She doesn't seem to have **proper regard** for all the help she received from her parents. 両親から受けたあらゆる援助をありがたいと思う気持ちが彼女にはないようだ

| regard | for A | Aへの敬意；Aへの配慮 |

▷I have a lot of **regard for** people who fight their way to the top. 苦労してトップに登り詰める人々にとても敬意を抱いている

in	this regard	この点に関して
in	that regard	その点に関して
with	regard to A	Aに関して
in	regard to A	
without	regard to A	Aに構わず，Aを
without	regard for A	無視して

▷Tom's so impatient! **In this regard** he makes life a little difficult for himself. トムはとても短気だ．この点で彼は自ら人生を難しくしている
▷Mike would like to talk to you **with regard to** the contract. マイクは契約の件できみと話したがっている
▷He took the decision **without** any **regard for** the consequences. 彼は後先考えずに決定を下した

regard /rigá:rd/ 動 …と見なす, 考える

highly	regarded	高く評価されて
well	regarded	
generally	regarded	一般に認められて
widely	regarded	広く認められて

▷He's **highly regarded** within the medical profession. 彼は医師界で高く評価されている
▷A degree from Harvard is **generally regarded** as the key to a good job. ハーバードの学位はよい仕事に就く鍵と一般に見なされている
▷She's **widely regarded** as an expert in her field. 彼女はその分野でのエキスパートと広く見なされている

| regard A | as C | AをCと見なす |
| regard A | with B | AをB(ある感情)をもって見る |

★B は suspicion, fear, respect, admiration など

▷Our boss **regards** you **as** a key person in our company. 上司はきみのことを会社の鍵となる人物と考えている
▷I've never trusted her. I've always **regarded** her **with suspicion**. 彼女を信用したことがない．いつも彼女を疑いの目で見てきた

region /rí:dʒən/ 名 地域, 地方

northern	region	北部地域
southern	region	南部地域
mountain	region	山岳地方
desert	region	砂漠地帯
central	region	中央部
an autonomous	region	自治区

▷In the **northern regions** of Canada temperatures can be terribly cold. カナダの北部地域では気温がひどく下がることがある
▷There are many mountains in the **central region** of Japan. 日本の中央部には多くの山がある
▷Tibet is an **autonomous region** of China. チベットは中国の自治区だ

| in | the region of A | 約A(数字)で |

| register |

▷He had to pay **in** the **region of** $500,000 for his house. 彼は家を買うのに50万ドルほど支払わなければならなかった

register /rédʒɪstər/ 名 記録簿, 名簿

keep	a register	記録をとっておく,
maintain	a register	記録を保存しておく
sign	a register	名簿にサインする

▷The hotel **keeps** a **register** of all its guests. そのホテルはすべての客の記録をとっている
▷Please **sign** the **register** when you enter and leave the building. 建物の出入りの際に名簿にサインをしてください

register /rédʒɪstər/ 動 登録する

| formally | register | 正式に登録する |
| officially | register | |

▷You are required to **formally register** at university before you can attend classes. 授業に出席する前に大学に正式に登録する必要がある

register A	as B	AをBとして登録する
register	for A	Aの登録をする
register	with A	Aに登録する

▷Would you like to come to my golf club? I can **register** you **as** a guest. 私のゴルフクラブにいらっしゃいませんか. あなたをゲストとして登録できますので
▷She loves J-pop. She's **registered with** lots of different fan clubs. 彼女はJポップが好きで，いろんなファンクラブに登録している

regret /rɪgrét/ 名 後悔, 遺憾

| express | regret | 遺憾の意を表す |
| have | no regrets | 後悔はない |

▷When he realized all the trouble he had caused did he **express** any **regret**? 自分がいろいろめんどうを引き起こしたのに気づいて，彼はすまなそうな顔をしたかい
▷He says he **has no regrets**. 後悔はないと彼は言っている

deep	regret	深い後悔, 強い遺憾
great	regret	の意
biggest	regret	最大の後悔
only	regret	唯一の後悔

▷It is *with* **great regret** that I announce my resignation from the board of directors. 誠に残念ですが，取締役を退任することを私はここに発表します

expression of	regret	遺憾の意の表明
a pang of	regret	痛恨の念
a tinge of	regret	かすかな後悔

▷He left his wife and children without any **expression of regret**. 妻子を捨てても彼はまったく後悔の念を示さなかった
▷It was with a **tinge of regret** that she split up with her boyfriend. ボーイフレンドと別れて彼女にはわずかに未練が残った

regret	about A	Aに対する後悔
regret	at A	
regret	for A	
to	A's regret	残念なことに

▷There's no point in having **regrets about** the past. 過去のことを後悔してもしようがない
▷She feels no **regret for** what she did. 彼女は自分がしたことを後悔していない
▷**To** his **regret**, the bank refused to lend him any more money. 残念なことに，銀行は彼にこれ以上の融資を断った

regret /rɪgrét/ 動 後悔する；残念に思う

| deeply | regret | 深く後悔する |
| bitterly | regret | ひどく後悔する |

▷He **deeply regrets** losing his temper. カッとなったことを彼は深く後悔している
▷She **bitterly regrets** not going to America when she had the chance. 機会があったのにアメリカに行かなかったことを彼女はひどく後悔している

| regret | that... | …が残念だ |

▷I **regret that** I never had the opportunity to study abroad. 留学する機会がなかったのが残念だ

| regret | doing | …したのを後悔する |
| regret | to do | 残念ながら…する |

★regret to do の do は say, inform, announce, advise, report など

▷I **regret** not going on the school trip. 遠足に行かなかったのを後悔している
▷I **regret to say** that there's nothing more I can do to help. 残念ですが私がお手伝いできることはもうありません
▷I **regret to inform** you that we are unable to offer

you a position. 残念ながら貴殿の採用は見合わせることになりました

live	to regret	一生後悔する

▷If you don't take this chance to go and work for a year in America you'll **live to regret** it! この機会を利用してアメリカで1年働かなかったら一生後悔することになるよ

regulation /règjuléiʃən/

名 規則, 法規；規制

make	a regulation	規則を設ける
enforce	a regulation	規則を実施する
comply with	a regulation	規則に従う
observe	a regulation	規則を守る
break	a regulation	規則を破る
have	a regulation	規則がある

▷The government is **making** new **regulations** about entry visas. 政府は入国ビザに関する新たな規定を設けつつある
▷If you don't **comply with** the **regulations** you'll be in trouble. 規則に従わなければやっかいなことになる
▷We **have** many **regulations** in this company concerning security. この会社にはセキュリティ面で多くの規定がある

strict	regulations	厳しい規則
new	regulations	新しい規則
detailed	regulations	詳細な規則
building	regulations	建築基準法規
traffic	regulations	交通法規
safety	regulations	安全規則
government	regulation	政府の規制
statutory	regulation	法的規制

▷We have **strict regulations** for club members. 会員に対する厳しい規則がある
▷There are **detailed regulations** about what to do in case of a hotel fire. ホテル火災時の対処法に関して詳細な規則がある
▷The **statutory regulation** against illegal entry into the country are very strict. 不法入国に対する法的規制はとても厳しい

regulations	on A	Aに関する規則
under	(the) regulations	規則のもとで

▷**Under** the **regulations** we can't serve alcoholic drinks to anybody under the age of 18. 法規では18歳未満の人にはアルコール飲料を提供できない

rules and regulations		規則・規定

▷When you join the army there are so many **rules and regulations**. 軍隊に入隊するには多くの規則・規定がある

reject /ridʒékt/ **動** 拒絶する, 退ける

explicitly	reject	はっきり拒否する
firmly	reject	きっぱり拒否する
immediately	reject	直ちに拒否する
totally	reject	全面的に拒否する

▷We **explicitly rejected** your proposal at the last meeting. 私たちは先回の会議であなたの提案をはっきりと拒否した
▷He **firmly rejects** everything that was written in the newspaper article. 彼は新聞記事の内容をすべてきっぱりと退けている
▷Her application was **immediately rejected**. 彼女の申請は直ちに拒否された

relate /riléit/ **動** 関連がある, 関係がある

closely	relate	密接に関連する
directly	relate	直接に関連する
relate	specifically	特に関係する

★directly は動詞の後でも用いる

▷The drop in cases of influenza **closely relates** to the increase in vaccinations. インフルエンザの症例の減少は予防接種の増加と密接に関連している
▷The rise in gas prices **relates directly** to the rise in oil prices. ガソリン価格の上昇は原油価格の値上がりと直接の関係がある
▷The change in the law **relates specifically** to foreign workers. 法律の変更点は特に外国人労働者に関係している

relate A	to B	AをBに関連づける

▷We can **relate** the rise in crime **to** the rise in unemployment. 犯罪の増加を失業増加と関連づけることができる

related /riléitid/ **形** 関連のある；親戚の

closely	related	密接に関連した
intimately	related	
strongly	related	強く関連した
directly	related	直接に関連した
clearly	related	明らかに関連した
closely	related	近い親戚で

| relation |

distantly	related	遠い親戚で

▷ I'm sure her success is **closely related** *to* all the hard work she's done. 彼女が成功したのはあんなにがんばったからこそだ
▷ It is well-known that smoking is **directly related** *to* cancer. 喫煙ががんと直接の関係があることはよく知られている
▷ Our new member of staff is **distantly related** *to* the boss's wife. 新しいスタッフは上司の奥さんの遠い親戚だ

relation /riléiʃən/ 名 関係, 関連; 親戚

establish	relations	関係を築く
have	relations	関係がある
bear	no relation to A	Aと関係がない
maintain	relations	関係を維持する
improve	relations	関係を改善する
restore	relations	関係を修復する

▷ She **has** close **relations** with many important people in the fashion world. 彼女はファッション界の多くの重要人物と親交がある
▷ It's important for us to **maintain** good **relations** with China. 中国との良好な関係を維持することが重要だ
▷ The two countries have finally **restored** diplomatic **relations** with each other. 両国はついに相互に外交関係を修復した

a close	relation	密接な関係
a direct	relation	直接の関係
friendly	relations	友好関係
good	relations	良好な関係
diplomatic	relations	外交関係
foreign	relations	
international	relations	国際関係
social	relations	社会的関係
industrial	relations	労使関係
public	relations	広報活動

▷ There's a **direct relation** between pollution and the greenhouse effect. 公害と温室効果には直接の関係がある
▷ It's essential to maintain **friendly relations** with our customers. 顧客と友好関係を維持するのが何より重要だ
▷ We have **good relations** with our sister university in Canada. カナダの姉妹大学とは良好な関係にある
▷ We need to maintain good **diplomatic relations** with all Arab countries. 全アラブ諸国と良好な外交関係を維持する必要がある
▷ At the moment **industrial relations** between trade unions and management are excellent. いまのところ労働組合と経営側の労使関係は良好だ
▷ He's an expert on **public relations**. 彼はPRの専門家だ

relation	between A	Aとの間の関係
relations	with A	Aとの関係
in relation	to A	Aに関して

▷ The **relation between** supply and demand determines price. 需要と供給の関係で価格が決まる
▷ Unfortunately she no longer has very good **relations with** her family. 不幸なことに彼女はもはや家族とはあまりよい関係にはない
▷ **In relation to** your second point, I'm afraid I totally disagree. 2点目に関してはまったく賛成しかねます

relationship /riléiʃənʃip/

名 関係, 関連

establish	a relationship	関係を築く
develop	a relationship	関係を発展させる
examine	the relationship	関連を探る
explore	the relationship	
show	the relationship	関連を示す

▷ This lecture will **explore** the **relationship** between politicians and the media. この講義では政治家とマスコミの関係を探ります
▷ This graph **shows** the **relationship** between advertising our product on TV and increases in sales. このグラフは当社製品のテレビ広告と売り上げ増の関係を示している

a good	relationship	良好な関係
a close	relationship	密接な関係
a special	relationship	特別な関係
a personal	relationship	個人的関係
a sexual	relationship	性的関係
human	relationships	人間関係
social	relationships	社会的関係

▷ Samantha and I have a **close relationship**. サマンサと私は親しい間柄です
▷ Britain and America have a **special relationship**. イギリスとアメリカは特別な関係だ
▷ She has an excellent **personal relationship** with her boss. 彼女は上司と個人的にすばらしい関係にある
▷ We think that they may have had a **sexual relationship**. 彼らには性的関係があったんじゃないかなあ
▷ **Human relationships** can be very complicated. 人間関係はとても複雑なところがある

relationship	between A	Aとの間の関係

| relationship | with A | Aとの関係 |

▷Do you think there's a **relationship between** violence on television and violence in the real world? テレビでの暴力と現実世界での暴力には関係があると思いますか
▷She has a really good **relationship with** her other classmates. 彼女は他のクラスメイトととてもよい関係だ

relax /rilǽks/ 動 くつろぐ

totally	relax	すっかりくつろぐ
completely	relax	
relax	a little	少しくつろぐ

▷I need to go on holiday and **totally relax**. 休暇に出かけて思いっ切り羽をのばさないといけない
▷Take your shoes off and sit down. **Relax a little**! 靴を脱いで座って，少しくつろぎなさい

| relax and enjoy | | くつろいで楽しむ |

▷When I get home I'm going to sit back, **relax and enjoy** a movie! 家に帰ったらゆったり腰掛けて映画を楽しむつもりだ

release /rilí:s/

名 解放，釈放；公表，発売，公開

announce	the release	解放を発表する；発売を発表する
be scheduled for	release	公開予定である
demand	the release	解放を要求する；公表を求める
secure	A's release	解放を勝ち取る

▷The Government has **announced** the **release** of six political prisoners. 政府は6名の政治犯の釈放を発表した
▷The film is **scheduled for release** in May. その映画は5月公開予定だ
▷The terrorists are **demanding** the **release** of their leader. テロリストたちはリーダーの釈放を求めている

general	release	一般公開
a new	release	新作
a press	release	新聞発表

▷This movie can now be seen on **general release**. この映画は一般公開中です

| release | from A | Aからの釈放 |

▷His **release from** prison is scheduled for next Saturday. 彼が刑務所を出るのは次の土曜日の予定だ

release /rilí:s/

動 解放する，釈放する；公表する，発売する，公開する

finally	released	ついに解放された；
eventually	released	ついに公開された
recently	released	最近解放された；最近発売された

▷There were many problems but the movie will be **finally released** next week. いろいろ問題があったが，その映画はようやく来週封切りになる
▷Six rare birds were **recently released** into the wild. 6羽の希少な鳥が最近野生に放たれた

| release A | from B | AをBから解放する |

▷They **released** my grandmother **from** hospital last week. 先週，祖母が退院した

relief /rilí:f/

名 安心，安堵；緩和；救済；救援物資

bring	relief	安心をもたらす；緩和する
provide	relief	
feel	relief	安心する

▷It **brought** her a lot of **relief** to hear that her daughter was safe. 娘が無事だと聞いて彼女はほっとした
▷If you take this medicine it will **provide relief** from the pain. この薬を飲めば痛みが和らぎます
▷She **felt** great **relief** that she had finally passed the driving test after 3 attempts! 3度目でやっと運転免許試験に合格して彼女はほっとした

a great	relief	大きな安心
(a) welcome	relief	うれしい息抜き
(a) light	relief	軽い息抜き
pain	relief	鎮痛
tax	relief	減税；免税

▷It was a **great relief** to everyone when she telephoned to say she was OK. 無事を知らせる彼女からの電話にみんなほっとした
▷It was a **welcome relief** when I finally got a seat on the train. ようやく列車で席に座れたときはほんとうに助かった
▷It came as a **light relief** to have a cup of coffee after the 2-hour lecture! 2時間の講義の後での1杯のコーヒーは軽い息抜きになった
▷You need to fill in this form to obtain **tax relief**. 免税を受けるにはこの用紙に記入する必要がある

| a sense of | relief | 安心感 |

| relieved |

| a sigh of | relief | 安堵のため息 |

▷ "It's OK. I've found my wallet!" He breathed a **sigh of relief**. 「よかった．財布が見つかった」と言って彼はほっとため息をついた

relief	from A	Aの軽減
in	relief	安心して，ほっとして
to	A's relief	ほっとしたことに

▷ You need to get some **relief from** all this stress. こういったストレスを少し減らさないといけないね
▷ When she got home the front door was open, but **to her relief** nothing had been stolen. 帰宅すると玄関のドアが開いていたが，盗まれたものは何もなかったので彼女はほっとした

PHRASES
What a relief! 😊 ああ，ほっとした

relieved /rilíːvd/ 形 ほっとして，安心して

| greatly | relieved | 大いにほっとして |
| immensely | relieved | |

▷ He was **immensely relieved** when he found the missing book. なくなっていた本が見つかって彼はとてもほっとした

| relieved | to do | …してほっとして |
| relieved | that... | …にほっとして |

▷ We're all **relieved to** hear that your operation was successful. あなたの手術がうまくいったと聞いて本当にほっとしている
▷ I'm **relieved that** you've decided to stay with the company. あなたが会社に残ることになって私はほっとしている

rely /rilái/

動 (rely on A, rely upon A で) Aに頼る

rely	heavily on A	大いにAに頼る
rely	entirely on A	すっかりAに頼る
rely	solely on A	
increasingly	rely on A	ますますAに頼る
always	rely on A	いつもAに頼る
no longer	rely on A	もはやAに頼らない

▷ I don't know what the boss would do if you left. He **relies** so **heavily on** you. きみがいなくなったら上司はどうするかわからないよ．きみに頼りっきりだもの
▷ We're **increasingly relying on** the Internet for up-to-date information. 最新の情報を得るためにインターネットに頼ることがますます多くなっている
▷ You can **always rely on** me for help at any time. 助けが必要なときはいつでも私に言ってきなさい

| rely on A | to do | Aが…するのを当てにする |
| rely on A | for B | AにBを当てにする |

▷ My family are **relying on** me **to** plan the whole trip. うちの家族は旅行プランをすっかり私に任せっきりだ
▷ I'm **relying on** you **for** up-to-date information. きみから最新情報をもらうのを当てにしている

remark /rimáːrk/ 名 意見, 発言

make	a remark	発言する
withdraw	one's remark	発言を撤回する
ignore	A's remark	発言を無視する

▷ "Did you **make a remark**?" "No, I didn't say anything." 「何かおっしゃいましたか」「いえ，何も言っていません」
▷ She refused to **withdraw** her **remarks**. 彼女は発言を撤回するのを拒んだ
▷ Don't be upset. Just **ignore** her **remarks**. 取り乱さないで．彼女の発言なんか無視しなさい

a casual	remark	何気ない発言
critical	remarks	批判的な発言
sarcastic	remarks	皮肉を込めた発言
racist	remarks	人種差別発言
sexist	remarks	性差別発言
introductory	remarks	前置きの話
a personal	remark	個人攻撃

▷ I didn't mean it seriously. It was just a **casual remark**. 本気じゃなかったの．何気なく言っただけ
▷ Welcome to our scuba-diving course. I'd like to start with a few **introductory remarks**. スキューバダイビング講習会へようこそ．最初にちょっと前置きさせていただきます
▷ This is a business meeting. Please don't make **personal remarks**. 仕事の打ち合わせなので，個人攻撃になるような発言はしないでください

| a remark | about A | Aについての意見 |
| a remark | on A | |

▷ Did anybody make any **remarks about** your new hairstyle? あなたの新しい髪型のことでだれか何か言ったかい

remarkable /rimáːrkəbl/

形 注目すべき；著しい，驚くべき

particularly	remarkable	とりわけ注目すべき
quite	remarkable	とても驚くべき
truly	remarkable	まさに驚くべき

▷Her progress in English has been **quite remarkable** since she went to London. ロンドンに行ってからの彼女の英語の上達はすごく著しい
▷His quick recovery after the accident was **truly remarkable**. 事故後の彼の急速な回復ぶりはまさに驚くほどだ

it is remarkable	that...	…には驚く

▷**It's remarkable that** nobody noticed that the money was missing. お金がなくなっていることにだれも気づかなかったのは驚きだ

remarkable	for A	Aの理由で注目すべき
remarkable	about A	Aの点で注目すべき

▷This department store is **remarkable for** its discounts. この百貨店は驚くほど値引きする

remember /rimémbər/

動 覚えている；思い出す

well	remember	よく覚えている
clearly	remember	はっきり覚えている
distinctly	remember	
vividly	remember	鮮やかに覚えている
vaguely	remember	ぼんやり覚えている
dimly	remember	かすかに覚えている
always	remember	ずっと忘れない
suddenly	remember	急に思い出す
remember	rightly	正確に覚えている
remember	correctly	
remember	exactly	正確に思い出す

▷I can **well remember** the first time I saw you. きみに初めて会ったときのことをよく覚えている
▷She **suddenly remembered** she hadn't locked the front door. 彼女は玄関の鍵をかけてこなかったのを急に思い出した
▷"Where's Peter's house?" "If I **remember rightly** it's the third on the left." 「ピーターの家はどこ？」「記憶に間違いがなければ左側の3つ目だよ」
▷Sorry, I can't **remember exactly** what she said. ごめん，彼女が何を言ったか正確に思い出せないや

remember	doing	…したのを覚えている
remember A	doing	A(人)が…したのを覚えている
remember	to do	忘れずに…する

▷I don't **remember** receiv**ing** an email from him. 彼からEメールを受け取った覚えはない
▷**Remember to** let us know you've arrived safely. 無事に着いたら忘れずに知らせてね

remember	that...	…を覚えている
remember	wh-	…か覚えている

★wh- は what, when, how など

▷Oh! You **remembered that** I take milk and sugar! あら，私がミルクと砂糖を入れるのを覚えていてくれたのね
▷I don't **remember what** she said. 彼女が何を言ったか覚えていない
▷I don't **remember how** to get to Bob's house. ボブの家への行き方を覚えていない

remind /rimáind/ 動 思い出させる

always	remind	いつも思い出させる
constantly	remind	絶えず思い出させる
frequently	remind	しばしば思い出させる

▷Getting emails from Sachiko **constantly reminds** me of my life before I left Japan. 幸子からEメールをもらうと日本を発つ前の生活をいつも思い出す

remind A	of B	A(人)にBを思い起こさせる
remind A	about B	A(人)にBのことで念を押す

▷That TV program about Sydney **reminded** me **of** my homestay in Australia. シドニーを取り上げたテレビ番組を見てオーストラリアでのホームステイを思い出した
▷Don't forget to **remind** Angus **about** the party on Saturday. 土曜日のパーティーの件でアンガスに忘れずに念を押しておいてね

remind A	that...	A(人)に…だと思い出させる
remind A	wh-	A(人)に…か思い出させる

★wh- は what, when, how など

▷Can I **remind** you **that** we have to leave in 5 minutes to catch the plane! 飛行機に乗るにはあと5分で出かけなきゃいけないんだよ，わかってるかい
▷Can you **remind** me **how** to get to your house? きみの家にどう行けばいいのかもう一度教えてくれないか

remind A	to do	A(人)に…するよう念を押す

▷Please **remind** me **to** call him later. 後で彼に電話するよう忘れずに私に念を押してね

PHRASES
Don't remind me. ☺ いやなことを思い出させるなよ

| remove |

That reminds me. 😊 それで思い出した ▷Speaking of money, that reminds me. You owe me $20! お金と言えば，思い出したよ．きみに20ドル貸しているよね

remove /rimúːv/ 動 取り除く，取り去る

carefully	remove	注意深く取り除く
effectively	remove	効果的に取り除く
be easily	removed	簡単に取り除ける
far	removed	遠くかけ離れた

▷The ink cartridge can **be easily removed** from the printer. インクカートリッジはプリンターから簡単に取り外せる
▷What he said is **far removed** from the truth. 彼が言ったことは事実とは遠くかけ離れている

remove A	from B	AをBから取り出す

▷He **removed** all his money **from** the safe. 彼は金庫からあり金を残らず取り出した

repair /ripéər/ 名 修理，修繕

carry out	repairs	修理する
do	repairs	
make	repairs	
need	repairs	修理を必要とする
be in need of	repair	

▷It'll take months to **carry out repairs**. 修理するのに何か月もかかるだろう
▷It's a lovely country cottage, but it's **in** constant **need of repair**. すてきな田舎の小別荘だが修理が絶えず必要だ（★needの前にgreat, desperate, constant, urgentなどの形容詞をしばしば伴う）

a major	repair	大規模な修理
a minor	repair	小規模な修理
necessary	repairs	必要な修理
urgent	repairs	緊急の修理

▷After the flood our apartment needed **major repairs**. 洪水の後，うちのアパートは大修理が必要だった
▷We've carried out all the **necessary repairs**. 必要な修理をすべて行った

repair and maintenance		修理と保守
repair or replacement		修理か交換

▷The landlord is responsible for the **repair and maintenance** of our apartment. うちのアパートの修理と保守は家主の責任だ
▷The insurance company will pay for the **repair or replacement** of goods damaged in the fire. 火事で破損した家財の修理や交換費は保険会社が払ってくれる

under	repair	修理中で
beyond	repair	修理できないほど
in good	repair	手入れが行き届いて
in poor	repair	手入れが行き届かなくて

▷We can't go over this bridge. It's **under repair**. この橋は渡れないな．修理中だ
▷I'm afraid this TV set is **beyond repair**. このテレビは修理してもむだなんじゃないかな
▷I've had this bicycle for nearly five years, but it's still **in good repair**. この自転車は5年近く乗っているが，いまでも手入れが行き届いた状態だ

repeat /ripíːt/ 名 繰り返し，反復

prevent	a repeat	繰り返しを避ける

▷We have to **prevent a repeat** of this disaster. このような災害が繰り返されるのは避けなければならない

replace /ripléis/

動 取って代わる；取り替える

completely	replace	完全に取って代わる
eventually	replace	結局は取って代わる
gradually	replace	徐々に取って代わる

▷DVDs will **eventually replace** videos entirely. DVDはいずれビデオに完全に取って代わるだろう
▷Hybrid cars may **gradually replace** cars run on gasoline. ハイブリッドカーは徐々にガソリンで動く車に取って代わるかもしれない

replace A	with B	AをBと取り替える
replace A	as B	BとしてAに取って代わる
be replaced	by A	Aに取って代わられる

▷We need to **replace** this old photocopying machine **with** a new one. この古いコピー機を新しいのと取り替える必要がある
▷Did you hear? Malcolm has **replaced** Tom **as** Managing Director! 聞いたか．マルコムがトムに代わって業務執行取締役になったよ
▷Hand written letters have largely been **replaced by** emails. 手書きの手紙は大部分がEメールに取って代わられた

reply /riplái/ 名 返事，応答

get	a reply	返事をもらう
have	a reply	
receive	a reply	返事を受け取る
make	no reply	返事しない
send	a reply	返事を送る

▷ We still haven't **got** a **reply** from them. 彼らからまだ返事をもらっていない
▷ So far they've **made no reply**. これまでのところ彼らから返事がない
▷ We should **send** a **reply** as soon as possible. できるだけ早く返信するほうがいい

a reply	from A	Aからの返事
a reply	to A	Aに対する返事
in reply	(to A)	(Aへの)返事として

▷ "How's your job-hunting going?" "Quite well. I've had a **reply from** six companies." 「職探しはどう?」「好調だよ。6社から返事をもらったよ」
▷ Have you had a **reply to** your letter? 手紙への返事はありましたか
▷ **In reply to** your letter of July 4, please find enclosed information. 7月4日付の手紙にお答えして情報を同封いたします

reply /riplái/ 動 返事する, 答える; 応じる

reply	firmly	きっぱり返事する
reply	immediately	即座に返事する
reply	quickly	急いで返事する
reply	quietly	静かに返事する
reply	shortly	そっけなく返事する

▷ This matter is really urgent. I think we should **reply immediately**. この問題は緊急だ。すぐ返事しなくてはいけない
▷ If you want the job you need to **reply quickly**. 仕事がほしいなら返事を急ぐ必要がある
▷ When I asked my boss for a raise he **replied shortly** that it was impossible. 上司に昇給を求めたら, 無理だとそっけなく返事された

reply	to A	Aに返事をする
reply	with A	Aで応じる

▷ They still haven't **replied to** our letter. 私たちの手紙にまだ返事がもらえていない

reply	(that...)	…と答える

▷ They **replied that** they needed more time to consider our proposal. われわれの提案を検討する時間がもっと必要だと彼らは返事してきた

report /ripɔ́:rt/ 名 報告; 報告書; 報道

give	a report	報告する
make	a report	
write	a report	報告書を書く
produce	a report	報告書を作成する
issue	a report	報告書を出す
publish	a report	報告書を発表する
submit	a report	報告書を提出する

▷ I have to **give** a **report** to the committee on Monday. 月曜日に委員会に報告しなくてはならない
▷ I still haven't **made** a **report** on my business trip. まだ出張報告をしていない
▷ We have to **submit** our **report** by the end of this month. 今月末までに報告書を提出しなければならない

a detailed	report	詳細な報告
a recent	report	最近の報告
an interim	report	中間報告
an annual	report	年次報告
a final	report	最終報告
a written	report	文書による報告
an official	report	公式の報告
a committee	report	委員会報告
a government	report	政府報告
a news	report	ニュース報道
a newspaper	report	新聞報道

▷ A **recent report** suggests that the number of unemployed is rising. 最近の報告では失業者数が増加していることがわかる
▷ According to our company's **annual report** profits are up again this year. 当社の年次報告によれば利益は今年また上昇している
▷ We're still waiting for the Government's **final report**. なお政府の最終報告を待っている

a report	by A	Aによる報告
a report	from A	Aからの報告
a report	on A	Aに関する報告

▷ This is a **report from** our branch in New York. これはニューヨーク支店からの報告です
▷ Have you read this **report on** the earthquake in Chile? チリ地震についてのこの報告書を読んだかい

report /ripɔ́:rt/ 動 報告する, 報道する

be widely	reported	広く報道される
be officially	reported	公式に報道される
falsely	report	誤って報道する

| represent |

correctly	report	正しく報道する
report	back	帰って報告する

▷ It has been **widely reported** that the Prime Minister is going to resign. 首相が近く辞任すると広く報道されている
▷ The marriage of Prince William and Kate Middleton was **officially reported** by newspapers all over the world. ウィリアム王子とケイト・ミドルトンの結婚が世界中の新聞で公式に報道された

report	on A	Aに関して報告する
report A	to B	AをBに通報する

▷ The TV program **reported on** recent events in India. そのテレビ番組はインドでの最近の出来事について報道した
▷ He **reported** the story **to** the newspapers. 彼はその話を新聞社に通報した

report	doing	…したと報告する

▷ She **reported** seeing a strange man in the building. 彼女はその建物で不審な男を見かけたと報告した

report	that...	…と報告する

▷ He went to the police station and **reported that** his car had been stolen. 彼は警察署に行って車の盗難届を出した

be reported	to be	…であると報道される

▷ A helicopter is **reported to** have crashed in a mountain area. ヘリコプターが山間部で墜落したと報道されている

represent /rèprizént/
動 代表する；表す；描く

adequately	represent	的確に代弁する
be well	represented	多くの人が集まる
be poorly	represented	少ない人が集まる

▷ We need to find someone who can **adequately represent** our views to the meeting. 私たちの見解を会議で的確に代弁できる人を見つける必要がある
▷ British film makers were **well represented** at the Cannes Film Festival this year. 今年のカンヌ映画祭にはイギリスの映画製作会社の代表が多く集まった

represent A	as B	AをBとして描く

▷ This newspaper report **represents** the latest drop in crime figures **as** encouraging. この新聞報道では最近の犯罪件数の減少を明るい材料と見ている

reputation /rèpjutéiʃən/ 名 評判；名声

have	a reputation	評判がある
acquire	a reputation	名声を得る
earn	a reputation	
gain	a reputation	
build	a reputation	名声を築く
establish	a reputation	
make	a reputation	
enhance	a reputation	名声を高める
damage	A's reputation	名声を傷つける
maintain	a reputation	名声を維持する
protect	one's reputation	名声を守る

▷ He **has a reputation** for working slowly. 彼は仕事が遅いという評判だ
▷ She's beginning to **gain a reputation** in the art world. 彼女は美術界で注目され出した
▷ Our company has **established** an excellent **reputation** for after sales service. 当社はアフターサービスが充実しているとの好評をいただいています
▷ The scandal **damaged** the Prime Minister's **reputation**. そのスキャンダルで首相の名前に傷がついた

an excellent	reputation	よい評判
a good	reputation	
a high	reputation	高い評判
a bad	reputation	悪い評判
a growing	reputation	高まる評判
an international	reputation	国際的名声
a worldwide	reputation	世界的名声

▷ He has a really **good reputation** as a manager. 彼はマネジャーとしてすごく評判がいい
▷ That young man's going to be successful. He has a **growing reputation**. あの若者は成功するだろう. 評判が高まりつつある
▷ She's a top golf player now. She has an **international reputation**. 彼女はいまやゴルフのトッププレーヤーで, 国際的にも有名だ

a reputation	as A	Aとしての評判
a reputation	for A	Aに対する評判

▷ He has a **reputation as** an expert in his field. 彼はその分野で専門家として評判だ
▷ He has a **reputation for** losing his temper. 彼はかんしゃくを起こすという評判だ

request /rikwést/ 名 要請, 要望

make	a request	要望する
have	a request	要望を受ける

receive	a request	
consider	a request	要望を検討する
accept	a request	要望を受け入れる
grant	a request	
respond to	a request	要望に応じる
ignore	a request	要望を無視する
refuse	a request	要望を拒絶する
reject	a request	
repeat	a request	要望を繰り返す

▷ Can I **make** a **request**? お願いしていいかな
▷ We've **had** a lot of **requests** to repeat this TV drama. このテレビドラマを再放送してほしいという多くの要望があった
▷ We've **received** a **request** for somebody to transfer from here to head office in Tokyo. ここから東京本社にだれか異動してほしいとの要望を受けた
▷ They **refused** her **request** for a new computer. 新しいコンピュータがほしいという彼女の要望は却下された

a reasonable	request	妥当な要望
a formal	request	正式な要望

▷ It's a **reasonable request** so I think there will be no problem. それはもっともな要望だから問題ないだろう
▷ If you want to take three days' holiday you need to make a **formal request**. 3日間の休暇をとりたいなら正式に申請する必要がある

a request	for A	Aを求める要望
at	the request of A	Aの要望で
by	request	要望に応えて
on	request	要望があれば

▷ We've received a **request for** more medical supplies. 医療物資がもっとほしいとの要望を受けた
▷ **At** the **request of** our members we're going to change some of the club rules. 会員の要望でクラブ規則の一部を変える予定です
▷ Further details are available **on request**. 要望があればさらに詳細をお見せできます

a request	that...	…という要望

▷ We've received a **request that** our canteen should have a smoking and a nonsmoking area. 社員食堂を分煙にしてほしいという要望を受け取った

PHRASES
Any requests? 😊 何かほしいものはありますか

require /rikwáiər/ 動 必要とする；求める

urgently	require	緊急に必要とする
normally	require	ふつうは必要とする
reasonably	require	正当に要求する

▷ We **urgently require** a van driver. 緊急にトラック運転手を求めている
▷ This teaching post **normally requires** a master's degree. この教職に就くにはふつう修士号が必要だ
▷ We can't **reasonably require** our employees to work 15 hours a day! 従業員に1日15時間労働を要求するなど許されない

require A	to do	A(人)に…するよう求める

▷ His manager **required** him **to** do 3 hours overtime every day for a month. 部長は彼に1か月間、毎日3時間の残業をするよう求めた

require	that...	…を要求する

▷ The new law **requires that** smoking is banned in public places. 新法は公共の場での禁煙を求めている

requirement /rikwáiərmənt/

名 必要条件，要求されること；必要事項

meet	the requirements	必要条件を満たす
fulfill	the requirements	
satisfy	the requirements	
comply with	the requirements	

▷ Sorry sir, your hand luggage doesn't **comply with** the **requirements** of the airline. I'm afraid it's too large. 申し訳ありませんが、お客様の手荷物は航空会社の基準に合っておりません。大きすぎます

a basic	requirement	基本的な必要条件
the minimum	requirement	最低必要条件

▷ A university degree is a **basic requirement** for this job. この仕事に就くには基本的に大学の学位が必要です

rescue /réskju:/ 名 救助

come to	A's rescue	救助に来る

▷ I would have drowned if you hadn't **come to** my **rescue**. あなたが救助に来てくれなかったら私はおぼれ死んでいただろう

research /rísə:rtʃ/ 名 研究, 調査

| resemble |

do	research	研究する
carry out	research	
conduct	research	
undertake	research	研究に取り組む
engage in	research	研究に従事する
fund	research	研究に資金を出す
support	research	研究を支援する

▷ My brother's **doing research** for his master's degree at London University. 兄はロンドン大学で修士号をとるために研究している
▷ She's **engaged in research** into the effects of long-distance space travel. 彼女は長距離宇宙旅行が与える影響について研究している
▷ It's difficult to find companies to **fund research** these days. 近ごろは研究に資金を出してくれる企業を見つけるのは難しい

research	shows	研究の示すところでは
research	suggests	

▷ Recent **research suggests** that consuming green or oolong tea may help prevent high blood pressure. 最近の研究によれば緑茶やウーロン茶を飲むと高血圧の予防につながるようだ

basic	research	基礎研究
recent	research	最近の研究
market	research	市場調査
medical	research	医学研究
scientific	research	科学研究

▷ We've done the **basic research** and we think we'll soon be able to produce an improved hybrid car. 基礎研究が終わり、まもなく改良ハイブリッド車を生産できると思う

research	into A	Aについての研究
research	on A	
research	in A	Aにおける研究

▷ Pete's doing **research into** the effects of pollution on marine life. ピートは汚染が海洋生物へ与える影響について研究している

an area of	research	研究分野

resemble /rizémbl/ 動 似ている

closely	resemble	よく似ている
strongly	resemble	
faintly	resemble	少し似ている
vaguely	resemble	

▷ Two of the girls in my class aren't identical twins, but they **closely resemble** each other. うちのクラスの女の子二人は一卵性双生児でもないのに、お互いにそっくりだ

reservation /rìzərvéiʃən/

名 予約；疑念, 懸念

make	a reservation	予約する
have	a reservation	予約してある
have	reservations	懸念がある
express	reservations	懸念を示す

▷ I **made a reservation** for you at the Hilton Hotel. あなたの名前でヒルトンホテルを予約しました
▷ I **have a reservation** for tonight. A table for two. 今夜2名のテーブルを予約してあります

reservations	about A	Aについての懸念

▷ I still have **reservations about** signing the contract. 契約書にサインするにはまだ懸念があります

resist /rizíst/ 動 抵抗する；耐える

fiercely	resist	激しく抵抗する
strongly	resist	強く抵抗する
successfully	resist	うまく抵抗する

▷ She fought back hard and **successfully resisted** her attacker. 彼女は懸命に反撃し、攻撃してくる相手を撃退した

resist	doing	…するのを我慢する

▷ I can't **resist** hav**ing** just one more piece of chocolate cake! もう一切れチョコレートケーキが食べたくてたまらない

be hard	to resist	我慢するのが難しい
be difficult	to resist	

▷ That lovely chocolate cake is **difficult to resist**! そのおいしそうなチョコレートケーキを見ると我慢できない

resistance /rizístəns/

名 抵抗, 反抗；抵抗力

put up	resistance	抵抗する
offer	resistance	
meet (with)	resistance	抵抗に遭う
face	resistance	
encounter	resistance	

▷ Surprisingly her boss **offered** no **resistance** to her request for a rise in salary. 驚いたことに彼女の賃上げ要求を上司はあっさりのんでくれた
▷ Management's plans to reorganize the department **met with** a lot of **resistance**. 部を再編しようとする経営側の計画は多くの抵抗に遭った

| resistance | to A | Aに対する抵抗 |

▷ At first there was a lot of **resistance to** the plans to relocate. 当初は移転計画にかなり抵抗があった

resolution /rìzəlúːʃən/

名 決議(案); 解決(策); 決意, 決心

support	a resolution	決議案を支持する
adopt	a resolution	決議案を採択する
pass	a resolution	決議案を通す
approve	a resolution	決議案を認める
reject	a resolution	決議案を否決する
make	a resolution	決心する

▷ I would never **support** a **resolution** to force staff members to retire early. 職員に早期退職を強要する決議など決して支持しない
▷ The meeting **adopted** a **resolution** to reduce the workforce by 10%. 従業員を1割削減する決議を会議で採択した
▷ We **made** a **resolution** to employ no more staff for the next 6 months. 向こう半年間は新しい職員を採用しないことに決めた

a draft	resolution	決議草案
an affirmative	resolution	賛成決議
a special	resolution	特別決議
a peaceful	resolution	平和的解決
conflict	resolution	紛争解決
New Year's	resolution(s)	新年の決意

▷ Both countries are seeking a **peaceful resolution** to their problems. 両国ともこの問題の平和的解決を求めている
▷ What are your **New Year's resolutions**? あなたの新年の決意は何ですか

| a resolution | on A | Aに関する決議案 |
| the resolution | to A | Aの解決 |

▷ The United Nations have passed a **resolution on** the situation in Libya. 国連はリビア情勢に関する決議案を可決した

resolve /rizálv | -zɔ́lv/

動 解決する; 決定する, 決議する

| fully | resolve | 完全に解決する |
| finally | resolve | ついに解決する |

▷ They've made some progress, but they still haven't **fully resolved** the situation. いくらか進展はあったが、まだ状況を完全に解決するには至っていない

| attempt to | resolve | 解決を試みる |
| try to | resolve | |

▷ I think you and Martin should **attempt to resolve** your differences. きみとマーチンは意見の違いを埋めるよう試みるべきだ

| resolve | to do | …することに決める |

▷ After the plane crash she **resolved** never **to** fly again. その航空機事故に遭ってから、彼女は二度と飛行機に乗らないと決めた

| resolve | that... | …と決める |

▷ She **resolved that** one day she would have her own business. いつの日か自分で会社を経営すると彼女は心に決めた

resource /ríːsɔːrs | rizɔ́ːs/

名 資源; 経済資源; 天然資源

have	the resources	資源がある
allocate	resources	資源を配分する
use	resources	資源を利用する

▷ We don't **have** the **resources to** offer any more help. これ以上支援する財源がない
▷ It's important to **allocate resources to** flood victims as soon as possible. できるだけ早く洪水の犠牲者に資金を配分するのが重要だ
▷ We need to think about the best way to **use** our **resources**. 資源を活用する最善の方策を考える必要がある

limited	resources	限られた資源
scarce	resources	希少資源
financial	resources	財源
human	resources	人的資源
natural	resources	天然資源
resources	available	利用可能な資源

▷ The **human resources** department deals with employment contracts. 人事部は雇用契約を扱う
▷ The USA is a country rich in **natural resources**. アメリカは天然資源の豊かな国だ

| respect |

the allocation	of resources	資源の配分

▷ We need to make sure that we have a fair system for the **allocation of resources**. 資源配分のための公平なシステムをつくるようにする必要がある

respect /rispékt/

名 尊敬, 敬意；尊重, 配慮

have	respect	尊敬する
earn	respect	尊敬を得る
gain	respect	尊敬を得る
command	respect	尊敬を集める
lose	respect	尊敬を失う
show	respect	敬意を示す

▷ I **have** a lot of **respect** *for* firefighters. 消防士をとても尊敬している
▷ You need to **earn respect** before you are accepted by the other team members. チームの仲間たちに受け入れられるには，まず尊敬を得る必要がある
▷ In Japanese society you should **show respect** when you meet a person senior to you. 日本社会では目上の人に会うときには敬意を示すほうがよい

deep	respect	深い尊敬
great	respect	
mutual	respect	相互の尊敬

▷ The President has **great respect** for the views of ordinary people. 大統領は世間一般の人たちの見解をとても重んじている

respect	for A	Aに対する尊敬
out of	respect	尊敬の念から；敬意を表して
with	respect	敬意をもって
with respect	to A	Aに関して
in respect	of A	

▷ I have a lot of **respect for** her. She never gives up. 彼女をとても尊敬している．決してあきらめない人だから
▷ **Out of respect**, everybody observed one minute's silence. 敬意を表してみんなで1分間の黙とうを献げた
▷ He always treated her **with** great **respect**. 彼はいつも大きな敬意をもって彼女に接した
▷ **With respect to** the wedding, we've decided to hold it in a five-star hotel. 結婚式のほうは5つ星ホテルで挙げることに決めました

in	this respect	この点で
in	some respects	いくつかの点で
in	all respects	あらゆる点で
in	one important respect	ある重要な点で

▷ **In some respects** what you say is correct, but that's not the whole story. いくつかの点できみの言うとおりだが，話はそれで終わりではない
▷ I disagree with you **in one important respect**. ある重要な点であなたに賛成しかねます

respond /rispánd | -spónd/

動 反応する, 応じる；答える, 返事する

respond	quickly	すばやく反応する
respond	immediately	
respond	positively	前向きに反応する
respond	well	うまく反応する
respond	appropriately	適切に反応する

▷ We can't waste time. We have to **respond quickly**. ぐずぐずしてはいられない．すばやく対応しなければ
▷ I think she **responded** really **well** to the situation. 彼女は状況に実にうまく対応したと思う
▷ Let's wait to see what they do. Then we can **respond appropriately**. 彼らの行動をまず静観しよう．そうすれば適切に対応できる

respond	to A	Aに反応する；Aに答える
respond	by doing	…して応える
respond	with A	Aで応じる

▷ How are you going to **respond to** her letter? 彼女の手紙にどう返事するつもりですか
▷ She **responded by** tearing up the letter into little pieces. 彼女が示した反応は手紙を細かく引きちぎることとだった
▷ He **responded with** a very angry reply. 怒りも露わな反応が彼から返ってきた

response /rispáns | -spóns/

名 反応；答え, 応答

make	a response	反応する；返事する
give	a response	
get	a response	反応がある；返事をもらう
receive	a response	
produce	a response	反応を引き起こす
provoke	a response	

▷ She just stood there and said nothing. She wasn't able to **make a response**. 彼女はそこにたたずんで一言も発しなかった．何とも反応できなかったのだ
▷ I've sent five emails and I still haven't **got a response**. Eメールを5通送ったのに返事がまだない

a good	response	よい反応
a positive	response	前向きな反応
a negative	response	否定的反応
an appropriate	response	適切な反応
a direct	response	直接の反応
an immediate	response	すばやい反応
a quick	response	
the initial	response	最初の反応
a public	response	大衆の反応
an emotional	response	感情的反応
a political	response	政治的反応
an immune	response	免疫反応

▷We're very much hoping for a **positive response**. 前向きな反応を大いに期待している
▷After my email I received an **immediate response**. メールしたらすぐに返事が来た
▷When the Government suggested a rise in the sales tax the **public response** was very negative. 政府が売上税アップを示唆すると，大衆の反応はとても否定的だった

a response	from A	Aからの反応
a response	to A	Aに対する反応

▷I left a message on her desk, but so far I haven't received any **response from** her. 彼女の机に伝言を残しておいたが，これまでのところ彼女から返事がない
▷The **response to** our survey was very encouraging. 調査に対する反応にとても勇気づけられた

in	response (to A)	(Aへの)答えとして

▷I put in a request for holiday leave, but so far I've heard nothing **in response**. 休暇願いを出したが，これまでのところ回答がない

responsibility /rispὰnsəbíləti | -spòn-/

名 責任，義務，責務

have	responsibility	責任がある
accept	responsibility	責任を負う
assume	responsibility	
take	responsibility	
share	responsibility	責任を共有する
claim	responsibility	犯行声明を出す

▷I'm looking for a job where I can **have responsibility**. 責任をもってやらせてもらえる仕事を探しています
▷I've asked Mr. Bean to **assume responsibility** for the office while I'm away. 留守中にビーンさんに事務所のことを頼んだ
▷We both **share** equal **responsibility** for the mistakes that were made. 誤りがあったら私たち二人とも同等に責任がある
▷So far nobody has **claimed responsibility** for yesterday's terrorist attack. 昨日のテロ攻撃の犯行声明はいまのところどこからも出ていない

full	responsibility	全責任
a great	responsibility	大きな責任
a heavy	responsibility	重い責任
a special	responsibility	特別な責任
personal	responsibility	個人の責任
social	responsibility	社会的責任
parental	responsibility	親の責任

▷It was my decision. I take **full responsibility**. 私が決めたことなので，私が全責任をとります
▷Some young couples these days don't show enough **parental responsibility**. 近ごろの若いカップルの中には親の責任を十分に果たさない者がいる

a sense of	responsibility	責任感
a position of	responsibility	責任ある立場

▷I know you have a deep **sense of responsibility**. あなたが責任感が強いのはわかっています

responsibility	for A	Aへの責任
a responsibility	to A	A(人)に対する
a responsibility	toward A	責任
on one's own responsibility		自分の責任で

▷We mustn't forget that we have a **responsibility to** our investors. 投資家に対してわれわれは責任があることを忘れてはならない
▷He acted entirely **on** his **own responsibility**. 彼はひたすら自分の責任で行動した

a responsibility	to do	…する責任

▷We all have a **responsibility to** help each other in a crisis. 危機に際してみんなが助け合う責任がある

responsible /rispʌ́nsəbl | -spɔ́n-/

形 責任がある

largely	responsible	大きな責任がある
primarily	responsible	おもに責任がある
directly	responsible	直接責任がある
personally	responsible	個人的に責任がある
ultimately	responsible	最終的に責任がある

▷Emma was **largely responsible** for the success of the project. エマにはプロジェクトを成功させる大きな責任があった
▷In my new job I'm **primarily responsible** for

| rest |

contacting new customers. 新しい仕事では新たな顧客と連絡をとることが私のおもな役割だ

▷If there is a serious problem the president of the company is **ultimately responsible**. 深刻な問題があれば社長が最終的に責任をとる

responsible	for A	Aに責任がある

▷Who was **responsible for** booking the hotels? だれが責任をもってホテルを予約したのか

| hold A | responsible | A(人)に責任を |
| find A | responsible | 問う |

▷Put on your safety helmets! I don't want to be **held responsible** *for* any accidents. 安全ヘルメットを着けろ。いかなる事故の責任も私は問われたくない

rest /rést/ 名 休息, 休憩；残り

get	some rest	少し休む
have	a rest	一休みする
take	a rest	
spend	the rest	残りを過ごす
finish	the rest	残りを終える
do	the rest	残りをする

▷Take care and **get some rest**. じゃあ，しばらく休んでね

▷You look tired. I think you should **have** a good **rest**. 疲れているみたいだね。ゆっくり休んだほうがいいよ

▷She **spent** the **rest** of the day relaxing on the beach. 彼女はその日の残りを海辺でゆったり過ごした

▷I'm too tired to do any more homework. I'll **finish** the **rest** of it tomorrow. 疲れてもう宿題はできないや．残りはあしたやろうっと

at	rest	静止して；永眠して

▷She had a difficult life, but now she's **at rest**. 彼女は辛い人生を送ったが，いまでは安らかに眠っている

restaurant /réstərənt | -rɔ̀nt/

名 レストラン, 料理店

go to	a restaurant	レストランに行く
run	a restaurant	レストランを経営する

▷Shall we **go to** a **restaurant** this evening? 今晩レストランに行こうか

an excellent	restaurant	いいレストラン
a good	restaurant	
a local	restaurant	地元のレストラン
a Chinese	restaurant	中華料理店
a French	restaurant	フランス料理店
a fast-food	restaurant	ファーストフード店

▷Last night we went to a really **good restaurant**. 昨夜とてもいいレストランに行った

▷I don't want to eat in the hotel. Let's eat in one of the **local restaurants**. ホテルでは食べたくない．地元のレストランに食べに行こうよ

▷Excuse me, is there a **Chinese restaurant** anywhere near here? すみません，この辺りに中華料理店はありますか

in	a restaurant	レストランで
at	a restaurant	

▷Do you want to go to a pub? Or shall we have dinner **in** a **restaurant**? パブに行きたいですか，それともレストランで食事しましょうか

restore /ristɔ́:r/

動 取り戻す；回復する；修復する

fully	restored	完全に回復した
recently	restored	最近回復した
carefully	restored	入念に修復された
extensively	restored	大幅に修復された

▷Electricity should be **fully restored** by tomorrow morning. 電気はあすの朝までには完全に復旧するはずだ

restore A	to B	AをBに回復させる；
		AをBに戻す

▷The electricity company **restored** power **to** the city late last night. 電力会社は昨夜遅く街に電力を復旧させた

result /rizʌ́lt/ 名 結果；成果, 業績

produce	a result	結果を生む
achieve	a result	結果を得る
get	a result	
announce	the result	結果を発表する
show	the result	成果を示す

▷We need to work harder to **produce** a **result**. 結果を生むためにもっと懸命に働く必要がある

▷They're going to **announce** the **results** at the end of this month. 今月末に結果が発表される予定だ

a good	result	よい結果
a positive	result	

the final	result	最終結果
the end	result	
a direct	result	直接の結果
election	results	選挙結果
examination	results	試験結果
research	results	研究結果
concrete	results	具体的な成果
tangible	results	目に見える成果

▷ You worked really hard for these exams. I hope you get a **good result**. 試験のために猛勉強したね。いい結果が出るといいね
▷ We need to get a **positive result**. われわれはよい成果を上げる必要がある
▷ We still don't know the **final result** of the election. 選挙の最終結果はまだわからない

as	a result (of A)	(Aの)結果として
with	the result that...	その結果…となって

▷ The referee sent him off. **As a result** he missed the next two matches. 審判は彼を退場させた。その結果, 彼は続く2試合に出られなくなった
▷ Kevin died **as a result of** the accident. ケビンは事故がもとで死んだ
▷ The meeting ended **with** the **result that** nothing was decided. 会議は何も決まらないまま終わった

return /ritə́ːrn/ 名 帰ること; 返却; 復帰

make	a return	復帰する
demand	a return	返却を求める

▷ Everybody thought his movie career was over, but he was able to **make a return**. だれもが彼の映画キャリアは終わったと思ったが, 彼は復帰できた
▷ He **demanded** the **return** of his money in two weeks. 彼は2週間以内に金を返すよう求めた

the return	to A	Aへ帰ること
the return	from A	Aから帰ること
the return	of A	Aが戻ること
on	A's return	A(人)が戻ってみると
on	return (of A)	(Aの)返却時に
upon	return (of A)	
in	return	お返しに

▷ We lost touch after his **return to** England. 彼がイギリスに帰ってから接触が途絶えた
▷ When the travel agency went bankrupt many people demanded the **return of** their money. その旅行代理店が倒産して多くの人が金の返還を要求した
▷ His friends held a big party for him **on** his **return** from the States. 米国から帰国した彼のために友

人たちは盛大なパーティーを開いた
▷ You've helped me so much. **In return** I'd like to cook dinner for you. ずいぶんと助けていただいて, お返しに夕食をつくって差し上げます

PHRASES
Many happy returns. ☺ お誕生日おめでとう(何度も巡って来ますように)

return /ritə́ːrn/ 動 戻る; 返す, 戻す

recently	returned	最近戻った
eventually	return	ついに戻る
finally	return	
return	home	家へ帰る
return	safely	無事に戻る

▷ My best friend **recently returned** from a year abroad in New Zealand. 私のいちばんの親友は1年間のニュージーランド滞在を終えて, 最近帰って来た
▷ I missed the last train so I couldn't **return home**. 終電に乗り遅れて帰宅できなかった
▷ You'd better call your parents to let them know you've **returned safely**. 無事に戻ったことを知らせるためにご両親に電話すべきです

return	from A	Aから戻る
return	to A	Aに戻る
return A	to B	AをBに戻す

▷ Have you met my cousin? He's just **returned from** South America. ぼくのいとこに会ったかい。彼は南米から戻って来たばかりなんだ
▷ My temperature's **returned to** normal so I think I'll be OK. 体温は平熱に戻ったので, だいじょうぶだと思います
▷ OK. You can borrow my lecture notes, but please don't forget to **return** them **to** me! わかった。講義のノートを貸してあげるけど忘れずに返してね

review /rivjúː/ 名 見直し; 批評

conduct	a review	見直しを行う
carry out	a review	
undertake	a review	見直しに着手する
read	a review	書評を読む

▷ The Government is going to **conduct** a **review** of the pensions system. 政府は年金制度の見直しをするつもりだ
▷ Our company has agreed to **undertake** a **review** of the pay structure. わが社は給与体系の見直しに着手することに同意した
▷ I **read** a really good **review** of the play we're

going to see.　これから見に行く予定の劇の，とてもよい書評を読んだ

a comprehensive	review	包括的見直し
a regular	review	定期的見直し
an annual	review	年次見直し
a good	review	好評
rave	reviews	絶賛
a bad	review	悪評，不評
a book	review	書評

▷The Government intends to carry out a **comprehensive review** of the tax system.　政府は税制の包括的な見直しを行う予定である
▷The **annual review** of salaries takes place this month.　給与の年度ごとの見直しは今月行われる
▷This new Broadway musical has got really **good reviews**!　ブロードウェイのこの新作ミュージカルは大好評だった

under	review	再検討中で

▷We keep businesses **under review**.　われわれは商取引を見直している

review /rivjú:/ 動 見直す；批評する

thoroughly	review	徹底的に見直す
carefully	review	注意深く見直す
briefly	review	簡単に見直す
constantly	review	絶えず見直す
regularly	review	定期的に見直す

▷Let us **briefly review** the most important point.　最重要点を簡単に見直しましょう
▷You should **regularly review** your lecture notes.　定期的に講義ノートを見直したほうがいい

reward /riwɔ́:rd/ 名 報酬；報奨金，謝礼

get	a reward	報酬を受ける
receive	a reward	
reap	the reward(s)	
bring	a reward	報酬をもたらす
offer	a reward	賞金を出す

▷I took the wallet I found to the police station. They told me I might **get a reward**.　拾った財布を警察署に届けた．謝礼がもらえるかもしれないという話だ
▷Well, you studied hard and now you're **reaping the reward**.　でも，きみは一生懸命勉強したおかげでいまや報われているよね
▷Well, Davis, all your hard work has finally **brought a reward**.　いやあデイビス，がんばった努力がようやく報われたね
▷They're **offering a reward** of $500.　5百ドルの報奨金が出ている

great	reward	大きな報酬
high	reward	
(a) rich	reward	
(a) just	reward	正当な報酬
financial	reward	経済的報酬
economic	reward	
monetary	reward	
a substantial	reward	多額の報奨金

▷Doing a job that you love can bring you **great reward**.　好きな仕事をやっていると大きな見返りがありうる
▷The **financial reward** isn't great, but I enjoy my job very much.　お金の面では見返りは少ないけれど，仕事を大いに楽しんでいる
▷The police are offering a **substantial reward** for information.　警察は情報提供に多額の報奨金を出している

reward	for A	Aに対する報酬

▷Tom's going to get a medal *as* a **reward for** his bravery.　勇敢な行為に対する報奨としてトムはメダルをもらうことになっている

reward /riwɔ́:rd/ 動 報酬を与える，報いる

be well	rewarded	十分報われた
be handsomely	rewarded	

▷If you help us I promise you'll be **well rewarded**.　助けてくれたらあなたに十分な報酬を約束します

reward A	for B	A(人)のBに報いる
reward A	with B	A(人)にBで報いる

▷How can we best **reward** him **for** all he's done for us?　彼がいろいろやってくれたことに対してどう報いるのがいちばんいいだろうか
▷They **rewarded** him **with** a check for $5,000.　彼らは彼に5千ドルの小切手で報いた

rich /rítʃ/ 形 金持ちの，裕福な；豊かな

get	rich	金持ちになる

▷Rich people seem to **get richer** in this country.　この国では金持ちはますます金持ちになっていくようだ

fabulously	rich	すごい金持ちの
immensely	rich	
seriously	rich	

▷Her husband isn't **fabulously rich**, but they're very happy together. 彼女の夫はすごい金持ちというわけではないが，とても幸せな夫婦生活を送っている

the rich and famous	金持ちで有名な人
(the) rich and (the) poor	貧富，金持ちと貧乏人

★×poor and rich とはふつういわない

▷Polo is a sport that is associated with the **rich and famous**. ポロというスポーツは富と名声のある人々を連想させる

▷The gap between **rich and poor** is getting wider. 貧富の差は次第に広がりつつある

rich	in A	Aが豊かな

▷Many Arab countries are **rich in** oil. 多くのアラブ諸国は原油が豊富だ

ride /ráid/ 名 乗ること

have	a ride	(乗り物に)乗る
take	a ride	
go for	a ride	乗り物で出かける
hitch	a ride	車に乗せてもらう
give A	a ride	A(人)を車に乗せてあげる

▷Can I **have a ride** on your bike? きみの自転車に乗ってもいいかい

▷They **went for a ride** on his new motorbike. 彼らは彼の新しいオートバイに乗って出かけた

▷He **hitched a ride** from Tokyo to Kyoto. 彼は東京から京都まで車に便乗させてもらった

▷I can **give** you **a ride** to the station. 駅まできみを車で送ってあげる

a bus	ride	バスに乗ること
a train	ride	列車に乗ること

▷It's only a 20-minute **bus ride** to the station. 駅までバスでほんの20分です

a ride	in A	Aに乗ること
a ride	on A	

▷Let's go for a **ride in** the car. 車でドライブに行こう

ridiculous /ridíkjuləs/ 形 ばかげた

absolutely	ridiculous	まったくばかげた
quite	ridiculous	
totally	ridiculous	

▷How can you say that? That's **absolutely ridiculous**! どうしてそんなことが言えるの．まったくばかげているよ

it is ridiculous	to do	…するのはばかげている
it is ridiculous	that...	…はばかげている

★it seems ridiculous もよく用いる

▷**It's ridiculous to** blame Kate. It wasn't her idea. ケイトを責めるのはばかげている．彼女の考えではなかったのだから

▷**It's ridiculous that** there's no one here to welcome us. ここではだれも私たちを歓迎してくれないなんて，ばかげている

PHRASES
That is ridiculous! / This is ridiculous! ☺ ばかげている ▷I can't find my car keys! This is ridiculous! 車のキーが見つからないや．こんなばかな

right /ráit/ 形 正しい；ふさわしい，適切な

prove	right	正しいとわかる
sound	right	正しそうだ

▷The rumor **proved** (to be) **right**. そのうわさは本当とわかった

absolutely	right	まったく正しい
quite	right	
exactly	right	
probably	right	おそらく正しい

▷What you said was **exactly right**! あなたが言ったことはまさにそのとおりだった

be right	in doing	…するのは正しい

★doing は saying, thinking, believing, suggesting など

▷Am I **right in thinking** that you don't really want to go out tonight? 今夜は本当に出かけたくないんだね？

it is right	to do	…するのは正しい

▷**It's right to** ask for more information from the Government. They still haven't told us enough.

right	
right	about A	Aについて正しい
right	for A	Aにふさわしい

▷You are **right about** that. その点はきみの言うとおりだ

▷I think a job in a travel agency would be just **right for** you. 旅行代理店の仕事はきみにうってつけだと思う

exactly	the right A	まさにぴったりのA

★Aはword, time, place, person, sizeなど

▷That is **exactly** the **right word**. それこそぴったりのことばだ

PHRASES
That's right. 😊 そのとおりです
You're right. 😊 きみの言うとおりだ ▷You're absolutely right. The bank's closed. まったくきみの言うとおりだ．銀行は閉まっている

right /ráit/

名 権利；正しさ，公正さ；右；(the rightで)右翼

have	the right	権利がある
reserve	the right	権利を保留する
give	the right	権利を与える
exercise	the right	権利を行使する
defend	the right	権利を守る
protect	the right	
take	a right	右に曲がる

▷You **have** the **right** to appeal against their decision. 彼らの決定に抗議する権利があなたにはある

▷We **reserve** the **right** to cancel the contract in case of nonpayment. 不払いの場合には契約を破棄する権利を保留します

▷It's important to **defend** the **right** to free speech. 言論の自由に対する権利を守るのが大事だ

▷We need to **protect** the **rights** of minority groups. 少数派の権利を守る必要がある

civil	rights	公民権，市民的権利
equal	rights	平等の権利
exclusive	rights	独占的権利
human	rights	人権
voting	rights	投票権
property	rights	財産権
the extreme	right	極右

▷We are talking about basic **civil rights** and **human rights**. 基本的な公民権と人権について話し合っている

▷Women still need to fight hard for **equal rights**. 女性はなお権利の平等を求めて激しく闘う必要がある

▷Regarding politics he's on the **extreme right**. 政治に関して彼は極右だ

in	the right	もっともな；正しい
on	A's right	A(人)の右側に
to	A's right	A(人)の右手方向に

▷**On** your **right** you can see the Tower of London. 右側にロンドン塔が見えます

the right	to do	…する権利

▷You don't have the **right to** say that. あなたにはそんなことを言う権利はない

rights and freedom	権利と自由
rights and obligations	権利と義務

▷We have to work hard to protect our **rights and freedom**. 権利と自由を守るために懸命に努力しなければならない

▷Please read this contract. It explains your **rights and obligations**. この契約書を読んでください．あなたの権利と義務が説明してあります

ring /ríŋ/ 名 指輪；輪；《英》電話をかけること

wear	a ring	指輪をしている
put on	a ring	指輪をはめる
give A	a ring	Aに電話する

▷She wasn't **wearing** a wedding **ring**. 彼女は結婚指輪をしていなかった

an engagement	ring	婚約指輪
a wedding	ring	結婚指輪
a diamond	ring	ダイヤの指輪
an inner	ring	内輪
an outer	ring	外輪

▷The President has an **inner ring** of trusted politicians. 大統領は自分の周りに信頼のおける政治家たちを置いている

a ring	on A	Aにはめた指輪
in	a ring	輪になって

▷The children were dancing around **in a ring**. 子どもたちは輪になって踊っていた

rise /ráiz/ 名 上昇，増加

a dramatic	rise	激増
a sharp	rise	急増
a steep	rise	
a rapid	rise	
a steady	rise	着実な増加
a pay	rise	賃上げ
a price	rise	値上げ
a tax	rise	増税

▷During the last month there's been a **sharp rise** in sales. 先月は売り上げが急上昇した
▷Recently there's been a **steep rise** in the cost of living. 近ごろ生活費が急に上がった
▷There's been a **rapid rise** in the number of cases of bird flu. 鳥インフルエンザの症例数が急増している
▷This year we've seen a **steady rise** in sales. 今年度は売り上げが着実に伸びている

a rise	in A	Aにおける増加
rise	to A	Aに登りつめること
on	the rise	上昇中で, 上向いて

★rise to A の A は power, fame, stardom, the top など

▷The latest figures show a large **rise in** unemployment. 最近の数字は失業の大幅増を示している
▷The government is considering a 2% **rise in** sales tax. 政府は売上税の2％アップを検討している
▷I have to write an essay on the reasons for Hitler's **rise to power**. ヒトラーが権力を掌握した理由についてレポートを書かなければならない
▷The number of accidents in the home is **on the rise**. 家庭での事故件数が上昇している

the rise and fall	of A	Aの上下；Aの盛衰

▷I'm studying the **rise and fall of** the Roman Empire. ローマ帝国の盛衰を研究している

rise /ráiz/

動 上昇する, 増加する；立ち上がる；昇る

rise	dramatically	劇的に上昇する
rise	sharply	急上昇する
rise	steeply	
rise	rapidly	
rise	slightly	わずかに上昇する
rise	steadily	着実に上昇する
rise	slowly	ゆっくり上昇する

▷Recently the cost of gas has been **rising sharply**. 最近ガソリンの値段が急騰してきている
▷The temperature has **risen slightly**, but it's still very cold. 気温がわずかに上昇したが, それでもまだかなり寒い
▷In the river the water level is **rising steadily**. 川の水位が着実に上がり始めている

rise	by A	A（数値・割合）だけ増加する
rise	from A to B	AからBに上昇する
rise	above A	Aを超える
rise	from A	Aから立ち上がる；Aから立ち昇る

▷Electricity prices have **risen by** 30% over the last 5 years. 電気料金がこの5年間で3割上がった
▷Last year the price of gas **rose from** $3 a gallon **to** nearly $4. 昨年はガソリン代が1ガロン3ドルから4ドル近くに値上がりした
▷The temperature still hasn't **risen above** freezing point. 気温はまだ氷点下だ

risk /rísk/ 名 危険, リスク

take	a risk	危険を冒す
run	the risk (of A)	(Aの)危険を冒す
carry	a risk	リスクを伴う
pose	a risk	リスクをもたらす
increase	the risk	リスクを高める
reduce	the risk	リスクを減らす
minimize	the risk	リスクを最小に抑える
avoid	the risk	リスクを避ける
assess	the risk	リスクを査定する

▷If we do that, we **run** the **risk of** losing everything. そんなことをすればすべてを失う危険がある
▷Overeating **poses** a serious health **risk**. 過食は健康に甚大なリスクをもたらす
▷Smoking **increases** the **risk** of lung cancer. 喫煙は肺がんのリスクを高める
▷Regular exercise **reduces** the **risk** of heart attacks. 定期的に運動すれば心臓麻痺の危険が減る

a great	risk	大きなリスク
a high	risk	高いリスク
a serious	risk	深刻なリスク
a low	risk	低いリスク
an increased	risk	増大したリスク
a potential	risk	潜在的リスク
the relative	risk	相対的リスク
a health	risk	健康リスク
a fire	risk	火災リスク

▷There's a **great risk** that the operation will be unsuccessful. 手術が成功しない危険が高い
▷Living in a city gives you an **increased risk** of

| river |

being a victim of crime.　都会暮らしをすると犯罪に巻き込まれるリスクも増す
▷ The higher the rate of interest, the greater (is) the **potential risk** to your investment.　金利が上がれば上がるほど投資に対する潜在的リスクが大きくなる

at	risk	危険な状態で
at	the risk of doing	…する危険を冒して

▷ Whatever we do we can't put our children **at risk**.　何があろうと子どもたちを危険にさらすわけにはいかない
▷ **At** the **risk of** sounding overcautious, I think we should check everything one more time.　慎重すぎるとの批判を覚悟の上で，もう一度すべてを点検すべきだと思う

river /rívər/ 名 川

cross	the river	川を渡る
overlook	the river	川を見下ろす

▷ You have to **cross** the **river** to get to our hotel.　ホテルまで来るのに川を渡らなくてはならない
▷ Tom's house **overlooks** the **river**.　トムの家からは川が見下ろせる

the river	flows	川が流れる

▷ The **river flows** through the center of town.　川が町の中心を流れている

a great	river	大きな川
a large	river	
a small	river	小さな川
the main	river	本流

▷ The Amazon is a **great river** which flows through South America.　アマゾン川は南米を流れる大河だ

across	the river	川を渡って
in	the river	川で；川に入って
into	the river	川へ
along	the river	川に沿って
on	the river	川で；川の上で
up	river	上流に
down	river	下流に

▷ We need to go **across** the **river** to get to the pub.　パブに行くには川を渡る必要がある
▷ Is it OK to swim **in** the **river**?　川で泳いでだいじょうぶですか
▷ Be careful! Don't fall **into** the **river**!　気をつけて．川に落ちないように
▷ Let's go for a walk **along** the **river**.　川沿いを散歩しよう
▷ I love to go canoeing **on** the **river**.　川でカヌーを漕ぐのが好きです

road /róud/ 名 道路，道；通り

cross	the road	道路を渡る

▷ Be careful when you **cross** the **road**.　道路を渡るときは気をつけなさい

a narrow	road	狭い道路
a wide	road	広い道路
a broad	road	
a busy	road	交通量の多い道路
a winding	road	曲がりくねった道路
the main	road	幹線道路
a major	road	主要道路
a national	road	国道
a private	road	私道
a public	road	公道
a country	road	田舎道
《英》the ring	road	環状道路

▷ Be careful! This is a really **busy road**.　気をつけて．この道路はすごく交通量が多いので
▷ According to the map it's a long **winding road** down the mountainside.　地図によればそれは山腹を下る長い曲がりくねった道路だ
▷ Our children have to cross the **main road** to get to school.　うちの子どもたちは学校へ行くのに幹線道路を渡らなければならない

down	the road	通りを下って
up	the road	通りを上って
along	the road	通りに沿って
on	the road	道路で；移動中で
in	the road	道路に
across	the road	道路の向かい側に
by	road	陸路で
the road	to A	Aへ行く道

▷ Walk **along** the **road** for 50 yards and the post office is on the right.　通りに沿って50ヤード歩くと，郵便局は右側にあります
▷ We've been **on** the **road** for over 10 hours. You must be exhausted.　もう10時間以上も移動しています．疲れたでしょう
▷ Tell the children not to play **in** the **road**.　子どもたちに道路で遊ばないように注意しなさい
▷ There's a really good hotel **across** the **road**.　道路の向かい側にとてもいいホテルがあります
▷ It takes much longer to get there **by road** than by

rail. そこに行くには鉄道より陸路のほうがずっと時間がかかる
▷ Is this the **road to** Cambridge? これはケンブリッジへ行く道ですか

role /róul/ 名 役割, 役目；(劇などの)役

have	a role	役割がある
perform	a role	役割を果たす；
play	a role	役を演じる
assume	a role	役割を担う；役
take	a role	を演じる
fulfill	a role	役割を果たす
fill	a role	役割を務める

▷ She **has** a very important **role** within the company. 彼女は社内でとても重要な役割を担っている
▷ She **performs** the **role** of both wife and mother really well. 彼女は妻と母親の両方の役をとてもうまくこなしている
▷ A woman often has to **fulfill** many **roles** — wife, mother, wage earner... 女性はしばしば多くの役割を果たさなければならない．妻，母親，稼ぎ手などだ

a lead	role	主役；指導的役割
a leading	role	
a starring	role	主役
the title	role	
a big	role	大役；大きな役割
a supporting	role	脇役
an important	role	重要な役割
a central	role	中心的な役割
a key	role	鍵となる役割
a major	role	大きな役割
a crucial	role	決定的な役割
a minor	role	小さな役割
an active	role	積極的な役割
gender	role	性別役割分担

▷ He played a **leading role** in the success of his college football team. 彼は大学のフットボールチームの成功に指導的役割を果たした
▷ China will play a **crucial role** in Asia's future. 中国はアジアの未来に決定的な役割を果たすだろう
▷ I'm not very important. I only have a very **minor role** within the company. 私はそれほど重きを置かれず，社内では大した役割も担っていない
▷ He played an **active role** in the meeting. 彼は会議で積極的な役割を果たした

roof /rú:f/ 名 屋根

climb up to	the roof	屋根まで登る
go up to	the roof	
climb up on	the roof	屋根の上に登る
go up on	the roof	
climb down from	the roof	屋根から下りる
fall off	the roof	屋根から落ちる
fall from	the roof	

▷ During the storm many tiles **fell off** the **roof**. 嵐の間に瓦がたくさん屋根から落ちた

a flat	roof	平屋根
a thatched	roof	かやぶき屋根

▷ Jon's country house has a nice **thatched roof**. ジョンの田舎の家はすてきなかやぶき屋根だ

on	the roof	屋根の上に

▷ He went up **on** the **roof** to fix the TV antenna. 彼はテレビのアンテナを直すために屋根に上がった

room /rú:m/ 名 部屋；空間；余地

enter	the room	部屋に入る
leave	the room	部屋を出る
tidy	A's room	部屋を片づける
share	a room	部屋を共同で使う
take up	room	場所をとる
make	room	場所を空ける

▷ Sorry, can I **leave** the **room** for a moment? 失礼，ちょっと退出してもよろしいですか
▷ It'll be cheaper if we **share** a **room** at the hotel. ホテルの部屋を共同で使ったらもっと安くなるだろう
▷ Sorry, could you **make room** for one more? 申し訳ないですがもう一人分空けていただけませんか

a bright	room	明るい部屋
a dark	room	暗い部屋
a darkened	room	暗くした部屋
a comfortable	room	快適な部屋
an empty	room	空室
a spare	room	空き部屋
a furnished	room	家具つきの部屋
a single	room	シングルの部屋
a double	room	ダブルの部屋
a twin	room	ツインの部屋
a storage	room	貯蔵室
a waiting	room	待合室
a lecture	room	講義室
a dining	room	食堂

| rough |

a living	room	居間
《英》a sitting	room	

▷She was sitting in a **dark room** with the curtains drawn. 彼女はカーテンが引かれた暗い部屋に座っていた
▷I stayed in a **comfortable room** with a good view of the sea. 海がよく見える快適な部屋に滞在した
▷If you like you can stay in the **spare room**. よければ空き部屋に泊まっていいよ
▷When I was a student I lived in just one small **furnished room**. 学生のころ家具つきの小さなワンルームに住んでいた

room	for A to do	A(人)が…する場所

▷There was no **room for** her **to** sit down. 彼女が座る場所はなかった

room	for A	Aの余地

▷There's always **room for** improvement. 常に改善の余地がある
▷It was definitely him. There was no **room for** doubt. 絶対に彼だった. 疑いの余地はなかった

rough /rʌ́f/ 形 ざらざらした；大ざっぱな

pretty	rough	かなりざらざらした
slightly	rough	少しざらざらした

▷Wow! Look at those waves! It's **pretty rough** out there. うわあ. あの波を見て. あそこはかなり荒れているね
▷He hadn't shaved for a day and his skin felt **slightly rough**. 彼は一日ひげをそっていなかったので, 肌に触ると少しざらざらしていた

rough and ready		間に合わせの

▷Can you build me a shed in the garden? Nothing grand. Just something **rough and ready**. 庭に小屋をつくってくれるかい. りっぱなのじゃなくていいんだ. 間に合わせでいい

row /róu/ 名 列

the front	row	1列目
the second	row	2列目

▷Can you try to get a seat in the **front row**? 1列目の席を取ってもらえませんか

in	a row	一列に；立て続けに

▷She hasn't eaten anything for three days **in a row**! 彼女は3日続けて何も食べていない

row	upon row	延々と続く列
rows	and rows	

▷From the top of the hill all you could see were **rows and rows** of houses. 丘の頂上から見えるのは延々と続く家並みだけだった

rude /rúːd/ 形 失礼な, 無作法な

extremely	rude	きわめて失礼な
downright	rude	とても失礼な

▷He was **extremely rude**. It was unbelievable! 彼はひどく失礼だった. 信じられなかった

rude	to A	A(人)に対して失礼な

▷I'm sorry I was so **rude to** you last time. このあいだは失礼なことをしてごめんなさい

it is rude	to do	…するのは失礼だ

▷**It's rude to** stare at people! 人をじろじろ見つめるのは失礼だ

rule /rúːl/ 名 規則；習慣；支配

make	a rule	規則をつくる
accept	a rule	規則を受け入れる
follow	the rules	規則に従う
obey	the rules	
have	a rule	規則がある
break	a rule	規則を破る
apply	a rule	規則を適用する
bend	the rules	規則を曲げる
change	the rules	規則を変える
know	the rules	規則を知っている

▷Make sure you **follow** the **rules**! 必ず規則に従ってください
▷If you **break** a **rule** you'll be in trouble! 規則を破るとめんどうなことになるよ
▷Do you **know** the **rules** of rugby? ラグビーのルールを知っていますか

a basic	rule	基本的な規則
a golden	rule	黄金律
a general	rule	一般的な規則
a new	rule	新しい規則
strict	rules	厳しい規則
a legal	rule	法的なルール

▷ As a **general rule** we don't allow pets in the apartment. 原則としてアパートでペットは許可されない
▷ The school I go to has very **strict rules**. 私が通っている学校は規則がとても厳格だ

against	the rules	規則に反して
under	... rule	…の支配下に
as	a rule	一般に

▷ Sorry, I can't help you. It's **against** the **rules**. ごめんなさい，あなたを助けられません。ルール違反ですので
▷ Some parts of Canada used to be **under** French **rule**, others **under** British **rule**. カナダにはかつてフランスの支配下にあった地域とイギリスの支配下にあった地域がある
▷ **As a rule**, she goes for lunch at 12:30. 彼女はふだんは12時半に昼食に出かける

| a set of rules | 一連の規則 |

▷ This is a **set of rules** for new club members. これがクラブの新会員向けの一連の規則です

| rules and regulations | 規則と規定 |

▷ What are the **rules and regulations** concerning fire safety? 火災予防に関する規則や規定はどうなっていますか

run /rÁn/ 動 走る；流れる；動く；立候補する

run	fast	速く走る
run	away	走り去る
run	upstairs	2階へ駆け上がる

▷ I tried to stop him, but he **ran away**. 止めようとしたが彼は走り去った

run	across A	Aを走って横切る
run	down A	Aを走って行く；Aを流れ落ちる
run	out of A	Aから走って出る
run	into A	Aにぶつかる；Aに偶然出会う
run	through A	Aを流れる
run	to A	Aに向かって走る
run	up A	Aを駆け上がる
run	on A	(機械が)Aで動く
run	for A	Aに立候補する

▷ She **ran across** the road when the lights were still red. まだ赤信号なのに彼女は道路を走って横切った
▷ He **ran down** the street, but the bus moved off before he could catch it. 彼は通りを走ったが，バスは発車してしまって間に合わなかった
▷ People were **running out of** the building shouting "Fire! Fire!" 「火事だ，火事だ」と叫びながら人々が建物の外に走り出ていた
▷ You'll never guess who I **ran into** last week! 先週ぼくがだれと偶然出会ったか聞いたらきっと驚くよ
▷ The River Seine **runs through** Paris. セーヌ川はパリを流れる
▷ We **ran to** the station to catch the last train. 終電に間に合うように駅へと走った
▷ She **ran up** the stairs. 彼女は階段を駆け上がった
▷ The motor **runs on** electricity. モーターは電気で動く
▷ Do we know yet who is **running for** President in the next election? 次の選挙でだれが大統領に立候補するかもうわかりますか

run /rÁn/

名 走ること；(野球の)得点；連続公演，興行

go for	a run	ランニングをする
score	a run	得点を上げる
extend	a run	興行を延長する

▷ He **goes for** a three-mile **run** before breakfast every morning! 彼は毎朝朝食前に3マイルのランニングをしているんだ

| at | a run | 駆け足で |
| on | the run | 逃亡して；急いで |

▷ According to the newspapers he'd been **on the run** for 3 weeks before the police caught him. 新聞によれば彼は警察に捕まるまで3週間逃亡していた

rush /rÁʃ/

名 突進；勢いよく流れること

| in | a rush | 急いで |

▷ Sorry, I have to go. I'm **in** a bit of a **rush**! ごめん，もう行かなくちゃ。ちょっと急いでいるの

| a rush of | A | Aの激しい流れ |

★Aは blood, water, air, wind など

▷ I'm sorry I lost my temper. It was a **rush of blood** to the head. かんしゃくを起こして悪かった。頭に血が上ったものだから
▷ A **rush of wind** caught his papers and sent them flying all over the garden. 突風が来て書類が庭中に吹き飛ばされた

S

sad /sæd/ 形 悲しい

feel	sad	悲しい

▷I **felt** very **sad** *about* leaving the party early. パーティーを早めに切り上げるのは悲しかった

extremely	sad	すごく悲しい
desperately	sad	ものすごく悲しい
particularly	sad	特に悲しい
terribly	sad	ひどく悲しい

▷Her mother died after a long illness. It was **extremely sad**. 長い病の末に彼女のお母さんは亡くなった。すごく悲しいことだった

be sad	to do	…するのは悲しい

▷I'm really **sad to** move away from all my friends. 友人たちみんなから離れるのがとても悲しい

it's sad	that...	…は悲しい
I'm sad	that...	

★it's sad は客観的描写で，I'm sad は個人的感情を表す

▷**It's sad that** we weren't able to help her. 彼女を助けられなかったのは悲しいことだ

safe /séif/ 形 安全な，安心な；無事な

completely	safe	まったく安全な
perfectly	safe	まったく安全な
really	safe	ほんとうに安全な
fairly	safe	かなり安全な
reasonably	safe	そこそこ安全な
relatively	safe	比較的安全な

▷Don't worry. It's **perfectly safe** to drink this water. 心配いらないよ。この水は飲んでもまったく安全だから

▷London is **reasonably safe** if you don't go out alone late at night. 夜遅く一人で外出しさえしなければロンドンはそこそこ安全だ

safe	from A	Aから安全な
safe	for A	A(人)にとって安全な

▷I always wear a helmet when I ride my bicycle. It keeps me **safe from** accidents. 自転車に乗るときはヘルメットを必ずかぶる。事故から身を守れるからね

▷It's not **safe for** children to play in the road. 子どもが道で遊ぶのは安全ではない

safe and sound	無事な
safe and well	
safe and secure	安全な
safe and effective	安全かつ有効な

▷I need to telephone my family to find out if they're **safe and well**. 家族の安否確認のために電話しなきゃ
▷It's great to know that your money is **safe and secure** after the financial crisis. 金融危機の後もあなたのお金が安全でよかったですね
▷My doctor says this new medicine is **safe and effective**. 掛かりつけの医者はこの新薬は安全で効き目があると言っている

be safe	to do	…しても安全な

▷It's **safe to** come out now, children. The big dog has gone away. もう出てきても安全だよ，みんな。大きな犬は行ってしまったから

salary /sæləri/ 名 給料

pay	a salary	給料を支払う
earn	a salary	給料を稼ぐ
receive	a salary	給料を受け取る
have	a salary	給料をもらう

▷I think I'm going to stop my part-time job. They don't **pay** a very high **salary**. アルバイトはやめようと思っている。給料は大してよくないし
▷She **earns** a really high **salary**. 彼女はすごい高給とりだ

salary	increases	給料が上がる

▷I'm really lucky. My **salary increases** every year. ついてるなあ。給料が毎年上がるんだもの

a good	salary	高給
a high	salary	
a low	salary	安月給
an annual	salary	年俸
a monthly	salary	月給
a base	salary	基本給
《英》a basic	salary	

▷Lawyers earn a really **high salary**. 弁護士はとても高給とりだ
▷Do you know what his **annual salary** is? 彼の年俸を知っていますか

a cut	in salary	減給
《英》a drop	in salary	
an increase	in salary	昇給
《英》a rise	in salary	

★ salary cut, salary increase も用いる

▷My boss has promised me an **increase in salary**. 上司は私に昇給を約束してくれた

sale /séil/ 名 販売, 売却;(sales で)売上高;バーゲン, 大売り出し

make	a sale	販売する
close	a sale	販売契約をまとめる
lose	a sale	売り損なう
approve	the sale	販売を承認する
ban	the sale	販売を禁止する

▷Finally we bought the house. It took us nearly 9 months to **close** the **sale**! ようやく家を購入したが,販売契約をまとめるのに9か月近くかかった
▷The local council hasn't **approved** the **sale** of that piece of land yet. 地方自治体はまだその土地の売却を承認していない
▷In Britain, the government has **banned** the **sale** of alcohol to people under the age of 18. イギリスでは18歳未満への酒類販売を政府が禁止した

sale	starts	バーゲンが始まる

▷The **sale starts** on Monday, December 28th. バーゲンは12月28日月曜日からです

a quick	sale	すぐ売れること
a winter	sale	冬物大売り出し
a clearance	sale	在庫一掃セール
a going-out-of-business	sale	閉店セール

▷They've reduced their prices for a **quick sale**! すぐ売れるよう価格を下げた

a sale	on A	Aのバーゲン
for	sale	売り物の
《米》on	sale	売り物の;特価の

▷They are having a **sale on** household goods. その店では家庭用品のバーゲンをやっている
▷I think they're going to offer their house **for sale**. 彼らは自宅を売りに出すだろうと思う ▷Sorry, it's not **for sale**. 申し訳ありません, 非売品です
▷I think the new 3-D TV goes **on sale** next week. 新しい3Dテレビが来週発売になるよ

salt /sɔ́ːlt/ 名 塩

add	salt	塩を加える
sprinkle A with	salt	Aに塩をかける
pass	the salt	塩を回す

▷Don't forget to **add salt** when you boil the potatoes. ジャガイモをゆでるときは必ず塩を加えなさい
▷Could you **pass** the **salt**, please? 塩を回していただけますか

salt and pepper		塩とこしょう

▷Help yourself. The **salt and pepper**'s on the table. 自由に取って食べてください. 塩とこしょうはテーブルに置いてあります

a pinch of	salt	一つまみの塩

▷Maybe you should add a **pinch of salt**. たぶん塩を一つまみ加えたほうがいいでしょう

same /séim/

形 同一の;同様の, 同じような

exactly	the same	まったく同じ
just	the same	
precisely	the same	
the very	same	
essentially	the same	本質的に同じ
roughly	the same	だいたい同じ
much	the same	

▷Your handbag and my handbag are **exactly** the **same**! あなたのハンドバッグは私のとまったく同じね
▷Ella and Emma are identical twins. They look **just** the **same**! エラとエマは一卵性双生児で, まったくそっくりだ
▷"I'm thinking of leaving my part-time job. The pay is so low." "Yes, I feel **much** the **same**." 「バイトをやめようと思っているんだ. 給料がとても安いから」「そうだね. ぼくもほぼ同感だ」

the same A	as B	Bと同じA

▷She's the **same** age **as** me. 彼女は私と同い年だ
▷Let's stay in the **same** hotel **as** last year. 昨年と同じホテルに泊まろう

the same	old A	いつもながらのA

▷It's the **same old** story. He always has some excuse for being late! いつものことだが, 彼はいつも遅刻の言い訳をする

satisfaction /sætisfǽkʃən/

名 満足, 満足感

find	satisfaction	満足する
get	satisfaction	
derive	satisfaction	
give	satisfaction	満足感を与える
express	satisfaction	満足感を表す
have	the satisfaction of doing	…して満足する

▷I think we should keep complaining until we **get satisfaction**. 満足がいくまでクレームをつけ続けたほうがいいと思う
▷It's most important to **give satisfaction** to our customers. 顧客に満足感を与えることが最も大事だ
▷At the meeting our boss **expressed** his **satisfaction** *with* the recent sales figures. 会議で上司は最近の売上データに満足の意を表した
▷He trained hard every day and **had** the **satisfaction of** being chosen as captain of the soccer team. 彼は毎日一生懸命練習し, サッカーチームのキャプテンに選ばれて満足した

complete	satisfaction	十分な満足感
deep	satisfaction	深い満足感
great	satisfaction	大きな満足感
personal	satisfaction	個人的満足
customer	satisfaction	顧客満足
job	satisfaction	職務満足
sexual	satisfaction	性的満足

▷Our aim is to give **complete satisfaction**. われわれの狙いは十分な満足感を与えることだ
▷Coming top in class gave her **great satisfaction**. クラスで一番になって彼女は大いに満足した

a feeling	of satisfaction	満足感
a sense	of satisfaction	
a smile	of satisfaction	満足の笑み
a level	of satisfaction	満足度

▷When I feel I've done my job well, I get a **feeling of satisfaction**. 仕事がうまくいったと感じると満足感がある
▷"That's the best cake I've ever made," she said with a **smile of satisfaction**. 「これまででいちばんできのいいケーキだわ」と彼女は会心の笑みを浮かべて言った

to	A's **satisfaction**	Aが満足するように

▷I can never seem to do anything **to** my boss's **satisfaction**. どんなことをやっても上司は満足してくれそうもない

satisfied /sǽtisfàid/ 形 満足した

completely	satisfied	すっかり満足した
entirely	satisfied	
well	satisfied	十分に満足した
fully	satisfied	
reasonably	satisfied	そこそこ満足した

▷Manchester United's manager was **well satisfied** with the result of the game. マンチェスターユナイテッドの監督は試合の結果に十分満足していた

satisfied	with A	Aに満足した

▷Apparently Tina's boss said he wasn't **satisfied with** her work. どうやらティナの上司は彼女の仕事に満足していないと言ったようだ

satisfied	(that)...	…を納得している

▷I'm afraid I'm not **satisfied that** he's telling the truth. あいにく彼がほんとうのことを言っているとは思えない

say /séi/ 動 言う; 書いてある

say	softly	優しく言う
say	gently	
say	quietly	静かに言う
say	quickly	急いで言う
say	slowly	ゆっくり言う
say	firmly	きっぱり言う
say	again	再び言う
said	earlier	前に言った

▷"It's so romantic sitting here, looking at the moon," she **said softly**. 「ここに座って月を見るのはとてもロマンチックね」と彼女は優しく言った
▷Sorry, I didn't hear. Could you **say** that **again**? すみません, 聞こえませんでした. もう一度言っていただけますか
▷Well, as I **said earlier**, we need to take a decision fairly soon. さて, 前に申し上げたように速やかに決定する必要があります

say	(that)...	…と言う
say	wh-	…か言う

★wh- は what, why, how など

▷The newspaper **says** the government is going to increase the tax on cigarettes. 新聞には政府がたばこ税を上げると書いてある
▷She didn't **say where** she was going. 彼女はどこ

へ行くのか言わなかった

say A	about B	BについてAを言う
say A	on B	
say A	to B	AをB(人)に言う

▷I hear that Tracy has been **saying** bad things **about** me. トレイシーは私の悪口を言い続けているそうだ
▷He **said** goodbye **to** her at the station. 彼は駅で彼女に別れを告げた

be said	to do	…すると言われている
it is said	(that)...	…と言われている
They say	(that)...	
People say	(that)...	

▷Japanese is **said to** be one of the most difficult languages to learn. 日本語は学ぶのが最も難しい言語の一つだと言われている
▷**They say** the economy is going to get worse. 経済はさらに悪化しそうだ

I would	say (that)...	まあ…でしょうね
I should	say (that)...	
I must	say (that)...	まったく…だ
I have to	say (that)...	
if I may	say (so)	言わせてもらえば

▷"How many people went to the live concert?" "Well, **I'd say** there were over five thousand." 「ライブ・コンサートの聴衆はどのくらいだったの？」「そうねえ、5千人は超えていたでしょうね」
▷Well, **I must say**, I really enjoyed that meal! いやあ、実においしい料理でした
▷**If I may say so**, I thought your lecture on Shakespeare was most interesting. 率直に言って先生のシェイクスピアに関する講義がいちばんおもしろかったです

PHRASES

How can you say that? / How can you say such a thing? 😊 よくもそんなことが言えるね
How do you say this in English? 😊 これは英語で何と言いますか
Say no more. 😊 それ以上言うな(言わなくてもわかるから) ▷"Do you think you could drive me to the hospital tomorrow morning?" "Say no more! No problem!" 「あすの朝、病院まで車で送ってもらえるかな?」「言わなくてもわかってるよ。だいじょうぶ」
What did you say? 😊 何と言いましたか
What do you say? 😊 どう思いますか、どうですか ▷"What do you say to a nice cup of coffee in that new coffee shop?" "OK. Good idea!" 「あの新しい喫茶店でおいしいコーヒーでもどうだい?」「うん、いいね」
You can say that again! 😊 まったくそのとおり ▷"What a terrible movie! The worst I've seen!" "You can say that again!" 「なんてひどい映画だ。い

ままで最悪だ」「まったく同感だ」
You don't say (so)! 😊 まさか、本当なのかい ▷"When I arrived at the airport I found I'd forgotten my passport" "You don't say!" 「空港に着いてパスポートを忘れたことに気づいたんだ」「まさか」

scale /skéil/ 名 規模

a large	scale	大規模
a massive	scale	
a grand	scale	壮大な規模
a small	scale	小規模
a global	scale	世界的規模

▷Higher temperatures are having an effect on a **global scale**. 気温の上昇は世界的規模で影響を及ぼしている

scared /skéərd/ 形 怖がる, おびえる

really	scared	とても怖がった
dead	scared	
too	scared	あまりに怖がった

★dead scared はくだけた言い方

▷I missed the last bus and had to walk home by myself. I was **really scared**. 最終バスに乗り遅れて一人で歩いて帰宅しなければならなかった。ほんとうに怖かった

scared	of A	Aが怖い

▷Apparently Dione is really **scared of** spiders! どうもディオンはクモがすごく怖いみたいだ

be scared	to do	…するのが怖い

▷I always think Peter drives too fast, but I'm **scared to** say anything. ピーターは車を飛ばしすぎだといつも思うけど、怖くて何も言えない

scene /síːn/ 名 (映画などの)場面；情景, 光景, 風景；(事件などの)現場；大騒ぎ

rehearse	a scene	場面のけいこをする
shoot	a scene	場面を撮影する
depict	a scene	情景を描く
describe	a scene	
imagine	a scene	情景を想像する
picture	a scene	情景を思い描く
survey	the scene	光景を見渡す

| schedule |

rush to	the scene	現場に駆けつける
arrive at	the scene	現場に到着する
leave	the scene	現場を去る
make	a scene	大騒ぎする
cause	a scene	

▷ The picture **depicts** a quiet country **scene** in the South of France. その絵は南仏の静かな田舎の情景を描いている

▷ Nobody saw the murderer **leave** the **scene** of the crime. 殺人犯が犯行現場を去るのをだれも目撃していない

▷ Don't **make** a **scene**! It's better to say nothing! 大騒ぎしないで．何も言わないほうがいい

the opening	scene	冒頭のシーン
the final	scene	ラストシーン
the last	scene	
a battle	scene	戦闘シーン
a love	scene	ラブシーン
the international	scene	国際舞台
the political	scene	政治の舞台
the domestic	scene	家庭の情景
a murder	scene	殺人現場
an accident	scene	事故現場

★最後の2つは the scene of the murder, the scene of the accident も用いられる

▷ Do you know what happens in the **final scene**? ラストシーンで何が起きるか知っているかい

▷ The **political scene** in many countries seems to be changing fast. 多くの国で政治情勢が急速に変わりつつあるようだ

▷ It was a painting of a happy family sitting at home by the fire. A peaceful **domestic scene**. 暖炉のそばに座る幸せな家庭を描いた絵で，平和な家庭の情景だ

at	the scene	現場に
on	the scene	
behind	the scenes	舞台裏で；陰で

▷ There were lots of police **at** the **scene** of the crime. 犯行現場にはたくさんの警官がいた

schedule /skédʒuːl | ʃédjuːl/

名 予定(表)，スケジュール

a busy	schedule	忙しいスケジュール
a hectic	schedule	
a full	schedule	いっぱいのスケジュール
a tight	schedule	きついスケジュール
work	schedule	仕事の予定

a train	schedule	列車の時刻表

▷ Sorry, I can't meet you until next week. I've got a very **busy schedule**. ごめん．来週まで会えません．ずっと忙しいので

▷ Sorry, I have to rush. I'm on a **tight schedule**. ごめん，急がなきゃ．予定がびっしりで

a schedule	for A	Aのスケジュール

▷ Here's your **schedule for** the next three months. 今後3か月のあなたのスケジュールです

ahead of	schedule	予定より早く
on	schedule	予定どおり
behind	schedule	予定より遅れて

▷ Fantastic! We're two months **ahead of schedule**! すばらしい．予定より2か月進んでいる

▷ The plane from New York was **on schedule**. ニューヨーク発の飛行機は予定どおりだった

▷ We mustn't fall **behind schedule**. 予定より遅れてはいけない

school /skúːl/ 名 学校；大学院

attend	school	学校へ通う
go to	school	
enter	school	学校に入る
start	school	
finish	school	学校を卒業する
graduate from	school	
leave	school	学校をやめる；学校を出る
be late for	school	学校に遅刻する
be absent from	school	学校を休む
miss	school	
skip	school	学校をサボる
teach (at)	school	学校で教える

▷ Did you know that your son has not been **attending school** recently? 息子さんが最近不登校なのをご存じでしたか

▷ My son **started school** in September. 息子は9月から学校へ入った

▷ Julie's been **absent from school** four times this week! ジュリーは今週4回も学校を休んでいる

▷ We'll be in trouble if they find out we've **skipped school**! 学校をサボったのがばれたら困ったことになるよ

▷ Ben **teaches at** a school in Sydney. ベンはシドニーの学校で教えている

a coeducational	school	共学の学校
《英》a mixed	school	

a single-sex	school	男女別々の学校
an elite	school	名門校
a prestigious	school	
an elementary	school	小学校
《英》a primary	school	
a junior high	school	中学校
a high	school	高等学校
a boarding	school	寄宿学校
a private	school	私立学校
a public	school	公立学校
《英》a state	school	
a graduate	school	大学院
a business	school	経営学大学院
a law	school	法科大学院
a driving	school	自動車学校

▷What do you think is best? A **coeducational school** or a single-sex school? どちらがいいかな，共学の学校か男女別々の学校か
▷Apparently he went to an **elite school**. どうも彼は名門校の出らしい

before	school	授業前に
after	school	放課後
in	school	学校で；《米》在学中で
at	school	学校で；《英》在学中で

▷Let's meet **after school** and go to the park. 放課後に待ち合わせて公園に行こう
▷I hear your son's doing really well **at school**! お宅の息子さんは学校の成績がとてもいいそうですね

science /sáiəns/ 名 科学

modern	science	近代科学
basic	science	基礎科学
applied	science	応用科学
biological	science	生物科学
cognitive	science	認知科学
human	science	人間科学
natural	science	自然科学
physical	science	(物理・天文学などの)自然科学
political	science	政治学
social	science	社会学；社会科学

▷**Modern science** is advancing really rapidly these days. 近代科学はこのところ急速に進歩している
▷She has a good knowledge of **basic science**. 彼女には基礎科学の知識が十分ある

science and technology	科学技術

▷Jack's studying at a college of **science and technology**. ジャックは科学技術大学で研究している

score /skɔ́:r/ 名 得点；点数

get	a score	得点する；点をとる
keep	(the) score	得点を記録する
level	the score	同点になる
tie	the score	

▷I **got** a good **score** in today's English test! きょうの英語の試験でとてもいい点をとった
▷Manchester United struck just before halftime to **level the score** at 2-2. マンチェスターユナイテッドがハーフタイム直前に同点ゴールを決めて2対2とした

a good	score	よい点
a high	score	高い点
the top	score	最高点
a bad	score	ひどい点
a low	score	低い点
an average	score	平均点
total	score	総得点
the final	score	最終得点

▷Apparently he got a really **high score** in the math test. 彼は数学の試験でかなり高得点をとったようだ
▷She got 84% and 92% in her last two tests. An **average score** of 88%. 彼女はここ2回の試験で84点と92点をとった．平均点は88点だ
▷28, 26, and 36. That's a **total score** of 90%. 28点と26点と36点で総得点は90点だ

on that score	その点では
on this score	この点では

▷"Did you hear the headmaster is going to resign?" "No. I don't know anything **on that score**."「校長先生がやめるって聞きましたか」「いいえ，そのことについては何も知りません」

PHRASES
What's the score? ☺ 得点はどうなっているの ▷"What's the score?" "3 - 0."「得点はどう？」「3対0さ」(★ 3 - 0 は《米》では three to nothing, 《英》では three-nil と読む)

sea /sí:/ 名 海

overlook	the sea	海を見渡す
look out to	sea	海を眺める
put to	sea	出航する
go to	sea	船乗りになる
cross	the sea	海を渡る

| search |

▷They live in a lovely cottage that **overlooks** the **sea**. 彼らは海を見渡すすてきな小さな家に住んでいる
▷He was standing on the cliff **looking out to sea**. 彼は崖の上に立って海を眺めていた
▷The ship's already left. It **put to sea** 2 hours ago. 船はすでに出ていた．2時間前の出航だった
▷My uncle Will **went to sea** when he was only 16 years old. おじのウィルはわずか16歳で船乗りになった

a calm	sea	穏やかな海
a heavy	sea	荒れた海
a rough	sea	
a stormy	sea	
the North	Sea	北海
the Mediterranean	Sea	地中海
the Red	Sea	紅海
the East China	Sea	東シナ海

▷Nobody could understand why the boat sank. There was a **calm sea** and no wind. なぜ船が沈んだのかだれにもわからなかった．海は穏やかで風もなかった
▷Look at that **rough sea**! I think there's a storm coming! あの荒れた海を見て．嵐が来そうだよ

in	the sea	海で
at	sea	海で，海上で
by	sea	船で，海路で

▷I know a lovely place where you can swim **in the sea**. 海で泳げるかっこうの場所を知っているよ
▷We were **at sea** when the typhoon struck. 台風が襲ってきたとき私たちは海上にいた
▷I don't like traveling **by sea**. I get seasick. 船旅は嫌いだ．船酔いするから

search /sə́ːrtʃ/ 名 捜索，調査；検索

make	a search	捜索する
conduct	a search	
carry out	a search	
begin	a search	捜索を始める
continue	a search	捜索を続ける
abandon	a search	捜索を打ち切る
call off	a search	
do	a search	検索する

▷The police **made** a **search** of the area, but found nothing. 警察はその地域を捜索したが，何も見つからなかった
▷It's too dark now. We'll have to **continue** the **search** tomorrow. 暗くなりすぎたので，あすも捜索を続けることになるだろう
▷The helicopter had to **abandon** the **search** for survivors because of bad weather. 悪天候のためヘリコプターは生存者の捜索を打ち切らなければならなかった

a desperate	search	必死の捜索
a thorough	search	徹底的な捜索
a search	party	捜索隊
a search	warrant	捜査令状

▷The rescue team carried out a **desperate search** for survivors. 救助隊は生存者がいないか必死の捜索を行った
▷The police carried out a **thorough search** of the building. 警察は建物を隈なく捜索した

search	for A	Aの捜索
in search	of A	Aを探して

▷We still haven't had any success in the **search for** the missing files. 行方不明のファイルをまだ探せないでいた

search /sə́ːrtʃ/ 動 探す，捜索する

search	desperately	必死に探す
search	in vain	探してもむだである
search	thoroughly	徹底的に探す

▷He **searched desperately** for his wallet but couldn't find it anywhere. 彼は財布を必死で探したがどこにも見つからなかった

search	for A	Aを求めて探す
search	through A	A(場所)を探す

▷The rescuers **searched for** bodies, but couldn't find any. 救助隊員は遺体を捜索したが，何も見つからなかった
▷He **searched through** his pockets, but he couldn't find his keys. 彼はポケットを探したが，鍵は見つからなかった

PHRASES
Search me! 😊 (質問に対して)知るものか

season /síːzn/ 名 季節，時期，シーズン

a dry	season	乾季
a rainy	season	雨季
the four	seasons	四季
peak	season	最盛期
high	season	
low	season	閑散期
off	season	シーズンオフ
breeding	season	繁殖期
mating	season	

the harvest	season	収穫期
the hunting	season	狩猟期
closed	season	禁漁期, 禁猟期
《英》close	season	

▷I hate the **rainy season**. It's so humid! 梅雨なんか嫌いだ。むしむしするんだもの
▷It's **high season** and all the hotels are fully booked. ハイシーズンでホテルはどこも予約でいっぱいだ

in	season	旬で；盛りがついて
out of	season	季節外れの；禁猟期で

▷You can't get fresh blueberries any more. They're **out of season**. 新鮮なブルーベリーはもう手に入りません。旬を過ぎましたから

seat /síːt/ 名 座席, 席；議席

take	a seat	席に着く
get	a seat	
have	a seat	
sit on	a seat	席に座る
sit in	a seat	
give up	one's seat	席を譲る
leave	one's seat	席を立つ
reserve	a seat	席を予約する
《英》book	a seat	
win	a seat	議席を獲得する
gain	a seat	
hold	a seat	議席を持つ
retain	one's seat	議席を維持する
lose	one's seat	議席を失う

▷Please **take a seat**. どうぞお座りください
▷Do you know that man **sitting on the seat** over there? 向こうの席に座っている男の人を知っていますか
▷I usually **give up** my **seat** if I see an old person standing. 高齢者が立っているのを見たらたいてい席を譲ります
▷She **left** her **seat** before the performance ended. 彼女は終演前に席を立った
▷I think our candidate will **win a seat** at the next election. われわれの候補者は次の選挙で議席を獲得すると思う

a front	seat	前部座席
a back	seat	後部座席
a rear	seat	
a driver's	seat	運転席
《英》a driving	seat	
a passenger	seat	助手席
a window	seat	窓側座席

an aisle	seat	通路側座席
an empty	seat	空席
a vacant	seat	
an extra	seat	補助席
a non-reserved	seat	自由席
a reserved	seat	指定席；予約席

▷I think there's an **empty seat** over there. 向こうに空席があると思うよ
▷That's a **reserved seat**. それは予約席です

seat belt /síːt bèlt/ 名 シートベルト

wear	a seat belt	シートベルトをしている
fasten	a seat belt	シートベルトを締める
unfasten	a seat belt	シートベルトを外す

▷You should always **wear** a **seat belt**. いつもシートベルトを締めていたほうがいい
▷Please **fasten** your **seat belts**. シートベルトをお締めください

secret /síːkrit/ 名 秘密, 機密；秘訣

have	a secret	秘密がある
keep	a secret	秘密を守る
keep A	a secret	Aを秘密にしておく
reveal	a secret	秘密を明かす
share	a secret	
let A in on	a secret	A(人)に秘密を打ち明ける
discover	a secret	秘密を知る
learn	a secret	
know	a secret	秘密を知っている
remain	a secret	秘密のままである

▷Can you **keep a secret**? 秘密を守れるかい
▷"Don't tell anyone!" "We have to **keep** this a **secret**!"「だれにも言わないでね」「このことは秘密にしなくちゃね」
▷Ellie had a little too much to drink last night and **revealed** some interesting **secrets**! エリーは昨夜少し飲みすぎて、おもしろい秘密をいくつか漏らした
▷I just **learnt** a **secret** about how Bob got the manager's job! ボブがどうやってマネジャー職を得たか秘密を知ったところだ

a big	secret	大きな秘密
a great	secret	重大な秘密
a little	secret	ささいな秘密
a well-kept	secret	極秘のこと
a closely-guarded	secret	

| security |

an open	secret	公然の秘密
a dark	secret	やましい秘密
a guilty	secret	罪深い秘密
top	secret	最高機密
a trade	secret	企業秘密
a state	secret	国家機密

▷I'm not surprised nobody knew about their engagement. It was a **closely-guarded secret**. 彼らの婚約をだれも知らなかったとしても別に驚かない。極秘だったろう

▷The fact that she's going to leave her job is an **open secret**. 彼女が仕事を辞めるのは公然の秘密だ

in	secret	密かに

▷Apparently they had a meeting **in secret**. どうも彼らは密かに打ち合わせたらしい

security /sikjúərəti/

名 安心(感); 安全, 警備; 保障

provide	security	安心させる; 安全をもたらす
ensure	security	安全を確保する
guarantee	security	安全を保証する
improve	security	安全性を高める
threaten	security	安全を脅かす

▷They managed to save a lot of money to **provide security** for their old age. 彼らは老後に安心して暮らせるよう大金をどうにか貯めた

▷We need to **improve security** in this office. この事務所の安全性を高める必要がある

▷If the newspapers print this story it will **threaten the security** of our country. 新聞にこの記事が載ったらわが国の安全は脅かされることになるだろう

tight	security	堅い警備
lax	security	緩い警備
collective	security	集団安全保障
social	security	社会保障
internal	security	国内の治安
national	security	国の安全
personal	security	身の安全

▷There was **tight security** during the Queen's visit. 女王の訪問中は警備が厳重だった

▷We should all take measures to ensure our **collective security**. 集団安全保障を確保するためのあらゆる措置を講じるべきだ

▷What's your **social security** number? あなたの社会保障番号は何番ですか

▷Terrorists are threatening our **national security**. テロリストがわが国の安全を脅かしている

a sense of	security	安心感
a feeling of	security	

▷Wearing a seat belt gives me a **sense of security**. シートベルトをしていると安心する

▷We don't want to give people a false **sense of security**. 人々に偽りの安全神話を抱かせたくはない

select /silékt/ **動** 選ぶ, 選択する

carefully	select	注意深く選ぶ
specially	select	特別に選ぶ
randomly	select	無作為に選ぶ
automatically	select	自動的に選ぶ

▷They **carefully selected** which guests they were going to invite. どの客を招待するか注意深く人選した

▷The wine we're going to drink this evening has been **specially selected** by a wine expert. 今晩お飲みいただくワインはワイン通が特別に選んだものです

▷The lottery winners were **randomly selected** by computer. 宝くじの当選者はコンピュータで無作為に選ばれた

select	A to do	Aを選んで…させる
select	A for B	AをBのために選ぶ

▷Our company is going to **select** two more people **for** management training. わが社では管理職教育のためにあと2名を選ぶ予定だ

selection /silékʃən/

名 選択, 選抜; 選ばれた物, 選ばれた人

make	a selection	選択する
have	a selection	取りそろえている

▷We need to **make a selection** from these three package tours. これら3つのパッケージツアーの中から選ぶ必要がある

▷This store **has a** good **selection** of computers. この店はコンピュータの品ぞろえがいい

a careful	selection	注意深い選択
a random	selection	無作為選択
the final	selection	最終選考
natural	selection	自然選択
a varied	selection	幅広い選択
a wide	selection	幅広い選択; 豊富な品ぞろえ
a large	selection	豊富な品ぞろえ

a good	selection	よい品ぞろえ

▷She made a **careful selection** of the best photos and put them in an album. 彼女はよく撮れた写真を注意深く選んでアルバムに入れた
▷Your name was chosen by **random selection** from a computer. あなたの名前はコンピュータによって無作為に選ばれました
▷This store has a **wide selection** of earrings and bracelets. この店はイアリングとブレスレットの品ぞろえが豊富だ

a selection	for A	Aのための選択
a selection	from A	Aからの選択

▷These wines are a special **selection for** our first-class passengers. これらのワインはファーストクラスのお客様のために特別に選んだ物です

sell /sél/ 動 売る, 販売する；売れる

sell	well	よく売れる

▷iPhones are beginning to **sell** really **well**. iPhone はとてもよく売れ始めている

sell	A B	A(人)にB(物)を売る
sell	B to A	

▷He **sold** his car really cheaply **to** his best friend. 彼はいちばんの親友に車をすごく安く売った

sell A	for B	AをB(ある金額)で売る
sell A	at B	
sell A	at a profit	Aを売ってもうける
sell A	at a loss	Aを売って損を出す

▷These DVDs are **selling for** less than $1 each! これらのDVDは1枚1ドル未満で売っている
▷They **sold** their house **at** a big **profit**. 家を売って大もうけした

send /sénd/ 動 送る；行かせる

immediately	send	ただちに送る
simply	send	単に送る
recently	sent	最近送った

▷I phoned the office and they **immediately sent** me an application form. 事務所に電話したらすぐ申込用紙を送ってくれた
▷If you don't have a credit card you can **simply send** us a check. クレジットカードをお持ちでなければ小切手を送っていただくだけで結構です

send	A B	A(人)にBを送る
send	B to A	
send	A to B	A(人)をB(場所)に行かせる, 派遣する
send	A to do	A(人)を…しに行かせる
send	A doing	Aを…させる

▷We **sent** the parcel **to** you last Thursday. 先週の木曜日にあなたに小包を送りました
▷Can you **send** someone **to** repair the roof? 屋根の修理にだれかよこしてくれるかい
▷He pushed me and **sent** me fly**ing** down the steps. 彼に押されて, 階段を転げ落ちた

sense /séns/

名 感覚；感じ；常識；正気；意味

have	a sense	感覚がある；感じがする；意味がある
lose	a sense	感覚を失う
get	a sense	感じがする
convey	a sense	感じを伝える
give	a sense	感じを与える
develop	a sense	感覚を身につける
lack	a sense	感覚がない；常識に欠ける
make	sense	意味が通る
see	sense	道理がわかる
come to	one's senses	正気に戻る
bring A to	one's senses	A(人)を正気に戻す

▷Sorry. I've no idea where to go. I've no **sense of** direction. ごめん, どっちへ行けばいいかわからないや. 方向感覚がないので
▷This poem **conveys** a **sense** of hope for the future. この詩からは未来への期待感が伝わってくる
▷The signpost points this way, but the map says that way. It doesn't **make sense**! 案内標識はこちらを示しているけど地図では向こうになっている. おかしいぞ
▷When he **came to** his **senses** he realized he'd been knocked down by a car. 正気に戻って彼はああ車にはねられたんだとわかった

a deep	sense	深い感覚
a strong	sense	強い感覚
common	sense	常識, 良識
good	sense	良識, 分別
business	sense	経営センス
fashion	sense	ファッションセンス
a wide	sense	広い意味
a broad	sense	
a narrow	sense	狭い意味

a strict	sense	厳密な意味
a general	sense	一般的な意味
the usual	sense	ふつうの意味
a literal	sense	文字どおりの意味

▷ Just think for a minute! Use your **common sense**! ちょっと考えて. 常識を働かせてみて
▷ In the **strict sense** of the word, 'twitter' is the noise that birds make when they sing — not an Internet comment! 厳密に言えばツイッターは鳥がさえずるときの音のことでインターネットのコメントではない

in	a sense	ある意味で
in	some senses	
in	no sense	決して…ない

▷ I'm glad I found a new part-time job, but **in some senses** I miss the old one. 新しいアルバイトが見つかってうれしいが, 前のアルバイトが懐かしい面もある
▷ I'm sorry. What I said was **in no sense** meant to upset you. ごめん. きみを怒らせるつもりで言ったんじゃないんだ

in every sense	of the word	あらゆる意味で

▷ He is, **in every sense of** the **word**, a gentleman. 彼はどこから見ても紳士だ

sensible /sénsəbl/ 形 分別のある, 賢明な

eminently	sensible	とても分別のある
sensible	enough	十分に分別がある

▷ I think all his suggestions were **eminently sensible**. 彼の提案はどれも実にもっともだと思う
▷ Luckily I was **sensible enough to** bring an umbrella with me before I left the house. 運よく出がけに気がついて傘を持ってきた

be sensible	to do	…するのが賢明だ

▷ If you're going to pack, it would be **sensible to** do it now. 荷造りするならますぐするのが賢明だろう

sensitive /sénsətiv/ 形 敏感な; 微妙な

highly	sensitive	きわめて敏感な; 非常に微妙な
particularly	sensitive	特に敏感な
environmentally	sensitive	環境にとって微妙な
politically	sensitive	政治的に微妙な

▷ Building a power station here is an **environmentally sensitive** issue. ここに発電所を建設することは環境にとって微妙な問題だ
▷ A dog's sense of smell is **particularly sensitive** compared to a human's. 犬の嗅覚は人間のそれに比べて特に敏感だ

sensitive	to A	Aに敏感な
sensitive	about A	Aを気にする

▷ She wears sunglasses because her eyes are very **sensitive to** bright light. 彼女は眼がまぶしい光にとても弱いので, サングラスをかけている
▷ When you meet him don't mention the scar on his face. He's very **sensitive about** it. 彼に会ったら顔の傷の話はしないように. とても気にしているから

sentence /séntəns/ 名 判決; 文

pass	sentence	判決を下す
pronounce	sentence	
receive	a sentence	判決を受ける
be given	a sentence	
serve	a sentence	刑に服する

▷ Everybody gasped as the judge **passed sentence**. 裁判官が判決を下したとき, だれもがはっと息をのんだ
▷ He's **serving** a 3-year **sentence** for robbery. 彼は強盗の罪で3年の刑に服している

a heavy	sentence	重い刑
a severe	sentence	
a light	sentence	軽い刑
a long	sentence	長い刑期
a short	sentence	短い刑期
a suspended	sentence	執行猶予
a prison	sentence	実刑判決
a jail	sentence	
a life	sentence	終身刑
a death	sentence	死刑
an interrogative	sentence	疑問文
a negative	sentence	否定文

▷ The judge gave him a 6 month **suspended sentence**. 裁判官は彼に6か月の執行猶予を与えた
▷ Considering what he did, he received a very **short sentence**. その行為を考慮して, 彼が受けた刑期はとても短いものだった

separate /sépərèit/
動 分ける; 分かれる; 別れる

completely	separated	完全に分かれた

entirely	separated	
totally	separated	
well	separated	きちんと分けた
widely	separated	遠く離れた

▷ We got **completely separated** in the crowd. 人混みの中ですっかり離れ離れになってしまった
▷ The white and yolk of the egg must be **well separated**. 卵の白身と黄身をきちんと分けてください
▷ Most of villages in these mountains are remote and **widely separated**. この山岳地帯の村々はほとんどが辺ぴなところにあり，互いに遠く離れている

separate	A from B	AとBを分ける
separate	A into B	AをBに分ける

▷ The twins are identical. I can't **separate** one **from** the other. その双子は瓜二つで見分けがつかない

series /síəri:z/ 名 連続；連続番組，シリーズ

a continuous	series	一続きのもの
a new	series	新シリーズ
a drama	series	連続ドラマ
a comedy	series	連続コメディー

▷ These stories were published as a **continuous series** in a monthly magazine. これらの話は月刊誌で連続ものとして発表された
▷ A **new series** of TV dramas starts next week. テレビドラマの新シリーズが来週から始まる

a series	of A	一連のA

★ A は articles, events, meetings, experiments, attacks, questions など

▷ A **series of meetings** about the crisis will take place in the coming weeks. 危機についての一連の会議が今後数週間内に開かれるだろう

serious /síəriəs/ 形 重大な，深刻な；本気の，真剣な

extremely	serious	きわめて深刻な
particularly	serious	特に深刻な
potentially	serious	潜在的に深刻な

▷ Luckily her injuries were not **particularly serious**. 幸い彼女のけがは特に深刻なものではなかった
▷ This is definitely a **potentially serious** situation. まさに深刻な状況になる可能性のある状態だ

serious	about A	Aについて真剣な

▷ Are you **serious about** starting your own rock band? 本気でロックバンドを立ち上げる気かい

PHRASES

Are you serious? ☺ 本気かい ▷ "I'm thinking of quitting my job and going on a trip around the world." "Are you serious?" 「仕事を辞めて世界一周旅行に行こうと思っているんだ」「本気かい」
It's not serious. ☺ 大したことはない ▷ I sprained my ankle, but it's not serious. 足首をくじいたが大したことはない

serve /sə́:rv/

動 (飲食物を)出す；奉仕する；役に立つ

serve	immediately	(料理を)すぐに出す
serve	well	よく役立つ

▷ When the dish is completed we should **serve immediately**. 料理ができたらすぐ出したほうがいい
▷ I've had this bicycle for over 10 years! It's **served** me really **well**. この自転車に10年以上は乗っているけど，とても役立ったよ

serve	A B	A(人)にB(飲
serve	B to A	物)を出す
serve	A with B	

▷ She **served** him bacon and eggs for breakfast. 彼女は彼にベーコンエッグを朝食に出した
▷ During 'happy hour' they **serve** drinks **to** their customers at half-price. サービスタイム中は客に半額で飲み物を出している
▷ To begin with they **served** us **with** delicious smoked salmon. まずおいしいスモークサーモンが出た

serve	as A	Aとして仕える；Aとして役立つ

▷ He **served as** Mayor of New York for many years. 彼は何年にもわたってニューヨーク市長を務めた
▷ This room **serves as** both a study and a spare room for guests. この部屋は書斎としても客間としても使えます

service /sə́:rvis/

名 公共事業，公益サービス；業務；サービス

do A	a service	Aのために尽くす
provide	service	サービスを提供する
offer	service	
give	service	サービスする
improve	service	サービスを向上させる

▷ The bus is late again. I wish the company would

| set |

provide a better **service**. バスがまた遅れた．会社はサービス改善に努めてほしいね
▷ I think we should come to this hotel again. They **give** really good **service**. またこのホテルに来ようよ．すごくサービスがいいから
▷ We have to **improve service** to our customers. 顧客へのサービスを向上させなければならない

public	service	公共サービス
medical	service	医療業務
postal	service	郵便事業
social	services	社会奉仕
financial	services	金融サービス
military	service	兵役
voluntary	service	ボランティア活動
customer	service	顧客サービス
good	service	よいサービス
poor	service	貧弱なサービス

▷ The **medical service** here is excellent. ここの医療業務はとりわけすばらしい
▷ She works overseas for a **voluntary service** organization. 彼女はボランティア活動団体のために海外で働いている

set /sét/ 名 一組, ひとそろい

| a set | of A | Aの一式 |

★Aには circumstances, conditions, criteria, data, principles, problems, questions, rules, values など

▷ They gave us a **set of** silver knives and forks as a wedding present! 結婚祝いに銀のナイフとフォークのセットをもらったんだ

settle /sétl/ 動 解決する；落ち着く

| finally | settle | ついに解決する |
| eventually | settle | |

▷ We've **finally settled** how many people we're going to invite to the wedding. 結婚式の招待人数がようやく決まった

PHRASES
That's settled (then). ☺ (じゃあ)それで決まりだ ▷ "I want to go to Hawaii for our honeymoon!" "Hawaii? OK! Me, too." "That's settled, then!" 「新婚旅行はハワイに行きたいわ」「ハワイか，いいよ．ぼくもだ」「それじゃ決まりね」

settlement /sétlmənt/

名 解決, 和解；決済；植民

negotiate	a settlement	和解に向けて交渉する
reach	a settlement	和解に達する
accept	a settlement	和解を受け入れる
pay	a settlement	和解金を支払う

▷ We're still trying to **negotiate** a **settlement** with the people who are sueing us. 私たちを訴えている人たちといまも和解交渉をしようとしている
▷ She's finally **reached** a **settlement** with her husband's lawyers. 彼女は夫の弁護士とようやく合意に達した

a final	settlement	最終的解決
a peaceful	settlement	平和的解決
a negotiated	settlement	交渉による解決
a political	settlement	政治的解決
a divorce	settlement	離婚調停
an out-of-court	settlement	法廷外の示談
a peace	settlement	和平調停

▷ We should do our best to negotiate a **peaceful settlement** over the disputed islands. われわれは争点となっている島々について交渉による平和的解決に最善を尽くすべきだ
▷ It took many years for the two countries to reach a **political settlement**. 両国が政治的決着に達するまで何年もかかった

| in | settlement (of A) | (Aの)支払いとして |

▷ They are offering $10,000 **in settlement of** our claim. こちらの請求に対して向こうは1万ドルの支払いを提示している

severe /səvíər/ 形 厳しい, 深刻な

exceptionally	severe	例外的に厳しい
increasingly	severe	ますます厳しい
particularly	severe	とりわけ厳しい

▷ This year's winter was **particularly severe**. 今年の冬は特に厳しかった

sex /séks/ 名 性, 性別；性交, セックス

| have | sex | セックスする |

▷ He didn't want to **have sex** with me. 彼は私とセックスしたくなかったの

the opposite	sex	異性
the same	sex	同性
both	sexes	男女, 両性

▷He's still too young to be interested in the **opposite sex**. 異性に興味をもつには彼はまだ若すぎる
▷A "coeducational" school is a school where **both sexes** attend. 共学校とは男女が通う学校のことだ

shade /ʃéid/ 名 陰；色合い

a dark	shade	濃い色合い
a deep	shade	
a light	shade	薄い色合い
pastel	shades	パステルふうの色合い
various	shades	さまざまな色合い

▷The dress she was wearing was a **dark shade** of blue. 彼女が着ている服は濃い色合いの青だった
▷I think **pastel shades** suit you best. あなたにはパステルふうの色合いがいちばん似合うと思う
▷There were **various shades** *of* blue to choose from. In the end we chose a very dark blue. さまざまな色合いの青から選べたが，結局はとても濃い青を選んだ

in	the shade	陰で, 日陰で

▷They were having their picnic **in** the **shade** *of* a tree. 彼らは木陰でピクニックをしていた

[PHRASES]
Shades of A! Aを思い出すなあ(★しばしば亡くなった人のことを思い出すときに用いる) ▷"Kate Middleton looked beautiful in her wedding dress!" "Yes. Shades of Lady Diana!"「ケイト・ミドルトンのウェディングドレス姿は美しかったなあ」「ええ, ダイアナ妃のことを思い出したわ」

shadow /ʃǽdou/ 名 影, 陰

cast	a shadow	影を落とす
throw	shadows	
emerge from	the shadows	陰から現れる
see	a shadow	影が見える

▷The death of her father **cast** a **shadow** *over* the wedding celebrations. 彼女の父親が亡くなったことは結婚式のお祝いに暗い影を落とした
▷A dark figure **emerged from** the **shadows** and came toward her. 黒い姿が陰から現れ彼女の方へやって来た

a dark	shadow	濃い影
(a) deep	shadow	
a black	shadow	黒い影
a long	shadow	長い影
a pale	shadow	淡い影

▷As the sun set, it cast a **long shadow** of the lighthouse across the beach. 太陽が沈むにつれて灯台の長い影が砂浜に伸びた
▷After his wife's death he was a **pale shadow** of what he used to be. 妻が亡くなってからの彼は見る影もなかった

in	the shadows	陰の中で
in	shadow	陰になって

▷He could just make out the figure of a tall man standing **in** the **shadows**. 陰の中に立つ背の高い男の姿を彼はなんとか見分けられた

shake /ʃéik/ 動 振る；揺れる；震える

shake	slightly	わずかに震える

▷It was Helen's first presentation. She was a little nervous and her voice **shook slightly**. ヘレンの最初の発表だったが，緊張気味で声がわずかに震えていた

shake	with A	A(感情)に震える

★Aは emotion, fear, frustration など

▷Her whole body was **shaking with** fear. 彼女は全身恐怖に震えていた

shaken /ʃéikən/ 形 動揺した

badly	shaken	ひどく動揺した
severely	shaken	
visibly	shaken	目に見えて動揺した

▷When her lawyer told her she might go to prison for 10 years she was **visibly shaken**. 弁護士から10年間の刑務所入りになるかもしれないと聞かされて彼女は動揺を隠せなかった

shallow /ʃǽlou/ 形 浅い

relatively	shallow	比較的浅い
comparatively	shallow	

▷It's quite safe to swim here. The water's **relatively shallow**. この辺は泳いでも安全だ．比較的浅いから

shame /ʃéim/

图 恥ずかしさ；恥ずべきこと；残念なこと

feel	shame	恥ずかしく思う
bring	shame	恥をかかせる
die of	shame	恥ずかしくて死にそうだ

▷He didn't seem to **feel** any **shame** at what he had done. 彼は自分がしたことを恥ずかしいと思っていないようだった
▷You've **brought shame** on the whole family. お前は家族のみんなに恥をかかせた
▷If that happened to me I would **die of shame**. そんなことになったら恥ずかしくて死にそうだ

a great	shame	すごく残念なこと
a terrible	shame	
a real	shame	
a crying	shame	

▷It's a **great shame**. My grandparents lost all their money in the financial crisis. ものすごく残念なんだけど祖父母が金融危機で全財産をなくしたの

a sense of	shame	羞恥心
a feeling of	shame	

▷Emma seems to have no **sense of shame**! エマには羞恥心というものがないようだ

to	A's shame	Aが恥ずかしいことには

▷**To** my **shame** I completely forgot her name. 恥ずかしいことに彼女の名前をすっかり忘れていた

it is a shame	(that)...	…は残念だ

▷**It's a shame** you can't come to my birthday party. あなたが私の誕生パーティーに来られなくて残念です

with	shame	恥ずかしくて
in	shame	
without	shame	恥じることもなく

▷He admitted he'd taken the money and hung his head **in shame**. 彼はお金を受け取ったことを認め、恥ずかしさにうなだれた
▷You did your best, so you can hold your head up **without shame**. 全力を尽くしたのだから堂々と胸を張っていいよ

〈PHRASES〉
(**It's a**) **shame really**! 😊 ほんとうに残念だ
Shame on you! 😊 恥を知れ ▷How could you do such a terrible thing! Shame on you! よくもそんなひどいことができたね. 恥を知れよ
What a shame! 😊 何たることだ；それは残念だ / **That's**

a shame. それは残念だ ▷"All the tickets were sold out." "Oh, no. That's a shame." 「チケットは売り切れだったよ」「まさか. それは残念」

shape /ʃéip/ 图 形, 形状；状態, 調子

take	shape	具体化する

▷Finally the plans for starting our own company are beginning to **take shape**. ついに自分たちの会社を立ち上げる計画が具体化し始めている

complex	shape	複雑な形
geometric	shape	幾何学的な形
overall	shape	全体の形
physical	shape	体調
good	shape	よい調子
bad	shape	悪い調子

▷Ben's in very good **physical shape**. ベンはとても体調がいい
▷"How's Pam after the accident?" "Well, she's in pretty **bad shape**." 「事故後のパムはどうなの」「そうね、かなり調子が悪そうね」

all shapes and sizes	さまざまな形や大きさ

▷Dogs come in **all shapes and sizes**. 犬は体型も大きさもさまざまだ

in	the shape of A	Aの形の
in	shape	体調がよく
out of	shape	体調が悪く

▷Human DNA is **in** the **shape of** a double helix. ヒトのDNAは二重螺旋の形をしている
▷I don't think I'm **in shape** to run a marathon! マラソンが走れる体調だとは思わない ▷I exercise as much as I can. I don't want to get **out of shape**. できるだけ運動しています. 体調を崩したくないから
♦**get in shape** 体を鍛える, 体調を整える ▷I'm getting really fat! I need to get in shape! すごく太ってきちゃって. 体を鍛えないと
♦**keep in shape** 体調を維持する ▷She goes to the gym three times a week to keep in shape. 彼女は体調を保つために週3回ジムに通っている

share /ʃéər/ 图 株；分け前；占有率

acquire	shares	株を取得する
buy	shares	株を買う
sell	shares	株を売る
have	shares	株を持っている

own	shares	株を所有する
hold	shares	株を保有する
receive	a share	分け前を受け取る
have	a share	分け前をもらう
take	a share	

▷I think we should **buy shares** in that company. その会社の株を買うべきだと思う
▷We **have shares** *in* an oil company. 私たちは石油会社の株を持っている
▷We're business partners so we each **take** a 50% **share** of the profit. われわれはビジネスパートナーなのでそれぞれが利益の5割を受け取ることになっている

shares	rise	株が上がる
shares	jump	株が急騰する
shares	fall	株が下がる

▷The **shares jumped** 21p to 330p. 株価は21ペンス急騰して330ペンスになった
▷The **shares fell** 7p to 250p yesterday. きのう株価が7ペンス下落して250ペンスになった

a share	in A	Aの分け前

▷You are entitled to receive a **share in** the profits. あなたには利益の分け前を受け取る資格がある

preferred	share	優先株
(英) preference	share	
outstanding	share	発行済株式
market	share	市場占有率

share /ʃéər/ 動 分け合う, 共有する

widely	shared	幅広く共有された

▷You're probably right. That's a view that's **widely shared**. あなたはたぶん間違っていません. 幅広く共有されている見方です

share	equally	等しく分ける

▷We both own the company and **share equally** in the profits. 私たちは二人で会社を経営して利益を均等に分けている

share A	between B	AをBの間で分ける
share A	among B	
share (A)	with B	(Aを)B(人)と分け合う
share	in A	Aを共有する

▷Can you **share** this cake **between** you? このケーキをきみたちで分けてくれるかい

▷Do you mind if I **share** a room **with** you? あなたと同室で構いませんか
▷After she won the lottery she wanted everybody to **share in** her good fortune. 宝くじが当たって彼女はみんなに自分の幸運を共有してほしかった

sharp /ʃɑ́ːrp/ 形 鋭い; 頭が切れる

sharp and clear	とても冷たくて澄んだ

▷It was very cold, the night air was **sharp and clear**. とても寒くて, 夜の空気は身を切るように冷たく澄んでいた

as sharp as	a razor	かみそりのように鋭い; 抜け目がない
as sharp as	a tack	頭が切れる
as sharp as	a needle	

▷He may be 90 years old, but his mind is still **as sharp as a razor**! 90歳ではあるものの彼はまだ頭がすごくしっかりしている

sheep /ʃíːp/ 名 羊

a flock of	sheep	羊の群れ

★「牛, シカ, 象の群れ」には herd を用いる

▷There's a **flock of sheep** crossing the road. 羊の群れが道路を渡っている

shine /ʃáin/ 動 輝く, 光る; 光らせる

shine	brightly	明るく輝く
shine	brilliantly	さんさんと輝く

▷The moon **shone brightly** in the cloudless sky. 月が雲ひとつない空に明るく輝いていた

shine	on A	(光が)Aに当たる
shine A	on B	A(光など)をBに当てる
shine A	at B	
shine	in A	A(光)が当たって輝く

▷The sea's really warm. The sun's been **shining on** it all day. その海はとても温かい. 太陽が一日中海に当たっている
▷It's too dark to read this road sign. Can you **shine** a light **on** it? 暗すぎて道路標識が読めないよ. 照らしてくれるかな

ship /ʃíp/ 名 船

board	a ship	船に乗る
get on	a ship	
get off	a ship	船を下りる
build	a ship	船を建造する
abandon	ship	船を捨てる
jump	ship	

▷My uncle left school at 14 and **boarded** a **ship** for Australia. 叔父は14歳で学校を出てオーストラリア行きの船に乗った

▷I don't trust Dobson. He'll be the first person to **jump ship** if our company runs into difficulties. ドブソンを信用しない. 彼は会社が傾いたら真っ先に逃げ出すだろう

by	ship	船で
on	a ship	船の上で
on board	(a) ship	

▷Do you think we should go **by ship** or by plane? 船と飛行機のどちらで行くのがいいかな

▷If you go on a world cruise there are lots of things that you can do **on board ship**. 世界一周クルーズに出たら船上でできることがたくさんある

the captain of	a ship	船長

▷He's the **captain of** a **ship** in the Royal Navy. 彼は王室海軍の船長だ

a passenger	ship	客船
a cruise	ship	クルーズ客船
a cargo	ship	貨物船
a merchant	ship	商船
a whaling	ship	捕鯨船

shirt /ʃə́ːrt/ 名 ワイシャツ；シャツ

a clean	shirt	洗濯したシャツ
an open-necked	shirt	開襟シャツ
a short-sleeved	shirt	半袖シャツ
a long-sleeved	shirt	長袖シャツ
a polo	shirt	ポロシャツ
a silk	shirt	絹のシャツ
a cotton	shirt	綿のシャツ
a denim	shirt	デニムのシャツ
a striped	shirt	ストライプのシャツ

▷You'd better put on a **clean shirt** for this evening. 今晩は洗濯済みのシャツを着なさい

a shirt and jeans	ワイシャツとジーンズ
a shirt and trousers	ワイシャツとズボン
a shirt and tie	ワイシャツとネクタイ

▷He was wearing a **shirt and jeans**. 彼はワイシャツにジーンズ姿だった

▷I'll put on a **shirt and tie**. ワイシャツを着てネクタイをします

shock /ʃák | ʃɔ́k/ 名 衝撃, ショック

get	a shock	衝撃を受ける
receive	a shock	
suffer (from)	a shock	
come as	a shock	衝撃となる
give A	a shock	Aに衝撃を与える
die of	shock	ショック死する
recover from	the shock	衝撃から立ち直る

▷She **got** a **shock** when she found she'd failed her exams. 試験に落ちたことがわかって彼女はショックを受けた

▷The news **came as** quite a **shock**. その知らせはとてもショックだった

▷I couldn't see you there! You **gave** me a **shock**! そこできみに会えなくてショックだったよ

▷When I heard the news I nearly **died of shock**! その知らせを聞いてショックで死にそうだった

a great	shock	大きなショック
a big	shock	
a severe	shock	
a terrible	shock	
a sudden	shock	突然のショック
an electric	shock	電気ショック, 感電

▷It was a **great shock** when he heard he'd lost his job. 職を失ったと聞いて彼はすごくショックだった

▷"Ow!" "What happened?" "I got an **electric shock**!"「うっ」「どうしたの」「感電しちゃった」

in	shock	ショック状態で

▷That car nearly ran me over! I'm still **in** a state of **shock**. もう少しであの車にひかれそうだった. いまだにショック状態だ

shock /ʃák | ʃɔ́k/ 動 衝撃を与える

really	shock	ものすごくショックを与える
deeply	shock	
slightly	shock	軽いショックを与える

▷ When she heard her husband had been in prison it **deeply shocked** her. 夫が刑務所にいたと聞いて彼女はすごくショックを受けた

shock A	by doing	…してAにショックを与える

▷ He **shocked** everybody **by** fail**ing** all his exams. 彼は試験に全部落ちてみんなを仰天させた

shocked /ʃákt | ʃɔ́kt/ 形 ショックを受けた

deeply	shocked	強く衝撃を受けた
genuinely	shocked	心から衝撃を受けた
visibly	shocked	明らかに衝撃を受けた

▷ When she heard that she had failed to get a place at university she was **visibly shocked**. 大学に落ちたと聞いて彼女ははた目にもわかるほどのショックを受けた

shocked	at A	Aにショックを受ける
shocked	to do	…してショックを受けた

★ do は see, hear, learn など

▷ We were **shocked at** the news of his death. 彼の死の知らせにショックを受けた

shoe /ʃúː/ 名 (ふつう shoes で)靴

put on	one's shoes	靴を履く
wear	shoes	靴を履いている
take off	one's shoes	靴を脱ぐ
remove	one's shoes	
clean	A's shoes	靴をきれいにする
polish	A's shoes	靴を磨く
shine	A's shoes	

▷ Wait a minute. I need to **put on** my **shoes**. ちょっと待って。靴を履かなくちゃ
▷ Would you like me to **polish** your **shoes**? 靴を磨いてさしあげましょうか

high-heeled	shoes	かかとの高い靴
low-heeled	shoes	かかとの低い靴
leather	shoes	革靴
training	shoes	トレーニングシューズ
walking	shoes	ウォーキングシューズ
tennis	shoes	テニスシューズ

▷ She was wearing **high-heeled shoes**. 彼女はハイヒールの靴を履いていた

a pair of	shoes	靴1足

▷ I need to buy a new **pair of shoes**. 新しい靴を買わなくては(★「靴2足」は two pairs of shoes という)

shoot /ʃúːt/ 動 撃つ, 射る

shoot	back	撃ち返す
shoot	down	撃ち殺す；撃ち落とす

▷ According to the news, the terrorists **shot down** a helicopter this morning. ニュースによるとテロリストたちがヘリコプターを撃墜したそうだ

shoot	at A	Aを(ねらって)撃つ
shoot A	in the B	A(人)のB(体の部位)を撃つ

★ B は head, leg, stomach など

▷ It's boring watching movies where people are **shooting at** each other all the time. 撃ち合いばかりやっている映画を見るのは退屈だ
▷ When he saw the police were coming he **shot** himself **in** the head. 警察がやって来るのを見て彼は自分の頭を中で撃ち抜いた

shoot A	dead	A(人)を射殺する
shot and killed		射殺された

▷ The terrorists were **shot dead** by the police. テロリストたちは警察に射殺された
▷ Her brother was **shot and killed** while fighting in Afghanistan. 彼女の弟はアフガニスタンでの戦争で撃たれて死んだ

shop /ʃáp | ʃɔ́p/ 名 店, 小売店

run	a shop	店を経営する
set up	shop	開店する；事業を始める
close up	shop	閉店する；店じまいする
shut up	shop	

▷ We don't get enough customers here. I think we should **set up shop** nearer the center of town. この辺りは客が少ないから、もっと中心街に近い場所に店を出したほうがいいよ
▷ We **shut up shop** at 6:00 p.m. うちは午後6時閉店です

a coffee	shop	喫茶店
a gift	shop	ギフトショップ
a pet	shop	ペットショップ

shopping /ʃɑ́pɪŋ | ʃɔ́p-/ 名 買い物

go	shopping	買い物に行く
do	the shopping	買い物をする

▷We need to **go shopping** this afternoon. きょうの午後に買い物に行かなくちゃ

short /ʃɔ́ːrt/ 形 短い；不足して

relatively	short	比較的短い
comparatively	short	
desperately	short	まったく足りない
far	short	はるかに足りない

▷We've managed to do a lot in a **relatively short** period of time. 比較的短い期間内に多くのことをなんとか成し遂げた
▷She was **desperately short** of cash. 彼女は手持ちの金がまったく足りなかった
▷The amount of money we've got is **far short** of what we need. 調達した金は必要な額よりはるかに少なかった

short	for A	Aの省略形で
short	of A	A(物)が不足して
short	on A	A(能力など)が不足して

▷"Blog" is **short for** weblog. ブログはウェブログの省略形だ
▷I'm a bit **short of** time. ちょっと時間が足りない
▷I like Tracy, but she's a bit **short on** common sense. トレイシーのことは好きだけど彼女は少し常識が欠けている

be $30	short	30ドル足りない

▷I couldn't buy the dress. I was $30 **short** and had forgotten my credit card. そのドレスを買えなかった。30ドル足りなかったし，クレジットカードを忘れてきてしまっていた

short and sweet		簡潔で要を得た

▷Ken's reply was **short and sweet**. ケンの返事は簡潔で要を得ていた

shortage /ʃɔ́ːrtɪdʒ/ 名 不足

cause	a shortage	不足を招く
create	a shortage	
face	a shortage	不足に直面する

▷The lack of rain this summer has **caused** a **shortage** of rice. 今夏の雨不足で米不足になった

an acute	shortage	深刻な不足
a severe	shortage	
a desperate	shortage	
a chronic	shortage	慢性的な不足
a general	shortage	全般的な不足
a labor	shortage	労働力不足
a staff	shortage	人員不足
a food	shortage	食糧不足
a water	shortage	水不足
a housing	shortage	住宅不足

▷After the earthquake there was an **acute shortage** of food, water and medical supplies. 地震後に食糧，水，医薬品が大幅に不足した

shot /ʃɑ́t | ʃɔ́t/ 名 発砲；射手；シュート，ショット；写真，撮影；試み；注射

fire	a shot	発砲する
take	a shot	ねらい撃つ
hit	a shot	シュートを放つ，ショットを打つ
play	a shot	
take	a shot	写真を撮る
have	a shot	やってみる，試してみる
get	a shot	
take	a shot	
get	a shot	注射してもらう
have	a shot	
give A	a shot	A(人)に注射する

▷Did you hear that? Somebody **fired** a **shot**. 聞こえたかい．だれかが発砲したよ
▷He **took** a **shot** at the deer, but missed! 彼は鹿をねらって撃ったが，外した
▷Tiger Woods **hit** a fantastic **shot**. タイガー・ウッズはすばらしいショットをした
▷She **took** a **shot** of the President waving to the crowds. 彼女は群衆に手を振る大統領の写真を撮った
▷I think this job would be perfect for you. Why don't you **take** a **shot** at it? この仕事はきみにぴったりだよ．やってみたらどうだい
▷There's a lot of flu about at the moment. I think you should **get** a **shot**. インフルエンザがはやっているから，注射を打ってもらったほうがいいよ

a good	shot	射撃のうまい人；うまいシュート，ナイスショット
a bad	shot	射撃のへたな人
a close-up	shot	クローズアップ
a long	shot	ロングショット

▷Dave's a **good shot**. He was in the army.　デイブは射撃の名手だ．軍隊にいたんだ
▷**Good shot**! Almost a hole in one!　ナイスショット．あわやホールインワン!!

a shot	in the arm	カンフル剤, 元気回復剤
a shot	in the dark	当てずっぽう

▷Winning that scholarship was a **shot in** the **arm** for her.　その奨学金を得たことは彼女の励みになった
▷It was just a lucky guess. A **shot in** the **dark**!　運がよかっただけです．当てずっぽうだったので

like	a shot	すぐに, 即座に

▷When I offered him $100 for his old computer he agreed **like a shot**.　彼の古いコンピュータを100ドルで買うと言ったら，彼は即答でOKした

shoulder /ʃóuldər/ 名 肩

shrug	one's shoulders	肩をすぼめる
hunch	one's shoulders	肩を丸める
square	one's shoulders	肩を怒らせる
touch	A's shoulder	肩に触れる
tap A	on the shoulder	Aの肩をたたく

▷When I asked her what had happened she just **shrugged** her **shoulders**.　何が起こったか彼女に尋ねたとき彼女は肩をすぼめただけだった (★無関心・当惑・あきらめなどを表すしぐさ)
▷He **hunched** his **shoulders** and tried to warm himself by the fire.　彼は肩を丸めて火のそばで暖を取ろうとした
▷He **squared** his **shoulders** and looked ready for a fight.　彼は肩を怒らせ，いまにも殴りかかってきそうな気配だった

over	one's shoulder(s)	肩に; 肩ごしに
on	A's shoulders	両肩に

▷He slung his coat **over** his **shoulders** and left the room.　彼はコートを肩にかけると部屋を出て行った

broad	shoulders	広い肩幅

▷He's a big man with **broad shoulders**.　彼は肩幅の広い大男だ

shoulder	to shoulder	肩を並べて; 協力して

▷We can rely on Richard. He'll stand **shoulder to shoulder** with us on this issue.　リチャードは信頼できる．この件で私たちに協力してくれるだろう

shout /ʃáut/ 動 叫ぶ; 大声を出す

shout	angrily	怒って叫ぶ
shout	excitedly	興奮して叫ぶ
shout	loudly	大声で叫ぶ
shout	out	叫び声を上げる

▷He **shouted angrily** at the children to go away and play somewhere else.　どこかへ行って遊べ，と彼は子どもにどなった
▷She **shouted out** for help but no one came.　彼女は助けを求めて大声を出したがだれも来てくれなかった

shout	at A	A(人)に向かってどなる

▷Stop **shouting at** me!　私にどなるのはやめて

show /ʃóu/ 名 ショー; 番組; 展覧会

hold	a show	ショーを開く; 出し物
put on	a show	を出す
see	a show	ショーを見る
watch	a show	
host	a show	ショーの司会を務める
make	a show of A	Aのふりをする
put on	a show of A	

▷The school drama club are **putting on** a **show** for Christmas.　学校の演劇部はクリスマスに出し物を出す予定だ
▷Let's go and **see** a **show** on Broadway!　ブロードウェイのショーを見に行こう
▷I don't really like Indian food, but I **made** a **show of** enjoying it.　インド料理はそう好きではないが好きなふりをした

the show	opens	ショーが開演する

▷The **show opens** at 10:00 on July 1.　ショーは7月1日10時に開幕します

on	show	展示されて

▷The latest fashionable dresses are going **on show** in Paris this autumn.　最新流行の服がパリで今秋発表になる

a fashion	show	ファッションショー
a motor	show	モーターショー
a flower	show	フラワーショー
a trade	show	見本市
a quiz	show	クイズ番組
a talk	show	トークショー
《英》a chat	show	

| show |

a game	show	ゲーム番組

show /ʃóu/ 動 見せる, 示す；見える

clearly	show	明確に示す
previously	shown	以前に示された
recently	shown	最近示した

▷ The results of the survey **clearly show** a fall in support for the government. 調査結果は政府への支持下落を明らかに示している
▷ This TV documentary was **previously shown** last year. このテレビドキュメンタリーは昨年放送されたものだ
▷ Our sales figures have **recently shown** an increase. うちの売上高は最近上昇を見せた

show	A B	A(人)にBを教える
show	A B	A(人)にBを見せる
show B	to A	
show A	to B	A(人)をB(場所)に案内する
show A	into B	

▷ Can you **show** me how to do this math problem? この数学の問題の解き方を教えて
▷ Have you seen the photo of my dog? I'll **show** it **to** you. うちの犬の写真を見たことあるかい. 見せてあげるよ
▷ Welcome to our house. I'll **show** you **to** your room. わが家にようこそ. あなたの部屋にご案内します

show (A)	(that)...	(A(人)に)…ということを示す
show (A)	wh-	(A(人)に)…かを示す

★ wh- は what, where, why, how, which など

▷ Research **shows that** the program's viewers dropped by 50% during the last 3 months. 番組視聴者がこの3か月で半減したことが調査でわかっている
▷ Can you **show** me **what** to do? 何をすべきか私に示してくれませんか
▷ These instructions **show how** to put together the bookcase. これらの取扱説明書に本棚の組み立て方が書いてある

shower /ʃáuər/ 名 シャワー；にわか雨

take	a shower	シャワーを浴びる
《英》have	a shower	

▷ I'm going to **take a shower**. シャワーを浴びてくるよ

a cold	shower	冷たいシャワー
a hot	shower	熱いシャワー
a heavy	shower	激しいにわか雨

▷ There's no hot water. You'll have to take a **cold shower**. 湯が出ないので冷たいシャワーで済ませて
▷ "My God! You're soaked!" "Yes, I just got caught in that **heavy shower**."「まあひどい, ずぶ濡れね」「ああ, ちょうど激しいにわか雨に遭っちゃって」

bath or shower	バスかシャワー
shower and toilet	シャワーとトイレ
shower and W.C.	

▷ It's an old country cottage with no **bath or shower**. 風呂もシャワーもない古い田舎の小さな家です

shy /ʃái/ 形 恥ずかしがりの, 内気な

painfully	shy	ひどく内気な
extremely	shy	
naturally	shy	生まれながらに内気な
rather	shy	どちらかと言えば内気な

▷ She was **painfully shy** when she was a child. 彼女は子どものときはひどく内気だった
▷ Emmy doesn't say very much. She's **naturally shy**. エミーはあまりものを言わない. 生来の内気だ

shy and retiring	内気で引っ込み思案の

▷ Your grandfather was a **shy and retiring** man. おじいさんは内気で遠慮がちな人だったの

shy	about A	Aをしたがらない
shy	of A	

▷ I feel **shy about** giving a presentation in class. 教室で発表するのは気が引ける

sick /sík/

形 病気の；吐き気がする；うんざりして

get	sick	病気になる
fall	sick	
be out	sick	病欠する
《英》be off	sick	
feel	sick	吐き気がする
make A	sick	Aに吐き気を催させる

▷ Tom was **off sick** for 2 weeks last month. トムは先月2週間病気で休んだ
▷ After the meal I **felt** physically **sick**. 食後に体調の異変を感じた
▷ Don't eat so many strawberries. They'll **make**

you sick! そんなにイチゴを食べるんじゃないよ．気分が悪くなるよ

chronically	sick	慢性の病気の
violently	sick	ひどい吐き気がする

▷ I'm afraid he'll never get better. He's **chronically sick**. 彼は回復しないのではないだろうか．慢性の病気だ
▷ It was a terrible storm. Everybody on the boat was **violently sick**. ひどい嵐でみんなひどい船酔いになった

sick	with A	ひどくAの状態で

★Aは anger, excitement, fear, worry など

▷ Where have you been? It's 2 o'clock in the morning! I was **sick with worry**! どこへ行っていたの．午前2時よ．もう心配していたんだから

side /sáid/ 名 側面, 横；側

take	A's side	Aの味方をする
take	sides	一方の味方をする

▷ Peter and Helen were having a big argument. I didn't want to **take sides**. ピーターとヘレンは大げんかをしていたが, 私はどちらの肩ももちたくなかった

opposite	side	向こう側
other	side	
far	side	
this	side	こちら側
right(-hand)	side	右側
left(-hand)	side	左側
north	side	北側
south	side	南側
both	sides	両側
either	side	
each	side	
right	side	正しい側
wrong	side	反対側
the dark	side	暗い面
the funny	side	おもしろい面

▷ My house is on the **opposite side** of the road. 私の家は道路の反対側です
▷ We need to get on the **other side** of the river. 川の向こう側に行かなくては
▷ We are now on the **north side** of the island. 私たちはいま島の北側にいる
▷ There are tall trees on **either side** of the road. 道の両側に高い木々がある
▷ Remember you're in the USA now. Don't drive on the **wrong side** of the road! いま米国にいることを

忘れないで．道路のどちら側を運転するか間違えるなよ
▷ He tripped and fell into the river. Everybody laughed. But he couldn't see the **funny side**! 彼はつまずいて川に落ちた．みんな笑ったが, 本人はおもしろくともなんともなかった

at	A's side	A(人)のそばに, 脇に
by	A's side	
by	the side of A	
from	side to side	左右に, 横に
side	by side	並んで, 一緒に
on	one side	脇に
to	one side	
on	A's side	Aの味方して

▷ When Paul goes jogging he always has his dog **by his side**. ポールはジョギングするときいつも犬をそばに連れている ▷ You can put your bicycle **by** the **side of** the house. 家の脇に自転車を置いていいよ
▷ The car was traveling fast **from side to side**. 車は右へ左へと動きながら猛スピードで走っていた
▷ They were sitting **side by side**. 彼らは並んで座っていた
▷ He put the newspaper **to one side** and turned on the TV. 彼は新聞を脇に置いてテレビをつけた
▷ "Whose **side** are you **on**?" "Your side, of course!" 「どちらの味方なの」「もちろんきみさ」

sigh /sái/ 名 ため息

give	a sigh	ため息をつく
breathe	a sigh	
heave	a sigh	

▷ "Talking about this makes me so sad," she said, **giving a** deep **sigh**. 「この話になると悲しくなる」と彼女は深いため息混じりに言った

a deep	sigh	深いため息
a heavy	sigh	
a huge	sigh	大きなため息
a big	sigh	
a long	sigh	長いため息

▷ "I'll never learn how to make a chocolate cake!" she said with a **long sigh**. 「いつまでたってもチョコレートケーキの作り方を覚えられないわ」と彼女は長いため息をついて言った

sigh /sái/ 動 ため息をつく

sigh	deeply	深くため息をつく
sigh	heavily	

sigh	happily	満足げにため息をつく
sigh	contentedly	
sigh	inwardly	心の中でため息をつく
sigh	wearily	疲れてため息をつく

▷ She **sighed deeply**. "It's too late to do anything now." 彼女は深くため息をついて言った。「もう手遅れだわ」

sight /sáit/

名 視力；見ること；光景，景色；(sights で)目標

lose	one's sight	視力を失う
catch	sight of A	Aを見る
lose	sight of A	Aを見失う
come into	sight	視界に入ってくる
disappear from	sight	視界から消える

▷ If you look out of the window you may **catch sight of** Mount Fuji. 窓の外を見れば富士山が見えるかもしれない

▷ There was a terrible snowstorm and we **lost sight of** the other climbers. ひどい吹雪でほかの登山者たちを見失ってしまった

▷ As the ship neared the shore the Statue of Liberty **came into sight**. 船が岸に近づくにつれて自由の女神像が見えてきた

▷ The sun sank below the horizon and **disappeared from sight**. 太陽が地平線の下に沈み視界から消えた

| set | one's sights on A | Aを目指す |

▷ She's **set** her **sights on** becoming a fashion model. 彼女はファッションモデルになる目標を立てた

a beautiful	sight	美しい光景
a common	sight	よくある光景
a familiar	sight	見慣れた光景
an impressive	sight	印象的な光景
a rare	sight	まれな光景

▷ It's a **common sight** to see people checking their mobile phones on buses and trains. バスや列車で携帯電話をチェックする人たちをよく見かける

▷ It's a **rare sight** to see a panda in the wild. 野生のパンダを見るのはまれな光景だ

| at | first sight | 一目で，一見したところ |

▷ Apparently Ray fell in love with her **at first sight**! どうもレイは彼女に一目ぼれしたようだ

| know A | by sight | Aに見覚えがある |

▷ I **know** him **by sight**, but I've never spoken to him. 見覚えのある人だが話しかけたことはない

in	sight	見える位置に
out of	sight	見えない位置に
within	sight	見える範囲に
on	sight	目にしたらすぐに

▷ She broke down in tears **in sight** of everybody. 彼女は人目もはばからず泣き崩れた ▷ Make sure you keep the children **in sight**! 子どもたちを目の届くところに置いておくように

▷ He watched her train leave until it was **out of sight**. 彼は彼女が乗った列車が見えなくなるまで見送った

▷ The chief of police gave orders to shoot any terrorists **on sight**. 警察署長はテロリストを見たら直ちに撃つように命じた

PHRASES
Get out of my sight! ☺ 消え失せろ(★失礼な言い方なので使用に注意)

sign /sáin/

名 記号；合図；標識；兆候，気配

show	signs	兆しを見せる
give	a sign	合図をする
make	a sign	
obey	a sign	標識に従う
ignore	a sign	標識を無視する
follow	the signs	標識のとおりに進む

▷ The doctors say he's **showing signs** *of* recovery. 医師たちの診断では彼は回復の兆しを見せている

▷ If the party gets boring I'll **give** a **sign** that we should leave. パーティーがつまらなくなってきたら出る合図をするよ

a clear	sign	明らかな兆候
an obvious	sign	
a visible	sign	
a sure	sign	確かな兆候
a good	sign	よい兆候
a bad	sign	悪い兆候
a road	sign	道路標識
a traffic	sign	交通標識
a warning	sign	警告標識

▷ I've never seen so many empty beer cans! It's an **obvious sign** that he has a drinking problem. ビールの空き缶をこんなにたくさん見たことはない．彼が飲酒の問題を抱えている明らかな兆候だ

▷ They're buying an engagement ring tomorrow. It's a **sure sign** they're in love! 二人はあす婚約指輪を買いに行く．彼らが愛し合っている確かな証拠だ

▷Your temperature has dropped back to normal. That's a **good sign**. 体温は平熱に下がりましたね。いい兆候です

a sign	that...	…という兆候

▷The Government are hoping for a **sign that** the economic situation will improve. 政府は経済状況改善の兆しを期待している

signal /sígnəl/ 名 合図；信号

give	a signal	合図する；信号を出す
send	a signal	出す
receive	a signal	信号を受ける
transmit	a signal	信号を伝える

▷He **gave** the **signal** *for* the race to start. 彼はレース開始の合図をした
▷I can't **receive** a **signal** here on my cellphone. ここでは携帯電話で受信できない

a clear	signal	明確な合図
a nonverbal	signal	ことばによらない合図
the wrong	signal(s)	間違った合図
a strong	signal	強い信号
a digital	signal	デジタル信号
an electrical	signal	電気信号

▷The satellite is still sending out a **clear signal**. その人工衛星からはいまもはっきり聞こえる信号が送られてくる
▷We live in a mountainous area so we don't get a **strong signal** for our TV. 山間部に住んでいるのでテレビの電波がうまく入らない

signal /sígnəl/ 動 合図する

clearly	signal	はっきり合図する
signal	frantically	必死に合図する

▷We have to try to help that swimmer. He's **clearly signaling** that he's in trouble. 泳いでいるあの人を何とか助けないと。明らかにトラブルが起きている合図を送っている

signal	A **to** do	Aに…するよう合図する

▷She **signaled** him **to** come and sit beside her. 自分の横に来て座るよう彼女は彼に合図した

signal	that...	…と合図する

▷She **signaled that** she was going to turn right. 彼女は右折の合図を出した

significant /signífikənt/

形 重大な，意義深い

highly	significant	非常に意義深い
equally	significant	同等に意義深い
particularly	significant	特に意義深い
statistically	significant	統計的に有意な

▷Archaeologists have made some **highly significant** findings in Peru. 考古学者たちはペルーできわめて意義のある発見をいくつかした
▷The results obtained from the experiment were not **statistically significant**. 実験から得られた結果は統計的に有意なものではなかった

it is significant	that...	…は重大である

▷**It's significant that** only five people attended the lecture. 講義に5人しか出席者がいなかったことの意味は重大だ

silence /sáiləns/ 名 静けさ；沈黙

break	the silence	沈黙を破る
lapse into	silence	黙り込む

▷It was really embarrassing. Nobody did anything to **break** the **silence** during the interview. 面接中だれも沈黙を破ろうとしなかったので，とても気まずかった
▷Everybody was very tired, so after a while the conversation **lapsed into silence**. みんなとても疲れていたので，しばらくすると会話が途絶えてしまった

silence	falls	沈黙が訪れる

▷When the headmaster arrived in the classroom **silence fell**. 校長先生が教室に到着すると急に静かになった

a long	silence	長い沈黙
a brief	silence	短い沈黙
a short	silence	
an awkward	silence	気まずい沈黙
complete	silence	まったくの静寂
dead	silence	
total	silence	
a tense	silence	張り詰めた静寂
a stunned	silence	驚きのあまり声も出ない状態

▷After a **long silence** she said, "I'm sorry, I don't

| silent |

know the answer." 長い沈黙の後, 彼女は答えた.「すみません, 答えがわかりません」
▷There must be **complete silence** during the examination. 試験中は一言もことばを発してはいけません
▷They watched in **stunned silence** as the tsunami swept through their village. 津波が村全体を押し流すのを, 彼らはあ然として声もなく見た

| in | silence | 黙って, 無言で |

▷They finished their meal **in silence**. 彼らは無言で食事を終えた
▷Everybody sat **in silence** waiting for the exam to begin. 試験の開始をみんな無言で座って待っていた

silent /sáilənt/ 形 静かな;無言の

fall	silent	沈黙する
keep	silent	静かにしている
remain	silent	
stay	silent	
stand	silent	黙って立っている

▷He **fell silent** for a moment. 彼は瞬間, 黙り込んだ
▷She **remained silent** and refused to answer any questions. 彼女は黙ったままで, 質問にいっさい答えようとしなかった

silly /síli/ 形 ばかな, 愚かな

| silly | little | あのばかな |

▷Stop asking stupid questions you **silly little** boy! くだらない質問はやめなさい, おばかさんだな(★ little は silly の強調)

PHRASES
Don't be silly! ☺ ばかなことを言うな ▷"I think there's a ghost in this house!" "Don't be silly!"「この家には幽霊がいると思う」「ばかなことを言うな」
How silly of me! ☺ 私はなんてばかなんだろう ▷I left my umbrella in the restaurant. How silly of me! レストランに傘を忘れちゃった. どうしてこうばかなんだろう

similar /símələr/ 形 似ている, 類似の

| broadly | similar | 大筋で似ている |
| remarkably | similar | すごく似ている |

▷These two essays are **remarkably similar**. I think one of them was copied. この2つのレポートは酷似している. 一方はコピーされたものだと思う

| similar | in A | Aが似ている |
| similar | to A | Aに似ている |

▷I think we're **similar in** many ways. 私たちは多くの点で似ていると思う
▷She's **similar to** her mother in character. 彼女は性格が母親と似ている

simple /símpl/ 形 単純な, 簡単な;質素な

extremely	simple	ごく単純な
fairly	simple	かなり単純な
perfectly	simple	まったく単純な
relatively	simple	比較的単純な
apparently	simple	見かけは単純な
deceptively	simple	単純に見えてそうではない
simple	enough	ごく簡単な

▷This math problem looks **relatively simple**. この数学の問題は比較的やさしそうだ
▷The **apparently simple** problem turned out to be extremely difficult. 一見やさしそうなその問題が実はとても難しかった
▷Hitting a golf ball looks **deceptively simple**! ゴルフボールを打つのは簡単そうに見えて難しい
▷Riding a bicycle is **simple enough**. You just have to concentrate! 自転車に乗るなんて簡単さ. 集中するだけでいいんだ

simple and effective	簡単で効果的な
simple and inexpensive	簡単で安価な
simple and straightforward	単純明快な

▷We need to find a **simple and effective** way of increasing our sales. 売り上げを伸ばす簡単で効果的な方法を見つける必要がある
▷It wasn't a difficult exam. The questions were **simple and straightforward**. 難しい試験ではなかった. 問題は単純明快だった

| simple | to do | …するのが簡単な |

▷The crossword was very **simple to** do. そのクロスワードパズルはとても簡単だった

PHRASES
It's as simple as that. ☺ ただそれだけのことだ ▷You put the money in, press the button and out comes your drink. It's as simple as that. お金を入れてボタンを押してください. すると飲み物が出てきます. それだけです
It's not that simple. ☺ それほど単純ではない
It's that simple. ☺ ほら簡単でしょ ▷"All I have to do is sign this form?" "Yes. It's that simple."「この用紙に署名するだけでいいのですか」「はい. 簡単でしょ」

sing /síŋ/ 動 歌う

sing	happily	うれしそうに歌う
sing	loudly	大きな声で歌う
sing	quietly	静かに歌う
sing	softly	優しく歌う
sing	gently	

▷Tom always **sings loudly** when he's in the bath! トムはいつも風呂で大声で歌う
▷Emma was **singing softly** to her baby. エマは赤ん坊に優しく歌っていた

sing and dance	歌って踊る

▷She's only 6 years old, but she can **sing and dance** really well! 彼女はまだ6歳だが歌も踊りもすごくうまい

sing	A B	A(人)にBを歌う
sing	B to A	

▷The group **sang** "Happy Birthday" **to** Bill. そのグループはビルに「ハッピーバースデイ」を歌った

single /síŋgl/

形 たった一つの；一人用の；独身の

single or double	シングルかダブルか
single or married	独身か既婚か

★ married or single も用いる

▷"I think I'll have a whiskey." "**Single or double?**" 「ウイスキーをください」「シングルですか，それともダブルですか」
▷Is Joe **single or married**? ジョーは独身ですか，それとも結婚していますか

every	single A	個々のA
the	single largest A	まさに最大のA

★ largest のほか best, biggest, greatest, worst など最上級形容詞がくる

▷He lifted his glass of whiskey and drank down **every single** drop. 彼はウイスキーグラスを傾けて最後の一滴まで飲み干した
▷Do you know who was the **single most** popular singer ever? いままででいちばん人気のあった歌手はだれか知っているかい

sink /síŋk/ 動 沈む；沈める

sink	slowly	ゆっくり沈む
sink	deep	深く沈む

▷The boat filled with water and **sank slowly** to the bottom of the river. ボートは水でいっぱいになり川底にゆっくりと沈んだ
▷He tried to move forward, but he just **sank deeper** into the mud. 彼は前に進もうとしたが，泥沼に沈み込むばかりだった

sink	into A	Aに沈み込む
sink	to A	Aに倒れ込む

▷The toy boat turned over, filled with water and **sank into** the pond. おもちゃのボートはひっくり返って浸水し，池に沈んだ
▷Totally exhausted, she **sank to** her knees. 疲れきって彼女はがっくりひざをついた

sink or swim	のるかそるか，一か八か

▷Even though he knew no English, his company sent him to their branch in Australia. It was a case of **sink or swim!** 彼は英語がまったくできなかったが，会社からオーストラリア支店に派遣された。一か八かというのが実のところだった

sister /sístər/ 名 姉，妹，姉妹

have	a sister	姉がいる，妹がいる

▷Do you **have** a **sister**? 女きょうだいはいるの

an older	sister	姉
an elder	sister	
a big	sister	
a younger	sister	妹
a little	sister	

▷My **older sister** goes to university. 姉は大学に通っています
▷My **younger sister** is in junior high school. 妹は中学生です

sit /sít/ 動 座る

sit	still	じっと座る
sit	comfortably	くつろいで座る
sit	cross-legged	足を組んで座る
sit	patiently	おとなしく座る
sit	quietly	静かに座る
sit	silently	黙って座る
sit	upright	背筋を伸ばして座る

| situation |

sit	down	座る，腰かける
sit	back	ゆったり座る；くつろぐ
sit	around	何もせずに座っている
sit	next to A	Aの隣に座る
sit	side by side	並んで座る
sit	together	いっしょに座る
simply	sit	ただ座る
just	sit	

▷Kelly **sat cross-legged** on the floor. ケリーは床にあぐらをかいた
▷Why don't you **sit down** for a moment? ちょっとおかけになりませんか
▷She **sat back** and switched on the TV. 彼女はゆったり座ってテレビのスイッチをつけた
▷He just **sits around** all day watching TV. 彼は一日中座ってテレビばかり見ている
▷Come and **sit next to** me. 来て私の隣に座りなさい
▷There's nothing we can do except **simply sit** and wait. ただ座って待つ以外に何もできない

sit	doing	座って…している

▷She's **sitting** at the table **doing** her homework. 彼女はテーブルに着いて宿題をしている ▷She was **sitting** in the garden **reading** a book. 彼女は庭に座って本を読んでいた

situation /sìtʃuéiʃən/ 名 状況, 情勢

create	a situation	状況を生み出す
understand	the situation	状況を理解する
review	the situation	状況を再検討する
explain	the situation	状況を説明する
describe	the situation	
handle	the situation	事態に対処する
cope with	the situation	
deal with	the situation	
improve	the situation	状況を改善する
remedy	the situation	状況を正す
resolve	the situation	
change	the situation	状況を変える
make	the situation worse	事態を悪化させる
make	the situation better	事態を好転させる

▷If he resigns it will **create** a very difficult **situation**. 彼が辞任したら困難な状況が生まれるだろう
▷I don't really know how to **handle** the **situation**. どう状況に対処すべきかよくわからない
▷We have to try to **remedy** the **situation**. 状況を正すべく努めなければならない
▷I'm afraid I just **made** the **situation worse**. さらに事態を悪化させただけではないかと心配だ

the present	situation	現在の状況
the current	situation	
a difficult	situation	困難な状況
a dangerous	situation	危険な状況
a social	situation	社会状況
the economic	situation	経済状況
the financial	situation	財政状況
the political	situation	政治状況
a particular	situation	特別な状況

▷What is the **present situation**? 現在の状況はどうですか
▷We've never had to deal with this **particular situation** before. これまでこういった状況に対処せざるをえなくなったことはない

in	this situation	この状況で

▷What should I do **in this situation**? この状況で何をしたらいいですか

size /sáiz/ 名 大きさ；サイズ，寸法

the right	size	ちょうどよい大きさ
the same	size	同じ大きさ
large	size	大きなサイズ
small	size	小さなサイズ
various	sizes	いろんなサイズ

▷Do you think this is the **right size** for me? これは私にぴったりの大きさかな
▷We're about the **same size**. 私たちはだいたい同じ背格好です

increase	the size	規模を拡大する
reduce	the size	規模を縮小する
double	the size	規模を倍にする
depend on	the size of A	Aの大きさによる

▷You should try to **reduce** the **size of** the food portions you eat. 1回の食事でとる量を減らすよう心がけたほうがいいですよ
▷I'm not sure how many wedding guests we can invite. It **depends on** the **size of** the room. 結婚式に何人くらい呼べるかわからない。部屋の大きさ次第だね

half	the size of A	Aの半分の大きさ
twice	the size of A	Aの2倍の大きさ
two times	the size of A	
three times	the size of A	Aの3倍の大きさ

▷Hamburgers in the USA are **three times** the **size of** the ones in my country! 米国のハンバーガーはぼくの国のより3倍も大きい

in	size	規模が；サイズが
the size	of A	Aの大きさ

▷I've been eating so much junk food recently that I've almost doubled **in size**! 最近たくさんジャンクフードを食べているので2倍ぐらいに太っちゃった
▷He had a bump on his head the **size of** a golf ball! 彼は頭にゴルフボール大のこぶがあった

shape and size		形と大きさ
size and shape		
size and weight		大きさと重さ

▷She's about the same **shape and size** as you. 彼女はあなたとだいたい同じ体型でサイズも同じだ
▷The airline has changed its rules about the **size and weight** of baggage. 航空会社は荷物の大きさと重さの規則を変えた

skill /skíl/ 名 技術, 技能, 手腕

have	a skill	技能がある
require	a skill	技能を必要とする
acquire	a skill	技能を身につける
develop	a skill	
learn	a skill	
show	a skill	技能を見せる
improve	one's skill	技能を磨く

▷This course will help you to **acquire** some basic communication **skills**. このコースは基本的なコミュニケーション技術を身につけるのに役立ちます
▷Her interest in yoga enabled her to **develop** her **skills** of concentration. ヨガに興味があるおかげで彼女は集中力が身についた
▷She practices the violin every day. She's **improved** her **skill** immensely. 彼女は毎日バイオリンを練習しており、ずいぶんうまくなった

basic	skills	基本的な技能
practical	skills	実用的技能
professional	skills	プロの技能
interpersonal	skills	対人能力
social	skills	社交術
special	skills	特殊技能

▷He has the **basic skills** required for the job. 彼はその仕事に必要な基本的技能がある
▷For this job, theory is not enough. You need **practical skills**. この仕事では理論だけは不十分で実用的技能が必要だ
▷I'm afraid he doesn't have very good **interpersonal skills**. 彼の対人能力はあまりよくないな

▷Bob needs to improve his **social skills**. ボブは社交術を磨く必要がある

skill(s)	at A	Aの技量
skill(s)	in A	

▷Even when he was a little boy, Messi showed incredible **skills at** the game of soccer. 少年のころでもメッシはサッカーの試合で信じられない技量を見せた
▷A salesman needs to have excellent **skills in communication**. セールスマンはコミュニケーション技術に長けている必要がある

a lack of	skill	技術不足
a level of	skill	技術レベル

▷He shows a **lack of skill** when it comes to dealing with people. 人と接するとなると彼は能力不足を示す
▷If you want to be a chess champion you'll have to develop a much higher **level of skill**. チェスチャンピオンになりたいならもっと技術レベルを上げなくては

with	great skill	非常に巧みに

▷Mao Asada usually performs the triple axel **with great skill**. 浅田真央はたいてい絶妙のトリプルアクセルをする

skin /skín/ 名 皮膚, 肌；皮

protect	one's skin	肌を守る

▷You need to put some sun cream on to **protect** your **skin**. 皮膚を守るために日焼け止めクリームの塗る必要がある

smooth	skin	滑らかな肌
sensitive	skin	敏感な肌
dry	skin	かさかさした肌
dark	skin	浅黒い肌
fair	skin	白い肌
pale	skin	青白い肌
tanned	skin	日焼けした肌
bare	skin	素肌
a thick	skin	厚い皮；鈍感
a thin	skin	薄い皮；敏感
an animal	skin	動物の皮
a banana	skin	バナナの皮
potato	skins	ジャガイモの皮

▷I can't stay out in the sun too long. I have very **sensitive skin**. あまり長く外で日光を浴びていられません。肌がとても敏感なので
▷I have **dry skin** so I use a lot of moisturizer. かさかさ肌なので保湿用クリームをたくさん使う

| skip |

▷Seals have a **thick skin** that keeps them warm in winter. アザラシは皮が厚くて，冬でも体を暖かく保てる

| skin | peels | 皮膚がむける |
| skin | crawls | 鳥肌が立つ |

▷She got so sunburned that her **skin peeled**. 彼女は日焼けして皮膚がむけた

| skin and bone(s) | | やせてがりがりの |

▷She's all **skin and bones** and probably weighs no more than 90 pounds. 彼女はやせこけており，体重はたぶんわずか90ポンドくらいだ

skip /skíp/ 動 軽く飛ぶ；飛ばし読みする

| skip | happily | うれしそうに飛び跳ねる |
| skip | lightly | 軽やかに飛び跳ねる |

▷The little girl **skipped happily** out of the room. 小さな女の子はうれしそうに飛び跳ねて部屋から出てきた

| skip | over A | A(不要な箇所)を飛ばす |
| skip | to A | A(次の事項)に飛ぶ |

▷For your homework, **skip over** the Introduction and start with Chapter one. 宿題では導入部は飛ばして第1章から始めなさい

PHRASES
Skip it! ☺ その話はやめろ

sky /skái/

名 (ふつう the sky で)空；(skies で)空模様

| look up at | the sky | 空を見上げる |

▷They **looked up at** the **sky** and saw that rain clouds were forming. 空を見上げると雨雲ができてくるのが見えた

| the sky | clears | 空が晴れる |
| the sky | darkens | 空が暗くなる |

▷Look! The **sky's clearing**! 見て．空が晴れてきた
▷The **sky darkened** and the moon was clearly visible. 空が暗くなって月がはっきり見えた

clear	sky	晴れた空
bright	sky	
cloudless	sky	雲ひとつない空
blue	sky	青い空
dark	sky	曇った空

black	sky	真っ暗な空；闇夜の空
gray	sky	灰色の空
the open	sky	広々とした空
the morning	sky	朝の空
the night	sky	夜の空
the summer	sky	夏の空
the winter	sky	冬の空
the northern	sky	北の空

▷Look! It's a **clear sky**. It'll be a sunny day again tomorrow. 見て．空が明るいからあしたも晴れだろう
▷She lay back on the grass, gazing up at the **cloudless sky**. 彼女は芝生に横になって雲ひとつない空を眺めていた
▷They were in the middle of the ocean. Nothing but **open sky** and sea. 大洋の真ん中にいて，周りは広々とした空と海だけだった

| in | the sky | 空に |
| the sky | above A | Aの上の空 |

▷The clouds **in** the **sky** are shaped like animals! 空の雲は動物みたいな形をしている
▷The **sky above** them was filled with a huge black cloud. 彼らの頭上の空は巨大な黒雲に覆われていた

sleep /slí:p/ 名 眠り，睡眠

have	a sleep	睡眠をとる
go to	sleep	眠りにつく
get to	sleep	
drift into	sleep	
fall into	a sleep	眠りに落ちる
get back to	sleep	再び眠りにつく
disturb	A's sleep	睡眠を妨げる
get	some sleep	少し睡眠をとる
get	enough sleep	十分睡眠をとる
get	much sleep	たっぷり睡眠をとる

▷I feel really tired. I'm going to **have** a **sleep** for a while. ひどく疲れたので，一眠りするよ
▷In winter I like to have a hot drink before I **go to sleep**. 冬は寝る前に温かい飲み物を飲むのが好きだ
▷It was two or three hours before she finally **drifted into sleep**. ようやく眠りに着くのに彼女は2，3時間かかった
▷He **fell into** a deep **sleep** and started snoring! 彼はぐっすり寝入っていびきをかき始めた
▷I woke up at 3:30 in the morning and couldn't **get back to sleep**. 朝の3時半に目が覚めてそれから眠れなかった
▷I'm sorry to **disturb** your **sleep**, but you've got a visitor. 眠っているところを邪魔してごめん．お客さんよ
▷Make sure you **get enough sleep**. We have to

get up early tomorrow! 必ず十分な睡眠をとるようにしてください．あすは早く起きなければなりません

a deep	sleep	深い眠り
a light	sleep	浅い眠り
a good	sleep	十分な睡眠
a dreamless	sleep	夢を見ない睡眠

▷He's in a **deep sleep**. We shouldn't wake him. 彼は熟睡しているから起こさないほうがいい
▷Have a **good sleep**. You'll feel better. ぐっすり眠ってね．そうすれば気分がよくなるから
▷I feel great this morning! I had a refreshing, **dreamless sleep**. けさはとても気分がいい．ぐっすり寝て夢も見なかったよ

in	one's **sleep**	眠っているときに

▷He talks a lot **in** his **sleep**. 彼は盛んに寝言を言う

lack of	sleep	寝不足

▷Her face looked old and tired through **lack of sleep**. 寝不足で彼女の顔は老けて疲れて見えた
PHRASES
Get a good night's sleep. ☺ ぐっすりお休みなさい

sleep /slíːp/ 動 眠る

sleep	well	よく眠る
sleep	soundly	熟睡する
sleep	like a baby	
sleep	badly	よく眠れない
sleep	peacefully	すやすや眠る
sleep	late	遅くまで寝る
hardly	sleep	ほとんど眠れない

▷"Morning Pete! Did you **sleep well**?" "Like a log!" 「おはよう，ピート．よく眠れたかい」「ぐっすり寝たよ」
▷I was totally exhausted when I got home and **slept like a baby** for 11 hours. 疲れ果てていたので家に帰ると11時間ぐっすり眠った
▷I've been **sleeping badly** recently. It's so hot and humid! 最近よく眠れない．とても暑くて湿気が多いから
▷I **hardly slept** at all last night. きのうの晩はほとんど眠れなかった

slice /sláis/ 名 一切れ，薄片

a thin	slice	薄切り

▷Could you cut this loaf into **thin slices** for me, please? このローフを薄く切っていただけますか

slide /sláid/ 動 滑る；滑らせる

slide	slowly	ゆっくり滑る
slide	smoothly	なめらかに滑る

▷Thanks for repairing the sliding door. It slides **really smoothly** now. 引き戸を直してくれてありがとう．とてもなめらかに滑るようになったよ

slide	open	スライドして開く

▷The door **slid open** slowly and silently. ドアはゆっくりと静かに開いた

slide	down A	Aを滑り降りる
slide	across A	Aを滑る
slide	into A	Aに滑り込む

▷Look it's snowing! We can **slide down** the hill on our toboggans! ほら雪だ．そりで丘を滑って遊ぼうよ
▷Exhausted, she **slid into** bed and was asleep in seconds. 疲れ果てていたので彼女はベッドにもぐりこむと数秒で眠り込んだ

slight /sláit/ 形 わずかな，ささいな

extremely	slight	非常にわずかな
only	slight	ほんのわずかな
relatively	slight	比較的わずかな
comparatively	slight	

▷His injuries after the car crash were **only slight**. 交通事故で彼が受けた傷はごく軽かった
▷The damage to his car was **relatively slight**. 彼の車の損害は比較的軽かった

slip /slíp/

動 滑る；滑るように動く；滑り込ませる

slip	quietly	静かに出て行く

▷They **slipped quietly** outside into the garden. 彼らは静かに庭へと出て行った

slip and fall		滑って転ぶ

▷She **slipped and fell** on the icy pavement. 彼女は凍結した歩道で滑って転んだ

slip	on A	A(場所など)で滑る

▷Don't **slip on** the floor! I've just washed it. 床で滑らないように．洗ったばかりだから

slip	into A	Aに滑り込む
slip	out of A	Aからそっと出る
slip	through A	Aを滑るように通る
slip A	into B	AをBにそっと入れる

▷She managed to **slip out of** the room without anyone seeing her. 彼女はだれにも見られずにうまく部屋から出た
▷The vase **slipped through** her fingers and crashed onto the floor. 花瓶は彼女の指からするりと落ちて床に砕けた
▷The man **slipped** a $10 bill **into** the waiter's hand. その男は10ドル紙幣をウェイターの手に滑り込ませた

slow /slóu/ 形 遅い

extremely	slow	非常に遅い
relatively	slow	比較的遅い
painfully	slow	ひどくのろい
notoriously	slow	遅いことで有名な

▷Compared to the other students her progress is **relatively slow**. 他の生徒と比べると彼女の進歩は比較的遅い

| slow | in doing | …するのが遅い |
| slow | to do | |

▷He was very **slow in** answering questions during the interview. 彼は面接の際に質問にてきぱき答えられなかった
▷We were too **slow to** deal with the problem. われわれは問題を処理するのが遅すぎた

| slow and steady | ゆっくり着実に |
| slow but steady | ゆっくりだが着実に |

▷She's out of hospital and making **slow but steady** progress. 彼女は退院して、ゆっくりだが着実に回復しつつある

small /smɔ́ːl/ 形 小さい；少ない

extremely	small	非常に小さい
relatively	small	比較的小さい
comparatively	small	

▷Our profits are **relatively small** compared with last year. わが社の利益は昨年に比べると少ない

smart /smάːrt/ 形 利口な；しゃれた

| look | smart | さっそうとして見える；《英》急ぐ |

▷You **look** really **smart** in that new suit. その新しいスーツを着るときはさっそうとして見えるね
▷You'd better **look smart** or you'll be late for your interview! 急がないと面接に遅れるよ

extremely	smart	すごく利口な；すごく
particularly	smart	おしゃれな
smart	enough	十分に利口な

▷You're looking **particularly smart** today! きょうはとてもすてきね
▷He was **smart enough** to refuse to answer any questions until his lawyer arrived. 彼は賢明にも弁護士が来るまで質問に答えるのを拒否した

| smart | new | おしゃれで新しい |
| smart | young | 賢くて若い；格好よくて若い |

▷I'm going to buy a **smart new** dress for the party. パーティーに着て行くおしゃれで新しい服を買おうと思う
▷Who's that **smart young** man over there? 向こうにいるあの格好いい若い男性はだれですか

smell /smél/ 名 におい；嗅覚

have	a smell	においがする
give off	a smell	においを放つ
can't stand	the smell	においに耐えられない

▷New rush mats **have** a lovely **smell**. 新しい畳はいいにおいがする
▷I **can't stand** the **smell**. Do you mind if I open the window? 耐えられないにおいだ. 窓を開けていいかな

a strong	smell	強いにおい
a faint	smell	かすかなにおい
a sweet	smell	甘いにおい
a bad	smell	いやなにおい
an unpleasant	smell	不快なにおい
a sour	smell	酸っぱい香り

▷There's a **strong smell** of gasoline in the car. 車の中はガソリンのにおいがぷんぷんしている
▷At last she was able to smell the **sweet smell** of success. ついに彼女は成功の甘い香りをかぐことができた
▷There's a **bad smell** coming from the drains. 排水口からいやなにおいがしている
▷There was the **sour smell** of old beer on his breath. 彼の息は飲んだビールの酸っぱいにおいがした

| smile |

sights and smells		光景とにおい
smell and taste		においと味

★ taste and smell も用いられる

▷I love the **sights and smells** of London. ロンドンの眺めとにおいが好きだ
▷I've got a terrible cold. I've completely lost my sense of **smell and taste**. ひどいかぜを引いてにおいと味の感覚がすっかりなくなった

a sense of	smell	嗅覚

▷When I get an allergy my nose runs and I lose my **sense of smell**. アレルギーになると鼻水が出て嗅覚がなくなる

smell /smél/

動 においがする；いやなにおいがする

smell	faintly	ほのかににおう
smell	strongly	強くにおう

▷Her perfume **smelt faintly** of lavender. 彼女の香水はほのかにラベンダーのにおいがした
▷The kitchen **smells strongly** of gas. 台所はものすごいガスのにおいがしている

smell	like A	Aのようなにおいがする

▷It **smells like** garlic. ニンニクのようなにおいがする

can	smell	においがする

▷I **can smell** something burning. 何か焦げているにおいがする

smile /smáil/ 名 ほほえみ, 微笑

flash	a smile	ほほえみを送る
give	a smile	
manage	a smile	やっと笑顔を見せる
return	A's smile	ほほえみ返す
hide	a smile	ほほえみを隠す
force	a smile	作り笑いをする

▷The security guard always **gives** me a **smile** when I go in to work. 警備員は私が出社するといつもほほえみかけてくれる
▷Ben's quite ill. When I saw him he could hardly **manage** a **smile**. ベンはかなり体調が悪く，会っても笑顔もつくれないほどだった
▷"Don't worry, I'll be fine," she said, **forcing** a **smile**. 「心配しないで，私はだいじょうぶだから」と彼女は無理にほほえみながら言った

have	a smile on one's face	顔に笑みを浮かべている
bring	a smile to A's face	A(人)を笑顔にさせる
put	a smile on A's face	

▷We should always **have** a **smile on** our **face** when we welcome customers. お客を迎えるときはいつも顔に笑みを絶やしてはいけない
▷I told him joke after joke, but I couldn't **bring** a **smile to** his **face**. 冗談を連発したが，彼をほほえませることはできなかった
▷Dave's just been promoted. That should **put** a **smile on** his **face**! デイブは昇進したばかりだからご機嫌のはずだよ

one's smile	broadens	笑みが満面に広がる
one's smile	fades	笑みが消える

▷When he saw that nobody else was laughing his **smile faded**. 他にだれもほほえんでいないのを見て彼の笑みは消えた

a smile	plays on A's lips	笑みがAの口元に浮かぶ

▷"So you think Bill and Tom are both in love with me?" she said, a **smile playing on** her **lips**. 「ビルもトムも私を愛していると思うの？」と彼女は口元に笑みを浮かべて言った

a bright	smile	明るい笑み
a broad	smile	満面の笑み
a big	smile	
a wide	smile	
a charming	smile	魅力的な笑み
a little	smile	かすかな笑み
a faint	smile	
a slight	smile	
a wry	smile	苦笑い

▷"I passed the university entrance exam," he said, with a **broad smile** on his face. 「大学入試に通ったよ」と彼は顔に満面の笑みを浮かべて言った
▷Come on. It's not as bad as all that. Give me a **little smile**! 元気を出して．そんなにひどくはないわよ．少しは笑ってよ

with	a smile	にっこりして

▷"I hope you'll enjoy your stay here," she said **with** a **smile**. 「ここでの滞在をお楽しみください」と彼女はほほえみを浮かべて言った

smile /smáil/ 動 ほほえむ, 微笑する

smile	broadly	満面に笑みを浮かべる
smile	faintly	かすかにほほえむ
smile	thinly	薄ら笑いを浮かべる
smile	sweetly	にっこり笑う
smile	wryly	苦笑いを浮かべる
smile	back	ほほえみ返す

▷"That's the third fish to escape from my line this morning," he said, **smiling wryly**. 「逃がした魚はこれでもう3匹目だ」と彼は言って苦笑いを浮かべた
▷She smiled at me and I **smiled back**. 彼女がほほえみかけてきたので,私はほほえみ返した

smile	at A	Aにほほえみかける
smile	with A	A(感情)を示してほほえむ

★with A の A は relief, delight, satisfaction など

▷He **smiled at** her and said, "Haven't we met somewhere before?" 彼は彼女にほほえみかけて言った。「以前どこかでお会いしていませんか」
▷Oh! Thank goodness you're OK, she said, **smiling with relief**. あなたが無事でよかった,と彼女はほっとしてほほえみながら言った

smile	to oneself	ひとりでほほえむ

▷"One day I'll get my revenge!" she said, **smiling to herself**. 「いつか仕返ししてやるわ」と彼女は言ってほくそ笑んだ

smoke /smóuk/ 名 煙; 喫煙

blow	smoke	煙を吹く
have	a smoke	たばこを吸う

▷I hate it when people **blow smoke** in my face. 顔に煙を吹きかけられるのはいやだ
▷I'm dying to **have a smoke**. たばこが吸いたくてたまらない

smoke	billows	煙が巻き上がる
smoke	drifts	煙が漂う
smoke	rises	煙が上がる

▷It was a terrible fire. **Smoke** was **billowing** from the windows. ひどい火事で,煙が窓から噴き出していた
▷Thick **smoke rose** from the bonfire and drifted across the garden. 濃い煙がたき火から上がって庭に漂った

thick	smoke	濃い煙
dense	smoke	
acrid	smoke	鼻を突く煙
cigarette	smoke	たばこの煙

▷**Thick smoke** started to pour out of the windows. 濃い煙が窓から流れ出した
▷People were coughing from the **acrid smoke** coming from the burning car tires. 燃えている車のタイヤから出る鼻を突く煙で人々はせき込んでいた

a cloud	of smoke	もうもうたる煙
a column	of smoke	立ち上る煙
a pall	of smoke	辺り一面の煙
a puff	of smoke	ひと吹きの煙
a wisp	of smoke	ひと筋の煙

▷A **cloud of smoke** rose from the factory chimney. 工場の煙突からもうもうと煙が上がった
▷Finally a **wisp of smoke** started to rise from the damp leaves. ようやくかすかな煙が湿った木の葉から上がり始めた

go up in	smoke	煙と消える;水泡に帰する

▷If we can't get the money all our plans will **go up in smoke**. 資金を得られなければわれわれの計画はすべて煙と消えるだろう

smoke /smóuk/ 動 たばこを吸う

smoke	heavily	たくさんたばこを吸う
smoke	regularly	いつもたばこを吸う

▷**Smoking heavily** is not good for your health. たばこの吸い過ぎは健康によくない

drink and smoke	酒を飲んでたばこを吸う

▷My boyfriend likes to **drink and smoke**. 私のボーイフレンドは酒を飲んでたばこを吸うのが好きだ

smooth /smú:ð/ 形 滑らかな;円滑な

fairly	smooth	かなり滑らかな
completely	smooth	まったく滑らかな
perfectly	smooth	

▷The surface of the glass is **completely smooth**. ガラスの表面はまったく滑らかだ
▷If you travel by bullet train the ride is **perfectly smooth**. 新幹線で移動すれば乗り心地は快適そのものです(★日本語では「乗り心地が滑らか」とはあまり言わないが英語では ride と smooth がしばしば連結する)

snow /snóu/ 名 雪

snow	falls	雪が降る
snow	melts	雪が解ける

▷ Later that evening **snow** began to **fall**. その夜遅く雪が降り始めた

be covered	in snow	雪に覆われる
be covered	with snow	

▷ The cars parked outside are completely **covered in snow**. 外に止めてある車はすっかり雪に覆われている

heavy	snow	大雪
deep	snow	深い雪
wet	snow	べた雪
fresh	snow	新雪

▷ There's **deep snow** outside the front door! 玄関の外は深く雪が積もっている
▷ **Fresh snow** fell during the night. 新雪が夜のあいだに降った

snow and ice		雪と氷

★ ice and snow も用いる

▷ I couldn't see anything but **snow and ice**. 雪と氷のほかは何も見えなかった

snow /snóu/ 動 雪が降る

snow	heavily	激しく雪が降る
snow	lightly	ちらちら雪が降る

▷ It's started to **snow heavily**. 激しく雪が降り始めた

society /səsáiəti/ 名 社会；会, 協会

create	a society	社会をつくる
transform	a society	社会を変革する
join	a society	団体に加わる

▷ It's difficult to **create** a **society** without any discrimination. いかなる差別もない社会をつくるのは難しい
▷ Amanda has **joined** a **society** for the protection of the environment. アマンダは環境保護の団体に加わった

(a) modern	society	現代社会
an affluent	society	豊かな社会
a capitalist	society	資本主義社会

a democratic	society	民主主義的社会
an industrial	society	産業社会

▷ Life in **modern society** can be very stressful. 現代社会の生活はストレスにあふれている
▷ The USA claims to be a **democratic society**. 米国は自国が民主主義的な社会だと自称している
▷ Some countries are still progressing from an agricultural to an **industrial society**. いまなお農業社会から産業社会への移行の段階にある国もある

a member of society		社会の一員

▷ I hope he grows up to be a useful **member of society**. 彼が成長して社会の役に立つ一員になることを望む

soft /sɔ́:ft | sɔ́ft/ 形 柔らかい；穏やかな

extremely	soft	非常に柔らかい
fairly	soft	かなり柔らかい

▷ I like to eat my boiled eggs **fairly soft**. ゆで卵はかなり柔らかめで食べるのが好きだ

soft	on A	Aに甘い, 手ぬるい

▷ We need to be stricter. We can't be **soft on** crime. もっと厳しくやらなくてはいけない. 犯罪に手ぬるい態度をとるべきではない

soft and warm		柔らかくて暖かい

★ warm and soft も用いる

▷ This bed feels **soft and warm**. このベッドは柔らかくて暖かい

soil /sɔ́il/ 名 土, 土壌, 土地；国土

fertile	soil	肥えた土壌
good	soil	
rich	soil	
poor	soil	やせた土壌
dry	soil	乾いた土壌
moist	soil	湿った土壌
wet	soil	
sandy	soil	砂地
clay	soil	粘土質の土

▷ This is very **fertile soil**. You'll be able to grow lots of vegetables. ここの土はとても肥えているから野菜がたくさん育つでしょう
▷ You need to put some **moist soil** into that flower

| solution |

pot. 湿った土を花瓶に入れてください

| on | British soil | 英国で |
| on | American soil | 米国で |

▷ If he sets foot on **American soil** he'll be arrested. 米国に足を踏み入れたら彼は逮捕されるだろう

solution /səlúːʃən/ 名 解決策；解答

seek	a solution	解決策を探る
find	a solution	解決策を見つける
come up with	a solution	
offer	a solution	解決策を出す
provide	a solution	

▷ We've been **seeking** a **solution** to this problem for weeks. われわれは何週間もこの問題の解決策を探っている
▷ We have to **find** a **solution** to this problem—and fast! この問題の解決策を見つけなくては。それも至急に
▷ During the meeting they **offered** several possible **solutions**. 会議中に彼らはいくつか可能な解決策を出した

a good	solution	よい解決策
an ideal	solution	理想的な解決策
the optimal	solution	最善の解決策
a possible	solution	可能な解決策
an alternative	solution	替わりの解決策
a practical	solution	実際的な解決策
a final	solution	最終的な解決策
a peaceful	solution	平和的な解決策
a political	solution	政治的な解決策

▷ I think that's a really **good solution**. それはとてもよい解決策だと思う
▷ The **optimal solution** would be to close down the company. 最善の解決策は会社を閉鎖することだろう
▷ We're trying to think of a **possible solution**. 可能な解決策を考えているところだ

| a solution | to A | Aの解決策 |
| a solution | for A | Aに対する解決策 |

▷ We still can't find a **solution to** the problem. まだ問題の解決策を見いだせない

solve /sálv | sɔ́lv/

動 解く，解答する，解決する

| completely | solve | 完全に解決する |
| easily | solve | 簡単に解く |

▷ I still haven't **completely solved** this crossword. まだこのクロスワードパズルを全部解けないでいる
▷ We can **easily solve** this problem. この問題は簡単に解ける

son /sʌ́n/ 名 息子

| have | a son | 息子がいる |

▷ I **have** a **son** and two daughters. 息子と娘が二人います

one's baby	son	男の赤ん坊
the eldest	son	長男
the oldest	son	
the younger	son	下の息子
the only	son	一人息子
five-year-old	son	5歳の息子

▷ Her **baby son** looks just like his father. 彼女が産んだ男の子は父親そっくりだ
▷ He's the **eldest son** of Mr. and Mrs. (John) Carter. 彼はカーター夫妻の長男
▷ They have two daughters, but Mike's the **only son**. 彼らには娘が二人いるが，男の子はマイクだけだ
▷ My **five-year-old son** wants to be a famous soccer player! 私の5歳の息子は有名サッカー選手になりたがっている

song /sɔ́ːŋ | sɔ́ŋ/ 名 歌

write	a song	歌をつくる
compose	a song	
play	a song	歌を流す；歌を演奏する
sing (A)	a song	(Aに)歌を歌う
record	a song	歌を録音する
listen to	a song	歌を聞く
hear	a song	歌が聞こえる

▷ One day I'd like to **write** a **song**. いつか歌をつくってみたい
▷ Come on! **Sing** us a **song**! さあ歌を歌って
▷ He likes to **sing songs** in the bath! 彼は風呂で歌を歌うのが好きだ

one's favorite	song	好きな歌
a great	song	すばらしい歌
a popular	song	流行歌
a hit	song	ヒット曲
a folk	song	フォークソング
a pop	song	ポップス
a love	song	ラブソング

▷ Sssshhh! Listen! They're playing my **favorite song**! しーっ，聞いて．私の好きな歌を演奏しているから
▷ John Lennon's song 'Imagine' is a really **great song**! ジョン・レノンの歌「イマジン」はとてもすばらしい曲だ

sorry /sɑ́ri | sɔ́ri/

形 すまないと思う；気の毒に思う；残念に思う

| feel | sorry | 気の毒に思う |

▷ I really **felt sorry** for her. 彼女を本当に気の毒だと思った

terribly	sorry	たいへん申し訳な
really	sorry	い；とても残念な
awfully	sorry	

▷ I'm **terribly sorry**. たいへん申し訳ありません

| sorry | about A | Aを気の毒に思う |

▷ I'm really **sorry about** what happened. こんなことが起きてほんとうにお気の毒です

| sorry | to do | …して申し訳ない；…して気の毒に思う |
| sorry | (that)... | …は申し訳ない；…は残念だ |

▷ "My girlfriend broke up with me last weekend." "Oh, I'm so **sorry to** hear that."「先週末ガールフレンドに振られちゃった」「まあかわいそうに」
▷ I'm **sorry** you can't come to the party. あなたがパーティーに来られなくて残念です ▷ (I'm) **sorry** I'm late. 遅くなってごめん

PHRASES

I'm sorry. ☺ 申し訳ありません；それは気の毒に ▷ "I'm so sorry." "That's OK."「ほんとうに申し訳ありません」「いいんですよ」▷ (I'm) sorry. I can't join you for lunch. ごめんなさい，昼食をごいっしょできません
I'm sorry to say that... / I'm sorry to tell you, but... 申し上げにくいのですが ▷ I'm sorry to say that you haven't passed this course. 残念だけどあなたはこの科目で合格点をとれなかった

sort /sɔ́:rt/ 名 種類

all sorts	of A	あらゆる種類のA
some sort	of A	何らかのA
A of	some sort	
the same sort	of A	同じ種類のA
a similar sort	of A	似た種類のA

▷ We met **all sorts of** interesting people when we went on holiday abroad. 休暇で外国に行っていろんなおもしろい人々に出会った
▷ "What's this? I've never had this before." "I think it's **some sort of** vegetable."「これ何？いまで食べたことないな」「何かの野菜じゃないかな」
▷ We need to get our boss a present **of some sort** for her birthday. 上司に何か誕生日プレゼントを買わなくちゃ

| this sort | of thing | このようなもの |
| that sort | of thing | そのようなもの |

▷ There's a total eclipse of the sun next week. **That sort of thing** happens only very rarely. 来週には皆既日食がある．めったにないことだ

soul /sóul/ 名 魂，霊魂；人

save	one's soul	魂を救う
sell	one's soul	魂を売り渡す
lose	one's soul	たいせつなものを失う
bare	one's soul	心の内を明かす
be good for	the soul	心が安らぐ

▷ I think he had a little too much to drink and **bared his soul** to her. 彼は少しばかり飲み過ぎたせいで，彼女に胸中を明かしたんだよ

an immortal	soul	不滅の魂
a brave	soul	勇敢な人
a poor	soul	かわいそうな人
a sensitive	soul	感受性の強い人

▷ She lost her house and everything in the earthquake, **poor soul**. かわいそうに彼女は地震で家も何もかも失ってしまった
▷ She's a **sensitive soul**. She always cries at the movies. 彼女は感受性が強い人で，映画を見ては泣いている

| not | a soul | 人っ子一人…でない |

▷ There was nobody there. **Not a soul**. そこにはだれも，人っ子一人いなかった

sound /sáund/ 名 音；響き

hear	a sound	音が聞こえる
listen to	the sound	音を聞く
make	a sound	音を立てる

▷ Wake up, Tony! I think I **heard** some **sounds** coming from downstairs! トニー起きて．下の階で何

| soup |

か音がしたと思うんだけど
▷ It's lovely by this stream. I love **listening to** the **sound** of water. この流れのそばにいると気持ちがいい。水のせせらぎを聞くのが好きなの
▷ Ssssh! Quiet! Don't **make a sound**! しっ, 静かに。音を立てるな

sound	travels	音が伝わる
a sound	comes	音が聞こえてくる
a sound	echoes	音が反響する
a sound	emerges	音が出る
a sound	dies away	音がだんだん消える

▷ **Sound travels** more slowly than light. 音は光よりゆっくり伝わる
▷ There's a strange **sound coming** from my car engine. 車のエンジンから変な音がしている
▷ The **sound** of our footsteps **echoed** in the empty church. 私たちの足音がだれもいない教会に反響した
▷ Gradually the **sound** of the marching band **died away**. 徐々にマーチングバンドの音は小さくなった

a loud	sound	大きな音
a faint	sound	かすかな音
a soft	sound	柔らかい音, 弱い音
a good	sound	よい音
a familiar	sound	聞き慣れた音
a strange	sound	奇妙な音
a distant	sound	遠くの音

▷ My bicycle is making a **strange sound**! 私の自転車は奇妙な音を立てている
▷ Later that evening we could hear the **distant sound** of church bells. その夜遅く教会の鐘の音が遠くから聞こえた

| a sound | from A | Aから聞こえる音 |

▷ After we complained about the noise we didn't hear a **sound from** our neighbors. 騒音のことで苦情を言ってからは, 隣から音がしなくなった

| the speed of | sound | 音速 |

soup /súːp/ 名 スープ

| have | soup | スープを飲む |
| eat | soup | |

▷ I **had soup** and toast for lunch. 昼食にスープとトーストをとった（★カップのスープの場合は drink を用いることもある）

| a bowl of | soup | 一杯のスープ |

▷ I would love a **bowl of** hot **soup**. 熱いスープを一杯飲みたいのですが

chicken	soup	チキンスープ
vegetable	soup	野菜スープ
tomato	soup	トマトスープ

sour /sáuər/

形 酸っぱい, 酸味のある; 不機嫌な

taste	sour	酸っぱい味がする
go	sour	酸っぱくなる; うまくいかなくなる
turn	sour	

▷ We'll have to throw this milk away. It's **gone sour**. この牛乳は捨てなくちゃ。酸っぱくなってしまった
▷ They were fine for a few months, but later their relationship **turned sour**. 2, 3か月はうまくいっていたが, やがて彼らの関係はうまくいかなくなった

source /sɔːrs/ 名 源, 根源; 情報源

| provide | a source | 源となる |

▷ This well has **provided** a **source** of water for hundreds of years. この井戸から何百年も水を汲んできた

| a source | says | 情報筋によると |

▷ A reliable **source said** that the minister had accepted a bribe. 信頼できる情報筋によると大臣は賄賂を受けとった

a good	source	よい情報源
the main	source	主要な情報源
a major	source	
an alternative	source	代替源
an energy	source	エネルギー源
a food	source	食糧源
a power	source	電源

▷ The British Library would be a **good source** of material for your research. 研究資料は大英図書館で探すと見つかるでしょう
▷ A **major source** of his information was the Internet. 彼の主要情報源はインターネットだった
▷ We need to find an **alternative source** of energy to nuclear power. 原子力の代替エネルギー源を見つける必要がある

according to	sources	情報筋によれば
at	source	元で；源泉で

▷**According to sources** close to the President, he intends to stand for election again next year.　大統領に近い情報筋によれば，大統領は来年再び選挙に立候補する予定だ
▷We need to stop these rumors **at source**.　このうわさを根元で絶つ必要がある

sources	close to A	Aに近い情報筋

▷**Sources close to** the Prime Minister confirmed that he was thinking of resigning.　首相に近い情報筋の証言によると首相は辞任を考えているようだ

space /spéis/

名 空き，空所，スペース，余白；空間；宇宙

have	space	スペースがある
make	space	スペースをつくる
create	space	
find	space	スペースを見つける
leave	space	スペースを空ける
save	space	スペースを節約する
take up	space	スペースを食う
look into	space	虚空を見つめる
stare into	space	

▷We don't **have** enough **space** in this office.　このオフィスには十分なスペースがない
▷If we take out that chair, it'll **make space** for our new TV.　椅子をどければ新しいテレビ用のスペースができるだろう

a limited	space	限られたスペース
an open	space	空き地，開放スペース
a confined	space	閉ざされたスペース
an enclosed	space	
a blank	space	余白，空欄，空き
an empty	space	ペース
a living	space	居住スペース
storage	space	収納スペース
a parking	space	駐車スペース
a public	space	公共スペース
outer	space	大気圏外，宇宙空間

▷This room has a lot of **open space** and huge windows.　この部屋は多くの開放スペースと大きな窓がある
▷It's not fair to keep dogs in a **confined space** all day.　犬を終日限られたスペースに置いておくのはよくない
▷If we move the sofa it'll leave an **empty space** by the bookcase.　ソファーを動かせば本棚のそばに空きスペースができる
▷One day maybe we'll all be able to take holidays in **outer space**!　いつの日かたぶんだれもが宇宙空間に遊びに行けるようになるだろう

space	between A	Aの間のスペース
space	for A	Aのためのスペース

▷Her earring had dropped down into the **space between** the bed and the wall.　彼女のイアリングはベッドと壁の間のスペースに落ちた
▷There's **space for** one more car to park outside the house.　家の外にもう1台車を止めるスペースがある

amount	of space	スペースの量
a waste	of space	スペースのむだ遣い

▷The new sofa takes up an enormous **amount of space**.　新しいソファーはずいぶんスペースを食う
▷I think we should rearrange the storeroom. At the moment it's a **waste of space**.　物置を整理し直したほうがいい．いまはスペースのむだ遣いだ

spare /spéər/ **動** (時間などを)割く

money	to spare	費やす金
time	to spare	割く時間

▷Tony will help you. He has got **money to spare**!　トニーがきみを助けてくれるよ．彼はお金に余裕があるから
▷She finished the exam with **time to spare**.　彼女は時間に余裕をもって試験を終えた

spare	A B	A(人)のためにBを
spare	B for A	割く

▷Could you **spare** me a moment?　少々お時間をいただいてよろしいでしょうか

speak /spíːk/ **動** 話す；会話する

speak	briefly	短く話す；簡潔に話す
speak	clearly	明確に話す
speak	quietly	静かに話す
speak	softly	穏やかに話す
speak	slowly	ゆっくり話す
speak	directly	じかに話す
speak	fluently	流ちょうに話す
hardly	speak	ほとんど話さない

▷If you're giving a presentation you need to **speak clearly**.　発表するのなら明確に話す必要があります
▷Could you **speak** a little more **quietly**!　もう少し小さな声で話していただけませんか

▷Could you **speak** more **slowly**, please? もう少しゆっくり話していただけますか
▷I think you should **speak directly** to your boss about the problem. その問題は上司にじかに言ったほうがいいよ
▷She had a terrible cold. She could **hardly speak**. 彼女はひどいかぜを引いていてほとんど話せなかった

generally	speaking	一般的に言えば
broadly	speaking	大まかに言えば

▷**Generally speaking** I prefer watching DVDs to going to the movies. 一般的に言って映画館で見るよりDVDで見るほうが好きだ

speak	to A	A(人)に話をする
speak	with A	
speak	of A	Aについて話す
speak	about A	
speak	on A	
speak	for A	Aを代弁する

▷Do you have a moment? I need to **speak with** you. ちょっと時間あるかい。きみと話があるんだ
▷**Speaking of** spaghetti, I'm really hungry! Let's go to an Italian restaurant. スパゲッティと言えば腹ペこだ。イタリアンの店に行こう

speak	ill of A	A(人)のことを
speak	badly of A	悪く言う
speak	well of A	A(人)のことを
speak	highly of A	よく言う

▷I know you shouldn't **speak ill of** the dead, but... 亡くなった人のことを悪く言うべきではないとわかっていますが…
▷Your headmaster **speaks** very **highly of** you. 校長先生はきみのことをとてもほめていたよ

PHRASES

Speak for yourself. ☺ 自分のことだけ言ってろ，勝手なことを言うな ▷"Everybody hates Tom Denver!" "What do you mean? I don't! Speak for yourself!" 「トム・デンバーのことはみんな嫌っているさ」「どういう意味？私はそうじゃないわ。勝手なこと言わないで」

special /spéʃəl/ 形 特別な；特殊な

special	to A	Aには大事な

▷You are so **special to** me. あなたは私にとってとてもたいせつな人です

nothing	special	特別なものはない
something	special	何か特別なこと
anything	special	

▷"What's the food like at that new Italian restaurant?" "**Nothing special**." 「あの新しいイタリアンレストランの料理はどうだったの」「どうってことないな」

specific /spɪsífɪk/

形 明確な；独特の，固有の

specific	about A	Aについてはっきり言う
specific	to A	Aに独特の

▷You need to be more **specific about** your future plans. 自分の将来計画をもっと明確にする必要がある

(more) specific		(もっと)はっきり言う

▷"I know you make tomato soup with tomatoes, but could you be **more specific**?" "Sure. You need fresh tomatoes, cream, parsley..." 「トマトスープをトマトでつくるのはわかるけど，もっと細かく教えてくれますか」「いいよ。新鮮なトマトとクリーム，パセリを使って…」

speech /spíːtʃ/

名 スピーチ，演説；話すこと，話す能力

make	a speech	スピーチをする
deliver	a speech	
give	a speech	

▷I'm not very good at **making speeches**. スピーチはあまり得意ではありません

a short	speech	短いスピーチ
a long	speech	長いスピーチ
a major	speech	重要な演説
an opening	speech	開会の辞
a closing	speech	閉会の辞
A's inaugural	speech	就任演説
everyday	speech	日常のことば
free	speech	自由な言論

▷We're hoping you'll give a **short speech** at our wedding. ぼくたちの結婚式できみにやってもらうスピーチは短くしてね
▷The President's **inaugural speech** was a great success. 大統領の就任演説は大成功だった
▷There was an article in the newspaper today on the right to **free speech**. 言論の自由に関する記事がきょうの新聞に載っていた

a speech	about A	Aに関するスピーチ
a speech	on A	

a speech	to A	Aへのスピーチ

▷He gave a **speech on** Japan's political and economic relations with Russia. 彼はロシアとの日本の政治的経済的関係についてスピーチした

freedom of	speech	言論の自由

▷In many countries there is still little or no **freedom of speech**. 言論の自由がほとんどあるいはまったくない国がまだ多い

speed /spíːd/ 图 速度, スピード

increase	speed	速度を上げる
pick up	speed	
gather	speed	
gain	speed	
maintain	speed	速度を保つ
reduce	speed	速度を落とす
measure	speed	速度を測る

▷The bullet train **increased speed** smoothly as it left the station. 新幹線は駅を出ると滑らかにスピードを上げた
▷This machine **measures** the **speed** and direction of the wind. この機械は風速と風向を測るものだ

great	speed	すごい速さ
high	speed	高速
low	speed	低速
top	speed	最高速度, 全速力
full	speed	
a maximum	speed	
an average	speed	平均速度
wind	speed	風速

▷The police chased him at **high speed** through the streets of London. 警察は彼を猛スピードで追ってロンドンの通りを走り抜けた
▷If we go at an **average speed** of 50 miles an hour we should arrive before dark. 時速50マイルの平均速度で行けば暗くなるまでに着くはずだ

speed and accuracy		スピードと正確さ
speed and efficiency		スピードと効率

▷When you take the test both **speed and accuracy** are important. 試験を受けるときはスピードも正確さも重要だ

at	speed	高速で

▷The two cyclists came round the bend **at speed** and nearly crashed into each other. 自転車に乗った2人がどちらも高速でカーブを曲がってきて, もう少しで衝突するところだった

spend /spénd/ 動 (金を)使う; (時間を)過ごす

spend	wisely	賢く使う
well	spent	うまく使った

▷Even though the price was high, I think it was money **well spent**. 値段は高かったものの, いい金の使い方だったと思う

spend A	doing	…するのにA(金・時間)を使う
spend A	on B	A(金・時間)をBに使う
spend A	with B	A(時間)をB(人)といっしょに過ごす

▷I **spent** most of the day ly**ing** on the beach. その日のほとんどを浜辺で寝そべって過ごした
▷She **spent** a lot of money **on** a Gucci handbag. 彼女はグッチのハンドバッグに大金を使った
▷We **spent** a couple of days **with** our friends in New York. 2, 3日友人とニューヨークで過ごした

spirit /spírit/ 图 精神, 心; (…の)精神をもった人; (spirits で)気分, 士気; 霊魂, 霊

capture	the spirit	精神をとらえる
enter into	the spirit	雰囲気に溶け込む
get into	the spirit	
lift	A's spirits	士気を高める
raise	A's spirits	
keep up	one's spirits	気分を高める
break	A's spirits	士気をくじく

▷I think this painting **captures** the **spirit** of life in 19th century Paris. この絵は19世紀パリの生活の精神をうまくとらえていると思う
▷Let's go out for a drink. You need to do something to **lift** your **spirits**! 飲みに行こうよ. 気分を高めるためにきみは何かしないとね
▷We sang as we walked through the rain to **keep up** our **spirits**. 気分を明るくしようと雨の中を歩きながら歌を歌った

the human	spirit	人間の精神
a free	spirit	自由な精神の持ち主
one's fighting	spirit	闘志
pioneering	spirit	開拓者精神
team	spirit	チームスピリット
community	spirit	共同体意識

| spirit |

ancestral	spirits	先祖の霊
evil	spirits	悪霊

▷She's a bit of a **free spirit**. If she wants to do something she just does it! 彼女は自由な精神の持ち主で，何かをやりたいときはひたすらやるだけだ
▷They say this house is haunted by **evil spirits**! この家は悪霊にとりつかれているという話だ

in	spirit	心は
in	good spirits	いい気分で，上機嫌で
in	high spirits	
in	the spirit of A	Aの精神で

▷I'm always with you **in spirit**. 心はいつもきみといっしょだ
▷What happened? You seem to be **in high spirits**! どうしたの．上機嫌みたいだけど
▷Man will continue to explore space **in the spirit of** previous great explorers. 人類はかつての偉大な探検家の精神で宇宙を探検し続けるだろう

PHRASES
That's the spirit. ☺ その調子だ ▷"I'm not going to give up!" "That's the spirit!"「あきらめないぞ」「その調子だ」

split /splít/ 動 裂く，裂ける；分裂させる，分裂する；分け合う，分ける

split	apart	割れる，裂ける
split	open	裂けて開く
split	in two	2つに割れる
split	in half	半分に割れる

▷The egg **split apart** in the nest and a young chick emerged. 巣の卵が割れてひな鳥が現れた
▷He hit the ball so hard that the baseball bat **split in two**. 彼が思い切りボールを打つと野球のバットは2つに裂けた

split A	between B	AをBの間で分け合う
split A	into B	AをBに分ける
(be) split	over A	Aを巡って分裂する
(be) split	on A	

▷The ax hit the wood, **splitting** it **into** three pieces. 斧は木材に当たって木材は3つに割れた
▷Bob and Tony used to be good friends, but apparently they **split over** a girl they both liked. ボブとトニーは以前は友人同士だったが，どうも同じ女の子を好きになって仲たがいしたようだ

sport /spɔ́ːrt/ 名 スポーツ，運動競技

play	sport(s)	スポーツをする
do	sport(s)	
enjoy	sport(s)	スポーツを楽しむ

★米国ではふつうsportsで用いられる

▷I **did** a lot of **sport** when I was at school, but now I've stopped. 学生のころはスポーツをよくやったが，もうやめてしまった
▷My brother's a very good athlete. He **enjoys** all kinds of **sports**. 兄はスポーツがとても得意で，あらゆるスポーツを楽しんでいる

an amateur	sport	アマチュアスポーツ
a professional	sport	プロスポーツ
a popular	sport	人気スポーツ
a spectator	sport	見るスポーツ
a national	sport	国民的スポーツ
one's favorite	sport	好きなスポーツ
a team	sport	団体スポーツ
winter	sports	冬のスポーツ

▷In Britain in summer cricket is the **national sport**. イギリスでは夏はクリケットが国民的スポーツだ

spot /spát | spɔ́t/ 名 場所，地点；斑点，染み

the very	spot	まさにその場所
the exact	spot	
a good	spot	よい場所
the right	spot	適当な場所
a tourist	spot	観光スポット
a trouble	spot	問題の起こりやすい場所
a weak	spot	弱点，不備な点
a sore	spot	痛いところ
a tender	spot	
a blind	spot	盲点，死角
a high	spot	ハイライト
the top	spot	首位
a bright	spot	明るいところ，救い
a tight	spot	窮地

▷Be careful when you're driving. The mirror has a **blind spot**. 運転に気をつけて．ミラーには死角がある
▷The arrival of Brad Pitt and Angelina Jolie was the **high spot** of the evening. ブラッド・ピットとアンジェリーナ・ジョリーの登場はその夜のハイライトだった
▷Roger Federer held the **top spot** as a tennis player for many years. ロジャー・フェデラーは何年間もテニスプレーヤーのトップに君臨した
▷It can't all be bad news. There must be a **bright spot** somewhere! 何から何まで悪いニュースなどありえない．どこかに明るいところがあるものだ

▷Can you help me out? I'm in rather a **tight spot**. 助けてくれないかな．かなり窮地に立たされているんだ

| on | the spot | 現場に；すぐに |

▷He wrote her a check **on** the **spot**. 彼はその場で彼女に小切手を書いた

spot /spάt | spɔ́t/ 動 見つける

be easy to	spot	見つけるのが簡単な
be difficult to	spot	見つけるのが難しい
be hard to	spot	

▷We'll meet Mike outside the football stadium. He'll be **easy to spot**. He's very tall and has got green hair! サッカー競技場の外でマイクに会うんだ．見つけるのは簡単さ．背が高くて髪が緑色だから

| spot | A doing | Aが…しているところを見つける |

▷I couldn't see our cat anywhere, but finally I **spotted** her climbing a tree. うちの猫がどこに行ったかわからなかったが，ようやく木に登っているところを見つけた

spread /spréd/

動 広げる，広がる；塗り広げる

spread	out	広げる
spread	rapidly	急速に広がる
spread	quickly	
spread	outward	ぱっと広がる
spread	evenly	均一に広がる
spread	thinly	薄く広がる
spread	widely	遠くまで広がる

★rapidly, quickly, evenly, thinly, widely は動詞の前でも用いる

▷He **spread** the map **out** across his knees. 彼は両ひざの上に地図を広げた

▷Opposition to the government is **spreading rapidly** throughout the country. 政府への反対は国中に急速に広がりつつある

▷The pot fell from the ladder and red paint **spread outward** over the floor. つぼがはしごから落ちて，赤いペンキがぱっと床の上に広がった

▷Cases of influenza are becoming more **widely spread**. インフルエンザの症例があちこちに広がりつつある

spread	across A	Aに広がる
spread A	over B	AをBに広げる
spread A	on B	AにBを塗る
spread B	with A	
spread	throughout A	A中に広がる
spread	to A	Aに広がる
spread	through A	

▷A big smile **spread across** her face. 満面の笑みが彼女の顔に広がった

▷She **spread** a plastic sheet **over** the wet grass. 彼女はビニールシートを濡れた芝に広げた

▷I've never seen anyone **spread** so much butter **on** their toast! トーストにこんなにバターを塗りまくる人は見たことがないよ

▷He **spread** his toast **with** the best caviar. 彼はトーストに極上のキャビアを塗った

▷People are worried that the bird flu may **spread to** other countries. 鳥インフルエンザが他の国々に広がることを人々は心配している

▷A wonderful smell of coffee **spread through** the kitchen. コーヒーのよいにおいが台所中に広がった

spring /spríŋ/ 名 春

early	spring	早春
late	spring	晩春
the following	spring	次の春

▷For me, the best time of the year is **early spring**. 一年で私がいちばん好きなのは早春だ

| in | (the) spring | 春に |
| in | the spring of 2012 | 2012年の春に |

▷I'm going to start university **in** the **spring**. 春に大学生になる予定です

square /skwéər/

名 正方形，四角；(四角い)広場；2乗，平方

| draw | a square | 正方形を描く |
| cross | the square | 広場を横切る |

▷You **cross** the **square** and take the second on the left. 広場を横切って2番目の角を左へ曲がってください

| a central | square | 中央広場 |
| the main | square | |

▷The **central square** of this town has a good shopping center. この町の中央広場にはいいショッピングセンターがある

| a square | of A | 四角いA |
| the square | of A | Aの2乗 |

▷ Take a **square of** paper, fold it in half and follow the instructions. 四角い紙をとって半分に折り曲げ, 指示に従ってください
▷ The **square of** 5 is 25. 5の2乗は25です

staff /stǽf | stάːf/ 名 (集合的に)職員, 社員, スタッフ(★個々の職員は a staff member という)

| join | the staff | スタッフに加わる |
| have | a staff of 20 | 20名のスタッフがいる |

▷ It's quite a big company. They **have** a **staff of** over 2,000. 大会社で2千名を超すスタッフがいる

full-time	staff	フルタイムの職員
part-time	staff	パートタイムの職員
permanent	staff	常勤職員
temporary	staff	臨時職員
experienced	staff	経験豊かな職員
qualified	staff	資格のある職員
trained	staff	訓練を受けた職員
senior	staff	幹部職員
hospital	staff	病院スタッフ
nursing	staff	看護スタッフ

▷ This room is for **senior staff** only. この部屋は幹部職員以外立ち入り禁止
▷ The **medical staff** are very positive. 医療スタッフはとても積極的だ

| on | the staff (of A) | (Aの)職員で |

▷ Sally was **on** the **staff of** a hospital before she took this job. この仕事に就く前にサリーは病院の職員だった

stage /stéidʒ/ 名 段階; 舞台, ステージ

reach	the stage	段階に達する
take	the stage	舞台に登場する
go on	stage	
come on	stage	
go on	the stage	俳優になる
leave	the stage	舞台から退場する
set	the stage	舞台をセットする; おぜん立てをする

▷ We've now **reached** the **stage** where we have to make a decision. いまや決断すべき段階に来た
▷ The audience went wild every time Michael Jackson **came on stage**. マイケル・ジャクソンがステージに出るたびに聴衆は熱狂した
▷ It seems our daughter wants to **go on** the **stage**. うちの娘は俳優になりたがっているようだ
▷ The audience applauded loudly as she **left** the **stage**. 彼女がステージから去るとき聴衆は大きな拍手を送った
▷ The problems at Fukushima **set** the **stage** for many countries to reconsider their nuclear power programs. フクシマの問題は多くの国が原子力発電計画を再考するきっかけとなった

an early	stage	早い段階
the initial	stage(s)	初期段階
a late	stage	遅い段階
the final	stage(s)	最終段階
the next	stage	次の段階
various	stages	さまざまな段階
the first	stage(s)	第1段階
the second	stage(s)	第2段階
an experimental	stage	実験段階
a planning	stage	計画段階
the world	stage	世界の舞台
the international	stage	国際舞台
the political	stage	政治の舞台

▷ The project is still *at* an **early stage**. その事業はまだ初期段階にある
▷ The doctors say that his illness has reached a **late stage**. 医師たちの話では彼の病状は末期だそうだ
▷ Babies pass through **various stages** as they learn their mother language. 赤ん坊はさまざまな段階を経て母語を学んでいく

at	this stage	この段階で
at	one stage	ある段階で
at	some stage	どこかの段階で
on	stage	舞台で

▷ **At one stage** I nearly gave up trying to pass the entrance exam. ある段階で入試に受かるための努力をほぼやめた
▷ It was an incredible one-man show. He was **on stage** for 3 hours! すごいワンマンショーだった. 3時間も舞台に上がりっぱなしさ

stair /stéər/ 名 (stairs で)階段

climb	the stairs	階段を上がる
go up	the stairs	
run up	the stairs	階段をかけ上がる
descend	the stairs	階段を下りる
go down	the stairs	
run down	the stairs	階段をかけ下りる

★ up the stairs は upstairs, down the stairs は

downstairs ともいう

▷My grandma is finding it more and more difficult to **climb** the **stairs**. 祖母は階段を上がるのがますます難しくなってきている

▷He **ran down** the **stairs** and into the garden. 彼は階段をかけ下りて庭に出た

steep	stairs	急な階段
narrow	stairs	狭い階段
spiral	stairs	らせん階段
the back	stairs	裏階段
wooden	stairs	木の階段
stone	stairs	石の階段

▷It's an old country house with **wooden stairs** leading to the bedrooms. 寝室に通じる木の階段がある古い田舎の家です

the bottom	of the stairs	階段のいちばん下
the foot	of the stairs	
the top	of the stairs	階段のいちばん上
the head	of the stairs	

▷The children left their toys *at* the **bottom of** the **stairs**. 子どもたちはおもちゃを階段のいちばん下に置きっぱなしにした

▷She called down *from* the **top of** the **stairs**. 彼女は階段の最上段から下に向かって呼んだ

a flight of	stairs	一続きの階段

▷She tripped and fell down a **flight of stairs**. 彼女はつまずいて階段を転げ落ちた

stamp /stǽmp/ 名 切手；スタンプ；印

put on	a stamp	切手を貼る
collect	stamps	切手を収集する
bear	the stamp of A	Aの刻印を帯びている

▷You don't need to **put** a **stamp on** that envelope. その封筒に切手を貼る必要はありません

▷His hobby is **collecting stamps**. 彼の趣味は切手収集だ

▷He was involved in a public scandal and **bore** the **stamp of** it for the rest of his life. 彼は周知となったスキャンダルに関わり、残りの人生にその影を引きずった

a commemorative	stamp	記念切手

▷Did you see the Olympic Games **commemorative stamp**? オリンピックの記念切手を見たかい

stand /stǽnd/ 動 立つ, 立っている；我慢する

stand	upright	まっすぐ立つ
stand	still	じっと立つ
stand	motionless	
stand	on tiptoe	つま先で立つ
stand	clear	離れて立つ
stand	alone	ひとりで立つ
stand	back	後ろへ下がる

▷That little boy is always running around. He won't **stand still** for a moment! あの坊やは走り回ってばかりいて、ちっともじっとしていない

▷"**Stand clear** *of* the doors, please!" shouted the guard and blew his whistle. 「ドアから離れて立ってください」と車掌は叫び, 笛を吹いた

▷**Stand back** from the platform edge! There's a train coming! ホームの端から下がってください. 列車が来ます

can't	stand A	Aは大嫌いだ
can't	stand (A) doing	（Aが）…するのは大嫌いだ
can't	stand to do	…するのは耐えられない

▷I **can't stand** this hot, humid weather any longer! 暑くて湿気の多いこの天候にはもううんざりだ

▷I **couldn't stand to** see her cry. 彼女が泣くのを見るのは耐えられない

stand	at A	Aに立つ
stand	on A	Aの上に立つ
stand	outside A	Aの外に立つ
stand	behind A	Aの後ろに立つ
stand	by A	Aのそばに立つ

▷Two policemen were **standing outside** the house. 2人の警察官が家の外に立っていた

▷The tall man **standing by** Amy's side is her new boyfriend. エイミーのそばに立っている背の高い男性が彼女の新しいボーイフレンドです

stand	doing	立って…している
stand and	do	立って…する

▷He **stood** there staring at her. 彼はそこに立って彼女を見ていた

standard /stǽndərd/

名 水準, 基準；規範

set	standards	水準を設定する

| star |

achieve	standards	水準に達する
reach	standards	
meet	standards	水準を満たす
raise	standards	水準を上げる
improve	standards	
lower	standards	水準を下げる
maintain	standards	水準を維持する

▷Sally is an amazing runner. She **sets** the **standards** for everyone else.　サリーはすごいランナーだ．みんな彼女を基準に設定する
▷It's difficult to **meet** the **standards** necessary to become a commercial airline pilot.　民間航空会社のパイロットになるために必要な基準を満たすのは難しい

a high	standard	高い水準
a low	standard	低い水準
a minimum	standard	最低水準
a professional	standard	専門的水準
an international	standard	国際水準
quality	standards	品質基準
living	standards	生活水準
safety	standards	安全基準
emission	standards	排出基準
moral	standards	道徳的規範
double	standards	二重規範

▷He's reached a **high standard** as a tennis player in a very short time.　彼は短期間でテニス選手として高い水準に達した
▷He's only an amateur photographer, but he has **professional standards**.　彼はアマチュア写真家にすぎないがプロ級の腕前だ
▷He's a very good golf player, but he hasn't yet reached **international standards**.　彼はとてもすばらしいゴルフ選手だが，まだ国際水準には達していない

above	standard	水準以上で
below	standard	水準以下で
up to	standard	水準に達して

▷I'm afraid that recently your work has not been **up to standard**.　近ごろきみの仕事は水準に達していないね

star /stάːr/

名　星，恒星；スター；(等級を表す)星印

see	the stars	星を眺める
look up at	the stars	星を見上げる

▷You can **see** the **stars** really clearly tonight.　今夜はとてもはっきり星が見える

the stars	are out	星が出ている
the stars	come out	星が出る
the stars	appear	
the stars	shine	星が輝く
the stars	twinkle	星がきらめく

▷Look! The **stars** are **coming out**!　見て，星が出てきたよ

a bright	star	明るい星
a distant	star	遠くの星
the morning	star	明けの明星
the evening	star	宵の明星
a shooting	star	流れ星
a big	star	大スター
a rising	star	売り出し中の新人
a movie	star	映画スター
《英》a film	star	
a pop	star	ポップスター
a rock	star	ロックスター

▷Can you see that **bright star** just above us?　頭上にあるあの明るい星が見えるかい
▷What's the name of that **big star** over there?　あそこにいる大スターの名前は何だっけ
▷Apparently he's a **rising star**. People think that one day he'll be Prime Minister.　どうやら売り出し中の新人のようで，あの人はいつか首相になると目されている

under	the stars	星空の下で

▷It was a great holiday. We spent every night camped out **under** the **stars**.　すばらしい休暇だった．毎夜星空の下でキャンプをして過ごした

stare /stéər/　動　じっと見る，見つめる

stare	fixedly	じっと見つめる
stare	intently	一心に見つめる
stare	blankly	ぼんやりと見る
stare	back	見つめ返す
stare	ahead	前を見つめる
stare	up	じっと見上げる

▷When his teacher asked if he had cheated during the exam Tom just **stared fixedly** at the floor.　試験でカンニングしたのかと先生に尋ねられたトムは床をじっと見つめるだけだった
▷If someone stares at me I just **stare back**!　だれかにじっと見られたら見つめ返してやる
▷She wouldn't look at me. She just **stared** straight **ahead**.　彼女は私を見ようとせず，ただまっすぐ前を見つめていた

stare	at A	Aをじっと見る
stare	into A	Aをじっと見つめる
stare	out of A	Aの外をじっと見つめる

▷Why is that man **staring at** me? あの男の人ったら，なぜ私をじっと見ているのかな
▷In class he spent most of his time **staring out of** the window. 授業中彼はほとんど窓の外ばかり見て過ごした

sit and stare	座ってじっと見る
stand and stare	立ってじっと見る
stop and stare	止まってじっと見る

▷She seems to be in shock. She just **sits and stares**. 彼女はショックを受けているみたいで，ただ座って見つめているだけだ

start /stá:rt/ 名 出発，スタート；開始

make	a start	スタートする
have	a start	
get off to	a start	スタートを切る
signal	the start	始まりを合図で知らせる

▷I suggest you **make** a **start** right away. すぐ始めたらどうかな
▷Luckily I **got off to** a good **start** with my new boss. 幸い新しい上司とさい先のいいスタートを切れた
▷A gunshot **signaled** the **start** of the race. 銃声がレース開始を告げた

a flying	start	好調なスタート
a good	start	よいスタート
a great	start	
a bad	start	悪いスタート
a poor	start	
a slow	start	遅れたスタート
a false	start	フライング；出だしの失敗
a fresh	start	新たなスタート
a new	start	

▷Robson was off to a **flying start** in the hundred meters and won easily. ロブソンは100メートルで好スタートを切って楽勝した
▷Ella has made a really **good start** in her new job. エラは新しい仕事でさい先のよいスタートを切った
▷Let's forget the past and make a **fresh start**. 過去のことは忘れて出直そう

at	the start (of A)	(Aの)初めに
from	the start	始めから
from	start to finish	始めから終わりまで

▷Things began to go wrong right **at** the **start of** our holiday. 休暇が始まるときからいろいろ手違いが生じた
▷I knew there'd be a problem **from** the **start**. 始めから問題があるとわかっていた
▷He led the race **from start to finish**. 彼はレースを終始リードした

start /stá:rt/ 動 始まる，始める；出発する

immediately	start	すぐに始まる
suddenly	start	急に始まる；急に動き出す
recently	started	最近始めた
start	off	出発する；始める
start	out	
start	up	始まる；始める
start	over	最初からやり直す

▷I've **recently started** taking tennis lessons. 最近テニスのレッスンを受け始めた
▷We need to **start off** early in the morning. 朝早く出発しなくては
▷They **started off** the celebrations with a firework display. 祝典は花火で始まった
▷We're thinking of **starting up** a reading circle. 読書会を始めようと思っている
▷I was interrupted in the middle of counting and had to **start over**. 数を数えている途中で邪魔が入って，最初からやり直さなければならなかった

start	with A	Aで始める

▷**Start with** something simple and just get the feel of it. 簡単なことから始めて感じをつかみなさい

start	to do	…し始める
start	doing	

▷She **started** pla**ying** the piano when she was 6 years old. 彼女は6歳でピアノを習い始めた

starve /stá:rv/ 動 飢える；餓死する

starve	to death	餓死する

▷The rice crop failed and many people **starved to death**. 米の不作で多くの人々が餓死した

be starved	for A	Aに飢えている
be starved	of A	

▷He was **starved of** affection when he was young. 彼は若いころ愛情に飢えていた

state /stéit/ 名 状態；国家；州

an emotional	state	感情の状態
a mental	state	精神状態
an awful	state	ひどい状態
a dreadful	state	
a terrible	state	
a sorry	state	
the present	state	現在の状態
the current	state	
a nation	state	国民国家
an independent	state	独立国家
a rogue	state	ならず者国家
a democratic	state	民主主義国家
the welfare	state	福祉国家

▷She was in a highly **emotional state**. 彼女は感情が高揚していた

▷She fell in the river with all her clothes on. She was in a **terrible state**. 彼女は服を着たまま川に落ちた．とてもひどいありさまだった

▷The **present state** is that nobody has any idea what to do next. 次に何をすればよいかだれもわからないというのが現在の状況だ

statement /stéitmənt/

名 声明，陳述；計算書

make	a statement	述べる，陳述する
issue	a statement	声明を出す
take	a statement	調書を取る

▷The President is going to **issue** a **statement** in 2 hours' time. 大統領は2時間後に声明を出す予定だ

▷The police wanted to **take** a **statement** from me. 警察は私から調書を取りたがった

a false	statement	虚偽の陳述
a sworn	statement	宣誓供述書
a joint	statement	共同声明
a public	statement	公式声明
an official	statement	
a financial	statement	財務諸表
a bank	statement	銀行取引明細書

▷She made a **false statement** to the police. 彼女は警察に虚偽の陳述をした

▷The leader of the Democrats and the leader of the Republicans are going to issue a **joint statement**. 民主党党首と共和党党首は共同声明を出す予定だ

▷An **official statement** said that the Prime Minister had decided to resign. 公式声明によると首相は辞任を決めたとのことだ

a statement	about A	Aについての声明
a statement	on A	陳述

▷The Ministry of Health, Labour and Welfare is going to issue a **statement about** the flu epidemic. 厚生労働省はインフルエンザの流行について声明を出す予定だ

a statement	that...	…という声明

▷The MP issued a **statement that** he had not committed any crime. 下院議員は自分はいかなる犯罪も犯していないとの声明を出した

in	a statement	声明で，陳述で

▷**In** a **statement** to the press the senator said that he was going to resign because of health reasons. 報道陣への声明で上院議員は健康上の理由で辞任するつもりであると語った

station /stéiʃən/ 名 駅，発着所；署，局

a train	station	鉄道の駅
a railroad	station	
《英》a railway	station	
a bus	station	長距離バスの発着所
《英》a coach	station	
a subway	station	地下鉄の駅
《英》a tube	station	
a fire	station	消防署
a police	station	警察署
a polling	station	投票所
a power	station	発電所
a gas	station	ガソリンスタンド
《英》a petrol	station	
a service	station	サービスエリア；ガソリンスタンド
a space	station	宇宙ステーション
a radio	station	ラジオ局
a TV	station	テレビ局

▷You'd better pull in at that **gas station**. We need some more petrol. あのガソリンスタンドに寄ろう．ガソリンを入れなくちゃ

statistics /stətístiks/

名 データ；統計学（★「データ」の意では複数扱い）

collect	statistics	データを集める
use	statistics	データを用いる

▷I need to **collect** more **statistics** for my research.

研究のためにもっとデータを集める必要がある

statistics	show	データの示すところ
statistics	indicate	では
statistics	reveal	
statistics	suggest	データの示唆すると ころでは

▷ **Statistics suggest** that the birthrate is decreasing more quickly than expected. データの示唆するところでは出生率が予想より速く減少している

official	statistics	公式データ

▷ These are the **official statistics** for traffic accidents during the past year. 昨年度中の交通事故の公式データです

status /stéitəs/ 名 地位, 身分

achieve	status	地位を得る
acquire	status	
raise	status	地位を向上させる

▷ Dave's more concerned about **achieving status** within the company than spending time with his family. デイブは家族と過ごすよりも会社内で地位を得ることのほうに関心がある

high	status	高い地位
low	status	低い地位
equal	status	対等の地位
social	status	社会的地位
marital	status	配偶者の有無

▷ If you want a job with **high status** you should be a doctor or a lawyer. ステータスの高い職業に就きたいなら医師か弁護士になるべきだ
▷ Generally speaking, teachers in Asia have a higher **social status** than those in the West. 一般的にアジアでは西洋より教師の社会的地位が高い
▷ What's your **marital status**? 配偶者はいますか

one's status	as A	Aとしての地位

▷ After the takeover, his **status as** company president was severely threatened. 買収後, 彼の社長の地位は非常に脅かされた

steady /stédi/ 形 しっかりした; 着実な

fairly	steady	かなりしっかりした
remarkably	steady	きわめて着実な
relatively	steady	比較的着実な

▷ Since he started his new school his progress has been **fairly steady**. 新しい学校へ行き始めてから彼は着実に進歩している

steep /stí:p/ 形 急な, 険しい

become	steep	急になる
get	steeper	
grow	steeper	

▷ It's **getting steeper** and steeper as you get to the peak. 頂上に近づくにつれだんだん急になる

step /stép/

名 歩み; (目標への)一歩; 階段, 段; 手段, 対策

take	a step	一歩踏み出す
move	a step	
retrace	one's **steps**	同じ道を引き返す
take	steps	手段を講じる

▷ As the dog came rushing toward her she hurriedly **took** a **step** back. 犬が自分の方へ走って来たので彼女はあわてて一歩後ずさった
▷ I think I dropped my keys. If I **retrace** my **steps** maybe I can find them. 鍵を落としたようだ. 来た道を引き返せば見つかるかもしれない
▷ We need to **take steps** to improve security. 安全性を高めるための対策を講じる必要がある

a small	step	小さな一歩
a big	step	大きな一歩
an important	step	重要な一歩
a major	step	
a further	step	さらなる一歩

▷ That's one **small step** for a man, one giant leap for mankind. 一人の人間にとっては小さな一歩だが人類にとっては大きな飛躍だ
▷ Passing this law will be a **major step** toward improving women's rights. この法律が通れば女性の権利向上への重要な一歩となるだろう

a step	toward A	Aへの一歩

▷ Reducing carbon dioxide emissions is a **step toward** preventing global warming. 二酸化炭素の排出を減らすことは地球温暖化を防ぐ第一歩だ

one step	ahead	一歩先んじて
a step	ahead	
one step	behind	一歩遅れて
a step	behind	

| step |

▷Tony wants to be boss of the company, too, so you'd better keep **one step ahead** of him! トニーも社長になりたがっているから，きみは一歩先んじていたほうがいいな

in	step	歩調を合わせて
out of	step	歩調を乱して

▷Everybody needs to be **in step** with each other. みんな互いに歩調を合わせる必要がある

step by step		一歩一歩

▷Don't try and do everything at once. Take it easy. **Step by step**. すべてを一度にやろうと思わないで気楽に構えろ．一歩一歩やりなさい

PHRASES
Watch your step. /《英》**Mind your step.** ☺ 足元に気をつけろ；ことばに気をつけろ

step /stép/ 動 一歩進む

step	aside	わきへ寄る
step	back	一歩下がる
step	forward	一歩前に出る
step	down	降りる
step	out	外へ出る

▷The police officer **stepped aside** to let the President's car pass through. その警察官は大統領の車を通すためにわきへ寄った
▷Stand up and **step back** to the starting position. 立って最初の位置まで下がってください
▷She fell as she **stepped down** off the bus. 彼女はバスから降りるとき転んだ

step	into A	Aに足を踏み入れる
step	out of A	Aから出る

▷She **stepped into** the shop doorway to shelter from the rain. 彼女は雨宿りしようと店の戸口へと入った

stiff /stíf/ 形 凝った，硬直した；堅い

stiff	with A	Aでこわばる

▷My hands are **stiff with** cold. 手が寒さでこわばっている

beat A	until stiff	A(卵白など)を固くなるまで泡立てる
whisk A	until stiff	

▷Don't forget. You have to **whisk** the egg whites **until stiff**. きちんと卵白を固くなるまで泡立てるんですよ

still /stíl/ 形 静止した，静かな

keep	still	じっとしている

▷**Keep still**! There's a bee in your hair! じっとして．髪にハチが止まっているよ

perfectly	still	まったく動かない
completely	still	
absolutely	still	

▷You should keep your head **perfectly still** when the dentist starts to drill! 歯医者さんがドリルを動かし始めたら頭をじっと動かさないでいなさい

stock /sták | stɔ́k/ 名 在庫；株式，株

have	a stock	在庫がある；Aを
hold	a stock	保有する
keep	a stock	備蓄する
buy	stocks	株を買う
sell	stocks	株を売る

▷The supermarket near us **has** a large **stock** of good wines. うちの近くのスーパーマーケットにはいいワインの在庫がたくさんある
▷Many people in Japan **keep** a **stock** of bottled water and tinned food in case of an earthquake. 多くの日本人は地震に備えて瓶入り飲料水や缶詰食品を貯蔵している

a large	stock	大量の在庫
a good	stock	
a low	stock	少ない在庫
existing	stock	いまある在庫
new	stock	新たな在庫
growth	stock	成長株
common	stock	普通株式

▷The bookshop near us is closing down. They're selling off their **existing stock** at half-price. 近所の書店が店を閉めるので，いまある在庫を半額で売る予定だ

in	stock	仕入れて，在庫して
out of	stock	在庫切れで

▷We always keep a lot of spare parts **in stock**. 予備部品は在庫を切らさず置いてある
▷There are no more 40-inch TVs. We're **out of stock**. 40インチテレビはもうありません．品切れです

stomach /stʌ́mək/ 名 胃；腹，腹部

hold	one's **stomach**	腹を押さえる
lie on	one's **stomach**	うつぶせになる

▷She might have food poisoning. She was **holding** her **stomach** in pain. 彼女は食中毒かもしれない。痛みで腹を押さえていた
▷The nurse told me to **lie on** my **stomach**. 看護師は私にうつぶせになるように言った

one's **stomach**	churns	胃がむかつく
one's **stomach**	lurches	

▷It was my first presentation. I was so nervous. I could feel my **stomach churn**. 初めての発表だったのでとても緊張して胃がむかつくのを感じた

an empty	**stomach**	空っぽの胃
a full	**stomach**	満腹の胃
an upset	**stomach**	胃のむかつき

▷It's not good to drink alcohol *on* an **empty stomach**. 空き腹にアルコールを飲むのはよくない
▷You shouldn't take a bath *on* a **full stomach**. 満腹で風呂に入らないほうがいい

the pit of	one's **stomach**	みぞおちのあたり

▷She woke up depressed with a sad feeling *in* the **pit of** her **stomach**. 彼女はみぞおちのあたりにいやな感じがして目が覚めた

kick A	in the **stomach**	Aの腹をける

★kick のほか shoot, hit, stab などとも連結する

▷Apparently the man was **kicked in** the **stomach**. その男は腹をけられたようすだった

stop /stάp | stɔ́p/

名 止まること，停止；滞在；停留所

make	a **stop**	停車する；立ち寄る
come to	a **stop**	止まる
put	a **stop** to A	Aを終わらせる

▷If we're flying from Paris to Tokyo why don't we **make** a **stop** for a couple of days in Hong Kong? パリから東京に飛ぶなら、香港に2, 3日立ち寄らないか
▷The golf ball hit a fence, bounced off a tree and finally **came to** a **stop** just in front of the hole! ゴルフボールはフェンスに当たり，木に当たって跳ね返り，最後はホール手前で止まった
▷We would like to **put** a **stop to** this kind of harassment as soon as possible. できるだけ早くこのような嫌がらせをやめさせたい

a brief	**stop**	少しの停止；ちょっと
a short	**stop**	立ち寄ること
an overnight	**stop**	一泊の滞在
a bus	**stop**	バス停
(the) next	**stop**	次の停留所

▷Let's make a **brief stop** to have a cup of coffee. コーヒーを飲みにちょっと立ち寄ろう
▷We can't drive all the way there in one day. We'll have to make an **overnight stop**. 1日ではそこまで車で行けないから一泊することになるだろう
▷I think we need to get off at the **next stop**. 次の駅で降りたほうがいいと思います

stop /stάp | stɔ́p/

動 止める，止まる；やめる；立ち寄る

stop	abruptly	急に止まる
stop	suddenly	
stop	immediately	すぐ止まる
stop	altogether	完全に止まる
stop	completely	

★suddenly は動詞の前でも用いる

▷The bus **stopped abruptly** and everybody fell forward. バスが急停車してみんな前倒しになった
▷My watch kept stopping and starting, and now it's **stopped altogether**. 私の時計は止まったり動いたりしていたが，とうとうすっかり止まった

stop	doing	…するのをやめる
stop	to do	…するために立ち止まる
cannot **stop**	doing	…するのをやめられない
stop A	(from) doing	A(人)が…するのをやめさせる

▷Has it **stopped** rain**ing** yet? 雨はもうやんだかい
▷The scenery along the coastal road was so beautiful that we **stopped** to have a picnic. 海岸道路沿いの景色はとてもきれいだったので，ピクニックをするために止まった
▷I **can't stop** eating this chocolate cake! It's so delicious! このチョコレートケーキは食べ出したら止まらない。とてもおいしいから
▷Her parents tried to **stop** her **from** stay**ing** out too late. 夜遅くまで彼女が出歩くのを両親はやめさせようとした

stop	at A	Aに立ち寄る；Aに泊まる；Aで停まる

| store |

▷ We **stopped at** a gas station to fill up. ガソリンを満タンにするためにガソリンスタンドに寄った　▷ I **stopped at** a small hotel for two days. 小さなホテルに2日間滞在した

PHRASES
Stop it! 😊 やめなさい

store /stɔ́ːr/ 名 店, 商店；蓄え；倉庫

open	a store	開店する
close	a store	閉店する
run	a store	店を経営する

▷ After he retired from his job my grandfather decided to **open** a **store** in his village. 祖父は退職後、村で店を開くことにした

a large	store	大きな店；大量の蓄積
a chain	store	チェーン店
a convenience	store	コンビニ
a department	store	百貨店, デパート
a grocery	store	食料雑貨店
a shoe	store	靴屋
a video	store	ビデオ店

▷ There's a **large store** *of* spare parts in the warehouse. 倉庫に予備の部品がたくさん置いてある

in	store	待ち構えて

▷ When he accepted the job he didn't realize what was **in store** for him. 仕事を引き受けたときこの先どんなことが待ち受けているか彼にはわかっていなかった

storm /stɔ́ːrm/ 名 嵐, 暴風雨；騒乱

a storm	hits	嵐が襲う
a storm	strikes	
a storm	breaks	嵐になる
a storm	is coming	嵐がやって来る
a storm	is brewing	
a storm	blows up	嵐が吹き荒れる

▷ A **storm hit** the southeast coast of the USA and caused a lot of damage. 嵐が米国南東岸を襲い、多くの損害を引き起こした
▷ It looks as if a **storm** is going to **break** soon. 嵐になりそうだ
▷ There's a **storm blowing up**. 嵐が吹き荒れている

cause	a storm	騒ぎを引き起こす
provoke	a storm	
weather	a storm	難局を切り抜ける

▷ If the story gets into the newspapers it'll **cause a storm**! その話が新聞に出たら大騒ぎになるだろう
▷ The rise in gasoline prices **provoked** a **storm** of protest from motorists. ガソリン価格の高騰はドライバーたちの抗議の嵐を呼び起こした

a bad	storm	ひどい嵐
a great	storm	
a violent	storm	
a severe	storm	
a terrible	storm	
a rain	storm	暴風雨
a snow	storm	吹雪
a political	storm	政治の動乱

▷ A **great storm** hit the island with almost no warning. 大嵐がほとんどなんの前触れもなく島を襲った
▷ A **political storm** followed the Prime Minister's resignation. 政治の動乱が首相の辞任に続いて起きた

the eye of	the storm	嵐の目

▷ Our plane was caught right in the **eye of** the **storm**. 私たちの乗った飛行機は台風の目に巻き込まれた

story /stɔ́ːri/ 名 物語, 話；記事

write	a story	物語を書く
read	a story	物語を読む；物語を読んで聞かせる
tell	a story	物語をして聞かせる
hear	a story	話を聞く
believe	the story	その話を信じる
know	the story	その話を知っている

▷ Chris and his brother **told** us some interesting **stories** about their father, Roger. クリスとその弟は父親ロジャーについてのおもしろい話を聞かせてくれた
▷ I **heard** a very strange **story** about a ghost in this house. この家に出る幽霊についてのとても奇妙な話を聞いた

the true	story	本当の話
an interesting	story	興味深い話
an old	story	昔の話
a strange	story	奇妙な話
a funny	story	おもしろい話
a sad	story	悲しい話
a success	story	成功物語
the full	story	話の全貌
the whole	story	
a short	story	短編
a bedtime	story	寝物語

an adventure	story	冒険物語
a detective	story	探偵物語
a fairy	story	おとぎ話, 童話
a ghost	story	幽霊物語, 怪談
a horror	story	怪奇物語
a love	story	恋愛物語
a front-page	story	一面記事
a news	story	ニュース記事
the main	story	主要記事

▷Maybe in 6 months from now we'll find out the **true story** of what really happened. 半年もたてばたぶん事の真相がわかるだろう
▷We know some of the facts, but I don't think we've heard the **whole story** yet. わかっている事実もあるが, まだ話の全貌は聞いていないと思う

a story	about A	Aについての話
the story	behind A	Aの背景にある話

▷The **story behind** how Helen got her job is quite interesting. ヘレンがどのように仕事にありついたかの裏話はとても興味深い

PHRASES
End of story. ☺ それだけの話, 以上
It's a long story. ☺ 話せば長くなる ▷"Why are you so late?" "Yes, I'm sorry. Well, it's a long story..." 「なぜこんなに遅くなったの」「ごめん, いろいろあって」
It's the same old story. ☺ よくある話だ
but that's another story ☺ だがそれはまた別の話だ
That's not the whole story. ☺ それだけではないんです

straight /stréit/

形 まっすぐな, 一直線の; 連続した

perfectly	straight	一直線の
《英》dead	straight	
almost	straight	ほぼまっすぐな

▷Stand **perfectly straight** while I measure your height. 身長を測る間, 背筋を伸ばして立ってください

three straight	days	3日連続で

▷She's eaten no food for three **straight days**. 彼女は3日間ずっと何も食べていない

strange /stréindʒ/

形 奇妙な, 変な, 不思議な

seem	strange	奇妙と思われる
feel	strange	奇妙に感じる
sound	strange	奇妙に聞こえる

▷It **seems strange** that Emma hasn't phoned yet. エマがまだ電話してこないのは奇妙だな
▷It **felt strange** at first, but now I really like it. 初めは奇妙だなと感じたが, いまではとても気に入っている

extremely	strange	非常に奇妙な
particularly	strange	特に変な
slightly	strange	少し奇妙な

▷There's something **slightly strange** about that man's accent. その男のなまりには少しおかしなところがある

it is strange	that...	…は奇妙だ
it seems strange	that...	

▷**It's strange that** your brother locks himself in his room for hours and won't come out. お兄さんが何時間も部屋に鍵をかけて出てこないのはおかしい

the strange thing	is...	奇妙なのは…だ

▷The **strange thing is**, that I dreamt I was sitting in this same restaurant with you last night! 不思議なんだけど, 昨夜あなたとこのレストランで食事している夢を見たの

PHRASES
Strange but true. ☺ 奇妙だが本当なんだ
That's strange. ☺ それは変だ ▷That's strange. I thought I put my wallet on the table. 変だな. 財布をテーブルの上に置いたはずなんだけど

stranger /stréindʒər/ 名 見知らぬ人

a complete	stranger	まったく知らない人
a total	stranger	
a perfect	stranger	

▷This man started talking to me on the train. He was a **complete stranger**. It was scary! まったく知らないこの男の人が列車で話しかけてきたの. 怖かった

a stranger	to A	Aを知らない人; A(土地)に不案内な人

▷My dad's a firefighter. He's no **stranger to** dangerous situations. 父は消防士で, 危険な状況には慣れている

strategy /strǽtədʒi/ 名 戦略, 戦術

have	a strategy	戦略がある
develop	a strategy	戦略を立案する
adopt	a strategy	戦略を採る

| stream |

| implement | a strategy | 戦略を実行に移す |

▷We need to **develop** a new **strategy** for increasing our sales. 売り上げを伸ばすための新戦略を立案する必要がある

▷We need to **adopt** a different **strategy** if we're going to win this contract. この契約をとるには異なる戦略を採用する必要がある

an effective	strategy	効果的な戦略
an alternative	strategy	代替戦略
a long-term	strategy	長期戦略
an overall	strategy	全体的戦略
a military	strategy	軍事戦略
a political	strategy	政治戦略
a business	strategy	事業戦略
an investment	strategy	投資戦略
an economic	strategy	経済戦略
an energy	strategy	エネルギー戦略

▷We need to have a **long-term strategy**, not just a short-term plan. 短期計画だけでなく長期戦略をもつ必要がある

▷The Government's **economic strategy** has not been very successful so far. 政府の経済戦略はこれまであまりうまくいっていない

| a strategy | for A | Aのための戦略 |

▷The World Champion's **strategy for** his next fight is simple. Attack! Attack! Attack! 次の戦いのための世界チャンピオンの戦略は単純で，ただ攻撃あるのみだ

stream /stríːm/ 名 小川；流れ

a little	stream	小川
a small	stream	
a mountain	stream	渓流
a steady	stream	絶え間ない流れ
a constant	stream	
an endless	stream	

▷A **little stream** runs through the garden. 小川が庭を流れている

▷There's been a **steady stream** *of* people buying tickets for the concert all day. コンサートのチケットを買い求める人たちの絶え間ない流れが一日中続いている

street /stríːt/ 名 街路，通り；…街

cross	the street	通りを渡る
walk	the streets	通りを歩く
wander	the streets	通りをぶらつく

▷Look both ways before **crossing** the **street**. 道路を渡る前に左右を見なさい

▷He had no money for a hotel so he **wandered** the **streets** all night. 彼はホテルに泊まる金がなかったので一晩中，通りをぶらついた

a narrow	street	狭い通り
a busy	street	にぎやかな通り
a cobbled	street	石畳の通り
the main	street	本通り
《英》the high	street	
a residential	street	住宅街

▷We want to move. Our house is on a really **busy street**. 引っ越ししたい．うちの家はとても交通量の多い通りにあるので

▷A shopping center is to be built on the **main street**. ショッピングセンターが本通りに建つ予定だ

across	the street	通りの向こう側に
on	the street	通りに，通りで
《英》in	the street	

▷The post office is just **across** the **street**. 郵便局はちょうど通りの向こう側です

▷You should tell the children not to play **in** the **street**. 子どもたちに通りで遊ばないように言いなさい

strength /stréŋkθ/

名 力，体力；強度；強さ；強み，長所；兵力

have	the strength	力がある
build up	one's strength	力をつける
gain	strength	力を得る
grow in	strength	力を増す
give	strength	力を与える
lose	one's strength	力を失う

▷She didn't **have** the **strength** *to* lift the suitcase onto the rack. 彼女にはスーツケースを棚に上げる力がなかった

▷You need to **build up** your **strength** after that long illness. 長患いしたんだから体力をつけないとね

▷Support for the antinuclear power movement is **growing in strength**. 反原発運動への支持が力を増しつつある

▷The support of all my friends and family really **gave** me **strength**. 友人たちや家族みんなの援助は本当に私に力を与えてくれた

great	strength	大きな力
competitive	strength	競争力
real	strength	本物の力
an inner	strength	内面の力

physical	strength	体力
muscular	strength	筋力
economic	strength	経済力
military	strength	軍事力

▷I think she showed **great strength** of character by not giving up. あきらめなかったのは彼女の性格の力強さを示すものだね
▷We need to increase our **competitive strength** if we want to survive as a company. 企業として生き残りたいなら競争力を増す必要がある

strengths and weaknesses	長所と短所

▷What are your **strengths and weaknesses**? あなたの長所と短所はどこですか

at	full strength	全員そろって
with	all one's strength	力いっぱい

▷Two of our players are injured, so the team won't be **at full strength**. うちのチームは選手が2名負傷していて, 戦力が万全ではない
▷I can't push any harder! I'm already pushing **with all** my **strength**! これ以上は強く押せないよ。もう力いっぱい押しているもの

stress /strés/

名 ストレス；強調；圧迫, 圧力

cause	stress	ストレスを引き起こす
reduce	stress	ストレスを和らげる
suffer from	stress	ストレスに悩む
cope with	stress	ストレスに対処する
lay	stress on A	Aに重点を置く
put	stress on A	

▷What are the top three things that **cause stress** for people? 人々にストレスを引き起こす原因の上位3つは何ですか
▷I asked the doctor to give me something to **reduce stress**. ストレスを和らげるために何かくれるよう医師に頼んだ
▷Brian's been **suffering from** a lot of **stress** recently. ブライアンは近ごろ多くのストレスに悩まされている
▷Our new boss **lays** a lot of **stress on** working as a team. 新しい上司はわれわれがチームとして働くことにかなり重点を置いている

considerable	stress	かなりのストレス
great	stress	大きなストレス
severe	stress	きびしいストレス
mental	stress	精神的ストレス

▷Dealing with complaints every day can cause **great stress**. 毎日のクレーム処理は大きなストレスになることがある

the stress	on A	Aへの圧力, Aへの負担
under	stress	ストレスを受けて

▷There's a lot of **stress on** us to complete the project by the end of the month. 今月末までに事業を完成させろとの大きな圧力がわれわれにかかっている
▷I've been **under** a lot of **stress** lately. 最近ストレスをいっぱい抱えている

stress and anxiety	ストレスと心配
stresses and strains	ストレスと緊張

★anxiety and stress も用いられる

▷He's a good tennis player, but I'm not sure how well he'll stand up to the **stresses and strains** of international competition. 彼はいいテニス選手だが, 国際競技のストレスと緊張に耐えられるだろうか

stress /strés/ 動 強調する

strongly	stress	しっかり強調する
repeatedly	stress	繰り返し強調する

▷The mountain guide **repeatedly stressed** that nobody should leave the main group. 山のガイドはグループから離れる人が出ないように繰り返し強調した

stress	that...	…であると強調する

▷Our teacher **stressed that** we should make notes before writing the essay. 先生はレポートを書く前にメモをとるのが大事だと強調した

be important	to stress	強調するのが重要だ

▷It is **important to stress** that people should consult their doctors before making any decision to stop treatment. 治療の中断を決める前に医師たちと相談するのが大事だと強調しておこう

stretch /strétʃ/ 名 広がり；ストレッチ

have	a stretch	伸びをする
give	a stretch	

▷When I wake up in the morning I need to **have a** good **stretch** before I get out of bed! 朝起きるとベッドから出る前によく伸びをする必要がある

a great	stretch	大きな広がり
a long	stretch	

| stretch |

▷There's a **great stretch** of sea to cross before we see land. 陸が見えるまでには大海原を渡らなくてはならない

at	a stretch	一気に，一息に
at	full stretch	全身を伸ばして；全力を出して

▷It's not good to drive for more than 2 hours **at a stretch** without taking a break. 休みもとらずに一気に2時間以上運転するのはよくない

stretch /strétʃ/ 動 伸ばす，伸びる；張る

stretch	tightly	ぴんと伸ばす
stretch	out	手足を伸ばす
stretch	luxuriously	ゆったり手足を伸ばす
stretch	away	遠くまで伸びる
stretch	back	さかのぼる
fully	stretch	十分に伸びる

▷The nurse **stretched** the bandage **tightly** round his leg. 看護師は包帯をぴんと伸ばして彼の足に巻いた
▷The road **stretched away** in front of them for miles and miles. 道は彼らの前方はるかへと伸びていた
▷His experience as a mountain climber **stretches back** for over 40 years. 登山家としての彼の経験は40年以上にさかのぼる
▷We can't take on any more work. Our resources are already **fully stretched**. これ以上仕事を引き受けることはできない．もう限度いっぱいだ

stretch	across A	Aを横切って伸びる
stretch	for A	A (距離) に延びる
stretch	from A to B	AからBに伸びる

▷The area that was flooded **stretched for** over 70 square miles. 浸水地域は70平方マイル以上に及んだ
▷The clothesline **stretched from** the side of our house **to** a tree in the garden. 物干し綱は家の横から庭の木まで伸びていた

strike /stráik/ 名 ストライキ；攻撃

be on	strike	スト中である
go on	strike	ストに入る
call	a strike	ストを呼びかける
call off	a strike	ストを中止する

▷They've been **on strike** for over two months and still no progress. 2か月以上にわたってストライキをしているが，まだ進展がない
▷The union **called** a **strike** for better wages and working conditions. 組合は賃金と労働条件の改善を求めストライキを呼びかけた

a one-day	strike	1日スト
a general	strike	ゼネスト
a national	strike	全国スト
a hunger	strike	ハンガーストライキ
a sit-down	strike	座り込みスト
a sympathy	strike	同情スト
a rail	strike	鉄道スト
an air	strike	空爆

▷A **general strike** was carried out on the 9th of June. ゼネストは6月9日に行われた

a strike	against A	Aに反対するスト
a strike	over A	Aを巡るスト

▷The airline staff are going to **strike over** wages. 航空会社の職員は賃金を巡ってストライキをする予定だ

strike /stráik/ 動 打つ，殴る；心に浮かぶ

strike	hard	激しく打つ
particularly	strike	特に心を打つ
suddenly	strike	突然心に浮かぶ

▷I was **particularly struck** by the beauty of Mozart's music. モーツァルトの音楽の美しさに特に心を打たれた
▷A great idea **suddenly struck** him. すばらしい考えが突然彼の心に浮かんだ

it strikes A	that...	…であることがA (人) の心に浮かぶ

▷Hi, Bob. **It struck** me **that** you might like these tickets. You're a baseball fan, aren't you? やあ，ボブ．ひょっとしてこの切符がほしいかなと思って．野球ファンだったよね

be struck	by A	Aにぶつかる；Aに感動する

▷I was **struck by** the beauty of the scenery. 景色の美しさに打たれた

strike	at A	Aに殴りかかる
strike A	with B	AをBで殴る

▷He **struck** the security guard over the head **with** a baseball bat. 彼は野球のバットで警備員の頭を殴った

strike A	as C	A (人) にCだと印象づける

★Cは形容詞・名詞

▷Your new boyfriend **strikes** me **as** a really interesting guy. あなたの新しいボーイフレンドはとてもおもしろい人だと思う

strong /strɔ́ːŋ | strɔ́ŋ/ 形 強い, 強力な

grow	strong	強くなる

▷She's recovering well — **growing stronger** every day. 彼女の回復は順調で, 日増しに体力がついてきている

extremely	strong	とても強い
exceptionally	strong	
immensely	strong	
fairly	strong	かなり強い
particularly	strong	とりわけ強い
strong	enough	十分強い

▷This rope is **exceptionally strong**. It's used by mountain climbers. このロープは非常に強く, 登山者たちが使っている
▷Ed's **particularly strong** for a boy of his age. エドはあの年齢の男の子にしてはとりわけじょうぶだ
▷Amy's still not **strong enough** to get out of bed. エイミーはまだベッドから出るだけの体力がない

structure /strʌ́ktʃər/ 名 構造；組織

examine	the structure	構造を調べる
determine	the structure	構造を決定する

▷Scientists are **examining** the **structure** of a rock found on the moon. 科学者たちは月で見つかった岩石の構造を調べている

(an) internal	structure	内部構造
(an) organizational	structure	組織構造
(a) management	structure	経営構造
(an) economic	structure	経済構造
a social	structure	社会構造
(an) industrial	structure	産業構造
(a) class	structure	階級構造
(a) data	structure	データ構造

▷There are too many departments and divisions in the company. We need to improve the **internal structure**. わが社には課や部門が多すぎる。内部構造を改善する必要がある
▷Sally is studying the **social structure** of primitive societies in Africa. サリーはアフリカの原始社会の社会構造を研究している

struggle /strʌ́gl/ 名 闘争, 闘い；奮闘

a bitter	struggle	激しい闘い
an uphill	struggle	苦しい闘い
a constant	struggle	絶え間ない闘い
(an) armed	struggle	武装闘争
(a) class	struggle	階級闘争
(a) political	struggle	政治闘争
a power	struggle	権力闘争

▷After a **bitter struggle** she finally won custody of the children. 激しい闘いの末に彼女はようやく子どもの養育権を勝ち取った
▷For a single parent to bring up two young children is an **uphill struggle**. 片親が小さな子どもを2人育てるのは大変な苦労だ

a struggle	against A	Aに対する闘い
a struggle	for A	Aを求める闘い
a struggle	with A	Aとの闘い
a struggle	between A	Aの間の闘い

▷We must continue the **struggle against** racism. 人種差別との闘いを続けねばならない
▷Life seems to be a constant **struggle between** good and evil. 人生は善と悪との絶え間ない闘いのように思える

struggle /strʌ́gl/ 動 もがく；奮闘する

desperately	struggle	必死でもがく
constantly	struggle	絶えず奮闘する

▷She fell through the ice on the pond and **desperately struggled** to climb out. 池の氷が割れて落ちた彼女は氷の上に上がろうと必死でもがいた

struggle	for A	Aを求めてもがく
struggle	through A	Aを苦労して進む
struggle	with A	Aと戦う
struggle	against A	

▷They are **struggling for** a better future. よりよい未来を求めて奮闘している
▷I can't solve this math problem. I've been **struggling with** it for hours. この数学の問題が解けなくて, 何時間も格闘している

struggle	to do	…しようと奮闘する

▷It was really hot on the day of the marathon. Many of the competitors **struggled to** finish the race. マラソン当日はとても気温が高く, 多くのランナーたちは完走しようと踏ん張った

stuck /stˊʌk/ 形 動かなくなった

get	stuck	動けなくなる

▷ We **got stuck** in a traffic jam for 3 hours at the weekend. 週末に交通渋滞で3時間動けなくなった

student /stjúːdnt | stjúː-/ 名 学生, 生徒

a college	student	大学生
a university	student	
a first-year	student	1年生
a second-year	student	2年生
a research	student	研究生
a foreign	student	留学生
《英》an overseas	student	
an exchange	student	交換留学生

▷ I'm a **third-year student** at Oxford University. オックスフォード大学3年生です
▷ The university is accepting more and more **overseas students**. 大学はますます多くの留学生を受け入れている

study /stˊʌdi/

名 勉強;(個々の)研究;(studies で)勉学, 学問

make	a study	研究する
carry out	a study	
conduct	a study	
undertake	a study	研究に着手する
continue	one's studies	勉学を続ける
complete	one's studies	勉学を修了する

▷ She's thinking of going to Canada to **continue** her **studies**. 彼女は勉学を続けるためにカナダに行こうと考えている

the study	finds	研究でわかる
the study	shows	研究は示している
the study	indicates	
the study	suggests	研究は示唆している

▷ The **study found** that generally speaking women live longer than men. その研究で一般的に女性は男性より長生きだとわかった
▷ The **study shows** that the number of homeless people is increasing. その調査はホームレスの数が増加していることを示している

the present	study	現在の研究
a recent	study	最近の研究
a previous	study	先行研究
a detailed	study	詳細な研究

▷ A **recent study** has shown that obesity is a major problem in the USA. 肥満が米国における重大な問題であることが最近の研究で示されている
▷ We need to carry out a **detailed study** of the causes of the train crash. 列車衝突事故の諸原因を詳細に研究する必要がある

an area of	study	研究分野

study /stˊʌdi/ 動 調べる;勉強する, 研究する

carefully	study	注意深く調べる
intensively	study	集中的に調べる
extensively	study	幅広く調べる

★3つの副詞いずれも動詞の後でも用いる

▷ He **carefully studied** the map. 彼は注意深く地図を調べた
▷ The effects of global warming have been **extensively studied**. 地球温暖化の影響が広範囲にわたって調べられた

study	at A	A(学校)で勉強する
study	for A	Aのために勉強する

▷ He **studied** French literature **at** Kyoto University. 彼は京都大学でフランス文学を勉強した
▷ Carolyn is **studying for** a degree at Cambridge. キャロリンはケンブリッジで学位をとるために勉強している

study	wh-	…かを研究する

★ wh- は how, why, when など

▷ Peter **studied how** the brain works. ピーターは脳の働きを研究した

stupid /stjúːpid | stjúː-/ 形 ばかな, 愚かな

incredibly	stupid	信じられないほどばかな
absolutely	stupid	まったくばかな
really	stupid	本当にばかな
so	stupid	すごくばかな
stupid	enough	十分にばかな

▷ I can't believe that Ben could say something so **incredibly stupid**! 信じられないくらいばかなことをベンが言ったなんてなあ
▷ I should never have believed what Peter said. I was **so stupid**! ピーターのことばを信じるべきじゃなかっ

た．すごくばかだった

▷I can't believe I was **stupid enough** to leave my wallet in the taxi! タクシーに財布を置き忘れるなんてぼくもばかだなあ

feel	stupid	ばかだと感じる
sound	stupid	ばかげて聞こえる

▷I was the only one to get the answer wrong in class and everybody looked at me. I **felt** pretty **stupid**! クラスの中で答えを間違えたのは私だけだったのでみんなが私を見た．自分がずいぶんばかだと感じた

be stupid	of A (to do)	(…するとは) A (人) はばかだ

▷It was **stupid of** me **to** argue with my boss. 上司と口げんかするなんて私はばかだった

PHRASES

How stupid! なんてばかなんだ ▷Oh, I left my umbrella on the train! How stupid! 列車に傘を忘れてしまった．なんてばかなんだ

style /stáil/

名 様式；型，スタイル；流行；文体；上品，気品

have	a style	様式がある
develop	a style	様式をつくり出す
adopt	a style	様式を取り入れる
change	A's style	様式を変える
have	style	品がある

▷Kazuo Ishiguro **has** a very interesting **style** of writing. カズオ・イシグロの文体はとても興味深い

▷After you've played golf for a while you **develop a style** of your own. しばらくゴルフをすれば自分なりのスタイルができてくるよ

▷Look at the way Melissa's dancing. She really **has style**! メリッサの踊りぶりを見てごらん．品があるね

(a) modern	style	現代的様式
(a) classical	style	古典的様式
(a) traditional	style	伝統的様式
(an) architectural	style	建築様式
one's own	style	自分のスタイル
a particular	style	特定のスタイル
leadership	style	指導スタイル
management	style	経営スタイル

▷Everyone has their **own style** of giving a presentation. だれもが自分の発表スタイルをもっている

▷Mr. Bean has his own **particular style** of comedy. ミスタービーンには特有のコメディースタイルがある

in	style	流行して；はでに

▷Maria and her partner won the ballroom dancing competition **in style**. マリアとそのパートナーは社交ダンス競技ではでに勝利を収めた

subject /sʌ́bdʒikt/

名 主題, 話題；科目, 教科

bring up	the subject	話題を持ち出す
raise	the subject	
broach	the subject	
get onto	the subject	話題になる
drop	the subject	話題をやめる
get off	the subject	話題から外れる
change	the subject	話題を変える
be related to	the subject	話題に関連する
choose	a subject	科目を選ぶ
take	a subject	科目をとる

▷I think we'd better **change** the **subject**. 話題を変えたほうがいいと思う

▷I'm afraid we've rather **got off** the **subject**. どうも話題がそれたようだ

▷What I have to say is **related to** the **subject** under discussion. 審議中の話題に関連して発言があります

▷How many **subjects** are you **taking** this year? 今年は何科目とっているの？

a complex	subject	複雑な話題
one's favorite	subject	得意の話題
the main	subject	主題；主要科目
a particular	subject	特定の話題

▷Is there any **particular subject** that you'd like to discuss today? きょう議論したい特定の話題はあるかい

on	the subject of A	Aのテーマについて；Aと言えば

▷**On** the **subject of** birthdays, it's my birthday tomorrow! 誕生日と言えば，あしたはぼくの誕生日だ

subway /sʌ́bwèi/ 名 地下鉄；《英》地下道

take	the subway	地下鉄に乗る
ride	the subway	

▷Ted **takes** the **subway** to work every day. テッドは毎日地下鉄に乗って仕事に出かける

by	subway	地下鉄で

▷Do you take a bus to work or go **by subway**? 仕

事に行くのにバスですか、それとも地下鉄ですか

succeed /səksíːd/

動 成功する；継承する，後を継ぐ

eventually	succeed	最終的にうまくいく
finally	succeed	最終的にうまくいく
nearly	succeed	ほぼうまくいく

▷ If you keep trying you'll **eventually succeed**. 挑戦し続ければ最後はうまくいくだろう

succeed	in (doing) A	Aに成功する
succeed	A as B	A(人)の後を継いでBに就く
succeed	to A	Aを継ぐ

▷ Peter **succeeded in** cooking us a really nice meal. ピーターはとてもおいしい食事を私たちにつくってくれた
▷ President Obama **succeeded** George W. Bush **as** President of the USA. オバマはG・W・ブッシュの後を継いで米国大統領になった
▷ One day Prince William will **succeed to** the throne. いつの日かウィリアム王子が王位を継ぐだろう

be likely to succeed	成功する可能性がある

▷ I'm trying to persuade my father to buy me a car, but I don't think I'm **likely to succeed**! 父親を説得して車を買ってくれるよう頼み込んでいるけど、うまくいきそうにない

success /səksés/

名 成功；うまくいったもの；成功した人

make	a success	成功する
score	a success	成功を収める
achieve	success	
enjoy	success	
have	success	
ensure	success	成功を確実にする
guarantee	success	成功を保証する

▷ I hope you **make** a **success** *of* your new job. あなたが新しい仕事で成功するよう祈ります
▷ Tiger Woods **enjoyed** great **success** as a golf player. タイガー・ウッズはゴルフ選手として大成功した
▷ I tried to persuade Tina to come to the party but I didn't **have** much **success**. ティナをパーティーに来るよう説得しようとしたが、あまりうまくいかなかった

a great	success	大きな成功
a huge	success	
a big	success	
(a) considerable	success	かなりの成功
(a) notable	success	注目すべき成功
(a) remarkable	success	目覚ましい成功
limited	success	まずまずの成功
moderate	success	
a complete	success	完全な成功
(a) commercial	success	商業的成功

▷ You're going to be a **big success**. きみはきっと大成功するよ
▷ He achieved only **limited success** as a basketball player. 彼はバスケットボールの選手としてまずまずの成功しか収められなかった
▷ The operation was a **complete success**. 作戦は完全な成功だった

a chance of	success	成功の見込み

▷ I don't think your **chances of success** are very high. あなたの成功の見込みはそう高いとは思えない

success	in (doing) A	Aでの成功
success	with A	Aにおける成功

▷ She had no **success in** getting him to change his mind. 彼に決心を変えさせることは彼女にはできなかった
▷ Terry doesn't have much **success with** women. テリーは女性にあまりもてない

successful /səksésfəl/

形 成功した，うまくいった

highly	successful	大成功した
hugely	successful	
extremely	successful	非常に成功した
remarkably	successful	驚くほど成功した

▷ She was **highly successful** in running her own business. 彼女は自分の事業の経営に大成功した
▷ The diet was **remarkably successful**. I lost 2 kilos in one month! ダイエットは驚くほどうまくいって、1か月で2キロ減った

successful	in (doing) A	Aに成功した

▷ There are so many books about how to be **successful in** business. ビジネスでいかに成功するかについて書かれた本は山ほどある

suffer /sʌ́fər/ 動 苦しむ；患う；被害を受ける

suffer	badly	ひどく苦しむ
suffer	greatly	

▷My grandfather **suffered greatly** during the war. 祖父は戦争中大いに苦しんだ

suffer	from A	A(病気)を患う；Aの被害を受ける

▷He **suffered from** depression. 彼はうつ病に苦しんだ

sugar /ʃúgər/ 名 砂糖

add	sugar	砂糖を加える
take	sugar	砂糖を入れる

▷**Add sugar** and stir into the mixture. 砂糖を加え、かき回して混ぜなさい
▷Do you **take sugar** in your coffee? コーヒーに砂糖を入れますか

a lump of	sugar	角砂糖1個
a cube of	sugar	
a spoonful of	sugar	砂糖さじ1杯
a teaspoon of	sugar	砂糖茶さじ1杯

▷He put three **spoonfuls of sugar** in his coffee. 彼はコーヒーに砂糖を3さじ入れた

suggest /səɡdʒést | sədʒést/

動 提案する；示唆する

strongly	suggest	強く提案する；強く示唆する
seriously	suggest	真剣に提案する

▷I **strongly suggest** you see a doctor before your cold gets worse. かぜが悪くなる前に医者に診てもらうよう強く勧めます

suggest	(that)...	…を提案する；…を示唆する
suggest	wh-	…かを提案する
suggest	doing	…するよう提案する

★wh- は how, what, why, where など

▷My dad **suggested** I should get a part-time job during the summer vacation. 父は夏休みの間アルバイトをするよう提案した
▷Can you **suggest how** we should deal with this situation? この状況にどのように対処したらよいか提案してくれませんか
▷She **suggested** hav**ing** a rest. 一休みしようと彼女は提案した

suggestion /səɡdʒéstʃən | sədʒés-/

名 提案；暗示；可能性，見込み

have	a suggestion	提案がある
make	a suggestion	提案する
offer	a suggestion	
accept	a suggestion	提案を受け入れる
reject	a suggestion	提案を拒否する
support	the suggestion	提案を支持する

▷Can I **make** a **suggestion**? 提案していいですか
▷The meeting decided to **accept** your **suggestion**. 会議できみの提案を受け入れることに決まった
▷He **rejected** the **suggestion** that membership fees should be increased. 彼は会費を上げるべきだという提案を却下した

a good	suggestion	よい提案
a constructive	suggestion	建設的提案
a helpful	suggestion	役立つ提案
a positive	suggestion	前向きな提案
a practical	suggestion	現実的提案
an alternative	suggestion	代替案

▷That's a **good suggestion**. それはよい提案だ
▷Has anybody got any **practical suggestions**? だれか現実的な提案はありますか
▷Do you have an **alternative suggestion**? 代替案はありますか

a suggestion	about A	Aに関する提案
a suggestion	for A	Aに対する提案

▷Do you have any **suggestions for** a place to hold our Christmas party? クリスマスパーティーを開く場所について何か提案はありますか

a suggestion	that...	…という提案

▷They made the **suggestion that** she should resign. 彼女は辞めるべきだと彼らは提案した

suicide /súːəsàid | sjúː-/ 名 自殺

commit	suicide	自殺する
attempt	suicide	自殺を図る

▷The gunman shot three people and then **committed suicide**. 武装犯は3人を射殺し，それから自殺を図った

attempted	suicide	自殺未遂
a suicide	attempt	

▷ The local newspaper reported 3 cases of **attempted suicide** this month.　地元の新聞は今月3件の自殺未遂を報じた

suit /súːt | sjúːt/ 名 スーツ；訴訟

wear	a suit	スーツを着ている
file	(a) suit	訴訟を起こす
bring	(a) suit	
win	a suit	訴訟に勝つ
lose	a suit	訴訟に負ける

▷ If you're going to a funeral you should **wear** a dark **suit**.　葬儀に行くならダークスーツを着て行きなさい
▷ He **filed** a **suit** *against* his company for unfair dismissal.　彼は自分のいた会社を相手どって不当解雇に対する訴訟を起こした

in	a suit	スーツを着た

▷ When I arrived at the cottage, a man **in** a **suit** answered the door.　別荘に着くとスーツを着た男が玄関まで応対に出てきた

suitable /súːtəbl | sjúːt-/

形 適した，ふさわしい

particularly	suitable	特にふさわしい
eminently	suitable	
especially	suitable	

▷ I think the last candidate for the job was **particularly suitable**.　仕事に応募してきた人たちの中で最後の人が適任だったと思う

suitable	for A	Aにふさわしい

▷ Do you think this dress is **suitable for** attending a wedding?　この服は結婚式に出るのにふさわしいと思いますか

sum /sám/ 名 合計，総計；金額

the sum	of A	Aの合計

▷ The **sum of** 4 and 6 is 10.　4プラス6は10

a large	sum	大金
a considerable	sum	かなりの金
a substantial	sum	相当な金額
a huge	sum	巨額の金
a vast	sum	
a small	sum	少額の金

▷ He spent a **huge sum** of money on an expensive sports car!　彼は高価なスポーツカーに巨額の金を使った
▷ His aunt left him a **small sum** of money in her will.　おばは遺言でわずかばかりの金を彼に残した

summer /sámər/ 名 夏

last	summer	前の夏
the following	summer	次の夏
next	summer	
this	summer	この夏
early	summer	初夏
late	summer	晩夏
high	summer	盛夏，真夏
a hot	summer	暑い夏
a dry	summer	乾燥した夏
an Indian	summer	小春日和
all	summer	夏じゅう
a summer	school	夏期講座
a summer	vacation	夏休み
《英》a summer	holiday	

▷ The **following summer** we went back to the same hotel.　次の夏，同じホテルに戻った
▷ The weather is much cooler in **late summer**.　夏の終わりには天候はずっと涼しい
▷ The children spent **all summer** playing on the beach.　子どもたちは夏じゅう浜辺で遊んで過ごした

in	(the) summer	夏に
during	(the) summer	夏の間

▷ I'm going to visit Canada **in** the **summer**.　夏にカナダを訪れるつもりだ
▷ **During** the **summer** I traveled a lot in Europe.　夏の間，ヨーロッパをたくさん旅した

sun /sán/ 名 (the sun で)太陽；日光

catch	the sun	少し日焼けする
soak up	the sun	日光浴をする

▷ Ooh! You've **caught** the **sun**. Your face is all red!　わあ，少し日焼けしたね．顔が真っ赤だ
▷ I love to **soak up** the **sun**.　日光浴が好きだ

the sun	rises	太陽が昇る
the sun	comes up	

the sun	sets	太陽が沈む
the sun	goes down	
the sun	shines	太陽が輝く
the sun	comes out	太陽が現れる

▷The **sun rises** in the east and **sets** in the west. 太陽は東から昇り西に沈む
▷It's getting colder. The **sun's going down**. だんだん寒くなってきた．太陽が沈んでいく
▷Look! The **sun's coming out**! 見て．太陽が出てくるよ

a bright	sun	明るい太陽
the rising	sun	昇る太陽, 朝日
a hot	sun	照りつける太陽
a blazing	sun	
full	sun	十分な日光
the morning	sun	朝日
the evening	sun	夕日

▷I don't like this **bright sun**! Where are my sunglasses? 日差しが明るくていやだな．サングラスはどこかな
▷Don't stay out in the **hot sun** too long. 照りつける太陽の下に長いこと出ていてはいけない
▷These plants grow really well in **full sun**. これらの植物は十分に日の当たる場所でよく育つ

under	the sun	太陽の下で；地上に

▷The car's really hot inside. It's been standing **under** the **sun** all day. 車の中がひどく暑い．一日じゅう太陽の下に止めてあったから
◆**everything under the sun** ありとあらゆること ▷It's an incredible shop! It sells everything under the sun. この店はすごいな．売っていない物がないよ

Sunday /sʌ́ndei/ 名 日曜日

each	Sunday	日曜日ごとに
every	Sunday	毎日曜日
the following	Sunday	次の日曜日
last	Sunday	先週の日曜日
next	Sunday	次の日曜日
this	Sunday	今週の日曜日
Sunday	morning	日曜の朝
Sunday	afternoon	日曜の午後
Sunday	evening	日曜の夕方
Sunday	night	日曜の夜

▷We go to church **every Sunday**. 毎週日曜日に教会へ行く
▷It was Tom's birthday **last Sunday**. 先週の日曜日はトムの誕生日だった

on	(a) Sunday	日曜日に
on	Sundays	日曜日はいつも

▷What are you doing **on Sunday**? 日曜日は何をしていますか

sunshine /sʌ́nʃàin/ 名 日光, 日差し

bright	sunshine	明るい日差し
brilliant	sunshine	まばゆい日差し
warm	sunshine	暖かい日差し
morning	sunshine	朝の日差し
afternoon	sunshine	午後の日差し
evening	sunshine	夕方の日差し
spring	sunshine	春の日差し
summer	sunshine	夏の日差し

▷You'd better take a sunshade. There's **bright sunshine** outside. 日傘を持って行ったほうがいいよ．外は日差しがきついから

in	(the) sunshine	日なたで

▷Doesn't the garden look beautiful **in** the **sunshine**? 日が降り注ぐ庭がきれいだこと

superior /səpíəriər | sjuː-/

形 より優れた；優秀な

clearly	superior	明らかに優れた
vastly	superior	ずっと優れた
greatly	superior	
infinitely	superior	はるかに優れた
technically	superior	技術的に優れた

▷They've redesigned the car and the new model is **vastly superior** to the old one. 設計し直された車の新モデルは前のよりずっといい

superior	to A	Aより優れた

▷Linda thinks she's **superior to** everyone else. リンダは自分が他のだれよりも優れていると思っている

supper /sʌ́pər/ 名 夕食, 晩ご飯

have	supper	夕食をとる
eat	supper	
cook	supper	夕食を料理する
make	supper	夕食をつくる

| supply |

▷ What time do you usually **have supper**? ふだんは何時に夕食をとりますか
▷ Our dad's **making supper** for us this evening! 今夜はパパが私たちのために夕食をつくってくれているの

for	supper	夕食に

▷ We're going to have fish **for supper** this evening. 今夜は夕食に魚を食べるつもりだ

■ supply /səplái/

名 供給, 補給; (supplies で)必需品

have	a supply	供給がある
provide	a supply	供給する
ensure	a supply	供給を確保する
increase	the supply	供給を増やす
reduce	the supply	供給を減らす
control	the supply	供給を制御する
exceed	(the) supply	供給を上回る

▷ The electricity companies are doing their best to **ensure** a regular **supply** of electricity. 電力会社各社は電力の定期的供給を確保するために全力を尽くしている
▷ We can **increase** the **supply** of electricity through the use of solar power. 太陽光発電を用いることで電気の供給を増やせる

a plentiful	supply	豊富な供給
an abundant	supply	
a good	supply	
an adequate	supply	適正な供給
a constant	supply	一定供給
a regular	supply	定期供給
a steady	supply	安定供給
food	supply	食糧供給
water	supply	水の供給
electricity	supply	電力供給
energy	supply	エネルギー供給
labor	supply	労働力の供給
money	supply	通貨供給量

▷ This year there will be a **plentiful supply** of rice. 今年はコメの供給は豊富だろう
▷ A dam was built to ensure a **steady supply** of fresh water. ダムが新鮮な水の安定供給を確保するために建設された

supply and demand	需要と供給
demand and supply	

▷ The price of a product is determined by **supply and demand**. 製品の価格は需要と供給で決まる

supply	to A	Aへの供給
in	short supply	不足して
in	limited supply	

▷ The gas company cut the **supply to** our house. うちはガス会社からガスの供給を止められた
▷ At the moment spare parts are **in short supply**. いまのところ予備の部品は不足している

■ supply /səplái/ **動** 提供する, 供給する

supply A	with B	A(人・場所)にBを
supply B	to A	供給する

▷ Our house is **supplied with** water and electricity, but not gas. うちの家は水道と電気は供給されているが, ガスは供給されていない
▷ We need to be able to **supply** our product quickly **to** our customers. 製品をすぐ顧客に供給する体制ができていなければならない

be well	supplied	十分にある
be generously	supplied	ふんだんにある
be poorly	supplied	あまりない
be kindly	supplied	好意で提供される

▷ Before you go on your camping trip make sure you're **well supplied** with food, water and medicine. キャンプに行く前に食料, 水, 薬が十分にあるか確かめなさい

■ support /səpɔ́:rt/ **名** 支援, 支持; 援助

receive	support	支援を受ける
win	support	支援を得る
gain	support	
mobilize	support	
provide	support	支援する
give	support	
lend	support	
offer	support	
need	support	支援を必要とする

▷ We've **received** a lot of **support** from the TV and the press. テレビや新聞から多くの支援を受けた
▷ This new organization **provides support** for homeless people. この新組織はホームレスを支援する
▷ The Government should **offer** more **support** to earthquake victims. 政府は地震の犠牲者たちにもっと支援の手を差し伸べるべきだ

full	support	全面的支援

strong	support	強力な支援
popular	support	大衆の支持
public	support	世論の支持
mutual	support	相互支援
emotional	support	精神的支援
financial	support	財政的支援
political	support	政治的支援
technical	support	技術的支援
customer	support	顧客サポート

▷You can be sure of my **full support**. 私は全面的に支援すると思ってくれていいよ
▷There's **strong support** *for* abandoning nuclear power as a source of energy. エネルギー源としての原子力利用をやめることを支持する声が強い
▷He gave her a lot of **emotional support** when she most needed it. 彼女がいちばん支援を必要とするときに彼は精神的に支えてあげた

support	for A	Aへの支援
support	from A	Aからの支援

▷We've managed to get quite a lot of **support for** our charity concert. 慈善コンサートへの多くの支援を何とか得ることができた

support /səpɔ́ːrt/

動 支える；支持する，支援する；養う

fully	support	十分に支える
strongly	support	強く支える
actively	support	積極的に支える
further	support	さらに支える
be well	supported	十分支持される

▷I **strongly support** everything you said in the meeting. 会議でのあなたの発言をすべて強く支持します
▷Our local soccer team is **well supported** by our fans. うちの地元サッカーチームはファンからの支持を十分に受けている

support A	in B	A(人)のBを支援する

▷We all **support** you **in** your aim to improve working conditions. 労働条件を改善するというあなたの目標をみんな支持しています

suppose /səpóuz/

動 思う，考える；仮定する

be commonly	supposed	一般に考えられる
be generally	supposed	

▷It is **commonly supposed** that older people find it harder to learn a new language. 年齢をとるほど新しい言語を学ぶのが難しくなると一般に考えられている

suppose	(that)...	…だと思う；…と仮定する

▷I **suppose** it's too late to do anything about it now. その件はもう手遅れだと思う

suppose A	to be	A(人)を…だと思う

▷Everybody **supposed** him **to** be her husband. みんな彼が彼女の夫だと思った

be reasonable	to suppose	…と思うのはもっともだ

▷If he walked out of the exam room after 5 minutes it's **reasonable to suppose** that he failed! 試験教室から彼が5分で出てきたなら，不合格だと考えるのが道理だ

reason	to suppose (that)...	…と思う理由

▷There's no **reason to suppose** there'll be any problems. 何か問題が生じると考える理由は何もない
PHRASES
I don't suppose (that)... ☺ (丁寧な依頼で)…というのは無理でしょうか ▷I don't suppose you could lend me $50 until tomorrow, could you? あしたまで50ドル貸してくださるのはご無理でしょうね
I suppose not. ☺ そうではないと思います
I suppose so. ☺ そう思います／**I don't suppose so.** ☺ そうは思いません ▷"Dad! Can I borrow your car this evening to go to a party?" "Well.... OK. I suppose so." 「お父さん，パーティーに出かけるので今夜，車を借りてもいいかな」「そうだなあ，まあ別にかまわないよ」
What do you suppose...? ☺ 何が…と思うか(★ who, where, why なども用いる) ▷What do you suppose they're going to do? 彼らは何をするつもりと思いますか

sure /ʃúər/ **形** 確信した；きっと…する

quite	sure	まったく確かな
absolutely	sure	絶対確かな
not entirely	sure	必ずしも確信がない
not really	sure	それほど確信がない
not so	sure	
fairly	sure	かなり確かな
pretty	sure	

▷Are you **quite sure** you've got everything? Tickets, passport, money... 間違いなくすべて持った

| surface |

かい？チケット，パスポート，お金…
▷Are you **absolutely sure** you locked the door before we went out.　出かける前にドアに鍵をかけたのは絶対確かですか
▷I'm **not entirely sure** where the hotel is.　ホテルがどこなのか必ずしも確信がない
▷I'm **pretty sure** that the parcel will arrive tomorrow.　小包はきっとあす着くと思います

| sure | of A | Aを確信して |
| sure | about A | |

▷Are you **sure about** wanting to go to university next year?　来年ほんとに大学に行きたいのかい

| sure | (that)... | きっと…だと思う |
| sure | wh- | …か確信して |

★wh- は what, whether, how, where など

▷I'm **sure** she'll like the birthday present you got her.　あなたが彼女に買った誕生プレゼントを彼女はきっと気に入ると思います
▷I'm not **sure what** to do.　何をしたらよいかわからない
▷I'm not **sure where** I parked the car.　どこに車を止めたかわからない

| sure | to do | きっと…する |

▷Mike is **sure to** be late. He's never on time for anything!　マイクはきっと遅刻するよ．何をするにも時間どおりだったことはないな
▷**Be sure to** let me know if there is anything I can do to help.　私に手伝えることがあったらぜひ知らせてください（★会話では be sure and do も用いる）

| feel | sure (that)... | …を確かだと感じる |
| make | sure (that)... | …を確かめる；…を確実にする |

▷I **feel sure** I've seen him somewhere before.　彼を以前どこかで見かけた確信がある
▷**Make sure** you turn all the lights off before you leave.　出かける前には必ず明かりをすべて消しなさい

| for | sure | 確かに，確実に |

▷I don't know **for sure** if I can take a holiday in July.　7月に休暇がとれるかどうかはっきりとはわからない
◆**That's for sure.** 😊 まったくそのとおりだ　▷"If I don't take my umbrella with me it's certain to rain." "That's for sure!"　「傘を持って行かないと決まって雨が降るんだ」「そうだよね」

PHRASES
Are you sure? 😊 確かですか　▷Are you sure you had your wallet with you when you left the house?　家を出るとき財布を持っていたのは確かですか

I'm not sure (about that). 😊 (それについては)よくわかりません　▷"What time will you be home this evening?" "I'm not sure. I'll call you later."　「今夜は何時に家に帰るの」「わからないな．後で電話するよ」
Well, I'm sure. 😊 おやおや，まあまあ

surface /sə́:rfis/ 名 表面；外観，うわべ

come to	the surface	表面に浮上する
rise to	the surface	
bring A	to the surface	Aを表面に浮上させる
scratch	the surface	表面だけをなぞる

▷The divers stayed deep in the sea and didn't **come to** the **surface** for many hours.　ダイバーたちは海深く潜水したまま，何時間も水面に浮かんでこなかった
▷The 300-year-old sunken ship was carefully **brought to** the **surface**.　300年前の沈没船が慎重に海上に引き上げられた

a flat	surface	平らな表面
a rough	surface	粗い表面
the water	surface	水面
the road	surface	路面

▷It's too hilly here. We need a **flat surface** to pitch the tent on.　ここは起伏がありすぎる．テントを張るための平らな表面が必要だ

beneath	the surface	水面下で；内面では
below	the surface	
under	the surface	
on	the surface	表面に；表面上は

▷The river looks calm and peaceful, but **under** the **surface** all kinds of creatures are living in another world.　川は穏やかで静かに見えるが，水面下ではあらゆる生き物が別世界で生きている
▷Immediately after the plane crash many pieces of wreckage were seen floating **on** the **surface** of the sea.　飛行機の墜落直後，多くの残骸が海面に浮かんでいるのが見られた

surprise /sərpráiz/

名 驚き；驚くべきこと；思いがけない贈り物

express	surprise	驚きを表す
show	surprise	
get	a surprise	驚く
have	a surprise	
hide	one's surprise	驚きを隠す

come as	a surprise	驚きである
come as	no surprise	驚くにあたらない
spring	a surprise	人を驚かす
be in for	a surprise	びっくりする

▷When he heard he'd failed his exams he **showed no surprise**. 自分が試験に落ちたと聞いても彼は驚いたようすを見せなかった
▷News about their wedding **came as no surprise**. 彼らの結婚の知らせは驚くにはあたらなかった

a great	surprise	大きな驚き
a big	surprise	
a real	surprise	まったくの驚き
a complete	surprise	
a pleasant	surprise	うれしい驚き
a nice	surprise	
a lovely	surprise	すてきな驚き

▷What a **nice surprise**! なんてうれしい驚きでしょう

in	surprise	驚いて
with	surprise	
to A's	surprise	A(人)が驚いたことに

▷She looked at him **in surprise**. 彼女は驚いて彼を見た
▷**To** my **surprise**, I passed the entrance exam first time. 驚いたことに一発で入試に受かった

PHRASES
Surprise, surprise! ☺ 驚くなかれ, びっくりだね(★予想どおりのことが起きたときに, ふざけて言う) ▷I walked into the room and, surprise, surprise, everybody sang 'Happy Birthday!' 部屋に入って行くと, 意外と意外, みんなが「ハッピーバースデー」を歌ってくれた

surprised /sərpráizd/ 形 驚いた

seem	surprised	驚いたようすだ
look	surprised	
sound	surprised	

▷Why do you **look surprised**? I said I'd be home early. どうしてびっくりした顔をしているの？早く家に帰るって言ったでしょ

genuinely	surprised	心底驚いた
really	surprised	実に驚いた
a little	surprised	少し驚いた
slightly	surprised	
pleasantly	surprised	うれしい驚きを覚えた
not at all	surprised	少しも驚かない
not in the least	surprised	

▷Last night I met an old friend from junior high school. I was **really surprised** she recognized me. 昨夜中学校時代の古い友人に会ったんだけど, 彼女が私のことを覚えていてくれて本当にびっくりした
▷Anna was **pleasantly surprised** to find that her husband had washed the dishes. 夫が皿を洗ってくれたことに気づいてアンナはうれしい驚きを覚えた

be surprised	to do	…して驚く
be surprised	that…	…に驚く

▷We hadn't met for over twelve years, so she was **surprised to** see me. 12年以上もお互い会っていなかったから, 彼女は私に会って驚いた
▷I'm **surprised that** you didn't receive a wedding invitation. きみに結婚式の招待状が来ないなんて驚きだ

be surprised	at A	Aに驚く
be surprised	by A	

▷He was **surprised at** the number of people who attended the lecture. 彼は講義に出てきた人の数に驚いた

surprising /sərpráiziŋ/

形 驚くべき, びっくりするほどの

hardly	surprising	驚くにあたらない
scarcely	surprising	

▷After walking all that way it's **hardly surprising** that you're tired. ずっと歩きっぱなしだったんだから, きみが疲れていても驚くにあたらない

it is surprising	that…	…は驚きだ
it is surprising	wh-	…かは驚きだ

★wh- は how, what, where など

▷**It** is perhaps not **surprising that** our sales figures have dropped during this period of economic recession. わが社の売り上げが落ちたのはこの景気後退下ではたぶん驚くに値しない
▷It's **surprising how** healthy he is for a man of 92. 92歳の男性にしては彼はいかに健康か驚くべきほどだ

survive /sərváiv/

動 生き残る, 生き延びる；長生きする

barely	survive	かろうじて生き残る
miraculously	survive	奇跡的に生き残る
still	survive	なお生き残る

▷They were lost on the mountain for three days

| suspect |

without food or water and **barely survived**. 彼らは食料も水もなく山で3日間道に迷ったが、かろうじて生き延びた
▷She was attacked by a shark but **miraculously survived**. 彼女はサメに襲われたが、奇跡的に助かった

survive	from A	Aから存続し続ける
survive	into A	Aまで存続し続ける

▷In some parts of the world some ancient traditions and customs still **survive into** the 21st century. 古い伝統や習慣の一部が21世紀までなお残る地域が世界にはいくつかある

suspect /səspékt/

動 疑う、あやしいと思う;《話》思う

strongly	suspect	強く疑う
rather	suspect	かなり疑う

▷His teacher **strongly suspected** him of cheating during the exam. 彼が試験中カンニングしたと先生は強く疑った

suspect	that...	…だと疑う

▷I **suspect that** it was one of our office staff who took the money. お金を取ったのは事務職員の一人だと疑っている

suspect A	of B	A(人)のBを疑う
suspect A	of doing	A(人)が…したと疑う

▷The police **suspect** him **of** be**ing** involved in the bank robbery. 警察は彼が銀行強盗に関わっていると疑っている

swear /swéər/ 動 ののしる、悪態をつく;誓う

swear	loudly	大声でののしる
swear	violently	激しくののしる

▷Tom dropped the hammer on his foot and **swore violently**! トムは自分の足に金づちを落としてしまい、「くそっ」とわめいた

swear	at A	A(人)をののしる
swear	by A	Aにかけて誓う
swear	to A	Aに誓う

▷I couldn't believe it! He actually **swore at** me! 信じられなかった。彼ったら私をののしったの
▷I **swear by** this bible that I'm telling the truth. 真実を語っていると聖書にかけて誓います

▷I **swear to** God that I'll never do it again. 神に誓って2度としません

swear	(that)...	…と誓う
swear	to do	…すると誓う

▷I **swear** I know nothing about it. それについて何も知らないと誓います
▷He **swore to** give up smoking and go on a diet. たばこをやめてダイエットすると彼は誓った

PHRASES
I could have sworn (that)... ☺ 絶対に…だと思っていた ▷I could have sworn I closed all the windows before I went out. 出かける前に窓はすべて閉めたと思っていた
I swear. ☺ 誓います

sweat /swét/ 名 汗;発汗

break out in	a sweat	汗をかき始める
be drenched in	sweat	汗だくになる
wipe	the sweat	汗を拭く

▷Look! You're **drenched in sweat**! You should take a shower. ほら、汗だくだよ。シャワーを浴びなよ
▷He **wiped** the **sweat** from his forehead. 彼は額の汗を拭いた

sweat	runs	汗が流れる
sweat	pours	
sweat	stands out	汗が噴き出す

▷The **sweat** started to **pour** off him as soon as he entered the sauna. サウナに入るとすぐ彼の体から汗がだらだら流れ出した
▷As they tried to push the car uphill the **sweat stood out** on their faces. 坂の上へと車を押そうとした彼らの顔から汗が噴き出した

beads of	sweat	玉の汗

▷It was so humid that **beads of sweat** began to form on his forehead. あまりに蒸し蒸ししたので玉のような汗が額に浮かんできた

in	a (cold) sweat	冷や汗をかいて

▷She had a nightmare and broke out **in** a **cold sweat**. 彼女は悪い夢を見て冷や汗をかいた

PHRASES
No sweat! ☺ 簡単です、お安いご用です

sweat /swét/ 動 汗をかく

sweat	profusely	すごく汗をかく

▷As he stood up to give his first lecture he noticed that he was **sweating profusely**. 初めての講義をするために立ち上がると，彼は自分がひどく汗をかいていることに気づいた

sweat	like a pig	大汗をかく

▷It's so hot and humid in here. I'm **sweating like a pig**! ここはとても蒸し暑くて，汗だくだ

sweet /swíːt/

形 甘い；優しい；かわいらしい

smell	sweet	甘いにおいがする
taste	sweet	甘い味がする

▷The flowers in that vase **smell sweet**. あの花瓶の花から甘いにおいがする

sweet and sour		甘酸っぱい

▷I love this Chinese **sweet and sour** sauce. この甘酸っぱい中華ソースが大好きです

slightly	sweet	やや甘い
so	sweet	とても甘い；とてもかわいい

▷This herb tea has a **slightly sweet** taste. このハーブティーは少し甘い味がする
▷Look at that little kitten. It's **so sweet**! あの子猫を見て. すごくかわいい

swing /swíŋ/

動 揺れる，揺らす；ぐるっと回る

swing	open	パタンと開く
swing	shut	パタンと閉まる

▷She pushed the door and it **swung open**. 彼女がドアを押すとパタンと開いた

swing	wildly	大きく揺れる
swing	from side to side	左右に揺れる
swing	back and forth	前後に揺れる
swing	to and fro	あちこち揺れる

▷It felt really dangerous. The roller coaster was **swinging** wildly **from side to side**! すごく危ないと思った．ジェットコースターは左右に大きく揺れていた

switch /swítʃ/ 名 スイッチ；急な変化

flick	a switch	スイッチを入れる；スイッチを切る
flip	a switch	イッチを切る

turn on	a switch	スイッチを入れる
turn off	a switch	スイッチを切る
press	a switch	スイッチを押す
make	the switch	切り替える

▷He **flicked a switch** and the lights came on. 彼がスイッチを入れると明かりがついた
▷Could you **turn on** the **switch**? スイッチをオンにしていただけますか
▷It's not easy to **make** the **switch** from amateur to professional golfer. アマチュアからプロのゴルファーに転身するのは簡単ではない

switch /swítʃ/

動 変える，変わる，変更する；切り替わる

automatically	switch	自動的に変わる
simply	switch	簡単に変わる
suddenly	switch	突然変わる

▷The car **automatically switches** from petrol to electric every time it stops. その車は停車するたびにガソリンから電気に自動的に切り替わる

switch	between A and B	AとBを切り替える
switch	from A to B	AからBに変える
switch	to A	Aに変える，変わる
switch A	to B	AをBに変える

▷My father really annoys me. He keeps **switching between** one TV channel and another! 父にはまったくいらいらする．テレビのチャンネルを次々と変えてばかりだ
▷I'd like to **switch** my day off **from** Wednesdays **to** Fridays, if possible. 可能なら非番を水曜から金曜に変えたい
▷A long time ago I used a typewriter but now I've **switched to** a computer. ずっと昔はタイプライターを使っていたが，いまはコンピューターに変えた
▷Please **switch** your cellphone **to** silent mode. 携帯電話をサイレントモードに切り替えてください

symbol /símbəl/

名 象徴，表象，シンボル；記号，符号

a potent	symbol	力強い象徴
a powerful	symbol	
a political	symbol	政治的象徴
a religious	symbol	宗教的象徴

▷The sword is a **potent symbol** of power. 剣は権力の力強い象徴だ
▷The cross is the most well-known Christian **religious symbol**. 十字架は最も有名なキリスト教の宗教

| sympathy |

的象徴だ

| a symbol | for A | Aを表す記号 |

▷A red rose or the shape of a heart are popular **symbols for** love.　赤いバラあるいはハート形は愛の一般的な象徴だ

sympathy /símpəθi/

名 同情；思いやり；共鳴

have	sympathy	同情する；共
feel	sympathy	感する
express	sympathy	同情を表す
show	sympathy	同情を示す
extend	one's sympathy	お悔やみを申
offer	one's sympathy	し上げる

▷I **have** a lot of **sympathy** with what she says.　彼女の発言に共感するところが多い
▷I'd like to **extend** my deepest **sympathy** to you.　心からお悔やみ申し上げます

deep	sympathy	深い同情
great	sympathy	
a little	sympathy	少しの同情
public	sympathy	人々の共感

▷You have my **deepest sympathy**.　心からお悔やみ申し上げます
▷My foot really hurts! I think you might show a **little sympathy**!　足がすごく痛いんだ．少しは同情してくれるよね
▷There's a lot of **public sympathy** for the President in this difficult situation.　この困難な状況で多くの人々が大統領へ共感を抱いている

sympathy	for A	A（人）への共感
sympathy	with A	
in	sympathy with A	Aに同調して
in	sympathy	共感して；共振して

▷I feel a lot of **sympathy for** her.　彼女にとても共感している
▷I have no **sympathy with** him at all.　彼には何ら共感できるところがない
▷I'm not really **in sympathy with** his ideas.　彼の考えには必ずしも同調しない
▷Peter nodded **in sympathy**.　ピーターは共感してうなずいた

system /sístəm/

名 システム，制度，体系，系

build	a system	システムを構築する
design	a system	システムを設計する
develop	a system	システムを開発する
have	a system	システムがある
adopt	a system	システムを採用する
introduce	a system	システムを導入する
operate	a system	システムを運用する
run	a system	

▷We're thinking of **developing** a new type of computer **system**.　新しいコンピュータシステムの開発を考えている
▷The new **system** will be **introduced** next month.　来月新しいシステムが導入される
▷Do you know how to **operate** this **system**?　このシステムの運用法がわかりますか

the political	system	政治体制
the economic	system	経済体制
the educational	system	教育制度
the legal	system	法律制度
the security	system	安全システム
the support	system	支援システム
an information	system	情報システム
the social	system	社会制度
an open	system	開かれた制度
the immune	system	免疫系
the circulatory	system	循環系

▷The **political system** in China seems to be gradually changing.　中国の政治体制は徐々に変化しているようだ
▷It's an **open system**. Anybody can use it.　開かれた制度だから，だれでも利用できる

| a system | for A | Aのためのシステム |

▷We need to create a better **system for** keeping track of orders.　注文を把握するよりよいシステムをつくる必要がある

| under | the system | システムのもとで |

▷**Under** the present **system** there's a new election every 4 years.　現在のシステムで4年ごとに新たな選挙がある

T

table /téibl/ 名 テーブル, 食卓；表, 一覧表

sit around	a table	テーブルを囲んで座る
sit (down) at	a table	テーブルにつく
leave	the table	席を立つ
set	the table	食卓の用意をする
《英》lay	the table	
clear	the table	食卓を片づける
reserve	a table	席を予約する
book	a table	
see	table	表を参照する

▷I think we should **sit around** the **table** and discuss things. テーブルを囲んで座り議論するのがいい
▷Dinner's ready! Come and **sit down at** the **table**. 食事が準備できたよ. 食卓について
▷Can you help me **clear** the **table**? テーブルを片づけるのを手伝ってくれるかい
▷I've **reserved a table** at that nice Italian restaurant. あのすてきなイタリアンレストランに席を予約した
▷**See table** below. 下の表を参照せよ

a round	table	丸テーブル
a wooden	table	木のテーブル
a dining	table	食卓
a kitchen	table	台所用テーブル
a dinner	table	ディナーテーブル
a corner	table	コーナーテーブル
a bedside	table	ベッドサイドテーブル
a statistical	table	統計表
a periodic	table	周期表

▷There's a beautiful, old **round table** for sale in the antique shop in town. 町の骨董品店にきれいな古い丸テーブルが売りに出ている
▷It's possible to work out how long you will live to by checking the relevant **statistical tables**. 関連の統計表を調べることで, あなたが何歳くらいまで生きられるか算出できる

on	the table	テーブルの上に
in	Table 3	表3に

▷You left your glasses **on** the **table**. テーブルの上に眼鏡を置き忘れたね
▷The results of the questionnaire are summarized **in Table** 3. アンケート結果は表3にまとめられている

talent /tǽlənt/ 名 才能

have	a talent	才能がある
display	a talent	才能を表す
show	a talent	才能を発揮する
discover	a talent	才能を発見する
develop	a talent	才能を伸ばす
use	a talent	才能を活用する
waste	a talent	才能を浪費する

▷He **has** a real **talent** *for* long-distance running. 彼は長距離走の才能がすごくある
▷She was beginning to **show** a **talent** *for* ballet even at the age of eight. 彼女は8歳にしてバレエの才能を示し始めた
▷Joining the tennis club enabled her to **develop** a **talent** she never knew she had. テニスクラブに入ることで, 彼女はそれまで知らなかった自分の才能を伸ばせた

a considerable	talent	大きな才能
a great	talent	
an exceptional	talent	非凡な才能
a rare	talent	
a hidden	talent	隠れた才能
a special	talent	特別な才能
a natural	talent	天賦の才能
a new	talent	新しい才能
a young	talent	若い才能
an artistic	talent	芸術的才能

▷Cindy has a **great talent** for drawing. シンディには絵を描く才能がとてもある
▷She has a **natural talent** for playing the piano. 彼女にはピアノを弾く天賦の才能がある
▷Air Kei is a **new talent** in the tennis world. エア・ケイはテニス界の新しい才能だ

a talent	for A	Aの才能

▷You don't have a **talent for** anything! Except making people laugh! あなたは何の才能もない. 人を笑わせること以外はね

talk /tɔ́ːk/

名 話；(くだけた)講演；(ふつう talks で)協議, 会談

have	a talk	話をする
hold	talks	会談を行う
have	talks	
give	a talk	講演をする

▷Finally the two countries have stopped fighting and are **holding talks** *with* each other. ようやく両国は戦闘をやめ, 互いに会談を行っている
▷The English Speaking Club has asked me to **give** a **talk** on British culture. 英会話クラブからイギリス文

513

| talk |

化に関する講演を頼まれている

a little	talk	少しの話
a long	talk	長話
small	talk	世間話, 雑談
direct	talks	直接協議
peace	talks	和平協議

▷ Our teacher wants us to give a **little talk** on some aspects of American culture. 先生は私たちにアメリカ文化の諸相について短い発表をしてほしいと思っている
▷ I'm not good at making **small talk** at formal parties. 改まったパーティーで雑談をするのは得意じゃない
▷ In this case I think **direct talk** is better than sending an email. この場合はEメールを送るより直接話し合うほうがいいよ

(a) talk	about A	Aについての話
(a) talk	on A	
(a) talk	with A	Aとの話
talks	on A	Aに関する協議
talks	between A	Aの間の協議
talks	with A	Aとの協議

▷ I had a **talk with** Bob about his future plans last night. 昨夜ボブと彼の将来の計画について話をした
▷ **Talks between** the employers and the unions are not going well. 労使間協議はうまく進んでいない

round of	talks	話し合い

▷ The next **round of talks** takes place next week. 次回の話し合いは来週行われる

talk /tɔ́ːk/ 動 話す, しゃべる

talk	directly	じかに話す
talk	quietly	静かに話す
talk	excitedly	興奮して話す
talk	endlessly	延々と話す
talk	freely	自由に話す
talk	openly	率直に話す
talk	seriously	真剣に話す

▷ When I came into the room she was **talking excitedly** about her wedding plans. 私が部屋に入ると彼女は結婚式の計画について興奮気味に話していた
▷ I think it's better if we **talk openly** about what went wrong. どこがまずかったか率直に話し合えばいいと思う

talk	about A	Aについて話す
talk	to A	A(人)と話す
talk	with A	

▷ Can we **talk about** this later? この件は後で話せるかな
▷ Can I **talk to** you for a moment? ちょっとお話できますか
▷ Nice **talking with** you. お話しできてよかったです

talking	of A	Aといえば

▷ **Talking of** pizza, I'm really hungry! Let's go eat! ピザと言えば, 腹ぺこだ. 食べに出かけよう

tall /tɔ́ːl/ 形 背が高い;高さが…の

five feet	tall	5フィートの高さの
five inches	tall	5インチの高さの

▷ She's five **feet tall**. 彼女の身長は5フィートだ
▷ He's one **meter** 62 **tall** and weighs about 75 kilos. 彼は身長1メートル62センチで体重75キロくらいだ

tall and thin		背が高くやせぎすの
tall and slim		背が高く細い

★ thin は否定的な意味に, slim は肯定的な意味に用いる

▷ Have you met Sarah's husband? He's so **tall and thin**. サラのだんなさんに会ったことがあるかい. とても背が高くやせぎすなんだ

taste /téist/ 名 味;味覚;好み, 趣味;ひと口

have	a taste	味がする;味わう;好む
leave	a taste	後味が残る
get	a taste	好きになる
develop	a taste	
acquire	a taste	
indulge	one's taste	趣味に興じる
suit	A's taste	好みに合う

▷ She said the way their friendship ended **left** a bitter **taste** in her mouth. 彼らの友情が迎えた破局には苦い後味が残ったと彼女は言った
▷ She seems to have **developed** a **taste** *for* eating at expensive restaurants. 彼女は高級レストランで食事するのが好きになったようだ
▷ Last night's concert certainly **suited** my **taste** in music. 昨夜のコンサートはまさに私の音楽の好みにぴったりだった

a bitter	taste	苦い味
a sour	taste	酸っぱい味
a sweet	taste	甘い味
a good	taste	いい味;いい趣味

personal	taste	個人の好み
popular	taste	大衆の好み
an acquired	taste	何度も味わって好きになるもの

▷This chocolate has a very **bitter taste**. このチョコレートはとても苦い味がする

▷Amanda's apartment shows that she has a really **good taste** *in* furnishings. アマンダのアパートを見ると彼女の調度品の趣味がとてもいいのがわかる

▷Some people prefer modern art to classical, and some don't. It's all down to **personal taste**. 古典より現代芸術が好きな人もいれば，そうでない人もいる．すべて個人の好みだ

▷Wine is an **acquired taste**. ワインの味は習い覚えるものだ

a taste	for A	Aへの好み
taste	in A	Aの好み；Aの趣味
a taste	of A	Aの少しの経験

▷She seems to have developed a **taste for** foreign travel. 彼女は海外旅行が好きになったようだ

▷What's your **taste in** music? あなたの音楽の趣味はどんなもの？

▷If you get a part-time job you'll get a **taste of** what it's like to do a full-time job. アルバイトをすればフルタイムの仕事がどんなものか一端を味わえるよ

sense of	taste	味覚
a matter of	taste	趣味の問題

▷If you have a bad cold it can affect your **sense of taste**. ひどいかぜを引くと味覚に影響が出ることがある

in good	taste	趣味のいい
in bad	taste	趣味の悪い
in poor	taste	

▷Tom told some jokes at the wedding, but they were **in** rather **poor taste**. トムは結婚式でジョークを言ったが，かなり趣味が悪かった

tax /tæks/ 名 税金

pay	(a) tax	税金を払う
impose	a tax	税金を課す，課税する
levy	a tax	
put	a tax	
introduce	a tax	税金を導入する
deduct	tax	税金を控除する
raise	taxes	税金を上げる，増税する
increase	taxes	
cut	taxes	税金を下げる，減税する
reduce	taxes	
lower	taxes	

▷I didn't earn enough to **pay** any **tax** last year. 去年は税金を払うほど稼がなかった

▷I don't agree with **putting** a **tax** *on* food. 食品に税金を課すのには反対だ

▷The Government is going to **introduce** a new **tax**. 政府は新しい税金を導入する予定だ

▷The Government is planning to **raise taxes**. 政府は増税を計画している

high	tax	高い税金
low	tax	低い税金
direct	tax	直接税
indirect	tax	間接税
local	tax(es)	地方税
income	tax	所得税
inheritance	tax	相続税
property	tax	固定資産税
consumption	tax	消費税
sales	tax	売上税
value added	tax	付加価値税
corporation	tax	法人税

▷There are usually very **high taxes** on gasoline, tobacco and alcohol. ガソリン，たばこ，アルコールには通常とても高い税がかかる

▷Income tax is a **direct tax** paid to the government, whereas sales tax is an **indirect tax** on goods and services. 所得税は政府に支払う直接税なのに対し，売上税は商品やサービスにかかる間接税である

tax	on A	Aに対する税金
before	tax	税引前の
after	tax	税引後の

▷There are plans to raise the **tax on** alcohol. アルコールに課す税金を上げる計画がある

taxi /tæksi/ 名 タクシー

take	a taxi	タクシーに乗る
call	a taxi	タクシーを呼ぶ
order	a taxi	
get	a taxi	タクシーを拾う
hail	a taxi	タクシーを呼び止める
get into	a taxi	タクシーに乗り込む
get out of	a taxi	タクシーから降りる

▷She **took** a **taxi** to the station. 彼女は駅までタクシーに乗った

▷Can you **call** a **taxi** for me? タクシーを呼んでくれるかい

▷It's getting late. We'd better **get** a **taxi**. 遅くなったのでタクシーを拾ったほうがいい

tea /tíː/ 名 お茶, 紅茶;《英》午後のお茶の時間

have	tea	お茶を飲む
drink	tea	
sip	one's **tea**	お茶をすする
make	tea	お茶を入れる
pour	the tea	お茶を注ぐ

▷ Would you like to **have** some **tea** or coffee? お茶かコーヒーはいかがですか
▷ Would you like me to **make** some **tea**? お茶を入れて差し上げましょうか
▷ Shall I **pour** the **tea**? お茶を注ぎましょうか

strong	tea	濃いお茶
weak	tea	薄いお茶
cold	tea	冷めたお茶
hot	tea	熱いお茶
iced	tea	アイスティー

▷ Mmmm! That looks good! **Hot tea** and toast! うーん, おいしそう。熱い紅茶とトーストだ

| a cup of | tea | 1杯のお茶 |
| a pot of | tea | ポット1杯のお茶 |

▷ Could I have a **cup of tea**? お茶を1杯いただけますか(★2杯のときは two cups of tea)

teach /tíːtʃ/ 動 教える

| teach | effectively | 効果的に教える |
| teach | privately | 個人的に教える |

▷ Mr. Jennings **teaches** very **effectively**. ジェニングズ先生は教えるのがとてもうまい

teach	A B	A(人)にBを教える
teach	B to A	
teach	A about B	A(人)にBについて教える
teach	A (how) to do	A(人)に…する仕方を教える

▷ Professor Aitchison used to **teach** linguistics **to** us at Oxford. エイチソン教授はかつてオックスフォードで私たちに言語学を教えていた
▷ His uncle **taught** him **to** play chess. 叔父さんが彼にチェスのやり方を教えてくれた
▷ Can you **teach** me **how to** play mahjong? 麻雀の仕方を教えてくれるかい

| teach | at A | A(場所)で教える |

▷ His wife **teaches at** Harvard. 彼の奥さんはハーバードで教えている

teacher /tíːtʃər/ 名 先生, 教師

a good	teacher	よい教師
a primary	teacher	小学校教員
a qualified	teacher	資格のある教師
an experienced	teacher	経験豊富な教師
an English	teacher	英語教師

▷ Our school needs to employ two or three more **qualified teachers**. うちの学校はあと2, 3人は資格のある先生を雇う必要がある

| teachers and pupils | 先生と生徒 |
| teachers and students | 先生と学生 |

★ pupils and teachers, students and teachers も用いる

▷ I had to change school last year and get used to new **teachers and pupils**. 昨年転校し, 新しい先生や生徒に慣れる必要があった

teaching /tíːtʃɪŋ/
名 教えること, 教職, 教育

| go into | teaching | 教職に就く |

▷ I'm going to **go into teaching**. 教職に就くつもりだ

| a method of | teaching | 教授法 |
| an approach to | teaching | 教え方 |

▷ She has a really interesting **method of teaching**. 彼女の教授法は実に興味深い
▷ Our principal has a very strict **approach to teaching**. 校長先生は教育に関してとても厳しいやり方をとっている

| teaching and learning | 教育と学習 |
| teaching and research | 教育と研究 |

▷ These days quite a lot of **teaching and learning** takes place over the Internet. 近ごろはインターネットを使っての教育と学習がとても多い

| language | teaching | 語学教育 |

team /tíːm/ 名 チーム;一団

be on	a team	チームの一員である
be in	a team	
play for	a team	

| television |

lead	a team	チームの指揮をとる
make	the team	チームのメンバーに選ばれる

▷Honda **plays for** the national **team**. 本田は国の代表チームの選手だ
▷She practiced really hard and **made** the lacrosse **team**. 彼女は一生懸命に練習してラクロスチームのメンバーに選ばれた

a strong	team	強いチーム
the winning	team	優勝チーム
an international	team	国際チーム
a local	team	地元のチーム
the national	team	国の代表チーム
a project	team	プロジェクトチーム
a research	team	研究チーム
a rescue	team	救助隊

▷The **winning team** was presented with a silver cup. 優勝チームには銀杯が贈られた
▷Are you interested in soccer? The **national team** is doing really well at the moment. サッカーに興味があるかい．ナショナルチームがいまとても好調だね

tear /tíər/ 名 (ふつう tears で)涙

shed	tears	涙を流す
wipe (away)	the tears	涙をぬぐう
fight back	(the) tears	涙をこらえる
hold back	(the) tears	
break down in	tears	泣き崩れる
burst into	tears	わっと泣き出す
move A to	tears	A(人)を泣かせる
reduce A to	tears	
fill with	tears	涙があふれる
end in	tears	泣きを見る

▷He lent her a handkerchief to **wipe away** the **tears**. 彼は涙をぬぐうためのハンカチを彼女に貸してあげた
▷I don't know why, but suddenly she **burst into tears**. なぜかわからないが，彼女は急にわっと泣き出した
▷That movie we saw last night was so sad. It **reduced** me **to tears**. 昨夜見た映画はとても悲しくて，感動で涙が出た
▷If you aren't honest with her, it'll all **end in tears**. 彼女に誠実に接しないと最後には泣きを見るよ

tears	come	涙が出る
a tear	falls	一粒の涙が落ちる
tears	flow	涙が流れる
tears	run down A	涙がAを流れ落ちる
tears	stream down A	

★Aは A's face, A's cheek など

▷Suddenly she felt the **tears coming** to her eyes. 彼女は急に目に涙があふれるのを感じた

floods of	tears	大泣き
tears	of A	Aの涙

★Aは joy, laughter, rage など

▷When he came home he found his wife in **floods of tears**. 家に帰ると妻が大泣きしていた
▷She wept **tears of joy** when her little girl was found safe. 彼女は幼い娘が無事に見つかって喜びの涙をぬぐった

close to	tears	いまにも泣き出しそうで
near to	tears	

▷Angela was **close to tears**. アンジェラはいまにも泣き出しそうだった

in	tears	涙を流して，泣いて
on the verge of	tears	いまにも泣き出しそうで

▷I returned home to find my wife **in tears**. 家に帰ると妻が涙を流していた
▷I think Helen was really upset. She was **on the verge of tears**. ヘレンはとても動揺していたと思う．いまにも泣き出しそうだった

telephone /téləfòun/ 名 電話；電話機

use	the telephone	電話を借りる
answer	the telephone	電話に出る
pick up	the telephone	受話器を取る
put down	the telephone	受話器を置く

▷May I **use** the **telephone**? 電話を借りていいですか
▷Can someone **answer** the **telephone**? だれか電話に出てくれるかい
▷When she **picked up** the **telephone** nobody answered. 彼女は受話器を取ったが，応答がなかった

the telephone	rings	電話が鳴る

▷The **telephone's ringing**! 電話が鳴っているよ

by	telephone	電話で
on	the telephone	

▷I couldn't get any reply **by telephone** so I sent her an email. 電話で返事をもらえなかったので彼女にEメールを送った

television /téləvìʒən/ 名 テレビ

watch	television	テレビを見る

| temper |

turn on	the television	テレビをつける
switch on	the television	
turn off	the television	テレビを消す
switch off	the television	
turn down	the television	テレビの音量を下げる

★× watch a [the] television とはいわない

▷I think I spend too much time **watching television**. どうもテレビを見る時間が長すぎるな
▷Can you **turn** the **television off**? テレビを消してくれるかい(★この語順も用いる)
▷Could you **turn down** the **television**? テレビの音量を下げていただけますか

satellite	television	衛星放送
live	television	テレビの生放送

▷The Olympic Games will be broadcast on **live television**. オリンピックは生放送で放送される

on	(the) television	テレビで

▷There's a really good film **on television** this evening. 今晩テレビでとてもいい映画を放送する ▷What's **on television** tonight? 今晩はどんな番組があるの

temper /témpər/

名 短気, かんしゃく; 気質; 気分, 機嫌

control	one's temper	短気を抑える
keep	one's temper	
lose	one's temper	短気を起こす

▷I tried to **keep** my **temper**, but it was impossible. 短気を抑えようとしたが, だめだった

a bad	temper	すごい短気; 不機嫌
a foul	temper	不機嫌
a good	temper	上機嫌
a fiery	temper	すごい短気
a terrible	temper	
a violent	temper	
a short	temper	短気
a quick	temper	

▷My husband has been in a **foul temper** all morning. 夫は午前中ずっと機嫌が悪い
▷I didn't know Tom had such a **violent temper**. トムがあんなに短気とは知らなかった
▷I have a rather **short temper**. 私はどちらかと言うと短気なほうだ

a fit of	temper	かんしゃく

▷She smashed the vase in a **fit of temper**. 彼女はかんしゃくを起こして花瓶を粉々に割った

in a	temper	かんしゃくを起こして

▷He rushed out of the room **in a temper**. 彼は怒って部屋を飛び出した

PHRASES〉
Temper! Temper! ☺ 落ち着いて

temperature /témpərətʃər/

名 温度, 気温; 体温, 熱

raise	the temperature	温度を上げる
increase	the temperature	
reduce	the temperature	温度を下げる
lower	the temperature	
reach	a temperature	温度に達する
control	the temperature	温度を調節する
measure	the temperature	温度を測る
have	a temperature	熱がある
take	A's temperature	熱を測る

▷Can you **raise** the **temperature**? It's really cold in here. 温度を上げてよ. ここはすごく寒いもの
▷It was so hot yesterday. It **reached** a **temperature** of over 35 degrees. 昨日はとても暑くて, 気温が35度を超えた
▷Do you **have** a **temperature**? You look very feverish. 熱があるの？熱っぽい顔だよ
▷The nurse **took** my **temperature**. 看護師は私の体温を測った

temperature	increases	気温が上がる
temperature	rises	
temperature	drops	気温が下がる
temperature	falls	

▷The **temperature fell** to minus 20 last night. 昨夜は気温が零下20度まで下がった

a high	temperature	高温
a low	temperature	低温
a normal	temperature	常温
maximum	temperature	最高気温
an average	temperature	平均気温
global	temperature	地球の気温
water	temperature	水温
air	temperature	気温
room	temperature	室温
body	temperature	体温

surface	temperature	表面温度
a high	temperature	高熱
a slight	temperature	微熱

▷Chris has got a **high temperature**. I think we should call a doctor. クリスは高熱だから，医者を呼んだほうがいい
▷The **average temperature** is much higher this summer compared with last summer. 今年の夏は平均気温が昨年の夏に比べてずっと高い

a change in	temperature	気温の変化
a drop in	temperature	気温の下降
a rise in	temperature	気温の上昇
an increase in	temperature	

▷When night fell there was a rapid **change in temperature**. 夜のとばりが降りると急激に気温が変化した

temperature and humidity		気温と湿度

▷**Temperature and humidity** are closely related. 気温と湿度は密接に関係している

temptation /temptéiʃən/ 名 誘惑

avoid	the temptation	誘惑を避ける
resist	the temptation	誘惑に耐える
succumb to	the temptation	誘惑に負ける

▷She couldn't **resist** the **temptation** to buy the Gucci shoes! 彼女はグッチの靴を買いたい衝動を抑えられなかった
▷That cake looks delicious! But I'm on a diet. I mustn't **succumb to** the **temptation**! おいしそうなケーキだ．でもダイエット中さ．誘惑に負けちゃいけない

a constant	temptation	絶え間ない誘惑
a great	temptation	強い誘惑
a strong	temptation	
an overwhelming	temptation	抗し難い誘惑

▷I was offered a really good job in California. It was a **great temptation**, but I decided to stay in New York. カリフォルニアで絶好の仕事のオファーがあった．すごく心が動いたけどニューヨークに残ることにした

tendency /téndənsi/ 名 傾向；性癖

have	a tendency	傾向がある
show	a tendency	傾向を示す
reinforce	a tendency	傾向を強める

▷My old car **has** a **tendency** to steer to the right. 私の古い車は右に切れる癖がある
▷Recently he's been **showing** a **tendency** to fall asleep in class. 近ごろ彼は授業中によく居眠りする

a strong	tendency	強い傾向
a growing	tendency	強まる傾向
an increasing	tendency	
a general	tendency	一般的傾向
a natural	tendency	自然な傾向

▷There's an **increasing tendency** for women to marry later in life. 女性の晩婚化が増える傾向がある
▷At the moment, as a **general tendency**, the stock market seems to be moving up. いまのところ全般として株式市場は上向きのようだ

a tendency	for A	Aの傾向
a tendency	toward A	

▷In the present economic climate there is a **tendency for** people to save rather than spend. 現在の経済情勢では人々は消費より貯蓄に傾いている
▷Recently in the Arab World there has been a **tendency toward** democracy. 近ごろアラブ世界には民主化へと向かう傾向がある

a tendency	to do	…する傾向

▷Tony has a **tendency to** overreact to criticism. トニーは批判に過剰反応する傾向がある

tense /téns/ 形 緊張した，緊迫した

feel	tense	緊張する
become	tense	緊迫する
remain	tense	緊迫したままである

▷The atmosphere in the meeting suddenly **became tense**. 会議の雰囲気は急に緊迫した
▷The situation in Afghanistan still **remains tense**. アフガニスタン情勢はなお緊迫している

extremely	tense	きわめて緊迫した

▷She was **extremely tense** during the interview. 彼女は面接の間とても緊張していた

tension /ténʃən/ 名 緊張

ease	the tension	緊張を緩める
reduce	the tension	
release	the tension	緊張を解く
increase	the tension	緊張を高める
heighten	the tension	

▷He **eased** the **tension** *between* the two countries. 彼は両国間の緊張関係を緩和した
▷Recent terrorist attacks have **increased** the **tension** in Afghanistan. 最近のテロ攻撃でアフガニスタンにおける緊張が高まっている

muscular	tension	筋肉の緊張
nervous	tension	神経の緊張
political	tension	政治的緊張
racial	tension	人種間の緊張
social	tension	社会的緊張

▷A good massage helps relieve **muscular tension**. うまくマッサージすると筋肉の緊張がほぐれる
▷**Political tension** always increases near election time. 選挙が近づくと政治的緊張はいつも増す

term /tɔ́:rm/ 名 (専門)用語;期間, 任期,《英》学期;(terms で)条件

use	a term	用語を使う
define	the term	用語を定義する
coin	a term	新語をつくる
accept	the terms	条件を受け入れる

▷How would you **define** the **term** "communication"? 「コミュニケーション」という語をどう定義しますか
▷I think we should **accept** the **terms** of the contract and sign it. 契約条件を受け入れて, 署名したほうがよいと思う

a technical	term	専門用語
a legal	term	法律用語
a medical	term	医学用語
a first	term	1期目
a second	term	2期目
the summer	term	夏学期
the autumn	term	秋学期

▷The President is hoping to win a **second term** of office. 大統領は2期目も政権を握ることを望んでいる
▷The **autumn term** begins in September. 秋学期は9月に始まる

on	good terms	よい間柄で, 親しい
on	friendly terms	間柄で
on	equal terms	対等の立場で
on	speaking terms	話をする間柄で

▷They're no longer boyfriend and girlfriend, but they're still **on friendly terms**. 二人はもう恋人同士ではないが, いまも親しい間柄だ
▷Men and women should be able to apply for a job **on equal terms**. 男女は対等の立場で仕事に応募できるべきだ

in	practical terms	実際的に
in	real terms	実質的に
in	general terms	一般論として
in	broad terms	
in	economic terms	経済面で
in	financial terms	財政面で
in	political terms	政治面で
in	the long term	長期的には
in	the medium term	中期的には
in	the short term	短期的には

▷He was only talking **in general terms**. He didn't mean you specifically. 彼は一般論で言っていただけで, 特にきみのことを指したわけじゃない
▷**In financial terms** the company has serious problems. 財政面でその会社は深刻な問題を抱えている
▷This part-time job is OK for me **in the short term**. このアルバイトは短期的には私にとってよい仕事だ

in	terms of A	Aの観点から
under	the terms of A	Aの条件のもとで

▷Adam Smith explains prices **in terms of** labor inputs. アダム・スミスは価格を労働投入量の観点から説明している
▷**Under the terms of** the agreement we have two weeks to repay the money. 契約条件ではお金を返すまでまだ2週間ある

terms and conditions	契約条件

▷You should check the **terms and conditions** of the contract carefully. 契約書の契約条件をよく確認すべきだ

terrible /térəbl/

形 猛烈な;ひどい;恐ろしい, 怖い

feel	terrible	ひどい気分だ;すまないと思う
look	terrible	ひどいようすだ
sound	terrible	ひどそうだ

▷Are you OK? You **look terrible**! だいじょうぶかい. ひどい顔だけど
▷"Her father was in a car accident. He's in hospital." "Oh, that **sounds terrible**." 「彼女のお父さんは自動車事故で入院中です」「それは大変ですね」

really	terrible	本当にひどい
truly	terrible	
absolutely	terrible	まったくひどい

▷I think the food in that restaurant was **really terri-**

ble. あのレストランの料理は本当にひどいよ
▷We went on holiday last week but the weather was **absolutely terrible**. 先週休暇に出かけたが，まったくひどい天気だった

test /tést/ 图 試験, テスト；検査

take	a test	試験を受ける
do	a test	
sit	a test	
pass	a test	試験に受かる
fail	a test	試験に落ちる
give	a test	試験をする
have	a test	検査を受ける
carry out	a test	検査する
run	a test	
put A to	the test	Aを試す

▷Our teacher says we have to **do a test** tomorrow. 先生が言うにはあしたテストだって
▷I **passed** my **test**! Yeeeeaaahh! 試験に受かったぞ．やったあ
▷I'm sure I'm going to **fail the test**. 私はきっと試験に落ちるだろう
▷Before the interview they **gave** me a personality **test**. 面接の前に性格テストをされた
▷During the interview they really **put** my knowledge of computers **to the test**. 面接で私はコンピュータの知識をかなり試された

an oral	test	口頭試験
a written	test	筆記試験
a driving	test	運転免許試験
a blood	test	血液検査
a DNA	test	DNA検査
an intelligence	test	知能テスト
a personality	test	性格テスト
a psychological	test	心理テスト
a nuclear	test	核実験

▷I have to go to hospital for **a blood test** tomorrow. 血液検査を受けにあした病院に行かなくてはならない
▷Another **nuclear test** will take place next week. 来週また核実験が行われる

a test	for A	Aの検査

▷My dad has to take a **test for** diabetes next week. 父は来週，糖尿病の検査を受けなければならない

on	a test	試験で
《英》in	a test	

▷I think I've done quite well **in the test**. 試験のできはとてもよかったと思う

thank /θǽŋk/ 動 感謝する，礼を言う

warmly	thank	心から感謝する
personally	thank	個人的に感謝する
publicly	thank	公に感謝の意を表す

▷I'd like to **warmly thank** everybody for all your hard work this year. 今年一生懸命に働いてくれた皆さんに心から感謝したいと思います

thank	A for (doing) B	BしてくれてA(人)に礼を言う

▷I want to **thank** you **for** all your help. いろいろ助けてくれてありがとう

PHRASES
I can't thank you enough. 😊 いくら感謝しても足りません
No, thank you. 😊 いいえ結構です
Thank you. 😊 ありがとう；ご清聴ありがとうございました；(助言・援助を断って)ありがとう ▷It was a wonderful meal. Thank you. とてもおいしい食事でした．ごちそうさまでした
Thank you again. 😊 重ねてお礼を言います

thanks /θǽŋks/ 图 感謝

sincere	thanks	心からの感謝
grateful	thanks	厚い感謝
special	thanks	特別な感謝

▷**Sincere thanks** to you all. みなさんに心から感謝します
▷You have my **grateful thanks**. 心から感謝します

express	one's thanks	感謝の意を表す
give	thanks	感謝する
accept	A's thanks	感謝のことばを受け入れる

▷I think we should **give thanks** for the wonderful harvest this year. 今年の豊作に感謝しようと思います
▷Please **accept** my **thanks**. 感謝申し上げます

thanks	for (doing) A	Aしてくれてありがとう

▷Many **thanks for** your letter of January 12th. 1月12日付けの手紙をどうもありがとう

PHRASES
No, thanks. 😊 いいえ結構です ▷"Would you like some more cake?" "No, thanks. I couldn't manage any more." 「もっとケーキはいかが？」「いいえ結構です．もうこれ以上は食べられません」
Thanks again (for A). 😊 改めて(Aを)ありがとう

| theme |

▷ Thanks again for a wonderful evening. 改めてすばらしい夜をありがとうございました
Thanks a lot. 😊 本当にありがとう

theme /θí:m/ 名 主題, テーマ；話題

choose	a theme	主題を選ぶ
explore	a theme	主題を探る
develop	a theme	主題を発展させる
take up	a theme	主題を取り上げる

▷ Today I'd like to **take up** the **theme** of passion in the novel *Wuthering Heights*. きょうは小説『嵐が丘』における情熱のテーマを取り上げたいと思います

the central	theme	中心テーマ
a dominant	theme	メインテーマ
the main	theme	
an underlying	theme	底に流れる主題
the general	theme	全体のテーマ
a common	theme	共通のテーマ
a recurrent	theme	反復される主題
a recurring	theme	

▷ The **main theme** of the lecture was the works of Charles Dickens. その講義のメインテーマはチャールズ・ディケンズの諸作品だった
▷ The **general theme** of the movie is romance. その映画の全体のテーマは恋愛だ
▷ Murder is a **common theme** in many of Shakespeare's plays. 殺人は多くのシェイクスピア劇の共通テーマだ

| a variation | on a theme | 主題の変奏 |

▷ Rachmaninov has written **variations on** a **theme** of Paganini. ラフマニノフはパガニーニの主題の変奏曲を書いた

theory /θí:əri | θíəri/ 名 学説, 理論

construct	a theory	理論を構築する
develop	a theory	理論を展開する
have	a theory	理論がある
prove	a theory	理論を証明する
support	the theory	理論を支持する

▷ Freud was the first person to **develop** a **theory** of personality. フロイトは人格の理論を発展させた最初の人だ
▷ There is much evidence to **support** the **theory** of global warming. 地球温暖化の説を支持する多くの証拠がある

a general	theory	一般理論
economic	theory	経済理論
literary	theory	文学理論
political	theory	政治理論

▷ Albert Einstein is famous for his **general theory** of relativity. アインシュタインは一般相対性理論で有名だ

| a theory | that... | …との説 |
| my theory is | that... | 私が思うに…だ |

▷ "You know Sally's really afraid of dogs?" "Well, **my theory is that** she was bitten when she was a child." 「サリーは本当に犬が怖いのかな？」「私が思うに、子どものころ犬にかまれたんだろう」

| in | theory | 理論的には |
| a theory | about A | Aについての理論, 説 |

▷ Taylor has the quickest time for the 100 meters this year so **in theory** he should win the race. テイラーは100メートル走の今年度記録をもっているので、順当なら彼がレースに勝つはずだ
▷ There are many **theories about** who killed President John F. Kennedy. ジョン・F・ケネディを殺したのはだれかについては諸説ある

| theory and practice | | 理論と実践 |

▷ There's a big difference between **theory and practice**. 理論と実践の間には大きな違いがある

thick /θík/

形 厚い, 厚さ…の；太い, 太さ…の；濃い

| thick | with A | Aでいっぱいの |

▷ The chocolate cake was **thick with** cream on top. そのチョコレートケーキにはクリームがいっぱいかかっていた

5 inches	thick	厚さ5インチ
5 centimeters	thick	厚さ5センチ
5 feet	thick	厚さ5フィート

▷ We need a rope that's at least 10 **centimeters thick**. 少なくとも太さ10センチのロープが必要だ

thin /θín/ 形 薄い；やせた；細い

extremely	thin	非常に薄い；とてもやせた
painfully	thin	ひどくやせた
relatively	thin	比較的薄い；比較的やせた

▷ When he came out of hospital Tom looked **painfully thin**. 退院したときトムはひどくやせて見えた
▷ I like my toast cut **relatively thin**. トーストは薄めに切ったほうが好きです

thing /θíŋ/

名 物；事，問題；(things で)事態，状況

things	change	事態が変わる
things	get better	事態が改善する
things	get worse	事態が悪化する
things	go wrong	
a thing	happens	物事が起こる

▷ Our business is not doing very well at the moment... but **things change**. うちの商売は今のところまくいっていないが，いつまでもこのままではない
▷ **Things** could **get worse**! 事態がさらに悪くなるかもしれないぞ
▷ "I think you were really unlucky to break your leg." "Well, **things happen**."「足を折るとはきみもついていなかったね」「まあ，いろんなことがあるよ」

a good	thing	よいこと
a bad	thing	悪いこと
a strange	thing	奇妙なこと
the amazing	thing	驚くべきこと
the important	thing	重要なこと
the first	thing	最初のこと
the last	thing	いちばんしたくないこと
the real	thing	本物
the whole	thing	全部のこと
the right	thing	正しいこと

▷ It's a **good thing** your friend was there to help you! 友人がそこにいて助けてくれたのはよかったね
▷ The **amazing thing** is that she said yes! 驚いたのは彼女がはいと言ったことだ
▷ The **important thing** is not to panic. 重要なことはパニックに陥らないことです
▷ The **first thing** I do every morning is take a shower. 毎朝まずするのはシャワーを浴びることだ
▷ They aren't imitation diamonds. This necklace is the **real thing**! 模造ダイヤではありません．このネックレスは本物です

the kind of	thing	そのようなこと，そのような
the sort of	thing	

▷ I think I'll buy this sweater. It's just the **kind of thing** I was looking for! このセーターを買おう，ちょうどこんなのを探していた

| as | things stand | 現状では |

▷ **As things stand**, we have a good chance of getting to the final. 現状では決勝に進出するチャンスはかなりある

〈PHRASES〉

How are things (with you)? / How are things going? 😊 いかがお過ごしですか ▷ "Ivan, how are things?" "Fine, thanks. And you?"「アイバン，いかがお過ごしですか」「元気ですよ．あなたは？」
That's the thing! 😊 まさにそこが問題なんだ ▷ "So why should you have to take the blame?" "Exactly! That's the thing! It wasn't my fault!"「で，なぜきみが責任をとらなくちゃいけないの」「そのとおり．まさにそこが問題なんだ．ぼくのせいじゃないのにさ」
There is no such thing as A. 😊 A のようなものはない ▷ My boss always says there's no such thing as "impossible"! 上司のいつもの口癖は「不可能なことはない」だ

think /θíŋk/ 動 思う，考える

think	carefully	じっくり考える
think	clearly	はっきり考える
think	seriously	真剣に考える
think	well	よく考える
think	again	考え直す
think	twice	熟考する
just	think	ちょっと考える

▷ **Think carefully** before you make a final decision. 最終決定をする前にじっくり考えなさい
▷ **Think well** before you do something you'll regret! 後になって後悔しないようによく考えなさい
▷ You should **think twice** before you drop out of university. 大学をやめる前によく考えたほうがいい
▷ **Just think!** Tom and Ellie are lying on the beach now in Hawaii having a great time! 考えてもみてよ．トムとエリーはいまごろハワイで浜辺に横になってすばらしい時を過ごしているんだよ

think	about A	A について考える
think	of A	A のことを考える

▷ What are you **thinking about**? 何を考えているの
▷ I'm **thinking about** getting a part-time job. アルバイトをやろうかと考えている
▷ I can't **think of** any reason why she's so late. 彼女がこんなに遅くなる理由が思い当たらない

| think | (that)... | …であると思う |

▷ I **think** it's time to leave. もうおいとまする時間です
▷ I don't **think** we're going to arrive in time. 間に合うとは思えないな

| it is thought | that... | …だと考えられている |

| thirsty |

▷ **It is thought that** exercising too hard can sometimes lead to a heart attack. 過度な運動は心臓発作を起こすことがあると考えられている

I think	so	そう思います

▷ "Is Nigel English?" "Yes, **I think so**."「ナイジェルはイギリス人ですか」「そう思うよ」

wh-	do you think...?	…かと思うか

★ wh- は what, how, why, where, when など

▷ **What do you think**? Does this dress look OK on me? どう思う？この服，私に似合ってるかな ▷ **How do you think** we should go? By bus or by train? どう行ったらいいかな？バスそれとも列車かな ▷ **When do you think** Dave will be back? デイブはいつ帰って来ると思いますか

I can't	think wh-	…かがわからない

★ wh- は why, who, where, what など

▷ **I can't think why** she got so angry. 彼女がなぜあんなに怒ったのかわからない

PHRASES

I wasn't thinking. ☺(謝罪で用いて)うっかりしていました ▷ Oh, sorry. Is this your umbrella? **I wasn't thinking.** あ，ごめんなさい．あなたの傘でしたか．うっかりしていました

Let me think (about A)! ☺(Aについて)考えさせてください

That's what you think ☺ それはあなたが考えていることでしょ(★ you のほか they なども用いる) ▷ "There's no way you'll complete a 50 kilometer walk!" "**That's what you think**!"「50キロも歩き通せるわけがないよ」「それはきみの勝手な思い込みさ」

What was A thinking of? ☺(驚きを表して)A(人)は何を考えていたんだ ▷ Tom kept interrupting during the meeting. I don't know **what he was thinking of**! トムったら会議中ずっとじゃまばかりして．いったい何を考えていたんだか

Who do you think you are? ☺ いったい自分を何様だと思っているんだ

Who would have thought...? ☺(驚きを表して)だれが…だと想像できただろう ▷ **Who would have thought** Ella and Steve would get married? エラとスティーブが結婚するなんてだれに想像できただろう

You know what I think? ☺(相手の注意を引いて)思うんだけど，何を考えてるかわかると思うけど ▷ **You know what I think**? Harry and Kate are the perfect couple! ねえ，思うんだけど，ハリーとケイトはお似合いのカップルね

thirsty /θɔ́ːrsti/ 形 のどが渇いた

feel	thirsty	のどが渇いている
get	thirsty	のどが渇く

▷ **I feel thirsty**. のどが渇いた

really	thirsty	すごくのどが渇いた
terribly	thirsty	

▷ I'm **really thirsty**. すごくのどが渇いた

thought /θɔ́ːt/

名 考え；意見；思考；思想；意図

have	a thought	考えがある
collect	one's thoughts	考えをまとめる
express	one's thoughts	考えを表明する
share	A's thoughts	考えを共有する
read	A's thoughts	心を読む
push	the thought away	考えを振り払う
give	thought	考える；思いやる
spare	a thought	

▷ I need some time to **collect** my **thoughts**. 私には考えをまとめる時間が必要だ

▷ It's almost as if she was able to **read** my **thoughts**. 彼女はまるで私の心を読めるみたいだ

▷ **Give** some **thought** to the people around you when you answer your cellphone in public. 人前で携帯電話に出るときは周りの人のことを考えなさい

▷ We should **spare** a **thought** for the victims of the earthquake. 地震の犠牲者たちに思いを馳せるべきだ

thought	comes to A	考えがAに浮かぶ
thought	occurs to A	
thought	strikes A	

▷ The **thought comes to** me that Peter didn't get the message to meet us here. ここで待ち合わせするとの伝言をピーターは受け取っていないのではないかと思う

be lost in	thought	考え込む
be deep in	thought	

▷ He sat at his desk **lost in thought**. 彼は机の前に座って考え込んでいた

a happy	thought	うまい考え，妙案
the first	thought	最初の考え
second	thoughts	再考
careful	thought	熟慮，真剣に考えること
a serious	thought	

▷ I was going to marry Ken, but then I had **second thoughts**. ケンと結婚するつもりだったが，考え直した

▷ You need to give some **serious thought** to what you're going to do after you graduate from university. 大学卒業後は何をするか真剣に考える必要がある

a thought	**on** A	Aについての考え
a thought	**about** A	Aについての考え
the thought	**of** A	Aの考え

▷ I felt sick at the **thought of** eating raw horsemeat! 生の馬肉を食べると考えると気分が悪くなった

the thought	**that...**	…という考え

▷ The **thought that** she heard everything we were saying is very embarrassing! 私たちの話を彼女がすべて聞いていたと考えるととても気まずい

thoughts and feelings	考えや気持ち

▷ He wrote all his **thoughts and feelings** down in a notebook. 彼は自分の考えや気持ちをすべてノートに書いた

a line of	**thought**	思考の道筋

threat /θrét/ 名 脅迫, 脅し；脅威

make	a threat	脅す
issue	a threat	
carry out	one's threat	脅しを実行に移す
pose	a threat	脅威となる
represent	a threat	
face	a threat	脅威にさらされる

▷ He **made** a lot of **threats**, but he didn't **carry them out**. 彼はたくさん脅しをかけてきたが、実行には移さなかった

▷ Many diseases that **posed** a **threat** 100 years ago no longer do so today. 100年前には脅威であった多くの病気は今日ではもはや脅威ではなくなっている

an empty	threat	ただの脅し
an idle	threat	
death	threats	殺すという脅し
a bomb	threat	爆破するとの脅し
a great	threat	大きな脅威
a big	threat	
a major	threat	
a real	threat	現実の脅威
a serious	threat	深刻な脅威
a potential	threat	潜在的脅威

▷ The police say that some leading politicians have received **death threats**. 警察の発表によると、殺すと脅された有力政治家もいる

▷ Earthquakes pose a **greater threat** if they cause a tsunami. 地震は津波を引き起こすとさらなる脅威となる

▷ Is global warming a **serious threat**? 地球温暖化は深刻な脅威なのか

a threat	**against** A	Aに対する脅威
a threat	**from** A	Aからの脅威
a threat	**to** A	Aへの脅威

▷ The **threat from** the sea is particularly bad along this part of the coast. この沿岸地域では海からの脅威が特に高い

under	**threat**	脅威にさらされて

▷ Over one fifth of the world's plants may be **under threat** of extinction. 世界の植物の5分の1以上が絶滅の脅威にさらされているかもしれない

threaten /θrétn/

動 脅す, 脅かす；脅威となる

constantly	threaten	絶えず脅す
seriously	threaten	ひどく脅かす

▷ All day it's been **constantly threatening** to rain. 一日中いつ雨が降ってもおかしくない雲行きだ

▷ Her injury **seriously threatens** her chances of winning the race. けがのせいで彼女がレースに勝つチャンスがひどく脅かされている

threaten	A **with** B	A(人)をBで脅す

▷ He came up behind her and **threatened** her **with** a knife. 彼は彼女の背後に歩み寄ってナイフで脅した

threaten	**to do**	…すると脅す；…する脅威がある

▷ Mummy! That big boy **threatened to** hit me if I didn't give him my sweets. ママ、お菓子をくれないと殴るぞってあのお兄ちゃんが脅したんだ

throat /θróut/ 名 のど

clear	one's throat	せき払いする

▷ He **cleared** his **throat** nervously. 彼は緊張してせき払いした

a sore	throat	のどの痛み

▷ I have a **sore throat**. のどが痛い

ticket /tíkit/

名 切符,入場券,券,チケット;反則切符

get	a ticket	切符を手に入れる
obtain	a ticket	
book	a ticket	切符を予約する
reserve	a ticket	
issue	a ticket	反則切符を切る
receive	a ticket	反則切符を切られる

▷It was impossible to **obtain** a **ticket**. 切符を手に入れることはできなかった
▷Would you like me to **book** a **ticket** for the concert? コンサートのチケットを予約して差し上げましょうか

a one-way	ticket	片道切符
《英》a single	ticket	
a round-trip	ticket	往復切符
《英》a return	ticket	
a season	ticket	通しの切符;定期券
a first-class	ticket	ファーストクラスの切符
a complimentary	ticket	招待券,無料券
a free	ticket	
an advance	ticket	前売り券
an airline	ticket	航空券
a train	ticket	列車の切符
a lottery	ticket	宝くじ券
a parking	ticket	駐車違反の切符
a speeding	ticket	スピード違反の切符

▷It's cheaper if you get a **return ticket**. 往復切符を買えば割安だ
▷I think we should try to get some **advance tickets**. 前売り券を手に入れるようにしたほうがいいと思う
▷Where's my **lottery ticket**? I think I've won a fortune! 私の宝くじ券はどこかな。大金を当てたと思うんだけど

a ticket	for A	Aのチケット;A行き
a ticket	to A	の切符

▷**Tickets for** the concert are $20. コンサートのチケットは20ドルだ
▷How much is **a ticket to** London? ロンドン行きの切符はいくらですか

tie /tái/

名 ネクタイ;(ふつう ties で)つながり,絆;同点

wear	a tie	ネクタイをしている
put on	a tie	ネクタイをする
loosen	one's tie	ネクタイを緩める
straighten	one's tie	ネクタイを直す
cut	one's ties	つながりを絶つ
end in	a tie	同点に終わる
result in	a tie	

▷Do you think I should **put on** a **tie** for the dinner party this evening? 今夜のディナーパーティーはネクタイをして出たほうがいいかな
▷Let me **straighten** your **tie** for you! ネクタイをまっすぐに直してあげる
▷Peter's family have completely **cut** their **ties** *with* him. ピーターの家族は完全に彼とのつながりを絶った

close	ties	密接なつながり
strong	ties	強いつながり
blood	ties	血のつながり
family	ties	家族のつながり
personal	ties	個人的つながり
economic	ties	経済的つながり
cultural	ties	文化的つながり
diplomatic	ties	外交上のつながり

▷He has **strong ties** with many influential politicians. 彼は多くの有力政治家と強いつながりがある
▷It's important to establish **personal ties** *with* our customers. 客と個人的な関係を築くのが大切だ
▷The two countries are hoping to strengthen their **economic ties**. 両国は経済関係の強化を望んでいる

the tie	between A	Aの間のつながり
ties	with A	Aとのつながり
ties	to A	

▷They are a very close family. The **ties between** them are very strong. よくまとまった家族で,互いのつながりがとても強い
▷Do you have **ties to** any political party? あなたはどこかの政党と関係がありますか

a jacket and tie	上着とネクタイ
a suit and tie	スーツとネクタイ

▷You'd better put on a **suit and tie**. スーツを着てネクタイをしたほうがいいですよ

tie /tái/ 動 結ぶ,結びつける;縛る;束縛する

tie	firmly	しっかり結ぶ
tie	tightly	
tie	together	まとめて縛る,束ねる
tie	up	縛りつける
neatly	tie	きちんと結ぶ
closely	tied	密接に関係した
inextricably	tied	密接不可分に関係した

▷Make sure you **tie** your shoelaces **firmly**. 靴ひもをしっかり結びなさい
▷He **tied** the boat **up** to the riverbank and jumped out. 彼はボートを土手にゆわえてから、水に飛び込んだ
▷His Christmas present was beautifully wrapped and **neatly tied** with a bow. 彼へのクリスマスプレゼントはきれいに包まれ、蝶結びできちんと結んであった
▷Do you believe that poverty is **inextricably tied to** crime? 貧困は犯罪と分かちがたく関係していると思いますか

tie	A **to** B	AをBに縛る

▷He **tied** the dog **to** a lamppost and went into the shop. 彼は犬を街灯柱につないで店に入って行った ▷I don't want to get married. I don't want to be **tied to** one person for the rest of my life! 結婚はしたくない。ひとりの人にこれからの人生を縛られたくないからね

tight /táit/ 形 きつい；固い；厳しい

feel	tight	きつく感じる
get	tight	きつくなる
hold	tight	しっかりつかまる

▷These new shoes **feel** a bit **tight**. 新しい靴なので少しきつい
▷These roller coasters go so fast. **Hold tight**! ジェットコースターはとても速いからしっかりつかまって

extremely	tight	とてもきつい；厳重な
fairly	tight	かなりきつい；厳重な
pretty	tight	

▷The cork in this wine bottle is **extremely tight**. I can't get it out! このワイン瓶のコルクはとてもきつくて抜けないよ

time /táim/ 名 時間；時刻；(しばしば times で)時代；時機；回数；倍

have	time	時間がある
need	time	時間を必要とする
take	time	時間がかかる
spend	time	時間を費やす
kill	time	時間をつぶす
pass	time	
devote	time	時間を割く
save	time	時間を節約する
waste	time	時間をむだにする
lose	time	時間をむだに費やす

▷Recently Kelley hasn't **had** much **time** to go out with her friends. 最近ケリーは友人たちと出かける時間があまりない
▷It'll **take time** before Kate gets out of hospital. ケイトは退院まで時間がかかるだろう
▷My plane's departure was delayed for 2 hours so I read a book to **kill time**. 飛行機の出発が2時間遅れたので時間つぶしに本を読んだ
▷Anna **devotes** a lot of **time** to her studies. アンナは勉強に多くの時間を割いている
▷It would **save time** if we took a taxi. タクシーに乗れば時間の節約になるだろう
▷We mustn't **waste** any more **time**. これ以上時間をむだにしてはいけない
▷Quick! There's no **time** to **lose**! 急いで。むだにする時間はないぞ
▷When he realized he'd won the lottery he **lost no time** in claiming his money! 宝くじに当たったことを知って、彼はすぐ賞金をもらいに行った

time	goes by	時間が過ぎ去る，時間
time	passes	がたつ

▷**Time goes by** much quicker than you think. 考えているより時間はずっと早く過ぎる
▷You'll feel better as **time goes by**. 時間がたつにつれて気分がよくなりますよ

a long	time	長時間
a short	time	短時間
a little	time	少しの時間
a limited	time	限られた時間
free	time	自由時間
spare	time	余暇，空き時間
a bad	time	悪い時代
a difficult	time	困難な時代
a hard	time	つらい時代
a tough	time	
a rough	time	
recent	times	最近，近年
an appropriate	time	適切な時機
the right	time	
a bad	time	悪い時機
the wrong	time	ふさわしくない時機
the first	time	初めて
the second	time	2回目
each	time	するたびに
every	time	
a good	time	楽しい時間
a great	time	すてきな時間
a wonderful	time	すばらしい時間
a marvelous	time	
local	time	現地時間
daylight saving	time	夏時間

| time |

▷I haven't seen you for a **long time**! 久しぶりだね
▷I can only stay for a **short time**. ほんの少ししかいられないんだ
▷What do you like to do in your **spare time**? 余暇には何をしたいですか
▷He had a **hard time** trying to persuade her to marry him! 彼女に結婚を承諾してもらうのに彼はとても苦労した
▷She had a **tough time** at school. She was bullied a lot. 彼女は学校でつらい目にあった．いじめをずいぶん受けた
▷In **recent times** the Internet has greatly changed society. 近年インターネットは大きく社会を変えた
▷You came at just the **right time**! ちょうどいいところに来たね
▷I went to New York for the **first time**. 初めてニューヨークに行った ▷For the **first time** in months I feel really healthy. こんなに体調がいいのは何か月ぶりかだ
▷It's the **second time** that I've left my umbrella on the train in a week! 1週間で列車に傘を置き忘れたのは2回目だ
▷I love him! My heart beats faster **every time** I see him! 彼が好き．会うたびに心臓の鼓動が高まるの
▷Have a **good time**! 楽しんでね
▷I had a **great time** with her. 彼女と過ごした時間はとても楽しかった
▷Thanks for inviting us out today. We had a **marvelous time**. 外食に誘ってくれてありがとう．楽しい時間を過ごせました
▷The plane arrives at 16:00 hours **local time**. 飛行機は現地時間の16時に到着します

a length of	time	時間の長さ
a period of	time	一定期間
a waste of	time	時間のむだ
a lot of	time	多くの時間
plenty of	time	

▷After a **period of time** I got used to living in the USA. しばらくすると米国での生活に慣れた
▷It took me a **lot of time** to write this report. このレポートを書くのにかなり時間がかかった

time and place	時間と場所
time and space	時間と空間
time and money	時間とお金
time and effort	時間と労力

★place and time, space and time も用いる

▷We still have not solved many mysteries of **time and space**. 時間と空間を巡る多くの謎はまだ解明されていない
▷Ellie and Joe spent a lot of **time and money** (on) redecorating their house. エリーとジョーは家の改装に多くの時間とお金を費やした
▷What a waste of **time and effort**! なんという時間と労力のむだだ

it's time	for A	Aの時間だ
it's time	to do	…する時間だ
it's time	A did B	AがBしていなければならないころだ

▷**It's time for** a cup of tea. お茶の時間だ
▷Come on! **It's time to** get up! さあ起きる時間だ
▷**It's time** you took that book back to the library. It's three days overdue! そろそろその本を図書館に返さなきゃ．返却期限を3日過ぎているよ

ahead of	time	定刻より早く
behind	time	定刻より遅れて
behind	the times	時代に遅れて
by	the time	その時までに
on	time	時間どおりに
out of	time	調子外れの
with	time	時間が経つにつれ

▷The plane landed **ahead of time**. 飛行機は定刻より早く着陸した
▷The plane's running **behind time** because of engine trouble. 飛行機はエンジントラブルのため定刻より遅れて飛行しています
▷**By the time** Rob gets here the party will be over. ロブがここに着くまでにパーティーは終わっているだろう
▷Here comes the bus. Right **on time**. バスが来たよ．時間ぴったりだ
▷Ben's terrible at karaoke! He always sings **out of time**! ベンのカラオケはひどい．いつも調子外れだ
▷Things will improve **with time**. 時間が経つにつれ事態は好転するだろう

at	a time	一度に，同時に
at	one time	かつて；一度に
at	times	ときどき
at	all times	いつも，常時
at	the same time	同時に
at	the present time	いまのところ，現在は
at	this time	
at	the time	そのころ，当時
at	that time	

▷I can only do one thing **at a time**! 私は一度に一つのことしかできない
▷**At one time** I could run the 100 meters in 12 seconds. Now it would take me 30 seconds! 以前なら100メートルを12秒で走れたが，いまは30秒かかるだろう
▷**At times** I wonder why I became a teacher! ときどき自分はなぜ教師になったのかと思う
▷When you're driving you need to concentrate on the road **at all times**. 車の運転中は常に道路に集中

していなければいけません

▷**At** the **present time** we have no information about the missing ship. いまのところ行方不明の船についての情報はない
▷**At this time** it's 3 o'clock in the morning in Australia. 現在オーストラリアは朝3時です
▷**At** the **time** I didn't know it, but actually my father was very ill. その時は知らなかったが、実は父はとても体調が悪かった

for	a time	しばらくの間
for	some time	かなり長い間
for	the time being	当分は，差し当たって

▷He stared silently out of the window **for some time**. かなり長いこと彼はじっと窓の外を眺めていた
▷That's all I wanted to say **for** the **time being**. 差し当たり言いたかったのはこれくらいです

in	time	間に合って；やがて
in	no time (at all)	すぐに，瞬時に
in	the course of time	そのうちに，やがて

▷We couldn't get to the airport **in time** to catch our plane. 飛行機に間に合う時間に空港に着けなかった
▷I finished the job **in no time at all**. あっという間に仕事を終えた
▷**In** the **course of time** the sea wore away large areas of coastline. やがて海は海岸線の大部分を浸食してしまった

PHRASES
Have you got the time? ☺ いま何時ですか ▷"Excuse me, have you got the time?" "Sure. It's five past six."「すみません、いま何時ですか」「6時5分です」
It's been a long time. ☺ 久しぶりです
Until next time. / Till next time. ☺ それではまた次回まで(★テレビ番組の終わりに用いる)

tiny /táini/ 形 とても小さい

extremely	tiny	ものすごく小さい
comparatively	tiny	比較的小さい

▷Computers these days are **comparatively tiny** when you look at the huge size of the early ones. 最近のコンピュータは初期のとても大きなサイズと比べると比較的小さい

tiny	little	とても小さな

★ little tiny ともいう

▷Can I have just a **tiny little** piece of that chocolate? そのチョコレートをちょっとだけもらっていいかな

tip /típ/ 名 先，先端；チップ；秘訣，助言

give (A)	a tip	(A)にチップを出す
leave (A)	a tip	(A)にチップを置く
get	a tip	チップをもらう
give	a tip	コツを教える

▷In the USA if you're in a taxi you should always **give** a **tip**. 米国でタクシーに乗ったら必ずチップをあげなさい
▷Don't forget to **leave** the waiter a **tip**. ウェーターにチップを置くのを忘れないように
▷I hear you're an expert skier. Can you **give** me a few **tips**? あなたはスキーの専門家だそうですね。少し助言をいただけますか

the southern	tip	南端
the northern	tip	北端
a good	tip	よい助言
a useful	tip	役に立つ助言
a hot	tip	確かな情報

▷The Atlantic and Pacific Oceans meet at the **southern tip** of South America. 大西洋と太平洋は南アメリカの南端で出会う
▷There are some **useful tips** in this magazine about how to lose weight. 減量の方法についてこの雑誌には有益な情報が載っている

tips	on A	Aについての秘訣，コツ，
tips	for A	助言

▷There are some good **tips** in this book **on** how to start your own business. この本にはビジネスをどうスタートさせるかに関していくつかよい助言が載っている

tired /táiərd/ 形 疲れた；飽きた，うんざりした

look	tired	疲れたようすだ
feel	tired	疲れを感じる
get	tired	疲れる

▷You **look tired**. Are you all right? 疲れているようだけど、だいじょうぶかい
▷She said she **felt tired** and went to bed. 疲れたので寝ると彼女は言った
▷I **got** very **tired** after six miles of walking. 6マイル歩いてとても疲れた

extremely	tired	非常に疲れた
really	tired	本当に疲れた
dead	tired	くたくたに疲れた
desperately	tired	ひどく疲れた

a bit	tired	少し疲れた
a little	tired	
rather	tired	かなり疲れた

★程度の副詞と連結する

▷I'm **really tired**. I think I'll go to bed. とても疲れたから寝るよ
▷I'm **dead tired**. I want to go home. くたくただ。家に帰りたい(★dead tired はくだけた言い方)
▷Are you OK? You look **rather tired**. だいじょうぶ？かなり疲れているようだけど

tired	from A	Aで疲れて
tired	of (doing) A	A(するの)に疲れて

▷You are probably very **tired from** the journey. 旅行でとてもお疲れでしょう
▷I'm **tired of** doing all the housework. あれやこれや家事をするのにうんざりしている ▷Paul never gets **tired of** playing video games. ポールは飽きずにテレビゲームをやっている
♦**sick and tired of** (doing) A A(するの)にほとほとうんざりして ▷I'm sick and tired of telling you to put away all your toys. おもちゃをみんな片づけなさいといやになるほど言ってるでしょ

tired and thirsty	疲れてのどが渇いた

▷After the long hike everybody was **tired and thirsty**. 長いハイキングの後みんな疲れてのどが渇いていた

title /táitl/

名 (競技の)タイトル；書名；称号，肩書き

win	the title	タイトルを獲得する
take	the title	
defend	one's title	タイトルを防衛する
retain	the title	タイトルを守る
give	the title	書名をつける；称号を与える
have	the title	称号をもっている

▷Real Madrid **won the** Spanish League **title** again this year. レアル・マドリードは今年もまたスペインリーグで優勝した
▷I think **defending the title** will be more difficult than winning it. タイトル防衛は獲得より難しいと思う

the world	title	世界タイトル

▷If he wins this match it will be his third **world title**. 彼がこの試合に勝てば3度目の世界タイトルになる

today /tədéi/ 名 きょう，本日；最近，現代

a week	from today	来週のきょう
a month	from today	来月のきょう
a year	from today	来年のきょう

▷It's Helen's birthday **a week from today**. 来週のきょうはヘレンの誕生日だ

PHRASES

That's all for today. ☺(授業の終わりに)きょうはここまで ▷That's all for today. You can all go home now. きょうはここまでにします。みんな帰ってよろしい
Today is Wednesday. ☺ きょうは水曜日です(★"What day is it today?" と聞かれたときは Today is Wednesday. ではなく It's Wednesday. と答える)

toilet /tɔ́ilit/

名 トイレ(★米国ではふつう bathroom を用いる)

go to	the toilet	トイレに行く
need	the toilet	
use	the toilet	トイレを借りる
clog	the toilet	トイレを詰まらせる
flush	a toilet	トイレの水を流す

▷Do you **need** the **toilet**? トイレに行かなくていい？
▷Could I **use** the **toilet**? トイレをお借りしていいですか

tomorrow /təmɔ́:rou | -mɔ́r-/

名 あした，あす；(近い)将来，未来

tomorrow	morning	あすの朝
tomorrow	afternoon	あすの午後
tomorrow	evening	あすの夕方
tomorrow	night	あすの夜

▷See you **tomorrow morning**. あすの朝会おう

the day after tomorrow	明後日

▷We're leaving the **day after tomorrow**. あさって出発します

PHRASES

Tomorrow is Sunday. ☺ あすは日曜日だ

tone /tóun/

名 口調，音色；調子；雰囲気；色調

change	the tone	口調を変える
set	the tone	雰囲気を決める
lower	the tone	雰囲気を悪くする

raise	the tone	雰囲気を盛り上げる

▷The President looked very relaxed and that set the whole **tone** *for* the TV interview. 大統領はとてもリラックスしているように見え、それでテレビインタビューの全体の雰囲気が定まった

a deep	tone	低い声の調子
a low	tone	
a flat	tone	淡々とした口調
a soft	tone	柔らかい口調
the general	tone	全体の雰囲気
a light	tone	明るい色調
a dark	tone	暗い色調

▷He answered all my questions in a **flat tone** of voice. 彼は私の質問すべてに淡々とした口調で答えた
▷She spoke in **a very soft tone**. 彼女は穏やかな口調で話した
▷The **general tone** of the meeting was very positive. 会議の全体の雰囲気は前向きだった

tongue /tʌ́ŋ/ 名 舌；国語；言語；話し方

stick	one's tongue out	舌を出す
click	one's tongue	舌打ちする
bite	one's tongue	口をつぐむ
hold	one's tongue	口をつぐんでいる

▷Someone should tell that child that it's rude to **stick** your **tongue out**! 舌を出すのは失礼だとだれかがその子どもに言ったほうがいい
▷He **clicked** his **tongue** in annoyance. 彼はいらだって舌打ちした
▷It's better to **hold** your **tongue** and say nothing. 口をつぐんで何も言わないほうがいいよ

a forked	tongue	二枚舌
a sharp	tongue	毒舌
one's mother	tongue	母語
one's native	tongue	
a foreign	tongue	外国語

▷Be careful when you talk to Jill. She has a very **sharp tongue**! ジルと話すときは気をつけて、すごく毒舌だから
▷She speaks several languages, but her **mother tongue** is French. 彼女は数か国語を話すが母語はフランス語だ

tooth /túːθ/ 名 歯（★複数形は teeth）

pull out	a tooth	歯を抜く
lose	a tooth	歯が抜ける
fill	a tooth	歯に詰め物をする
cut	a tooth	歯が生え始める
brush	one's teeth	歯を磨く
clean	one's teeth	
bare	one's teeth	（犬などが）歯をむき出す
show	one's teeth	
grit	one's teeth	歯を食いしばる
clench	one's teeth	
grind	one's teeth	歯ぎしりする
gnash	one's teeth	

▷Babies usually **cut** their **teeth** at around 3 or 4 months. 赤ちゃんはふつう3，4か月で歯が生え始める
▷Have you **brushed** your **teeth**? 歯を磨いたかい
▷The dog growled, **showing** it's sharp yellow **teeth**. その犬は鋭い黄色い歯をむき出して、うなり声をあげた
▷Some people **grind** their **teeth** when they are asleep. 睡眠中に歯ぎしりする人もいる

one's **teeth**	chatter	歯がたがたいう

▷It's so cold my **teeth** are **chattering**. とても寒くて歯がたがたいっている

a decayed	tooth	虫歯
a canine	tooth	犬歯
a wisdom	tooth	親知らず
back	teeth	奥歯
front	teeth	前歯
baby	teeth	乳歯
permanent	teeth	永久歯
false	teeth	義歯，入れ歯
sharp	teeth	鋭い歯

▷My dentist says I have to have a **wisdom tooth** removed. 親知らずを抜くよう歯医者さんに言われている
▷One of my **front teeth** came out this morning. 前歯の1つがけさ抜けた

between	one's teeth	声をひそめて

▷"Ow! That really hurts," he said **between** his **teeth**. 「あう，痛い」と彼は声をひそめて言った

top /tʌ́p | tɔ́p/ 名 頂上，最上部；最上位

reach	the top	頂上まで行く；頂点
get to	the top	まで行く

▷They **reached** the **top** of Mount Fuji just before dawn. 夜明け直前に富士山頂に達した
▷Chris worked really hard to **get to** the **top** of the class. クリスはクラスの首席になるよう懸命に勉強した

at	the top	上(部)に; 最高位で
on	top	
on	top of A	Aの上に; Aに加えて
from top	to bottom	上から下まで
from top	to toe	頭の先からつま先まで

▷ Your name was **at** the **top** of the list. あなたの名前はリストのいちばん上にあった
▷ I like these London double-decker buses. Let's go and sit **on top**! ロンドンのダブルデッカーバスが好きだ．上の座席に座ろう
▷ You left your glasses **on top of** the bookcase. 書棚の上に眼鏡を置き忘れているよ
▷ In this department store you can dress yourself well **from top to toe** without spending too much money. この百貨店ではそれほどお金を使わなくても頭のてっぺんからつま先までおしゃれな服が買える

topic /tápik | tɔ́p-/ 名 話題, 論題, 題目

cover	a topic	話題を扱う
deal with	a topic	
discuss	the topic	話題を論じる
choose	a topic	話題を選ぶ
introduce	the topic	話題を導入する

▷ I really liked this class. We **covered** so many interesting **topics**. この授業がとても好きだった．とても多くの興味深い話題を扱ったからだ
▷ We have to **choose** a **topic** and write a report. 話題を選んでレポートを1つ書かなければならない

| topics | include | 話題は…を含む |

▷ It was a great program of lectures. **Topics included** black American culture, history of hip-hop, Madonna and so on. すばらしいプログラムの講演だった．題目にはアメリカの黒人文化，ヒップホップの歴史，マドンナなどが含まれていた

a particular	topic	特定の話題
a specific	topic	
a related	topic	関連の話題
an important	topic	重要な話題
the main	topic	主要な話題

▷ Is there a **particular topic** that you would like to write about? 書いてみたい特定の話題はありますか
▷ The **main topic** of conversation was who is going to win the next election. 会話の主要な話題はだれが次の選挙に勝つかということだった

| a topic | for A | Aの話題, 題目 |

▷ For most of the evening the **topic for** discussion was where to go for our summer holidays. その晩はほとんど，夏休みにどこへ行くかを話し合った

total /tóutl/ 名 合計, 総額, 総計

| make | a total | 合計する |
| bring | the total to A | 合計でAになる |

▷ Your $25 **brings** the **total** received for charity **to** over $2,000. あなたの25ドルでチャリティに集まったお金の合計は2千ドルを超える

a grand	total	総計
an overall	total	
a combined	total	合計, 通算

▷ The London Olympic Stadium seats **a grand total** of 80,000 people. ロンドンのオリンピックスタジアムには総計8万人が収容できる
▷ The Korean ice skater's **combined total** from the short and free programs meant that she won the World Championship. ショートとフリーの合計点で韓国のアイススケート選手は世界チャンピオンとなった

| in | total | 合計で, 全部で |

▷ Including Barack Obama there have been **in total** 44 presidents of the USA. バラク・オバマを含む全部で44人の米国大統領がいる

touch /tʌ́tʃ/

名 触覚; 感触; 接触; 手法, 手際

feel	a touch	触れるのを感じる
get in	touch	連絡をとる
keep in	touch	連絡をとり続ける
stay in	touch	
lose	touch	接触がなくなる

▷ She **felt a touch** on her shoulder from behind. 彼女は後ろから何かが肩に触れるのを感じた
▷ I'll **get in touch** *with* you later in the week. 週の後半に連絡します
▷ Let's **stay in touch**. 連絡をとり続けようね
▷ Over the years I **lost touch** *with* my school friends. 何年も学校の友人たちと連絡をとらなくなっていた

a gentle	touch	そっと触れること
a light	touch	軽い接触; 軽いタッチ
a magic	touch	魔法のような手際
finishing	touch(es)	最後の仕上げ
final	touch	

close	touch	緊密な連絡

▷I like your drawings. They have a very **light touch**. あなたの絵が好きです。タッチがとても軽妙だ
▷You made a good job of painting the fence. Just let me put the **finishing touches**. フェンスにうまくペンキを塗ったね。最後の仕上げだけ私にやらせて
▷We were in junior high school together and we've kept in **close touch** ever since. 私たちは中学校がいっしょで、それ以来緊密に連絡をとり合っている

a touch	of A	少しの A

▷The doctor says I may have a **touch of** flu. 医師が言うには私は軽いインフルエンザかもしれない

touch /tʌtʃ/ 動 触れる, さわる；接触する

barely	touch	ほとんど触れない
hardly	touch	ほとんど触れない
never	touch	まったく触れない

▷I **hardly touched** the vase but it fell to the ground. ほとんど触れなかったのに花瓶が地面に落ちた
▷"Why is your little brother crying?" "I don't know. I **never touched** him!" 「なぜ弟が泣いているの」「さあ。弟にはさわっていないよ」

touch A	on B	A(人)の B(体の部位)に触れる
touch A	with B	A に B(物)で触れる

▷Someone came up behind me in the street and **touched** me **on** the shoulder. 通りでだれかが後ろから近づいてきて私の肩に触れた
▷He **touched** the snake **with** a stick to see if it was still alive. まだ生きているか確かめようと彼は棒で蛇にさわった

reach out and touch		手を伸ばして触れる

▷The little baby **reached out and touched** her mother's face. 小さな赤ちゃんは手を伸ばして母親の顔に触れた

tough /tʌf/
形 困難な, 難しい；厳格な；じょうぶな, タフな；堅い

extremely	tough	非常に難しい；非常に厳しい
pretty	tough	厳格な, すごく堅い
particularly	tough	とりわけ難しい；とりわけ厳格な
remarkably	tough	驚くほどじょうぶな

▷You have to be **extremely tough** to survive winter in the South Pole. 南極の冬を生き延びるにはすごくタフでないといけない

tough	on A	A に厳しい, きつい

▷Don't be too **tough on** him. He's only a child. 彼にそう厳しくするな。まだ子どもなんだから

tour /túər/ 名 旅行；一巡；見学, 見物

do	a tour	旅行する；一巡する,
make	a tour	周遊する
go on	a tour	ツアーに出かける

▷We want to **do a tour** of Oxford when we're in England. イングランド滞在中にオックスフォードを回りたい
▷We **made a tour** of all the interesting places in Edinburgh. エジンバラのおもしろい場所をすべて巡った
▷We'll be in New York for three weeks so we'll have plenty of time to **go on tours**. ニューヨークに3週間いる予定なので, あちこち出かける時間はたっぷりあります

a national	tour	全国ツアー
a world	tour	世界ツアー
a package	tour	パック旅行
a bus	tour	バスツアー
a concert	tour	コンサートツアー
a guided	tour	ガイドつき見学
a conducted	tour	
a factory	tour	工場見学

▷The musical was so successful on Broadway that it went on **national tour**. そのミュージカルはブロードウェーで大ヒットしたので, 全国ツアーに出た
▷We did a **guided tour** of the Tower of London. ロンドン塔をガイドつきで見学した

on	(a) tour	旅行中で；巡業中で

▷My favorite boy band will be **on tour** in our area next month. 私のお気に入りのボーイバンドが来月この地域にツアーにやって来る
▷I'll take you **on a tour** of the local beauty spots. 地元の名所をご案内します

town /táun/ 名 町；繁華街, 商業地区

come to	town	町へやって来る
leave	town	町を出る
go into	town	繁華街へ行く

▷The last bus **leaves town** at 10:15. 最終バスは10時15分に町を出ます
▷I'm **going into town** to do some shopping this afternoon. きょうの午後町へ買い物に行く

a nearby	town	近くの町
a medieval	town	中世の町
an industrial	town	産業都市
a provincial	town	地方の町
a coastal	town	海岸沿いの町

▷Manchester started as an **industrial town** in the late 18th century. マンチェスターは18世紀後半に産業都市として始まった
▷Brighton is a **coastal town** in the south of England. ブライトンはイングランド南部の海岸沿いの町です

the center of	(the) town	町の中心
the outskirts of	(the) town	町の郊外
the edge of	(the) town	

▷There's a really good shopping mall in the **center of town**. 町の中心にとてもいいショッピングモールがある

trade /tréid/

名 貿易, 売買, 取引；商売；職業, 仕事

ply	one's trade	商売に励む
learn	one's trade	商売を学ぶ
carry on	a trade	商売を営む

▷The police are trying to stop drug sellers from **plying** their **trade** in the city center. 警察は繁華街で麻薬の売人が商売に精を出すのを止めようとしている

foreign	trade	外国貿易
international	trade	国際貿易
overseas	trade	海外取引
free	trade	自由貿易
fair	trade	公正取引；公正な貿易
agricultural	trade	農業貿易
a roaring	trade	商売繁盛

▷**Foreign trade** has increased by nearly 30% this year. 外国貿易は今年3割ほど増えた
▷The EU is a **free trade** area. EUは自由貿易圏だ

trade	in A	Aの取引
trade	with A	Aとの取引

▷Many people think that the **trade in** animal furs is wrong. 動物の毛皮取引は悪いことだと考える人が多い
▷The USA is hoping to increase **trade with** China. 米国は中国との取引が増えるのを望んでいる

the tricks of	the trade	商売のこつ

▷Can you teach me some of the **tricks of** the **trade**? 商売のこつをいくつか教えてくれるかい

trade /tréid/ 動 取引する, 貿易する, 売買する

actively	trade	活発に取引する
widely	trade	広く取引する
trade	profitably	取引で利益を出す

▷At first there were problems, but now his company is **trading profitably**. 当初は問題があったものの, いまは会社は取引で利益を出している

trade	in A	A(商品)を取引する
trade	with A	Aと取引する

▷Tony **trades in** antique furniture. トニーは骨董家具の売買をしている
▷The USA is hoping to **trade** more **with** China. 米国は中国とのさらなる取引を望んでいる

tradition /trədíʃən/ 名 伝統, 慣習

have	a tradition	伝統がある
continue	a tradition	伝統を続ける
follow	a tradition	伝統に従う
maintain	a tradition	伝統を維持する
preserve	a tradition	伝統を守る
break with	tradition	伝統を破る

▷The English **have** a **tradition** of eating roast turkey for Christmas lunch. イギリス人は焼いた七面鳥をクリスマスランチに食べる伝統がある
▷We don't want to **break with tradition**. We're going to have a white wedding. 伝統を破りたくはない．(花嫁が純白の衣装を着る)ホワイトウェディングをするつもりだ

an old	tradition	古い伝統, 昔からの伝統
an ancient	tradition	
a long	tradition	長い伝統
a great	tradition	偉大な伝統
a strong	tradition	根強い伝統
an oral	tradition	口伝えによる伝承

▷Celebrating Halloween is a very **old tradition** in the West. ハロウィーンを祝うのは西洋のとても古い伝統だ
▷Our company has a **long tradition** of making whiskey. わが社にはウィスキーづくりの長い伝統がある
▷Joining the army is a **strong tradition** in our

family. 軍隊入りはうちの家系の根強い伝統だ

| by | tradition | 昔からの伝統で |
| in | the tradition of A | Aの伝統に基づいて |

▷Nigel is going into the army **in** the **tradition of** his family. ナイジェルは家族の伝統を継いで軍隊に入る予定だ

traffic /trǽfik/ 名 交通, 通行；交通量

| stop | the traffic | 交通を止める |
| get stuck in | traffic | 交通渋滞にはまる |

▷The police are **stopping** the **traffic** ahead of us. 警察が前方の交通を止めている
▷Sorry we're late. We **got stuck in** traffic. 遅れてごめん. 交通渋滞に巻き込まれちゃって

heavy	traffic	多い交通量
light	traffic	少ない交通量
increased	traffic	増加した交通量
motor	traffic	自動車交通
road	traffic	道路交通

▷We were stuck in **heavy traffic** for hours. 何時間もひどい交通渋滞に巻き込まれた
▷This road has become quite dangerous because of **increased traffic**. 交通量の増加のため, この道路はかなり危険になってきた

| the volume of | traffic | 交通量 |

▷During the rush hour the **volume of traffic** passing through the town is enormous. ラッシュ時に町を通り過ぎる車の量は膨大だ

tragedy /trǽdʒədi/

名 悲劇, 惨事；悲劇作品

end in	tragedy	悲劇に終わる
prevent	a tragedy	惨事を防ぐ, 悲劇が
avert	a tragedy	起こらないようにする

▷The recent expedition to climb Mount Everest **ended in tragedy**. 最近のエベレスト登山は悲劇に終わった

a great	tragedy	大きな悲劇
a terrible	tragedy	
a real	tragedy	本物の悲劇
a personal	tragedy	個人的な悲劇
a Greek	tragedy	ギリシャ悲劇

▷I think there was some **great tragedy** in Peter's life. ピーターの人生には何か大きな悲劇があったのだと思う

train /tréin/ 名 列車, 電車

catch	a train	列車に乗る
get	a train	
take	a train	列車で行く
miss	the train	列車に乗り遅れる
get on	a train	列車に乗り込む
board	a train	
get off	a train	列車を降りる
change	trains	列車を乗り換える

▷Sorry, I have to run to **catch a train**! ごめん. 急いで列車に乗らなくちゃいけないんだ
▷We'll have to hurry or we'll **miss** the **train**! 急がないと列車に乗り遅れるぞ
▷I **got off** the **train** at the wrong station. 列車を降りる駅を間違えた
▷Do I need to **change trains** to get from London to Edinburgh? ロンドンからエジンバラに行くには列車を乗り換える必要がありますか

a local	train	普通列車
an express	train	急行列車
a special	train	特別列車
a crowded	train	混雑した列車
a full	train	満員列車
a high-speed	train	高速列車
an overnight	train	夜行列車
a passenger	train	旅客列車
a freight	train	貨物列車

▷I hate traveling on **crowded trains** during the rush hour. ラッシュアワーに混んだ列車で移動するのはいやだ

by	train	列車で
on	a train	列車に乗って；車内で
a train	to A	A行きの列車
a train	for A	

▷It's too expensive to fly there. Let's go **by train**. 飛行機で行くのは高すぎるから列車で行こう
▷The children are so excited. It's the first time they've traveled **on** a **train**! 子どもたちはすごく興奮している. 列車で旅行するのは初めてだからね
▷The **train for** Liverpool leaves at 10:10. リバプール行きの列車は10時10分に出る

train /tréin/ 動 訓練する, しつける

| trained |

| properly | train | しっかり訓練する |

▷ I'm not going to do well in the marathon. I didn't have time to **properly train**. マラソンでいいタイムは出ないだろう．しっかり練習する時間がなかったから

be trained	as A	Aになる訓練を受ける
train	as A	
train	for A	Aの訓練を受ける

▷ He was **trained as** a doctor in the USA. 彼は米国で医師になる訓練を受けた

| train A | to do | Aに…する訓練をする |

▷ Tim's **trained** his dog **to** do lots of tricks. ティムは飼い犬にたくさん芸を教え込んだ

trained /tréind/ 形 訓練された，熟練した

highly	trained	高度の訓練を受けた
fully	trained	十分に訓練された
adequately	trained	
well	trained	よく訓練された
specially	trained	特別に訓練された

▷ We need to bring in some **highly trained** experts to solve this problem. この問題を解決するには高度の訓練を受けた専門家に来てもらう必要がある

training /tréiniŋ/

名 訓練，研修；トレーニング

do	training	訓練を受ける；トレーニングする
receive	training	訓練を受ける
undergo	training	
give	training	訓練を施す
provide	training	
require	training	訓練を必要とする

▷ When she was in the police force they **gave** her **training** *in* first aid. 警察隊にいたとき彼女は応急処置の訓練を受けた

▷ The company will **provide** some **training** during your internship. 会社はインターンシップ期間中に研修を行う

basic	training	基本的な訓練
initial	training	初期訓練
intensive	training	集中訓練
formal	training	正規の訓練
vocational	training	職業訓練

| in-service | training | 現職研修 |
| on-the-job | training | 実地研修 |

▷ Helen has a beautiful voice, but she's never received any **formal training**. ヘレンはきれいな声をしているが，正式な訓練を受けていない

| in | training | 訓練中で；トレーニング中で |

▷ I can't play in Saturday's match. I hurt my ankle **in training**. 土曜日の試合には出られない．トレーニング中に足首を痛めてしまって

| training and qualification(s) | 訓練と資格 |

▷ You'll find it difficult to get a better job without proper **training and qualifications**. 相応の訓練と資格なしにさらによい仕事に就くのは難しいことがあなたはわかるでしょう

translate /trænsléit/

動 翻訳する；訳せる；解釈する

| literally | translate | 文字どおりに訳す |
| roughly | translate | おおざっぱに訳す |

▷ The word "manga" **roughly translates** as "comic" but the meaning is a little different. 「漫画」という語はおおざっぱに「コミック」と訳せるが，意味は少し違う

| translate | A into B | AをBに翻訳する |
| translate | as A | Aと訳せる |

▷ Can you **translate** this **into** English for me? これを英語に翻訳してもらえませんか

▷ The word "karaoke" literally **translates as** "empty orchestra." 「カラオケ」という語は文字どおり訳すと「空のオーケストラ」だ

translation /trænsléiʃən/ 名 翻訳

| make | a translation | 翻訳する |

▷ We need someone to **make** a **translation** of this report for us. このレポートを翻訳してくれる人が必要だ

an accurate	translation	正確な翻訳
a literal	translation	直訳
a word-for-word	translation	逐語訳
an English	translation	英訳
machine	translation	機械翻訳
automatic	translation	自動翻訳

▷ This is an **English translation** of Natsume Soseki's *Botchan*. これは夏目漱石の『坊っちゃん』の英訳

です

a translation	from A	Aからの翻訳
a translation	into A	Aへの翻訳
in	translation	翻訳で

▷This is a **translation into** English of the Japanese contract. これは日本語で書かれた契約を英語に翻訳したものです

travel /trǽvəl/

名 旅行, 旅;移動;(travels で)長期の旅行

foreign	travel	海外旅行
business	travel	出張
space	travel	宇宙旅行

▷If you're thinking of **foreign travel** you'll need to do a lot of preparation before you leave. 海外旅行を考えているなら出かける前に準備を十分する必要がある

travel	(from A) to B	(Aから)Bへの旅行

▷Rail **travel to** Paris costs only slightly less than going by air. パリへ鉄道で移動すると飛行機で移動するより少しだけ安い

travel /trǽvəl/

動 旅行する, 移動する;進む, 動く;伝わる

travel	widely	広く旅する
travel	extensively	あちこち旅行する
travel	abroad	海外旅行をする
travel	fast	早く伝わる

▷She **traveled extensively** when she was in Europe. 彼女はヨーロッパにいたときあちこち旅行した
▷I spent the last 6 months **traveling abroad**. この半年, 海外旅行をして過ごした
▷It seems highly unlikely that anything can **travel faster** than light. 光より早く進むものなどありそうもない

travel	(from A) to B	(Aから)Bへ旅行する
travel	in A	Aを旅行する
travel	around A	Aじゅうを旅する
travel	through A	Aを通って旅行する
travel	by A	Aで旅行する

▷It takes a long time to **travel from** Japan **to** the US even by air. 日本から米国に行くには飛行機でも長時間かかる
▷A good way to **travel in** America is to use the Greyhound bus network. 米国を旅行するよい方法はグレイハウンド社のバス網を利用することだ

▷After I graduate from university I want to **travel around** the world. 大学を卒業したら世界じゅうを旅行したい
▷I prefer to **travel by** car rather than **by** bus or **by** train. バスや列車でよりも車で旅行するのが好きだ

treasure /tréʒər/

名 宝物, 財宝;貴重品, 大切なもの

buried	treasure	埋蔵された財宝
hidden	treasure	隠された財宝
a great	treasure	貴重な宝物
an art	treasure	貴重な美術品
a national	treasure	国宝

▷There are many **great treasures** in the British Museum. 大英博物館には多くの貴重な宝物がある
▷The Golden Pavilion Temple in Kyoto is a **national treasure**. 京都の金閣寺は国宝だ

treat /tríːt/ 名 楽しみ;ごちそう;おごり

give A	a treat	A(人)を喜ばせる

▷Go on! Have another piece of chocolate cake! **Give** yourself a **treat**! さあ, チョコレートケーキをもうひとつどうぞ. 存分に召し上がれ

a real	treat	本当の楽しみ
a special	treat	特別な楽しみ

▷You did so well in your exams that we think you deserve a **special treat**! 試験のできがよかったので特別にお祝いしてあげよう

PHRASES

(It's) my treat. 😊 私のおごりです ▷"That meal was really expensive! How much do I owe you?" "No, no. Nothing. It's my treat." 「すごく高い料理でしたね. いくらお支払いすればよいですか」「いえ, いいんです. 私のおごりです」

treat /tríːt/ 動 扱う;治療する

treat	equally	平等に扱う
treat	fairly	公平に扱う
treat	seriously	真剣に扱う
treat	differently	異なる扱いをする
treat	separately	別々に扱う
well	treat	よい扱いをする
badly	treat	ひどい扱いをする
treat	successfully	治療がうまくいく

▷ Of course men and women should be **treated equally**. もちろん男性と女性は平等に扱われるべきだ
▷ Dave was seriously ill, but he was **successfully treated** in hospital. デイブは重病だったが、病院での治療がうまくいった

treat	A as B	AをBのように扱う
treat	A like B	
treat	A with B	AにBをもって接する
treat	A for B	A(人)のB(病気)を治療する

▷ The people I stayed with **treated** me **as** a member of their own family. 滞在先の人たちは私を家族の一員のように扱ってくれた
▷ In England pets are **treated like** family members. イングランドではペットは家族の一員のように扱われる
▷ You should **treat** your parents **with** more respect. 両親にもっと敬意をもって接するべきだ
▷ Anna went into hospital to be **treated for** a heart problem. アンナは心臓病の治療を受けるために入院した

treatment /tríːtmənt/

名 治療；取り扱い，待遇

get	treatment	治療を受ける；待遇
receive	treatment	を受ける
undergo	treatment	治療を受ける
give	treatment	治療する；待遇を与える
require	treatment	治療を必要とする
respond to	treatment	治療の効果が現れる

▷ Ben has gone into hospital to **receive treatment** for a broken leg. ベンは骨折した脚の治療を受けるために入院した
▷ I hurt my foot playing soccer, but I don't think it's serious enough to **require treatment**. サッカーをしていて脚をけがしたけど、治療が必要なほどではない

effective	treatment	効果的な治療
hospital	treatment	病院治療
medical	treatment	医療，診療
dental	treatment	歯科治療
preferential	treatment	優遇
special	treatment	特別待遇
equal	treatment	平等な待遇

▷ Are you insured? **Medical treatment** can be incredibly expensive. 保険には入っていますか。信じられないほど高額な医療費がかかることがあります
▷ Just because he's the boss's son I don't think he should receive **special treatment**. 上司の息子だからと言って、彼が特別待遇を受けていいとは思わない

| treatment | for A | Aの治療 |

▷ A lot of progress is being made in the **treatment for** AIDS. エイズ治療は大きく進歩した

tree /tríː/ 名 木，樹木

grow	a tree	木を育てる
plant	a tree	木を植える
climb	a tree	木に登る
cut down	a tree	木を切る

▷ I'm going to **plant** a **tree** by that fence over there. 向こうのフェンスのそばに木を植えるつもりだ
▷ Can you help me **cut down** a dead **tree** in the garden? 庭の枯木を切るのを手伝ってくれるかい

a deciduous	tree	落葉樹
an evergreen	tree	常緑樹
a fruit	tree	果樹
an apple	tree	リンゴの木
a cherry	tree	桜の木

▷ There's a beautiful old **cherry tree** in our garden. うちの庭には桜の古木がある

| under | a tree | 木の下で |

▷ Let's sit in the shade **under** the **tree** over there. 向こうの木陰で座ろう

trend /trénd/ 名 傾向；流行

set	a trend	流行を決める
follow	a trend	流行を追う
buck	a trend	流行に逆らう
reverse	a trend	傾向を反転させる

▷ Amy wears really cool clothes. She always **follows** the latest **trends** in fashion. エイミーはとてもすてきな服を着ている。いつも最新ファッションを追っている
▷ Profits have fallen this year so we need to **reverse** the **trend** as quickly as possible. 今年は利益が下がったので、できるだけ早く反転に転じる必要がある

| a trend | continues | 傾向が続く |

▷ The **trend** for joining Facebook is still **continuing**. フェイスブックに加入する傾向はなお続いている

the current	trend	現在の傾向
a recent	trend	最近の傾向
a general	trend	一般的な傾向

an upward	trend	上昇傾向
a downward	trend	下降傾向
an economic	trend	景気動向

▷I can't keep up with the **current trends** in teenage fashion. 10代ファッションのいまの傾向についていけない
▷Sales of smartphones are on an **upward trend** at the moment. スマートフォンの売り上げはいまのところ上昇傾向だ
▷At the moment the **economic trend** seems to be toward slow recovery. 当面の景気動向はゆっくり回復の方向にあると思われる

a trend	toward A	Aへの傾向
a trend	to A	
a trend	for A	
a trend	in A	Aの傾向, 流行

▷This autumn there's a **trend toward** high boots and short skirts in women's fashion. 今年の秋の女性ファッションはハイブーツとミニスカートが流行するだろう
▷What are the latest **trends in** computer game software? 最新のコンピュータのゲームソフトの流行はどんなふうですか

trial /tráiəl/ 名 裁判；試み；試験

come to	trial	公判に付される
go to	trial	
go on	trial	裁判を受ける
stand	trial	
bring A to	trial	Aを裁判にかける
put A on	trial	

▷Ben has been waiting for 6 months to **go on trial**. ベンは公判が始まるまで半年待たされている
▷The terrorists will be **put on trial** next month. テロリストたちは来月裁判にかけられる

a criminal	trial	刑事裁判
a fair	trial	公正な裁判
a murder	trial	殺人事件の裁判
a clinical	trial	臨床試験
field	trial	実地試験

▷A **criminal trial** is brought against someone by the police. 刑事裁判が警察からある人物に対して起こされている

on	trial	審理中で, 公判中で

▷She is **on trial** for murder. 彼女は殺人の容疑で公判中だ

trial and error	試行錯誤

▷After much **trial and error** a much improved car engine was developed. 多くの試行錯誤の末に，大幅に改良された車両エンジンが開発された

trick /trík/

名 策略, いたずら；手品, 芸当, トリック；こつ

play	a trick	いたずらする, だます
use	a trick	
fall for	a trick	策略にはまる
perform	a trick	手品をする
do	a trick	

▷I think Bob's crazy. He's always **playing tricks** *on* people. ボブは頭がどうかしているよ．いつも人にいたずらしてばかりだ

a dirty	trick	汚い策略
a cruel	trick	卑劣な策略
a nasty	trick	
a cheap	trick	小細工
a clever	trick	巧みな芸当

▷Politicians often use **dirty tricks** to stay in power. 政治家は権力の座にとどまるために汚いやり方をしばしば使う
▷Bob's dog can do all kinds of **clever tricks**! ボブの犬はいろんな賢い芸ができる

PHRASES
Trick or treat! ☺ お菓子をくれないといたずらするぞ（★子どもたちがハロウィーンで家を回りながら言うセリフ）

trip /tríp/

名 旅行；ちょっと近くまで行ってくること

plan	a trip	旅行を計画する
make	a trip	旅行する
take	a trip	
go on	a trip	
enjoy	a trip	旅行を楽しむ
return from	a trip	旅行から戻る

▷We're **planning** a **trip** to Tibet. チベットへの旅行を計画している
▷I **made** a **trip** to China last summer. 前の夏に中国を旅行した ▷I have to **make** a **trip** into town to do some shopping. 買い物をしに町へ行かなくちゃ

a long	trip	長旅
a short	trip	小旅行
a day	trip	日帰り旅行
a round	trip	往復旅行；《英》周遊旅行

| trouble |

a foreign	trip	外国旅行
a business	trip	出張
a school	trip	遠足, 修学旅行
a field	trip	現地調査, 社会見学

▷We went on a **day trip** to London. 日帰りでロンドンへ行った
▷I have to go on a **business trip** next week. 来週出張しなければならない

| a trip | to A | Aへの旅行 |

▷The **trip to** Spain was my first time abroad. スペイン旅行は私にとって初めての海外だった

trouble /trʌ́bl/

名 困難, めんどう, 苦労；心配, 悩み事

have	trouble	苦労する
cause	trouble	問題を引き起こす；
make	trouble	手間をかける
run into	trouble	問題を抱える, 困ったことになる
get into	trouble	
get A into	trouble	A(人)をめんどうに巻き込む
be asking for	trouble	めんどうなことになる
take	the trouble	労を惜しまない
save A	the trouble	A(人)の手間を省く

▷I told him he had to hand his homework in on time and I've **had** no **trouble** with him since. 彼に宿題をきちんと期限までに提出するよう言ってからは, 彼には苦労をかけられていない ◆**have trouble** doing … するのに苦労する ▷I had no trouble finding the address. その住所を見つけるのに苦労しなかった
▷Why does Sarah always **cause trouble**? サラはなぜいつもめんどうを引き起こすのか
▷Most of the math exam was OK, but I **ran into trouble** with the last two questions. 数学の試験のほとんどはうまくいったが, 最後の2問には苦労した
▷He didn't even **take** the **trouble** to apologize. 彼は謝ろうとさえしなかった
▷This dishwasher is great! It **saves** you the **trouble** of doing the washing up after meals! この食器洗い機はすごい. 食後の皿洗いの手間を省いてくれる

big	trouble	大きな問題
serious	trouble	深刻な問題
real	trouble	
terrible	trouble	
deep	trouble	
financial	trouble	財政問題
engine	trouble	エンジン故障

▷I don't think it's a **serious trouble**. 深刻な問題ではないと思う

| in | trouble | 困って；問題を起こして |
| trouble | with A | Aの問題；Aとの問題 |

▷"What's wrong?" "I'm **in** deep **trouble**, Mom."「どうしたの」「すごく困っているの, お母さん」
▷I'm having a bit of **trouble with** this homework. この宿題に少し苦労している
◆**the trouble** (**with** A) **is** (**that**)... (Aの)問題は…なことだ ▷The trouble is, the baby just won't stop crying. 問題は赤ちゃんがどうにも泣きやまないことだ

true /trúː/ 形 真実の, 本当の；本物の；誠実な

come	true	実現する
hold	true	当てはまる
remain	true	依然として真実だ

▷Water freezes at 0 degrees centigrade, but this does not **hold true** if it has salt in it. 水は摂氏0度で凍るが, 塩分を含む水にはこのことは当てはまらない

particularly	true	とりわけ真実の
especially	true	
quite	true	まったく真実の
perfectly	true	
certainly	true	確かに真実の
partly	true	部分的に真実の
equally	true	同様に真実の

▷Older people become forgetful and this is **particularly true** of your grandfather. 年配の人たちは忘れっぽくなるものだが, きみのおじいさんは特にそうだ
▷**Quite true**! You're absolutely right! まったくそうだ. まさにきみの言うとおりだ
▷I know Clare has her bad points, but it's **equally true** that she has some good ones. クレアには悪いところもあるが, 同じようにいいところもある

| true | of A | Aについて当てはまる |

▷The same is **true of** me. I get angry easily, too! 私も同じです. 私も怒りやすいんです

| true or false | | 正しいか誤りか |
| true or not | | 本当か本当でないか |

▷Butter is more fattening than margarine, **true or false**? バターはマーガリンより肥満の原因になる. 正しいか間違いか
▷**True or not**, that rumor could cause a lot of damage. 真実であろうとなかろうとそんなうわさが立つだけで大打撃だ

it's true	(that)...	…は本当だ
that may be true,	but	そうかもしれ
that might be true,	but	ないが、でも

▷**Is it true that** people who quit smoking gain weight? たばこをやめると太るって本当ですか
▷**That might be true, but** nobody will believe you! なるほどそうかもしれないが、だれもあなたを信じないだろう

(PHRASES)
That's true. 😊 それは本当だ / **That's not true.** 😊 それは違います ▷"I've never been in any trouble before." "That's true." 「これまで困ったことにはなっていません」「それはそうです」

trust /trʌ́st/ 名 信頼, 信用；委託

put	(one's) **trust**	信頼する, 信用
place	(one's) **trust**	を置く
establish	a **trust**	信頼を築く
create	a **trust**	
build up	**trust**	
win	the **trust**	信頼を得る
gain	the **trust**	
betray	A's **trust**	信頼を裏切る
abuse	A's **trust**	
lose	**trust**	信頼を失う

▷I'm sure Richard is someone you can **put** your **trust** in. リチャードは信用できる人だと思うよ
▷It's important to **establish** a **trust** with our clients. 顧客との信頼を築くことが大事だ
▷We don't want to promote someone who will **betray** our **trust** later. 後になって信頼を裏切るような人を昇進させたくない

mutual	**trust**	相互信頼
complete	**trust**	全幅の信頼
investment	**trust**	投資信託

▷Marriage should be based on **mutual trust**. 結婚は相互信頼に基づくべきだ

in	**trust**	委託して；信託にして

▷Her parents are going to hold the money **in trust** for her until she comes of age. 両親は彼女が成人するまで彼女のためにお金を委託管理するつもりだ

a lack of	**trust**	信頼の欠如
a position of	**trust**	信頼される立場

▷The main problem between the management and staff was a **lack of trust**. 労使間の主要な問題は信頼の欠如だった

trust /trʌ́st/ 動 信用する, 信頼する

fully	**trust**	全面的に信用する
really	**trust**	本当に信用する
never	**trust**	決して信用しない
no longer	**trust**	もはや信用しない
not entirely	**trust**	完全には信用しない

▷Would you **really trust** a man like Greg? グレッグのような男に全幅の信頼を置けますか
▷I can **no longer trust** you. きみはもう信用できない

trust	A **to** do	A(人)に…するのを任せる

▷"Can I **trust** you **to** remember to post this letter for me?" "Sure mom. No problem." 「この手紙を忘れずに投函してくれる？」「わかったよ、ママ。だいじょうぶ」

trust	A **with** B	A(人)にBを委ねる

▷I'd **trust** him **with** my last penny! 彼に有り金を残らず預けよう

trust	**in** A	Aを信じる
trust	**to** A	Aを当てにする

▷He has a lot of experience. **Trust in** what he tells you. 彼は経験豊富だから彼のことばを信じなさい
▷We've done everything we can. Now we have to **trust to** luck! できることはすべてやった、あとは運に任せるしかない

truth /trúːθ/ 名 真実, 事実；真理；真実味

know	the **truth**	真実を知っている
admit	the **truth**	真実を認める
tell	the **truth**	真実を語る
speak	the **truth**	
discover	the **truth**	真実を発見する
find out	the **truth**	真実を見いだす
get at	the **truth**	真実をつかむ
learn	the **truth**	真実を知る
reveal	the **truth**	真実を明らかにする
accept	the **truth**	真実を受け入れる
face (up to)	the **truth**	事実を直視する

▷Nobody really **knows** the **truth** about what happened. 何が起きたか本当にはだれも知らない
▷I don't think she's **telling** the **truth**. 彼女が本当のことを話しているとは思わない

| try |

▷ One day somebody will **discover** the **truth**. いつかだれかが真実を発見するだろう
▷ Maybe nobody ever really **found out** the **truth** about the assassination of President John F. Kennedy. ケネディ大統領の暗殺の真実を見つけ出した人はおそらくだれもいない
▷ I'm trying to **get at** the **truth**, but it's not easy. 真実をつかもうとしているが簡単ではない
▷ It took her a long time to **accept** the **truth** about her son. 息子についての真実を受け入れるに彼女には長い時間がかかった

(the) absolute	truth	絶対的な真理
the whole	truth	真相，全容
the simple	truth	ありのままの真実
the naked	truth	
a universal	truth	普遍的真実
an eternal	truth	永遠の真実

▷ What I'm telling you is the **absolute truth**. あなたに話していることはまったくの真実です
▷ You're not telling us the **whole truth**. あなたは真相を語ってくれていない
▷ The **simple truth** is you never really loved me! ありていに言うと，あなたは私のことを愛してくれてなどいなかった

the truth	about A	Aについての真実
the truth	in A	Aの真実
in	truth	本当は，実は

▷ Tell us the **truth about** what happened. 何が起きたのか真実を話してください
▷ I can't decide what is the **truth in** his story and what are lies. 彼の話で何が真実で何がうそなのか，決められない
▷ Well, **in truth**, I think I should have kept quiet and said nothing. 実のところ黙って何も言わずにいるべきだったと思う

the quest	for truth	真理の追求
the search	for truth	
an element	of truth	いくぶんかの真実
a grain	of truth	
the moment	of truth	正念場，決定的な瞬間

▷ Many people believe that our journey through life is the **search for truth**. 人生の旅は真理の追求であると信じる人が多い
▷ There is an **element of truth in** what you say. あなたのことばにはいくらか真実がある
▷ OK. The **moment of truth**! Will you marry me? さあ真実の瞬間だ．ぼくと結婚してくれるかい

| the truth | is (that)... | 実を言うと |

▷ **The truth is**, I wish I was back home in the USA! 実を言うと米国に帰りたい

try /trái/ 名 試み；(ラグビーで)トライ

have	a try	試みる
give A	a try	Aをやってみる
be worth	a try	やってみる価値がある
score	a try	トライを決める

▷ "I can't unscrew the top off this bottle." "OK. Let me **have** a **try**!"「この瓶のふたが開かないんだけど」「じゃあ，ぼくがやってみよう」
▷ "Do you think I should apply for this job?" "Yes. Go on. It's **worth** a **try**."「この仕事に応募してみるべきだろうか？」「うん，やってごらんよ．試す価値はあるよ」
▷ Jones **scored** three **tries** against New Zealand. ジョーンズはニュージーランド戦でトライを3つ決めた

try /trái/ 動 試みる；試す；努める

try	desperately	懸命に試みる
try	hard	
try	in vain	試みるがむなしい
try	unsuccessfully	

★ desperately は動詞の前でも用いる

▷ I **tried desperately** to get a ticket for the Olympics, but they were all sold out. オリンピックの切符を必死で手に入れようとしたが，完売だった
▷ I **tried hard** not to cry, but it was no good. 泣くまいとがんばったが，だめだった
▷ The doctors **tried in vain** to save her life, but she was too seriously injured. 医師たちは彼女の命を救おうとしたが，けがの程度はあまりにひどかった

try	to do	…しようと試みる
try	doing	…することを試みる
try	and do	《話》…しようとする

★ try doing は実際に動作が行われることを暗示するのに対し，try to do は「試みる」だけで，次に続き動作が行われない場合も多い．try and do は try to do より強い切迫感がある

▷ I **tried to** open the window, but I couldn't. 窓を開けようとしたがだめだった
▷ You look really tired. Why don't you **try going** to bed earlier? すごく疲れているみたいだね．早めに寝るようにしたら？

▷I'll **try and** arrange a meeting for tomorrow morning. あすの朝に会議を開くよう設定します

turn /tə́ːrn/

名 回転, 方向転換；曲がり角；順番

make	a left turn	左へ曲がる
make	a right turn	右へ曲がる
wait	one's turn	自分の番を待つ

▷You need to **make** a **left turn** at the traffic lights. 信号で左に曲がらなくては

a sharp	turn	急カーブ
an unexpected	turn	予期せぬ展開

▷Everything looked OK, but then things took an **unexpected turn** and we lost the contract. すべて順調に見えたが, 事態は予期せぬ展開を見せ契約はとれなかった

by	turns	代わる代わる, 交替で
in	turn	交替で, 順に

▷The suitcase was really heavy so we carried it **by turns**. スーツケースがすごく重かったので交替で運んだ
▷The students answered the questions **in turn**. 生徒たちは順番に質問に答えた

A's turn	to do	…する順番

▷It's your **turn to** do the washing up. きみが食器を洗う順番だ

turn /tə́ːrn/

動 回す, 回る；向きを変える；曲がる；変える

turn	abruptly	不意に向きを変える
turn	quickly	急いで向きを変える
turn	slowly	ゆっくり向きを変える
turn	slightly	ちょっと向きを変える

▷Stella heard someone call out her name and **turned abruptly** to see who it was. ステラはだれかに名前を呼ばれ, あわててだれかなと振り返った

turn	to A	Aの方を向く
turn	around	向きを変える；振り向く
turn	round	
turn	away	目をそらす

▷She **turned to** him in surprise. "Tom! I thought you weren't coming!" 彼女は驚いて彼の方を見て言った. 「トム, あなたは来ないと思っていたわ」

▷Don't **turn around** yet! I've got a surprise for you. まだ振り返らないでよ. きみを驚かせることがあるんだ

type /táip/ **名** 型, タイプ, 種類

identify	the type	型を識別する
include	types	型を含む
depend on	the type	型による

▷We need to **identify** the **type** of flu virus you have. あなたがかかっているインフルエンザウイルスの型を特定する必要がある
▷I don't know if you can use this software. It **depends on** the **type** of computer you have. きみがこのソフトウエアを使えるかどうかはわからない. きみのコンピュータの型によるよ

a certain	type	あるタイプ
a particular	type	特定のタイプ
various	types	さまざまなタイプ
the same	type	同じタイプ

▷I always seem to be attracted by a **certain type** of person: tall, handsome, intelligent and rich! 私が魅力を感じるのはいつもあるタイプの人みたい. 背が高くて, ハンサムで, 知的でお金持ちの人ね
▷Do you have any **particular type** of perfume? 何か特別なタイプの香水をお使いですか
▷My boyfriend and I both have the **same type** of character. ボーイフレンドと私は2人とも同じ性格なの

typical /típikəl/ **形** 典型的な

fairly	typical	かなり典型的な
quite	typical	実に典型的な
entirely	typical	まったく典型的な

▷She's a **fairly typical** Japanese high school student. She loves cute things and Tokyo Disney Land! 彼女はかなり典型的な日本の高校生だ. かわいいものが好きで東京ディズニーランドが好きだ
▷That's **entirely typical** of Annabel! まったくいかにもアナベルらしいよ

typical	of A	典型的なAの；いかにもAらしい

▷"Cindy keeps changing her mind about where she wants to go on holiday." "Yes! That's **typical of** her!" 「シンディは休暇にどこに行くか, ころころ考えを変えるんだ」「そうだよ. いかにも彼女らしいね」

U

umbrella /ʌmbrélə/ 名 傘；保護

open	an umbrella	傘をさす
put up	an umbrella	傘をさす
hold	an umbrella	傘をさしている
fold	an umbrella	傘をたたむ
carry	an umbrella	傘を持って行く

▷They say it's unlucky to **open** an **umbrella** indoors. 室内で傘をさすのは不吉とされる
▷I **carried** the **umbrella** around with me all day, but it didn't rain. 一日中傘を持ち歩いたが、雨は降らなかった

a folding	umbrella	折りたたみ傘
a beach	umbrella	ビーチパラソル
a nuclear	umbrella	核の傘

▷A **nuclear umbrella** means that it protects countries from a nuclear attack by other countries. 核の傘とは他国による核攻撃から国を守るという意味だ

under	the umbrella	保護の下に

▷Soldiers from many countries were sent in to keep the peace **under** the **umbrella** of the United Nations. 国連の保護の下、多くの国々から兵士たちが平和維持のために送り込まれた

uncertain /ʌnsə́ːrtn/

形 確信がもてない；不確実な

rather	uncertain	いくぶん確信がない
somewhat	uncertain	いくぶん不確実な
still	uncertain	まだ不確実な

▷Emma is still **rather uncertain** whether to apply for the job or not. その職に応募するかどうかエマはまだ気持ちが固まっていない

uncertain	wh-	…かわからない

★ wh-は how, what, why, whether など

▷She was **uncertain how** to reply to his email. 彼のEメールにどう返事すべきか彼女にはわからなかった
▷We're **uncertain what** to do next. 次に何をすべきかわからない
▷It's **uncertain whether** we'll be able to finish the project on time. プロジェクトを時間どおりに終えられるかどうかわからない

uncertain	about A	Aについて確信が
uncertain	of A	もてない

▷I'm **uncertain of** whether to have my watch repaired or buy a new one. 時計を修理してもらうか新しいのを買うか決めかねている

understand /ʌ̀ndərstǽnd/

動 理解する、わかる

clearly	understand	はっきり理解する
well	understand	よく理解する
fully	understand	十分に理解する
quite	understand	
not really	understand	よく理解できない
properly	understand	きちんと理解する
easily	understand	容易に理解する
readily	understand	
understand	correctly	正しく理解する
understand	perfectly	完璧に理解する

▷I can **well understand** why you were so embarrassed! きみがなぜそんなに困惑したのかよく理解できる
▷I **fully understand** your point of view. あなたの見方は十分にわかります
▷I couldn't **properly understand** what he said. 彼が言ったことをきちんと理解できなかった
▷I can **easily understand** why you got so angry! きみがなぜそんなに怒ったのかすぐわかるよ

begin to	understand	理解し始める
try to	understand	理解しようとする
help (A) to	understand	(A(人)の)理解を助ける

▷Ah! Now I **begin to understand**! ああ、やっとわかり始めたよ
▷Can you **help** me **to understand** this math problem? この数学の問題がわかるよう手伝ってくれるかい

be difficult to	understand	理解するのが難しい
be easy to	understand	理解するのが簡単だ

▷It's really **difficult to understand** these instructions! この説明書を理解するのはとても難しい

understand	wh-	…かを理解する
understand	(that)...	…を理解する

★ wh-は what, why, how など

▷I can't **understand why** you didn't tell me before. きみがなぜ事前に私に言わなかったのか理解できない
▷I **understand that** you have a lot of experience as

a waitress. あなたにウエートレスとしての経験が豊富なのはわかります

understand	A to do	Aが…すると解釈する

★do はふつう be, mean, say など

▷I **understood** him **to** say that there were no more problems. もう問題はないと彼が言っていると理解した

PHRASES
Do you understand? ☺ わかりますか ▷"Do you understand?" "Yes, I see what you mean."「わかりますか」「はい、おっしゃりたいことはわかります」
(**Is that**) **understood?** ☺ (脅しで)わかったか、言うとおりにしろ
I understand. ☺ わかります、わかりました ▷"So, it's really important you keep it a secret." "OK. Don't worry. I understand."「だから、絶対に秘密にしてくれよ」「ああ、心配しないで. わかってるから」

understanding /ʌ̀ndərstǽndiŋ/

名 理解, 知識；合意；思いやり

have	an understanding	理解する
show	an understanding	理解を示す
gain	an understanding	理解を得る
develop	an understanding	理解を深める
improve	A's understanding	理解を高める
increase	A's understanding	
come to	an understanding	合意に達する
reach	an understanding	

▷He **has** no **understanding** of the importance of human relationships. 彼には人間関係の大事さがわかっていない
▷She quickly **gained** a good **understanding** of our new accounting system. 彼女はうちの新しい会計システムをすぐによく理解した

a full	understanding	十分な理解
a thorough	understanding	
sufficient	understanding	
a clear	understanding	明確な理解
a deep	understanding	深い理解
a proper	understanding	適切な理解
a real	understanding	本当の理解
a better	understanding	よりよい理解
a greater	understanding	いっそうの理解
(a) mutual	understanding	相互理解

▷I don't think they have a **full understanding** of the situation. 彼らが状況を十分に理解しているとは思えない
▷I think we should be able to come to a **mutual understanding**. 互いにわかり合えるようになるべきだよ

a lack of	understanding	理解不足

▷There was a **lack of understanding** between the boss and his staff. 上司とスタッフとの間に理解不足があった

an understanding	between A	Aの間の合意
an understanding	with A	Aとの合意

▷I have a good **understanding with** my boss. 上司との意思疎通がうまくいっている

on	the understanding that...	…との条件で

▷I'll lend you $5,000 **on** the **understanding that** you pay me back within six months. 半年以内に返す条件で5千ドル貸してあげよう

unhappy /ʌnhǽpi/

形 不幸な, 惨めな；不満な

feel	unhappy	不幸と感じる
look	unhappy	不幸なようすだ

▷Emma **feels unhappy** living by herself alone in New York. エマはひとりでニューヨークに住んでいるのを悲しく思っている

deeply	unhappy	ひどく不幸な
desperately	unhappy	
really	unhappy	とても不幸な

▷Melissa has been **deeply unhappy** since her divorce. メリッサは離婚以来, 不幸のどん底だ

unhappy	about A	Aに不満な
unhappy	with A	
unhappy	at A	

▷I'm a little **unhappy about** leaving all my school friends and moving to Chicago. 学校の友人たちみんなと別れてシカゴに引っ越すのが少し悲しい

union /júːnjən/

名 労働組合；連合；結合, 団結

form	a union	組合をつくる
organize	a union	組合を組織する
join	a union	組合に入る
belong to	a union	組合に入っている

▷Some people at work are thinking of **forming** a **union**. 職場には組合をつくろうと考えている人もいる
▷Do you think it's a good idea to **join** a **union**? 組

a labor	union	労働組合
《英》a trade	union	
economic	union	経済同盟
monetary	union	通貨統合
political	union	政治統合
the European	Union	欧州連合

▷ Many European countries formed a **monetary union** which uses the euro as a currency. 欧州諸国の多くは通貨としてユーロを使う通貨統合を築いた
▷ England and Scotland formed a **political union** in the 17th century. イングランドとスコットランドは17世紀に政治統合した

unique /juːníːk/

形 独特な, ユニークな；唯一の

quite	unique	まったくユニークな
totally	unique	
truly	unique	まさにユニークな
almost	unique	ユニークと言ってよい

▷ This writer's style of writing is **quite unique**. この作家の執筆スタイルはまったく独特だ
▷ This 12th century coin is **almost unique**. この12世紀のコインはほとんど他に類を見ない

unique	to A	Aに特有の, 固有の

▷ This species of lizard is **unique to** the Galapagos Islands. トカゲのこの種はガラパゴス諸島に固有だ

unit /júːnit/ 名 単位；事業部；設備一式

a basic	unit	基本単位
the family	unit	家族単位
a business	unit	事業部門
control	unit	制御装置

▷ The centimeter is a **basic unit** of measurement. センチメートルは計測の基本単位だ
▷ The **unit cost** of electricity is going to go up again this year. 電力の単位当たり原価は今年また上がる

university /jùːnəvə́ːrsəti/ 名 大学

go to	(the) university	大学に行く
graduate from	university	大学を卒業する

▷ I'm hoping to **go to** (the) **university** next year. 来年大学に行きたいと思っている

at (the)	university	大学で

▷ Do you have a job or are you still **at university**? あなたは仕事に就いていますか, それともまだ大学に在学中ですか
▷ Her father is a professor **at** Stanford **university**. 彼女の父親はスタンフォード大学の教授です

unknown /ʌnnóun/

形 知られていない, 未知の

remain	unknown	依然わからない

▷ The cause of the car crash **remains unknown**. 車の衝突事故の原因は依然わからない

virtually	unknown	ほとんど知られていない
almost	unknown	
still	unknown	まだ知られていない
hitherto	unknown	これまで知られていない
previously	unknown	

▷ In 6 months she went from being a **virtually unknown** singer to famous pop star. 半年で彼女はほとんど無名の歌手から有名なポップスターになった
▷ We've found a **previously unknown** species of spider. これまで知られていないクモの種を発見した

unknown	to A	A(人)に知られていない

▷ There are still many species of animals and insects that are **unknown to** man. 人間に知られていない動物や昆虫の種がまだたくさんある

unlikely /ʌnláikli/ 形 ありそうもない

most	unlikely	まずありそうもない
highly	unlikely	
extremely	unlikely	

▷ We'll be **most unlikely** to finish by 6:00 this evening. 今晩の6時までにはまず終わりそうもない

unlikely	to do	…しそうにない
unlikely	(that)...	

▷ It's **unlikely** (**that**) I'll be home before 10:00. The boss asked me to work late this evening. 10時前には家に帰れそうもない. 上司から今晩の残業を命じられたんだ

unusual /ʌnjúːʒuəl/

形 普通でない，まれな，珍しい

highly	unusual	きわめてまれな
most	unusual	
somewhat	unusual	いささかまれな

▷ Forty years ago it was **highly unusual** for women to play soccer. 40年前には女性がサッカーをするのはきわめてまれだった

it is unusual	(for A) to do	(Aが)…するのは普通でない

▷ **It's not unusual to** feel nervous before an exam. 試験の前に緊張するのは珍しいことではない

nothing	unusual	変わったことはない

▷ There's **nothing unusual** about having more than one part-time job at the same time. 同時に2つ以上のアルバイトをするのは何も珍しいことではない

upset /ʌpsét/ 形 動揺した，取り乱した

get	upset	取り乱す
feel	upset	動揺する
look	upset	動揺したようすだ

▷ Calm down! There's no need to **get upset**! 落ち着いて．取り乱さなくていいから

really	upset	すごく動揺した
extremely	upset	
terribly	upset	

▷ After the interview Bella looked **really upset**. 面接のあとベラはとても動揺して見えた

upset	about A	Aのことで動揺する
upset	with A	A(人)に気分を害した

▷ Tina's really **upset about** what you said to her. ティナはきみのことばにとても動揺している

upset	(that)...	…に動揺した

▷ Cleo was **upset that** no one remembered her birthday. だれも自分の誕生日を覚えてくれていないことにクレオは気分を害した

urge /ə́ːrdʒ/ 動 強く勧める；強く主張する

constantly	urge	絶えず勧める
repeatedly	urge	何度も勧める
strongly	urge	強く勧める

▷ His doctor **strongly urged** him to give up smoking. 彼は医師から禁煙するよう強く勧められた

urge	A to do	A(人)に…するよう強く勧める

▷ Our teacher **urged** us **to** work hard to pass the entrance exam. 入試に受かるよう一生懸命に勉強しろと先生は私たちに強く勧めた

urge	that...	…と強く主張する

▷ As your doctor, I **urge that** you give up smoking and go on a diet immediately. 医者として，すぐたばこをやめてダイエットするよう強く勧めます

use /júːs/ 名 使用，用途；役に立つこと

make	use	利用する
come into	use	使われるようになる
go out of	use	使われなくなる
put A to	use	Aを活用する
encourage	the use	使用を勧める
be of	use	役に立つ

▷ You need to **make** the best **use** *of* your time during the summer holidays. 夏休み中の時間を最大限に利用する必要があります
▷ Our company **encourages** the **use** *of* eco-friendly cars. わが社は環境に優しい車の使用を勧めている
▷ Don't hesitate to call me if I can be **of use** (to you). もしお役に立てるのでしたら遠慮なく声をかけてください

in	use	使われて
out of	use	使われなくなって

▷ "I thought the elevator was **out of use**." "No, it's been **in use** again since last Friday." 「エレベーターは稼働していないと思っていた」「いや，先週の金曜日から再稼働しています」

increased	use	ますます使うこと
regular	use	恒常的な使用
widespread	use	幅広い使用
effective	use	効果的な使用
efficient	use	効率的な使用

▷ **Increased use** of air-conditioning can bring health problems. エアコンをますます使うようになると健康に問題が生じる可能性がある
▷ Antibiotics are becoming less effective because of their **widespread use**. 抗生物質は使われすぎてだんだん効かなくなりつつある
▷ To avoid power cuts this winter we shall all need to make more **efficient use** of electricity. この冬の停電を避けるためより効率的に電気を使う必要がある

use /júːz/ 動 使う，使用する

frequently	use	頻繁に使う
normally	use	普通に使う
regularly	use	定期的に使う
rarely	use	まれに使う
commonly	used	よく使われる
widely	used	幅広く使われる
use	effectively	有効に使う
use	mainly	おもに使う
use	up	使い果たす
used	extensively	広く使われる

▷ I **regularly use** the bus to go into town. 町へ行くのにバスを定期的に使っている
▷ In Holland bicycles are **commonly used** as a method of transport. オランダでは自転車は交通手段として普通に使われている
▷ We've **used up** all the toothpaste. 練り歯磨きを使い切った

use	A for B	AをBのために使う
use	A as B	AをBとして使う

▷ It was a valuable antique vase and he just **used** it **for** keeping pens and pencils in! 高価な骨董の花瓶なのに，彼はペンや鉛筆を入れるのに使っていた

use	A to do	Aを…するのに使う

▷ Can I **use** your cellphone **to** make a quick call? 急いで電話したいからきみの携帯電話を貸してくれるかな

used /júːst/ 形 慣れて

be used	to A	Aに慣れている
get used	to A	Aに慣れる
become used	to A	

★Aは名詞・動名詞

▷ I'm **used to** getting up at 5:00 in the morning now. いまは朝5時に起きるのに慣れている
▷ You'll soon **get used to** living abroad. すぐに外国暮らしに慣れるでしょう
▷ I've **become used to** commuting two hours to work every day. 毎日2時間の通勤に慣れた

useful /júːsfəl/ 形 有用な，役に立つ

extremely	useful	非常に役に立つ
especially	useful	特に役に立つ
particularly	useful	
really	useful	すごく役に立つ

▷ That book you lent me was **extremely useful**. きみが貸してくれた本は非常に役に立った
▷ I found your advice **especially useful**. あなたの助言が特に有益でした

useful	for A	Aに役立つ
useful	to A	

▷ This penknife is **useful for** all sorts of things. このペンナイフは何にでも使える

prove	useful	役に立つとわかる
find A	useful	Aは役立つと思う
make oneself	useful	手伝う，役に立つ

▷ I **find** this dictionary very **useful**. この辞書はとても役に立つと思う
▷ Don't just stand there! **Make** yourself **useful**! そんなところに突っ立っていないで，手伝いなさい

useful	to do	…するのは有益な

▷ It's **useful to** live so close to the supermarket. 家のすぐそばにスーパーマーケットがあると役に立つ

useless /júːslis/ 形 役に立たない，むだな

prove	useless	役に立たないとわかる

▷ I've tried many kinds of diet but they've all **proved useless**. いろいろダイエットを試したがすべてむだだった

quite	useless	まったく役に立たない
completely	useless	
absolutely	useless	
totally	useless	

▷ The thin coats were **quite useless** against the cold. その薄手のコートは防寒にまったく役立たなかった

useless	as A	Aとして役立たない
useless	for A	Aに役立たない
useless	to A	A(人)に役立たない

▷ Our dog is friendly to everyone – even strangers! He's **useless for** protecting the house. うちの犬はだれにでも，知らない人にでもなつくので，防犯に役立たない
▷ All this information is out of date. It's **useless to** us. この情報はすべて古くて私たちには役立たない

V

vacation /veikéiʃən | və-/

名 《おもに米》休暇

go on	(a) vacation	休暇に出かける
take	a vacation	休暇をとる
spend	a vacation	休暇を過ごす
plan	a vacation	休暇を計画する
enjoy	one's vacation	休暇を楽しむ

▷Tim and Sue have **gone on vacation**. ティムとスーは休暇に出かけている
▷I'd love to **spend** a **vacation** in Hawaii. ハワイで休暇を過ごしたい

summer	vacation	夏休み
winter	vacation	冬休み

▷I'm going to do a part-time job during the **summer vacation**. 夏休み中はアルバイトをするつもりだ

on	vacation	休暇で

▷Kate and Lesley are **on vacation** in Switzerland. ケイトとレズリーはスイスで休暇中だ

valuable /væljuəbl/

形 高価な；貴重な，価値のある，役に立つ

prove	valuable	価値があるとわかる

▷Thanks so much for your advice. I'm sure it will **prove valuable**. アドバイスをありがとう．きっと役立つよ

extremely	valuable	とても高価な；とても貴重な
particularly	valuable	とりわけ貴重な
especially	valuable	
potentially	valuable	潜在的に貴重な

▷I think this old stamp is **extremely valuable**. この古い切手はとても高価だと思う
▷This piece of land isn't worth very much now, but it's **potentially** very **valuable**. この土地はいまはそれほど価値がないが，潜在的には価値がある

valuable	for A	Aにとって貴重な
valuable	to A	Aに貴重な

▷This training course has been very **valuable for** me. この訓練コースは私にはとても有益だった
▷The ring was **valuable to** her for sentimental reasons. その指輪は心情的な理由から彼女には大切なものだった

value /vælju:/

名 価値；重要性；(values で)価値観

add	value	価値を増す
increase	the value	価値を上げる
reduce	the value	価値を下げる
have	a value	価値がある
show	the value	価値を示す
know	the value	価値を知る

▷If you add an extension it will **increase** the **value** *of* your house. 増築すれば家の価値が上がるだろう
▷I don't think she **knows** the true **value** *of* this painting. 彼女はこの絵の本当の価値を知らないと思う

high	value	高い価値
low	value	低い価値
good	value	お値打ち
face	value	額面(額)
market	value	市場価格
nutritional	value	栄養価
cultural	values	文化的価値観
social	values	社会的価値観
moral	values	倫理的価値観

▷If you shop at the new supermarket you get very **good value**. あの新しいスーパーマーケットで買い物するととてもお値打ちだ

drop	in value	価値が下がる
fall	in value	
rise	in value	価値が上がる

▷The dollar has **fallen in value** against the yen. 円に対してドルが急落した

of	value	価値のある，貴重な

★ great, real や little, no などを伴う

▷Your suggestions have been **of great value**. あなたの提案はとても貴重だった

value	for money	費用対効果，値段に見合った価値

▷If you go somewhere else you'll get better **value for money**. ほかへ行けばもっと値段に見合った価値の品物が得られるだろう

a set of	values	価値体系

▷When I lived abroad in an African village I expe-

| variety |

rienced a completely different **set of values**. アフリカの村で海外暮らしをしたとき，まったく異なる価値体系を体験した

variety /vəráiəti/

名 多様性，変化に富むこと；種類，変種

add	variety	変化を与える
offer	variety	

▷Traveling **adds variety** to life. 旅行は人生に変化を与える

a wide	variety	幅広い多様性
a great	variety	大きな多様性
a rich	variety	豊富な多様性
an infinite	variety	無限の多様性
an astonishing	variety	驚くほどの多様性
a bewildering	variety	
different	varieties	さまざまな種類
new	varieties	新しい種類

▷Our department store stocks a **wide variety** *of* brand goods. うちの百貨店は幅広いブランド品を取りそろえています
▷You've got a **great variety** *of* flowers in your garden. あなたの庭にはずいぶんいろんな花がありますね
▷There's a **rich variety** *of* desserts to choose from. 豊富なデザートの中からお選びいただけます
▷An almost **infinite variety** of beautiful tropical fish live on this coral reef. このサンゴ礁にはほとんど無限と言ってよい多種多様な美しい熱帯魚が生息している

vegetable /védʒətəbl/ 名 野菜

plant	vegetables	野菜を植える
grow	vegetables	野菜を育てる
cook	vegetables	野菜を加熱調理する

▷We **grow vegetables** in our garden. 庭で野菜を育てています
▷I need to **cook** some **vegetables** to go with the meat. 肉に添える野菜を調理しなくちゃ

green	vegetables	緑色野菜
leafy	vegetables	葉の多い野菜
fresh	vegetables	新鮮な野菜

▷Are you sure you're eating enough **fresh vegetables**? 新鮮な野菜を十分食べていますか

verdict /və́ːrdikt/ 名 評決

reach	a verdict	評決に達する
return	a verdict	評決を下す
deliver	a verdict	

▷The jury **returned** a guilty **verdict** after half an hour. 陪審員は30分後に有罪の評決を下した

video /vídiòu/ 名 ビデオ

make	a video	ビデオを制作する
rent	a video	ビデオを借りる
watch	a video	ビデオを見る
see	a video	

▷Let's **rent** a **video** and **watch** it this evening. ビデオを借りて今晩見よう

| a home | video | 家庭用ビデオ |

▷Look! I've found some old **home videos**! ほら，古いホームビデオを見つけたよ

| on | video | ビデオに |

▷The concert was recorded **on video**. そのコンサートはビデオに録画された

view /vjúː/ 名 見解，見方；視界；眺め，景色

have	a view	見解がある
hold	a view	
take	the view	見解をとる
share	the view	見解を共有する
support	the view	見解を支持する
reflect	the views	見解を反映する
have	a view	眺めがある
block	A's view	視界を遮る
come into	view	視界に入ってくる
disappear from	view	視界から消える

▷You may think that, but I **hold** a very different **view**. きみはそう考えるかもしれないが，私の見方はまったく違う
▷That idea does not **reflect** the **views** of the majority of Australians. その考えはオーストラリア人の大多数の見解を反映したものではない
▷We got great tickets for the live concert so we **had** a really good **view** of the band. ライブコンサートのとてもいいチケットを入手したのでバンドがとてもよく見えた
▷The crowd cheered as the marathon runner **came into view**. そのマラソン走者が見えてくると群衆は声援を送った

a general	view	一般的な見解
one's personal	view	個人的な見解
a clear	view	明快な見解
political	views	政治的な見解
a traditional	view	伝統的な見解
a breathtaking	view	息をのむ眺め
a clear	view	遮るもののない眺め
a panoramic	view	全景

▷My **personal view** is that he should apologize. 私の個人的な意見だが, 彼は謝ったほうがいい
▷Your grandfather has very **traditional views**. きみのおじいさんはとても伝統的な考えをしているね
▷There's a wonderful **panoramic view** from the top of the tower. 塔の上からみごとな全景が見渡せる

a view	on A	Aについての見解
a view	about A	
a view	from A	Aからの眺め
in	A's view	Aの見方では
in	view	見えるところに
on	view	展示されて

▷What are your **views on** nuclear power? 原子力についてあなたはどう考えていますか
▷There's a wonderful **view** of the sea **from** the bedroom window. 寝室の窓から見る海の眺めがすばらしい
▷**In** my **view** we should accept their offer. 私の見るところ彼らの申し出を受け入れるべきだ
▷A kindergarten teacher always needs to keep the little children **in view**. 幼稚園の先生は常に小さな子どもたちから目を離さないことが必要だ

a point of	view	観点, 視点

▷From his **point of view** there was nothing more he could have done. 彼の目から見れば, あれ以上彼にできることは何もなかった

violence /váiələns/ 名 暴力, 暴動；激しさ

resort to	violence	暴力に訴える
use	violence	暴力を振るう
incite	violence	暴力をそそのかす
end	the violence	暴力を終わらせる

▷You mustn't **resort to violence**. 暴力に訴えてはならない
▷The police were forced to **use violence** against the demonstrators. 警察はデモ参加者たちに武力を行使することを余儀なくされた
▷United Nations troops were sent in to **end** the **violence**. 暴動を終結させるために国連軍が送り込まれた

violence	erupts	暴動が勃発する
violence	breaks out	
violence	escalates	暴動が拡大する

▷**Violence erupted** in Karachi. カラチで暴動が勃発した

domestic	violence	家庭内暴力
physical	violence	肉体的暴力
sexual	violence	性的暴力

▷**Domestic violence** is still a major problem in many countries. 家庭内暴力は多くの国でなお大きな問題になっている

violence	against A	Aに対する暴力

▷The police claimed that they did not use too much **violence against** the demonstrators. 警察はデモ参加者たちに対して行きすぎた暴力は使っていないと主張した

an act of	violence	暴力行為
a victim of	violence	暴力の犠牲者
an outbreak of	violence	暴動の勃発

▷Just one punch is an **act of violence**. 1回殴るだけでも暴力行為だ

violent /váiələnt/ 形 暴力的な；激しい

become	violent	暴力的になる
turn	violent	
get	violent	

▷At first the demonstration was peaceful, but later the crowd **turned violent**. 初めのうちは平和的なデモだったが, そのうち群衆が暴力を振るいだした

vision /víʒən/

名 先見の明, 予見力, ビジョン；視力, 視覚

have	a vision	ビジョンがある
lack	vision	ビジョンに欠ける
create	a vision	ビジョンを作り出す
share	a vision	ビジョンを共有する
blur	A's vision	視界を曇らせる
cloud	A's vision	

▷I **had** a **vision** of myself running my own company at the age of 30. 30歳で自分の会社を経営するというビジョンが私にはあった
▷Helen was crying and the tears **blurred** her **vision**. ヘレンは泣いていた. 涙で視界がぼんやりした

| visit |

great	vision	すぐれたビジョン
strategic	vision	戦略的ビジョン
a common	vision	共通のビジョン
excellent	vision	よい視力
poor	vision	弱い視力

▷ You showed **great vision** to invest in gold at that time! あの時に金に投資するなんて，あなたは先を見る目がありますね
▷ An investor needs to have good **strategic vision**. 投資家には優れた戦略的ビジョンが必要だ
▷ You need to have **excellent vision** to be an airline pilot. パイロットになるには視力がよくないといけない

a field of	vision	視野，視界
a line of	vision	視線の方向

▷ Generally speaking, women have a wider **field of vision** than men. 一般的に言って女性は男性より視野が広い

visit /vízit/ 名 訪問；見舞い；見物，視察

make	a visit	訪問する
pay	a visit	
receive	a visit	訪問を受ける
have	a visit	
arrange	a visit	訪問の予定を組む
be (well) worth	a visit	訪れる価値がある

▷ We **paid** a **visit** to the Golden Pavilion Temple in Kyoto. 京都の金閣寺を見学した
▷ When I was in hospital I **had** many **visits** from friends. 入院中に多くの友人たちが見舞いに来てくれた
▷ When you're in Paris you should go to the Eiffel Tower. It's **well worth a visit**. パリに行ったらエッフェル塔に行くべきだ．訪れる価値があるよ

a brief	visit	ちょっと訪れること
a short	visit	
regular	visits	定期的な訪問
a three-day	visit	3日間の訪問
a recent	visit	最近の訪問
a previous	visit	前回の訪問
an official	visit	公式訪問

▷ When we were in Paris we made a **brief visit** to the Louvre Museum. パリ滞在中にルーブル美術館にちょっと立ち寄った
▷ I make **regular visits** to the dentist. 歯科医に定期的に行っている
▷ We went on a **five-day visit** to Paris. 5日間パリに滞在した

▷ The President of the USA is in our country on an **official visit**. 米国大統領はわが国を公式訪問中だ

during	one's visit	訪問中に
on	a visit	
a visit	to A	Aへの訪問

▷ I made so many friends **during** my **visit** to Australia. オーストラリア訪問中に友人がたくさんできた
▷ Sorry. Tom's not here. He's **on** a **visit** to some friends in California. すみませんがジムは留守です．カリフォルニアの友人のところへ行っています

visit /vízit/ 動 訪問する，訪れる；見舞う

frequently	visit	頻繁に訪れる
often	visit	しばしば訪れる
regularly	visit	定期的に訪れる
rarely	visit	めったに訪れない

▷ Sally **regularly visited** her mother in hospital. サリーは入院中の母を定期的に見舞った（★ visit regularly も用いられる）

come to	visit	やって来る
come and	visit	

▷ Some old school friends are **coming to visit** next weekend. 次の週末に昔の学校仲間たちがやって来る
▷ Please **come and visit** us again. どうぞまたいらしてください

voice /vɔ́is/ 名 声

hear	A's voice	Aの声が聞こえる
raise	one's voice	声を上げる
lower	one's voice	声を下げる
lose	one's voice	声が出なくなる
recognize	A's voice	Aの声だとわかる

▷ It's really nice to **hear** your **voice**. あなたの声が聞けて本当にうれしい
▷ Can you **raise** your **voice** a little? The people at the back can't hear you. 声を少し上げてくれますか．後ろの方の人に聞こえません
▷ Sorry, I've caught a cold and **lost** my **voice**. すみません，かぜを引いて声が出なくなっていて
▷ I **recognized** your **voice** over the phone immediately! 電話ですぐきみの声だとわかったよ

one's voice	rises	声が大きくなる
a voice	comes from A	Aから声が聞こえる

| one's **voice** | **sounds angry** | 怒った声に聞こえる |

★ angry のほか excited, sad, strange などの形容詞もくる

▷A **voice came** from the back of the room: "Speak up! We can't hear you!" 部屋の後ろの方から声がした.「大きな声で話してください.声が聞こえません」
▷Hello? Is that you Ben? Your **voice sounds strange**! もしもし,ベンかい? 声が変だね

a loud	voice	大きな声
a small	voice	小さな声
a little	voice	
a low	voice	低い声
a deep	voice	太い声
a quiet	voice	静かな声
a gentle	voice	やさしい声
a flat	voice	抑揚のない声
a female	voice	女性の声
a male	voice	男性の声

★ in a ... voice でよく用いる

▷We could hear **loud voices** coming from the apartment next door. アパートの隣から大きな声が聞こえてきた
▷"This play is really boring!" she whispered **in a low voice**. 「本当に退屈な芝居だこと」と彼女は低い声でささやいた
▷She spoke **in a soft voice**. 彼女は穏やかな声で話した

| a tone of | voice | 声の調子,口調 |

▷Never mind. I'll find someone else to help, she said in a disappointed **tone of voice**. 気にしないで.だれかほかに手伝ってくれる人を見つけます,と彼女はがっかりした口調で言った

| at the top of | one's **voice** | 声を限りに |

▷Dave shouted **at the top of** his voice. "Look out! There's a car coming!" デイブは声を限りに叫んだ.「気をつけて.車が来たよ」

vote /vóut/ 名 投票;投票権;票;得票

take	a vote	投票で決める
have	a vote	
give	one's vote	投票する
cast	a vote	票を投じる
put A to	the vote	Aを採決する
count	the votes	票を数える

| have | the vote | 投票権がある |

▷I **gave** my **vote** to the Liberal Democrat. 民主党に投票した
▷I wish I was old enough to **have** the **vote**. 投票権がある年齢ならいいのになあ

get	... percent of the vote	投票総数の…%を獲得する
win	20 votes	20票を獲得する
receive	20 votes	

★ get ... percent of the vote は get のほか win, receive, poll なども用いる

▷Nigel **got** only 5 **percent of** the **vote**. ナイジェルは投票総数の5%しか獲得できなかった

a majority	vote	過半数の投票
a unanimous	vote	満場一致の投票
the popular	vote	一般投票
the swing	vote	浮動票
《英》the floating	vote	
the female	vote	女性票

▷It wasn't unanimous, but Tony won by a **majority vote**. 全会一致ではなかったが,トニーは過半数の投票を得て勝った

a vote	on A	Aについての投票
a vote	for A	Aへの賛成票
a vote	in favor of A	
a vote	against A	Aへの反対票
by	vote	投票で

▷I cast my **vote in favor of** spending the school's money on building a swimming pool. 学校の予算をプール建設に使うことに賛成票を投じた
▷I think we should decide this **by vote**. これは投票で決めたほうがいいと思う

vote /vóut/ 動 投票する;投票で決める

vote	on A	Aについて投票する
vote	for A	Aに賛成投票する
vote	against A	Aに反対投票する

▷Tomorrow the soccer club is meeting to **vote on** who's going to be captain. あしたサッカークラブはだれをキャプテンにするか投票するために集まります

| vote | to do | …すると投票で決める |

▷We **voted to** go to Hawaii for our school trip next year. 来年の修学旅行の行き先をハワイにするほうに投票した

W

wage /wéidʒ/ 名 賃金, 給料

earn	a wage	賃金を稼ぐ
make	a wage	
pay	a wage	賃金を払う
raise	wages	賃金を引き上げる
lower	wages	賃金を引き下げる
cut	wages	賃金をカットする

▷She **earns** a **wage** of about $500 a week. 彼女は週500ドルほどの賃金を得ている
▷They're going to **raise** our **wages** next month. 来月に給料の引き上げがある

wage	increases	賃金が上がる
wage	rises	

▷Our **wages increased** by 10% last year. 賃金は昨年10％上がった

a good	wage	よい賃金
high	wages	高い賃金
low	wages	低い賃金
a weekly	wage	週給
nominal	wages	名目賃金
real	wages	実質賃金
a basic	wage	基本給
(a) minimum	wage	最低賃金
an average	wage	平均賃金
unpaid	wages	未払い賃金

▷I want to find a job with **high wages** and good working conditions. 賃金が高くて労働条件のよい仕事を見つけたい

wait /wéit/ 動 待つ

wait	quietly	おとなしく待つ
wait	patiently	我慢強く待つ
wait	anxiously	心配して待つ
wait	impatiently	いらいらして待つ
wait	nervously	
wait	expectantly	わくわくして待つ
wait	outside	外で待つ

▷You'll just have to **wait patiently** for the results of the interview. 面接の結果を我慢強く待つしかないよ
▷We **waited anxiously** at the hospital to hear if Chris was going to be OK. クリスが治るかどうか聞こうと病院で心配して待った
▷Could you **wait outside** for a moment, please? 外で少々お待ちいただけますか

wait	for A	Aを待つ
wait	until A	Aまで待つ
wait	till A	

▷I'll **wait for** you here. あなたをここで待っています
▷I think we should **wait until** Tom arrives before we start the meeting. トムが到着するのを待って会議を始めたほうがいいと思います

can't	wait	待ち遠しくてたまらない
can hardly	wait	

▷I **can't wait** to open my Christmas presents! クリスマスプレゼントを開けたくてうずうずするよ

wait and see	ようすを見る

▷"So what happens at the end of the film?" "**Wait and see!**" 「で, 映画の最後はどうなるの」「おとなしく見てて」

wait	for A to do	Aが…するのを待つ

▷Oh! It's raining! Can you **wait for** me **to** get my umbrella? あ, 雨だ. 傘を取って来るから待ってくれるかい

[PHRASES]
Wait a minute. / Wait a second. ☺ ちょっと待って

walk /wɔ́ːk/ 名 散歩, 歩くこと；歩行距離

go for	a walk	散歩に出かける
take	a walk	散歩する
have	a walk	
take A	for a walk	Aを散歩に連れて行く

▷Do you feel like **going for** a **walk** along the beach? 浜辺を散歩しないかい
▷Let's **take** a **walk** in the park. 公園を散歩しよう

a short	walk	短い道のり
a long	walk	長い道のり
a ten-minute	walk	徒歩10分

▷It's only a **short walk** to the post office. 郵便局までは歩いてすぐです
▷My house is a **five-minute walk** *from* the station. 私の家は駅から徒歩5分です

walk /wɔ́ːk/ 動 歩く, 歩いて行く

walk	quickly	足早に歩く
walk	slowly	ゆっくり歩く
walk	quietly	静かに歩く
walk	backward	後ろへ歩く
walk	forward	前へ歩く
walk	around	歩き回る
walk	away	歩いて立ち去る
walk	off	立ち去る
walk	in	歩いて入って来る
walk	out	歩いて出て行く

▷Do you think we could **walk** a bit more **quickly**? もう少し速く歩きませんか
▷Don't **walk away** when I'm talking to you! きみに話しかけているんだから，逃げるなよ
▷The movie was so bad that we **walked out**. あんまりひどい映画だったので，出てしまった

walk	across A	Aを歩いて横切る
walk	along A	Aを歩いて行く
walk	up A	
walk	down A	
walk	around A	Aを歩き回る
walk	into A	歩いてAに入る
walk	out of A	歩いてAから出る
walk	to A	Aへ歩いて行く
walk	toward A	Aの方へ歩いて行く

▷She was **walking across** the road when the car hit her. 道路を横断中に彼女は車にはねられた
▷Let's **walk along** the riverbank. 川の土手沿いに歩こう
▷She **walked** angrily **out of** the room. 彼女は怒って部屋から出て行った
▷It only takes 5 minutes to **walk to** the station. 駅まで歩いて5分しかかからない

▎wall /wɔ́:l/ 名 壁；塀

build	a wall	塀を築く；壁をつくる
climb	a wall	塀をよじ登る
lean against	a wall	壁に寄りかかる

▷We're **building** a **wall** at the bottom of the garden. 庭のいちばん奥に塀を築いています
▷Tom was **leaning against** a **wall**, smoking. トムは壁に寄りかかってたばこを吸っていた

a high	wall	高い壁
a low	wall	低い壁
a brick	wall	れんが塀
a stone	wall	石垣
the city	wall	町の城壁

▷The castle was surrounded by a **high wall**. 城は高い壁に囲まれていた
▷This is where the old **city wall** used to be. ここはかつて古い町の城壁があったところだ

on	a [the] wall	壁に
against	a [the] wall	壁にぶつかって

▷The light switch is **on** the **wall** over there. 明かりのスイッチは向こうの壁にあります
▷Every evening he goes out to kick a ball **against** a **wall**. 夕方になるといつも彼は外へ出て，壁に向かってボールをける

▎wander /wάndər | wɔ́n-/

動 ぶらつく，歩き回る；迷う

wander	aimlessly	あてもなく歩き回る
wander	off	はぐれる
wander	away	

▷We got lost and spent 2 hours **wandering** around **aimlessly**. 道に迷ってあてもなく2時間ぶらぶら歩いた

wander	along A	Aをぶらつく
wander	around A	
wander	through A	

▷We had a great time **wandering around** the night market. 夜の市場をぶらぶら歩き回って楽しんだ
▷We **wandered through** the beautiful temple gardens. 美しいお寺の庭をぶらついた

▎want /wάnt | wɔ́nt/ 動 したい；ほしい

desperately	want	どうしても…したい
really	want	
simply	want	単に…したい
particularly	want	特に…したい
always	want	いつも…したい

▷I **desperately want** to go to the toilet! どうしてもトイレに行きたい
▷I won't stay long. I **simply wanted** to check you were OK. 長居はしません．きみがだいじょうぶか確かめたかっただけです
▷She **particularly wants** to talk to you. 彼女はきみと特に話したがっている

want	to do	…したい
want	A to do	Aに…してほしい

| war |

| want | A done | Aが…されるのを望む |

▷I don't **want** you **to** be angry. 怒らないでほしい
▷Tom **wants** his photo **taken** with you. トムはきみといっしょに写真を撮りたがっている

PHRASES
Who wants A? Aがほしい人はいますか ▷Who wants a piece of birthday cake? 誕生日のケーキを一切れほしい人はいますか

war /wɔ́:r/ 名 戦争；闘争

fight	the war	戦争する
make	war	
wage	war	
win	the war	戦争に勝つ
lose	the war	戦争に負ける
declare	war	宣戦布告する
go to	war	戦争に行く
end	the war	戦争を終結させる
prevent	war	戦争を回避する
be killed in	the war	戦死する

▷They don't have enough weapons to **fight the war**. 彼らには戦争をするのに十分な武器がない
▷After 9/11 America **declared war** *against* Saddam Hussein's Iraq. 9.11後に米国はサダム・フセインのイラクに宣戦布告した
▷In the end it was impossible to **prevent war**. 最終的には戦争を回避できなかった
▷Tom's brother was **killed in the war**. トムの兄は戦死した

a holy	war	聖戦
a civil	war	市民戦争, 内戦
a nuclear	war	核戦争
the cold	war	冷戦
the First World	War	第一次世界大戦
the Second World	War	第二次世界大戦
a price	war	価格競争

▷The Spanish **Civil War** began in July 1936. スペイン内戦は1936年7月に始まった
▷A **nuclear war** must be avoided at all costs. 核戦争は何としても避けねばならない

a war	on A	Aとの戦い
a war	against A	
a war	with A	
at	war	戦争状態で

▷After 9/11 America declared **war on** terrorism. 9.11後に米国はテロとの戦いを宣言した
▷After the **war against** Iraq no weapons of mass destruction were found. イラクとの戦争後, いかなる大量破壊兵器も見つからなかった
▷Many soldiers are still **at war** in Afghanistan. アフガニスタンでなお戦争状態にある兵士は多い

warm /wɔ́:rm/ 形 暖かい；温かい

feel	warm	暖かい
get	warm	暖かくなる
keep	warm	暖かく保つ
stay	warm	

▷We lit a campfire to cook some food and **keep warm**. キャンプファイヤーをたいて調理して暖まった

pleasantly	warm	心地よく暖かい
really	warm	すごく暖かい
slightly	warm	やや暖かい
warm	enough	十分に暖かい

▷It's **pleasantly warm** today, isn't it? きょうは心地よい暖かさですね
▷Are you **warm enough**? 十分に暖かいですか

warm and comfortable	暖かく快適な
warm and dry	暖かく乾燥した
warm and sunny	暖かくて晴天の
warm and friendly	温かくて親切な

▷The hotel we stayed in was **warm and comfortable**. 滞在したホテルは暖かくて快適だった
▷The forecast for tomorrow is **warm and sunny**. あすの天気予報は暖かくて晴天です
▷The host family I stayed with in Australia was **warm and friendly**. オーストラリアで滞在したホストファミリーは温かくて親切だった

warn /wɔ́:rn/ 動 警告する

always	warn	いつも警告する
constantly	warn	絶えず警告する
repeatedly	warn	繰り返し警告する

▷Tim was **repeatedly warned** about arriving late for class. ティムは授業への遅刻のことで何度も警告された

warn	A about B	A(人)にB(危険など)を警告する
warn	A against B	
warn	A of B	

▷We **warned** them **about** the dangers of swimming in that part of the sea. その辺りの海で泳ぐことの危険性について彼らに警告した

▷We were **warned against** drinking the tap water. 水道水は飲まないよう警告された

warn	(A) that...	(A(人)に)…と警告する
warn	A to do	A(人)に…するよう警告する

▷The firefighters **warned that** the building could collapse at any moment. 消防隊員たちは建物がいつ崩壊するかわからないと警告した
▷I **warned** him not **to** drive too fast. 彼に車のスピードを出しすぎないよう警告した

warning /wɔ́ːrniŋ/ 名 警告, 警報

give	(a) warning	警告を出す
issue	(a) warning	警告を出す
sound	a warning	警鐘を鳴らす
receive	a warning	警告を受ける
ignore	(a) warning	警告を無視する
heed	the warning	警告に従う
carry	(a) warning	警告を載せる

▷The local government has **issued** a **warning** about serious flooding. 地方自治体は大洪水警報を出した
▷The problems caused by nuclear power **sound** a **warning** to us all. 原子力が引き起こした問題はわれわれみんなに警鐘を鳴らすものだ
▷Many people **ignored** the **warning**. 多くの人々は警告を無視した
▷It's required by law to **carry** a **warning** on every pack of cigarettes. たばこのどの箱にも警告を載せるように法律で義務づけられている

a stern	warning	厳しい警告
advance	warning	事前の警告
fair	warning	余裕をもった予告
an early	warning	早期警戒
a final	warning	最後の警告

▷You need to give him a **stern warning**. 彼に厳しく警告しなくてはだめですね
▷I gave you **fair warning**. You've been absent six times, so you've failed the course. 前もって警告しましたよね。6回欠席したので, この科目は落第ですよ
▷It's not possible to give an **early warning** of an earthquake. 地震の早期警戒を出すのは不可能だ
▷This is your **final warning**! これがあなたへの最後の警告です

without	warning	警告なしに

▷The stupid dog jumped up and bit me **without warning**. 変な犬が前触れもなく飛びかかってきて私をかんだ

waste /wéist/ 名 廃棄物, くず；むだ

dump	waste	廃棄物を捨てる
recycle	waste	廃棄物を再生利用する
reduce	waste	廃棄物を減らす
go to	waste	むだになる
reduce	waste	むだを減らす

▷These days people are much better at **recycling waste**. 近ごろ人々は廃棄物の再生利用がずっとうまくなりつつある
▷It's such a shame to let all this food **go to waste**. この食料を全部むだにするなんて本当にひどい
▷We need to do more to **reduce waste** of electricity. 電気のむだを減らすためにもっとやることがある

hazardous	waste	危険廃棄物
toxic	waste	有毒廃棄物
industrial	waste	産業廃棄物
nuclear	waste	核廃棄物
radioactive	waste	放射性廃棄物
a complete	waste	まったくのむだ

▷Finding an acceptable place to dump **nuclear waste** can be a big problem. 核廃棄物の受け入れ場所を見つけるのは大変だろう
▷Buying this exercise machine was a **complete waste** of money! この運動器具を買うなんてまったくお金のむだだった

a waste	of A	Aのむだ

★Aに time, money, effort など

▷It's a **waste of time** talking to her. 彼女に話しても時間のむだだ

watch /wátʃ | wɔ́tʃ/ 名 時計；監視

check	one's watch	時計を見る
consult	one's watch	時計を見る
look at	one's watch	時計を見る
set	a watch	時計を合わせる
wear	a watch	時計をしている
take off	one's watch	時計を外す
keep	(a) watch	監視する

▷I **checked** my **watch**. It was 3:00 in the morning. 時計を見たら朝の3時だった
▷She **took off** her **watch** and put it on the desk in front of her. 彼女は時計を外して, 前にある机に置いた
▷**Keep** close **watch** *on* him. 彼をしっかり見張っていろ

a digital	watch	デジタル時計

▷ It's just a cheap **digital watch**. ほんの安物のデジタル時計です

on	watch	当直で, 監視して
on	the watch (for A)	(Aを)見張って

▷ The security guard fell asleep while he was **on watch**. 警備員は当直中に眠り込んだ
▷ We need to be **on the watch for** anything suspicious. 何か不審なことがないか見張る必要がある

watch /wátʃ | wɔ́tʃ/

動 じっと見る; 見守る; 注意する

watch	carefully	注意して見る
watch	closely	じっと見る
watch	intently	熱心に見る
watch	anxiously	不安げに見る

▷ OK. Let's do some origami. **Watch carefully**. では折り紙をしましょう。よく見てね
▷ I'll show you how to operate the cash register. **Watch closely**. レジをどう操作するか見せてあげる。よく見ていてね
▷ They **watched intently** as the magician performed his incredible card trick. 手品師が信じられないほどのカード手品をするのを彼らは一心に見た

watch	A do	A(人)が…するのを見る
watch	A doing	A(人)が…しているのを見る

▷ She **watched** him open his birthday present. 彼女は彼が誕生日の贈り物を開けるのをじっと見ていた
▷ He **watched** the bird build**ing** its nest. 彼は鳥が巣をつくっているのを観察した

watch	wh-	…かを見る; …かに気をつける
watch	that...	…に気をつける

★ wh- は how, who, what など

▷ **Watch what** I do and then do the same. 私がすることをよく見て, 同じようにしなさい
▷ **Watch that** your dog doesn't run into the road! きみの犬が道路に飛び出さないよう用心しなさい

watch and listen		よく見て聞く

▷ Please **watch and listen** to this video very carefully. このビデオを注意深く見てよく聞いてください

water /wɔ́:tər/

名 水, 湯; (waters で)海, 領海

pour	water	水を注ぐ
boil	water	湯を沸かす
heat	water	水を熱する
pump	water	水をポンプでくむ
be filled with	water	水があふれる

▷ **Pour** hot **water** into the teapot to warm it first. 湯を注いでまずティーポットを温めなさい
▷ It had rained heavily and the pond was **filled with water**. 大雨が降って池は水でいっぱいだった

water	pours	水が流れ出る
water	runs	水が流れる
water	flows	
water	drips	水がぽたぽた落ちる
water	evaporates	水が蒸発する

▷ **Water** was **pouring** out of the burst pipe. 破裂した水道管から水があふれ出ていた
▷ Look at the **water running** under that bridge! The level is really high! 橋の下を流れている水を見て。水位がすごく上がっている
▷ There's **water dripping** from the kitchen tap. 台所の蛇口から水がぽたぽた落ちている

boiling	water	熱湯
cold	water	冷水
hot	water	湯
warm	water	温水
iced	water	氷水
clean	water	きれいな水
dirty	water	汚い水
fresh	water	淡水; 新鮮な水
sea	water	海水
hard	water	硬水
soft	water	軟水
running	water	水道水
drinking	water	飲料水
tap	water	蛇口から出る水道水
bottled	water	ボトル入り飲料水
mineral	water	ミネラルウォーター
territorial	waters	領海

▷ She spilt **boiling water** on her foot. 彼女は煮立った湯を足の上にこぼした
▷ The hotel room was dirty and there was no **hot water**. ホテルの部屋は汚くて湯も出なかった
▷ Both countries claim that this area is within their **territorial waters**. 両国ともこの地域は領海内であると主張している

a glass of	water	コップ1杯の水

▷ Could I have a **glass of water**, please? 水をコッ

プ1杯いただけませんか

| by | water | 船(便)で, 海路で |

▷You can get to the island by bridge or go **by water**.　島へは橋を渡っても船でも行けます

wave /wéiv/ 名 波；手を振ること

a wave	breaks	波が砕ける
a wave	crashes	波が激しく砕ける
a wave	hits A	波がAにぶつかる

▷It was very stormy and the **waves** were **crashing** against the rocks.　すごい嵐で, 波が岩にぶつかって激しく砕けていた

▷A big **wave hit** the side of the ship.　大きな波が船腹にぶつかった

| give (A) | a wave | (A(人)に)手を振る |

▷The President and his wife **gave** the crowds a **wave** from their open car.　大統領夫妻はオープンカーから群衆に手を振った

a big	wave	大波
a mountainous	wave	山のような波
a tidal	wave	津波
a tsunami	wave	
electromagnetic	waves	電磁波
radio	waves	電波
seismic	waves	地震波
shock	waves	衝撃波
sound	waves	音波
a new	wave	新しい波
a crime	wave	犯罪の急増

▷The **tidal wave** caused horrific damage.　その津波はひどい被害をもたらした

▷News of the death of Michael Jackson sent **shock waves** through the pop world.　マイケル・ジャクソン死亡のニュースはポップスの世界に衝撃を与えた

▷We are in the middle of a serious **crime wave**.　犯罪の深刻な急増にさらされている

| in | waves | 波状的に, 次から次へと |

▷The pain came and went **in waves**.　痛みは断続的に強くなったり弱まったりした

wave /wéiv/ 動 手を振る；振る

| wave | back | 手を振り返す |
| wave | aside | 手で払いのける |

| wave | away | 手を振って追い払う |

▷He waved at her and she **waved back**.　彼が彼女に手を振ると彼女は手を振り返した

| wave | to A | Aに手を振る |
| wave | at A | |

▷Look! There's someone **waving at** you.　ほら, きみにだれかが手を振っているよ

way /wéi/

名 道, 通り；道のり；方法；習慣, 流儀；意味, 点

make	one's way	進む, 前進する
feel	one's way	手探りで進む
grope	one's way	
edge	one's way	少しずつ進む
push	one's way	押し分けて進む
work	one's way	骨折って進む
fight	one's way	押しのけて進む
force	one's way	強引に進む
pick	one's way	慎重に進む
clear	the way	道を開ける, 道を切り開く
pave	the way	
make	way	道を譲る
give	way	
lose	one's way	道に迷う
find	one's way	やっとたどり着く
ask	the way	道を聞く
tell A	the way	A(人)に道を教える
show A	the way	
lead	the way	先導する
know	the way	道を知っている
keep out of	A's way	A(人)に近づかない
stay out of	A's way	
stand in	A's way	A(人)のじゃまをする
change	one's ways	やり方を改める
mend	one's ways	

▷Finally she **made** her **way** *to* the top of her profession.　彼女はついに同業者仲間のトップに登りつめた

▷When you start a new job you need to **feel** your **way**.　新しい仕事を始めるときには手探りでやる必要がある

▷She **pushed** her **way** *through* the crowd.　彼女は群衆を押し分けて進んだ

▷We had to **fight** our **way** *through* the crowd.　群衆を押しのけて進まなければならなかった

▷The police **forced** their **way** *into* the house.　警察はその家に突入した

▷The police motorcyclists went ahead to **clear** the **way** *for* the President's car.　警察のオートバイは大統

| way |

領の車に道を開けるために先導した
▷We pulled over to the side of the road to **make way** *for* the ambulance. 救急車が通れるよう路肩に車を寄せた
▷I've no idea where we are. We've completely **lost our way**. ここがどこかわからない. すっかり道に迷った
▷Why don't we stop and **ask** the **way**? 止まって道を聞いたらどうかな
▷Can you **tell** me the **way** *to* the station? 駅への道を教えてくれるかい
▷Would you like me to **show** you the **way**? 道を教えて差し上げましょうか
▷You **lead** the **way**, I'll follow. 先導して. ついて行くから
▷I'd **keep out of** the boss's **way**, if I were you. He's in a terrible mood! 私なら上司に近づかないな. とても機嫌が悪いからね
▷If you want to marry him we won't **stand in** your **way**. あなたが彼と結婚したいのならじゃまはしません
▷If he doesn't **mend** his **ways** he'll get into big trouble. やり方を改めないと彼は困ったことになるだろう

get	one's **way**	思いどおりにする
have	one's **way**	
go	one's **own way**	自分の道を行く

▷**Have** it your **way**. 好きなようにしろ

an easy	way	簡単な方法
a convenient	way	便利な方法
an effective	way	効果的な方法
a good	way	よい方法
a quick	way	手っ取り早い方法
a simple	way	単純な方法
a proper	way	ふさわしい方法
the right	way	正しい方法
the wrong	way	誤った方法
a traditional	way	伝統的な方法
an alternative	way	代わりの方法
a different	way	異なる方法
various	ways	さまざまな方法
the same	way	同じ方法
a similar	way	似た方法
an odd	way	奇妙な方法
the right	way	正しい道
the wrong	way	間違った道
a long	way	長い道のり
a short	way	短い道のり
separate	ways	別々の道

▷There's no **easy way** to learn English! 英語を学ぶ楽な方法などない
▷I think I've done it the **wrong way**. やり方を間違えたと思う
▷Watch me and do it in the **same way**. 私を見て私と同じようにしなさい
▷Mike holds his chopsticks in an **odd way**. マイクのはしの持ち方は変だ
▷We came the **wrong way**. 道を間違えた
▷I don't think we can walk back to my house. It's quite a **long way**. 家まで歩いて帰るのは無理だよ. かなり距離があるから
▷I think it's better if we go our **separate ways**. 私たち, 別々の人生を歩むほうがいいわ

in	a way	ある意味では
in	a certain way	ある点で
in	every way	すべての点で
in	some ways	いくつかの点で
(in)	one way or another	何とかして;どちらにしろ
in	a big way	大規模に, はでに
(in)	one's own way	自分なりに

▷**In a way** I feel quite sorry for Tony. ある意味ではトニーにとても申し訳ないと思います
▷Tina's determined to become a famous pop star **one way or another**! ティナは何とかして有名なポップスターになろうと決めている
▷If we're going to expand our business we need to do it **in a big way**. ビジネスを拡大するなら大きく打って出る必要がある
▷Let me do it **in** my **own way**. 私流にやらせてね

on	the [one's] way	途中で
out of	the [one's] way	道筋から離れて
under	way	進行中で

▷Hi, Mike. I'm **on** my **way**. See you in ten minutes. やあ, マイク. いま向かっているところだ. 10分後に会おう
▷Plans for the new building are **under way**. 新ビルの計画が進行中だ

all	the way	途中ずっと, はるばる
all	this way	
all	that way	

▷He ran **all** the **way** home. 彼は家までずっと走って帰った

a [the] way	of doing	…する方法
a [the] way	to do	
the way	(that)...	…の仕方

▷We need to find a new **way of** promoting our product. うちの製品の販売を促進する新しい方法を見つける必要がある
▷Swimming is a nice **way to** relax. 泳ぐのはリラックスするよい方法です
▷I don't like the **way** he looks at me. 彼が私を見るときのようすが気に入らない

weak /wíːk/ 形 弱い；劣った

extremely	weak	非常に弱い
relatively	weak	比較的弱い
too	weak	あまりにも弱い

▷After the operation I felt **too weak** to do anything. 手術後，体力がすっかり落ちて何もできなかった

weak	at the knees	ひざがくがくして

▷Every time I see Rod I go **weak at** the **knees**! ロッドに会うたびにひざがかくがくする

wealth /wélθ/ 名 富, 財産；豊富

create	wealth	富を築く

▷Pete has a magic touch. He seems to be able to **create wealth** out of nothing. ピートの手際は魔法のようで，まるでゼロから富を築けるみたいだ

great	wealth	巨大な富
national	wealth	国富
personal	wealth	個人資産
household	wealth	家計資産

▷My grandfather was a man of **great wealth**. 祖父は大富豪だった
▷His **personal wealth** amounted to over a million pounds. 彼の個人資産は百万ポンドを超える額だった

a wealth	of A	豊富なA，多量のA

▷The Internet provided me with a **wealth of** information. インターネットから大量の情報が入手できた

the distribution of	wealth	富の分配

▷Communism is based on equal **distribution of wealth**. 共産主義は富の平等な分配に基づいている

wealth and power	富と権力

★ power and wealth も用いられる

▷Throughout history men have fought for **wealth and power**. 歴史を通して人間は富と権力を得るために戦ってきた

wear /wéər/

動 身に着けている；擦り切れる；長持ちする

wear	thin	擦り切れて薄くなる

wear	well	長持ちする

▷My jacket is beginning to **wear thin** at the elbows. 私の上着はひじの部分が擦り切れて薄くなり始めている
▷These boots have **worn** very **well**. このブーツはとても長持ちしている

weather /wéðər/ 名 天気, 天候

the weather	holds	天気がもつ
the weather	changes	天気が変わる
the weather	breaks	天気が崩れる
the weather	worsens	天気が悪くなる
the weather	improves	天気がよくなる
the weather	gets cold	天気が寒くなる
the weather	gets warm	天気が暖かくなる
the weather	allows	天気が許す
the weather	permits	

▷The English **weather changes** so often. イギリスの天気はしょっちゅう変わる
▷If the **weather improves** we can go for a hike. 天気がよくなったらハイキングに行ける
▷**Weather permitting**, we can climb to the top of the mountain. 天候が許せば山頂まで登れる

beautiful	weather	すばらしい天気
good	weather	よい天気
fine	weather	
lovely	weather	
perfect	weather	最高の天気
bad	weather	悪い天気
poor	weather	
rough	weather	荒れた天気
hot	weather	暑い天気
warm	weather	暖かい天気
mild	weather	穏やかな天気
sunny	weather	晴天
wet	weather	雨天
severe	weather	厳しい天気
cold	weather	寒い天気
stormy	weather	大荒れの天気
windy	weather	風の強い天気
summer	weather	夏の天候
winter	weather	冬の天候

▷We had **beautiful weather** and a marvelous time. 天気がよく，すばらしい時間を過ごした
▷We're hoping for **good weather** tomorrow. あすは天気がよくなるよう願っている
▷Are you sure you want to go out in the boat? It looks like **rough weather**. 本当にボートで出かけたいの？ 天気が荒れるようだけど

▷ They've forecast **wet weather** again for tomorrow. あすもまた雨との予報だ
▷ Typical English **summer weather**. Rain, rain and more rain! 典型的なイギリスの夏の天気だ。雨, 雨また雨だ

in	all weather(s)	どんな天気でも
whatever	the weather	天気がどうであれ

▷ The lifeboat men go out **in all weathers**. 救命艇の乗組員はどんな天候でも出動する
▷ Emma's determined to go jogging **whatever the weather**. 天気がどうであれジョギングに行くとエマは決めている

because of	bad weather	悪天候のため
due to	bad weather	

▷ Our flight was canceled **because of bad weather**. フライトは悪天候のため欠航になった

wedding /wédiŋ/ 名 結婚式, 婚礼

have	a wedding	結婚式を挙げる
attend	a wedding	結婚式に出席する

▷ Have you decided when you're going to **have** your **wedding**? 結婚式の日取りを決めたかい
▷ Over 300 guests **attended** the **wedding**. 300人以上が結婚式に出席した

week /wíːk/ 名 週

this	week	今週
last	week	先週
next	week	来週
the previous	week	その前の週
the following	week	次の週
a whole	week	丸1週間
a five-day	week	週5日制

▷ Bob came back from Canada **last week**. ボブは先週カナダから帰って来た
▷ I can't meet **next week**. How about the **following week**? 来週は会えません。その次の週はどうですか
▷ It took me a **whole week** to write that report. その報告書を書くのに丸1週間かかった
▷ Everybody's working a **five-day week**. みんな週5日制で働いている

the week	before last	先々週
the week	after next	再来週

▷ A friend from Japan came to stay with us the **week before last**. 日本からの友人が先々週やって来てうちに泊まった
▷ I start my new job the **week after next**. 再来週, 新しい仕事を始めます

every other	week	1週間おきに
every two	weeks	2週間おきに

▷ I go to visit my grandparents **every other week**. 1週間おきに祖父母のところへ行きます
▷ I have to go for a hospital checkup **every two weeks**. 2週間おきに病院に検査に行かなくてはならない

once	a week	1週間に1度
twice	a week	1週間に2度

▷ I go to the fitness club **twice a week**. 1週間に2回フィットネスクラブに行きます

earlier	this week	今週の前半
later	this week	今週の後半

▷ We had a letter from Carrie **earlier this week**. 今週前半にキャリーから手紙をもらった

by	the week	週ぎめで
during	the week	平日は
for	a week	1週間
in	a week	1週間したら
within	a week	1週間以内に

▷ In my part-time job I get paid **by the week**. アルバイト代は週ぎめでもらっている
▷ Weekends are our busiest time. We're not so busy **during the week**. 週末がいちばん忙しくて, 平日はそれほどでもありません
▷ We're going on holiday to France **for a week**. 1週間休暇をとってフランスへ出かけます

weekend /wíːkènd/ 名 週末

last	weekend	前の週末
next	weekend	次の週末
a whole	weekend	週末ずっと
a long	weekend	長い週末

▷ I spent the **whole weekend** revising for my exams. 週末はずっと試験に備えて復習をした
▷ Monday's a holiday so it's a **long weekend**. 月曜日は休日なので長い週末だ

on	the weekend	週末に
《英》at	the weekend	
over	the weekend	週末ずっと

▷ Do you want to go to Sydney **at** the **weekend**? 週末にシドニーに行きませんか
▷ Some friends came to stay with us **over** the **weekend**. 友人が何人か週末ずっとうちに泊まりに来た
〈PHRASES〉
Have a nice weekend. ☺ よい週末を ▷ "Have a nice weekend." "You, too." 「よい週末を」「あなたもね」

weigh /wéi/

動 重さがある；重さをはかる；よく考える

carefully	weigh	入念に検討する
weigh	up	じっくり検討する
weigh	heavily	重くのしかかる

▷ You should **carefully weigh** his advice. 彼の助言の重みを考えたほうがいい
▷ She **weighed** it **up** in her mind and finally said: "OK. Let's do it!" 心の中でじっくり考えてから彼女は最後に言った。「ではそうしましょう」

weigh	A against B	AをBと比較検討する

▷ We have to **weigh** the pros **against** the cons. 賛否両論を比較検討しなければならない

weight /wéit/ **名** 重さ, 体重；重み, 重要性

put on	weight	体重が増える
gain	weight	
lose	weight	体重が減る
watch	one's **weight**	体重に気をつける
carry	weight	重みがある
add	weight	重みを加える
lend	weight	
give	weight	重きを置く

▷ You've **lost** a lot of **weight** since I saw you last! この前会ってからずいぶんやせたね
▷ "Another piece of chocolate cake?" "I'd better not. I need to **watch** my **weight**!" 「チョコレートケーキをもう1ついかが？」「やめておくよ。体重に気をつけないと」
▷ People respect him so his words **carry** a lot of **weight**. 彼は人から尊敬されているので，彼のことばには重みがある
▷ I think the interviewers **give** as much **weight** *to* experience as qualifications. 面接官は資格と同じくらい経験を重視していると思う

ideal	weight	理想体重
body	weight	体重

▷ You can use a special formula to calculate your **ideal weight**. 理想体重を計算するのに特別な式を使える
▷ The relationship between your height and your **body weight** gives you your BMI. 身長と体重の関係から体格指数が求められる

in	weight	重さが
under	the weight of A	Aの重みで

▷ It was a big fish. Nearly 5 kilos **in weight**. 大きな魚で，重さが5キロ近くあった
▷ The little bridge collapsed **under** the **weight of** the truck. その小さな橋はトラックの重みで壊れた

welcome /wélkəm/ **名** 歓迎

a warm	welcome	温かい歓迎
a hearty	welcome	心からの歓迎

▷ I'd now like to extend a **warm welcome** to our guest speaker: Mr Owen! それでは来賓の講演者を温かく迎えたいと思います。オーウェンさんです

extend	a welcome	歓迎する
give	a welcome	
receive	a welcome	歓迎を受ける

▷ Would you please **give** a warm **welcome** to: Santa Claus! どうか温かくお迎えください。サンタクロースです
▷ We **received** a very warm **welcome**. 私たちはとても温かい歓迎を受けた

welcome /wélkəm/ **形** 歓迎される

always	welcome	いつでも歓迎だ
very	welcome	とても歓迎だ
more than	welcome	大歓迎だ
most	welcome	
particularly	welcome	特に歓迎だ

▷ Come and see us again soon. You know you're **always welcome**. いつでもまた会いに来てね。いつでも歓迎だから
▷ You are **very welcome** to telephone me this evening. 今夜私に電話してくれていいよ
▷ "It's really nice of you to let me stay the night." "No problem. You're **most welcome**!" 「泊めていただいて本当にありがとう」「どういたしまして。大歓迎です」

make A	welcome	A(人)を歓迎する

▷ The host family I stayed with **made** me very **welcome**. 滞在したホストファミリーは私をとても歓迎

| welcome |

してくれた

be welcome	to do	自由に…してよい

▷You're most **welcome to** use any of these computers. どのコンピュータでもどうぞ自由にお使いください

PHRASES
You're welcome. 😊 どういたしまして ▷"Thanks very much for your help." "You're welcome."「助けてくれてありがとう」「どういたしまして」

welcome /wélkəm/

動 歓迎する, 快く受け入れる

warmly	welcome	温かく歓迎する
particularly	welcome	特に歓迎する
be widely	welcomed	広く受け入れられる

▷We were **warmly welcomed** by everybody we met. 出会っただれからも温かく迎えられた
▷The news about tax cuts was **widely welcomed** by the public. 減税のニュースは大衆に広く受け入れられた

be delighted to	welcome	迎えてうれしい

▷Today we are **delighted to welcome** three new members of staff. きょう新人スタッフ3名をお迎えできてうれしく思います

well /wél/ 形 健康で, 元気で

well	enough	十分元気で

▷She isn't **well enough** to leave hospital yet. 彼女はまだ退院できるほど元気ではない

PHRASES
That is all very well, but... 😊 それはまことに結構ですが… ▷That's all very well, but what happens if there's a problem? それはまことに結構ですが, 問題が生じたらどうなりますか

wet /wét/ 形 湿った, ぬれた; 雨降りの

get	wet	ぬれる

▷I don't mind **getting wet**. ぬれても構いません

soaking	wet	びしょぬれの
dripping	wet	

▷There was a sudden downpour. I'm **soaking wet**. 突然の土砂降りでびしょぬれだ

wet and windy		雨で風のある

▷We walked along the cliff. It was really **wet and windy**. 崖に沿って歩いた。すごい雨と風だった

wet	with A	Aでぬれた

▷Her face was **wet with** tears. 彼女の顔は涙でぬれていた

while /hwáil | wáil/ 名 時間, 間

a little	while	少しの間
a short	while	
a long	while	長い間

▷Can you wait **a little while** longer? あともう少し待ってくれるかい
▷We queued a **long while** for tickets to the concert. コンサートのチケットを買おうと長いこと列に並んだ

after	a while	しばらくして
for	a while	しばらくの間
in	a while	少ししたら, 間もなく
quite	a while	かなり長いこと
a while	ago	少し前に

▷**After** a while my eyes got used to the dark. しばらくすると目が暗さに慣れた
▷Let's take a break **for** a **while**. しばらく休憩しよう
▷We'll be there **in** a little **while**. もう少しで着きます
▷It'll take **quite** a **while** to get there. そこに着くまでにかなり長くかかるだろう
▷There was a phone call for you a **while ago**. 少し前にあなたに電話がありました

whisper /hwíspər | wís-/ 名 ささやき, 小声

a low	whisper	低いささやき
a stage	whisper	聞こえよがしのささやき

▷"I told you so, Paul," he added in a **stage whisper** so that everybody could hear. 「だから言ったのに, ポール」と彼はみんなに聞こえよがしにつぶやいた

in	a whisper	小声で

▷"Sssssh! They mustn't hear us," he said, speaking **in** a **whisper**. 「しっ, 私たちの話を聞かれないようにしなくちゃ」と彼は小声で言った

whisper /hwíspər | wís-/ 動 ささやく

| whisper | softly | 優しくささやく |
| whisper | urgently | せっぱ詰まったようにささやく |

▷"There's a fire! We need to evacuate everybody from the hotel," she **whispered urgently**. 「火事だわ．ホテルからみんなを避難させなくては」とせっぱ詰まったようすで彼女はささやいた

| whisper | in A's ear | Aの耳元でささやく |
| whisper | into A's ear | |

▷What did he **whisper in** your **ear**? あなたの耳元で彼は何をささやいたの

| whisper | (A) to B | (Aを)B(人)にささやく |

▷She **whispered** something **to** me, but I couldn't hear what she said. 彼女は私に何かささやいたが，何と言ったか聞こえなかった

| whisper | that... | …と小声で言う；…とうわさする |

▷She **whispered that** the lecture was really boring. とても退屈な講義だわと彼女は小声で言った

whole /hóul/ 名 全体，全部

| the whole | of A | Aの全部 |

▷The weather was terrible. We spent the **whole of** the time in the hotel. ひどい天気で，ずっとホテルで過ごしたよ

| as | a whole | 全体として |
| on | the whole | 全体的に言えば，概して |

▷We should look at the situation **as** a **whole**, not just how it affects individuals. 全体として状況を見たほうがいいね．個々人にどう影響があるかだけじゃなく
▷**On** the **whole** I prefer classical music to pop. 概してポップスよりクラシック音楽が好きだ

wide /wáid/ 形 幅の広い；幅が…ある

extremely	wide	とても幅が広い
increasingly	wide	ますます幅が広い
relatively	wide	比較的幅が広い
sufficiently	wide	十分に幅が広い

▷The gap between rich and poor in this country is becoming **increasingly wide**. この国の貧富の格差はますます広がりつつある

three inches	wide	3インチの幅
three feet [foot]	wide	3フィートの幅
three meters	wide	3メートルの幅

▷There was a hole in the fence three **foot wide**. フェンスに幅3フィートの穴があった

wife /wáif/ 名 妻

have	a wife	妻がいる
leave	one's wife	妻と別れる
lose	one's wife	妻を亡くす
love	one's wife	妻を愛する

▷Tom **has** a **wife** and three children. トムには妻と3人の子どもがいる
▷He **left** his **wife** three years ago. 彼は3年前に妻と別れた
▷He **lost** his **wife** in a car accident. 彼は自動車事故で妻を亡くした

A's new	wife	新妻
A's future	wife	未来の妻
A's former	wife	前妻
A's estranged	wife	別居中の妻
A's late	wife	亡き妻
A's pregnant	wife	妊娠中の妻

▷Did you hear? I've become engaged. This is my **future wife**. もう聞いてるかな．ぼく婚約したんだ．こちらが未来の妻です
▷His **former wife** was a top fashion model. 彼の前妻はトップファッションモデルだった(★ ex-wife ともいう：Actually she's my ex-wife. 実を言うと彼女はぼくの前の奥さんなんだ)

| one's wife and children | | 妻と子どもたち |
| Bob and his wife | | ボブ夫妻 |

▷Did you know that Alex has a **wife and children** back in Canada? アレックスにはカナダに奥さんと子どもがいると知ってたかい
▷Bob **and his wife** are coming to the party. ボブ夫妻がパーティーに来ます

wild /wáild/

形 野生の；未開の；猛烈な；乱暴な

| go | wild | 熱狂する；したい放題する |
| run | wild | |

▷She **went wild** with joy after she won the gold medal in the Olympics. オリンピックで金メダルをとっ

て彼女は大喜びした
▷They let their children **run wild** all over the place. 子どもたちにどこでも自由にさせた

wild and crazy	荒れ狂った

▷He has some really **wild and crazy** ideas. 彼は実に大それたとんでもない考えをもっている

willing /wíliŋ/ 形 自ら進んでする

perfectly	willing	心から喜んで
always	willing	いつも喜んで
no longer	willing	もう喜んで…しない

▷Joe says he's going to quit his part-time job. He's **no longer willing** *to* work for such low wages. ジョーはバイトを辞めると言っている.あんな低賃金の仕事をやる気はもうない

willing	to do	喜んで…する

▷He says he's **willing to** do anything to help. 喜んで何でも手伝うと彼は言っている

a willing	helper	進んで手伝う人

★ worker, volunteer なども用いる

▷We need lots of **willing helpers** to prepare for the festival. 祭りの準備を進んで手伝ってくれる人がたくさん必要だ

win /wín/ 名 勝利

a big	win	圧勝
a convincing	win	
an easy	win	楽勝
a good	win	快勝
successive	win(s)	連勝
consecutive	win(s)	

▷I just had a **big win** on the national lottery! 全国宝くじで大当たりしたよ
▷Serena Williams was hoping for a third **successive win** at Wimbledon. セリーナ・ウィリアムズはウィンブルドンでの3連覇をねらっていた(★ three successive wins も用いる)

a win	over A	Aへの勝利

▷Manchester United had a 3–1 **win over** Liverpool on Saturday. マンチェスター・ユナイテッドは土曜日リバプールに3対1で勝った

win /wín/ 動 勝つ;勝ち取る,手に入れる

easily	win	簡単に勝つ
narrowly	win	きわどく勝つ
eventually	win	最終的に勝つ
finally	win	

▷Lucy **easily won** the race. ルーシーはレースに楽勝した
▷At halftime we were losing 2–0, but we **eventually won** 3–2. ハーフタイムでは2対0で負けていたが,最終的に3対2で勝った

win or lose	勝っても負けても

▷**Win or lose**, let's make sure we play our best. 勝とうが負けようが全力を尽くそう

PHRASES
You win! 😊 きみの勝ちだ

wind /wínd/ 名 風;動向,傾向

the wind	blows	風が吹く
the wind	gusts	突風が吹く
the wind	howls	風がうなる
the wind	drops	風がやむ

▷The **wind's blowing** really hard outside. 外は風がすごく激しく吹いている
▷Listen! Can you hear the **wind howling**? ほら,風がうなっているのが聞こえるかい
▷Let's shelter somewhere until the **wind drops**. 風がやむまでどこかに避難しよう

a strong	wind	強風
a high	wind	
a light	wind	そよ風
a warm	wind	暖かい風
a biting	wind	身を切るような冷たい風
a bitter	wind	い風
a cold	wind	冷たい風
a chill	wind	
an icy	wind	氷のように冷たい風
a howling	wind	うなる風
the prevailing	wind	卓越風
the solar	wind	太陽風

▷The forecast is for **strong winds** and rain. 予報では強風と雨だ
▷The temperature outside was below zero and there was a **biting wind**. 外の気温は氷点下で,身を切るような冷たい風が吹いていた
▷A snowstorm had begun and an **icy wind** was

blowing. 吹雪が吹き始め，氷のような冷たい風が吹いていた
▷The **prevailing wind** is usually from the south-west. 卓越風はたいてい南西から吹く

against	the wind	風に逆らって
in	the wind	風の中を

▷It was difficult to cycle uphill **against** the **wind**. 風に逆らって自転車で坂を上るのは難しかった

a gust of	wind	突風

▷A **gust of wind** blew all the papers off my desk. 一陣の風で机の上の書類がみんな吹き飛んだ

wind and rain		風と雨，風雨

▷I don't like driving through all this **wind and rain**. この風雨の中を車を走らせるのはいやだ

wind /wáind/ 動 巻く；曲がる

wind	tightly	しっかり巻く

▷Don't **wind** the watch too **tightly**. It'll break. 時計のねじを巻きすぎないように。壊れるから

wind	A around B	AをBに巻く
wind	A round B	

▷The nurse **wound** a bandage **around** his leg. 看護師は包帯を彼の脚に巻いた

window /wíndou/ 名 窓, 窓ガラス

open	a window	窓を開ける
close	a window	窓を閉める
shut	a window	
look out (of)	the window	窓から外を見る
look through	the window	窓を通して見る
break	a window	窓を割る
smash	a window	窓をたたき割る

▷Could somebody **open** a **window**? だれか窓を開けていただけませんか
▷Quick! **Look out** (**of**) the **window**! 急いで。窓の外を見てごらん
▷Who **broke** the **window**? 窓を割ったのはだれだ
▷They had to **smash** a **window** to get out of the car. 車から出るために彼らは窓をたたき割らなくてはならなかった

a large	window	大きな窓
a big	window	
a small	window	小さな窓
a bay	window	張り出し窓
a French	window	フランス窓
an open	window	開いている窓
a broken	window	割れた窓
a bedroom	window	寝室の窓
a kitchen	window	台所の窓
a show	window	ショーウインドー

▷The study has two **large windows** so there's plenty of light. 書斎には大きな窓が2つあるので，日の光がよく入る
▷The thief climbed in through an **open window**. 泥棒は開いた窓からよじ登って中に入った

wine /wáin/ 名 ワイン

pour	wine	ワインを注ぐ
produce	wine	ワインを生産する

▷I **poured** some **wine** in a glass. グラスにワインを注いだ

red	wine	赤ワイン
white	wine	白ワイン
dry	wine	辛口ワイン
sweet	wine	甘口ワイン
chilled	wine	よく冷えたワイン

▷**Dry** white **wine**, please. 辛口の白ワインをください
▷I'd love a glass of **chilled** white **wine**. よく冷えた白ワインを1杯飲みたい

a glass of	wine	1杯のワイン
a bottle of	wine	ワイン1本

▷Could I have another **glass of wine**? ワインをもう1杯いただけますか

winter /wíntər/ 名 冬, 冬季

last	winter	前の冬
next	winter	今度の冬
early	winter	初冬
late	winter	晩冬
a long	winter	長い冬
a cold	winter	寒い冬
a severe	winter	厳しい冬
a hard	winter	
a mild	winter	穏やかな冬

▷This year we're going to take our holiday in late

| wipe |

autumn or **early winter**. 今年は晩秋か初冬に休暇をとるつもりだ
▷ It's going to be a **cold winter** this year. 今年は寒い冬になるだろう
▷ It was a **severe winter** with temperatures well below zero. 気温が零度をはるかに下回る厳しい冬だった
▷ We had a very **mild winter** this year. 今年はとても穏やかな冬だった

in	(the) winter	冬に
during	(the) winter	冬の間
through	the winter	冬を通して
throughout	the winter	冬の間ずっと

▷ It gets very cold here **in** the **winter**. ここは冬にはとても寒くなる
▷ We had some really heavy snow **during** the **winter**. 冬の間かなりの大雪が降った
▷ Tony went jogging every day **through** the **winter**. トニーは冬を通して毎日ジョギングに出かけた

wipe /wáip/ 動 ふく

carefully	wipe	注意深くふく
gently	wipe	そっとふく
quickly	wipe	さっとふく

▷ He took off his glasses and **carefully wiped** them with his clean handkerchief. 彼は眼鏡を外してきれいなハンカチでていねいにふいた

wipe	away	ふきとる
wipe	up	

▷ She tried to **wipe away** her tears. 彼女は涙をふきとろうとした

wipe	A from B	AをBからふきとる
wipe	A off B	

▷ I need a tissue to **wipe** this egg **off** my tie. ネクタイについた卵をふきとるのにティッシュがいる

wisdom /wízdəm/ 名 知恵, 賢明さ

conventional	wisdom	世間の常識
received	wisdom	
accepted	wisdom	

▷ According to **conventional wisdom** a red sky at night means good weather the following day. 夕焼けの翌日は晴れになると一般に信じられている

words of	wisdom	名言；賢明な教え

▷ Let me give you some **words of wisdom**. きみにいい助言をさせてくれ

wise /wáiz/ 形 賢明な, 賢い

grow	wise	賢くなる
seem	wise	賢明と思われる

▷ What we did **seemed wise** at the time, but now I'm not so sure. われわれがやったことはその時は賢明だと思ったが, いまでは確信がない

wise	enough	十分に賢い

▷ Luckily she was **wise enough** to say nothing. 幸い彼女には何も言わないだけの分別があった

wise	to do	…するのは賢明な

▷ It's **wise to** take out travel insurance when you go on holiday abroad. 海外へ休暇に出かけるときは旅行保険に入るのが賢明だ

wish /wíʃ/ 名 願い, 願望

express	a wish	願いを口にする
get	one's wish	願いがかなう
grant	A's wish	願いをかなえる
respect	A's wishes	願いを尊重する
make	a wish	願いごとをする

▷ You always said you wanted to go abroad to study and now you've **got** your **wish**. きみはいつも留学したいと言っていたけど, やっと願いがかなったね
▷ We're prepared to **grant** your **wish** under three conditions. 3つの条件のもとであなたの願いをかなえる用意がある
▷ You should **respect** your father's **wishes** and try to enter university. お父さんの願いを尊重して大学に入るようにしたほうがいい
▷ You throw a coin into the well and **make** a **wish**. 井戸にコインを投げて願いごとをします

give A	one's best wishes	A(人)によろしくと伝える
send A	one's best wishes	

▷ **Give** Clare my **best wishes** when you see her. クレアに会ったらよろしく伝えて

A's wish	comes true	望みがかなう

▷ I always wanted to ride in a hot-air balloon and now my **wish** has **come true**! ずっと熱気球に乗りたかったが, やっと望みがかなった

a wish	for A	Aを求める願い

▷Emily always had a **wish for** fame and now she's a pop star. エミリーはいつも名声を求めていたが、いまやポップスターだ

a wish	to do	…したいという願望

▷I've always had a **wish to** travel to South America. ずっと南アメリカに旅行したいと思っていた

against	A's wishes	願いに反して
according to	A's wishes	願いどおり

▷She left school at 16 **against** the **wishes of** her parents. 彼女は両親の願いに反して16歳で学校をやめた

wit /wít/ 名 機知

a biting	wit	辛辣な機知
an acerbic	wit	

▷He was known for his **biting wit**. 彼は辛辣な機知で知られていた

wit and humor		機知とユーモア

▷He was often praised for his **wit and humor**. 彼はよくその機知とユーモアをほめられた

woman /wúmən/ 名 女性

a young	woman	若い女性
an old	woman	高齢の女性
an elderly	woman	
an attractive	woman	魅力的な女性
a beautiful	woman	美しい女性
a married	woman	既婚女性
a single	woman	独身女性
a pregnant	woman	妊婦
a working	woman	働く女性

▷You can see by her ring that she's a **married woman**. 指輪で彼女が既婚だとわかる

▷It's difficult to be a **working woman** and a mother at the same time. 仕事と育児を両立させるのは難しい

wonder /wʌ́ndər/

名 驚き；不思議なこと、驚くべきこと

do	wonders	驚くほど効果がある
work	wonders	

▷Take some of this medicine. It **works wonders**. この薬を飲んでみて。驚くほど効くから

in	wonder	驚いて

▷He gazed **in wonder** at the beautiful view before him. 彼は目の前の美しい風景を驚嘆して見つめた

a sense of	wonder	驚嘆の念

▷Kate looked up at the stars above with a **sense of wonder**. ケイトは驚嘆の念で星を見上げた

wonder /wʌ́ndər/ 動 …かと思う、だろうか

wonder	wh-	…かどうかと思う

★wh- は why, where, what, who, how など

▷**I wonder why** she said that. なぜ彼女はそんなことを言ったのかな
▷**I wonder what** she's going to do. 彼女は何をするつもりなんだろう
▷**I wonder how** she found out. 彼女はどのようにして知ったのだろう

wonder	if	…かと思う
wonder	whether	

▷**I wonder if** Pete will come to the party. ピートはパーティーに来るかな
▷**I wonder whether** Alan and Lea are still dating. アランとリーはまだつきあっているのかな
♦**I wonder if / I wonder whether** …してもらえませんか；…しないかなと思う ▷**I wonder if you would** open the window. 窓を開けていただけませんか ▷**I was wondering if you'd like to** see a movie this weekend? この週末に映画を見ませんか

wonder	about A	Aのことを考える；Aを変だと思う

▷I was **wondering about** the wedding. How many people do you want to invite? 結婚式のことを考えていたんだけど、きみは何人招待したい？

wonderful /wʌ́ndərfəl/

形 すばらしい、すてきな

sound	wonderful	すばらしそうだ

| wood |

▷ "We're going to a Justin Bieber live concert this weekend!" "Wow! That **sounds wonderful!**"「今週末ジャスティン・ビーバーのライブコンサートに行くの」「へえ，それはすばらしいね」

really	wonderful	実にすばらしい
absolutely	wonderful	まったくすばらしい
quite	wonderful	とてもすばらしい

▷ It was a **really wonderful** party. Thanks for inviting us. 実にすばらしいパーティーでした。招待していただいてありがとう

PHRASES

How wonderful! 😊 まあすてき ▷ "Tom's asked me to marry him!" "Oh! How wonderful!"「結婚してってトムに言われたの」「まあすてき」

That's wonderful! 😊 すばらしい ▷ "I got two tickets for a Purple Days concert!" "Wow! That's wonderful!"「パープルデイズのコンサートのチケットを2枚手に入れたよ」「わあ，それはすばらしい」

▌wood /wúd/

名 木材；(the woods で)(小さな)森

cut	wood	木材を切る
chop	wood	木材を割る
be made of	wood	木でできている

▷ This old saw isn't sharp enough to **cut wood**. この古いのこぎりは鈍くて木材を切れない

▷ Bill's outside **chopping wood** for the fire. ビルは外で暖炉用の薪を割っている

▷ It was a beautifully carved statue **made of wood**. 美しく彫られた像で，木でできていた

hard	wood	硬材
soft	wood	軟材
natural	wood	天然木

▷ The floor in the hall is made of **natural wood**. 玄関ホールの床は天然木でできている

through	the woods	森を抜けて

▷ I often take my dog for a walk **through** the **woods**. よく犬を連れて森を散歩する

a piece of	wood	木片

▷ We need a longer **piece of wood**. もう少し長い木片が必要だ

▌word /wə́ːrd/

名 語；ことば，ひとこと，会話；口論；知らせ；約束

use	a word	語を使う
look up	a word	語を調べる
understand	a word	語を理解する
find	the word	語を見つける
say	a word	ひとこと言う
speak	a word	
hear	a word	ことばが聞こえる
choose	one's words	ことばを選ぶ
want	a word	話をしたい
have	a word	話をする
have	words	口論する
exchange	words	
remember	the words	発言を覚えている
eat	one's words	前言を取り消す
keep	one's word	約束を守る
break	one's word	約束を破る
send	word	知らせる

▷ I can't understand these instructions. Why don't they **use** simple **words**? この説明書はわからない。なぜ簡単な語を使わないのかな

▷ **Look up** any **words** you don't know in a dictionary. 知らない語は辞書で調べなさい

▷ Remember. Don't **say a word**! It's a secret! いいかい，ひとことも言っちゃだめだ。秘密だから

▷ Can I **have a word** with your father? お父さんと話できるかな

▷ She **had words** with her sister and they haven't spoken to each other ever since. 彼女は妹と口論し，それ以来お互いに話をしていない

▷ She made him **eat his words**. 彼女は彼に前言を取り消させた

▷ He **kept** his **word** and repaid all the money he owed me. 彼は約束を守って，私に借りていた金を全部返した

▷ Can you **send word** to Thompson that the meeting is ready to start? 会議が始まる準備が整ったとトンプソンに知らせてくれるかい

an English	word	英単語
a long	word	長い語
a big	word	難解な語
the right	word	ぴったりの語
a dirty	word	汚いことば
the magic	word	魔法のことば
the spoken	word	話しことば
the written	word	書きことば

▷ Our four-year-old daughter has started to use some **big words**! 4歳になるうちの娘は難しい語を使い始めた

▷ Yes. "Delicious." That's exactly the **right word**. そうだ。「デリシャス」こそぴったりの語だ

▷Don't use that word. It's a **dirty word**. その語を使っちゃだめだ。汚いことばだから
▷The **spoken word** is often more powerful than the **written word**. 話しことばはしばしば書きことばよりも力強い

sense of	the word	語の意味
a meaning of	the word	

▷My grandfather was using "gay" in the original **sense of** the **word** to mean happy. 祖父は「うれしい」というもとの意味で "gay" という語を使っていた

in	a word	ひとことで言えば
without	a word	ひとことも言わずに
in other	words	言い換えれば
in one's own	words	自分のことばで

▷That meal was, **in a word**, scrumptious! その食事はひとことで言えばとてもおいしかった
▷She turned and walked out of the room **without a word**. 彼女は振り返り、ひとことも言わずに部屋を出て行った

word	for word	一語一語そのまま

▷This is a **word for word** translation of what was said. これは発言の逐語訳だ

work /wə́ːrk/ 名 仕事, 労働; 職; 作品

do	the work	仕事する
carry out	the work	
get down to	work	仕事に取りかかる
set to	work	
continue	the work	仕事を続ける
have	work	仕事がある
look for	work	仕事を探す
seek	work	
find	work	仕事を見つける
go to	work	仕事に行く
start	work	仕事を始める
finish	work	仕事を終える
return to	work	仕事に戻る

▷Come on. Finish your tea. It's time we **got down to work**! さあお茶を飲んでしまって、もう仕事に取りかかる時間だ
▷We still **have** lots of **work** to do. やる仕事がまだたくさんある
▷She didn't **go to work** this morning. 彼女はけさは仕事に行かなかった
▷Sharon **starts work** in a supermarket next week. シャロンは来週スーパーマーケットで働き始める

▷What time do you **finish work**? 仕事は何時に終わるの？
▷I'm still not well enough to **return to work**. まだ仕事に戻れるほどは体が回復していない

hard	work	骨の折れる仕事
heavy	work	重労働
light	work	軽い仕事
extra	work	余分な仕事
dirty	work	人のいやがる仕事
practical	work	実習
paid	work	有給の仕事
well-paid	work	賃金の高い仕事
full-time	work	常勤の仕事
part-time	work	パートの仕事
voluntary	work	ボランティア活動

▷I like my job but it's **hard work**. 仕事は好きだが、大変だ
▷This university course contains a lot of **practical work**. この大学のコースでは実習が多くある
▷My sister is doing some **voluntary work** to help the homeless. 姉はホームレスの人を助けるボランティア活動をしている

the works	by A	Aの作品

▷An exhibition of the **works by** Picasso starts next week. ピカソの作品の展覧会が来週始まる

at	work	仕事中の; 働いている
out of	work	失業して

▷My husband's still **at work**. 夫はまだ仕事中です
▷My brother's been **out of work** for three months. 兄は3か月間、失業中だ

PHRASES

Good work! / **Nice work!** ☺ よくやったね！ ▷"I got an A for my essay!" "Good work!" 「レポートでAをもらったよ」「よくがんばったね」

work /wə́ːrk/

動 働く, 働かせる; 動く, 動かす; 勉強する

work	hard	一生懸命働く
work	full-time	フルタイムで働く
work	part-time	パートで働く
work	overtime	残業する
work	closely	親しく働く
work	together	いっしょに働く
work	effectively	うまく作動する
work	properly	正常に作動する
work	well	うまく機能する

| worker |

▷ You'll need to **work hard** to get into university. 大学へ入るには一生懸命勉強する必要があるだろう
▷ Tom **works part-time** at a gas station. トムはガソリンスタンドでアルバイトをしている
▷ We share the same office and **work closely** *with* each other. 私たちは共同で事務所を使い, 互いに親しく仕事している
▷ Our new management system is **working** very **effectively**. うちの新しい経営システムはとても効率的に機能している
▷ This flashlight doesn't **work properly**. この懐中電灯は正常に作動しない

work	as A	Aとして働く
work	at A	A(場所)で働く
work	for A	A(会社・業種)で働く
work	on A	Aに取り組む
work	with A	A(人)と働く

▷ She **works as** a nurse in the city hospital. 彼女は市民病院で看護師として働いている
▷ He's **worked for** the same company for nearly 30 years. 彼は同じ会社で30年近く働いている
▷ I'm still **working on** my Ph.D. まだ博士号に取り組んでいる
▷ Colin is a difficult person to **work with**. コリンといっしょに働くのは難しい

worker /wə́ːrkər/ 名 労働者

a hard	worker	よく働く人
a good	worker	
a slow	worker	仕事の遅い人
a part-time	worker	パートタイマー
a temporary	worker	臨時労働者
a skilled	worker	熟練労働者
an unskilled	worker	未熟練労働者
a manual	worker	単純労働者
an office	worker	事務職員
a clerical	worker	
a factory	worker	工場労働者
a farm	worker	農場労働者
a health	worker	医療従事者
a rescue	worker	救助員

▷ We need to employ some more **temporary workers**. 臨時雇いをもっと増やす必要がある
▷ My elder sister's going to be an **office worker**. 姉は事務職員になるつもりだ

world /wə́ːrld/ 名 世界；世の中

create	the world	世界を創造する
travel	the world	世界を旅する
see	the world	世界を見る；見聞を広める
change	the world	世の中を変える
come into	the world	生まれる
bring A into	the world	A(子)を生む

▷ Who do you believe **created** the **world**? 世界を創造したのはだれだと思いますか
▷ Take the opportunity to **travel** the **world** while you're still young. まだ若いうちに世界を旅行する機会をもちなさい
▷ I want to travel and **see** the **world**. 世界を旅して, 見てみたい
▷ She **came into** the **world** weighing only 1.8 kilograms. 彼女は体重たった1.8キロで生まれた
▷ It's a big responsibility to **bring** a child **into** the **world**. 子どもを産むのは大きな責任が伴う

the whole	world	全世界
the Arab	world	アラブ世界
the Islamic	world	イスラム世界
the Western	world	西洋世界
the ancient	world	古代世界
the modern	world	現代世界
the outside	world	外の世界
the real	world	現実の世界
the animal	world	動物界
the natural	world	自然界
the business	world	経済界
the sports	world	スポーツ界

▷ My grandmother lived in a little village all her life and knows very little about the **outside world**. 祖母は一生を小さな村で暮らしてきたので, 外の世界をほとんど知らない
▷ You don't know anything about the **real world**! きみには現実の世界のことが何もわかっていない

all over	the world	世界中で
throughout	the world	
all around	the world	

▷ Visitors came from **all over** the **world**. 観光客が世界中からやって来た
▷ The Beatles became famous **throughout** the **world**. ビートルズは世界中で有名になった
▷ The flu epidemic spread quickly **all around** the **world**. インフルエンザの流行はすぐ世界中に広まった

in	the world	世界で

▷ This is one of the tallest buildings **in** the **world**. これは世界一高いビルの一つです

♦**go up in the world** 出世する ▷She's president of the company now. She's really gone up in the world. 彼女はいまや会社社長だ。実に出世したものだ

| the rest of | the world | 世界の他の地域 |

▷I've been to South America and Africa and now I want to travel around the **rest of the world**. 南米とアフリカに行ったことがあるが、次は世界の他の地域を旅行したい

PHRASES
It's a small world. ☺ 世の中は狭い

worried /wə́ːrid | wʌ́r-/ 形 心配している

| get | worried | 心配になる |

▷She **gets worried** very easily. 彼女は心配症だ

desperately	worried	ひどく心配している
extremely	worried	
deeply	worried	
slightly	worried	少し心配している

▷The family is **desperately worried**. Dave had a terrible car crash and is in hospital. デイブが大きな車の衝突事故にあって入院しているので、家族はひどく心配している

| worried | about A | Aのことで心配している |

▷It's after midnight! I was **worried about** you! 真夜中を過ぎているんだよ。きみのこと、心配しちゃったじゃないか

| worried | that... | …を心配している |

▷I was **worried that** you hadn't got my message. きみがぼくの伝言を受け取っていないんじゃないかと心配した

worse /wə́ːrs/ 形 より悪い

| get | worse | さらに悪くなる |

▷I feel terrible. My cold's **got worse**. 気分がすぐれない。かぜはさらに悪化した

| much | worse | はるかに悪い |
| far | worse | |

▷The sales figures are **much worse** than we thought. 売上高は思っていたよりずっと悪かった
▷Things have got **far worse** since we last spoke. 前回話してから事態はさらに悪くなっている

| worth |

| worse and worse | | どんどん悪くなる |

▷The children's behavior is getting **worse and worse**. 子どもたちの態度はどんどん悪くなりつつある

worst /wə́ːrst/ 形 最悪の、最も悪い

| one of | the worst A | 最悪のAの一つ |
| the worst | possible A | 起こりうる最悪のA |

▷That's **one of the worst** movies I've ever seen. いままでに見た最悪の映画の一つだ
▷That's **the worst possible** outcome. それは起こりうる最悪の結果だ

worst /wə́ːrst/ 名 最悪の状態

| fear | the worst | 最悪の事態を恐れる |
| prepare for | the worst | 最悪の事態に備える |

▷I'm not sure what's going to happen, but I think we should **prepare for the worst**. 何が起こるかわからないが、最悪の事態に備えておいたほうがいいと思う

| the worst | of it | 最悪なのは |

▷**The worst of it** is that I still haven't told my mother. 最悪なのは母にまだ話していないことだ

| at | worst | 最悪でも |
| at | one's worst | 最悪の状態で |

▷I think we'll make a really good profit this year. **At worst** it will still be better than last year. 今年はかなりの利益を出すと思う。最悪でも昨年よりさらにいいだろう
▷**At his worst** Nigel is still a better tennis player than Mike. 最悪の状態でもナイジェルはマイクより優れたテニス選手だ

worth /wə́ːrθ/ 形 価値がある

| well | worth | 十分に価値がある |
| really | worth | 本当に価値がある |

▷We paid a lot extra to go on some special tours but it was **well worth** doing it. 特別ツアーに参加するのに余分にかなり払ったが、それだけの価値はあった

| be worth | doing | …する価値がある |

▷If you have time it's well **worth** visiting the Tower of London. 時間があるならロンドン塔は訪れる

| write |

価値が十分あります

worth	A	Aの価値がある
worth	it	それだけの価値がある

★A は ten dollars などの金額や，a lot, a visit など

▷ This contract is **worth** more than 10 million US dollars. この契約は1千万米ドル以上の価値がある
▷ All that effort was **worth it**. いろいろがんばってみただけの価値はあった

write /ráit/ 動 書く；手紙を書く

write	clearly	はっきり書く；わかりやすく書く
write	properly	きちんと書く
write	down	書き留める
write	back	返事を書く

▷ My young son isn't old enough to **write properly**, but he can use a word processor! うちの息子はまだきちんと文字が書ける年ではないんだが，ワープロは使えるんだ
▷ I've written to him several times, but he hasn't **written back**. 彼に数回手紙を書いたが，返事が来ない

write	about A	Aについて書く
write	on A	
write	for A	Aのために書く
write	to A	Aに手紙を書く

▷ I have to **write** an essay **about** my summer holidays. 夏休みについて作文を書かなくてはいけない
▷ The Peter Rabbit stories were **written for** children. ピーターラビットの物語は子どもたちのために書かれた
▷ Promise you'll **write to** me. 私に手紙を書くと約束して

write	A B	A(人)にB(手紙など)を書く
write	B to A	
write	A on B	AをB(紙など)に書く

▷ I need to **write** a letter **to** my parents. 両親に手紙を書かなくちゃ
▷ I'll **write** my address **on** the back of this envelope. この封筒の裏に私の住所を書きます

write	that...	…と手紙で知らせる

▷ Kevin **wrote that** he was well and happy in Australia. ケビンはオーストラリアで元気で幸せに暮らしていると書いてきた

PHRASES
Write your name and address here, please. 😊 名前と住所をここにお書きください

wrong /rɔ́ːŋ | rɔ́ŋ/

形 間違った，誤った；悪い；調子が悪い

seriously	wrong	ひどく間違っている
totally	wrong	まったく間違っている
completely	wrong	
entirely	wrong	
morally	wrong	道徳的に間違っている

▷ I'm useless at math. I always get the answer **totally wrong**! 私は数学がだめだ．いつも答えを完全に間違える

it is wrong	to do	…するのは悪い

▷ Do you think **it**'s **wrong to** download pop music from the Internet? ポップミュージックをインターネットからダウンロードするのは間違っていると思いますか

PHRASES
Correct me if I'm wrong, but... 私が間違っていれば訂正してほしいのですが… / **Correct me if I'm wrong, but haven't we met somewhere before?** 間違っていたら申し訳ないですが，以前どこかでお会いしましたか
There is nothing wrong (with A) (Aには)何も悪いところがない / **There is something wrong (with A)** (Aには)何かおかしなところがある ▷ There's something wrong with the refrigerator. 冷蔵庫はどこかおかしい
What's wrong? 😊 どうかしましたか；(…して)どうして悪いのか

Y

year /jíər/ 名 年；歳；学年

spend	one year	1年を過ごす
take	one year	1年かかる

▷ Kumiko **spent** three **years** living in Australia. 久美子は3年オーストラリアで過ごした
▷ This university course **takes** four **years** to complete. この大学の課程は終えるのに4年かかる

last	year	昨年
this	year	今年
next	year	来年
the year	after next	再来年
the year	before last	一昨年
the previous	year	前年
recent	years	近年
a calendar	year	暦年
a leap	year	うるう年

the academic	year	学年度
the school	year	
the fiscal	year	会計年度;
《英》the financial	year	営業年度

▷I'm hoping to go to university **next year**. 来年大学へ行きたいと思っている
▷I'm going to graduate the **year after next**. 再来年に卒業する予定だ
▷I left school the **year before last**. 一昨年学校を出た
▷This year's exam results are much better than those from the **previous year**. 今年の試験結果は前年よりずっとよい
▷**In recent years** people have become much more aware of the environment. 近年は人々はずっと環境を意識するようになってきている
▷This is the timetable for the **academic year**. これが学年度の時間割です

early in	the year	年の初め
late in	the year	年の暮れ
the beginning of	the year	年度初め
the end of	the year	年度末

▷I got a new job **early in** the year. 年の初めに新しい仕事を得た
▷We won't know the results of our exams until the **end of** the year. 年度末まで試験の結果はわからない

| year | after year | 来る年も来る年も |
| year | by year | 年ごとに, 年々 |

▷I don't want to do the same job **year after year**. 毎年同じ仕事をしていたくない
▷He saved up his money **year by year**. 彼は年々お金を蓄えた

a year	from today	来年のきょう
a year	ago today	去年のきょう
three years	ago	3年前に
three years	later	3年後に

▷Let's meet again a **year from today**. 来年のきょうまた会いましょう
▷Sharon and Kevin got divorced three **years ago**. シャロンとケビンは3年前に離婚した

in	the year 2025	西暦2025年に
for	years	何年も
over	the years	長年にわたって

▷I wonder what the world will be like **in** the **year** 2025. 2025年の世界はどんなだろうか
▷I haven't seen Bill **for years**. ビルには何年も会っていない
▷I think I've grown a little wiser **over** the **years**. 長年の間に私も少しは賢くなったと思う

| all (the) | year around | 年中 |
| all (the) | year round | |

▷We're so far north here that there's snow **all year round**. この辺りは最北に位置するので年中雪が降ります

yesterday /jéstərdèi/ 名 昨日

yesterday	afternoon	昨日の午後
yesterday	evening	昨日の夜
yesterday	morning	昨日の朝

★night は ×yesterday night ではなく last night という

▷This letter arrived **yesterday morning**. この手紙は昨日の朝に届きました（★×last morning, last afternoon とはいわない）

| the day before | yesterday | 一昨日 |

▷We had lunch together the **day before yesterday**. 私たちはおととい昼食をいっしょにとった

young /jʌ́ŋ/ 形 若い, 年少の; 若々しい

| look | young | 若く見える |

▷She **looks young** for her age. 彼女は年の割に若く見える

fairly	young	かなり若い
pretty	young	とても若い
quite	young	
relatively	young	比較的若い

▷Sixteen is **pretty young** to get married. 16歳は結婚するには若すぎる
▷He became a top golf player when he was still **relatively young**. 彼はまだ比較的若いときにトップゴルフ選手になった

| young and old | | 老いも若きも |

★日本語とは順序が逆. old and young も用いられるが頻度ははるかに低い

▷Everybody, **young and old**, loved the Beatles. 老いも若きもみなビートルズが大好きだった

プログレッシブ
英語コロケーション辞典

2012年 5月16日	初版　第1刷発行
2014年12月10日	初版　第3刷発行

著　者	塚本　倫久
発行者	神永　曉
発行所	株式会社　小学館
	〒101-8001 東京都千代田区一ツ橋2－3－1
	電話　編集　03-3230-5169
	販売　03-5281-3555
印刷所	萩原印刷株式会社
製本所	株式会社若林製本工場

© Shogakukan 2012

造本には十分注意しておりますが、印刷・製本など製造上の不備がございましたら、「制作局コールセンター」(フリーダイヤル 0120-336-340) にご連絡ください。
(電話受付は、土・日・祝休日を除く 9:30～17:30)

Ⓡ＜公益社団法人日本複製権センター委託出版物＞
本書を無断で複写 (コピー) することは、著作権法上の例外を除き、禁じられています。本書をコピーされる場合は、事前に公益社団法人日本複製権センター (JRRC) の許諾を受けてください。
JRRC　　URL: http://www.jrrc.or.jp
　　　　 email: jrrc_info@jrrc.or.jp
　　　　 電話 03-3401-2382

本書の電子データ化等の無断複製は著作権法上の例外を除き禁じられています。代行業者等の第三者による本書の電子的複製も認められておりません。

★小学館外国語編集部のウェブサイト『小学館ランゲージワールド』
　http://www.l-world.shogakukan.co.jp/

Printed in Japan　　ISBN 978-4-09-511009-7